BRITISH POLITICAL
1900–1994

Also by David Butler

THE BRITISH GENERAL ELECTION OF 1951
THE ELECTORAL SYSTEM IN BRITAIN 1918–1951
THE BRITISH GENERAL ELECTION OF 1955
THE STUDY OF POLITICAL BEHAVIOUR
ELECTIONS ABROAD (*editor*)
THE BRITISH GENERAL ELECTION OF 1959 (*with Richard Rose*)
THE BRITISH GENERAL ELECTION OF 1964 (*with Anthony King*)
THE BRITISH GENERAL ELECTION OF 1966 (*with Anthony King*)
POLITICAL CHANGE IN BRITAIN (*with Donald Stokes*)
THE BRITISH GENERAL ELECTION OF 1970 (*with Michael Pinto-Duschinsky*)
THE CANBERRA MODEL
THE BRITISH GENERAL ELECTION OF FEBRUARY 1974 (*with Dennis Kavanagh*)
THE BRITISH GENERAL ELECTION OF OCTOBER 1974 (*with Dennis Kavanagh*)
THE 1975 REFERENDUM (*with Uwe Kitzinger*)
COALITIONS IN BRITISH POLITICS (*editor*)
POLICY AND POLITICS (*with A. H. Halsey*)
THE BRITISH GENERAL ELECTION OF 1979 (*with Dennis Kavanagh*)
REFERENDUMS (*with A. Ranney*)
EUROPEAN ELECTIONS AND BRITISH POLITICS (*with David Marquand*)
DEMOCRACY AT THE POLLS (*with H. Penniman and A. Ranney*)
THE BRITISH GENERAL ELECTION OF 1983 (*with Dennis Kavanagh*)
DEMOCRACY AND ELECTIONS (*with V. Bogdanor*)
PARTY STRATEGIES IN BRITAIN (*with Paul Jowett*)
GOVERNING WITHOUT A MAJORITY
INDIA DECIDES (*with Ashok Lahiri and Prannoy Roy*)
THE BRITISH GENERAL ELECTION OF 1987 (*with Dennis Kavanagh*)
THE BRITISH GENERAL ELECTION OF 1992 (*with Dennis Kavanagh*)
ELECTIONEERING (*with A. Ranney*)
FAILURE IN BRITISH GOVERNMENT (*with A. Adonis and T. Travers*)
BRITISH ELECTIONS SINCE 1945
CONGRESSIONAL REDISTRICTING (*with B. Cain*)

BRITISH POLITICAL FACTS 1900–1994

BY

DAVID BUTLER

AND

GARETH BUTLER

SEVENTH EDITION

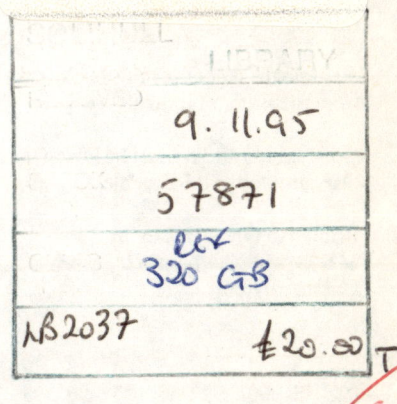

M

First edition 1963
Reprinted with corrections 1964
Second edition 1968
Third edition 1969
Fourth edition 1975
Fifth edition 1980
Sixth edition 1986
Reprinted 1987
Seventh edition 1994

Published by
THE MACMILLAN PRESS LTD
Houndmills, Basingstoke, Hampshire RG21 2XS
and London
Companies and representatives
throughout the world

ISBN 0–333–52616–3 hardcover
ISBN 0–333–52617–1 paperback

A catalogue record for this book is available
from the British Library.

Copy-edited and typeset by Povey–Edmondson
Okehampton and Rochdale, England

Printed in Great Britain by
Mackays of Chatham PLC
Chatham, Kent

9   8   7   6   5   4   3   2   1
02 01 00 99 98 97 96 95 94

CONTENTS

INTRODUCTION to the Seventh Edition   XV

I. MINISTRIES

Complete Ministries   1
Ministerial Salaries   49
Opposition Salaries   49
Ministerial Offices: the Offices   50
               the Holders   52
Leaders of the House of Commons and the House of Lords   65
Government Chief Whips in the House of Commons and the House of
     Lords   65
Size of Cabinets and Governments   66
Social and Educational Composition of Cabinets   66
Durability of Prime Ministers   67
Long Tenure of Office   67
Oldest and Youngest Ministers   67
Cabinet Members Dying in Office   68
Cabinet Members Suffering Electoral Defeat   68
Ministerial Resignations   68
Parliamentary Private Secretaries to Prime Ministers   70
Biographical Notes on Prime Ministers, Chancellors of the Exchequer,
     Foreign Secretaries, and Leaders of the Opposition   71
Index of Ministers   77

II. PARTIES

Conservative Party:
     Leaders of the Party   127
     Leadership Elections   127
     Deputy Leaders   127
     Leaders in the House of Lords   128
     Party Officials   128
     Chief Whips in the House of Commons and House of Lords   130
     Chairmen of the 1922 Committee   130
     Shadow Cabinets   130
     Party Membership   132
     Party Finance   132
     Party Conferences and their Chairmen   133
Labour Party:
     Leaders and Deputy Leaders of the Party   135
     Election of Leaders   135
     Leaders in the House of Lords   138
     Chief Whips in the House of Commons and House of Lords   138
     Labour Representation Committee and National Executive
         Committee Office-holders   138
     Parliamentary Labour Party   139
     Parliamentary Committee members   140
     Party Conferences and Party Chairmen   144
     Party Membership Statistics   146

Labour Party Organisation and Constitutions   148
Sponsored M.P.s   149
Party Finance   151
Liberal Party:
    Leaders and Deputy Leaders of the Party   152
    Leaders in the House of Lords   152
    Principal Office-holders   152
    Chief Whips in the House of Commons and House of Lords   154
    Party Conferences and their Presidents   154
(Social and) Liberal Democrats:
    Leaders and Deputy Leaders of the Party   156
    Principal Office-holders   156
    Party Conferences   156
    Party Finance   156
Minor Parties:
    Minor Parties Contesting Elections   157
    Common Wealth   159
    Communist Party   159
    Co-operative Party   159
    Independent Labour Party   160
    Irish Nationalist Party up to 1922   160
    Irish Parties since 1922   161
    Liberal National Party   162
    Liberal Unionist Party   163
    National Democratic Party   163
    National Front and British National Party   164
    National Party   164
    National Labour Party   164
    New Party, British Union of Fascists, Union Movement   165
    Plaid Cymru   165
    Scottish Labour Party   166
    Scottish National Party   166
    Social Democratic Party   167
    Independent M.P.s   167
    Representation of Minor Parties in the House of Commons   169
    Political Pressure Groups   169

III. PARLIAMENT

House of Commons:
    Speakers and their Deputies   171
    Officers of the House of Commons   172
    Parliamentary Sessions   172
    Parliamentary Hours of Sitting   172
    Emergency Recalls of the House of Commons   173
    Government and Private Members' Time   173
    Broadcasting of Parliament   173
    Main Occupation of M.P.s   174
    Education of M.P.s   175
    Dates of Sessions, Use of Parliamentary Time, Parliamentary Bills,
        and Questions to Ministers   176

Fathers of the House of Commons   179
Long-service M.P.s   179
Oldest and Youngest M.P.s   180
Family Connections of M.P.s   180
Spouse's Succession   181
Filial Succession   182
Dual Mandates   182
Critical Votes in the House of Commons   183
Confidence Motions since 1945   186
Guillotine Motions since 1945   187
Suspension of M.P.s   187
Regnal Years   187
Select Committees: 188
    Powers   188
    Duration   188
    Chairmen   188
    Chairmen's Liaison Committee   189
    Selection   189
    Public Accounts   190
    Estimates   190
    National Expenditure   191
    Expenditure   191
    Nationalised Industries   192
    Agriculture   192
    Science and Technology   192
    Education and Science   193
    Race Relations and Immigration   193
    Overseas Aid, Overseas Development 193
    Scottish Affairs   193
    European Secondary Legislation   194
    European Standing Committee   194
    Procedure   194
    House of Commons Services   194
    House of Commons Commission   195
    Domestic Committees   195
        Accommodation   195
        Administration   195
        Finance and Services 195
        Information   195
        Members' Interests 196
    Privileges   196
    Statutory Instruments   198
    Public Petitions   199
    Committee on Parliamentary Commissioner for
        Administration   200
Parliamentary Commissioner for Administration   200
House of Commons Commission   201
Public Accounts Commission   201
Specialist Select Committees since 1979   201
Payment of M.P.s   203
Seats Forfeited   204

House of Lords:
    Lord Chairmen of Committees   205
    Officers of the House of Lords   205
    Composition of the House of Lords   205
    Creation of Peerages   206
    Party Organisation   206
    Party Strengths   207
    Attendance   207
    Sittings and Business   208
    Critical Votes   210
    Reform of the House of Lords   211

IV. ELECTIONS

General Election Statistics   213
1975 E.E.C. Referendum Result   220
Direct Elections to European Parliament   220
General Election Results by Regions   222
Party Changes between Elections   224
M.P.s' Changes of Allegiance   225
M.P.s Elected under New Label   231
M.P.s Denied Renomination   232
By-elections   234
M.P.s seeking Re-election   238
Ministers seeking Re-election   238
Electoral Administration, Franchise and Redistribution   239
Election Expenses   241
European Referendum Expenses   242
Lost Deposits   242
Women Candidates and M.P.s   243
Election Petitions   243
Sources on Electoral Matters   244
Public Opinion Polling Organisations   245
Polls on Voting Intention   246
Accuracy of Forecasts in General Elections   259

V. POLITICAL ALLUSIONS

Political Place-names   263
Political Quotations   265
Political Scandals   276
Major Civil Disturbances and Demonstrations   277
Political Assassinations   277

VI. CIVIL SERVICE

Heads of Departments and Public Offices   279
Top Civil Service Salary Level   284
Prime Minister's Staff   285
Political Advisers   286
Size of Civil Service   286
Next Steps   289

VII. ROYAL COMMISSIONS, COMMITTEES OF INQUIRY AND TRIBUNALS

Investigatory Processes	291
Royal Commissions Listed Chronologically	291
Permanent and Operating Commissions	295
Other Crown Committees	296
Irish Vice-Regal Commissions	297
Departmental Committees	297
Select Chronological List	297
Inquiries Held under the Tribunals of Inquiry (Evidence) Act, 1921	301
Tribunals and Commissions	302
Political Honours Scrutiny Committee	303

VIII. JUSTICE AND LAW ENFORCEMENT

Criminal Justice Legislation	305
Legislation Relating to Administration of Civil Justice	308
Cases of Political Significance	309
Principal Judges	312
Other Legal and Law Enforcement Officials	315
Security Services	316
Security Commission	317
Number of Judges	317
Civil Proceedings	317
Judicial Review	318
Criminal Statistics:	
Higher Courts	318
Summary Courts: Indictable Offences	319
Recorded Crime	319
Traffic Offences	320
Prison Sentences and Prison Populations	320
Parole Board	320
Police Force	321

IX. SOCIAL CONDITIONS

Population:	
U.K. Population 1901–	323
Intercensal Changes in Population	323
Population of Components of U.K.	324
Birth Rates, Death Rates, and Marriages in the U.K.	324
Age Distribution of the Population of the U.K.	325
Expectation of Life	325
Main Causes of Death	325
Average Age at First Marriage	326
Divorces	326
Net Emigration from Great Britain and Ireland	326
People Born Overseas	327
Naturalisation	327
Commonwealth Immigration:	
1956–62 Commonwealth Immigration	327
Acceptances for Settlement	328

        Commonwealth Immigrants in the U.K.   328
        Race Relations Legislation   329
Housing:
        Major Housing Acts   330
        Major Rent and Mortgage Interest Restriction Acts   331
        Permanent Dwellings Completed   332
        Tenancy   333
        Council House Sales   334
Social Security:
        Legislation   334
        Old Age Pensions   337
        Women's Rights   337
        Equal Opportunities Commission   338
        Maternity and Child Welfare   339
        Rates of Child Benefit   340
        Legal Abortions   340
Education:
        Legislation   341
        Pupils in Schools   342
        Percentage Receiving Full-time Education   343
        Students in Full-time Higher Education   343
        Expenditure on Education   343
Public Library Service   344
Pressure Groups   344
Transport and Communications:
        Current Vehicle Licences   348
        Railways   349
        Shipping   349
        Volume of Air Traffic   349
        Volume of Postal Traffic   350
        Cost of Letter Mail   350
        Telephones   351

X. EMPLOYMENT AND TRADE UNIONS

Major Employment and Trade Union Litigation   353
Major Trade Union Litigation   356
Earnings and Hours Worked   358
Size of Labour Force   360
Rates of Unemployment Benefit   360
Industrial Analysis of the Occupied Population   361
Trades Union Congresses, with Presidents and General
        Secretaries   362
The Largest Unions:
        Formation and Officers   364
        Membership Figures   368
Income, Expenditure and Funds of Registered Trade Unions   370
Density of Union Membership in Total Labour Force   370
Major Industrial Disputes   370
Emergency Powers   372
Unemployment, Industrial Disputes and Trade Union Statistics   373

XI. THE ECONOMY

Some Landmarks in British Economic Policy 377
Sources of Government Economic Advice:
    Economic Section of the Cabinet Office 380
    Economic Adviser to the Government 380
    Head of Government Economic Service 380
    Bank of England 380
    Economic Advisory Council 380
    Import Duties Advisory Council 380
    Economic Planning Board 380
    National Economic Development Office 381
    Council on Pay, Productivity and Incomes 381
    National Incomes Commission 381
    Prices and Incomes Board 381
    Prices Commission 381
    Pay Board 381
    Industrial Adviser to the Government 381
    Committee of Pay Comparability 381
Economic Interest Groups 381
Statistics:
    National Income 383
    Income Tax 383
    Amount Retained of Bachelor's Income after Tax 383
    Wholesale and Retail Prices Indices 383
    Purchasing Power of the Pound in 1900 Terms 383
    Real Gross Domestic Product per head 383
    Indices of Industrial Production 385
    Steel, Car and Coal Production 385
    Raw Cotton Consumption 385
    Agriculture, Output and Employment 385
    Price of 2½% Consols 385
    Bank Rate 385
    Net Balance of Payments 387
    Terms of Trade 387
    Imports and Exports: Volume Indices 387
    Foreign Exchange Rates 387
    Total National Revenue 390
    Main Sources of Revenue 390
    Main Heads of Expenditure 393
    Specimen Tariffs 393
    National Debt 393
    Percentage Shares in Net National Income 396
    Selected Items of Consumer Expenditure 396
    Income Distribution after Tax 396
    Percentage of Personal Net Capital owned by Groups of Population 397
    Output per Man 397
    Industrial Output of the U.K. 397
    Surtax 398
    Capital Transfer Tax 398
    Consumer Credit 398
Budget Dates 399

XII. THE PUBLIC SECTOR

Main Landmarks	401
Privatisation since 1979	402
Nationalised Industries: Chairmen and Responsible Ministers, 1950–	405
Nationalised Industries: Assets and Employees, 1950–	415
External Financing of Nationalised Industries, 1977–	415
Inquiries into Nationalised Industries	416
Central Government Trading Bodies	416
Other Quasi-governmental Organisations	416
White Papers on Nationalised Industry Policy	418

XIII. ROYALTY

British Kings and Queens	419
Use of Royal Power	419
Regency Acts	420
The Royal Family	420
Private Secretaries to the Sovereign	422
Lord Chamberlains	422
Poets Laureate	422
Civil List of the Crown	422

XIV. BRITISH ISLES

Scotland	425
Wales	426
Ireland 1900–1922	427
Northern Ireland 1922–72	428
Governors and Prime Ministers of Northern Ireland	429
Northern Ireland Ministers 1921–72	429
General Elections of Northern Ireland 1921–69	431
Northern Ireland 1972–	431
Channel Islands	433
Isle of Man	434
Devolution	435

XV. LOCAL GOVERNMENT

Structure	437
Number of Councils	437
Local Government Finance	438
Major Legislation Affecting Local Government	438
Local Authority Interest Groups	441
New Towns	441
Local Government Elections:	443
Borough Council Election Results 1949–72	443
Party Control in Major Cities 1945–	444
Local Government Elections 1973–	445
Party Representation on the London County Council and Greater London Council	448

XVI. THE COMMONWEALTH

Main Territories under British rule since 1900	451
Independent Self-Governing Members of the Commonwealth	458

Commonwealth Prime Ministers' Meetings 459
Commonwealth Secretariat 460
Viceroys and Governors-General 460

XVII. INTERNATIONAL RELATIONS

Major Treaties and Documents Subscribed to by Britain 465
League of Nations 467
United Nations 467
Foreign Affairs Pressure Groups 467
British Ambassadors to Leading Powers and International
    Organisations 467

XVIII. BRITAIN AND EUROPE

A Chronology of Events 471
Summits 1973– 472
European Organisations with British Membership 472
    Western European Union 473
    European Free Trade Association 473
    Council of Europe 473
    European Court of Human Rights 474
    European Community; European Union 474
    U.K. Contributions and Receipts 475
    European Coal and Steel Community 475
    Euratom 475
    European Parliament 476
    European Court of Justice 476
British Representation in Europe 476

XIX. ARMED FORCES

Service Chiefs 479
Defence Organisation:
    Committee of Imperial Defence 480
    Ministry of Defence 480
Defence Pressure Groups 481
Total Forces Serving 481
Total Expenditure on Defence 481
Conscription 482
Rationing 482
Principal Military Operations, with Costs and Casualties 482
Major War Commanders 486

XX. THE PRESS

National Daily Newspapers 489
National Sunday Newspapers 493
London Evening Newspapers 495
National Newspapers Printing in More than One City 497
Partisan Tendencies in General Elections 498
Circulations 500
Provincial Morning Daily Newspapers 501

Main Political Weeklies   503
The Press Council   503
Press Complaints Commission   504

XXI. BROADCASTING AUTHORITIES

The British Broadcasting Corporation: 505
    British Broadcasting Company Board   505
    British Broadcasting Corporation Board   505
    B.B.C. Radio   507
    B.B.C. Local Radio   507
    B.B.C. Television   508
    Licences and Expenditure   508
Independent Broadcasting   510
    Chairmen of ITA, IBA, ITC, and Radio Authority   510
    Programme Contracting Companies – Television   511
    Finance of Independent Broadcasting   512
    Cable Television   513
    Satellite Television   513
    Programme Contracting Companies – Radio   513
    Broadcasting Complaints Commission   515
    Broadcasting Standards Council   515
Inquiries into Broadcasting   515

XXII. RELIGION

Church Membership Statistics   517
The Church of England: 518
    Membership Statistics   518
    Archbishops and Leading Bishops of the five Principal Dioces in the
        Church of England   518
The Church in Wales   519
Episcopal Church in Scotland   519
Baptist Union   520
Congregational Union   520
Presbyterian Church   520
United Reformed Church   521
Methodist Church   521
The Church of Scotland   521
The Roman Catholic Church   522
Northern Ireland, Religious Affiliations   522
Other Christian Denominations   523
The Jewish Community   523
Buddhists, Hindus, Muslims and Sikhs   523
Marriages by Manner of Solemnisation   524

BIBLIOGRAPHICAL NOTE   525

INDEX   529

INTRODUCTION TO THE SEVENTH EDITION

THE table of contents offers the simplest justification for this book – but inevitably it is a book that must justify itself in different ways to different readers. The scholar, the journalist, the politician and the everyday pedant were each in the authors' minds at some point during its compilation. Some of those who look at this book will, we hope, be delighted to find in compact and reliable form data that might still have eluded them after searching through a dozen standard works of reference; others will at least discover from our pages where the information they seek may be found: a few, we fear, will be infuriated by our omissions and, despite all our efforts at checking, by our errors.

The idea of writing this book grew gradually in the mind of one of its authors as, in the course of his years as a student and a teacher at Nuffield College (which is devoted to research in contemporary subjects), he noticed the amount of time that he and others wasted in searching for seemingly obvious facts about twentieth-century Britain. If, therefore, any reader has been especially in our minds, he is the graduate student writing a thesis on any domestic theme in the last century. We hope he will find here not only an expeditious way of checking basic facts but also, if he finds time to browse through our lists and tables, a stimulating reminder of people and considerations that must have played a part, perhaps only as background, in the situations he is analysing.

Bur we are not concerned solely with academic needs. Experience of checking facts in newspaper offices and broadcasting studios, and the anecdotes of friends in Whitehall and Westminster, have made plain to us how much elementary political data is annoyingly elusive. Many admirable works of reference exist but the right one is not always to hand; most of them, moreover, are compiled on an annual basis – which can be very frustrating for those who are trying to trace an office or a statistic over a number of years.

The compiler of any work of reference is limited by space and time. How much data shall be included? How far shall other works be duplicated? How many hours is it worth devoting to any particular entry? In this book we have had to exclude interesting information either because it would fill a disproportionate number of pages or because it could not be obtained without more labour than we thought justified. We have consoled ourselves for setting out data in abbreviated form by giving references to more exhaustive sources.

Indeed, since the compilation of reference books is, even more than other research, systematised plagiarism, perhaps the most valuable part of these pages lies in these citations. We have not attempted an exhaustive bibliography – except for as compilation of bibliographies and general reference books – but we have throughout tried to list all major authorities.

The title, *British Political Facts 1900–1994*, provides a reasonably close delimitation of the scope of this book. *British* indicates that we have been concerned with the domestic history of the United Kingdom. But it is not possible to set precise boundaries to the term 'domestic' and we have perhaps strayed beyond them by listing Colonies, Governors-General, and some Ambassadors, as well as including a chapter on Britain's relations with Europe.

Political is potentially ambiguous, but we have used it to stress that our interest is in the power of the state. We have tried to list the principal people who were involved in the government of Britain at any moment in this century; we have recorded election results – as providing the basis for political authority – and major legislation – as representing its use; we have assembled, in summary form, statistical data which show some of the social and economic background to all political action.

Facts indicates that we have tried to eschew political judgements as far as possible. Some value judgements may be implicit in our selection of material, but we believe that virtually everything here would be acceptable as non-controversial evidence in debates over the nature of twentieth-century British history. It is a waste of time to argue about verifiable questions of fact. But it is also a waste of time to assemble facts except as a basis for argument. Because in this book we have stuck rigidly to facts, it does not mean that we overrate them. Analysis of our past and present situation is far more important than mere fact-gathering. Unlike Martha we are fully aware which is the better part.

1900–1994 is a somewhat arbitrary period – but any historical period must be arbitrary. Our terminal date is simply as near to the present as publishing allows. Our opening date was a numerological accident – but it would be hard to find a better watershed without going back at least to 1885, which because of space, and still more because of the availability of data, was impracticable. We have endeavoured to treat every one of our ninety-four years equally, providing as full and exact data about 1901 as about 1991. With some statistics this has proved impossible and some of our time-series are regrettably discontinuous. But in general it will be found that we have resisted the temptation to make a special favourite of the more recent past; it is not our fault that there was no Gallup polls before 1938 and that local election results cannot usefully be pursued very far back.

In compiling this book we have become very conscious of the strengths and weaknesses of other reference books – and particularly of the importance of pedantic accuracy and clear presentation. We have certainly not avoided all the pitfalls into which we have observed others falling; therefore, by way both of excuse and of warning, it may be worth describing a few of the difficulties we have faced.

The general problems of finding exact data on British politics were best exemplified in the gathering of complete lists of ministries over the last ninety-four years – the most time-consuming of all our operations. There are a number of publications which purport to list all ministerial appointments – the most useful of these are the two Parliamentary handbooks, *Dod* and *Vacher*. There is also the Stationery Office publication *H.M. Ministers and Heads of Public Departments* which used to appear four to five times a year. Lists of ministers are also printed in *Hansard* once a fortnight during sessions. But all these sources have the same disadvantage – no indication is given of the date when a minister was appointed or left office. A man may indeed be appointed and leave office between the publication of these lists, so that there is no record whatever of his elevation. Since 1931 *Keesing's Contemporary Archives* and, since 1988, *Keesing's UK Record*, have recorded most government appointments – but they depend on newspaper sources and are not altogether infallible. The Indexes to *The Times* are the best means of checking on ministerial changes, though here too there are problems. *Palmer's Index to The Times* which was not superseded by the *Official Index* until 1906 is far from satisfactory; under the heading 'Official Appointments' is the depressing injunction 'See every issue'. From 1906 the *Official Index* is much more thorough, although misprints and references to different editions of the paper do occur. Even *The Times*, moreover, has occasionally missed a minor government change. An additional complication lies in the range of possible days which might be considered the date of appointment: there is the announcement from Downing Street, the press report the following day, the official gazetting a week or more later, the exchange of seals and the kissing of hands. None of these may represent the precise date on which the new minister took over his duties, but, wherever possible, we have used the earliest and most public announcement. Until 1960 this was usually the date of *The Times* report, but more recently most resignations or reshuffles have been widely publicised by the broadcast media on the day they actually take place, and this is the date we have used. Peerages sometimes cause further confusion, since weeks usually elapse before a newly elevated minister's title is announced. Care has also to be taken when a familiar minister disappears behind a new name – the fact that Mr Ivor Guest, Lord Ashby St Ledgers, and Viscount Wimborne were one and the same person is not immediately apparent. Another snag arises, particularly in wartime and since the late 1960s, when the titles and functions of departments changed kaleidoscopically.

In many other fields the sources of confusion were almost equally numerous. The search for reliable and consistent evidence about newspaper circulations, religious affiliations and trade disputes caused us particular trouble. But it would be tedious to quote all the gaps in existing works of reference which we have – with very varying success – tried to fill. We must, however, mention the complications which arise from the structure of the United Kingdom. The changes in Ireland in 1922 inevitably cause a break in all national statistical time-series and since then many tables have, perforce, to exclude Northern Ireland as well as Eire; but the administrative separation of Scotland causes almost as many difficulties. Statistics are compiled independently north and south of the Border, quite often on different bases. Sometimes this arises from the different legal or administrative systems – as with education; but in the case of population and vital statistics the Registrars-General seem unnecessarily perverse in presenting their census findings in differing forms.

This book was first compiled at the beginning of the 1960s. It has been checked, updated and modified through successive editions in response to the reactions of its readers. It is the people who have used the book most – academics, civil servants, librarians, journalists, party officials and officers of the Houses of Parliament – who have been its keenest and most constructive critics.

The preparation and revision of this book has indeed depended on a vast amount of help from many quarters, ranging from scholars and friends who have spent many hours assisting us to check on obscure details, to unidentified voices at the end of official telephones. We must thank above all Jennie Freeman, who in 1961 bore so much of the brunt of preparing the First Edition, and Ann Sloman who co-authored the Fourth and Fifth editions, introducing valuable new features. After them come the Warden, Fellows and Students of Nuffield College, who have made so many contributions over the years. But we owe a deep debt of gratitude to officials in Parliament, in Party Headquarters, in Government Departments and newspaper offices, to many colleagues in the academic world and in the B.B.C., especially to those in News Information and the Reference Library, to complete strangers who have sent us corrections and suggestions, and to our publisher. We must also acknowledge what we owe to anonymous compilers of the many works of reference from which we have so freely drawn. We give here an incomplete list of those who have supplied information or emendations in the preparation of one or more of the successive editions of this book and, although many have given unstinted help, we must draw special attention to the encyclopaedic precision of Mr S. M. Lees and Mr P. C. Thompson who have saved us from so many errors.

P. Addison
R. K. Alderman
R. F. Allen
L. Anderson
J. M. Austen
G. S. Bain
Miss P. Baines
F. M. Barlow
C. J. Bartlett
E. Batstone
D. Beamish
M. Beloff
M. Berlins
F. Berman

H. B. Berrington
N. Birnbaum
N. Blewett
G. D. M. Block
V. Bogdanor
J. M. Bouen
D. Brack
K. Britto
P. Brierley
M. G. Brock
P. A. Bromhead
B. Bush
E. E. Butler
Sir Robin Butler

R. Butt
P. Campbell
T. J. .M. Cartwright
A. N. Cass
J. Chesshire
Sir N. Chester
D. M. Clark
H. A. Clegg
R. Clements
P. C. Collison
Miss S. J. Conwill
D. Cowling
F. W. S. Craig

M. Crick
B. Criddle
J. A. Cross
S. Cursley
J. K. Curtice
P. Davies
C. Dawson
N. Deakin
A. Devermond
C. Dobson
Mrs M. Dowley
G. Drewry
C. Driver
B. Dye
Miss D. Edmunds
N. D. Ellis
Sir T. Evans
H. R. M. Farmer
Sir E. Fellowes
A. Flanders
A. Fox
Lord Fraser of Kilmorack
Yash Ghai
M. Gilbert
S. Gordon
B. Gosschalk
A. H. Halsey
T. Harris
B. H. Harrison
M. Harrison
A. J. Hastings
S. C. Hawtrey
C. G. Hazlehurst
D. Heald
J. Hemingway
R. Hetherington
A. E. Holmans
C. C. Hood
A. Hunt
R. J. Jackson
D. Jeffcock
Miss J. Jeger

R. Jenkins
L. Keillor
B. Keith-Lucas
Miss C. Kennedy
A. S. King
U. W. Kitzinger
A. L. Lamaison
F. Lawson
S. M. Lees
T. O. Lloyd
A. B. Lyons
Lord MacCarthy
J. C. McCrudden
B. MacDonald
K. MacDonald
Sir D. MacDougall
A. MacIntyre
R. McKibbin
D. McKie
A. F. Madden
G. Marshall
J. Maule
Miss E. Meehan
J. S. Milner
B. R. Mitchell
Miss J. P. Morgan
J. Morland Craig
J. Muellbauer
D. L. Munby
R. Neuss
H. G. Nicholas
P. Norton
C. O'Leary
P. Oppenheimer
J. Palmer
Lord Pannell
J. Paxton
H. Pelling
Dame M. Perham
M. Pinto-Duschinsky
A. M. Potter
D. Prysor-Jones

G. Pyatt
C. Rallings
C. Raphael
R. A. Rempel
N. Rees
Miss A. Rhodes
P. G. Richards
Mrs P. Ryan
M. Ryle
J. C. Sainty
S. Sargent
Miss K. Schott
Miss O. Seligman
C. Seymour-Ure
D. M. Shapiro
L. J. Sharpe
Mrs A. Skeats
K. J. A. Skidelsky
M. G. M. Sloman
M. Steed
D. Stephen
S. Symes
Mrs A. Taylor
A. J. P. Taylor
A. Teasdale
M. Thrasher
T. Travers
Mrs R. Wagner
R. Watford
N. D. Walker
W. Wallace
A. H. Warren
Miss N. Watts
P. Way
Mrs J. Wigan
P. M. Williams
Mrs B. Williams
T. Wilson
R. Worcester
R. Wybrow

While we could not have completed this book without these far-flung helpers (not to mention the indefatigable assistance of our secretaries) we should stress our sole responsibility for its inevitable errors. Our readers are earnestly invited to let us know of any that they may detect.

I

MINISTRIES

The following list contains the names of all those who have held paid and political ministerial office since 1900. It leaves out some office-holders, since from time to time various offices in the Royal Household have ceased to be political appointments. The list also omits some politicians with government posts, since various other offices, such as the Second Church Estates Commissioner, are not regarded as part of the Ministry. Assistant Government Whips were unpaid until 1964 and are not listed before that date. Parliamentary Private Secretaries are also unlisted.

The problems of compiling this list are discussed in the introduction. As far as possible the date cited is the one on which the announcement of the appointment appeared in *The Times*, except where it is plain that the news received wide publicity the previous day. Where more that one person holds the same title the starting and finishing dates are given. In almost all other cases it may be assumed that the starting date of the new appointment represents the vacating of the office.

Ministers in the Cabinet are printed in bold type capitals throughout this section. Ministers outside the Cabinet and Ministers of State are printed in capitals. Junior ministers are in ordinary print. The seven leading offices are placed first in each Ministry; the remainder are arranged alphabetically, except for the Law Officers and the political appointments to the Royal Household which are placed at the end together with the Treasury appointments reserved for whips.

In these lists – and throughout the book – titles are placed in brackets if acquired during the tenure of office or on transfer to the next office. U-S. denotes Under-Secretary; F.S. Financial Secretary; P.S. Parliamentary Secretary.

This section has been sub-divided chronologically at changes of Prime Minister, except when few other offices changed hands as in 1902, 1923, 1937, 1955, 1963 and 1976; further divisions are made for the drastic reconstructions of 1915, 1931 and May 1945.

CONSERVATIVE GOVERNMENT, 1900–1905

P.M.	**M of SALISBURY** (*3rd*)	1900–11 Jul 02	*Foreign O.*	**M of SALISBURY** (*3rd*) (*P.M.*)	1900	
	A. BALFOUR	12 Jul 02–4 Dec 05		**M of LANSDOWNE**	1 Nov 00	
1st Ld of	**A. BALFOUR**	1900	*U-S.*	St J. Brodrick	1900	
Treasury	(*office combined with P.M. when*			Vt Cranborne	7 Nov 00	
	Balfour succeeded Salisbury)			(*4th M of Salisbury*)		
Ld Pres.	**D of DEVONSHIRE**	1900		Earl Percy[1]	9 Oct 03	
	M of LONDONDERRY	13 Oct 03	*Home O.*	**SIR M. WHITE RIDLEY**	1900	
Ld Chanc.	**E of HALSBURY**	1900		**C. RITCHIE**	1 Nov 00	
Privy S.	**VT CROSS**	1900		**A. AKERS-DOUGLAS**	8 Aug 02	
	M of SALISBURY (*3rd*) (*P.M.*)		*U-S.*	J. Collings	1900	
		Nov 00		T. Cochrane	8 Aug 02	
	A. BALFOUR (*P.M.*)	12 Jul 02	*Admiralty*	**G. GOSCHEN**	1900	
	M of SALISBURY (*4th*)	11 Oct 03		**E of SELBORNE**	1 Nov 00	
Exchequer	**SIR M. HICKS BEACH**	1900		**EARL CAWDOR**	5 Mar 05	
	C. RITCHIE	8 Aug 02	*P. & F.S.*	Sir W. Macartney	1900	
	A. CHAMBERLAIN	6 Oct 03		H. Arnold-Forster	7 Nov 00	
F.S.	R. Hanbury	1900		E. Pretyman	11 Oct 03	
	A. Chamberlain	7 Nov 00	*Civil Ld*	A. Chamberlain	1900	
	W. Hayes Fisher	8 Aug 02		E. Pretyman	7 Nov 00	
	A. Elliot	10 Apr 03		A. Lee	11 Oct 03	
	V. Cavendish	9 Oct 03	*B. Ag. & Fish.*	**W. LONG**	1900	

[1] M.P. Not a Member of the House of Lords

CONSERVATIVE GOVERNMENT, 1900–1905 (contd.)

B.Ag.& Fish. (contd.)	R. HANBURY	14 Nov 00
	E of ONSLOW	19 May 03
	A. FELLOWES	12 Mar 05
Colonies	J. CHAMBERLAIN	1900
	A. LYTTELTON	6 Oct 03
U-S.	E of Selborne	1900
	E of Onslow	12 Nov 00
	D of Marlborough	23 Jul 03
B. Educ.	(office not established)	
	D of DEVONSHIRE	1 Apr 00
	M of LONDONDERRY	8 Aug 02
V.-Pres. of Com. of Council on Education	Sir J. Gorst	1900
	(office abolished 8 Aug 02)	
P.S.	Sir W. Anson	8 Aug 02
India	LD G. HAMILTON[1]	1900
	ST J. BRODRICK	6 Oct 03
U-S.	E of Onslow	1900
	E of Hardwicke	12 Nov 00
	Earl Percy[1]	8 Aug 02
	E of Hardwicke	15 Oct 03
	M of Bath	19 Jan 05
Ld Lieut. Ireland	EARL CADOGAN	1900
	(office not ministerial 8 Aug 02)	
Chief Sec. Ireland	G. BALFOUR	1900
	G. WYNDHAM	7 Nov 00
	(office in cabinet)	
	G.WYNDHAM	8 Aug 02
	W. LONG	12 Mar 05
V. Pres. Dept. Agric. for Ireland	(Sir) H. Plunkett	1900
Ld Chanc. Ireland	LD ASHBOURNE	1900
D. Lanc.	LD JAMES of HEREFORD	1900
	(office not in cabinet)	
	SIR W. WALROND	8 Aug 02
Loc. Govt. B.	H. CHAPLIN	1900
	W. LONG	7 Nov 00
	G. BALFOUR	12 Mar 05
P.S.	T. Russell	1900
	(Sir) J. Lawson	11 Nov 00
	A. Jeffreys	27 Jun 05
Paym.-Gen.	D of MARLBOROUGH	1900
	SIR S. CROSSLEY	11 Mar 02
Postm.-Gen.	D of NORFOLK	1900
	M of LONDONDERRY	2 Apr 00
	(office in cabinet)	
	M of LONDONDERRY	7 Nov 00
	A. CHAMBERLAIN	8 Aug 02
	LD STANLEY[1]	6 Oct 03
Scotland	LD BALFOUR of BURLEIGH	1900
	A. MURRAY	6 Oct 03
	M of LINLITHGOW	2 Feb 05
B. Trade	C. RITCHIE	1900
	G. BALFOUR	7 Nov 00
	M of SALISBURY (4th)	12 Mar 05
P.S.	E of Dudley	1900
	A. Bonar Law	8 Aug 02
War	M of LANSDOWNE	1900
	ST J. BRODRICK	1 Nov 00
	H. ARNOLD-FORSTER	6 Oct 03
F.S.	J. Powell Williams	1900
	Ld Stanley	7 Nov 00
	W. Bromley-Davenport	11 Oct 03
U-S.	G. Wyndham	1900
	Ld Raglan	12 Nov 00
	E of Hardwicke	8 Aug 02
	E of Donoughmore	15 Oct 03
Works	A. AKERS-DOUGLAS	1900
	(office not in cabinet)	
	Ld WINDSOR	8 Aug 02

Law Officers

Att.-Gen.	SIR R. WEBSTER	1900
	SIR R. FINLAY	7 May 00
Sol.-Gen.	SIR R. FINLAY	1900
	SIR E. CARSON	7 May 00
Ld Advoc.	A. MURRAY	1900
	S. DICKSON	18 Oct 03
Sol.-Gen. Scotland	S. DICKSON	1900
	D. DUNDAS	18 Oct 03
	E. SALVESEN	30 Jan 05
	J. CLYDE	16 Oct 05
Att.-Gen. Ireland	J. ATKINSON	1900
	J. CAMPBELL	4 Dec 05
Sol.-Gen. Ireland	D. BARTON	1900
	G. WRIGHT	30 Jan 00
	J. CAMPBELL	8 Jul 03

Whips

P.S. to Treasury	Sir W. Walrond	1900
	Sir A. Acland Hood	8 Aug 02
Lds of Treasury	W. Hayes Fisher	1900–8 Aug 02
	H. Anstruther	1900–11 Oct 03
	Ld Stanley[1]	1900–7 Nov 00
	A. Fellowes	7 Nov 00–15 Mar 05
	H. Forster	8 Aug 02–4 Dec 05
	Ld Balcarres[1]	11 Oct 03–4 Dec 05
	G. Loder	29 Mar 05–8 Apr 05
	Ld E. Talbot[1]	16 Jun 05–4 Dec 05

H.M. Household

Treasurer	Vt CURZON[1] (Earl Howe)	1900
	V. CAVENDISH	3 Dec 00
	M of HAMILTON[1]	11 Oct 03
Compt.	VT VALENTIA[1]	1900
V. Chamb.	A. FELLOWES	1900
	SIR A. ACLAND HOOD	3 Dec 00
	LD WOLVERTON	17 Nov 00
Ld Chamb.	E of HOPETOUN	1900
	E of CLARENDON	12 Nov 00
Ld Steward	E of PEMBROKE	1900
Cap Gents at Arms	LD BELPER	1900
Cap Yeo. of Guard	EARL WALDEGRAVE	1900
Master of Horse	D of PORTLAND	1900

[1] M.P. Not a Member of the House of Lords

CONSERVATIVE GOVERNMENT, 1900–1905 (contd.)

Master of	E of COVENTRY	1900	*Lds in*	Ld Bagot	1900–2 Jul 01
Buckhounds	LD CHESHAM	2 Nov 00	*Waiting*	E of Kintore	1900–4 Dec 05
	(*office abolished 1901*)		(*contd.*)	E of Denbigh	1900–4 Dec 05
Lds in	E of Clarendon	1900–30 Oct 00		Earl Howe	30 Oct 00–1 Oct 03
Waiting	Ld Harris	1900–4 Dec 00		Ld Kenyon	4 Dec 00–4 Dec 05
	Ld Churchill (*Vt*)	1900–4 Dec 05		E of Erroll	19 Oct 03–4 Dec 05
	Ld Lawrence	1900–4 Dec 05			

LIBERAL GOVERNMENT, 1905–1908

P.M.	**SIR H. CAMPBELL-BANNERMAN**		*Law Officers (contd.)*		
		5 Dec 05–5 Apr 08	*Att.-Gen.*	SIR W. ROBSON	28 Jan 08
Ld Pres.	**E of CREWE**	10 Dec 05	*Sol.-Gen.*	SIR W. ROBSON	12 Dec 05
Ld Chanc.	**LD LOREBURN**	10 Dec 05		SIR S. EVANS	28 Jan 08
Privy S.	**M of RIPON**	10 Dec 05	*Ld Advoc.*	T. SHAW	12 Dec 05
Exchequer	**H. ASQUITH**	10 Dec 05	*Sol.-Gen.*	A. URE	18 Dec 05
F.S.	R. McKenna	12 Dec 05	*Scotland*		
	W. Runciman	29 Jan 07	*Att.-Gen.*	R. CHERRY	20 Dec 05
Foreign 0.	**SIR E. GREY**	10 Dec 05	*Ireland*		
U.-S.	Ld E. Fitzmaurice[1] (*Ld*)	18 Dec 05	*Sol.-Gen.*	R. BARRY	20 Dec 05
Home 0.	**H. GLADSTONE**	10 Dec 05	*Ireland*		
U.-S.	H. Samuel	12 Dec 05	***Whips***		
Admiralty	**LD TWEEDMOUTH**	10 Dec 05	*P.S. to*	G. Whiteley	12 Dec 05
P.& F.S	E. Robertson	12 Dec 05	*Treasury*		
Civil Ld	G. Lambert	18 Dec 05	*Lds of*	H. Lewis	18 Dec 05–5 Apr 08
B. Ag.&	**EARL CARRINGTON**	10 Dec 05	*Treasury*	J. Pease	18 Dec 05–5 Apr 08
Fish.				F. Freeman-Thomas	
Colonies	**E of ELGIN**	10 Dec 05			21 Dec 05–2 Feb 06
U.-S.	W. Churchill	12 Dec 05		C. Norton	21 Dec 05–5 Apr 08
B. Educ.	**A. BIRRELL**	10 Dec 05		J. Fuller	2 Feb 06–27 Feb 07
	R. MCKENNA	23 Jan 07		J. Whitley	27 Feb 07–5 Apr 08
P.S.	T. Lough	18 Dec 05	***H.M. Household***		
India	**J. MORLEY**	10 Dec 05	*Treasurer*	SIR E. STRACHEY	18 Dec 05
U.-S.	J. Ellis	12 Dec 05	*Compt.*	MASTER of ELIBANK	18 Dec 05
	C. Hobhouse	29 Jan 07	*V. Chamb.*	W BEAUMONT	
Chief Sec.	**J. BRYCE**	10 Dec 05		(*Ld Allendale*)	18 Dec 05
Ireland	**A. BIRRELL**	23 Jan 07		J. FULLER	27 Feb 07
V.-Pres.	Sir H. Plunkett	12 Dec 05	*Ld Chamb.*	VT ALTHORP	18 Dec 05
Dept. Agric.	T. Russell	21 May 07	*Ld Steward*	LD HAWKESBURY	
for Ireland				(*1st E of Liverpool*)	18 Dec 05
D. Lanc.	**SIR H. FOWLER**	10 Dec 05		EARL BEAUCHAMP	31 Jul 07
Loc.Govt.B.	**J. BURNS**	10 Dec 05	*Master*	E of SEFTON	18 Dec 05
P.S.	W. Runciman	18 Dec 05	*of Horse*	E of GRANARD	6 Sep 07
	T. Macnamara	29 Jan 07	*Cap. Gents*	EARL BEAUCHAMP	18 Dec 05
Paym.-Gen.	R. CAUSTON	12 Dec 05	*at Arms*	LD DENMAN	31 Jul 07
Postm.-Gen.	**S. BUXTON**	10 Dec 05	*Cap.Yeo.*	D of MANCHESTER	18 Dec 05
Scotland	**J. SINCLAIR**	10 Dec 05	*of Guard*	LD ALLENDALE	29 Apr 07
B. Trade	**D. LLOYD GEORGE**	10 Dec 05	*Lds in*	Ld Denman	18 Dec 05–31 Jul 07
P.S.	H. Kearley	18 Dec 05	*Waiting*	E of Granard	18 Dec 05–21 Aug 07
War	**R. HALDANE**	10 Dec 05		Ld Acton	18 Dec 05–5 Apr 08
U.-S.	E of Portsmouth	12 Dec 05		Earl Granville	18 Dec 05–5 Apr 08
F.S.	T. Buchanan	14 Dec 05		Ld Hamilton of	
Works	L. HARCOURT	10 Dec 05		Dalzell	18 Dec 05–5 Apr 08
	(*office in cabinet*)			Ld Colebrooke	20 Dec 05–5 Apr 08
	L. HARCOURT	27 Mar 07		Ld Herschell	31 Jul 07–5 Apr 08
Law Officers				Ld O'Hagan	1 Nov 07–5 Apr 08
Att.-Gen.	SIR J. WALTON	12 Dec 05			

[1] M.P. Not a Member of the House of Lords

LIBERAL GOVERNMENT, 1908–1915

P.M.	H. ASQUITH	5 Apr 08–25 May 15
Ld Pres.	LD TWEEDMOUTH	12 Apr 08
	VT WOLVERHAMPTON	13 Oct 08
	EARL BEAUCHAMP	16 Jun 10
	VT MORLEY	3 Nov 10
	EARL BEAUCHAMP	5 Aug 14
Ld Chanc.	LD LOREBURN (*Earl*)	12 Apr 08
	VT HALDANE	10 Jun 12
Privy S.	M of RIPON	12 Apr 08
	E of CREWE	9 Oct 08
	EARL CARRINGTON	23 Oct 11
	M of CREWE	13 Feb 12
Exchequer	D. LLOYD GEORGE	12 Apr 08
F.S.	C. Hobhouse	12 Apr 08
	T. McKinnon Wood	23 Oct 11
	C. Masterman	13 Feb 12
	E. Montagu	11 Feb 14
	F. Acland	3 Feb 15
Foreign O.	SIR E. GREY	12 Apr 08
U-S.	Ld Fitzmaurice	12 Apr 08
	T. McKinnon Wood	19 Oct 08
	F. Acland	23 Oct 11
	N. Primrose	4 Feb 15
Home O.	H. GLADSTONE	12 Apr 08
	W. CHURCHILL	14 Feb 10
	R. MCKENNA	23 Oct 11
U-S.	H. Samuel	12 Apr 08
	C. Masterman	7 Jul 09
	E. Griffith	19 Feb 12
	C. Harmsworth	4 Feb 15
Admiralty	R. MCKENNA	12 Apr 08
	W. CHURCHILL	23 Oct 11
P. & F.S.	T. Macnamara	13 Apr 08
Civil Ld	G. Lambert	12 Apr 08
B. Ag. & Fish.	EARL CARRINGTON	12 Apr 08
	W. Runciman	23 Oct 11
	LD LUCAS	6 Aug 14
P.S.	(*post not established*)	
	Sir E. Strachey	
	(*Ld Strachie*)	20 Dec 09
	Ld Lucas	23 Oct 11
	Sir H. Verney	10 Aug 14
Colonies	E of CREWE	12 Apr 08
	L. HARCOURT	3 Nov 10
U-S.	J. Seely	12 Apr 08
	Ld Lucas	23 Mar 11
	Ld Emmott	23 Oct 11
	Ld Islington	10 Aug 14
B. Educ.	W. RUNCIMAN	12 Apr 08
	J. PEASE	23 Oct 11
P.S.	T. McKinnon Wood	13 Apr 08
	C. Trevelyan	19 Oct 08
	C. Addison	10 Aug 14
India	J. MORLEY (*Vt*)	12 Apr 08
	E of CREWE	3 Nov 10
	VT MORLEY	7 Mar 11
	E of CREWE (*M of*)	25 May 11
U-S.	T. Buchanan	12 Apr 08
	Master of Elibank	25 Jun 09
	E. Montagu	20 Feb 10
	C. Roberts	17 Feb 14

Chief Sec. Ireland	A. BIRRELL	12 Apr 08
V. Pres. Dept. Agric. Ireland	T. Russell	12 Apr 08
D. Lanc.	SIR H. FOWLER	12 Apr 08
	(*Vt Wolverhampton*)	
	LD FITZMAURICE	13 Oct 08
	H. SAMUEL	25 Jun 09
	J. PEASE	14 Feb 10
	C. HOBHOUSE	23 Oct 11
	C. MASTERMAN	11 Feb 14
	E. MONTAGU	3 Feb 15
Loc. Govt B.	J. BURNS	12 Apr 08
	H. SAMUEL	11 Feb 14
P.S.	C. Masterman	12 Apr 08
	H. Lewis	7 Jul 09
Paym-Gen.	R. CAUSTON	12 Apr 08
	(*Ld Southwark*)	
	I. GUEST	23 Feb 10
	(*Ld Ashby St Ledgers*)	
	LD STRACHIE	23 May 12
Post.-Gen.	S. BUXTON	12 Apr 08
	H. SAMUEL	14 Feb 10
	C. HOBHOUSE	11 Feb 14
Ass.	(*post not established*)	
	Sir H. Norman	3 Jan 10
	C. Norton	20 Feb 10
Scotland	J. SINCLAIR (*Ld Pentland*)	12 Apr 08
	T. MCKINNON WOOD	13 Feb 12
B. Trade	W. CHURCHILL	12 Apr 08
	S. BUXTON	14 Feb 10
	J. BURNS	11 Feb 14
	W. RUNCIMAN	5 Aug 14
P.S.	(Sir) H. Kearley	12 Apr 08
	H. Tennant	10 Jan 09
	J. Robertson	25 Oct 11
War	R. HALDANE (*Vt*)	12 Apr 08
	J. SEELY	12 Jun 12
	H. ASQUITH (*P.M.*)	30 Mar 14
	EARL KITCHENER	5 Aug 14
F.S.	F. Acland	12 Apr 08
	C. Mallet	4 Mar 10
	F. Acland	31 Jan 11
	H. Tennant	25 Oct 11
	H. Baker	14 Jun 12
U-S.	Ld Lucas	12 Apr 08
	J. Seely	23 Mar 11
	H. Tennant	14 Jun 12
Works	L. HARCOURT	12 Apr 08
	EARL BEAUCHAMP	3 Nov 10
	LD EMMOTT	6 Aug 14
Law Officers		
Att.-Gen.	SIR W. ROBSON	12 Apr 08
	SIR R. ISAACS	7 Oct 10
	(*office in cabinet*)	
	SIR R. ISAACS	4 Jun 12
	SIR J. SIMON	19 Oct 13
Sol.-Gen.	SIR S. EVANS	12 Apr 08
	SIR R. ISAACS	6 Mar 10
	SIR J. SIMON	7 Oct 10

LIBERAL GOVERNMENT, 1908–1915 *(contd.)*

Sol.-Gen.	SIR S. BUCKMASTER	19 Oct 13	*Lds of*	F. Guest	16 Apr 11–21 Feb 12
Ld Advoc.	T. SHAW	12 Apr 08	*Treasury*	Sir A. Haworth	23 Feb 12–16 Apr 12
	A. URE	14 Feb 09	*(contd.)*	H. Webb	16 Apr 12–25 May 15
	R. MUNRO	30 Oct 13		C. Beck	3 Feb 15–25 May 15
Sol.-Gen.	A. URE	12 Apr 08		W. Rea	3 Feb 15–25 May 15
Scotland	A. DEWAR	18 Feb 09	***H.M. Household***		
	W. HUNTER	18 Apr 10	*Treasurer*	SIR E. STRACHEY	12 Apr 08
	A. ANDERSON	3 Dec 11		W. DUDLEY WARD	20 Dec 09
	T. MORISON	30 Oct 13		F. GUEST	21 Feb 12
Att.-Gen.	R. CHERRY	12 Apr 08	*Compt.*	MASTER of ELIBANK	12 Apr 08
Ireland	R. BARRY	2 Dec 09		E of LIVERPOOL (*2nd*)	12 Jul 09
	C. O'CONNOR	26 Sep 11		LD SAYE & SELE	1 Nov 12
	I. O'BRIEN	24 Jun 12	*V. Chamb.*	(SIR) J. FULLER	12 Apr 08
	T. MOLONY	10 Apr 13		G. HOWARD	6 Feb 11
	J. MORIARTY	20 Jun 13	*Ld Chamb.*	Vt ALTHORP	12 Apr 08
	J. PIM	1 Jul 14		(*Earl Spencer*)	
Sol.-Gen.	R. BARRY	12 Apr 08		LD SANDHURST	14 Feb 12
Ireland	C. O'CONNOR	2 Dec 09	*Ld Steward*	EARL BEAUCHAMP	12 Apr 08
	I. O'BRIEN	19 Oct 11		E of CHESTERFIELD	22 Jun 10
	T. MOLONY	24 Jun 12	*M. of Horse*	E of GRANARD	12 Apr 08
	J. MORIARTY	25 Apr 13	*Cap. Gents*	LD DENMAN	12 Apr 08
	J. PIM	20 Jun 13	*at Arms*	LD COLEBROOKE	26 Jun 11
	J. O'CONNOR	1 Jul 14	*Cap. Yeo.*	LD ALLENDALE (*Vt*)	12 Apr 08
Whips			*of Guard*	E of CRAVEN	2 Oct 11
P.S. to	G. Whiteley	12 Apr 08	*Lds in*	Ld O'Hagan	12 Apr 08–15 Apr 10
Treasury	J. Pease	3 Jun 08	*Waiting*	Ld Hamilton of Dalzell	
	Master of Elibank	14 Feb 10			12 Apr 08–2 Oct 11
	P. Illingworth	7 Aug 12		Ld Colebrooke	12 Apr 08–26 Jun 11
	J. Gulland	24 Jan 15		Ld Herschell	12 Apr 08–25 May 15
Lds of	J. Pease	12 Apr 08–3 Jun 08		Ld Acton	12 Apr 08–25 May 15
Treasury	H. Lewis	12 Apr 08–7 Jul 09		Earl Granville	12 Apr 08–25 May 15
	C. Norton	12 Aor 08–7 Jul 09		Ld Tweedmouth	15 Apr 10–4 Dec 11
	J. Whitley	12 Apr 08–20 Feb 10		Ld Willingdon	19 Jul 11–31 Jan 13
	O. Partington	6 Jul 09–19 Jan 11		Vt Allendale	2 Oct 11–25 May 15
	J. Gulland	7 Jul 09–24 Jan 15		Ld Loch	4 Dec 11–1 May 14
	W. Benn	20 Feb 10–25 May 15		Ld Ashby St Ledgers	
	E. Soares	20 Feb 10–16 Apr 11		(*Ld Wimborne*)	31 Jan 13–8 Feb 15
	P. Illingworth	28 Feb 10–7 Aug 12		Ld Stanmore	1 May 14–25 May 15
	W. Jones	19 Jan 11–25 May 15		Ld Ranksborough	8 Feb 15–25 May 15

COALITION GOVERNMENT, 1915–1916

P.M.	H. ASQUITH (Lib)		*U.-S. Ass.*	Ld Newton (C)	18 Aug 16
		25 May 15–5 Dec 16	*Home O.*	SIR J. SIMON (Lib)	25 May 15
Ld Pres.	M of CREWE (Lib)	25 May 15		SIR H. SAMUEL (Lib)	10 Jan 16
Ld Chanc.	LD BUCKMASTER (Lib)	25 May 15	*U.-S.*	W. Brace (Lab)	30 May 15
Privy S	EARL CURZON (C)	25 May 15	*Admiralty*	A. BALFOUR (C)	25 May 15
Exchequer	R. MCKENNA (Lib)	25 May 15	*P. & F.S.*	T. Macnamara (Lib)	30 May 15
F.S.	E. Montagu (Lib)	26 May 15	*Civil Ld*	D of Devonshire (C)	9 Jun 15
	(*also D. Lanc.*)			E of Lytton (C)	26 Jul 16
	(*office in cabinet*)		*B. Ag. &*	E of SELBORNE (C)	25 May 15
	E. MONTAGU (Lib)	16 Jan 16	*Fish.*	E of CRAWFORD (C)	11 Jul 16
	T. MCKINNON WOOD (Lib)		*P.S.*	F. Acland (Lib)	30 May 15
		9 Jul 16	*Blockade*	LD R. CECIL[1] (C)	23 Feb 16
Foreign O.	SIR E. GREY (*Vt*) (Lib)	25 May 15		(*also U.-S. at F.O.*)	
U.-S.	Ld R. Cecil[1] (C)	30 May 15	*Colonies*	A. BONAR LAW (C)	25 May 15
	(*also Blockade*)		*U.-S.*	A. Steel-Maitland (C)	30 May 15
	(*office in cabinet*)		*B. Educ.*	A. HENDERSON (Lab)	25 May 15
	LD R. CECIL[1] (C)	23 Feb 16		M of CREWE (Lib)	18 Aug 16

[1] M.P. Not a Member of the House of Lords

COALITION GOVERNMENT, 1915–1916 (contd.)

B. Educ. P.S.	H. Lewis (Lib)	30 May 15	*F.S.*	H. Forster (C)	30 May 15
Health &	**W. LONG** (C)	25 May 15	*Works*	**L. HARCOURT** (*Vt*) (Lib)	25 May 15
L. Govt. B.			***Law Officers***		
P.S.	W. Hayes Fisher (C)	30 May 15	*Att.-Gen.*	**SIR E. CARSON** (C)	25 May 15
India	**A. CHAMBERLAIN** (C)	25 May 15		**SIR F. SMITH** (C)	3 Nov 15
U-S.	Ld Islington (Lib)	30 May 15	*Sol.-Gen.*	SIR F. SMITH (C)	2 Jun 15
Chief Sec.	A. BIRRELL (Lib)	25 May 15		(SIR) G. CAVE (C)	8 Nov 15
Ireland	(*office vacant 3 May 16*)		*Ld Advoc.*	R. MUNRO (Lib)	8 Jun 15
	H. DUKE (C)	31 Jul 16	*Sol.-Gen.*	T. MORISON (Lib)	8 Jun 15
V. Pres.	T. Russell (Lib)	30 May 15	*Scotland*		
Dept. Agric.			*Att.-Gen.*	J. GORDON (C)	8 Jun 15
for Ireland			*Ireland*	J. CAMPBELL (C)	9 Apr 16
D. Lanc.	**W. CHURCHILL** (Lib)	25 May 15	*Sol.-Gen.*	J. O'CONNOR (Nat)	8 Jun 15
	H. SAMUEL (Lib)	25 Nov 15	*Ireland*		
	E. MONTAGU (Lib)	11 Jan 16	***Whips***		
	(*also F.S. at Treasury*)		*P.S. to*	J. Gulland (Lib)	30 May 15–5 Dec 16
	T. MCKINNON WOOD (Lib)	9 Jul 16	*Treasury*	Ld E. Talbot[1] (C)	30 May 15–5 Dec 16
	(*also F.S. at Treasury*)		*Lds of*	G. Howard (Lib)	27 May 15–5 Dec 16
Munitions	**D. LLOYD GEORGE** (Lib)	25 May 15	*Treasury*	G. Roberts (Lab)	27 May 15–5 Dec 16
	E. MONTAGU (Lib)	9 Jul 16		W. Bridgeman (C)	27 May 15–5 Dec 16
P.S.	C. Addison (Lib)	30 May 15–8 Dec 16		W. Rea (Lib)	27 May 15–5 Dec 16
	A. Lee (C)	11 Nov 15[2]–9 Jul 16	***H. M. Household***		
Nat. Service	N. CHAMBERLAIN	19 Aug 16	*Treasurer*	J. HOPE (C)	30 May 15
Paym.-Gen.	**LD NEWTON** (C)	9 Jun 15	*Compt.*	C. ROBERTS (Lib)	30 May 15
	(*office in cabinet*)		*V. Chamb.*	C. BECK (Lib)	30 May 15
	A. HENDERSON (Lab)	18 Aug 16	*Ld Chamb.*	LD SANDHURST (Lib)	9 Jun 15
Min. without	**M of LANSDOWNE** (C)	25 May 15	*Ld Steward*	LD FARQUHAR (C)	9 Jun 15
Portfolio			*Master*	E of CHESTERFIELD (Lib)	
Postm. Gen.	**H. SAMUEL** (Lib)	26 May 15	*of Horse*		9 Jun 15
	J. PEASE (Lib)	18 Jan 16	*Cap. Gents*	LD COLEBROOKE (Lib)	9 Jun 15
Ass.	H. Pike Pease (C)	30 May 15	*at Arms*		
Scotland	**T. MCKINNON WOOD** (Lib)		*Cap. Yeo.*	LD SUFFIELD (C)	9 Jun 15
		25 May 15	*of Guard*		
	H. TENNANT (Lib)	9 Jul 16	*Lds in*	Ld Herschell (Lib)	9 Jun 15–5 Dec 16
B Trade	**W. RUNCIMAN** (Lib)	25 May 15	*Waiting*	Vt Allendale (Lib)	9 Jun 15–5 Dec 16
P.S.	E. Pretyman (C)	30 May 15		Ld Stanmore (Lib)	9 Jun 15–5 Dec 16
War	**EARL KITCHENER**	25 May 15		Ld Ranksborough (Lib)	
	D. LLOYD GEORGE (Lib)	6 Jul 16			9 Jun 15–5 Dec 16
U-S.	H. Tennant (Lib)	30 May 15		Vt Valentia[1] (C)	9 Jun 15–5 Dec 16
	E of Derby (C)	6 Jul 16		Ld Hylton (C)	9 Jun 15–5 Dec 16

COALITION GOVERNMENT, 1916–1922

From 6 Dec 1916 to 31 Oct 1919 there was an inner war cabinet of 5–7 ministers.

Three were members throughout:

    D. LLOYD GEORGE
    EARL CURZON
    A. BONAR LAW

The other members were:

A. HENDERSON (Lab)	10 Dec 16–12 Aug 17	
VT MILNER (C)	10 Dec 16–18 Apr 18	
J. SMUTS[2]	22 Jun 17–10 Jan 19	
G. BARNES (Lab)	29 May 17–3 Aug 17	
	13 Aug 17–10 Jan 19	
A. CHAMBERLAIN (C)	18 Apr 18–31 Oct 19	
SIR E. GEDDES (C)	10 Jan 19–31 Oct 19	

P.M.	**D. LLOYD GEORGE** (Lib)	
		6 Dec 16–19 Oct 22
Ld Pres.	**EARL CURZON** (C)	10 Dec 16
	A. BALFOUR (C)	23 Oct 19
Ld Chanc.	**LD FINLAY** (C)	10 Dec 16
	LD BIRKENHEAD (*Vt*) (C)	10 Jan 19
Privy S.	**E of CRAWFORD** (C)	15 Dec 16
	A. BONAR LAW (C)	10 Jan 19
	A. CHAMBERLAIN (C)	23 Mar 21
Exchequer	**A. BONAR LAW** (C)	10 Dec 16
	A. CHAMBERLAIN (C)	10 Jan 19
	SIR R. HORNE (C)	1 Apr 21
F.S.	Sir H. Lever (Lib)	15 Dec 16–19 May 19
	S. Baldwin (C)	18 Jun 17–1 Apr 21

[1] M.P. Not a Member of the House of Lords
[2] Not a Member of the House of Commons

COALITION GOVERNMENT, 1916–1922 (contd.)

F.S. (contd.)	E. Young (Lib)	1 Apr 21–19 Oct 22
Foreign O.	**A. BALFOUR** (C)	10 Dec 16
	EARL CURZON (*Marq.*) (C)	
		23 Oct 19
U-S.	Ld R. Cecil[1] (C)	10 Dec 16
	C. Harmsworth (Lib)	10 Jan 19
Ass. U-S.	Ld Newton (C)	10 Dec 16
	(*post abolished 10 Jan 19*)	
Home O.	**SIR G. CAVE** (*Vt*) (C)	10 Dec 16
	E. SHORTT (Lib)	10 Jan 19
U-S.	W. Brace (Lab)	10 Dec 16
	Sir H. Greenwood (Lib)	10 Jan 19
	(Sir) J. Baird (C)	29 Apr 19
Admiralty	**SIR E. CARSON** (C)	10 Dec 16
	SIR E. GEDDES (C)	17 Jul 17
	W. LONG (C)	10 Jan 19
	LD LEE (C)	13 Feb 21
P.& F.S	T. Macnamara (Lib)	10 Dec 16
	Sir J. Craig (C)	2 Apr 20
	L. Amery (C)	1 Apr 21
Add. P.S	E of Lytton (C)	7 Feb 17
	(*post abolished 27 Jan 19*)	
Civil Ld	E. Pretyman (C)	14 Dec 16
	E of Lytton (C)	27 Jan 19
	E of Onslow (C)	26 Oct 20
	B. Eyres-Monsell (C)	1 Apr 21
2nd. Civil Ld	A. Pease (C)	10 Dec 16
	(*post abolished 10 Jan 19*)	
Ag. & Fish.	**R. PROTHERO**	10 Dec 16
	(*Ld Ernle*) (C)	
	LD LEE (C)	15 Aug 19
	(*Board renamed Min. 15 Aug 19*)	
	SIR A. GRIFFITH-BOSCAWEN (C)	
		13 Feb 21
P.S.	Sir R. Winfrey (Lib)	
		14 Dec 16–10 Jan 19
	D of Marlborough (C)	
		18 Feb 17–21 Mar 18
	Vt Goschen (C)	26 Mar 18–18 Jun 18
	Ld Clinton (C)	18 Jun 18–10 Jan 19
	Sir A. Griffith-Boscawen (C)	
		10 Jan 19–13 Feb 21
	(*& Dep. Min. Fisheries 18 Nov 19*)	
	E of Onslow (C)	5 Apr 21–7 Apr 21
	E of Ancaster (C)	7 Apr 21–19 Oct 22
	(*& Dep. Min. Fisheries 28 Oct 21*)	
Air	**LD COWDRAY** (Lib)	3 Jan 17
	LD ROTHERMERE (Lib)	26 Nov 17
	LD WEIR (Lib)	26 Apr 18
	(*War & Air combined 10 Jan 19–13 Feb 21*)	
	W. CHURCHILL (Lib)	10 Jan 19
	(*office not in cabinet*)	
	F. GUEST (Lib)	1 Apr 21
P.S. Air	J. Baird (C)	14 Dec 16
Council	(*post abolished 10 Jan 19*)	
U-S.	J. Seely (Lib)	10 Jan 19
	G. Tryon (C)	22 Dec 19
	M of Londonderry (C)	2 Apr 20
	Ld Gorell (Lib)	18 Jul 21

Blockade	LD R. CECIL[1] (C)	10 Dec 16
	(*also U-S. at Foreign O.*)	
	SIR L. WORTHINGTON-EVANS (C)	
		18 Jul 18
	(*office abolished 10 Jan 19*)	
P.S.	F. Leverton Harris (C)	22 Dec 16
	(*post abolished 10 Jan 19*)	
Colonies	**W. LONG** (C)	10 Dec 16
	VT MILNER (C)	10 Jan 19
	W. CHURCHILL (Lib)	13 Feb 21
U-S.	(Sir) A. Steel-Maitland (C)	10 Dec 16
	W. Hewins (C)	26 Sep 17
	L. Amery (C)	10 Jan 19
	E. Wood (C)	1 Apr 21
B. Educ.	**H. FISHER** (Lib)	10 Dec 16
P.S.	(Sir) H. Lewis (Lib)	10 Dec 16
Food	**VT DEVONPORT** (Lib)	10 Dec 16
Control	**LD RHONDDA** (*Vt*) (Lib)	19 Jun 17
	J. CLYNES (Lab)	9 Jul 18
	G. ROBERTS (Lab)	10 Jan 19
	C. McCURDY (Lib)	19 Mar 20
	(*office abolished 31 Mar 21*)	
P.S.	(Sir) C. Bathurst (C)	12 Dec 16
	J. Clynes (Lab)	2 Jul 17
	W. Astor (C)	18 Jul 18
	C. McCurdy (Lib)	27 Jan 19
	Sir W. Mitchell-Thomson (C)	
		19 Apr 20
Health	(*Dept under Loc. Govt Bd*)	
	C. ADDISON (Lib)	24 Jun 19
	SIR A. MOND (Lib)	1 Apr 21
P.S. (Loc.	W. Hayes Fisher (C)	10 Dec 16
Govt Bd.)	S. Walsh (Lab)	28 Jun 17
	W. Astor (*Vt*) (C)	27 Jan 19
	E of Onslow (C)	7 Apr 21
India	**A. CHAMBERLAIN** (C)	10 Dec 16
	E. MONTAGU (Lib)	17 Jul 17
	VT PEEL (C)	19 Mar 22
U-S.	Ld Islington (Lib)	10 Dec 16
	Ld Sinha (Lib)	10 Jan 19
	E of Lytton (C)	22 Sep 20
	Earl Winterton (C)	20 Mar 22
Ld Lieut.	(*not usually min. office*)	
Ireland	Vt FRENCH	6 May 18
	(*office in cabinet*)	
	VT FRENCH (*E of Ypres*)	28 Oct 18
	(*office not in cabinet 2 Apr 21*)	
Chief Sec.	(Sir) H. DUKE (C)	10 Dec 16
Ireland	E. SHORTT (Lib)	5 May 18
	I. MACPHERSON (Lib)	10 Jan 19
	SIR H. GREENWOOD (Lib)	
		2 Apr 20
V. Pres.	(Sir) T. Russell (Lib)	10 Dec 16
Dept. Agric.	H. Barrie (C)	15 Jan 19
Ireland		
Labour	**J. HODGE** (Lab)	10 Dec 16
	G. ROBERTS (Lab)	17 Aug 17
	SIR R. HORNE (C)	10 Jan 19
	T. MACNAMARA (Lib)	19 Mar 20

[1] M.P. Not a Member of the House of Lords

COALITION GOVERNMENT, 1916–1922 (contd.)

Labour P.S.	W. Bridgeman (C)	22 Dec 16	*Min.*	**SIR E. CARSON** (C)	
	G. Wardle (Lab)	10 Jan 19	*without*		17 Jul 17–21 Jan 18
	Sir A. Montague-Barlow (C)	2 Apr 20	*Portfolio*	**G. BARNES** (Lab)	
D. Lanc.	**SIR F. CAWLEY** (Lib)	10 Dec 16	*(contd.)*		13 Aug 17–27 Jan 20
	LD BEAVERBROOK (C)	10 Feb 18		**A. CHAMBERLAIN** (C)	
	(*& Min. of Propaganda/Information*)				18 Apr 18–10 Jan 19
	LD DOWNHAM (C)	4 Nov 18		**SIR E. GEDDES** (C)	
	(office not in cabinet)				10 Jan 19–19 May 19
	E of CRAWFORD (C)	10 Jan 19		**SIR L. WORTHINGTON-EVANS** (C)	
	VT PEEL (C)	1 Apr 21			2 Apr 20–13 Feb 21
	SIR W. SUTHERLAND (Lib)			**C. ADDISON** (Lib) 1 Apr 21–14 Jul 21	
		7 Apr 22	*Reconstruc.*	C. ADDISON (Lib)	17 Jul 17
Loc. Govt B.	**LD RHONDDA** (Lib)	10 Dec 16		*(office combined with Nat. Service*	
	W. HAYES FISHER	28 Jun 17		*10 Jan 19; for junior Ministers see*	
	(*Ld Downham*) (C)			*National Service & Reconstruction*)	
	SIR A. GEDDES (C)	4 Nov 18	*Scotland*	R. MUNRO (Lib)	10 Dec 16
	C. ADDISON (Lib)	10 Jan 19	*P.S. Min. of*	(Sir) J. Pratt (Lib)	8 Aug 19
	(24 Jun 19 became Min. of Health)		*Health for*		
Munitions	**C. ADDISON** (Lib)	10 Dec 16	*Scotland*		
(Supply)	**W. CHURCHILL** (Lib)	17 Jul 17	*Shipping*	SIR J. MACLAY (*Ld*) (Lib)	10 Dec 16
	(office not in cabinet)			*(office abolished 31 Mar 21)*	
	Ld Inverforth (C)	10 Jan 19	*P.S.*	Sir L. Chiozza Money (Lib)	22 Dec 16
P.S.	Sir L. Worthington-Evans (C)			L. Wilson (C)	10 Jan 19
		14 Dec 16–30 Jan 18	*Supply*	LD INVERFORTH (C)	10 Jan 19
	F. Kellaway (Lib) 14 Dec 16–1 Apr 20			*(office abolished 31 Mar 21)*	
	J. Seely (Lib) 10 Jul 18–10 Jan 19		*B. Trade*	**SIR A. STANLEY** (Lib)	10 Dec 16
	J. Baird (C) 10 Jan 19–29 Apr 19			**SIR A. GEDDES** (C)	26 May 19
P. & F. S.	Sir L. Worthington-Evans (C)			**SIR R. HORNE** (C)	19 Mar 20
		30 Jan 18–18 Jul 18		**S. BALDWIN** (C)	1 Apr 21
	J. Hope (C) 27 Jan 19–31 Mar 21		*P.S.*	G. Roberts (Lab)	14 Dec 16
National	N. CHAMBERLAIN[1] (C)	15 Dec 16		G. Wardle (Lab)	17 Aug 17
Service	SIR A. GEDDES (C)	17 Aug 17		W. Bridgeman (C)	10 Jan 19
	(office held jointly with			Sir P. Lloyd-Greame (C)	22 Aug 20
	Reconstruction Jan–May 19 & with			Sir W. Mitchell-Thomson (C)	1 Apr 21
	B. of Trade May–Aug 19; formally		*Sec.*	Sir A. Steel-Maitland (C)	14 Sep 17
	abolished 19 Dec 19)		*Overseas*	Sir H. Greenwood (Lib)	29 Apr 19
P.S.	S. Walsh (Lab) 17 Mar 17–28 Jun 17		*Trade*	F. Kellaway (Lib)	2 Apr 20
	C. Beck (Lib) 28 Jun 17–19 Dec 19			Sir P. Lloyd-Greame (C)	1 Apr 21
	Vt Peel (C) 15 Apr 18–10 Jan 19			*(Director Overseas Trade)*	
	(post abolished 19 Dec 19)		*P.S. Mines*	W. Bridgeman (C)	22 Aug 20
Paym.-Gen.	SIR J. COMPTON-RICKETT (Lib)		*Transport*	*(office not established)*	
		15 Dec 16		**SIR E. GEDDES** (C)	19 May 19
	SIR T. WALTERS (Lib)	26 Oct 19		*(office not in cabinet)*	
Pensions	G. BARNES (Lab)	10 Dec 16		Vt Peel (C)	7 Nov 21
	J. HODGE (Lab)	17 Aug 17		*(office in cabinet)*	
	SIR L. WORTHINGTON-EVANS (C)			**E of CRAWFORD** (C)	12 Apr 22
		10 Jan 19	*P.S.*	Sir R. Williams (Lib)	23 Sep 19
	I. MACPHERSON (Lib)	2 Apr 20		A. Neal (Lib)	28 Nov 19
P.S.	Sir A. Griffith-Boscawen (C)		*War*	**E of DERBY** (C)	10 Dec 16
		22 Dec 16		**VT MILNER** (C)	18 Apr 18
	Sir J. Craig (C)	10 Jan 19		*(10 Jan 19 War O.& Air Min. combined)*	
	G. Tryon (C)	2 Apr 20		**W. CHURCHILL** (Lib)	10 Jan 19
Postm.-Gen.	A. ILLINGWORTH (Lib)	10 Dec 16		*(13 Feb 21 War only)*	
	F. KELLAWAY (Lib)	1 Apr 21		**SIR L. WORTHINGTON-EVANS** (C)	
Ass.	H. Pike Pease (C)	10 Dec 16			13 Feb 21
Min.	**A. HENDERSON** (Lab)		*U-S.*	I. Macpherson (Lib)	14 Dec 16
without		10 Dec 16–12 Aug 17		Vt Peel (C)	10 Jan 19
Portfolio	**VT MILNER** (C) 10 Dec 16–18 Apr 18			Sir R. Sanders (C)	1 Apr 21
	J. SMUTS[1] 22 Jun 17–10 Jan 19		*F.S.*	H. Forster (*Ld*) (C)	10 Dec 16

[1] Not a Member of the House of Commons

COALITION GOVERNMENT, 1916–1922 (contd.)

F.S.	Sir A. Williamson (Lib)	18 Dec 19		*Lds of*	J. Hope (C)	14 Dec 16–27 Jan 19
(contd.)	G. Stanley (C)	1 Apr 21		*Treasury*	J. Pratt (Lib)	14 Dec 16–8 Aug 19
P.S.	Earl Stanhope (C)	14 Dec 16			S. Baldwin (C)	29 Jan 17–18 Jun 17
	(post abolished 10 Jan 19)				J. Parker (Lab)	29 Jan 17–19 Oct 22
Works	SIR A. MOND (Lib)	10 Dec 16			J. Towyn Jones (Lib)	29 Jan 17– 4 Jul 22
	E of CRAWFORD (C)	1 Apr 21			(Sir) R. Sanders (C)	5 Feb 19–1 Apr 21
	(office in cabinet)				Sir G. Collins (Lib)	8 Aug 19–10 Feb 20
	E OF CRAWFORD (C)	7 Apr 22			W. Edge (Lib)	18 Aug 19–1 Aug 22
					Sir W. Sutherland (Lib)	
Law Officers						15 Feb 20– 7 Apr 22
Att.-Gen.	SIR F. SMITH (C)	10 Dec 16			Sir J. Gilmour (C)	1 Apr 21–19 Oct 22
	(Ld Birkenhead)				T. Lewis (Lib)	4 Jul 22–26 Jul 22
	SIR G. HEWART (Lib)	10 Jan 19				
	(office in cabinet)			*H. M Household*		
	SIR G. HEWART (Lib)	7 Nov 21		*Treasurer*	(SIR) J. CRAIG (C)	14 Dec 16
	SIR E. POLLOCK (C)	6 Mar 22			*(office vacant 22 Jan 18)*	
Sol.-Gen.	SIR G. HEWART (Lib)	10 Dec 16			R. SANDERS (C)	11 Jun 18
	SIR E. POLLOCK (C)	10 Jan 19			B. EYRES-MONSELL (C)	5 Feb 19
	(SIR) L. SCOTT (C)	6 Mar 22			G. GIBBS (C)	1 Apr 21
Ld Advoc.	J. CLYDE (C)	10 Dec 16		*Compt.*	SIR E. CORNWALL (Lib)	14 Dec 16
	T. MORISON (Lib)	25 Mar 20			G. STANLEY (C)	28 Feb 19
	C. MURRAY (C)	5 Mar 22			H. BARNSTON (C)	7 Apr 21
Sol.-Gen.	T. MORISON (Lib)	10 Dec 16		*V. Chamb.*	C. BECK (Lib)	14 Dec 16
Scotland	C. MURRAY (C)	25 Mar 20			W. DUDLEY WARD (Lib)	9 Dec 17
	A. BRIGGS CONSTABLE (C)			*Ld Chamb.*	LD SANDHURST (*Vt*) (Lib)	
		16 Mar 22				14 Dec 16
	W. WATSON (C)	24 Jul 22			D of ATHOLL (C)	20 Nov 21
Ld Chanc.	SIR J. O'BRIEN (Lib)	10 Dec 16		*Ld Steward*	LD FARQUHAR (*Vt*) (C)	14 Dec 16
Ireland	SIR J. CAMPBELL (C)	4 Jun 18		*Master*	E of CHESTERFIELD (Lib)	14 Dec 16
	SIR J. ROSS (C)	27 Jun 21		*of Horse*		
Att.-Gen.	J. O'CONNOR (Nat)	8 Jan 17		*Cap. Gents*	LD COLEBROOKE (Lib)	14 Dec 16
Ireland	A. SAMUELS (C)	7 Apr 18		*at Arms*		
	D. HENRY (C)	6 Jul 19		*Cap. Yeo.*	LD SUFFIELD (C)	14 Dec 16
	T. BROWN (C)	5 Aug 21		*of Guard*	LD HYLTON (C)	21 May 18
	(office vacant from 16 Nov 21)			*Lds in*	Ld Herschell (Lib)	14 Dec 16–11 Feb 19
Sol.-Gen.	J. CHAMBERS (C)	19 Mar 17		*Waiting*	Ld Stanmore (Lib)	14 Dec 16–19 Oct 22
Ireland	A. SAMUELS (C)	12 Sep 17			Ld Ranksborough (Lib)	
	J. POWELL[2] (C)	7 Apr 18				14 Dec 16– 4 Apr 21
	D. HENRY (C)	27 Nov 18			Vt Valentia (C)	14 Dec 16–19 Oct 22
	D. WILSON (C)	6 Jul 19			Ld Hylton (C)	14 Dec 16–18 May 18
	T. BROWN (C)	12 Jun 21			Ld Kenyon (C)	14 Dec 16–11 Sep 18
	(office vacant from 5 Aug 21)				Ld Somerleyton (C)	
Whips						18 May 18–19 Oct 22
P.S. to	Ld E. Talbot[1] (C)	14 Dec 16–1 Apr 21			E of Jersey (C)	11 Jan 19–17 Aug 19
Treasury	N. Primrose (Lib)	14 Dec 16–2 Mar 17			E of Bradford (C)	11 Feb 19–19 Oct 22
	F. Guest (Lib)	2 Mar 17–1 Apr 21			E of Onslow (C)	17 Aug 19–21 Nov 20
	C. McCurdy (Lib)	1 Apr 21–19 Oct 22			E of Lucan (C)	12 Nov 20–19 Oct 22
	L. Wilson (C)	1 Apr 21–19 Oct 22			E of Clarendon (C)	4 Apr 21–19 Oct 22

CONSERVATIVE GOVERNMENT, 1922–24

P.M.	**A. BONAR LAW**			*Privy S.*	LD R. CECIL[1]	25 May 23
		23 Oct 22–20 May 23		*(contd.)*		
	S. BALDWIN	22 May 23–22 Jan 24		*Exchequer*	**S. BALDWIN**	27 Oct 22
Ld Pres.	**M of SALISBURY**	24 Oct 22			*(& P.M. from 22 May)*	
Ld Chanc.	**VT CAVE**	24 Oct 22			**N. CHAMBERLAIN**	27 Aug 23
Privy S.	*(office vacant)*					

[1] M.P. Not a Member of the House of Lords
[2] Not a Member of the House of Commons

CONSERVATIVE GOVERNMENT, 1922–24 (contd.)

F.S.	J. Hills	6 Nov 22
	A. Boyd-Carpenter	12 Mar 23
	(office in cabinet)	
	SIR W. JOYNSON-HICKS	25 May 23
	(office not in cabinet)	
	W. Guinness	5 Oct 23
Foreign O.	MARQUESS CURZON	24 Oct 22
U-S.	R. McNeill	31 Oct 22
Home O.	W. BRIDGEMAN	24 Oct 22
U-S.	G. Stanley	31 Oct 22
	G. Locker-Lampson	12 Mar 23
Admiralty	L. AMERY	24 Oct 22
P. & F.S.	B. Eyres-Monsell	31 Oct 22
	A. Boyd-Carpenter	25 May 23
Civil Ld	M of Linlithgow	31 Oct 22
Ag. & Fish.	SIR R. SANDERS	24 Oct 22
P.S. Ag. & Deputy Min. Fisheries	E of Ancaster	31 Oct 22
Air	Sir S. Hoare	31 Oct 22
	(office in cabinet)	
	SIR S. HOARE	25 May 23
U-S.	D of Sutherland	31 Oct 22
Colonies	D of DEVONSHIRE	24 Oct 22
U-S.	W. Ormsby-Gore	31 Oct 22
B. Educ.	E. WOOD	24 Oct 22
P.S.	Ld E. Percy[1]	21 Mar 23
	E of Onslow	25 May 23
Health	SIR A. GRIFFITH-BOSCAWEN	24 Oct 22
	N. CHAMBERLAIN	7 Mar 23
	SIR W. JOYNSON-HICKS	27 Aug 23
P.S.	E of Onslow	31 Oct 22
	Ld E. Percy[1]	25 May 23
India	VT PEEL	24 Oct 22
U-S.	Earl Winterton	31 Oct 22
Labour	SIR A. MONTAGUE-BARLOW	31 Oct 22
P.S.	A. Boyd-Carpenter	6 Nov 22
	H. Betterton	12 Mar 23
D. Lanc.	M of SALISBURY	24 Oct 22
	(office not in cabinet)	
	J. DAVIDSON	25 May 23
Paym.-Gen.	(office vacant)	
	N. CHAMBERLAIN	5 Feb 23
	SIR W. JOYNSON-HICKS	15 Mar 23
	A. BOYD-CARPENTER	25 May 23
Pensions	G. TRYON	31 Oct 22
P.S.	C. Craig	13 Feb 23
Postm.-Gen.	N. CHAMBERLAIN	31 Oct 22
	SIR W. JOYNSON-HICKS	7 Mar 23
	(office in cabinet)	
	SIR L. WORTHINGTON-EVANS	28 May 23
Scotland	VT NOVAR	24 Oct 22
P.S. Min. of Health for Scotland	J. Kidd	31 Oct 22
	W. Elliot	15 Jan 23
B. Trade	SIR P. LLOYD-GREAME	24 Oct 22
P.S.	Vt Wolmer[1]	31 Oct 22
Sec. Overseas Trade	Sir W. Joynson-Hicks	31 Oct 22–12 Mar 23
	A. Buckley	12 Mar 23–18 Nov 23
Sec. Mines	G. Lane Fox	6 Nov 22
Transport	SIR J. BAIRD	31 Oct 22
P.S. Off. of Works & Min. of Transport	W. Ashley	31 Oct 22
	J. Moore-Brabazon	8 Oct 23
	(to Min. Transp. only)	
War	E of DERBY	24 Oct 22
U-S.	W. Guinness	31 Oct 22
	W. Ashley	8 Oct 23
F.S.	S. Jackson	31 Oct 22
	R. Gwynne	15 Mar 23
Works	SIR J. BAIRD	31 Oct 22

Law Officers

Att.-Gen.	SIR D. HOGG	24 Oct 22
Sol.-Gen.	SIR T. INSKIP	31 Oct 22
Ld Advoc.	W. WATSON	24 Oct 22
Sol.-Gen. Scotland	D. FLEMING[2]	6 Nov 22
	F. THOMSON	5 Apr 23

Whips

P.S. to Treasury	L. Wilson	31 Oct 22
	B. Eyres-Monsell	25 Jul 23
Lds of Treasury	D. King	31 Oct 22–22 Jan 24
	A. Buckley	31 Oct 22–12 Mar 23
	G. Hennessy	11 Dec 22–22 Jan 24
	F. Thomson	7 Feb 23–10 Apr 23
	W. Cope	20 Mar 23–22 Jan 24
	P. Ford	10 Apr 23–20 Dec 23
	Sir J. Gilmour	20 Dec 23–22 Jan 24

H. M. Household

Treasurer	G. GIBBS	6 Nov 22
Compt.	H. BARNSTON	31 Oct 22
V. Chamb.	D. HACKING	20 Nov 22
Ld Chamb.	E of CROMER	20 Nov 22
Ld Steward	E of SHAFTESBURY	20 Nov 22
Master of Horse	M of BATH	20 Nov 22
Cap. Gents at Arms	E of CLARENDON	20 Nov 22
Cap. Yeo. of Guard	LD HYLTON	20 Nov 22
Lds in Waiting	Vt Valentia	20 Nov 22–22 Jan 24
	Ld Somerleyton	20 Nov 22–22 Jan 24
	E of Bradford	20 Nov 22–22 Jan 24
	E of Lucan	20 Nov 22–22 Jan 24
	E of Malmesbury	20 Nov 22–22 Jan 24
	E of Albemarle	20 Nov 22–22 Jan 24

[1] M.P. Not a Member of the House of Lords
[2] Not a Member of the House of Commons

LABOUR GOVERNMENT, 1924

P.M.	**R. MACDONALD**		*Scotland*	**W. ADAMSON**	22 Jan 24
		22 Jan 24–3 Nov 24	*P.S. Health*	J. Stewart	23 Jan 24
Ld Pres.	**LD PARMOOR**	22 Jan 24	*for Scotland*		
Ld Chanc.	**VT HALDANE**	22 Jan 24	*B.Trade*	**S.WEBB**	22 Jan 24
Privy S.	**J. CLYNES**	22 Jan 24	*P.S.*	A. Alexander	23 Jan 24
Exchequer	**P. SNOWDEN**	22 Jan 24	*Sec.*	W. Lunn	23 Jan 24
F.S.	W. Graham	23 Jan 24	*Overseas*		
Foreign O.	**R. MACDONALD** (*P.M.*)	22 Jan 24	*Trade*		
U-S.	A. Ponsonby	23 Jan 24	*Sec. Mines*	E. Shinwell	23 Jan 24
Home O.	**A. HENDERSON**	22 Jan 24	*Transport*	**H. GOSLING**	24 Jan 24
U-S.	R. Davies	23 Jan 24	*War*	**S.WALSH**	22 Jan 24
Admiralty	**VT CHELMSFORD**	22 Jan 24	*U-S.*	C. Attlee	23 Jan 24
P.& F.S.	C. Ammon	23 Jan 24	*F.S.*	J. Lawson	23 Jan 24
Civil Ld	F. Hodges	24 Jan 24	*Works*	**F. JOWETT**	22 Jan 24
Ag. & Fish.	**N. BUXTON**	22 Jan 24	***Law Officers***		
P.S.	W. Smith	23 Jan 24	*Att.-Gen.*	**SIR P. HASTINGS**	23 Jan 24
Air	**LD THOMSON**	22 Jan 24	*Sol.-Gen.*	**SIR H. SLESSER**	23 Jan 24
U-S.	W. Leach	23 Jan 24	*Ld Advoc.*	H. MACMILLAN[1]	8 Feb 24
Colonies	**J.THOMAS**	22 Jan 24	*Sol.-Gen.*	J. FENTON[1]	18 Feb 24
U-S.	Ld Arnold	23 Jan 24	*Scotland*		
B Educ.	**C. TREVELYAN**	22 Jan 24	***Whips***		
P.S.	M. Jones	23 Jan 24	*P.S. to*	B. Spoor	23 Jan 24
Health	**J.WHEATLEY**	22 Jan 24	*Treasury*		
P.S.	A. Greenwood	23 Jan 24	*Lds of*	F. Hall	2 Feb 24
India	**LD OLIVIER**	22 Jan 24	*Treasury*	T. Kennedy	2 Feb 24
U-S.	R. Richards	23 Jan 24		J. Robertson	2 Feb 24
Labour	**T. SHAW**	22 Jan 24		G. Warne	24 Feb 24
P.S.	Miss M. Bondfield	23 Jan 24	***H.M. Household***		
D. Lanc.	**J.WEDGWOOD**	22 Jan 24	*Treasurer*	**T. GRIFFITHS**	2 Feb 24
Paym.-Gen.	H. GOSLING	6 May 24	*Compt.*	**J. PARKINSON**	2 Feb 24
P.S.	J. Muir	28 Jan 24	*V. Chamb.*	**J. DAVISON**	2 Feb 24
Pensions	**F. ROBERTS**	23 Jan 24	*Lds in*	Earl De La Warr	8 Feb 24
P.S.	(*vacant*)		*Waiting*	Ld Muir-Mackenzie	8 Feb 24
Postm.-Gen.	**V. HARTSHORN**	22 Jan 24			

CONSERVATIVE GOVERNMENT, 1924–1929

P.M.	**S. BALDWIN**	4 Nov 24–4 Jun 29	*P.& F.S*	C. Headlam	16 Dec 26
Ld Pres.	**MARQUESS CURZON**	6 Nov 24	(*contd.*)		
	E of BALFOUR	27 Apr 25	*Civil Ld*	Earl Stanhope	11 Nov 24
Ld Chanc.	**VT CAVE**	6 Nov 24	*Ag. & Fish.*	**E.WOOD**	6 Nov 24
	LD HAILSHAM (*Vt*)	28 Mar 28		**W. GUINNESS**	4 Nov 25
Privy S.	**M of SALISBURY**	6 Nov 24	*P.S.*	Ld Bledisloe	11 Nov 24
Exchequer	**W. CHURCHILL**	6 Nov 24		E of Stradbroke	5 Feb 28
F.S.	W. Guinness	11 Nov 24	*Air*	**SIR S. HOARE**	6 Nov 24
	R. McNeill	5 Nov 25	*U-S.*	Sir P. Sassoon	11 Nov 24
	(*Ld Cushendun*)		*Colonies*	**L. AMERY**	6 Nov 24
	A. Samuel	1 Nov 27	*U-S.*	W. Ormsby-Gore	12 Nov 24
Foreign O.	**(SIR) A. CHAMBERLAIN**	6 Nov 24	*Dom. O.*	**L. AMERY**	11 Jun 25
U-S.	R. McNeill	11 Nov 24	*U-S.*	E of Clarendon	5 Aug 25
	G. Locker-Lampson	7 Dec 25		Ld Lovat	5 May 27
Home O.	**SIR W. JOYNSON-HICKS**	6 Nov 24		E of Plymouth	1 Jan 29
U-S.	G. Locker-Lampson	11 Nov 24	*B Educ.*	**LD E. PERCY**	6 Nov 24
	D. Hacking	8 Dec 25	*P.S.*	Duchess of Atholl	11 Nov 24
	Sir V. Henderson	9 Nov 27	*Health*	**N. CHAMBERLAIN**	6 Nov 24
Admiralty	**W. BRIDGEMAN**	6 Nov 24	*P.S.*	Sir K. Wood	11 Nov 24
P.& F.S.	J. Davidson	11 Nov 24	*India*	**E of BIRKENHEAD**	6 Nov 24

[1] Not a Member of the House of Commons

CONSERVATIVE GOVERNMENT, 1924–29 (contd.)

India (contd.)	VT PEEL	18 Oct 28
U-S.	Earl Winterton[1]	11 Nov 24
Labour	SIR A. STEEL-MAITLAND	6 Nov 24
P.S.	H. Betterton	11 Nov 24
D. Lanc.	VT CECIL of CHELWOOD	10 Nov 24
	LD CUSHENDUN	19 Oct 27
Paym.-Gen.	(office vacant)	
	D of SUTHERLAND	28 Jan 25
	E of ONSLOW	2 Dec 28
Pensions	G. TRYON	11 Nov 24
P.S.	G. Stanley	11 Nov 24
Postm.-Gen.	SIR W. MITCHELL-THOMSON	11 Nov 24
Ass.	Vt Wolmer[1]	11 Nov 24
Scotland	SIR J. GILMOUR	6 Nov 24
	(S. of State for Scotland 15 Jul 26)	
U-S.	W. Elliot	26 Jul 26
P.S. Health for Scotland		
	W. Elliot	11 Nov 24
	(post abolished 26 Jul 26)	
B.Trade	SIR P. LLOYD-GREAME	6 Nov 24
	(changed name to Sir P. Cunliffe-Lister 27 Nov 24)	
P.S.	Sir B. Chadwick	11 Nov 24
	H. Williams	13 Jan 28
Sec. Overseas	A. Samuel	11 Nov 24
Trade	D. Hacking	9 Nov 27
Sec.	G. Lane-Fox	11 Nov 24
Mines	D. King	13 Jan 28
Transport	W. ASHLEY	11 Nov 24
P.S.	J. Moore-Brabazon	11 Nov 24
	(post vacant from 14 Jan 27)	
War	SIR L. WORTHINGTON-EVANS	6 Nov 24
U-S.	E of Onslow	11 Nov 24
	D of Sutherland	2 Dec 28
F.S.	D. King	11 Nov 24
	A. Duff Cooper	13 Jan 28
Works	VT PEEL	10 Nov 24
	M of LONDONDERRY	18 Oct 28

Law Officers		
Att.-Gen.	SIR D. HOGG	6 Nov 24
	(Ld Hailsham)	
	(office not in cabinet)	
	SIR T. INSKIP	28 Mar 28
Sol.-Gen.	SIR T. INSKIP	11 Nov 24
	SIR F. MERRIMAN	28 Mar 28
Ld Advoc.	W. WATSON	11 Nov 24
	A. MACROBERT	23 Apr 29
Sol.-Gen. Scotland	D. FLEMING	11 Nov 24
	A. MACROBERT	30 Dec 25
	W. NORMAND	23 Apr 29
Whips		
P.S. to Treasury	B. Eyres-Monsell	7 Nov 24
Lds of Treasury	G. Hennessy	13 Nov 24–10 Dec 25
	Ld Stanley[1]	13 Nov 24–9 Nov 27
	F. Thomson	13 Nov 24–14 Jan 28
	(Sir) W. Cope	13 Nov 24–14 Jan 28
	Vt Curzon[1]	13 Nov 24–15 Jan 29
	D. Margesson	28 Aug 26–4 Jun 29
	G. Bowyer	28 Dec 27–4 Jun 29
	F. Penny	13 Jan 28–4 Jun 29
	M of Titchfield[1]	13 Jan 28–4 Jun 29
	E. Wallace	1 Jan 29–4 Jun 29
H.M. Household		
Treasurer	G. GIBBS	13 Nov 24
	SIR G. HENNESSY	13 Jan 28
Compt.	SIR H. BARNSTON	13 Nov 24
	SIR W. COPE	13 Jan 28
V. Chamb.	D. HACKING	13 Nov 24
	(SIR) G. HENNESSY	10 Dec 25
	(SIR) F. THOMSON	13 Jan 28
Cap. Gents at Arms	E of CLARENDON	1 Dec 24
	E of PLYMOUTH	26 Jun 25
	E of LUCAN	1 Jan 29
Cap. Yeo. of Guard	LD DESBOROUGH	1 Dec 24
Lds in Waiting	Vt Gage	1 Dec 24–4 Jun 29
	Ld Somers	1 Dec 24–23 Mar 26
	E of Lucan	1 Dec 24–1 Jan 29
	E of Airlie	1 Apr 26–4 Jun 29
	Ld Templemore	1 Jan 29–4 Jun 29

LABOUR GOVERNMENT, 1929–1931

P.M.	R. MACDONALD	5 Jun 29–24 Aug 31
Ld Pres.	LD PARMOOR	7 Jun 29
Ld Chanc.	LD SANKEY	7 Jun 29
Privy S.	J. THOMAS	7 Jun 29
	V. HARTSHORN	5 Jun 30
	T. JOHNSTON	24 Mar 31
Exchequer	P. SNOWDEN	7 Jun 29
F.S.	F. Pethick-Lawrence	11 Jun 29
Foreign O.	A. HENDERSON	7 Jun 29
U-S.	H. Dalton	11 Jun 29

Home O.	J. CLYNES	7 Jun 29
U-S.	A. Short	11 Jun 29
Admiralty	A. ALEXANDER	7 Jun 29
P. & F.S.	C. Ammon	11 Jun 29
Civil Ld	G. Hall	11 Jun 29
Ag. & Fish.	N. BUXTON	7 Jun 29
	C. ADDISON	5 Jun 30
P.S.	C. Addison	11 Jun 29
	Earl De La Warr	5 Jun 30
Air	LD THOMSON	7 Jun 29
	LD AMULREE	14 Oct 30

[1] M.P. Not a Member of the House of Lords

LABOUR GOVERNMENT, 1929–1931 (contd.)

Air U-S.	F. Montague	11 Jun 29		Transport	H. MORRISON	7 Jun 29
Colonies	**LD PASSFIELD**	7 Jun 29			(office in cabinet)	
U-S.	W. Lunn	11 Jun 29			**H. MORRISON**	19 Mar 31
	D. Shiels	1 Dec 29		P.S.	Earl Russell	11 Jun 29
Dom. O.	**LD PASSFIELD**	7 Jun 29			A. Ponsonby (Ld)	1 Dec 29
	J. THOMAS	5 Jun 30			J. Parkinson	1 Mar 31
U-S.	A. Ponsonby	11 Jun 29		War	**T. SHAW**	7 Jun 29
	W. Lunn	1 Dec 29		U-S.	Earl De La Warr	11 Jun 29
B Educ.	**SIR C. TREVELYAN**	7 Jun 29			Ld Marley	5 Jun 30
	H. LEES-SMITH	2 Mar 31		F.S.	E. Shinwell	11 Jun 29
P.S.	M. Jones	11 Jun 29			W. Sanders	5 Jun 30
Health	**A. GREENWOOD**	7 Jun 29		Works	**G. LANSBURY**	7 Jun 29
P.S.	Miss S. Lawrence	11 Jun 29		***Law Officers***		
India	**W. BENN**	7 Jun 29		Att.-Gen.	SIR W. JOWITT	7 Jun 29
U-S.	D. Shiels	11 Jun 29		Sol.-Gen.	SIR J. MELVILLE	7 Jun 29
	Earl Russell	1 Dec 29			SIR S. CRIPPS	22 Oct 30
	Ld Snell	13 Mar 31		Ld Advoc.	C. AITCHISON	17 Jun 29
Labour	**MISS M. BONDFIELD**	7 Jun 29		Sol.-Gen.	J. WATSON[2]	17 Jun 29
P.S.	J. Lawson	11 Jun 29		Scotland		
D. Lanc.	SIR O. MOSLEY	7 Jun 29		***Whips***		
	C. ATTLEE	23 May 30		P.S. to	T. Kennedy	14 Jun 29
	LD PONSONBY	13 Mar 31		Treasury		
Paym.-Gen.	LD ARNOLD	7 Jun 29		Lds of	C. Edwards	11 Jun 29–13 Mar 31
	(office vacant 6 Mar 31)			Treasury	J. Parkinson	11 Jun 29–24 Aug 31
Pensions	F. ROBERTS	7 Jun 29			A. Barnes	11 Jun 29–23 Oct 30
P.S.	(post vacant)				W. Whiteley	27 Jun 29–24 Aug 31
Postm.-Gen.	H. LEES-SMITH	7 Jun 29			W. Paling	27 Jun 29–24 Aug 31
	C. ATTLEE	2 Mar 31			E. Thurtle	23 Oct 30–24 Aug 31
Ass.	S. Viant	7 Jul 29			H. Charleton	13 Mar 31–23 Aug 31
Scotland	**W. ADAMSON**	7 Jun 29		***H.M. Household***		
U-S.	T. Johnston	7 Jun 29		Treasurer	B. SMITH	24 Jun 29
	J. Westwood	25 Mar 31		Compt.	T. HENDERSON	24 Jun 29
B. Trade	**W. GRAHAM**	7 Jun 29		V. Chamb.	J. HAYES	24 Jun 29
P.S.	W. Smith	11 Jun 29		Lds in	Earl De La Warr	18 Jul 29–24 Aug 31
Sec. Over-	G. Gillett	7 Jul 29		Waiting	Ld Muir-Mackenzie	
seas Trade						18 Jul 29–22 May 30
Sec.	B. Turner	1 Jun 29			Ld Marley	17 Jun 30–24 Aug 31
Mines	E. Shinwell	5 Jun 30				

NATIONAL GOVERNMENT, 1931–1935

P.M.	**R. MACDONALD** (N.Lab)			U-S.	A. Eden (C)	3 Sep 31
		24 Aug 31–7 Jun 35			Earl Stanhope (C)	18 Jan 34
Ld Pres.	**S. BALDWIN** (C)	25 Aug 31		Home O.	**SIR H. SAMUEL** (Lib)	25 Aug 31
Ld Chanc.	**LD SANKEY** (Vt) (N.Lab)	25 Aug 31			**SIR J. GILMOUR** (C)	28 Sep 32
Privy S.	**EARL PEEL** (C)	3 Sep 31		U-S.	O. Stanley (C)	3 Sep 31
	(office in cabinet)				D. Hacking (C)	22 Feb 33
	VT SNOWDEN (N. Lab)	5 Nov 31			H. Crookshank (C)	29 Jun 34
	S. BALDWIN (C)	29 Sep 32		Admiralty	SIR A. CHAMBERLAIN (C)	
	(office not in cabinet)					25 Aug 31
	A. EDEN (C)	31 Dec 33			(office in cabinet)	
Exchequer	**P. SNOWDEN** (Vt) (N.Lab)	25 Aug 31			**SIR B. EYRES-MONSELL** (C)	
	N. CHAMBERLAIN (C)	5 Nov 31				5 Nov 31
F.S.	W. Elliot (C)	3 Sep 31		P. & F.S.	Earl Stanhope (C)	3 Sep 31
	L. Hore-Belisha (L.Nat)	29 Sep 32			Ld Stanley[1] (C)	10 Nov 31
	A. Duff Cooper (C)	29 Jun 34		Civil Ld	E. Wallace (C)	10 Nov 31
Foreign O.	**M of READING** (Lib)	25 Aug 31		Ag. & Fish.	SIR J. GILMOUR (C)	25 Aug 31
	SIR J. SIMON (L.Nat)	5 Nov 31			(office in cabinet)	

[1] M.P. Not a Member of the House of Lords

NATIONAL GOVERNMENT, 1931–1935 *(contd.)*

Ag.& Fish.		
(contd.)	**SIR J. GILMOUR** (C)	5 Nov 31
P.S.	**W. ELLIOT** (C)	28 Sep 32
	(vacant)	
	Earl De La Warr (N.Lab)	10 Nov 31
Air	LD AMULREE (N.Lab)	25 Aug 31
	(office in cabinet)	
	M of LONDONDERRY (C)	5 Nov 31
U-S.	Sir P. Sassoon (C)	3 Sep 31
Colonies	**J. THOMAS** (N.Lab)	25 Aug 31
	SIR P. CUNLIFFE-LISTER (C)	5 Nov 31
U-S.	Sir R. Hamilton (Lib)	3 Sep 31
	E of Plymouth (C)	29 Sep 32
Dom. O.	**J. THOMAS** (N.Lab)	25 Aug 31
U-S.	M. MacDonald (N.Lab)	3 Sep 31
B.Educ.	Sir D. Maclean (Lib)	25 Aug 31
	(office in cabinet)	
	SIR D. MACLEAN (Lib)	5 Nov 31
	LD IRWIN (*Vt Halifax*) (C)	15 Jun 32
P.S.	Sir K. Wood (C)	3 Sep 31
	H. Ramsbotham (C)	10 Nov 31
Health	**N. CHAMBERLAIN** (C)	25 Aug 31
	SIR E. YOUNG (C)	5 Nov 31
P.S.	E. Simon (Lib)	22 Sep 31
	E. Brown (L.Nat.)	10 Nov 31
	G. Shakespeare (L.Nat)	30 Sep 32
India	**SIR S. HOARE** (C)	25 Aug 31
U-S.	*(vacant)*	
	M of Lothian (Lib)	10 Nov 31
	R. Butler (C)	29 Sep 32
Labour	**SIR H. BETTERTON** (C)	25 Aug 31
	(office in cabinet)	
	SIR H. BETTERTON (C)	5 Nov 31
	O. STANLEY (C)	29 Jun 34
P.S.	M. Gray (Lib)	3 Sep 31
	R. Hudson (C)	10 Nov 31
D.Lanc.	**M OF LOTHIAN** (Lib)	25 Aug 31
	(SIR) J. DAVIDSON (C)	10 Nov 31
Paym.-Gen.	**SIR T. WALTERS** (Lib)	4 Sep 31
	LD ROCHESTER (N.Lab)	23 Nov 31
Pensions	G. TRYON (C)	3 Sep 31
P.S.	*(vacant)*	
	C. Headlam (C)	10 Nov 31
	(vacant from 29 Sep 32)	
Post.-Gen.	W. ORMSBY-GORE (C)	3 Sep 31
	SIR K. WOOD (C)	10 Nov 31
	(office in cabinet)	
	SIR K. WOOD (C)	20 Dec 33
Ass.	G. White (Lib)	3 Sep 31
	Sir E. Bennett (N.Lab)	21 Oct 32
Scotland	Sir A. Sinclair (Lib)	25 Aug 31
	(office in cabinet)	
	SIR A. SINCLAIR (Lib)	5 Nov 31
	SIR G. COLLINS (L.Nat)	28 Sep 32
U-S.	N. Skelton (C)	3 Sep 31
B. Trade	**SIR P. CUNLIFFE-LISTER** (C)	25 Aug 31
	W. RUNCIMAN (L.Nat)	5 Nov 31

P.S.	G. Lloyd-George (Lib)	3 Sep 31
	L. Hore-Belisha (L.Nat)	10 Nov 31
	L. Burgin (L.Nat)	29 Sep 32
Sec.	Sir E. Young (C)	3 Sep 31
Overseas Trade	J. Colville (C)	10 Nov 31
Sec.	I. Foot (Lib)	3 Sep 31
Mines	E. Brown (L.Nat)	30 Sep 32
Transport	J. PYBUS (L.Nat)	3 Sep 31
	O. STANLEY (C)	22 Feb 33
	L. HORE-BELISHA (L.Nat)	29 Jun 34
P.S.	(Sir) G. Gillett (N. Lab)	4 Sep 31
	E of Plymouth (C)	25 Nov 31
	C. Headlam (C)	29 Sep 32
	(vacant from 5 Jul 34)	
	A. Hudson (C)	12 Apr 35
War	M of CREWE (Lib)	26 Aug 31
	(office in cabinet)	
	VT HAILSHAM (C)	5 Nov 31
U-S.	*(vacant)*	
	Earl Stanhope (C)	10 Nov 31
	Ld Strathcona (C)	24 Jan 34
F.S.	A. Duff Cooper (C)	3 Sep 31
	D. Hacking (C)	29 Jun 34
Works	M of LONDONDERRY (C)	
	(office in cabinet)	25 Aug 31
	W. ORMSBY-GORE (C)	5 Nov 31

Law Officers

Att.-Gen.	**SIR W. JOWITT** (N.Lab)	3 Sep 31
	SIR T. INSKIP (C)	26 Jan 32
Sol.-Gen.	**SIR T. INSKIP** (C)	3 Sep 31
	SIR F. MERRIMAN (C)	26 Jan 32
	SIR D. SOMERVELL (C)	29 Sep 33
Ld Advoc.	C. AITCHISON (N Lab)	3 Sep 31
	W. NORMAND (C)	2 Oct 33
	D. JAMIESON (C)	28 Mar 35
Sol.-Gen.	J WATSON[2] (N.Lab)	4 Sep 31
Scotland	W. NORMAND (C)	10 Nov 31
	D. JAMIESON (C)	2 Oct 33
	T. COOPER (C)	15 May 35

Whips

P.S. to	Sir B. Eyres-Monsell (C)	3 Sep 31
Treasury	D. Margesson (C)	10 Nov 31
Lds of	D. Margesson (C)	26 Aug 31–10 Nov 31
Treasury	Sir F. Penny (C)	3 Sep 31–12 Nov 31
	A. Glassey (Lib)	14 Sep 31–12 Nov 31
	M of Titchfield[1] (C)	3 Sep 31–12 Nov 31
	E. Wallace (C)	3 Sep 31–12 Nov 31
	(Sir) W. Womersley (C)	12 Nov 31–7 Jun 35
	Sir V. Warrender (C)	12 Nov 31–30 Sep 32
	G. Shakespeare (L.Nat)	12 Nov 31–30 Sep 32
	A. Hudson (C)	12 Nov 31–12 Apr 35
	Sir L. Ward (C)	12 Nov 31–1 May 35

[1] M.P. Not a Member of the House of Lords
[2] Not a Member of the House of Commons

NATIONAL GOVERNMENT, 1931–1935 (contd.)

Treasury	G. Davies (C)	11 Oct 32–7 Jun 35		*V. Chamb.*	SIR F. THOMSON (C)	3 Sep 31
(contd.)	J. Blindell (L.Nat)	30 Sep 32–7 Jun 35			SIR F. PENNY (C)	12 Nov 31
	J. Stuart (C)	1 May 35–7 Jun 35			SIR V. WARRENDER (C)	30 Sep 32
	A. Southby (C)	23 Apr 35–7 Jun 35			SIR L. WARD (C)	1 May 35
				Cap. Gents	E OF LUCAN (C)	12 Nov 31
H.M. Household				*at Arms*		
Treasurer	SIR G. HENNESSY (C)	3 Sep 31		*Cap. Yeo.*	LD STRATHCONA(C)	12 Nov 31
	SIR F. THOMSON (C)	12 Nov 31		*of Guard*	LD TEMPLEMORE (C)	24 Jan 34
	SIR F. PENNY (C)	1 May 35		*Lds in*	Ld Templemore (C) 12 Nov 31–24 Jan 34	
Compt.	G. OWEN (Lib)	14 Sep 31		*Waiting*	Vt Gage (C)	12 Nov 31–7 Jun 35
	W. REA (Lib)	12 Nov 31			Vt Allendale (Lib)	12 Nov 31–28 Sep 32
	SIR F. PENNY (C)	30 Sep 32			E of Munster (C)	24 Jan 34–7 Jun 35
	SIR V. WARRENDER (C)	1 May 35			E of Feversham (C)	24 Jan 34–7 Jun 35

NATIONAL GOVERNMENT, 1935–40

P.M.	S. BALDWIN	7 Jun 35–28 May 37		*Admiralty*	SIR B. EYRES-MONSELL	7 Jun 35
	N. CHAMBERLAIN[2]				(Vt Monsell)	
		28 May 37–10 May 40			SIR S. HOARE	5 Jun 36
Ld Pres.	R. MACDONALD	7 Jun 35			A. DUFF COOPER	28 May 37
	VT HALIFAX	28 May 37			EARL STANHOPE	27 Oct 38
	VT HAILSHAM	9 Mar 38			W. CHURCHILL[2]	3 Sep 39
	VT RUNCIMAN	31 Oct 38		*P. & F.S.*	Sir V. Warrender	18 Jun 35
	EARL STANHOPE	3 Sep 39			Ld Stanley[1]	28 Nov 35
Ld Chanc.	VT HAILSHAM	7 Jun 35			G. Shakespeare	28 May 37
	LD MAUGHAM	9 Mar 38			Sir V. Warrender	3 Apr 40
	VT CALDECOTE	3 Sep 39		*Civil Ld*	K. Lindsay	18 Jun 35
Privy S.	M OF LONDONDERRY	7 Jun 35			J. Llewellin	28 May 37
	VT HALIFAX	22 Nov 35			A. Hudson	14 Jul 39
	EARL DE LA WARR	28 May 37		*Ag. & Fish.*	W. ELLIOT	7 Jun 35
	SIR J. ANDERSON	31 Oct 38			W. MORRISON	29 Oct 36
	SIR S. HOARE[2]	3 Sep 39			SIR R. DORMAN-SMITH	29 Jan 39
	SIR K. WOOD	3 Apr 40		*P.S.*	Earl De La Warr	18 Jun 35
Exchequer	N. CHAMBERLAIN	7 Jun 35			H. Ramsbotham	28 Nov 35
	SIR J. SIMON[2]	28 May 37			E of Feversham	30 Jul 36
F.S.	A. Duff Cooper	18 Jun 35			Ld Denham	19 Sep 39
	W. Morrison	22 Nov 35		*Air*	SIR P. CUNLIFFE-LISTER	7 Jun 35
	J. Colville	29 Oct 36			(Vt Swinton)	
	E. Wallace	16 May 38			SIR K. WOOD[2]	16 May 38
	H. Crookshank	21 Apr 39			SIR S. HOARE	3 Apr 40
Foreign O.	SIR S. HOARE	7 Jun 35		*U-S.*	Sir P. Sassoon	18 Jun 35
	A. EDEN	22 Dec 35			A. Muirhead	28 May 37
	VT HALIFAX[2]	21 Feb 38			H. Balfour	16 May 38
U-S.	Earl Stanhope	18 Jun 35–16 Jun 36		*Colonies*	M. MACDONALD	7 Jun 35
	Vt Cranborne[1]	6 Aug 35–20 Feb 38			J. THOMAS	22 Nov 35
	E of Plymouth	30 Jul 36–12 May 39			W. ORMSBY-GORE	28 May 36
	R. Butler	25 Feb 38–10 May 40			M. MACDONALD	16 May 38
Home O.	SIR J. SIMON	7 Jun 35		*U-S.*	E of Plymouth	18 Jun 35
	SIR S. HOARE	28 May 37			Earl De La Warr	30 Jul 36
	SIR J. ANDERSON	3 Sep 39			M of Dufferin & Ava	28 May 37
U-S.	E. Wallace	18 Jun 35		*Min. for*	(office not established)	
	G. Lloyd	28 Nov 35		*Co-ord.*	SIR T. INSKIP	13 Mar 36
	O. Peake	21 Apr 39		*of Def.*	LD CHATFIELD[2]	29 Jan 39
P.S. Min.	A. Lennox-Boyd	6 Sep 39			(office abolished 3 Apr 40)	
Home	W. Mabane	24 Oct 39		*Dom. O.*	J. THOMAS	7 Jun 35
Security					M. MACDONALD	22 Nov 35

[1] M.P. Not a Member of the House of Lords

[2] Denotes a member of the war cabinet. On 3 Sep 39 all ministers formally surrendered their portfolios to the Prime Minister. That evening the formation of a war cabinet was announced.

NATIONAL GOVERNMENT, 1935–40 (contd.)

Dom. O. (contd.)	LD STANLEY[1]	16 May 38
	M. MACDONALD	31 Oct 38
	SIR T. INSKIP (Vt Caldecote)	29 Jan 39
	A. EDEN	3 Sep 39
U.-S.	Ld Stanley[1]	18 Jun 35
	D. Hacking	28 Nov 35
	M of Hartington[1] (D of Devonshire)	4 Mar 36
Ec. Warfare	R. CROSS	3 Sep 39
B. Educ.	O. STANLEY	7 Jun 35
	EARL STANHOPE	28 May 37
	EARL DE LA WARR	27 Oct 38
	H. RAMSBOTHAM	3 Apr 40
P.S.	H. Ramsbotham	18 Jun 35
	Earl De La Warr	28 Nov 35
	G. Shakespeare	30 Jul 36
	K. Lindsay	28 May 37
Food (combined with D. Lanc. 4 Sep 39)	LD WOOLTON	3 Apr 40
P.S.	A. Lennox-Boyd	11 Oct 39
Health	SIR K. WOOD	7 Jun 35
	W. ELLIOT	16 May 38
P.S.	G. Shakespeare	18 Jun 35
	R. Hudson	30 Jul 36
	R. Bernays	28 May 37
	Miss F. Horsbrugh	14 Jul 39
India (& Burma 1937–)	M of ZETLAND	7 Jun 35
U.-S.	R. Butler	18 Jun 35
	Ld Stanley[1]	28 May 37
	A. Muirhead	16 May 38
	Sir H. O'Neill	11 Sep 39
Information	(office not established)	
	LD MACMILLAN	4 Sep 39
	SIR J. REITH	5 Jan 40
P.S.	Sir E. Grigg	19 Sep 39
	(office vacant 3 Apr 40)	
Labour	E. BROWN (3 Sep 39 Lab. & Nat S.)	7 Jun 35
P.S.	A. Muirhead	18 Jun 35
	R. Butler	28 May 37
	A. Lennox-Boyd	25 Feb 38
	R. Assheton	6 Sep 39
D. Lanc.	SIR J. DAVIDSON	18 Jun 35
	EARL WINTERTON[1] (office in cabinet)	28 May 37
	EARL WINTERTON[1]	11 Mar 38
	W. MORRISON (4 Sep 39–3 Apr 40 combined with Min. of Food)	29 Jan 39
	LD TRYON	3 Apr 40
Paym.-Gen.	LD ROCHESTER	18 Jun 35
	LD HUTCHISON	6 Dec 35
	E OF MUNSTER	2 Jun 38
	EARL WINTERTON[1] (office vacant from Nov 39)	29 Jan 39
Pensions	R. HUDSON	18 Jun 35
	H. RAMSBOTHAM	30 Jul 36
	SIR W. WOMERSLEY	7 Jun 39
Min. without Portfolio for League of Nations Affairs	A. EDEN	7 Jun 35–22 Dec 35
Min. without Portfolio	LD E. PERCY[1]	7 Jun 35–31 Mar 36
	L. BURGIN	21 Apr 39–14 Jul 39
	LD HANKEY[2]	3 Sep 39–10 May 40
Postm.-Gen.	G. TRYON	7 Jun 35
	W. MORRISON	3 Apr 40
Ass.	Sir E. Bennett	18 Jun 35
	Sir W. Womersley	6 Dec 35
	W. Mabane	7 Jun 39
	C. Waterhouse	24 Oct 39
Scotland	SIR G. COLLINS	7 Jun 35
	W. ELLIOT	29 Oct 36
	J. COLVILLE	16 May 38
U.-S.	N. Skelton	18 Jun 35
	J. Colville	28 Nov 35
	H. Wedderburn	29 Oct 36
	J. McEwen	6 Sep 39
Shipping	(office not established)	
	SIR J. GILMOUR	13 Oct 39
	R. HUDSON	3 Apr 40
P.S.	Sir A. Salter	13 Nov 39
Supply	(office not established)	
	L. BURGIN	14 Jul 39
P.S.	J. Llewellin	14 Jul 39
B. Trade	W. RUNCIMAN	7 Jun 35
	O. STANLEY	28 May 37
	SIR A. DUNCAN	5 Jan 40
P.S.	L. Burgin	18 Jun 35
	E. Wallace	28 May 37
	R. Cross	16 May 38
	G. Lloyd-George	6 Sep 39
Sec.	J. Colville	18 Jun 35
Overseas Trade	E. Wallace	28 Nov 35
	R. Hudson	28 May 37
	G. Shakespeare	3 Apr 40
Sec. Mines	H. Crookshank	18 Jun 35
	G. Lloyd	21 Apr 39
Transp.	L. HORE-BELISHA (office in cabinet)	18 Jun 35
	L. HORE-BELISHA	29 Oct 36
	L. BURGIN	28 May 37
	E. WALLACE	21 Apr 39
P.S.	A. Hudson	18 Jun 35
	R. Bernays	14 Jul 39
War	VT HALIFAX	7 Jun 35
	A. DUFF COOPER	22 Nov 35
	L. HORE-BELISHA[2]	28 May 37
	O. STANLEY	5 Jan 40
U.-S.	Ld Strathcona	18 Jun 35
	E of Munster	29 Jan 39
	Vt Cobham	19 Sep 39

[1] M.P. Not a Member of the House of Lords

[2] Denotes a member of the war cabinet. On 3 Sep 39 all ministers formally surrendered their portfolios to the Prime Minister. That evening the formation of a war cabinet was announced.

NATIONAL GOVERNMENT, 1935–40 (contd.)

F.S.	D. Hacking	18 Jun 35		*Lds of*	S. Furness	20 May 38-10 May 40
	Sir V. Warrender	28 Nov 35		*Treasury*	Sir J. Edmondson	4 Apr 39–13 Nov 39
	Sir E. Grigg	3 Apr 40			P. Buchan-Hepburn	
Works	**W. ORMSBY-GORE**	7 Jun 35				13 Nov 39–10 May 40
	EARL STANHOPE	16 Jun 36			W. Boulton	12 Feb 40–10 May 40
	(office not in cabinet)					
	Sir P. Sassoon	28 May 37		***H.M. Household***		
	H. RAMSBOTHAM	7 Jun 39		*Treasurer*	SIR F. PENNY	18 Jun 35
	EARL DE LA WARR	3 Apr 40			SIR L. WARD	28 May 37
					A. HOPE	18 Oct 37
Law Officers					C. WATERHOUSE	4 Apr 39
Att.-Gen.	SIR T. INSKIP	18 Jun 35			R. GRIMSTON	12 Nov 39
	SIR D. SOMERVELL	18 Mar 36		*Compt.*	SIR G. BOWYER	21 Jun 35
Sol.-Gen.	SIR D. SOMERVELL	18 Jun 35			SIR L. WARD	6 Dec 35
	SIR T. O'CONNOR	19 Mar 36			SIR G. DAVIES	28 May 37
Ld Advoc.	D. JAMIESON	18 Jun 35			C. WATERHOUSE	18 Oct 37
	T. COOPER	25 Oct 35			C. KERR	4 Apr 39
Sol.-Gen.	T. COOPER	18 Jun 35		*V. Chamb.*	SIR L. WARD	18 Jun 35
Scotland	A. RUSSELL[1]	29 Nov 35			(SIR) G. DAVIES	6 Dec 35
	J. REID	25 Jun 36			A. HOPE	28 May 37
					R. CROSS	18 Oct 37
Whips					R. GRIMSTON	18 May 38
P.S. to	D. Margesson	18 Jun 35			SIR J. EDMONDSON	12 Nov 39
Treasury				*Cap. Gents*	E OF LUCAN	18 Jun 35
Lds of	J. Stuart	18 Jun 35–10 May 40		*at Arms*		
Treasury	(Sir) A. Southby	18 Jun 35–28 May 37		*Cap. Yeo.*	LD TEMPLEMORE	18 Jun 35
	Sir W. Womersley	18 Jun 35–6 Dec 35		*of Guard*		
	G. Davies	18 Jun 35–6 Dec 35		*Lds in*	Vt Gage	18 Jun 35– 11 Apr 39
	(Sir) J. Blindell	18 Jun 35–28 May 37		*Waiting*	E of Munster	18 Jun 35–2 Jun 38
	A. Hope	6 Dec 35–28 May 37			E of Feversham	18 Jun 35–30 Jul 36
	(Sir) H. Morris-Jones				M of Dufferin & Ava	
		6 Dec 35–28 May 37				29 Oct 36–28 May 37
	C. Kerr	28 May 37–4 Apr 39			E of Erne	29 Oct 36–25 Jul 39
	T. Dugdale	28 May 37–12 Feb 40			Earl Fortescue	26 Aug 37–10 May 40
	C. Waterhouse	28 May 37–18 Oct 37			E of Birkenhead	12 Jul 38–10 May 40
	R. Cross	28 May 37–18 Oct 37			Vt Bridport	11 Apr 39–10 May 40
	P. Munro	18 Oct 37–10 May 40			Ld Ebury	25 Jul 39–10 May 40
	R. Grimston	18 Oct 37–18 May 38				

COALITION GOVERNMENT, 1940–1945

P.M. and	**W. CHURCHILL**[2] (C)			*Exchequer*	**SIR J. ANDERSON**[2] (Nat)	24 Sep 43
Defence		10 May 40–23 May 45		*(contd.)*		
Ld Pres.	**N. CHAMBERLAIN**[2] (C)	11 May 40		*F.S.*	H. Crookshank (C)	15 May 40
	SIR J. ANDERSON[2] (Nat)	3 Oct 40			R. Assheton (C)	7 Feb 43
	C. ATTLEE[2] (Lab)	24 Sep 43			O. Peake (C)	29 Oct 44
Ld Chanc.	LD SIMON (L.Nat)	12 May 40		*Foreign O.*	**VT HALIFAX**[2] (C)	11 May 40
Privy S.	**C. ATTLEE**[2] (Lab)	11 May 40			**A. EDEN**[2] (C)	22 Dec 40
	SIR S. CRIPPS[2] (Lab)	19 Feb 42		*U-S.*	R. Butler (C)	15 May 40
	(office not in war cabinet)				R. Law (C)	20 Jul 41
	VT CRANBORNE (C)	22 Nov 42			G. Hall (Lab)	25 Sep 43
	LD BEAVERBROOK[2] (C)	24 Sep 43		*Home O.*	SIR J. ANDERSON (Nat)	
Exchequer	SIR K. WOOD (C)	12 May 40				12 May 40
	(office in war cabinet)			*& Home*	H. MORRISON[2] (Lab)	3 Oct 40
	SIR K. WOOD[2] (C)	3 Oct 40		*Security*	*(office in war cabinet)*	
	(office not in war cabinet)				**H. MORRISON** (Lab)	22 Nov 42
	SIR K. WOOD (C)	19 Feb 42		*U-S.*	O. Peake (C)	15 May 40
	(office in war cabinet)				E of Munster (C)	31 Oct 44

[1] Not a Member of the House of Commons
[2] Denotes a member of the war cabinet. (Although Vt Halifax became an Ambassador to the United States on 24 Jan 41, he remained nominally a member of the War Cabinet until 1945.)

COALITION GOVERNMENT, 1940–1945 (*contd.*)

P.S. Home Security	W. Mabane (L.Nat)	15 May 40–3 Jun 42
	Miss E. Wilkinson (Lab)	8 Oct 40–23 May 45
Admiralty	A. ALEXANDER (Lab)	11 May 40
P.& F.S.	Sir V. Warrender (C)	17 May 40
	(*Ld Bruntisfield*)	
Civil Ld	A. Hudson (C)	15 May 40
	R. Pilkington (C)	4 Mar 42
F.S.	G. Hall (Lab)	4 Feb 42
	J. Thomas (C)	25 Sep 43
Ag.& Fish.	R. HUDSON (C)	14 May 40
P.S.	Ld Moyne (C)	15 May 40–8 Feb 41
	T. Williams (Lab)	15 May 40–23 May 45
	D of Norfolk (C)	8 Feb 41–23 May 45
Air	SIR A. SINCLAIR (Lib)	11 May 40
P.S.	H. Balfour (C)	15 May 40–21 Nov 44
	Ld Sherwood (Lib)	20 Jul 41–23 May 45
	R. Brabner (C)	21 Nov 44–27 Mar 45
	Q. Hogg (C)	12 Apr 45–23 May 45
Aircraft Production	LD BEAVERBROOK (C)	14 May 40
	(*office in war cabinet*)	
	LD BEAVERBROOK[3] (C)	2 Aug 40
	(*office not in war cabinet*)	
	J. MOORE-BRABAZON (C)	1 May 41
	J. LLEWELLIN (C)	22 Feb 42
	SIR S. CRIPPS (Lab)	22 Nov 42
P.S.	J. Llewellin (C)	15 May 40
	F. Montague (Lab)	1 May 41
	B. Smith (Lab)	4 Mar 42
	A. Lennox-Boyd (C)	11 Nov 43
Civil Av.	(*office not established*)	
	VT SWINTON(C)	8 Oct 44
P.S.	R. Perkins (C)	22 Mar 45
Colonies	LD LLOYD (C)	12 May 40
	LD MOYNE (C)	8 Feb 41
	VT CRANBORNE (C)	22 Feb 42
	O. STANLEY (C)	22 Nov 42
U-S.	G. Hall (Lab)	15 May 40
	H. Macmillan (C)	4 Feb 42
	D of Devonshire (C)	1 Jan 43
Dom. O.	VT CALDECOTE (C)	14 May 40
	VT CRANBORNE[1] (C)	3 Oct 40
	(*office in war cabinet*)	
	C. ATTLEE[3] (Lab)	19 Feb 42
	(*office not in war cabinet*)	
	VT CRANBORNE (C)	24 Sep 43
U-S.	G. Shakespeare (L.Nat)	15 May 40
	P. Emrys-Evans (C)	4 Mar 42
Economic Warfare	H. DALTON (Lab)	15 May 40
	VT WOLMER (C)	22 Feb 42
	(*E of Selborne*)	
P.S.	D. Foot (Lib)	17 May 40
B. Educ.	H. RAMSBOTHAM (C)	14 May 40
	R. BUTLER (C)	20 Jul 41
	(*3 Aug 44 becomes Min. of Education*)	
P.S.	C. Ede (Lab)	15 May 40
Food	LD WOOLTON (C)	13 May 40
	J. LLEWELLIN (C)	11 Nov 43
P.S.	R. Boothby (C)	15 May 40
	G. Lloyd-George (Ind.L)	22 Oct 40
	W. Mabane (L.Nat)	3 Jun 42
Fuel, Light & Power	(*office not established*)	
	G. LLOYD-GEORGE (Ind.L)	3 Jun 42
P.S.	G. Lloyd (C)	3 Jun 42–23 May 45
	T. Smith (Lab)	3 Jun 42–23 May 45
Health	M. MACDONALD (N.Lab)	13 May 40
	E. BROWN (L.Nat)	8 Feb 41
	H. WILLINK (C)	11 Nov 43
P.S.	Miss F. Horsbrugh (C)	15 May 40
India & Burma	L. AMERY (C)	13 May 40
P.S.	D of Devonshire (C)	17 May 40
	E of Munster (C)	1 Jan 43
	E of Listowel (Lab)	31 Oct 44
Information	A. DUFF COOPER (C)	12 May 40
	(*attended war cabinet from 28 May 40*)	
	B. BRACKEN (C)	20 Jul 41
P.S.	H. Nicolson (N. Lab)	17 May 40
	E. Thurtle (Lab)	20 Jul 41
Labour & Nat. S.	E. BEVIN (Lab)	13 May 40
	(*office in war cabinet*)	
	E. BEVIN[3] (Lab)	3 Oct 40
P.S.	R. Assheton (C)	15 May 40–4 Feb 42
	G. Tomlinson (Lab)	8 Feb 41–23 May 45
	M. McCorquodale (C)	4 Feb 42–23 May 45
D Lanc.	LD HANKEY (Ind)	14 May 40
	A. DUFF COOPER (C)	20 Jul 41
	E. BROWN (L.Nat)	11 Nov 43
Min. resident NW. Africa	H. MACMILLAN (C)	30 Dec 42
Min. resident Mid. East	**O. LYTTELTON**[3] (C)	19 Feb 42
	R. CASEY[2,3] (Ind)	19 Mar 42
	(*office not in war cabinet 23 Dec 43*)	
	LD MOYNE (C)	28 Jan 44
	SIR E. GRIGG (C)	21 Nov 44
Deputy Min. of State	Ld Moyne (C)	27 Aug 42–28 Jan 44
Min. resident Washington for Supply	J. LLEWELLIN (C)	22 Nov 42
	B. SMITH (Lab)	11 Nov 43
Min. resident W. Africa	VT SWINTON (C)	8 Jun 42
	H. BALFOUR (C)	21 Nov 44

[1] M.P. Not a Member of the House of Lords. (Vt Cranborne was promoted to the House of Lords by writ of acceleration in January 1941).

[2] Not a Member of the House of Commons

[3] Denotes a member of the war cabinet.

COALITION GOVERNMENT, 1940–1945 (contd.)

Min. without Portfolio	A. GREENWOOD² (Lab)	11 May 40–22 Feb 42
	(not in war cabinet)	
	SIR W. JOWITT (Lab)	
		30 Dec 42–8 Oct 44
Paym.-Gen.	VT CRANBORNE¹ (C)	15 May 40
	(office vacant 3 Oct 40)	
	LD HANKEY (Ind)	20 Jul 41
	SIR W. JOWITT (Lab)	4 Mar 42
	LD CHERWELL (C)	30 Dec 42
Pensions	SIR W. WOMERSLEY (C)	15 May 40
P.S.	Miss E. Wilkinson (Lab)	17 May 40
	Ld Tryon (C)	8 Oct 40
	W. Paling (Lab)	8 Feb 41
Post.-Gen.	W. MORRISON (C)	15 May 40
	H. CROOKSHANK (C)	7 Feb 43
Ass.	C. Waterhouse (C)	17 May 40
	A. Chapman (C)	1 Mar 41
	R. Grimston (C)	4 Mar 42
Reconstruc.	(office not established)	
	LD WOOLTON² (C)	11 Nov 43
Scotland	E. BROWN (L. Nat)	14 May 40
	T. JOHNSTON (Lab)	8 Feb 41
P.S.	J. Westwood (Lab)	
		17 May 40–23 May 45
	H. Wedderburn (C)	8 Feb 41–4 Mar 42
	A. Chapman (C)	4 Mar 42–23 May 45
Shipping	R. CROSS (C)	14 May 40
	(1 May 41 combined with Min. of Transport as Min. of War Transport)	
P.S.	Sir A. Salter (Ind)	15 May 40
Soc.	(office not established)	
Insurance	SIR W. JOWITT (Lab)	8 Oct 44
	(renamed Nat. Insurance 17 Nov 44)	
P.S.	C. Peat (C)	22 Mar 45
State (Min. of)	LD BEAVERBROOK² (C)	1 May 41
	O. LYTTELTON² (C)	29 Jun 41
	(office vacant 12 Mar 42)	
	R. LAW (C)	24 Sep 43
Supply	H. MORRISON (Lab)	12 May 40
	SIR A. DUNCAN (C)	3 Oct 40
	(office in war cabinet)	
	LD BEAVERBROOK²	29 Jun 41
	(office not in war cabinet)	
	SIR A. DUNCAN (C)	4 Feb 42
P.S.	H. Macmillan (C)	15 May 40–4 Feb 42
	Ld Portal (C)	4 Sep 40–4 Mar 42
	R. Assheton (C)	4 Feb 42–7 Feb 43
	C. Peat (C)	4 Mar 42–22 Mar 45
	D. Sandys (C)	7 Feb 43–21 Nov 44
	J. Wilmot (Lab)	21 Nov 44–23 May 45
	J. de Rothschild (Lib)	
		22 Mar 45–23 May 45
T. & C. Planning	(office not established)	
	W. MORRISON (C)	30 Dec 42
	(Minister designate until 7 Feb 43)	
P.S.	H. Strauss (C)	30 Dec 42
	A. Jenkins (Lab)	22 Mar 45
B Trade	SIR A. DUNCAN (C)	12 May 40
	O. LYTTELTON (C)	3 Oct 40
	SIR A. DUNCAN (C)	29 Jun 41
	J. LLEWELLIN (C)	4 Feb 42
	H. DALTON (Lab)	22 Feb 42
P.S.	G. Lloyd-George (Ind L.)	
	(& P.S. Food 22 Oct 40)	15 May 40
	C. Waterhouse (C)	8 Feb 41
Sec.	H. Johnstone (Lib)	15 May 40
Overseas Trade	S. Summers (C)	22 Mar 45
Sec. Mines	D. Grenfell (Lab)	15 May 40
Sec. Petrol	G. Lloyd (C)	15 May 40–3 Jun 42
	(3 Jun 42 combined in Min. of Fuel, Light & Power)	
Transport	SIR J. REITH (Nat)	14 May 40
	J. MOORE-BRABAZON (C)	3 Oct 40
	(1 May 41 became Min. of War Transport)	
(War) Production	LD BEAVERBROOK² (C)	4 Feb 42
	(office vacant 19 Feb 42)	
	O. LYTTELTON² (C)	12 Mar 42
	(Minister of Production)	
P.S.	G. Garro-Jones (Lab)	10 Sep 42
War	A. EDEN (C)	11 May 40
	D. MARGESSON (C)	22 Dec 40
	SIR J. GRIGG (Nat)	22 Feb 42
U-S.	Sir H. Page Croft (C)	
	(Ld Croft)	17 May 40–23 May 45
	Sir E. Grigg (C)	17 May 40–4 Mar 42
	A. Henderson (Lab)	
		4 Mar 42–7 Feb 43
F.S.	R. Law (C)	17 May 40
	D. Sandys (C)	20 Jul 41
	A. Henderson (Lab)	7 Feb 43
War Transp	LD LEATHERS (C)	1 May 41
P.S.	F. Montague (Lab)	
		18 May 40–1 May 41
	(renamed War Transport 1 May 41)	
	J. Llewellin (C)	1 May 41–4 Feb 42
	Sir A. Salter (Ind)	29 Jun 11–4 Feb 42
	P. Noel-Baker (Lab)	
		4 Feb 42–23 May 45
Works	LD TRYON (C)	18 May 40
	SIR J. REITH (Ld) (Nat)	3 Oct 40
	(Min. of Works & Buildings & 1st Com. Works 3 Oct 40)	
	LD PORTAL (C)	22 Feb 42
	(Min. of Works and Planning 11 Feb 42 Min. of Works Feb 43)	

¹ M.P. Not a Member of the House of Lords. (Vt Cranborne was promoted to the House of Lords by writ of acceleration in January 1941.)
² Denotes a member of the war cabinet.

COALITION GOVERNMENT, 1940–1945 (contd.)

Works (contd.)		
	D. SANDYS (C)	21 Nov 44
P.S.	G. Hicks (Lab)	19 Nov 40–23 May 45
	H. Strauss (C)	4 Mar 42–30 Dec 42
Law Officers		
Att.-Gen.	SIR D. SOMERVELL (C)	15 May 40
Sol.-Gen.	SIR W. JOWITT (Lab)	15 May 40
	SIR D. MAXWELL FYFE(C)	4 Mar 42
Ld Advoc.	T. COOPER (C)	15 May 40
	J. REID (C)	5 Jun 41
Sol.-Gen. Scotland	J. REID (C)	15 May 40
	(SIR) D. MURRAY (C)	5 Jun 41
Whips		
P.S. to Treasury	D. Margesson (C)	17 May 40–22 Dec 40
P.S. to Treasury	Sir C. Edwards (Lab)	17 May 40–12 Mar 42
	J. Stuart (C)	14 Jan 41–23 May 45
	W. Whiteley (Lab)	12 Mar 42–23 May 45
Lds of Treasury	S. Furness (L.Nat)	12 May 40–18 May 40
	J. Stuart (C)	12 May 40–14 Jan 41
	P. Munro (C)	12 May 40–13 Mar 42
	P. Buchan-Hepburn (C)	12 May 40–26 Jun 40
	W. Boulton (C)	12 May 40–13 Mar 42
	W. Paling (Lab)	18 May 40–8 Feb 41
	J. Thomas (C)	26 Jun 40–25 Sep 43
	T. Dugdale (C)	8 Feb 41–23 Feb 42

Lds of Treasury (contd.)	W. Adamson (Lab)	1 Mar 41–2 Oct 44
	A. Young (C)	23 Feb 42–3 Jul 44
	J. McEwen (C)	13 Mar 42–6 Dec 44
	L. Pym (C)	13 Mar 42–23 May 45
	A. Beechman (L. Nat)	25 Sep 43–23 May 45
	C. Drewe (C)	3 Jul 44–23 May 45
	W. John (Lab)	2 Oct 44–23 May 45
	P Buchan-Hepburn (C)	6 Dec 44–23 May 45
H.M. Household		
Treasurer	R. GRIMSTON (C)	17 May 40
	SIR J. EDMONDSON (C)	12 Mar 42
Compt.	W. WHITELEY (Lab)	17 May 40
	W. JOHN (Lab)	12 Mar 42
	G. MATHERS (Lab)	2 Oct 44
V. Chamb.	SIR J. EDMONDSON (C)	17 May 40
	W. BOULTON (C)	12 Mar 42
	A. YOUNG (C)	13 Jul 44
Cap. Gents at Arms	LD SNELL (Lab)	31 May 40–21 Apr 44
	EARL FORTESCUE (C)	22 Mar 45
Cap. Yeo. of Guard	LD TEMPLEMORE (C)	31 May 40
Lds in Waiting	Earl Fortescue (C)	31 May 40–22 Mar 45
	Vt Clifden (Lib)	31 May 40–22 Mar 45
	Ld Alness (L.Nat)	31 May 40–23 May 45
	M of Normanby (C)	22 Mar 45–23 May 45

CARETAKER GOVERNMENT, 1945

P.M. and Min of Defence	**W. CHURCHILL**	23 May 45–26 Jul 45
Ld Pres.	**LD WOOLTON**	25 May 45
Ld Chanc.	VT SIMON	25 May 45
Privy S.	**LD BEAVERBROOK**	25 May 45
Exchequer	**SIR J. ANDERSON**	25 May 45
F.S.	O. Peake	26 May 45
Foreign O.	**A. EDEN**	25 May 45
Min. of State	W. Mabane	25 May 45
U-S.	Ld Dunglass[1]	26 May 45
	Ld Lovat	26 May 45
Home O.	**SIR D. SOMERVELL**	25 May 45
U-S.	E of Munster	26 May 45
Admiralty	**B. BRACKEN**	25 May 45
P.& F.S.	Ld Bruntisfield	26 May 45
Civil Ld	R. Pilkington	26 May 45
F.S.	J. Thomas	26 May 45
Ag. & Fish.	**R. HUDSON**	25 May 45
P.S.	D of Norfolk	26 May 45
	D. Scott	26 May 45
Air	**H. MACMILLAN**	25 May 45
U-S.	Q. Hogg	26 May 45

Air U-S.	Earl Beatty	26 May 45
Aircraft Production	E. BROWN	25 May 45
P.S.	A. Lennox-Boyd	26 May 45
Civil Av.	VT SWINTON	25 May 45
P.S.	R. Perkins	26 May 45
Colonies	**O. STANLEY**	25 May 45
U-S.	D of Devonshire	26 May 45
Dom. O.	**VT CRANBORNE**	25 May 45
U-S.	P. Emrys-Evans	26 May 45
Educ.	R. LAW	25 May 45
P.S.	Mrs T. Cazalet-Keir	26 May 45
Food	**J. LLEWELLIN**	25 May 45
P.S.	Miss F. Horsbrugh	26 May 45
Fuel & Power	**G. LLOYD-GEORGE**	25 May 45
P.S.	Sir A. Hudson	26 May 45
Health	**H. WILLINK**	25 May 45
P.S.	H. Kerr	26 May 45
India & Burma	**L. AMERY**	25 May 45
P.S.	E of Scarbrough	26 May 45

[1] Not a Member of the House of Commons

CARETAKER GOVERNMENT, 1945 (contd.)

Information	G. LLOYD	25 May 45	*War*	**SIR J. GRIGG**	25 May 45
Labour &	**R. BUTLER**	25 May 45	*U.-S.*	Ld Croft	26 May 45
National S.			*F.S.*	M. Petherick	26 May 45
P.S.	M. McCorquodale	26 May 45	*War Transp.*	**LD LEATHERS**	25 May 45
D. Lanc.	SIR A. SALTER	25 May 45	*P.S.*	P. Thorneycroft	26 May 45
Min. resident	SIR E. GRIGG	25 May 45	*Works*	D. SANDYS	25 May 45
Mid. East			*P.S.*	R. Manningham-Buller	26 May 45
Min. resident	H. BALFOUR	25 May 45			
W. Africa			***Law Officers***		
Nat.	L. HORE-BELISHA	25 May 45	*Att.-Gen.*	**SIR D. MAXWELL FYFE**	25 May 45
Insurance			*Sol.-Gen.*	**SIR W. MONCKTON**[1]	25 May 45
P.S.	C. Peat	36 May 45	*Ld Advoc.*	J. REID	25 May 45
Paym.-Gen.	**LD CHERWELL**	25 May 45	*Sol.-Gen*	**SIR D. MURRAY**	25 May 45
Pensions	SIR W. WOMERSLEY	25 May 45	*Scotland*		
P.S.	W. Sidney (*Ld De L'Isle*)	26 May 45			
Postm.-Gen.	H. CROOKSHANK	25 May 45	***Whips***		
Ass.	W. Anstruther-Gray	26 May 45	*P.S. to*	J. Stuart	26 May 45
Production	**O. LYTTELTON**	25 May 45	*Treasury*		
	(*& Pres. B Trade*)		*Lds of*	A. Beechman	28 May 45
			Treasury	C. Drewe	25 May 45
P.S.	J. Maclay	28 May 45		P. Buchan-Hepburn	25 May 45
Scotland	**E OF ROSEBERY**	25 May 45		R. Cary	28 May 45
P.S.	A. Chapman	26 May 45		C. Mott-Radclyffe	28 May 45
	T. Galbraith	26 May 45			
Supply	**SIR A. DUNCAN**	25 May 45	***H.M. Household***		
P.S.	R. Grimston	26 May 45	*Treasurer*	**SIR J. EDMONDSON**	28 May 45
Town &	W. MORRISON	25 May 45	*Compt.*	L. PYM	28 May 45
Country			*V. Chamb.*	A. YOUNG	28 May 45
Planning			*Cap. Gents*	**EARL FORTESCUE**	28 May 45
P.S.	R. Tree	26 May 45	*at Arms*		
B. Trade	**O. LYTTELTON**	25 May 45	*Cap. Yeo.*	**LD TEMPLEMORE**	28 May 45
	(*& Min. of Production*)		*of Guard*		
P.S.	C. Waterhouse	26 May 45	*Lds in*	Ld Alness	28 May 45
Sec. Over-	S. Summers	26 May 45	*Waiting*	M of Normanby	28 May 45
seas Trade				D of Northumberland	28 May 45

LABOUR GOVERNMENT, 1945–1951

P.M.	**C. ATTLEE**	26 Jul 45–26 Oct 51	*Econ S.*	D. Jay	5 Dec 47
Ld Pres.	**H. MORRISON**	27 Jul 45		(*office vacant 2 Mar 50*)	
	VT ADDISON	9 Mar 51		J. Edwards	19 Oct 50
Ld Chanc.	**LD JOWITT**	27 Jul 45	*Foreign O.*	**E. BEVIN**	27 Jul 45
Privy S.	**A. GREENWOOD**	27 Jul 45		**H. MORRISON**	9 Mar 51
	LD INMAN	17 Apr 47	*Min. of*	P. NOEL-BAKER	3 Aug 45
	VT ADDISON	7 Oct 47	*State*	H. McNEIL	4 Oct 46
	E. BEVIN	9 Mar 51		K. YOUNGER	28 Feb 50
	R. STOKES	26 Apr 51	*U.-S.*	H. McNeil	4 Aug 45–4 Oct 46
	(*also Min. of Materials 6 Jul 51*)			C. Mayhew	4 Oct 46–2 Mar 50
Exchequer	**H. DALTON**	27 Jul 45		Ld Henderson	7 Jun 48–26 Oct 51
	SIR S. CRIPPS	13 Nov 47		E. Davies	2 Mar 50–26 Oct 51
	H. GAITSKELL	19 Oct 50	*Home O.*	**C. EDE**	3 Aug 45
Min. Econ.	(*office not established*)		*U.-S.*	G. Oliver	4 Aug 45
Affairs	**SIR S. CRIPPS**	29 Sep 47		K. Younger	7 Oct 47
	(*office combined with Exch. 13 Nov 47*)			G. de Freitas	2 Mar 50
	H. GAITSKELL	28 Feb 50–19 Oct 50	*Admiralty*	**A. ALEXANDER**	3 Aug 45
F.S.	W. Glenvil Hall	4 Aug 45		(*office not in cabinet*)	
	D. Jay	2 Mar 50		**VT HALL**	4 Oct 46

[1] Not a Member of the House of Commons

LABOUR GOVERNMENT, 1945–1951 (contd.)

Admiralty (contd.)	LD PAKENHAM	24 May 51
P. & F.S.	J. Dugdale	4 Aug 45
	J. Callaghan	2 Mar 50
Civil Ld	W. Edwards	4 Aug 45
Ag. & Fish.	**T. WILLIAMS**	3 Aug 45
P.S.	E of Huntingdon	4 Aug 45–22 Nov 50
	P. Collick	5 Sep 45–7 Oct 47
	G. Brown	7 Oct 47–26 Apr 51
	E of Listowel	22 Nov 50–26 Oct 51
	A. Champion	26 Apr 51–26 Oct 51
Air	**VT STANSGATE**	3 Aug 45
	(office not in cabinet)	
	P. NOEL-BAKER	4 Oct 46
	A. HENDERSON	7 Oct 47
U-S.	J. Strachey	4 Aug 45
	G. de Freitas	27 May 46
	A. Crawley	2 Mar 50
Aircraft Production	J. WILMOT (office abolished 1 Apr 46)	4 Aug 45
P.S.	A. Woodburn	4 Aug 45
Civil Av.	LD WINSTER	4 Aug 45
	LD NATHAN	4 Oct 46
	(office in cabinet)	
	LD PAKENHAM	31 May 48
	(office not in cabinet)	
	Ld Pakenham	28 Feb 50
	LD OGMORE	1 Jun 51
P.S.	I. Thomas	10 Aug 45
	G. Lindgren	4 Oct 46
	F. Beswick	2 Mar 50
Colonies	**G. HALL**	3 Aug 45
	A. CREECH JONES	4 Oct 46
	J. GRIFFITHS	28 Feb 50
Min.	E of Listowel	4 Jan 48
	J. DUGDALE	28 Feb 50
U-S.	A. Creech Jones	4 Aug 45
	I. Thomas	40 Oct 46
	D. Rees-Williams	7 Oct 47
	T. Cook	2 Mar 50
C.R.O.	(office not established)	
	VT ADDISON	7 Jul 47
	P. NOEL-BAKER	7 Oct 47
	P. GORDON WALKER	28 Feb 50
Min.	A. HENDERSON	14 Aug 47–7 Oct 47
U-S.	A. Bottomley	7 Jul 47
	P. Gordon Walker	7 Oct 47
	Ld Holden	2 Mar 50
	D. Rees-Williams (Ld Ogmore)	4 Jul 50
	E of Lucan	1 Jun 51
Defence	**C. ATTLEE** (P.M.)	27 Jul 45
	A. ALEXANDER (Vt)	20 Dec 46
	E. SHINWELL	28 Feb 50
Dom. O.	**VT ADDISON**	3 Aug 45
	(became C.R.O. 7 Jul 47)	
U-S.	J. Parker	4 Aug 45
	A. Bottomley	10 May 46
Educ.	**MISS E. WILKINSON**	3 Aug 45
	G. TOMLINSON	10 Feb 47
P.S.	A. Jenkins	4 Aug 45
	D. Hardman	30 Oct 45

Food	SIR B. SMITH	3 Aug 45
	J. STRACHEY	27 May 46
	M. WEBB	28 Feb 50
P.S.	Edith Summerskill	4 Aug 45
	S. Evans	2 Mar 50
	F. Willey	18 Apr 50
Fuel & Power	**E. SHINWELL**	3 Aug 45
	(office not in cabinet)	
	H. GAITSKELL	7 Oct 47
	P. NOEL-BAKER	28 Feb 50
P.S.	W. Foster	4 Aug 45
	H. Gaitskell	10 May 46
	A. Robens	7 Oct 47
	H. Neal	26 Apr 51
Health	**A. BEVAN**	3 Aug 45
	(office not in cabinet)	
	H. MARQUAND	17 Jan 51
P.S.	C. Key	4 Aug 45
	J. Edwards	12 Feb 47
	A. Blenkinsop	1 Feb 49
India & Burma	**LD PETHICK-LAWRENCE**	3 Aug 45
	E of LISTOWEL	17 Apr 47
	(14 Aug 47/4 Jan 48 offices abolished)	
U-S.	A. Henderson	4 Aug 45–14 Aug 47
Information	E. WILLIAMS	4 Aug 45
	E of LISTOWEL	26 Feb 46
	(office wound up 31 Mar 46)	
Lab. & Nat. S.	**G. ISAACS**	3 Aug 45
	A. BEVAN	17 Jan 51
	A. ROBENS	24 Apr 51
P.S.	N. Edwards	4 Aug 45
	F. Lee	2 Mar 50
D. Lanc.	J. HYND	4 Aug 45
	LD PAKENHAM	17 Apr 47
	(office in cabinet)	
	H. DALTON	31 May 48
	VT ALEXANDER	28 Feb 50
Nat. Ins.	**J. GRIFFITHS**	4 Aug 45
	EDITH SUMMERSKILL	28 Feb 50
P.S.	G. Lindgren	4 Aug 45
	T. Steele	4 Oct 46
	H. Taylor	2 Mar 50
Paym.-Gen.	(office vacant)	
	A. GREENWOOD	9 Jul 46
	(office not in cabinet)	
	H. Marquand	5 Mar 47
	(office in cabinet)	
	VT ADDISON	2 Jul 48
	(office not in cabinet)	
	LD MACDONALD of GWAENYSGOR	1 Apr 49
Min. without Portfolio	**A. ALEXANDER**	4 Oct 46–20 Dec 46
	A. GREENWOOD	17 Apr 47–29 Sep 47
Pensions	W. PALING	3 Aug 45
	J. HYND	17 Apr 47
	G. BUCHANAN	7 Oct 47
	H. MARQUAND	2 Jul 48
	G. ISAACS	17 Jan 51
P.S.	Mrs J. Adamson	4 Aug 45

LABOUR GOVERNMENT, 1945–1951 (contd.)

P.S.	A. Blenkinsop	10 May 46
(Pensions)	C. Simmons	1 Feb 49
Postm.-Gen.	E of LISTOWEL	4 Aug 45
	W. PALING	17 Apr 47
	N. EDWARDS	28 Feb 50
Ass.	W. Burke	10 Aug 45
	C. Hobson	7 Oct 47
Scotland	J. WESTWOOD	3 Aug 45
	A. WOODBURN	7 Oct 47
	H. MCNEIL	28 Feb 50
U-S.	G. Buchanan	4 Aug 45–7 Oct 47
	T. Fraser	4 Aug 45–26 Oct 51
	J. Robertson	7 Oct 47–2 Mar 50
	Miss M. Herbison	2 Mar 50–26 Oct 51
Supply	J. WILMOT	3 Aug 45
	G. STRAUSS	7 Oct 47
P.S.	W. Leonard	4 Aug 45–7 Oct 47
	A. Woodburn	1 Apr 46–7 Oct 47
	J. Freeman	7 Oct 47–23 Apr 51
	J. Jones	7 Oct 47–2 Mar 50
	M. Stewart	2 May 51–26 Oct 51
T. & C.	L. SILKIN	4 Aug 45
Planning	(office in cabinet)	
	H. DALTON	28 Feb 50
	(recast as Local Government & Planning 31 Jan 51)	
P.S.	F. Marshall	10 Aug 45
	E. King	7 Oct 47
	G. Lindgren	2 Mar 50
B. Trade	SIR S. CRIPPS	27 Jul 45
	H. WILSON	29 Sep 47
	SIR H. SHAWCROSS	24 Apr 51
P.S.	E. Smith	4 Aug 45
	J. Belcher	12 Jan 46
	J. Edwards	1 Feb 49
	H. Rhodes	2 Mar 50
Sec.	H. Marquand	4 Aug 45
Overseas	H. Wilson	5 Mar 47
Trade	A. Bottomley	7 Oct 47
Transp.	A. BARNES	3 Aug 45
P.S.	G. Strauss	4 Aug 45
	J. Callaghan	7 Oct 47
	Ld Lucas of Chilworth	2 Mar 50
War	J. LAWSON	3 Aug 45
	(office not in cabinet)	
	F. BELLENGER	4 Oct 46
	E. SHINWELL	7 Oct 47
	J. STRACHEY	28 Feb 50
U-S.	Ld Nathan	4 Aug 45
	Ld Pakenham	4 Oct 46–17 Apr 47
F.S.	F. Bellenger	4 Aug 45
	J. Freeman	4 Oct 46–17 Apr 47
U-& F.S	J. Freeman	17 Apr 47
	M. Stewart	7 Oct 47
	W. Wyatt	2 May 51
Works	G. TOMLINSON	4 Aug 45
	C. KEY	10 Feb 47
	R. STOKES	28 Feb 50
Works	G. BROWN	26 Apr 51

P.S.	H. Wilson	4 Aug 45
	E. Durbin	5 Mar 47
	Ld Morrison	26 Sep 48
Law Officers		
Att.-Gen.	SIR H. SHAWCROSS	4 Aug 45
	SIR F. SOSKICE	24 Apr 51
Sol.-Gen.	SIR F. SOSKICE	4 Aug 45
	SIR L. UNGOED-THOMAS	24 Apr 51
Ld Advoc.	G. THOMSON	10 Aug 45
	J. WHEATLEY	7 Oct 47
Sol.-Gen.	D. BLADES[1]	10 Sep 45
Scotland	J. WHEATLEY	19 Mar 47
	D. JOHNSTON	24 Oct 47
Whips		
P.S to	W. Whiteley	3 Aug 45
Treasury		
Lds of	R. Taylor	4 Aug 45–26 Oct 51
Treasury	J. Henderson	4 Aug 45–1 Jan 50
	M. Stewart	10 Aug 45–30 Mar 46
	A. Blenkinsop	10 Aug 45–10 May 46
	F. Collindridge	10 Aug 45–9 Dec 46
	C. Simmons	30 Mar 46–1 Feb 49
	W. Hannan	10 May 46–26 Oct 51
	J. Snow	9 Dec 46–3 Mar 50
	R. Adams	1 Feb 49–23 Apr 50
	W. Wilkins	1 Jan 50–26 Oct 51
	H. Bowden	3 Mar 50–26 Oct 51
	C. Royle	23 Apr 50–26 Oct 51
H.M. Household		
Treasurer	G. MATHERS	4 Aug 45
	A. PEARSON	30 Mar 46
Compt.	A. PEARSON	4 Aug 45
	M. STEWART	30 Mar 46
	F. COLLINDRIDGE	9 Dec 46
V. Chamb.	J. SNOW	10 Aug 45
	M. STEWART	9 Dec 46
	E. POPPLEWELL	16 Oct 47
Cap. Gents	LD AMMON	4 Aug 45
at Arms	LD SHEPHERD	18 Oct 49
Cap. Yeo.	LD WALKDEN	4 Aug 45
of Guard	LD SHEPHERD	6 Jul 49
	LD LUCAS of CHILWORTH	18 Oct 49
	E of LUCAN	5 Mar 50
	LD ARCHIBALD	8 Jun 51
Lds in	Ld Westwood	10 Sep 45–17 Jan 47
Waiting	Ld Pakenham	14 Oct 45–4 Oct 46
	Ld Henderson	21 Oct 45–7 Jun 48
	Ld Chorley	11 Oct 46–31 Mar 50
	Ld Morrison	17 Jan 47–26 Sep 48
	Ld Lucas of Chilworth	9 Jul 48–18 Oct 49
	Ld Shepherd	14 Oct 48–6 Jul 49
	Ld Kershaw	6 Jul 49–26 Oct 51
	Ld Darwen	18 Oct 49–26 Dec 50
	Ld Burden	31 Mar 50–26 Oct 51
	Ld Haden-Guest	13 Feb 51–26 Oct 51

[2] Not a Member of the House of Commons

CONSERVATIVE GOVERNMENT, 1951–1957

P.M.	(SIR) W. CHURCHILL	26 Oct 51–5 Apr 55
	SIR A. EDEN	6 Apr 55–9 Jan 57
Ld Pres.	LD WOOLTON	28 Oct 51
	M of SALISBURY	24 Nov 52
Ld Chanc.	LD SIMONDS	30 Oct 51
	VT KILMUIR	18 Oct 54
Privy S.	M of SALISBURY	28 Oct 51
	H. CROOKSHANK	7 May 52
	R. BUTLER	20 Dec 55
Exchequer	R. BUTLER	28 Oct 51
	H. MACMILLAN	20 Dec 55
Min. Econ.	SIR A. SALTER	31 Oct 51
Affs	(24 Nov 52 office abolished)	
F.S.	J. Boyd-Carpenter	31 Oct 51
	H. Brooke	28 Jul 54
Econ. S.	R. Maudling	24 Nov 52
	Sir E. Boyle	7 Apr 55
	D. Walker-Smith	11 Nov 56
Foreign O.	(SIR) A. EDEN	28 Oct 51
	H. MACMILLAN	7 Apr 55
	S. LLOYD	20 Dec 55
Min. of	S. LLOYD	30 Oct 51–18 Oct 54
State	M of READING	11 Nov 53–9 Jan 57
	A. NUTTING	18 Oct 54–3 Nov 56
	A. NOBLE	9 Nov 56–9 Jan 57
U-S.	M of Reading	31 Oct 51–11 Nov 53
	A. Nutting	31 Oct 51–18 Oct 54
	D. Dodds-Parker	11 Nov 53–18 Oct 54
	R. Turton	18 Oct 54–20 Dec 55
	D. Dodds-Parker	20 Dec 55–9 Jan 57
	Ld J. Hope[1]	18 Oct 54–9 Nov 56
	D. Ormsby-Gore	9 Nov 56–9 Jan 57
Home O.	SIR D. MAXWELL FYFE	28 Oct 51
& Welsh	(Vt Kilmuir)	
Affs	G. LLOYD-GEORGE	18 Oct 54
U-S.	D. Llewellyn	5 Nov 51–14 Oct 52
	Sir H. Lucas-Tooth	3 Feb 52–20 Dec 55
	Ld Lloyd	24 Nov 52–18 Oct 54
	Ld Mancroft	18 Oct 54–9 Jan 57
Admiralty	J. THOMAS (Vt Cilcennin)	31 Oct 51
	VT HAILSHAM	2 Sep 56
P.& F.S.	A. Noble	5 Nov 51
	G. Ward	20 Dec 55
Civil Ld	S. Wingfield Digby	5 Nov 51
Ag. & Fish.	SIR T. DUGDALE	31 Oct 51
	(office in cabinet)	
	SIR T. DUGDALE	3 Sep 53
	D. HEATHCOAT AMORY	28 Jul 54
	(18 Oct 54 Min. of Ag. & Fish. combined with Min. of Food)	
P.S.	W. Deedes	20 Dec 55–9 Jan 57
	Ld Carrington	5 Nov 51–18 Oct 54
	R. Nugent	5 Nov 51–9 Jan 57
	Earl St Aldwyn	18 Oct 54–9 Jan 57
	H. Nicholls	7 Apr 55–9 Jan 57
Air	LD DE L'ISLE AND DUDLEY	31 Oct 51
Air (contd.)	N. BIRCH	20 Dec 55
U-S.	N. Birch	3 Nov 51
	G. Ward	29 Feb 52
	C. Soames	20 Dec 55
Colonies	O. LYTTELTON	28 Oct 51
	A. LENNOX-BOYD	28 Jul 54
Min.	A. LENNOX-BOYD	2 Nov 51
	H. HOPKINSON	7 May 52
	J. HARE	20 Dec 55
	J. MACLAY	18 Oct 56
U-S.	E of Munster	5 Nov 51
	Ld Lloyd	18 Oct 54
C.R.O.	LD ISMAY	28 Oct 51
	M of SALISBURY	12 Mar 52
	VT SWINTON	24 Nov 52
	E of HOME	7 Apr 55
U-S.	J. Foster	3 Nov 51
	D. Dodds-Parker	18 Oct 54
	A. Noble	20 Dec 55
	Ld J. Hope[1]	9 Nov 56
Co-ord. of	LD LEATHERS	30 Oct 51
Transport	(3 Sep 53 office abolished)	
Fuel & Power		
Defence	W. CHURCHILL (P.M.)	28 Oct 51
	EARL ALEXANDER of TUNIS	1 Mar 52
	H. MACMILLAN	18 Oct 54
	S. LLOYD	7 Apr 55
	SIR W. MONCKTON	20 Dec 55
	A. HEAD	18 Oct 56
P.S.	N. Birch	28 Feb 52
	Ld Carrington	18 Oct 54
	E of Gosford	26 May 56
Education	MISS F. HORSBRUGH	2 Nov 51
	(office in cabinet)	
	MISS F. HORSBRUGH	3 Sep 53
	SIR D. ECCLES	18 Oct 54
P.S.	K. Pickthorn	5 Nov 51
	D. Vosper	18 Oct 54
Food	G. LLOYD-GEORGE	31 Oct 51
	(office in cabinet)	
	G. LLOYD-GEORGE	3 Sep 53
	D. HEATHCOAT AMORY	18 Oct 54
	(& combined with Min. of Ag. & Fish.)	
P.S.	C. Hill	31 Oct 51
Fuel & Power	G. LLOYD	31 Oct 51
	A. JONES	20 Dec 55
P.S.	L. Joynson-Hicks	5 Nov 51
	D. Renton	20 Dec 55
Health	H. CROOKSHANK	30 Oct 51
	(office not in cabinet)	
	I. MACLEOD	7 May 52
	R. TURTON	20 Dec 55
P.S.	Miss P. Hornsby-Smith	3 Nov 51
Housing &	H. MACMILLAN	30 Oct 51
Loc. Govt	D. SANDYS	18 Oct 54
P.S.	E. Marples	3 Nov 51
	W. Deedes	18 Oct 54
	E. Powell	20 Dec 55

[1] M.P. Not a Member of the House of Lords

CONSERVATIVE GOVERNMENT, 1951–1957 (contd.)

Lab. &	**SIR W. MONCKTON**	28 Oct 51
Nat. S.	**I. MACLEOD**	20 Dec 55
P.S.	Sir P. Bennett	31 Oct 51
	H. Watkinson	28 May 52
	R. Carr	20 Dec 55
D. Lanc.	VT SWINTON	31 Oct 51–24 Nov 52
	(also Min. of Materials)	
	(office in cabinet)	
	LD WOOLTON (Vt)	24 Nov 52
	(Sep 53–Aug 54 also Min. of Materials)	
	E of SELKIRK	20 Dec 55
Materials	VT SWINTON	31 Oct 51–24 Nov 52
	(also D. Lancaster)	
	SIR A. SALTER	24 Nov 52–1 Sep 53
	(1 Sep 53–16 Aug 54 Ld Woolton	
	combined Materials with D. Lanc. in	
	cabinet. 16 Aug 54 Min. of Materials	
	wound up)	
Min. without	E OF MUNSTER	18 Oct 54–8 Jan 57
Portfolio		
Nat. Ins.	O. PEAKE	31 Oct 51
	(3 Sep 53 combined with Min. of	
	Pensions)	
Paym.-Gen.	**LD CHERWELL**	30 Oct 51
	(office not in cabinet)	
	E of SELKIRK	11 Nov 53
	(20 Dec 55 office vacant)	
	(office in cabinet)	
	SIR W. MONCKTON	18 Oct 56
Pensions	D. HEATHCOAT AMORY	5 Nov 51
(& Nat. Ins.)	(1 Sep 53 mins combined)	
	O. PEAKE	3 Sep 53
	(office in cabinet)	
	O. PEAKE	18 Oct 54
	(office not in cabinet)	
	J. BOYD-CARPENTER	20 Dec 55
P.S.	J. Smyth	5 Nov 51–20 Dec 55
	R. Turton	5 Nov 51–18 Oct 54
	E. Marples	18 Oct 54–20 Dec 55
	Miss E. Pitt	20 Dec 55–9 Jan 57
	R. Wood	20 Dec 55–9 Jan 57
Post.-Gen.	EARL DE LA WARR	5 Nov 51
	C. HILL	7 Apr 55
Ass.	D. Gammans	5 Nov 51
	C. Alport	20 Dec 55
Power	(see Fuel & Power above)	
Scotland	**J. STUART**	30 Oct 51
Min.	E OF HOME	2 Nov 51
	T. GALBRAITH	7 Apr 55
	(Ld Strathclyde)	
U-S.	T. Galbraith	2 Nov 51–5 Apr 55
	W. Snadden	2 Nov 51–13 Jun 55
	J. Henderson Stewart	
		4 Feb 52–9 Jan 57
	J. Browne	7 Apr 55–9 Jan 57
	N. Macpherson	13 Jun 55–9 Jan 57
Supply	D. SANDYS	31 Oct 51
	S. LLOYD	18 Oct 54
	R. MAUDLING	7 Apr 55

P.S.	T. Low	3 Nov 51
	Sir E. Boyle	28 Jul 54
	F. Erroll	7 Apr 55
	I. Harvey	11 Nov 56
B. Trade	**P. THORNEYCROFT**	30 Oct 51
Min.	D. HEATHCOAT AMORY	3 Sep 53
	T. LOW	28 Jul 54
P.S.	H. Strauss	3 Nov 51
	D. Kaberry	7 Apr 55
	D. Walker-Smith	19 Oct 55
	F. Erroll	11 Nov 56
Sec.	H. Hopkinson	3 Nov 51
Overseas	H. Mackeson	28 May 52
Trade	(3 Sep 53 office abolished, Min. of State	
	took over)	
Transport	J. MACLAY	31 Oct 51
(& Civil Av.)	A. LENNOX-BOYD	7 May 52
	(Ministries of Transport & Civil	
	Aviation merged 1 Oct 53)	
	J. BOYD-CARPENTER	28 Jul 54
	H. WATKINSON	20 Dec 55
P.S.	J. Braithwaite	5 Nov 51–1 Nov 53
	R. Maudling	18 Apr 52–24 Nov 52
	J. Profumo	24 Nov 52–9 Jan 57
	H. Molson	11 Nov 53–9 Jan 57
War	A. HEAD	31 Oct 51
	J. HARE	18 Oct 56
U-S. & F.S.	J. Hutchison	5 Nov 51
	F. Maclean	18 Oct 54
Works	(SIR) D. ECCLES	1 Nov 51
	N. BIRCH	18 Oct 54
	(office in cabinet)	
	P. BUCHAN-HEPBURN	20 Dec 55
P.S.	H. Molson	3 Nov 51
	R. Bevins	11 Nov 53

Law Officers

Att.-Gen.	SIR L. HEALD	3 Nov 51
	SIR R. MANNINGHAM-BULLER	
		18 Oct 54
Sol.-Gen.	SIR R. MANNINGHAM-BULLER	
		3 Nov 51
	SIR H. HYLTON-FOSTER	18 Oct 54
Ld Advoc.	J. CLYDE	2 Nov 51
	W. MILLIGAN	30 Dec 54
Sol.-Gen.	W. MILLIGAN[2]	3 Nov 51
Scotland	W. GRANT	10 Jan 55

Whips

P.S. to	P. Buchan-Hepburn	30 Oct 51
Treasury	E. Heath	30 Dec 55
Lds of	H. Mackeson	7 Nov 51–28 May 52
Treasury	(Sir) H. Butcher	7 Nov 51–3 Jul 53
	E. Heath	7 Nov 51–20 Dec 55
	T. Galbraith (Jnr)	7 Nov 51–4 Jun 54
	D. Vosper	7 Nov 51–18 Oct 54
	H. Oakshott	28 May 52–13 Jun 55
	M. Redmayne	3 Jul 53–9 Jan 57
	R. Thompson	28 Jul 54–8 Apr 56
	G. Wills	26 Oct 54–9 Jan 57

[1] M.P. Not a Member of the House of Lords

CONSERVATIVE GOVERNMENT, 1951–1957 (*contd.*)

Lds of	P. Legh	13 Jun 55–9 Jan 57	*Cap. Gents*	EARL FORTESCUE		5 Nov 51
Treasury	E. Wakefield	24 Jan 56–9 Jan 57	*at Arms*			
(*contd.*)	H. Harrison	8 Apr 56–9 Jan 57	*Capt.Yeo.*	E of ONSLOW		5 Nov 51
H.M. Household			*of Guard*			
Treasurer	(SIR) C. DREWE	7 Nov 51	*Lds in*	E of Birkenhead	5 Nov 51–28 Jan 55	
	T. GALBRAITH (Jnr)	13 Jun 55	*Waiting*	E of Selkirk	5 Nov 51–11 Nov 53	
Compt.	R. CONANT	7 Nov 51		Ld Lloyd	7 Nov 51–24 Nov 52	
	T. GALBRAITH (Jnr)	7 Jun 54		Ld Mancroft	15 Dec 52–18 Oct 54	
	H. OAKSHOTT	13 Jun 55		Ld Hawke	11 Nov 53–9 Jan 57	
V. Chamb.	H. STUDHOLME	7 Nov 51		Ld Fairfax	18 Oct 54–9 Jan 57	
	R. THOMPSON	8 Apr 56		Ld Chesham	28 Jan 55–9 Jan 57	

CONSERVATIVE GOVERNMENT, 1957–1964

P.M.	**H. MACMILLAN**		*Min. of State*	P. THOMAS	27 Jun 63–16 Oct 64
		10 Jan 57–13 Oct 63	*U-S.*	E of Gosford	18 Jan 57–23 Oct 58
	SIR A. DOUGLAS-HOME			I. Harvey	18 Jan 57–24 Nov 58
	(*formerly E of Home*)			M of Lansdowne	23 Oct 58–20 Apr 62
		18 Oct 63–16 Oct 64		J. Profumo	28 Nov 58–16 Jan 59
1st. Sec.	**R. BUTLER**	13 Jul 62		R. Allan	16 Jan 59–7 Oct 60
of State	(*office wound up 18 Oct 63*)			J. Godber	28 Oct 60–27 Jun 61
Ld Pres.	**M of SALISBURY**	13 Jan 57		P. Thomas	27 Jun 61–27 Jun 63
	E of HOME	29 Mar 57		P. Smithers	16 Jul 62–29 Jan 64
	VT HAILSHAM	17 Sep 57		R. Mathew	30 Jan 64–16 Oct 64
	E of HOME	14 Oct 59	*Home O.*	**R. BUTLER**	13 Jan 57
	VT HAILSHAM (*Q. Hogg*)	27 Jul 60		**H. BROOKE**	13 Jul 62
	(*also Min. for Science*)		*Min. Home*	D. VOSPER	28 Oct 60
Ld Chanc.	**VT KILMUIR**	14 Jan 57	*Affs*	D. RENTON	27 Jun 61
	LD DILHORNE	13 Jul 62		EARL JELLICOE	17 Jul 62
Privy S.	**R. BUTLER**	13 Jan 57		LD DERWENT	21 Oct 63
	(*also Home Sec.*)		*U-S.*	Miss P. Hornsby-Smith	
	VT HAILSHAM	14 Oct 59			18 Jan 57–22 Oct 59
	(*also Min. for Science*)			J. Simon	18 Jan 57–6 Jan 58
	E. HEATH	27 Jul 60		D. Renton	17 Jan 58–27 Jun 61
	S. LLOYD	20 Oct 63		D. Vosper	22 Oct 59–28 Oct 60
Exchequer	**P. THORNEYCROFT**	13 Jan 57		Earl Bathurst	8 Feb 61–16 Jul 62
	D. HEATHCOAT AMORY	6 Jan 58		C. Fletcher-Cooke	27 Jun 61–27 Feb 63
	S. LLOYD	27 Jul 60		C. Woodhouse	16 Jul 62–16 Oct 64
	R. MAUDLING	13 Jul 62		Miss M. Pike	1 Mar 63–16 Oct 64
	(*see also Paymaster-General*)		*Admiralty*	E of SELKIRK	16 Jan 57
F.S.	E. Powell	16 Jan 57		LD CARRINGTON	16 Oct 59
	J. Simon	6 Jan 58		EARL JELLICOE	22 Oct 63
	Sir E. Boyle	22 Oct 59		(*1 Apr 64, reorganised under Min. of*	
	A. Barber	16 Jul 62		*Defence*)	
	A. Green	23 Oct 63	*P. & F.S.*	C. Soames	18 Jan 57
Econ. S.	N. Birch	16 Jan 57		R. Allan	17 Jan 58
	(*office vacant 6 Jan 58*)			C. Orr Ewing	16 Jan 59
	F. Erroll	23 Oct 58		(*16 Oct 59 office vacant*)	
	A. Barber	22 Oct 59	*Civil Ld*	T. Galbraith	18 Jan 57
	E. du Cann	16 Jul 62		C. Orr Ewing	16 Oct 59
	M. Macmillan	21 Oct 63		J. Hay	3 May 63
Foreign O.	**S. LLOYD**	14 Jan 57	*Ag. Fish*	**D. HEATHCOAT AMORY**	14 Jan 57
	E of HOME	27 Jul 60	*& Food*	**J. HARE**	6 Jan 58
	R. BUTLER	20 Oct 63		**C. SOAMES**	27 Jul 60
Min. of	A. NOBLE	16 Jan 57–16 Jan 59	*P.S.*	Earl St Aldwyn	18 Jan 57–27 Jun 58
State	D. ORMSBY-GORE			J. Godber	18 Jan 57–28 Oct 60
		16 Jan 57–27 Jun 61		Earl Waldegrave	27 Jun 58–16 Jul 62
	J. PROFUMO	16 Jan 59–27 Jul 60		W. Vane	28 Oct 60–16 Jul 62
	J. GODBER	27 Jun 61–27 Jun 63		Ld St. Oswald	16 Jul 62–16 Oct 64
	E of DUNDEE	9 Oct 61–16 Oct 64		J. Scott-Hopkins	16 Jul 62–16 Oct 64

CONSERVATIVE GOVERNMENT, 1957–1964 (contd.)

Air	G. WARD	16 Jan 57
	J. AMERY	28 Oct 60
	H. FRASER	16 Jul 62
	(1 Apr 64, reorganised under Min. of Defence)	
U-S.	C. Orr Ewing	18 Jan 57
	A. Neave	16 Jan 59
	W. Taylor	16 Oct 59
	J. Ridsdale	16 Jul 62
Aviation	(see Transp. & Civil Av.)	
	D. SANDYS	14 Oct 59
	P. THORNEYCROFT	27 Jul 60
	(office not in cabinet)	
	J. AMERY	16 Jul 62
	(for Junior Ministers see below Trans. & Civil Av.)	
P.S	G. Rippon	22 Oct 59
	C. Woodhouse	9 Oct 61
	B. de Ferranti	16 Jul 62
	N. Marten	3 Dec 62
Colonies	**A. LENNOX-BOYD**	14 Jan 57
	I. MACLEOD	14 Oct 59
	R. MAUDLING	9 Oct 61
	(joint minister with C.R.O. 13 Jul 62)	
	D. SANDYS	13 Jul 62
Min.	E of PERTH	16 Jan 57
	M of LANSDOWNE	20 Apr 62
	(joint with C.R.O. 21 Oct 63)	
U-S.	J. Profumo	18 Jan 57
	J. Amery	28 Nov 58
	H. Fraser	28 Oct 60
	N. Fisher	16 Jul 62–16 Oct 64
	R. Hornby	24 Oct 63–16 Oct 64
	(joint with C.R.O 21 Oct 63)	
C.R.O.	**E of HOME**	14 Jan 57
	D. SANDYS	27 Jul 60
	(joint with Col. O. 13 Jul 62)	
Min.	C. ALPORT	22 Oct 59–8 Feb 61
	D of DEVONSHIRE	6 Sep 62–16 Oct 64
	(joint with Col. O. 21 Oct 63)	
U-S.	C. Alport	18 Jan 57
	R. Thompson	22 Oct 59
	D of Devonshire	28 Oct 60–6 Sep 62
	B. Braine	8 Feb 61–16 Jul 62
	J. Tilney	16 Jul 62–16 Oct 64
	(joint with Col. O. 21 Oct 63)	
Defence	**D. SANDYS**	13 Jan 57
	H. WATKINSON	14 Oct 59
	P. THORNEYCROFT	13 Jul 62
P.S.	Ld Mancroft	18 Jan 57
	(11 Jun 57 office vacant)	
	(Defence Dept. reorganised 1 Apr 64)	
Min. of State		
Air	H. FRASER	1 Apr 64
Army	J. RAMSDEN	1 Apr 64
Navy	EARL JELLICOE	1 Apr 64
U-S. Air Force	J. Ridsdale	1 Apr 64
U-S. Army	P. Kirk	1 Apr 64
U-S. Navy	J. Hay	1 Apr 64

Education.	**VT HAILSHAM**	13 Jan 57
	G. LLOYD	17 Sep 57
	SIR D. ECCLES	14 Oct 59
	SIR E. BOYLE	13 Jul 62
	(Educ. & Science 1 Apr 64)	
	Q. HOGG	1 Apr 64
	(formerly Vt Hailsham)	
Min. of State	**SIR E. BOYLE**	1 Apr 64
	(office not in cabinet)	
	LD NEWTON	1 Apr 64
P.S.	Sir E. Boyle	18 Jan 57
	K. Thompson	22 Oct 59
	C. Chataway	16 Jul 62
	(reorganisation 1 Apr 64)	
U-S.	E of Bessborough	1 Apr 64
	C. Chataway	1 Apr 64
Health	D. VOSPER	16 Jan 57
	D. WALKER-SMITH	17 Sep 57
	E. POWELL	27 Jul 60
	(office in cabinet)	
	E. POWELL	13 Jul 62
	A. BARBER	20 Oct 63
P.S.	J. Vaughan-Morgan	18 Jan 57
	R. Thompson	17 Sep 57
	Miss E. Pitt	22 Oct 59
	B. Braine	16 Jul 62–16 Oct 64
	Ld Newton	6 Sep 62–1 Apr 64
	M of Lothian	24 Mar 64–16 Apr 64
Housing,	**H. BROOKE**	13 Jan 57
Loc. Govt	**C. HILL**	9 Oct 61
& Welsh Affs	**SIR K. JOSEPH**	13 Jul 62
Min. of State for Welsh Affs	LD BRECON	12 Dec 57
P.S.	R. Bevins	18 Jan 57
	Sir K. Joseph	22 Oct 59–9 Oct 61
	Earl Jellicoe	27 Jun 61–16 Jul 62
	G. Rippon	9 Oct 61–16 Jul 62
	F. Corfield	16 Jul 62–16 Oct 64
	Ld Hastings	3 Dec 62–16 Oct 64
Labour &	**I. MACLEOD**	14 Jan 57
Nat. S.	**E. HEATH**	14 Oct 59
	(12 Nov 59 – Min. of Labour)	
	J. HARE	27 Jul 60
	J. GODBER	20 Oct 63
P.S.	R. Carr	19 Jan 57
	R. Wood	14 Apr 58
	P. Thomas	22 Oct 59
	A. Green	27 Jun 61
	W. Whitelaw	16 Jul 62
D. Lanc.	**C. HILL**	13 Jan 57
	I. MACLEOD	9 Oct 61
	VT BLAKENHAM	20 Oct 63
	(J. Hare)	
Paym.-Gen.	R. MAUDLING	16 Jan 57
	(office in cabinet)	
	R. MAUDLING	17 Sep 57
	LD MILLS	14 Oct 59
	(after 9 Oct 61 Chief Sec. to Treasury & Paym.-Gen.)	
	H. BROOKE	9 Oct 61
	J. BOYD-CARPENTER	13 Jul 62

CONSERVATIVE GOVERNMENT, 1957–1964 (contd.)

Pensions & Nat. Ins.	J. BOYD-CARPENTER	16 Jan 57
	N. MACPHERSON	16 Jul 62
	R. WOOD	21 Oct 63
P.S.	Miss E. Pitt	19 Jan 57–22 Oct 59
	R. Wood	19 Jan 57–14 Apr 58
	W. Vane	14 Apr 58–28 Oct 60
	Miss P. Hornsby-Smith	22 Oct 59–31 Aug 61
	B. Braine	28 Oct 60–8 Feb 61
	R. Sharples	8 Feb 61–16 Jul 62
	Mrs M. Thatcher	9 Oct 61–16 Oct 64
	S. Maydon	16 Jul 62–16 Oct 64
Min. without Portfolio	E of MUNSTER	16 Jan 57
	LD MANCROFT	11 Jun 57
	E of DUNDEE	23 Oct 58
	(office in cabinet)	
	LD MILLS	9 Oct 61–14 Jul 62
	W. DEEDES	13 Jul 62–16 Oct 64
	LD CARRINGTON	20 Oct 63–16 Oct 64
Post.-Gen.	E. MARPLES	16 Jan 57
	R. BEVINS	22 Oct 59
Ass.	K. Thompson	18 Jan 57
	Miss M. Pike	22 Oct 59
	R. Mawby	1 Mar 63
Power	**LD MILLS**	13 Jan 57
	(office not in cabinet)	
	R. WOOD	14 Oct 59
	(office in cabinet)	
	F. ERROLL	20 Oct 63
P.S.	D. Renton	18 Jan 57
	Sir I. Horobin	17 Jan 58
	J. George	22 Oct 59
	J. Peyton	25 Jun 62
Science	**VT HAILSHAM**	14 Oct 59
	(1 Apr 64 Educ. & Science)	
P.S.	D. Freeth	8 Feb 61
	E of Bessborough	24 Oct 63
	(1 Apr 64. Educ. & Science)	
Scotland	**J. MACLAY**	13 Jan 57
	M. NOBLE	13 Jul 62
Min. of State	LD STRATHCLYDE	17 Jan 57
	LD FORBES	23 Oct 58
	J. BROWNE *(Ld Craigton)*	22 Oct 59
U-S.	J. Browne	18 Jan 57–22 Oct 59
	N. Macpherson	19 Jan 57–28 Oct 60
	Ld J. Hope	18 Jan 57–22 Oct 59
	T. Galbraith	22 Oct 59–8 Nov 62
	G. Leburn	22 Oct 59–15 Aug 63
	R. Brooman-White	28 Oct 60–12 Dec 63
	Lady Tweedsmuir	3 Dec 62–16 Oct 64
	A. Stodart	19 Aug 63–16 Oct 64
	G. Campbell	12 Dec 63–16 Oct 64
Supply	A. JONES	16 Jan 57
	(office wound up 22 Oct 59)	
P.S.	W. Taylor	18 Jan 57
	(office wound up 22 Oct 59)	

Technical Co-op.	*(office not established)*	
	D. VOSPER	27 Jun 61
	R. CARR	9 May 63
B. Trade	**SIR D. ECCLES**	13 Jan 57
	R. MAUDLING	14 Oct 59
	F. ERROLL	9 Oct 61
	E. HEATH	20 Oct 63
	(also Sec. of State for Industry, Trade & Regional Development)	
Min. of State	D. WALKER-SMITH	16 Jan 57
	J. VAUGHAN-MORGAN	17 Sep 57
	F. ERROLL	22 Oct 59
	SIR K. JOSEPH	9 Oct 61
	A. GREEN	16 Jul 62–23 Oct 63
	LD DERWENT	6 Sep 62–23 Oct 63
	LD DRUMALBYN	23 Oct 63–16 Oct 64
	(formerly N. Macpherson)	
	E. DU CANN	21 Oct 63–16 Oct 64
P.S.	F. Erroll	18 Jan 57
	J. Rodgers	24 Oct 58
	N. Macpherson	28 Oct 60
	D. Price	17 Jul 62
Transport & Civil Av.	**H. WATKINSON**	13 Jan 57
	(14 Oct 59 Min. of Trans. only)	
	E. MARPLES	14 Oct 59
	(see above, Min. of Aviation)	
P.S.	R. Nugent	18 Jan 57–22 Oct 59
	A. Neave	18 Jan 57–16 Jan 59
	J. Hay	16 Jan 59–3 May 63
	Ld Chesham	22 Oct 59–16 Oct 64
	J. Hughes-Hallett	26 Apr 61–16 Oct 64
	T. Galbraith	3 May 63–16 Oct 64
War	J. HARE	16 Jan 57
	C. SOAMES	6 Jan 58
	J. PROFUMO	27 Jul 60
	J. GODBER	27 Jun 63
	J. RAMSDEN	21 Oct 63
	(1 Apr 64 reorganised under Min. of Defence)	
U-S. & F.S.	J. Amery	18 Jan 57
	H. Fraser	28 Nov 58
	J. Ramsden	28 Oct 60
	P. Kirk	24 Oct 63
Works	H. MOLSON	16 Jan 57
	LD J. HOPE[1]	22 Oct 59
	(16 Jul 62 Min. of Public Building & Works)	
	G. RIPPON	16 Jul 62
	(office in cabinet)	
	G. RIPPON	20 Oct 63
	(Min. of Public Building & Works)	
P.S.	H. Nicholls	18 Jan 57
	R. Thompson	28 Oct 60
	R. Sharples	16 Jul 62
Law Officers		
Att.-Gen.	SIR R. MANNINGHAM-BULLER	17 Jan 57
	SIR J. HOBSON	16 Jul 62

[1] M.P. Not a Member of the House of Lords

CONSERVATIVE GOVERNMENT, 1957–1964

Sol.-Gen.	SIR H. HYLTON-FOSTER	17 Jan 57
	SIR J. SIMON	22 Oct 59
	SIR J. HOBSON	8 Feb 62
	SIR P. RAWLINSON	19 Jul 62
Ld. Advoc.	W. MILLIGAN	17 Jan 57
	W. GRANT	5 Apr 60
	I. SHEARER[1]	12 Oct 62
Sol.-Gen.	W. GRANT	17 Jan 57
Scotland	D. ANDERSON	11 May 60
	N. WYLIE	27 Apr 64

Whips

P.S. to	E. HEATH	17 Jan 57
Treasury	M. REDMAYNE	14 Oct 59
Lds of	M. Redmayne	21 Jan 57–14 Oct 59
Treasury	P. Legh	21 Jan 57–17 Sep 57
	E. Wakefield	21 Jan 57–23 Oct 58
	H. Harrison	21 Jan 57–16 Jan 59
	A. Barber	9 Apr 57–19 Feb 58
	R. Brooman-White	28 Oct 57–21 Jun 60
	P. Bryan	19 Feb 58–9 Feb 61
	M. Hughes-Young	23 Oct 58–6 Mar 62
	G. Finlay	16 Jan 59–28 Oct 60
	D. Gibson-Watt	22 Oct 59–29 Nov 61
	R. Chichester-Clark	21 Jun 60–29 Nov 61
	J. Hill	28 Oct 60–16 Oct 64
	W. Whitelaw	6 Mar 61–16 Jul 62
	J. Peel	29 Nov 61–16 Oct 64
	M. Noble	29 Nov 61–13 Jul 62
	F. Pearson	6 Mar 62–19 Oct 63
	G. Campbell	6 Sep 62–12 Dec 63
	M. Hamilton	6 Sep 62–16 Oct 64

	M. McLaren	21 Nov 63–16 Oct 64
	I. MacArthur	12 Dec 63–16 Oct 64

H.M. Household

Treasurer	H. OAKSHOTT	19 Jan 57
	P. LEGH (Ld Newton)	16 Jan 59
	E. WAKEFIELD	21 Jun 60
	M. HUGHES-YOUNG	6 Mar 62
Compt.	(SIR) G. WILLS	19 Jan 57
	E. WAKEFIELD	23 Oct 58
	H. HARRISON	16 Jan 59
	R. CHICHESTER-CLARK	29 Nov 61
V. Chamb.	R. THOMPSON	21 Jan 57
	P. LEGH	17 Sep 57
	F. WAKEFIELD	16 Jan 59
	R. BROOMAN-WHITE	21 Jun 60
	G. FINLAY	28 Oct 60
Cap. Gents	EARL FORTESCUE	21 Jan 57
at Arms	EARL ST ALDWYN	27 Jun 58
Cap. Yeo.	E of ONSLOW	21 Jan 57
of Guard	LD NEWTON	28 Oct 60
	VT GOSCHEN	6 Sep 62
Lds in	Ld Hawke	21 Jan 57–11 Jun 57
Waiting	Ld Fairfax	21 Jan 57–21 Jun 57
	Ld Chesham	21 Jan 57–22 Oct 59
	M of Lansdowne	11 Jun 57–23 Oct 58
	Earl Bathurst	17 Sep 57–8 Feb 61
	E of Gosford	23 Oct 58–22 Oct 59
	Ld St Oswald	22 Oct 59–16 Jul 62
	Earl Jellicoe	8 Feb 61–27 Jun 61
	Ld Hastings	6 Mar 61–3 Dec 62
	Ld Denham	27 Jun 61–16 Oct 64
	M of Lothian	6 Sep 62–3 Mar 64
	Earl Ferrers	3 Dec 62–10 Oct 64

LABOUR GOVERNMENT, 1964–1970

P.M.	H. WILSON	16 Oct 64–19 Jun 70
1st. Sec.	G. BROWN	16 Oct 64
of State	M. STEWART	11 Aug 66–18 Mar 68
	(office linked to Dept. of Econ. Affairs 16 Oct 64–29 Aug 67)	
	MRS B. CASTLE	6 Apr 68
	(office linked to Min. of Employment)	
Ld Pres.	H. BOWDEN	16 Oct 64
	R. CROSSMAN	11 Aug 66
	F. PEART	18 Oct 68
Ld Chanc.	LD GARDINER	16 Oct 64
Privy S.	E of LONGFORD	18 Oct 64
	SIR F. SOSKICE	23 Dec 65
	E of LONGFORD	6 Apr 66
	LD SHACKLETON	16 Jan 68
	F. PEART	6 Apr 68
	LD SHACKLETON	18 Oct 68
Exchequer	J. CALLAGHAN	16 Oct 64
	R. JENKINS	30 Nov 67
Chief Sec	J. DIAMOND	20 Oct 64
	(office in cabinet)	
	J. DIAMOND	1 Nov 68

Min. of	D. TAVERNE	6 Apr 68
State	W. RODGERS	13 Oct 69
F.S.	N. MacDermot	21 Oct 64
	H. Lever	29 Aug 67
	D. TAVERNE	13 Oct 69
Econ. S.	A. Crosland	19 Oct 64
	(de facto Min. of State, Econ. Affs office abolished 22 Dec 64)	
Economic	G. BROWN	16 Oct 64
Affs	M. STEWART	11 Aug 66
	P. SHORE	29 Aug 67
	(office abolished 6 Oct 69)	
Min. of	A. CROSLAND	20 Oct 64
State	(until 22 Dec 64 nominally Econ. Sec. to Treasury)	
	A. ALBU	27 Jan 65–7 Jan 67
	T. URWIN	6 Apr 68–6 Oct 69
U-S.	M. Foley	21 Oct 64–6 Apr 66
	W. Rodgers	21 Oct 4–7 Jan 67
	H. Lever	7 Jan 67–29 Aug 67
	P. Shore	7 Jan 67–29 Aug 67
	A. Williams	29 Aug 67–6 Oct 69

[1] Not a Member of the House of Commons

LABOUR GOVERNMENT, 1964–1970 (contd.)

U-S. (contd.)	E. Dell	29 Aug 67–6 Apr 68
Foreign O. (& C.R.O.)	**P. GORDON WALKER**[2]	16 Oct 64
	M. STEWART	22 Jan 65
	G. BROWN	11 Aug 66
Foreign O. (& C.R.O.)	**M. STEWART**	16 Mar 68
	(merged with Comm. O. 17 Oct 68)	
Min. of State	LD CARADON	16 Oct 64–19 Jun 70
	G. THOMSON	19 Oct 64–6 Apr 66
		& 7 Jan 67–29 Aug 67
	W. PADLEY	19 Oct 64–7 Jan 67
	LD CHALFONT	23 Oct 64–19 Jun 70
	MRS E. WHITE	11 Apr 66–7 Jan 67
	F. MULLEY	7 Jan 67–6 Oct 69
	G. ROBERTS	29 Aug 67–13 Oct 69
	LD SHEPHERD	17 Oct 68–19 Jun 70
U-S.	Ld Walston	20 Oct 64–7 Jan 67
	W. Rodgers	7 Jan 67–3 Jul 68
	M. Foley	3 Jul 68–19 Jun 70
	W. Whitlock	17 Oct 68–13 Oct 69
	E. Luard	13 Oct 69–19 Jun 70
Home O.	**SIR F. SOSKICE**	18 Oct 64
	R. JENKINS	23 Dec 65
	J. CALLAGHAN	30 Nov 67
Min. of State	MISS A. BACON	19 Oct 64
	LD STONHAM	29 Aug 67
	MRS S. WILLIAMS	13 Oct 69
U-S.	Ld Stonham	20 Oct 64–29 Aug 67
	G. Thomas	20 Oct 64–6 Apr 66
	M. Foley	6 Apr 66–7 Jan 67
	D. Taverne	6 Apr 66–6 Apr 68
	D. Ennals	7 Jan 67–1 Nov 68
	E. Morgan	6 Apr 68–19 Jun 70
	M. Rees	1 Nov 68–19 Jun 70
Ag. Fish. & Food	**F. PEART**	18 Oct 64
	C. HUGHES	6 Apr 68
P.S.	J. Mackie	20 Oct 64–19 Jun 70
	J. Hoy	21 Oct 64–19 Jun 70
Aviation	R. JENKINS	18 Oct 64
	F. MULLEY	23 Dec 65
	J. STONEHOUSE	7 Jan 67
	(office abolished 15 Feb 67)	
P.S.	J. Stonehouse	20 Oct 64–7 Jan 67
	J. Snow	6 Apr 66–7 Jan 67
Colonies	**A. GREENWOOD**	18 Oct 64
	E of LONGFORD	23 Dec 65
	F. LEE	6 Apr 66
	(came under Dept. of Comm. Affs 1 Aug 66, office abolished 7 Jan 67)	
U-S.	Mrs E. White	20 Oct 64–11 Oct 65
	Ld Taylor	20 Oct 64–11 Apr 66
	Ld Beswick	11 Oct 65–1 Aug 66
	(Ld Taylor & Ld Beswick were also U-S. at C.R.O.)	
	J. Stonehouse	6 Apr 66–7 Jan 67
C.R.O.	**A. BOTTOMLEY**	18 Oct 64
	(re-named Commonwealth Affs 1 Aug 66)	
C.R.O. (contd.)	**H. BOWDEN**	11 Aug 66
	G. THOMSON	29 Aug 67
	(merged with Foreign O. 17 Oct 68)	
Min. of State	C. HUGHES	19 Oct 64–6 Apr 66
	MRS J. HART	6 Apr 66–26 Jul 67
	G. THOMAS	7 Jan 67–6 Apr 68
	LD SHEPHERD	26 Jul 67
U-S.	Ld Taylor	20 Oct 64
	Ld Beswick	11 Oct 65
	(held jointly with U-S. at Colonies until 1 Aug 66)	
	W. Whitlock	26 Jul 67
Defence	**D. HEALEY**	16 Oct 64
Min. Army & Dep. Sec. of State	F. MULLEY	19 Oct 64
	G. REYNOLDS	24 Dec 65
	(no Dep. Sec. of State after 24 Dec 65 office abolished 7 Jan 67)	
U-S. Army	G. Reynolds	20 Oct 64
	M. Rees	24 Dec 65
	D. Ennals	6 Apr 66
	J. Boyden	7 Jan 67
	I. Richard	13 Oct 69
Min. Navy	C. MAYHEW	19 Oct 64
	J. MALLALIEU	19 Feb 66
	(office abolished 7 Jan 67)	
U-S. Navy	J. Mallalieu	21 Oct 64
	Ld Winterbottom	6 Apr 66
	M. Foley	7 Jan 67
	D. Owen	3 Jul 68
Min. Air Force	LD SHACKLETON	19 Oct 64
	(office abolished 7 Jan 67)	
U-S. Air Force	B. Millan	20 Oct 64
	M. Rees	16 Apr 66
	Ld Winterbottom	1 Nov 68
Min. of Defence for Admin.	G. REYNOLDS	7 Jan 67
	R. HATTERSLEY	15 Jul 69
Min. of Defence for Equipment	R. MASON	7 Jan 67
	J. MORRIS	16 Apr 68
Educ. & Science	**M. STEWART**	18 Oct 64
	A. CROSLAND	22 Jan 65
	P. GORDON WALKER	29 Aug 67
	E. SHORT	6 Apr 68
Min. of State	LD BOWDEN	19 Oct 64–11 Oct 65
	R. PRENTICE	20 Oct 64–6 Apr 66
	E. REDHEAD	11 Oct 65–7 Jan 67
	G. ROBERTS	6 Apr 66–29 Aug 67
	MRS S. WILLIAMS	7 Jan 67–13 Oct 69
	MISS A. BACON	29 Aug 67–19 Jun 70
	G. FOWLER	13 Oct 69–19 Jun 70
Min. of State (Arts)	MISS J. LEE	17 Feb 67–19 Jun 70
U-S.	J. Boyden	20 Oct 64–24 Feb 65
	D. Howell	20 Oct 64–13 Oct 69
	Miss J. Lee (Arts)	24 Feb 65–17 Feb 67
	Miss J. Lestor	13 Oct 69–19 Jun 70

[1] M.P. Not a Member of the House of Lords
[2] Not a Member of the House of Commons

LABOUR GOVERNMENT, 1964–1970 (*contd.*)

Employment	**MRS B. CASTLE**	6 Apr 68
& Productivity		
Min.of State	E. DELL	13 Oct 69
U-S.	E. Fernyhough	6 Apr 68–13 Oct 69
	R. Hattersley	6 Apr 68–15 Jul 69
	H. Walker	6 Apr 68–19 Jun 70
Health	K. ROBINSON	18 Oct 64
	(*office abolished 1 Nov 68*)	
P.S.	Sir B. Stross	20 Oct 64
	C. Loughlin	24 Feb 65
	J. Snow	7 Jan 67
Health & Soc. Sec. (known as S. of S. for Social Services)		
	R. CROSSMAN	1 Nov 68
Min.of State	S. SWINGLER	Nov 68–19 Feb 69
	D. ENNALS	1 Nov 68–19 Jun 70
	LADY SEROTA	25 Feb 69–19 Jun 70
U-S.	N. Pentland	1 Nov 68–13 Oct 69
	C. Loughlin	1 Nov 68–20 Nov 68
	J. Snow	1 Nov 68–13 Oct 69
	B. O'Malley	13 Oct 69–19 Jun 70
	J. Dunwoody	13 Oct 69–19 Jun 70
Housing	**R. CROSSMAN**	18 Oct 64
& Loc. Govt	**A. GREENWOOD**	11 Aug 66
	(*office not in cabinet*)	
	A. GREENWOOD	6 Oct 69
	R. MELLISH	31 May 70
Min.of	F. WILLEY	17 Feb 67
State	N. MACDERMOT	
		29 Aug 67–28 Sep 68
	D. HOWELL	13 Oct 69
Min.for	K. ROBINSON	1 Nov 68
Planning and Land	(*office abolished 6 Oct 69*)	
P.S.	R. Mellish	18 Oct 64–29 Aug 67
	J. MacColl	20 Oct 64–13 Oct 69
	Ld Kennet	6 Apr 66–19 Jun 70
	A. Skeffington	17 Feb 67–19 Jun 70
	R. Freeson	13 Oct 69–19 Jun 70
P.S.	R. Marsh	20 Oct 64–11 Oct 65
	E. Thornton	21 Oct 64–6 Apr 66
	Mrs S. Williams	6 Apr 66–7 Jan 67
	E. Fernyhough	7 Jan 67–6 Apr 68
	R. Hattersley	7 Jan 67–6 Apr 68
Labour	**R. GUNTER**	18 Oct 64
	(*6 Apr 68 reorganised as Min.of Employment & Productivity*)	
D. Lanc.	**D. HOUGHTON**	18 Oct 64
	(*office not in cabinet*)	
	G. THOMSON	6 Apr 66
	F. LEE	7 Jan 67
	(*office in cabinet*)	
	G. THOMSON	6 Oct 69
Local Govt & Regional Planning		
	(*office created 6 Oct 69*)	
	A. CROSLAND	6 Oct 69
Min.of State	T. URWIN	6 Oct 69
Land & Nat. Res.	F. WILLEY	18 Oct 64
	(*office wound up 17 Feb 67*)	
P.S.	Ld Mitchison	20 Oct 64–6 Apr 66
	A. Skeffington	21 Oct 64–17 Feb 67
Overseas	**MRS B. CASTLE**	18 Oct 64
Dev.	**A. GREENWOOD**	23 Dec 65
	A. BOTTOMLEY	11 Aug 66
	(*office not in cabinet*)	
	R. PRENTICE	29 Aug 67
	MRS J. HART	6 Oct 69
P.S.	A. Oram	21 Oct 64
	B. Whitaker	13 Oct 69
Paym.-Gen.	G. WIGG	19 Oct 64–12 Nov 67
	(*office vacant 12 Nov 67*)	
	(*office in cabinet*)	
	LD SHACKLETON	6 Apr 68
	MRS J. HART	1 Nov 68
	H. LEVER	6 Oct 69
Pensions	MISS M. HERBISON	18 Oct 64
& Nat. Ins.	(*6 Aug 66 became Min. of Social Security*)	
P.S.	H. Davies	20 Oct 64–6 Aug 66
	N. Pentland	21 Oct 64–6 Aug 66
Min. without	SIR E. FLETCHER	19 Oct 64–6 Apr 66
Portfolio	LD CHAMPION	21 Oct 64–7 Jan 67
	D. HOUGHTON	6 Apr 66–7 Jan 67
	LD SHACKLETON	7 Jan 67–16 Jan 68
	P. GORDON WALKER	7 Jan 67–21 Aug 67
	G. THOMSON	17 Oct 68–6 Oct 69
	P. SHORE	6 Oct 69–19 Jun 70
Post.-Gen.	A. BENN	19 Oct 64
	E. SHORT	4 Jul 66
	R. MASON	6 Apr 68
	J. STONEHOUSE	1 Jul 68
	(*1 Oct 69 Post Office became a Public Corporation*)	
Ass.	J. Slater	20 Oct 64
Posts & Tel.	J. STONEHOUSE	1 Oct 69
P.S.	J. Slater	1 Oct 69
	N. Pentland	13 Oct 69
Power	**F. LEE**	18 Oct 64
	R. MARSH	6 Apr 66
	R. GUNTER	6 Apr 68
	R. MASON	1 Jul 68
	(*office abolished 6 Oct 69*)	
P.S.	J. Morris	21 Oct 64
	Ld Lindgren	10 Jan 66
	J. Bray	6 Apr 66
	R. Freeson	7 Jan 67–6 Oct 69
Public	C. PANNELL	19 Oct 64
Building	R. PRENTICE	6 Apr 66
& Works	R. MELLISH	29 Aug 67
	J. SILKIN	30 Apr 69
P.S.	Miss J. Lee (*Arts*)	20 Oct 64
	J. Boyden	24 Feb 65
	Ld Winterbottom	7 Jan 67
	C. Loughlin	20 Nov 68

LABOUR GOVERNMENT, 1964–1970 (contd.)

Scotland	**W. ROSS**	18 Oct 64
Min. of	G. WILLIS	20 Oct 64–7 Jan 67
State	D. MABON	7 Jan 67–19 Jun 70
	LD HUGHES	13 Oct 69–19 Jun 70
U-S.	Ld Hughes	21 Oct 64–13 Oct 69
	Mrs J. Hart	20 Oct 64–6 Apr 66
	D. Mabon	21 Oct 64–7 Jan 67
	B. Millan	6 Apr 66–19 Jun 70
	N. Buchan	7 Jan 67–19 Jun 70
Social	MISS M. HERBISON	6 Aug 66
Sec.	MRS J. HART	26 Jul 67
	(office abolished 1 Nov 68, see Health & Soc. Security)	
P.S.	H. Davies	6 Aug 66–7 Jan 67
	N. Pentland	6 Aug 66–1 Nov 68
	C. Loughlin	7 Jan 67–1 Nov 68
Tech.	**F. COUSINS**	18 Oct 64
	A. BENN	4 Jul 66
Min. of	J. STONEHOUSE	15 Feb 67–1 Jul 68
State	J. MALLALIEU	1 Jul 68–13 Oct 69
	R. PRENTICE	6 Oct 69–10 Oct 69
	LD DELACOURT-SMITH	13 Oct 69–19 Jun 70
	E. VARLEY	13 Oct 69–19 Jun 70
P.S.	Ld Snow	19 Oct 64–6 Apr 66
	R. Marsh	11 Oct 65–6 Apr 66
	P. Shore	6 Apr 66–7 Jan 67
	E. Dell	6 Apr 66–29 Aug 67
	J. Bray	7 Jan 67–24 Sep 69
	G. Fowler	29 Aug 67–13 Oct 69
	A. Williams	6 Oct 69–19 Jun 70
	N. Carmichael	13 Oct 69–19 Jun 70
	E. Davies	13 Oct 69–19 Jun 70
B. Trade	**D. JAY**	18 Oct 64
	A. CROSLAND	29 Aug 67
	R. MASON	6 Oct 69
Min. of	G. DARLING	20 Oct 64–6 Apr 68
State	E. REDHEAD	20 Oct 64–11 Oct 65
	R. MASON	20 Oct 64–7 Jan 67
	LD BROWN	11 Oct 65–19 Jun 70
	J. MALLALIEU	7 Jan 67–1 Jul 68
	E. DELL	6 Apr 68–13 Oct 69
	W. RODGERS	1 Jul 68–13 Oct 69
	G. ROBERTS	13 Oct 69–19 Jun 70
P.S.	Ld Rhodes	20 Oct 64
	Ld Walston	7 Jan 67
	Mrs G. Dunwoody	29 Aug 67
Transport	**T. FRASER**	18 Oct 64
	MRS B. CASTLE	23 Dec 65
	R. MARSH	6 Apr 68
	(office not in cabinet)	
	F. MULLEY	6 Oct 69
Min. of	S. SWINGLER	29 Aug 67
State	(office vacant)	1 Nov 68
P.S.	Ld Lindgren	20 Oct 64–10 Jan 66
	S. Swingler	20 Oct 64–29 Aug 67
	J. Morris	10 Jan 66–6 Apr 68
	N. Carmichael	29 Aug 67–13 Oct 69
	R. C. Brown	6 Apr 68–19 Jun 70

P.S. (contd.)	A. Murray	13 Oct 69–19 Jun 70
Wales	**J. GRIFFITHS**	18 Oct 64
	C. HUGHES	6 Apr 66
	G. THOMAS	6 Apr 68
Min. of	G. ROBERTS	20 Oct 64
State	G. THOMAS	6 Apr 66
	MRS E. WHITE	7 Jan 67
U-S.	H. Finch	21 Oct 64
	I. Davies	6 Apr 66
	E. Rowlands	13 Oct 69

Law Officers

Att.-Gen.	SIR E. JONES	18 Oct 64
Sol.-Gen.	SIR D. FOOT	18 Oct 64
	SIR A. IRVINE	24 Aug 67
Ld Advoc.	G. STOTT[1]	20 Oct 64
	H. S. WILSON (LD)[1]	26 Oct 67
Sol.-Gen.	J. LEECHMAN[1]	20 Oct 64
Scotland	H. S. WILSON[1]	11 Oct 65
	E. STEWART[1]	26 Oct 67

Whips

P.S. to	E. SHORT	18 Oct 64
Treasury	J. SILKIN	4 Jul 66
	R. MELLISH	30 Apr 69
	(office vacant)	31 May 70
Lds of	G. Rogers	21 Oct 64–11 Jan 66
Treasury	G. Lawson	21 Oct 64–1 Apr 67
	J. McCann	21 Oct 64–11 Apr 66
		29 Jul 67–13 Oct 69
	I. Davies	21 Oct 64–6 Apr 66
	Mrs H. Slater	21 Oct 64–6 Apr 66
	J. Silkin	11 Jan 66–11 Apr 66
	A. Fitch	16 Apr 66–13 Oct 69
	J. Harper	16 Apr 66–19 Jun 70
	W. Whitlock	11 Apr 66–7 Jul 66
		1 Apr 67–28 Jul 67
	W. Howie	16 Apr 66–1 Apr 67
	H. Gourlay	7 Jul 66–29 Oct 68
	B. O'Malley	1 Apr 67–13 Oct 69
	W. Harrison	29 Oct 68–19 Jun 70
	N. McBride	13 Oct 69–19 Jun 70
	E. Perry	13 Oct 69–19 Jun 70
	E. Armstrong	13 Oct 69–19 Jun 70
Ass.	A. Fitch	22 Oct 64 1–16 Apr 66
Whips	H. Gourlay	22 Oct 64–7 Jul 66
	J. Harper	22 Oct 64–16 Apr 66
	W. Howie	22 Oct 64–16 Apr 66
	B. O'Malley	22 Oct 64–1 Apr 67
	J. Silkin	22 Oct 64–11 Jan 66
	C. Morris	25 Jan 66–29 Jul 67
	E. Bishop	16 Apr 66–1 Apr 67
	R. W. Brown	16 Apr 66–20 Jan 67
	W. Harrison	16 Apr 66–28 Oct 68
	N. McBride	16 Apr 66–13 Oct 69
	I. Evans	7 Jul 66–6 Feb 68
	E. Armstrong	20 Jan 67–13 Oct 69
	H. Walker	1 Apr 67–5 Apr 68
	E. Varley	29 Jul 67–30 Nov 68
	E. Perry	6 Feb 68–13 Oct 69

[1] M.P. Not a Member of the House of Lords

LABOUR GOVERNMENT, 1964–1970 (contd.)

Ass.Whips	D. Concannon	11 Apr 68–19 Jun 70		*V. Chamb.*	W.WHITLOCK	21 Oct 64
(contd.)	M. Miller	29 Oct 68–13 Oct 69			J. McCANN	11 Apr 66
	T. Boston	13 Oct 69–19 Jun 70			C. MORRIS	29 Jul 67
	J. Hamilton	13 Oct 69–19 Jun 70			A. FITCH	13 Oct 69
	R. Dobson	13 Oct 69–19 Jun 70		*Cap. Gents*	LD SHEPHERD	21 Oct 64
	W. Hamling	13 Oct 69–19 Jun 70		*at Arms*	LD BESWICK	29 Jul 67
				Cap.Yeo.	LD BOWLES	28 Dec 64
H.M. Household				*of Guard*		
Treasurer	S. IRVING	21 Oct 64		*Lds in*	Ld Hobson	21 Oct 64–17 Feb 66
	J. SILKIN	11 Apr 66		*Waiting*	Ld Beswick	28 Dec 64–11 Oct 65
	C. GREY	7 Jul 66			Ld Sorensen	28 Dec 64–20 Apr 68
	C. MORRIS	13 Oct 69			Lady Phillips	10 Dec 65–19 Jun 70
Compt.	C. GREY	21 Oct 64			Ld Hilton	6 Apr 66–19 Jun 70
	W.WHITLOCK	7 Jul 66			Lady Serota	23 Apr 68–25 Feb 69
	W. HOWIE	1 Apr 67			Lady Llewelyn-Davies	
	I. EVANS	6 Feb 68				13 Mar 69–19 Jun 70

CONSERVATIVE GOVERNMENT, 1970–1974

P.M.	**E. HEATH**	19 Jun 70–4 Mar 74		*Min. of*	R. SHARPLES	23 Jun 70–7 Apr 72
P.S. Civil	D. Howell[2]	23 Jun 70–26 Mar 72		*State*	LD WINDLESHAM	
Service	K. Baker	7 Apr 72–4 Mar 74				23 Jun 70–26 Mar 72
Dept	G. Johnson-Smith	5 Nov 72–4 Mar 74			M. CARLISLE	7 Apr 72–4 Mar 74
Ld Pres.	**W.WHITELAW**	20 Jun 70			VT COLVILLE	21 Apr 72–4 Mar 74
	R. CARR	7 Apr 72		*U-S.*	M. Carlisle	24 Jun 70
	J. PRIOR	5 Nov 72			D. Lane	7 Apr 72
Ld. Chanc.	**Q. HOGG** (*Ld Hailsham*)	20 Jun 70		*Ag. Fish.*	**J. PRIOR**	20 Jun 70
Privy S.	**EARL JELLICOE**	20 Jun 70		*& Food*	**J. GODBER**	5 Nov 72
	LD WINDLESHAM	5 Jun 73		*Min. of State*	A. STODART	7 Apr 72
Exchequer	**I. MACLEOD**	20 Jun 70		*P.S.*	A. Stodart	24 Jun 70–7 Apr 72
	A. BARBER	25 Jul 70			P. Mills	7 Apr 72–5 Nov 72
Chief	M. MACMILLAN	23 Jun 70			Mrs P. Fenner	5 Nov 72–4 Mar 74
Sec.	P. JENKIN	7 Apr 72			Earl Ferrers	8 Jan 74–4 Mar 74
	T. BOARDMAN	8 Jan 74		*Aviation*	F. CORFIELD	15 Oct 70
Min. of	T. HIGGINS	23 Jun 70		*Supply*	(*abolished 1 May 71; functions*	
State	J. NOTT	7 Apr 72			*transferred to Procurement Executive,*	
F.S.	P. JENKIN	23 Jun 70			*Min. of Defence*)	
	T. HIGGINS	7 Apr 72		*Defence*	**LD CARRINGTON**	20 Jun 70
For. &	**SIR A. DOUGLAS-HOME**	20 Jun 70			**I. GILMOUR**	8 Jan 74
Comm. O.				*Min. of*	LD BALNIEL[1]	23 Jun 70
Min. of	J. GODBER	23 Jun 70–5 Nov 72		*State*	I. GILMOUR	5 Nov 72
State	LADY TWEEDSMUIR				G. YOUNGER	8 Jan 74
		7 Apr 72–4 Mar 74		*Min. of*	I. GILMOUR	7 Apr 71
	J. AMERY	5 Nov 72–4 Mar 74		*State for*	(*office abolished 5 Nov 72*)	
	LD BALNIEL[1]	5 Nov 72–4 Mar 74		*Procurement*		
U-S.	M of Lothian	24 Jun 70–7 Apr 72		*U-S.*	P. Kirk	24 Jun 70
	A. Royle	24 Jun 70–8 Jan 74		*Navy*	A. Buck	5 Nov 72
	A. Kershaw	15 Oct 70–5 Jun 73		*U-S.*	Ld Lambton	24 Jun 70
	P. Blaker	8 Jan 74–4 Mar 74		*Air*	A. Kershaw	5 Jun 73
Min. for	R. WOOD	15 Oct 70			Ld Strathcona	8 Jan 74
Overseas				*U-S.*	I. Gilmour	24 Jun 70
Development[3]				*Army*	G. Johnson-Smith	7 Apr 71
Home O.	**R. MAUDLING**	20 Jun 70			P. Blaker	5 Nov 72
	R. CARR	18 Jul 72			D. Smith	8 Jan 74

[1] M.P. Not a Member of the House of Lords
[2] Also Junior Lord of Treasury 24 Jun 70–6 Jan 71; P.S. Dept of Employment 5 Jan 71–26 Mar 72.
[3] The Ministry of Overseas Development formally came under the Foreign Office 12 Nov 70.

CONSERVATIVE GOVERNMENT, 1970–1974 (contd.)

Educ. & Science	**MRS M. THATCHER**	20 Jun 70
Min. of State	N. ST. JOHN-STEVAS (*Arts*)	2 Dec 73
U-S.	Ld Belstead	24 Jun 70–5 Jun 73
	W. Van Straubenzee	24 Jun 70–5 Nov 72
	N. St. John-Stevas	5 Nov 72–2 Dec 73
	Ld Sandford	5 Jun 73–4 Mar 74
	T. Raison	2 Dec 73–4 Mar 74
Emp. (*& Productivity to 12 Nov 70*)	**R. CARR**	20 Jun 70
	M. MACMILLAN	7 Apr 72
	W. WHITELAW	2 Dec 73
Min. of State	P. BRYAN	23 Jun 70
	R. CHICHESTER-CLARK	7 Apr 72
U-S.	D. Smith	24 Jun 70–8 Jan 74
	D. Howell	5 Jan 71–26 Mar 72
	N. Scott	8 Jan 74–4 Mar 74
Energy	**LD CARRINGTON** (*S. of S*)	8 Jan 74
Min.	**P. JENKIN** (*Minister*)	8 Jan 74
Min. of State	D. HOWELL	8 Jan 74
U-S.	P. Emery	8 Jan 74
Env.	**P. WALKER**	15 Oct 70
	G. RIPPON	5 Nov 72
Min. for Loc. Govt & Development	G. PAGE	15 Oct 70
Min. for Housing & Construction	J. AMERY	15 Oct 70
	P. CHANNON	5 Nov 72
Min. for Transport Industries	J. PEYTON	15 Oct 70
U-S.	E. Griffiths	15 Oct 70–4 Mar 74
	P. Channon	15 Oct 70–26 Mar 72
	M. Heseltine	15 Oct 70–7 Apr 72
	Ld Sandford	15 Oct 70–5 Jun 73
	K. Speed	7 Apr 72–4 Mar 74
	R. Eyre	7 Apr 72–4 Mar 74
	Lady Young	5 Jun 73–4 Mar 74
	H. Rossi	8 Jan 74–4 Mar 74
Health & Soc. Security	**SIR K. JOSEPH**	20 Jun 70
Min. of State	LD ABERDARE	23 Jun 70–8 Jan 74
P.S.	P. Dean	24 Jun 70–4 Mar 74
	M. Alison	24 Jun 70–4 Mar 74
Housing & Local Govt	**P. WALKER**	20 Jun 70–15 Oct 70
	(*15 Oct 70 office reorganised under Environment*)	
Min. of State	G. PAGE	23 Jun 70–15 Oct 70
P.S.	P. Channon	24 Jun 70–15 Oct 70
	E. Griffiths	24 Jun 70–15 Oct 70
	Ld Sandford	24 Jun 70–15 Oct 70
D. Lanc.	(*with special responsibility for Europe*)	
	A. BARBER	20 Jun 70
	G. RIPPON	28 Jul 70
	J. DAVIES	5 Nov 72
Northern Ireland	**W. WHITELAW**	24 Mar 72
	F. PYM	2 Dec 73
Min. of State	P. CHANNON	26 Mar 72–5 Nov 72
	LD WINDLESHAM	26 Mar 72–5 Jun 73
	W. VAN STRAUBENZEE	5 Nov 72–4 Mar 74
	D. HOWELL	5 Nov 72–8 Jan 74
U-S.	D. Howell	26 Mar 72–5 Nov 72
	P. Mills	5 Nov 72–4 Mar 74
	Ld Belstead	5 Jun 73–4 Mar 74
Overseas Development	R. WOOD	23 Jun 70–15 Oct 70
	(*came under Foreign Office 15 Oct 70*)	
Paym.-Gen.	VT ECCLES (*Min. for Arts*)	23 Jun 70
	(*office in cabinet*)	
	M. MACMILLAN	2 Dec 73
Min. without Portfolio	LD DRUMALBYN	15 Oct 70
	LD ABERDARE	8 Jan 74
Posts & Tel.	C. CHATAWAY	24 Jun 70
	SIR J. EDEN	7 Apr 72
Public Buildings & Works	J. AMERY	23 Jun 70–15 Oct 70
	(*15 Oct 70 office reorganised under Dept of Environment*)	
P.S.	A. Kershaw	24 Jun 70–15 Oct 70
Scotland	**G. CAMPBELL**	20 Jun 70
Min. of State	LADY TWEEDSMUIR	23 Jun 70
	LD POLWARTH	7 Apr 72
U-S.	A. Buchanan-Smith	24 Jun 70–4 Mar 74
	G. Younger	24 Jun 70–8 Jan 74
	E. Taylor	24 Jun 70–28 Jul 71
	H. Monro	28 Jul 71–4 Mar 74
	E. Taylor	8 Jan 74–4 Mar 74
Tech.	**G. RIPPON**	20 Jun 70
	J. DAVIES	28 Jul 70–15 Oct 70
	(*15 Oct 70 office reorganised under Trade and Industry*)	
Min. of State	SIR J. EDEN	23 Jun 70–15 Oct 70
	E OF BESSBOROUGH	24 Jun 70–15 Oct 70
P.S.	D. Price	24 Jun 70–15 Oct 70
	N. Ridley	24 Jun 70–15 Oct 70
Trade	**M. NOBLE**	20 Jun 70–15 Oct 70
Trade & Industry	**J. DAVIES**	15 Oct 70
	P. WALKER	5 Nov 72
Trade & Consumer Affairs	**SIR G. HOWE**	5 Nov 72
Min. of State	F. CORFIELD	24 Jun 70–15 Oct 70
P.S.	A. Grant	24 Jun 70–15 Oct 70
Min. for Trade	M. NOBLE	15 Oct 70
	(*Sir G. Howe & in cabinet 5 Nov 72*)	
U-S.	A. Grant	15 Oct 70
	E of Limerick	7 Apr 72
Min. for Industry	SIR J. EDEN	15 Oct 70
	T. BOARDMAN	7 Apr 72–8 Jan 74
U-S.	N. Ridley	15 Oct 70
	P. Emery	7 Apr 72–8 Jan 74
Min. for Aerospace (*and Shipping 5 Nov 72*)	F. CORFIELD	1 May 71
	M. HESELTINE	7 Apr 72

CONSERVATIVE GOVERNMENT, 1970–1974 (contd.)

U-S.	D. Price	1 May 71	*Ass. Whips*	H. Rossi	21 Oct 70–7 Apr 72	
	C. Onslow	7 Apr 72	*(contd.)*	H. Gray	8 Nov 71–30 Oct 73	
Min. for	C. CHATAWAY	7 Apr 72		J. Thomas	8 Nov 71–30 Oct 73	
Industrial				M. Jopling	8 Nov 71–30 Oct 73	
Development				O. Murton	8 Nov 71–7 Apr 72	
U-S.	A. Grant	7 Apr 72		M. Fox	13 Apr 72–2 Dec 73	
P.S.	M. Heseltine	24 Jun 70–15 Oct 70		K. Clarke	13 Apr 72–8 Jan 74	
Wales	**P. THOMAS**	20 Jun 70		D. Walder	30 Oct 73–4 Mar 74	
Min. of State	D. GIBSON-WATT	23 Jun 70		A. Hall-Davis	30 Oct 73–4 Mar 74	
				R. Hicks	30 Oct 73–4 Mar 74	
Law Officers				A. Butler	8 Jan 74–4 Mar 74	
Att.-Gen.	SIR P. RAWLINSON	23 Jun 70		C. Parkinson	8 Jan 74–4 Mar 74	
Sol.-Gen.	SIR G. HOWE	23 Jun 70				
	SIR M. HAVERS	5 Nov 72	***H.M. Household***			
Ld Advoc.	N WYLIE	23 Jun 70	*Treasurer*	H. ATKINS	24 Jun 70	
Sol.-Gen.	D. BRAND	23 Jun 70		B. WEATHERILL	2 Dec 73	
Scotland	I. STEWART[1]	5 Nov 72	*Compt.*	W. ELLIOTT	24 Jun 70	
				R. EYRE	24 Sep 70	
Whips				B. WEATHERILL	7 Apr 72	
P.S. to	F. PYM	20 Jun 70		W. CLEGG	2 Dec 73	
Treasury	H. ATKINS	2 Dec 73	*V. Chamb.*	J. MORE	24 Jun 70	
Lds of	R. Eyre	24 Jun 70–23 Sep 70		B. WEATHERILL	17 Oct 71	
Treasury	D. Howell[2]	24 Jun 70–6 Jan 71		W. CLEGG	7 Apr 72	
	H. Monro	24 Jun 70–28 Jul 71		P. HAWKINS	2 Dec 73	
	B. Weatherill	24 Jun 70–17 Oct 71	*Cap. Gents*	EARL ST ALDWYN	24 Jun 70	
	W. Clegg	24 Jun 70–7 Apr 72	*at Arms*			
	V. Goodhew	21 Oct 70–9 Oct 73	*Cap. Yeo.*	VT GOSCHEN	24 Jun 70	
	P. Hawkins	5 Jan 71–2 Dec 73	*of Guard*	LD DENHAM	20 Nov 71	
	T. Fortescue	8 Nov 71–21 Sep 73	*Lds in*	Ld Mowbray	24 Jun 70–4 Mar 74	
	K. Speed	8 Nov 71–7 Apr 72	*Waiting*	Ld Denham	24 Jun 79–20 Nov 71	
	H. Rossi	7 Apr 72–8 Jan 74		Ld Bethell	24 Jun 70–5 Jan 71	
	O. Murton	7 Apr 72–30 Oct 73		Earl Ferrers	5 Jan 71–8 Jan 74	
	M. Jopling	30 Oct 73–4 Mar 74		M of Lothian	7 Apr 72–27 Jul 73	
	H. Gray	30 Oct 73–4 Mar 74		E of Gowrie	7 Apr 72–4 Mar 74	
	J. Thomas	30 Oct 73–4 Mar 74		Lady Young	21 Apr 72–5 Jun 73	
	M. Fox	2 Dec 73–4 Mar 74		Ld Strathcona	27 Jun 73–8 Jan 74	
	K. Clarke	8 Jan 74–4 Mar 74		Ld Sandys	8 Jan 74–4 Mar 74	
Ass.	V. Goodhew	29 Jun 70–21 Oct 70		Earl Cowley	8 Jan 74–4 Mar 74	
Whips	P. Hawkins	29 Jun 70–5 Jan 71		Earl Alexander of Tunis		
	T. Fortescue	29 Jun 70–8 Nov 71			8 Jan 74–4 Mar 74	
	K. Speed	29 Jun 70–8 Nov 71				

LABOUR GOVERNMENT, 1974–1979

P.M.	**H. WILSON**	4 Mar 74–5 Apr 76	*Paym.-Gen.*	E. DELL	7 Mar 74
	J. CALLAGHAN			*(Mrs S. Williams and office combined*	
		5 Apr 76–4 May 79		*with Prices & Consumer Protection*	
Civil Service	R. SHELDON	7 Mar 74		*8 Apr 76 and then with Education*	
Dept Min.	C. MORRIS	18 Oct 74		*10 Sep 76)*	
of State			*Ld Chanc.*	**LD ELWYN-JONES**	5 Mar 74
P.S.	J. Grant	7 Mar 74–18 Oct 74	*Privy S.*	**LD SHEPHERD**	7 Mar 74
Ld Pres.	**E. SHORT**	5 Mar 74		**LD PEART**	10 Sep 76
	M. FOOT	8 Apr 76	*Exchequer*	**D. HEALEY**	5 Mar 74
Privy	G. FOWLER	18 Oct 74	*Chief*	J. BARNETT	7 Mar 74
Council	LD CROWTHER-HUNT	23 Jan 76	*Sec.*	*(office in cabinet)*	
Office,	J. SMITH	8 Apr 76		**J. BARNETT**	21 Feb 77
Min. of State	LADY BIRK	3 Jan 79	*F.S.*	J. GILBERT	7 Mar 74
P.S.	W. Price	18 Oct 74		R. SHELDON	17 Jun 75

[1] Not a Member of the House of Commons
[2] Also P.S. Civil Service Dept. 23 Jun 70-26 Mar 72.

LABOUR GOVERNMENT, 1974–1979 (contd.)

Min. of State	R. SHELDON	18 Oct 74
State	D. DAVIES	17 Jun 75
For. & Comm. O.	**J. CALLAGHAN**	5 Mar 74
	A. CROSLAND	8 Apr 76
	D. OWEN	21 Feb 77
Min. of State	D. ENNALS	7 Mar 74–8 Apr 76
	R. HATTERSLEY	7 Mar 74–10 Sep 76
	LD GORONWY-ROBERTS	4 Dec 75–4 May 79
	E. ROWLANDS	14 Apr 76–4 May 79
	D. OWEN	10 Sep 76–21 Feb 77
	F. JUDD	21 Feb 77–4 May 79
U-S.	Miss J. Lestor	8 Mar 74–12 Jun 75
	Ld Goronwy-Roberts	8 Mar 74–4 Dec 75
	E.Rowlands	12 Jun 75–14 Apr 76
	J.Tomlinson	17 Mar 76–4 May 79
	(see also Overseas Development)	
	E. Luard	14 Apr 76–4 May 79
Home O.	**R. JENKINS**	5 Mar 74
	M. REES	10 Sep 76
Min. of State	LD HARRIS	8 Mar 74–3 Jan 79
	A. LYON	8 Mar 74–14 Apr 76
	B. JOHN	14 Apr 76–4 May 79
	LD BOSTON	3 Jan 79–4 May 79
U-S.	Dr S. Summerskill	8 Mar 74
Ag. Fish. & Food	**F. PEART**	5 Mar 74
	J. SILKIN	10 Sep 76
Min. of State	N. BUCHAN	8 Mar 74
	E. BISHOP	18 Oct 74
P.S.	R. Moyle	11 Mar 74
	E. Bishop	28 Jun 74
	G. Strang	18 Oct 74
Defence	**R. MASON**	5 Mar 74
	F. MULLEY	10 Sep 76
Min. of State	W. RODGERS	8 Mar 74
	J. GILBERT	10 Sep 76
U-S. Navy	F. Judd	8 Mar 74
	P. Duffy	14 Apr 76
U-S. Army	Ld Brayley	8 Mar 74
	R. C. Brown	18 Oct 74
U-S. Air Force	B. John	8 Mar 74
	J. Wellbeloved	14 Apr 76
Educ. & Science	**R. PRENTICE**	5 Mar 74
	F. MULLEY	10 Jun 75
	MRS S. WILLIAMS	10 Sep 76
Min. of State	G. FOWLER	8 Mar 74
	LD CROWTHER-HUNT	18 Oct 74
	G. FOWLER	23 Jan 76
	G. OAKES	10 Sep 76
Min. of State	LD DONALDSON (Arts)	14 Apr 76
U.S.	E. Armstrong	7 Mar 74–12 Jun 75
	H. Jenkins (Arts)	8 Mar 74–14 Apr 76
	Miss J. Lestor	12 Jun 75–21 Feb 76
	Miss M. Jackson	12 Mar 76–4 May 79
Emp.	**M. FOOT**	5 Mar 74
	A. BOOTH	8 Apr 76
Min. of State	A. BOOTH	8 Mar 74
	H. WALKER	14 Apr 76
U-S.	J. Fraser	8 Mar 74–14 Apr 76
Emp. U-S.	H. Walker	11 Mar 74–14 Apr 76
Emp. U-S. (contd.)	J. Grant	14 Apr 76–4 May 79
	J. Golding	14 Apr 76–4 May 79
Energy	**E. VARLEY**	5 Mar 74
	A. BENN	10 Jun 75
Min. of State	LD BALOGH	7 Mar 74
	J. SMITH	4 Dec 75
	D. MABON	14 Apr 76
U-S.	G. Strang	7 Mar 74–18 Oct 74
	A. Eadie	7 Mar 74–4 May 79
	J. Smith	18 Oct 74–4 Dec 75
	Ld Lovell-Davis	4 Dec 75–14 Apr 76
	G. Oakes	14 Apr 76–10 Sep 76
	J. Cunningham	10 Sep 76–4 May 79
Env.	**A. CROSLAND**	5 Mar 74
	P. SHORE	8 Apr 76
Min. for Planning & Loc. Govt	**J. SILKIN**	7 Mar 74
	(office in cabinet & in Dept of Environment)	
	J. SILKIN	18 Oct 74
	(office abolished 10 Sep 76)	
Min. for Transport	**F. MULLEY**	7 Mar 74
	J. GILBERT	12 Jun 75
	(separate Department and office in cabinet 10 Sep 76)	
Min. for Planning & Loc. Govt	**J. SILKIN**	7 Mar 74
	(office in cabinet 18 Oct 74)	
Min. for Housing & Construction	**R. FREESON**	7 Mar 74
Min. of State (Urban Affs)	C. MORRIS	7 Mar 74
	(post abolished 18 Oct 74)	
Min. of State	(Sport, Recreation and Water Resources 24 Aug 76)	
	D. HOWELL	7 Mar 74
U-S.	N. Carmichael	8 Mar 74–4 Dec 75
	G. Kaufman	8 Mar 74–12 Jun 75
	G. Oakes	8 Mar 74–14 Apr 76
	Lady Birk	18 Oct 74–3 Jan 79
	E.Armstrong	12 Jun 75–4 May 79
Health & Soc. Security (Soc. Serv.)	**MRS B.CASTLE**	5 Mar 74
	D. ENNALS	8 Apr 76
Min. of State	B. O'MALLEY	8 Mar 74–6 Apr 76
	D. OWEN	26 Jul 74–10 Sep 76
	S. ORME	8 Apr 76–10 Sep 76
	S. ORME	10 Sep 76–4 May 79
	(in cabinet as Min. for Soc. Security)	
	R. MOYLE	10 Sep 76–4 May 79
U-S.	D. Owen	8 Mar 74–26 Jul 74
	R. C. Brown	8 Mar 74–18 Oct 74
	A. Jones	18 Oct 74–12 Jun 75
	M. Meacher	12 Jun 75–14 Apr 76
	E. Deakins	14 Apr 76–4 May 79
	Ld Wells-Pestell	3 Jan 79–4 May 79
U-S. (Disabled)	A. Morris	11 Mar 74–4 May 79
Industry	**A. BENN**	5 Mar 74
	(also 7 Mar 74–29 Mar 74 Min. for Posts and Telecommunications)	
	E. VARLEY	10 Jun 75

LABOUR GOVERNMENT, 1974–1979 (contd.)

Min. of	E. HEFFER	7 Mar 74–9 Apr 75
State	LD BESWICK	11 Mar 74–4 Dec 75
	G. MACKENZIE	10 Jun 75–14 Apr 76
	G. KAUFMAN	4 Dec 75–4 May 79
	A. WILLIAMS	14 Apr 76–4 May 79
U-S.	G. Mackenzie	7 Mar 74–10 Jun 75
	M. Meacher	7 Mar 74–12 Jun 75
	G. Kaufman	12 Jun 75–4 Dec 75
	Ld Melchett	4 Dec 75–10 Sep 76
	N. Carmichael	4 Dec 75–14 Apr 76
	L. Huckfield	4 Apr 76–4 May 79
	R. Cryer	10 Sep 76–20 Nov 78
D. Lanc.	H. LEVER	5 Mar 74
Northern	M. REES	5 Mar 74
Ireland	R. MASON	10 Sep 76
Min. of	S. ORME	7 Mar 74–8 Apr 76
State	R. MOYLE	27 Jun 74–10 Sep 76
	D. CONCANNON	
		14 Apr 76–4 May 79
	LD MELCHETT	10 Sep 76–4 May 79
U-S.	Ld Donaldson	11 Mar 74–14 Apr 76
	D. Concannon	27 Jun 74–14 Apr 76
	J. Dunn	14 Apr 76–4 May 79
	R. Carter	14 Apr 76–4 May 79
	T. Pendry	11 Nov 78–4 May 79
Overseas	Mrs J. HART	7 Mar 74
Development	(office in cabinet)	
	R. PRENTICE	10 Jun. 75
	(office not in cabinet)	
	F. JUDD	21 Dec 76
	MRS J. HART	21 Feb 77
P.S.	W. Price	11 Mar 74
	J. Grant	18 Oct 74
	F. Judd	14 Apr 76
	J. Tomlinson (also at For. O.)	3 Jan 77
Prices &	MRS S. WILLIAMS	5 Mar 74
Consumer	R. HATTERSLEY	10 Sep 76
Protection		
Min. of	A. WILLIAMS	8 Mar 74
State	J. FRASER	14 Apr 76
U-S.	R. Maclennan	11 Mar 74
Scot O.	W. ROSS	5 Mar 74
	B. MILLAN	8 Apr 76
Min. of	B. MILLAN	8 Mar 74–8 Apr 76
State	LD HUGHES	8 Mar 74–8 Aug 75
	LD KIRKHILL	8 Aug 75–15 Dec 78
	G. MACKENZIE	14 Apr 76–4 May 79
U-S.	R. Hughes	11 Mar 74–22 Jul 75
	H. Brown	28 Jun 74–4 May 79
	H. Ewing	18 Oct 74–4 May 79
	F. McElhone	12 Sep 75–4 May 79
Soc.	(office not in cabinet)	
Security	S. ORME	10 Sep 76
	(in Dept. of Health & Soc. Security)	
U-S.	K. Marks	5 Dec 75–4 May 79
	G. Barnett	14 Apr 76–4 May 79
	Lady Stedman	3 Jan 79–4 May 79
Trade	P. SHORE	5 Mar 74

Trade	E. DELL	8 Apr 76
(contd.)	J. SMITH	11 Nov 78
U-S.	E. Deakins	8 Mar 74–14 Apr 76
	S. Clinton Davis	8 Mar 74–4 May 79
	M. Meacher	14 Apr 76–4 May 79
Transport	W. RODGERS	10 Sep 76
U-S.	J. Horam	12 Sep 76
Wales	J. MORRIS	5 Mar 74
U-S.	E. Rowlands	7 Mar 74–12 Jun 75
	B. Jones	7 Mar 74–4 May 79
	A. Jones	12 Jun 75–4 May 79

Law Officers

Att.-Gen.	S. SILKIN	7 Mar 74
U-S.	A. Davidson	26 Jul 74
Sol.-Gen.	P. ARCHER	7 Mar 74
Ld Advoc.	R. KING-MURRAY	8 Mar 74
Sol.-Gen. Scotland	J. McCLUSKEY[1] (Ld)	14 Mar 74

Whips

P.S. to	R. MELLISH	5 Mar 74
Treasury	(office in cabinet 26 Jul 74–8 Apr 76)	
	M. COCKS	8 Apr 76
Lds of	D. Coleman	8 Mar 74–6 Jul 78
Treasury	J. Dunn	8 Mar 74–14 Apr 76
	J. Golding	8 Mar 74–18 Oct 74
	T. Pendry	8 Mar 74–18 Jan 77
	J. Hamilton	8 Mar 74–28 Jun 74
	M. Cocks	28 Jun 74–8 Apr 76
	J. Dormand	18 Oct 74–4 May 79
	D. Stoddart	4 Apr 76–18 Nov 77
	E. Graham	14 Apr 76–4 May 79
	T. Cox	19 Jan 77–4 May 79
	P. Snape	23 Nov 77–4 May 79
	A. Stallard	5 Jul 78–17 Jan 79
	A. Bates	17 Jan 79–4 May 79
Ass. Whips	M. Cocks	8 Mar 74–24 Jun 74
	T. Cox	8 Mar 74–19 Jan 77
	E. Perry	8 Mar 74–24 Oct 74
	J. Dormand	14 Mar 74–18 Oct 74
	L. Pavitt	14 Mar 74–5 Feb 76
	W. Johnson	22 Jun 74–23 Jan 75
	Miss B. Boothroyd	
		24 Oct 74–4 Nov 75
	J. Ellis	24 Oct 74–8 Nov 76
	Miss M. Jackson	27 Jan 75–12 Mar 76
	D. Stoddart	27 Jan 75–14 Apr 76
	P. Snape	20 Nov 75–23 Nov 77
	A. Stallard	5 Feb 76–5 Jul 78
	A. Bates	12 Mar 76–17 Jan 79
	F. White	14 Apr 76–31 Oct 78
	J. Tinn	16 Jun 76–4 May 79
	J. Ashton	8 Nov 76–9 Nov 77
	Mrs A. Taylor	19 Jan 77–4 May 79
	J. Marshall	23 Nov 77–4 May 79
	J. Dean	6 Jul 78–4 May 79
	J. Evans	31 Oct 78–4 May 79
	B. Davies	17 Jan 79–4 May 79

[1] Not a Member of the House of Commons

LABOUR GOVERNMENT, 1974–1979 *(contd.)*

H.M. Household				*Lds in*	Lady Birk	14 Mar 74–18 Oct 74
Treasurer	W. HARRISON	7 Mar 74		*Waiting*	Ld Wells-Pestell	14 Mar 74–3 Jan 79
Compt.	J. HARPER	8 Mar 74		*(contd.)*	Ld Winterbottom	
	J. HAMILTON	5 Jul 78				29 Oct 74–27 Oct 78
V. Chamb.	D. CONCANNON	8 Mar 74			Ld Lovell-Davis	29 Oct 74–4 Dec 75
	J. HAMILTON	28 Jun 74			Ld Melchett	29 Oct 74–4 Dec 75
	D. COLEMAN	5 Jul 78			Lady Stedman	4 Dec 75–3 Jan 79
Cap. Gents	LADY LLEWELYN-DAVIES				Ld Oram	23 Jan 76–23 Mar 78
at Arms		11 Mar 74			Ld Wallace of Coslany	
Cap. Yeo.	LD STRABOLGI	11 Mar 74				28 Feb 77–4 May 79
of Guard					Lady David	27 Oct 78–4 May 79
Lds in	Ld Jacques	14 Mar 74–19 Jan 77			Ld Leonard	27 Oct 78–4 May 79
Waiting	Ld Garnsworthy	14 Mar 74–4 Sep 74			Ld Jacques	11 Jan 79–4 May 79

CONSERVATIVE GOVERNMENT, 1979–1990

P.M.	**MRS M. THATCHER**		*Econ. Sec.*	P. LILLEY	13 Jun 87
		4 May 79–28 Nov 90	*(contd.)*	R. RYDER	24 Jul 89
Min. of State	P. CHANNON	7 May 79		J. MAPLES	24 Jul 90
Civil Service	B. HAYHOE	5 Jan 81	*Min. of*	P. REES	6 May 79–14 Sep 81
Dept	*(Department abolished 12 Nov 81)*		*State*	LD COCKFIELD	
Ld Pres.	**LD SOAMES**	5 May 79			6 May 79–6 Apr 82
	F. PYM	14 Sep 81		J. BRUCE-GARDYNE	
	J. BIFFEN	7 Apr 82			15 Sep 81–11 Nov 81
	VT WHITELAW	11 Jun 83		B. HAYHOE	11 Nov 81–2 Sep 85
	J. WAKEHAM	10 Jan 88		J. WAKEHAM	6 Apr 82–13 Jun 83
	SIR G. HOWE	24 Jul 89		I. GOW	2 Sep 85–19 Nov 85
	J. MACGREGOR	2 Nov 90		P. BROOKE	19 Nov 85–13 Jun 87
Min. of	E. of GOWRIE	11 Jun 83		*(office vacant)*	
State, Privy	*(office vacant 11 Sept 84)*		*For. &*	**LD CARRINGTON**	5 May 79
Council	R. LUCE	2 Sep 85	*Comm. O.*	**F. PYM**	6 Apr 82
Office	D. MELLOR	24 Jul 90		**SIR G. HOWE**	11 Jun 83
Ld Chanc.	**LD HAILSHAM**	5 May 79		**J. MAJOR**	24 Jul 89
	LD HAVERS	13 Jun 87		**D. HURD**	26 Oct 89
	LD MACKAY	26 Oct 87	*Min. of*	D. HURD	6 May 79–11 Jun 83
Privy S.	**SIR I. GILMOUR**	5 May 79	*State*	N. RIDLEY	6 May 79–29 Sep 81
	H. ATKINS	14 Sep 81		P. BLAKER	6 May 79–29 May 81
	LADY YOUNG	6 Apr 82		R. LUCE	30 Sep 81–5 Apr 82
	J. BIFFEN	11 Jun 83		LD BELSTEAD	5 Apr 82–13 Jun 83
	J. WAKEHAM	13 Jun 87		C. ONSLOW	5 Apr 82–13 Jun 83
	LD BELSTEAD	10 Jan 88		R. LUCE	11 Jun 83–2 Sep 85
Exchequer	**SIR G. HOWE**	5 May 79		LADY YOUNG	13 Jun 83–13 Jun 87
	N. LAWSON	11 Jun 83		M. RIFKIND	13 Jun 83–11 Jan 86
	J. MAJOR	26 Oct 89		T. RENTON	2 Sep 85–13 Jun 87
Chief Sec.	**J. BIFFEN**	5 May 79		MRS L. CHALKER	
	L. BRITTAN	5 Jan 81			11 Jan 86–24 Jul 89
	P. REES	11 Jun 83		LD GLENARTHUR	
	J. MACGREGOR	2 Sep 85			13 Jun 87–24 Jul 89
	J. MAJOR	13 Jun 87		D. MELLOR	13 Jun 87–26 Jul 88
	N. LAMONT	24 Jul 89		W. WALDEGRAVE	
F.S.	N. LAWSON	6 May 79			26 Jul 88–2 Nov 90
	N. RIDLEY	30 Sep 81		LD BRABAZON of TARA	
	J. MOORE	18 Oct 83			24 Jul 89–24 Jul 90
	N. LAMONT	21 May 86		F. MAUDE	24 Jul 89–14 Jul 90
	P. LILLEY	24 Jul 89		T. GAREL-JONES	
	F. MAUDE	14 Jul 90			14 Jul 90–28 Nov 90
Econ. Sec.	J. BRUCE-GARDYNE	11 Nov 81		E of CAITHNESS	
	J. MOORE	13 Jun 83			14 Jul 90–28 Nov 90
	I. STEWART	18 Oct 83		D. HOGG	2 Nov 90–28 Nov 90

CONSERVATIVE GOVERNMENT, 1979–1990 (*contd.*)

Min. of State (*Overseas Dev.*)	N. MARTEN	8 Oct 79	*Min. for the Arts*	N. ST JOHN-STEVAS (*office out of cabinet*)	5 May 79
	T. RAISON	6 Jan 83		P. CHANNON	5 Jan 81
	C. PATTEN	10 Sep 86		E of GOWRIE	13 Jun 83
	MRS L. CHALKER	24 Jul 89		(*D. Lanc. & office in cabinet 11 Sep 84*)	
U-S.	R. Luce	6 May 79		**E of GOWRIE** (*office out of cabinet*)	11 Sep 84
	Ld Trefgarne	14 Sep 81		R. LUCE	2 Sep 85
	M. Rifkind	6 Apr 82		D. MELLOR	23 Jul 90
	R. Whitney	13 Jun 83	*Defence*	**F. PYM**	5 May 79
	T. Renton	11 Sep 84		**J. NOTT**	5 Jan 81
	T. Eggar	2 Sep 85		**M. HESELTINE**	6 Jan 83
	T. Sainsbury	24 Jul 89		**G. YOUNGER**	9 Jan 86
	M. Lennox-Boyd	24 Jul 90		**T. KING**	24 Jul 89
Home O.	**W. WHITELAW**	5 May 79	*Min. of State*	LD STRATHCONA VT TRENCHARD	6 May 79
	L. BRITTAN	11 Jun 83			5 Jan 81–29 May 81
	D. HURD	3 Sep 85	*Min. of State* (*Armed Forces*)	P. BLAKER	29 May 81
	D. WADDINGTON	26 Oct 89		J. STANLEY	13 Jun 83
Min. of State	T. RAISON	6 May 79–6 Jan 83		I. STEWART	13 Jun 87
	L. BRITTAN	6 May 79–5 Jan 81		A. HAMILTON	25 Jul 88
	P. MAYHEW	5 Jan 81–13 Jun 83	*Min. of State* (*Defence Procure.*)	VT TRENCHARD	29 May 81
	D. WADDINGTON	6 Jan 83–13 Jun 87		G. PATTIE	6 Jan 83
				A. BUTLER	11 Sep 84
	D. HURD	13 Jun 83–11 Sep 84		N. LAMONT	2 Sep 85
	LD ELTON	11 Sep 84–25 Mar 85		LD TREFGARNE	21 May 86
	G. SHAW	11 Sep 84–10 Sep 86		I. STEWART	13 Jun 87
	E of CAITHNESS	10 Sep 86–10 Jan 88		A. CLARK	24 Jul 89
	D. MELLOR	10 Sep 86–13 Jun 87	*Min. of State* (*Defence Support*)	LD TREFGARNE	2 Sep 85–21 May 86
	J. PATTEN	13 Jun 87–28 Nov 90	*U-S. Army*	B. Hayhoe	6 May 79
	T. RENTON	13 Jun 87–28 Oct 89		P. Goodhart	5 Jan 81–29 May 81
	EARL FERRERS	10 Jan 88–28 Nov 90	*U-S. Navy*	K. Speed	6 May 79–18 May 81
	D. MELLOR	27 Oct 89–22 Jul 90	*U-S. Air*	G. Pattie	6 May 79–29 May 81
	MRS A. RUMBOLD	23 Jul 90–28 Nov 90		(*Defence Dept reorganised May 81*)	
U-S.	Ld Belstead	7 May 79–6 Apr 82	*U-S.* (*Armed Forces*)	P. Goodhart	29 May 81–30 Sep 81
	Ld Elton	6 Apr 82–11 Sep 84		J. Wiggin	15 Sep 81–11 Jun 83
	D. Mellor	6 Jan 83–10 Sep 86		Ld Trefgarne	13 Jun 83–1 Sep 85
	Ld Glenarthur	27 Mar 85–10 Sep 86		R. Freeman	21 May 86–15 Dec 88
	D. Hogg	10 Sep 86–26 Jul 89		M. Neubert	19 Dec 88–23 Jul 90
	P. Lloyd	25 Jul 89–28 Nov 90	*U-S.* (*Def. Procure.*)	G. Pattie	29 May 81
Ag. Fish. & Food	**P. WALKER**	5 May 79		I. Stewart	6 Jan 83
	M. JOPLING	11 Jun 83		J. Lee	18 Oct 83
	J. MACGREGOR	13 Jun 87		A. Hamilton	10 Sep 86
	J. S. GUMMER	24 Jul 89		T. Sainsbury	13 Jun 87
Min. of State	EARL FERRERS	7 May 79–13 Jun 83		E of Arran	25 Jul 89
	A. BUCHANAN-SMITH	7 May 79–13 Jun 83		K. Carlisle	26 Jul 90
	J. MACGREGOR	13 Jun 83–2 Sep 85	*Educ. & Science*	**M. CARLISLE**	5 May 79
	J. S. GUMMER	2 Sep 85–26 Jul 88		**SIR K. JOSEPH**	14 Sep 81
	LD BELSTEAD	13 Jun 83–13 Jun 87		**K. BAKER**	21 May 86
	LADY TRUMPINGTON	28 Sep 89–28 Nov 90		**J. MACGREGOR**	24 Jul 89
U-S.	J. Wiggin	7 May 79–29 Sep 81		**K. CLARKE**	2 Nov 90
	Mrs. P. Fenner	14 Sep 81–10 Sep 86	*Min. of State*	LADY YOUNG	7 May 79–14 Sep 81
	D. Thomson	10 Sep 86–25 Sep 87		P. CHANNON	5 Jan 81–13 Jun 83
	Lady Trumpington	13 Jun 87–28 Sep 89		C. PATTEN	5 Sep 85–10 Sep 86
	R. Ryder	25 Jul 88–24 Jul 89		MRS A. RUMBOLD	10 Sep 86–24 Jul 90
	D. Curry	26 Jul 89–28 Nov 90		T. EGGAR	24 Jul 90–28 Nov 90
	D. Maclean	26 Jul 89–28 Nov 90			

CONSERVATIVE GOVERNMENT, 1979–1990 (contd.)

U-S.	R. Boyson	7 May 79–13 Jun 83
	N. Macfarlane	7 May 79–15 Sep 81
	W. Shelton	15 Sep 81–13 Jun 83
	W. Waldegrave	15 Sep 81–13 Jun 83
	P. Brooke	13 Jun 83–19 Nov 85
	R. Dunn	13 Jun 83–26 Jul 88
	G. Walden	19 Nov 85–13 Jun 87
	Lady Hooper	13 Jun 87–26 Jul 88
	R. Jackson	13 Jun 87–24 Jul 90
	J. Butcher	26 Jul 88–24 Jul 89
	A. Howarth	24 Jul 89–28 Nov 90
	M. Fallon	24 Jul 90–28 Nov 90
Emp.	**J. PRIOR**	5 May 79
	N. TEBBIT	14 Sep 81
	T. KING	16 Oct 83
	LD YOUNG of GRAFFHAM	2 Sep 85
	N. FOWLER	13 Jun 87
	M. HOWARD	3 Jan 90
Min. of State	E of GOWRIE	7 May 79–15 Sep 81
	M. ALISON	15 Sep 81–13 Jun 83
	P. MORRISON	13 Jun 83–2 Sep 85
	J. S. GUMMER	18 Oct 83–11 Sep 84
	K. CLARKE	2 Sep 85–13 Jun 87
	(Paym.-Gen. and in cabinet)	
	J. COPE	13 Jun 87–25 Jul 89
	T. EGGAR	25 Jul 89–23 Jul 90
	(office vacant)	
U-S.	J. Lester	7 May 79–5 Jan 81
	P. Mayhew	7 May 79–5 Jan 81
	D. Waddington	5 Jan 81–6 Jan 83
	P. Morrison	5 Jan 81–13 Jun 83
	J. S. Gummer	6 Jan 83–18 Oct 83
	A. Clark	13 Jun 83–24 Jan 86
	P. Bottomley	11 Sep 84–23 Jan 86
	D. Trippier	2 Sep 85–13 Jun 87
	I. Lang	31 Jan 86–10 Sep 86
	J. Lee	10 Sep 86–26 Jul 89
	P. Nicholls	13 Jun 87–28 Jul 90
	Ld Strathclyde	26 Jul 89–24 Jul 90
	R. Jackson	24 Jul 90–28 Nov 90
	Vt Ullswater	24 Jul 90–28 Nov 90
	E. Forth	24 Jul 90–28 Nov 90
Energy	**D. HOWELL**	5 May 79
	N. LAWSON	14 Sep 81
	P. WALKER	11 Jun 83
	C. PARKINSON	13 Jun 87
	J. WAKEHAM	24 Jul 89
Min. of State	H. GRAY	7 May 79
	A. BUCHANAN-SMITH	13 Jun 83
	P. MORRISON	13 Jun 87
	(office vacant 26 Jul 90)	
U-S.	N. Lamont	7 May 79–5 Sep 81
	J. Moore	7 May 79–13 Jun 83
	D. Mellor	15 Sep 81–6 Jan 83
	E of Avon	6 Jan 83–11 Sep 84
	G. Shaw	13 Jun 83–11 Sep 84
	A. Goodlad	11 Sep 84–13 Jun 87
	D. Hunt	11 Sep 84–13 Jun 87
	M. Spicer	13 Jun 87–3 Jan 90
	Lady Hooper	26 Jul 88–28 Jul 89

U-S. (contd.)	T. Baldry	3 Jan 90–28 Nov 90
	C. Moynihan	24 Jul 90–28 Nov 90
Env.	**M. HESELTINE**	5 May 79
	T. KING	6 Jan 83
	P. JENKIN	11 Jun 83
	K. BAKER	2 Sep 85
	N. RIDLEY	21 May 86
	C. PATTEN	24 Jul 89
Min. of State (Loc. Govt)	T. KING	6 May 79
	LD BELLWIN	6 Jan 83
	K. BAKER	11 Sep 84
	W. WALDEGRAVE	2 Sep 85
	R. BOYSON	10 Sep 86
	M. HOWARD	13 Jun 87
	J. S. GUMMER	25 Jul 88
	D. HUNT	25 Jul 89
	M. PORTILLO	4 May 90
Min. of State (Housing)	J. STANLEY	7 May 79
	I. GOW	13 Jun 83
	J. PATTEN	2 Sep 85
	W. WALDEGRAVE	13 Jun 87
	E of CAITHNESS	25 Jul 88
	M. HOWARD	25 Jul 89
	M. SPICER	3 Jan 90
Min. of State	LD ELTON	27 Mar 85
	W. WALDEGRAVE	10 Sep 86
	LD BELSTEAD	13 Jun 87
	E of CAITHNESS	10 Jan 88
	M. HOWARD	25 Jul 88
	D. TRIPPIER	24 Jul 89
U-S. (Sport)	H. Monro	7 May 79–30 Sep 81
	N. MacFarlane	15 Sep 81–2 Sep 85
	R. Tracy	7 Sep 85–13 Jun 87
	C. Moynihan	22 Jun 87–26 Jul 90
	R. Atkins	26 Jul 90–28 Nov 90
U-S.	M. Fox	7 May 79–5 Jan 81
	G. Finsberg	7 May 79–15 Sep 81
	Ld Bellwin	7 May 79–6 Jan 83
	G. Shaw	5 Jan 81–13 Jun 83
	Sir G. Young	15 Sep 81–10 Sep 86
	W. Waldegrave	13 Jun 83–2 Sep 85
	E of Avon	11 Sep 84–27 Mar 85
	Mrs A. Rumbold	2 Sep 85–10 Sep 86
	Ld Skelmersdale	10 Sep 86–13 Jun 87
	C. Chope	10 Sep 86–22 Jul 89
	Mrs M. Roe	13 Jun 87–26 Jul 88
	D. Trippier	13 Jun 87–23 Jul 89
	Mrs V. Bottomley	25 Jul 88–28 Oct 89
	Ld Hesketh	31 Jan 89–2 Nov 90
	D. Heathcoat-Amory	28 Oct 89–28 Nov 90
	P. Nicholls	26 Jul 90–12 Oct 90
	Ld Strathclyde	26 Jul 90–7 Sep 90
	Lady Blatch	7 Sep 90–28 Nov 90
	R. Key	12 Oct 90–28 Nov 90
Health & Soc. Security (Social Services)	**P. JENKIN**	5 May 79
	N. FOWLER	14 Sep 81
	J. MOORE	13 Jun 87
	(Social Security a separate Dept 25 Jul 88)	

CONSERVATIVE GOVERNMENT, 1979–1990 (*contd.*)

Health	**K. CLARKE**	25 Jul 88	*Northern*	**H. ATKINS**	5 May 79
	W. WALDEGRAVE	2 Nov 90	*Ireland*	**J. PRIOR**	14 Sep 81
Min. of State	G. VAUGHAN	7 May 79		**D. HURD**	11 Sep 84
(Health)	K. CLARKE	5 Mar 82		**T. KING**	3 Sep 85
	B. HAYHOE	2 Sep 85		**P. BROOKE**	24 Jul 89
	A. NEWTON	10 Sep 86	*Min. of*	M. ALISON	7 May 79–15 Sep 81
	D. MELLOR	25 Jul 88	*State*	H. ROSSI	7 May 79–5 Jan 81
	LD TRAFFORD	25 Jul 89		A. BUTLER	5 Jan 81–11 Sep 84
	Mrs V. BOTTOMLEY	28 Oct 89		E of GOWRIE	15 Sep 81–10 Jun 83
Min. of State	R. PRENTICE	7 May 79		E of MANSFIELD	
(Social	H. ROSSI	5 Jan 81			13 Jun 83–12 Apr 84
Security)	R. BOYSON	12 Jun 83		R. BOYSON	11 Sep 84–10 Sep 86
	A. NEWTON	11 Sep 84		N. SCOTT	10 Sep 86–13 Jun 87
	J. MAJOR	10 Sep 86		J. STANLEY	13 Jun 87–25 Jul 89
	N. SCOTT	13 Jun 87		I. STEWART	25 Jul 88–25 Jul 89
U-S.	Sir G. Young	7 May 79–15 Sep 81		J. COPE	25 Jul 89–28 Nov 90
	Mrs. L. Chalker	7 May 79–5 Mar 82	*U-S.*	Ld Elton	7 May 79–15 Sep 81
	G. Finsberg	15 Sep 81–14 Jun 83		P. Goodhart	7 May 79–5 Jan 81
	Ld Elton	15 Sep 81–6 Apr 82		G. Shaw	7 May 79–5 Jan 81
	A. Newton	5 Mar 82–11 Sep 84		D. Mitchell	5 Jan 81–13 Jun 83
	Ld Trefgarne	6 Apr 82–14 Jun 83		J. Patten	5 Jan 81–13 Jun 83
	J. Patten	14 Jun 83–2 Sep 85		N. Scott	15 Sep 81–11 Sep 86
	Ld Glenarthur	14 Jun 83–26 Mar 85		C. Patten	14 Jun 83–2 Sep 85
	R. Whitney	11 Sep 84–10 Sep 86		Ld Lyell	12 Apr 84–25 Jul 89
	Lady Trumpington			R. Needham	3 Sep 85–28 Nov 90
		30 Mar 85–13 Jun 87		P. Viggers	10 Sep 86–26 Jul 89
	J. Major	2 Sep 85–10 Sep 86		B. Mawhinney	10 Sep 86–28 Nov 90
	N. Lyell	10 Sep 86–13 Jun 87		P. Bottomley	24 Jul 89–28 Jul 90
	Mrs E. Currie	10 Sep 86–16 Dec 88		Ld Skelmersdale	24 Jul 89–28 Nov 90
	M. Portillo	13 Jun 87–25 Jul 88	*Paym.-Gen.*	**A. MAUDE**	5 May 79
	Ld Skelmersdale	13 Jun 87–25 Jul 89		**F. PYM**	5 Jan 81
	R. Freeman	16 Dec 88–4 May 90		**C. PARKINSON**	14 Sep 81
	Lady Hooper	29 Sep 89–28 Nov 90		(*office vacant 11 Jun 83*)	
	S. Dorrell	4 May 90–28 Nov 90		(*office not in cabinet*)	
Industry	**SIR K. JOSEPH**	7 May 79		**J. GUMMER**	11 Sep 84
	P. JENKIN	14 Sep 81		(*office in cabinet*)	
	(*12 Jun 83 office reorganised as Trade*			**K. CLARKE** (*also Min. Emp.*)	2 Sep 85
	and Industry)			(*office not in cabinet*)	
Min. of	A. BUTLER	6 May 79–5 Jan 81		P. BROOKE	13 Jun 87
State	VT TRENCHARD	6 May 79–5 Jan 81		E of CAITHNESS	24 Jul 89
	N. TEBBIT	5 Jan 81–14 Sep 81		R. RYDER	14 Jul 90
	N. LAMONT	14 Sep 81–12 Jun 83	*Min. without*	**LD YOUNG OF GRAFFHAM**	
Min. of State	K. BAKER	5 Jan 81–12 Jun 83	*Portfolio*		11 Sep 84–3 Sep 85
(Industry &			*Scot. O.*	**G. YOUNGER**	5 May 79
Info. Tech.)				**M. RIFKIND**	11 Jan 86
U-S.	D. Mitchell	6 May 79–5 Jan 81	*Min. of*	E of MANSFIELD	
	M. Marshall	6 May 79–15 Sep 81	*State*		7 May 79– 13 Jun 83
	J. MacGregor	5 Jan 81–14 Jun 83		LD GRAY of CONTIN	
	J. Wakeham	15 Sep 81–6 Apr 82			13 Jun 83–11 Sep 86
	J. Butcher	6 Apr 82–14 Jun 83		LD GLENARTHUR	
D. Lanc.	**N. ST JOHN STEVAS** (*Arts*)	5 May 79			10 Sep 86– 13 Jun 87
	F. PYM	5 Jan 81		I. LANG	13 Jun 87–28 Nov 90
	LADY YOUNG	27 Oct 81		LD SANDERSON	13 Jun 87–7 Sep 90
	C. PARKINSON	6 Apr 82		M. FORSYTH	7 Sep 90–28 Nov 90
	LD COCKFIELD	11 Jun 83	*U-S.*	A. Fletcher	7 May 79–14 Jun 83
	E of GOWRIE (*Arts*)	11 Sep 84		R. Fairgrieve	7 May 79–15 Sep 81
	N. TEBBIT	3 Sep 85		M. Rifkind	7 May 79–6 Apr 82
	K. CLARKE	13 Jun 87		A. Stewart	15 Sep 81–10 Sep 86
	(*also Min. Trade*)			J. Mackay	6 Apr 82–14 Jun 87
	A. NEWTON	25 Jul 88		M. Ancram	13 June 83–14 Jun 87
	K. BAKER	24 Jul 89		I. Lang	10 Sep 86–13 Jun 87

CONSERVATIVE GOVERNMENT, 1979–1990 (contd.)

Scot. O. (contd.)	Ld J. Douglas-Hamilton[1]	13 Jun 87–28 Nov 90
	M. Forsyth	13 Jun 87–7 Sep 90
	Ld Strathclyde	7 Sep 90–28 Nov 90
Soc.	**J. MOORE**	25 Jul 88
Security	**A. NEWTON**	23 Jul 89
Min. of State	N.SCOTT	25 Jul 88
U.-S.	Ld Skelmersdale	24 Jul 88–26 Jul 89
	P. Lloyd	25Jul 88–28 Jul 89
	Ld Henley	25 Jul 89–28 Nov 90
	Mrs G. Shephard	25 Jul 89–28 Nov 90
Trade	**J. NOTT**	5 May 79
	J. BIFFEN	5 Jan 81
	LD COCKFIELD	6 Apr 82
	(office reorganised as Trade & Industry)	
	C. PARKINSON	12 Jun 83
	N. TEBBIT	16 Oct 83
	L. BRITTAN	2 Sep 85
	P. CHANNON	24 Jan 86
	LD YOUNG of GRAFFHAM	13 Jun 87
	N. RIDLEY	24 Jul 89
	P. LILLEY	14 Jul 90
Min. for	MRS S. OPPENHEIM	6 May 79
Consumer	G. VAUGHAN	5 Mar 82
Affairs	(office abolished 13 Jun 83)	
Min. of	N. LAMONT	13 Jun 83–2 Sep 85
State	G. SHAW	10 Sep 86–13 Jun 87
Min. for	C. PARKINSON	7 May 79
Trade	P. REES	14 Sep 81
	P. CHANNON	13 Jun 83
	A. CLARK	24 Jan 86
	LD TREFGARNE	25 Jul 89
	T. SAINSBURY	23 Jul 90
Min. for	K. BAKER	13 Jun 83
Industry &	G. PATTIE	11 Sep 84
Info. Tech.	(office vacant 13 Jun 87)	
Min. for	D. HOGG	24 Jul 89
Industry	LD HESKETH	2 Nov 90
Min. for	J. REDWOOD	24 Jul 89
Corporate		
Affairs		
U.-S.	N. Tebbit	7 May 79–5 Jan 81
	R. Eyre	7 May 79–5 Mar 82
	Ld Trefgarne	5 Jan 81–15 Sep 81
	I. Sproat	15 Sep 81–12 Jun 83
	J. Butcher	14 Jun 83–26 Jul 88
	A. Fletcher	14 Jun 83–2 Sep 85
	D. Trippier	14 Jun 83–2 Sep 85
	Ld Lucas of Chilworth	11 Sep 84–13 Jun 87
	M. Howard	2 Sep 85–13 Jun 87
	R. Atkins	13 Jun 87–26 Jul 89
	F. Maude	13 Jun 87–26 Jul 89
	E. Forth	26 Jul 88–24 Jul 90
	J. Redwood	26 Jul 89–1 Nov 90
	E. Leigh	2 Nov 90–28–Nov 90

Transport	N. FOWLER (Minister)	11 May 79
	(office in cabinet 5 Jan 81)	
	N. FOWLER (Sec. of S)	5 Jan 81
	D. HOWELL	14 Sep 81
	T. KING	11 Jun 83
	N. RIDLEY	16 Oct 83
	J. MOORE	21 May 86
	P. CHANNON	13 Jun 87
	C. PARKINSON	24 Jul 89
Min. of	MRS L. CHALKER	18 Oct 83–10 Jan 86
State	D. MITCHELL	23 Jan 86–25 Jul 88
	M. PORTILLO	25 Jul 88– 4 May 90
	R. FREEMAN	4 May 90–28 Nov 90
	LD BRABAZON of TARA	23 Jul 90–28 Nov 90
P.S.	K. Clarke	7 May 79–5 Jan 81
U.-S.	K. Clarke	5 Jan 81–5 Mar 82
	Mrs. L. Chalker	5 Mar 82–18 Oct 83
	R. Eyre	5 Mar 82–11 Jun 83
	D. Mitchell	11 Jun 83–23 Jan 86
	M. Spicer	11 Sep 84–13 Jun 87
	E of Caithness	2 Sep 85–10 Sep 86
	P. Bottomley	23 Jan 86–24 Jul 89
	Ld Brabazon of Tara	10 Sep 86–23 Jul 89
	R. Atkins	25 Jul 89–22 Jul 90
	P. McLoughlin	25 Jul 89–28 Nov 90
	C. Chope	23 Jul 90–28 Nov 90
Wales	**N. EDWARDS**	5 May 79
	P. WALKER	13 Jun 87
	D. HUNT	4 May 90
Min. of	J. S. THOMAS	17 Feb 83
State	W. ROBERTS	15 Jun 87
U.-S.	M. Roberts	7 May 79–6 Jan 83
	M. Robinson	3 Oct 85–15 Jun 87
	W. Roberts	7 May 79–13 Jun 87
	I. Grist	15 Jun 87– 28 Nov 90

Law Officers

Att.-Gen.	SIR M. HAVERS	6 May 79
	SIR P. MAYHEW	13 Jun 87
Sol.-Gen.	SIR I. PERCIVAL	6 May 79
	SIR P. MAYHEW	11 Jun 83
	SIR N. LYELL	15 Jun 87
Ld Advoc.	J. MACKAY[2] (LD)	7 May 79
	LD CAMERON of LOCHBROOM	16 May 84
	P.(LD) FRASER	4 Jan 89
Sol.-Gen.	N. FAIRBAIRN	7 May 79
Scotland	P. FRASER[2]	28 Jan 82
	A. RODGER[2]	4 Jan 89
P.S. to	M. JOPLING	5 May 79
Treasury	J. WAKEHAM	11 Jun 83
	D. WADDINGTON	13 Jun 87
	T. RENTON	28 Oct 89
Lds of	C. Mather	7 May 79–1 Oct 81
Treasury	P. Morrison	7 May 79–5 Jan 81

[1] M.P. Not a Member of the House of Lords
[2] Not a Member of the House of Commons

CONSERVATIVE GOVERNMENT, 1979–1990 (contd.)

Lds of Treasury	Ld J. Douglas-Hamilton[1]	
		7 May 79–1 Oct 81
	J. MacGregor	7 May 79–5 Jan 81
	D. Waddington	16 May 79–5 Jan 81
	R. Boscawen	9 Jan 81–17 Feb 83
	J. Wakeham	9 Jan 81–15 Sep 81
	J. Cope	9 Jan 81–13 Jun 83
	A. Newton	1 Oct 81–5 Mar 82
	P. Brooke	1 Oct 81–13 Jun 83
	J. S. Gummer	1 Oct 81–6 Jan 83
	A. Goodlad	16 Feb 82–10 Sep 84
	D. Thompson	14 Jan 83–10 Sep 86
	D. Hunt	23 Feb 83–10 Sep 84
	I. Lang	11 Jun 83–1 Feb 86
	T. Garel-Jones	11 Jun 83–16 Oct 86
	J. Major	3 Oct 84–1 Nov 85
	A. Hamilton	3 Oct 84–10 Sep 86
	T. Sainsbury	7 Oct 85–23 Jun 87
	M. Neubert	10 Feb 86–26 Jul 88
	T. Durant	16 Oct 86–19 Dec 88
	M. Lennox-Boyd	16 Oct 86–25 Jul 88
	P. Lloyd	16 Oct 86–24 Jul 88
	D. Lightbown	26 Jun 87–24 Jul 90
	K. Carlisle	27 Jul 88–22 Jul 90
	A. Howarth	27 Jul 88–24 Jul 89
	D. Maclean	27 Jul 88–24 Jul 89
	S. Dorrell	20 Dec 88–3 May 90
	J. Taylor	26 Jul 89–28 Nov 90
	D. Heathcoat-Amory	
		26 Jul 89–28 Oct 89
	T. Sackville	30 Oct 89–28 Nov 90
	M. Fallon	10 May 90–22 Jul 90
	S. Chapman	25 Jul 90–28 Nov 90
	G. Knight	25 Jul 90–28 Nov 90
	I. Patnick	25 Jul 90–28 Nov 90
Ass. Whips	R. Boscawen	16 May 79–9 Jan 81
	J. Cope	16 May 79–9 Jan 81
	A. Newton	16 May 79–30 Sep 81
	J. Wakeham	16 May 79–9 Jan 81
	P. Brooke	16 May 79–30 Sep 81
	J. S. Gummer	9 Jan 81–30 Sep 81
	A. Goodlad	9 Jan 81–5 Feb 82
	D. Thompson	9 Jan 81–14 Jan 83
	N. Budgen	30 Sep 81–8 May 82
	D. Hunt	30 Sep 81–22 Feb 83
	I. Lang	30 Sep 81–10 Jun 83
	T. Garel-Jones	16 Mar 82–10 Jun 83
	A. Hamilton	11 May 82–3 Oct 84
	J. Major	14 Jan 83–2 Oct 84
	D. Hogg	22 Feb 83–10 Oct 84
	M. Neubert	15 Jun 83–9 Feb 86
	T. Sainsbury	15 Jun 83–7 Oct 85
	T. Durant	3 Oct 84–16 Oct 86
	P. Lloyd	3 Oct 84–16 Oct 86
	M. Lennox-Boyd	3 Oct 84–16 Oct 86
	F. Maude	7 Oct 85–15 Jun 87
	G. Malone	10 Feb 86–15 Jun 87
	M. Portillo	16 Oct 86–15 Jun 87
	D. Lightbown	16 Oct 86–25 Jun 87

Ass. Whips (contd.)	R. Ryder	16 Oct 86–24 Jul 88
	K. Carlisle	18 Jun 87–25 Jul 88
	A. Howarth	18 Jun 87–25 Jul 88
	D. Maclean	18 Jun 87–25 Jul 88
	S. Dorrell	26 Jun 87–19 Dec 88
	J. Taylor	26 Jul 88–25 Jul 89
	D. Heathcoat-Amory	
		26 Jul 88–25 Jul 89
	T. Sackville	26 Jul 88–29 Oct 89
	M. Fallon	26 Jul 88–10 May 90
	S. Chapman	20 Dec 88–25 Jul 90
	G. Knight	28 Jul 89–25 Jul 90
	I. Patnick	28 Jul 89–25 Jul 90
	N. Baker	2 Nov 89–28 Nov 90
	T. Wood	10 May 90–28 Nov 90
	T. Boswell	25 Jul 90–28 Nov 90
	N. Hamilton	25 Jul 90–28 Nov 90
	T. Kirkhope	25 Jul 90–28 Nov 90

H.M. Household

Treasurer	J. S. THOMAS	6 May 79
	A. BERRY	17 Feb 83
	J. COPE	11 Jun 83
	D. HUNT	15 Jun 87
	T. GAREL-JONES	25 Jul 89
	A. GOODLAD	22 Jul 90
Compt.	S. LE MARCHANT	7 May 79
	A. BERRY	30 Sep 81
	C. MATHER	17 Feb 83
	R. BOSCAWEN	16 Oct 86
	T. GAREL-JONES	26 Jul 88
	A. GOODLAD	25 Jul 89
	SIR G. YOUNG	23 Jul 90
V. Chamb.	A. BERRY	7 May 79
	C. MATHER	30 Sep 81
	R. BOSCAWEN	17 Feb 83
	T. GAREL-JONES	16 Oct 86
	M. NEUBERT	26 Jul 88
	T. DURANT	20 Dec 88
	D. LIGHTBOWN	25 Jul 90
Cap. Gents at Arms	LORD DENHAM	6 May 79
Cap. Yeo. of Guard	LD SANDYS	6 May 79
	E of SWINTON	20 Oct 82
	VT DAVIDSON	10 Sep 86
Lds in Waiting	Vt Long	9 May 79–28 Nov 90
	Ld Mowbray and Stourton	
		9 May 79–22 Sep 80
	Ld Lyell	9 May 79–12 Apr 84
	Ld Cullen of Ashbourne	
		9 May 79–27 May 82
	Ld Trefgarne	9 May 79–5 Jan 81
	E of Avon	22 Sep 80–6 Jan 83
	Ld Skelmersdale	9 Jan 81–10 Sep 86
	Ld Glenarthur	27 May 82–10 Jun 83
	Ld Lucas of Chilworth	
		6 Jan 83–9 Sep 84
	Lady Trumpington	
		11 Jun 83–25 Mar 85
	E of Caithness	8 May 84–2 Sep 85

---

[1] M.P. Not a Member of the House of Lords

CONSERVATIVE GOVERNMENT, 1979–1990 (*contd.*)

Lds in	Ld Brabazon of Tara	
Waiting		19 Sep 84–10 Sep 86
(*contd.*)	Lady Cox	3 Apr 85–2 Aug 85
	Vt Davidson	17 Sep 85–10 Sep 86
	Lady Hooper	17 Sep 85–14 Jun 87
	Ld Hesketh	10 Sep 86–31 Jan 89
	Ld Beaverbrook	10 Sep 86–28 Jul 89
	E of Dundee	3 Oct 86–26 Jul 89
	E of Arran	18 Jun 87–24 Jul 89

Lds in	Ld Strathclyde	12 Aug 88–24 Jul 89
Waiting	Ld Henley	13 Feb 89–24 Jul 90
(*contd.*)	Vt Ullswater	26 Jul 89–22 Jul 90
	Ld Reay	2 Aug 89–28 Nov 90
	E of Strathmore	2 Aug 89–28 Nov 90
	Lady Blatch	15 Jan 90–7 Sep 90
	Ld Cavendish	14 Sep 90–28 Nov 90
	Vt Astor	11 Oct 90–28 Nov 90

CONSERVATIVE GOVERNMENT 1990–

P.M.	**J. MAJOR**	28 Nov 90
Ld Pres.	**J. MACGREGOR**	28 Nov 90
	A. NEWTON	10 Apr 92
U.-S.	R. Jackson	28 Nov 90
	(*office under Min. for Public Service 11 Apr 92*)	
Ld. Chanc.	**LD MACKAY**	28 Nov 90
U.-S.	J. Taylor	14 Apr 92
Privy S.	**LD WADDINGTON**	28 Nov 90
	LD WAKEHAM	10 Apr 92
	VT CRANBORNE	20 Jul 94
Exchequer	**N. LAMONT**	28 Nov 90
	K. CLARKE	27 May 93
Chief Sec.	**D. MELLOR**	28 Nov 90
	M. PORTILLO	10 Apr 92
	J. AITKEN	20 Jul 94
F.S.	F. MAUDE	28 Nov 90
	S. DORRELL	14 Apr 92
	SIR G. YOUNG	20 Jul 94
E.S.	J. MAPLES	28 Nov 90
	A. NELSON	14 Apr 92
	(*Min. of State 20 Jul 94*)	
Min. of	Mrs G. SHEPHARD	28 Nov 90
State	(*office vacant 11 Apr 92–20 Jul 94*)	
	A. NELSON	20 Jul 94
For. &	**D. HURD**	28 Nov 90
Comm. O.		
Min. of	E of CAITHNESS	
State		28 Nov 90–15 Apr 92
	D. HOGG	28 Nov 90–
	T. GAREL-JONES	
		28 Nov 90–27 May 93
	A. GOODLAD	14 Apr 92–
	D. HEATHCOAT-AMORY	
		27 May 93–20 Jul 94
	D. DAVIS	20 Jul 94–
Min. of State (*Overseas Development*)		
	MRS L. (LADY) CHALKER	
		28 Nov 90
U.-S.	M. Lennox-Boyd	28 Nov 90
	A. Baldry	20 Jul 94
Home O.	**K. BAKER**	28 Nov 90
	K. CLARKE	10 Apr 92
	M. HOWARD	27 May 93
Min. of	J. PATTEN	28 Nov 90–14 Apr 92
State	EARL FERRERS	28 Nov 90–20 Jul 94
	MRS A. RUMBOLD	
		28 Nov 90–14 Apr 92

Min. of	P. LLOYD	15 Apr 92–20 Jul 94
State	M. JACK	15 Apr 92–27 May 93
(*contd.*)	D. MACLEAN	27 May 93–
	LADY BLATCH	20 Jul 94–
	M. FORSYTH	20 Jul 94–
U.-S.	P. Lloyd	28 Nov 90
	C. Wardle	15 Apr 92
	N. Baker	20 Jul 94
Ag. Fish.	**J. S. GUMMER**	28 Nov 90
& Food	**MRS G. SHEPHARD**	27 May 93
	W. WALDEGRAVE	20 Jul 94
Min. of	**LADY TRUMPINGTON**	28 Nov 90
State	D. CURRY	14 Apr 92
	M. JACK	27 May 93
U.-S.	D. Curry	28 Nov 90–14 Apr 92
	D. Maclean	28 Nov 90–15 Apr 92
	Earl Howe	14 Apr 92–
	N. Soames	14 Apr 92–20 Jul 94
	Miss A. Browning	20 Jul 94
Min. for	T. RENTON	28 Nov 90–11 Apr 92
the Arts	(*11 Apr 92 See National Heritage*)	
Office of Minister for Public Service and Science		
Min.	**W. WALDEGRAVE**	10 Apr 92
	D. HUNT	20 Jul 94
	(*D. Lanc.*)	
P.S.	R. Jackson	14 Apr 92
	D. Davis	27 May 93
Defence	**T. KING**	28 Nov 90
	M. RIFKIND	10 Apr 92
Min. of State	A. CLARK	28 Nov 90
(*Def.*	J. AITKEN	14 Apr 92
Procure.*)	R. FREEMAN	20 Jul 94
Min. of State	A. HAMILTON	28 Nov 90
(*Armed	J. HANLEY	27 May 93
Services*)	N. SOAMES	20 Jul 94
U.-S.	K. Carlisle	28 Nov 90–15 Apr 92
	E of Arran	28 Nov 90–15 Apr 92
	Vt Cranborne	22 Apr 92–20 Jul 94
	Ld Henley	20 Jul 94
Educ. &	**K. CLARKE**	28 Nov 90
Science	(*Became Dept for Educ. 10 Apr 1992*)	
	J. PATTEN	10 Apr 92
	MRS G. SHEPHARD	20 Jul 94
Min. of	T. EGGAR	28 Nov 90
State	LADY BLATCH	14 Apr 92
	E. FORTH	20 Jul 94
U.-S.	A. Howarth	28 Nov 90–14 Apr 92
	M. Fallon	28 Nov 90–14 Apr 92

Educ. &	R. Atkins (*Sport*)	28 Nov 90–14 Apr 92
Science	E. Forth	14 Apr 92–20 Jul 94
U-S.	N. Forman	14 Apr 92–11 Dec 92
(contd.)	T. Boswell	19 Dec 92–
	R. Squire	27 May 93–
Emp.	**M. HOWARD**	28 Nov 90
	MRS G. SHEPHARD	11 Apr 92
	D. HUNT	27 May 93
	M. PORTILLO	20 Jul 94
Min. of State	M. FORSYTH	14 Apr 92
	MISS A. WIDDECOMBE	20 Jul 94
U-S.	R. Jackson	28 Nov 90–14 Apr 92
	E. Forth	28 Nov 90–14 Apr 92
	Vt Ullswater	28 Nov 90–16 Sep 93
	P. McLoughlin	14 Apr 92–27 May 93
	Miss A. Widdecombe	
		27 May 93–20 Jul 94
	Ld Henley	16 Sep 93–20 Jul 94
	J. Paice	20 Jul 94–
	P. Oppenheim	20 Jul 94–
Energy	**J. WAKEHAM**	28 Nov 90
	(*office abolished 11 Apr 92*)	
U-S.	D. Heathcoat-Amory	
		28 Nov 90–11 Apr 92
	C. Moynihan	28 Nov 90–11 Apr 92
Env.	**M. HESELTINE**	28 Nov 90
	M. HOWARD	11 Apr 92
	J. S. GUMMER	27 May 93
Min. for	M. PORTILLO	28 Nov 90
Loc. Govt	J. REDWOOD	15 Apr 92
	D. CURRY	27 May 93
Min. for Env.	D. TRIPPIER	28 Nov 90
	D. MACLEAN	14 Apr 92
	T. YEO	27 May 93
	R. ATKINS	11 Jan 94
Min. for	SIR G. YOUNG	28 Nov 90
Housing	VT ULLSWATER	20 Jul 94
Min. of State	LADY BLATCH	21 May 91–13 Apr 92
U-S.	Lady Blatch	28 Nov 90–21 May 91
	R. Key	28 Nov 90–15 Apr 92
	T. Yeo	28 Nov 90–15 Apr 92
	T. Baldry	28 Nov 90–20 Jul 94
	Ld Strathclyde	15 Apr 92–20 Jul 94
	R. Squire	15 Apr 92–27 May 93
	Lady Denton	16 Sep 93–11 Jan 94
	E of Arran	11 Jan 94–20 Jul 94
	Sir P. Beresford	20 Jul 94
	R. Jones	20 Jul 94
Health	**W. WALDEGRAVE**	28 Nov 90
	MRS V. BOTTOMLEY	10 Apr 92
Min. of	MRS V. BOTTOMLEY	28 Nov 90
State	B. MAWHINNEY	14 Apr 92
	G. MALONE	20 Jul 94
U-S.	Lady Hooper	28 Nov 90–14 Apr 92
	S. Dorrell	28 Nov 90–14 Apr 92
	T. Sackville	14 Apr 92–
	T. Yeo	15 Apr 92–27 May 93
	Lady Cumberlege	14 Apr 92–
	J. Bowis	27 May 93–

D. Lanc.	**C. PATTEN**	28 Nov 90
	(*from 12 April 92 also Min. for Public*	
	Service)	
	W. WALDEGRAVE	10 Apr 92
	D. HUNT	20 Jul 94
P.S.	R. Jackson	15 Apr 92–27 May 93
	D. Davis	27 May 93
	R. Hughes	20 Jul 94
Min.	**J. HANLEY**	20 Jul 94
without		
Portfolio		
Nat.	**D. MELLOR**	11 Apr 92
Heritage	**P. BROOKE**	25 Sep 92
	S. DORRELL	20 Jul 94
U-S.	R. Key	14 Apr 92–27 May 93
	I. Sproat	27 May 93–
	Vt Astor	20 Jul 94
Northern	**P. BROOKE**	28 Nov 90
Ireland	**SIR P. MAYHEW**	10 Apr 92
Min. of	B. MAWHINNEY	
State		28 Nov 90–14 Apr 92
U-S.	LD BELSTEAD	28 Nov 90–14 Apr 92
	(*also Paym.-Gen.*)	
	M. MATES	15 Apr 92–24 Jun 93
	R. ATKINS	14 Apr 92–11 Jan 94
	SIR J. WHEELER	25 Jun 93–
	M. ANCRAM	11 Jan 94–
U-S.	R. Needham	28 Nov 90–15 Apr 92
	J. Hanley	28 Nov 90–27 May 93
	E of Arran	22 Apr 92–11 Jan 94
	M. Ancram	27 May 93–11 Jan 94
	Lady Denton	20 Jul 94–
	T. Smith	20 Jul 94–
Paym.-Gen.	LD BELSTEAD	28 Nov 90
	SIR J. COPE	14 Apr 92
	D. HEATHCOAT-AMORY	20 Jul 94
Scot. O.	**I. LANG**	28 Nov 90
Min. of	M. FORSYTH	28 Nov 90
State	LD FRASER of CARMYLLIE	
		14 Apr 92
U-S.	Ld J. Douglas-Hamilton[1]	28 Nov 90–
	A. Stewart	28 Nov 90–
	Ld Strathclyde	28 Nov 90–14 Apr 92
	Sir H. Munro	14 Apr 92–
Soc.	**A. NEWTON**	28 Nov 90
Security	**P. LILLEY**	10 Apr 92
Min. of	N. SCOTT	28 Nov 90–20 Jul 94
State	W. HAGUE	20 Jul 94–
	LD MACKAY of ARDBRECKNISH	
		20 Jul 94–
U-S.	Ld Henley	28 Nov 90–16 Sep 93
	M. Jack	28 Nov 90–14 Apr 92
	Miss A. Widdecombe	
		30 Nov 90–27 May 93
	A. Burt	14 Apr 92–
	W. Hague	27 May 93–20 Jul 94
	Vt Astor	16 Sep 93–20 Jul 94
	J. Arbuthnot	20 Jul 94–
	R. Evans	20 Jul 94–

[1] M.P. Not a Member of the House of Lords

CONSERVATIVE GOVERNMENT, 1990– (contd.)

Trade	**P. LILLEY**	28 Nov 90
	M. HESELTINE	10 Apr 92
Min.for Trade	T. SAINSBURY	28 Nov 90
	R. NEEDHAM	14 Apr 92
Min.for Industry	LD HESKETH	28 Nov 90–21 May 91
	(*office vacant 23 May 91–15 Apr 92*)	
	T. SAINSBURY	15 Apr 92
	(*office vacant 20 Jul 94*)	
Min.for Corporate Affairs	J. REDWOOD	28 Nov 90–13 Apr 92
Min. for Energy (and Industry 20 Jul 94)	T. EGGAR	15 Apr 92
Min. for Consumer Affairs	EARL FERRERS	20 Jul 94
Min.	LD STRATHCLYDE	11 Jan 94–20 Jul 94
U-S.	Ld Reay	22 May 91–14 Apr 92
	E. Leigh	28 Nov 90–27 May 93
	N. Hamilton	14 Apr 92–
	Lady Denton	14 Apr 92–16 Sep 93
	P. McLoughlin	27 May 93–20 Jul 94
	Ld Strathclyde	16 Sep 93–11 Jan 94
	C. Wardle	20 Jul 94
Transport	**M. RIFKIND**	28 Nov 90
	J. MACGREGOR	10 Apr 92
	B. MAWHINNEY	20 Jul 94
Min. of State	LD BRABAZON of TARA	28 Nov 90–14 Apr 92
	R. FREEMAN	28 Nov 90–20 Jul 94
	E of CAITHNESS	14 Apr 92–11 Jan 94
	J. WATTS	20 Jul 94
U-S.	C. Chope	28 Nov 90–14 Apr 92
	P. McLoughlin	28 Nov 90–14 Apr 92
	S. Norris	14 Apr 92–
	K. Carlisle	14 Apr 92–27 May 93
	R. Key	27 May 93–20 Jul 94
	Ld Mackay of Ardbrecknish	11 Jan 94–20 Jul 94
	I. Taylor	20 Jul 94–
	Vt Goschen	20 Jul 94–
Wales	**D. HUNT**	28 Nov 90
	J. REDWOOD	27 May 93
Min. of State	SIR W. ROBERTS	28 Nov 90–20 Jul 94
U-S.	N. Bennett	3 Dec 90–14 Apr 92
	G. Jones	14 Apr 92–
	R. Richards	20 Jul 94–
Law Officers		
Att. Gen.	SIR P. MAYHEW	28 Nov 90
	SIR N. LYELL	10 Apr 92
Sol. Gen.	SIR N. LYELL	28 Nov 90
	SIR D. SPENCER	14 Apr 92
Ld. Adv.	LD FRASER of CARMYLLIE	28 Nov 90
	LD RODGER	14 Apr 92
Sol. Gen. Scotland	A. RODGER[1]	28 Nov 90
	T. DAWSON[1]	14 Apr 92

Whips		
P.S. to Treas.	R.RYDER	28 Nov 90
Lds of Treasury	T. Sackville	28 Nov 90–14 Apr 92
	S. Chapman	28 Nov 90–14 Apr 92
	G. Knight	28 Nov 90–27 May 93
	I. Patnick	28 Nov 90–20 Jul 94
	N. Baker	3 Dec 90–20 Jul 94
	T. Wood	15 Apr 92–
	T. Boswell	15 Apr 92–10 Dec 92
	T. Kirkhope	11 Jan 93–
	A. Mackay	27 May 93–
	A. Mitchell	20 Jul 94–
	D. Conway	20 Jul 94–
Ass. Whips	T. Wood	28 Nov 90–14 Apr 92
	T. Boswell	28 Nov 90–14 Apr 92
	N. Hamilton	28 Nov 90–14 Apr 92
	T. Kirkhope	28 Nov 90–11 Jan 93
	D. Davis	3 Dec 90–27 May 93
	R. Hughes	15 Apr 92–20 Jul 94
	J. Arbuthnot	15 Apr 92–20 Jul 94
	A. Mackay	15 Apr 92–27 May 93
	A. Mitchell	11 Jan 93–20 Jul 94
	M. Brown	27 May 93–7 May 94
	D. Conway	27 May 93–20 Jul 94
	B. Wells	10 May 94–
	M. Bates	20 Jul 94–
	S. Burns	20 Jul 94–
	D. Willetts	20 Jul 94–
	L. Fox	20 Jul 94–
H.M.Household		
Treasurer	A. GOODLAD	28 Nov 90
	D. HEATHCOAT-AMORY	15 Apr 92
	G. KNIGHT	27 May 93
Compt.	D. LIGHTBOWN	28 Nov 90
Vice-Chamb.	J. TAYLOR	28 Nov 90
	S. CHAPMAN	15 Apr 92
Cap. Gent at Arms	LD DENHAM	28 Nov 90
	LD HESKETH	22 May 91
	VT ULLSWATER	16 Sep 93
	LD STRATHCLYDE	20 Jul 94
Cap. Yeo. of Guard	VT DAVIDSON	28 Nov 90
	E of STRATHMORE	30 Sep 91
	E of ARRAN	20 Jul 94–
Lords in Waiting	Vt Long	28 Nov 90–
	Ld Reay	28 Nov 90–21 May 91
	E of Strathmore	28 Nov 90–30 Dec 92
	Ld Cavendish	28 Nov 90–22 Apr 92
	Vt Astor	28 Nov 90–16 Sep 93
	Earl Howe	28 Nov 90–15 Apr 92
	Lady Denton	19 Dec 91–15 Apr 92
	Vt St.Davids	22 Apr 92–20 Jul 94
	Vt Goschen	28 Apr 92–20 Jul 94
	Lady Trumpington	22 Apr 92–
	Ld Mackay of Ardbrecknish	15 Oct 93–11 Jan 94
	Ld Annaly	18 Mar 94–20 Jul 94
	Ld Lucas of Crudwell	20 Jul 94–
	Lady Miller of Hendon	20 Jul 94–
	Ld Inglewood	21 Jul 94–

[1] Not a Member of the House of Commons

MINISTRIES
(for addenda)

Ministerial Salaries

	Prime Minister[a]	Secretaries of State[a]	Other Dept. Ministers[a]	Reduced Parl. Salary
1831	£5,000	£5,000	£2,000	–
1937	£10,000	£5,000	£5,000	–
1965	£14,000	£8,500	£8,500	£1,250
1972	£20,000	£13,000	£7,500	£3,000
1978	£22,000	£14,300	£8,250	£3,529[c]
1979	£23,500	£19,650	£12,625	£5,265[c]
1980	£34,650[b]	£23,500	£16,250	£6,130[c]
1981	£36,725[b]	£23,500	£19,775	£6,930
1982	£38,200[b]	£28,950	£20,575	£8,130
1983	£38,200[b]	£28,950	£20,575	£8,460
1984	£38,987[b]	£29,367	£20,867	£11,443
1985	£40,808[b]	£30,188	£20,708	£12,792
1986	£42,745[b]	£31,625	£21,795	£13,375
1987	£44,775[b]	£33,145	£22,875	£13,875
1988	£45,787[b]	£34,157	£23,887	£16,911
1989	£46,109[b]	£34,479	£24,209	£18,148
1990	£46,750[b]	£35,120	£24,850	£20,101
1991	£50,724	£38,105	£26,962	£21,809
1992	£53,007	£39,820	£28,175	£23,227
1994	£54,438	£40,895	£28,936	£23,854
1995	£55,900	£41,994	£29,713	£24,495

[a] Not including the salary Ministers receive as members of Parliament in the fourth column. Until 1946 they received no pay as MPs. From 1946 to 1955 they were allowed to take £500 of their MPs salary as tax-free expenses.
[b] Throughout her period as Prime Minister Margaret Thatcher opted only to collect the same salary as other Cabinet Ministers.
[c] A minimum figure. From 1975 to 1980 some ministers were paid up to £1000 more.

Opposition Salaries

		Chief Opposition Whip	
	Leader of the Opposition*	House of Commons*	House of Lords
1937	£2,000	–	–
1957	£3,000	–	–
1965	£4,500	£3,750	£1,500
1972	£9,500	£7,500	£2,500
1978	£10,450	£8,250	£3,248
1979	£16,225	£12,625	£7,124
1980	£20,950	£16,250	£9,950
1981	£20,950	£16,250	£9,950
1982	£24,100	£18,650	£16,925
1983	£26,575	£20,575	£17,840
1984	£26,947	£20,867	£18,770
1985	£27,518	£20,798	£19,710
1986	£28,825	£21,795	£20,645
1987	£30,225	£22,875	£21,570
1988	£31,237	£23,887	£25,618
1989	£31,559	£24,209	£27,377
1990	£32,200	£24,850	£29,971
1991	£34,937	£26,962	£32,519
1992	£36,509	£28,175	£33,982
1994	£37,495	£28,936	£35,099
1995	£38,502	£29,713	£36,239

* Not including the Parliamentary salary – see above.

Ministerial Offices, 1900-

This list includes all specifically named ministerial offices held by Ministers or Ministers of State, apart from appointments in the Royal Household or, after 1950, Ministers of State without a functional title. It does not include offices held by junior ministers. In the 1980s it became increasingly common to give specific titles to Ministers of State in the larger departments, especially in Defence, Environment, Trade, and Transport. Minor variations in these labels were frequent and are not listed here.

Admiralty. First Lord of the Admiralty, 1900–64

Aerospace. Minister, 1971–72; Aerospace and Shipping, 1972–74

Agriculture. President of the Board of Agriculture, 1900–2; President of the Board of Agriculture and Fisheries, 1903–19; Minister of Agriculture and Fisheries, 1919–1955; Minister of Agriculture, Fisheries and Food, 1955–

Air. President of the Air Board, 1917; President of the Air Council, 1917–1918; Secretary of State, 1918–64

Aircraft Production. Minister. 1940–1946

Armed Forces. Minister for, 1981–

Arts. Under Secretary of State, 1965–67; Minister of State, 1967–70; Paymaster-General, 1970–73; Minister of State, 1973–74; Under Secretary of State, 1974–76; Minister of State, 1976–79: Minister for Arts, 1979–92; Secretary of State for the National Heritage 1992–

Attorney-General, 1900–

Attorney-General for Ireland, 1900–22

Aviation. Minister, 1959–67 (under *Transport*) (see *Civil Aviation*), Minister of State for Aviation and Shipping 1990–1994

Aviation Supply. Minister, 1970–71

Blockade. Minister, 1916–19

Burma. Secretary of State for India and Burma, 1937–47; Secretary of State for Burma, 1947–48

Citizen's Charter. Minister for, 1994–

Civil Aviation. Minister, 1944–53: Minister of Transport and Civil Aviation, 1953–59; Minister of Aviation, 1959–67; Minister of State for Aviation 1990–

Civil Service. Minister for the, 1968–

Colonies. Secretary of State, 1900–67

Commonwealth. Secretary of State for Dominions, 1925–47; Secretary of State for Commonwealth Relations, 1947–66; Secretary of State for Commonwealth Affairs, 1966–68

Consumer Affairs. Minister for 1979–1983 (under *Trade*).

Co-ordination of Defence. Minister, 1936–40

Co-ordination of Transport, Fuel and Power; Secretary of State, 1951–53

Corporate Affairs. Minister for 1989–(under *Trade*)

Defence. Minister, 1940–64; Secretary of State, 1964–

Defence. Minister for the Armed Forces, 1981–

Defence Procurement. Minister for, 1971–72, 1981–

Defence Support. Minister, 1985–6

Defence for Administration. Minister of, 1967–70

Defence for Air Force. Minister of, 1964–67

Defence for Army. Minister of, 1964–67

Defence for Equipment. Minister of, 1967–70

Defence for Navy. Minister of, 1964–67

Dominions. Secretary of State, 1925–47

Duchy of Lancaster. Chancellor, 1900–

Economic Affairs. Minister, Sep–Nov 1947, Feb–Oct 1950, 1951–52; Secretary of State, 1964–69. Minister of State for Economic Affairs, 1957–64

Economic Warfare. Minister, 1939–45

Education. President of the Board of Education, 1900–44; Minister of Education, 1944–64; Secretary of State for Education and Science, 1964–92; Secretary of State for Education 1992–

Employment and Productivity. Secretary of State, 1968–70

Employment. Secretary of State, 1970–

Energy. Secretary of State, 1974–92; also Minister for, Jan–Mar 1974, 1992– (under *Trade)*

Environment. Secretary of State, 1970–; Minister for 1985–

First Secretary of State. 1962–63, 1964–70

Food. Minister, 1916–21, and 1939–54 (see *Agriculture*)

Foreign Affairs. Secretary of State, 1900–68

Foreign and Commonwealth Affairs. Secretary of State, 1968–

Fuel and Power. Minister, 1944–57 (see *Power*)

Fuel, Light and Power. Minister, 1942–44 (see *Fuel and Power*)

Health. Minister, 1919–68; Minister of State, 1968–70; also Minister for 1979–; Secretary of State, 1988–

Health and Social Security. 1968–1988 (see *Social Services*)

Heritage. Minister for 1991–2. Secretary of State 1992–

Home Affairs. Secretary of State, 1900–

Home Security. Minister, 1939–45

Housing and Local Government. Minister of Town and Country Planning, 1943–51; Minister of Local Government and Planning, 1951; Minister of Housing and Local Government, 1951–70 (see *Local Government)* Minister, 1970– (under *Environment*)

India. Secretary of State for India, 1900–37; Secretary of State for India and Burma, 1937–47

Industrial Development. Minister, 1972–74

Industry. Secretary of State for Industry, Trade and Regional Development, 1963–64; Minister, 1970–74, 1983–; Secretary of State, 1974–83 (see *Trade*)

Information. Minister, Mar–Nov 1918 and 1939–46

Information Technology. Minister for Industry and Information Technology, 1981–3; Minister for Information Technology, 1983–7

Ireland. Chief Secretary to the Lord Lieutenant of Ireland, 1900–22 (Irish Office wound up 1924)

Labour. Minister of Labour, 1916–39; Minister of Labour and National Service, 1939–59; Minister of Labour, 1959–68

Land and Natural Resources. Minister, 1964–67

Local Government. President of the Local Government Board, 1900–19 (see *Housing and Local Government*)

Local Government. Minister, 1970– (under *Environment*)

Local Government and Planning. Minister, 1951 (see *Housing and Local Government*)

Local Government and Regional Planning. Secretary of State, 1969–70 (see *Planning and Local Government*)

Lord Advocate, 1900–

Lord Chancellor, 1900–

Lord Chancellor of Ireland, 1900–22

Lord President of the Council, 1900–

Lord Privy Seal, 1900–

Materials. Minister, 1951–54

Mines. Secretary for Mines Department, 1920–42

Ministers Resident Overseas. Allied H.Q., North Africa, 1942–5; Washington for Supply, 1942–5; West Africa, 1942–5; Middle East, 1942–3, 1944–5.

Munitions. Minister, 1915–19 (see *Supply*)

National Insurance. Minister, 1944–53; Minister of Pensions and National Insurance, 1953–66

National Service. Minister, 1916–19; Minister of Labour and National Service, 1939–59

Northern Ireland. Secretary of State, 1972–

Overseas Development. Minister, 1964–

Overseas Trade. Secretary for Overseas Trade, 1917–53

Paymaster-General, 1900–

Pensions. Minister of Pensions, 1916–53; Minister of Pensions and National Insurance, 1953–66

Petroleum. Secretary for Petroleum Department, 1940–42

Planning and Land. Minister, 1968–69

Planning and Local Government. Minister for Planning and Local Government, 1974–76

Portfolio. Minister without Portfolio, 1915–21, 1935–36, 1939–42, 1942–44, 1946, 1947, 1954–68, 1968–74, 1984–5

Post Office. Postmaster-General, 1900–69

Post and Telecommunications. Minister, 1969–74

Power. Minister, 1957–69 (see *Fuel and Power*)

Prices and Consumer Protection. Secretary of State, 1974–79

Prime Minister, 1900–

Privy Council Office. Minister of State, 1974–79, 1983–4, 1985–90

Production. Minister, 1942–45

Public Building and Works. Minister, 1962–70 (see *Housing and Construction*)

Public Service and Science, Minister, 1992–

Public Transport, Minister for, 1988– (under *Transport*)

Reconstruction. Minister, 1917–19 and 1944–45

Science. Minister, 1959–64

Scotland. Secretary, 1900–26; Secretary of State, 1926–

Shipping. Minister, 1916–21 and 1939–41 (see *War Transport*)

Social Insurance. Minister, Oct–Nov 1944 (see *National Insurance*)

Social Security. Minister, 1966–68, (See *Health and Social Security*); Secretary of State 1988–; also Minister for Social Security 1976–

Social Services. Secretary of State, 1968–88

Solicitor-General, 1900–

Solicitor-General for Ireland, 1900–22

Solicitor-General for Scotland, 1900–

Sport (and Recreation). Minister of State, 1974–79

State. Minister of (at Foreign Office), 1941–42, 1943–50

State, First Secretary of. 1962–63, 1964–70

Supply. Minister, 1919–21 and 1939–59

Technical Cooperation. Secretary for, 1961–64

Technology. Minister, 1964–70

Town and Country Planning. Minister of Town and Country Planning, 1943–51 (see *Local Government and Planning*)

Trade. President of the Board of Trade, 1900–70, 1992–; Secretary of State of Trade and Industry, 1970–74, 1983–92; Secretary of State for Trade, 1974–83. also Minister for Trade, 1970–72, 1983–94; Minister for Export and Trade 1994; Minister for Trade and Consumer Affairs, 1972–74

Transport. Minister of Transport, 1919–41; Minister of War Transport, 1941–46; Minister of Transport, 1946–53; Minister of Transport and Civil Aviation, 1953–59; Minister of Transport, 1959–70; Minister for Transport Industries, 1970–74; Minister for Transport, 1974–76; Secretary of State, 1976–79, 1981–; Minister of Transport, 1979–81

Treasury. Chancellor of the Exchequer, 1900–; Chief Secretary, 1961–; Financial Secretary, 1900–; Economic Secretary, 1947–50, 1950–51, 1952–8, 1958–64, 1981–; Minister of State, 1964–9, 1970–87, 1990–92

Urban Affairs. Minister of State, 1974–74

Wales. Minister for Welsh Affairs, 1951–64; Secretary of State for Wales, 1964–; also Minister of State for Welsh Affairs, 1957–64

War. Secretary of State, 1900–64

War Transport. Minister, 1941–46 (see *Shipping and Transport*)

Works. First Commissioner of Works, 1900–40; Minister of Works and Buildings, 1940–42; Minister of Works and Planning, 1942–43; Minister of Works, 1943–62; Minister of Public Building and Works, 1962–70

Holders of Ministerial Offices

Prime Minister

1900		M of Salisbury(3rd)
12 Jul	02	A. Balfour
5 Dec	05	Sir H. Campbell-Bannerman
5 Apr	08	H. Asquith
6 Dec	16	D. Lloyd George
23 Oct	22	A. Bonar Law
22 May	23	S. Baldwin
22 Jan	24	R. MacDonald
4 Nov	24	S. Baldwin
5 Jun	29	R. MacDonald
7 Jun	35	S. Baldwin
28 May	37	N. Chamberlain
10 May	40	W. Churchill
26 Jul	45	C. Attlee
26 Oct	51	(Sir) W. Churchill
6 Apr	55	Sir A. Eden
10 Jan	57	H. Macmillan
18 Oct	63	Sir A. Douglas-Home
16 Oct	64	H. Wilson
19 Jun	70	E. Heath
4 Mar	74	H. Wilson
5 Apr	76	J. Callaghan
4 May	79	Mrs M. Thatcher
28 Nov	90	J. Major

Deputy Prime Minister

19 Feb 42–23 May 45	C. Attlee
26 Jul 45–24 Feb 51	H. Morrison
26 Oct 51– 6 Apr 55	(Sir) A. Eden
13 Jul 62–18 Oct 63	R. Butler
4 May 79–10 Jan 88	W. Whitelaw
24 Jul 89– 1 Nov 90	Sir G. Howe

Lord President of the Council

1900		D of Devonshire
13 Oct	03	M of Londonderry
10 Dec	05	E of Crewe
12 Apr	08	Ld Tweedmouth
13 Oct	08	Vt Wolverhampton
16 Jun	10	Earl Beauchamp
3 Nov	10	Vt Morley
5 Aug	14	Earl Beauchamp
25 May	15	M of Crewe
10 Dec	16	Earl Curzon
23 Oct	19	(Sir) A. Balfour (E of Balfour)
24 Oct	22	M of Salisbury (4th)
22 Jan	24	Ld Parmoor
6 Nov	24	Marquess Curzon
27 Apr	25	E of Balfour
7 Jun	29	Ld Parmoor
25 Aug	31	S. Baldwin

7 Jun	35	R. MacDonald
28 May	37	Vt Halifax
9 Mar	38	Vt Hailsham(1st)
31 Oct	38	Vt Runciman
3 Sep	39	Earl Stanhope
11 May	40	N. Chamberlain
3 Oct	40	Sir J. Anderson
24 Sep	43	C. Attlee
25 May	45	Ld Woolton
27 Jul	45	H. Morrison
9 Mar	51	Vt Addison
28 Oct	51	Ld Woolton
24 Nov	52	M of Salisbury (5th)
29 Mar	57	E of Home
17 Sep	57	Vt Hailsham (2nd)
14 Oct	59	E of Home
27 Jul	60	Vt Hailsham (2nd) (Q. Hogg)
16 Oct	64	H. Bowden
11 Aug	66	R. Crossman
18 Oct	68	F. Peart
20 Jun	70	W. Whitelaw
7 Apr	72	R. Carr
5 Nov	72	J. Prior
5 Mar	74	E. Short
8 Apr	76	M. Foot
5 May	79	Ld Soames
14 Sep	81	F. Pym
5 Apr	82	J. Biffen
11 Jun	83	Vt Whitelaw
10 Jan	88	J. Wakeham
24 Jul	89	Sir G. Howe
2 Nov	90	J. MacGregor
10 Apr	92	A. Newton

Lord Chancellor

1900		E of Halsbury
10 Dec	05	Ld Loreburn(E)
10 Jun	12	Vt Haldane
25 May	15	Ld Buckmaster
10 Dec	16	Ld Finlay
10 Jan	19	Ld Birkenhead (Vt)
24 Oct	22	Vt Cave
22 Jan	24	Vt Haldane
6 Nov	24	Vt Cave
28 Mar	28	Ld Hailsham(Vt)
7 Jun	29	Ld Sankey (Vt)
7 Jun	35	Vt Hailsham
9 Mar	38	Ld Maugham (Vt)
3 Sep	39	Vt Caldecote
12 May	40	Vt Simon
27 Jul	45	Ld Jowitt
30 Oct	51	Ld Simonds
18 Oct	54	Vt Kilmuir
13 Jul	62	Ld Dilhorne
16 Oct	64	Ld Gardiner
20 Jun	70	Ld Hailsham
5 Mar	74	Ld Elwyn-Jones
5 May	79	Ld Hailsham
13 Jun	87	Ld Havers
26 Oct	87	Ld Mackay

Lord Privy Seal

1900		Vt Cross
1 Nov	00	M of Salisbury (3rd)
12 Jul	02	A. Balfour
11 Oct	03	M of Salisbury (4th)
10 Dec	05	M of Ripon
9 Oct	08	E of Crewe
23 Oct	11	Earl Carrington
13 Feb	12	M of Crewe
25 May	15	Earl Curzon
15 Dec	16	E of Crawford
10 Jan	19	A. Bonar Law
23 Mar	21	A. Chamberlain
24 Oct	22	(office vacant)
25 May	23	Ld R. Cecil
22 Jan	24	J. Clynes
6 Nov	24	M of Salisbury (4th)
7 Jun	29	J. Thomas
5 Jun	30	V. Hartshorn
24 Mar	31	T. Johnston
3 Sep	31	Earl Peel
5 Nov	31	Vt Snowden
29 Sep	32	S. Baldwin
31 Dec	33	A. Eden
7 Jun	35	M of Londonderry
22 Nov	35	Vt Halifax
28 May	37	Earl De La Warr
31 Oct	38	Sir J. Anderson
3 Sep	39	Sir S. Hoare
3 Apr	40	Sir K. Wood
11 May	40	C. Attlee
19 Feb	42	Sir S. Cripps
22 Nov	42	Vt Cranborne (5th M of Salisbury)
24 Sep	43	Ld Beaverbrook
27 Jul	45	A. Greenwood
17 Apr	47	Ld Inman
7 Oct	47	Vt Addison
9 Mar	51	E. Bevin
26 Apr	51	R. Stokes
28 Oct	51	M of Salisbury (5th)
7 May	52	H. Crookshank
20 Dec	55	R. Butler
14 Oct	59	Vt Hailsham
27 Jul	60	E. Heath
20 Oct	63	S. Lloyd
18 Oct	64	E of Longford
23 Dec	65	Sir F. Soskice
6 Apr	66	E of Longford
16 Jan	68	Ld Shackleton
6 Apr	68	F. Peart
18 Oct	68	Ld Shackleton
20 Jun	70	Earl Jellicoe
5 Jun	73	Ld Windlesham
7 Mar	74	Ld Shepherd
10 Sep	76	Ld Peart
5 May	79	Sir I. Gilmour
14 Sep	81	H. Atkins
6 Apr	82	Lady Young
11 Jun	83	J. Biffen

13 Jun 87   J. Wakeham
10 Jan 88   Ld Belstead
28 Nov 90   Ld Waddington
11 Apr 92   Ld Wakeham
20 Jul 94   Vt Cranborne

Secretary of State for Economic Affairs

16 Oct 64   G. Brown
11 Aug 66   M. Stewart
29 Aug 67   P. Shore
(office wound up 8 Oct 69)

Chancellor of the Exchequer

1900   Sir M. Hicks-Beach
8 Aug 02   C. Ritchie
6 Oct 03   A. Chamberlain
10 Dec 05   H. Asquith
12 Apr 08   D. Lloyd-George
25 May 15   R. McKenna
10 Dec 16   A. Bonar Law
10 Jan 19   A. Chamberlain
1 Apr 21   Sir R. Horne
24 Oct 22   S. Baldwin
27 Aug 23   N. Chamberlain
22 Jan 24   P. Snowden
6 Nov 24   W. Churchill
7 Jun 29   P. Snowden
5 Nov 31   N. Chamberlain
28 May 37 Sir J. Simon
12 May 40 Sir K. Wood
24 Sep 43 Sir J. Anderson
27 Jul 45 H. Dalton
13 Nov 47 Sir S. Cripps
19 Oct 50 H Gaitskell
28 Oct 51 R. Butler
20 Dec 55 H. Macmillan
13 Jan 57 P. Thorneycroft
6 Jan 58   D. Heathcoat Amory
27 Jul 60 S. Lloyd
13 Jul 62 R. Maudling
16 Oct 64 J. Callaghan
30 Nov 67 R. Jenkins
20 Jun 70 I. Macleod
25 Jul 70 A. Barber
25 Mar 74 D. Healey
5 May 79 Sir G. Howe
11 Jun 83 N. Lawson
26 Oct 89 J. Major
28 Nov 90 N. Lamont
27 May 93 K. Clarke

Secretary of State for Foreign Affairs

1900   M of Salisbury (3rd)
1 Nov 00   M of Lansdowne
10 Dec 05   Sir E. Grey (Vt)
10 Dec 16   A. Balfour
23 Oct 19   Earl Curzon (M)
22 Jan 24   R. MacDonald
6 Nov 24   (Sir) A. Chamberlain
7 Jun 29   A. Henderson

25 Aug 31   M of Reading
5 Nov 31   Sir J. Simon
7 Jun 35   Sir S. Hoare
22 Dec 35   A. Eden
21 Feb 38   Vt Halifax
22 Dec 40   A. Eden
27 Jul 45   E. Bevin
9 Mar 51   H. Morrison
28 Oct 51   (Sir) A. Eden
7 Apr 55   H. Macmillan
20 Dec 55   S. Lloyd
27 Jul 60   E of Home
20 Oct 63   R. Butler
16 Oct 64   P. Gordon Walker
22 Jan 65   M. Stewart
11 Aug 66   G. Brown
16 Mar 68   M. Stewart

(Secretary of State for Foreign and Commonwealth Affairs)

17 Oct 68   M. Stewart
20 Jun 70   Sir A. Douglas-Home
5 Mar 74   J. Callaghan
8 Apr 76   A. Crosland
21 Feb 77   D. Owen
5 May 79   Ld Carrington
5 Apr 82   F. Pym
11 Jun 83   Sir G. Howe
14 Jun 89   J. Major
26 Oct 89   D. Hurd

Secretary of State for the Home Department

1900   Sir M. White-Ridley
1 Nov 00   C. Ritchie
8 Aug 02   A. Akers-Douglas
10 Dec 05   H. Gladstone
14 Feb 10   W. Churchill
23 Oct 11   R. McKenna
25 May 15   Sir J. Simon
10 Jan 16   H. Samuel
10 Dec 16   Sir G. Cave (Vt)
10 Jan 19   E. Shortt
24 Oct 22   W. Bridgeman
22 Jan 24   A. Henderson
6 Nov 24   Sir W. Joynson-Hicks
7 Jun 29   J. Clynes
25 Aug 31   Sir H. Samuel
28 Sep 32   Sir J. Gilmour
7 Jun 35   Sir J. Simon
28 May 37 Sir S. Hoare
3 Sep 39   Sir J. Anderson
3 Oct 40   H. Morrison
25 May 45   Sir D. Somervell
3 Aug 45   C. Ede
28 Oct 51   Sir D. Maxwell-Fyfe
18 Oct 54   G. Lloyd-George
13 Jan 57   R. Butler
13 Jul 62   H. Brooke
18 Oct 64   Sir F. Soskice

23 Dec 65   R. Jenkins
30 Nov 67   J. Callaghan
20 Jun 70   R. Maudling
19 Jul 72   R. Carr
5 Mar 74   R. Jenkins
10 Sep 76   M. Rees
5 May 79   W. Whitelaw
11 Jun 83   L. Brittan
2 Sep 85   D. Hurd
26 Oct 89   D. Waddington
28 Nov 90   K. Baker
11 Apr 92   K. Clarke
27 May 93   M. Howard

First Lord of the Admiralty

1900   G. Goschen
1 Nov 00   E of Selborne
5 Mar 05   Earl Cawdor
10 Dec 05   Ld Tweedmouth
12 Apr 08   R. McKenna
23 Oct 11   W. Churchill
25 May 15   A. Balfour
10 Dec 16   Sir E. Carson
17 Jul 17   Sir E. Geddes
10 Jan 19   W. Long
13 Feb 21   Ld Lee
24 Oct 22   L. Amery
22 Jan 24   Vt Chelmsford
6 Nov 24   W. Bridgeman
7 Jun 29   A. Alexander
25 Aug 31   Sir A. Chamberlain
5 Nov 31   Sir B. Eyres-Monsell
                (Vt Monsell)
5 Jun 36   Sir S. Hoare
28 May 37 A. Duff Cooper
27 Oct 38   Earl Stanhope
3 Sep 39   W. Churchill
11 May 40   A. Alexander
25 May 45   B. Bracken
3 Aug 45   A. Alexander
4 Oct 46   Vt Hall
24 May 51   Ld Pakenham
31 Oct 51   J. Thomas (Vt
                Cilcennin)
2 Sep 56   Vt Hailsham
16 Jan 57   E of Selkirk
16 Oct 59   Ld Carrington
22 Oct 63   Earl Jellicoe
(office wound up 1 Apr 64)

Minister for Aerospace (and Shipping)

1 May 71   F. Corfield
7 Apr 72   M. Heseltine
(office wound up 5 Mar 74)

President of the Board of Agriculture (and Fisheries 1903)

1900   W. Long
14 Nov 00   R. Hanbury

19 May 03	E of Onslow
12 Mar 05	A. Fellowes
10 Dec 05	Earl Carrington
23 Oct 11	W. Runciman
6 Aug 14	Ld Lucas
25 May 15	E of Selborne
11 Jul 16	E of Crawford
10 Dec 16	R. Prothero
	(Ld Ernle)·

(Minister of Agriculture and Fisheries)
(and *Food, 18 Oct 54*)

15 Aug 19	Ld Lee
13 Feb 21	Sir A. Griffith-Boscawen
24 Oct 22	Sir R. Sanders
22 Jan 24	N. Buxton
6 Nov 24	E. Wood
4 Nov 25	W. Guinness
7 Jun 29	N. Buxton
5 Jun 30	C. Addison
25 Aug 31	Sir J. Gilmour
28 Sep 32	W. Elliot
29 Oct 36	W. Morrison
29 Jan 39	Sir R. Dorman-Smith
14 May 40	R. Hudson
3 Aug 45	T. Williams
31 Oct 51	Sir T. Dugdale
28 Jul 54	D. Heathcoat Amory
6 Jan 58	J. Hare
27 Jul 60	C. Soames
18 Oct 64	F. Peart
6 Apr 68	C. Hughes
20 Jun 70	J. Prior
5 Nov 72	J. Godber
5 Mar 74	F. Peart
10 Sep 76	J. Silkin
5 May 79	P. Walker
11 Jun 83	M. Jopling
13 Jun 87	J. MacGregor
24 Jul 89	J. S. Gummer
27 May 93	Mrs G. Shephard
20 Jul 94	W. Waldegrave

President of the Air Board

3 Jan 17	Ld Cowdray

(President of the Air Council)

26 Nov 17	Ld Rothermere
26 Apr 18	Ld Weir

(Secretary of State for Air)

10 Jan 19	W. Churchill
1 Apr 21	F. Guest
31 Oct 22	Sir S. Hoare
22 Jan 24	Ld Thomson
6 Nov 24	Sir S. Hoare
7 Jun 29	Ld Thomson
14 Oct 30	Ld Amulree
5 Nov 31	M of Londonderry

7 Jun 35	Sir P. Cunliffe-Lister (Vt Swinton)
16 May 38	Sir K. Wood
3 Apr 40	Sir S. Hoare
11 May 40	Sir A. Sinclair
25 May 45	H. Macmillan
3 Aug 45	Vt Stansgate
4 Oct 46	P. Noel-Baker
7 Oct 47	A. Henderson
31 Oct 51	Ld De L'Isle
20 Dec 55	N. Birch
16 Jan 57	G. Ward
28 Oct 60	J. Amery
16 Jul 62	H. Fraser
	(*office wound up 1 Apr 64*)

Minister of Aircraft Production

14 May 40	Ld Beaverbrook
1 May 41	J. Moore-Brabazon
22 Feb 42	J. Llewellin
22 Nov 42	Sir S. Cripps
25 May 45	E. Brown
4 Aug 45	J. Wilmot
	(*office wound up 1 Apr 46*)

Minister of State for the Armed Forces

29 May 81	P. Blaker
13 Jun 83	J. Stanley
13 Jun 87	A. Clark
25 Jul 88	A. Hamilton
27 May 93	J. Hanley

Minister for the Arts

20 Oct 64	Miss J. Lee
17 Feb 67	Miss J. Lee
23 Jun 70	Vt Eccles
2 Dec 73	N. St John-Stevas
8 Mar 74	H. Jenkins
14 Apr 76	Ld Donaldson
5 May 79	N. St John-Stevas
5 Jun 81	P. Channon
13 Jun 83	E of Gowrie
2 Sep 85	R. Luce
26 Jul 90	D. Mellor
28 Nov 90	T. Renton
	(*11 Apr 92 under National Heritage*)

Attorney-General

1900	Sir R. Webster
7 May 00	Sir R. Finlay
12 Dec 05	Sir J. Walton
28 Jan 08	Sir W. Robson
7 Oct 10	Sir R. Isaacs
19 Oct 13	Sir J. Simon
25 May 15	Sir E. Carson
3 Nov 15	Sir F. Smith
10 Jan 19	Sir G. Hewart
6 Mar 22	Sir E. Pollock
24 Oct 22	Sir D. Hogg

23 Jan 24	Sir P. Hastings
6 Nov 24	Sir D. Hogg
28 Mar 28	Sir T. Inskip
7 Jun 29	Sir W. Jowitt
26 Jan 32	Sir T. Inskip
18 Mar 36	Sir D. Somervell
25 May 45	Sir D. Maxwell-Fyfe
4 Aug 45	Sir H. Shawcross
24 Apr 51	Sir F. Soskice
3 Nov 51	Sir L. Heald
18 Oct 54	Sir R. Manningham-Buller
16 Jul 62	Sir J. Hobson
1 Oct 64	Sir E. Jones
23 Jun 70	Sir P. Rawlinson
7 Mar 74	S. Silkin
5 May 79	Sir M. Havers
13 Jun 87	Sir P. Mayhew
15 Apr 92	Sir N. Lyell

Minister of Blockade

10 Dec 16	Ld R. Cecil
18 Jul 18	Sir L. Worthington-Evans
	(*office wound up 10 Jan 19*)

Minister of Civil Aviation

8 Oct 44	Vt Swinton
4 Aug 45	Ld Winster
4 Oct 46	Ld Nathan
31 May 48	Ld Pakenham
1 Jun 51	Ld Ogmore
31 Oct 51	J. Maclay
7 May 52	A. Lennox-Boyd

(Minister of Transport and Civil Aviation)

1 Oct 53	A. Lennox-Boyd
28 Jul 54	J. Boyd-Carpenter
20 Dec 55	H. Watkinson

(Minister of Aviation)

14 Oct 59	D. Sandys
27 Jul 60	P. Thorneycroft
16 Jul 62	J. Amery
18 Oct 64	R. Jenkins
23 Dec 65	F. Mulley
7 Jan 67	J. Stonehouse
	(*office absorbed into Min. of Technology 15 Feb 67*)

Minister for Aviation
(under *Transport*)

23 Jul 90	Ld Brabazon
15 Apr 92	E of Caithness
12 Jan 94	(*office reduced to U-S level*)

Minister of Aviation Supply

15 Oct 70 F. Corfield
*(office absorbed into Min. of
Defence 1 May 71)*

Minister for the Civil Service

1 Nov 68 H. Wilson
19 Jun 70 E. Heath
4 Mar 74 H. Wilson
5 Apr 76 J. Callaghan
4 May 79 Mrs M. Thatcher
28 Nov 90 J. Major

Secretary of State for the Colonies

1900 J. Chamberlain
6 Oct 03 A. Lyttelton
10 Dec 05 E of Elgin
12 Apr 08 E of Crewe
3 Nov 10 L. Harcourt
25 May 15 A. Bonar Law
10 Dec 16 W. Long
10 Jan 19 Vt Milner
13 Feb 21 W. Churchill
24 Oct 22 D of Devonshire
22 Jan 24 J. Thomas
6 Nov 24 L. Amery
7 Jun 29 Ld Passfield
25 Aug 31 J. Thomas
5 Nov 31 Sir P. Cunliffe-Lister
7 Jun 35 M. MacDonald
22 Nov 35 J. Thomas
28 May 36 W. Ormsby-Gore
16 May 38 M. MacDonald
12 May 40 Ld Lloyd
8 Feb 41 Ld Moyne
22 Feb 42 Vt Cranborne
22 Nov 42 O. Stanley
3 Aug 45 G. Hall
4 Oct 46 A. Creech Jones
28 Feb 50 J. Griffiths
28 Oct 51 O. Lyttelton
28 Jul 54 A. Lennox-Boyd
14 Oct 59 I. Macleod
9 Oct 61 R. Maudling
13 Jul 62 D. Sandys
18 Oct 64 A. Greenwood
23 Dec 65 E of Longford
6 Apr 66 F. Lee
*(office came under Commonwealth
Affairs 1 Aug 66 and abolished
6 Jan 67)*

Minister for Consumer Affairs
(under *Trade*)

8 May 79 Mrs S. Oppenheim
5 Mar 82 G. Vaughan
(office wound up 13 Jun 83)

Minister for Corporate Affairs
(under *Trade*)

24 Jul 89 J. Redwood
(office vacant 15 Apr 92)

Minister for Co-ordination of Defence

13 Mar 36 Sir T. Inskip
29 Jan 39 Ld Chatfield

(Minister of Defence)

10 May 40 W. Churchill
27 Jul 45 C. Attlee
20 Dec 46 A. Alexander
28 Feb 50 E. Shinwell
28 Oct 51 W. Churchill
1 Mar 52 Earl Alexander of Tunis
18 Oct 54 H. Macmillan
7 Apr 55 S. Lloyd
20 Dec 55 Sir W. Monckton
18 Oct 56 A. Head
13 Jan 57 D. Sandys
14 Oct 59 H. Watkinson
13 Jul 62 P. Thorneycroft

(Secretary of State)

1 Apr 64 P. Thorneycroft
16 Oct 64 D. Healey
20 Jun 70 Ld Carrington
8 Jan 74 I. Gilmour
5 Mar 74 R. Mason
10 Sep 76 F. Mulley
5 May 79 F. Pym
5 Jan 81 J. Nott
8 Jan 83 M. Heseltine
9 Jan 86 G. Younger
24 Jul 89 T. King
15 Apr 92 M. Rifkind

Minister of Defence for Administration

7 Jan 67 G. Reynolds
15 Jul 69 R. Hattersley
(office wound up 19 Jun 70)

Minister of State (Armed Forces)

29 May 81 P. Blaker
13 Jun 83 J. Stanley
13 Jun 87 A. Clark
25 Jul 88 A. Hamilton
27 May 92 J. Hanley
20 Jul 94 N. Soames

Minister of State for Defence Procurement

7 Apr 71 I. Gilmour
(office vacant 5 Nov 72)
29 May 81 Vt Trenchard
6 Jan 83 G. Pattie

11 Sep 84 A. Butler
2 Sep 85 N. Lamont
21 May 86 Ld Trefgarne
13 Jun 87 I. Stewart
24 Jul 89 A. Clark
15 Apr 92 J. Aitken
20 Jul 94 R. Freeman

Minister for Defence Support

2 Sep 85 Ld Trefgarne
(office wound up 10 Sep 86)

Minister of Defence for Air Force

1 Apr 64 H. Fraser
19 Oct 64 Ld Shackleton
(office wound up 7 Jan 67)

Minister of Defence for Army

1 Apr 64 J. Ramsden
19 Oct 64 F. Mulley
24 Dec 65 G. Reynolds
(office wound up 7 Jan 67)

Minister of Defence for Navy

1 Apr 64 Earl Jellicoe
19 Oct 64 C. Mayhew
19 Feb 66 J. Mallalieu
(office wound up 7 Jan 67)

Minister of Defence for Equipment

7 Jan 67 R. Mason
6 Apr 68 J. Morris
(office wound up 19 Jun 70)

Secretary of State for Dominion Affairs

11 Jun 25 L. Amery
7 Jun 29 Ld Passfield
5 Jun 30 J. Thomas
22 Nov 35 M. MacDonald
16 May 38 Ld Stanley
31 Oct 38 M. MacDonald
29 Jan 39 Sir T. Inskip (Vt Caldecote)
3 Sep 39 A. Eden
14 May 40 Vt Caldecote
3 Oct 40 Vt Cranborne
19 Feb 42 C. Attlee
24 Sep 43 Vt Cranborne
3 Aug 45 Vt Addison

(Secretary of State for Commonwealth Relations)

7 Jul 47 Vt Addison
7 Oct 47 P. Noel-Baker

28 Feb	50	P. Gordon Walker
28 Oct	51	Ld Ismay
12 Mar	52	M of Salisbury
24 Nov	52	Vt Swinton
7 Apr	55	E of Home
27 Jul	60	D. Sandys
18 Oct	64	A. Bottomley

(Secretary of State for Commonwealth Affairs)

1 Aug	66	A. Bottomley
11 Aug	66	H. Bowden
29 Aug	67	G. Thomson

(17 Oct 68 office merged with Foreign Office)

Minister of Economic Warfare

3 Sep	39	R. Cross
15 May	40	H. Dalton
22 Feb	42	Vt Wolmer (E of Selborne)

(office wound up 23 May 45)

President of the Board of Education

1 Jan	00	D of Devonshire
8 Aug	02	M of Londonderry
10 Dec	05	A. Birrell
23 Jan	07	R. McKenna
12 Apr	08	W. Runciman
23 Oct	11	J. Pease
25 May	15	A. Henderson
18 Aug	16	M of Crewe
10 Dec	16	H. Fisher
24 Oct	22	E. Wood
22 Jan	24	C. Trevelyan
6 Nov	24	Ld E. Percy
7 Jun	29	Sir C. Trevelyan
2 Mar	31	H. Lees-Smith
25 Aug	31	Sir D. Maclean
15 Jun	32	Ld Irwin (Vt Halifax)
7 Jun	35	O. Stanley
28 May	37	Earl Stanhope
27 Oct	38	Earl De La Warr
3 Apr	40	H. Ramsbotham
20 Jul	41	R. Butler

(Minister of Education)

3 Aug	44	R. Butler
25 May	45	R. Law
3 Aug	45	Miss E. Wilkinson
10 Feb	47	G. Tomlinson
2 Nov	51	Miss F. Horsbrugh
18 Oct	54	Sir D. Eccles
13 Jan	57	Vt Hailsham (2nd)
17 Sep	57	G. Lloyd
14 Oct	59	Sir D. Eccles
13 Jul	62	Sir E. Boyle

(Secretary of State for Education and Science)

1 Apr	64	Q. Hogg
18 Oct	64	M. Stewart
22 Jan	65	A. Crosland
29 Aug	67	P. Gordon Walker
6 Apr	68	E. Short
20 Jun	70	Mrs M. Thatcher
5 Mar	74	R. Prentice
10 Jun	75	F. Mulley
10 Sep	76	Mrs S. Williams
5 May	79	M. Carlisle
14 Sep	81	Sir K. Joseph
21 May	86	K. Baker
24 Jul	89	J. MacGregor
2 Nov	90	K. Clarke

(Secretary of State for Education)

15 Apr	92	J. Patten
20 Jul	94	Mrs G. Shephard

Secretary of State for Employment and Productivity

6 Apr	68	Mrs B. Castle
20 Jun	70	R. Carr

(Secretary of State for Employment)

12 Nov	70	R. Carr
7 Apr	72	M. Macmillan
2 Dec	73	W. Whitelaw
5 Mar	74	M. Foot
8 Apr	76	A. Booth
5 May	79	J. Prior
14 Sep	81	N. Tebbit
16 Oct	83	T. King
2 Sep	85	Ld Young of Graffham
13 Jun	87	N. Fowler
3 Jan	90	M. Howard
12 Apr	92	Mrs G. Shephard
27 May	93	D. Hunt
20 Jul	94	M. Portillo

Secretary of State for Energy

8 Jan	74	Ld Carrington
5 Mar	74	E. Varley
10 Jun	75	A. Benn
5 May	79	D. Howell
14 Sep	81	N. Lawson
11 Jun	83	P. Walker
13 Jun	87	C. Parkinson
24 Jul	89	J. Wakeham

(office merged with Trade 15 Apr 92)

Minister for Energy
(under *Trade*)

15 Apr	92	T. Eggar

Secretary of State for the Environment

15 Oct	70	P. Walker
5 Nov	72	G. Rippon
5 Mar	74	A. Crosland
8 Apr	76	P. Shore
5 May	79	M. Heseltine
6 Jan	83	T. King
11 Jun	83	P. Jenkin
2 Sep	85	K. Baker
21 May	86	N. Ridley
24 Jul	89	C. Patten
28 Nov	90	M. Heseltine
11 Apr	92	M. Howard
27 May	93	J. S. Gummer

Minister for Environment
(under *Environment*)

27 Mar	85	Ld Elton
10 Sep	86	W. Waldegrave
13 Jun	87	Ld Belstead
25 Jul	88	M. Howard
24 Jul	89	D. Trippier
14 Apr	92	D. Maclean
27 May	93	T. Yeo
8 Jan	94	R. Atkins

Minister of Food Control

10 Dec	16	Vt Devonport
19 Jun	17	Ld Rhondda (Vt)
9 Jul	18	J. Clynes
10 Jan	19	G. Roberts
19 Mar	20	C. McCurdy

(office wound up 31 Mar 21)

Minister of Food

4 Sep	39	W. Morrison
3 Apr	40	Ld Woolton
11 Nov	43	J. Llewellin
3 Aug	45	Sir B. Smith
27 May	46	J. Strachey
28 Feb	50	M. Webb
31 Oct	51	G. Lloyd-George
18 Oct	54	D. Heathcoat Amory

(and combined with Agriculture and Fisheries)

Foreign Affairs
(*See p. 53*)

Minister of Fuel, Light and Power

3 Jun	42	G. Lloyd-George

(Minister of Fuel and Power)

25 May	45	G. Lloyd-George
3 Aug	45	E. Shinwell
7 Oct	47	H. Gaitskell

28 Feb 50	P. Noel-Baker
31 Oct 51	G. Lloyd
20 Dec 55	A. Jones

(Minister of Power)

13 Jan 57	Ld Mills
14 Oct 59	R. Wood
20 Oct 63	F. Erroll
18 Oct 64	F. Lee
6 Apr 66	R. Marsh
6 Apr 68	R. Gunter
6 Jul 68	R. Mason

(office absorbed into Technology 6 Oct 69)

Minister of Health

(See below, under Local Government and under Social Services)

Minister for Health
(under *Social Services*)

7 May 79	G. Vaughan
5 Mar 82	K. Clarke
2 Sep 85	B. Hayhoe
11 Sep 84	A. Newton
10 Sep 86	D. Mellor (under Health)
25 Jul 89	Ld Trafford
28 Oct 89	Mrs V. Bottomley
15 Apr 92	B. Mawhinney

Home Office
(See p. 53)

Minister of Housing

(See below, under Local Government and under Environment)

7 May 79	J. Stanley
13 Jun 83	I. Gow
2 Sep 85	J. Patten
13 Jun 87	W. Waldegrave
25 Jul 88	E of Caithness
25 Jul 89	M. Howard
3 Jan 90	M. Spicer
28 Nov 90	Sir G. Young

Secretary of State for India
(and Burma 1937–48)

1900	Ld G. Hamilton
6 Oct 03	St J. Brodrick
10 Dec 05	J. Morley (Vt)
3 Nov 10	E of Crewe
7 Mar 11	Vt Morley
25 May 11	E of Crewe (M)
25 May 15	A. Chamberlain
17 Jul 17	E. Montagu
19 Mar 22	Vt Peel
22 Jan 24	Ld Olivier
6 Nov 24	E of Birkenhead

18 Oct 28	Vt Peel
7 Jun 29	W. Benn
25 Aug 31	Sir S. Hoare
7 Jun 35	M of Zetland
13 May 40	L. Amery
3 Aug 45	Ld Pethick-Lawrence
17 Apr 47	E of Listowel

(4 Jan 1948 India and Burma Offices wound up)

Minister for Industrial Development

7 Apr 72	C. Chataway

(office abolished 5 Mar 74)

Minister for Industry
(under *Trade and Industry*)

15 Oct 70	Sir J. Eden
7 Apr 72	T. Boardman

(office abolished 8 Jan 74)

Secretary of State for Industry, Trade and Regional Development

20 Oct 63	E. Heath

(office abolished 16 Oct 64)

Secretary of State for Industry

5 Mar 74	A. Benn
10 Jun 75	E. Varley
5 May 79	Sir K. Joseph
14 Sep 81	P. Jenkin

(11 Jun 83 office merged with Trade)

Minister for Industry and Information Technology

13 Jun 83	K. Baker
11 Sep 84	G. Pattie

(office wound up 13 Jun 87)

Minister for Industry

(under Trade and Industry)

13 Jun 83	N. Lamont
2 Sep 85	P. Morrison
13 Jun 87	K. Clarke
24 Jul 88	A. Newton
25 Jul 89	D. Hogg
2 Nov 90	Ld Hesketh

(office vacant 23 May 91)

15 Apr 92	T. Sainsbury

(office vacant 20 Jul 94)

Minister of Information

10 Feb 18	Ld Beaverbrook
4 Nov 18	Ld Downham

(office wound up 10 Jan 19)

4 Sep 39	Ld Macmillan
5 Jan 40	Sir J. Reith
12 May 40	A. Duff Cooper
20 Jul 41	B. Bracken
25 May 45	G. Lloyd
4 Aug 45	E. Williams
24 Feb 46	E of Listowel

(office abolished 31 Mar 46)

Chief Secretary for Ireland

1900	G. Balfour
7 Nov 00	G. Wyndham
12 Mar 05	W. Long
10 Dec 05	J. Bryce
23 Jan 07	A. Birrell
31 Jul 16	(Sir) H. Duke
5 May 18	E. Shortt
10 Jan 19	I. Macpherson
2 Apr 20	Sir H. Greenwood

(post vacant 19 Oct 22, office abolished 6 Dec 22)

Lord Chancellor of Ireland

1900	Ld Ashbourne
12 Dec 05	Sir S. Walker
26 Sep 11	K. Barry
10 Apr 13	(Sir) I. O'Brien
4 Jun 18	Sir J. Campbell
27 Jun 21	Sir J. Ross

(ceased to be executive office 27 Jun 21)

Lord Lieutenant of Ireland

(office in Cabinet only Jun 95– 8 Aug 02 and 28 Oct 19–2 Apr 21)

Attorney-General for Ireland

1900	J. Atkinson
4 Dec 05	J. Campbell
20 Dec 05	R. Cherry
2 Dec 09	R. Barry
26 Sep 11	C. O'Connor
24 Jun 12	I. O'Brien
10 Apr 13	T. Molony
20 Jun 13	J. Moriarty
1 Jul 14	J. Pim
8 Jun 15	J. Gordon
9 Apr 16	J. Campbell
8 Jan 17	J. O'Connor
7 Apr 18	A. Samuels
6 Jul 19	D. Henry
5 Aug 21	T. Brown

(post vacant 16 Nov 21)

Solicitor-General for Ireland

1900	D. Barton
30 Jan 00	G. Wright

8 Jan 03	J. Campbell
20 Dec 05	R. Barry
2 Dec 09	C. O'Connor
19 Oct 11	I. O'Brien
24 Jun 12	T. Molony
25 Apr 13	J. Moriarty
20 Jun 13	J. Pim
1 Jul 14	J. O'Connor
19 Mar 17	J. Chambers
12 Sep 17	A. Samuels
7 Apr 18	J. Powell
27 Nov 18	D. Henry
6 Jul 19	D. Wilson
2 Jun 21	T. Brown

(post vacant 5 Aug 21)

Minister of Labour

10 Dec 16	J. Hodge
17 Aug 17	G. Roberts
10 Jan 19	Sir R. Horne
19 Mar 20	T. Macnamara
31 Oct 22	Sir A. Montague-Barlow
22 Jan 24	T. Shaw
6 Nov 24	Sir A. Steel-Maitland
7 Jun 29	Miss M. Bondfield
25 Aug 31	Sir H. Betterton
29 Jun 34	O. Stanley
7 Jun 35	E. Brown

(Minister of Labour and National Service)

3 Sep 39	E. Brown
13 May 40	E. Bevin
25 May 45	R. Butler
3 Aug 45	G. Isaacs
17 Jan 51	A. Bevan
24 Apr 51	A. Robens
28 Oct 51	Sir W. Monckton
20 Dec 55	I. Macleod
14 Oct 59	E. Heath

(Minister of Labour)

12 Nov 59	E. Heath
27 Jul 60	J. Hare
20 Oct 63	J. Godber
18 Oct 64	R. Gunter

(6 Apr 68 office reorganised as Ministry of Employment and Productivity)

Chancellor of the Duchy of Lancaster

1900	Ld James of Hereford
8 Aug 02	Sir W. Walrond
10 Dec 05	Sir H. Fowler (Vt Wolverhampton)
13 Oct 08	Ld Fitzmaurice

15 Jun 09	H. Samuel
14 Feb 10	J. Pease
23 Oct 11	C. Hobhouse
11 Feb 14	C. Masterman
3 Feb 15	E. Montagu
25 May 15	W. Churchill
25 Nov 15	H. Samuel
11 Jan 16	E. Montagu
9 Jul 16	T. McKinnon Wood
10 Dec 16	Sir F. Cawley
10 Feb 18	Ld Beaverbrook
4 Nov 18	Ld Downham
10 Jan 19	E of Crawford
1 Apr 21	Vt Peel
7 Apr 22	Sir W. Sutherland
24 Oct 22	M of Salisbury
25 May 23	J. Davidson
22 Jan 24	J. Wedgwood
10 Nov 24	Vt Cecil
19 Oct 27	Ld Cushendun
7 Jun 29	Sir O. Mosley
23 May 30	C. Attlee
13 May 31	Ld Ponsonby
25 Aug 31	M of Lothian
10 Nov 31	(Sir) J. Davidson
28 May 37	Earl Winterton
29 Jan 39	W. Morrison
3 Apr 40	G. Tryon
14 May 40	Ld Hankey
20 Jul 41	A. Duff Cooper
11 Nov 43	E. Brown
25 May 45	Sir A. Salter
4 Aug 45	J. Hynd
27 Apr 47	Ld Pakenham
11 May 48	H. Dalton
28 Feb 50	Vt Alexander
31 Oct 51	Vt Swinton
24 Nov 52	Ld Woolton
20 Dec 55	E of Selkirk
13 Jan 57	C. Hill
9 Oct 61	I. Macleod
20 Oct 63	Ld Blakenham
18 Oct 64	D. Houghton
6 Apr 66	G. Thomson
7 Jan 67	F. Lee
6 Oct 69	G. Thomson
20 Jun 70	A. Barber
28 Jul 70	G. Rippon
5 Nov 72	J. Davies
5 Mar 74	H. Lever
5 May 79	N. St John-Stevas
5 Jan 81	F. Pym
14 Sep 81	Lady Young
6 Apr 82	C. Parkinson
11 Jun 83	Ld Cockfield
11 Sep 84	E of Gowrie
3 Sep 85	N. Tebbit
13 Jun 87	K. Clarke
25 Jul 88	A. Newton
24 Jul 89	K. Baker
28 Nov 90	C. Patten
11 Apr 92	W. Waldegrave
20 Jul 94	D. Hunt

President of the Local Government Board

1900	H Chaplin
7 Nov 00	W. Long
12 Mar 05	G. Balfour
10 Dec 05	J. Burns
11 Feb 14	H. Samuel
25 May 15	W. Long
10 Dec 16	Ld Rhondda
28 Jun 17	W. Hayes Fisher
4 Nov 18	Sir A. Geddes
10 Jan 19	C. Addison

(24 Jun 19 the Local Government Board became the Ministry of Health)

(Minister of Health)

24 Jun 19	C. Addison
1 Apr 21	Sir A. Mond
24 Oct 22	Sir A. Griffith-Boscawen
7 Mar 23	N. Chamberlain
27 Aug 23	Sir W. Joynson-Hicks
22 Jan 24	J. Wheatley
6 Nov 24	N. Chamberlain
7 Jun 29	A. Greenwood
25 Aug 31	N. Chamberlain
5 Nov 31	Sir E. Young
7 Jun 35	Sir K. Wood
16 May 38	W. Elliot
13 May 40	M. MacDonald
8 Feb 41	E. Brown
11 Nov 43	H. Willink
3 Aug 45	A. Bevan
17 Jan 51	H. Marquand
30 Oct 51	H. Crookshank
7 May 52	I. Macleod
20 Dec 55	R. Turton
16 Jan 57	D. Vosper
17 Sep 57	D. Walker-Smith
27 Jul 60	E. Powell
20 Oct 63	A. Barber
18 Oct 64	K. Robinson

(combined with Ministry of Social Security 1 Nov 68–25 Jul 88 See Social Services and Health)

Secretary of State for Health and Social Security

5 May 79	P. Jenkin
14 Sep 81	N. Fowler
13 Jun 87	J. Moore

Secretary of State for Health

25 Jul 88	K. Clarke
2 Nov 90	W. Waldegrave
11 Apr 92	Mrs. V. Bottomley

Minister of Land and Natural Resources

17 Oct 64 F. Willey
  (*17 Feb 67 office wound up*)

Minister for Planning and Land

1 Nov 68 K. Robinson
  (*6 Oct 69 office wound up*)

Minister of Local Government and Planning

1 Jan 51 H. Dalton
  (*30 Oct 51 office wound up*)

(Minister of Housing and Local Government)

30 Oct 51 H. Macmillan
18 Oct 54 D. Sandys
13 Jan 57 H. Brooke
9 Oct 61 C. Hill
13 Jul 62 Sir K. Joseph
18 Oct 64 R. Crossman
11 Aug 66 A. Greenwood
31 May 70 R. Mellish
20 Jun 70 P. Walker
  (*15 Oct 70 reorganised as Local Government and Development under Dept. of Environment*)

Minister for Local Government and Development

15 Oct 70 G. Page
  (*office wound up 5 Mar 74*)

Minister for Planning and Local Government

7 Mar 74 J. Silkin
  (*office abolished 10 Sep 76*)

Minister for Housing and Construction

15 Oct 70 J. Amery
5 Nov 72 P. Channon
7 Mar 74 R. Freeson
7 May 79 J. Stanley
13 Jun 83 I. Gow
2 Sep 85 J. Patten
13 Jun 87 W. Waldegrave
13 Jul 88 E of Caithness
25 Jul 89 M. Spicer
28 Nov 90 Sir G. Young
20 Jul 94 Vt Ullswater

Minister for Local Government (under Environment)

6 May 79 T. King
6 Jan 83 Ld Bellwin

11 Sep 84 K. Baker
2 Sep 85 W. Waldegrave
10 Sep 86 R. Boyson
13 Jun 87 M. Howard
25 Jul 88 J. S. Gummer
25 Jul 89 D. Hunt
4 May 90 M. Portillo
15 Apr 92 J. Redwood
27 May 93 D. Curry

Minister of Materials

6 Jul 51 R. Stokes
31 Oct 51 Vt Swinton
24 Nov 52 Sir A. Salter
1 Sep 53 Ld Woolton
  (*16 Aug 54 office wound up*)

Minister of Munitions

25 May 15 D. Lloyd George
9 Jul 16 E. Montagu
10 Dec 16 C. Addison
17 Jul 17 W. Churchill
10 Jan 19 Ld Inverforth
  (*and Minister designate for Ministry of Supply. Office abolished 21 Mar 21*)

Secretary of State for National Heritage

11 Apr 92 D. Mellor
24 Sep 92 P. Brooke

Minister of National Service

19 Aug 16 N. Chamberlain
17 Aug 17 Sir A. Geddes
  (*office abolished Aug 19*)

Secretary of State for Northern Ireland

24 Apr 72 W. Whitelaw
2 Dec 73 F. Pym
5 Mar 74 M. Rees
10 Sep 76 R. Mason
5 May 79 H. Atkins
14 Sep 81 J. Prior
11 Sep 84 D. Hurd
3 Sep 85 T. King
24 Jul 89 P. Brooke
15 Apr 92 Sir P. Mayhew

Minister of (for) Overseas Development

18 Oct 64 Mrs B. Castle
23 Dec 65 A. Greenwood
11 Aug 66 A. Bottomley
29 Aug 67 R. Prentice
6 Oct 69 Mrs J. Hart

23 Jun 70 R. Wood
7 Mar 74 Mrs J. Hart
10 Jun 75 R. Prentice
21 Dec 76 F. Judd
21 Feb 77 Mrs J. Hart
6 May 79 N. Marten
6 Jan 83 T. Raison
10 Sep 86 C. Patten
24 Jul 89 Mrs L. (Lady) Chalker
  (*from 10 Jun 75 the Foreign Secretary became technically Minister of Overseas Development while the Minister for Overseas Development took day-to-day charge of the Department. It ceased to be a separate Department 5 May 79*)

Paymaster-General

1900 D of Marlborough
11 Mar 02 Sir S. Crossley
12 Dec 05 R. Causton (Ld Southwark)
23 Feb 10 I. Guest (Ld Ashby St Ledgers)
23 May 12 Ld Strachie
9 Jun 15 Ld Newton
18 Aug 16 A. Henderson
15 Dec 16 Sir J. Compton-Rickett
26 Oct 19 Sir T. Walters
24 Oct 22 (*office vacant*)
5 Feb 23 N. Chamberlain
15 Mar 23 Sir W. Joynson-Hicks
25 May 23 A. Boyd-Carpenter
22 Jan 24 (*office vacant*)
6 May 24 H. Gosling
6 Nov 24 (*office vacant*)
28 Jul 25 D of Sutherland
2 Dec 28 E of Onslow
7 Jun 29 Ld Arnold
6 Mar 31 (*office vacant*)
4 Sep 31 Sir T. Walters
23 Nov 31 Ld Rochester
6 Dec 35 Ld Hutchison
2 Jun 38 E of Munster
29 Jan 39 Earl Winterton
Nov 39 (*office vacant*)
15 May 40 Vt Cranborne
3 Oct 40 (*office vacant*)
20 Jul 41 Ld Hankey
4 Mar 42 Sir W. Jowitt
30 Dec 42 Ld Cherwell
3 Aug 45 (*office vacant*)
9 Jul 46 A. Greenwood
5 Mar 47 H. Marquand
2 Jul 48 Vt Addison
1 Apr 49 Ld Macdonald
30 Oct 51 Ld Cherwell
11 Nov 53 E of Selkirk
20 Dec 55 (*office vacant*)

18 Oct	56	Sir W. Monckton
16 Jan	57	R. Maudling
14 Oct	59	Ld Mills
9 Oct	61	H. Brooke
13 Jul	62	J. Boyd-Carpenter
19 Oct	64	G. Wigg
12 Nov	67	(office vacant)
6 Apr	68	Ld Shackleton
1 Nov	68	Mrs J. Hart
6 Oct	69	H. Lever
23 Jun	70	Vt Eccles
2 Dec	73	M. Macmillan
7 Mar	74	E. Dell
8 Apr	76	Mrs S. Williams
5 May	79	A. Maude
5 Jan	81	F. Pym
14 Sep	81	C. Parkinson
11 Jun	83	(office vacant)
11 Sep	84	J. S. Gummer
2 Sep	85	K. Clarke
13 Jun	87	H. Brooke
24 Jul	89	E of Caithness
14 Jul	90	R. Ryder
28 Nov	90	Ld Belstead
15 Apr	92	Sir J. Cope
20 Jul	94	D. Heathcoat-Amory

Minister of Pensions

10 Sep	16	G. Barnes
17 Aug	17	J. Hodge
10 Jan	19	Sir L. Worthington-Evans
2 Apr	20	I. Macpherson
31 Oct	22	G. Tryon
23 Jan	24	F. Roberts
11 Nov	24	G. Tryon
7 Jun	29	F. Roberts
3 Sep	31	G. Tryon
18 Jun	35	R. Hudson
30 Jul	36	H. Ramsbotham
7 Jun	39	Sir W. Womersley
3 Aug	45	W. Paling
17 Apr	47	J. Hynd
7 Oct	47	G. Buchanan
2 Jul	48	H. Marquand
17 Jan	51	G. Isaacs
5 Nov	51	D. Heathcoat Amory

(Minister of Pensions and National Insurance)

3 Sep	53	O. Peake
20 Dec	55	J. Boyd-Carpenter
16 Jul	62	N. Macpherson
21 Oct	63	R. Wood
18 Oct	64	Miss M. Herbison
		(6 Aug 66 recast as Social Security)

Minister of Social Insurance

8 Oct	44	Sir W. Jowitt

(Minister of National Insurance)

17 Nov	44	Sir W. Jowitt
25 May	45	L. Hore-Belisha
4 Aug	45	J. Griffiths
28 Feb	50	Edith Summerskill
31 Oct	51	O. Peake
		(3 Sep 53 combined with Ministry of Pensions)

Minister without Portfolio

25 May	15–5 Dec 16	
		M of Lansdowne
10 Dec	16–12 Aug 17	
		A. Henderson
10 Dec	16–18 Apr 18	Vt Milner
22 Jun	17–10 Jan 19	J. Smuts
17 Jul	17–21 Jan 18	
		Sir E. Carson
13 Aug	17–27 Jan 20	G. Barnes
28 Apr	18–10 Jan 19	
		A. Chamberlain
10 Jan	19–19 May 19	
		Sir E. Geddes
2 Apr	20–13 Feb 22	
		Sir L. Worthington-Evans
1 April–14 Jul 21		C. Addison
7 Jun	35–22 Dec 35	A. Eden
7 Jun	35–31 Mar 36	Ld E. Percy
21 Apr	39–14 Jul 39	L. Burgin
3 Sep	39–10 May 40	
		Ld Hankey
11 May	40–22 Feb 42	
		A. Greenwood
30 Dec	42– 8 Oct 44	
		Sir W. Jowitt
4 Oct	46–20 Dec 46	
		A. Alexander
17 Apr	47–29 Sep 47	
		A. Greenwood
18 Oct	54–11 Jun 57	
		E of Munster
11 Jun	57–23 Oct 58	
		Ld Mancroft
23 Oct	58– 9 Oct 61	
		E of Dundee
9 Oct	61–14 Jul 62	Ld Mills
13 Jul	62–16 Oct 64	W. Deedes
20 Oct	63–16 Oct 64	
		Ld Carrington
19 Oct	64–6 Apr 66	E. Fletcher
21 Oct	64–7 Jan 67	
		Ld Champion
6 Apr	66– 7 Jan 67	
		D. Houghton
7 Jan	67–29 Aug 67	
		P. Gordon Walker
7 Jan	67–16 Jan 68	
		Ld Shackleton
17 Oct	68–6 Oct 69	G. Thomson
6 Oct	69–19 Jun 70	P. Shore

15 Oct	70–8 Jan 74	
		Ld Drumalbyn
8 Jan	74–4 Mar 74	
		Ld Aberdare
11 Sep	84–2 Sep 85	
		Ld Young of Graffham
20 Jul	94	J. Hanley

Secretary of State for Prices and Consumer Protection

5 Mar	74	Mrs S. Williams
10 Sep	76	R. Hattersley
		(office wound up 5 May 79)

Minister for Consumer Affairs
(under Trade)

6 May	79	Mrs S. Oppenheim
5 Mar	82	G. Vaughan
		(13 Jun 83 office wound up)

Postmaster-General

1900		D of Norfolk
2 Apr	00	M of Londonderry
8 Aug	02	A. Chamberlain
6 Oct	03	Ld Stanley
10 Dec	05	S. Buxton
14 Feb	10	H. Samuel
11 Feb	14	C. Hobhouse
26 May	15	H. Samuel
18 Jan	16	J. Pease
10 Dec	16	A. Illingworth
1 Apr	21	F. Kellaway
31 Oct	22	N. Chamberlain
7 Mar	23	Sir W. Joynson-Hicks
28 May	23	Sir L. Worthington-Evans
22 Jan	24	V. Hartshorn
11 Nov	24	Sir W. Mitchell-Thomson
7 Jun	29	H. Lees-Smith
2 Mar	31	C. Attlee
3 Sep	31	W. Ormsby-Gore
10 Nov	31	Sir K. Wood
7 Jun	35	G. Tryon
3 Apr	40	W. Morrison
30 Dec	42	H. Crookshank
4 Aug	45	E. of Listowel
17 Apr	47	W. Paling
28 Feb	50	N. Edwards
5 Nov	51	Earl De La Warr
7 Apr	55	C. Hill
16 Jan	57	E. Marples
22 Oct	59	R. Bevins
19 Oct	64	A. Wedgwood Benn
4 Jul	66	E. Short
6 Apr	68	R. Mason
1 Jul	68	J. Stonehouse
		(Post Office became a Public Corporation 1 Oct 69)

(Minister of Posts and Telecommunications)

1 Oct	69	J. Stonehouse
24 Jun	70	C. Chataway
7 Apr	72	Sir J. Eden
9 Mar	74	T. Benn

(*29 Mar 74 office wound up*)

Minister of Public Building and Works

16 Jul	62	G. Rippon
18 Oct	64	C. Pannell
6 Apr	66	R. Prentlce
29 Aug	67	R. Mellish
30 Apr	69	J. Silkin
23 Jun	70	J. Amery

(*15 Oct 70 reorganised as Housing and Construction under Environment. See Local Government*)

Minister of Public Transport

(under *Transport*)

23 Jul	88	M. Portillo
4 May	90	R. Freeman

Minister Resident in Middle East

19 Feb	42	O. Lyttelton
19 Mar	42	R. Casey

(Minister of State in Middle East)

28 Jan	44	Ld Moyne
21 Nov	44	Sir E. Grigg

(*office abolished 27 Jul 45*)

Minister Resident at Allied H.Q. in N.W. Africa

30 Dec	42	H. Macmillan

(*office abolished 23 May 45*)

Minister Resident in W. Africa

8 Jun	42	Vt Swinton
21 Nov	44	H. Balfour

(*office abolished 27 Jul 45*)

Minister Resident in Washington for Supply

22 Nov	42	J. Llewellin
11 Nov	43	B. Smith

(*office abolished 23 May 45*)

Minister of Reconstruction

17 Jul	17–10 Jan	19
		C. Addison
10 Jan	19–Aug	19
		Sir A. Geddes
11 Nov	43–23 May	45
		Ld Woolton

Minister for Science

14 Oct	59	Vt Hailsham

(*1 Apr 64 combined with Dept. of Education*)

Secretary for Scotland

1900		Ld Balfour
6 Oct	03	A. Murray
2 Feb	05	M of Linlithgow
10 Dec	05	J. Sinclair (Ld Pentland)
13 Feb	12	T. McKinnon Wood
9 Jul	16	H. Tennant
10 Dec	16	R. Munro
24 Oct	22	Vt Novar
22 Jan	24	W. Adamson
6 Nov	24	Sir J. Gilmour

(Secretary of State for Scotland)

15 Jul	26	Sir J. Gilmour
7 Jun	29	W. Adamson
25 Aug	31	Sir A. Sinclair
28 Sep	32	Sir G. Collins
29 Oct	36	W. Elliot
16 May	38	J. Colville
14 May	40	E. Brown
8 Feb	41	T. Johnston
25 May	45	E of Rosebery
3 Aug	45	J. Westwood
7 Oct	47	A. Woodburn
28 Feb	50	H. McNeil
30 Oct	51	J. Stuart
13 Jan	57	J. Maclay
13 Jul	62	M. Noble
18 Oct	64	W. Ross
19 Jun	70	G. Campbell
5 Mar	74	W. Ross
8 Apr	76	B. Millan
5 May	79	G. Younger
11 Jan	86	M. Rifkind
28 Nov	90	I. Lang

Lord Advocate

1900		A. Murray
18 Oct	03	S. Dickson
12 Dec	05	T. Shaw
14 Feb	09	A. Ure
30 Oct	13	R. Munro
10 Dec	16	J. Clyde
25 Mar	20	T. Morison
5 Mar	22	C. Murray

24 Oct	22	W. Watson
8 Feb	24	H. Macmillan
11 Nov	24	W. Watson
23 Apr	29	A. MacRobert
17 Jun	29	C. Aitchison
2 Oct	33	W. Normand
28 Mar	35	D. Jamieson
25 Oct	35	T. Cooper
5 Jun	41	J. Reid
10 Aug	45	G. Thomson
7 Oct	47	J. Wheatley
2 Nov	51	J. Clyde
30 Dec	54	W. Milligan
5 Apr	60	W. Grant
12 Oct	62	I. Shearer
20 Oct	64	G. Stott
26 Oct	67	H. S. Wilson (Ld)
23 Jun	70	N. Wylie
8 Mar	74	R. King Murray
7 May	79	J. Mackay (Ld)
16 May	84	Ld Cameron of Lochbroom
4 Jan	89	Ld Fraser of Carmyllie
15 Apr	92	A. Rodger (Ld)

Solicitor-General for Scotland

1900		S. Dickson
18 Oct	03	D. Dundas
30 Jan	05	E. Salvesen
16 Oct	05	J. Clyde
18 Dec	05	A. Ure
18 Feb	08	A. Dewar
18 Apr	10	W. Hunter
3 Dec	11	A. Anderson
30 Oct	13	T. Morison
25 Mar	20	C. Murray
16 Mar	22	A. Briggs Constable
24 Jul	22	W. Watson
6 Nov	22	D. Fleming
5 Apr	23	F. Thomson
18 Feb	24	J. Fenton
11 Nov	24	D. Fleming
30 Dec	25	A. MacRobert
23 Apr	29	W. Normand
17 Jun	29	J. Watson
10 Nov	31	W. Normand
2 Oct	33	D. Jamieson
15 May	35	T. Cooper
29 Nov	35	A. Russell
25 Jun	36	J. Reid
5 Jun	41	(Sir) D. Murray
10 Sep	45	D. Blades
19 Mar	47	J. Wheatley
24 Oct	47	D. Johnston
3 Nov	51	W. Milligan
10 Jan	55	W. Grant
11 May	60	D. Anderson
27 Apr	64	N. Wylie
20 Oct	64	J. Leechman
11 Oct	65	H.S. Wilson
26 Oct	67	E. Stewart

23 Jun 70	D. Brand	
5 Nov 72	I. Stewart	
14 Mar 74	J. McCluskey (Ld)	
7 May 79	N. Fairbairn	
28 Jan 82	P. Fraser	
4 Jan 89	A. Rodger	
15 Apr 92	T. Dawson	

Minister of Shipping

10 Dec 16	Sir J. Maclay (Ld)

(office wound up 31 Mar 21)

13 Oct 39	Sir J. Gilmour
3 Apr 40	R. Hudson
14 May 40	R. Cross

(1 May 41 combined with Ministry of Transport to form Ministry of War Transport)

Minister of Social Security

6 Aug 66	Miss M. Herbison
26 Jul 67	Mrs J. Hart

(Secretary of State for Social Services)

17 Oct 68	R. Crossman
20 Jun 70	Sir K. Joseph
5 Mar 74	Mrs B. Castle
8 Apr 76	D. Ennals
5 May 79	P. Jenkin
14 Sep 81	N. Fowler
13 Jun 87	J. Moore

(office recast 25 Jul 88)

Secretary of State for Social Security

25 Jul 88	J. Moore
23 Jul 89	A. Newton
11 Apr 92	P. Lilley

Minister for Social Security
(under *Social Services*)

10 Sep 76	S. Orme
7 May 79	R. Prentice
8 Jan 81	H. Rossi
13 Jun 83	R. Boyson
11 Sep 84	A. Newton
10 Sep 86	J. Major
13 Jun 87	N. Scott
20 Jul 94	W. Hague

Solicitor-General

1900	Sir R. Finlay
7 May 00	Sir E. Carson
12 Dec 05	Sir W. Robson
28 Jan 08	Sir S. Evans
6 Mar 10	Sir R. Isaacs
7 Oct 10	Sir J. Simon
19 Oct 13	Sir S. Buckmaster
2 Jun 15	Sir F. Smith
18 Jan 15	Sir G. Cave
10 Dec 16	Sir G. Hewart
10 Jan 19	Sir E. Pollock
6 Mar 22	Sir L. Scott
31 Oct 22	Sir T. Inskip
23 Jan 24	Sir H. Slesser
11 Nov 24	Sir T. Inskip
28 Mar 28	Sir F. Merriman
7 Jun 29	Sir J. Melville
22 Oct 30	Sir S. Cripps
3 Sep 31	Sir T. Inskip
26 Jan 32	Sir F. Merriman
29 Sep 33	Sir D. Somervell
19 Mar 36	Sir T. O'Connor
15 May 40	Sir W. Jowitt
4 Mar 42	Sir D. Maxwell-Fyfe
25 May 45	Sir W. Monckton
4 Aug 45	Sir F. Soskice
24 Apr 51	Sir L Ungoed-Thomas
3 Nov 51	Sir R. Manningham-Buller
18 Oct 54	Sir H. Hylton-Foster
22 Oct 59	Sir J. Simon
8 Feb 62	Sir J. Hobson
19 Jul 62	Sir P. Rawlinson
18 Oct 64	Sir D. Foot
24 Aug 67	Sir A. Irvine
23 Jun 70	Sir G. Howe
5 Nov 72	Sir M. Havers
7 Mar 74	P. Archer
5 May 79	Sir I. Percival
13 Jun 83	Sir P. Mayhew
13 Jun 87	Sir N. Lyell
15 Apr 92	Sir D. Spencer

Minister with Responsibility for Sport

(U-S., Educ. & Sci.)

20 Oct 64	D. Howell

(M. of S., Housing & Local Govt.)

13 Oct 69	D. Howell

(U-S., Housing & Local Govt.)

24 Jun 70	E. Griffiths

(U-S., Environment)

15 Oct 70	E. Griffiths

(M. of S., Environment)

7 Mar 74	D. Howell

(U-S., Environment)

7 May 79	H. Monro
15 Sep 81	N. MacFarlane
7 Sep 85	R. Tracy
22 Jun 87	C. Moynihan
26 Jul 90	R. Atkins

(U-S., Educ. & Sci.)

28 Nov 90	R. Atkins

(U-S., Nat. Heritage)

14 Apr 92	R. Key
27 May 93	I. Sproat

Minister of State

1 May 41	Ld Beaverbrook
29 Jun 41	O. Lyttelton

(office abolished 12 Mar 42)

24 Sep 43	R. Law
25 May 45	W. Mabane
3 Aug 45	P. Noel Baker
4 Oct 46	H. McNeil
28 Feb 50	K. Younger

(office came formally under Foreign Office May 50)

First Secretary of State

13 Jul 62	R. Butler
18 Oct 63	*(office vacant)*
16 Oct 64	G. Brown
11 Aug 66	M. Stewart
6 Apr 68	Mrs B. Castle
19 Jun 70	*(office vacant)*

Minister of Supply

10 Jan 19	Ld Inverforth

(office vacant 31 Mar 21)

14 Jul 39	L. Burgin
12 May 40	H. Morrison
3 Oct 40	Sir A. Duncan
29 Jun 41	Ld Beaverbrook
4 Feb 42	Sir A. Duncan
3 Aug 45	J. Wilmot
7 Oct 47	G. Strauss
31 Oct 51	D. Sandys
18 Oct 54	S. Lloyd
7 Apr 55	R. Maudling
16 Jan 57	A. Jones

(office wound up 22 Oct 59)

Secretary for Technical Cooperation

27 Jun 61	D. Vosper
9 May 63	R. Carr

(office abolished 16 Oct 64)

Ministry of Technology

18 Oct 64	F. Cousins
4 Jul 66	A. Benn
20 Jun 70	G. Rippon
28 Jul 70	J. Davies

(15 Oct 70 office reorganised under Trade and Industry)

Minister of Town and Country Planning

30 Dec 42	W. Morrison
4 Aug 45	L. Silkin
28 Feb 50	H. Dalton

(recast as Local Government and Planning 31 Jan 51)

President of the Board of Trade

1900		C. Ritchie
7 Nov	00	G. Balfour
12 Mar	05	M of Salisbury
10 Dec	05	D. Lloyd George
12 Apr	08	W. Churchill
14 Feb	10	S. Buxton
11 Feb	14	J. Burns
5 Aug	14	W. Runciman
10 Dec	16	Sir A. Stanley
26 May	19	Sir A. Geddes
19 Mar	20	Sir R. Horne
1 Apr	21	S. Baldwin
24 Oct	22	Sir P. Lloyd-Greame
22 Jan	24	S. Webb
6 Nov	24	Sir P. Lloyd-Greame
		(*changed name to*
		Cunliffe-Lister
		27 Nov 24)
7 Jun	29	W. Graham
25 Aug	31	Sir P. Cunliffe-Lister
5 Nov	31	W. Runciman
28 May	37	O. Stanley
5 Jan	40	Sir A. Duncan
3 Oct	40	O. Lyttelton
29 Jun	41	Sir A. Duncan
4 Feb	42	J. Llewellin
22 Feb	42	H. Dalton
25 May	45	O. Lyttelton
27 Jul	45	Sir S. Cripps
29 Sep	47	H. Wilson
24 Apr	51	Sir H. Shawcross
30 Oct	51	P. Thorneycroft
13 Jan	57	Sir D. Eccles
14 Oct	59	R. Maudling
9 Oct	61	F. Erroll
20 Oct	63	E. Heath[1]
18 Oct	64	D. Jay
29 Aug	67	A. Crosland
6 Oct	69	R. Mason
20 Jun	70	M. Noble

(Secretary of State for Trade and Industry)

15 Oct	70	J. Davies
5 Nov	72	P. Walker

(Secretary of State for Trade)
(see also *Industry*)

5 Mar	74	P. Shore
8 Apr	76	E. Dell
12 Nov	78	J. Smith
5 May	79	J. Nott
14 Sep	81	J. Biffen
5 Apr	82	Ld Cockfield

(Secretary of State for Trade and Industry)

11 Jun	83	C. Parkinson
16 Oct	83	N. Tebbit

2 Sep	85	L. Brittan
24 Jan	86	P. Channon
13 Jun	87	Ld Young of
		Graffham
24 Jul	89	N. Ridley
14 Jul	90	P. Lilley

(President of the Board of Trade)

11 Apr	92	M. Heseltine

Minister for Trade
(under *Trade and Industry*)

15 Oct	70	M. Noble

(Minister for Trade and Consumer Affairs)

5 Nov	72	Sir G. Howe
		(*office wound up 5 Mar 74*)

Minister for Trade

7 May	79	C. Parkinson
14 Sep	81	P. Rees
13 Jun	83	P. Channon
24 Jan	86	A. Clark
25 Jul	89	Ld Trefgarne
23 Jul	90	T. Sainsbury
15 Apr	92	R. Needham

Minister of Transport

19 May	19	Sir E. Geddes
7 Nov	21	Vt Peel
12 Apr	22	E of Crawford
31 Oct	22	Sir J. Baird
24 Jan	24	H. Gosling
11 Nov	24	W. Ashley
7 Jun	29	H. Morrison
3 Sep	31	J. Pybus
22 Feb	33	O. Stanley
29 Jun	34	L. Hore-Belisha
28 May	37	L. Burgin
21 Apr	39	E. Wallace
14 May	40	Sir J. Reith
3 Oct	40	J. Moore-Brabazon

(Minister of War Transport)

1 May	41	Ld Leathers
3 Aug	45	A. Barnes

(Minister of Transport)

6 Mar	46	A. Barnes
31 Oct	51	J. Maclay
7 May	52	A. Lennox-Boyd

(Minister of Transport and Civil Aviation)

1 Oct	53	A. Lennox-Boyd
28 Jul	54	J. Boyd-Carpenter
20 Dec	55	H. Watkinson

(Minister of Transport)

14 Oct	59	E. Marples
18 Oct	64	T. Fraser
23 Dec	65	Mrs B. Castle
6 Apr	68	R. Marsh
6 Oct	69	F. Mulley
23 Jun	70	J. Peyton

(Minister for Transport Industries)

15 Oct	70	J. Peyton

(Minister for Transport)

7 Mar	74	F. Mulley
12 Jun	75	J. Gilbert

(Secretary of State for Transport)

10 Sep	76	W. Rodgers

(Minister of Transport)

5 May	79	N. Fowler

(Secretary of State for Transport)

5 Jan	81	N. Fowler
14 Sep	81	D. Howell
11 Jun	83	T. King
16 Oct	83	N. Ridley
21 May	86	J. Moore
13 Jun	87	P. Channon
24 Jul	89	C. Parkinson
28 Nov	90	M. Rifkind
15 Apr	92	J. MacGregor
20 Jul	94	B. Mawhinney

Treasury
(*see p. 53 for Chancellor of the Exchequer*)

Chief Secretary

9 Oct	61	H. Brooke
13 Jul	62	J. Boyd-Carpenter
20 Oct	64	J. Diamond
23 Jun	70	M. Macmillan
7 Apr	72	P. Jenkin
8 Jan	74	T. Boardman
7 Mar	74	J. Barnett
5 May	79	J. Biffen
5 Jan	81	L. Brittan
11 Jun	83	P. Rees
2 Sep	85	J. MacGregor
13 Jun	87	J. Major
24 Jul	89	N. Lamont
28 Nov	90	D. Mellor
10 Apr	92	M. Portillo
20 Jul	94	J. Aitken

Secretary of State for War

1900		M of Lansdowne
1 Nov	00	St J. Brodrick
6 Oct	03	H. Arnold-Forster
10 Dec	05	R. Haldane (Vt)

---

[1] Also Sec. of State for Industry and Regional Development

12 Jun	12	J. Seely
30 Mar	14	H. Asquith
5 Aug	14	Earl Kitchener
6 Jul	16	D. Lloyd George
10 Dec	16	E of Derby
18 Apr	18	Vt Milner
10 Jan	19	W. Churchill
13 Feb	21	Sir L. Worthington-Evans
24 Oct	22	E of Derby
22 Jan	24	S. Walsh
6 Nov	24	Sir L. Worthington-Evans
7 Jun	29	T. Shaw
26 Aug	31	M of Crewe
5 Nov	31	Vt Hailsham
7 Jun	35	Vt Halifax
22 Nov	35	A. Duff Cooper
28 May	37	L. Hore-Belisha
5 Jan	40	O. Stanley
11 May	40	A. Eden
22 Dec	40	D. Margesson
22 Feb	42	Sir J. Grigg
3 Aug	45	J. Lawson
4 Oct	46	F. Bellenger
7 Oct	47	E. Shinwell
28 Feb	50	J. Strachey
31 Oct	51	A. Head
18 Oct	56	J. Hare
6 Jan	58	C. Soames
27 Jul	60	J. Profumo
27 Jun	63	J. Godber
21 Oct	63	J. Ramsden

(office abolished 1 Apr 64)

Minister for Welsh Affairs

28 Oct	51	Sir D. Maxwell-Fyfe
18 Oct	54	G. Lloyd-George
13 Jan	57	H. Brooke
9 Oct	61	C. Hill
13 Jul	62	Sir K. Joseph

(Secretary of State for Wales)

18 Oct	64	J. Griffiths
6 Apr	66	C. Hughes
6 Apr	68	G. Thomas
20 Jun	70	P. Thomas
5 Mar	74	J. Morris
5 May	79	N. Edwards
13 Jun	87	P. Walker
4 May	90	D. Hunt
27 May	93	J. Redwood

First Commissioner of Works

1900		A. Akers-Douglas
8 Aug	02	Ld Windsor
10 Dec	05	L. Harcourt
3 Nov	10	Earl Beauchamp
6 Aug	14	Ld Emmott
25 May	15	L. Harcourt (Vt)
10 Dec	16	Sir A. Mond
1 Apr	21	E of Crawford
31 Oct	22	Sir J. Baird
22 Jan	24	F. Jowett
10 Nov	24	Vt Peel
18 Oct	28	M of Londonderry
7 Jun	29	G. Lansbury

25 Aug	31	M of Londonderry
5 Nov	31	W. Ormsby-Gore
16 Jun	36	Earl Stanhope
28 May	37	Sir P. Sassoon
7 Jun	39	H. Ramsbotham
3 Apr	40	Earl De La Warr
18 May	40	Ld Tryon
3 Oct	40	Sir J. Reith (Ld)

(Minister of Works and Buildings and First Commissioner of Works)

23 Oct	40	Ld Reith

(Minister of Works and Planning)

11 Feb	42	Ld Reith
21 Feb	42	Ld Portal

(Minister of Works)

Feb	43	Ld Portal
21 Nov	44	D. Sandys
4 Aug	45	G. Tomlinson
10 Feb	47	C. Key
28 Feb	50	R. Stokes
26 Apr	51	G. Brown
18 Nov	51	(Sir) D. Eccles
1 Oct	54	N. Birch
20 Dec	55	P. Buchan-Hepburn
16 Jan	57	H. Molson
22 Oct	59	Ld J. Hope

(16 Jul 62 recast as Public Building and Works)

---

[1] Although Mr Attlee fulfilled the role of Leader of the House of Commons during this period he was technically only Deputy Leader to Mr Churchill

Leaders of the House of Commons

1900	A. Balfour
5 Dec 05	Sir H. Campbell-Bannerman
5 Apr 08	H. Asquith
10 Dec 16	A. Bonar Law
23 Mar 21	A. Chamberlain
23 Oct 22	A. Bonar Law
22 May 23	S. Baldwin
22 Jan 24	J. R. MacDonald
4 Nov 24	S. Baldwin
5 Jun 29	J. R. MacDonald
7 Jun 35	S. Baldwin
28 May 37	N. Chamberlain
11 May 40	C. Attlee[1]
19 Feb 42	Sir S. Cripps
22 Nov 42	A. Eden
27 Jul 45	H. Morrison
9 Mar 51	C. Ede
30 Oct 51	H. Crookshank
7 Apr 55	R. Butler
9 Oct 61	I. Macleod
20 Oct 63	S. Lloyd
16 Oct 64	H. Bowden
11 Aug 66	R. Crossman
6 Apr 68	F. Peart
20 Jun 70	W. Whitelaw
7 Apr 72	R. Carr
5 Nov 72	J. Prior
5 Mar 74	E. Short
8 Apr 76	M. Foot
5 May 79	N. St John-Stevas
5 Jan 81	F. Pym
5 Apr 82	J. Biffen
13 Jun 87	J. Wakeham
24 Jul 89	Sir G. Howe
3 Nov 90	J. MacGregor
11 Apr 92	A. Newton

Leaders of the House of Lords

1900	3rd M of Salisbury
12 Jul 02	D of Devonshire
13 Oct 03	M of Lansdowne
10 Dec 05	M of Ripon
14 Apr 08	E of Crewe (M)[8]
10 Dec 16	Earl Curzon (M)
22 Jan 24	Vt Haldane
6 Nov 24	Marquess Curzon
27 Apr 25	4th M of Salisbury
7 Jun 29	Ld Parmoor
25 Aug 31	M of Reading
5 Nov 31	1st Vt Hailsham
7 Jun 35	M of Londonderry
22 Nov 35	Vt Halifax
27 Oct 38	Earl Stanhope
14 May 40	Vt Caldecote
3 Oct 40	Vt Halifax
22 Dec 40	Ld Lloyd
8 Feb 41	Ld Moyne
21 Feb 42	Vt Cranborne (5th M of Salisbury)
3 Aug 45	Vt Addison
28 Oct 51	5th M of Salisbury
29 Mar 57	E of Home
27 Jul 60	2nd Vt Hailsham
20 Oct 63	Ld Carrington
18 Oct 64	E of Longford
16 Jan 68	Ld Shackleton
20 Jun 70	Earl Jellicoe
5 Jun 73	Ld Windlesham
7 Mar 74	Ld Shepherd
10 Sep 76	Ld Peart
5 May 79	Ld Soames
14 Sep 81	Lady Young
11 Jun 83	Vt Whitelaw
10 Jan 88	Ld Belstead
28 Nov 90	Ld Waddington
11 Apr 92	Ld Wakeham

Government Chief Whip
(Parliamentary Secretary to the Treasury)

1900	Sir W. Walrond
8 Aug 02	Sir A. Acland Hood
12 Dec 05	G. Whiteley
3 Jun 08	J. Pease
14 Feb 10	Master of Elibank
7 Aug 12	P. Illingworth
24 Jan 15	J. Gulland
30 May 15	{ J. Gulland
30 May 15	{ Ld E. Talbot
14 Dec 16	{ Ld E. Talbot
14 Dec 16	{ N. Primrose
2 Mar 17	{ Ld E. Talbot
2 Mar 17	{ F. Guest
1 Apr 21	{ C. McCurdy
1 Apr 21	{ L. Wilson
31 Oct 22	L. Wilson
25 Jul 23	B. Eyres-Monsell
23 Jan 24	B. Spoor
7 Nov 24	B. Eyres-Monsell
14 Jun 29	T. Kennedy
3 Sep 31	Sir B. Eyres-Monsell
10 Nov 31	D. Margesson
17 May 40	{ D. Margesson
17 May 40	{
	Sir C. Edwards
14 Jan 41	Sir C. Edwards
14 Jan 41	{ J. Stuart
12 Mar 42	{ J. Stuart
12 Mar 42	{ W. Whiteley
26 May 45	J. Stuart
3 Aug 45	W. Whiteley
30 Oct 51	P. Buchan-Hepburn
30 Dec 55	E. Heath
14 Oct 59	M. Redmayne
18 Oct 64	E. Short
4 Jul 66	J. Silkin
30 Apr 69	R. Mellish
20 Jun 70	F. Pym
2 Dec 73	H. Atkins
5 Mar 74	R. Mellish
8 Apr 76	M. Cocks
5 May 79	M. Jopling
11 Jun 83	J. Wakeham
13 Jun 87	D. Waddington
28 Oct 89	T. Renton
28 Nov 90	R. Ryder

Government Chief Whip in the House of Lords
(usually Captain of the Gentlemen at Arms – see footnotes for exceptions)

1900	Earl Waldegrave[1]
18 Dec 05	Ld Ribblesdale[2]
29 May 07	Ld Denman[3]
15 Mar 11	Ld Colebrooke[4]
9 Jun 15	{ Ld Colebrooke[4]
9 Jun 15	{ D of Devonshire[5]
26 Jul 16	{ Ld Colebrooke[4]
26 Jul 16	{ Ld Hylton[6]
20 Nov 22	E of Clarendon
22 Jan 24	Ld Muir-Mackenzie[7]
1 Dec 24	E of Clarendon
26 Jun 25	E of Plymouth
1 Jan 29	E of Lucan
18 Jul 29	Earl de le Warr[7]
17 Jan 30	Ld Marley[7]
12 Nov 31	E of Lucan
31 May 40	Ld Templemore[1]
4 Aug 45	Ld Ammon
18 Oct 49	1st Ld Shepherd
5 Nov 51	Earl Fortescue
27 Jun 58	Earl St Aldwyn
21 Oct 64	2nd Ld Shepherd
29 Jul 67	Ld Beswick
24 Jun 70	Earl St Aldwyn
11 Mar 74	Lady Llewelyn-Davies
6 May 79	Ld Denham
23 May 91	Ld Hesketh
16 Sep 93	Vt Ullswater

---

[1] Captain of the Yeomen of the Guard.
[2] Without office.
[3] Lord in Waiting 1907; Captain of Gentlemen at Arms 1907–11.
[4] Lord in Waiting 1911; Captain of Gentlemen at Arms 1911–22.
[5] Civil Lord of the Admiralty.
[6] Lord in Waiting 1916–18; Captain of Gentlemen at Arms 1918–22.
[7] Lord in Waiting.
[8] During the summer of 1911 Vt Morley was temporarily Leader of the House of Lords

Size of Cabinets and Governments
(at 1 Jan)

	1900	1910	1917	1920	1930	1940	1950	1960	1970	1980	1990
Cabinet Mins.	19	19	5	19	19	9	18	19	21	22	22
Non-Cabinet Mins	10	7	33	15	9	25	20	20	33	38	33
Junior Mins	31	36	47	47	30	40	43	43	48	47	48
No.of M.P.s in paid Govt. Posts	33	43	60	58	50	58	68	65	85	86	80
No.of Peers in paid Govt. posts	27	19	25	23	8	16	13	17	17	21	22
Total paid Govt. Posts	60	62	85	81	58	74	81	82	102	107	103
Parliamentary Private Secs in Commons	9	16	12	13	26	25	27	36	30	28	30
Total no. of MPs involved in Govt	42	59	72	71	76	83	95	101	115	114	111

Social and Educational Composition of British Cabinets 1895–[1]

					No.	Class			Education			
						Arist.	Middle	Work	Public School	Eton	Univ	Ox-bridge
Aug	1895	Con.	Salisbury		19	8	11	–	16	7	15	14
Jul	1902	Con.	Balfour		19	9	10	–	16	9	14	13
Dec	1905	Lib.	Campbell-Bannerman		19	7	11	1	11	3	14	12
Jul	1914	Lib.	Asquith		19	6	12	1	11	3	15	13
Jan	1919	Coal.	Ll.George		21	3	17	1	12	2	13	8
Nov	1922	Con.	Bonar Law		16	8	8	–	14	8	13	13
Jan	1924	Lab.	MacDonald		19	3	5	11	8	–	6	6
Nov	1924	Con.	Baldwin		21	9	12	–	21	7	16	16
Jan	1929	Lab.	MacDonald		18	2	4	12	5	–	6	3
Aug	1931	Nat.	MacDonald		20	8	10	2	13	6	11	10
Jun	1935	Con.	Baldwin		22	9	11	2	14	9	11	10
May	1937	Con.	Chamberlain		21	8	13	–	17	8	16	13
May	1945	Con.	Churchill		16	6	9	1	14	7	11	9
Aug	1945	Lab.	Attlee		20	–	8	12	5	2	10	5
Oct	1951	Con.	Churchill		16	5	11	–	14	7	11	9
Apr	1955	Con.	Eden		18	5	13	–	18	10	16	14
Jan	1957	Con.	Macmillan		18	4	14	–	17	8	16	15
Oct	1963	Con.	Home		24	5	19	–	21	11	17	17
Oct	1964	Lab.	Wilson		23	1	14	8	8	1	13	11
Jun	1970	Con.	Heath		18	4	14	–	15	4	15	15
Mar	1974	Lab.	Wilson		21	1	16	4	7	–	16	11
Apr	1976	Lab.	Callaghan		22	1	13	7	7	–	15	10
May	1979	Con.	Thatcher		22	3	19	–	20	6	18	17
Nov	1990	Con.	Major		22	3	17	2	14	2	20	17
Average 24 Cabinets					20	5	13	3	13	5	14	12
		14 Con. Cabinets			19	7	$12\frac{1}{2}$	–	17	$7\frac{1}{2}$	14	13
		6 Lab. Cabinets			$20\frac{1}{2}$	$1\frac{1}{2}$	$9\frac{1}{2}$	9	7	$\frac{1}{2}$	$11\frac{1}{2}$	$7\frac{1}{2}$
		2 Lib. Cabinets			19	6	$11\frac{1}{2}$	1	11	3	$14\frac{1}{2}$	$12\frac{1}{2}$

[1] This table is largely based on W. L. Guttsman, *The British Political Elite* (1963). *Aristocrats* are those who had among their grandparents the holder of a hereditary title. *Working class* are those whose fathers appear to have had a manual occupation when they were growing up. *Schools* are classified as public schools if members of the Headmasters' Conference.

Durability of Prime Ministers 1900–

	Years as P.M.	No. of Times P.M.	Age	Pre-P.M. Years in HC	Years Post-P.M. in HC	Years Lived after P.M.
M of Salisbury	13.9	3	55	15[1]	0	1
M. Thatcher (Mrs)	11.6	1	53	20	2	–
H. Asquith	8.8	1	55	22	6	11
(Sir) W. Churchill	8.8	2	65	38	9	10
H. Wilson	7.9	2	48	19	7	–
S. Baldwin	7.2	3	56	15	0	11
J. R. MacDonald	6.9	2	58	14	2	2
H. Macmillan	.6.9	1	62	29	1	22
C. Attlee	6.3	1	62	23	4	16
D. Lloyd George	5.10	1	53	26	22	22
E. Heath	3.8	1	53	20	–	–
A. Balfour	3.5	1	53	28	17	24
J. Callaghan	3.1	1	64	31	8	–
N. Chamberlain	2.11	1	68	19	$\frac{1}{2}$	$\frac{1}{2}$
Sir H. Campbell-Bannerman	2.4	1	69	37	0	0
Sir A. Eden	1.9	1	58	32	0	20
Sir A. Douglas-Home	1.0	1	60	15[2]	10	–
A. Bonar Law	0.7	1	63	22	0	0
J. Major	–	1	47	11	–	–

[1] Plus 17 years in the House of Lords
[2] Plus 13 years in the House of Lords

Long Tenure of Ministerial Office

The following are the only twentieth century British politicians to have served more than 20 years in ministerial office:

Years		Period	Years		Period
29	Sir W. Churchill	1905–1955	22	Vt Swinton	1920–1957
28	E of Balfour	1885–1929	21	M of Salisbury	1866–1902
26	R. Butler	1932–1964	21	Sir M. Hicks-Beach	1868–1902
24	D of Devonshire	1863–1903	20	Ld G. Hamilton	1874–1903
22	E of Halsbury	1875–1905	20	Ld Ashbourne	1877–1905
22	W. Long	1886–1921	20	Sir J. Simon	1910–1945
22	Sir A. Chamberlain	1895–1931	20	Vt Hailsham	1945–1987

Oldest and Youngest Ministers

The oldest M.P. to hold Cabinet office was Sir W. Churchill (80 in 1955): the oldest peers were Vt Halsbury (82 in 1905) and Vt Addison (82 in 1951) and the only other octogenarians were M of Ripon (80 in 1908) and Earl Balfour (80 in 1929). The oldest holder of any ministerial office was Ld Muir-Mackenzie (85 in 1930). The youngest Cabinet minister was H. Wilson (31 in 1947). The youngest M.P. to hold any office was H. Wilson (29 in 1945). R. Butler (1932), E. Rowlands (1969), and Mrs A. Taylor (1977) also held office at 29; the youngest peer was Earl de la Warr (23 in 1924).

Cabinet Members Dying in Office[1]

5 Jun	1916	Earl Kitchener	30 Mar 1940	Sir J. Gilmour
20 Mar	1925	Marquess Curzon	21 Sep 1943	Sir K. Wood[2]
5 Oct	1930	Lord Thomson	6 Feb 1947	Miss E. Wilkinson
13 Mar	1931	V. Hartshorn	14 Apr 1951	E. Bevin
15 Jun	1932	Sir D. Maclean	20 Jul 1970	I. Macleod
13 Oct	1936	Sir G. Collins	19 Feb 1977	A. Crosland

[1] H. Gaitskell, the official Leader of the Opposition died on 18 Jan 63. J. Smith, the official Leader of the Opposition died on 19 May 1994.
[2] Chancellor of the Exchequer but not actually in the War Cabinet.

Cabinet Members Suffering Electoral Defeat while Holding Office

Apr	1908	W. Churchill[1]	Jul	1945	L. Amery, B. Bracken, Sir J. Grigg,
Feb	1914	C. Masterman[1]			H. Macmillan, Sir D. Somervell
May	1914	C. Masterman[2]	Feb	1950	A. Creech Jones
Mar	1921	Sir A. Griffith-Boscawen[1]	Oct	1964	A. Barber
Nov	1922	Sir A. Griffith-Boscawen[2]	Jan	1965	P. Gordon-Walker[2]
Mar	1923	Sir A. Griffith-Boscawen	Jun	1970	J. Diamond
Dec	1923	Sir A. Montague-Barlow	Feb	1974	G. Campbell
Oct	1924	F. Jowett	May	1979	Mrs S. Williams
May	1929	Sir A. Steel-Maitland	Apr	1992	C. Patten
Nov	1935	R. MacDonald[1] M. MacDonald[1]			

[1] Sought another seat and continued in office.
[2] By-election defeat followed by resignation.

In Jan 1906 8 members of the Conservative Cabinet that left office in Dec 1905 were defeated, including A. Balfour who had been Prime Minister.

In Dec 1918 10 Asquithian Liberals who had left office in Dec 1916 were defeated including H. Asquith.

In Nov 1922 2 National Liberal members of the Coalition Cabinet that left office in Oct 1922 were defeated.

In Oct 1931 13 members of the Labour Cabinet that left office in Aug 1931 were defeated, including A. Henderson, the Party Leader.

On two occasions the Government Chief Whip was defeated (J. Pease in Jan 1910 and L. Wilson in Nov 1922). On both occasions a new seat was very speedily found.

These Ministers of Cabinet rank were found seats in by-elections:- 1916: H. Fisher, Sir A. Stanley; 1917: Sir A. Geddes, Sir E. Geddes: 1924: A. Henderson; 1940: E. Bevin, O. Lyttelton, Sir J. Reith, Sir A. Duncan; 1942: Sir J. Grigg; 1963: Sir A. Douglas-Home, Q. Hogg; 1965: F. Cousins.

(See also p. 238 for defeated Ministers' attempts at re-election.)

Ministerial Resignations

Resignations from ministerial office are not easy to classify. A retirement on the ground of ill-health may always conceal a protest or a dismissal. However, there are some cases where ministers have unquestionably left office because they were not willing to continue to accept collective responsibility for some part of Government policy and some cases where the individual actions of ministers have been thought impolitic or unworthy. The following list does not include resignations made necessary because of private scandals, except when the resignation became the subject of public comment. Nor does it include even the most publicised 'refusals to serve' (e.g. I. Macleod and E. Powell in 1963).

16 Sep	03	J. Chamberlain (Imperial preference)
4–15 Sep	03	C. Ritchie, Ld Balfour of Burleigh, Ld G. Hamilton, D of Devonshire, A. Elliot (Free Trade)
6 Mar	05	G. Wyndham (Ireland)
30 Mar	14	J. Seely (Curragh Mutiny)
2 Aug	14	Vt Morley, J. Burns (entry into war)
5 Aug	14	C. Trevelyan (entry into war)
19 Oct	15	Sir E. Carson (conduct of war in the Balkans)
31 Dec	15	Sir J. Simon (Compulsory National Service)
3 May	16	A. Birrell (Irish Rebellion)
25 Jun	16	E of Selborne (Irish policy)
12 Jul	17	A. Chamberlain (Campaign in Mesopotamia)
8 Aug	17	N. Chamberlain (Ministry of National Service)
17 Nov	17	Ld Cowdray (Conduct of the Air Ministry)
21 Jan	18	Sir E. Carson (Ireland)
25 Apr	18	Ld Rothermere (Air Force)
22 Nov	18	Ld R. Cecil (Welsh disestablishment)
12 Nov	19	J. Seely (role of Air Ministry)
14 Jul	21	C. Addison (Housing)
9 Mar	22	E. Montagu (Turkey)
18 Nov	23	A. Buckley (abandonment of Free Trade)
28 Aug	27	Vt Cecil (Disarmament)
19 May	30	Sir O. Mosley (unemployment)
2 Mar	31	Sir C. Trevelyan (Education)
6 Mar	31	Ld Arnold (Free Trade)
9 Oct	31	G. Lloyd-George, G. Owen (Calling of election)
28 Sep	32	Sir H. Samuel, Sir A. Sinclair, Vt Snowden, M of Lothian, I. Foot, Sir R. Hamilton, G. White, W. Rea, Vt Allendale (Free Trade)
18 Dec	35	Sir S. Hoare (Laval Pact)
22 May	36	J. Thomas (Budget leak)
20 Feb	38	A. Eden, Vt Cranborne (negotiations with Mussolini)
12–16 May	38	Earl Winterton, Vt Swinton (Air Force strength)
16 May	38	Ld Harlech (partition of Palestine)
1 Oct	38	A. Duff Cooper (Munich)
21 Jan	41	R. Boothby (Blocked Czechoslovakian assets)
1 Mar	45	H. Strauss (treatment of Poles by Yalta Conference)
26 May	46	Sir B. Smith (overwork and criticism)
13 Nov	47	H. Dalton (Budget leak)
13 Dec	48	J. Belcher (Lynskey Tribunal)
16 Apr	50	S. Evans (agricultural subsidies)
23 Apr	51	A. Bevan, H. Wilson, J. Freeman (Budget proposals)
20 Jul	54	Sir T. Dugdale (Crichel Down)
31 Oct	56	A. Nutting (Suez)
5 Nov	56	Sir E. Boyle (Suez)
29 Mar	57	M of Salisbury (release of Archbishop Makarios)
6 Jan	58	P. Thorneycroft, E. Powell, N. Birch (econ. policy)
24 Nov	58	I. Harvey (private scandal)
8 Nov	62	T. Galbraith (Security) (*exonerated and given new office 5 May 63*)
5 Jun	63	J. Profumo (lying to the House of Commons)
23 Oct	63	D. Freeth (private scandal)
19 Feb	66	C. Mayhew (Defence estimates)
3 Jul	66	F. Cousins (incomes policy)
26 Jul	67	Miss M. Herbison (Social Services policy)
16 Jan	68	E of Longford (delay in of raising school age)
5 Feb	68	W. Howie (Enforcement of Party discipline)
16 Mar	68	G. Brown (conduct of Government business)
1 Jul	68	R. Gunter (general dissatisfaction)
24 Sep	69	J. Bray (permission to publish)
28 Jul	71	E. Taylor (entry into the E.E.C.)
17 Oct	71	J. More (entry into the E.E.C.)
18 Jul	72	R. Maudling (Poulson Inquiry)
22 May	73	Ld Lambton (private scandal)
23 May	73	Earl Jellicoe (private scandal)
25 Sep	74	Ld Brayley (former business interests)

17 Oct	74	N. Buchan (Agricultural policy)
9 Apr	75	E. Heffer (opposing E.E.C. membership in Commons)[1]
10 Jun	75	Dame J. Hart (dissatisfaction with P.M.)
21 Jul	75	R. Hughes (incomes policy)
21 Feb	76	Miss J. Lestor (Education cuts)
21 Dec	76	R. Prentice (disenchantment with Government)
9 Nov	77	J. Ashton (Government's handling of power dispute)
20 Nov	78	R. Cryer (failure to support Kirkby Coop.)
17 Jan	79	A. Stallard (Extra Seats for Northern Ireland)
18 May	81	K. Speed (Defence estimates)[1]
21 Jan	82	N. Fairbairn (handling of a Scottish prosecution)
5 Apr	82	Ld Carrington, H. Atkins, R. Luce (Falklands)
8 May	82	N. Budgen (Northern Ireland policy)
11 Oct	83	C. Parkinson (private scandal)
16 Nov	85	I. Gow (Anglo-Irish Accord)
7 Jan	86	M. Heseltine (Westland affair)
22 Jan	86	L. Brittan (Westland affair)
16 Dec	88	Mrs E. Currie (remarks on salmonella scare)
29 Oct	89	N. Lawson (P.M.'s economic advice)
13 Jul	90	N. Ridley (remarks about Germany)
1 Nov	90	Sir G. Howe (P.M.'s attitude to Europe)
22 Sep	92	D. Mellor (private scandal)
24 Jun	93	M. Mates (links with Asil Nadir)
7 Jan	94	T. Yeo (private scandal)
11 Jan	94	E of Caithness (private scandal)
7 May	94	M. Brown (private scandal)

[1] Technically a dismissal, not a resignation.

Parliamentary Private Secretaries to Prime Ministers

1900–02	E. Cecil		1952–55	C. Soames
1906–08	H. Carr-Gomm		1955–55	R. Carr
1908–10	G. Howard		1955–58	R. Allan
1910–15	C. Lyell		1958–59	A. Barber
1915–16	Sir J. Barran		1959–63	K. Cunningham
1916–17	D. Davies		1963–64	F. Pearson
1918–18	W. Astor		1964–66 {	P. Shore
1918–20	(Sir) W. Sutherland		1964–67 {	E. Fernyhough
1940–41	B. Bracken		1967–68	H. Davies
1920–22	Sir P. Sassoon		1968–69 {	H. Davies
1922–23	J. Davidson		1969–69 {	E. Varley
1923–24	S. Herbert		1969–70	H. Davies
1924–24	L. MacNeil Weir		1970–74	T. Kitson
1924–27	S. Herbert		1974–75	W. Hamling
1927–29	C. Rhys		1975–75	K. Marks
1929–31 {	L. MacNeil Weir		1975–76	J. Tomlinson
1929–31 {	R. Morrison		1976–76	J. Cunningham
1931–32 {	R. Glyn		1976–79	R. Stott
1931–32 {	F. Markham		1979–83	I. Gow
1932–35 {	(Sir) R. Glyn		1983–87	M. Alison
1932–35 {	J. Worthington		1987–88	A. Hamilton
1935–35	G. Lloyd		1988–90	M. Lennox-Boyd
1935–37	T. Dugdale		1990–90	P. Morrison
1937–40	Ld Dunglass		1990–94	G. Bright
1941–45	G. Harvie-Watt		1994– {	J. Ward
1945–46	G. de Freitas			Ld McColl
1946–51	A. Moyle			

Biographical Notes

Prime Ministers, Chancellors of the Exchequer, Foreign Secretaries, and Leaders of the Opposition.

(Virtually all the most eminent politicians of this century have held one of these four positions, but, common sense being more important than consistency, two of the most outstanding exceptions have been added to the list – Joseph Chamberlain and Aneurin Bevan).

Adamson, William
> b. 1863. *Educ.* Elementary. Miner. Union official. M.P. (Lab.) for West Fife 1910–31. Leader of Opposition 1918–21. Sec. for Scotland 1924, Sec of State for Scotland 1929–31. d. 1945.

Anderson, John (Sir). 1st Vt Waverley (1952)
> 1882. *Educ.* George Watson's Coll., Edin., Edinburgh and Leipzig Univs. Entered Col. O.,1905. Sec. to Min. of Shipping, 1917–19. K. C. B., 1919. Addit. Sec. to Loc. Govt. Bd 1919. 2nd Sec. to Min. of Health, 1919. Ch. of Bd. of Inland Revenue, 1919–22. Joint U- S. to Ld. Lieut. of Ireland, 1920–22. P. U-S. Home O., 1922–32. Gov. of Bengal, 1932–37. M.P. (Nat.) for Scottish Univs., 1938–50. Ld. Privy S., 1938–39. Home Sec. and Min. of Home Security, 1939–40. Ld. Pres. of Council, 1940–43. Chanc. of Exch., 1943–45. d. 1958.

Asquith, Herbert Henry, 1st E of Oxford and Asquith (1925)
> b. 1852. *Educ.* City of London School; Oxford. Barrister, 1876. M.P. (Lib.) for E. Fife, 1886–1918. M.P. for Paisley, 1920–24. Home Sec., 1892–95. Chanc. of Exch., 1905–8. P.M. 1908–16. Leader of Lib. party, 1908–1926. Sec. for War, 1914. Formed Coalition Govt., 1915. Resigned as P.M., became Leader of Opposition, 1916. Resigned Leadership of Lib. party, 1926. d. 1928.

Attlee, Clement Richard. 1st Earl Attlee (1955)
> b. 1883. *Educ.* Haileybury; Oxford. Barrister, 1906; practised, 1906–9. Lecturer at L. S. E., 1913–23. M.P. (Lab.) for Limehouse, Stepney, 1922–50. M.P. for W. Walthamstow, 1950–55. P.P.S. to J. R. MacDonald, 1922–24. U-S. for War, 1924. Chanc. of D. of Lanc., 1930–31. Postm.-Gen., 1931. Dep. Leader of Lab. party in Commons, 1931–35. Leader of Lab. party, 1935–55. Leader of Opposition, 1935–40. Ld Privy S., 1940–42. Sec. for Dominions, 1942–43. Ld Pres. of Council, 1943–45. Leader of Opposition, 1945. Dep. P.M., 1942–45. P.M., 1945–51. Min. of Def., 1945–46. Leader of Opposition, 1951–1955. d. 1967.

Baldwin, Stanley. 1st Earl Baldwin of Bewdley (1937)
> b. 1867. *Educ.* Harrow; Cambridge. Family business. M.P. (Con.) for Bewdley div. of Worcs., 1908–37. Joint F. S. to Treas., 1917–21; Pres. of Bd. of Trade, 1921–22; Chanc. of Exch., 1922–23. Leader of Con. party, 1923–37. P.M., 1923–24, 1924–29 and 1935–37. Leader of Opposition, 1924, 1929–31. Ld Pres. of Council, 1931–35. Ld Privy S., 1932–33. d. 1947.

Balfour, Arthur James (Sir). 1st Earl of Balfour (1922)
> b. 1848. *Educ.* Eton; Cambridge. M.P. (Con.) for Hertford, 1874–85. M.P. for E. Manchester, 1885–1906. M.P. for City of London, 1906–22. P.P.S. to Ld Salisbury, 1878–80. Pres. of Loc. Govt. Bd., 1885. Sec. for Scotland, 1886. (Member of Cabinet, Nov 1886.) Ch. Sec. for Ireland, 1887–91. Leader of Commons and 1st Ld of Treas., 1891–92 and 1895–1905. P.M., 1902–5. Leader of Con. party, 1902–11. Member of Committee of Imperial Defence, 1914. Attended war cabinet meetings, 1914–15. 1st Ld of Admir., 1915–16. For. Sec., 1916–19. Ld Pres. of Council, 1919–22 and 1925–29. K.G. 1922. d. 1930.

Barber, Anthony Perrinott Lysberg, Ld Barber (Life Peer 1974)
> b. 1920. *Educ.* Retford G. S.; Oxford. Barrister, 1948. M.P. (Con.) for Doncaster, 1951–64. M.P. for Altrincham and Sale, 1965–74. Con. Whip, 1955–58; P.P.S. to P.M., 1958–59. Econ. S. to Treasury, 1959–62. F. S., 1962–63. Min. of Health, 1963–64. Ch. of Con. Party Organisation, 1967–70. Chanc. of D. of Lanc., 1970. Chanc. of Exch., 1970–74.

Bevan, Aneurin
> b. 1897. *Educ.* Elem.; Central Labour College. Miner. M.P. (Lab.) for Ebbw Vale, 1929–60. Deputy Leader of Lab. party, 1959–60. Min. of Health, 1945–51. Min. of Lab. and Nat. Service, 1951. Resigned, 1951. Treasurer of Lab. party, 1956–60. d. 1960.

Bevin, Ernest
> b. 1881. *Educ.* Elem. National Organiser of Dockers' Union, 1910–21. Gen. Sec. of T. & G. W. U., 1921–40. Member of General Council for T. U. C., 1925–40. M.P. (Lab.) for Cent. Wandsworth, 1940–50. M.P. for E. Woolwich, 1950–51. Min. of Lab. and Nat. Service, 1940–45. For. Sec., 1945–51. Ld Privy S., Mar–Apr 1951. d. 1951.

Blair, Tony
> b. 1953. *Educ.* Fettes and Oxford. Barrister. M.P. (Lab) for Sedgefield 1983–. Leader of the Opposition 1994–.

Bonar Law, Andrew
> b 1858. *Educ.* Canada and Glasgow H.S. Family business. M.P. (Con.) for Blackfriars, Glasgow, 1900–6. M.P. for Dulwich, 1906–10. M.P. for Bootle, 1911–18. M.P. for C. Glasgow, 1918–23. P. S. to Bd. of Trade, 1902–5.

Leader of Con. party in Commons, 1911–21. Col. Sec., 1915–16. Chanc. of Exch., 1916–19. Ld Privy S. and Leader of Commons, 1919–21. Resigned, 1921. P.M. and Leader of Con. party, 1922–23. Resigned, 1923. d. 1923.

Brown, George Alfred. Ld George-Brown (Life Peer 1970)

b. 1914. *Educ.* Secondary. M.P. (Lab.) for Belper 1945–70. P.P.S. to Min. of Lab. and Nat. Service, 1945–47, and to C. of Exchequer, 1947. Joint Parliamentary Secretary, Min. of Ag. and Fish., 1947–51. Min. of Works, Apr–Oct 1951. First Sec. of State and Sec. of State for Econ. Affairs, 1964–66. For. Sec. 1966–68. Resigned, 1968. Deputy Leader of the Labour Party, 1960–70. d. 1985.

Butler, Richard Austen, Ld Butler of Saffron Walden (Life Peer 1965)

b. 1902. *Educ.* Marlborough; Cambridge. M.P. (Con.) for Saffron Walden, 1929–65. U. S. India O., 1932–37. P. S. Min. of Lab., 1937–38. U-S. For. O., 1938–41. Pres. Bd. of Educ.,1941–44. Min. of Educ., 1944–45. Min. of Lab., 1945. Chanc. of Exch., 1951–55. Leader of Commons, 1955–61. Ld Privy S., 1955–59. Hom. Sec., 1957–62. First Sec. of State and Min. in charge of C. African O., 1962–63. For. Sec., 1963–64. Ch. of Con. party organisation 1959–61. Master of Trinity College, Cambridge, 1965–78. d. 1982.

Callaghan, (Leonard) James, Ld Callaghan of Cardiff(Life Peer 1987)

b. 1912. *Educ.* Elem. and Portsmouth Northern Secondary Schools. M.P. (Lab.) for S. Cardiff 1945–50. M.P. for S. E. Cardiff 1950–83. M.P. for S. Cardiff and Penarth 1983–7. P. S. Min. of Transport, 1947–50. P. S. and F. S. Admiralty, 1950–51. Chanc. of the Exch., 1964–67. Home Sec., 1967–70. For. Sec., 1974–76. P.M., 1976–79. Leader of Opposition 1979–80. K.G. 1987.

Campbell-Bannerman, Henry (Sir)

b. 1836. *Educ.* Glasgow H.S.; Glasgow Univ. and Cambridge. Family business. M.P. (Lib.) for Stirling Burghs, 1868–1908. F. S. to War O., 1871–74 and 1880–82. Sec. to Admir., 1882–84. Ch. Sec. for Ireland (without seat in cabinet), 1884–85. Sec. for War, 1886 and 1892–95. G. C. B., 1895. Leader of Lib. party in Commons, 1899–1908. P.M., 1905–8. Resigned, 1908. d. 1908.

Carrington, 6th Ld (1938), Peter Alexander Rupert Carington

b. 1919. *Educ.* Eton; Sandhurst. Army 1939–45. Banker. P. S. Min. of Ag. and Fish., 1951–54. P. S. Min. of Defence, 1954–56. High Commissioner to Australia, 1956–59. 1st Ld of Admiralty, 1959–63. Leader of House of Lords, 1963–64. Sec. of State for Defence, 1970–74. Sec. of State for Energy, 1974. Ch. of Con. Party Organisation, 1972–74. For. Sec.,1979–82. Secretary-General of N. A. T. O., 1984–9. European peace negotiator in former Yugoslavia 1991–2.

Chamberlain, (Arthur) Neville

b. 1869. *Educ.* Rugby; Mason Science College, Birmingham. Business career. Ld Mayor of Birmingham, 1915–16. Dir.-Gen. of Nat. Service, 1916–17. M.P. (Con.) for Ladywood, Birmingham, 1918–29. M.P. for Edgbaston, Birmingham, 1929–40. Postm.-Gen., 1922–23. Paym.-Gen., 1923. Min. of Health, 1923. Chanc. of Exch., 1923–24. Min. of Health, 1924–29 and 1931. Ch. of Con. party organisation, 1930–31. Chanc. of Exch., 1931–37. P.M. and Leader of Con. party, 1937–40. Ld Pres. of Council, 1940. Resigned, 1940. d. 1940.

Chamberlain, Joseph

b. 1836. *Educ.* University College School. Family business. Mayor of Birmingham, 1873–75. M.P. (Lib.) for Birmingham, 1876–85. M.P. for W. Birmingham, 1885–86, M.P. (Lib. U.) for W. Birmingham, 1886–1914. Pres. of Bd. of Trade, 1880–85. Pres. of Loc. Govt. Bd., 1886. Col. Sec., 1895–1903. d. 1914.

Chamberlain, (Joseph) Austen (Sir)

b. 1863. *Educ.* Rugby; Cambridge. M.P. (Lib. U.) for E. Worcs., 1892–1914. M.P. (Un.) for W. Birmingham, 1914–37. Lib. U. Whip, 1892. Civil Ld of Admir., 1895–1900. F. S. to Treas.,1900–2. Postm.-Gen., 1902–3. Chanc. of Exch., 1903–5. Sec. for India, 1915–17. Resigned, 1917. Min. without Portfolio in war cabinet, 1918–19. Chanc. of Exch., 1919–21. Ld Privy S. and Leader of Con. party in Commons, 1921–22. For. Sec., 1924–29. K.G., 1925. 1st Ld of Admir., 1931. d. 1937.

Churchill, Winston Leonard Spencer (Sir)

b. 1874. *Educ.* Harrow; Sandhurst. Army, 1895–1900. M.P. (Con.) for Oldham, 1900–4. M.P. (Lib.) for Oldham, 1904–6. M.P. (Lib.) for N. W. Manchester, 1906–8. M.P. (Lib.) for Dundee, 1908–22. M.P. (Const.) for Epping, 1924–29. M.P. (Con.) for Epping, 1924–45; M.P. (Con.) for Woodford, 1945–64. U-S. for Col. O., 1905–8. Pres. of Bd. of Trade, 1908–10. Home Sec.,1910–11. 1st Ld of Admiralty, 1911–15. Chanc. of D. of Lanc., 1915. Min. of Munitions, 1917–19. Sec. for War and Air, 1919–21. Sec. for Air and Col., 1921. Col. Sec., 1921–22. Chanc. of Exch., 1924–29. 1st Ld of Admir., 1939–40. P.M. and Min. of Def. 1940–45. Leader of Con. party, 1940–55. Leader of Opposition, 1945–51. Min. of Def., 1951–52. P.M., 1951–55. K.G., 1953. d. 1965.

Clarke,Kenneth

b. 1940. Educ. Nottingham H.S.; Cambridge. Barrister. M.P. (Con.) Rushcliffe 1970–. Asst. Whip, 1972–4. Ld. Com.,1974, P. S. Transport 1979–82. Min. Health 1982–5. Paym. Gen. and Emp. Min.,1985–7. Chanc. of Duchy and Min. Trade 1987–8. Sec. of State Health 1988–90, . Sec. of State Educ.,1990–2. Home Sec. 1992–3. Chanc. of Exch.,1993–.

Clynes, John Richard

b. 1869. *Educ.* Elementary. Cotton worker; union official. M.P. (Lab) for N. E. Manchester 1906–18; for Manchester, Platting 1918–31,1935–45. Food controller 1918. Leader of Opposition 1921–2. Lord Privy Seal 1924. Home Sec. 1929–31. d. 1949.

Cripps, (Richard) Stafford (Sir)
   b. 1889. *Educ.* Winchester; London. Barrister. M.P. (Lab.) for E. Bristol, 1931–50. M.P. for S. E. Bristol, 1950. Kt., 1930. Sol.-Gen., 1930–31. Brit. Amb. to U. S. S. R., 1940–42. Ld Privy S. and Leader of Commons, 1942. Min. of Aircraft Prod., 1942–45. Pres. of Bd. of Trade, 1945–47. Min. for Econ. Affairs, 1947. Chanc. of Exch., 1947–50. d. 1952.

Crosland, (Charles) Anthony Raven
   b. 1918. *Educ.* Highgate; Oxford. M.P. (Lab.) for South Glos., 1950–55; M.P. for Grimsby, 1959–77. Min. of State, Econ. Affairs, 1964–65. Sec. of State Educ. and Science, 1965–67. President of the Bd. of Trade, 1967–69. Sec. of State for Local Govt. and Regional Planning, 1969–70. Sec. of State for the Environment, 1974–76. For. Sec., 1976–77. d. 1977.

Curzon, George Nathaniel. Ld Curzon (1898), 1st Earl (1911), 1st Marquess Curzon of Kedleston (1921)
   b. 1859. *Educ.* Eton; Oxford. M.P. (Con.) for Southport, 1886–98. U-S. India O., 1891–92. U-S. For. 0., 1895–98. Viceroy of India, 1899–1905. Entered H. of Lords as Irish Representative Peer, 1908. Ld Privy Seal, 1915–16. Ld Pres. of Council, 1916–19. Member of war cabinet, Leader of Lords, 1916–24. For. Sec., 1919–24. Ld Pres. of Council, 1924–25. Leader of Con. Party, Lords, 1916–25. d. 1925.

Dalton, (Edward) Hugh John Neale. Ld Dalton (Life Peer 1960)
   b. 1887. *Educ.* Eton; Cambridge, L. S. E. Barrister, 1914. Univ. Lecturer, London, 1919–36. M.P. (Lab.) for Peckham, 1924–29. M.P. Bishop Auckland, 1929–31 and 1935–59. U-S. For. O., 1929–31. Min. of Econ. Warfare, 1940–42. Pres. of Bd. of Trade, 1942–45. Chanc. of Exch., 1945–47. Chanc. of D. of Lanc., 1948–50. Min. of Town and Country Planning, 1950–51. Min. of Loc. Govt. and Planning, 1951. d. 1962.

Douglas-Home, Sir Alec (Alexander Frederick), Ld Dunglass (1918–51), 14th E of Home (1951–63). Ld Home of the Hirsel (Life Peer 1974)
   b. 1903. *Educ.* Eton; Oxford. M.P. (Con.) for S. Lanark, 1931–45. M.P. for Lanark, 1950–51. M.P. for Kinross and W. Perthshire, 1963–74. P.P.S. to N. Chamberlain, 1937–40. Joint U-S. For. O., 1945. (Succ. to Earldom 1951) Min. of State Scottish O., 1951–55. Sec. Commonwealth Relations, 1955–60. Dep. Leader of Lords, 1956–57. Ld Pres. of Council, 1957 and 1959–60. Leader of Lords, 1957–60. For. Sec., 1960–63. K. T., 1962. P.M., 1963–64 (Renounced peerage 1963). Leader of Con. Party, 1963–65. For Sec., 1970–74.

Eden, (Robert) Anthony (Sir). 1st E of Avon (1961)
   b. 1897. *Educ.* Eton; Oxford. M.P. (Con.) for Warwick and Leamington, 1923–57. P.P.S. to Sir A. Chamberlain (For. Sec.), 1926–29. U-S. For. O., 1931–33. Ld Privy S., 1933–35. Min. without Portfolio for League of Nations Affairs, 1935. For. Sec., 1935–38. Resigned, 1938. Sec. for Dominions, 1939–40. Sec. for War, 1940. For. Sec., 1940–45. Leader of Commons, 1942–45. Dep. Leader of Opposition, 1945–51. For. Sec., 1951–55. K.G., 1954. P.M. and Leader of Con. party, 1955–57. d. 1977.

Foot, Michael Mackintosh
   b. 1913. *Educ.* Leighton Park Sch., Reading; Oxford. Journalist. M.P. (Lab) for Plymouth Devonport, 1945–55. M.P. for Ebbw Vale, 1960–83. M.P. for Blaenau Gwent, 1983–92. Sec. for Employment 1974–76; Lord Pres. of Council and Leader of House of Commons, 1976–79. Leader of Opposition, 1980–83. Dep. Leader of Labour Party, 1976–80. Leader of Labour Party, 1980–83.

Gaitskell, Hugh Todd Naylor
   b. 1906. *Educ.* Winchester; Oxford. M.P. (Lab.) for S. Leeds, 1945–63. Princ. Private Sec. to Min. of Econ. Warfare, 1940–42. Princ. Asst. Sec. Bd. of Trade, 1942–45. P. S. Min. of Fuel and Power, 1946–47. Min. of Fuel and Power, 1947–50. Min. of State for Econ. Affairs, 1950. Chanc. of Exch., 1950–51. Leader of Lab. party, 1955–63. d. 1963.

Gordon Walker, Patrick Chrestien. Ld Gordon-Walker (Life Peer 1974)
   b. 1907. *Educ.* Wellington; Oxford. University Teacher. M.P. (Lab.) for Smethwick, 1945–64. M.P. (Lab.) Leyton, 1966–74. P.P.S. to H. Morrison, 1946. Parl. U-S., Commonwealth Relations O., 1947–50. Sec. of State for Commonwealth Relations, 1950–51. For. Sec., 1964–65. Min. without Portfolio, 1967. Sec. for Educ. and Science, 1967–68. d. 1980.

Grey, Edward (Sir). 1st Vt Grey of Fallodon (1916)
   b. 1862. *Educ.* Winchester; Oxford. Succ. to Btcy., 1882. M.P. (Lib.) for Berwick-on-Tweed, 1885–1916. U-S. For. O., 1892–95. For. Sec., 1905–16. (For. Sec. in Lords, 1916). Leader of Lib. party, Lords, 1923–24. d. 1933.

Halifax, 3rd Vt (1934). Edward Frederick Lindley Wood. 1st Ld Irwin (1925), 1st E of (1944)
   b. 1881. *Educ.* Eton; Oxford. M.P. (Con.) for Ripon, 1910–25. U-S. Col. O., 1921–22. Pres. of Bd. of Educ., 1922–24. Min. of Agric., 1924–25. Viceroy of India, 1926–31. Pres. of Bd. of Educ., 1932–35. Sec. for War, 1935. Ld Privy S., 1935–37. Leader of Lords, 1935–38. Ld Pres. of Council, 1937–38. For. Sec., 1938–40. Leader of Lords, 1940. Brit. Amb. to U. S. A., 1941–46. d. 1959.

Healey, Denis Winston, Lord Healey (Life Peer 1992)
   b. 1917. *Educ.* Bradford G. S.; Oxford. M.P. (Lab.) for Leeds South-East, 1952–55. M.P. for Leeds East, 1955–. Sec. for Defence, 1964–70. Chanc. of Exch., 1974–79. Dep. Leader of Lab. Party, 1980–83.

Heath, Edward Richard George (Sir)
   b. 1916. *Educ.* Chatham House School, Ramsgate; Oxford. M.P. (Con.) for Bexley, 1950–74. M.P. for Sidcup 1974–83. M.P. for Old Bexley and Sidcup 1983– . Con. Whip, 1951–55. Chief Whip, 1955–59. Min. of Labour,

1959–60. Lord Privy Seal, 1960–63. Sec. for Trade & Industry, 1963–64. Leader of the Con. Party, 1965–75. Leader of the Opposition, 1965–70. P.M., 1970–74. Leader of the Opposition, 1974–75. K.G. 1992.

Heathcoat Amory, Derick. 1st Vt Amory (1960)

b. 1899. *Educ.* Eton; Oxford. M.P. (Con.) for Tiverton, 1945–60. Min. of Pensions, 1951–53. Min. of State for Bd. of Trade, 1953–54. Min. of Ag., Fish. and Food, 1954–58. Chanc. of Exch., 1958–60. High Commissioner for the U. K. in Canada, 1961–63. d. 1981.

Henderson, Arthur

b. 1863. *Educ.* Elem. M.P. (Lab.) for Barnard Castle, 1903–18. M.P. for Widnes, 1919–22. M.P. for Newcastle E., 1923. M.P. for Burnley, 1924–31. M.P. for Clay Cross, 1933–35. Sec. of Lab. party, 1911–34. Treasurer of Lab. party, 1930–35. Leader of Lab. party in Commons, 1908–10 and 1914–17. Chief Whip, 1914. Pres. Bd. of Educ., 1915–16. Paym.-Gen., 1916. Min. without portfolio and member of war cabinet, 1916–17. Resigned from cabinet, 1917. Chief Lab. party Whip, 1920–24 and 1925–27. Home Sec., 1924. For. Sec., 1929–31. Leader of Lab. Opposition, 1931–32. d. 1935.

Hicks Beach, Michael Edward (Sir). 1st Vt St Aldwyn (1906), 1st Earl (1915)

b. 1837. *Educ.* Eton; Oxford. Succ. to Btcy., 1854. M.P. (Con.) for E. Gloucs., 1864–85. M.P. for W. Bristol, 1885–1906. Sec. of Poor Law Bd., 1868. U-S. Home O., 1868. Ch. Sec. for Ireland, 1874–78. (Seat in cabinet, 1876.) Sec. for Col., 1878–80. Chanc. of Exch. and Leader of Commons, 1885–86. Leader of Opposition in Commons, 1886. Ch. Sec. for Ireland, 1886–87. Resigned, 1887, but remained in cabinet without portfolio. Pres. of Bd. of Trade, 1888–92. Chanc. of Exch., 1895–1902. Resigned 1902. d. 1916.

Hoare, Samuel John Gurney (Sir). 1st Vt Templewood (1944)

b. 1880. *Educ.* Harrow; Oxford. M.P. (Con.) for Chelsea, 1910–44. Succ. to Btcy., 1915. Sec. for Air, 1922–24 and 1924–29. Sec. for India, 1931–35. For. Sec., 1935. 1st Ld of Admir., 1936–37. Home Sec., 1937–39. Ld Privy S., 1939–40. Sec. for Air, 1940. Brit. Amb. to Spain, 1940–44. d. 1959.

Horne, Robert Stevenson (Sir). 1st Vt Horne of Slamannan (1937)

b. 1871. *Educ.* George Watson's Coll., Edin.; Glasgow Univ. Member of Faculty of Advocates, 1896. K. B. E., 1918. M.P. (Con.) for Hillhead, Glasgow, 1918–37. Min. of Lab., 1919–20. Pres. of Bd. of Trade, 1920–21. Chanc. of Exch., 1921–22. d. 1940.

Howard, Michael

b. 1941. Educ. Llanelli G. S.; Cambridge. Barrister. M.P. for Folkestone and Hythe 1983–. U-S Dept. of Trade and Industry, 1985–87; Min. of State Dept. of Env. 1987–90; Sec of State for Emp. 1990–92; Sec of State for Env. 1992–93; Home Sec. 1993–.

Howe, (Richard Edward) Geoffrey (Sir),Ld Howe of Aberavon (Life Peer 1992)

b. 1926. *Educ.* Winchester; Cambridge. Barrister. M.P. (Con.) for Bebington, 1964–66. M.P. for Reigate, 1970–74. M.P. for Surrey East, 1974–92. Sol.-Gen., 1970–72. Min. for Trade and Consumer Affairs, 1972–74. Chanc. of Exch., 1979–83. For. Sec., 1983–9. Ld Pres. and Deputy P.M. 1989–90. Resigned 1990.

Hurd, Douglas Richard

b. 1930. *Educ.* Eton; Cambridge. Diplomat. Pol. Sec. to E. Heath 1968–73. M.P. (Con.) for Mid-Oxon 1974–83, for Witney 1983–. Min. of State Foreign Office 1979–83, Home Office 1983–4; Sec. of State for N. Ireland, 1984–5; Home Sec., 1985–9; For. Sec., 1989–.

Jenkins, Roy Harris. Ld Jenkins of Hillhead (Life Peer 1987)

b. 1920. *Educ.* Abersychan G. S.; Oxford. Army, 1939–45. M.P. (Lab.) for Central Southwark, 1948–50. M.P. (Lab.) For Stechford, Birmingham, 1950–76. M.P. (S. D. P.) for Glasgow Hillhead, 1982–87. P.P.S. Commonwealth Relations O., 1949–50. Min. of Aviation, 1964–65. Home Sec., 1965–67. Chanc. of Exch., 1967–70. Deputy Leader of Lab. party, 1970–72. Home Sec., 1974–76. President of European Commission, 1977–81. Leader of SDP, 1982–83. Leader of (Social and) Liberal Democrat Peers 1987–.

Kinnock, Neil Gordon

b. 1942 *Educ.* Lewis Sch., Pengam; U. of Wales (Cardiff). M.P. (Lab.) for Bedwellty, 1970–83. M.P. for Islwyn, 1983–. P.P.S. to Sec. of State for Employment, 1974–75. Chief Opposition Spokesman on Education, 1979–83. Leader of the Opposition, and Leader of Labour Party, 1983–92.

Lamont, Norman Stewart Hughson

b. 1942. *Educ.* Loretto; Cambridge. Merchant banker. M.P. (Con.) for Kingston-on-Thames 1972–. U-S Energy 1979–81; Min. of State for Industry, 1981–5; Min. of State (Defence Procurement) 1985–6; Fin. Sec. Treasury 1986–9; Chief Sec. 1989–90; Chanc. of Exch. 1990–93.

Lansbury, George

b. 1859. *Educ.* Elem. M.P. (Lab.) for Bow and Bromley, 1910–12 and 1922–35. First Comm. of Works, 1929–31. Leader of the Opposition, 1931–35. Leader of the Labour Party, 1932–35. d. 1940.

Lansdowne, 5th M of (1866), Henry Charles Keith Petty-Fitzmaurice, Vt Clanmaurice (1845–63), E of Kerry (1863–66)

b. 1845. *Educ.* Eton; Oxford. Succ. to M. 1866. Junior Ld of Treas. (Lib.), 1869–72. U-S. for War, 1872–74. U-S. India O.,1880. Resigned and opposed Lib. Govt. in Lords, 1880. Gov.-Gen. of Canada, 1883–88. Viceroy of India, 1888–94. Sec. for War (Con.), 1895–1900. For. Sec., 1900–5. Leader of Con. party in Lords, 1903–16. Min. without portfolio, member of war cabinet, 1915–16. Left Con. party, 1917. d. 1927.

Lawson, Nigel. Ld Lawson (Life Peer 1992)

b. 1932. *Educ.* Westminster; Oxford. Journalist. M.P. (Con.) for Blaby, Feb. 1974–1992. Opposition Spokesman on Treasury and Economic Affairs, 1977–79. F. S. to Treasury, 1979–81. Sec. for Energy, 1981–83; Chanc. of Exch., 1983–89. Resigned 1989.

Lloyd, (John) Selwyn Brooke, Ld Selwyn-Lloyd (Life Peer 1976)

b.1904. *Educ.* Fettes; Cambridge. Barrister, 1930. M.P. (Con.) for Wirral, 1945–76. Min. of State For. O., 1951–54. Min. of Supply, 1954–55. Min. of Def., 1955. For. Sec., 1955–60. Chanc. of Exch., 1960–62. Lord Privy Seal and Leader of the House of Commons, 1963–64. Speaker of the House of Commons, 1971–76. d. 1978.

Lloyd George, David. 1st Earl Lloyd George of Dwyfor (1945)

b. 1863. *Educ.* Church School. Solicitor, 1884. M.P. (Lib.) for Caernarvon Boroughs, 1890–1945 (Ind. L., 1931–35). Pres. of Bd. of Trade, 1905–8. Chanc. of Exch., 1908–15. Min. of Munitions, 1915–16. Sec. for War, 1916. P.M., 1916–22. Leader of Lib. party, 1926–31. d. 1945.

MacDonald, James Ramsay

b. 1866. *Educ.* Drainie School. M.P. (Lab.) for Leicester, 1906–18. M.P. for Aberavon, Glamorganshire, 1922–29. M.P. for Seaham, 1929–35. (Nat. Lab., 1931–35.) M.P. (Nat. Lab.) for Scottish Univs., 1936–37. Sec. of L. R. C. and Lab. party, 1900–12. Treas. of Lab. party, 1912–29. Chairman of I. L. P., 1906–9. Ch. of Lab. party, 1911–14. Resigned Chairmanship, 1914. Ch. of P. L. P. and Leader of official Opposition, 1922. Leader of Lab. party, 1922–31. P.M. and For. Sec., 1924. P.M., 1929–31. P.M. of National Govt., 1931–35. Ld Pres. of Council, 1935–37. d. 1937.

McKenna, Reginald

b. 1863. *Educ.* St. Malo, Ebersdorf and King's Coll. School; Cambridge. Barrister, 1887. M.P. (Lib.) for N. Monmouthshire, 1895–1918. F. S. to Treas., 1905–7. Pres. Bd. of Educ., 1907–8. 1st Ld of Admir., 1908–11. Home Sec., 1911–15. Chanc. of Exch., 1915–16. Ch. of Midland Bank, 1919–43. d. 1943.

Macleod, Iain Norman

b. 1913. *Educ.* Fettes; Cambridge. Journalist. M.P. (Con.) for Enfield West, 1950–70. Min. of Health, 1952–55. Min. of Labour, 1955–59. Sec. of State for Colonies, 1959–61. Chanc. of D. of Lanc. and Leader of House of Commons, 1961–63. Ch. of Con. party organisation, 1961–63. Editor of Spectator, 1963–65. Chanc. of Exch., 1970. d. 1970.

Macmillan, (Maurice) Harold. 1st E of Stockton (1984)

b. 1894. *Educ.* Eton; Oxford. M.P. (Con.) for Stockton-on-Tees, 1924–29 and 1931–45. M.P. (Con.) for Bromley, 1945–64. P. S. Min. of Supply, 1940–42. U-S. Col. O., 1942. Min. Resident at Allied H. Q. in N. W. Africa, 1942–45. Sec. for Air, 1945. Min. of Housing and Loc. Govt., 1951–54. Min. of Def., 1954–55. For. Sec., 1955. Chanc. of Exch., 1955–57. P.M. and Leader of Con. party, 1957–63. d. 1986.

Major, John

b. 1943. *Educ.* Rutlish G. S. Banker. M.P. (Con.) for Huntingdon 1979–. Whip, 1983–5. U-S Soc. Sec., 1985–6; Min. of State D. H.S. S.,1986–7; Chief Sec. Treasury, 1987–89; For. Sec., 1989; Ch. of Exch., 1989–90; P.M. and Leader of the Conservative Party, 1990–.

Maudling, Reginald

b. 1917. *Educ.* Merchant Taylors'; Oxford. Barrister, 1940. M.P. (Con.) for Barnet, 1950–74. M.P. for Chipping Barnet, 1974–79. P. S. Min. of Civil Aviation, 1952. Econ. Sec. to Treasury, 1952–55. Min. of Supply, 1955–57. Paym.-Gen., 1957–59. Pres. Bd. of Trade, 1959–61. Sec. of State for Colonies, 1961–62. Chanc. of Exch., 1962–64. Deputy Leader of Con. party, 1965–72. Home Sec., 1970–72. Resigned, 1972. d. 1979.

Morrison, Herbert Stanley, Ld Morrison of Lambeth (Life Peer 1959)

b. 1888. *Educ.* Elem. Member of L. C. C., 1922–45. Leader of Council, 1934–40. M.P. (Lab.) for S. Hackney, 1923–24, 1929–31, 1935–45. M.P. for E. Lewisham, 1945–50. M.P. for S. Lewisham, 1950–59. Min. of Transport, 1929–31. Min. of Supply, 1940. Home Sec. and Min. of Home Security, 1940–45. Member of war cabinet, 1942–45. Dep. P.M., 1945–51. Ld Pres. of Council and Leader of Commons, 1945–51. For. Sec., 1951. Dep. Leader of Opposition, 1951–55. d. 1965.

Owen, David Anthony Llewellyn, Lord Owen (Life Peer 1992)

b. 1938. *Educ.* Bradfield; Cambridge. Doctor, 1962. M.P. (Lab.) Plymouth Sutton, 1966–74. Plymouth Devonport, 1974–92. U-S. for Navy, 1968–70. U. S. Health and Social Security, 1974. Min. of State Health and Social Security, 1974–76. Min. of State For. O., 1976–77. For. Sec., 1977–79. Leader of SDP, 1983–.

Pym, Francis Leslie, Ld Pym (Life Peer 1987)

b. 1922 *Educ.* Eton; Cambridge. M.P. (Con) for Cambridgeshire, 1961–83. M.P. for Cambridgeshire S. E., 1983–87. Parl. Sec. to the Treasury and Government Chief Whip, 1970–73. Sec. for Northern Ireland, 1973–74. Sec. for Defence, 1979–81. Chanc. of D. of Lancaster, Paym.-Gen. and Leader of House of Commons, 1981. Lord Pres. of Council and Leader of House of Commons, 1981–82. For. Sec., 1982–83.

Reading, 1st M of (1926). Rufus Daniel Isaacs (Sir), 1st Ld (1914), 1st Vt (1916) 1st E of (1917)

b. 1860. Educ. Brussels, Anglo-Jewish Acad., London, University College Sch. Family business. Barrister, 1887. M.P. (Lib.) for Reading, 1904–13. Kt., 1910. Sol.-Gen , 1910. Att. Gen., 1910–13 (seat in cabinet, 1912). Ld Chief Justice, 1913–21. Brit Amb. to U. S. A., 1918–19. Viceroy of India, 1921–26. For. Sec , 1931. Leader of Lords, 1931; Leader of Lib. party, Lords, 1930–35. d 1935.

Ritchie, Charles Thomson. 1st Ld Ritchie of Dundee (1905)
b. 1838. *Educ.* City of London School. M.P. (Con.) for Tower Hamlets, 1874–85. M.P. for St. George's in the East, 1885–92. M. P for Croydon, 1895–1903. F. S. to Admir., 1885–86 Pres. of Loc. Govt. Bd., 1886–92. Pres. of Bd. of Trade, 1895–1900. Home Sec., 1900–2. Chanc. of Exch., 1902–3. Resigned, 1903. d. 1906.

Salisbury, 3rd M of (1868). Robert Arthur Talbot Gascoyne-Cecil, Vt Cranborne (1865–68)
b. 1830. *Educ.* Eton; Oxford. M. P (Con.) for Stamford, 1853–68. Sec. for India, 1866. Resigned, 1867. Succ. to M. 1868. Sec. for India, 1874–76. For. Sec., 1878–80. Leader of Opposition in Lords, 1881–85. Leader of the Con. party, 1885–1902. P.M. and For. Sec., 1885–86. P.M., 1886–87. P.M. and For. Sec., 1887–92 and 1895–1900. P. M and Ld Privy S., 1900–2. d 1903.

Simon, John Allsebrook (Sir), 1st Vt Simon (1940)
b. 1873. *Educ.* Fettes; Oxford. Barrister. M.P. (Lib.) for Walthamstow 1906–18 M.P. for Spen Valley, 1922–31 M.P. (L. Nat.) for Spen Valley, 1931–40. Kt., 1910. Sol.-Gen., 1910–13. Att.-Gen. (with seat in cabinet), 1913–15. Home Sec, 1915–16. For. Sec., 1931–35. Leader of L. Nat. party, 1931–40. Home Sec. and Dep. Leader of Commons, 1935–37. Chanc. of Exch., 1937–40. Ld. Chanc., 1940–45. d. 1954.

Smith, John
b. 1938. *Educ.* Dunoon G. S.; Edinburgh Univ. Barrister. M.P. (Lab.)for N. Lanarkshire, 1970–83. M.P. for Monklands E. 1983–. U-S for Energy, 1974–5. Min. of State Energy, 1975–6. Min. of State, Energy, 1975–6. Min. Privy Council Off., 1976–8; Sec. of State Trade, 1978–9. Leader of Opposition 1992–4. d. 1994.

Snowden, Philip. 1st Vt Snowden (1931)
b. 1864. *Educ.* Bd. School M. P (Lab.) for Blackburn, 1906–18. M.P. for Colne Valley, 1922–31. Ch. of I. L. P. 1903–6 and 1917–20. Chanc. of Exch., 1924, 1929–31, and 1931. Ld Privy S., 1931–32. Resigned, 1932. d 1937.

Stewart, (Robert) Michael Maitland. Ld Stewart of Fulham (Life Peer 1979)
b. 1906. *Educ.* Christ's Hospital; Oxford. Teacher. M.P. (Lab.) Fulham East, 1945–55 and for Fulham, 1955–79. Vice-Chamberlain, H. M. Household, 1946. Comptroller, H. M. Household, 1946–47. U-S. for War, 1947–51. P. S. Min. of Supply, 1951. Sec. for Educ. and Science, 1964–65. For. Sec., 1965–66. Sec. of State for Econ. Affairs, 1966–67. First Sec. of State, 1966–68. For. (and Commonwealth) Sec., 1968–70. d. 1990

Thatcher, Mrs Margaret Hilda (née Roberts). Lady Thatcher (Life Peeress 1992)
b. 1925. *Educ.* Grantham Girls' School; Oxford. Research Chemist. Barrister. M.P. (Con) for Finchley, 1959–92. P. S. to Min. of Pensions and Nat. Insurance, 1961–64. Sec. of State for Education and Science, 1970–74. Leader of the Conservative Party, 1975–90. P.M., 1979–90.

Thorneycroft, (George Edward) Peter. Ld Thorneycroft of Dunston (Life Peer 1967)
b. 1909. *Educ.* Eton; Woolwich. Barrister, 1935. M.P. (Con.) for Stafford, 1938–45. M P. (Con.) for Monmouth, 1945–66. P. S Min. of War Transport, 1945. Pres. of Bd. of Trade, 1951–57. Chanc. of Exch., 1957–58. Resigned, 1958. Min. of Aviation, 1960–62. Min. of Defence, 1962–64. Sec. of State for Defence, 1964. Ch. of Con. party organisation 1975–81. d. 1994.

Wilson, (James) Harold (Sir). Ld Wilson of Rievaulx. (Life Peer 1983)
b. 1916. *Educ.* Wirral G. S.; Oxford. University teacher. Director of Economics and Statistics, Min. of Fuel and Power, 1943–44. M.P. (Lab.) for Ormskirk, 1945–50, and for Huyton (Lab.), 1950–83. P. S. Min. of Works, 1945–47. Sec. for Overseas Trade, 1947. Pres. Bd. of Trade, 1947–51. Resigned 1951. Leader, Lab. party, 1963–76. Leader of the Opposition 1963–64. P.M. 1964–70. Leader of the Opposition, 1970–74. P.M. . 1974–76. K.G., 1976.

Wood, (Howard) Kingsley (Sir)
b. 1881. *Educ.* Central Foundation Boys School. Solicitor, 1903. Kt. . 1918. M.P. (Con.) for W. Woolwich, 1918–43. P.P.S. to Min. of Health, 1919–22. P. S. Min. of Health. 1924–29. P. S. Bd. of Educ., 1931. Postm.-Gen., 1931–35 (seat in cabinet, 1933). Min. of Health, 1935–38. Sec. for Air, 1938–40 Ld Privy S., 1940. Chanc. of Exch., 1940–43. d. 1943.

Index of Ministers

This Index covers every reference to a Minister given in the Tables of Ministries, pp. 1–46. It does not cover the supplementary information on Ministers and Ministries, pp. 49–76.

The educational information is necessarily incomplete. It is not always possible to trace the name or status of an elementary or secondary school. When several schools are recorded, the last is normally named here. All schools that are unstarred are public schools' or, more precisely, are in the 1990s members of the Headmasters' Conference. However this can be misleading, particularly for Ministers educated in the 19th century. RNC Dartmouth is also unstarred. By courtesy, we have listed the Royal Military College (Sandhurst) and the Royal Military Academy (Woolwich) in the University column.

In this index promotion from a knighthood to a higher order of chivalry or to a baronetcy is not recorded.

† denotes a Privy Councillor.

When an individual appears more than once on a page, the number is indicated. Double entries are given when an individual held office under different names, and where a title was acquired after office had been held.

	Born	Died	School	University	Page reference
Abercorn, 3rd D of (1913). J. Hamilton, M of Hamilton (1885)	1869	1953	Eton		2
† Aberdare, 4th Ld (1957). M. G. L. Bruce	1919	. .	Winchester	Oxford	34^2
† Acland, Sir F. D. (14th Bt 1926)	1874	1939	Rugby	Oxford	4^4, 5
† Acland Hood, Sir A. F. (4th Bt (1892). 1st Ld St Audries (1911)	1853	1917	Eton	Oxford	2^2
Acton, 2nd Ld (1902). R. M. Dalberg-Acton	1870	1924	Privately	Oxford	3, 5
Adams, (H.) R.	1912	1978	Emanuel	London	23
Adamson, Mrs J. L.	1882	1962	Elementary		22
† Adamson, W.	1863	1936	Elementary		11, 13
Adamson, W. M.	1881	1945	Elementary		20
† Addison, 1st Vt (1945). C. Addison, 1st Ld (1937)	1869	1951	Trinity Coll., Harrogate*	London	4, 6, 7, 8^4, 12^2, 21, 22^3
† Ailwyn, 1st Ld (1921). Sir A. E. Fellowes (K.C.V.O. 1911)	1855	1924	Eton	Cambridge	2^3
Airlie, 12th E of (1900). D. L. G. W. Ogilvy	1893	1968	Eton		12
Aitchison, Ld (Scot. Judge 1933). C. M. Aitchison	1882	1941	Falkirk H.S.*	Edinburgh	13, 14
Aitken, J. W. P.	1942	. .	Eton	Oxford	44^2
† Akers-Douglas, A., 1st Vt Chilston (1911)	1851	1926	Eton	Oxford	1, 2
Albemarle, 8th E of (1884). A. A. C. Keppel	1858	1942	Eton		10
Albu, A. H.	1903	. .	Tonbridge	London	29
† Aldington, 1st Ld (1962). Sir T. A. R. W. Low (K.C. M.G. 1957)	1914	. .	Winchester	Oxford	25^2
† Alexander of Hillsborough, 1st E (1963). A. V. Alexander 1st Vt (1950)	1885	1965	Elementary		11, 12, 18, 21, 22^3
† Alexander of Tunis, 1st E (1952). H. R. L. G. Alexander, 1st Vt (1946)	1891	1969	Harrow	Sandhurst	24

Alexander of Tunis, 2nd E (1969). S. W. D. Alexander, Ld Rideau (1952)	1935	. .	Harrow		35
† Alison, M. J. H.	1926	. .	Eton	Oxford	34, 40, 41
Allan, of Kilmahew, Ld (Life Peer 1973). R. A. Allan	1914	1979	Harrow	Cambridge	26^2
† Allendale, 1st Vt (1911). W. C. B. Beaumont, 2nd Ld Allendale (1907)	1860	1923	Eton	Cambridge	$3^2, 5^2, 6$
Allendale, 2nd Vt (1923). W. H. C. Beaumont	1890	1956	Eton	Cambridge	15
† Alness, 1st Ld (1934). R. Munro	1868	1955	Aberdeen G.S.*	Edinburgh	5, 6, 8, 20, 21
† Alport, Ld (Life Peer 1961). C. J. M. Alport	1912	. .	Haileybury	Cambridge	25, 27^2
† Althorp, 1st Vt (1905). C. R. Spencer, Vt Althorp (1857). 6th Earl of Spencer (1910)	1857	1922	Harrow	Cambridge	3, 5
† Altrincham, 1st Ld (1945). Sir E. W. M. Grigg (K.V.C.O. 1920)	1879	1955	Winchester	Oxford	16, 17, 18, 19, 21
† Alverstone, 1st Vt (1913). Sir R. E. Webster (G.C.M.G. 1893). 1st Ld Alverstone (1900)	1842	1915	King's Coll. S.	Cambridge & Charterhouse	2
† Amery, Ld (Life Peer 1992). J. Amery	1919	. .	Eton	Oxford	27^3, 28, 33, 34^2
† Amery, L. S.	1873	1955	Harrow	Oxford	7^2, 10, 11^2, 18, 20
† Ammon, 1st Ld (1944). C. G. Ammon	1875	1960	Elementary		11, 12, 23
† Amory, 1st Vt (1960). D. Heathcoat Amory	1899	1981	Eton	Oxford	$24^2, 25^2, 26^2$
Amulree, 1st Ld (1929). Sir W. W. Mackenzie (K.B.E. 1918)	1860	1942	Perth Academy*	Edinburgh & London	12, 14
Amwell, 1st Ld Montague (1947). F. Montague	1876	1966	Elementary		13, 18, 19
† Ancaster, 2nd E (1910). G. H. D. Willoughby	1867	1951	Eton	Cambridge	7, 10
Ancram (E of) (1965). M. A. F. J. Kerr	1945	. .	Ampleforth	Oxford & Edinburgh	41, 45^2
Anderson, Ld (Scot. Judge 1913). A. M. Anderson	1862	1936	Dundee H.S.*	Edinburgh	5
Anderson, D.C.	1916	. .	Glenalmond	Oxford & Edinburgh	29
† Anderson, Sir J. (K.C.B. 1919). 1st Vt Waverley (1952)	1882	1958	George Watson's Edinburgh	Edinburgh & Leipzig	$15^2, 17^3, 20$
Annaly, 6th Ld (1994). L. H. White	1953	. .	Eton	Sandhurst	46
Anson, Sir W. (3rd Bt 1873)	1843	1914	Eton	Oxford	2
Anstruther, H.T.	1860	1926	Eton	Edinburgh	2
† Anstruther-Gray, Sir W. J. (1st Bt 1956). Ld Kilmany (Life Peer 1966)	1905	1985	Eton	Oxford	21
Arbuthnot, J. N.	1952	. .	Eton/Glasgow*	Cambridge	46
† Archer of Sandwell, Ld (Life Peer 1992). P. K. Archer	1926	. .	Wednesbury Boys' H.S.*	London	37
Archibald, 1st Ld (1949). G. Archibald	1898	1975	Allan Glen's H.S		23
† Armstrong, E.	1915	. .	Wolsingham G.S.*		$32^2, 36^2$
Arnold, 1st Ld (1924). S. Arnold	1878	1945	Manchester G.S.		11, 13
† Arnold-Forster, H. O.	1855	1909	Rugby	Oxford	1, 2
Arran, 9th E of, (1983). A. D. C. Gore	1938	. .	Eton	Oxford	39, $44^2, 45^2$, 46

† Ashbourne, 1st Ld (1885).   1837   1913   Dublin   2
    E. Gibson
† Ashby St Ledgers, 1st Ld (1910). 1873   1939   Eton   Cambridge   4, 5
    I. C. Guest, 2nd Ld
    Wimborne (1914), 1st Vt
    Wimborne (1918)
† Ashfield, 1st Ld (1920). Sir   1874   1948   American Schs.   8
    A. H. Stanley (Kt 1914)
† Ashley, W.W. 1st Ld Mount   1867   1939   Harrow   Oxford 10^2, 12
    Temple (1932)
  Ashton, J.W.   1933   ..   High Storrs   37
                                                  G.S.*
† Asquith, H. H. 1st E of Oxford   1852   1928   City of London Oxford   3, 4^2, 5
    & Asquith (1925)
† Assheton, R. 1st Ld Clitheroe   1901   1984   Eton   Oxford   16, 17, 18, 19
    (1955)
  Astor, 2nd Vt (1919). W.W. Astor 1879   1952   Eton   Oxford 7^2
  Astor, 4th Vt (1966). W.W. Astor 1952   ..   Eton   44, 45, 46
† Atholl, 8th D of (1917).   1871   1942   Eton   9
    J.G. Stewart-Murray, M of
    Tullibardine (1871)
  Atholl, Duchess of, K. M.   1874   1960   Wimbledon H.S.   11
† Atkins, Sir H. E. (K.C.M.G.   1922   ..   Wellington 35^2, 38, 41
    1983) Ld Colnbrook (Life
    Peer 1987)
  Atkins, R. J.   1948   ..   Highgate   40, 42^2, 44, 45
† Atkinson, Ld (Ld of Appeal   1844   1932   Royal Belfast   Galway   2
    1905). J. Atkinson   Acad. Inst.
† Attlee, 1st E (1955). C. R. Attlee 1883 1967   Haileybury   Oxford   11, 13^2, 17^2, 18, 21,
                                                                                         22
† Avon, 1st E of (1961). Sir (R.) A. 1897 1977   Eton   Oxford 13^2, 15, 16^2, 17, 19,
    Eden (K.G. 1954)   20, 24^2
  Avon, 2nd E of (1977). Vt Eden   1930   1985   Eton 40^2, 43
    (1961). N. Eden
† Avonside, Ld (Scot. Judge   1914   ..   Dunfermline   Glasgow &   29
    1964). I. H. Shearer   H.S.*   Edinburgh
† Aylestone Ld (Life Peer 1967).   1905   1994   Secondary   23, 29, 30
    H.W. Bowden
† Bacon. Lady (Life Peer 1970).   1911   1993   Normanton   London 30^2
    Miss A. M. Bacon   H.S.*
  Bagot. 4th Ld (1887) W. Bagot   1857   1932   Eton   3
† Baird, Sir J. L. (2nd Bt 1920). 1874   1941   Eton   Oxford 7^2, 8, 10^2
    1st Ld Stonehaven (1925).
    1st Vt (1938)
† Baker. H.T.   1877   1960   Winchester   Oxford   4
† Baker, K.W.   1934   ..   St Paul's   Oxford   33, 39, 40^2, 41^2,
                                                                                         42, 44
  Baker, N. B.   1938   ..   Clifton   Oxford   43, 44, 46
† Balcarres, Ld (1880).   1871   1940   Eton   Oxford   2, 5, 6, 8^2, 9^2
    D. A. E. Lindsay, 27th E of
    Crawford (1913)
  Baldry, A. B.   1950   ..   Leighton Park   Sussex   40, 44, 45
† Baldwin of Bewdley, 1st E   1867   1947   Harrow   Cambridge   6, 8, 9^3, 11, 13^2, 15
    (1937). S. Baldwin
† Balfour, 1st E of (1922).   1848   1930   Eton   Cambridge 1^3, 5, 6, 7, 11
    A. J. Balfour
† Balfour. 2nd E of (1930).   1853   1945   Eton   Cambridge 2^3
    G.W. Balfour
† Balfour of Burleigh. 6th Ld   1849   1921   Eton   Oxford   2
    (1869). A. H. Bruce
† Balfour of Inchrye, 1st Ld   1897   1988   R. N. Coll.,   15, 18^2, 21
    (1945). H. H. Balfour   Osborne

Name	Born	Died	School	University	Pages
† Balniel. Ld (1940) (Life Peer 1974). 29th E of Crawford (1975) R. A. Lindsay	1927	..	Eton	Cambridge	33[2]
Balogh, Ld (Life Peer 1968). T. Balogh	1905	1985	The Gymnasium, Budapest*	Budapest, Berlin & Harvard	36
† Barber, Ld (Life Peer 1974). A. P. L. Barber	1920	..	Retford G.S.*	Oxford	26[2], 27.29, 33, 34
† Barnes. A.	1887	1974	Northampton Inst.*		13, 23
† Barnes. G. N.	1859	1940	Elementary		6, 8[2]
† Barnett, Ld (Life Peer). J. Barnett	1923	..	Manchester Central H.S.*		35[2]
Barnett, (N.) G.	1928	1986	Highgate	Oxford	37
Barnston, Sir H. (1st Bt 1924)	1870	1929	Private Schs.	Oxford	9, 10, 12
Barrie, H.T.	1860	1922	Secondary		7
Barry, R.	1866	1913	Secondary	Dublin	3, 5[2]
Barton, Sir D. P. (1st Bt 1918)	1853	1937	Harrow	Oxford	2
Bates, M.	1961	..	Heathfield H.S.		46
Bates, A.	1944	..	Stretford G.S.	Manchester	37[2]
† Bath, 5th M of (1896). T. H. Thynne, Vt Weymouth (1862)	1862	1946	Eton	Oxford	2, 10
Bathurst. 8th E (1943). H. A. J Bathurst	1927	..	Canada & Eton	Oxford	26, 29
† Bathurst, Sir C. (K.B.E. 1917). 1st Ld Bledisloe (1918). 1st Vt (1935)	1867	1958	Sherborne & Eton	Oxford	7, 11
† Bayford, 1st Ld (1929). Sir R. A. Sanders (1st Bt 1920)	1867	1940	Harrow	Oxford	8, 9[2], 10
Beatty, 2nd E (1936). D. F. Beatty, Vt Borodale (1919)	1905	1972	R.N.C. Osborne & Dartmouth		20
† Beauchamp, 7th E (1891). W. Lygon	1872	1938	Eton	Oxford	3[2], 4[3], 5
Beaumont, W. C. B. 2nd Ld Allendale (1907). 1st Vt (1911)	1860	1923	Eton	Cambridge	3[2], 5[2], 6
† Beaverbrook, 1st Ld (1917). Sir W. M. Aitken (Kt 1911)	1879	1964	Hawkins Acad.*		8, 17, 18[2], 19[3], 20
Beaverbrook, 3rd Ld (1985). M. W. H. Aitken	1951	..	Charterhouse	Cambridge	44
Beck, Sir (A.) C.T. (Kt 1920)	1878	1932	Haileybury	Cambridge	5, 6, 8, 9
Beckett, Mrs M. (formerly Miss M. Jackson)	1943	..	Notre Dame H.S.	Manchester	36, 37
Beechman, (N.) A.	1896	1965	Westminster	Oxford	20, 21
Belcher, J. W.	1905	1964	Latymer Upper	London	23
† Bellenger, F. J.	1894	1968	Elementary		23[2]
Bellwin. Ld (Life Peer 1979) I. Bellow	1923	..	Leeds G.S.	Leeds	40[2]
† Belper, 2nd Ld (1880). H. Strutt	1840	1914	Harrow	Cambridge	2
† Belstead, 2nd Ld (1958). J. J. Ganzoni	1932	..	Eton	Oxford	34[2], 38[2], 39[2], 40, 45[2]
† Benn, A. Wedgwood	1925	..	Westminster	Oxford	31, 32, 36[2]
† Benn, W. Wedgwood, 1st Vt Stansgate (1941)	1877	1960	Paris Lycée	London	5, 13, 22
Bennett of Edgbaston, 1st Ld (1953). Sir P. F Bennett (Kt 1941)	1880	1957	King Edward's, Birmingham		25
Bennett, Sir E. N. (Kt 1930)	1868	1947	Durham	Oxford	14, 16
Bennett, N. J.	1949	..	Prenton G.S. Birkenhead*	London & Sussex	45
Beresford, Sir P. (Kt 1990)	1946	..	N.Z. Schools*	Dunedin & Lond.	45
Bernays, R. H.	1902	1945	Rossall	Oxford	16[2]
Berry, Sir A. G. (Kt 1983)	1925	1984	Eton	Oxford	43[3]
Bessborough. 10th E of (1956). F. E. N. Ponsonby, Vt Duncannon (1920)	1913	1993	Eton	Cambridge	27, 28, 34

Name	Born	Died	School	University	References
† Beswick, Ld (Life Peer 1964). F. Beswick	1912	1987	Elementary		22, 30[2], 33[2], 37
Bethell. 4th Ld (1967) N.W. Bethell	1938	. .	Harrow	Cambridge	35
† Betterton, Sir H. B. (1st Bt 1929). 1st Ld Rushcllffe (1935)	1872	1949	Rugby	Oxford	10, 12 14[2]
† Bevan, A.	1897	1960	Elementary		22[2]
† Bevin, E.	1881	1951	Elementary		18[2], 21[2]
† Bevins. (J.) R.	1908	. .	Liverpool Coll		25, 27, 28
† Biffen (W.) J.	1930	. .	Dr Morgan's G.S.*	Cambridge	38[3], 42
† Bingley 1st Ld (1933). G. R. Lane-Fox	1870	1947	Eton	Oxford	10, 12
† Birch, (E.) N.C., Ld Rhyl (Life Peer 1970)	1906	1981	Eton		24[3], 25, 26
Birk, Lady (Life Peeress 1967). Alma Blrk	1921	. .	Hampstead H.S.*	London	35, 36, 38
† Birkenhead. 1st E of (1922) Sir F. E. Smith (Kt 1915). 1st Ld Birkenhead (1919). 1st Vt (1921)	1872	1930	Birkenhead	Oxford	6[3], 9, 11
Birkenhead, 2nd E of (1930) F. W. F. Smith. Vt Furneaux (1922)	1907	1975	Eton	Oxford	17, 26
Birnam, Ld (Scot. judge 1945). Sir (T.) D. K. Murray (Kt 1941)	1884	1955	Hamilton Acad.* & Glasgow H.S.*	Glasgow	20, 21
† Birrell, A.	1850	1933	Amersham Hall*	Cambridge	3[2], 4, 6
Bishopston, Ld (Life Peer 1981). E. S. Bishop	1920	1984	S. Bristol C.S.*	Bristol	32, 36[2]
Blades. Ld (Scot. judge 1947). D. P. Blades	1888	1959	Berwickshire	Edinburgh	23
† Blakenham. 1st Vt (1963). J. H. Hare	1911	1982	Eton		24, 25, 26, 27[2], 28
† Blaker, Sir P. A. R. (K.C.M.G 1983)	1922	. .	Shrewsbury	Toronto & Oxford	33[2], 38, 39
† Blatch, Lady (Life Peeress 1987) Emily Blatch	1937	. .	Secondary		40, 44[3], 45[2]
† Bledisloe, 1st Vt (1935), Sir C. Bathurst (K.B.E 1917), 1st Ld Bledisloe (1918)	1867	1958	Sherborne & Eton	Oxford	7, 11
Blenkinsop, A.	1911	1979	R.G.S. Newcastle upon Tyne		22, 23[2]
Blindell, Sir J. (Kt 1936)	1884	1937	St. Mary's, Hitchin		15, 17
Boardman, Ld (Life Peer 1980). T. G. Boardman	1919	. .	Bromsgrove		33, 34
Bondfield. Miss M. G.	1873	1953	Elementary		11, 13
† Booth, A. E.	1928	. .	St. Thomas S. Winchester*		36[2]
† Boothby, Ld (Life Peer 1958), Sir R. J. G. Boothby (K.B.E. 1953)	1900	1986	Eton	Oxford	18
† Boothroyd, Miss B.	1929	. .	Dewsbury Tech.C.*		37
† Boscawen, R. T.	1923	. .	Eton	Cambridge	43[4]
Boston of Faversham, Ld (Life Peer 1976). T. G. Boston	1930	. .	Woolwich Poly- technic Sch.*	London	33, 36
Boswell, T. E.	1944	. .	Marlborough	Oxford	43, 45, 46[2]
† Bottomley, Ld (Life Peer). A. G. Bottomley	1907	. .	Elementary		22[2], 23, 30, 31
Bottomley, P. J.	1944	. .	Westminster	Cambridge	40, 41, 42
† Bottomley, Mrs V. H. B. M.	1948	. .	Putney H.S.	Essex & London	40, 41, 45[2]
Boulton, Sir W. W. (1st Bt 1944)	1873	1949	Privately		17, 20[2]
Bowden, Ld (Life Peer 1964). B. V. Bowden	1910	1989	Chesterfield G.S.*	Cambridge	30

Name	Born	Died	School	University	Pages
† Bowden, H. W., Ld Aylestone (Life Peer 1967)	1905	1994	Secondary		23, 29, 30
Bowis, J. C.	1945	. .	Tonbridge	Oxford	45
Bowles, Ld (Life Peer 1964). F. G. Bowles	1902	1970	Highgate	London	33
Bowyer, Sir G. E. W. (Kt 1929). 1st Ld Denham (1937)	1886	1948	Eton	Oxford	12, 15, 17
† Boyd, 1st Vt (1960). A. T. Lennox-Boyd	1904	1983	Sherborne	Oxford	15, 16^2, 18, 20, 24^2, 25, 27
Boyd-Carpenter, Sir A. B. (Kt 1926)	1873	1937	Harrow	Oxford	10^4
† Boyd-Carpenter, Ld (Life Peer 1972). J. A. Boyd-Carpenter	1908	. .	Stowe	Oxford	24, 25^2, 27, 28
Boyden, H. J.	1910	. .	Tiffin*	London	30^2, 31
† Boyle, Ld Boyle of Handsworth (Life Peer 1970), Sir E. C. G. (3rd Bt 1945)	1923	1981	Eton	Oxford	24, 25, 26, 27^3
† Boyson, R. R.	1925	. .	Haslingden G.S.*	Manchester & Cambridge	40^2, 41^2
† Brabazon, 1st Ld (1942). J. T. C. Moore-Brabazon	1884	1964	Harrow	Cambridge	10, 12, 18, 19
Brabazon, 3rd Ld (1974) I. A. Moore-Brabazon	1946	. .	Harrow		38, 42^2, 44, 46
Brabner, R. A.	1911	1945	Felstead	Cambridge	18
† Brace, W.	1865	1947	Elementary		5, 7
† Bracken, 1st Vt (1952). B. Bracken	1901	1958	Sedbergh		18, 20
Bradford, 5th E of (1915). O. Bridgeman, Vt Newport (1898)	1873	1957	Harrow	Cambridge	9, 10
† Braine, Ld. (Life Peer 1992) Sir B. R. Braine (Kt 1972)	1914	. .	Hendon C.S.*		27^2, 28
Braithwaite, Sir J. G. (1st Bt 1954)	1895	1958	Bootham		25
Brand, Ld (Scot. judge 1972). D. W. R. Brand	1923	. .	Stonyhurst	Edinburgh	35
Bray, J. W.	1930	. .	Kingswood	Cambridge	31, 32
Brayley, Ld (Life Peer 1973). Sir J. D. Brayley (Kt 1970)	1917	1977	Secondary		36
† Brecon, 1st Ld (1957) D. V. P. Lewis	1905	1976	Monmouth*		27
† Brentford, 1st Vt (1929). Sir W. Joynson-Hicks (1st Bt 1919.)	1865	1932	Merchant Taylors' Sch.		10^4, 11
Brentford, 3rd Vt (1958). L. W. Joynson-Hicks	1902	1983	Winchester	Oxford	24
† Brldgeman, 1st Vt (1929). W. C. Bridgeman	1864	1935	Eton	Cambridge	6, 8^3, 11
Bridport, 3rd Vt (1924). R. A. H. N. Hood	1911	1969	R.N. Coll., Dartmouth		17
† Brittan, Sir L. (Kt 1986)	1939	. .	Haberdasher's Aske's	Cambridge	38, 39^2, 42
† Brodrick. (W) St J. 9th Vt Midleton (1907). 1st E of (1920)	1856	1942	Eton	Oxford	1, 2^2
Bromley-Davenport, Sir W. (K.C.B. 1924)	1862	1949	Eton	Oxford	2
† Brooke of Cumnor, Ld (Life Peer 1966). H. Brooke	1903	1984	Marlborough	Oxford	24, 26, 27^2
† Brooke, P. L	1934	. .	Marlborough	Oxford	38, 40, 41^2, 43^2, 45^2
Brooman-White, R. C.	1912	1964	Eton	Cambridge	28, 29^2
† Brown, (A.) E.	1881	1962	Torquay*		14^2, 16, 18^2, 19, 20

† Brown, G. A., Ld George-Brown (Life Peer 1970)	1914	1985	Secondary		22, 23, 29², 30
Brown, H. D.	1919	..	Whitehill S.S.*		37
Brown, M. R.	1951	..	Littlehampton Boys. S*	York	46
Brown, R. C.	1921	..	Elementary		32, 36²
Brown, R. W.	1921	..	Elementary		32
Brown, T. W.	1879	1944	Campbell Coll.	Belfast	9²
† Brown. Ld (Life Peer 1964). W. Brown	1908	1985	Rossall	..	32
† Browne, J. N., Ld Craigton (Life Peer 1959)	1904	1993	Cheltenham		25, 28²
Browning, Mrs. Angela F.	1946	..	Reading		44
† Broxbourne, Ld (Life Peer 1983). Sir D. C. Walker-Smith (Bt 1960)	1910	1992	Rossall	Oxford	24, 25, 27, 28
Bruce-Gardyne, Ld (Life Peer 1983). J. Bruce-Gardyne	1930	1990	Winchester	Oxford	38²
Bruntisfield, 1st Ld (1942). Sir V. A. G. A. Warrender (8th Bt 1917)	1899	1993	Eton		14, 15⁴, 17, 18, 20
Bryan, Sir P. E. O. (Kt 1972)	1913	..	St John's, Leatherhead	Cambridge	29, 34
† Bryce, 1st Vt (1914). J. Bryce	1838	1922	Glasgow H.S.*	Glasgow & Oxford	3
Buchan, N.	1922	1990	Kirkwall G.S.*	Glasgow	32, 36
† Buchan-Hepburn, P. G. T. 1st Ld Hailes (1957)	1901	1974	Harrow	Cambridge	17, 20², 21, 25²
† Buchanan, G.	1890	1955	Elementary		22, 23
† Buchanan, T. R.	1846	1911	Sherborne	Oxford	3, 4
† Buchanan-Smith, A. L.	1932	1991	Edinburgh Acad.	Cambridge	34, 39, 40
Buck, Sir (P.) A. F. (Kt 1983)	1928	..	King's Sch., Ely	Cambridge	33
Buckley, A.	1877	1965	Merchant Taylor's, Crosby		10²
† Buckmaster, 1st Vt (1933). Sir S. O. Buckmaster (Kt 1913). 1st Ld (1915)	1861	1934	Aldenham	Oxford	5²
Budgen, N.	1937	..	St Edward's	Cambridge	43
Burden, 1st Ld (1950). T. W. Burden	1885	1970	Elementary	London	23
† Burgin, (E.) L.	1887	1945	Christ's Coll., Finchley*	Lausanne & Paris	14, 16⁴
Burke, W. A.	1890	1968	Secondary		23
† Burns, J.	1858	1943	Elementary		3, 4²
Burns, S. H. M.	1952	..	Stamford*	Oxford	46
Burntwood, Ld (Life Peer 1970). J. W. Snow	1910	1982	Haileybury		23², 30, 31²
Burt, A. J. H.	1955	..	Bury G.S.	Oxford	45
Butcher, Sir H. W. (Kt 1953)	1901	1966	Hastings G.S.*		25
Butcher, J. P.	1946	..	Huntingdon G.S.*	*Birmingham & London	40, 41, 42
† Butler of Saffron Walden, Ld (Life Peer 1965). R. A. Butler	1902	1982	Marlborough	Cambridge	14, 15, 16², 17, 18, 21, 24², 26⁴
† Butler, Sir A. C.(Kt 1986)	1931	..	Eton	Cambridge	35, 39, 41²
† Buxton, 1st E (1920). S. C. Buxton, 1st Vt (1914)	1853	1934	Clifton	Cambridge	3, 4²
† Buxton, N. E. N. 1st Ld Noel-Buxton (1930)	1869	1948	Harrow	Cambridge	11, 12
† Cadogan, 5th E (1873). Vt Chelsea (1864)	1840	1915	Eton	Oxford	2
† Caithness, 20th E (1965). M. I. Sinclair	1948	..	Marlborough		38, 39, 40, 41, 42, 43, 44, 46

† Caldecote, 1st Vt (1939). Sir T.W.H. Inskip (Kt 1922)	1876	1947	Clifton	Cambridge	10, 12^2, 14^2, 15^2, 16, 17, 18
† Callaghan of Cardiff, Ld (Life Peer 1987). (L.) J. Callaghan	1912	..	Portsmouth N.Sec.*		22, 23, 29, 30, 35, 36
† Cameron of Lochbroom, Ld (Life Peer 1984). K. J. Cameron	1931	..	Edinburgh Acad.	Oxford & Edinburgh	42
† Campbell, of Croy, Ld (Life Peer 1974). G.T.C. Campbell	1921	..	Wellington		28, 29, 34
† Campbell, Sir J. H. M. (1st Bt 1916). 1st Ld Glenavy (1921)	1851	1931	Kingstown*	Dublin	2^2, 6, 9^2
† Campbell-Bannerman, Sir H. (G.C.B. 1895)	1836	1908	Glasgow H.S.*	Glasgow	3
† Caradon, Ld (Life Peer 1964). Sir H. Foot (K.C.M.G. 1951)	1907	1990	Leighton Park	Cambridge	30
Carlisle, K. M.	1941	..	Eton		39, 43^2, 44, 46
† Carlisle of Bucklow, Ld (Life Peer 1987) M. Carlisle	1929	..	Radley	Manchester	33^2, 39
Carmichael, Ld (Life Peer 1983). N. G. Carmichael	1921	..	Estbank Acad.*		32^2, 36, 37
† Carr of Hadley, Ld (Life Peer 1975) R. Carr	1916	..	Westminster	Cambridge	25, 27, 28, 33^2, 34
† Carrington, 1st E (1895). C. R. Wynn-Carrington, 3rd Ld Carrington (1868), 1st M of Lincolnshire (1912)	1843	1928	Eton	Cambridge	3, 4^2
† Carrington, 6th Ld (1938) P. A. R. Carington	1919	..	Eton	Sandhurst	24^2, 26, 28, 33, 34, 38
† Carson, Ld (Lord of Appeal 1921). Sir E. H. Carson (Kt 1900)	1854	1935	Portarlington*	Dublin	2, 6, 7, 8
Carter, Ld (Life Peer 1987) R. J. Carter	1935	..	Mortlake Co. S.S.*		37
Cary, Sir R. A. (1st Bt 1955)	1898	1979	Ardingly	Sandhurst	21
† Casey, Ld (Life Peer 1960). R. G. Casey	1890	1976	Melbourne G.S.	Melbourne & Cambridge	18
† Castle of Blackburn, Lady (Life Peeress 1990) Mrs B. A. Castle	1911	..	Bradford G.G.S.	Oxford	29, 31^2, 32, 36
† Causton, R. K. 1st Ld Southwark (1910)	1843	1929	Privately		3, 4
† Cave. 1st Vt (1918). Sir G. Cave (Kt 1915)	1856	1928	Merchant Taylors'	Oxford	6, 7, 9, 11
† Cavendish, V. C. W. 9th D of Devonshire (1908)	1868	1938	Eton	Cambridge	1, 2, 5, 10
† Cawdor, 3rd E (1898). F. A. V. Campbell. Vt Emlyn (1847)	1847	1911	Eton	Oxford	1
† Cawley, 1st Ld (1918). Sir F. Cawley (1st Bt 1906)	1850	1937	Secondary		8
Cazalet-Keir, Mrs T.	1899	1989	Privately		20
† Cecil of Chelwood, 1st Vt (1923). Ld R. Cecil	1864	1958	Eton	Oxford	5^3, 7^2, 9, 12
Chadwick. Sir (R.) B. (Kt 1920)	1869	1951	Birkenhead & Privately		12
† Chalfont, Ld (Life Peer 1964). A. Gwynne-Jones	1919	..	W. Monmouth S.*		30
† Chalker, Lady (Life Peeress 1992). Mrs. L Chalker	1942	..	Roedean	London	38, 39, 41, 42^2, 44
† Chamberlain, (A.) N.	1869	1940	Rugby	Birmingham	6, 8, 9, 10^3, 11, 13, 15^2, 17
† Chamberlain, J.	1836	1914	University Coll. Sch.		2
† Chamberlain, Sir (J.) A. (K.G. 1925)	1863	1937	Rugby	Cambridge	1^3, 2, 6^4, 7, 8, 11, 13

Name	Born	Died	School	University	Pages
Chambers, J.	1863	1917	Royal Acad. Institution	Belfast	9
† Champion, Ld (Life Peer 1962) A. J. Champion	1897	1985	St. John's. Glastonbury*		22, 31
† Chandos, 1st Vt (1954). O. Lyttelton	1893	1972	Eton	Cambridge	18, 19^3, 21^2, 24
† Channon. (H) P.G.	1935	. .	Eton	Oxford	34^4, 38, 39^2, 42^3
† Chaplin. 1st Vt (1916), H. Chaplin	1840	1923	Harrow	Oxford	2
Chapman, A.	1897	1966	Secondary	Cambridge	19^2, 21
Chapman, S. B.	1935	. .	Rugby	Manchester	43^2, 46^2
Charleton, H C.	1870	1959	Elementary		13
† Chataway, C. J	1931	. .	Sherborne	Oxford	27^2, 34, 35
† Chatfield, 1st Ld (1937). Sir A. E. M. Chatfield (K.C.M.G. 1919)	1873	1967	H.M.S., Britannia*		15
† Chelmsford, 1st Vt (1921). F. J. N. Thesiger. 3rd Ld Chelmsford (1905)	1868	1933	Winchester	Oxford	11
Cherry, R. R.	1859	1923	Secondary	Dublin	3, 5
† Cherwell.,1st Vt (1956). F. A. Lindemann. 1st Ld Cherwell (1941)	1886	1957	Blair Lodge* & Darmstadt	Berlin	19, 21, 25
Chesham, 3rd Ld (1882)	1850	1907	Eton		3
† Chesham. 5th Ld (1952). J. C. C. Cavendish	1916	1989	Eton	Cambridge	26, 28, 29
† Chesterfield, 10th E of (1887) E. F. S.-Stanhope	1854	1933	Eton	Oxford	5, 6, 9
Chichester-Clark, Sir R. (Kt 1974)	1928	. .	R.N. College*	Cambridge	29^2, 34
† Chilston, 1st Vt (1911). A. Akers-Douglas	1851	1926	Eton	Oxford	1, 2
Chope, C. R.	1947	. .	Marlborough	St.Andrews	40, 42, 46
Chorley, 1st Ld (1945). R. S.T. Chorley	1895	1978	Kendal*	Oxford	23
Churchill, 1st Vt (1902). V. A. F. S. Churchill, 3rd Ld (1886)	1864	1934	Eton	Sandhurst	3
† Churchill, Sir W. L. S. (K.G. 1953)	1874	1965	Harrow	Sandhurst	3, 4^3, 6, 7^2, 8^2, 11, 15, 17, 20, 24^2
† Chuter-Ede, Ld (Life Peer 1964) J.C. Ede	1882	1965	Dorking H.S.*	Cambridge	18, 21
† Cilcennin, 1st Vt (1955). J. P. L. Thomas	1903	1960	Rugby	Oxford	18, 20^2, 24
Clarendon 5th E of (1870). E. H. Villiers, Ld Hyde (1846)	1846	1914	Harrow	Cambridge	2, 3
Clarendon, 6th E of (1914). G. H. H. Villiers, Ld Hyde (1877)	1877	1955	Eton		9, 10, 11, 12
† Clark, A. K. M.	1928	. .	Eton	Oxford	39, 40, 42, 44
† Clarke, K. H.	1940	. .	Nottingham H.S.	Cambridge	35^2, 39, 40, 41^4, 42^2, 44^3
† Cledwyn of Penrhos, Ld (Life Peer 1979). C. Hughes	1916	. .	Holyhead G.S.	Aberystwyth	30^2, 32
Clegg, Sir W. (Kt 1980)	1920	1994	Bury G.S.	Manchester	35^3
Clifden, 7th Vt (1930). F. G. Agar-Robartes	1883	1966	Eton	Oxford	20
† Clinton, 21st Ld (1904). C. J. R. H.-S.-F.-Trefusis	1863	1957	Eton		7
Clinton Davis, Ld (Life Peer 1990) S. C. Davis	1928	. .	Mercer's Sch.*	London	37
† Clitheroe, 1st Ld (1955). R. Assheton	1901	1984	Eton	Oxford	16, 17, 18, 19

† Clyde, Ld (Scot. judge 1920). J. A. Clyde	1863	1944	Edinburgh Academy	Edinburgh	2, 9
† Clyde, Ld (Scot.judge 1954). J. L. M. Clyde	1898	1975	Edinburgh Academy	Oxford & Edinburgh	25
† Clydesmuir, 1st Ld (1947). Sir D. J. Colville (G.C.I.E. 1943)	1894	1954	Charterhouse	Cambridge	14, 15, 16³
† Clynes, J. R.	1869	1949	Elementary		7², 11, 12
Cobham, 9th Vt (1922). J. C. Lyttelton	1881	1949	Eton		16
Cochrane of Cults, 1st Ld (1919). T. H. A. E. Cochrane	1857	1951	Eton		1
† Cockfield, Ld (Life Peer 1978). Sir A. C. Cockfield (Kt 1973)	1916	. .	Dover County*	London	38, 41, 42
† Cocks of Hartcliffe, (Life Peer 1987) M. F. L. Cocks	1929	. .	Secondary	Bristol	37³
† Colebrooke, 1st Ld (1906). Sir E. A. Colebrooke (5th Bt 1890)	1861	1939	Eton		3, 5², 6, 9
Coleman, D. R.	1925	1991	Cadoxton Boys' S.*		37, 38
† Coleraine, 1st Ld (1954). R. K. Law	1901	1980	Shrewsbury	Oxford	17, 19², 20
Collick, P. H.	1897	1984	Elementary		22
Collindridge, F.	1890	1951	Elementary		23²
† Collings, J.	1831	1920	Plymouth*		1
† Collins, Sir G. P. (K.B.E. 1919)	1875	1936	H.M.S. Britannia*		9, 14, 16
† Collins, V. J. Ld Stonham (Life Peer 1958)	1903	1971	Regent St. Poly.*	London	30²
Colnbrook, Ld. (Life Peer 1987) Atkins, Sir H. E. (K.C.M.G. 1983)	1922	. .	Wellington		35², 38, 41
† Colville, Sir D. J. (G.C.I.E. 1943). 1st Ld Clydesmuir (1947)	1894	1954	Charterhouse	Cambridge	14, 15, 16³
Colville of Culross, 4th Vt. (1945). J. M A. Colville	1933	. .	Rugby	Oxford	33
† Colyton, 1st Ld (1956). H. L D. Hopkinson	1902	. .	Eton	Cambridge	24, 25
† Compton-Rickett, Sir J. (Kt 1907)	1847	1919	K. Edward VI, Bath*		8
Conant, Sir R. J. E. (1st Bt 1954)	1899	1973	Eton	Sandhurst	26
† Concannon, (J.) D.	1930	. .	Rossington S.S *		33, 37², 38
Conesford, 1st Ld (1955). H. G. Strauss	1892	1974	Rugby	Oxford	19, 20, 25
Constable, Ld (Scot. judge 1922). A. H. B. Constable	1865	1928	Dollar*	Edinburgh	9
Conway, D.	1953	. .	Beacon Hill*		46²
Cook, T. F.	1908	1952	Cardenden*		22
† Cooper. A. Duff, 1st Vt Norwich (1952)	1890	1954	Eton	Oxford	12, 13, 14, 15², 16, 18²
† Cooper of Culross, 1st Ld (1954). T. M. Cooper	1892	1955	George Watson's Edinburgh	Edinburgh	14, 17, 20
Cope, 1st Ld (1945). Sir W. Cope (1st Bt 1928)	1870	1946	Repton	Cambridge	10, 12²
† Cope, Sir J. A. (Kt 1991)	1937	. .	Oakham		40, 41, 43³, 45
† Corfield, Sir F. V. (Kt 1974)	1915	. .	Cheltenham	Woolwich	27.33, 34²
† Cornwall, Sir E (Kt 1905)	1863	1953	Elementary		9
† Cousins, F.	1904	1986	Elementary		32
† Coventry, 9th E of (1843)	1838	1930	Eton	Oxford	3
† Cowdray, 1st Vt (1916). Sir W. D. Pearson, 1st Bt (1894). 1st Ld (1910)	1856	1927	Privately		7
Cowley, 6th E (1968). R. F. Wellesley	1946	1975	Eton	Birmingham	35
Cox, Lady (Life Peeress 1982). Mrs C. A. Cox	1937	. .	Channing Sch.*	London	44

Cox, T. M.	1930	..	Secondary	London	37[2]
† Craig, C. C.	1869	1960	Clifton		10
† Craig, Sir J. (Bt 1918). 1st Vt Craigavon (1927)	1871	1940	Merchiston Castle		7, 8, 9
† Craigavon, 1st Vt (1927). Sir J. Craig (1st Bt 1918)	1871	1940	Merchiston Castle		7, 8, 9
Craigmyle, 1st Ld (1929). T. Shaw. Ld Shaw (Ld of Appeal 1909)	1850	1937	Dunfermline H.S.*	Edinburgh	3, 5
† Craigton, Ld (Life Peer 1959). J. N. Browne	1904	1993	Cheltenham		25, 28[2]
† Cranborne, Vt (1865). R. A. T. Gascoyne-Cecil, 3rd M of Salisbury (1868)	1830	1903	Eton	Oxford	1[3]
† Cranborne, Vt (1868). J. E. H. Gascoyne-Cecil, 4th M of Salisbury (1903)	1861	1947	Eton	Oxford	1[2], 2, 9, 10, 11
† Cranborne, Vt (1903). R. A. J. Gascoyne-Cecil, 5th M of Salisbury (1947)	1893	1972	Eton	Oxford	15, 17, 18[3], 19, 20, 24[3], 26
† Cranborne, Vt (1972) R. M. J. Gascoyne-Cecil, (sits as Ld Cecil of Essendon by writ of acceleration 1992)	1946	..	Eton	Oxford	44[2]
† Crathorne, 1st Ld (1959). Sir T. L. Dugdale (1st Bt 1945)	1897	1977	Eton	Sandhurst	17, 20, 20, 24[2]
Craven, 4th E of (1883). W. G. R. Craven	1868	1921	Eton		5
† Crawford, 27th E of (1913). D. A. E. Lindsay, Ld Balcarres (1880)	1871	1940	Eton	Oxford	2, 5, 6, 8[2], 9[2]
† Crawford, 29th E of (1975). R. A. Lindsay. Ld Balniel (1940) (Life Peer 1974)	1927	..	Eton	Cambridge	33[2]
Crawley, A. M.	1908	1993	Harrow	Oxford	22
† Crewe, 1st M of (1911). R. O. A. Crewe-Milnes, 2nd Ld Houghton (1885). 1st E of Crewe (1895)	1858	1945	Harrow	Cambridge	3, 4[2], 5[2], 14
† Crickhowell, Ld (Life Peer 1987). (R.) N. Edwards	1934	..	Westminster	Cambridge	42
† Cripps, Sir (R.) S. (Kt 1930)	1889	1952	Winchester	London	13, 17, 18, 21[2], 23
Croft, 1st Ld (1940). Sir H. Page Croft (1st Bt 1924)	1881	1947	Eton & Shrewsbury	Cambridge	19, 21
† Cromer, 2nd E of (1917). R. T. Baring, Vt Errington (1901)	1877	1953	Eton		10
† Crookshank, 1st Vt (1956). H. F. C. Crookshank	1893	1961	Eton	Oxford	13, 15, 16, 17, 19, 21, 24[2]
† Crosland, (C.) A. R.	1918	1977	Highgate	Oxford	29[2], 30, 31, 32, 36[2]
† Cross, 1st Vt (1886). R. Cross	1823	1914	Rugby	Cambridge	1
† Cross, Sir R. H. (1st Bt 1941)	1896	1968	Eton		16[2], 17[2], 19
† Crossley, Sir S. B. (2nd Bt 1872). 1st Ld Somerleyton (1916)	1857	1935	Eton	Oxford	2, 9, 10
† Crossman, R. H. S.	1907	1974	Winchester	Oxford	29, 31[2]
Crowther-Hunt, Ld (Life Peer 1973). N. C. Hunt	1920	1987	Bellevue H.S. Bradford*	Cambridge	35, 36
Cryer, (G.) R.	1934	1994	Salt H.S.*	Hull	37
Cullen of Ashbourne, (2nd Ld 1932). C. B. M. Cokayne	1912	..	Eton		43

Name	Born	Died	School	University	Pages
Cumberlege, Lady (Life Peeress 1990) Mrs J. Cumberlege	1943	. .	Sacred Heart Tunbridge Wells*		45
† Cunliffe-Lister, Sir P. (K.B.E.) 1920). (*Born Lloyd-Greame, changed name to Cunliffe-Lister 1924*). 1st Vt Swinton (1935). 1st E of Swinton (1955)	1884	1972	Winchester	Oxford	8^2, 10, 12, 14^2, 15, 18^2, 20, 24, 25^2
† Cunningham, J. A.	1939	. .	Jarrow G.S.*	Durham	36
Currie, Mrs E.	1946	. .	Liverpool Inst.for Girls*	Oxford	41
Curry, D. M.	1944	. .	Ripon G.S.	Oxford	39, 44^2, 45
† Curzon, 1st M (1921). G. N. Curzon. 1st Ld Curzon of Kedleston (1898). 1st E (1911)	1859	1925	Eton	Oxford	5, 6^2, 7, 10, 11
Curzon, Vt (1876). R. G. P. Curzon. 4th Earl Howe (1900)	1861	1929	Eton	Oxford	2, 3
Curzon. Vt (1900). F. R. H. P. Curzon, 5th Earl Howe (1929)	1884	1964	Eton	Oxford	12
Cushendun, 1st Ld (1927). R. J. McNeill	1861	1934	Harrow	Oxford	10, 11^2, 12
† Dalton, Ld (Life Peer 1960). (E.) H. J. N. Dalton	1887	1962	Eton	Cambridge	12, 18, 19, 21, 22, 23
† Darling of Hillsborough, Ld (Life Peer 1974). G. Darling	1905	1985	Elementary	Liverpool & Cambridge	32
Darwen, 1st Ld (1946). J. P. Davies	1885	1950	Bootham		23
† Daryngton, 1st Ld (1923). H. Pike Pease	1867	1949	Brighton Coll	Cambridge	6, 8
David, Lady (Life Peeress 1978). Mrs N. R. David	1913	. .	St Felix S.	Cambridge	38
† Davidson, 1st Vt(1937). Sir J. C. C. Davidson (G.C.V.O. 1935)	1889	1970	Westminster	Cambridge	10, 11, 14, 16
Davidson, 2nd Vt (1970). J. A. Davidson	1928	. .	Westminster	Cambridge	43, 44, 46
Davidson, A.	1928	. .	King George Sch., Southport*	Cambridge	37
Davies, B.	1939	. .	Redditch H.S.*	London	37
† Davies, (D. J.) D.	1938	. .	Carmarthen G.S.*	Oxford	36
Davies, E. A.	1926	1991	Coventry Tech. Sch.*	St.Andrews' & Cambridge	32
Davies, E. A. J.	1902	1985	Wycliffe Coll.	London	21
Davies, Sir G. F. (Kt 1936)	1875	1950	Uppingham	Cambridge	15, 17^3
† Davies of Leek, Ld (Life Peer 1970). H. Davies	1904	1984	Lewis Sch.*	London	31, 32
Davies, I.	1910	1984	Elementary		32^2
† Davies, J. E. H. (Life Peer 1979)	1916	1979	St. Edward's		34^3
Davies, R. J.	1877	1954	Elementary		11
Davis, S. C., Ld Clinton-Davies (Life Peer 1990)	1928	. .	Mercers' Sch.*	London	37
Davis, D. M.	1945	. .	Bec G.S.*	London & Harvard	44^2, 45, 46
Davison, J. E.	1870	1927	Elementary		11
Dawson, T.	1948	. .	R.High S. Edinburgh*	Edinburgh	45
Deakins, E. P.	1932	. .	Tottenham G.S.*	London	36, 37
† Dean, Sir (A.) P. (Kt 1985)	1924	. .	Ellesmere Coll.	Oxford	34

Dean of Beswick, Ld (Life Peer 1983). J. Dean	1923	..	St. Anne, Ancoats*		37
Deedes, Ld (Life Peer 1986). W. F. Deedes	1913	..	Harrow		24^2, 28
de Ferranti, B. R. Z.	1930	1988	Eton	Cambridge	27
de Freitas, Sir G. S. (K.C.M.G. 1961)	1913	1982	Haileybury	Cambridge	21, 22
Delacourt-Smith, Ld (Life Peer 1967). C. G. P. Smith	1917	1972	County Boys Sch. Windsor*	Oxford	32
De La Warr, 9th E (1915). H. E. D. B. Sackville, Ld Buckhurst (1900)	1900	1976	Eton	Oxford	11, 12, 13^2, 14, 15^3, 16^2, 17, 25
† De L'Isle, 1st Vt (1956). W. P. Sydney, 6th Ld De L'Isle & Dudley (1945)	1909	1991	Eton	Cambridge	21, 24
† Dell, E.	1921	..	Owen's Sch.*	Oxford	30, 31, 32^2, 35, 37
Denbigh, 9th E of (1892). R. B. A. A. Fielding	1859	1939	Oscott Coll., Birmingham*	Woolwich	3
Denham, 1st Ld (1937). Sir G. E. W. Bowyer (Kt 1929).	1886	1948	Eton	Oxford	12, 15, 17
† Denham, 2nd Ld (1948). B. S. M. Bowyer	1927	..	Eton	Cambridge	29, 35^2, 43, 46
† Denman, 3rd Ld (1894). T. Denman	1874	1954	Wellington	Sandhurst	3^2, 5
Denton of Wakefield, Lady, (Life Peeress 1991). Miss J. Denton	1935	..	Rothwell G.S.*	London	45^2, 46^2
Derby, 17th E of (1908). E. G. V. Stanley, Ld Stanley (1893)	1865	1948	Wellington		2^3, 6, 8, 10
Derwent, 4th Ld (1949). P. V. B. Johnstone	1901	1986	Charterhouse	Sandhurst	26, 28
Desborough, 1st Ld (1905) W. H. Grenfell	1855	1945	Harrow	Oxford	12
† Devonport, 1st Vt (1917). Sir H. E. Kearley (1st Bt 1908), 1st Ld Devonport (1910)	1856	1934	Cranleigh		3, 4, 7
† Devonshire, 8th D of (1891). S. C. Cavendish, M of Hartington (1858)	1833	1908	Privately	Cambridge	1, 2
† Devonshire, 9th D of (1908). V. C. W. Cavendish	1868	1938	Eton	Cambridge	1, 2, 5, 10
Devonshire, 10th D of (1938). E. W. S. Cavendish, M of Hartington (1908)	1895	1950	Eton	Cambridge	16, 18^2, 20
† Devonshire, 11th D of (1950). A. R. B. Cavendish, M of Hartington (1944)	1920	..	Eton	Cambridge	27^2
Dewar, Ld (Scot. judge 1910). A. Dewar	1860	1917	Perth Academy*	Edinburgh	5
† Diamond, Ld Diamond (Life Peer 1970). J. Diamond	1907	..	Leeds G.S.		29^2
Dickson, Ld (Scot. judge 1915). S. Dickson	1850	1922	Glasgow H.S.*	Glasgow & Edinburgh	2^2
Digby, (K.) S. D W.	1910	..	Harrow	Cambridge	24
† Dilhorne, 1st Ld (1962). 1st Vt (1964). Sir R. E. Manningham-Buller (Kt 1951) (4th Bt 1956)	1905	1980	Eton	Oxford	21, 25^2, 26, 28
Dobson, R. F. H.	1925	..	Purbrook Park G.S.*	Oxford	33
Dodds-Parker, Sir A. D. (Kt 1973)	1909	..	Winchester	Oxford	24^3

Name	Born	Died	School	University	Pages
Donaldson, Ld (Life Peer 1967). J. G. S. Donaldson	1907	. .	Eton	Cambridge	36, 37
† Donoughmore, 6th E of (1900). R. W. J. Hely-Hutchinson	1875	1948	Eton	Oxford	2
Dormand, Ld (Life Peer 1987). J. D. Dormand	1919	. .	Bede Coll.*	Oxford & Harvard	37^2
† Dorman-Smith, Sir R. H. (Kt 1937)	1899	1977	Harrow	Sandhurst	15
† Dorrell, S. J.	1952	. .	Uppingham	Oxford	41, 43^2, 44, 45^2
Douglas-Hamilton, Ld J.	1942	. .	Eton	Oxford	42, 43, 45
† Douglas-Home, Sir A. F., (K.T. 1962) Ld Dunglass (1918), 14th E of Home (1951–63). Ld Home of the Hirsel (Life Peer 1974)	1903	. .	Eton	Oxford	20, 24, 25, 26^4, 27, 33
Doverdale, 2nd Ld (1925). O. Partington	1872	1935	Rossall		5
† Downham, 1st Ld (1918). W. Hayes Fisher	1853	1920	Haileybury	Oxford	1, 2, 6, 7, 8^2
Drewe, Sir C. (K.C.V.O 1953)	1896	1971	Eton	Woolwich	20, 21, 26
† Drumalbyn, 1st Ld (1963). N. M. S. Macpherson	1908	1987	Fettes	Oxford	25, 28^4, 34
† du Cann, Sir E. D. L. (K.B.E. 1985)	1924	. .	Woodbridge*	Oxford	26, 28
† Dudley, 2nd E (1885). W. H. Ward, Vt Ednam (1867)	1867	1932	Eton		2
Dufferin & Ava, 4th M of (1930). B. S. H.-T.-Blackwood, E of Ava (1918)	1909	1945	Eton	Oxford	15, 17
Duffy, Sir (A. E.) P. (Kt 1991)	1920	. .	Secondary	London & Columbia, N.Y.	36
† Dugdale, J.	1905	1963	Wellington	Oxford	22^2
† Dugdale, Sir T. L. (1st Bt 1945) 1st Ld Crathorne (1959)	1897	1977	Eton	Sandhurst	17, 20, 24^2
† Duke, Sir H. E. (Kt 1918). 1st Ld Merrivale (1925).	1855	1939	Elementary		6, 7
† Duncan, Sir A. R. (Kt 1921)	1884	1952	Secondary	Glasgow	16, 19^4, 21
† Duncan-Sandys, Ld (Life Peer 1974). D. Sandys	1908	1987	Eton	Oxford	19^2, 20, 21, 24, 25, 27^4
Dundas, Ld (Scot.judge 1905). D. Dundas	1854	1922	Edinburgh Academy	Oxford & Edinburgh	2
† Dundee, 11th E of (1953). H. J. Scrymgeour-Wedderburn, Vt Dudhope (1952)	1902	1983	Winchester	Oxford	16, 19, 26, 28
Dundee, 12th E of (1983). A. H. Scrymgeour, Vt Scrymgeour (1949)	1949	. .	Eton	St Andrews	44
Dunedin, 1st Vt (1926). A. G. Murray, 1st Ld Dunedin (1905)	1849	1942	Harrow	Cambridge	2^2
† Dunglass, Ld (1918). Sir A. F. Douglas-Home (K.T. 1962). 14th E of Home (1951–63). Ld Home of the Hirsel (Life Peer 1974)	1903	. .	Eton	Oxford	20, 24, 25, 26^4, 27, 33
Dunn, J. A.	1926	. .	St. Theresa's Sch.*	London	37^2
Dunn, R. J.	1946	. .	Cromwell Rd., Pendlebury*	Salford	40
† Dunrossil, 1st Vt (1959). W. S. Morrison	1893	1961	George Watson's Edinburgh	Edinburgh	15^2, 16^2, 19^2, 21
Dunwoody, Mrs G.	1930	. .	Notre Dame Convent*		32
Dunwoody, J. E. O.	1929	. .	St. Paul's	London	31
Durant, Sir (R.) T. (Kt 1991)	1928	. .	Bryanston		43^3

Name	Born	Died	School	University	Pages
Durbin, E. F. M.	1906	1948	Taunton	Oxford	23
Eadie, A.	1920	..	Buckhaven S.S.*		36
Ebury, 5th Ld (1932). R. E. Grosvenor	1914	1957	Harrow		17
† Eccles, 1st Ld (1962). 1st Vt (1964) Sir D. M. Eccles (K.C.V.O. 1953)	1904	..	Winchester	Oxford	24, 25, 27, 28, 34
† Ede, J. C., Ld Chuter-Ede (Life Peer 1964)	1882	1965	Dorking H.S.*	Cambridge	18, 21
† Eden of Winton, Ld (Life Peer 1983). Sir J. B. (9th Bt 1963)	1925	..	Eton		34^3
† Eden, Sir (R.) A. (K.G. 1954). 1st E of Avon (1961)	1897	1977	Eton	Oxford	13^2, 15, 16^2, 17, 19, 20, 24^2
Edge, Sir W. (Kt 1922)	1880	1948	Bolton G.S.*		9
Edmondson, Sir A. J. (Kt 1934). 1st Ld Sandford (1945)	1887	1959	University Coll. Sch.		17^2, 20^2, 21
Edwards, Sir C. (Kt 1935)	1867	1954	Elementary		13, 20
Edwards, (L.) J.	1904	1959	Aylesbury G.S.*	Leeds	21, 22, 23
Edwards, N.	1897	1968	Elementary		22, 23
† Edwards, (R.) N., Ld Crickhowell (Life Peer 1987)	1934	..	Westminster	Cambridge	42
Edwards, W. J.	1900	1964	Secondary		22
Eggar, T. J. C.	1951	..	Winchester	Cambridge	39^2, 40, 44, 46
Elgin, 9th E of (1863). V. A. Bruce	1849	1917	Eton	Oxford	3
Elibank, Master of (1st Ld Murray of Elibank 1912). A. W. C. O. Murray	1870	1920	Cheltenham		3, 4, 5^2
Elliot, W. E.	1888	1958	Glasgow Academy	Glasgow	10, 12, 13, 14, 15, 16^2
Elliott, A.	1846	1923	Privately	Edinburgh & Cambridge	1
Elliott of Morpeth, Ld (Life Peer 1985). Sir R. W. Elliott (Kt 1974)	1920	..	Morpeth G.S.*		35
Ellis, J.	1934	..	Rastrick G.S.*		37
Ellis, J. E.	1841	1910	Friends' Schs.*		3
Elton, 2nd Ld (1973). R. Elton	1930	..	Eton	Oxford	39^2, 40, 41^2
† Elwyn-Jones, Ld (Life Peer 1974). Sir F. E. Jones (Kt 1964)	1909	1989	Llanelli G.S.*	Aberystwyth & Cambridge	32, 35
Elystan-Morgan, Ld (Life Peer 1981). (D.) E. Morgan	1932	..	Ardwyn G.S.*	Aberystwyth	30
† Emery, Sir P. F. H. (Kt 1982)	1926	..	Scotch Plains U.S.A.*	Oxford	34^2
Emmott, 1st Ld (1911). A. Emmott	1858	1926	Grove House, Tottenham*	London	4^2
Emrys-Evans, P. V.	1894	1967	Harrow	Cambridge	18, 20
† Ennals, Ld (Life Peer 1983) D. H. Ennals	1922	..	Q. Mary's G.S. Walsall*		30^2, 31, 36^2
Erne, 5th E of (1914) J. H. G. Crichton	1907	1940	Eton	Sandhurst	17
Ernle 1st Ld (1919) R. E. Prothero	1851	1937	Marlborough	Oxford	7
Erroll, 20th E of (1891)	1852	1927	Harrow		3
† Erroll of Hale, 1st Ld (1964) F. J. Erroll	1914	..	Oundle	Cambridge	25^2, 26, 28^4
Evans, I. L.	1927	1984	Llanelli G.S.*	Swansea	32
Evans J.	1930	..	Jarrow Cent. S.*		37
Evans, R.	1947	..	Bristol G.S.	Cambridge	45
Evans, S. N.	1898	1970	Elementary		22
† Evans, Sir S. T. (G.C.B. 1916)	1859	1929	Secondary	London	3, 4

Name	Born	Died	School	University	Pages
Ewing, Lord (Life Peer 1992) H. Ewing	1931	..	Beith H. S.*		37
Eyre, Sir R. E. (Kt 1983)	1924	..	K.Edward VI Birmingham	Cambridge	34, 35^2, 42^2
† Eyres-Monsell, Sir B. M. (G.B.E. 1929). 1st Vt Monsell (1935)	1881	1969	H.M.S. Britannia*		7, 9, 10^2, 12, 13, 14, 15
Fairbairn, Sir N.	1933	..	Loretto	Edinburgh	42
Fairfax, 13th Ld (1939). T. B. M. Fairfax	1923	1964	Eton		26, 29
Fairgrieve, Sir(T.) R. (Kt 1981)	1924	..	Sedbergh		41
Fallon, M.	1952	..	Epsom	St.Andrews	40, 43^2, 44
Fanshawe, Ld (Life Peer 1983). Sir A. H. F. Royle (K.C.M.G. 1974)	1927	..	Harrow	Sandhurst	33
† Farquhar, 1st E (1922). Sir H. B. Farquhar (1st Bt 1892), 1st Ld (1898), 1st Vt (1917)	1844	1922	Privately		6, 9
† Fellowes, Sir A. E. (K.C.V.O. 1911), 1st Ld Ailwyn (1921)	1855	1924	Eton	Cambridge	2^3
Fenner, Dame P. E.	1922	..	Ide Hill S.*		33, 39
Fenton, Sir J.C. (Kt 1945)	1880	1951	George Watson's Edinburgh	Edinburgh & Sorbonne	11
† Fernyhough, E.	1908	1993	Elementary		31^2
† Ferrers, 13th E (1954). R. W. S. Shirley	1929	..	Winchester	Cambridge	29, 33, 35, 39^2, 44, 45
Feversham, 3rd E of (1916). C. W. S. Duncombe	1906	1964	Eton		15^2, 17
Finch, Sir H. J. (Kt 1976)	1898	1979	Elementary		32
† Finlay, 1st Vt (1919). Sir R. Finlay (Kt 1895), 1st Ld (1916)	1842	1929	Edinburgh Acad.	Edinburgh	2^2, 6
Finlay, Sir G. B. (1st Bt 1964)	1917	1987	Marlborough		29^2
Finsberg, Sir G. (Kt 1984)	1926	..	C.of London		40, 41
† Fisher, H. A. L.	1865	1940	Winchester	Oxford, Paris & Göttingen	7
Fisher, Sir N.T. L. (Kt 1974)	1913	..	Eton	Cambridge	27
Fitch, (E.) A.	1915	1985	Kingswood		32^2, 33
† Fitzalan, 1st Vt (1921). E. B. Fitzalan-Howard. Assumed name of Talbot(1876). Ld E.Talbot	1855	1947	Oratory Sch.		2, 6, 9
† Fitzmaurice, 1st Ld (1906). Ld E. G. P.-Fitzmaurice	1846	1935	Eton	Cambridge	3, 4^2
Fleming, Ld (Scot. judge 1926). D. Fleming	1877	1944	Glasgow H.S.	Edinburgh & Glasgow	10, 12
Fletcher, Sir A. M.	1929	1989	Greenock H. S.*		41, 42
† Fletcher, Ld (Life Peer 1970). Sir E. G. M. Fletcher (Kt 1964)	1903	1990	Radley	London	31
Fletcher-Cooke, Sir C. (Kt 1981)	1914	..	Malvern	Cambridge	26
Foley, M. A.	1925	1978	St.Mary's Coll. Middlesboro'*		29, 30^3
Foot, Sir D. M. (Kt 1964)	1905	1978	Bembridge	Oxford	18, 32
† Foot I.	1880	1960	Hoe G.S. Plymouth*		14
† Foot, M. M.	1913	..	Leighton Park	Oxford	35, 36
Forbes, 22nd Ld (1953). N. I. Forbes	1918	..	Harrow	Sandhurst	28
Ford, Sir P. J. (Kt 1926)	1880	1945	Edinburgh Academy	Oxford & Edinburgh	10

Name	Born	Died	School	University	Pages
Forman, (F.) N.	1943	..	Shrewsbury	Oxford	45
† Forres, 1st Ld (1922). Sir A. Williamson (1st Bt 1909)	1860	1931	Craigmont*	Edinburgh	9
† Forster, 1st Ld (1919). H.W. Forster	1866	1936	Eton	Oxford	2, 6, 8
Forsyth, M. B.	1954	..	Arbroath H.S.*	St.Andrews	40, 42, 44, 45²
Fortescue, 5th E (1932). H.W. Fortescue	1888	1958	Eton	Sandhurst	17, 20², 21, 26, 29
Fortescue. T. V. N.	1916	..	Uppingham	Cambridge	2, 6, 8, 9
Forth, E.	1944	..	Jordanhill H.S.*	Glasgow	41, 42, 44, 45²
Foster, Sir J. G. (K.B.E. 1964)	1904	1982	Eton	Oxford	24
Foster, W.	1887	1947	Elementary		22
Fowler, G.T.	1935	1993	Northampton G.S.*	Oxford	30, 35, 36²
† Fowler, Sir H. H. (G.C.S.I. 1895). 1st Vt Wolverhampton (1908)	1830	1911	St Saviour's G.S., Southwark*		3, 4
† Fowler, Sir (P.) N.	1938	..	K. Ed. VI, Chelmsford *	Cambridge	40², 42²
Fox, Sir (J.) M. (Kt 1986)	1927	..	Wheelwright G.S. Dewsbury*		35², 40
Fox, L.	1961	..	St Bride's H.S.	Glasgow	46
Fraser, Sir H. C. P. J. (Kt 1980)	1918	1984	Ampleforth	Oxford & Paris	27³, 28
Fraser, J. D.	1934	..	Sloane G.S.*		36, 37
† Fraser of Carmyllie, Ld (Life Peer 1989). P. D. Fraser	1945	..	Loretto	Cambridge & Edinburgh	42², 45²
† Fraser, T.	1911	1988	Lesmahagow*		23, 32
† Freeman, J.	1915	..	Westminster	Oxford	23⁴
† Freeman, R. N.	1942	..	Whitgift	Oxford	39, 41, 42, 44, 46
† Freeman-Thomas, F., 1st Ld Willingdon (1910), 1st Vt (1924), 1st E of (1931), 1st M of (1936)	1866	1941	Eton	Cambridge	3, 5
† Freeson, R. Y.	1926	..	Jewish Orphanage, W. Norwood*		31², 36
Freeth, D. K.	1924	..	Sherborne	Oxford	28
† French, Sir J. D. P. (K.C.B 1900). 1st Vt French of Ypres (1915). 1st E of Ypres (1921)	1852	1925	H.M.S. Britannia*		7²
Fuller. Sir J. M. F. (1st Bt 1910)	1864	1915	Winchester	Oxford	3², 5
Furness, S. N.	1902	1974	Charterhouse	Oxford	17, 20
Gage, 6th Vt (1912). H. R. Gage	1895	1982	Eton	Oxford	12, 15, 17
† Gainford, 1st Ld (1917). J. A. Pease	1860	1943	Tottenham*	Cambridge	3, 4², 5², 6
† Gaitskell, H. T. N.	1906	1963	Winchester	Oxford	21², 22²
† Galbraith, T. D. 1st Ld Strathclyde (1955)	1891	1985	Glasgow Acad., R.N.C. Osborne & Dartmouth		21, 25², 28
Galbraith, Sir T. G. D. (K.B.E. 1982)	1917	1982	Wellington	Oxford	25, 26³, 28²
Gammans, Sir (L.) D. (1st Bt 1955)	1895	1957	Portsmouth G.S.	London	25
† Gardiner, Ld (Life Peer 1964). G. A. Gardiner	1900	1990	Harrow	Oxford	29
† Garel-Jones, T.	1941	..	King's Sch. Canterbury		38, 43⁵, 44
Garnsworthy, Ld (Life Peer 1967). C. J. Garnsworthy	1906	1974	Wellington		38
Garro-Jones, G. M. 1st Ld Trefgarne (1947). *Surname changed to Trefgarne in 1954*	1894	1960	Caterham		19
† Geddes, 1st Ld (1942). Sir A. C. Geddes (K.C.B. 1917)	1879	1954	George Watson's Edinburgh	Edinburgh	8³
† Geddes, Sir E. C. (Kt 1916)	1875	1937	Merchiston Castle		6, 7, 8²

† Geoffrey-Lloyd, Ld (Life Peer 1974). G. Lloyd	1902	1984	Harrow	Cambridge	15, 16, 18, 19, 21, 24, 27
George, Sir J. C. (K.B.E. 1963)	1901	1972	Ballingry, Fife		28
† George-Brown, Ld (Life Peer 1970). G. A. Brown	1914	1985	Secondary		22, 23, 29^2, 30
† Gibbs, G. A. 1st Ld Wraxall (1928)	1873	1931	Eton	Oxford	9, 10, 12
† Gibson-Watt, Ld (Life Peer 1979). (J.) D. Gibson-Watt	1918	. .	Eton	Cambridge	29, 35
† Gilbert, J. W.	1927	. .	Merchant Taylors' Sch.	Oxford & New York	35, 36^2
Gillett, Sir G. M. (Kt 1931)	1870	1939	Secondary		13, 14
† Gilmour, Sir J. (2nd Bt 1920)	1876	1940	Trinity Coll. Glenalmond	Edinburgh & Cambridge	9, 10, 12, 13^2, 14, 16
† Gilmour of Craigmillar, Ld (Life Peer 1992), Sir I. H. J. L. Gilmour (3rd Bt 1977)	1926	. .	Eton	Oxford	33^3, 38
† Gladstone, 1st Vt (1910). H. J. Gladstone	1854	1930	Eton	Oxford	3, 4
Glassey, A. E.	1887	1971	Penistone G.S.*		14
† Glenamara, Ld (Life Peer 1976). E. Short	1912	. .	Secondary	Durham	30, 31, 32, 35
Glenarthur, 4th Ld (1976). S. M. Arthur	1944	. .	Eton		38, 39, 41^2, 43
† Glenavy, 1st Ld (1921), Sir J. H. M. Campbell (1st Bt 1916)	1851	1931	Kingstown*	Dublin	2^2, 6, 9^2
† Glendevon, 1st Ld (1964). Ld J. A. Hope	1912	. .	Eton	Oxford	24^2, 28^2
Glenkinglas, Ld (Life Peer 1974) M. A. C. Noble	1913	1984	Eton	Oxford	28, 29, 34^2
† Godber, Ld (Life Peer 1979). J. B. Godber	1914	1980	Bedford		26^3, 27, 28, 33^2
Golding, J.	1931	. .	Chester G.S.*	London & Keele	36, 37
Goodhart, Sir P. C. (Kt 1981)	1925	. .	Hotchkiss (USA)	Cambridge	39^2, 41
Goodhew, Sir V. H. (Kt 1982)	1919	. .	King's Coll.Sch.		35^2
† Goodlad, A.	1943	. .	Marlborough	Cambridge	40, 43^4, 44, 46
Gordon, J.	1849	1922	Royal Acad. Institution	Belfast	6
† Gordon Walker, Ld (Life Peer 1974). P. C. Gordon Walker	1907	1980	Wellington	Oxford	22^2, 30^2, 31
Gorell, 3rd Ld (1917). R. G. Barnes	1884	1963	Winchester & Harrow	Oxford	7
† Goronwy-Roberts, Ld (Life Peer 1974), G. O. Roberts	1913	1981	Bethesda G.S.*	Wales & London	30^2, 32^2, 36^2
† Gorst, Sir J. Eldon (Kt 1885)	1835	1916	Preston G.S.*	Cambridge	2
† Goschen, 1st Vt (1900). G. J. Goschen	1831	1907	Rugby	Oxford	1
† Goschen, 2nd Vt (1907). G. J. Goschen	1866	1952	Rugby	Oxford	7
Goschen, 3rd Vt (1952). J. A. Goschen	1906	1977	Harrow	Oxford	29, 35
Goschen, 4th Vt (1977). G. J. H. Goschen	1965	. .	Eton		46^2
Gosford. 6th E of (1954). A. A. J. S. Acheson. Vt Acheson (1922)	1911	1966	Harrow	Cambridge	24, 26, 29
Gosling. H.	1861	1930	Elementary		11^2
Gourlay, H.	1916	. .	Kirkcaldy H.S.*		32^2
Gow, I. R. E.	1937	1990	Winchester		38, 40
† Gowrie, 2nd E of (1955). A. P. G. Ruthven	1939	. .	Eton	Oxford	35, 38, 39^2, 40, 41^2

Name	Born	Died	School	University	Pages
† Graham of Edmonton, Ld (Life Peer 1983). (T.) E. Graham	1925	..	Elementary	Open Univ.	37
† Graham, W.	1887	1932	George Heriot's, Edin.	Edinburgh	11, 13
† Granard, 8th E of (1889) B. A. W. P. H. Forbes	1874	1948	Oratory Sch.		3^2, 5
Grant, Ld (Scot. judge 1962). W. Grant	1909	1972	Fettes	Oxford	25, 29^2
Grant, Sir (J.) A. (Kt 1983)	1925	..	St. Paul's	Oxford	34^2, 35
Grant, J. D.	1932	..	Stationers' Company's Sch *		35, 36, 37
Granville, 3rd E (1891). G. G. L. Gower	1872	1939	Eton		3, 5
† Gray of Contin, Ld (Life Peer 1983). (J.) H. M. Gray	1927	..	Inverness Royal Acad.*		35^2, 40, 41
Gray, M.	1871	1943	Greenwich*		14
Green, A.	1911	1991	Brighton Coll.	London	26, 27, 28
† Greenwood. 1st Vt (1937). Sir H. Greenwood (1st Bt 1915). 1st Ld (1929)	1870	1948	Canadian Sch *	Toronto	7^2, 8
† Greenwood, A.	1880	1954	Beverley St*	Leeds	11, 13, 19, 22, 22^2
† Greenwood of Rossendale, Ld (Life Peer 1970). A. W. Greenwood	1911	1982	Merchant Taylors'	Oxford	30, 31^3
† Grenfell D R.	1881	1968	Elementary		19
† Grey of Fallodon, 1st Vt (1916). Sir E. Grey (3rd Bt 1882)	1862	1933	Winchester	Oxford	3, 4, 5
Grey. C F.	1903	1984	Elementary		33^2
† Griffith, Sir E. J. E. (1st Bt 1918)	1860	1926	Secondary	Aberystwyth & Cambridge	4
† Griffith-Boscawen, Sir A. S. T. (Kt 1911)	1865	1946	Eton	Oxford	7^2, 8, 10
Griffiths, Sir E. W. (Kt 1985)	1925	..	Ashton G.S.*	Cambridge	34^2
† Griffiths, J.	1890	1975	Elementary		22^2, 32
Griffiths, T.	1867	1955	Elementary		11
† Grigg, Sir E. W. M. 1st Ld Altrincham (1945)	1879	1955	Winchester	Oxford	16, 17, 18, 19, 21
† Grigg, Sir (P.) J. (K.C.B. 1932)	1890	1964	Bournemouth*	Cambridge	19, 21
Grimston, 1st Ld (1964). Sir R. V. Grimston (1st Bt 1952)	1897	1979	Repton	London	17^3, 19, 20, 21
Grist, I.	1938	..	Repton	Oxford	42
† Guest. F. E.	1875	1937	Winchester		5^2, 7, 9
† Guest, I.C. . 1st Ld Ashby St Ledgers (1910), 2nd Ld Wimborne (1914), 1st Vt (1918)	1873	1939	Eton	Cambridge	4, 5
† Guinness. W. E. 1st Ld Moyne (1932)	1880	1944	Eton		10^2, 11^2, 18^4
† Gulland, J.W.	1864	1927	Edinburgh H.S*	Edinburgh	5^2, 6
† Gummer, J. S.	1939	..	King's Sch. Rochester	Cambridge	39^2, 40^3, 41, 43^2, 44, 45
† Gunter, R. J.	1909	1977	Newbridge S.S.*		31^2
Gwynne, R. S.	1873	1924	Shrewsbury	Cambridge	10
† Hacking, 1st Ld (1945). Sir D. H. Hacking (1st Bt 1938)	1884	1950	Giggleswick	Manchester	10, 11, 12^2, 13, 14, 16, 17
Haden-Guest, 1st Ld (1950). L. H. Haden-Guest	1877	1960	Hulme's G.S.*	Manchester	23
Hague, W.	1961	..	Wath-on-Dearne*	Oxford	45^2
† Hailes, 1st Ld (1957) P.G.T. Buchan-Hepburn	1901	1974	Harrow	Cambridge	17, 20^2, 21, 25^2

Name	Born	Died	School	University	Pages
† Hailsham. 1st Vt (1929). Sir D. M. Hogg (Kt 1922), 1st Ld Hailsham (1928)	1872	1950	Eton		10, 11, 12, 14, 15[2]
† Hailsham, 2nd Vt (1950–63). Q. M. Hogg. Ld Hailsham of St. Marylebone (Life Peer 1970)	1907	..	Eton	Oxford	18, 20, 24, 26[3], 27[2], 28, 33, 38
† Haldane. 1st Vt (1911). R. B. Haldane	1856	1928	Edinburgh Academy	Edinburgh & Gottingen	3, 4[2], 11
† Halifax, 1st E of (1944). E. F. L Wood. 1st Ld Irwin (1925), 3rd Vt Halifax (1934)	1881	1959	Eton	Oxford	7, 10, 11, 14, 15[3], 16, 17
† Hall, 1st Vt (1946). G. H. Hall	1881	1965	Elementary		12, 17, 18[2], 21, 22
Hall, F.	1855	1933	Elementary		11
† Hall, W. G.	1887	1962	Ellesmere		22
Hall-Davis, Sir A. G. F. (Kt 1979)	1924	1979	Clifton Coll.		35
† Halsbury, 1st E (1898). H. S. Giffard, 1st Ld Halsbury (1885)	1823	1921	Privately	Oxford	1
† Hamilton, A.	1941	..	Eton	Oxford	39, 43[2], 44
† Hamilton, M of (1885). J A. E. Hamilton, 3rd D of Abercorn (1913)	1869	1953	Eton		2
† Hamilton, Ld G. F.	1845	1927	Harrow		2
Hamilton of Dalzell, 2nd Ld (1900). G. G. Hamilton	1872	1952	Eton	Sandhurst	3, 5
Hamilton, J.	1918	..	St. Mary's, High Whifflet*		33, 37, 38[2]
Hamilton, Sir M. A. (Kt 1983)	1918	..	Radley	Oxford	29
Hamilton, M. N.	1949	..	Repton	Oxford	43, 46[2]
Hamilton, Sir R. W. (Kt 1918)	1867	1946	St Paul's	Cambridge	14
Hamling, W.	1912	1975	Liverpool Inst. H.S.*	Liverpool	33
† Hanbury, R.	1845	1903	Rugby	Oxford	1, 2
† Hankey, 1st Ld (1939). M. P. A. Hankey	1877	1963	Rugby		16, 18, 19
† Hanley, J. J.	1945	..	Rugby		44, 45[2]
Hannan, W.	1906	1987	N. Kelvinside S.S.*		23
† Hanworth. 1st Vt (1936). Sir E. M. Pollock (K.B.E. 1917), 1st Ld Hanworth(1926)	1861	1936	Charterhouse	Cambridge	9[2]
† Harcourt, 1st Vt (1916). L. Harcourt	1863	1922	Eton		3[2], 4[2], 6
Hardman, D. R.	1901	1987	Coleraine Acad. Inst.*	Cambridge	22
Hardwicke, 6th E (1897). A. E. P. H. Yorke. Vt Royston (1873)	1867	1904	Eton		2[3]
† Hare. J. H. 1st Vt Blakenham (1963)	1911	1982	Eton		24, 25, 26, 27[2], 28
† Harlech, 4th Ld (1938). W. G. A. Ormsby-Gore	1885	1964	Eton	Oxford	10, 11, 14[2], 15, 17
† Harlech. 5th Ld (1964). Sir (W.) D. Ormsby-Gore (K.C.M.G. 1961)	1918	1985	Eton	Oxford	24, 26
Harmar-Nicholls. Ld (Life Peer 1974). Sir H. Nicholls (1st Bt 1960)	1912	..	Q. Mary's G.S., Walsall		24, 28
Harmsworth. 1st Ld (1939). C. B. Harmsworth	1869	1948	Marylebone G.S.*	Dublin	4, 7
Harper, J.	1914	1978	Elementary		32[2], 38
Harris. 4th Ld (1872). G. R. C. Harris	1851	1932	Eton	Oxford	3

† Harris, F. L.	1864	1926	Winchester	Cambridge	7
† Harris of Greenwich, Ld (Life Peer 1974). J. H. Harris	1930		Pinner G.S.*		36
Harrison. Sir (J.) H. (1st Bt 1961)	1907	1980	Northampton G.S.*	Oxford	26, 29²
† Harrison, W.	1921	. .	Dewsbury Tech*		32², 38
† Hart, Lady (Life Peeress 1988) Dame J. C. M. (D.B.E. 1979)	1924	1991	Clitheroe R.G.S.*	London	30, 31², 32², 37²
Hartington, M of (1908). E. W. S. Cavendish, 10th D of Devonshire (1938)	1895	1950	Eton	Cambridge	16, 18², 20
† Hartshorn, V.	1872	1931	Elementary		11, 12
Harvey, I. D	1914	1987	Fettes	Oxford	25, 26
Hastings, 22nd Ld (1956). E. D. H. Astley	1912	. .	Eton		27, 29
Hastings. Sir P. (Kt 1924)	1880	1952	Charterhouse		11
† Hattersley, R. S. G.	1932	. .	Sheffield City G.S.*	Hull	30, 31², 36, 37
† Havers, Ld (Life Peer 1987). Sir (R.) M. O. Havers (Kt 1973)	1923	1992	Westminster	Cambridge	35, 38, 42
Hawke, 9th Ld (1939). B. W. Hawke	1901	1985	Winchester	Cambridge	26, 29
Hawkesbury, 1st Ld (1893). C. G. S. Foljambe, 1st E of Liverpool (1905)	1846	1907	Eton		3
Hawkins, Sir P. (Kt 1982)	1912	. .	Cheltenham		35³
Haworth, Sir A. A. (1st Bt 1911)	1865	1944	Rugby		5
Hay, J. A.	1919	. .	Hove & Sussex G.S.*		26, 27, 28
Hayes, J. H.	1889	1941	Tech. S., Wolverhampton		13
† Hayes Fisher, W., 1st Ld Downham (1918)	1853	1920	Haileybury	Oxford	1, 2, 6, 7, 8²
† Hayhoe, Ld (Life Peer 1992). Sir B. J. Hayhoe (Kt 1987)	1927	. .	Stanley T.S.*		38², 39, 41
† Head, 1st Vt (1960). A. H. Head	1906	1981	Eton	Sandhurst	24, 25
† Headlam, Sir C. M. (1st Bt 1935)	1876	1964	King's Sch., Canterbury	Oxford	11, 14²
† Heald, Sir L. F. (Kt 1951)	1897	1981	Charterhouse	Oxford	25
† Healey Ld (Life Peer 1992) D. W. Healey	1917	. .	Bradford G.S.	Oxford	30, 35
† Heath, Sir E. R. G. (K.G. 1992)	1916	. .	Chatham House*	Oxford	25², 26, 27, 28, 29, 33
† Heathcoat Amory, D. 1st Vt Amory (1960)	1899	1981	Eton	Oxford	24², 25², 26²
Heathcoat-Amory, D. P.	1949	. .	Eton	Oxford	40, 43², 44, 45², 46
Heffer, E. S.	1922	1991	Longmore Sch.*		37
† Henderson, 1st Ld (1945). W. W. Henderson	1891	1984	Q. Elizabeth G.S., Darlington*		21, 23
Henderson of Ardwick, 1st Ld (1950). J. Henderson	1884	1950	Elementary		23
† Henderson, A.	1863	1935	Elementary		5, 6², 8, 11, 12
† Henderson, A., Ld Rowley (Life Peer 1966)	1893	1968	Queen's Coll., Taunton*	Cambridge	19², 22³
Henderson, T.	1867	1960	Elementary		13
Henderson, Sir V. L. (Kt 1927)	1884	1965	Uppingham	Sandhurst	11
Henderson-Stewart, Sir J. (1st Bt 1957)	1897	1961	Morrison's Acad., Crieff*	Edinburgh	25
Henley, 8th Ld (1977) O. M. R. Eden	1953	. .	Clifton	Durham	42, 44, 45²
Hennessy, Sir G. R. J. (1st Bt 1927). 1st Ld Windlesham (1937)	1877	1953	Eton		10, 12³, 15
Henry, Sir D. S. (1st Bt 1922)	1864	1925	Mount St Mary's Coll.	Belfast	9²

Name	Born	Died	School	University	References
† Herbison, Miss M. M.	1907	. .	Bellshill Acad.*	Glasgow	23, 31, 32
Herschell, 2nd Ld (1899). R. F. Herschell	1878	1929	Eton	Oxford	3, 5, 6, 9
† Heseltine, M. R. D.	1933	. .	Shrewsbury	Oxford	34², 35, 39, 40, 45, 46
† Hesketh, 3rd Ld (1955). T. A. Fermor-Hesketh	1950	. .	Ampleforth		40, 42, 44, 46²
† Hewart, 1st Vt (1940). Sir G. Hewart (Kt 1916), 1st Ld (1922)	1870	1943	Manchester G.S.	Oxford	9³
Hewins, W. A. S.	1865	1931	Wolverhampton G.S.	Oxford	7
Hicks, (E.) G.	1879	1954	Elementary		20
Hicks, R.	1938	. .	Queen Elizabeth G.S. Crediton*	London	35
† Hicks Beach, Sir M. E., 1st Vt St Aldwyn (1906), (9th Bt 1854), 1st E (1915)	1837	1916	Eton	Oxford	1
† Higgins, Sir T. L. (K.B.E. 1993)	1928	. .	Alleyn's	Cambridge	33²
† Hill of Luton, Ld (Life Peer 1963). C.Hill	1904	1991	St.Olave's	Cambridge	24, 25, 27²
Hill, J. E. B.	1912	. .	Charterhouse	Oxford	29
† Hills, J. W.	1867	1938	Eton	Oxford	10
Hilton of Upton, Ld (Life Peer 1965). A.V. Hilton	1908	1970	Elementary		33
† Hoare, Sir S. J. G. (2nd Bt 1915). 1st Vt Templewood (1944)	1880	1959	Harrow	Oxford	10², 11, 14, 15⁵
† Hobhouse, Sir C. E. H. (4th Bt 1916)	1862	1941	Eton	Oxford	3, 4²
Hobson, Ld (Life Peer 1963) C. R. Hobson	1904	1966	Elementary		23, 33
† Hobson, Sir J. G. S. (Kt 1962)	1912	1967	Harrow	Oxford	28, 29
† Hodge. J.	1855	1937	Hutchesontown G.S.*		7, 8
Hodges, F.	1887	1947	Elementary		11
† Hogg, Sir D. M. (Kt 1922). 1st Ld Hailsham (1928), 1st Vt (1929)	1872	1950	Eton		10, 11, 12, 14, 15²
† Hogg, D. M.	1945	. .	Eton	Oxford	38, 39, 42, 43, 44
† Hogg, Q. M., 2nd Vt Hailsham (1950–63), Ld Hailsham of St Marylebone (Life Peer 1970)	1907	. .	Eton	Oxford	18, 20, 24, 26³, 27², 28, 33, 38
Holden, 3rd Ld (1937). A.W. E. Holden	1898	1951	Eton	Oxford	22
† Holderness Ld (Life Peer 1979). R. F. Wood	1920	. .	Eton	Oxford	25, 27, 28³, 33, 34
† Home, 14th E of (1951–63). Sir A. F. Douglas-Home (Kt 1962), Ld Dunglass. (1918), Ld Home of the Hirsel (Life Peer 1974)	1903	. .	Eton	Oxford	20, 24, 25, 26⁴, 27, 33
Hooper, Lady (Life Peeress 1985) Miss G. Hooper	1935	. .	Royal Ballet School*	Southampton	40², 41, 44, 45
† Hope, Ld J. A., 1st Ld Glendevon (1964)	1912	. .	Eton	Oxford	24², 28²
† Hope, J. F., 1st Ld Rankeillour (1932)	1870	1949	Oratory Sch.	Oxford	6, 8, 9
Hope, A. O. J., 2nd Ld Rankeillour (1949)	1897	1958	Oratory Sch.	Sandhurst	17³
Hopetoun, 7th E of (1873). 1st M of Linlithgow (1902). J. A. L. Hope	1860	1908	Eton		2²

† Hopkinson, H. L. D., 1st Ld Colyton (1956)	1902	..	Eton	Cambridge	24, 25
Horam, J. R.	1939	..	Silcoates Sch.*	Cambridge	37
† Hore-Belisha, 1st Ld (1954). L. Hore-Belisha	1893	1957	Clifton	Paris, Heidelberg & Oxford	13, 14^2, 16^3, 21
Hornby, R.	1922	..	Winchester	Oxford	27
† Horne, 1st Vt (1937). Sir R. S. Horne (K.B.E. 1918)	1871	1940	George Watson's Edinburgh	Glasgow	6, 7, 8
† Hornsby-Smith, Lady (Life Peeress 1974). Dame (M.) P. Hornsby-Smith (D.B.E. 1961)	1914	..	Richmond*		24, 26, 28
Horobin, Sir I. M. (Kt 1955)	1899	1976	Highgate	Cambridge	28
† Horsbrugh, Lady (Life Peeress 1959). (G.B.E. 1954) Dame F. Horsbrugh	1889	1969	St Hilda's Folkestone*		16, 18, 20, 24^2
† Houghton, of Sowerby, Ld (Life Peer 1974). (A. L. N.) D. Houghton	1898	..	Secondary		31^2
Howard, G. W. A.	1877	1935	Privately	Cambridge	5, 6
† Howard, M.	1941	..	Llanelli G.S.*	Cambridge	40^4, 42, 44, 45^2
Howarth, A. T.	1944	..	Rugby	Cambridge	40, 43^2, 44
Howe, 4th E (1900). R. G. P. Curzon, Vt Curzon (1876)	1861	1929	Eton	Oxford	2, 3
† Howe, 5th E (1929). F. R. H. P. Curzon, Vt Curzon (1900)	1884	1964	Eton	Oxford	12
Howe, 7th E (1984). F. R. P. Curzon	1951	..	Rugby	Oxford	44, 46
† Howe of Aberavon, Ld (Life Peer 1992) Sir (R. E.) G. Howe (Kt 1970)	1926	..	Winchester	Cambridge	34, 35, 38^3
† Howell, D. A. R.	1936	..	Eton	Cambridge	33, 34^4, 35, 40, 42
† Howell, Ld (Life Peer 1992) D. H. Howell	1923	..	Handsworth G.S.*		30, 31, 36
Howie of Troon, Ld (Life Peer 1978). W. Howie	1924	..	Marr Coll., Troon*		32^2, 33
† Hoy, Ld (Life Peer 1970). J. H. Hoy	1909	1976	Secondary		30
Huckfield, L.	1942	..	Prince Henry's G.S.*	Oxford	37
† Hudson, 1st Vt (1952). R. S. Hudson	1886	1957	Eton	Oxford	14, 16^4, 18, 20
Hudson, Sir A. U. M. (1st Bt 1942)	1897	1956	Eton	Sandhurst	14^2, 15, 16, 18, 21
† Hughes, Ld (Life Peer 1961). W. Hughes	1911	..	Elementary		32^2, 37
† Hughes, C., Ld Cledwyn of Penrhos (Life Peer 1979)	1916	..	Holyhead G.S.*	Aberystwyth	30^2, 32
Hughes, R.	1932	..	Robert Gordon's C., Aberdeen		37
Hughes, R. G.	1946	..	Spring Grove G.S.*		45, 46
Hughes-Hallett, J.	1901	1972	Bedford & Osborne	Cambridge	28
Hughes-Young, M. H. C., 1st Ld St Helens (1964)	1912	1980	Harrow	Sandhurst	29^2
† Hunt, D.	1942	..	Liverpool Coll.	Bristol	40^2, 42, 43^3, 44, 45^2, 46
Hunter, Ld (Scot. judge 1911). W. Hunter	1865	1957	Ayr Academy*		5
Huntingdon, 15th E of (1939). F. J. C. W. P. Hastings, Vt Hastings (1901)	1901	1990	Eton	Oxford	22
† Hurd, D. R.	1930	..	Eton	Cambridge	38^2, 39^2, 41, 44
† Hutchison of Montrose, 1st Ld (1932). R. Hutchison	1873	1950	Secondary		16

Name	Born	Died	School	University	Pages
Hutchison, Sir J. R. H. (1st Bt 1956)	1893	1979	Harrow		25
Hylton, 3rd Ld (1899). H. G. H. Jolliffe	1862	1945	Eton	Oxford	6, 9^2, 10
† Hylton-Foster, Sir H. B. H. (Kt 1954)	1905	1965	Eton	Oxford	25, 29
Hynd, J. B.	1902	1971	St Ninian's Park*		22^2
† Illingworth, 1st Ld (1921). A. H. Illingworth	1865	1942	London Internat. Coll.* & Switzerland		8
Illingworth, P. H.	1869	1915		Cambridge	5^2
† Ingleby, 1st Vt (1955). O. Peake	1897	1966	Eton	Sandhurst & Oxford	15, 17^2, 20, 25^3
Inglewood, 1st Ld (1964). W. M. F. Vane	1909	1989	Charterhouse	Cambridge	26, 28
Inglewood, 2nd Ld (1989) (W.) R. F. Vane	1951	. .	Eton	Cambridge	46
† Inman, 1st Ld (1946). P. A. Inman	1892	1979	Harrogate*	Leeds	21
† Inskip, Sir T. W. H. (Kt 1922). 1st Vt Caldecote (1939)	1876	1947	Clifton	Cambridge	10, 12^2, 14^2, 15^2, 16, 17, 18
† Inverforth, 1st Ld (1919). A. Weir	1865	1955	Kirkcaldy H.S.*		8^2
† Irvine, Sir A. (Kt 1967)	1909	1978	Angusfield S. Aberdeen*	Edinburgh	32
† Irving, Ld (Life Peer 1979). S. Irving	1918	. .	Pendower*	London	33
† Irwin, 1st Ld (1925). E. F. L. Wood. 3rd Vt Halifax (1934). 1st E of Halifax (1944)	1881	1959	Eton	Oxford	7, 10, 11, 14, 15^3, 16, 17
† Isaacs, G. A.	1883	1979	Elementary		22^2
† Isaacs, Sir R. D. (Kt 1910). 1st Ld Reading (1914), 1st Vt (1916), 1st E of (1917), 1st M of (1926)	1860	1935	University Coll. Sch.		4^3, 13
† Islington, 1st Ld (1910). J. P. Dickson-Poynder	1866	1936	Harrow	Oxford	4, 6, 7
† Ismay, 1st Ld (1947). H. L. Ismay	1887	1965	Charterhouse	Sandhurst	24
Jack, J. M.	1946	. .	Bradford G.S.	Leicester	44^2, 45
† Jackson. Sir (F.) S. (G.C.I.E. 1927)	1870	1947	Harrow	Cambridge	10
Jackson, Miss M. M. (Mrs M. M. Beckett)	1943	. .	Notre Dame H.S. Norwich*	Manchester	36, 37
Jackson, R. V.	1946	. .	Falcon Coll. Rhodesia	Oxford	40^2, 44, 45
Jacques, Ld (Life Peer 1968). J. H. Jacques	1905	. .	Secondary	Manchester	38^2
† James of Hereford, 1st Ld (1895). H. James	1828	1911	Cheltenham		2
† Jamieson, Ld (Scot. judge 1935). D. Jamieson	1880	1952	Fettes	Glasgow & Edinburgh	14^2, 17
† Jay, Ld (Life Peer 1987) D. P. T. Jay	1907	. .	Winchester	Oxford	21^2, 32
† Jeffreys, A. F.	1848	1906	Privately	Oxford	2
† Jellicoe, 2nd E (1935). G. P. J. R. Jellicoe	1918	. .	Winchester	Cambridge	26^2, 27^2, 29, 33
† Jenkin, Ld (Life Peer 1987) (C.) P. F. Jenkin	1926	. .	Clifton	Cambridge	33^2, 34, 40^2, 41
Jenkins, A.	1884	1946	Elementary		19, 22
Jenkins of Putney, Ld (Life Peer 1981). H. G. Jenkins	1908	. .	Enfield G.S.*		36
† Jenkins of Hillhead (Life Peer 1987). R. H. Jenkins	1920	. .	Abersychan G.S.*	Oxford	29, 30^2, 36

Jersey 8th E of (1915). G. H. R. C. Villiers, Vt Grandison (1873)	1873	1923	Eton	Oxford	9
John. B. T.	1934	1988	Pontypridd Boys' G.S.*	London	36^2
John. W.	1878	1955	Elementary		20^2
John-Mackie, Ld (Life Peer 1981). J. Mackie	1916	. .	Aberdeen G.S.*		30
Johnson, W.	1917	. .	Devon Ho., Margate*		37
Johnson-Smith, Sir G. (Kt 1981)	1924	. .	Charterhouse	Oxford	33^2
† Johnston, Ld (Scot. judge 1961) D H. Johnston	1907	1985	Aberdeen G.S.*	Oxford & Edinburgh	23
† Johnston, T.	1882	1965	Lenzie Academy*	Glasgow	12, 13, 19
† Johnstone, H.	1895	1945	Eton	Oxford	19
† Jones, A.	1911	1983	Cyfarthfa S.S.*	London	24, 28
† Jones, A. Creech	1891	1964	Elementary		22^2
† Jones. Sir F. E. (Kt 1964) Ld Elwyn-Jones (Life Peer 1974)	1909	1989	Llanelli G.S.*	Aberystwyth & Cambridge	32, 35
Jones, G. H.	1947	. .	Secondary		45
Jones, J. H.	1894	1962	Rotherham*		23
Jones, J. T.	1858	1925	Elementary		9
Jones, M.	1885	1939	Elementary	Reading	11, 13
Jones, R. B.	1950	. .	Merchant Taylors	St. Andrews	45
Jones, (S.) B.	1938	. .	Hawarden G.S.*		37
† Jones. (T.) A.	1924	1983	Porth Cty G.S.*		36, 37
Jones, W.	1860	1915	Bangor Normal Coll.*	Aberystwyth & Oxford	5
† Jopling. (T.) M.	1930	. .	Cheltenham	Newcastle	35^2, 39, 42
† Joseph, Ld (Life Peer 1987). Sir K. S. Joseph (2nd Bt 1944)	1918	. .	Harrow	Oxford	27^2, 28, 34, 39, 41
† Jowett, F. W.	1864	1944	Elementary		11
† Jowitt. 1st E (1951). Sir W. A. Jowitt (Kt 1929), 1st Ld (1945), 1st Vt (1947)	1885	1957	Marlborough	Oxford	13, 14, 19^3, 20, 21
† Joynson-Hicks, Sir W. (1st Bt 1919). 1st Vt Brentford (1929)	1865	1932	Merchant Taylors' Sch.		10^4, 11
Joynson-Hicks, L. W. 3rd Vt Brentford (1958)	1902	1983	Winchester	Oxford	24
Judd, Ld (Life Peer 1991) F. A. Judd	1935	. .	City of London Sch.	London	36^2, 37^2
Kaberry, Ld (Life Peer 1983). Sir D. Kaberry (1st Bt 1960)	1907	1991	Leeds G.S.		25
† Kaufman, G. B.	1930	. .	Leeds G.S.	Oxford	36, 37^2
† Kearley, Sir H. E. (1st Bt 1908). 1st Ld Devonport (1910), 1st Vt (1917)	1856	1934	Cranleigh		3, 4, 7
† Kellaway, F. G.	1870	1933	Bishopstoun*		8^3
† Kennedy, T.	1876	1954	Secondary		11, 13
† Kennet, 1st Ld (1935). Sir E. H. Young (G.B.E. 1927)	1879	1960	Eton	Cambridge	7, 14^2
Kennet, 2nd Ld (1960). W. Young	1923	. .	Stowe	Cambridge & Harvard	31
Kenyon, 4th Ld (1869). L. Tyrrell-Kenyon	1864	1927	Eton	Oxford	3, 9
Kerr, C. I. 1st Ld Teviot (1940)	1874	1968	S. Hawtrey's, Windsor*		17^2
Kerr, Sir H. W. (1st Bt 1957)	1903	1974	Eton	Oxford	20
Kershaw, 1st Ld (1947). F. Kershaw	1881	1962	Elementary		23
Kershaw, Sir (J.) A. (Kt 1981)	1915	. .	Eton	Oxford	33^2, 34

Name	Born	Died	School	University	Pages
† Key, C. W.	1883	1964	Chalfont St Giles*		22, 23
Key, (S.) R.	1945	..	Sherborne	Cambridge	40, 45², 46
Kidd, J.	1872	1928	Carriden*	Edinburgh	10
† Kilmany, Ld (Life Peer 1966). Sir W. J. Anstruther-Gray (1st Bt 1956)	1905	1985	Eton	Oxford	21
† Kilmuir, 1st E (1962). Sir D. P. Maxwell Fyfe (Kt 1942). 1st Vt Kilmuir (1954)	1900	1967	George Watson's Edinburgh	Oxford	20, 21, 24², 26
King, E. M.	1907	1994	Cheltenham	Cambridge	23
King, (H.) D.	1877	1930	Christ's Hospital		10, 12²
† King, T. J.	1933	..	Rugby	Cambridge	39, 40³, 41, 42, 44
† Kintore, 10th E of (1880). A. H. T. Keith-Falconer	1852	1930	Eton	Cambridge	3
Kirk, Sir P. M. (Kt 1976)	1928	1977	Marlborough	Oxford	27, 28, 33
Kirkhill, Ld. (Life Peer 1975). J. F. Smith	1930	..	Robert Gordon's C., Aberdeen*		37
Kirkhope, T.	1945	..	R.G.S Newcastle	Leicester	43, 46²
† Kitchener of Khartoum, 1st E (1914). H. H. Kitchener, 1st Ld (1898), 1st Vt (1902)	1850	1916	France	Woolwich	4, 6
Knight, G.	1949	..	Newton's G.S. Leicester*		43², 46
† Lambert, 1st Vt (1945). G. Lambert	1866	1958	Privately		3, 4
Lambton, Vt (1941–69). A. C. F. Lambton (6th E of Durham, 1969, disclaimed 1970)	1922	..	Harrow		33
† Lamont, N. S. H.	1942	..	Loretto	Cambridge	38², 39, 40, 41, 42, 44
Lane, Sir D. W. S. S. (Kt 1983)	1922	..	Eton	Cambridge	33
† Lane-Fox, G. R. 1st Ld Bingley (1933)	1870	1947	Eton	Oxford	10, 12
† Lang, I. B.	1940	..	Rugby	Cambridge	40, 41, 43², 45
† Lansbury, G.	1859	1940	Elementary		13
† Lansdowne, 5th M of (1866). H. C. K. Petty-Fitzmaurice, Vt Clanmaurice (1845). E of Kerry (1863)	1845	1927	Eton	Oxford	1, 2, 6
† Lansdowne, 8th M of (1944). G. J. C. M. N. Petty-Fitzmaurice	1912	..	Eton	Oxford	26, 27, 29
† Law, A. Bonar	1858	1923	Glasgow H.S.*		2, 5, 6³, 9
† Law, R. K. 1st Ld Coleraine (1954)	1901	1980	Shrewsbury	Oxford	17, 19², 20
Lawrence, 2nd Ld (1879). J. H. Lawrence	1846	1913	Wellington	Cambridge	3
Lawrence, Miss (A.) S.	1871	1947	Privately	Cambridge	13
† Lawson, 1st Ld (1950). J. J. Lawson	1881	1965	Elementary		11, 13, 23
Lawson, G. M.	1906	1978	Elementary		32
Lawson, Sir J. G. 1st Bt (1905)	1856	1919	Harrow	Oxford	2
† Lawson of Blaby. Ld (Life Peer 1992) N. Lawson	1932	..	Westminster	Oxford	38², 40
Leach, W.	1870	1949	Bradford G.S.		11
† Leathers, 1st Vt (1954). F. J. Leathers, 1st Ld (1941)	1883	1965	Elementary		19, 21, 24
Leburn (W.) G.	1913	1963	Strathallan*		28
† Lee of Asheridge, Lady (Life Peer 1970). Miss J. Lee (Mrs A. Bevan)	1904	1988	Benton*	Edinburgh	30², 31
† Lee of Fareham, 1st Vt (1922). Sir A. Lee (K.C.B. 1916). 1st Ld (1918)	1868	1947	Cheltenham	Woolwich	1, 6, 7²

† Lee of Newton, Ld (Life Peer 1974). F. Lee	1906	1984	Langworthy Rd.*		22, 30, 31[2]
Lee, J. R. L.	1942	..	Hulme's G.S. Manchester		39, 40
Leechman, Ld (Scot. judge 1965). J. G. Leechman	1906	1986	Glasgow H.S.*	Glasgow	32
† Lees-Smith, H. B.	1878	1941	Aldenham		13[2]
Legh, P. R. 4th Ld Newton (1960)	1915	1992	Eton	Oxford	26, 27[2], 29[4]
Leigh, E. J. E.	1950	..	Oratory Sch.	Durham	42, 46
Le Marchant, Sir S. (Kt 1984)	1931	..	Eton		43
† Lennox-Boyd, A. T. 1st Vt Boyd of Merton (1960)	1904	1983	Sherborne	Oxford	15, 16[2], 18, 20, 24[2], 25, 27
Lennox-Boyd, Sir M. A. (Kt 1994)	1943	..	Eton	Oxford	39, 43[2], 44
Leonard, Ld (Life Peer 1978) J. D. Leonard	1909	1983	Boys Nat. S., Leitrim*		38
Leonard, W.	1887	1969	Elementary		23
Lester, J. T.	1932	..	Nottingham H.S.		40
Lestor, Miss J.	1931	..	William Morris S.S.*	London	30, 36[2]
Lever, Sir (S.) H. (K.C.B. 1917)	1869	1947	Merchant Taylors' Sch., Crosby		6
† Lever of Manchester, Ld (Life Peer 1979) (N.) H. Lever	1914	..	Manchester G S.		29[2], 31, 37
† Lewis, Sir (J.) H. (G.B.E. 1922)	1858	1933	Secondary	McGill & Oxford	3, 4, 5, 6, 7
Lewis, T. A.	1881	1923	Denbigh G.S.*	Cardiff	9
Lightbown, D. L.	1932	..	Derby Sch. of Art*		43[3], 46
† Lilley, P. B.	1943	..	Dulwich	Cambridge	38[2], 42, 45, 46
Limerick, 6th E of (1967). P. E. Pery. Vt Glentworth (1930)	1930	..	Eton	Oxford	34
† Lincolnshire, 1st M of (1912). C. R. Wynn-Carrington, 3rd Ld Carrington (1868), 1st E (1895)	1843	1928	Eton	Cambridge	3, 4[2]
Lindgren, Ld (Life Peer 1961). G. S. Lindgren	1900	1971	Elementary		22[2], 23, 31, 32
Lindsay, K.	1897	1991	St Olave's	Oxford	15, 16
† Linlithgow, 1st M of (1902). J. A. L. Hope, 7th E of Hopetoun (1873)	1860	1908	Eton		2[2]
Linlithgow, 2nd M of (1908). V. A. J. Hope, E of Hopetoun (1902)	1887	1952	Eton		10
† Listowel, 5th E of (1931). W. F. Hare, Vt Ennismore (1924)	1906	..	Eton	Oxford	18, 22[4], 23
† Liverpool, 1st E of (1905). C. G. S. Foljambe, 1st Ld Hawkesbury (1893)	1846	1907	Eton		3
† Liverpool, 2nd E of (1907). A. W. D. S. Foljambe, Vt Hawkesbury (1905)	1870	1941	Eton	Sandhurst	5
† Llewellin, 1st Ld (1945). J. J. Llewellin	1893	1957	Eton	Oxford	15, 16, 18[4], 19[2], 20
Llewellyn, Sir D. T. (Kt 1960)	1916	1992	Eton	Cambridge	24
† Llewelyn-Davies of Hastoe, Lady (Life Peeress 1967). Mrs (A.) P. Llewelyn-Davies	1915	..	Liverpool Coll.	Cambridge	33, 38
† Lloyd, 1st Ld (1925). Sir G. A. Lloyd (G.C.I.E. 1918)	1879	1941	Eton	Cambridge	18

Lloyd, 2nd Ld (1941). A. D. F. Lloyd	1912	1985	Eton	Cambridge	24^2, 26
† Lloyd, G., Ld Geoffrey-Lloyd (Life Peer 1974)	1902	1984	Harrow	Cambridge	15, 16, 18, 19, 21, 24, 27
† Lloyd, (J.) S. B. Ld Selwyn-Lloyd (Life Peer 1976)	1904	1978	Fettes	Cambridge	24^3, 25, 26^3
Lloyd, P. R. C.	1937	. .	Tonbridge	Oxford	39, 42, 43^2, 44^2
† Lloyd George of Dwyfor, 1st E (1945). D. Lloyd George	1863	1945	Llanystumdwy Church Sch.*		3, 4, 6^4
† Lloyd-George, G. 1st Vt Tenby (1957)	1894	1967	Eastbourne	Cambridge	14, 16, 18^2, 19, 20, 24^2
† Lloyd-Greame, Sir P. (K.B.E. 1920). Changed name to Sir P. Cunliffe-Lister in 1924, 1st Vt Swinton (1935). 1st E of Swinton (1955)	1884	1972	Winchester	Oxford	8^2, 10, 12, 14^2, 15, 18^2, 20, 24, 25^2
Loch, 2nd Ld (1900). E. D. Loch	1873	1942	Winchester		5
† Lochee of Gowrie, 1st Ld (1908). E. Robertson	1846	1911	Secondary	St Andrews & Oxford	3
Locker-Lampson, G. L. T.	1875	1946	Eton	Cambridge	10, 11^2
† Londonderry, 6th M of (1884). C. S. Vane-Tempest-Stewart. Vt Castlereagh (1872)	1852	1915	Eton	Oxford	1, 2^3
† Londonderry, 7th M of (1915). C. S. H. Vane-Tempest-Stewart. Vt Castlereagh (1884)	1878	1949	Eton	Sandhurst	7, 12, 14^2, 15
† Long, 1st Vt (1921). W. H. Long	1854	1924	Harrow	Oxford	1, 2^2, 6, 7^2
Long, 4th Vt (1967). R. G. Long	1929	. .	Harrow		43, 46
† Longford, 7th E of (1961). F. A. Pakenham, 1st Ld Pakenham (1945)	1905	. .	Eton	Oxford	22^4, 23^2, 29^2, 30
† Loreburn, 1st E (1911). Sir R. T. Reid (Kt 1894), 1st Ld Loreburn (1906)	1846	1923	Cheltenham	Oxford	3, 4
† Lothian, 11th M of (1930). P. H. Kerr	1882	1940	Oratory Sch.	Oxford	14^2
Lothian, 12th M of (1940). P. F. W. Kerr	1922	. .	Ampleforth	Oxford	27, 29, 33, 35
† Lough, T.	1850	1922	Wesleyan Sch., Dublin*		3
Loughlin, C. W.	1914	. .	Elementary		31^3, 32
Lovat, 16th Ld (1887). S. J. Fraser	1871	1933	Fort Augustus Abbey	Oxford	11
Lovat, 17th Ld (1933). S. C. J. Fraser	1911	. .	Ampleforth	Oxford	20
Lovell-Davis, Ld (Life Peer 1974). P. L. Davis	1925	. .	Stratford upon Avon G.S.*	Oxford	36, 38
† Low, Sir T. A. R. W. (K.C.M.G. 1957). 1st Ld Aldington (1962)	1914	. .	Winchester	Oxford	25^2
Luard, (D.) E. T.	1926	1991	Felsted	Cambridge	30, 36
† Lucan, 5th E of (1914). G. C. Bingham, Ld Bingham (1888)	1860	1949	Harrow	Sandhurst	9, 10, 12^2, 15, 17
Lucan, 6th E of (1949). G. C. P. Bingham, Ld Bingham (1914)	1898	1964	Eton	Sandhurst	22, 23
Lucas of Chilworth, 1st Ld (1946). G. W. Lucas	1896	1967	Elementary		23^3
Lucas of Chilworth, 2nd Ld (1967). M. W. G. Lucas	1926	. .	Peter Symond's Winchester*		42, 43

Name	Born	Died	School	University	Pages
Lucas of Crudwell, 10th Ld (1992), R. M. Palmer	1951	..	Eton	Oxford	46
Lucas & Dingwall, 8th & 11th Ld (1905). A. T. Herbet	1876	1916	Bedford	Oxford	4[4]
Lucas-Tooth, Sir H. V. H. D. (Munro) 1st Bt (1920)	1903	1985	Eton	Oxford	24
† Luce, Sir R. N.(Kt 1991)	1936	..	Wellington	Cambridge & Oxford	38[3], 39[2]
Lunn, W.	1872	1942	Elementary		11, 13[2]
Lyell, 3rd Ld (1943). C. Lyell	1939	..	Eton	Oxford	41, 43, 45
† Lyell, Sir N. (Kt 1987)	1938	..	Stowe	Oxford	41, 42, 45[2]
Lyon, A. W.	1931	1993	West Leeds H.S.*	London	36
† Lyttelton, A.	1857	1913	Eton	Cambridge	2
† Lyttelton, O. 1st Vt Chandos (1954)	1893	1972	Eton	Cambridge	18, 19[3], 21[2], 24
† Lytton, 2nd E of (1891). V. A. G. R. Lytton	1876	1947	Eton	Cambridge	5, 7[3]
† Mabane, 1st Ld (1962). Sir W. Mabane (K.B.E. 1954)	1895	1969	Woodhouse Grove*	Cambridge	15, 16, 18[2], 20
† Mabon, J. D.	1925	..	N. Kelvinside*	Glasgow	32[2], 36
Macarthur. I.	1925	..	Cheltenham	Oxford	29
† Macartney, Sir W. (K.C.M.G. 1913)	1852	1924	Eton	Oxford	1
McBride, N.	1910	1974	Elementary		32[2]
McCann, J.	1910	1972	Elementary		32, 33
McCluskey, Ld (Life Peer 1976). J. McCluskey	1929	..	Holy Cross Academy*	Edinburgh	37
MacColl, J. E.	1908	1971	Sedbergh	Oxford	31
† McCorquodale, 1st Ld (1955). M. S. McCorquodale	1901	1971	Harrow	Oxford	18, 21
† McCurdy, C. A	1870	1941	Loughboro'G.S.*	Cambridge	7[2], 9
MacDermot, N.	1916	..	Rugby	Cambridge	29, 31
Macdonald, of Gwaenysgor, 1st Ld (1949). G. Macdonald	1888	1966	Elementary		22
† MacDonald, J. Ramsay	1866	1937	Elementary		11[2], 12, 13, 15
† MacDonald, M. J.	1901	1981	Bedales*	Oxford	14, 15[3], 16, 18
McElhone, F.	1929	1982	St Bonaventure's S.S. .*	Glasgow	37
McEwen, Sir J. H. F. (lst Bt 1953)	1894	1962	Eton	Oxford	16, 20
Macfarlane, (D.) N.	1936	..	Bancroft's Sch.		40[2]
† MacGregor, J. R. R.	1937	..	Merchiston Castle	St.Andrews & London	38[2], 39[3], 41, 43, 44, 46, 47
† Mackay of Ardbrecknish (Life Peer 1991) J. J. Mackay	1938	..	Campbelltown G.S.*	Glasgow	41, 45, 46
† Mackay of Clashfern, Ld (Life Peer 1979). J. P. H. Mackay	1927	..	George Heriot's	Edinburgh	38, 42, 44
Mackay, A. J.	1949	..	Solihull		46[2]
† McKenna, R.	1863	1943	Privately	London	3[2], 4[2], 5
Mackenzie (J.) G.	1927	1992	Queen's Park S.*	Glasgow	37[3]
Mackeson, Sir H. R. (lst Bt 1954)	1905	1964	Rugby	Sandhurst	25[2]
Mackie, J., Ld John-Mackie (Life Peer 1981)	1909	1994	Aberdeen G.S.*		30
McLaren, M.	1914	1980	Sedbergh	Oxford	29
† Maclay, 1st Ld (1922). Sir J. P. Maclay (1st Bt 1914)	1857	1951	Glasgow H.S.*		8
† Maclay, J. S. lst Vt Muirshiel (1964)	1905	1992	Winchester	Cambridge	21, 24, 25, 28
† Maclean, Sir D. (K.B.E. 1917)	1864	1932	Haverfordwest G.S.*		14[2]
Maclean, D. J.	1953	..	Fortrose Acad.*	Aberdeen	39, 43[2], 44[2], 45
Maclean, Sir F. (1st Bt 1957)	1911	..	Eton	Cambridge	25
† Macleod, I. N.	1913	1970	Fettes	Cambridge	24, 25, 27[3], 33

Name	Born	Died	School	University	Pages
Maclennan, R. A. R.	1936	..	Glasgow Academy	Cambridge & Oxford	37
McLoughlin, P. A.	1957	..	Griffin Comp. Cannock*		42, 45, 46²
† Macmillan, Ld (Ld of Appeal 1930). H. P. Macmillan	1873	1952	Coll.H.S. Greenock*	Edinburgh & Glasgow	11, 16
† Macmillan, (M.) H. 1st E of Stockton (1984)	1894	1986	Eton	Oxford	18², 19, 20, 24⁴, 25
† Macmillan of Ovenden, Vt (1984). M. V. Macmillan	1921	1984	Eton	Oxford	26, 33, 34²
† Macnamara, T.J.	1861	1931	St Thomas', Exeter*		3, 4, 5, 7²
† McNeil, H.	1907	1955	Woodside, Glas.*	Glasgow	21², 23
† McNeill, R. J. 1st Ld Cushendun (1927)	1861	1934	Harrow	Oxford	10, 11², 12
† Macpherson, Sir I. (1st Bt 1933). 1st Ld Strathcarron (1936)	1880	1937	George Watson's Edinburgh	Edinburgh	7, 8²
Macpherson, N. M. S. 1st Ld Drumalbyn (1963)	1908	1987	Fettes	Oxford	25, 28⁴, 34
† MacRobert, A. M.	1873	1930	Paisley Acad.*	Glasgow & Edinburgh	12²
† Major, J.	1943	..	Rutlish G.S.*		38³, 41², 43², 44
Mallalieu, Sir J. P. W. (Kt 1979)	1908	1980	Cheltenham	Oxford	30², 32²
Mallet, Sir C. E. (Kt 1917)	1862	1947	Harrow	Oxford	4
Malmesbury, 5th E of (1899). J. E. Harris	1872	1950	Privately	Oxford	10
Malone P. B.	1950	..	St. Aloysius, Glasgow*	Glasgow	43, 45
† Manchester, 9th D of (1892). W. A. D. Montagu	1877	1947	Eton	Cambridge	3, 5
Mancroft, 1st Ld (1937). Sir A. M. Samuel (1st Bt 1932)	1872	1942	Norwich G.S.*		11, 12
Mancroft, 2nd Ld (1942). S. M. S. Mancroft	1914	1987	Winchester	Oxford	24, 26, 27, 28
† Manningham-Buller, Sir R. E. (Kt 1951). 1st Ld Dilhorne (1962). 1st Vt (1964)	1905	1980	Eton	Oxford	21, 25², 26, 28
Mansfield, 8th E of (1971), Vt Stormont (1935). W. D. M. J. Murray	1930	..	Eton	Oxford	41²
Maples, J. C.	1943	..	Marlborough	Cambridge	38, 44
† Marchamley, 1st Ld (1908). G. Whiteley	1855	1925	Abroad	Zurich	3
Marchwood. 1st Vt (1945). Sir F. G. Penny (Kt 1929). 1st Ld Marchwood (1937)	1876	1955	K.Edward VI G.S., Southampton*		12, 14, 15³
† Margesson, 1st Vt (1942). (H.) D. R. Margesson	1890	1965	Harrow	Cambridge	12, 14², 17, 19, 20
Marks, K.	1920	..	Central H.S., * Manchester		37
† Marlborough, 9th D of (1892). C. R. J. Spencer-Churchill, M of Blandford (1883)	1871	1934	Winchester	Cambridge	2², 7
Marley, 1st Ld (1930). D. L. Aman	1884	1952	Marlborough & R.N.C. Greenwich		13²
† Marples, Ld (Life Peer 1974). (A.) E. Marples	1907	1978	Stretford G.S.*		24, 25, 28²
† Marquand, H. A.	1901	1972	Cardiff H.S.*	Cardiff	22³, 23
† Marsh, Ld (Life Peer 1981). Sir R. W. Marsh (Kt 1976) ..	1928	..	Elementary		31², 32²
Marshall, F.	1883	1962	Elementary		23

Marshall, J.	1941	..	City G.S., Sheffield*	Leeds	37
Marshall, Sir (R.) M.(Kt 1990)	1930	..	Bradfield	Harvard	41
Marten, Sir (H.) N. (Kt 1983)	1916	1985	Rossall		27, 39
† Mason of Barnsley, Ld (Life Peer 1987) R. Mason	1924	1985	Royston*		30, 31², 32², 36, 37
† Masterman, C. F. G.	1873	1927	Weymouth*	Cambridge	4⁴
Mates, M. J.	1934	..	Blundells	Cambridge	45
Mather, (D.) C. M.	1919	..	Harrow	Oxford	42, 43²
† Mathers, lst Ld (1951). G. Mathers	1886	1965	Elementary		20, 23
Mathew, R.	1911	1966	Eton	Cambridge	26
† Maude, Ld (Life Peer 1983). Sir A. E. U. Maude (Kt 1981)	1912	1993	Rugby	Oxford	41
† Maude, F.	1953	..	Abingdon	Cambridge	38, 42, 43, 44
† Maudling, R.	1917	1979	Merchant Taylors'	Oxford	24, 25², 26, 27³, 28, 33
† Maugham, 1st Vt (1939). Sir F. H. Maugham (Kt 1928), Ld (Ld of Appeal 1935)	1866	1958	Dover Coll.	Cambridge	15
Mawby, R. L.	1922	1990	Long Lawford S.*		28
† Mawhinney, B. S.	1940	..	R. Belfast A.I.	Belfast	41, 45³
† Maxwell Fyfe, D. P. lst Vt Kilmuir (1954). 1st E (1962)	1900	1967	George Watson's Edinburgh	Oxford	20, 21, 24², 26
Maydon, S. L. C.	1913	1971	Twyford*		28
Mayhew, Ld (Life Peer 1981). C. P. Mayhew	1915	..	Haileybury	Oxford	21, 30
Mayhew, Sir P. B. B. (Kt 1983)	1929	..	Tonbridge	Oxford	39, 40, 42², 45²
Meacher, M. H.	1939	..	Berkhamsted	Oxford	36, 37²
† Melchett, 1st Ld (1928). Sir A. M. Mond (1st Bt 1910)	1868	1930	Cheltenham	Cambridge & Edinburgh	7, 9
Melchett, 4th Ld (1973). P. R. H. Mond	1948	..	Eton	Cambridge & Keele	37², 38
† Mellish, Ld (Life Peer 1985). R. J. Mellish	1913	..	Elementary		31³, 32, 37
† Mellor, D. J.	1949	..	Swanage G.S.*	Cambridge	38², 39⁴, 40, 41, 44, 45
Melville, Sir J. B. (Kt 1929)	1885	1931	Secondary		13
Merlyn-Rees, Ld (Life Peer 1992) M. Rees	1920	..	Harrow Weald	London	30³, 36, 37
† Merriman, 1st Ld (1941). Sir F. B. Merriman (Kt 1928)	1880	1962	Winchester		12, 14
† Merrivale, 1st Ld (1925). Sir H. E. Duke (Kt 1918)	1855	1939	Elementary		6, 7
† Midleton, 1st E of (1920). (W.) St. J. Brodrick, 9th Vt Midleton (1907)	1856	1942	Eton	Oxford	1, 2²
† Millan, B.	1927	..	Harris Acad., Dundee*		30, 32, 37²
† Milligan, Ld (Scot. Judge 1960). W. R. Milligan	1898	1975	Sherborne	Oxford & Glasgow	25², 29
Miller, Lady (Life Peer 1994). Doreen Miller	1933	..	Kilburn H.S.*	London	46
Miller, M. S.	1920	..	Shawland's Acad.*	Glasgow	33
† Mills, 1st Ld (1957). Sir P. H. Mills (Kt 1942)	1890	1968	Barnard Castle		27, 28²
Mills, Sir P. M. (Kt 1982)	1921	1993	Epsom		33, 34
† Milner, 1st Vt (1902). Sir A. Milner (K.C.B. 1895). 1st Ld (1901)	1854	1925	German Schs.	London & Oxford	6, 7, 8², 9
Mitchell, A.	1953	..	Rugby	Cambridge	46²
Mitchell, Sir D. B. (Kt 1988)	1928	..	Aldenham		41², 42²
† Mitchell-Thomson, Sir W. (2nd Bt 1918). 1st Ld Selsdon (1932)	1877	1938	Winchester	Oxford	7, 8, 12

Mitchison, Ld (Life Peer 1964). G. R. Mitchison	1890	1970	Eton	Oxford	31
Molony, Sir T. F. (1st Bt 1925)	1865	1949	Secondary	Dublin	5^2
† Molson, Ld (Life Peer 1961). (A.) H. E. Molson	1903	1991	Lancing, R.N.C. Osborne & Dartmouth	Oxford	25^2, 28
† Monckton, 1st Vt (1957). Sir W.T. Monckton (K.C.V.O. 1937)	1891	1965	Harrow	Oxford	21, 24, 25^2
† Mond, Sir A. M. (1st Bt 1910). 1st Ld Melchett (1928)	1868	1930	Cheltenham	Cambridge & Edinburgh	7, 9
Money, Sir L. G. C. (Kt 1915)	1870	1944	Privately		8
Monro, Sir H. S. P. (Kt 1981)	1922	. .	Canford Sch.	Cambridge	34, 35, 40
† Monsell, 1st Vt (1935). Sir B. M. Eyres-Monsell (G.B.E. 1929)	1881	1969	H.M.S. Britannia*		7, 9, 10^2, 12, 13, 14, 15
† Montagu, E. S.	1879	1924	Clifton & City of London	Cambridge	4^3, 5^2, 6^2, 7, 8
Montague, F. 1st Ld Amwell (1947)	1876	1966	Elementary		13, 18, 19
† Montague-Barlow, Sir (C.) A. (K.B.E. 1918)	1868	1951	Repton	Cambridge	8, 10
Moore of Lower Marsh, Ld (Life Peer 1992) J. E. M. Moore	1937	. .	Victualler's S. Slough*	London	38^2, 40^2, 42^2
† Moore-Brabazon, J.T. C., 1st Ld Brabazon (1942)	1884	1964	Harrow	Cambridge	10, 12, 18, 19
More, Sir J. (Kt 1979)	1907	1988	Eton	Cambridge	35
Morgan, (D.) E., Ld Elystan-Morgan (Life Peer 1981)	1932	. .	Ardwyn G.S.*	Aberystwyth	30
Moriarty, J. F.	1854	1915	Stonyhurst	Dublin	5^2
† Morison, Ld (Scot. Judge 1922). T. B. Morison	1868	1945	Secondary	Edinburgh	5, 6, 9^2
† Morley, 1st Vt (1908). J. Morley	1838	1923	Cheltenham	Oxford	3, 4^3
† Morris, A.	1928	. .	Elementary	Oxford & Manchester	36
† Morris, C. R.	1926	. .	Elementary		32, 33^2, 35, 36
† Morris, J.	1931	. .	Ardwyn G.S.*	Aberystwyth & Cambridge	30, 31, 32, 37
Morris-Jones, Sir (J.) H. (Kt 1937)	1884	1972	Menai Bridge G.S.*		17
† Morrison, Sir P. H. (Kt 1990)	1944	. .	Eton	Oxford	40^3, 42
† Morrison, 1st Ld (1945). R. C. Morrison	1881	1953	Aberdeen*		23^2
† Morrison of Lambeth, Ld (Life Peer 1959). H. S. Morrison	1888	1965	Elementary		13^2, 17^2, 19, 21^2
† Morrison, W. S., 1st Vt Dunrossil (1959)	1893	1961	George Watson's Edinburgh	Edinburgh	15^2, 16^2, 19^2, 21
Mosley, Sir O. E. (6th Bt 1928)	1896	1980	Winchester	Sandhurst	13
† Mottistone, 1st Ld (1933). J. E. B. Seely	1868	1947	Harrow	Cambridge	4^3, 7, 8
Mott-Radclyffe, Sir C. E. (Kt 1957)	1911	1992	Eton	Oxford	21
† Mount Temple, 1st Ld (1932). W.W. Ashley	1867	1939	Harrow	Oxford	10^2, 12
Mowbray and Stourton, 26th Ld (1965). C. E. Stourton	1923	. .	Ampleforth	Oxford	35, 43
† Moyle, R. D.	1928	. .	Llanidloes County Sch.*	Aberystwyth & Cambridge	36^2, 37
† Moyne, 1st Ld (1932). W. E. Guinness	1880	1944	Eton		10^2, 11^2, 18^4
Muir, J. W.	1879	1931	Elementary		11

Name	Born	Died	School	University	Pages
† Muir-Mackenzie, 1st Ld (1915). Sir K. A. Muir-Mackenzie (K.C.B. 1898).	1845	1930	Charterhouse	Oxford	11, 13
Muirhead, A. J.	1890	1939	Eton	Oxford	15, 16[2]
† Muirshiel, 1st Vt (1964). J. S. Maclay	1905	1992	Winchester	Cambridge	21, 24, 25, 28
† Mulley, Ld (Life Peer 1984). F. W. Mulley	1918	..	Warwick Sch.*	Cambridge & Oxford	30[3], 32, 36[3]
Munro, P.	1883	1942	Leeds G.S.	Oxford	17, 20
† Munro, R. 1st Ld Alness (1934)	1868	1955	Aberdeen G.S.*	Edinburgh	5, 6, 8, 20, 21
† Munster, 5th E of (1928). G. W. R. H. FitzClarence	1906	1975	Charterhouse		15, 16[2], 17[2], 18, 20, 24, 25, 28
† Murray, Ld (Scot. judge 1922). C. D. Murray	1866	1936	Edinburgh Acad.	Edinburgh	9[2]
† Murray of Elibank, 1st Ld (1912). A. W. C. O. Murray	1870	1920	Cheltenham		3, 4, 5[2]
Murray, A. G. 1st Ld Dunedin (1905). 1st Vt (1926)	1849	1942	Harrow	Cambridge	2[2]
Murray of Gravesend, Ld (Life Peer 1976). A. J. Murray	1930	1980	Elementary		32
Murray, Sir (T.) D. K. (Kt 1941). Ld Birnam (Scot. judge 1945)	1884	1955	Hamilton Acad.* & Glasgow H.S.*	Glasgow	20, 21
† Murray, Ld (Scot. judge 1979). R. K. Murray	1922	..	George Watson's Edinburgh	Edinburgh & Oxford	37
† Murton, Ld (Life Peer 1974). (H.) O. Murton	1914	..	Uppingham		35[2]
† Nathan, 1st Ld (1940). H. L. Nathan	1889	1964	St. Paul's		8
Neal, A.	1862	1933	Wesley Coll., Sheffield*		22, 23
Neal, H.	1897	1972	Elementary		22
Neave, A. M. S.	1916	1979	Eton	Oxford	27, 28
† Needham, R. F.	1942	..	Eton		41, 45, 46
Nelson, R. A.	1948	..	Harrow	Cambridge	44
Neubert, Sir M. J. (Kt 1990)	1933	..	Bromley G.S.*	Cambridge	39, 43[2]
Newton, A. H.	1937	..	Friends Sch., Saffron Walden*	Oxford	41[4], 42, 43[2], 44, 45
Newton, 2nd Ld (1899). T. W. Legh	1857	1942	Eton	Oxford	5, 6, 7
Newton, 4th Ld (1960). P. R. Legh	1915	1992	Eton	Oxford	26, 27[2], 29[4]
Nicholls, Sir H. (1st Bt 1960). Ld Harmar-Nicholls (Life Peer 1974)	1912	..	Q. Mary's G.S., Walsall*		24, 28
Nicholls, P. C. M.	1948	..	Redrice, Andover*		40[2]
Nicolson, Sir H. G. (K.C.V.O. 1953)	1886	1968	Wellington	Oxford	18
Noble, Sir A. H. P. (K.C.M.G. 1959)	1908	1982	Radley		24[3], 26
† Noble, M. A. C. Ld Glenkinglas (Life Peer 1974)	1913	1984	Eton	Oxford	28, 29, 34[2]
† Noel-Baker, Ld (Life Peer 1977) P. J. Noel-Baker	1889	1982	Bootham	Cambridge	19, 21, 22[3]
† Noel-Buxton, 1st Ld (1930). N. E. N. Buxton	1869	1948	Harrow	Cambridge	11, 12
† Norfolk, 15th D of (1860). H. FitzAlan-Howard, E of Arundel (1847)	1847	1917	Oratory Sch.		2
† Norfolk, 16th D of (1917). B. M. Fitz Alan-Howard, E of Arundel (1908)	1908	1975	Oratory Sch.		18, 20

Name	Born	Died	School	University	Refs
† Norman, Sir H. (Kt 1906)	1858	1939	Privately	Harvard & Leipzig	4
Normanby, 4th M of (1932). O. C. J. Phipps, E of Mulgrave (1912)	1912	. .	Eton	Oxford	20, 21
† Normand, Ld (Ld of Appeal 1947). W. G. Normand	1884	1962	Fettes	Oxford, Paris & Edinburgh	12, 14^2
Norris, S. J.	1945	. .	Liverpool Inst.*	Oxford	46
Northumberland, 10th D of (1940). H. A. Percy	1914	1988	Eton	Oxford	21
Norton, C. W., 1st Ld Rathcreedan (1916)	1845	1930	Abroad	Dublin & Sandhurst	3, 4, 5
† Norwich, 1st Vt (1952). A. Duff Cooper	1890	1954	Eton	Oxford	12, 13, 14, 15^2, 16, 18^2
† Nott, Sir J. W. F. (K.C.B. 1983)	1932	. .	Bradfield	Cambridge	33, 39, 42
† Novar, 1st Vt (1920). Sir R. C. Munro-Ferguson (G.C.M.G. 1914)	1860	1935	Privately	Sandhurst	10
† Nugent of Guildford, Ld (Life Peer 1966), Sir (G.) R. H. Nugent (1st Bt 1960)	1907	1994	Imperial Service Coll.	Woolwich	24, 28
† Nutting, Sir (H.) A. (3rd Bt 1972)	1920	. .	Eton	Cambridge	24^2
† Oakes, G. J.	1931	. .	Wade Deacon Sch., Widnes*	Liverpool	36^2
Oakshott, Ld (Life Peer 1964). Sir H. D. Oakshott (1st Bt 1959)	1904	1975	Rugby	Cambridge	25, 26, 29
O'Brien, Sir I. J. (1st Bt 1916) 1st Ld Shandon (1918)	1857	1930	Vincentian Sch. Cork*	Dublin	5^2, 9
O'Connor, C. A.	1854	1928	St. Stanislaus Coll.*	Dublin	5^2
O'Connor, Sir J. (Kt 1925)	1872	1931	Blackrock Coll.*		5, 6, 9
O'Connor, Sir T. J. (Kt 1936)	1891	1940	Secondary		17
† Ogmore, 1st Ld (1950). D. R. Rees-Williams	1903	1976	Mill Hill	Wales	22^3
O'Hagan, 3rd Ld (1900). M. H. T. Townley-O'Hagan	1882	1961	Marlborough	Cambridge	3, 5
Oliver, G. H.	1888	1984	Bolton*		21
† Olivier, 1st Ld (1924). S. Olivier	1859	1943	Tonbridge	Oxford	11
† O'Malley, B. K.	1930	1976	Mexborough G.S.*	Manchester	31, 32^2, 36
† O'Neill, Sir (R. W.) H. (1st Bt 1929). 1st Ld Rathcavan (1953)	1883	1982	Eton	Oxford	16
† Onslow, 4th E of (1870). W. H. Onslow, Vt Cranley (1855)	1853	1911	Eton	Oxford	2^3
Onslow 5th E of (1911). R. W. A. Onslow, Vt Cranley (1876)	1876	1945	Eton	Oxford	7^3, 9, 10^2, 12^2
Onslow, 6th E of (1945). W. A. B. Onslow. Vt Cranley (1913)	1913	. .	Winchester	Sandhurst	26, 29
† Onslow, Sir C. (K.C.M.G. 1993)	1926	. .	Harrow	Oxford	35, 38
Oppenheim, P. A. C. L.	1956	. .	Harrow	Oxford	45
† Oppenheim-Barnes, Lady (Life Peeress 1989), Mrs S. Oppenheim	1928	. .	Sheffield H.S.*		42
Oram, Ld (Life Peer 1975). A. E. Oram	1913	. .	Brighton G.S.*	London	31, 38
† Orme, S.	1923	. .	Elementary		36, 37^2
† Ormsby-Gore, W. G. A. 4th Ld Harlech (1938)	1885	1964	Eton	Oxford	10, 11, 14^2, 15, 17
† Ormsby-Gore, Sir (W) D. (K.C.M.G. 1961). 5th Ld Harlech (1964)	1918	1985	Eton	Oxford	24, 26

Orr-Ewing, Ld (Life Peer 1971). Sir C. I. Orr-Ewing (Bt 1963)	1912	..	Harrow	Oxford	26[2], 27
† Owen, Ld (Life Peer 1992) D. Owen	1938	..	Bradfield	Cambridge	30, 36[4]
Owen, Sir G. (Kt 1944)	1881	1963	Ardwyn G.S.*	Aberystwyth	15
† Oxford & Asquith, 1st E of (1925). H. H. Asquith	1852	1928	City of London	Oxford	3, 4[2], 5
Padley, W. E.	1916	1984	Chipping Norton G.S.*		30
† Page, Sir R. G. (Kt 1980)	1911	1981	Magdalen Coll.	London	34[3]
Page Croft, Sir H. (1st Bt 1924) 1st Ld Croft (1940)	1881	1947	Eton & Shrewsbury	Cambridge	19, 21
Paice, J. E. T.	1949	..	Framlingham		45
† Pakenham, 1st Ld (1945). F. A. Pakenham, 7th E of Longford (1961)	1905	..	Eton	Oxford	22[4], 23[2], 29[2], 30
† Paling, W.	1883	1971	Elementary		13, 19, 20, 22, 23
† Pannell, Ld (Life Peer 1974). T. C. Pannell	1902	1980	Elementary		31
Parker, J.	1863	1948	Wesleyan Sch.*		9
Parker, J.	1906	1987	Marlborough	Oxford	22
† Parkinson, Ld (Life Peer 1992). C. Parkinson	1931	..	R.G.S., Lancaster*	Cambridge	35, 40, 41[2], 42[2]
Parkinson. J. A.	1870	1941	Elementary		11, 13[2]
† Parmoor, 1st Ld (1914). Sir C. A. Cripps (K.C.V.O. 1908)	1852	1941	Winchester	Oxford	10, 12
Partington, O., 2nd Ld Doverdale (1925)	1872	1935	Rossall		5
† Passfield, 1st Ld (1929). S. J. Webb	1859	1947	Switzerland & Secondary		11, 13[2]
Patnick, Sir C. I. (Kt 1994)	1929	..	Tech.S. Sheffield*		43[2], 46
† Patten, C. F.	1944	..	St. Benedict's, Ealing*	Oxford	39[2], 40, 41, 44
† Patten, J. H. C.	1945	..	Wimbledon	Cambridge	39, 40, 41[2], 44, 45
† Pattie, Sir G. E. (Kt 1987)	1936	..	Durham	Cambridge	39[3], 42
Pavitt, L. A.	1914	1987	Secondary		37
† Peake, O., 1st Vt Ingleby (1955)	1897	1966	Eton	Sandhurst & Oxford	15, 17[2], 20, 25[3]
Pearson, A.	1898	1980	Elementary		23[2]
Pearson, Sir F. F. (1st Bt 1964)	1911	1991	Uppingham	Cambridge	29
† Pearson, W. D., 1st Bt (1894). Ld Cowdray (1910). 1st Vt (1916)	1856	1927	Privately		7
† Peart, Ld (Life Peer 1976). (T.) F. Peart	1914	1980	Wolsingham G.S.*	Durham	29[2], 30, 35, 36
Pease, Sir A. F. (1st Bt 1920)	1866	1927	Brighton Coll.	Cambridge	7
† Pease, J. A. 1st Ld Gainford (1917)	1860	1943	Tottenham*	Cambridge	3, 4[2], 5[2], 6
Peat, C. U.	1892	1979	Sedbergh	Oxford	19[2], 21
† Peel, 1st E (1929). W. R. W. Peel, 2nd Vt (1912)	1867	1937	Harrow	Oxford	7, 8[4], 9[2], 10, 12[2], 13
Peel, Sir J. (Kt 1973)	1912	..	Wellington	Cambridge	29
† Pembroke & Montgomery, 14th E of (1895). S. Herbert	1853	1913	Eton	Oxford	2
Pendry, T.	1934	..	St Augustine's*	Oxford	37[2]
Penny, Sir F. G. (Kt 1929). 1st Ld Marchwood (1937), 1st Vt (1945)	1876	1955	K. Edward VI G.S. Southampton*		12, 14, 15[3]
† Pentland, 1st Ld (1909). J. Sinclair	1860	1925	Edinburgh Acad.	Sandhurst & Wellington	3, 4
Pentland, N.	1912	1972	Elementary		31[3], 32
† Percival Sir (W.) I. (Kt 1979)	1921	..	Latymer Upper	Cambridge	42
Percy, Earl (1899), H.A.G. Percy	1871	1909	Eton	Oxford	1, 2

Name	Born	Died	School	University	Pages
† Percy of Newcastle, 1st Ld (1953). Ld E. Percy	1887	1958	Eton	Oxford	10^2, 11, 16
Perkins, Sir R. D. (Kt 1954)	1903	. .	Eton	Cambridge	18, 20
Perry, E. G.	1910	. .	Elementary		37
† Perth, 17th E of (1951). Vt Strathallan (1937)	1907	. .	Downside	Cambridge	27
† Pethick-Lawrence, 1st Ld (1945). F. W. Pethick-Lawrence	1871	1961	Eton	Cambridge	12, 22
Petherick, M.	1894	1985	Marlborough	Cambridge	21
† Peyton, Ld (Life Peer 1983). J. W. W. Peyton	1919	. .	Eton	Oxford	28, 34
Phillips, Lady (Life Peeress 1964). Mrs N. M. Phillips	1910	1992	Marist Convent*		33
† Pickthorn, Sir K. W. M. (1st Bt 1959)	1892	1975	Aldenham	Cambridge	24
Pike, Lady (Life Peeress 1974). Miss M. Pike	1918	. .	Hunmanby Hall*	Reading	26, 28
Pike Pease, H. 1st Ld Daryngton (1923)	1867	1949	Brighton Coll.	Cambridge	6, 8
Pilkington, Sir R. A. (K.B.E. 1961)	1908	1976	Charterhouse	Oxford	18, 20
Pim, J.	1859	1949	Secondary	Dublin	5^2
Pitt, Dame E. M. (D.B.E. 1962)	1906	1966	Bordesley Green, Birmingham*		25, 27, 28
† Plunkett, Sir H. C. (K.C.V.O. 1903)	1854	1932	Eton	Oxford	2, 3
Plymouth, 1st E of (1905). R. G. Windsor-Clive, 14th Ld Windsor(1869)	1857	1923	Eton	Cambridge	2
Plymouth, 2nd E of (1923). I. M. Windsor-Clive	1889	1943	Eton	Cambridge	11, 12, 14^2, 15
† Pollock, Sir E. M. (K.B.E. 1917). 1st Ld Hanworth (1926). 1st Vt (1936)	1861	1936	Charterhouse	Cambridge	9^2
Polwarth, 10th Ld (1944). H. A. Hepburne-Scott	1916	. .	Eton	Cambridge	34
Ponsonby of Shulbrede, 1st Ld (1930). A. A. W. H. Ponsonby	1871	1946	Eton	Oxford	11, 13^3
Popplewell, Ld (Life Peer 1966). E. Popplewell	1899	1977	Elementary		23
† Portal, 1st Vt (1945). Sir W. R. Portal (3rd Bt 1931). 1st Ld (1935)	1885	1949	Eton	Oxford	19^2
† Portillo, M. D. X.	1953	. .	Harrow C.S.*	Cambridge	40, 41, 42, 43, 44^2, 45
† Portland, 6th D of (1879). W. J. A. C. J. Cavendish-Bentinck	1857	1943	Eton		2
Portland, 7th D of (1943). W. A. Cavendish-Bentinck, M of Titchfield (1893)	1893	1977	Eton	Sandhurst	12, 14
Portsmouth, 6th E of (1891). N. Wallop, Vt Lymington (1856)	1856	1917	Eton	Oxford	3
Powell, J. B.	1862	1923	Secondary	Dublin	9
† Powell, (J.) E.	1912	. .	King Edward's, Birmingham	Cambridge	24, 27, 27^2
Pratt, Sir J. W. (Kt 1922)	1873	1952	S.Shields*	Glasgow	8, 9
† Prentice, Ld (Life Peer 1992) Sir R. E. Prentice (Kt 1987)	1923	. .	Whitgift	London	30, 31^2, 32, 36, 37, 41
† Pretyman, E. G.	1860	1931	Eton	Woolwich	1^2, 6, 7
Price, Sir D. E. C. (Kt 1980)	1924	. .	Eton	Cambridge & Yale	28, 34
Price, W. G.	1934	. .	Forest of Dean		35^2, 37

					Tech.Coll.*
Primrose, N. J. A.	1882	1917	Eton	Oxford	4, 9
† Prior, Ld (Life Peer 1987) J. M. L. Prior	1927	..	Charterhouse	Cambridge	33^2, 40, 41
(†) Profumo, J. D.	1915	..	Harrow	Oxford	25, 26^2, 27, 28
† Prothero, R. E. 1st Ld Ernle	1851	1937	Marlborough	Oxford	7
Pybus, Sir (P.) J. (1st Bt 1934)	1880	1935			14
Pym, L. R.	1884	1945	Bedford	Cambridge	20, 21
† Pym, Ld (Life Peer 1987) F. L. Pym	1922	..	Eton	Cambridge	34, 35, 38^2, 39, 41^2
Raglan, 3rd Ld (1884). G. F. H. Somerset	1857	1921	Eton	Sandhurst	2
† Raison, Sir T. H. F. (Kt 1991)	1929	..	Eton	Oxford	34, 39^2
† Ramsbotham, H. 1st Ld Soulbury (1941), 1st Vt (1954)	1887	1971	Uppingham	Oxford	14, 15, 16^3, 17, 18
† Ramsden, J. E.	1923	..	Eton	Oxford	27, 28
† Rankeillour, 1st Ld (1932). J. F. Hope	1870	1949	Oratory Sch.	Oxford	6, 8, 9
Rankeillour, 2nd Ld (1949). A. O. J. Hope	1897	1958	Oratory Sch.	Sandhurst	17^3
Ranksborough, 1st Ld (1914). J. F. Brocklehurst	1852	1921	Rugby	Cambridge	5, 6, 9
† Rathcavan, 1st Ld (1953). Sir (R. W.) H.O'Neill (1st Bt 1929)	1883	1982	Eton	Oxford	16
Rathcreedan, 1st Ld (1916). C. W. Norton	1845	1930	Abroad	Dublin & Sandhurst	3, 4, 5
† Rawlinson of Ewell, Ld (Life Peer 1978). Sir P. Rawlinson (Kt 1962)	1919	..	Downside	Oxford	29, 35
Rea, 1st Ld (1937). Sir W. R. Rea (1st Bt 1935)	1873	1948	University Coll Sch.		5, 6, 15
† Reading, 1st M of (1926). Sir R. D. Isaacs (Kt 1910), 1st Ld Reading (1914), 1st Vt (1916), 1st E of (1917)	1860	1935	University Coll Sch.		4^3, 13
Reading, 2nd M of (1935). G. R. Isaacs, Vt Erleigh (1917)	1889	1960	Rugby	Oxford	24^2
Reay, 14th Ld (1963) H. W. Mackay	1937	..	Eton	Oxford	44, 46^2
Redhead, E. C.	1902	1967	Elementary		30, 32
† Redmayne, Ld (Life Peer 1966). Sir M. Redmayne (1st Bt 1964)	1910	1983	Radley		25, 29^2
† Redwood, J. A.	1951	..	Oxford		42^2, 45^2, 46
† Rees, M., Ld Merlyn-Rees (Life Peer 1992)	1920	..	Harrow Weald G.S.*	London	30^3, 36, 37
† Rees, Ld (Life Peer 1987) P. W. I. Rees	1926	..	Stowe	Oxford	38^2, 42
† Rees-Williams, D R. 1st Ld Ogmore (1950)	1903	1976	Mill Hill	Wales	22^3
† Reid, Ld (Ld of Appeal 1948). J. S. C. Reid	1890	1975	Edinburgh Acad.	Cambridge	17, 20^2, 21
† Reid, Sir R. T. 1st Ld Loreburn (1906), 1st E (1911)	1846	1923	Cheltenham	Oxford	3, 4
† Reigate, Ld (Life Peer 1970). Sir J. K. Vaughan-Morgan (1st Bt 1960)	1906	..	Eton	Oxford	27, 28
† Reith, 1st Ld (1940). Sir J. C. W. (Kt 1927)	1889	1971	Glasgow Acad & Gresham's		16, 19^2
† Renton, Ld (Life Peer 1979). Sir D. L. Renton (K.B.E. 1964)	1908	..	Oundle	Oxford	24, 26^2, 28
† Renton, (R.) T.	1932	..	Eton	Cambridge	38, 39^2, 42, 44

				& McGill	
† Reynolds, G. W.	1927	1969	Acton G.S.*		30^3
† Rhodes, Ld (Life Peer 1964). H. Rhodes	1895	1987	Elementary		23, 32
† Rhondda, 1st Vt (1918). 1st Ld (1916). D. A. Thomas	1856	1918	Privately	Cambridge	7, 8
† Rhyl, Ld (Life Peer 1970). (E.) N. C. Birch	1906	1981	Eton		24^3, 25, 26
Richard, Ld (Life Peer 1992). I. S. Richard	1932	. .	Cheltenham	Cambridge	30
Richards, R.	1884	1954	Elementary		11
Richards, R.	1947	. .	Llandovery	Swansea	45
† Ridley, 1st Vt (1900). Sir M. White Ridley (5th Bt 1877)	1842	1904	Harrow	Oxford	1
† Ridley of Liddesdale, Ld (Life Peer 1992). N. Ridley	1929	1993	Eton	Oxford	34^2, 38^2, 40, 42^2
Ridsdale, Sir J. E. (Kt 1981)	1915	. .	Tonbridge	Sandhurst	27^2
† Rifkind, M.	1946	. .	Geo. Watson's Edinburgh	Edinburgh	38, 39, 41^2, 44, 46
† Ripon, 1st M of (1871). G. F. S. Robinson, Vt Goderich (1833), 2nd E of Ripon (1859)	1827	1909	Privately		3, 4
† Rippon of Hexham, Ld (Life Peer 1987) (A.) G. F. Rippon	1924	. .	King's, Taunton	Oxford	27^2, 28^2, 34^3
† Ritchie of Dundee, 1st Ld (1905). C. T. Ritchie	1838	1906	City of London		1^2, 2
† Robens, Ld (Life Peer 1961). A. Robens	1910	. .	Secondary		22^2
Roberts, C. H.	1865	1959	Marlborough	Oxford	4, 6
† Roberts, F. O.	1876	1941	Elementary		11, 13
† Roberts, G. H.	1869	1928	Elementary		6, 7^2, 8
† Roberts, G. O., Ld Goronwy-Roberts (Life Peer 1974)	1913	1981	Bethesda G.S.*	Wales	30^2, 32^2, 36^2
Roberts, M. H. A.	1927	1983	Neath G.S.*	Cardiff	42
Roberts, Sir (I.) W. P. (Kt 1990)	1930	. .	Harrow	Oxford	42^2
† Robertson, E., 1st Ld Lochee of Gowrie (1908)	1846	1911	Secondary	St Andrews & Oxford	3
Robertson, J.	1867	1926	Elementary		11
Robertson, J. J.	1898	1955	Elementary		23
† Robertson, J. M.	1856	1933	Stirling*		4
† Robinson, Sir K. (Kt 1983)	1911	. .	Oundle		31^2
Robinson, M. N. F.	1946	. .	Harrow	Oxford	42
† Robson, Ld (Ld of Appeal 1910). Sir W. S. Robson (Kt 1905)	1852	1918	Privately	Cambridge	3^2, 4
Rochester, 1st Ld (1931). Sir E. H. Lamb (Kt 1914)	1876	1955	Dulwich & Wycliffe Coll.		14, 16
† Rodger of Earlsferry, Ld (Life Peer 1992) A. F. Rodger	1944	. .	Kelvinside Acad.	Glasgow & Oxford	42, 45^2
Rodgers, Sir J. C. (1st Bt 1964)	1906	1993	St Peter's, York	Oxford	28
† Rodgers of Quarry Bank (Life Peer 1992). W. T. Rodgers	1928	. .	Quarry Bank H.S. Liverpool*	Oxford	29^2, 30, 32, 36, 37
Roe, Mrs M. A.	1936	. .	Croydon H.S.		40
Rogers, G. H. R.	1906	1983	Secondary		32
† Rosebery, 6th E of (1929). A. E. H. M. A. Primrose, Ld Dalmeny (1882)	1882	1974	Eton	Sandhurst	21
Ross, Sir J. (1st Bt 1919)	1854	1935	Foyle Coll.*	Dublin	9
† Ross of Marnock, Ld (Life Peer 1979). W. Ross	1911	1988	Ayr Academy*	Glasgow	32, 37
Rossi, Sir H. A. L. (Kt 1983)	1927	. .	Finchley Cath.	London	34, 35^2, 41^2

			G.S.*		
† Rothermere, 1st Vt (1919). Sir H. S. Harmsworth (1st Bt 1910), 1st Ld Rothermere (1914)	1868	1940	Secondary		7
Rothschild, J. A. de	1878	1957	Lyceé Louis le Grand*	Cambridge	19
Rowlands, E.	1940	. .	Wirral G.S.*	London	32, 36, 37
† Rowley, Ld (Life Peer 1966). A. Henderson	1893	1968	Queen's Coll., Taunton*	Cambridge	19², 22³
Royle, Ld (Life Peer 1964). C. Royle	1896	1975	Stockport G.S.*		23
Royle, Sir A. H. F. (K C.M.G. 1974). Ld Fanshawe (Life Peer 1983)	1927	. .	Harrow	Sandhurst	33
† Rumbold, Dame A. (D.B.E. 1992)	1932	. .	Perse Girls S.	London	39², 40, 44
† Runciman, of Doxford 1st Vt (1937). W. Runciman	1870	1949	S.Shields H.S.* & privately	Cambridge	3², 4³, 6, 14, 15, 16
† Runcorn, Ld (Life Peer 1964). D. F. Vosper	1916	1968	Marlborough	Cambridge	24, 25, 26², 27, 28
† Rushcliffe, 1st Ld (1935). Sir H. B. Betterton (1st Bt 1929)	1872	1949	Rugby	Oxford	10, 12, 14²
Russell, 2nd E (1878). J. F. S. Russell	1865	1931	Winchester	Oxford	13²
Russell, Ld (Scot. judge 1936). A. Russell	1884	1975	Glasgow Acad.	Glasgow	17
Russell, Sir T. W. (1st Bt 1917)	1841	1920	Madras Acad., Fife*		2, 3, 4, 6, 7
† Ryder, R. A.	1949	. .	Radley	Oxford	38, 39, 41, 43, 46
† St Aldwyn, 1st E (1915). M. E. Hicks Beach, 1st Vt St Aldwyn (1906)	1837	1916	Eton	Oxford	1
† St Aldwyn, 2nd E (1916). M. J. Hicks Beach	1912	1992	Eton	Oxford	24, 26, 29, 35
† St Audries, 1st Ld (191 1). Sir A. F. Acland Hood (4th Bt 1892)	1853	1917	Eton	Oxford	22
St Davids, 3rd Vt (1991). C. J. J. Philipps	1939	. .	Sevenoaks	London	46
St Helens, 1st Ld (1964). M. H. C. Hughes-Young	1912	1980	Harrow	Sandhurst	29²
† St John of Fawsley, Ld (Life Peer 1987) N. A. F. St John-Stevas	1929	. .	Ratcliffe	Cambridge & Oxford	34², 39, 41
St Oswald, 4th Ld (1957). R. D. G. Winn	1916	1984	Stowe	Bonn & Freiburg	26, 29
Sackville, T. G.	1950	. .	Eton	Oxford	43², 45, 46
† Sainsbury, T. A. G.	1932	. .	Eton	Oxford	39², 42, 43², 46²
† Salisbury, 3rd M of (1868). R. A. T. Gascoyne-Cecil, Vt Cranborne (1865)	1830	1903	Eton	Oxford	13
† Salisbury, 4th M of (1903). J. E. H. Gascoyne-Cecil, Vt Cranborne (1868)	1861	1947	Eton	Oxford	1², 2, 9, 10, 11
† Salisbury, 5th M of (1947). R. A. J. Gascoyne-Cecil, Vt Cranborne (1903)	1893	1972	Eton	Oxford	15, 17, 18³, 19, 20, 24³, 26
† Salter, 1st Ld (1953). Sir (J.) A. Salter (K.C.B. 1922)	1881	1975	Oxford H.S.*	Oxford	16, 19², 21, 24, 25
† Salvesen, Ld (Scot. judge 1905). E. Salvesen	1857	1942	Collegiate Sch. Edin.*	Edinburgh	2

Name	Born	Died	School	University	References
† Samuel, 1st Vt (1937). Sir H. L. Samuel (G.B.E. 1920)	1870	1963	University Coll. Sch.	Oxford	3, 4[4], 5, 6[2], 13
Samuel, Sir A. M. (1st Bt 1932). 1st Ld Mancroft (1937)	1872	1942	Norwich G.S.*		11, 12
Samuels, A. W.	1852	1925	Royal Sch., Dungannon*	Dublin	9[2]
† Sanders, Sir R. A. (1st Bt 1920). 1st Ld Bayford (1929)	1867	1940	Harrow	Oxford	8, 9[2], 10
Sanders, W. S.	1871	1941	Elementary	Berlin	13
Sanderson of Bowden, Ld (Life Peer 1985) C. R. Sanderson	1933	..	Glenalmond		41
Sandford, 1st Ld (1945). Sir A. J. Edmondson (Kt 1934)	1887	1959	University Coll. Sch.		17[2], 20[2], 21
Sandford, 2nd Ld (1959). Rev J. C. Edmondson	1920	..	Eton	Cambridge	34[3]
† Sandhurst, 1st Vt (1917). W. Mansfield, 2nd Ld Sandhurst (1876)	1855	1921	Rugby		5, 6, 9
† Sandys, D. Ld Duncan-Sandys (Life Peer 1974)	1908	1987	Eton	Oxford	19[2], 20, 21, 24, 25, 27[4]
Sandys, 7th Ld (1961). R. M. O. Hill	1931	..	R. Naval Coll. Dartmouth		35, 43
† Sankey, 1st Vt (1932). Sir J. Sankey (Kt 1914), 1st Ld (1929)	1866	1948	Lancing	Oxford	12, 13
† Sassoon, Sir P. A. G. D. (3rd Bt 1912)	1888	1939	Eton	Oxford	11, 14, 15, 17
Saye & Sele, 18th Ld (1907). G. C. T.-W.-Fiennes	1858	1937	Eton		5
† Scarbrough, 11th E of (1945). L. R. Lumley	1896	1969	Eton	Sandhurst & Oxford	20
† Scott, Sir L. F. (Kt 1922)	1869	1950	Rugby	Oxford	9
Scott, Sir (R.) D. (Kt 1955)	1901	1974	Mill Hill	Cambridge	20
† Scott, N. P.	1933	..	Clapham Coll*		34, 41[3]
Scott-Hopkins, Sir J. S. R. (Kt 1981)	1921	..	Eton	Oxford	26
† Seely. J. E. B. 1st Ld Mottistone (1933)	1868	1947	Harrow	Cambridge	4[3], 7, 8
† Sefton, 6th E of (1901). O. C. Molyneux	1871	1930			3
† Selborne, 2nd E of (1895). W. W. Palmer, Vt Wolmer (1882)	1859	1942	Winchester	Oxford	1, 2, 5
† Selborne, 3rd E of (1942). R. C. Palmer, Vt Wolmer (1895)	1887	1971	Winchester	Oxford	10, 12, 18
† Selkirk, 10th E of (1940). Ld G. N. Douglas-Hamilton	1906	..	Eton	Oxford	25[2], 26[2]
† Selsdon, 1st Ld (1932). Sir W. Mitchell-Thomson (2nd Bt 1918)	1877	1938	Winchester	Oxford	7, 8, 12
† Selwyn-Lloyd. Ld (Life Peer 1976). (J.) S. B. Lloyd	1904	1978	Fettes	Cambridge	24[3], 25, 26[3]
Serota, Lady (Life Peeress 1967). Mrs B. S. Serota	1919	..	J.C. Howard Sch.*	London	31, 33
† Shackleton, Ld (Life Peer 1958). E. A. A. Shackleton	1911	..	Radley	Oxford	29[2], 30, 31[2]
† Shaftesbury, 9th E of (1886). A. Ashley-Cooper	1869	1961	Eton	Sandhurst	10
† Shakespeare, Sir G. H. (1st Bt 1942)	1893	1980	Highgate	Cambridge	14[2], 15, 16[3], 18
Shandon, 1st Ld (1918). Sir I. J. O'Brien (1st Bt 1916)	1857	1930	Vincentian Schs, Cork*	Dublin	5[2], 9

Name	Born	Died	School	University	Pages
Sharples, Sir R. C. (K.C.M.G 1972)	1916	1973	Eton	Sandhurst	28^2, 33
Shaw, Sir (J.) G.D.	1931	. .	Sedbergh	Cambridge	40^2, 41, 42
† Shaw, Ld (Ld of Appeal 1909). T. Shaw, 1st Ld Craigmyle (1929)	1850	1937	Dunfermline H.S.*	Edinburgh	3, 5
† Shaw, T.	1872	1938	Elementary		11, 13
† Shawcross, Ld (Life Peer 1959). Sir H. W. Shawcross (Kt 1945)	1902	. .	Dulwich	Geneva	23^2
† Shearer, I. H., Ld Avonside (Scot. judge 1964)	1914	. .	Dunfermline H.S.*	Glasgow & Edinburgh	29
† Sheldon, R. E.	1923	. .	Secondary		35^2, 36
Shelton, Sir W. J. M.(Kt 1989)	1929	. .	Radley	Oxford	40
† Shephard, Mrs G.	1940	. .	N. Walsham G.S.*	Oxford	42, 44^2, 45
† Shepherd, 1st Ld (1946). G. R. Shepherd	1881	1954	Elementary		23^3
† Shepherd, 2nd Ld (1954). M. N. Shepherd	1918	. .	Friends' Sch., Saffron Walden*		30^2, 33, 35
Sherwood, 1st Ld (1941). Sir H. M. Seely (3rd Bt 1926)	1898	1971	Eton		18
Shiels, Sir (T.) D. (Kt 1939)	1881	1953	Elementary	Edinburgh	13
† Shinwell, Ld (Life Peer 1970). E. Shinwell	1884	1986	Elementary		11, 13^2, 22^2, 23
† Shore, P. D.	1924	. .	Quarry Bank H.S., Liverpool*	Cambridge	29^2, 31, 32, 36, 37
Short, A.	1882	1938	Elementary		12
† Short, E. W., Ld Glenamara (Life Peer 1976)	1912	. .	Secondary	Durham	30, 31, 32, 35
† Shortt, E.	1862	1935	Durham	Durham	7^2
† Sidney, W. P. 6th Ld De L'Isle & Dudley (1945). 1st Vt De L'Isle (1956)	1909	1991	Eton	Cambridge	21, 24
† Silkin, 1st Ld (1950). L. Silkin	1889	1972	Secondary	London	23
† Silkin, J. E.	1923	1987	Dulwich	Wales & Cambridge	31, 32^3, 33, 36^4
† Silkin of Dulwich, Ld (Life Peer 1985). S. C. Silkin	1918	1988	Dulwich	Cambridge	37
Simmons, C. J.	1893	1975	Elementary	.	23^2
† Simon, 1st Vt (1940). Sir J. A. Simon (Kt 1910)	1873	1954	Fettes	Oxford	4^2, 5, 13, 15^2, 17, 20
Simon of Wythenshawe, 1st Ld (1947). Sir E. D. Simon (Kt 1932)	1879	1960	Rugby	Cambridge	14
† Simon of Glaisdale, Ld (Life Peer 1971). Simon, Sir J. E. S. (Kt 1959)	1911	. .	Gresham's	Cambridge	26^2, 29
† Simonds, 1st Vt (1954). G. T. Simonds, Ld (Ld of Appeal 1944). 1st Ld (1952)	1881	1971	Winchester	Oxford	24
† Sinclair, Sir A. H. M. (4th Bt 1912). 1st Vt Thurso (1952)	1890	1970	Eton	Sandhurst	14^2, 18
† Sinclair, J., 1st Ld Pentland (1909)	1860	1925	Edinburgh Acad. & Wellington	Sandhurst	3, 4
† Sinha, 1st Ld (1919). Sir S. P. Sinha (Kt 1915)	1864	1928	Indian Sch.		7
Skeffington, A. M.	1909	1971	Streatham G.S.*	London	31^2
Skelmersdale, 7th Ld (1973). R. Bootle-Wilbraham	1945	. .	Eton		40, 41^2, 42, 43
Skelton, (A.) N.	1880	1935	Glenalmond	Oxford	14, 16
Slater, Mrs H.	1903	1976	Hanley H.S.*		32
Slater, Ld (Life Peer 1970). J. Slater	1904	1977	Elementary		31^2

Name	Born	Died	School	University	Pages
† Slesser, Sir H. (Kt 1924)	1883	1979	Oundle & St Paul's	London	11
† Smith, Sir B. (K.B.E. 1945)	1879	1964	Elementary		13, 18[2], 22
Smith, Sir D. G. (Kt 1983)	1926	. .	Chichester H.S.*		33, 34
Smith, E.	1896	1969	Elementary		23
† Smith, Sir F. E. (Kt 1915). 1st Ld Birkenhead (1919), 1st Vt (1921), 1st E of (1922)	1872	1930	Birkenhead	Oxford	6[2], 9, 11
† Smith, J.	1938	. .	Dunoon G.S.*	Glasgow	35, 36[2], 37
Smith, T.	1886	1953	Elementary		18
Smith, W. R.	1872	1942	Norwich		13
Smithers, Sir P. H. B. O. (Kt 1970)	1913	. .	Harrow	Oxford	26
† Smuts, J. C.	1870	1950	S. Africa	Stellenbosch & Cambridge	6, 8
† Smyth, Sir J. G. (1st Bt 1955)	1893	1983	Repton	Sandhurst	25
Snadden, Sir W. M. (1st Bt 1955)	1896	1959	Dollar Academy		25
Snape, P. C.	1942	. .	St Winifred's S. Stockport*		37[2]
† Snell, 1st Ld (1931). H. Snell	1865	1944	Elementary	Nottingham	13, 20
Snow, Ld (Life Peer 1964). Sir C. P. Snow (Kt 1957)	1905	1980	Newton's*	Leicester & Cambridge	32
Snow, J. W., Ld Burntwood (Life Peer 1970)	1910	1982	Haileybury		23[2], 30, 31[2]
† Snowden, 1st Vt (1931). P. Snowden	1864	1937	Elementary		10, 12, 13[2]
† Soames, Ld (Life Peer 1978). Sir (A.) C. J. Soames (G.C.M.G. 1972)	1920	1987	Eton	Sandhurst	24, 26[2], 28, 38
Soames, A. N. W.	1948	. .	Eton		44[2]
Soares, Sir E. J. (Kt 1911)	1864	1926	Privately	Cambridge	5
† Somerleyton, 1st Ld (1916). Sir S. B. Crossley (2nd Bt 1872)	1857	1935	Eton	Oxford	2, 9, 10
Somers, 6th Ld (1899). A. H. T. S. Cocks	1887	1944	Charterhouse	Oxford	12
† Somervell of Harrow, Ld (Ld of Appeal 1954). Sir D. B. Somervell (Kt 1933)	1889	1960	Harrow	Oxford	14, 17[2], 20[2]
Sorensen, Ld (Life Peer 1964). R. W. Sorensen	1891	1971	Elementary		33
† Soskice, Sir F. (Kt 1945). Ld Stow Hill (Life Peer 1966)	1902	1979	St Paul's	Oxford	23[2], 29, 30
† Soulbury, 1st Vt (1954). H. Ramsbotham, 1st Ld Soulbury (1941)	1887	1971	Uppingham	Oxford	14, 15, 16[3], 17, 18
Southby, Sir A. R. J. (1st Bt 1937)	1886	1969	H.M.S. Britannia*		15, 17
† Southwark, 1st Ld (1910). R. K. Causton	1843	1929	Privately		3, 4
Speed, Sir (H.) K. (Kt 1992)	1934	. .	Bedford		34, 35[2], 39
† Spencer, 6th E (1910). C. R. Spencer, Vt Althorp (1857), 1st Vt Althorp (1905)	1857	1922	Harrow	Cambridge	3, 5
Spencer, Sir D.	1936	. .	Clitheroe G.S.*	Oxford	45
Spicer, (W.) M. H.	1943	. .	Wellington	Cambridge	40[2], 42
† Spoor, B C.	1878	1928	Secondary		11
Sproat, I. M.	1938	. .	Winchester	Oxford	42, 45
Squire, R. C.	1944	. .	Tiffin*		44, 45[2]
Stallard, Ld (Life Peer 1983). A. W. Stallard	1921	. .	Hamilton Acad.*		37[2]
† Stanhope, 7th E (1905). J R. Stanhope, Vt Mahon (1880)	1880	1967	Eton	Oxford	9, 11, 13, 14[2], 15[2], 16, 17

† Stanley, Ld (1893). E. G. V. Stanley, 17th E of Derby (1908)	1865	1948	Wellington		2^3, 6, 8, 10
† Stanley, Ld (1908). E. M. C. Stanley	1894	1938	Eton	Oxford	12, 13, 15, 16^3
† Stanley, Sir A. H. (Kt 1914). 1st Ld Ashfield (1920)	1874	1948	American Schs		8
† Stanley, Sir G. F. (G.C.I.E. 1929)	1872	1938	Wellington	Woolwich	9^2, 10, 12
Stanley, Sir J. P. (Kt 1988)	1942	. .	Repton	Oxford	39, 40, 41
† Stanley, O. F. G.	1896	1950	Eton		13, 14^2, 16^3, 20
† Stanmore, 2nd Ld (1912). G. A. M. Hamilton-Gordon	1871	1957	Winchester	Cambridge	5, 6, 9
† Stansgate, 1st Vt (1941). W. Wedgwood Benn	1877	1960	Paris Lycée	London	5, 13, 22
Stedman, Lady (Life Peeress 1974). P. Stedman	1916	. .	County G.S., Peterborough*		37, 38
Steel-Maitland, Sir A. H. D. R. (1st Bt 1917)	1876	1935	Rugby	Oxford	5, 7, 8, 12
Steele, T.	1905	1979	Elementary		22
† Stewart, (B. H.) I. H.	1935	. .	Haileybury	Cambridge	38, 39, 40, 41
Stewart, Ld (Scot. judge 1975). E. G. F. Stewart	1923	. .	George Watson's Edinburgh	Edinburgh	32
Stewart, J.	1863	1931	Normal Sch., Glasgow*		11
Stewart, (J.) A.	1942	. .	Baxter H.S., Coupar*	St Andrew's & Harvard	41, 45
† Stewart of Fulham, Ld (Life Peer 1979). (R.) M. M. Stewart	1906	1990	Christ's Hospital	Oxford	23^5, 29^2, 30^3
Stewart, (W.) I.	1925	. .	Loretto	Glasgow & Edinburgh	35
† Stockton, 1st E of (1984). H. Macmillan	1894	1986	Eton	Oxford	18^2, 19, 20, 24^4, 26
† Stodart of Leaston, Ld (Life Peer 1981). (J.) A. Stodart	1916	. .	Wellington		28, 33^2
Stoddart of Swindon, Ld (Life Peer 1983). D. L. Stoddart	1926	. .	Henley G.S.*		37^2
† Stokes, R. R.	1897	1957	Downside	Cambridge	21, 23
† Stonehaven, 1st Vt (1938). Sir J. L. Baird (2nd Bt 1920). 1st Ld Stonehaven (1925)	1874	1941	Eton	Oxford	7^2, 8, 10^2
(†) Stonehouse, J. T.	1925	1988	Taunton's, Southampton*	London	30^3, 31^2, 32
† Stonham, Ld (Life Peer 1958). V. J. Collins	1903	1971	Regent St. Poly.	London	30^2
† Stott, Ld (Scot. judge 1967). G. Stott	1909	. .	Edinburgh Acad.	Edinburgh	32
† Stow Hill, Ld (Life Peer 1966). Sir F. Soskice (Kt 1945)	1902	1979	St Paul's	Oxford	23^2, 29, 30
Strabolgi, 11th Ld (1953) D. M de D. K. Strabolgi	1914	. .	Gresham's Sch.		38
Strachey, Sir E. (4th Bt 1901). 1st Ld Strachie (1911)	1858	1936	Privately	Oxford	3, 4^2, 5
† Strachey, (E.) J. St. L.	1901	1963	Eton	Oxford	22^2, 23
† Strachie, 1st Ld (1911). Sir E. Strachey (4th Bt 1901)	1858	1936	Privately	Oxford	3, 4^2, 5
Stradbroke, 3rd E of (1886). G. E. J. M. Rous	1862	1947	Harrow	Cambridge	11
Strang, G. S.	1943	. .	Secondary	Edinburgh & Cambridge	36^2
† Strathcarron, 1st Ld (1936). Sir I. Macpherson (1st Bt 1933)	1880	1937	George Watson's Edinburgh	Edinburgh	7, 8^2

Name	Born	Died	School	University	Pages
† Strathclyde, 1st Ld (1914) (Scot. judge 1913). A. Ure	1853	1928	Larchfield Acad.*	Glasgow & Edinburgh	3, 5[2]
Strathclyde, 1st Ld (1955). T. D. Galbraith	1891	1985	Glasgow Acad.& Dartmouth		21, 25[2], 28
Strathclyde, 2nd Ld (1985) T. G. D. Galbraith	1960	..	Wellington	East Anglia	40[2], 42, 44, 46[3]
Strathcona & Mount Royal, 3rd Ld (1926). D. S. P. Howard	1891	1959	Eton	Cambridge	14, 15, 16
Strathcona & Mount Royal, 4th Ld (1959). D. E. P. Howard	1923	..	Eton	Cambridge & McGill	33, 35[2], 39
Strathmore, 16th E of (1987). M. F. Bowes-Lyon	1957	..		Aberdeen	44, 46[2]
† Strauss, Ld (Life Peer 1979). G. R. Strauss	1901	1993	Rugby		23[2]
Strauss, H. G., 1st Ld Conesford (1955)	1892	1974	Rugby	Oxford	19, 20, 25
Stross, Sir B. (Kt 1964)	1899	1967	Leeds	Leeds	31
† Stuart, of Findhorn, 1st Vt (1959) J. G. Stuart	1897	1971	Eton		15, 17, 20[2], 21, 25
Studholme, Sir H. G. (1st Bt 1956)	1899	1988	Eton	Oxford	26
Suffield, 6th Ld (1914). C. Harbord	1855	1924	Eton		6, 9
† Summerskill, Lady (Life Peeress 1961). Edith Summerskill	1901	1980	Secondary	London	22[2]
Summerskil,. Shirley	1931	..	St Paul's Girls Sch.	Oxford	36
† Sutherland. 5th D of (1913). G. G. S.-L.-Gower	1888	1963	Eton		9, 12[2]
† Sutherland, Sir W (K.C.B. 1919)	1880	1949	Secondary	Glasgow	8, 9
† Swingler, S. T	1915	1969	Stowe	Oxford	31, 32[2]
† Swinton. 1st E of (1955). Sir P. Lloyd-Greame (changed name to Cunliffe-Lister in 1924), 1st Vt Swinton (1935)	1884	1972	Winchester	Oxford	8[2], 10, 12, 14[2], 15, 18[2], 20, 24, 25[2]
Swinton, 2nd E of (1972). J. Cunliffe-Lister, Ld Masham (1955)	1937	..	Winchester		43
† Talbot, Ld E. B. Fitzalan-Howard. assumed name of Talbot in 1876. 1st Vt Fitzalan (1921)	1855	1947	Oratory Sch.		2, 6, 9
Taverne, D.	1928	..	Charterhouse	Oxford	29[2], 30
Taylor. Ld (Life Peer 1958). S. J. L. Taylor	1910	1988	Stowe	London	30[2]
Taylor, Sir E. M.(Kt 1991)	1937	..	Glasgow H.S.	Glasgow	34[2]
Taylor, H. B., Ld Taylor of Mansfield (Life Peer 1966)	1895	1991	Elementary		22
Taylor, I.	1945	..	Whitby Abbey*	Keele	45
Taylor, J. M.	1941	..	Bromsgrove		43[2], 44, 46
† Taylor, R. J.	1881	1954	Elementary		22
Taylor, Mrs (W.) A.	1947	..	Bolton Sch.*	Bradford	37
Taylor, Sir W. J. (1st Bt 1963)	1902	1972	Archb.Holgate's G.S.*	Sheffield	27, 28
† Tebbit, Ld (Life Peer 1992) N. B. Tebbit	1931	..	Edmonton CGS*		40, 41[2], 42[2]
† Templemore, 4th Ld (1924). A. C. S. Chichester	1880	1953	Harrow	Sandhurst	12, 15[2], 17, 20, 21
† Templewood, 1st Vt (1944). Sir S. J. G.Hoare (2nd Bt 1915)	1880	1959	Harrow	Oxford	10[2], 11, 14, 15[5]
† Tenby, 1st Vt (1957). G. Lloyd George	1894	1967	Eastbourne	Cambridge	14, 16, 18[2], 19, 20, 24[2]

Name	Born	Died	School	University	Pages
Tennant, H. J.	1865	1935	Eton	Cambridge	43, 62
Teviot, Ld 1st Ld (1940). C. I. Kerr	1874	1968	S.Hawtrey's Windsor*		17^2
Thankerton, Ld (Ld of Appeal 1929). W. Watson	1873	1948	Winchester	Cambridge	9, 10, 12
Thatcher, Lady (Life Peeress 1992). Mrs. M. H. Thatcher	1925	. .	Grantham G.S.*	Oxford	28, 34, 38
Thomas, I. (later Bulmer-Thomas)	1905	1993	W.Monmouth*	Oxford	22^2
Thomas, J. H.	1874	1949	Elementary		11, 12, 13, 14^2, 15^2
† Thomas, J. P. L., 1st Vt Cilcennin (1955)	1903	1960	Rugby	Oxford	18, 20^2, 24
Thomas, Sir J. S.(Kt 1985)	1925	1991	Rugby	London	35^2, 42, 43
† Thomas of Gwydir, (Life Peer 1987) P. J. M. Thomas	1920	. .	Epworth Coll., Rhyl*	Oxford	26^2, 27, 35
Thomas, T. G. 1st Vt Tonypandy (1983)	1909	. .	Tonypandy Sec.S.*	Southampton	30^2, 32^2
Thompson, Sir D. (Kt 1992)	1931	. .	Hipperholme G.S.*		39, 43^2
Thompson, Sir K. P. (1st Bt 1963)	1909	1984	Bootle G.S.*		27, 28
Thompson, Sir R. H. M. (1st Bt 1963)	1912	. .	Malvern		25, 26, 27^2, 28, 29
† Thomson, 1st Ld (1924). C. B. Thomson	1875	1930	Cheltenham	Woolwich	11, 12
† Thomson, Ld (Scot. judge 1947). G. R. Thomson	1893	1962	South African Coll.	Cape Town Oxford & Edinburgh	23
Thomson, Sir F. C. (lst Bt 1929)	1875	1935	Edinburgh Academy	Oxford & Edinburgh	10^2, 12^2, 15^2
† Thomson of Monifieth, Ld (Life Peer 1977). G. M Thomson	1921	. .	Grove Academy, Dundee		30^3, 31^3
† Thorneycroft, Ld (Life Peer 1967). (G. E.) P. Thorneycroft	1909	1994	Eton	Woolwich	21, 25, 26, 27^2
Thornton, E.	1905	1992	Elementary		31
† Thurso, 1st Vt (1952) Sir A. H. M. Sinclair (4th Bt 1912)	1890	1970	Eton	Sandhurst	14^2, 18
Thurtle, E.	1884	1954	Elementary		13, 18
Tilney, Sir J. (Kt 1972)	1907	1994	Eton	Oxford	27
Tinn, J.	1922	. .	Elementary	Oxford	37
Titchfield, M of (1893). W. A. H. Cavendish-Bentinck, 7th D of Portland (1943)	1893	1977	Eton	Sandhurst	12, 14
† Tomlinson. G.	1890	1952	Rishton Wesleyan*		18, 22, 23
Tomlinson, J. E.	1939	. .	Westminster City Sch.*	Nottingham	36, 37
† Tonypandy, 1st Vt (1983). (T.) G. Thomas	1909	. .	Tonypandy Sec.S.*	Southampton	$30^2 32^2$
Tracey, R. P.	1948	. .	K.Ed.VI, Stratford*		40
Trafford, Ld (Life Peer 1987). Sir J. A. Trafford (Kt 1985)	1932	1989	Charterhouse	London	41
† Tranmire, Ld (Life Peer 1974). Sir R. H. Turton (Kt 1971)	1903	1994	Eton	Oxford	24^2, 25
Tree, R.	1897	1976	Winchester		21
Trefgarne, 1st Ld (1947). G. M. Garro-Jones. Surname changed to Trefgarne in 1954	1894	1960	Caterham		19
† Trefgarne, 2nd Ld (1960) D. G. Trefgarne	1941	. .	Haileybury	Princeton	39^4, 41, 42^2, 43
Trenchard, 2nd Vt (1956). T. Trenchard	1923	1987	Eton		39^2, 41

Name	Born	Died	School	University	Pages
† Trevelyan, Sir C. P. (3rd Bt 1928)	1870	1958	Harrow	Cambridge	4, 11, 13
Trippier, D. A.	1946	. .	Bury G. S.		40^3, 42, 45
† Trumpington, Lady (Life Peeress 1980). Mrs J. A. Barker	1922	. .	Privately		39^2, 41, 43, 44, 46
† Tryon, 1st Ld (1940). G. C. Tryon	1871	1940	Eton	Sandhurst	7, 8, 10, 12, 14, 16^2, 19^2
Turner, Sir B. (Kt 1931)	1863	1942	Elementary		13
† Turton, Sir R. H. (Kt 1971). Ld Tranmire (Life Peer 1974)	1903	1994	Eton	Oxford	24^2, 25
† Tweedmouth, 2nd Ld (1894). E. Majoribanks	1848	1909	Harrow	Oxford	3, 4
Tweedmouth, 3rd Ld (1909). D. C. Majoribanks	1874	1935	Harrow		5
† Tweedsmuir of Belhelvie, Lady (Life Peeress 1970). Lady Tweedsmuir (1948). Lady P. J. F. Grant	1915	1978	Abroad		28, 29, 34
Ullswater, 2nd Vt (1949) N. J. C. Lowther	1942	. .	Eton	Cambridge	44, 45, 46
Ungoed-Thomas, Sir (A.) L. (Kt 1951)	1904	1972	Haileybury	Oxford	23
† Ure, A. Ld Strathclyde (Scot. judge 1913). 1st Ld (1914)	1853	1928	Larchfield Academy	Glasgow & Edinburgh	3, 5^2
† Urwin, T.	1912	. .	Elementary		29, 31
Valentia, 11th Vt (1863). A. Annesley (U.K. Ld Annesley 1917)	1843	1927	Privately	Woolwich	2, 6, 9, 10
Vane, W. M. F., 1st Ld Inglewood (1964)	1909	. .	Charterhouse	Cambridge	26, 28
Van Straubenzee, Sir W. R. (Kt 1981)	1924	. .	Westminster		34^2
† Varley, Ld (Life Peer 1990). E. G. Varley	1932	. .	Poolsbrook Sec. Mod.S.*		32^2, 34^2
Vaughan, Sir G. F. (Kt 1983)	1933	. .	Kenya*	London	41, 42
† Vaughan-Morgan, Sir J. K. (1st Bt 1960) Ld Reigate (Life Peer 1970)	1906	. .	Eton	Oxford	27, 28
Verney, Sir H. C. W. (4th Bt 1910)	1881	1974	Harrow	Oxford	4
Viant, S. P.	1882	1964	Devonport*		13
Viggers, P. J.	1938	. .	Portsmouth G.S.	Cambridge	41
† Vosper, D. F., Ld Runcorn (Life Peer 1964)	1916	1968	Marlborough	Cambridge	24, 25, 26^2, 27, 28
† Waddington, Ld (Life Peer 1990) D. C. Waddington	1929	. .	Sedbergh	Oxford	39^2, 40, 42, 43^2, 44, 45
Wakefield, Sir E. B.(1st Bt 1962)	1903	1969	Haileybury	Oxford	26, 29^4
† Wakeham, Ld (Life Peer 1992) J. Wakeham	1932	. .	Charterhouse		38^3, 40, 41, 42, 43^2, 44, 45
† Waldegrave, 9th E (1859). W. F. Waldegrave	1851	1930	Eton	Cambridge	2
Waldegrave, 12th E (1936). G. N. Waldegrave, Vt Chewton (1933)	1905	. .	Winchester	Cambridge	26
† Waldegrave, W.	1946	. .	Eton	Oxford & Harvard	38, 40^5, 41, 45^2
Walden, G. G. H.	1939	. .	Latymer Upper	Cambridge	40
Walder, (A.) D.	1928	1978	Latymer Upper	Oxford	35
† Waleran, 1st Ld (1905). Sir W. H. Walrond (2nd Bt 1889)	1849	1925	Eton		2^2
Walkden, 1st Ld (1945). A. G. Walkden	1873	1951	Merchant Taylors' Sch. Ashwell		23
† Walker, Sir H. (Kt 1992)	1927	. .	Secondary		31, 32, 36^2
† Walker of Worcester (Life Peer 1992) P. E. Walker	1932	. .	Latymer Upper		34^3, 39, 40, 42

† Walker-Smith, Sir D. C. (1st Bt 1960). Ld Broxbourne (Life Peer 1983) — 1910 — 1992 — Rossall — Oxford — 24, 25, 27, 28

† Wallace, (D.) E. — 1892 — 1941 — Harrow — Sandhurst — 12, 13, 14, 15², 16³

Wallace of Coslany, Ld (Life Peer 1974). G. D. Wallace — 1906 — .. — Central Sch. Cheltenham* — 38

Walrond, Sir W. H. (2nd Bt 1889). 1st Ld Waleran (1905) — 1849 — 1925 — Eton — 2²

† Walsh, S. — 1859 — 1929 — Elementary — 7, 8, 11

Walston, Ld (Life Peer 1961). H. D. L. Walston — 1912 — 1991 — Eton — Cambridge — 30, 32

† Walters, Sir (J.) T. (Kt 1912) — 1868 — 1933 — Clitheroe G.S.* — 8, 14

Walton, Sir J. L. (Kt 1905) — 1852 — 1908 — Merchant Taylors' Crosby* — London — 3

† Ward of Witley, 1st Vt (1960). G. R. Ward — 1907 — 1988 — Eton — Oxford — 24², 27

Ward, Sir (A.) L. (1st Bt 1929) — 1875 — 1956 — St. Paul's — Paris & Darmstadt — 14, 15, 17³

† Ward, W. D. — 1877 — 1946 — Eton — Cambridge — 5, 9

Wardle, C. F. — 1939 — .. — Tonbridge — Oxford — 44, 45

Wardle, G. J. — 1865 — 1947 — Elementary — 8²

Warne, G. H. — 1881 — 1928 — Elementary — 11

Warrender, Sir V. A. G. A. (8th Bt 1917). 1st Ld Bruntisfield (1942) — 1899 — 1993 — Eton — 14, 15⁴, 17, 18, 20

† Waterhouse, C. — 1893 — 1975 — Cheltenham — Cambridge — 16, 17³, 19², 21

† Watkinson, 1st Vt (1964) H. A. Watkinson — 1910 — .. — Queen's Coll., Taunton* — London — 25², 27, 28

Watson, Sir J. C. (Kt 1931) — 1883 — 1944 — Neilson Instit., Paisley* — Glasgow & Edinburgh — 13, 14

† Watson, W., Ld Thankerton (Ld of Appeal 1929) — 1873 — 1948 — Winchester — Cambridge — 9, 10, 12

Watts, J. A. — 1947 — .. — Bishophalt Sch.* — Cambridge — 45

† Waverley, 1st Vt (1952). Sir J. Anderson (K.C.B. 1919) — 1882 — 1958 — George Watson's Edinburgh — Edinburgh & Leipzig — 15², 17³, 20

† Weatherill, Ld, (Life Peer 1992) B. B. Weatherill — 1920 — .. — Malvern — 35⁴

Webb, Sir H. (1st Bt 1916) — 1866 — 1940 — Privately — 5

† Webb, M. — 1904 — 1956 — Christ Ch., Lancaster* — 22

† Webb, S. J. 1st Ld Passfield (1929) — 1859 — 1947 — Switzerland & Secondary — 11, 13²

† Webster, Sir R. E. (G.C.M.G. 1893). 1st Ld Alverstone (1900). 1st Vt (1913) — 1842 — 1915 — King's Coll. S. & Charterhouse — Cambridge — 2

† Wedderburn, H. J. S., 13th Vt Dudhope (1952). 11th E of Dundee (1953) — 1902 — 1983 — Winchester — Oxford — 16, 19, 26, 28

† Wedgwood, 1st Ld (1942). J. C. Wedgwood — 1872 — 1943 — Clifton & R.N.C. Greenwich — 11

† Weir, 1st Vt (1938). Sir W. D. Weir (Kt 1917). 1st Ld (1918) — 1877 — 1959 — Glasgow H.S.* — 7

Wellbeloved, (A.) J. — 1926 — .. — Elementary — 36

Wells, (P.) B. — 1935 — .. — St. Paul's — Exeter — 46

Wells-Pestell, Ld (Life Peer 1965). R. A. Wells-Pestell — 1910 — 1991 — Secondary — London — 36, 38

† Westwood, 1st Ld (1944). W. Westwood — 1880 — 1953 — Elementary — 23

† Westwood, J. — 1884 — 1948 — Elementary — 13, 19, 23

† Wheatley, Ld (Scot. judge 1954) (Life Peer 1970). J. Wheatley — 1908 — 1988 — Mount St Mary's C., Chesterfield* — Glasgow — 23²

† Wheatley, J. — 1869 — 1930 — Elementary — 11

† Wheeler, Sir J. (Kt 1990) — 1940 — .. — Suffolk county sch. — 45

Name	Born	Died	School	University	Pages
Whitaker, B. C. G	1934	..	Eton	Oxford	31
White, Lady (Life Peeress 1970). Mrs E. L. White	1909	..	St Paul's Girls Sch.	Oxford	30^2, 32
White, F.	1939	..	Elementary		37
† White. (H.) G.	1880	1965	Birkenhead	Liverpool	14
† Whitelaw, 1st Vt (1983). W. S. I. Whitelaw	1918	..	Winchester	Cambridge	27, 29, 33, 34^2, 38, 39
† Whiteley, G. 1st Ld Marchamley (1908)	1855	1925	Abroad	Zurich	3, 5
† Whiteley, W.	1882	1955	Elementary		13, 20^3, 23
† Whitley, J. H.	1866	1935	Clifton	London	3, 5
Whitlock, W. C.	1918	..	Itchen G.S.*	Southampton	30^2, 32, 33^2
Whitney, R.	1930	..	Wellingborough	London	39, 41
Widdecombe, Miss A.	1947	..	Overseas	Birmingham & Oxford	44, 45^2
† Wigg, 1st Ld (1967). G. Wigg	1900	1983	Q Mary's, Basingstoke*		31
Wiggin, Sir (A.W.) J. (Kt 1993)	1937	..	Eton	Cambridge	39^2
† Wilkins, W. A.	1899	1987	Elementary		23
† Wilkinson, Miss E. C.	1891	1947	Stretford Rd*	Manchester	18, 19, 22
Willetts, D.	1956	..	K. Edward VI Sch Birmingham	Oxford	46
† Willey, F. T.	1910	1987	Johnston Sch*	Cambridge	22, 31^2
Williams, A. J.	1930	..	Cardiff H.S.	Oxford	29, 32, 37^2
† Williams, Sir E. J.	1890	1963	Elementary		22
Williams, Sir H. G. (Kt 1939)	1884	1954	Privately	Liverpool	12
Williams, J. P.	1840	1904	Elementary		2
Williams, Sir R. R. (1st Bt 1918)	1865	1955	Eton	Oxford	8
† Williams of Crosby, Lady (Life Peeress 1993). Mrs S. V. T. B. Williams	1930	..	St Paul's Girls' S.	Oxford	30^2, 31, 35, 36, 37
† Williams of Barnburgh, Ld (Life Peer 1961). T. Williams	1888	1967	Elementary		18, 22
† Williamson, Sir A. (1st Bt 1909). 1st Ld Forres (1922)	1860	1931	Craigmont*	Edinburgh	9
† Willingdon, 1st M of (1936). F. Freeman-Thomas, 1st Ld Willingdon (1910). 1st Vt (1924). 1st E (1931)	1866	1941	Eton	Cambridge	3, 5
† Willink, Sir H. U. (1st Bt 1957)	1894	1973	Eton	Cambridge	18, 20
† Willis, (E.) G.	1903	1987	C.of Norwich S.S.		32
Wills, Sir G. (Kt 1958)	1905	1969	Privately	Cambridge	25, 29
† Wilmot, 1st Ld (1950). J. Wilmot	1895	1964	Secondary	London	19, 22, 23
Wilson, D. M.	1862	1932	R. Belfast Acad.Inst.	Dublin	9
† Wilson of Langside. Ld (Life Peer 1969). H. S. Wilson	1916	..	Glasgow H.S.*	Glasgow	32
† Wilson of Rievaulx (Life Peer 1983). Sir (J.) H. Wilson (K.G. 1976)	1916	..	Wirral G.S.*	Oxford	23^3, 29, 35
† Wilson, Sir L. O. (G.C.I.E. 1923)	1876	1955	St Paul's		8, 9, 10
† Wimborne, 1st Vt (1918). I. C. Guest. 1st Ld Ashby St Ledgers (1910), 2nd Ld Wimborne (1914)	1873	1939	Eton	Cambridge	4, 5
Windlesham, 1st Ld (1937). Sir G. R. J. Hennessy (1st Bt 1927)	1877	1953	Eton		10, 12^3, 15
† Windlesham, 3rd Ld (1962). D. J. G. Hennessy	1932	..	Ampleforth	Oxford	33^2, 34
† Windsor, 14th Ld (1869). R. G. Windsor-Clive, 1st E of Plymouth (1905)	1857	1923	Eton	Cambridge	2

Name	Born	Died	School	University	Pages
Winfrey, Sir R. (Kt 1914)	1858	1944	King's Lynn G.S.*		7
† Winster, 1st Ld (1942). R.T.H. Fletcher	1885	1961	H.M.S. Britannia*		22
Winterbottom, Ld (Life Peer 1965). I. Winterbottom	1913	1992	Charterhouse	Cambridge	30^2, 31, 38
† Winterton, 6th E (1907). E. Turnour (U.K. Ld Turnour 1952)	1883	1962	Eton	Oxford	7, 10, 11, 14, 15^3, 16
† Wolmer, Vt (1895). R.C. Palmer. 3rd E of Selborne (1942)	1887	1971	Winchester	Oxford	10, 12, 18
† Wolverhampton, 1st Vt (1908). Sir H. H. Fowler (G.C.S.I. 1895)	1830	1911	St Saviour's G.S., Southwark*		3, 4
Wolverton, 4th Ld (1888). F. G. Wolverton	1864	1932	Eton	Oxford	2
† Womersley, Sir W. J. (Kt 1934)	1878	1961	Elementary		14, 16^2, 17, 19, 21
† Wood. E F. L. 1st Ld Irwin (1925). 3rd Vt Halifax (1934). 1st E of (1944)	1881	1959	Eton	Oxford	7, 10, 11, 14, 15^3, 16
† Wood, Sir (H.) K. (Kt 1918)	1881	1943	Cent. Foundation B.S.*		11, 14^2, 15^2, 16, 17
† Wood, R. F. Ld Holderness (Life Peer 1979)	1920	. .	Eton	Oxford	25, 27, 28^3, 33, 34
† Wood, T.M.	1855	1927	Mill Hill	London	4^4, 5, 6^2
† Woodburn, A.	1890	1978	Heriot-Watt Coll.*		22, 23^2
Woodhouse, C.M.	1917	. .	Winchester	Oxford	26, 27
† Woolton, 1st E of (1955). Sir F. J. Marquis (Kt 1935). 1st Ld Woolton (1939). 1st Vt (1953)	1883	1964	Manchester G.S.	Manchester	16, 18, 19, 20, 24, 25
† Worthington-Evans, Sir L. (1st Bt 1916)	1868	1931	Eastbourne		7, 8^5, 9, 10, 12
† Wraxall, 1st Ld (1928) G. A. Gibbs	1873	1931	Eton	Oxford	9, 10, 12
Wright, G.	1847	1913		Dublin	2
Wyatt of Weeford, Ld (Life Peer 1987) Sir W. L. Wyatt (Kt 1983)	1918	. .	Eastbourne	Oxford	23
† Wylie, Ld (Scot. judge 1974). N. R. Wylie	1923	. .	Paisley G.S.*	Oxford & Glasgow	29, 35
† Wyndham, G.	1863	1913	Eton	Sandhurst	2^3
Yeo, T. S. K.	1945	. .	Charterhouse	Cambridge	45^3
Young, Sir A S. L. (1st Bt 1945)	1889	1950	Fettes		20^2, 21
† Young of Graffham, Ld (Life Peer 1984). D. I. Young	1932	. .	Christ's Coll., Finchley*	London	40, 42
† Young, Sir E. H. (G.B.E 1927). 1st Ld Kennet (1935)	1879	1960	Eton	Cambridge	7, 14^2
† Young, Sir G. S. K. (6th Bt 1960)	1941	. .	Eton	Oxford	40, 41, 43, 44, 45
† Young, Lady (Life Peeress 1971). Mrs J. M. Young	1926	. .	Headington Sch.	Oxford	34, 35, 38^2, 39, 41
† Younger of Prestwick, Ld (Life Peer 1992), G. K. H. Younger	1931	. .	Winchester	Oxford	33, 34, 39, 41
† Younger, Sir K. G. (K.B.E. 1973)	1908	1976	Winchester	Oxford	21^2
† Ypres, 1st E of (1921), Sir J. D. P. French (K.C.B. 1900). 1st Vt French (1915)	1852	1925	H.M.S. Britannia*		7
† Zetland, 2nd M of (1929). L. J. L. Dundas, E of Ronaldshay (1892)	1876	1961	Harrow	Cambridge	16

II

PARTIES

Conservative Party

Party Leaders

1900	M of Salisbury	9 Oct	40	(Sir) W. Churchill
14 Jul	02	A. Balfour	21 Apr	55	Sir A. Eden
13 Nov	11	A. Bonar Law[1]	22 Jan	57	H. Macmillan
21 Mar	21	A. Chamberlain[1]	11 Nov	63	Sir A. Douglas-Home
23 Oct	22	A. Bonar Law[1]	2 Aug	65	E. Heath
28 May	23	S. Baldwin	11 Feb	75	Mrs. M. Thatcher
31 May	37	N. Chamberlain[2]	28 Nov	90	J. Major

Conservative Party Leadership Elections

In 1965 The Conservative Party introduced a procedure for the leader to be elected by a ballot of M.P.s. If there was no clear winner on the first ballot (defined by having over 50% of the votes, and being 15% clear of the second placed candidate), the rules stated that the election should go to a second ballot; if there was still no winner with over 50%, it should go to a run-off between the best-placed candidates. This procedure has been used four times – in Aug 1965, when E. Heath was elected; in Feb 1975, when Mrs M. Thatcher was elected; in Nov 1989, when Sir A. Meyer unsuccessfully challenged Mrs M. Thatcher; and in Nov 1990, when J. Major was elected.

Date	1st ballot		Date	2nd ballot	
28 Jul 65	E. Heath[3]	150			
	R. Maudling	133			
	E. Powell	15			
4 Feb 75	Mrs M. Thatcher	130	11 Feb 75	Mrs M. Thatcher	110
	E. Heath	119		W. Whitelaw	79
	H. Fraser	16		Sir G. Howe	19
				J. Prior	19
				J. Peyton	11
5 Dec 89	Sir A. Meyer	33			
	Mrs M. Thatcher	314			
20 Nov 90	M. Heseltine	152	27 Nov 90	J. Major[4]	185
	Mrs M. Thatcher	204		M. Heseltine	131
				D. Hurd	56

Deputy Leaders

4 Aug 65–18 Jul 72	R. Maudling
12 Feb 75–4 Aug 91	W. Whitelaw (Vt)

[1] A Bonar Law, 1911–21, and A. Chamberlain, 1921–22, were leaders of the Conservative Party in the House of Commons. Formerly, when the party was in opposition, there were separate Leaders in the Commons and the Lords; and the present title 'Leader of the Conservative and Unionist Party' did not officially exist. It was first conferred, in Oct 1922, on A. Bonar Law when he was selected for his second term of office.

[2] N. Chamberlain remained the Leader of the Conservative Party until 4 Oct 40, though he was succeeded as Prime Minister by W. Churchill on 10 May 40, and resigned from the Government on 30 Sep 40.

[3] Although the rules required a larger majority, R. Maudling immediately withdrew in favour of E. Heath.

[4] Although the rules require an overall majority, both D. Hurd and M. Heseltine withdrew in favour of J. Major when the results of the second ballot were known.

Leaders in the House of Lords

1900	3rd M of Salisbury	1957	E of Home
1902	D of Devonshire	1960	2nd Vt Hailsham
1903	M of Lansdowne	1963	Ld Carrington
1916	Earl Curzon (M)	1970	Earl Jellicoe
1925	4th M of Salisbury	1973	Ld Windlesham
1930	1st Vt Hailsham	1974	Ld Carrington
1935	M of Londonderry	1979	Ld Soames
1935	Vt Halifax	1981	Lady Young
1938	Earl Stanhope	1983	Vt Whitelaw
1940	Vt Caldecote	1988	Ld Belstead
1940	Vt Halifax	1990	Ld Waddington
1941	Ld Lloyd	1992	Ld Wakeham
1941	Ld Moyne	1994	Vt Cranborne
1942	Vt Cranborne (5th M of Salisbury)		

Principal Party Officials

Chairmen of the Party Organisation

Jun 11–Dec 16	A. Steel–Maitland	Oct 63–Jan 65	Vt Blakenham
Dec 16–Mar 23	Sir G. Younger	Jan 65–Sep 67	E. du Cann
Mar 23–Nov 26	S. Jackson	Sep 67–Jul 70	A. Barber
Nov 26–May 30	J. Davidson	Jul 70–Apr 72	P. Thomas
Jun 30–Apr 31	N. Chamberlain	Apr 72–Jun 74	Ld Carrington
Apr 31–Mar 36	Ld Stonehaven	Jun 74–Feb 75	W. Whitelaw
Mar 36–Mar 42	(Sir) D. Hacking	Feb 75–Sep 81	Ld Thorneycroft
Mar 42–Sep 44	T. Dugdale	Sep 81–Sep 83	C. Parkinson
Oct 44–Jul 46	R. Assheton	Oct 83–Sep 85	J. S. Gummer
Oct 46–Jul 55	Ld Woolton (Vt)	Sep 85–Jun 87	N. Tebbit
Jul 55–Sep 57	O. Poole	Jun 87–Jul 89	P. Brooke
Sep 57–Oct 59	Vt Hailsham	Jul 89–Nov 90	K. Baker
Oct 59–Oct 61	R. Butler	Nov 90–Apr 92	C. Patten
Oct 61–Apr 63	I. Macleod	Apr 92–Jul 94	Sir N. Fowler
Apr 63–Oct 63 ⎰	I. Macleod	Jul 94–	J. Hanley
Apr 63–Oct 63 ⎱	Ld Poole		

Deputy Chairman

May 24–Jan 26	M of Linlithgow	Sep 85–Oct 86	J. Archer
Sep 57–Oct 59	O. Poole (Ld)	Sep 85–Jul 89	P. Morrison
Oct 59–Oct 63	Sir T. Low (Ld Aldington)	Jul 89–May 90	Ld Young of Graffham
Oct 64–Oct 75	Sir M. Fraser (Ld)	May 90–Nov 90	D. Trippier
Apr 72–Jun 74	J. Prior	Nov 90–Apr 92	Sir J. Cope
Mar 75–Nov 77	W. Clark	Apr 92–	Dame A. Rumbold
Mar 75–May 79	A. Maude	May 92–Jul 94	G. Malone
Nov 77–May 79	Lady Young	Jul 94–	M. Dobbs
May 79–Jun 83	A. McAlpine (Ld)	Jul 94–	J. Maples
Jun 83–Sep 84	M. Spicer		

Treasurers[1]

Aug 11–Mar 23	Earl Farquhar	Aug 66–Apr 74	Sir T. Brinton
Mar 23–Apr 29	Vt Younger	Apr 74–Jul 77	Sir A. Silverstone
Jan 30–Jul 31	Sir S. Hoare		(Ld Ashdown)
Jul 31–Nov 33	Ld Ebbisham	Apr 74–Mar 75	W. Clark
Nov 33–Jun 38	Vt Greenwood	Aug 75–Nov 90	A. McAlpine (Ld)
Jun 38–Feb 47	Vt Marchwood	May 79–Jun 83	Ld Boardman
Feb 47–Apr 60	C. Holland-Martin	Apr 82–Apr 90	Sir O. Wade
Feb 48–Mar 52	Ld De L'Isle	Dec 84–Jan 88	Sir C.(Ld) Johnston
Mar 52–Oct 55	O. Poole	Jan 88–Mar 93	Ld Laing
Oct 55–Jan 62	Sir H. Studholme	Apr 90–Jul 92	Ld Beaverbrook
Oct 60–Nov 65	R. Allan	Apr 91–Apr 92	Sir J. Cope
Jan 62–Aug 66	R. Stanley	Jul 92–Feb 93	T. Smith
Nov 65–Apr 77	Ld Chelmer	Mar 93–	C. Hambro

Chairman of Executive Committee of the Party

Oct 30	Sir H. Kingsley Wood		Feb 57	Sir E. Edwards (Ld Chelmer)
Mar 32	G. Herbert		Sep 65	Sir C. Hewlett
Apr 37	Sir G. Stanley		Jul 71	(Sir) J. Taylor
Apr 38	Sir E. Ramsden		Jul 76	Sir C. Johnston
Apr 43	R. Proby		Jul 81	Sir R. (Ld) Sanderson
Apr 46	N. Colman		Jul 86	Sir P. (Ld) Lane
Apr 51	A. Nutting		Jul 91	Sir B. Feldman
Apr 52	Sir E. Errington			

Principal Agent

Mar 1885–Jul 03	R. Middleton		Apr 20–Dec 20	W. Jenkins
Jul 03–Nov 05	L. Wells		Dec 20–Mar 23	(Sir) M. Fraser
Nov 05–Dec 06	A. Haig		Mar 23–Feb 24	Sir R. Hall
Dec 06–Jan 12	P. Hughes		Mar 24–Jan 27	(Sir) H. Blain
May 12–Jun 15	J. Boraston		Jan 27–Feb 28	Sir L. Maclachlan
Jun 15–Apr 20	(Sir) J. Boraston		Feb 28–Feb 31	R. Topping
Jun 15–Apr 20	W. Jenkins			

General Directors

Feb 31–Sep 45	(Sir) R. Topping		Aug 57–Jun 66	(Sir) W. Urton
Oct 45–Aug 57	(Sir) S. Pierssene			

Director of Organisation

Jun 66–Jan 76	(Sir) R. Webster		Feb 76–Jun 88	(Sir) A. Garner

Director of Organisation and Campaigning

Jun 88–May 92	(Sir) J. Lacy

Director of Campaigning

Jun 92–	T. Garrett

Director-General

Apr 74–Mar 75	M. Wolff		Nov 92–	P. Judge

Director of Publicity & Communications

1945	E. O'Brien		1966	T. Rathbone	1980	Sir H. Boyne
1946	M. Chapman Walker		1968	G. Tucker	1982	A. Shrimsley
1955	G. Schofield		1970	R. Lewis	1985	H. Thomas
1957	R. Sims		1971	D. Harker	1986	M. Dobbs
1961	G. Hutchinson		1975	A. Todd	1989	B. Bruce
1964	J. Pemberton		1977	T. Hooson	1991	S. Woodward
1965	(office vacant)		1978	G. Reece	1992	T. Collins

Conservative Research Department

Chairman

1930	N. Chamberlain[2]		1945	R. Butler	1975	A. Maude
1940	Sir K. Wood		(1964)	post vacant	(1979)	post abolished)
1943	Sir J. Ball		1970	Sir M. (Ld) Fraser		
	(Acting Chairman)		1974	I. Gilmour		

Director

1930–39	(Sir) J. Ball		1948–59	P. Cohen (joint)	1979–82	A. Howarth
(1939–45	post vacant)		1951–64	M. Fraser	1982–84	P. Cropper
1945–51	D. Clarke			(joint to 59)	(1984–85	post vacant)
1948–51	D. Clarke (joint)		1964–70	B. Sewill	1985–89	R. Harris
1948–50	H. Hopkinson		1970–74	J. Douglas	1989–	A. Lansley
	(joint)		1974–79	C. Patten		

SOURCES. – *Annual Conference Reports of the National Union of Conservative and Unionist Associations*, and information from the Conservative Research Department.

[1] From Feb 1948 to Jul 1977 and from May 1979 to Mar 1993 the office of Treasurer was held jointly.
[2] The Conservative Research Department was organised by Lord E. Percy in 1929 but there was no Chairman until Feb 1930.

Chief Whip in the House of Commons

1900	Sir W. Walrond	1941	J. Stuart	1979	M. Jopling
1902	Sir A. Acland Hood	1948	P. Buchan-Hepburn	1983	J. Wakeham
1911	Ld Balcarres	1955	E. Heath	1987	D. Waddington
1912	Ld E. Talbot	1959	M. Redmayne	1989	T. Renton
1921	L. Wilson	1964	W. Whitelaw	1990	R. Ryder
1923	(Sir) B. Eyres-Monsell	1970	F. Pym		
1931	D. Margesson	1973	H. Atkins		

Chief Whip in the House of Lords

1900	Earl Waldegrave	1925	E of Plymouth	1958	Earl St Aldwyn
1911	D of Devonshire	1929	E of Lucan (5th)	1977	Ld Denham
1916	Ld Hylton	1940	Ld Templemore	1991	Ld Hesketh
1922	E of Clarendon	1945	Earl Fortescue	1993	Vt Ullswater
				1994	Ld Strathclyde

SOURCES. – *Dod's Parliamentary Companion, 1900-*. For a full list of whips see F.M.G. Wilson, 'Some Career Patterns in British Politics; Whips in the House of Commons, 1906–66', *Parliamentary Affairs*, 24 (Winter 1970–1) pp. 33–42.

Chairman of 1922 Committee[1]

Jan 23–Nov 32	(Sir) G. Rentoul	Nov 51–Nov 55	D. Walker-Smith
Dec 32–Dec 35	W. Morrison	Nov 55–Nov 64	J. Morrison
Dec 35–Jul 39	Sir H. O'Neill	Nov 64–Mar 66	Sir W Anstruther-Gray
Sep 39–Nov 39	Sir A. Somerville	May 66–Jul 70	Sir A. Harvey
Dec 39–Dec 40	W. Spens	Jul 70–Nov 72	Sir H. Legge-Bourke
Dec 40–Dec 44	A. Erskine Hill	Nov 72–Nov 84	E. du Cann
Dec 44–Jun 45	J. McEwen	Nov 84–Apr 92	C. Onslow
Aug 45–Nov 51	Sir A. Gridley	Apr 92–	Sir M. Fox

SOURCES. – *The Times Index, 1923–*, information from the 1922 Committee, R. T. Mackenzie, *British Political Parties* (1955) pp. 57–61, P. Goodhart, *The 1922* (1973) and Conservative Research Department.

Conservative Shadow Cabinets

Little has been published about the Conservative arrangements when in opposition. The situation appears to have been as follows:–

1906–14   After the 1906 defeat, Conservative ex-ministers met regularly in what was known as a 'Shadow' Cabinet. Only after 1910 was new blood brought in, e.g. F. E. Smith and Sir A. Steel-Maitland.

1924   S. Baldwin summoned a formal Shadow Cabinet of all ex-ministers which met weekly during the Session and which had a secretariat.

1929–31   There was a Consultative Committee which met regularly and was serviced by the Research Department.

1945–51   The Chief Whip sent out notices to a regular Shadow Cabinet meeting, formally known as the Consultative Committee. Names were added but never subtracted and W. Churchill allowed the numbers to grow to about 24. No formal minutes were kept. The following seem to have attended regularly.

[1] Or the Conservative (Private) Members' Committee. This is an organisation of the entire backbench membership of the Conservative Party in the Commons. It acts as a sounding board of Conservative opinion in the House, but has no official role in formulating policy for the party.

W. Churchill
————

Sir J. Anderson	A. Eden	O. Stanley
R. Assheton	W. Elliot	J. Stuart
B. Bracken	R. Law	H. Willink
P. Buchan-Hepburn	O. Lyttelton	Vt Woolton
R. Butler	H. Macmillan	
Ld Cherwell	D. Maxwell Fyfe	*Secretary*
H. Crookshank	W. Morrison	H. Hopkinson 1945–50
	M of Salisbury	D. Clarke 1950–51

1964   A Leaders' Consultative Committee met regularly as soon as the party went into opposition and formal minutes were kept.

Sir A. Douglas-Home	J. Godber	E. Powell
(1964–5)	E. Heath	M. Redmayne
————	Q. Hogg	D. Sandys
Lord Blakenham	Sir K. Joseph	C. Soames
J. Boyd-Carpenter	S. Lloyd	P. Thorneycroft
Sir E. Boyle	I. Macleod	
R. Butler	E. Marples	*Secretary*
Ld Carrington	R. Maudling	Sir M. Fraser
Vt Dilhorne	M. Noble	

E. Heath (1965–70)	J. Godber	E. Powell
————	(1965–70)	(1965–8)
Lord Balniel	Ld Harlech	M. Redmayne
(1967–70)	(1966–7)	(1965–6)
A. Barber	Q. Hogg	G. Rippon
(1966–70)	(1965–70)	(1966–70)
J. Boyd-Carpenter	Earl Jellicoe	D. Sandys
(1965–6)	(1967–70)	(1965–6)
Sir E Boyle	Sir K. Joseph	C. Soames
(1965–9)	(1965–70)	(1965–6)
G. Campbell	S. Lloyd	Mrs M. Thatcher
(1969–70)	(1965–6)	(1967–70)
R. Carr	I. Macleod	P. Thorneycroft
(1967–70)	(1965–70)	(1965–6)
Ld Carrington	E. Marples	P. Walker
(1965–70)	(1965–6)	(1966–70)
Vt Dilhorne	R. Maudling	
(1965–6)	(1965–70)	(W. Whitelaw
Sir A. Douglas-Home	M. Noble	*Chief Whip*)
(1965–70)	(1965–9)	(1966–70)
E. du Cann	Miss M. Pike	*Secretary*
(1965–7)	(1966–7)	Sir M. Fraser

1974   Procedures followed the general pattern of 1964–70

E. Heath (1974–5)	Ld Hailsham	Mrs M. Thatcher
	Sir G. Howe	P. Thomas
A. Barber (–74)	P. Jenkin	W. Van Straubenzee
A. Buchanan-Smith	Sir K. Joseph	W. Whitelaw
P. Walker	M. Macmillan (–74)	Ld Windlesham (–74)
R. Carr	J. Peyton	
Ld Carrington	J. Prior	
P. Channon	T. Raison	(H. Atkins
Sir A. Douglas-Home	G. Rippon	*Chief Whip*)
(–74)	N. St. John-Stevas	*Secretary*
I. Gilmour	N. Scott	Sir M. Fraser (Ld)

Mrs M. Thatcher (1975–9)	P. Jenkin	N. St. John-Stevas
———	(1975–9)	(1975–9)
J. Biffen	Sir K. Joseph	E. Taylor
(1976–7, 1978–9)	(1975–9)	(1976–9)
A. Buchanan Smith	T. King	Ld Thorneycroft
(1975–6)	(1976–9)	(1975–9)
M. Carlisle	A. Maude	W. Whitelaw
(1978–9)	(1975–9)	(1975–9)
Ld Carrington	R. Maudling	G. Younger
(1975–9)	(1975–6)	(1975–9)
J. Davies	A. Neave	
(1976–8)	(1975–9)	
N. Edwards	J. Nott	
(1975–9)	(1976–9)	
N. Fowler	Mrs S. Oppenheim	
(1975–6)	(1975–9)	(H. Atkins, *Chief*
(Sir) I. Gilmour	J. Peyton	*Whip*, 1975–9)
(1975–9)	(1975–9)	*Secretary*
Ld Hailsham	J. Prior	Ld Fraser
(1975–9)	(1975–9)	(1975–6)
M. Heseltine	F. Pym	C. Patten
(1975–9)	(1975–9)	(1976–8)
Sir G. Howe	T. Raison	D. Wolfson
(1975–9)	(1975–6)	(1978–9)

Party Membership

The Conservative Party has seldom published figures of its total membership. Membership is a loose term, usually associated with the payment of an annual subscription, but exact records are not always kept locally, let alone nationally. In 1953 it was claimed that the party had reached an all-time record membership of 2,805,832, but this was a temporary peak. One estimate for 1969–70 suggests that the party's membership in Great Britain was then $1\frac{1}{2}$ to $1\frac{3}{4}$ million. The Houghton Committee estimated that in 1975 the Conservatives had an average membership of 2,400 per constituency, which is equal to about $1\frac{1}{2}$ million. Membership of the Young Conservatives fell from a peak of 157,000 in 1949 to 80,000 in 1959 and to 50,000 in 1968. In 1982 an internal study suggested that the membership was just under 1.2m. and a similar figure was found in 1984. Estimates in the press in 1993 suggested that previous suggested membership totals had been greatly exaggerated, and that the figure had in any case fallen sharply, so that there might now be as few as quarter of a million members.

SOURCES. – Nuffield Election Studies; *Committee on Financial Aid to Political Parties* (Cmnd 6601/ 1976 p.31); M. Pinto-Duschinsky, *British Political Finance*(1980).

Party Finance

The Conservative Party did not publish its central accounts until 1968.[1] In 1912 Sir A. Steel-Maitland, the Party Chairman, put the party's annual income centrally at £80,000 and suggested that the extra expenses of a general election, centrally, were £80,000 to £120,000. In 1929 J. Davidson, then Chairman, put the cost of the general election at £290,000 (although this including some grants to local campaigns).

The Houghton Committee estimated that in 1975–76 the Conservative parties raised £1.8m. at the centre and £4.5m. in the constituencies, a total of £6.3m.

In the year ending March 1983, the Conservative Party raised £4.8m.centrally and about £8.0m. locally. In the year ending March 1984 (containing a general election), central income totalled almost £10m.

The routine expenditure annually reported since 1968 has been:

1967–68	£1,071,000	1976–77	£2,177,000	1985–86	£5,500,000
1968–69	£1,054,000	1977–78	£2,754,000	1986–87	£7,500,000
1969–70	£1,052,000	1978–79	£4,800,000	1987–88	£15,600,000
1970–71	£1,668,000	1979–80	£6,200,000	1988–89	£10,200,000
1971–72	£1,249,000	1980–81	£5,500,000	1989–90	£10,800,000
1972–73	£1,481,000	1981–82	£4,200,000	1990–91	£14,900,000
1973–74	£2,134,000	1982–83	£4,700,000	1991–92	£23,400,000
1974–75	£2,867,000	1983–84	£8,600,000	1992–93	£11,500,000
1975–76	£1,874,000	1984–85	£5,600,000		

SOURCES. – *Annual Conference Reports of the National Union of Conservative and Unionist Associations*; N. Blewett, *The Peers, the Parties and the People: The General Elections of 1910* (1972), p 291; R. Rhodes James, *Memoirs of a Conservative* (1969); M. Harrison, in R. Rose and A. Heidenhammer (eds.), *Comparative Political Finance* (1963); R. Rose, *Influencing Voters* (1967) pp. 260–8; M. Pinto-Duschinsky, *The British General Election of 1970* (1971), pp. 282–3, and 'Central Office and "Power" in the Conservative Party', *Political Studies*, 20 (Mar 72) pp. 1–16; *Committee on Financial Aid to Political Parties* (Cmnd 6601/1976 p. 31); M. Pinto-Duschinsky, *British Political Finance, 1830–1980* (1981); Conservative Party Headquarters; M. Linton *Money and Votes* (Institute for Public Policy Research 1994).

National Union of Conservative and Unionist Associations –

Annual Conferences, 1900–[1]

Date		Place	President	Chairman
19 Dec	00	London	M of Zetland	Ld Windsor
26–27 Nov	01	Wolverhampton	Ld Llangattock	Sir A. Hickman
14–15 Oct	02	Manchester	E of Dartmouth	Sir C. Cave
1–2 Oct	03	Sheffield	E of Derby	F. Lowe
28–29 Oct	04	Southampton	D of Norfolk	H. Bowles
14–15 Nov	05	Newcastle	Ld Montagu	Sir W. Plummer
27 Jul	06	London	D of Northumberland	H. Imbert-Terry
14–15 Nov	07	Birmingham	D of Northumberland	D of Rutland
19–20 Nov	08	Cardiff	E of Plymouth	Sir R. Hodge
17–18 Nov	09	Manchester	Earl Cawdor	Sir T. Wrightson
17 Nov	10	Nottingham	E of Derby	H. Chaplin
16–17 Nov	11	Leeds	D of Portland	Ld Kenyon
14–15 Nov	12	London	Ld Faber	Sir W. Crump
12–14 Nov	13	Norwich	Ld Farquhar	A. Salvidge
1914–16		*No conference held*	Sir A. Fellowes	Sir H. Samuel
1917		London	Sir A. Fellowes	Sir H. Samuel
1918–19		*No conference held*	Sir A. Fellowes	Sir H. Samuel
10–11 Jun	20	Birmingham	Sir A. Fellowes	J. Williams
17–18 Nov	21	Liverpool	A. Chamberlain	Sir A. Benn
15–16 Dec	22	London	E of Derby	Sir A. Leith
25–26 Oct	23	Plymouth	Ld Mildmay of Flete	Sir H. Nield
2–3 Oct	24	Newcastle	D of Northumberland	E of Selborne
8–9 Oct	25	Brighton	G. Loder	Sir P. Woodhouse
7–8 Oct	26	Scarborough	G. Lane-Fox	Dame C. Bridgeman
6–7 Oct	27	Cardiff	Vt Tredegar	Sir R. Sanders
27–28 Sep	28	Great Yarmouth	Ld Queenborough	J. Gretton
21–22 Nov	29	London	Ld Faringdon	G. Rowlands
1 Jul	30	London	N. Chamberlain	C'tess of Iveagh
1931		*No conference held*	N. Chamberlain	G. Herbert
6–7 Oct	32	Blackpool	Ld Stanley	Earl Howe
5–6 Oct	33	Birmingham	E of Plymouth	Sir G. Ellis
4–5 Oct	34	Bristol	Ld Bayford	Miss R. Evans
3–4 Oct	35	Bournemouth	G. Herbert	Sir W. Cope
1–2 Oct	36	Margate	Ld Ebbisham	Sir L. Brassey
7–8 Oct	37	Scarborough	Ld Bingley	Mrs C. Fyfe
1938		*No conference held*	M of Londonderry	Sir E. Ramsden
1939		*No conference held*	M of Londonderry	N. Colman
1940		*No conference held*	Ld Queenborough	Lady Hillingdon

Date		Place	President	Chairman
1941		*No conference held*	Ld Queenborough	Sir C. Headlam
1942		*No conference held*	M of Salisbury	R. Catterall
20–21 May	43	London	M of Salisbury	R. Catterall
1944		*No conference held*	M of Salisbury	Mrs L. Whitehead
14–15 Mar	45	London	Ld Courthope	R. Butler
3–5 Oct	46	Blackpool	O. Stanley	R. Proby
2–4 Oct	47	Brighton	H. Macmillan	Mrs Hornyold-Strickland
7–9 Oct	48	Llandudno	G. Summers	Sir H. Williams
12–14 Oct	49	London	Vt Swinton	D. Graham
12–14 Oct	50	Blackpool	Sir D. Maxwell Fyfe	A. Nutting
1951		*No conference held*	Ld Ramsden	Mrs L. Sayers
9–11 Oct	52	Scarborough	Sir T. Dugdale	C. Waterhouse
8–10 Oct	53	Margate	M of Salisbury	Mrs J. Warde
7–9 Oct	54	Blackpool	A. Eden	Sir G. Llewellyn
6–8 Oct	55	Bournemouth	Mrs L. Sayers	Mrs E. Emmet
11–13 Oct	56	Llandudno	R. Butler	Sir E. Edwards
10–12 Oct	57	Brighton	E of Woolton	Mrs W. Elliot
8–11 Oct	58	Blackpool	Sir R. Proby	Sir S. Bell
1959		*No conference held*	H. Brooke	E. Brown
12–15 Oct	60	Scarborough	H. Brooke	E. Brown
11–14 Oct	61	Brighton	Vt Hailsham	Sir D. Glover
10–13 Oct	62	Llandudno	Sir G. Llewellyn	Sir J. Howard
8–11 Oct	63	Blackpool	E of Home	Mrs T. Shepherd
1964		*No conference held*	Vtess Davidson	Sir M. Bemrose
12–15 Oct	65	Brighton	Vtess Davidson	Sir M. Bemrose
13–16 Oct	66	Blackpool	S. Lloyd	Sir D. Mason
18–21 Oct	67	Brighton	Ld Chelmer	Mrs A. Doughty
9–12 Oct	68	Blackpool	R. Maudling	Sir T. Constantine
8–11 Oct	69	Brighton	Lady Brooke	D. Crossman
7–10 Oct	70	Blackpool	(I. Macleod)	Sir E. Leather
13–16 Oct	71	Brighton	W. Whitelaw	Miss U. Lister
11–14 Oct	72	Blackpool	Dame M. Shepherd	W. Harris
10–13 Oct	73	Blackpool	A. Barber	Mrs R. Smith
1974		*No conference held*	P. Thomas	Sir A. Graesser
7–10 Oct	75	Blackpool	P. Thomas	Sir A. Graesser
5–8 Oct	76	Brighton	Ld Hewlett	Miss S. Roberts
11–14 Oct	77	Blackpool	Ld Carrington	D. Sells
10–14 Oct	78	Brighton	Dame A. Doughty	Sir H. Redfearn
9–12 Oct	79	Blackpool	F. Pym	D. Davenport-Handley
11–15 Oct	80	Brighton	Sir T. Constantine	Dame A. Springman
13–16 Oct	81	Blackpool	E. du Cann	F. Hardman
12–15 Oct	82	Brighton	Sir J. Taylor	D. Walters
11–14 Oct	83	Blackpool	Sir G. Howe	P. Lane
9–12 Oct	84	Brighton	Sir A. Graesser	Dame P. Hunter
8–11 Oct	85	Blackpool	Sir H. Atkins	Sir B. Feldman
7–10 Oct	86	Bournmouth	P. Lawrence	
6–9 Oct	87	Blackpool	G. Younger	Dame J. Seccombe
11–14 Oct	88	Brighton	Dame S. Roberts	Sir I. McLeod
10–13 Oct	89	Blackpool	Vt Whitelaw	Sir S. Odell
9–12 Oct	90	Bournmouth	Sir D. Davenport-Handley	Dame M. Fry
7–10 Oct	91	Blackpool	J. Wakeham	Sir J. Barnard
6–9 Oct	92	Brighton	Sir D. Walters	J. Mason
5–8 Oct	93	Blackpool	Dame W. Mitchell	Sir B. Feldman

SOURCES. – *National Union Gleanings 1900–12, Gleanings and Memoranda 1912–33, Politics in Review 1934–39,* all published by the National Union of Conservative Associations; *National Union of Conservative and Unionist Associations, Annual Conference Reports, 1958-* ; for Conservative Party Manifestos and major reports, pamphlets etc from 1950s and early 60s, see G.D.M. Block, *A Source Book of Conservatism* (1964). See also I. Bulmer-Thomas, *The Growth of the British Party System* (1965).

[1] 1900–12, National Union of Conservative and Constitutional Associations; 1912–17 National Unionist Association of Conservative and Liberal-Unionist Associations; 1917–24 National Unionist Association; 1924– National Union of Conservative and Unionist Associations.

Labour Party

Party Leaders and Deputy Leaders

Chairman of the Parliamentary Party

1906	K. Hardie
1908	A. Henderson
1910	G. Barnes
1911	R. MacDonald
1914	A. Henderson
1917	W. Adamson
1921	J. Clynes

Chairman and Leader of the Parliamentary Party

1922	R. MacDonald[1]
1931	A. Henderson[2]
1932	G. Lansbury
1935	C. Attlee[1]
1955	H. Gaitskell
1963	H. Wilson

Leader of the Parliamentary Party[1]

1970	H. Wilson
1976	J. Callaghan

Leader of the Labour Party

1978	J. Callaghan
1980	M. Foot
1983	N. Kinnock
1992	J. Smith
1994	T. Blair

Vice Chairman

1906	D. Shackleton
1908	G. Barnes
1910	J. Clynes
1911	W. Brace
1912	J. Parker
1914	A. Gill
1915	J. Hodge *Acting*
1916	G. Wardle *Chairmen*
1918	J. Clynes
1921	J. Thomas *Joint*
	S. Walsh *Joint*

Deputy Leader

1922	S. Walsh *Joint*
	J. Wedgwood *Joint*
1923	J. Clynes
1931	J. Clynes *Joint*
	W. Graham *Joint*
1931	C. Attlee
1935	A. Greenwood
1945	H. Morrison
1956	J. Griffiths
1959	A. Bevan
1960	G. Brown
1970	R. Jenkins
1972	E. Short
1976	M. Foot
1980	D. Healey
1983	R. Hattersley
1992	Mrs. M. Beckett
1994	J. Prescott

Leadership Elections

From 1922 to 1981 the Parliamentary Labour Party, when in opposition, elected its Leader and Deputy Leader at the beginning of each session. Most elections were uncontested, but there were these exceptions. (The figures in brackets show the result of the first ballot. The date is for the final ballot.)

	Leader				Deputy Leader	
21 Nov 22	R. MacDonald		61	11 Nov 52	H. Morrison	194
	J. Clynes		56		A. Bevan	82
3 Dec 35	C. Attlee	(58)	88	29 Oct 53	H. Morrison	181
	H. Morrison	(44)	48		A. Bevan	76
	A. Greenwood	(33)	–			
				2 Feb 56	J. Griffiths	141
14 Dec 55	H. Gaitskell		157		A. Bevan	111
	A. Bevan		70		H. Morrison	40

[1] When the Labour Party was in power in 1924, 1929–31, 1945–51, and 1964–70, a Liaison Committee was set up. After 1970 the Parliamentary Party elected a separate Chairman. See p. 000.

[2] A. Henderson lost his seat in the 1931 election. The acting leader of the Parliamentary Labour Party in 1931 was G. Lansbury.

Leader					*Deputy Leader*			
3 Nov 60	H. Gaitskell			166	10 Nov 60	G. Brown	(118)	146
	H. Wilson			81		F. Lee	(73)	83
						J. Callaghan	(55)	–
2 Nov 61	H. Gaitskell			17	12 Nov 61	G. Brown		169
	A. Greenwood			59		Mrs B Castle		56
14 Feb 63	H. Wilson		(115)	144	8 Nov 62	G. Brown		133
	G. Brown		(88)	103		H. Wilson		103
	J. Callaghan		(41)	–				
					8 Jul 70	R. Jenkins		133
5 Apr 76	J. Callaghan	(84)	(141)	176		M. Foot		67
	M. Foot	(90)	(133)	137		F. Peart		48
	R. Jenkins	(56)	–					
	A Benn	(37)	–		17 Nov 71	R. Jenkins	(140)	140
	D. Healey	(30)	(38)	–		M. Foot	(96)	126
	A. Crosland	(17)	–			A. Benn	(46)	–
					25 Apr 72	E. Short	(111)	145
3 Nov 80	M. Foot		(83)	139		M. Foot	(89)	116
	D. Healey		(112)	129		A. Crosland	(61)	–
	J. Silkin		(38)	–				
	P. Shore		(32)	–	21 Oct 76	M. Foot		166
						Mrs S. Williams		128

At a special conference at Wembley, 24 Jan 1981, the Labour Party endorsed a procedure by which the Party's Leader and Deputy Leader should be re-elected each year by the Party Conference with 40% of the vote allocated to the Trade Unions, 30% to the Parliamentary Party and 30% to the constituency parties.

The system was first used on 1 Sep 1981 when D. Healey defeated A. Benn for the Deputy Leadership.

Deputy Leader

	1st ballot						*2nd ballot*			
	TU	CLP	MP	Total			TU	CLP	MP	Total
A. Benn	6.410	23.483	6.734	36.627		A. Benn	15.006	24.327	10.241	49.574
D. Healey	24.696	5.367	15.306	45.369		D. Healey	24.994	5.673	19.759	50.426
J. Silkin	8.894	1.150	7.959	18.004						

The first time the procedure was used for electing both Leader and Deputy Leader was on 2 Oct 83.

Leader

	1st ballot			
	TU	CLP	MP	Total
N. Kinnock	29.042	27.452	14.778	71.272
R. Hattersley	10.878	0.577	7.833	19.288
E. Heffer	0.046	1.971	4.286	6.303
P. Shore	0.033	0.000	3.103	3.137

Deputy Leader

	1st ballot			
	TU	CLP	MP	Total
R. Hattersley	35.237	15.313	16.716	67.266
M. Meacher	4.730	14.350	8.806	27.886
D. Davies	0.000	0.241	3.284	3.525
Ms G. Dunwoody	0.033	0.096	1.194	1.323

There was another leadership election on 2 Oct 88, when A. Benn challenged N. Kinnock for the leadership and E. Heffer and J. Prescott challenged R. Hattersley for the deputy leadership.

Leader

| | 1st ballot | | | |
	TU	CLP	MP	Total
N. Kinnock	39.660	24.128	24.842	88.630
A. Benn	0.340	5.872	5.158	11.370

Deputy Leader

| | 1st ballot | | | |
	TU	CLP	MP	Total
R. Hattersley	31.339	18.109	17.376	66.823
J. Prescott	8.654	7.845	7.195	23.694
E. Heffer	0.007	4.046	5.430	9.483

After the 1992 election N. Kinnock and R. Hattersley stood down as leader and deputy leader. An election was held on 18 Jul 92, at a special conference in London.

Leader

| | 1st ballot | | | |
	TU	CLP	MP	Total
J. Smith	38.518	29.311	23.187	91.016
B. Gould	1.482	0.689	6.813	8.984

Deputy Leader

| | 1st ballot | | | |
	TU	CLP	MP	Total
Mrs M. Beckett	25.394	19.038	12.871	57.303
J. Prescott	11.627	7.096	9.406	28.129
B. Gould	2.979	3.866	7.723	14.568

At the 1993 Party Conference the Party approved a change in the rules under which trade unions and constituency parties were obliged to ballot members individually in leadership elections and divide their votes accordingly (One Member One Vote). In addition the proportions in the electoral college were adjusted to three equal thirds for each of the constituent elements. This new procedure was used for the first time in July 1994 following the death of J. Smith. The results were declared on 21 July 94.

Leader

| | 1st ballot | | | |
	TU	CLP	MP	Total %
T. Blair	52.3	58.2	60.5	57.0
J. Prescott	28.4	24.4	19.6	24.1
Mrs M. Beckett	19.3	17.4	19.9	18.9

Deputy Leader

| | First ballot | | | |
	TU	CLP	MP	Total %
J. Prescott	55.6	59.4	53.7	56.5
Mrs M. Beckett	43.4	40.6	46.3	43.5

SOURCES. – *Labour Party Annual Conference Reports*, Labour Year Books; H. Pelling, *A Short History of the Labour Party* (4th Ed., 1972), p. 130. *Keesing's Contemporary Archive*, Keesing's U.K. Record 1988-.

Leaders in the House of Lords

1924	Vt Haldane	1952	Earl Jowitt	1974	Ld Shepherd
1928	Ld Parmoor	1955	Vt (Earl) Alexander of	1976	Ld Peart
1931	Ld Ponsonby		Hillsborough	1982	Ld Cledwyn
1935	Ld Snell	1964	E of Longford	1992	Ld Richard
1940	Ld (Vt) Addison	1968	Ld Shackleton		

Chief Whips in the House of Commons

1906	D. Shackleton	1919	W. Tyson Wilson	1955	H. Bowden
1906	A. Henderson	1920	A. Henderson	1964	E. Short
1907	G. Roberts	1924	B. Spoor	1966	J. Silkin
1914	A. Henderson	1925	A Henderson	1969	R. Mellish
1914	F. Goldstone	1927	T. Kennedy	1976	M. Cocks
1916	G. Roberts	1931	(Sir) C. Edwards	1985	D. Foster
1916	J. Parker	1942	W. Whiteley		

SOURCE. – For a full list of whips see F.M.G. Wilson, 'Some Career Patterns in British Politics; Whips in the House of Commons, 1906–66', *Parliamentary Affairs*, 24 (Winter 1970–1) pp. 33–42.

Chief Whips in the House of Lords

1924	Ld Muir-Mackenzie	1944	Ld Southwood	1967	Ld Beswick
1924	E De La Warr	1945	Ld Ammon	1973	Lady Llewelyn-Davies
1930	Ld Marley	1949	Ld Shepherd (1st)	1982	Ld Ponsonby
1937	Ld Strabolgi	1954	E of Lucan (6th)	1990	Ld Graham of Edmonton
1941	E of Listowel	1964	Ld Shepherd (2nd)		

SOURCES. – *Dod's Parliamentary Companion, 1900- ; Labour Party Annual Conference Reports.*

Labour Representation Committee – National Executive Officers

Chairman		*Treasurer*		*Secretary*	
1900	F. Rogers	1902	F. Rogers	1900	R. MacDonald
1902	R. Bell	1903	A. Gee		
1904	D. Shackleton	1904	A. Henderson		

Labour Party – National Executive Committee

Chairman
(listed as Chairman of Annual Conference at end of year in office; see pp. 143–4)

Secretary

1906	R. MacDonald	*(General Secretary)*		1972	R. Hayward
1912	A. Henderson	1959	M. Phillips	1982	J. Mortimer
1935	J. Middleton	1962	A. Williams	1985	L. Whitty
1944	M. Phillips	1968	(Sir) H. Nicholas		

Treasurer

1906	A. Henderson	1956	A. Bevan	1981	E. Varley
1912	R. MacDonald	1960	H. Nicholas	1984	A. Booth
1929	A. Henderson	1964	D. Davies (*acting*)	1984	S. McCluskie
1936	G. Lathan	1965	D. Davies	1992	T. Burlison
1943	A. Greenwood	1967	J. Callaghan		
1954	H. Gaitskell	1976	N. Atkinson		

National Agent

1908	A. Peters	1951	A. Williams	1979	D. Hughes
1919	E. Wake	1962	Miss S. Barker	1985	Mrs J. Gould
1929	E. Shepherd	1969	R. Hayward	1993	P. Coleman
1946	R. Windle	1972	R. (Ld) Underhill		

Research Secretary[1]

1942	M. Phillips	1952	D. Ginsburg	1974	G. Bish
1945	M. Young	1960	P. Shore	1993	R. Wales
1950	W. Fienburgh	1965	T. Pitt		

Director of Publicity (Communications)

1921	W. Henderson	1979	M. Madden	1990	J. Underwood
1945	A. Bax	1982	N. Grant	1990	D. Hill[2]
1962	J. Harris	1983	*office vacant*		
1964	P. Clark	1985	P. Mandelson		

[1] From 1922 to 1942 A. Greenwood acted as Secretary to the Research Department which was established in 1922 (at first as Joint Research and Information Department).
[2] In 1993 D. Hill took the title 'Chief Spokesperson.'
SOURCES. – *Labour Representation Committee Annual Conference Reports, 1900–5*, and *Labour Party Annual Conference Reports, 1906–*.

Parliamentary Labour Party – Parliamentary Committee

This committee was originally known as the Executive Committee of the Parliamentary Labour Party. Its name was changed in 1951 to avoid confusion with the N.E.C. The committee was first elected in 1923 to take the place of the Policy Committee of the P.L.P. It consists of 18 Commons' members (12 until 1981, 15 from 1981 to 1988), elected at the opening of every session of Parliament by members of the P.L.P. with seats in the House of Commons. There are six ex officio members: the Leader and Deputy Leader of the Party, the Chief Whip in the House of Commons, the Leader of the Labour Peers, the Chief Whip of the Labour Peers and their elected representative. The elected Commons' members of the Parliamentary Committee sit on the Front Bench with the Party's Leader, Deputy Leader, Chief Whip and the Assistant Whips. Ex-Labour Ministers have the right, by custom of the House, to sit on the Front Bench, but usually prefer a place on the Back Benches. The officers and the elected 18 are joined on the Front Benches by a number of other members who have been allotted the responsibility of looking after particular subjects. After 1955 it became the practice of the Leader of the P.L.P. to invite members to take charge of particular subjects, and these members included some who are not members of the Parliamentary Committee. In 1924 and 1929 when the Labour Party was in office a Consultative Committee of twelve was appointed representative of both Front and Back Benches. During the wartime coalition the P.L.P. elected an Administrative Committee of twelve, with Peers' representation, all of whom were non-Ministers. When the Labour Party was in office from 1945 to 1951, and from 1964 to 1970, the P.L.P. set up a small Liaison Committee of three elected backbench M.P.s, the Leader of the House, the Government Chief Whip, and an elected backbench Labour Peer. Until 1964 the Leader acted as Chairman at P.L.P. meetings when the party was in Opposition. Since 1970 the P.L.P. has elected a separate chairman.

Parliamentary Labour Party – Executive Committee
The figures denote the order of successful candidates in the ballot.

1923–29

	Feb 1923	Dec 1924	Dec 1925	Dec 1926	Dec 1927	1928[a]
W. Adamson	9	..	11	11	8	
H. Dalton	..	..	12	3	7	
R. Davies	12	..	..	..	..	
W. Graham	..	8	2	2	3	
A. Henderson	..	10	..	12	2	
T. Johnston	3	..	..	4	4	
F. Jowett	6	..	..	..	..	
G. Lansbury	2	1	10	9	10	
H. Lees-Smith	..	11	4	6	6	
J. Maxton	..	6	..	..	..	
E. Morel	5	..	..	..	..	
F. Roberts	..	12	..	..	..	
T. Shaw	11	..	7	..	12	
E. Shinwell	7	..	..	..	..	
R. Smillie	..	2	5	7	..	
P. Snowden	1	3	1	1	1	
J. Thomas	4	4	3	5	5	
C. Trevelyan	..	7	6	8	11	
S. Walsh	..	..	8	..	..	
S. Webb	10	..	9	10	9	
J. Wedgwood	..	9	..	..	..	
J. Wheatley	8	5	..	..	..	

[a] There is no record of an Executive Committee election in 1928.

1931

On 28 Aug 31 officers were elected to the P.L.P.:

A. Henderson (Leader), J. Clynes (Deputy Leader), W. Graham (2nd Deputy Leader), T. Kennedy (Chief Whip).

On 8 Sep 31 the following were elected to the P.L.P. Committee (in order)

T. Johnston	C. Addison	H. Lees-Smith
G. Lansbury	A. Alexander	D. Grenfell
H. Dalton	E. Edwards	Mary Hamilton
A. Greenwood	F. Pethick Lawrence	
J. Barr	E. Shinwell	

All but G. Lansbury and D. Grenfell were defeated in the Oct 31 election.

1931–35

	Nov 1931	Nov 1932	Nov 1933	Nov 1934
Sir S. Cripps	1	1	2	1
D. Grenfell	2	2	1	2
G. Hicks	4	3	3	5
M. Jones	7	7	4	6
W. Lunn	5	4	6	4
N. Maclean	6	6	7	7
T. Williams	3	5	5	3

1935–40

	Nov 1935	Nov 1936	Nov 1937	Nov 1938	Nov 1939
A. Alexander	6	5	2	2	1
W. Wedgwood Benn	..	..	7	5	2
J. Clynes	1	6	..	..	..
H. Dalton	2	3	5	3	10
D. Grenfell	5	4	4	4	4
G. Hall	..	..	..	..	7
T. Johnston	3	2	3	6	..
M. Jones	10	8	11	12	..
J. Lawson	..	..	..	..	12
H. Lees-Smith	9	11	8	8	5
W. Lunn	11	..	..	..	..
N. Maclean	12	..	..	..	..
H. Morrison	4	1	1	1	8
P. Noel-Baker	..	10	12	10	11
F. Pethick-Lawrence	8	9	9	9	6
D. Pritt	..	12	..	..	..
E. Shinwell	..	..	10	11	9
T. Williams	7	7	6	7	3

Parliamentary Labour Party (Parliamentary Committee)
(number indicates position in ballot)

1951–63

	Nov 51	Nov 52	Nov 53	Nov 54	Jun 55	Nov 56	Nov 57	Nov 58	Nov 59	Nov 60	Nov 61	Nov 62	Nov 63
A. Bevan	12	9[a]	..	7	3	3	1	..	..	..	..	..	
A. Bottomley	..	..	..	..	.	..	12	9	..	..	..	..	..
G. Brown	..	..	..	..	8	10	9	..	8	..	..	..	..
J. Callaghan	7	6	4	10	3	5	5	5	2	1	7	1	2
R. Crossman	..	..	..	..	..	..	..	..	13[d]	..	..	..	..
H. Dalton	8	5	5	4	..	..	..	..	..	..	..	..	..
J. Chuter Ede	5	2	6	9	..	..	..	..	..	..	..	..	..
T. Fraser	..	..	..	..	14[c]	12	8	12	7	6	9	5	6
H. Gaitskell	3	3	2	1[b]	2[c]	..	..	..	..	..	..	..	
P. Gordon Walker	..	..	..	..	..	11	6	9[d]	8	11	6	5	..
A. Greenwood	12	..	..	..	10	6	7	8	6[d]	..	..	..	..
J. Griffiths	1	1	1	1[b]	1[c]	..	..	..	..	..	..	..	
R. Gunter	..	..	..	..	..	..	..	..	..	7	6	10	8
W. Glenvil Hall	2	9	12	11	..	..	..	..	..	..	..	..	..
D. Healey	..	..	..	..	..	..	..	..	12	5	4	9	7
D. Houghton	..	..	..	..	..	..	..	..	..	10	3	4	3
D. Jay	..	..	..	..	..	..	..	..	..	..	..	13[e]	11
F. Lee	..	..	..	..	..	..	..	..	5	12	12	12	10
G. Mitchison	..	..	..	..	12	4	2	3	10	3	8	7	12
P. Noel-Baker	9	8	10	8	9	8	10	10	..	..	..	..	..
A. Robens	4	4	7	6	4	2	6	7	4	..	..	..	..
E. Shinwell	11	11	11	7	..	..	..	..	..	..	..	..	..
Sir F. Soskice	..	7	3	3	..	7	4	4	3	2	2	2	4
M. Stewart	..	..	..	..	..	..	..	..	..	4	5	8	..
R. Stokes	6	..	..	..	11	..	..	..	..	..	..	..	..
E. Summerskill	10	10	8	5	6	9	..	11	..	..	..	..	..
F. Willey	..	..	..	..	..	..	..	..	11	11	10	11	9
H. Wilson	..	..	13[a]	12	5	1	1	2	1	9	1	3	..
K. Younger	..	..	..	..	13[c]	11	..	..	..	..	..	..	..

[a] A. Bevan resigned from the Parliamentary Committee on 14 Apr 54; H. Wilson, who was 13th in order of votes obtained, took his place on the Committee on 28 Apr 54.
[b] H. Gaitskell and J. Griffiths both obtained 170 votes and tied for first place.
[c] H. Gaitskell and J. Griffiths were elected Leader and Deputy Leader of the Labour Party on 14 Dec 55 and 2 Feb 56, K. Younger and T. Fraser as runners-up filled the vacant places on the Parliamentary Committee.
[d] A. Greenwood resigned from the Parliamentary Committee on 13 Oct 60. R. Crossman, who was 13th in order of votes obtained, took his place on the Committee for a few weeks until the 1960–61 sessional elections in November.
[e] D. Jay joined the Committee when H. Wilson was elected Leader.

PARLIAMENTARY LABOUR PARTY

1970–73

	Jul 1970	Nov 1971	Nov 1972	Nov 1973
A. Benn	5	10	11	8
J. Callaghan	1	4	5	1
Mrs B. Castle	2	15[a]	..	..
A. Crosland	3	8	3	4
M. Foot	6	2	4	2
D. Healey	2	12	6	7
D. Houghton	4	..	..	..
R. Jenkins	..	..	..	5
H. Lever	8	7[a]	9	8
F. Peart	10	6	8	..
R. Prentice	..	13[a]	1	3
M. Rees	..	..	10	10
W. Ross	..[c]	5	7	12
P. Shore	..	11	12[b]	11
E. Short	9	1	..	..
J. Silkin	..	14[a]	(12[b])	(13)
G. Thomson	11	9[a]	..	..
Mrs S. Williams	7	3	1	6

[a] H. Lever and G. Thomson resigned on 10 Apr 72. They were replaced by R. Prentice and J. Silkin, who had 13th and 14th place respectively in the original ballot. When E. Short became Deputy Leader, Mrs B. Castle beat E. Heffer 111–89, to take his place on the Committee on 3 May 72.
[b] J. Silkin, who tied with P. Shore for 12th place, withdrew, making a second ballot unnecessary.
[c] W. Ross joined the committee in Nov 70 when D. Houghton became Chairman of the P.L.P.

1979–88

	Jun 1979	Nov 1980	Nov 1981[b]	Nov 1982	Nov 1983	Oct 1984	Oct 1985	Oct 1986	Jun 1987	Nov 1988
P. Archer	..	..	14	9	8	7	10	9	..	..
A. W. Benn	..	(13)[a]	..	..	..	..	..	..	..	..
A. Booth	7	8	8	6	..	..	..	..	..	..
G. Brown	..	..	..	..	..	..	..	..	11	1
D. Clark	..	..	..	..	..	..	..	11	14	4
R. Cook	..	..	..	..	10	15	5	..	8	5
J. Cunningham	..	..	..	..	5	3	9	8	11	14
D. Davies	..	..	..	..	..	12	13	3	6*	..
F. Dobson	..	..	..	..	..	..	..	..	10	7
Ms G. Dunwoody	..	..	15	13	12	10	..	..	..	..
B. Gould	..	..	..	..	..	..	..	14	1	7
R. Hattersley	4	1	3	4	..	..	..	..	..	..
D. Healey	1	..	..	..	1	2	3	4	..	..
E. Heffer	..	..	13	15	11	..	..	..	..	..
R. Hughes	..	..	..	..	..	..	15	..	7	..
B. John	..	..	10	12	..	..	..	..	..	..
B. Jones	..	..	..	..	9	8	11	6	..	12
G. Kaufman	..	3	2	1	2	1	1	1	4	3
N. Kinnock	..	12	7	2	..	..	..	..	..	..
R. Mason	11	10	..	..	..	..	..	..	..	..
M. Meacher	..	..	..	..	13	11	12	15	3	10
B. Millan	..	..	12	14	..	..	..	..	..	..
S. Orme	6	6	11	10	15	4	2	5	..	..
D. Owen	10	..	..	..	..	..	..	..	..	..
J. Prescott	..	..	..	..	6	8	4	12	2	13
G. Radice	..	..	..	..	14	13	8	10	..	..
M. Rees	9	4	6	11	..	..	..	..	..	..
Miss J. Richardson	..	..	..	..	..	..	..	..	11	15
W. Rodgers	8	9	..	..	..	..	..	..	..	..
P. Shore	3	5	1	3	3	6	..	..	..	..
J. Silkin	2	7	4	7	7	..	..	..	..	..
J. Smith	12	11	9	8	4	5	7	2	5	2
J. Straw	..	..	..	..	..	..	..	..	15	11
E. Varley	5	2	5	5	..	..	..	..	..	..

[a] A. Benn took over the place vacated by W. Rodgers when he joined the SDP.
[b] The PLP Committee was enlarged from 12 to 15 elected members in 1981.

1988–

In 1989 the rules for the election of the Parliamentary Committee were changed in favour of women M.P.s; the total size was increased to 18, at least three of whom had to be women. In 1993 the rules were further amended so that M.P.s had to vote for at least four women candidates.

	Nov 1989	Nov 1990	Nov 1991	Jul 1992	Oct 1993
Mrs M. Beckett	17	3	6	..	..
T. Blair	4	8	8	2	6
D. Blunkett	..	..	..	15	17
G. Brown	1	2	1	1	4
D. Clark	1	7	10	18	7
T. Clarke	..	..	..	17	13
Ms A. Clwyd	14	11	4	10	..
R. Cook	3	4	2	3	1
J. Cunningham	8	13	12	12	18
R. Davies	..	..	..	(19)[a]	11
D. Dewar	15	8	10	14	11
F. Dobson	10	16	6	4	2
B. Gould	9	17	5	6	..
Mrs H. Harman	..	..	..	6	..
B. Jones	16	13	17	..	..
G. Kaufman	5	5	12	..	..
Ms J. Lestor	6	..	..	..	15
M. Meacher	12	10	15	13	10
Ms M. Mowlam	..	..	..	6	5
J. Prescott	11	18	15	5	2
G. Robertson	..	..	..	..	16
Ms J. Richardson	7	15	18	..	..
C. Smith	..	..	..	6	9
J. Smith	2	1	3	..	..
J. Straw	18	6	14	16	8
Ms A. Taylor	..	12	9	11	14

[a] R. Davies was elected to the Shadow Cabinet as a result of a by-election in Nov 92 following the resignation of B. Gould.

Chairmen of Parliamentary Committee with Labour in power 1924–70

1924   *Parliamentary Executive Committee*

1924   R. Smillie

1929–31   *Consultative Committee*

1929	H. Snell	1930	J. Barr

1940–45   *Administrative Committee*

1940	H. Lees-Smith (*acting*)[1]	1942	A. Greenwood (*acting*)[1]
1941	H. Lees-Smith (*acting*)[1]	1943	A. Greenwood (*acting*)[1]
1942	F. Pethick-Lawrence (*acting*)[1]	1944	A. Greenwood (*acting*)[1]

1945–51   *Liaison Committee*

1945	N. Maclean	1948	M. Webb
1946	M. Webb	1949	M. Webb
1947	M. Webb	1950	W. Glenvil Hall

1964–70   *Liaison Committee*

1964	E Shinwell	1967	D. Houghton

[1] During C. Attlee's membership of the war-time Coalition, the Labour Party appointed an Acting Chairman each session.

Chairmen of Parliamentary Labour Party, 1970–

1970 (Nov)	D. Houghton		1983 (Nov)	J. Dormand
1974 (Mar)	I. Mikardo		1987 (Jul)	S. Orme
1974 (Nov)	C. Hughes		1992 (Jul)	D. Hoyle
1979 (Jun)	F. Willey			

Secretary, Parliamentary Labour Party

1943	C. Johnson		1979	B. Davies
1959	(Sir) G. Barlow		1992	A. Haworth

SOURCES. – 1923–29, *Daily Herald* and *Directory for National Council of Labour, TUC General Council, Labour Party and the Parliamentary Labour Party* (published annually by the Labour Party); 1931–, *Labour Party Annual Conference Reports; The Times*; and *Labour Party Directory.*

Labour Representation Committee–Annual Conferences, 1900–1905

Date	Place	Chairman
27–28 Feb 00	London	W. Steadman
1 Feb 01	Manchester	J. Hodge
20–22 Feb 02	Birmingham	W. Davies
19–21 Feb 03	Newcastle upon Tyne	J. Bell
4–5 Feb 04	Bradford	J. Hodge
26–29 Jan 05	Liverpool	A. Henderson

Labour Party–Annual Conferences, 1906–

Date	Place	Chairman
15–17 Feb 06	London	A. Henderson
24–26 Jan 07	Belfast	J. Stephenson
20–22 Jan 08	Hull	W. Hudson
27–29 Jan 09	Portsmouth	J. Clynes
9–11 Feb 10	Newport	J. Keir Hardie
1–3 Feb 11	Leicester	W. Robinson
24–26 Jan 12	Birmingham	B. Turner
29–31 Jan 13	London	G. Roberts
27–30 Jan 14	Glasgow	T. Fox
1915	*No conference held*	
26–28 Jan 16	Bristol	W. Anderson
23–26 Jan 17	Manchester	G. Wardle
23–25 Jan 18[1]	Nottingham	W. Purdy
26–28 Jun 18	London	W. Purdy
25–27 Jun 19	Southport	J. McGurk
22–25 Jun 20	Scarborough	W. Hutchinson
26–29 Jun 23	London	S. Webb
7–10 Oct 24	London	R. MacDonald
29 Sep–2 Oct 25	Liverpool	C. Cramp
11–15 Oct 26	Margate	R. Williams
3–7 Oct 27	Blackpool	F. Roberts
1–5 Oct 28	Birmingham	G. Lansbury
30 Sep–4 Oct 29	Brighton	H. Morrison
6–10 Oct 30	Llandudno	Susan Lawrence
5–8 Oct 31	Scarborough	S. Hirst
3–7 Oct 32	Leicester	G. Lathan
2–6 Oct 33	Hastings	J. Compton
1–5 Oct 34	Southport	W. Smith
30 Sep–4 Oct 35	Brighton	W. Robinson
5–9 Oct 36	Edinburgh	Jennie Adamson
4–8 Oct 37	Bournemouth	H. Dalton
1938	*No conference held*	

[1] Adjourned for one month. Resumed 26 Feb 18 in London.

29 May–2 Jun 39	Southport	G. Dallas
13–16 May 40	Bournemouth	Barbara Gould
2–4 Jun 41	London	J. Walker
25–28 May 42	London	W. Green
14–18 Jun 43	London	A. Dobbs
11–15 Dec 44	London	G. Ridley
21–25 May 45	Blackpool	Ellen Wilkinson
10–14 Jun 46	Bournemouth	H. Laski
26–30 May 47	Margate	P. Noel-Baker
17–21 May 48	Scarborough	E. Shinwell
6–10 Jun 49	Blackpool	J. Griffiths
2–6 Oct 50	Margate	S. Watson
1–3 Oct 51	Scarborough	Alice Bacon
29 Sep–3 Oct 52	Morecambe	H. Earnshaw
28 Sep–2 Oct 53	Margate	Arthur Greenwood
27 Sep–1 Oct 54	Scarborough	W. Burke
10–14 Oct 55	Margate	Edith Summerskill
1–5 Oct 56	Blackpool	E. Gooch
30 Sep–4 Oct 57	Brighton	Margaret Herbison
29 Sep–3 Oct 58	Scarborough	T. Driberg
28–29 Nov 59	Blackpool	Barbara Castle
3–7 Oct 60	Scarborough	G. Brinham
2–6 Oct 61	Blackpool	R. Crossman
2–5 Oct 62	Brighton	H. Wilson
30 Sep–4 Oct 63	Scarborough	D. Davies
12–13 Dec 64	Brighton	Anthony Greenwood
27 Sept Oct 65	Blackpool	R. Gunter
3–7 Oct 66	Brighton	W. Padley
2–6 Oct 67	Scarborough	J. Boyd
30 Sep–4 Oct 68	Blackpool	Jennie Lee
29 Sep–3 Oct 69	Brighton	Eirene White
28 Sep 2 Oct 70	Blackpool	A. Skeffington
4–8 Oct 71	Brighton	I. Mikardo
2–6 Oct 72	Blackpool	A. Benn
1–5 Oct 73	Blackpool	W. Simpson
27–30 Nov 74	London	J. Callaghan
26 Apr 75[2]	London	F. Mulley
29 Sept Oct 75	Blackpool	F. Mulley
27 Sep–1 Oct 76	Blackpool	T. Bradley
3–7 Oct 77	Brighton	Joan Lestor
2–6 Oct 78	Blackpool	Joan Lestor
1–5 Oct 79	Brighton	F. Allaun
29 Sep–3 Oct 80	Blackpool	Lady Jeger
27 Sep–2 Oct 81	Brighton	A. Kitson
27 Sep–1 Oct 82	Blackpool	Dame J. Hart
3–8 Oct 83	Brighton	S. McCluskey
1–5 Oct 84	Blackpool	E. Heffer
29 Sep–4 Oct 85	Bournemouth	A. Hadden
28 Sep–3 Oct 86	Blackpool	N. Hough
27 Sep–2 Oct 87	Brighton	S. Tierney
2–7 Oct 88	Blackpool	N. Kinnock
1–6 Oct 89	Brighton	D. Skinner
30 Sep–5 Oct 90	Blackpool	Jo Richardson
29 Sep–4 Oct 91	Brighton	J. Evans
27 Sep–2 Oct 92	Blackpool	T. Clarke
26 Sep–1 Oct 93	Brighton	D. Blunkett

SOURCES. – *1900–5 Reports of the Labour Representation Committee Annual Conferences, Labour Party Annual Conference Reports 1906-*.

[2] Special conference on the Common Market.

LABOUR PARTY MEMBERSHIP

Labour Party–Membership Statistics

Year	No. Constit & Central Parties	Total Indiv. Members ('000s)	T.U.s No.	T.U.s Members ('000s)	Soc. & Co-op Socs. No.	Soc. & Co-op Socs. Members ('000s)	Total Membership ('000s)
1900–01	7	..	41	353	3	23	376
1901–02	21	..	65	455	2	14	469
1902–03	49	..	127	847	2	14	861
1903–04	76	..	165	956	2	14	970
1904–05	73	..	158	855	2	15	900
1905–06	73	..	158	904	2	17	921
1906–07	83	..	176	975	2	21	998
1907	92	..	181	1,050	2	22	1,072
1908	133	..	176	1,127	2	27	1,159
1909	155	..	172	1,451	2	31	1,486
1910	148	..	151	1,394	2	31	1,431
1911	149	..	141	1,502	2	31	1,539
1912	146	..	130	1,858	2	31	1,895
1913	158	..	a	a	2	33	a
1914	179	..	101	1,572	2	33	1,612
1915	177	..	111	2,054	2	33	2,093
1916	199	..	119	2,171	3	42	2,220
1917	239	..	123	2,415	3	47	2,465
1918	389	b	131	2,960	4	53	3,013
1919	418	..	126	3,464	7	47	3,511
1920	492	..	122	4,318	5	42	4,360
1921	456	..	116	3,974	5	37	4,010
1922	482	..	102	3,279	5	32	3,311
1923	503	..	106	3,120	6	36	3,156
1924	529	..	108	3,158	7	36	3,194
1925	549	..	106	3,338	8	36	3,374
1926	551	..	104	3,352	8	36	3,388
1927	532	..	97	3,239	6	55[c]	3,294
1928	535	215	91	2,025[d]	7	52	2,292[d]
1929	578	228	91	2,044	6	59	2,331
1930	607	277	89	2,011	7	58	2,347
1931	608	297	80	2,024	7	37	2,358
1932	608	372	75	1,960	9	40	2,372
1933	612	366	75	1,899	9	40	2,305
1934	614	381	72	1,858	8	40	2,278
1935	614	419	72	1,913	9	45	2,378
1936	614	431	73	1,969	9	45	2,444
1937	614	447	70	2,037	8	43	2,528
1938	614	429	70	2,158	9	43	2,630
1939	614	409	72	2,214	6	40	2,663
1940	614	304	73	2,227	6	40	2,571
1941	585	227	68	2,231	6	28	2,485
1942	581	219	69	2,206	6	29	2,454
1943	586	236	69	2,237	6	30	2,503

[a] Owing to the operation of the Osborne Judgement it was made impossible to compile membership statistics for 1913.
[b] Individual membership statistics were not compiled 1918–27.
[c] The Royal Arsenal Co-operative Society, through its Political Purposes Committee, continued its affiliation with the Labour Party; its membership is included in the 1927–60 totals.
[d] From 1928 to 1946 inclusive, trade unionist members of the Labour Party had to 'contract in' to payment to party political funds.

Year	No. Constit & Central Parties	Total Indiv. Members ('000s)	T.U.s		Soc. & Co-op Socs.		Total Membership ('000s)
			No.	Members ('000s)	No.	Members ('000s)	
1944	598	266	68	2,375	6	32	2,673
1945	649	487	69	2,510	6	41	3,039
1946	649	645	70	2,635[d]	6	42	3,322[d]
1947	649	608	73	4,386	6	46	5,040
1948	656	629	80	4,751	6	42	5,422
1949	660	730	80	4,946	5	41	5,717
1950	661	908	83	4,972	5	40	5,920
1951	667	876	82	4,937	5	35	5,849
1952	667	1,015	84	5,072	5	21	6,108
1953	667	1,005	84	5,057	5	34	6,096
1954	667	934	84	5,530	5	35	6,498
1955	667	843	87	5,606	5	35	6,484
1956	667	845	88	5,658	5	34	6,537
1957	667	913	87	5,644	5	26	6,583
1958	667	889	87	5,628	5	26	6,542
1959	667	84B	87	5,564	5	25	6,437
1960	667	790	86	5,513	5	25	6,328
1961	667	751	86	5,550	5	25	6,326
1962	667	767	86	5,503	5	25	6,296
1963	667	830	83	5,507	6	21	6,358
1964	667	830	83	5,502	6	21	6,353
1965	659	817	79	5,602	6	21	6,440
1966	658	776	79	5,539	6	21	6,336
1967	657	734	75	5,540	6	21	6,295
1968	656	701	68	5,364	6	21	6,087
1969	656	681	68	5,462	6	22	6,164
1970	656	680	67	5,519	6	24	6,223
1971	659	700	67	5,559	6	25	6,284
1972	659	703	62	5,425	9	40	6,169
1973	651	665	60	5,365	9	42	6,073
1974	623	692	63	5,787	9	39	6,518
1975	623	675	61	5,750	9	44	6,469
1976	623	659	59	5,800	9	48	6,459
1977	623	660	59	5,913	9	43	6,616
1978	623	676	59	6,260	9	55	6,990
1979	623	666	59	6,511	9	58	7,236
1980	623	348	54	6,407	10	56	6,811
1981	623	277	54	6,273	10	58	6,608
1982	623	274	50	6,185	10	57	6,516
1983	633	295	47	6,101	10	59	6,456
1984	633	323	46	5,844	9	60	6,227
1985	633	313	44	5,827	9	60	6,200
1986	633	297	44	5,778	9	58	6,133
1987	633	289	44	5,564	9	55	5,908
1988	633	266	44	5,481	9	56	5,804
1989	633	294	44	5,335	9	53	5,682
1990	633	311	44	4,922	9	54	5,287
1991	634	261	34	4,811	13	54	5,126
1992	634	280	38	4,634	14	51	4,965

SOURCE. – *Labour Party Annual Conference Reports.*

[d] From 1928 to 1946 inclusive, trade unionist members of the Labour Party had to 'contract in' to payment to party political funds.

The Labour Party – Organisation and Constitutions

The Labour Representation Committee was formed on 27 Feb 1900 to promote a distinct Labour group in Parliament, representing the affiliated trade unions and socialist socie- ties. After the General Election of 1906 the L.R.C. group of M.P.s decided to assume the title of 'Labour Party' and elected their first officers and whips. Policy was determined by the Labour Party through the annual conference and its executive authority, the National Executive Committee. There was no official party leader, but an annually elected chair- man of the parliamentary party. There were scarcely any official Labour Party constitu- ency organisations (except for those provided by local trades councils, groups of miners' lodges, and local branches of the I.L.P.). In 1914 there were only two constituency associa- tions with individual members, Woolwich and Barnard Castle, which Will Crooks and Arthur Henderson had built up on their own.

The Reorganisation of the Labour Party, 1918

The reorganisation of the Labour Party was projected by Arthur Henderson in collabora- tion with Sidney Webb. Their main aims were to provide local Labour Parties in every constituency or group of constituencies. These local Labour Parties were to be based fun- damentally on individual subscribing membership, though representation was provided for Trades Councils, trade union branches, and socialist societies. The members of the N.E.C. were to be elected by the annual conference as a whole (though eleven were to be elected from candidates nominated by the trade unions and socialist societies as a single group, five were to represent the Local Labour Parties, and four were to be women). the scheme also involved an increase in affiliation fees.

    The original plan was amended, so that the N.E.C. was increased to a membership of 23 (adding two to the number specified for affiliated organisations). It was agreed that the election programme should be produced by the N.E.C. and P.L.P. jointly subject to the aims of the Party and the decisions of the annual conferences. The object of the pre-war Party had been to 'organise and maintain in Parliament and in the country a political Labour Party'. In 1918 this was changed to a new formula: 'to secure for the producers by hand and by brain the full fruits of their industry, and the most equitable distribution thereof that may be possible, upon the basis of the common ownership of the means of production and the best obtainable system of popular administration and control of each industry and service'.[1]

Modifications since 1918

The 1918 constitution was modified in 1937 in favour of the local constituency Labour Parties, which had repeatedly demanded a greater share in the control of party affairs. Representation of the constituency parties on the N.E.C. was increased from five to seven. The seven were to be elected by the vote of the constituency delegates alone. The twelve trade union representatives and one representative of the socialist societies were to be elected separately by their respective conference delegations. The five women members may be nominated by any affiliated organisation and are elected by a vote of the whole party conference. The Leader (since 1929) and the Deputy Leader (since 1953) are ex

---

[1] The 1914 and 1918 Labour Party constitutions are set out and compared in G. D. H. Cole, *A History of the Labour Party from 1914* (1948), pp. 71–81.

officio members of the N.E.C. The Treasurer of the Party may be nominated by any affiliated organisation, and is elected by the vote of the whole party conference. In 1972 a Young Socialist elected by the National Conference of Labour Party Young Socialists was added to the N.E.C. In 1981 the procedure for the election of Leader and Deputy Leader was changed (see p. 136).

SOURCES. – H. Pelling, *The Origins of the Labour Party, 1880–1900* (1954); F. Bealey and H. Pelling, *Labour and Politics, 1900–1906* (1958); P. Poirier, *The Advent of the Labour Party* (1958); G.D.H. Cole, *A History of the Labour Party from 1914* (1948); R.T. McKenzie, *British Political Parties* (1955); L. Minkin, *The Labour Party Conference* (1978). Since 1918 complete lists of Labour Party publications have been given in the Labour Party Annual Conference Reports. See also I. Bulmer-Thomas, *The Growth of the British Party System* (1965).

Sponsored M.P.s

The tables on p. 150 summarise information on sponsored Labour M.P.s. M.P.s have also been sponsored by organisations which are not affiliated to the Labour Party. The two major instances of this are the National Union of Teachers and the National Farmers' Union.

National Union of Teachers

The N.U.T. sponsored and assisted parliamentary candidates from 1895 to 1974. The number of sponsored candidates varied, but a strict parity between the parties was always attempted. The practice ceased after 1974.

N.U.T. adopted and supported M.P.s, 1900–1974

Election	Total	Con.	Lab.	Lib.
1910 (Jan)	Total	Con.	Lab.	Lib.
1900	3	1	..	2
1906	2	..	..	2
1910 (Jan)	1	..	..	
1910 (Dec)	2	..		
1918	1	1	..	..
1922	3	1	2	..
1923	3	..	3	..
1924	4	1	3	..
1929	5	..	5	..
1931	3	1	2	..
1935	5	1	4	..
1945	2	..	2	..
1950	4	..	4	..
1951	4	..	4	..
1955	6	2	4	..
1959	6	2	4	..
1964	5	1	4	..
1966	4	1	3	..
1970	5	2	3	..
1974 (Feb)	5	1	4	..
1974 (Oct)	4	1	3	..

SOURCES. – Information received from the National Union of Teachers; J.D. Stewart, *British Pressure Groups* (1958).

Sponsored M.P.s (Labour) 1918–

	1918	1922	1923	1924	1929	1931	1935	1945	1950	1951	1955	1959	1964	1966	1970	Feb 1974	Oct 1974	1979	1983	1987	1992
NUM	25	41	43	40	42	26	32	34	37	36	34	31	28	26	20	18	18	16	14	13	14
TGW	3	7	10	10	13	1	7	17	16	14	14	14	21	25	19	23	22	22	25	33	38
NUR (RMT)	1	3	4	3	8	..	5	12	10	9	8	5	6	7	5	6	6	12	10	8	12
TSSSA	..	..	..	7	..	6	9	7	7	5	5	7	6	4	3	3	3	2	2	2	2
GMW	4	5	5	4	6	2	6	10	6	6	4	4	9	11	12	13	13	14	11	11	17
ASW	1	1	3	2	6	1	2	3	3	2	1	..	..	..	2	3	1	1	..	..	..
USDAW	..	1	4	4	4	1	6	8	8	9	9	9	10	8	7	6	5	5	2	8	3
I&S	..	2	1	3	4	1	1	2	2	2	2	2	1	1	2	2	1	2	2	1	..
UTFWA	4	3	3	2	4	..	..	3	2	..	1	1	1	..	..	..	..	..	1	..	..
AEU	1	7	4	4	3	2	3	4	8	8	6	8	18	18	16	22	21	21	17	12	13
ASSET	..	..	..	..	..	..	..	..	..	..	..	..	..	1	2	2	6	10	8	10	13
ETU	..	..	..	..	..	..	..	..	1	1	1	..	2	..	1	3	3	6	4	3	3
APEX	..	..	..	..	..	..	..	..	..	1	1	2	2	3	4	3	3	6	5	3	..
NUPE	..	..	..	..	..	..	..	..	1	1	2	2	1	2	5	6	6	6	7	4	12
Others	10	16	25	16	17	1	10	15	9	9	6	9	12	18	12	11	9	11	12	21	16
Sponsored M.P.s																					
TU	49	86	102	88	114	35	78	120	111	108	95	92	120	127	112	127	126	134	115	129	143
Co-op	1	4	6	5	9	1	9	23	18	16	18	16	20	18	17	16	16	17	8	10	14
Unsupported M.P.s	7	52	83	58	164	10	67	250	186	171	164	150	177	218	158	143	177	118	86	139	157
Total Labour M.P.s	57	142	191	151	287	46	154	393	315	295	277	258	317	363	387	301	319	269	209	229	271

SOURCES. – 1918–24, *Labour Party Annual Conference Reports*; 1929–59, *Trade Unions and the Labour Party since 1945*, by M. Harrison (1960) (these figures are also based on the Labour Party Conference Reports but modified by examination of union accounts); J. Bailey, *The British Co-operative Movement* (1955); W. Muller, *The Kept Men* (1977) and information from Walworth Road.

National Farmers' Union

In 1909 the N.F.U. set up a Parliamentary Fund with the object of sending two sponsored M.P.s to Parliament from each side of the House. Although sometimes 'independent on agricultural questions' all N.F.U. M.P.s have been Conservatives. Since 1945 the N.F.U. has not sponsored any candidates and has adopted a position of strict neutrality between the political parties.

N.F.U.-sponsored M.P.s 1921–1935

Election	No. of M.P.s
1922	4
1923	3
1924	2
1929	No candidates
1931	No candidates
1935	2

SOURCES. – *National Farmers' Union Yearbooks, 1900–60*; P. Self and H. Storing, *The State and the Farmer* (1962), pp. 42–7,204; J.D. Stewart, *British Pressure Groups* (1958), pp. 173–4.

Party Finance

Labour Party Central Income (excluding special General Election Funds):

1910*	£12,000
1920	£55,000
1930	£44,000
1940	£51,000
1950*	£197,000
1960	£225,000
1970*	£1,034,000
1980	£2,801,000
1990	£6,274,000

* Asterisks denote general election years. For details of the Party's expenditure in recent general elections see p. 000. In 1912, the annual affiliation fee for constituency parties and trade unions was set at 1d per member. It was raised by stages: 1918 – 2d, 1920 – 3d, 1931 – 4d, 1937 – 4½d, 1940 – 5d, 1948 – 6d, 1957 – 9d, 1963 – 1/-, 1970 – 7½p, and thereafter almost every year: the affilation fee was 32p in 1980, and by 1992 it was £1.60. In 1990 Trade Union affiliation fees provided 67% of the Labour Party's routine annual income.

SOURCES. – The Labour Party has always published Accounts in its Annual Conference Reports. M. Harrison, *Trade Unions and the Labour Party* (1960); R. Rose, *Influencing Voters* (1967); M. Harrison's chapter in R. Rose and A. Heidenheimer, 'Comparative Political Finance', *Journal of Politics* (1963); *Committee on Financial Aid to Political Parties* (Cmnd 6601/1976); M. Pinto-Duschinsky, *British Political Finance 1830–1980* (1981); *Labour Party Annual Reports*; M. Linton, *Money and Votes* (Institute for Public Policy Research 1994).

Liberal Party

The Liberal Party split, following D. Lloyd George's supplantation of H. Asquith as Prime Minister in 1916. The two wings merged again following the 1922 election. In 1931 the party split once more between the National Liberals (who gradually merged with the Conservatives), the Liberals, and the Independent Liberals (a Lloyd George family group); the Independent Liberals rejoined the Liberals in the mid 1930s.

The Alliance and the Merger

From 1981 to 1987 the Liberal party was linked in the Alliance with the newly formed Social Democratic Party (see p. 167). On 14 Jun 87 the Liberal leader D. Steel proposed merging the two parties. On 17 Sep 87 the Liberal Conference in Harrogate voted to start negotiations. On 23 Jan 88 a special Liberal Assembly convened in Blackpool voted to proceed with merger. This took place on 3 Mar 88 following an affirmative ballot by the membership of both parties (see below for Social and Liberal Democrats).

Leaders[1]

1900		Sir H. Campbell-Bannerman	26 Nov	35	Sir A. Sinclair
30 Apr	08	H. Asquith (E of Oxford and Asquith)[2]	2 Aug	45	C. Davies
			5 Nov	56	J. Grimond
14 Oct	26	D. Lloyd George[3]	18 Jan	67	J Thorpe
4 Nov	31	Sir H. Samuel[4]	7 Jul	76	D. Steel[5]

Deputy Leaders

1929–31	H. Samuel	1962–64	D. Wade
1949–51	Lady M. Lloyd George	1985–88	A. Beith

Leaders in the House of Lords

1900	E of Kimberley	1924	Earl Beauchamp	1967	Ld Byers
1902	Earl Spencer	1931	M of Reading	1984	Lady Seear
1905	M of Ripon	1936	M of Crewe	1987	Lord Jenkins
1908	E (M) of Crewe	1944	Vt Samuel		
1923	Vt Grey	1955	Ld Rea		

National Liberal Federation, 1900–1936

Chairman of Committee		Treasurer		Secretary	
1900	(Sir) E. Evans	1901	W. Hart	1893	(Sir) R. Hudson
1918	Sir G. Lunn	1903	J. Massie	1922	F. Barter
1920	A. Brampton	1907	R. Bird	1925	H. Oldman
1931	R. Muir	1910	F. Wright	1930	H. Oldman & W. Davies
1933	R. Walker	1923	Sir R. Hudson	1931	W. Davies
1934	M. Gray	1927	Sir F. Layland-Barratt		
		1934	P. Heffer		

[1] All were Liberal 'Leaders in the House of Commons'. Sir H. Campbell-Bannerman from 1905 to 1908 and H. Asquith from 1908 to 1926 were formally the only 'Leaders of the Liberal Party' from 1900 until the 1969 Constitution came into force.
[2] After H. Asquith's defeat at the 1918 General Election, Sir D. Maclean was elected chairman of the Parliamentary Party but relinquished the post on H. Asquith's return to the Commons in Mar 1920.
[3] D. Lloyd George was Chairman of the Parliamentary Liberal party from Dec 1924.
[4] After the General Election in 1931 there were three Liberal groups in the House of Commons. Sir H. Samuel led the main group of Liberal M.P.s. D. Lloyd George led a small family group of Independent Liberals, and Sir J.Simon led the Liberal National group (see *Minor Parties*).On 25 Nov 35 D. Lloyd George and the other Independent Liberals rejoined the Liberal Party in the House of Commons.
[5] An electoral college representing all constituency associations voted: D. Steel 12,541; J.Pardoe 7,032. J. Grimond was acting Leader 12 May 76–7 Jul 76.

Liberal Party Organisation, 1936–88

Head

1936	W. Davies (Secretary)
1952	H. Harris (General Director)
1960	D. Robinson (Directing Secretary)
1961	P. Kemmis (Secretary)
1965	T. Beaumont (Head of Liberal Party Organisation)
1966	P. Chitnis (Head of Liberal Party Organisation)[1]
1970	E. Wheeler (Head of Liberal Party Organisation)[2]
1977	H. Jones (Sec.-General)[3]
1983	J. Spiller (Sec.-General)
1985	A. Ellis (Sec.-General)

Chairman of Executive Committee		Chairman	
1936	M. Gray	1966	Ld Byers
1946	P. Fothergill	1967	T. Beaumont (Ld)
1949	Ld Moynihan	1968	Ld Henley
1950	F. Byers	1969	D. Banks
1952	P. Fothergill	1970	R. Wainwright
1954	G. Acland	1972	C. Carr
1957	D. Abel	1973	K. Vaus
1959	L. Behrens	1976	G. Tordoff
1961	D. Banks	1980	R. Pincham
1963	B. Wigoder	1983	Mrs J. Rose
1965	G. Evans	1984	P. Tyler
1968–69	J. Baker	1986	T. Clement-Jones

Treasurer[4]

1937–50	Sir A. McFadyean	1962–65	R. Gardner-Thorpe
1937–41	P. Heffer	1962–66	Sir A Murray
1941–47	Ld Rea	1963–65	T. Beaumont
1942–47	H. Worsley	1966–67	J. Thorpe
1947–53	Ld Moynihan	1967–69	L. Smith
1950–58	W. Grey	1968–69	J. Pardoe
1950–52	Vt Wimborne	1969–72	Sir F. Medlicott
1953–62	Sir A. Suenson-Taylor (Ld Grantchester)	1972–77	P. Watkins
1955–59	P. Fothergill	1977–83	Ld Lloyd of Kilgerran
1959–62	Miss H. Harvey	1977–83	M. Palmer
1983–86	Sir H. Jones	1983–86	A. Jacobs
1959–60	P. Lort-Phillips	1986–88	C. Fox
1961–62	J. McLaughlin	1986–88	T. Razzall

SOURCES. – *Liberal Magazine 1900–1950; Liberal Year Book 1900–1939; Dod's Parliamentary Companion 1950-; Annual reports of the Liberal Party 1956-.*

[1] P. Chitnis resigned in 1969. From Oct 69 to Nov 70 E. Wheeler was Director of Organisation. From Dec 69 to Jun 70 Mrs D. Gorsky was General Election Campaign Editor.
[2] In 1969 the post of Chairman of the Executive Committee was combined with the Chairmanship of the Party.
[3] E. Wheeler left in 1976. From Aug 76 until Mar 77 Mrs M. Wingfield was acting head of the Liberal Party Organisation.
[4] Until 1965 the post of Treasurer was held jointly by two or three officers. This practice was reverted to in 1977.

Chief Whips in House of Commons

1900	H. Gladstone	1935	Sir P. Harris	*Coalition Liberal*	
1905	G Whiteley	1945	T. Horabin	1916	N. Primrose
1908	J. Pease	1946	F. Byers	1917	F. Guest
1910	Master of Elibank	1950	J. Grimond	1921	C. McCurdy
1912	P. Illingworth	1956	D. Wade	1922	E. Hilton Young
1915	J. Gulland	1962	A. Holt		
1919	*vacant*[1]	1963	E. Lubbock		
1923	V. Phillipps	1970	D. Steel		
1924	Sir G. Collins	1976	C. Smith		
1926	Sir R. Hutchinson	1977	A. Beith		
1930	Sir A. Sinclair	1985	D. Alton		
1931	G. Owen	1987	J. Wallace		
1932	W. Rea				

Chief Whips in House of Lords

1896	Ld Ribblesdale	1949	M of Willingdon
1907	Ld Denman	1950	Ld Moynihan
1911–22	Ld Colebrooke	1950	Ld Rea
1919	Ld Denman (Ind. Lib.)	1955	Ld Amulree
1924	Ld Stanmore	1977	Ld Wigoder
1944	Vt Mersey	1984	Ld Tordoff

SOURCE. – *Dod's Parliamentary Companion 1900–*.

National Liberal Federation – Annual Conferences, 1900–1935

Date	Place	President
27–28 Mar 00	Nottingham	R. Spence Watson
14–15 May 01	Bradford	"
13–14 May 02	Bristol	A. Birrell
14–15 May 03	Scarborough	"
12–13 May 04	Manchester	"
18–19 May 05	Newcastle upon Tyne	"
23–24 May 06	Liverpool	A. Acland
6–7 Jun 07	Plymouth	"
18–19 Jun 08	Birmingham	Sir W. Angus
1–2 Jul 09	Southport	"
25 Nov 10	Hull	"
23–24 Nov 11	Bath	Sir J. Brunner
21–22 Nov 12	Nottingham	"
26–27 Nov 13	Leeds	"
1914–1918	*No conference held*	
27–28 Nov 19	Birmingham	Sir G. Lunn
25–26 Nov 20	Bradford	J. Robertson
24–25 Nov 21	Newcastle upon Tyne	"
17–18 May 22	Blackpool	"
30 May–1 Jun 23	Buxton	Sir D. Maclean
22–23 May 24	Brighton	"
14–15 May 25	Scarborough	"
17–18 Jun 26	Weston-super-Mare	J. Spender
26–27 May 27	Margate	Sir C. Hobhouse
11–12 Oct 28	Great Yarmouth	"
3–4 Oct 29	Nottingham	"
16–17 Oct 30	Torquay	A. Brampton
14–15 May 31	Buxton	"
28–29 Apr 32	Clacton-on-Sea	"
18–19 May 33	Scarborough	R. Muir
2–5 May 34	Bournemouth	"
23–25 May 35	Blackpool	"

[1] J. Hogge and G. Thorne were elected joint whips, not chief whip, in Feb 1919.

Liberal Party – Assemblies[1] 1936–1988

Date		Place	President
18–19 Jun	36	London	Ld Meston
27–31 May	37	Buxton	"
19–20 May	38	Bath	"
11–12 May	39	Scarborough	"
1940		*No assembly held*	
18–19 Jul	41	London	"
4–5 Sep	42	London	"
15–17 Jul	43	London	"
1944		*No assembly held*	
1–3 Feb	45	London	Lady V. Bonham-Carter
9–11 May	46	London	"
24–26 Apr	47	Bournemouth	I. Foot
22–24 Apr	48	Blackpool	E. Dodds
24–26 Mar	49	Hastings	Sir A. MacFadyean
27–28 Jan	50	London	"
29–30 Sep	50	Scarborough	P. Fothergill
1951		*No assembly held*	
15–17 May	52	Hastings	R. Walker
9–11 Apr	53	Ilfracombe	L. Robson
22–24 Apr	54	Buxton	H. Graham White
14–16 Apr	55	Llandudno	Ld Rea
27–29 Sep	56	Folkestone	L. Behrens
19–21 Sep	57	Southport	N. Micklem
18–21 Sep	58	Torquay	Sir A. Comyns Carr
1959		*No assembly held*	
29 Sep–1 Oct	60	Eastbourne	H. Glanville
21–23 Sep	61	Edinburgh	E. Malindine
19–22 Sep	62	Llandudno	Sir F. Brunner
10–14 Sep	63	Brighton	Ld Ogmore
4–5 Sep	64	London	R. Fulford
22–25 Sep	65	Scarborough	Miss N. Seear
21–24 Sep	66	Brighton	Ld Henley
20–23 Sep	67	Blackpool	Ld Wade
18–21 Sep	68	Edinburgh	D. Banks
17–20 Sep	69	Brighton	Ld Beaumont of Whitley
23–26 Sep	70	Eastbourne	"
15–18 Sep	71	Scarborough	Mrs S. Robson
19–23 Sep	72	Margate	S. Terrell
18–22 Sep	73	Southport	T. Jones
17–21 Sep	74	Brighton	Ld Lloyd of Kilgerran
16–20 Sep	75	Scarborough	A. Holt
12 Jun	76	Manchester (Special Assembly)	Mrs M. Wingfield
14–18 Sep	76	Llandudno	"
26 Sep–1 Oct	77	Brighton	B. Goldstone
21 Jan	78	Blackpool (Special Assembly)	G. Evans
12–16 Sep	78	Southport	Ld Evans of Claughton
28–29 Sep	79	Margate	M. Steed
8–13 Sep	80	Blackpool	Mrs J. Rose
14–19 Sep	81	Llandudno	R. Holme
20–25 Sep	82	Bournemouth	V. Bingham
19–24 Sep	83	Harrogate	J. Griffiths
17–22 Sep	84	Bournemouth	Ld Tordoff
16–21 Sep	85	Dundee	A. Watson
21–26 Sep	86	Eastbourne	D. Penhaligon
13–18 Sep	87	Harrogate	D. Wilson
22–23 Jan	88	Blackpool (Special Assembly)	A. Slade

[1] Liberal Presidents normally held office from Annual Assembly to Annual Assembly. Until 1970 they were instituted at the beginning of the Assembly which marked the start of their term, and performed the President's duties at that Assembly. From 1970 on they have been instituted at the end of the Assembly and no longer actually presided over debates. Presidents are listed on that basis here.

SOURCES. – *Liberal Year Book 1902–1939; The Liberal Magazine 1900–1950; National Liberal Federation, Annual Reports 1900–1936; Keesing's Contemporary Archives 1900–1988.*

The Liberal Publication Department published miscellaneous collections of *Pamphlets and Leaflets, 1908–30. The Liberal Magazine* was published from 1893 to 1950. J. S. Rasmussen, *The Liberal Party, A Study of Retrenchment and Revival* (1965); Alan Watkins, *The Liberal Dilemma* (1966); Trevor Wilson, *The Downfall of the Liberal Party 1914–35* (1966); C. Cook, *A Short History of the Liberal Party* (1976); and A. Cyr, *Liberal Party Politics in Britain* (1977).

(Social and) Liberal Democrats

On 2 Mar 88 the result of a ballot was published in which Liberal Party members voted by 46,376 to 6,365 to merge with the Social Democratic Party (which voted by 18,722 to 9,929 to do the same). The new party was officially launched the following day (3 Mar 88). Its full title was the Social and Liberal Democrats (SLD), with the short title 'the Democrats'. On 16 Oct 89, following a membership ballot, the party announced that it was henceforth to be known as the Liberal Democrats (although for formal, legal purposes, it retained its full title).

Leader

1988   P. Ashdown

(In a postal ballot of party members P. Ashdown was elected Leader by 41,401 votes to 16,202 over A. Beith).

Deputy Leader of Parliamentary Party

1988   A. Beith

President

1988–90   I. Wrigglesworth
1990–   C. Kennedy

Treasurer

1988   T. Razzall

General Secretary

1988   A. Ellis
1989   G. Elson

Party Conferences

25–29 Sep 88	Blackpool
3–5 Mar 89	Bournemouth
9–15 Sep 89	Brighton
10–11 Mar 90	Cardiff
15–20 Sep 90	Blackpool
15–17 Mar 91	Nottingham
9–12 Sep 91	Bournemouth
7–8 Mar 92	Glasgow
13–17 Sep 92	Harrogate
29–31 May 93	Nottingham
19–23 Sep 93	Torbay

Party Finance
Total net central income

1988–89	£1.2m
1989–90	£1.4m
1990–91	£1.6m
1991–92	£1.9m
1992–93	£3.0m

Minor Parties

Minor parties contesting Parliamentary Elections in England, Scotland and Wales 1900–1993
(for parties that split from major parties see pp. 159–169)

Name	Date of founding	Principal founder or key policy	M.P.s elected	Candidates First	Candidates Last	Candidates No.	Lost deposits
Action Party	1953	Mosley's Union Movement (1948) renamed (see p. 165)		1959	1972	8	8
Agricultural	1931	Formed as Norfolk farmers party 1931		1933	1933	1	0
All-Party Alliance	1967	J. Creasey		1967	1968	3	3
Anti-Federalist Lgue	1991	A. Sked		1992	1993	19	19
Anti-Partition Lgue	1948			1950	1951	5	5
Anti Waste League	1921	Ld Rothermere	(2)	1921	1921	4	0
British Empire Party	1951			1951	1951	1	1
British Movement	1968	C. Jordan		1969	1974	3	3
British National Party (1)	1961	Merger of Whites Defence League and Nat. Lab. Party		1964	1966	4	4
British National Party (2)	1982	Merger of New National Front and other groups led by John Tyndall		1983	1992	68	68
British People's Pty	1939	D of Bedford		1939	1946	2	2
British Socialist Pty	1911	H. Hyndman		1913	1918	19	2
British Union of Fascists	1932	Sir O. Mosley (see p. 165)		1940	1941	3	3
Campaign for Social Democracy	1973	D. Taverne	(1)	1974	1974	6	4
Common Wealth	1942	Sir R. Acland (see p. 159)	(4)	1943	1945	35	16
Commonwealth Land Pty	1919	J. Peace		1931	1931	2	2
Communist Party of England (Marxist Leninist)	1972			1973	1974	16	
Communist Party of GB	1920	(see p. 159)	(5)	1922	1992	571	534
Cooperative Party	1917	Allied with Lab. Party after 1918	(1)	1918	1918	11	0
Cornish Nationalist Party	1975	J. Whetter		1979	1983	2	2
Democratic Party (1)	1942	N. Leith-Hay-Clark		1945	1945	5	5
Democratic Party (2)	1969	D. Donnelly		1969	1970	7	6
Ecology Party	1975	Successor to People		1976	1984	170	170
Empire Free Trade Crusade	1929	Ld Beaverbrook	(1)	1930	1931	2	0
English National Party	1974	F. Hansford-Miller		1974	1976	4	4
Fellowship Party	1955			1959	1979	8	8
Fife Socialist League	1953			1959	1959	1	1
Green Party	1985	Successor to Ecology		1986	1993	408	407
Highland Land League	1909			1918	1918	4	3
Ind. Democratic Alliance	1973	Successor to All-Party Alliance		1974	1974	6	6
Independent Labour Party	1893	Broke with Lab.Party from 1930 onwards (see p. 160)	(11)	1930	1970	82	35
Ind. Nuclear Disarmament Election Committee	1962	Miss P. Arrowsmith		1964	1964	2	2
Ind. Parliamentary Group	1920	H. Bottomley	(5)	1920	1921	7	3
International Marxist G.	1966			1974	1977	4	4
Irish Civil Rights Assn.	1972			1974	1974	7	7
Irish National Movement	1882		(9)[1]	1900	1929	12	0
Islamic Party	1989			1990	1992	5	5
Labour Independent Group	1949	Expelled Lab. M.P.s		1950	1950	5	2
League of Empire Loyalists	1954	A. Chesterton, merged with Nat. Front 1967		1957	1964	4	4
Liberal Party	1988	M. Meadowcroft		1988	1992	79	78
Liverpool Protestant Party	1903			1931	1945	3	0
Mebyon Kernow	1951	Cornish Independence		1970	1983	6	6
Mudiad Gweriniaethol Cymru	1950	Welsh Republican Movement		1950	1950	1	1
National Democratic and Labour Party	1915	To support war and later Coalition (see p. 164)	(10)	1918	1920	29	6

[1] All of these victories were by T.P. O'Connor in Liverpool (Scotland).

Name	Date of founding	Principal founder or key policy	M.P.s elected	Candidates			Lost deposits
				First	Last	No.	
National Democratic Party	1963	D. Brown		1964	1974	8	7
National Farmers Union	1908	(see p. 156)		1918	1922	10	3
National Federation of Discharged and Demobilised Sailors and Soldiers	1917			1917	1918	6	3
National Fellowship	1962	E. Martell		1963	1967	1	0
National Front	1967	Merger of British Nat. Party and League of Empire Loyalists (see p. 151)		1968	1992	565	564
National Independence P.	1972	National Front breakaway		1972	1974	3	3
National Labour Party	1958	J. Bean merged 1960 with White Defence League		1959	1959	1	1
National Party	1917	H. Page Croft	(2)	1917	1920	29	13
National Party	1966	E. Martell		1967	1967	1	1
National Prohibition P.	1887			1923	1923	1	1
National Socialist Party	1916	Breakaway from British Socialist Party		1918	1918	4	1
National Union of Small Shopkeepers	1943			1959	1968	3	3
Natural Law Party	1992	Transcendental meditation		1992	1993	311	311
New Conservative Party	1960	J. Dayton		1960	1961	4	4
New Party	1931	Sir O. Mosley (see p. 165)		1931	1931	25	3
Patriotic Party	1962	R. Hilton		1964	1966	3	3
People	1973			1974	1974	11	11
People's League for the Defence of Freedom	1956	E. Martell		1957	1957	1	1
Plaid Cymru	1925	(see p. 165)	(16)	1929	1992	338	245
Radical Alliance	1965	From supporters of C.N.D.		1966	1966	2	2
Red Front	1987	Alliance of left groups		1987	1987	14	14
Revolutionary Communist Party (1)	1944			1945	1945	1	1
Revolutionary Communist Party (2)	1981			1983	1992	15	15
Scottish Labour Party (1)	1900			1900	1908	10	0
Scottish Labour Party (2)	1975	J. Sillars (see p. 166)		1978	1979	4	3
Scottish Militant Labour	1992	Militant tendency		1992	1992	1	0
Scottish National Party	1928	(see p. 166)	(31)	1929	1992	526	141
Scottish Party	1932	From supporters of S.N.P.		1933	1933	1	0
Scottish Prohibition Party	1901	E. Scrymgeour	(4)	1908	1931	10	0
Social Credit	1935	J. Hargrave		1935	1950	2	2
Social Democratic Federation	1881	H. Hyndman		1900	1910	37	0
Social Democratic Party	1988	D. Owen – opponents of merger between SDP and Liberals		1988	1991	9	5
Socialist Labour Party	1903			1918	1918	3	1
Socialist Party of Great Britain	1904			1945	1979	15	15
Socialist Workers Party	1976	Formerly International Socialist Group		1976	1978	8	8
Union Movement	1948	(see Action Party) (see p. 165)					
United Country Party	1979	P. Moore		1979	1979	2	2
United Democratic Party	1974			1974	1974	13	13
United Empire Party	1930	Ld Beaverbrook. Merged with Empire Free Trade Crusade		1930	1930	3	1
Vectis National Party	1969			1970	1970	1	1
Wessex Regional Party	1979	A. Thynne		1979	1983	16	16
Women's Party	1917	Mrs Pankhurst		1918	1918	1	0
Workers' Party of Scotland	1966			1969	1969	1	1
Workers' Revolutionary Party	1959			1974	1992	114	114

SOURCES. – F.W.S. Craig, *Minor Parties at British Parliamentary Elections 1885–1974* (1975). BBC Political Research Unit.

Notes on the Principal Minor Parties

Common Wealth

This party was founded in 1942 by Sir Richard Acland (Liberal M.P. for Barnstaple) during the war-time electoral truce. Its immediate aim was to contest all by-elections where a 'reactionary' candidate was in the field, and was not opposed by a Labour or other 'progressive' candidate. Seats were won at Eddisbury (J. Loverseed, 1943), Skipton (H. Lawson, 1944), and Chelmsford (E. Millington, 1945). In 1943 membership of Common Wealth was proscribed by the Labour Party. In the 1945 General Election Common Wealth put up twenty-three candidates but were only successful in Chelmsford, where no Labour candidate stood: the victor there, E. Millington, joined the Labour Party. Sir R. Acland joined the Labour Party as soon as the 1945 results were known. Common Wealth survived as an organisation but contested no further parliamentary elections.

Communist Party

The Communist Party of Great Britain was founded in July 1920. In its early years it sought to affiliate to the Labour Party but was rebuffed. In 1922 J.T.W. Newbold (Motherwell) was elected to Parliament; S. Saklatvala (N. Battersea) was also elected in 1922 as a Labour M.P. (although a member of the Communist Party). After defeat in 1923, he was elected again in 1924 as a Communist. Since 1924 the Labour Party has ruled that no member of the Communist Party could be an individual member of the Labour Party and in 1935, 1943, and 1946 the Labour Party turned down further Communist requests for affiliation. In 1935 and again in 1945 W. Gallacher was elected as a Communist for W. Fife; and in 1945 P. Piratin was elected for the Mile End division of Stepney. In 1991 the party voted narrowly to change its name to Democratic Left and concentrate on political debate rather than contesting elections, although four candidates using the former party's full title did contest the 1992 General Election.

Secretaries of the Communist Party: 1920–29 A. Inkpin, 1929–56 H.Pollitt, 1956–75 J. Gollan, 1975–90 G. McLennan, 1990–91 Nina Temple.

Communist Candidates

1922	5	1935	2	1959	18	Oct 1974	29
1923	8	1945	21	1964	36	1979	38
1924	8	1950	100	1966	57	1983	35
1929	25	1951	10	1970	58	1987	19
1931	26	1955	17	Feb 1974	44		

SOURCE: – H. Pelling, *The British Communist Party* (1958).

Co-operative Party

In 1917 the Co-operative Congress agreed to organise as a political party. In the 1918 General Election one Co-operative M.P. was elected; he joined with the Labour Party in the House of Commons. Labour and Co-operative candidates never opposed each other at elections but it was not till 1926 that a formal understanding was reached and Co-operative Parties were made eligible for affiliation to divisional Labour Parties. In 1938 the Co-operative Party adopted a written constitution and in 1941 its representatives were invited to attend meetings of the National Council of Labour on equal terms with the Labour Party and the T.U.C. In 1946, the 1926 agreement with the Labour Party was replaced; Co-operative candidates were to run formally as Co-operative and Labour Candidates,[1] and after the General Election of 1959 it was agreed that the number of Co-operative candidates should be limited to 30.[2] In 1951 the Co-operative Party adopted a new constitution to prevent its members from joining organisations proscribed by the Labour Party.

Co-operative M.P.s and Candidates

1918	1	(10)	1945	23	(33)	1970	17	(27)
1922	4	(11)	1950	18	(33)	Feb 1974	16	(25)
1923	6	(10)	1951	16	(37)	Oct 1974	16	(22)
1924	5	(10)	1955	18	(38)	1979	17	(25)
1929	9	(12)	1959	16	(30)	1983	8	(17)
1931	1	(18)	1964	19	(27)	1987	10	(20)
1935	9	(21)	1966	18	(24)	1992	14	(26)

SOURCES. – J. Bailey, *The British Co-operative Movement* (1955); *Reports of the Annual Co-operative Congress 1900–*. The *People's Year Book 1932*.

Independent Labour Party

The Independent Labour Party, formed in 1893, was one of the founding bodies of the Labour Representation Committee in 1900. The I.L.P. was affiliated to the Labour Party but it held its own conferences, sponsored its own parliamentary candidates, and maintained its own policies, even after the 1918 revision of the Labour Party constitution. Differences with the Labour Party grew in the late 1920's and the 37 I.L.P. Members among the 288 Labour M.P.s elected in 1929 provided some of the second Labour Government's strongest critics. At the 1930 conference of the I.L.P., it was agreed that I.L.P. members should vote against the Labour Government when its actions conflicted with I.L.P. policy. The I.L.P. was disaffiliated by the 1932 Labour Party Conference. In 1935 17 I.L.P. candidates stood, all against Labour candidates, and four (all in Glasgow) were successful. In 1945 three of the five I.L.P. candidates won but, after the death of the party's leader James Maxton in 1946, the I.L.P. M.P.s one by one rejoined the Labour Party. In the elections of 1950 and 1951 there were three I.L.P. candidates and in 1955 and 1959 two candidates. All lost their deposits. There were no candidates after 1959.

M.P.s (since 1931)

1932–46	J. Maxton	1932–33	R. Wallhead
1932–47	J. McGovern	1935–47	C. Stephen
1932–39	G. Buchanan	1946–47	J. Carmichael
1932–33	D. Kirkwood		

SOURCE. – R.E. Dowse, *Left in the Centre* (1966).

Irish Nationalist Party up to 1922

From the days of Parnell until the First World War between 80 and 86 Irish Nationalists sat in the House of Commons at times divided by internal frictions but with a safe control of more than three-quarters of the seats in Ireland. Divisions over support for the war and the Easter Rebellion broke the party's hold and in 1918 only 7 of its 58 candidates were elected (while Sinn Fein candidates won 73 seats). T.P. O'Connor, from 1885 the solitary Irish Nationalist Member representing an English constituency, continued to be returned unopposed for the Scotland Division of Liverpool until his death in 1929.

Chairmen of the Irish Parliamentary Party

1900	J. Redmond
1917	J. Dillon

SOURCE. – F.S.L. Lyons, *The Irish Parliamentary Party 1890–1910* (1951).

[1] Labour Party Annual Report, 1946, pp. 229–31.
[2] Labour Party Annual Report, 1960, p. 24.

Irish Parties since 1922

Since 1922 candidates under the label 'Irish Nationalist' have fought only two or three of the Northern Ireland seats, but from 1922 to 1924 they held one of the two Fermanagh and Tyrone Seats (the other was held by Sinn Fein) and from 1929 to 1955 they held both. T.P. O'Connor continued to represent the Scotland division of Liverpool until 1929 and the Exchange division of Liverpool was fought by Nationalists on three occasions. Sinn Fein reappeared as a political force in 1955 and 1959, contesting all 12 Northern Ireland seats. In 1955 Sinn Fein candidates won Mid-Ulster and Fermanagh and South Tyrone but they were disqualified as felons. From 1943 to 1950, from 1951 to 1955 and from 1966 onwards Belfast West was held by candidates using the label 'Eire Labour', 'Republican Labour', and then 'Social Democratic and Labour'. The S.D.L.P. founded in 1970 became the main party representing the Republican or Nationalist aspirations of the Roman Catholic minority.

Nationalist M.P.s

1922–29	T.P. O'Connor	1929–34	J. Devlin
1922–24	T. Harbison	1934–35	J. Stewart
1922–24	C. Healy	1935–50	P. Cunningham
1931–35	C. Healy	1935–51	A. Mulvey
1950–55	C. Healy	1951–55	M. O'Neill

Sinn Fein M.P.s

1955–55	P. Clarke
1955–56	T. Mitchell
1983–92	G. Adams

Eire Labour M.P.s

1943–50	J. Beattie
1951–55	J. Beattie

Republican Labour M.P.

1966–70	G. Fitt

Independent Socialist M.P.

1979–83	G. Fitt

S.D.L.P. M.P.s

1970–9	G. Fitt
1983–	J. Hume
1986–	S. Mallon
1987–	E. McGrady
1992–	J. Hendron

Independent Republican M.P.s

1969–Feb 1974	Bernadette Devlin (Mrs B. McAliskey) (*Independent Unity*)
1970–Feb 1974	F. McManus (*Independent Unity*)
Oct 1974–81	F. Maguire (*Independent Unity*)
1981–81	R. Sands (*Anti H-Block*)
1981–83	O. Carron (*Anti H-Block*)

After 1969 increasing fissures developed in the Ulster Unionist Party which had dominated Northern Ireland's representation at Westminster. In 1970 I. Paisley standing as a Protestant Unionist defeated the Official Unionist Candidate in North Antrim. In 1971 he formed the Democratic Unionist Party. In 1970 W. Craig formed the Vanguard Movement and in January 1974 the Unionists split further. In the February 1974 election, 11 of the 12 Ulster seats were won by candidates standing under the banner of a new United Ulster Unionist Council in opposition to those Unionists who supported Mr Faulkner's Executive Council and the Sunningdale proposals for a Council of Ireland. Of the 11, 8 were members of the Unionist party under H. West, 2 carried the Vanguard label and I. Paisley was successful as a Democratic Unionist. In October 1974 H. West who had acted as Unionist Leader was the only one of the 11 to be defeated. J. Molyneaux succeeded him as parliamentary leader. Vanguard was wound up in September 1977. In 1979 3 Paisleyites, 1 Independent Unionist (J. Kilfedder), 1 U.U.U.P. and 5 official Unionists were successful. In 1983 3 Paisleyites, 11 Official Unionists and J. Kilfedder were successful. In 1986 all 15 Unionists resigned their seats to force by-elections in protest at the Anglo-Irish agreement; one, the Official Unionist M. Robinson in Newry and Armagh, lost his seat to the SDLP. At the 1987 election 9 Official Unionists, 3 Democratic Unionists and J. Kilfedder were elected; all these seats were retained in 1992, despite a strong challenge in North Down from the Conservative Party, which had been organising in the area since 1987 and received official blessing at the 1991 Conservative Party Conference.

Alliance Party of Northern Ireland

The non-Sectarian Alliance Party, founded in 1970, was joined by S.Mills, a Unionist M.P., in 1972. He did not stand in February 1974. The Alliance Party Leader 1973–84 was O. Napier, followed by J. Cushnahan (1984–1987) and J. Alderdice (1987–).

Election	Candidates	Lost Deposits	Share of vote
Feb 1974	3	2	n.a.
Oct 1974	5	1	6.4
1979	12	7	11.9
1983	11	7	8.0
1987	16	4	9.9
1992	16	5	8.7

Liberal National Party (National Liberal Party after 1948)

In October 1931 23 Liberal Members broke with the party and formed the Liberal National Group. The subsequent electoral history of the Liberal National Party falls into three periods: at the 1931 General Election some of the Liberal National candidates were opposed by Conservatives but none of them by Liberals. After 1931, a Conservative only once opposed a Liberal National (Scottish Universities 1946) but they were not opposed by Liberals (except in Denbigh 1935 and St. Ives 1937) until 1945. Of 41 candidates in 1931, 35 were returned as Members of Parliament and when the 'Samuelite' Liberals left the government over the Ottawa Agreements in 1932, the 'Simonite' Liberal Nationals remained. In 1935 33 of 44 candidates were returned, and in 1945 13 of 51 candidates. E. Brown, however, who had succeeded Sir J. Simon as leader on 4 December 1940 was defeated. In May 1947 the Woolton-Teviot agreement was signed, which urged the combination of Conservative and Liberal National Constituency Associations, and in 1948 the party was renamed the National Liberal Party. After the 1966 General Election only two M.P.s styled themselves Conservative and National Liberal. Two other members of the Group were elected as Conservatives by Joint Associations. In 1966 these four M.P.s relinquished the room assigned to them in the House of Commons to the Liberal Party. The group became an integral part of the Conservative Party.

Chairmen of the Parliamentary Party		Chief Whips	
1931	Sir J. Simon	1931	A. Glassey
1940	E. Brown	1931	G. Shakespeare
1945	(Sir) J. Henderson-Stewart	1932	(Sir) J. Blindell
1946	Sir S. Holmes	1937	C. Kerr
1947	J. Maclay	1940	H. Holdsworth
1956	(Sir) J. Duncan	1945–66	(Sir) H. Butcher
1959	Sir J. Henderson-Stewart		
1961–4	Sir C. Thornton Kemsley		

SOURCES. – Information from the National Liberal Party, and *Dod's Parliamentary Companion, 1931–66.*

Liberal Unionist Party

The Liberal Unionist Party was based upon those Liberals who, under J. Chamberlain and the M of Hartington, broke with the party over Irish Home Rule in 1886. After they accepted office in Ld Salisbury's 1895 government, they became increasingly fused with the Conservative Party and, although they had preserved a separate organisation with separate funds, the final merger in 1912 was to some extent a recognition of a *fait accompli.* The President between 1886 and 1904 was M of Hartington (D of Devonshire) and between 1904 and 1912 J. Chamberlain. The Organising Secretary between 1895 and 1912 was J. Boraston.

Liberal Unionist M. P.s

1900	68	Jan 1910	31
1906	23	Dec 1910	35

Militant

Militant, known internally as the Revolutionary Socialist League, secretly infiltrated the Labour Party for almost forty years, using the Trotskyist tactic of 'entryism'. The R.S.L. was established in 1955, a democratic centralist Marxist-Leninist Party with its own central committee and annual conference. The Militant newspaper was founded in 1964. Leading figures were its General Secretary P. Taaffe, and T. Grant. At its peak in the mid 1980s, Militant had more than 8,000 members, and achieved prominence in leading Liverpool City Council's resistance to Government spending controls. Two Militant members, D. Nellist and T. Fields, were elected as Labour M.P.s in 1983, and a third P. Wall in 1987. Both Taaffe and Grant were expelled from the Labour Party in 1983, the first of around 200 expulsions over the next decade culminating in the two surviving M.P.s in 1991 (both lost their seats to official Labour candidates at the 1992 election). In 1992 Grant and several of his followers were expelled from Militant itself for opposing its decision to abandon 'entryism' and work mainly outside the Labour Party under the name Militant Labour. In Scotland it has since had several local councillors elected.

National Democratic Party

The National Democratic Party was formed in 1915 to unite support amongst the Labour Movement for the Lloyd George Government. The N.D.P. had its origins in the dispute within the Labour Movement during the war and its greatest strength in the jingoist trade unions the Liverpool Dockers, the Musicians' Union, some of the Textile Workers, and parts of the Miners Federation. It was also, in part, the successor to the projected anti-socialist Trade Union Labour Party and included among its members the Labour Ministers who refused to resign from the Government in 1918. G. Barnes, Labour member of the

War Cabinet, was its accepted leader. In the 1918 Election the Party put up 28 candidates, all for working-class constituencies, and returned 15 to Parliament. Before the 1922 Election the surviving N.D.P. M.P.s joined the National Liberal Party, but only one (G. Roberts) was re-elected. The Party ceased to exist in 1923.

SOURCES. – G.D.H. Cole, *A History of the British Labour Party from 1914* (1945); G.N. Barnes, *From Workshop to War Cabinet* (1924); *Labour Party Annual Conference Reports, 1916–18; Trades Union Congress Reports, 1916–18.*

The National Front and British National Party

The National Front was formed by a merger of the League of Empire Loyalists and the British National Party in 1966. The Greater Britain Movement joined in 1967. The leader of the League of Empire Loyalists, A. K. Chesterton, President of the British National Party, became Executive Director. In 1970 A. K. Chesterton was succeeded by J. O'Brien, who was succeeded in 1972 by J. Tyndall (previously leader of the Greater Britain Movement). In 1974 J. Read ousted J. Tyndall but the courts ruled the ouster illegal. J. Read formed the National Party and J. Tyndall resumed as leader with M. Webster as National Activities Organiser. In 1982 a breakaway faction under J. Tyndall, the New National Front, merged with other groups to form the British National Party.

	National Front Candidates		
	No.	*Av. % vote*	*Highest vote*
1970	10	3.6	5.6
Feb 1974	54	3.3	7.8
Oct 1974	90	3.1	9.5
1979	303	1.3	7.6
1983	60	1.1	2.4
1987	–	–	–
1992	14	0.8	1.2

	British National Party Candidates		
	No.	*Av % vote*	*Highest vote*
1983	54	0.5	1.2
1987	2	0.6	0.8
1992	13	1.2	3.6

National Party

A small group of dissident Conservatives led by H. Page Croft, formed this party in September 1917, with a programme described by one historian as of 'xenophobic imperialism'. Most of its members drifted back to the Conservative fold and fought under the Conservative label in 1918: only Sir H. Page Croft and Sir R. Cooper survived the election (when they made a special point of attacking the sale of honours) and in 1921 it was decided not to maintain a separate parliamentary party.

SOURCES. – Ld Croft, *My Life of Strife* (1948); M. Foot, 'Henry Page Croft, Baron Croft', *Dictionary of National Biography 1941–50.*

National Labour Party

The party was formed in 1931 from the small group of Labour M.P.s who supported the National Government under Ramsay MacDonald. In the 1931 General Election 13 of its 20 candidates were elected. In 1935 8 of its 20 candidates were elected. The party wound itself up just before the 1945 election and in 1945 of the 7 surviving National Labour members 3 retired, 2 stood unsuccessfully as National candidates, and 2 as Independents (one, K. Lindsay, stood successfully–but in a new constituency, English Universities).

New Party, British Union of Fascists, Union Movement

Sir Oswald Mosley (Conservative, then Independent M.P. 1918–24, Labour M.P. 1926–31) resigned from the Labour Government in May 1930 after his Memorandum for dealing with unemployment had been rejected by the Cabinet. In October 1930 a resolution calling upon the National Executive to consider the Memorandum was narrowly defeated at the Labour Party Conference. On
6 December 1930 the Mosley Manifesto summarising the main proposals in the Memorandum was published, signed by 17 Labour M.P.s. Six of the 17 signatories of the Manifesto resigned from the Labour Party to form the new Party in February 1931 (Sir Oswald and Lady Cynthia Mosley, O. Baldwin, W. J. Brown, R. Forgan, and J. Strachey), but Baldwin and Brown remained members for only one day and Strachey resigned in June. The New Party received two further recruits before the 1931 General Election, W. E. D. Allen (Conservative) and R. Dudgeon (Liberal). In the Election the New Party contested 24 seats but failed to win a single one, the New Party M.P.s all losing their seats, and, apart from Sir Oswald Mosley, their deposits.

In 1932 the New Party was renamed the British Union of Fascists after Mosley had been to Italy to study the 'modern movements'. The Director of Organisation and Deputy Leader was R. Forgan. In the 1935 General Election, the B.U.F. put up no candidates and, with the slogan 'Fascism next Time', advised their supporters not to vote. The B.U.F. fought a number of by-elections in 1939 and 1940, before it was proscribed by the Government on 30 May 1940.

In 1948, Sir Oswald Mosley formed the Union Movement. Its first Parliamentary contest was in the 1959 General Election, when he fought North Kensington, losing his deposit. The Union Movement fought two by-elections in the 1959 Parliament and in the 1966 General Election Sir Oswald Mosley and 3 other candidates stood; they gained on average 3.7% of the vote.

SOURCES. – C. Cross, *The Fascists in Britain* (1961); R. Skidelsky, *Oswald Mosley* (1975).

Plaid Cymru (Welsh Nationalist Party)

The party was founded in 1925 and has fought elections consistently since then, but without any success at the Parliamentary level until a by-election victory in Carmarthen in 1966. The seat was lost in 1970 but in the February 1974 election, two seats, Caernarvon and Merioneth were won. Carmarthen was recaptured in October 1974 but lost in 1979. In 1987 Plaid Cymru gained Ynys Mon (Anglesey), and in 1992 Ceredigion and Pembroke North.

Welsh Nationalist Candidates

	Candidates		Candidates	Seats	% of Welsh vote
1929	1	1970	36	–	11.5
1931	2	Feb 1974	36	2	10.7
1935	1	Oct 1974	36	3	10.8
1945	6	1979	36	2	8.1
1950	7	1983	38	2	7.8
1951	4	1987	38	3	7.3
1955	11	1992	38	4	8.8
1959	20				
1964	23				
1966	20				

Plaid Cymru M.P.s

1966–70	G. Evans	1987	W. Jones
Feb 1974–	D. Wigley	1992	E. Llwyd
Feb 1974–92	D. Thomas	1992	C. Dafis
Oct 1974–79	G. Evans		

Scottish Labour Party

The Scottish Labour Party was formed in January 1976 by Scots, mostly members of the Labour Party, who were dissatisfied with the Government's proposals for devolution to Scotland. Two Labour M.P.s, J. Sillars (Ayrshire South) and J. Robertson (Paisley), became members of the S.L.P., but did not resign the Labour Whip until 26 July 76. They then indicated that theS.L.P. would act as an independent party within Parliament. At the S.L.P.'s first Congress at Stirling in October 1976, the leadership suspended the credentials of one delegation and expelled four others for being under the influence of the extreme Left, mainly the International Marxist Group. This led to a walk-out by one third of the delegates. The S.L.P. won three district council seats in May 1977. It fought 3 seats in the 1979 General Election. Only J. Sillars saved his deposit but he narrowly lost his seat. In 1981 the party was wound up and J. Sillars joined the Scottish National Party.

SOURCE. – H. Drucker, *Breakaway: the Scottish Labour Party* (1978).

Scottish National Party

The party was formed in 1928 as the National Party of Scotland. In 1934 it merged with a body called the Scottish Party (founded 1932) and the name was then changed to the Scottish National Party. Its first success was in the Motherwell by-election of April 1945; but the victor, R. McIntyre, was defeated in the General Election three months later. In 1967 a seat was won in the Hamilton by-election but lost in 1970. In 1970, however, a Scottish Nationalist won Western Isles. In November 1973 the Govan, Glasgow, seat was won in a by-election but lost four months later. In the General Elections of 1974 the Scottish Nationalists made great advances in votes and seats, but fell back sharply in 1979.

Scottish National Party Candidates

	Candidates			Candidates	Seats	% of Scottish vote
1929	2		1970	65	1	11.4
1931	3		Feb 1974	70	7	21.9
1935	6		Oct 1974	71	11	30.4
1945	8		1979	71	2	17.3
1950	3		1983	72	2	11.8
1951	2		1987	71	3	14.0
1955	2		1992	72	3	21.5
1959	5					
1964	15					
1966	23					

Scottish National Party M.P.s

1945–45	R. McIntyre
1967–70, 74 Feb–79	Mrs W. Ewing
1970–87	D. Stewart
1973–74 Feb	Mrs M. Macdonald
1974 Feb–79	D. Henderson
1974 Feb–79	I. MacCormick
1974 Feb–79	G. Reid
1974 Feb–79	H. Watt
1974 Feb–87	G. Wilson
1974 Oct–79, 87–	Mrs M. Bain (Mrs M. Ewing)
1974 Oct–79	G. Crawford
1974 Oct–79	G. Thompson
1974 Oct–79, 87–	A. Welsh
1987–	A. Salmond
1988–92	J. Sillars
1990–92	D. Douglas

Social Democratic Party

The Social Democratic Party was launched by four former Labour Cabinet Ministers in protest, following the Labour Party Special Conference on 24 Jan 81. In its first year it recruited a total of 25 sitting Labour M.P.s and one Conservative M.P. and two of its founders (Mrs S. Williams and R. Jenkins) won parliamentary by-elections. It formed an Alliance with the Liberal party and shared out constituencies with them in the 1983 general election, when the two parties jointly won 260% of the votes and 23 seats (6 SDP). The SDP won two further seats in by-elections in 1984 and early 1987 but in the General Election of 1987 only 6 SDP M.P.s survived. The party was seriously split over the Liberal Party's proposal in June 1987 that the two parties should merge. On 6 Aug 87 the membership voted narrowly to proceed with merger negotiations, whereupon D. Owen resigned as leader. R. Maclennan (one of only two SDP M.P.s to support merger) was elected leader unopposed on 29 Aug 88. A draft constitution for a new merged party was published on 11 Dec 87, and an amended version on 18 Jan 88; both were rejected by D. Owen and his supporters. The Council for Social Democracy voted to put the merger proposals to the party membership on 31 Jan 88 and a vote in favour of merger was announced on 2 Mar 88. The Social Democratic Party was formally subsumed into the Social and Liberal Democrats on 3 Mar 88.

Three of the five SDP M.P.s – D. Owen, J. Cartwright and Rosie Barnes – refused to be involved in the merged party and relaunched a continuing SDP on 8 Mar 88. The party had limited success in by elections and after disappointing results in local elections in May 1989 the party wound down its operations, conceding it could no longer operate as a national party. It formally suspended operations in Jun 90. Although attempts were later made to revive it, from this time on the three M.P.s sat as independent Social Democrats. D. Owen did not contest his seat in the 1992 General Election. J. Cartwright and Rosie Barnes fought the 1992 election as Independent Social Democrats but lost.

Leader

1982	R. Jenkins
1983	D. Owen

Independent M.P.s

The number of Independent M.P.s has been small and, even among those few elected without the label of one of the parties already listed, a substantial proportion were in fact elected with the tacit support of a major party or in default of its candidate. M.P.s elected as Independents fall into six broad categories.

Independents in University Seats

1922	J. Butler	1937	Sir A. Salter
1923	G. Davies	1945	Sir A. Salter
1924	(Sir) E. Graham-Little	1935	(Sir) A. Herbert
1929	(Sir) E. Graham-Little	1945	Sir A. Herbert
1931	(Sir) E. Graham-Little	1937	T. Harvey
1935	(Sir) E. Graham-Little	1940	A. Hill
1945	(Sir) E. Graham-Little	1945	W. Harris
1929	Miss E. Rathbone	1945	K. Lindsay
1931	Miss E. Rathbone	1945	Sir J. Boyd-Orr
1935	Miss E. Rathbone	1945	W. Harris
1945	Miss E. Rathbone		

Independents emerging from war-time situations

1917	N. Billing	1942	W. Brown
1918	N. Billing	1945	W. Brown
1918	H. Bottomley	1942	G. Reakes
1918	R. Barker	1942	T. Driberg[1]
1941	W. Kendall	1944	C. White[1]
1941	W. Kendall		

Dissident Conservatives

1902	T. Sloan	1922	O. Mosley
1906	T. Sloan	1923	O. Mosley
1903	E. Mitchell	1929	Sir R. Newman
1910	F. Bennett-Goldney[2]	1930	E. Taylor[2]
1920	Sir C. Townshend	1937	D. Lipson
1920	C. Palmer	1940	Sir C. Headlam[2]
1921	Sir T. Polson	1945	D. Lipson[3]
1922	J. Erskine[2]	1945	J. McKie[3]
1922	J. Erskine	1945	J. Little
1922	H. Becker[2]	1959	Sir D. Robertson
1922	G. Hall Caine[2]		

Dissident Liberal

1900	Sir J. Austin	1922	A. Hopkinson
1902	J. Wason	1923	A. Hopkinson
1922	G. Roberts[3]	1924*	A. Hopkinson[3]
		1931*	A. Hopkinson[3]
		1935*	A. Hopkinson[3]
		1929*	Sir T. Robinson

Dissident Labour

1915	C. Stanton	1972	D. Taverne
1922	Sir O. Thomas	Feb 1974	D. Taverne
1929	N. Maclean	Feb 1974	E. Milne
1945	D. Pritt		
1970	S. Davies		

Supported by the Left

1922	E. Scrymgeour	1938	V. Bartlett
1923	E. Scrymgeour	1945	V. Bartlett
1924	E. Scrymgeour		
1929	E. Scrymgeour		

[1] Later accepted Labour Whip.
[2] Later accepted Conservative Whip.
[3] These later candidacies might be put into a different category.

Minor Parties – Representation in the House of Commons

Year	Total	Ir. Nat	SNP	PC	Uls Uni	Comm	ILP	Ind Con	Ind Lab	Other
1900	82	82	..	..	..	..	..	..	..	..
1906	83	83	..	..	..	..	..	..	..	..
1910J	82	84	..	..	..	..	..	..,	..	2
1910D	84	84	..	..	..	..	..	..	..	..
1918	83	80[1]	..	..	..	..	..	..	..	3
1922	12	3	..	..	..	..	1	4	1	3
1923	7	3	..	..	..	..	..	..	..	4
1924	5	1	..	..	..	..	1	..	..	3
1929	8	3	1	..	..	..	..	..	..	4
1931	5	2	..	..	..	..	..	..	..	3
1935	9	2	..	..	..	1	4	..	..	2
1945	22	3	..	..	1	2	3	4	1	8
1950	3	2	..	..	..	..	..	..	..	1
1951	3	3	..	..	..	..	..	..	..	..
1955	2	2	..	..	..	..	..	..	..	..
1959	1	..	1							
1964	..	..	..	..	..	..	..	..	..	..
1966	1	1	..	..	..	..	..	..	..	..
1970	6	3	1	..	1	..	..	..	1	..
1974F	24	1	7	2	11	..	..	2	1	..
1974O	26	2	11	3	10	..	..	..	..	..
1979	16	2	2	2	10	..	..	..	..	..
1983	21	2	2	2	15	..	..	..	..	..
1987	23	3	3	3	14	..	..	..	..	..
1992	24	4	3	4	13	..	..	..	..	..

[1] There were 73 Sinn Fein candidates elected in Ireland in 1918 who never took their seats. There were also 7 Irish Nationalists who did not sit.

SOURCES. – *The Constitutional Year Book, 1919*; D. E. Butler, *The Electoral System in Britain since 1918* (1963); G. Thayer, *The British Political Fringe* (1965); F.W.S. Craig, *British Parliamentary Election Statistics, 1918–70* (1970); F.W.S. Craig, *Minor Parties at British Parliamentary Elections, 1885–1974* (1975).

Political Pressure Groups

Specialist pressure goups are listed at a number of other points in the book. (See p. xr., p.xx, p.xx, and p.xx). The following is a selection of pressure groups with a more generalised remit:

Centre for Policy Studies 1974–
Fabian Society 1884–
Insitute for Public Policy Research 1989–
P.E.P. (Political and Economic Planning) 1931–
P.S.I. (Policy Studies Institute) 1978–

III

PARLIAMENT

House of Commons

Speaker of the House of Commons

1895	W. Gully (Vt Selby)	Lib.	21 Oct	59	Sir H. Hylton-Foster[1]	Con.
20 Jun 05	J. Lowther (Vt Ullswater)	Con.	26 Oct	65	H. King	
28 Apr 21	J. Whitley	Co. Lib.			(Ld Maybray-King)	Lab.
21 Jun 28	E. Fitzroy[1]	Con.	12 Jan	71	S. Lloyd (Ld Selwyn-Lloyd)	Con.
9 Mar 43	D. Clifton Brown		3 Feb	76	G. Thomas (Vt Tonypandy)	Lab.
	(Vt Ruffside)	Con.	15 Jun	83	B. Weatherill (Ld Weatherill)	Con.
1 Nov 51	W. Morrison (Vt Dunrossil)	Con.	17 Apr	92	Miss B. Boothroyd	Lab.

Chairman of Ways and Means

1900	J. Lowther	Con.	1951	Sir C. MacAndrew	Con.
1905	G. Lawson	Con.	1959	Sir G. Touche	Con.
1906	A. Emmott	Lib.	1962	Sir W. Anstruther-Gray	Con.
1911	J. Whitley	Lib.	1964	H. King	Lab.
1921	J. Hope	Con.	1965	Sir S. Storey	Con.
1924	R. Young	Lab.	1966	Sir E. Fletcher	Lab.
1924	J. Hope	Con	1968	S. Irving	Lab.
1929	R. Young	Lab.	1970	Sir R. Grant-Ferris	Con.
1931	Sir D. Herbert	Con.	1974	G. Thomas	Lab.
1943	D. Clifton Brown	Con.	1976	O. Murton	Con.
1943	J. Milner	Lab.	1979	B. Weatherill	Con.
1945	C. Williams	Con.	1983	(Sir) H. Walker	Lab.
1945	J. Milner	Lab.	1992	M. Morris	Con.

Deputy Chairman of Ways and Means
(office created 1902)

1902	A. Jeffreys	Con.	1950	Sir C. MacAndrew	Con.
1905	L. Hardy	Con.	1951	Sir R. Hopkin Morris[1]	Lib.
1906	J. Caldwell	Lib.	1956	Sir G. Touche	Con.
1910	J. Whitley	Lib.	1959	Sir W. Anstruther-Gray	Con.
1911	D. Maclean	Lib.	1962	Sir R. Grimston	Con.
1919	Sir E. Cornwall	Lib.	1964	Sir S. Storey	Con.
1922	E. Fitzroy	Con.	1965	R. Bowen	Lib.
1924	C. Entwistle	Lib.	1966	S. Irving	Lab.
1924	E. Fitzroy	Con.	1968	H. Gourlay	Lab.
1928	D. Herbert	Con.	1970	Miss B. Harvie Anderson	Con.
1929	H. Dunnico	Lab.	1973	E. Mallalieu	Lab.
1931	R. Bourne[1]	Con.	1974	O. Murton	Con.
1938	D. Clifton Brown	Con.	1976	Sir M. Galpern	Lab.
1943	J. Milner	Lab.	1979	G. Irvine	Con.
1943	C. Williams	Con.	1982	E. Armstrong	Lab.
1945	Sir C. MacAndrew	Con.	1987	Sir P. Dean	Con.
1945	H. Beaumont	Lab.	1992	G. Lofthouse	Lab.
1948	F. Bowles	Lab.			

Second Deputy Chairman of Ways and Means
(office created 1971)

1971	E. Mallalieu	Lab.	1979	R. Crawshaw	Lab.
1973	O. Murton	Con.	1981	E. Armstrong	Lab.
1974	*(office vacant)*		1982	(Sir) P. Dean	Con.
1974	Sir M. Galpern	Lab.	1987	Miss B. Boothroyd	Lab.
1976	G. Irvine	Con.	1993	Dame J. Fookes	Con.

[1] Died in office.

Officers of the House of Commons

Clerk		Librarian	
1900	(Sir) A. Milman	1887	R. Walpole
1902	Sir C. Ilbert	1908	A. Smyth
1921	(Sir) T. Webster	1937	V. Kitto
1930	(Sir) H. Dawkins	1946	H. Saunders
1937	(Sir) G. Campion	1950	S. Gordon
1948	(Sir) F. Metcalfe	1968	D. Holland
1954	(Sir) E. Fellowes	1976	D. Menhennet
1962	(Sir) B. Cocks	1991	D. Englefield
1974	(Sir) D. Lidderdale	1993	Miss J. Tanfield
1976	(Sir) R. Barlas		
1979	(Sir) C. Gordon		
1983	(Sir) K. Bradshaw		
1987	(Sir) C. Boulton		

Parliamentary Sessions

Around 1900 sessions of Parliament lasted from February to July or August. Occasionally Parliament sat through the summer. In 1930 both Houses agreed that they should adjourn between July and October, and that the session should last from September or October to the September or October of the following year. During the adjournments the Speaker or the Lord Chancellor has the power to give notice of an earlier meeting of his House if it is in the national interest.

Parliamentary Hours of Sitting

In 1902 the House of Commons met from 2 p.m. until 11.30 p.m., but this was altered in 1906 to 2.45 until 11.30, to allow more time for lunch. During the 1939–45 war the time for rising in the evening was changed to 10.30 p.m. Since 1945 the normal hours for sitting have been 2.30 until 10.30 p.m. on every weekday except Friday although the House usually sits later than this. From 1900 to 1939 the House met on Fridays from noon to 5.30 p.m. From 1939 the House met on Fridays at 11 a.m. and normally adjourned for the weekend at 4.30 p.m. In 1967 as an experiment, the House also met from 10 a.m. to 1 p.m. on Mondays and Wednesdays but these morning sittings were discontinued from October 1967. From 1980 the House normally met at 9.30 a.m. on Friday and adjourned at 3 p.m.

If the House sits for more than 24 hours (or 19 hours on a Thursday) the next day's business is lost. This has happened on these occasions since 1900:

19 Jul 04	Finance Bill
20 Mar 07	Consolidated Fund Bill
22 Jul 36	Unemployment Assistance Regulations
11 Jun 51	Finance Bill
13 Jul 67	Abortion Bill
12 Jun 69	Divorce Reform Bill
24 Jul 75	Remuneration Bill
21 Jun 77	Price Commission Bill
28 Jul 77	Consolidated Fund Bill
4 Aug 80	Consolidated Fund Bill
1 Apr 81	Br. Telecommunications Bill
22 May 84	Local Government Bill
5 Mar 85	Water (Fluoridation) Bill
10 Dec 86	Teachers' Pay Bill
10 Nov 87	Felixstowe Dock and Railway Bill
14 Jun 88	Housing Bill

Emergency Recalls of the House of Commons

Under Standing Order No 12, which dates from 1948, the Speaker may give notice that the House of Commons will sit earlier than the date agreed on adjournment if the public interest requires it, following representations from Ministers. This Standing Order has been used sixteen times:

27–29 Sep 49	Devaluation
12–19 Sep 50	Korean War
4 Oct 51	Prorogation and dissolution
12–14 Sep 56	Suez crisis
18 Sep 59	Prorogation and dissolution
17–23 Oct 61	Berlin crisis
16 Jan 68	Government expenditure cuts
26–27 Aug 68	Czechoslovakia, Nigeria
26–29 May 70	Prorogation and dissolution
22–23 Sep 71	Northern Ireland
9–10 Jan 74	Fuel
3–4 Jun 74	Northern Ireland
3 Apr, 14 Apr 82	Falkland Islands
6–7 Sep 90	Kuwait
24–25 Sep 92	Exchange rate policy, UN operations

Government and Private Members' Time

Until 1939 Government business had precedence at every sitting of the House of Commons except certain Wednesdays and Fridays and Tuesday evenings after 8.15 p.m. until Easter. This generally gave Private Members about 8 Wednesdays and 13 Fridays on which they had precedence. This was always subject to the possibility that the House, or Government, might direct that the time was needed for Government business. Between 1914 and 1918 and between 1939 and 1948 Private Members' time was abolished completely. When Private Members' time was restored, the Government retained precedence on all days except for 20 Fridays. Private members motions are also allowed on some Mondays. In the nine sessions 1950–51 to 1958–59 an average of ten days was allotted to Private Members' Bills and 9 days to Private Members' motions. In 1960 four extra half-days (two Mondays and two Wednesdays) were allotted for consideration of Private Members' motions in addition to the twenty Fridays. From 1967 to 1970 sixteen of the twenty Fridays were given to Bills and four to motions. Since 1970 the number of Fridays for Bills has been between ten and twelve and usually ten for motions.

Broadcasting of Parliament

Television cameras were first allowed into Parliament for the opening of the session and the Queen's Speech on 28 Oct 58. On 11 Dec 67 the Commons approved without a division a proposal for a closed-circuit experiment in radio only. This was carried out in Apr and May 68. In Feb 68 the House of Lords engaged in a three-day radio and television closed-circuit experiment. But the House of Commons on a free vote rejected the idea of broadcasting Parliament on 24 Nov 66 (131–130), on 19 Oct 72 (191–165) and on 30 Jan 74 (189–164). On 24 Feb 75 the House of Commons approved (354–152) a 4-week experiment in the live radio broadcasting of its proceedings and this took place from 9 Jun to 4 Jul 75. On

16 Mar 76 the House approved (299–124) the idea of permanent sound broadcasting. A select committee of six M.P. s (Chairmen: 1978: R. Mellish; 1979: Sir A. Royle; 1983: Sir P. Goodhart) was set up on 6 Feb 78 to supervise the arrangements to be made with the broadcasting authorities. A similar Lords Committee was also set up (Chairman: 1978: Ld Aberdare). Amendments proposing the appointment of a manager of broadcasting operations and a House of Commons broadcasting unit to control the scheme were defeated (64–53) and (68–49). Regular sound broadcasting began on 3 Apr 1978. Private members then introduced Ten Minute Rule Bills to test opinion on televising proceedings, as follows:

4 Jul 78	defeated (181–161).
30 Jan 80	first reading carried (202–201) on Deputy Speaker's casting vote.
15 Dec 81	defeated (176–158).
13 Apr 83	(select committees only): first reading carried (153–138).
2 Nov 83	first reading carried (164–159).

On 8 Dec 1983, the Lords voted (74–24) for the public televising of some of its proceedings for an experimental period, and the select committee recommended a six-month experiment which began on 23 Jan 1985. On 22 Jul 1985 the House of Lords extended the experiment and on 12 May 1986 agreed to make television a permanent feature.

There were regular attempts by supporters of the televising of the House of Commons to air the issue, using Ten Minute Rule bills. On 20 Nov 85 a motion moved by Dame J. Fookes to allow the televising of proceedings was narrowly defeated (275–263). On 9 Feb 1988 the House voted, 318–264, to allow a limited experiment in televising proceedings under strict conditions, laid down by a newly appointed select committee on televising the proceedings of the House. Televising began on 21 Nov 1989. The Select Committee reviewed the first six months of the experiment, and when the House approved their report (19 Jul 1990) it effectively ended the debate on whether televising was desirable; it was formally made permanent on 1 May 1991. Under the permanent arrangements put in place in 1991, integrated coverage of both Houses of Parliament was undertaken by the Parliamentary Broadcasting Unit Limited (PARBUL), financed by the broadcasting companies. Although the strict conditions laid down by the House of Commons when it first approved the televising experiment were subsequently relaxed slightly, television directors are still not allowed to show reaction shots during question time or ministerial statements, or to show any scenes of disturbances.

Main Occupations of Members of Parliament 1918– (percentages)

	Conservative				Labour			
	Average 1918–35	1945	1950	1951	Average 1918–35	1945	1950	1951
Professional	52	61	62	58	24	49	47	46
Business	32	33	31	33	4	10	10	9
Unoccupied	12	3	5	6	–	–	–	–
Workers	4	3	3	5	72	41	43	45
	100	100	100	100	100	100	100	100

Main Occupations of Members of Parliament 1918– (percentages)
Conservative

	51	55	59	64	66	70	Feb 74	Oct 74	79	83	87	92
Profess'l	41	46	46	48	46	45	44	46	45	45	42	39
Business	37	30	30	26	29	30	32	33	34	36	37	38
Misc.	22	24	23	25	23	24	23	20	20	19	20	22
Workers	–	–	1	1	1	1	1	1	1	1	1	1
	100	100	100	100	100	100	100	100	100	100	100	100

Labour

	51	55	59	64	66	70	Feb 74	Oct 74	79	83	87	92
Professional	35	36	38	41	43	48	46	49	43	42	40	42
Business	9	12	10	11	9	10	9	8	7	9	10	8
Misc.	19	17	17	16	18	16	15	15	14	16	21	28
Workers	37	35	35	32	30	26	30	28	36	33	29	22
	100	100	100	100	100	100	100	100	100	100	100	100

Education of Conservative and Labour M.P.s 1906–1992 (percentages)

		Conservative		Labour	
		Public School	University Educated	Public School	University Educated
	1906	67	57	0	0
Jan	1910	74	58	0	0
Dec	1910	76	59	0	0
	1918	81	49	3	5
	1922	78	48	9	15
	1923	79	50	8	14
	1924	78	53	7	14
	1929	79	54	12	19
	1931	77	55	8	17
	1935	81	57	10	19
	1945	85	58	23	32
	1950	85	62	22	41
	1951	75	65	23	41
	1955	76	64	22	40
	1959	72	60	18	39
	1964	75	63	18	46
	1966	80	67	18	51
	1970	74	64	17	53
Feb	1974	74	68	17	56
Oct	1974	75	69	18	57
	1979	77	73	17	57
	1983	70	71	14	53
	1987	68	70	14	56
	1992	62	73	14	61

House of Commons Business

Sessions		Allocation of Time			Bills		Questions		
Date of Meeting	Date Prorogued	Sitting Days	Length of Day	Private MP's Days	Total Introduced	Royal Assent	Daily Av. Starred Yes	No	Total
3 Dec 00	15 Dec 00	11	5h 38m	3	–	–	–		314
23 Jan 01	17 Aug 01*	121	9h 5m	14	303	127	69		6,448*
16 Jan 02	18 Dec 02	181	8h 51m	17	300	121			7,168
17 Feb 03	14 Aug 03	115	9h 8m	14	311	311	28	18	4,536
2 Feb 04	15 Aug 04	124	9h 19m	13	308	121	38	18	5,933
14 Feb 05	11 Aug 05	114	9h 12m	12	309	86	47	19	6,244

Dissolution 8 Jan 06. Duration 5 years, 2 months, 7 days.

13 Feb 06	21 Dec 06	156	8h 32m	16	346	121	70	22	11,865
12 Feb 07	28 Aug 07	131	8h 28m	13	294	116	72	21	10,147
29 Jan 08	21 Dec 08	171	7h 39m	18	364	129	75	21	13,811
16 Feb 09	3 Dec 09	179	8h 38m	14	325	110	62	19	12,251

Dissolution 10 Jan 10. Duration 3 years, 10 months, 28 days.

15 Feb 10	28 Nov 10	103	6h 36m	9	289	101	81	24	8,201

Dissolution 28 Nov 10. Duration 9 months, 3 days.

31 Jan 11	16 Dec 11	172	7h 49m	11	373	134	87	21	15,439
14 Feb 12	7 Mar 13	206	8h 1m	14	343	101	97	19	19,913
10 Mar 13	15 Aug 13	102	7h 55m	10	315	108	88	18	18,936
10 Feb 14	18 Sep 14	130	7h 14m	16	391	168	55	16	7,705
11 Nov 14	27 Jan 16	155	6h 40m	–	162	152	72	16	12,976
15 Feb 16	22 Dec 16	127	7h 11m	–	112	105	108	20	15,743
7 Feb 17	6 Feb 18	181	7h 21m	–	102	91	92	16	19,146
12 Feb 18	21 Nov 18	119	7h 16m	–	99	86	89	15	12,025

Dissolution 25 Nov 18. Duration 7 years, 9 months, 25 days.

4 Feb 19	23 Dec 19	163	7h 16m	16	203	152	126	27	20,523
10 Feb 20	23 Dec 20	167	8h 20m	17	215	138	110	22	18,652
15 Feb 21	10 Nov 21	141	8h 0m	12	202	125	} 101	19	14,133
14 Dec 21	19 Dec 21	4	6h 5m	–	–	–		†	
7 Feb 22	4 Aug 22	113	8h 3m	11	196	105			

Dissolution 26 Oct 22. Duration 3 years, 9 months, 5 days.

20 Nov 22	15 Dec 22	20	7h 54m	10	–	10	103	18	12,860
13 Feb 23	16 Nov 23	114	8h 34m	17	181	78	107	21	12,370

Dissolution 16 Nov 23. Duration 11 months, 27 days.

8 Jan 24	9 Oct 24	129	7h 50m	21	248	79	101	25	13,092

Dissolution 9 Oct 24. Duration 9 months, 1 day.

2 Dec 24	22 Dec 25	148	8h 17m	22	247	145	91	23	14,035
2 Feb 26	15 Dec 26	151	7h 55m	21	180	105	71	17	10,713
8 Feb 27	22 Dec 27	144	7h 53m	19	195	91	74	14	10,536
7 Feb 28	3 Aug 28	115	7h 34m	24	168	79	67	13	7,559
6 Nov 28	10 May 29	100	7h 0m	..	115	64	68	17	7,074

Dissolution 10 May 29. Duration 4 years, 7 months, 2 days.

* Although the session of 1901 was not due to begin until 14 Feb, Parliament sat for three days between 23 and 25 Jan to discuss business arising out of the death of Queen Victoria.
† The figures for questions in the first 1922 session are included in those for the second 1922 session.

Sessions		Allocation of Time			Bills		Questions		
Date of Meeting	Date Prorogued	Sitting Days	Length of Day	Private MP's Days	Total Introduced	Royal Assent	Daily Av. Starred Yes	No	Total
25 Jun 29	1 Aug 30	189	7h 57m	31	237	132	93	24	18,327
28 Oct 30	7 Oct 31	187	7h 47m	21	212	106	78	15	14,373

Dissolution 8 Oct 31 Duration 2 years, 4 months, 28 days.

3 Nov 31	17 Nov 32	155	7h 32m	1	125	103	69	10	9,667
22 Nov 32	17 Nov 33	143	7h 33m	26	147	92	58	8	7,559
21 Nov 33	16 Nov 34	156	7h 49m	22	173	111	58	9	8,768
20 Nov 34	25 Oct 35	151	7h 36m	–	116	98	59	9	8,449

Dissolution 25 Oct 35. Duration 3 years, 11 months, 21 days.

26 Nov 35	30 Oct 36	137	7h 55m	19	149	111	82	13	10,215
3 Nov 36	22 Oct 37	157	7h 47m	24	170	126	79	11	11,769
26 Oct 37	4 Nov 38	168	7h 42m	26	179	113	85	14	13,787
8 Nov 38	23 Nov 39	200	7h 34m	14	227	171	92	17	18,460
28 Nov 39	20 Nov 40	127	6h 53m	–	80	73	84	27	13,536
21 Nov 40	11 Nov 41	113	5h 50m	–	55	54	77	23	10,825
12 Nov 41	10 Nov 42	116	6h 23m	–	46	46	80	23	11,592
11 Nov 42	23 Nov 43	122	7h 1m	–	59	58	83	22	11,911
24 Nov 43	28 Nov 44	153	7h 14m	–	55	52	77	17	11,498
29 Nov 44	15 Jun 45	95	6h 51m	–	57	48	91	18	7,856

Dissolution 15 Jun 45. Duration 9 years, 5 months, 20 days.

1 Aug 45	6 Nov 46	212	7h 45m	–	106	104	128	30	7,313
12 Nov 46	20 Oct 47	164	8h 38m	–	73	71	108	22	17,310
21 Oct 47	13 Sep 48	171	8h 13m	–	92	89	97	21	16,303
14 Sep 48	25 Oct 48	10	7h 2m	–	–	–	132	41	853
26 Oct 48	16 Dec 49	208	7h 48m	10	146	125	86	18	17,334

Dissolution 3 Feb 50. Duration 4 years, 4 months, 15 days.

1 Mar 50	26 Oct 50	105	7h 50m	5	58	57	105	19	9,861
31 Oct 50	4 Oct 51	153	8h 20m	19	107	81	108	18	15,720

Dissolution 5 Oct 51. Duration 1 year, 7 months, 4 days.

31 Oct 51	30 Oct 52	157	8h 48m	18	113	88	99	17	14,192
4 Nov 52	29 Oct 53	162	8h 12m	20	78	62	91	16	13,878
3 Nov 53	25 Nov 54	187	8h 11m	19	113	95	89	15	15,990
30 Nov 54	6 May 55	84	7h 58m	10	72	33	90	17	7,262

Dissolution 6 May 55. Duration 3 years, 6 months, 6 days.

7 Jun 55	5 Nov 56	219	7h 57m	25	126	101	86	16	18,285
6 Nov 56	1 Nov 57	159	7h 40m	20	93	75	90	20	14,259
5 Nov 57	23 Oct 58	156	7h 54m	20	112	89	84	18	12,734
28 Oct 58	18 Sep 59	159	7h 48m	20	113	89	89	21	14,518

Dissolution 18 Sep 59. Duration 4 years, 3 months, 11 days.

20 Oct 59	27 Oct 60	160	8h 2m	22	103	80	81	21	13,471
1 Nov 60	24 Oct 61	168	8h 30m	22	117	79	73	22	13,778
31 Oct 61	25 Oct 62	160	8h 23m	22	108	75	65	23	12,226
30 Oct 62	8 Nov 63	162	8h 15m	22	105	72	67	31	13,948
12 Nov 63	25 Sep 64	155	8h 14m	22	155	102	66	37	14,291

Dissolution 25 Sep 64. Duration 4 years, 11 months, 5 days.

27 Oct 64	10 Mar 66	177	9h 0m	22	158	94	74	46	19,148
9 Nov 65	8 Nov 65	65	8h 15m	22	74	21	67	56	7,978

Dissolution 10 Mar 66. Duration 1 year, 5 months, 13 days.

Sessions		Allocation of Time			Bills		Questions		
				Private			Daily Av.		
Date of	Date	Sitting	Length	MP's	Total	Royal	Starred		
Meeting	Prorogued	Days	of Day	Days	Introduced	Assent	Yes	No	Total
18 Apr 66	27 Oct 67	246	9h 50m	25	210	127	69	69	33,965
31 Oct 67	25 Oct 68	176	9h 2m	22	142	76	64	77	24,910
30 Oct 68	22 Oct 69	164	9h 26m	24	158	73	81	78	23,464
28 Oct 69	29 May 70	122	8h 16m	24	152	60	81	78	17,461

Dissolution 29 May 70. Duration 4 years, 1 month, 11 days.

29 Jun 70	28 Oct 71	206	8h 16m	24	164	110	83	99	33,946
2 Nov 71	26 Oct 72	180	9h 17m	24	149	84	77	97	28,946
31 Oct 72	25 Oct 73	164	8h 53m	24	153	83	47	109	25,788
30 Oct 73	8 Feb 74	60	8h 21m	6	77	17	41	104	8,690

Dissolution 8 Feb 74. Duration 3 years, 7 months, 10 days.

6 Mar 74	20 Sep 74	87	8h 28m	10	86	50	48	133	15,738

Dissolution 20 Sep 74. Duration 6 months, 14 days.

22 Oct 74	12 Nov 75	198	9h 20m	22	183	99	47	137	36,652
19 Nov 75	22 Nov 76	191	9h 13m	22	174	100	49	167	41,460
24 Nov 76	26 Oct 77	149	9h 10m	22	141	56	46	163	31,269
3 Nov 77	24 Oct 78	169	9h 24m	24	136	60	49	175	37,775
31 Oct 78	7 Apr 79	86	8h 17m	15	115	50	54	153	17,851

Dissolution 7 Apr 79. Duration 4 years, 5 months, 16 days.

9 May 79	13 Nov 80	244	8h 55m	25	217	102	51	164	52,635
20 Nov 80	30 Oct 81	163	9h 7m	22	145	78	50	139	30,863
4 Nov 81	28 Oct 82	174	8h 8m	22	143	59	52	135	32,430
3 Nov 82	13 May 83	115	8h 34m	17	134	56	53	149	23,220

Dissolution 13 May 1983. Duration 4 years, 4 days.

15 Jun 83	31 Oct 84	213	8h 59m	24	178	73	65	188	53,995
6 Nov 84	30 Oct 85	172	9h 6m	25	154	75	86	183	46,314
6 Nov 85	7 Nov 86	172	8h 56m	25	165	70	101	185	49,140
12 Nov 86	18 May 87	109	8h 32m	19	124	51	121	196	34,537

Dissolution 18 May 87. Duration 3 years 11 months 4 days

17 Jun 87	15 Nov 88	218	9h 4m	26	168	62	110	219	72,666
22 Nov 88	16 Nov 89	176	9h 4m	25	179	46	136	225	63,472
21 Nov 89	1 Nov 90	167	8h 48m	25	164	45	148	248	66,045
7 Nov 90	22 Oct 91	160	8h 35m	24	173	69	30[c]	205	37,664
31 Oct 91	16 Mar 92	83	8h 23m	12	97	46	29	193	18,433

Dissolution 16 Mar 1992. Duration 4 years 8 months 30 days

27 Apr 92	5 Nov 93	240	8h 16m	25	220	68	30	236	63,684
18 Nov 93	–								

[a] 'Notional' days on which Private Members' business had precedence. The idea of parliamentary 'days' must be treated with caution since actual days vary in length. Private Members' days are usually Fridays and only 5 hours long whereas Government 'days' are usually at least 6½ hours long and are frequently extended by suspension of the ten o'clock rule and by the practice of taking the affirmative and negative resolutions after ten o'clock.
[b] Including oral questions receiving a written reply.
[c] From 7 Nov 90, only the highest-placed questions for oral answer are printed on the order-paper.

SOURCES.–Information from the '*Black Book*', a compilation of Parliamentary statistics at the House of Commons, and the *Sessional Returns of the House of Commons*. Questions to Ministers taken from D.N. Chester and N. Bowring, *Questions in Parliament* (1962), pp. 87–8, and 316; and information from the Journal Office, House of Commons.

Fathers of the House of Commons

	M.P. until	Length of service			
		as M.P.		as Father	
		y.	m.	y.	m.
(Sir) W. Bramston Beach	Aug 1901	44	4	2	4
Sir M. Hicks Beach	Jan 1906	41	6	4	5
G. Finch	May 1907	39	6	1	4
Sir H. Campbell-Bannerman	Apr 1908	39	6		11
Sir J. Kennaway	Jan 1910	39	9	1	9
T. Burt	Nov 1918	44	10	8	11
T. P. O'Connor	Nov 1929	49	7	10	11
D. Lloyd George	Dec 1944	54	8	15	1
Earl Winterton	Oct 1951	46	11	6	10
Sir H. O'Neill	Oct 1952	37	8	1	0
D. Grenfell	Sep 1959	37	2	6	11
Sir W. Churchill	Sep 1964	62	0[a]	5	0
R. Butler	Jan 1965	35	8		4
(Sir) R. Turton	Feb 1974	44	8	9	1
G. Strauss	Apr 1979	46	11[a]	5	0
J. Parker	May 1983	47	6	4	1
J. Callaghan	May 1987	41	10	4	0
Sir B. Braine	Mar 1992	42	1	3	10
Sir E. Heath	(elected February 1950)				

[a] By tradition the title of Father of the House goes to the member with the longest continuous service. Sir W. Churchill's service was broken in 1908 and again in 1922–4. His continuous service was therefore exactly 40 years. G. Strauss sat 1929–31 and then 1934–79.

Long-service M.P.s

Apart from the Fathers of the House (all but three of whom served over 38 years) the following M.P.s served 38 years or more:

Years		
49	G. Lambert	91–24, 29–45
48	A. Balfour	74–06, 06–22
47	J. Gretton	95–06, 07–43
47	H. Chaplin	68–06, 07–16
45	Sir A. Chamberlain	92–14, 14–37
42	J. Talbot	68–78, 78–10
42	M. Foot	45–55, 60–92
41	Sir W. Hart Dyke	65–06
40	Sir W. Lawson	59–65, 68–85, 86–00, 03–06
40	E. Shinwell	22–24, 28–31, 35–70
40	W. Long	80–92, 93–21
40	D. Healey	52–92
39	Sir G. Courthope	06–45
39	W. Thorne	06–45
39	Sir T. Moore	25–64
39	Sir C. Taylor	35–74
39	Sir L. Ropner	23–29, 31–64
39	Sir H. Fraser	45–84
39	J. Amery	50–66, 69–92
38	Sir J. Pease	65–03
38	J. Round	68–06

Years		
38	Sir J. Agg-Gardner	74–80, 85–95 00–06, 11–28
38	J. Chamberlain	76–14
38	J. Collings	80–86, 86–18
38	J. Lowther	83–21
38	Ld H. Cecil	95–06, 10–37
38	W. Nicholson	97–35
38	E. Fitzroy	00–06, 10–43
38	W. Elliott	18–23, 24–45, 46–58
38	G. Oliver	22–31, 35–64
38	H. Macmillan	24–29, 31–45, 45–64
38	Dame I. Ward	31–45, 50–74
38	G. Lloyd	31–45, 50–74
38	Sir J. Langford-Holt	45–83
38	A. Lewis	45–83
38	G. Thomas	45–83
38	J. Silverman	45–83
38	F. Willey	45–83
38	Sir H. Wilson	45–83
38	Sir D. Walker-Smith	45–83

In 1994 Sir E. Heath (50–) and T. Benn (50–60, 63–83, 84–) were the only M.P.s to have sat for over 38 years.

Sir J. Fergusson (55–7, 59–68, 85–06), Sir F. Powell (57–9, 63–8, 72–4, 80–1, 85–10), and Lord C. Hamilton (65–8, 69–88, 10–18) with substantially interrrupted service, can be listed with Sir W. Churchill, D. Lloyd George, G. Lambert, Sir J. Agg-Gardner and G. Strauss as the only members to leave the House fifty years after entering it.

Oldest and Youngest M.P.s

The oldest M.P.s have been S. Young (96 in 1918); D. Logan (92 in 1964); Sir W. Churchill (89 in 1964); W. Thorne (88 in 1945); R. Cameron (87 in 1913); J. Collings (86 in 1918); Sir S. Chapman (86 in 1945); E. Shinwell (85 in 1970); and S. O. Davies (85 in 1972).

The youngest M.P.s have been Vt Turnour (Earl Winterton) (21 in 1904); J. Esmonde (21 in 1915); P. Whitty (21 in 1916); J. Sweeney (21 in 1918); E. Harmsworth (21 in 1919); Sir H. Lucas-Tooth (21 in 1924); P. Clarke (21 in 1955); and Miss B. Devlin (21 in 1969).

Family Connections of M.P.s

Many M.P.s have had extended family connections with other present or past M.P.s. Often, when through the female line, these are difficult to check. However, the following include the most outstanding examples of parliamentary families.

Acland	Sir R. Acland (1935–45, 1947–55); s. of Sir F. Acland (1906–22, 1923–4, 1932–39); s. of Sir A. Acland (1885–99); s. of Sir T. Acland (1837–47, 1865–85).
Astor	W. W. Astor (1935–45, 1951–2) and his brothers J. J. Astor (1951–9) and M. Astor (1945–51) were sons of Vtess Astor (1919–45) and W. Astor (1910–19). W. Astor's brother J. J. Astor (1922–45) and his son J. Astor (1964–74) also sat.
Baldwin	(E Baldwin of Bewdley). O. Baldwin (1929–31, 1945–7); s. of S. Baldwin (1908–37); s. of A. Baldwin (1892–1908).
Benn	(Vt Stansgate) A. Wedgwood Benn (1950–60, 63–83, 84–); s. of W. Benn (1906–31, 1937–41); s. of Sir J. Benn (1892–5, 1904–10).
Cavendish	(D of Devonshire) M. of Hartington (1923–38); s. of V. Cavendish (1865–8, 1880–91); s. of Ld E. Cavendish (1865–74, 1880–91) b. of M of Hartington (1857–91). Four of the sisters of the M of Hartington (1923–38) were married to M.P.s – H. Macmillan (1924–9, 1931–45, 1945–64); J. Stuart (1923–59); H. Hunloke (1938–44); F. Holland-Martin (1951–60) and then Vt Hinching-brooke (1941 –62).
Cecil	(M of Salisbury) Vt Cranborne (1979–87); s. of Vt Cranborne (1950–54); s. of Vt Cranborne (1929–41); s. of Vt Cranborne (1885–92, 1893–1903); s. of Vt Cranborne (1853–68); s. of Vt Cran-borne (1813–23); s. of Vt Cranborne (1774–80).
Chamberlain	N. Chamberlain (1918–40); b. of Sir A. Chamberlain (1892–1937); s. of J. Chamberlain (1876 1914).
Channon	(Sir) P. Channon (1959-); s. of Sir H. Channon (1935–58) and g.s. of Countess of Iveagh (1927–35) and Vt Elveden (1908–10, 1912–27). This is the only example of a seat, Southend, being held successively by four members of one family.
Churchill	(D of Marlborough) W. Churchill (1970-); s. of R. Churchill (1940–5); s. of Sir W. Churchill (1900–22, 1924–64); s. of Ld R. Churchill (1874–94); s. of M of Blandford (1844–5, 1847–57); s. of M of Blandford (1818–20, 1826–30, 1832–5, 1838–40); s. of M of Blandford (1790–96, 1802–4).
Clifton Brown	G. Clifton Brown (1992-); grandson of G. Clifton Brown (1945–50); nephew of H. Clifton Brown (1922–23, 1924–45); sons of J. Clifton Brown (1918–23, 1924–51); sons of J. Clifton Brown (1876–80); Grandson of Sir W. Brown (1846–59)
Dickinson	Vtess Davidson (1937–59); wife of Sir J. Davidson (1920–37) and daughter of Sir W. Dickinson (1906–18), S. of S. Dickinson (1868–74)
Foot	M. Foot (1945–55, 1960–92); b. of (Sir) D. Foot (1931–45, 1957–70) and s. of I. Foot (1922–4, 1929–35)

Guest	(Vt Wimborne) I. Guest (1935–45); s. of I. Guest (Vt Wimborne) (1906–10) who was b. of F. Guest (1910–22, 1923–9, 1931–37), O. Guest (1918–22, 1935–45) and C. Guest (1910–18, 1922–3, 1937–45).
Henderson	A. Henderson (1903–18, 1919–22, 1923, 1924–31, 1933–5), sat in the House with two sons, Arthur (1923–4, 1929–31, 1935–66) and William (1923–4, 1929–31).
Hogg	(Vt Hailsham) D. Hogg (1979–); s. of Q. Hogg (1938–50, 1963–70); s. of Sir D. Hogg (1922–8); nephew of Sir J. Hogg (1865–8, 1871–87), and grandson of Sir. J. Hogg (1835–57).
Hurd	D. Hurd (1974-); s. of Sir A. Hurd (1945–64); s. of (Sir) P. Hurd (1918–23, 1924–45).
Lindsay	(E of Crawford and Balcarres) Ld Balniel (1955–74); s. of Ld Balniel (1924–40) and nephew of J. Lindsay (1955–59); sons of Ld Balcarres (1895–1913); s. of Ld Balcarres (1874–80).
Lloyd George	D. Lloyd George (1890–1944) sat in the House with his son Gwilym (1924–50, 1951–7) and his daughter Megan (1929–51, 1957–66).
Montagu-Douglas-Scott	(D of Buccleuch) E of Dalkeith (1960–73); s. of E of Dalkeith (1923–35) and nephew of Ld W. Scott (1935–50); s. of E of Dalkeith (1895–1906); s. of E of Dalkeith (1853–60, 1874–80).
Morrison	C. Morrison (1963–92); b. of P. Morrison (1974–92); s. of J. Morrison (1942–64); s. of H. Morrison (1918–23, 1924–31); b. of J. Morrison (1900–06, 1910–12).
Nicholson	Miss E. Nicholson (1987-); d. of Sir G. Nicholson (1931–5, 1937–66); nephew of J. Nicholson (1921–4) and O. Nicholson (1924–31); sons of W. Nicholson (1897–1935); s.of W. Nicholson (1866–74, 1880–85).
Ormsby-Gore	(Ld Harlech). D.Ormsby-Gore (1950–61); s.of W. Ormsby-Gore (1910–38); s. of G. Ormsby Gore (1901–4); s.of W. Ormsby-Gore (1847–52, 1858–76) and nephew of J. Ormsby-Gore (1837–41, 1859–76); sons of W. Ormsby-Gore (1806–7, 1830–1, 1835–7).
Stanley	(E of Derby) R. Stanley (1950–66); s. of Ld Stanley (1917–18, 1922–38) and nephew of O. Stanley (1924–50); s. of Ld Stanley (1892–1900) and nephew of A. Stanley (1898–1918); s. of Ld Stanley (1865–86); s. of Ld Stanley (1824–44); s. of Ld Stanley (1796–1832).

Spouse's Succession

In the following cases a wife took over at a by-election the seat being left vacant by her husband's death, elevation to the peerage, disqualification, or resignation.

1919	Lady Astor (Plymouth, Sutton)
1921	Mrs M. Wintringham (Louth)
1923	Mrs H. Philipson (Berwick-on-Tweed)
1927	Countess of Iveagh (Southend)
1930	Lady Noel-Buxton (Norfolk North)
1937	Mrs A. Hardie (Glasgow, Springburn)
1937	Lady Davidson (Hemel Hempstead)
1941	Mrs B. Rathbone (Bodmin)
1943	Lady Apsley (Bristol Central)
1953	Mrs L. Jeger (Holborn & St. Pancras, S.)
1957	Lady Gammans (Hornsey)
1982	Mrs H. McElhone (Glasgow, Queen's Park)
1986	Mrs L. Golding (Newcastle-under-Lyme)
1990	Mrs I. Adams (Paisley North)

In 1931 Sir O. Mosley failed to take over his wife's seat at Stoke. In 1958 Mrs W. Elliot was defeated at Glasgow, Kelvingrove, when seeking to succeed her husband. In 1969 Mrs G. Forrest was defeated in Mid-Ulster when seeking to succeed her husband.

In 1929 H. Dalton took over the seat at Bishop Auckland which his wife had won in a 1929 by-election. In 1929 W. Runciman took over the seat – St Ives – which his wife had won in a 1928 by-election.

The Duchess of Atholl (1923–38) sat for the West Perthshire seat which her husband (M of Tullibardine) had occupied (1910–17). In 1984 Mrs C. Jackson succeeded R. Jackson as M.E.P. for Wiltshire.

The only cases of husband and wife sitting together in the House of Commons have been

W. and H. Runciman	1928–9	J. and F. Paton	1945–50
H. and R. Dalton	1929–9	R. and A. Kerr	1966–70
Sir O. and Lady C. Mosley	1929–31	J. and G. Dunwoody	1966–70
A. Bevan and Jennie Lee	1929–31	N. and A. Winterton	1983–
(married in 1934)	1945–60	P. and V. Bottomley	1984–
W. and J. Adamson	1938–45	G. and B. Prentice	1992–

A. Lyon (1966–83) and Clare Short (1983–), though married, did not sit in the same House. Some M.P.s have married after one had left the House: N.Fisher (1950–83) and Mrs P. Ford (1953–5); J. Sillars (1970–9, 1988–92) and Mrs M. Macdonald (1973–4); C. Stephen (1935–47) and Miss D. Jewson (1923–4).

Shirley Summerskill (1964–83) sat with her ex-husband J. Ryman (1974–87).

E. and E. Kellett-Bowman sat together as M.E.P.s (1979–84).

Filial Succession

In the following cases a son or daughter was nominated to fill a vacancy left by a parent.

1908	S. Baldwin (Bewdley)
1909	T. Lundon (Limerick E.)
1913	R. McCalmont (Antrim E.)
1913	P. Meehan (Queens Co., Leix)
1914	A. Chamberlain (Birmingham)
1940	N. Grattan-Doyle (Newcastle N.) (defeated)
1945	G. Lambert (South Molton)
1946	J. Little (Down) (defeated)
1953	Mrs P. Ford (Sir W. Smiles) (Down N.)
1959	P. Channon (Southend W.)
1970	G. Janner (Leicester N.W.)
1983	S. Palmer (Bristol N.W.) (defeated)
1987	Miss H. Armstrong (Durham N.W.)

Dual Mandates

From 1973 to 1979 all the UK members of the European Assembly were nominated from the House of Commons or the House of Lords. In the first direct elections, 10 M.P.s were elected as MEPs as well as 4 Peers. Since then the following M.P.s have served simultaneously at Westminster and Strasbourg.

1979–	I. Paisley (Dem.U.)		1983–84	J. Taylor (Con)
1979–	J. Hume (SDLP)		1983–84	R. Boyes (Lab)
1979–89	J. Taylor (UU)		1983–84	R. Caborn (Lab)
1979–84	Sir B. Rhys-Williams (Con)		1983–84	Mrs A. Clwyd (Lab)
1979–84	Mrs E. Kellett-Bowman (Con)		1983–84	W. Griffiths (Lab)
1979–87	T. Normanton (Con)		1983–84	A. Rogers (Lab)
1983–84	D. Curry (Con)		1987–89	Miss J. Quin (Lab)
1983–84	E. Forth (Con)		1992–94	G. Hoon (Lab)
1983–84	D. Harris (Con)		1992–94	L. Smith (Lab)
1983–84	R. Jackson (Con)		1992–94	G. Stevenson (Lab)

Critical Votes in the House of Commons since 1900

Votes in the House of Commons have only rarely disturbed or threatened to disturb a government or to prevent its implementing its programme. Moreover prudent governments have retreated rather than face the risk of defeat (e.g. over *In Place of Strife*, 1969). The following occasions do not constitute an exhaustive list (e.g. only 5 of the 9 minor defeats inflicted on the Labour Government of 1924 are included) but they probably include all that caused any serious stir.

15 Feb	1904	327–276	Government majority (on Liberal Free Trade motion) cut by desertion of 26 Unionist Free Traders.
20 Jul	1905	199–196	Government defeated on Estimates for Irish Land Commission.
11 Nov	1912	227–206	Government defeated on Amendment to financial resolution of the Government of Ireland Bill.
7 Jul	1914	269–246	Government wins guillotine on Budget despite 22 Lib. abstentions, one Lib. No; setback leads to abandonment of Revenue Bill.
8 Nov	1916	213–117	Government survives challenge on sale of German property in Nigeria but 65 Cons rebelled, provoking Bonar Law to think of Cabinet reconstruction.
9 May	1918	293–106	Lloyd George victory over Maurice affair. Coupons in Dec 1918 election issued largely on basis of how Libs voted in this division.
23 Oct	1919	185–113	Amendment to Alien Restriction Bill carried on report stage against Government.
25 Feb	1920	123–57	Motion for increased police pensions carried against Government.
19 Jul	1921	137–135	Amendment to Finance Bill exempting Provident Societies from Corporation Profits Tax carried against Government.
10 Apr	1923	145–138	Government defeated on procedural motion over ex-Servicemen's salaries.
21 Jan	1924	328–256	Baldwin Government, meeting new parliament, defeated by Lib. and Lab. votes.
7 Apr	1924	221–212	Government defeated on second reading of Rent Restriction Bill.
16 Jun	1924	189–126	New Clause to London Traffic Bill carried against Government.
18 Jul	1924	171–149	Government defeated on amendment to Unemployment Insurance Bill.
8 Oct	1924	364–198	MacDonald Government defeated on Lib. amendment for enquiry into Campbell case. Dissolution follows at once.
27 Feb	1930	280–271	Government defeats key Amendment to Coal Bill, saved by support of 4 Libs and abstention of 8 Libs.
21 Jan	1931	282–249	Government defeat on Report Stage over subsidy to Catholic schools (41 Lab. Noes).
14 Mar	1931	173–168	Government survives challenge over appointment of Sir E. Gowers to chair Mines Reorganisation Commission.
16 Mar	1931	277–273	Government defeated over abolition of University M.P.s (2 Lab. M.P.s voted with Opposition and 20 abstained).
8 Sep	1931	309–250	National Government wins first vote (on procedural motion); Ayes 243 Con., 53 Lib., 12 Lab., 3 Ind.; Noes: 241, Lab., 9 Ind.
11 Feb	1935	404–133	Government wins Second Reading for Government of India Bill (with 80 Con. Noes).
1 Apr	1936	156–148	Government defeated on adjournment motion over equal pay for civil servants (vote reversed 6 Apr 1936).
8 May	1940	281–200	Chamberlain survives censure motion but Con. Noes (33) and abstentions (about 65) force his resignation.
18 Mar	1943	335–119	Government wins motion on Beveridge Report but 97 Lab. M.P.s out of 99 non-ministers voting defy Whip.
28 Mar	1944	117–116	Government defeated on equal pay for women (vote reversed 30 May 1944, 429–23).
13 Dec	1945	345–98	Government obtains approval for the American Loan. Cons officially abstained, but 74 Con. and 23 Lab. M.P.s voted No; 8 Cons also voted Aye.
1 Apr	1947	386–85	Government obtains Second Reading for National Service Bill (72 Lab. and one Con. Noes).
9 Mar	1950	310–296	First division in new parliament (on Steel Nationalisation) showed Government with nominal majority of five could carry on.

29 Mar 1950	283–257	Government defeated on adjournment motion following debate on Fuel and Power.
9 Apr 1951	237–219	Motion to annul a Rationing Order carried against the Government.
5 Jul 1951	157–141	Motion to annul a Prices Order carried against the Government.
16 Jul 1951	232–229	Government defeated on amendment to the Forestry Bill.
6 Dec 1956	313–260	Government wins confidence vote on Suez action (15 Con. abstentions).
17 Jun 1963	321–252	Government survives adjournment debate on Profumo Affair (27 Con. abstentions).
10 Mar 1964	287–20	Government secures Second Reading of Resale Prices Bill with Labour abstaining (20 Con. Noes and about 20 abstentions).
24 Mar 1964	204–203	Government defeats Amendment excluding medicines from Resale Prices Bill (31 Con. voting against Government and over 20 abstaining).
6 May 1965	310–306	Approval for White Paper on Steel Nationalisation.
6 Jul 1965	180–167	New Clause to Finance Bill carried against Government.
21 Dec 1965	276–48	Rhodesia oil embargo order approved. Cons officially abstained but 48 Cons voted No and 31 Aye.
30 May 1968	129–52	Reintroduction of prescription charges approved but 49 Lab.Noes and over 150 Lab. abstentions.
3 Mar 1969	224–62	Motion approving In Place of Strife White Paper carried but 55 Lab. Noes and 40 Lab. abstentions.
28 Oct 1971	356–244	Approval for negotiated terms on European entry. 69 Lab.M.P.s voted for and 20 abstained. 39 Con. M.P.s voted against and 2 abstained.
17 Feb 1972	309–301	Government secures Second Reading of European Communities Bill (15 Con. Noes and 4 Con. abstentions; there were 4 Lab. abstentions; Libs divided 5–1 Aye).
13 Jul 1972	301–284	Government secures Third Reading of European Communities Bill (16 Con. Noes; 4 Con. and 13 Lab. abstentions).
22 Nov 1972	275–240	Government defeated on immigration rules (7 Con. Noes and 49 Con. abstentions).
13 Jun 1973	267–250	Government defeated on new Clause to Maplin Development Bill (17 Con. Ayes and 10 Con. abstentions).
13 Jun 1973	255–246	Government secures Third Reading of Maplin Development Bill.
12 Jul 1973	285–264	Government defeated on export of live animals for slaughter (23 Cons voted Aye).
20 Jun 1974	311–290	Government defeated in debate on industrial policy.
27 Jun 1974	298–289	Opposition motion on Rates carried against Government. [The above were only two of the seventeen government defeats during the short Parliament of 1974.]
29 Jan 1975	280–265	Government defeated on amendment to the Social Security Benefits Bill (9 Lab. Ayes).
17 Jul 1975	108–106	Government defeated on Opposition amendment to Finance Bill reducing V.A.T. on TV sets.
4 Aug 1975	268–261	Government defeated on clause to the Housing Finance (Special Provisions) Bill.
10 Mar 1976	284–256	Government defeated on motion approving public expenditure plans. (Next day Government won confidence motion 297–280.)
27 May 1976	304–303	In disputed vote Government set aside Standing Order rule on hybridity of Aircraft and Shipbuilding Nationalisation Bill. (Government won retaken vote on 29 Jun 311–297 with 14 Nationalists abstaining.)
28 Jun 1976	259–0	Government defeated on motion for adjournment (through failing to contest it) following debate on its child benefits scheme.
8 Nov 1976	311–310	Government secures guillotine on Lords amendments on Aircraft and Shipbuilding Acts.
10 Nov 1976	310–308	Key clause in Dock Labour Bill defeated through two Lab.abstentions (J. Mackintosh and B. Walden).
7 Feb 1977	130–129	Government lost Second Reading of the Redundancy Rebates Bill by one vote, due to unpaired absence of the P. M. (Subsequently reintroduced in modified form.)
22 Feb 1977	312–283	Government defeated over guillotine on Scotland and Wales Bill (with 22 Lab. Noes and 21 abstentions).

17 Mar	1977	293–0	Government defeated on adjournment motion to discuss public expenditure plans (all Lab. M.P.s abstained).
23 Mar	1977	322–298	Government survives Con. motion of censure with Lib. votes, following Lib-Lab Pact.
5 Apr	1977	203–185	Government defeated on adjournment motion following debate on training colleges in Scotland, through Lab. abstentions.
22 Nov	1977	199–184	Government loses first clause of the Scotland Devolution Bill.
5 Dec	1977	158–126	Government defeated on adjournment motion on Crown Agents' affair by M.P.s demanding public inquiry.
7 Dec	1977	161–160	Government defeated over Scotland Devolution Bill provision for Secretary of State to have regard to national pay policy (2 Lab. Noes).
13 Dec	1977	319–222	Government recommendation of proportional representation for European Parliament elections rejected on Free Vote (Lab 147 for, 115 against; Con.61 for, 198 against).
23 Jan	1978	291–281	Motion to devalue Green Pound by 7.5%, not 5%, carried against Government.
25 Jan	1978	166–151	Amendment to Scotland Devolution Bill, making 40% of electorate voting 'Yes' in referendum a precondition for the Bill taking effect carried against Government (34 Lab. in majority).
25 Jan	1978	204–118	Amendment to Scotland Devolution Bill, excluding Orkney and Shetland, carried against Government.
14 Feb	1978	298–243	Referendum decision of 25 Jan 78 confirmed on Report Stage (40 Lab. in majority).
8 May	1978	312–304	Amendment to reduce standard rate of Income Tax from 34p. to 33p. carried against Government.
10 May	1978	288–286	Amendment to raise threshold for higher tax rates from £7,000 to £8,000 carried against Government.
19 Jul	1978	293–260	Amendment to Wales Bill barring M.P.s from standing for Welsh Assembly carried against Government.
24 Jul	1978	291–281	Government defeated on clause in Dock Labour Bill giving dock workers local priority in jobs.
26 Jul	1978	276–275	Lords Amendment to Scotland Bill concerning non-Scottish legislation decided by Scottish M.P.s votes upheld against Government. (Lords amendment on Forestry powers also carried 288–266.)
13 Dec	1978	285–283	Government defeated on retention of powers to use sanctions against firms breaching pay policy.
28 Mar	1979	311–310	Government defeated on Conservative vote of No Confidence.
23 Apr	1980	477–49	Government faces rebellion on closed shop.
15 Dec	1982	290–272	Government defeated on amendment to immigration rules (51 Cons voting with Opposition or abstaining).
19 Jul	1983	226–218	Government advice on delaying M.P.s pay increase rejected.
11 Apr	1984	300–208	Government win against challenge on TU ballot rules but 90 M.P.s cross vote.
14 Apr	1986	296–282	Government defeated on Second Reading of Shops Bill (Sunday trading)
16 Jul	1986	172–128	Government defeated on Members' pay motion.
13 Mar	1990	256–253	Government defeat on social security benefits for elderly.
4 Nov	1992	319–316	Government win paving motion on Maastricht Treaty.
22 Jul	1993	324–316	Defeat of Government motion on Social Policy Protocol of Maastricht Treaty. (On the next day the decision was reversed 339–301 on a confidence motion).

In the Parliament of 1970–74 there were 6 government defeats in the House of Commons; in Mar–Jul 1974 there were 17 defeats; in 1974–79 there were 42 defeats; in 1979–83 there was one defeat; and in the 1983–87 Parliament there were two defeats; in the 1987–92 there was one defeat.

Confidence Motions

Many motions before the House of Commons are implicitly treated as questions of confidence. Between 1900 and 1945 two such motions were carried against the Government:

| | Voting | | |
	For Government	Against Government	Issue
21 Jan 24	151	328	General confidence
8 Oct 24	198	359	Campbell case

Since 1945 the question of confidence has only been put explicitly to the House on the following occasions. On 14 Dec 1978, 24 Sep 92 and on 23 Jul 1993 the motion expressed confidence. All the other motions expressed no confidence. The only one carried against the Government was on 28 Mar 1979.

| | Voting | | |
	For Government	Against Government	Issue
5 Dec 45	381	197	Nationalisation
4 Dec 52	304	280	Handling of parliamentary business
1 Nov 56	323	255	Suez intervention
6 Dec 56	312	260	Suez intervention
5 Feb 62	326	228	Attitude to United Nations
26 Jul 62	351	256	Government reshuffle
10 Nov 64	315	294	General confidence
2 Aug 65	303	290	General confidence
26 Jul 66	325	246	Economic management
1 Dec 66	329	246	Economic management
24 Jul 67	333	200	Economic management
6 Mar 72	317	270	European Community bill
19 Nov 73	304	286	Economic management
11 Mar 76	297	280	General confidence
9 Jun 76	309	290	Economic management
23 Mar 77	322	298	General confidence
20 Jul 77	312	282	Economic management
14 Dec 78	300	290	Economic management
28 Mar 79	310	311	General confidence
28 Feb 80	327	268	Economic management
27 Jul 81	334	262	Economic management
28 Oct 81	312	250	Economic management
31 Jan 85	395	222	Economic management
22 Nov 90	367	247	General confidence
27 Mar 91	358	238	Poll tax
24 Sep 92	322	296	Economic management
23 Jul 93	339	299	Maastricht treaty

Guillotine Motions since 1945

From 1945 to 1993 the average number of guillotine motions was betwen two and three per year. All were carried except one (the Scotland and Wales Bill 22 Feb 1977). The session numbers are:

Session	Guillotine motions	Session	Guillotine motions	Session	Guillotine motions
1946–7	2	1963–4	–	1979–80	7
1947–8	–	1964–5	–	1980–1	4
1948–9	1	1965–6	–	1981–2	5
1950–1	–	1966–7	1	1982–3	3
1951–2	2	1967–8	2	1983–4	3
1952–3	2	1968–9	1	1984–5	2
1953–4	2	1969–70	1	1985–6	3
1954–5	–	1970–1	2	1986–7	3
1955–6	–	1971–2	5	1987–8	9
1956–7	1	1972–3	1	1988–9	13
1957–8	1	1973–4	–	1989–90	6
1958–9	–	1974–5	5	1990–1	3
1959–60	–	1975–6	10	1991–2	6
1960–1	2	1976–7	1	1992–3	3
1960–2	5	1977–8	4		
1962–3	2	1978–9	–		

M.P.s' Suspension

Members acting in sustained defiance of the chair can be named and suspended from the service of the House of Commons for five sitting days. The following list includes all that have occurred since 1945:

18 Jul	49	E. Smith	12 Nov	87	T. Dalyell
27 Nov	51	S. Silverman	24 Nov	87	D. Wigley
26 Mar	52	Mrs E. Braddock	11 Jan	88	J. Hughes
23 May	68	Dame I. Ward	25 Jan	88	K. Livingstone
13 Mar	72	C. Loughlin	18 Feb	88	H. Cohen
12 Feb	81	I. Paisley	15 Mar	88	A. Salmond
8 Apr	81	R. Brown	13 Apr	88	D. Nellist
15 Jul	81	R. Brown	20 Apr	88	R. Brown
16 Nov	81	J. McQuade, P. Robinson, I. Paisley	25 Jul	88	T. Dalyell
26 May	82	A. Faulds	14 Mar	89	J. Sillars
2 May	84	T. Dalyell	24 Jul	89	T. Dalyell
17 Jul	84	D. Skinner	7 Mar	90	J. Browne
31 Jul	84	M. Flannery	23 Jul	90	D. Douglas
11 Nov	85	B. Sedgemore	2 Jul	92	D. Skinner
20 Jan	86	D. Wigley	20 Nov	93	I. Paisley

Regnal Years

Until 1962 the dates of Acts of Parliament were recorded in terms of the regnal years during the session in which they were passed. Regnal years date from the accession of the sovereign. Thus the act listed as 11 & 12 Geo. VI, c. 65 was passed in the parliamentary session during the eleventh and twelfth regnal year of George VI (1948). The parliamentary session of 1948–49 covered three regnal years, and its acts appear under the style 12, 13 & 14 Geo.VI. Since 1963 Acts of Parliament have been recorded by the calendar year and the chapter number, e.g. Finance Act 1963, c. 25.

Sovereign	Regnal Year	Date
Victoria	63	20 Jun 1899–19 Jun 1900
	64	20 Jun 00–22 Jan 01
Edward VII	1	22 Jan 01–21 Jan 02
	10	22 Jan 10–6 May 10
George V	1	6 May 10–5 May 11
	26	6 May 35–20 Jan 36
Edward VIII	1	20 Jan 36–11 Dec 36
George VI	1	11 Dec 36–10 Dec 37
	16	11 Dec 51–6 Feb 52
Elizabeth II	1	6 Feb 52–5 Feb 53
	10	6 Feb 61–5 Feb 62

Select Committees

Select Committees have been appointed for many purposes and have a long history in both Houses. In the Commons Select Committees have long been used in connection with public expenditure, parliamentary procedure, legislation, and for *ad hoc* enquiries, sometimes of a quasi-judicial character. In the nineteenth century and up to 1914 Select Committees were also used for a wide range of specific enquiries, many of which would now be undertaken by a Government Inquiry or even a Royal Commission. Between the wars Select Committees were also occasionally used to examine Empire matters. Select Committees may be set up for a session or part of a session to consider a specific matter e.g. the Select Committee on Patent Medicines in 1914, the Select Committee on Tax-Credit in 1972–73, or the Select Committee on Conduct of Members in 1975–76 and 1976–77. Others are set up more regularly by custom.[1]

The Public Accounts Committee has existed continuously since 1862.

An Estimates Committee later subsumed in the Expenditure Committee, was set up in one form or another most sessions from 1912 to 1979.

Although the Nationalised Industries Committee existed from 1956 to 1979, other 'specialist Committees' to consider either a subject area e.g. Race Relations and Immigration or a Department e.g. Education and Science were appointed after the 'Crossman Reforms' in 1966 for each session until 1979. In 1979 a new structure of Select Committees was established to cover the work of each major Government Department.

Powers: In their order of reference, and under Standing Orders, Commons Select Committees have had powers of varying extent given to them by the House.

Except for Select Committees on Bills or procedure committees both Sessional Committees and specialist committees are now usually given powers to send for persons, papers and records (although only the House can act to punish contempt of such summons), to sit at times when the House is adjourned, to meet outside the Palace of Westminster ('to adjourn from place to place'), to report from time to time ('to report to the House and publish as many reports as they wish'), to appoint sub-committees from among their own members, and to appoint expert advisers.

Duration: Some Select Committees are more permanent than others. All share a degree of impermanence in that their membership needs to be reappointed every session. In March 1974 for the first time the membership of a Select Committee (the Expenditure Committee) was appointed for the duration of a Parliament and all Select Committees are now appointed on this basis.

Chairmen: Apart from the Public Accounts Committee, the Committee on Statutory Instruments, the Committee on the Parliamentary Commissioner and latterly the Select

---

[1] Since 1968–69 Select Committee returns showing membership and attendance etc. have been published regularly at House of Commons Papers.

Committee on European Secondary Legislation, the Chairmen of the Select Committees used until 1979 normally to be from the Government Party. This no longer applies nor did it ever apply necessarily to sub-committees.

Chairmen's Liaison Committee: In recent decades the practice grew up for Chairmen of Select Committees to meet in an informal Committee from time to time to discuss subjects of common interest such as the allocation of funds available for overseas visits. The Committee was not a Select Committee of the House until 1980.

Committee of Selection, 1840–

Chairman (since 1945)

1945	T. Smith	1964	C. Kenyon	1979	(Sir) P. Holland
1947	G. Mathers	1969	G. Rogers	1984	(Sir) M. Fox
1951	Sir G. Touche	1970	H. Gurden	1992	Sir F. Montgomery
1956	Sir R. Conant	1974	H. Delargy		
1960	Sir P. Agnew	1976	F. Willey		

Although the task of the Committee of Selection has for many years been predominantly the selection of Members to serve on Standing Committees on Bills, the Committee was originally set up to appoint Committees on Private Bills and is still appointed under Private Business S.O. 109. It has 11 Members.

The Committee of Selection nominates:

Public Business

(1)   Members of Standing Committees;
(2)   Some or all members of Select Committees on hybrid Bills (if the House orders);
(3)   The Commons members of Joint Committees on hybrid Bills (if the House orders);
(4)   The two members whom Mr Speaker is to consult, if practicable, before giving his certificate to a money bill;
(5)   Since 1979 all members of Select Committees

Private Business

(1)   The panel of members to serve on committees on unopposed bills;
(2)   Committees on unopposed bills;
(3)   Members of committees on opposed bills;
(4)   Eight members to serve on the Standing Orders Committee under S.O. 103;
(5)   The panel of members to act as commissioners under the Private Legislation Procedure (Scotland) Act 1936;
(6)   Commons Members on Joint Committees on special procedure petitions.

Terms of Reference: The Committee would appear to interpret its instructions in S.O. 62 to have 'regard . . . to the composition of the House' by choosing Standing Committees as far as possible in direct ratio to the size of the parties in the House, except that since the 1930s the Liberal Party has usually been given a higher representation than its size would merit on this basis – a Liberal member being appointed to all Committees of 5 members and above. In the three Parliaments since the war in which the size of the Government majority has been small the Committee of Selection has usually selected Members so as to give the Government a majority of one. In the 1974 Parliament, with a minority Government, no party had a majority on any standing Committee. The Committee tends to appoint those Members who spoke on the second reading of the Bill. In recent times of heavy legislation and expanding parliamentary activity it would appear that the position of the whips to offer advice as to which members are anxious, willing, or available to serve on a particular Committee has been strengthened.

Although no Government whip is appointed to the Committee a senior opposition whip was always appointed until 1974.

Committee of Public Accounts, 1862–

Chairman

1896	A. O'Connor	1931	M. Jones	1959	H. Wilson
1901	Sir A. Hayter	1938	F. Pethick-Lawrence	1962	D. Houghton
1906	V. Cavendish	1941	W. Elliot	1964	J. Boyd-Carpenter
1908	(Sir) R. Williams	1943	Sir A. Pownall	1970	H. Lever
1919	F. Acland	1945	O. Peake	1973	E. Dell
1921	A. Williams	1948	R. Assheton	1974	E. du Cann
1923	F. Jowett	1950	Sir R. Cross	1979	J. Barnett
1924	W. Guiness	1950	C. Waterhouse	1983	R. Sheldon
1924	W. Graham	1951	J. Edwards		
1929	A. Samuel	1952	(Sir) G. Benson		

The Committee is made up of no more than 15 members, including the Chairman, and meets on about 30 days each session. The Chairman is usually a member of the Opposition.

Usual Terms of Reference: 'for the examination of the accounts showing the appropriation of the sums granted by parliament to meet the public expenditure', 'and of such other accounts laid before parliament as the committee may think fit' (added 15 Nov 34). 'The Committee shall have power to send for persons, papers and records, and to report from time to time' (added 14 Nov 33). The Committee is aided in its work by the Comptroller and Auditor General whose staff audit the accounts of government departments. These audits and the Comptroller's subsequent report to the House of Commons provide the basic materials for the Committee's enquiries. In 1978 the Committee began to hear evidence in public.

See also Public Accounts Commission (p. 201).

Comptroller and Auditor-General

1896	R. Mills	1921	(Sir) G. Upcott	1976	Sir D. Henley
1900	D. Richmond	1946	Sir F. Tribe	1981	(Sir) G. Downey
1904	(Sir) J. Kempe	1958	Sir E. Compton	1989	(Sir) J. Bourn
1911	(Sir) H. Gibson	1966	Sir B. Fraser		
1921	Sir M. Ramsay	1971	Sir D. Pitblado		

Estimates Committee, 1912–1970

Chairman

1912	Sir F. Banbury	1935	Sir I. Salmon
1914	*(suspended)*	1939	*(see National Expenditure Committee)*
1917	*(see National Expenditure Committee)*	1945	B. Kirby
1920	Sir F. Banbury	1950	A. Anderson
1924	Sir J. Marriott	1951	Sir R. Glyn
1926	(Sir) V. Henderson	1953	C. Waterhouse
1927	A. Bennett	1957	R. Turton
1929	H. Charleton	1961	Sir G. Nicholson
1930	H. Romeril	1964–70	W. Hamilton
1931	Sir V. Henderson		

The Committee originally consisted of 15 members. In 1921 this was increased to 24, and in 1924 to 28. From 1948 to 1960 it had 36 members and from 1960 to 1970 43 members. The Chairman was usually a Government supporter.

Terms of Reference: 'to examine and report upon such of the Estimates presented to the Committee as may seem fit to the Committee' (7 Apr 12 original terms), 'and to suggest the form in which the estimates shall be presented for examination, and to report what if any economies consistent with the policy implied in those estimates may be effected therein' (added in 1921). Until 1939 the Estimates Committee seldom appointed sub-committees, although power to do so had been given in 1924; after 1945, however, following the example set by the Select Committee on National Expenditure, it invariably did so. In 1956 the wording of the terms of reference was rearranged but the substance remained unchanged.

In 1960 the terms were altered to read: 'to examine such of the estimates presented to this House as may seem fit to the committee and report how, if at all, the policy implied in those estimates may be carried out more economically and, if the committee think fit, to consider the principal variations between the estimates and those relating to the previous financial year, and the form in which the estimates are presented to the House'. The committee had power to send for persons, papers, and records, and sit notwithstanding any adjournment of the House, to adjourn from place to place, and to report from time to time: to appoint sub-committees and to refer to such sub-committees any of the matters referred to the committee [each sub-committee has the same powers of sending for persons, etc., sitting and adjourning as the main committee], and to report from time to time the minutes of evidence taken before sub-committees and reported by them to the committee.

In Sessions 1965 and 1966 the House gave the Estimates Committee the power 'to appoint persons with technical or scientific knowledge for the purpose of particular enquiries, either to supply information which is not readily available or to elucidate matters of complexity within the Committee's order of reference'. From 1965–70 the practice was to appoint sub-committees specialising in particular fields. The Select Committee was replaced by the Expenditure Committee in 1971.

Committee on National Expenditure, 1917–1920 and 1939–1945

Chairman

1917	H. Samuel	1939–45	Sir J. Wardlaw-Milne
1919–20	Sir F. Banbury		

No Estimates were presented to Parliament during the two wars, and the Committee on Estimates lapsed. A Committee on National Expenditure was established each year. It consisted of 26 members 1917–20, and 32 members 1939–45. It met about 13 days a session between 1917–20, and about 19 days a session between 1939–45.

1939–45 *Terms of Reference*: 'to examine the current expenditure defrayed out of moneys provided by Parliament for the Defence Services, for Civil Defence, and for other services directly connected with the war, and to report what, if any, economies, consistent with the execution of the policy decided by the Government, may be effected therein'.

Expenditure Committee, 1971–1979

Chairman

1971	E. du Cann	1974–9	J. Boyden
1973	Sir H. D'Avigdor-Goldsmid		

The Committee consisted of 49 members with a quorum of 9.

Terms of Reference: 'to consider how, if at all, the policies implied in the figures of expenditure and in the estimates may be carried out more economically, and to examine the form of the paper and of the estimates presented to this House'. The Committee's work was carried out through seven largely autonomous sub-committees (General; Defence and External Affairs; Employment and Social Services; Trade and Industry; Environment; Education; Arts and Home Affairs).

Nationalised Industries Committee, 1956–1979

Chairman

1956	Sir P. Spens		1966	I. Mikardo
1957	Sir T. Low		1970	Sir H. D'Avigdor-Goldsmid
1961	Sir R. Nugent		1972	(Sir) J. Hall
1964	E. Popplewell		1974–9	R. Kerr

The Committee was appointed on a sessional basis; it had 13 members (1956–66), 18 members (1966–70), 14 members (1970–74), 13 members (1974) and 15 members (1974–9). The Chairman was always a Government supporter.

Terms of Reference: 'to examine the reports and accounts of the nationalised industries established by statute, whose controlling boards are wholly appointed by Ministers of the Crown and whose annual receipts are not wholly or mainly derived from moneys provided by Parliament or advanced by the Exchequer'. In the 1965–66 and 1966–67 Sessions the Committee's terms of reference were amended to enable them to enquire into the Post Office. From 1968–69 the Committee's terms of reference were extended to include the Independent Television Authority, Cable and Wireless Ltd, the Horserace Totalisator Board and certain activities of the Bank of England.

Committee on Agriculture, 1966–1969

Chairman

1966–69   T. Watkins

Terms of Reference: 'To consider the activities in England and Wales of the Ministry of Agriculture, Fisheries and Food'. The Committee had power to send for persons, papers, and records, to sit notwithstanding any adjournment of the House, to adjourn from place to place, and to admit strangers during the examination of witnesses unless they otherwise order. The Committee ceased to exist in Feb 1970.

Committee on Science and Technology, 1966–1979

Chairman

1966	A. Palmer	1974–9	A. Palmer
1970	A. Neave		

Terms of Reference: 'To consider Science and Technology.' The Committee had power to send for persons, and papers.

Committee on Education and Science, 1968–1970

Chairman

1968–70   F. Willey

Terms of Reference: 'To consider the activities of the Department of Education and Science and the Scottish Education Department.' The Committee ceased to exist in 1970.

Committee on Race Relations and Immigration, 1968–79

Chairman

1968	A. Bottomley
1970	W. Deedes
1974–9	F. Willey

The Committee had 12 Members, and a quorum of 4.

Terms of Reference: 'To review policies, but not individual cases, in relation to: (a) the operation of the Race Relations Act 1968 with particular reference to the work of the Race Relations Board and the Community Relations Commission, and (b) the admission into the United Kingdom of Commonwealth citizens and foreign nationals for settlement.'

Committee on Overseas Aid, 1968–1971
(Overseas Development, 1973–1979)

Chairman

1968	Miss M. Herbison	1974	Sir G. de Freitas
1970–71	B. Braine	1978–9	K. McNamara
1973	Sir B. Braine		

The first Committee had between 10 and 18 Members, with a quorum of between 4 and 9. After 1973 it had 9 Members.

Terms of Reference: 'To consider the activities of the Ministry of Overseas Development'. The Committee ceased to exist in 1971. It was re-established under a new title in 1973, 'to consider United Kingdom assistance for overseas development'.

Committee on Scottish Affairs, 1969–1972

Chairman

1969	T. Steele
1970	Sir J. Gilmour
1971–2	J. Brewis

The Committee had 16 Members and a quorum of 8.

Terms of Reference: 'To consider Scottish Affairs'.

Committee on European Secondary Legislation, 1974–76;
European Legislation etc., 1976–

Chairman

1974	J. Davies	1983	N. Spearing
1976	Sir J. Eden	1992	J. Hood
1979	J. Silverman		

The Committee's membership since 1974 has been 16. There are currently three subcommittees.

Terms of Reference: To consider draft proposals of EC secondary legislation and to 'report their opinion as to whether such proposals or other documents raise questions of legal and political importance' . . . 'and to what extent they may affect the law of the United Kingdom'. Expanded in 1976 to cover documents submitted to the Council of Ministers 'whether or not such documents originate from the Commission'. The Committee has powers to send for persons, papers and records, to sit during the Adjournment, and to adjourn from place to place.

Procedure, 1961–76; Procedure (Sessional) Committee, 1976–

Chairman

1961	I. Macleod	1970	(Sir) R. Turton
1963	S. Lloyd	1974	S. Irving
1964	A. Irvine	1979	T. Higgins
1965	A. Blenkinsop	1983	Sir P. Emery
1966	D. Chapman		

The Committee has 15 Members and a quorum of 4.

It was long the practice of the House to set up Committees from time to time to make recommendations on its procedure. But since 1961 a Select Committee on Procedure has been appointed every Session to report on matters which the House refers to it. It came to be referred to as the 'Sessional Committee' to distinguish it from a Procedure Committee set up for the lifetime of the 1974 Parliament which reported in Aug 1978. It has powers to send for persons, papers and records and to report from time to time. It lapsed between Feb 74 and Nov 74 and in the 1978–79 Session. In the 1979–83 Parliament the full committee did not meet, although T. Higgins chaired Committees on Procedure (Supply) and Procedure (Finance).

House of Commons Services Committee, 1965–1992

Chairman

1965	H. Bowden	1976	M. Foot
1966	R. Crossman	1979	N. St John-Stevas
1968	F. Peart	1981	F. Pym
1970	W. Whitelaw	1982	J. Biffen
1972	R. Carr	1987	J. Wakeham
1972	J. Prior	1989	Sir G. Howe
1974	A. Bottomley	1990	J. MacGregor

Terms of Reference: 'To advise Mr Speaker on the control of the accommodation and services in that part of the Palace of Westminster and its precincts occupied by or on behalf of the House of Commons and to report thereon to this House'. This Committee was set up as a result of a recommendation of the Select Committee on the Palace of Westminster of Session 1964–65, whose main task had been to consider the arrangements to be made by the Commons following the transfer on 26 Apr 1965 of control of the Palace from the Lord Great Chamberlain on behalf of the Crown to the two Houses.

The Committee consisted of 19 members appointed by the House. It had power to send for persons, papers, and records, to sit notwithstanding the adjournment of the House, to report from time to time, and to appoint Sub-Committees, each of which consists of three members. Each Sub-Committee has similar powers to the main Committee (except of course power to nominate Sub-Committees). The Committee usually appointed four main Sub-Committees: the Accommodation and Administration Sub-Committee, the Catering Sub-Committee, the Library Sub-Committee and the Computer Sub-Committee. The Catering Sub-Committee replaced the 'Select Committee on Kitchen and Refreshment Rooms' appointed every session since the late nineteenth century.

The Leader of the House has always been appointed Chairman of the Committee (except in 1974–76).

See also House of Commons Commission (p. 195), and Domestic Committees.

House of Commons Commission 1978–

Under the House of Commons (Administration) Act of 1978, a House of Commons Commission was appointed to control the internal finances of the House. Independent of Government, it comprises the Speaker, the Leader of the House, one M.P. nominated by the Leader of the Opposition, and three other non-ministerial M.P.s (including one, in practice, nominated by the minority parties).

Following the Ibbs report (HC 38/ 1990–1991) the House of Commons drastically revised its administrative arrangements and four 'Domestic' committees were set up to oversee them under the general supervision of the House of Commons Commission.

Domestic Committees 1991–

Accommodation Committee 1991–

Chairman

1991–   R. Powell

Administration Committee 1991–

Chairman

1991–   J. Hood

Finance and Services Committee 199

Chairman

1991–   (Sir) P. Channon

Information Committee 1991–

Chairman

1991–   G. Waller

Committee on Members' Interests, 1975–

This Committee was established following a 1974 report (pp. 108/1974–5) to scrutinise a new Register of Members' outside interests. Since 1985 it has also looked at Members' staff and lobbyists.

Chairman

1975	F. Willey
1983	(Sir) G. Johnson-Smith

Committee of Privileges, c. 1630–

The Committee of Privileges only meets when *prima facie* breaches of privileges are referred to it by the House. Unlike other committees it includes senior members from both the Front Benches. It is ordered to be appointed by long-standing tradition on the first day of every session. Until 1940 it was chaired by the Prime Minister. from 1940 to 1945 C. Attlee, as Deputy Prime Minister, took the chair. Since 1945 the Chairman has usually but not always been the Leader of the House.

Chairman

1940	C. Attlee	1965	H. Bowden	1979	N. St John Stevas		
1945	H. Morrison	1967	R. Crossman	1981	F. Pym		
1946	A. Greenwood	1968	F. Peart	1982	J. Biffen		
1947	H. Morrison	1971	W. Whitelaw	1987	J. Wakeham		
1948	C. Ede	1972	R. Carr	1989	Sir G. Howe		
1952	H. Crookshank	1973	J. Prior	1990	J. MacGregor		
1956	R. Butler	1974	G. Strauss	1992	A. Newton		
1964	S. Lloyd	1979	J. Barnett				

The Committee currently has 17 members.

The following include all Reports of the Select Committee of Privileges and a few from *ad hoc* Committees.

1902	Imprisonment of a Member: C. O'Kelly.
1902	Imprisonment of a Member: P. McHugh.
1909	D of Norfolk: alleged interference in an election.
1911	E of Aberdeen and E of Roden: alleged interference in an election.
1924	*Daily Herald*: reflection on the impartiality of the Chairman of Committees.
1926	*Daily Mail*: allegations of corrupt motives against M.P.s.
1929–30	E. Sandham: allegations of drunkenness and acceptance of bribes against M.P.s.
1932–33	H. Bowles and E. Huntsman: reflections on a Private Bill Committee's impartiality.
1933–4	Sir S. Hoare and E of Derby: alleged improper pressure on witnesses to a Committee.
1937–8	D. Sandys: summons to Military court of Inquiry.
1937–8	Official Secrets Act.
1938–9	Official Secrets Act.
1939–40	Detention of A. Ramsay under Section 18B of Defence of the Realm Act.
1939–40	Conduct of R. Boothby.
1940–1	Conduct of R. Boothby.
1940–1	*Observer* publication of Secret Session debate.
1940–1	Grampian electricity supply bill: Highland Development League circular to M.P.s alleging irregularities in bill procedure.
1941–2	Disclosure of Secret Session proceedings by J. McGovern.
1942–3	H. Metcalf and J. Reid: payment of expense cheque to M.P. to attend prosecution by Board of Trade.
1943–4	N.U.D.A.W.: withdrawal of Trade Union financial support from W. Robinson on ground of refusal to resign seat.
1944–5	G. Reakes and D. Henderson. Offer to make donation to constituency association in return for M.P.s' help.
1945–6	Writ of Summons served on officer of House within precincts.
1945–6	Disclosure in conversation of Secret Session information by E. Granville.
1945–6	Posters threatening publication of names of M.P.s voting for bread rationing.

1946–7	Assault on P. Piratin in precincts of the House.
1946–7	Action by Civil Service Clerical Association calculated to influence W. Brown.
1946–7	G. Schofield and S. Dobson (Editor and Political Correspondent of *Evening News*): refusal to reveal source of information to Committee.
1946–7	Article by G. Allighan alleging disclosure to newspapers of information from party meetings.
1946–7	Disclosure of party meeting information by E. Walkden in return for payment.
1947–8	H. Dalton: Budget disclosure.
1947–8	The Chairman of Ways and Means (J. Milner): personal explanation that he acted professionally as a solicitor against a Member.
1947–8	Broadcast and interview in *Daily Mail* by C. Brogan alleging that Secret Session information would be given to Russia.
1948–9	Alleged misrepresentation by *Daily Worker* of Member's speech (R. Blackburn).
1950	J. MacManaway: election of a Member, being a clergyman of the Church of Ireland.
1951	Abuse of members not related to transactions in House (S. Silverman, I. Mikardo). Comment on B.B.C. 'Any Questions' programme on matter referred to Committee.
1951	Report in *Sutton Coldfield News* of speech by Lady Mellor criticising ruling by the Chair.
1951	Obstruction of J. Lewis by the police.
1952–3	Amendment of the law relating to the disability of some clergy from sitting and voting in the House of Commons.
1953	Article by Mrs P. Ford in *Sunday Express* (Mrs Braddock).
1953	*Daily Worker* article (M.P.s vote money into their own pockets).
1955	Action by Bishop against chaplain after communication with M.P.
1956	*Sunday Graphic* advocates telephone campaign against A. Lewis.
1956	*Sunday Express* article on M.P.s' petrol rationing allowances.
1956	*Evening News* cartoon on petrol rationing.
1956–7	G. Strauss: threat of libel action by the London Electricity Board, following letter from the Member to the Paymaster General.
1957	Comment on B.B.C. 'Any Questions' programme on matter referred to Committee: report of speech in *Romford Recorder* on petrol rationing.
1957–8	Order in Council directing that the Report of the Judicial Committee on a Question of Law concerning the Parliamentary Privilege Act 1770 be communicated to the House of Commons.
1957–8	G. Strauss: recommendations of the Committee arising out of the case involving the London Electricity Board.
1958–9	Report of an Inquiry into the methods adopted by the London Electricity Board for the disposal of scrap cable.
1959–60	C. Pannell: allegation of threat in a letter from C. Jordan.
1960–1	A. Wedgwood Benn: petition for redress of grievances regarding the disqualification of peers.
1963–4	Q. Hogg: complaint by G. Wigg concerning a speech at the Town Hall, Chatham, on 19 Mar 64.
1964–5	P. Duffy: complaint concerning speech at Saddleworth on 12 Feb 65 alleging drunkenness among Conservative Members.
1964–5	F. Allaun: complaint concerning letter addressed to Members and advocating racial and anti-semitic views.
1964–5	The Chancellor of the Exchequer: complaint by Sir R. Cary concerning passages of speech reported in the *Daily Telegraph* 5 Jul 65, on Members' business interests.
1966–7	G. Fitt: complaint concerning allegations of treachery in *Protestant Telegraph*.
1967–8	E. Hooson: complaint concerning allegations of treachery in interview published in *Town* magazine.
1967–8	W. Hannan: complaint concerning letter in the Scotsman by Mrs W. Ewing, M.P., reflecting on the conduct of members.
1967–8	A. Palmer: complaint concerning article about biological warfare published in the *Observer* from information allegedly supplied by T. Dalyell, M.P.
1968–9	Mrs R. Short: report in *Wolverhampton Press and Star* of a speech by Alderman Peter Farmer imputing partial conduct to a Member.
1968–9	Sir D. Glover: certain events attending to a visit of a Sub-Committee of the Select Committee on Education and Science to the University of Essex.
1968–9	R. Maxwell: article published in the *Sunday Times* reflecting on the conduct of a Member as Chairman of the Catering Sub-Committee of the Select Committee on House of Commons Services and as a member of that Committee.
1969–70	J. Mackintosh: matter reported in the *Times* which disclosed a breach of privilege.
1970–1	D. Steel: report in the *Sun* of alleged attempt by a trade union to influence actions of certain Members. (Report made in following Session.)
1970–1	A. Lewis: assault upon a servant of the House.
1970–1	W. Hamilton: publication by the *Daily Mail* of an article purporting to give an account of proceedings in a Select Committee not yet reported to the House. (Report made in following Session.)

1970–1	On a Motion moved by the Leader of the House. Rights of Members detained in prison.
1971–2	On a Motion moved by a member of the Government. Matter of the style and title of the Member for Berwick upon Tweed.
1972–3	R. Carter: serving of writ within the precincts of the House of Commons.
1973–4	A. Wedgwood Benn: alleged intimidation by Aims of Industry.
1973–4	J. Ashton: allegations about Members' financial interests.
1974–5	Eric Ogden: allegations made in Liverpool and West Derby on conduct of a member.
1974–5	G. Cunningham: words alleged to have been spoken by A. Scargill and other matters relating to N.U.M. conditions to be placed on M.P.s sponsored by them.
1974–5	J. Rooker: disclosure of evidence in the *Economist* from Select Committee on a Wealth Tax, before evidence reported to House.
1975–6	Sir B. Braine: reported accusation of bias in a Select Committee by National Abortion Campaign Steering Committee and threatened refusal to give evidence.
1975–6	J. Harper: possible contempt by National Coal Board in dismissing W. Grimshaw, a witness before the Select Committee on Nationalised Industries.
1976–7	M. Lipton: newspaper report alleging interference of the Totalisation Board on members.
1976–7	R. Adley: Press Association report of threat by the National Union of Public Employees to withdraw sponsorship from 6 members if they did not take certain action.
1977–8	F. Willey: *Daily Mail* and *Guardian* reports of proceedings of the Select Committee on Race Relations and Immigration.
1977–8	M. Foot: Publication of proceedings of the House and application of the *sub judice* rule (Colonel B.).
1978–9	C. Price: Court citation of *Hansard* without permission of House.
1980–1	D. Campbell-Savours: conversation about British Steel policy towards Workington.
1980–1	R. Parry: important letter from solicitors to M.P.
1982–3	T. Davis: behaviour of witnesses before Select Committee on Abortion (Amendment) Bill.
1982–3	R. Brown: comments by K. Livingstone and other GLC members.
1982–3	Sir A. Kershaw: leak of Foreign Affairs Committee report on Falklands.
1983–4	T. Jessel: threat by GLC Chairman to penalise constituencies of London members voting in a particular way.
1984–5	Sir E. Gardner: publication by the *Times* of Home Affairs Committee draft report on police special powers.
1985–6	Environment Committee: Leak of draft report of Evironment Committee on radio-active waste.
1986–7	Mr. Speaker: showing of Zircon film within the Palace of Westminster
1988–9	Clare Short: Alleged misconduct of a Parliamentary Agent.
1989–90	Education Committee: Premature disclosure of proceedings of Education Committee.
1989–90	Public Accounts Committee: Premature disclosure of proceedings of Public Accounts Committee.
1990–1	K. Barron: Guidelines issued by Yorkshire N.U.M.
1991–2	Health Committee: Premature disclosure of proceedings.
1992–3	T. Benn: Court interference with European Communities (Amendment) Bill.
1993–4	Mr. Speaker: members interests.

Statutory Instruments, 1947 (Statutory Rules and Orders, 1944–1947) (since 1972 a Joint Committee of both Houses)

Chairman

1944	Sir C. MacAndrew	1970	A. Booth	1987	R. Cryer
1950	G. Nicholson	1974	G. Page	1994	A. Bennett
1951	E. Fletcher	1979	R. Cryer		
1964	G. Page	1983	A. Bennett		

The Committee has had between 7 and 11 members, meeting fortnightly on about 16 days each session. The Chairman has always been an opposition member.

Terms of Reference: The original terms of 21 Jun 44 have been considerably enlarged by additional powers conferred in subsequent years.

In 1972 the procedure for considering Statutory Instruments was changed. The vast majority of instruments are now considered by a Joint Committee of Members of both Houses. However, the Statutory Instruments Committee still exists to consider instruments on which proceedings are subject to proceedings in the House of Commons only. The Joint Committee has power to consider every instrument which is laid before each House of Parliament and upon which proceedings may be or might have been taken in either House of Parliament in pursuance of an Act of Parliament. It also has power to draw the attention of the House of Commons to other Statutory Instruments on any of the following grounds:

(i) that they involve public money; (ii) that they are immune from challenge in the courts; (iii) that they have effect retrospectively; (iv) that there seems to have been an unjustifiable delay in publication of the S.I. or in laying it before Parliament; (v) that there seems to have been an unjustifiable delay in sending notification to the Speaker; (vi) that it appears to make unusual or unexpected use of the powers conferred by the Statute under which it is made; (vii) if elucidation is considered necessary; (viii) that the drafting appears to be defective.

Committee has powers to sit when it wishes, to report from time to time, to call for witnesses and to appoint sub-committees. It is obliged to give any government department an opportunity to explain an S.I. or other document before drawing it to the attention of the House.

Since 1890 the Statutory Rules and Orders, and since 1948 the S.I.s, have been published in annual volumes.

The distinction between 'General' and 'Local' follows that adopted between public Acts and local and personal Acts of Parliament. The documents registered as Statutory Instruments do not include rules of an executive character, or rules made by other bodies, e.g. local authorities, unless confirmed by a government department. Statutory Instruments also include some rules made by statutory authorities which are not government departments, e.g. the Law Society, General Dental Council, Rule Committee of Church Assembly.

Statutory Instruments

Year	Total	Annual General	Local
1900	995	174	821
1910	1,368	218	1,150
1920	2,475	916	1,559
1929	1,262	391	871
1940	2,222	1,626	596
1950	2,144	1,211	933
1960	2,495	733	1,762
1970	2,044	1,040	1,004
1980	2,051	1,197	854
1990	2,667		

Committee on Public Petitions, 1842–1974

Chairman (1945–1974)

1945	S. Viant	1966	D. Griffiths
1951	C. Lancaster	1970	J. Jennings
1964	G. Pargiter		

The Committee was appointed during most sessions since April 1842. It had 10 members, and a quorum of 3. It had power to send for persons, papers and records. It was abolished in 1974.

Terms of Reference: To clarify and prepare abstracts of Petitions 'in such form and manner as shall appear to them best suited to convey to the House all requisite information respecting their contents'. 'All Petitions presented to the House, with the exception of such as are deposited in the Private Bill Office' are referred to the Committee. The Committee was required in its reports to state the number of signatures to each petition. It had no power to consider the merits of the petitions.

Committee on Parliamentary Commission for Administration, 1967–

Chairman

1967	Sir H. Munro-Lucas-Tooth	1974	(Sir) A. Buck
1970	M. Stewart	1992	J. Pawsey
1974	C. Fletcher-Cooke		

The Committee has 10 members and a quorum of 4.

Terms of Reference: 'To examine the reports laid before this House by the Parliamentary Commissioner for Administration and Matters in Connection therewith.' The Committee has power to send for persons and papers.

Parliamentary Commissioner for Administration (Ombudsman)

The Parliamentary Commissioner for Administration is appointed by Letters Patent under the provisions of the Parliamentary Commissioner Act, 1967, which came into force on 7 Apr 67. His function is to investigate complaints referred to him by Members of the House of Commons from members of the public who claim to have sustained injustice in consequence of maladministration in connection with actions taken by or on behalf of Government Departments. (Other public bodies such as the nationalised industries and local government are outside his jurisdiction.)[1] Under the Act the Commissioner is required to report the results of each investigation to the Member who referred the complaint to him and also to make an annual report to each House of Parliament on the performance of his functions. In addition he may make other reports to Parliament with respect to those functions if he thinks fit; and he may make a special report to Parliament if he considers that injustice caused to the complainant by maladministration has not been or will not be remedied. The Commissioner may be removed from office only upon an Address from both Houses of Parliament.

Parliamentary Commissioners

1 Apr	67	Sir E. Compton	3 Jan	79	(Sir) C. Clothier
1 Apr	71	Sir A. Marre	1 Jan	85	A. Barrowclough
1 Apr	76	Sir I. Pugh	1 Jan	90	W. Reid

[1] Under the National Health Service (Scotland) Act 1972, and the National Health Service Reorganisation Act, 1973, provision was made for the appointment of Health Service Commissioners for Scotland, England and Wales. Sir A. Marre was appointed to these three posts with effect from 1 Oct 73, in addition to his post as Parliamentary Commissioner for Administration, and

Ombudsman Cases

Year	No. of cases disposed of during the year	Member informed case outside jurisdiction	Member informed case is discontinued	Investigation completed and result reported to Member
1967[1]	849	561	100	188
1968	1,181	727	80	374
1969	790	445	43	302
1970	651	362	30	259
1971	516	295	39	182
1972	596	318	17	261
1973	536	285	12	239
1974	653	374	27	252
1975	916	576	19	321
1976	863	505	29	329
1977	846	528		318
1978	1,305	927	35	343
1979	801	541	22	238
1980	927	686	16	225
1981	929	694	7	228
1982	784	574	8	202
1983	809	605	6	198
1984	850	658	9	183
1985	788	606	5	177
1986	719	549	2	168
1987	656	509	2	145
1988	657	529	8	120
1989	639	502	11	126
1990	724	535	12	177
1991	769	580	6	183
1992	851	661	6	190
1993	923	715	3	208

SOURCE: – Annual Reports of the Parliamentary Commissioner for Administration.

Public Accounts Commission 1984–

The Public Accounts Commission was set up by National Audit Act 1983. It is composed of nine members of the House of Commons of whom two–the Chairman of the Public Accounts Committee and the Leader of the House–are ex-officio. The remaining seven, none of whom may be Ministers of the Crown, are appointed by the House. The Commission was appointed to take office on 1 Jan 1984. The Act gave the Commission three main functions: to appoint an accounting officer for the National Audit Office; to appoint an auditor for the National Audit Office; and to examine the National Audit Office Estimates and lay them before the House, with such modifications as it thinks fit. In this last capacity, the Commission can examine all the expenses of the Office, including such things as accommodation, salaries of staff, superannuation provision.

Chairman

1984	(Sir) E. du Cann
1987	Sir P. Hordern

Select Committees since 1979

Fourteen Select Committees were appointed in 1979 'to examine the expenditure, administration and policy of the principle government departments ... and associated public bodies'. In Jan 1980 a Liaison Select Committee, comprising the chairman of the Committees (and some additional members) was appointed. Their membership varied between 9 and 11 until 1983 when all Committees except Scottish Affairs (13) were allotted 11 members. Only the Foreign Affairs, Home Affairs, and Treasury Committees were empowered to appoint a sub-committee.

Agriculture (9) (11)

1979	Sir W. Elliott
1983	J. Spence
1986	Sir R. Body
1987	(Sir) J. Wiggin

Defence (10) (11)

1979	Sir J. Langford-Holt
1981	C. Onslow
1982	Sir T. Kitson
1983	Sir H. Atkins
1987	M. Mates
1992	Sir N. Bonsor

Education, Science and Arts (9) (11)
(Education, 1992–)

1979	C. Price
1983	Sir W. Van Straubenzee
1987	T. Raison
1989	(Sir) M. Thornton

Employment (9) (11)

1979	J. Golding
1982	J. Craigen
1983	R. Leighton
1992	G. Janner

Energy (10) (11) 1981–92

1979	(Sir) I. Lloyd
1989	M. Clark

Environment (10) (11)

1979	B. Douglas-Mann
1981	R. Freeson
1983	Sir H. Rossi
1992	R. Jones

Foreign Affairs (11)

1979	Sir A. Kershaw
1987	D. Howell

Foreign Affairs Overseas Development Sub-committee (5)

1979	K. McNamara
1982	F. Hooley
1983	(not reconstituted)

Health

1991	N. Winterton
1992	Mrs M. Roe

Home Affairs (11)

1979	Sir G. Page
1981	Sir J. Eden
1983	Sir E. Gardner
1987	Sir J. Wheeler
1992	Sir I. Lawrence

Home Affairs Sub-committee on Race Relations and Immigration (5)

1979	J. Wheeler
1992	J. Greenway

National Heritage

1992	G. Kaufman

Northern Ireland

1994	Sir J. Kilfedder

Science and Technology

1992	Sir G. Shaw

Scottish Affairs (13)

1979	D. Dewar
1981	R. Hughes
1982	D. Lambie
	(In abeyance 1987–92)
1992	W. McKelvey

Social Services (9) (11)
(Social Security and Health 1988–1991)
Social Security 1991–)

1979	Mrs R. Short
1987	F. Field

Trade and Industry (11)
(Industry and Trade 1979–83)

1979	Sir D. Kaberry
1983	K. Warren
1992	R. Caborn

Transport (10) (11)

1979	T. Bradley
1983	H. Cowans
1985	G. Bagier
1987	D. Marshall
1992	R. Adley
1993	P. Channon

Treasury and Civil Service (11)

1979	E. du Cann
1983	T. Higgins
1992	J. Watts

Treasury and Civil Service Sub-committee (5)

1979	R. Sheldon
1981	J. Bray
1982	M. Meacher
1983	A. Mitchell
1987	G. Radice

Welsh Affairs (11)

1979	L. Abse
1981	D. Anderson
1983	G. Wardell

Payment of M.P.s

1912   M.P.s receive first salary; £400 per year paid to all members not receiving salaries as Ministers or officers of the House.

1913   £100 of M.P.s ' salaries made tax-exempt in respect of parliamentary expenses. This remained in force until 1954.

1924   M.P.s allowed free rail travel between London and their constituencies.

1931   Salary cut to £360 as an economy measure.

1934   Salary restored to £380 and then to £400.

1937   Salary increased to £600.

1946   Salary increased to £1,000 and salaries of £500 authorised for M.P.s who, as Ministers or Leaders of the Opposition, had an official salary of less than £5,000. Free travel was granted between M.P.s' homes and Westminster as well as to their constituencies.

1953   A sessional allowance of £2 per day introduced for every day (except Friday) on which the House sat: this was payable to all M.P.s including Ministers.

1957   The sessional allowance (usually amounting to about £280 p. a.) was replaced by an annual £750 to cover parliamentary expenses. The whole £1,750 drawn by ordinary M.P.s was subject to tax but M.P.s could claim as tax free any expenses up to £1,750 incurred in respect of parliamentary duties.

1964   Salary increased to £3,250 per year, following Lawrence Committee Report.

1965   Members' Pensions Act. First comprehensive pensions scheme introduced for M.P.s and dependants. Members contribute £150 per year and the Exchequer an amount equal to the aggregate of the Members' contributions. Members receive pensions from the age of 65 or on ceasing to be an M.P. if later, provided they have served for 10 years or more. The pension of £600 per year for 10 years' service increases to £900 after 15 years' service and by £24 for each further year thereafter.

1969   Secretarial allowance of up to £500 introduced. Members to have free telephone calls within the U.K.

1972   M.P.s' pay increased to £3,500 following Boyle Committee recommendations. Secretarial allowance increased to up to £1,000. An allowance of up to £750 for additional cost of living away from main residence and London members to receive a London supplement of £175 p. a. Travel allowances extended and a terminal grant equivalent to 3 months' salary established for M.P.s who lose their seats at a General Election.

1972   Parliamentary and Other Pensions Act. Existing pensions scheme revised. Minimum qualifying period reduced from 10 years to 4. M.P.s' benefits based on 1/60th of final salary for each year of reckonable service. Contributions to be 5% of salary. Early retirement option available from 60 onwards on an actuarially reduced pension.

1976   Pension scheme amended to provide for pensions to be based on a notional pensionable salary of £8,000.

1977   M.P.s' pay increased to £6, 270. Secretarial allowance (also research assistance and general office expenses) increased to up to £3,687. London supplement increased to £385 p. a. Travel allowances further extended and allowance introduced for overnight stays away from home of up to £1,814.

1983   M.P.s pay linked to Civil Service rates. Secretarial allowance raised to £12,000 and other allowances increased.

1992   Following a Top Salaries Review Board enquiry into office costs, the House voted for a substantial increase in the allowance for Office, Research and Secretarial Costs. MPs with constituencies in Inner London are entitled to a payment of £1,222 a year; MPs with constituencies outside London are entitled to claim up to £10,958 a year for staying overnight away from home.

	M.P.s' basic pay	Office costs		M.P.s' basic pay	Office costs
1911	£400		1981	£13,950	£8,480
1931	£360		1982	£14,510	£8,820
1934	£380		1983	£15,308	£11,364
1935	£400		1984	£16,106	£12,437
1937	£600		1985	£16,904	£13,211
1954	£1,250		1986	£17,702	£20,140
1964	£3,250		1987	£18,500	£21,302
1969	£3,250	£500	1988	£22,548	£22,588
1972	£4,500	£1,000	1989	£24,107	£24,903
1974	£4,500	£1,750	1990	£26,701	£27,166
1975	£5,750	£3,200	1991	£28,970	£28,986
1976	£5,750	£3,512	1992	£30,854	£39,960
1977	£6,270	£3,687	1993	£30,854	£40,380
1978	£6,897	£4,200	1994	£31,687	
1979	£9,450	£4,600	1995	£32,538	
1980	£11,750	£8,000			

See p. 49 for Ministers' pay, and reduced parliamentary salaries payable to Ministers and other paid office-holders.

Seats Forfeited

These members left or were expelled from the House before or after their conviction and imprisonment on criminal charges.

2 Mar	03	A. Lynch	Nat.	Galway
1 Aug	22	H. Bottomley	Ind.	Hackney South
31 Jul	41	Sir P. Latham	Con.	Scarborough & Whitby
6 Dec	54	P. Baker	Con.	S. Norfolk
27 Aug	76	J. Stonehouse	Lab.	(Ind) Walsall South

These members forfeited their seats as a result of being adjudged bankrupt.

17 Sep	03	P. McHugh	Nat.	N. Leitrim (re-elected)
15 Jul	09	N. Murphy	Nat.	S. Kilkenny
1 Oct	28	C. Homan	Con.	Ashton under Lyne

In addition, H. Bottomley resigned his seat 16 May 12 after filing his bankruptcy petition.

These members forfeited their seats when it transpired that they held a government contract. All but one were re-elected in the ensuing by-election.

2 Feb	04	A. Gibbs	City of London (re-elected)
2 Feb	04	V. Gibbs	St Albans (defeated)
21 Apr	12	Sir S. Samuel	Whitechapel (re-elected)
10 Feb	25	W. Preston	Walsall (re-elected)

In Nov 1924, J. Astor (Dover) forfeited his seat for inadvertently voting before taking the oath. He was re-elected unopposed in the ensuing by-election.

These members gave up their seats when under censure for some aspect of their parliamentary conduct.

26 Feb	31	T. Mardy Jones	Lab.	Pontypridd (*abuse of travel voucher*)
11 Jun	36	J. Thomas	Nat.Lab.	Derby (*Budget leak*)
11 Jun	36	Sir A. Butt	Con.	Balham & Tooting (*Budget leak*)
30 Oct	47	G. Allighan	Lab.	Gravesend (*expelled by a vote of 187–75 for breach of privilege*)
3 Feb	49	J. Belcher	Lab.	Sowerby (*following Lynskey Tribunal*)
5 Jun	63	J. Profumo	Con.	Stratford-on-Avon (*lying to the House*)
25 Jul	77	J. Cordle	Con.	Bournemouth E. (*Poulson affair*)

On 16 Aug 1916 C. Leach (Colne Valley) was deprived of his seat under the Lunacy (Vacating of Seats) Act 1886.

A. Ramsay, Con. Peebles and Southern, remained an M.P. from 1940 to 1945 although, being detained under Regulation 18B of the Defence of the Realm Act until Dec 1944, he was unable to sit from May 40 to Dec 44.

Various other members have resigned their seats while under the shadow of some minor private or public scandal but in almost every case it seems that they could well have remained as members had they chosen to do so. For a list of successful election petitions, which led to the original result being disallowed by the courts see p. 243.

House of Lords

Lord Chairmen of Committees

(Deputy Speaker of the House of Lords. The Lord Chancellor (see p. 52) acts as Speaker.)

1889	E of Morley	1944	Ld Stanmore	1965	E of Listowel
1905	4th E of Onslow	1944	Ld Stanmore	1977	Ld Aberdare
1911	E of Donoughmore	1946	E of Drogheda	1992	Ld Ampthill
1931	5th E of Onslow	1957	Ld Merthyr		

Principal Deputy Chairman of Committees

(Salaried Chairman of Select Committee on European Communities)

1974	Ld Diamond	1983	Lady Llewelyn-Davies of Hastoe
1974	Lady Tweedsmuir of Belhelvie	1986	Lady Serota
1977	Ld Greenwood of Rossendale	1992	Ld Boston of Faversham
1980	Lady White		

Officers of the House of Lords

Clerk of the Parliaments

1885	(Sir) H. Graham	1949	(Sir) R. Overbury	1974	(Sir) P. Henderson
1917	Sir A. Thring	1953	(Sir) F. Lascelles	1983	(Sir) J. Sainty
1930	Sir E. Alderson	1959	(Sir) V. Goodman	1990	M. Wheeler-Booth
1934	(Sir) H. Badeley	1963	(Sir) D. Stephens		

Librarian

1897	A. Strong	1922	C. Clay	1991	D. Jones
1904	E. Gosse	1956	C. Dobson		
1914	A. Butler	1977	R. Morgan		

SOURCES. – *Dod's Parliamentary Companion; Whitaker's Almanack; Hansard.*

Composition of the House of Lords
(including minors)

Year	Duke[a]	Marq	Earl	Vt.	Baron	Life Peer[b]	Law Ld[c]	Rep. Peers Sc.[d]	Ir.	Bishops	Total
1901	26	22	123	32	314	..	4	16	28	26	591
1910	25	23	124	42	334	..	4	16	28	26	622
1920	26	29	130	64	393	..	6	16	27	26	716
1930	24	26	134	73	428	..	7	16	18	26	753
1939	24	28	139	84	456	..	7	16	13	26	785
1950	23	30	137	95	503	..	11	16	6	26	847
1960	25	30	132	111	531	31	8	16	1	26	908
1970	29	30	163	110	530	163	11	..	..	26	1,057
1980	28	29	157	105	477	330	19	..	..	26	1,171
1990	27	27	156	102	471	358	19	..	..	26	1,186

[a] Including Peers of the Blood Royal.
[b] Created by the Life Peerages Act, 1958.
[c] Life Peers under the Appellate Jurisdiction Acts.
[d] Scottish and Irish peers sitting by virtue of UK title are listed under the latter. In 1963 all Scottish peers became entitled to sit and are listed under their senior title.

SOURCES. – *Constitutional Year Books, 1900–39; Dod's Parliamentary Companion, 1940–.*

Creation of Peerages

Administration[a]		New Hereditary Creations[a]	Life Peers		Advanced in Rank	Ministry		Average Annual Creations[b]
			Law	Other		Total	Yrs.	
Salisbury	1895–02	42	2	..	n.a.	44	7	6
Balfour	1902–05	17	1	..	5	23	3½	5
Cambell-Bannerman	1905–08	20	1	..	..	21	2⅔	9
Asquith	1908–15	61	6	..	13	80	7	9
Asquith	1915–16	17	..	..	2	19	1½	11
Lloyd George	1916–22	90	1	..	25	116	5¾	16
Bonar Law	1922–23	3	..	..	..	3	½	6
Baldwin	1923–24	7	1	..	1	9	⅔	10
MacDonald	1924	4	..	..	1	5	¾	5
Baldwin	1924–29	37	5	..	10	52	4½	18
MacDonald	1929–31	18	2	..	..	20	2⅔	8
MacDonald	1931–35	43	1	..	6	50	3¾	12
Baldwin	1935–37	27	2	..	5	34	2	14
Chamberlain	1937–40	18	2	..	4	24	3	6
Churchill	1940–45	60	2	..	9	71	5¾	11
Attlee	1945–51	75	11	..	8	94	6¾	10
Churchill	1951–55	31	2	..	6	39	3½	9
Eden	1955–57	19	..	..	3	22	1¾	11
Macmillan	1957–63	42	9	47	6	104	6	7
Douglas–Home	1963–64	14	1	16	1	32	1	30
Wilson	1964–70	6	2	152	1	161	5¾	29
Heath	1970–74	..	4	30	..	34	3½	9
Wilson	1974–76	..	3	81	..	84	2	40
Callaghan	1976–79	..	2	58	..	60	3	20
Thatcher	1979–90	4	11	193	..	208	11½	18
Major[c]	1990–93	..	4	88	..	92	3	31

[a] these figures can be misleading as dissolution honours created by an outgoing ministry fall , in fact, into the following ministry. E.g., of H. Wilson's new creations 6 were those of Sir A. Douglas-Home.
[b] Excluding the creation of Law Lords and advancements in rank.
[c] Up to and including 1994 New Year honours.

See p. 304 for Political Honours Scrutiny Committee.

Party Organisation in the House of Lords

From the early 1920s Conservative peers met weekly in an Association of Independent Unionist Peers, much on the lines of the 1922 Committee. In 1982 it was renamed the Association of Conservative Peers. From 1945 to 1974 Liberal peers held their weekly meetings jointly with Liberal M.P.s. After 1974 they held their own weekly meetings, but Liberal Peers who were members of the Liberal 'shadow administration' formed in 1977 met Liberal M.P.s on a regular basis. Labour peers are entitled to attend the meetings of the Parliamentary Labour Party, but since the 1930s they have also had their own weekly meetings.

Party Strengths in the House of Lords

Year		Con.	Lib.U.	Lib.	Lab.	Irish Nat.	Not stated	Minors	Total
1 Dec	00	354	111	69	..	1	39	15	589
31 Mar	16	360	107	93	..	1	51	11	623
10 Feb	20	491	..	130	1	1	67	26	716
31 Dec	30	489	..	79	17	..	140	27	753
31 Oct	38	519	23	55	13	..	141	24	785

SOURCE. – *Constitutional Year Book.*

Vacher's *Parliamentary Companion,* which has always been more sparing in giving party labels, suggests that in 1945 there were 400 Conservatives, 63 Liberals and 16 Labour among the 769 adult peers. For Aug 1955 the figures were Conservative 507, Liberal 42 and Labour 55 (out of 855). According to the House of Lords Information Office, the state of the parties in the House of Lords on 1 Jan 94 was Conservative 475, Liberal Democrat 56, Labour 115 and Association of Cross-bench peers 275. More exhaustive information on party membership was provided by the 1968 White Paper on House of Lords Reform.

Attendance at the House of Lords by Party
(for the period 31 Oct 67 to 1 Aug 68)

	Peers who attended more than 33% ('working House')			Peers who attended more than 5% but less than 33%			Peers who attended up to 5%			Peers who do not attend[a]			Total		
	C	S	Total	C	S	Total	C	S	Total	C	S	Total	C	S	Total
Lab.	81	14	95	8	5	13	4	1	5	2	1	3	95	21	116
Con.	38	87	125	24	86	110	9	70	79	6	31	37	77	274	351
Lib.	8	11	19	2	6	8	2	8	10	1	3	4	13	28	41
Other	26	26	52	61	24	85	22	56	78	32	307	339	141	413	554
Total	163	138	291	95	121	216	37	135	172	41	342	383	326	736	1,062

C = created peers. S = peers by succession. Attendance at Committees of the House (other than the Appellate Committee) has been taken into account.

[a] Including 192 peers with leave of absence; 81 peers without writ of summons.

SOURCE: – *House of Lords Reform* (Cmnd. 3799/ 1968).

House of Lords Sittings and Business

	Sessions and Sittings		Membership and Attendance				Work of the House					
Session[a]	Sittings	Average sitting	Total membership[b]	Without writ of summons[bc]	On leave of absence[b]	Average attendance	Public bills first in Lords	Gov. bills first in Lords	Divisions	Starred questions	Written questions	Unstarred (debatable questions)
L1955–56	136	3hrs 34m.	876	78	n.a.	104	20	9	26	203	82	11
1956–57	103	3hrs 54m.	871	73	n.a.	112	20	7	32	209	55	9
1957–58	103	3hrs 50m.	885	70	n.a.	124	22	8	19	184	28	6
1958–59	109	4hrs 15m.	e	e	232	134	25	g	26	244	32	11
1959–60	113	3hrs 59m.	907	76	192	136	17	9	16	264	48	12
1960–61	125	4hrs 48m.	918	57	193	142	11	7	48	290	73	12
1961–62	115	4hrs 44m.	932	74	203	143	17	8	47	275	72	12
1962–63	127	5hrs 30m.	965	100	202	140	19	5	158	297	84	9
1963–64	110	4hrs 51m.	976	85	207	151	23	11	25	340	77	23
1964–65	124	4hrs 47m.	1,018	91	186	194	34	6	34	370	73	37
S1965–66	50	5hrs 16m.	1,020	94	195	191	13	7	16	151	33	12
L1966–67	191	5hrs 17m.	1,045	99	182	241	48	18	BS	660	96	61
1967–68	139	5hrs 47m.	1,061.	83	190	225	44	14	72	437	92	28
1968–69	109	5hrs 03m.	1,064	91	193	235	28	9	47	363	92	35
S1969–70	83	4hrs 47m.	1,062	93	199	225	28	12	18	287	108	33
L1970–71	153	6hrs 19m.	1,078	101	171	264	37	11	196	511	283	37
1971–72	141	5hrs 46m.	1,073	98	169	249	40	15	171	494	315	26
1972–73	128	5hrs 38m.	1,080	101	173	240	32	13	73	460	281	31
S1973–74	45	5hrs 51m.	1,079	105	193	245	22	7	19	139	92	5
S1974	64	5hrs 28m.	1,108	100	171	246	31	13	21	192	171	23
1974–75	162	5hrs 44m.	1,121	110	170	262	49	20	119	560	350	35
1975–76	155	6hrs 15m.	1,139	95	143	275	51	27	146	553	517	41
1976–77	105	5hrs 41m.	1,140	90	135	2B1	40	11	45	385	380	36
1977–78	126	5hrs 51m.	1,154	88	128	282	30	22	96	439	544	46
S1978–79	59	5hrs 51m.	1,155	88	130	292	38	27	21	217	432	23
1979–80	206	6hrs 9m.	1,171	85	172	290	50	11	303	765	1277	68
1980–81	143	6hrs 43m.	1,179	87	160	296	48	12	184	537	857	31
1981–82	147	6hrs 20m.	1,174	91	150	284	42	10	146	531	1098	50

S1982–83	94	6hrs 35m.	1,181	97	143	294	40	11	89	357	619	36
L1983–84	178	7hrs 13m.	1,183	99	153	321	48	14	237	691	1350	60
1984–85	151	6hrs 47m.	1,174	95	142	320	40	12	145	573	1142	45
1985–86	165	7hrs 21m.	1,171	89	135	317	34	16	250	631	1182	44
S1986–87	84	6hrs 38m.	1,185	89	133	325	26	14	80	317	622	24
L1987–88	192	7hrs 6m.	1,185	84	169	333	21	9	279	742	1405	51
1988–89	153	7hrs 2m.	1,183	93	149	316	24	12	189	572	1202	35
1989–90	147	7hrs 18m.	1,186	86	139	318	23	8	186	551	1204	31
1990–91	137	6hrs 28m.	1,196	78	136	324	26	10	104	531	1304	42
S1991–92	74	7hrs 1m.	1,196	80	133	337	28	5	83	276	664	22
L1992–93	194	6hrs 52m.	1,208	85	82	379	39	12	165	739	2567	90

[a] S beside the date of a session indicates a shortened session drawn to an early conclusion by a General Election. L shows a prolonged session usually following an election.
[b] Figures at the end of the session in question.
[c] Includes minors and bankrupts.
[d] Excludes Consolidation Bills, on average an extra 7 per session.
[e] Records not kept.

SOURCE. – House of Lords Information Office.

Critical Votes in the House of Lords since 1900

The following represent outstanding occasions when the House of Lords has set itself against the House of Commons. In cases of repeated defiance on the same issue the final vote alone is normally recorded. One notable instance of the Lords yielding to the Commons (10 Aug 11) is also included.

27 Nov 08	272–96	2nd Reading refused for Licensing Bill.
30 Nov 09	350–75	2nd Reading refused for Finance Bill.
10 Aug 11	131–114	3rd Reading for Parliament Bill.
30 Jan 13	326–69	2nd Reading refused for Government of Ireland Bill (refusal repeated 15 Jul 13 by 302–64).
13 Feb 13	251–51	2nd Reading refused for Established Church (Wales) Bill (refusal repeated 22 Jul 13 by 243–48).
24 Jul 13	166–42	2nd Reading refused For Plural Voting Bill (refusal repeated 15 Jul 14 by 119–49).
22 Jan 18	131–42	P. R. Amendment to Representation of the People Bill carried.
3 Feb 30	156–42	Insistence on one year limit to Unemployment Act.
24 Jun 30	208–13	Insistence on 'quota' amendment to Coal Mines Bill.
15 Jul 30	168–36	Insistence on 'spreadover' amendment to Coal Mines Bill.
18 Feb 31	168–22	2nd Reading refused for Education (School Attendance) Bill.
2 Jul 31	80–29	Amendment restricting Alt. Vote in Representation of the People Bill carried.
2 Jun 48	181–28	Capital punishment amendment to Criminal Justice Bill rejected.
8 Jun 48	177–81	2nd Reading refused for Parliament Bill (refusal repeated 23 Sep 48 by 204–34 and 29 Nov 49 by 110–37).
8 Jun 49	103–29	Insistence on amendment delaying Vesting Day under Iron and Steel Act (compromise later reached and Royal Assent to Act 16 Dec 49).
10 Jul 56	238–95	2nd Reading refused for Death Penalty (Abolition) Bill.
18 Jun 68	193–184	Rhodesia Sanctions Order rejected (but passed without division 18 Jul 68).
16 Oct 69	229–78	Insistence on Amendments to Bill delaying redistribution of seats.
11 Nov 75	186–86	Insistence on Amendments to Trade Union and Labour Relations Bill that barred Closed Shop in Journalism.
22 Oct 76	147–71	3rd Reading refused for British Transport Docks (Felixstowe) Bill, a Private Bill designed to bring Felixstowe Harbour into public ownership.
22 Nov 76	197–90	Insistence on Amendments to Aircraft and Shipbuilding Bill that excluded ship-repairing.
13 Mar 80	216–112	Clause of the Education (No. 2) Bill to give local authorities power to charge for home-to-school transport rejected.
9 Apr 84	235–153	Amendment to 2nd Reading of Rates Bill (stating that it would 'result in damaging constitutional changes in the relationship between central and local government', etc.) rejected.
11 Jun 84	238–217	Amendment to 2nd Reading of Local Government (Interim Provisions Bill (stating that the Bill was a 'dangerous precedent', etc.) rejected.
28 Jun 84	191–143	Amendment carried to insert a clause postponing the coming into force of the Local Government (Interim Provisions) Bill until the passing of the main Act to abolish the GLC and Metropolitan County Councils.
7 May 85	152–135	Amendment to Local Government Bill preserving some environmental powers of GLC. This was the first of four amendments to the Bill carried against the Government.
23 May 88	317–184	Amendment to Local Government Finance Bill on poll tax carried against the Government.
8 Nov 88	257–207	Lords did not insist on earlier amendment on charges for eye-testing rejected by the commons.
18 Apr 91	177–79	Amendment to Criminal Justic Bill on mandatory life sentence for murder carried against Government.

Main Landmarks in the Reform of the House of Lords, 1900–

In 1900 the legislative powers of the two Houses were in theory equal, with the exception of the privileges of the House of Commons in relation to financial measures.

1908   *Rosebery Committee's Report.* The House approved the following principal recommendations:
(1) That a strong and efficient second Chamber was necessary for the balance of Parliament;
(2) That this objective should be achieved by the reform and reconstitution of the House of Lords;
(3) That, as a necessary preliminary to reform, it should be accepted that the possession of a peerage should no longer of itself entail the right to sit and vote in the House.
No action was taken to implement these recommendations.

1911   *Parliament Act.* Provided that
(1) Bills certified by the Speaker of the House of Commons as Money Bills were to receive the Royal Assent one month after being sent to the House of Lords, even without the consent of the latter House; and
(2) any other Public Bill (except one for extending the life of a Parliament) passed by the House of Commons in three successive Sessions and rejected by the House of Lords was nevertheless to receive the Royal Assent, provided that 2 years had elapsed between the second reading in the first session and the third reading in the third session of the House of Commons.

1918   *Bryce Report.* Recommended that the differences between the 2 Houses should be settled by some means of joint consultation. Proposed that the House should consist of two elements. (i) 246 members elected by members of the House of Commons arranged in geographical areas and voting by Proportional Representation with a single transferable vote. (ii) 80 peers to be elected for a period of 12 years by a joint Committee of both Houses of Parliament on which all parties should be represented. No action was taken to implement this Report.

1922   Government proposed House of Lords of 350 members consisting of some 'elected either directly or indirectly from the outside', hereditary peers elected by their order, and members nominated by the Crown. Resolutions criticised for vagueness, debate adjourned and not renewed.

1927   Further proposals introduced by government but later dropped.

1929   Vt Elibank's Life Peers Bill withdrawn before Second Reading.

1934   M of Salisbury's Parliament (Reform) Bill read a second time but not proceeded with in committee.

1935   Ld Rockley's Life Peers Bill read a second time but not proceeded with in committee.

1946   *Travelling Expenses.* Agreed that regular attenders at the House of Lords should be reimbursed for their travelling expenses. In practice made to apply to peers attending at least one-third of the sittings of the House.

1948   *Agreed Statement of Party Leaders.* A statement of nine principles agreed to but not acted upon. The most important of these were:
(1) The second Chamber should be complementary to and not a rival to the lower House, and
(2) The revised constitution of the House of Lords should be such as to secure as far as practicable that a permanent majority was not assured for any one political party.

1948   *Criminal Justice Act.* Privileges of Peers in Criminal Proceedings abolished.

1949   *Parliament Act.* Reduced the delaying powers of the House to two sessions and one year.

1956   *Swinton Committee Report.* Recommended provision of official Leave of Absence. This was put into effect in 1958. There are normally about 200 members of the House who have Leave of Absence at any one time.

1957   *Expenses.* Provision made for Peers to claim a maximum of three guineas a day for expenses incurred in attendance at the House. This was in addition to travelling expenses and claims were not subject to any minimum number of attendances.

1958   *Life Peerages Act.* Provided for the creation by the Sovereign, on the advice of the Prime Minister, of Life Peers and Peeresses. Women were thus for the first time enabled to become Members of the House of Lords. One of the objectives of this Act was to provide more balance of parliamentary representation in the House of Lords. This is achieved by the convention enabling recommendations for Life Peerages made by Opposition party leaders to be conveyed to the Queen through the agency of the Prime Minister.

1963   *Peerage Act.* Provided for
(1) the option for Peers to disclaim within one year (one month in the case of Members of the House of Commons) their peerages for life without such a disclaimer affecting the subsequent devolution of the peerage; [1]
(2) the abolition of elections for Scottish Representative Peers and the admission of all Scottish Peers to membership of the House;
(3) the removal from Irish Peers of certain disabilities relating to their voting and candidature at parliamentary elections;
(4) the admission of all female holders of hereditary peerages to membership of the House of Lords.

1964   *Expenses.* Provision made for increasing the maximum expenses to which Peers were entitled from three guineas to four-and-a-half guineas per day (increased to £6 10s. in 1969, to £8.50 in 1972, and to £13.50 in 1977).

1967   The Government announced their intention of introducing legislation to reform the House of Lords and an all-party committee was established.

1968   Formal discussions were broken off after the Lords' rejection of the Southern Rhodesia Sanctions order in June and the government introduced their own Parliament (No. 2) Bill dealing with both powers and composition.

1969   The Bill was dropped in April. Though the Peers themselves approved of the proposals, it met with strong opposition in the House of Commons from sections of both the Labour and Conservative parties.

1977   At the Labour Party Conference a motion was carried by 6,248,000 votes to 91,000 for the 'total abolition of the House of Lords and the reform of Parliament into an efficient single-chamber legislating body without delay'.

[1] These peers have in fact disclaimed their titles:

1963	Vt Stansgate (A. Wedgwood Benn)
	Ld Altrincham (J. Grigg)
	Ld Hailsham (Q. Hogg)
	E of Home (Sir A. Douglas -Home)
1964	Ld Southampton (E. Fitzroy) (d. 1989 His son resumed the title)
	Ld Monkswell (W. Collier (d. 1980 His son resumed the title)
	Ld Beaverbrook (M. Aitken (d. 1985 His son resumed the title)
	E of Sandwich (V. Montagu)
1966	Ld Fraser of Allander (Sir H. Fraser d.1987; peerage extinct)
1970	E of Durham (A. Lambton)
1971	Ld Sanderson of Ayot (A. Sanderson)
1972	Ld Reith (C. Reith)
1973	Ld Silkin (A. Silkin)
1975	Ld Archibald (G. Archibald)
1977	Ld Merthyr (T. Lewis)

SOURCES. – 1908 (H.L. 234), *Select Committee Report on the House of Lords*; Cd. 9038/ 1918, *The Reform of the Second Chamber* (Conference: Vt Bryce); Cmd. 7380/ 1948, *Report of the Inner Party Conference on the Parliament Bill*; H.M.S.O. (24 Jan 56), *Report of the Select Committee on the Power of the House in Relation to the Attendance of its Members*; Cmnd.3779/ 1968, *House of Lords Reform*; P. A. Bromhead, *The House of Lords and Contemporary Politics, 1911–1957* (1958); Sir I. Jennings, *Parliament* (2nd ed., 1957); *10th Report of the House of Lords Select Committee on Procedure* (Aug 1971); J. Morgan, *The House of Lords and the Labour Government, 1964–70* (1975); D. Shell, *The House of Lords (1991).*

IV

ELECTIONS

General Election Statistics

It is impossible to present election statistics in any finally authoritative way. British statutes make no acknowledgement of the existence of political parties, and in most general elections the precise allegiance of at least a few of the candidates has been in doubt. This, far more than arithmetic error, explains the discrepancies between the figures provided in various works of reference. Such discrepancies, however, are seldom on a serious scale (except, perhaps, for 1918). Election figures suffer much more from being inherently confusing than from being inaccurately reported. The complications that arise from unopposed returns, from plural voting, from two-member seats, and, above all, from variations in the number of candidates put up by each party are the really serious hazards in psephological interpretation. In the figures which follow an attempt is made to allow for these factors by a column which shows the average vote won by each opposed candidate (with the vote in two-member seats halved, and with University seats excluded). This still gives a distorted picture, especially when, as in 1900 or 1931, there were many unopposed candidates or when, as in 1929, 1931, or 1950, there was a sharp change in the number of Liberals standing; in 1918 the situation was so complicated that any such statistics are omitted, as they are likely to confuse more than to clarify; for other elections they should be regarded as corrective supplements to the cruder percentages in the previous column rather than as substitutes for them. The turn-out percentages are modified to allow for the distorting effect of the two-member seats which existed up to 1950. To simplify classification, some arbitrary decisions have been made. Before 1918 candidates have been classified as Conservative, Liberal, or Irish Nationalist, even if their designation had a prefix such as Tariff Reform or Independent, but only officially sponsored candidates are classed as Labour. From 1918 onwards candidates not officially recognised by their party have been classified with 'Others' (except that in 1935 Ind. Lib. are placed with Lib.). Liberal Unionists have been listed as Conservatives throughout. Liberal National, National Labour, and National candidates are listed with Conservatives except in 1931.

General Election Results, 1900–1992

	Total Votes	MPs Elected	Candidates	Unopposed Returns	% Share of Total Vote	Vote per Opposed Candidate
1900. 28 Sept–24 Oct						
Conservative	1,797,444	402	579	163	51.1	52.5
Liberal	1,568,141	184	406	22	44.6	48.2
Labour	63,304	2	15	..	1.8	26.6
Irish Nat.	90,076	82	100	58	2.5	80.0
Others	544	..	2	..	0.0	2.2
Elec. 6,730,935	3,519,509	670	1,102	243	100.0	..
Turnout 74.6%						

	Total Votes	MPs Elected	Candidates	Unopposed Returns	% Share of Total Vote	Vote per Opposed Candidate
1906. 12 Jan–7 Feb						
Conservative	2,451,454	157	574	13	43.6	44.1
Liberal	2,757,883	400	539	27	49.0	52.6
Labour	329,748	30	51	..	5.9	39.9
Irish Nat.	35,031	83	87	74	0.6	63.1
Others	52,387	..	22	..	0.9	18.8
Elec. 7,264,608 Turnout 82.6%	5,626,503	670	1,273	114	100.0	..
1910. 14 Jan–9 Feb						
Conservative	3,127,887	273	600	19	46.9	47.5
Liberal	2,880,581	275	516	1	43.2	49.2
Labour	505,657	40	78	..	7.6	38.4
Irish Nat.	124,586	82	104	55	1.9	77.7
Others	28,693	..	17	..	0.4	15.4
Elec. 7,694,741 Turnout 86.6%	6,667,404	670	1,315	75	100.0	..
1910. 2–19 Dec						
Conservative	2,420,566	272	550	72	46.3	47.9
Liberal	2,295,888	272	467	35	43.9	49.5
Labour	371,772	42	56	3	7.1	42.8
Irish Nat.	131,375	84	106	53	2.5	81.9
Others	8,768	..	11	..	0.2	9.1
Elec. 7,709,981 Turnout 81.1%	5,228,369	670	1,190	163	100.0	..
1918. Sat., 14 Dec[1]						
Coalition Unionist	3,504,198	335	374	42	32.6	
Coalition Lib.	1,455,640	133	158	27	13.5	
Coalition Lab.	161,521	10	18	..	1.5	
(Coalition)	(5,121,359)	(478)	(550)	(69)	(47.6)	
Conservative	370,375	23	37	..	3.4	
Irish Unionist	292,722	25	38	..	2.7	
Liberal	1,298,808	28	253	..	12.1	
Labour	2,385,472	63	388	12	22.2	
Irish Nat.	238,477	7	60	1	2.2	
Sinn Fein	486,867	73	102	25	4.5	
Others	572,503	10	197	..	5.3	
Elec.21,392,322 Turnout 58.9%	10,766,583	707	1,625	107	100.0	

[1] Result announced 28 Dec 1918.

	Total Votes	MPs Elected	Candidates	Unopposed Returns	% Share of Total Vote	Vote per Opposed Candidate
1922. Wed., 15 Nov						
Conservative	5,500,382	345	483	42	38.2	48.6
National Lib.	1,673,240	62	162	5	11.6	39.3
Liberal	2,516,287	54	328	5	17.5	30.9
Labour	4,241,383	142	411	4	29.5	40.0
Others	462,340	12	59	1	3.2	28.3
Elec. 21,127,663	14,393,632	615	1,443	57	100.0	..
Turnout 71.3%						
1923. Thu., 6 Dec						
Conservative	5,538,824	258	540	35	38.1	42.6
Liberal	4,311,147	159	453	11	29.6	37.8
Labour	4,438,508	191	422	3	30.5	41.0
Others	260,042	7	31	1	1.8	27.6
Elec.21,281,232	14,548,521	615	1,446	50	100.0	..
Turnout 70.8%						
1924. Wed., 29 Oct						
Conservative	8,039,598	419	552	16	48.3	51.9
Liberal	2,928,747	40	340	6	17.6	30.9
Labour	5,489,077	151	512	9	33.0	38.2
Communist	55,346	1	8	..	0.3	25.0
Others	126,511	4	16	1	0.8	29.1
Elec. 21,731,320	16,639,279	615	1,428	32	100.0	..
Turnout 76.6%						
1929. Thu., 30 May						
Conservative	8,656,473	260	590	4	38.2	39.4
Liberal	5,308,510	59	513	..	23.4	27.7
Labour	8,389,512	288	571	..	37.1	39.3
Communist	50,614	..	25	..	0.3	5.3
Others	243,266	8	31	3	1.0	21.2
Elec. 28,850,870	22,648,375	615	1,730	7	100.0	..
Turnout 76.1 %						
1931. Tue., 27 Oct						
Conservative	11,978,745	473	523	56	55.2}	
Nat. Labour	341,370	13	20	..	1.6}	62.9
Liberal Nat.	809,302	35	41	..	3.7}	
Liberal	1,403,102	33	112	5	6.5	28.8
(Nat.Govt.)	(14,532,519)	(554)	(696)	(61)	(67.0)	..
Ind.Liberal	106,106	4	7	..	0.5	35.8
Labour	6,649,630	52	515	6	30.6	33.0
Communist	74,824	..	26	..	0.3	7.5
New Party	36,377	..	24	..	0.2	3.9
Others	256,917	5	24	..	1.2	21.9
Elec. 29,960,071	21,656,373	615	1,292	67	100.0	..
Turnout 76.3%						

	Total Votes	MPs Elected	Candidates	Unopposed Returns	% Share of Total Vote	Vote per Opposed Candidate
1935. Thu., 14 Nov						
Conservative	11,810,158	432	585	26	53.7	54.8
Liberal	1,422,116	20	161	..	6.4	23.9
Labour	8,325,491	154	552	13	37.9	40.3
Ind.Lab.Party	139,577	4	17	..	0.7	22.2
Communist	27,117	1	2	..	0.1	38.0
Others	272,595	4	31	1	1.2	21.3
Elec. 31,379,050	21,997,054	615	1,348	40	100.0	..
Turnout 71.2%						
1945. Thu., 5 Jul[1]						
Conservative	9,988,306	213	624	1	39.8	40.1
Liberal	2,248,226	12	306	..	9.0	18.6
Labour	11,995,152	393	604	2	47.8	50.4
Communist	102,780	2	21	..	0.4	12.7
Common Wealth	110,634	1	23	..	0.4	12.6
Others	640,880	19	104	..	2.0	15.4
Elec. 33,240,391	25,085,978	640	1,682	3	100.0	..
Turnout 72.7%						
1950. Thu., 23 Feb						
Conservative	12,502,567	298	620	2	43.5	43.7
Liberal	2,621,548	9	475	..	9.1	11.8
Labour	13,266,592	315	617	..	46.1	45.7
Communist	91,746	..	100	..	0.3	2.0
Others	290,218	3	56	..	1.0	12.6
Elec. 33,269,770	28,772,671	625	1,868	2	100.0	..
Turnout 84.0%						
1951. Thu., 25 Oct						
Conservative	13,717,538	321	617	4	48.0	48.6
Liberal	730,556	6	109	..	2.5	14.7
Labour	13,948,605	295	617	..	48.8	49.2
Communist	21,640	..	10	..	0.1	4.4
Others	177,329	3	23	..	0.6	16.8
Elec. 34,645,573	28,595,668	625	1,376	4	100.0	..
Turnout 82.5%						
1955. Thu., 26 May						
Conservative	13,286,569	344	623	..	49.7	50.2
Liberal	722,405	6	110	..	2.7	15.1
Labour	12,404,970	277	620	..	46.4	47.3
Communist	33,144	..	17	..	0.1	4.2
Others	313,410	3	39	..	1.1	20.8
Elec. 34,858,263	26,760,498	630	1,409	..	100.0	..
Turnout 76.7%						

[1] Votes counted 26 Jul 45

	Total Votes	MPs Elected	Candidates	Unopposed Returns	% Share of Total Vote	Vote per Opposed Candidate
1959. Thu., 8 Oct						
Conservative	13,749,830	365	625	..	49.4	49.6
Liberal	1,638,571	6	216	..	5.9	16.9
Labour	12,215,538	258	621	..	43.8	44.5
Communist	30,897	..	18	..	0.1	4.1
Plaid Cymru	77,571	..	20	..	0.3	9.0
Scot Nat. P.	21,738	..	5	..	0.1	11.4
Others	12,464	1	31	..	0.4	11.0
Elec. 35,397,080 Turnout 78.8%	27,859,241	630	1,536	..	100.0	..
1964. Thu., 15 Oct						
Conservative	12,001,396	304	630	..	43.4	43.4
Liberal	3,092,878	9	365	..	11.2	18.5
Labour	12,205,814	317	628	..	44.1	44.1
Communist	45,932	..	36	..	0.2	3.4
Plaid Cymru	69,507	..	23	..	0.3	8.4
Scot Nat. P.	64,044	..	15	..	0.2	10.7
Others	168,422	..	60	..	0.6	6.4
Elec. 35,892,572 Turnout 77.1%	27,655,374	630	1,757	..	100.0	..
1966. Thu., 31 Mar						
Conservative	11,418,433	253	629	..	41.9	41.8
Liberal	2,327,533	12	311	..	8.5	16.1
Labour	13,064,951	363	621	..	47.9	48.7
Communist	62,112	..	57	..	0.2	3.0
Plaid Cymru	61,071	..	20	..	0.2	8.7
Scot Nat. P.	128,474	..	20	..	0.2	14.1
Others	201,302	2	49	..	0.6	8.6
Elec. 35,964,684 Turnout 75.8%	27,263,606	630	1,707	..	100.0	..
1970. Thu., 18 Jun						
Conservative	13,145,123	330	628	..	46.4	46.5
Liberal	2,117,035	6	332	..	7.5	13.5
Labour	12,179,341	287	624	..	43.0	43.5
Communist	37,970	..	58	..	0.1	1.1
Plaid Cymru	175,016	..	36	..	0.6	11.5
Scot Nat. P.	306,802	1	65	..	1.1	12.2
Others	383,511	6	94	..	1.4	9.1
Elec. 39,342,013 Turnout 72.0%	28,344,798	630	1,837	..	100.0	..

	Total Votes	MPs Elected	Candidates	Unopposed Returns	% Share of Total Vote	Vote per Opposed Candidate
1974. Thu., 28 Feb						
Conservative	11,868,906	297	623	..	37.9	38.8
Liberal	6,063,470	14	517	..	19.3	23.6
Labour	11,639,243	301	623	..	37.1	38.0
Communist	32,741	..	44	..	0.1	1.7
Plaid Cymru	171,364	2	36	..	0.6	10.7
Scot Nat. P.	632,032	7	70	..	2.0	21.9
National Front	76,865	..	54	..	0.3	3.2
Others (G.B.)	131,059	2	120	..	0.4	2.2
Others (N.I.)[1]	717,986	12	48	..	2.3	25.0
Elec. 39,798,899 Turnout 78.7%	31,333,226	635	2,135	..	100.0	..
1974. Thu., 10 Oct						
Conservative	10,464,817	277	623	..	35.8	36.7
Liberal	5,346,754	13	619	..	18.3	18.9
Labour	11,457,079	319	623	..	39.2	40.2
Communist	17,426	..	29	..	0.1	1.5
Plaid Cymru	166,321	3	36	..	0.6	10.8
Scot Nat. P.	839,617	11	71	..	2.9	30.4
National Front	113,843	..	90	..	0.4	2.9
Others(G.B.)	81,227	..	118	..	0.3	1.5
Others (N.I.)[1]	702,094	12	43	..	2.4	27.9
Elec. 40,072,971 Turnout 72.8%	29,189,178	635	2,252	..	100.0	..
1979. Thu., 3 May						
Conservative	13,697,690	339	622	..	43.9	44.9
Liberal	4,313,811	11	577	..	13.8	14.9
Labour	11,532,148	269	623	..	36.9	37.8
Communist	15,938	..	38	..	0.1	0.9
Plaid Cymru	132,544	2	36	..	0.4	8.1
Scot Nat. P.	504,259	2	71	..	1.6	17.3
National Front	190,747	..	303	..	0.6	1.6
Ecology	38,116	..	53	..	0.1	2.0
Workers Rev. P.	13,535	..	60	..	0.1	0.5
Others (G.B.)	85,338	..	129	..	0.3	1.3
Others (N.I.)[1]	695,889	12	64	..	2.2	18.8
Elec. 41,093,264 Turnout 76.0%	31,220,010	635	2,576	..	100.0	..

[1] From 1974 onwards, no candidates in Northern Ireland are included in the major party totals although it might be argued that some independent Unionists should be classed with the Conservatives and that Northern Ireland Labour candidates should be classed with Labour.

	Total Votes	MPs Elected	Candidates	Unopposed Returns	% Share of Total Vote	Vote per Opposed Candidate
1983. Thu., 9 Jun						
Conservative	13,012,315	397	633	..	42.4	43.5
Liberal	4,210,115	17	322	..	13.7	27.7
Social Democrat	3,570,834	6	311	..	11.6	24.3
(Alliance)	(7,780,949)	(23)	(633)	..	(25.4)	(26.0)
Labour	8,456,934	209	633	..	27.6	28.3
Communist	11,606	..	35	..	0.04	0.8
Plaid Cymru	125,309	2	36	..	0.4	7.8
Scottish Nat. P.	331,975	2	72	..	1.1	11.8
National Front	27,065	..	60	..	0.1	1.0
Others(G.B.)	193,383	..	282	..	0.6	1.4
Others (N.I.)[1]	764,925	17	95	..	3.1	17.9
Elec. 42,197,344 Turnout 72.7%	42,197,344	650	2,579	..	100.0	..
1987. Thu., 11 Jun						
Conservative	13,763,066	376	633	..	43.4	42.3
Liberal	4,173,450	17	327	..	25.5	12.8
Social Democrat	3,168,183	5	306	..	20.6	9.7
(Alliance)	(7,341,290)	(22)	(63)	..	(23.2)	(22.5)
Labour	10,029,778	229	633	..	31.7	30.8
Plaid Cymru	123,599	3	38	..	0.3	7.3
Scot Nat. P.	416,473	3	71	..	1.3	14.0
Others (G.B.)	151,519	..	241	..	0.5	1.2
Others (N.I.)[1]	730,152	17	77	..	2.2	22.1
Elec. 43,181,321 Turnout 75.3%	32,529,568	650	2,325	..	100.0	..
1992. Thu.9 Apr						
Conservative	14,092,891	336	645	..	42.3	41.9
Liberal Dem.	5,999,384	20	632	..	18.3	17.8
Labour	11,559,735	271	634	..	35.2	34.4
Plaid Cymru	154,439	4	38	..	8.8	0.5
Scot.Nat.P.	629,552	3	72	..	21.5	1.9
Others (G.B.)	436,207	..	841	..	1.0	1.3
Others (N.I.)[1]	740,485	17	89	..	2.2	18.0
Elec. 43,249,721 Turnout 77.7%	33,612,693	651	2,325	..	100.0	..

[1] From 1974 onwards, no candidates in Northern Ireland are included in the major party totals although it might be argued that some independent Unionists should be classed with the Conservatives and that Northern Ireland Labour candidates should be classed with Labour. In 1987 and 1992 some explicitly Conservative candidates in Northern Ireland are still excluded from the UK party totals.

Referendum on E.E.C. Membership
(Thursday 5 Jun 1975)

'Do you think that the United Kingdom should stay in the European Community (the Common Market)?'

	Total electorate[1]	Total votes[2]	% turnout[1]	%[2] 'yes'	Highest 'yes'	Lowest 'yes'
England	33,339,959	21,722,222	64.6	68.7	76.3	62.9
Wales	2,015,766	1,345,545	66.7	64.8	74.3	56.9
Scotland	3,698,462	2,286,676	61.7	58.4	72.3	29.5
N. Ireland[2]	1,032,490	498,751	47.4	52.1	52.1	
U.K.[1]	40,086,677	29,453,194	64.5	64.5	76.3	29.5

[1] The electorate and turnout figures are for the civilian electorate only. The 370,200 service votes are only in the total votes and in the 'Yes' percentages.
[2] The votes were counted on a county basis except in Northern Ireland which was treated as a single unit. In 66 of the 68 counties there was a 'yes' majority. (Shetland voted 56.3% 'No' and Western Isles 70.5% 'No'.)

(For 1979 referendums in Scotland and Wales see pp. 426, 427)

Direct Elections to European Parliament

1979. Thu., 7 Jun

	% Turnout	% votes					Seats				
		Con.	Lab.	Lib.	Nat.	Oth.	Con.	Lab.	Lib.	Nat.	Oth.
England	31.3	53.4	32.6	13.2	–	0.8	54	12	–	–	–
Wales	34.4	36.6	41.5	9.6	11.7	0.6	1	3	–	-	–
Scotland	33.7	33.7	33.0	13.9	19.4	–	5	2	–	1	–
G.B.	32.1	50.6	33.1	13.1	2.5	0.7	60	17	–	1	–
N.Ireland[3]	55.7	–	–	0.2	–	99.8	–	-	–	-	3
U.K.	32.7	48.4	31.6	12.6	2.5	4.9	60	17	–	1	3

Electorate 41,152,763   Votes cast 13,446,083

1984 Thu., 7 Jun

	% Turnout	% votes					Seats				
		Con.	Lab.	Lib.	Nat.	Oth.	Con.	Lab.	Lib.	Nat.	Oth.
England	31.6	43.1	35.0	20.4	–	1.5	42	24	–	–	–
Wales	39.7	25.4	44.5	17.4	12.2	0.5	1	3	–	–	–
Scotland	33.0	25.7	40.7	15.6	17.8	0.2	2	5	–	1	–
G.B.	31.8	40.8	36.5	19.5	2.5	0.8	45	32	–	1	–
N.Ireland[3]	63.5	–	-	–	–	100.0	–	-	–	-	3
U.K.	32.6	39.9	36.0	19.1	2.4	5.6	45	32	–	1	3

Electorate 42,493,274   Votes cast 13,998,274

[3] In Northern Ireland the election was conducted by Single Transferable Vote.

1989. Thu., 15 Jun

	% Turnout	Con.	Lab.	% votes Lib.	Nat.	Oth.	Con.	Lab.	Seats Lib.D.	Nat.	Oth.
England	35.8	37.2	29.2	6.6	–	16.9	32	34	–	–	–
Wales	41.1	23.1	49.7	3.2	12.2	13.0	–	4	–	–	–
Scotland	40.8	20.5	40.8	4.4	26.9	7.3	–	7	–	1	–
G.B.	35.9	34.7	40.1	6.4	–	19.0	32	45	–	1	–
N. Ireland	48.4	–	–	–	–	100.0	–	–	–	–	3
U.K.	36.8	33.5	38.7	6.2	3.2	2.8	32	45	–	–	4

Electorate 43,180,720   Votes cast 15,893,408

1994. Thu., 9 Jun

	% Turnout	Con.	Lab.	% votes Lib.	Nat.	Oth.	Con.	Lab.	Seats Lib.D.	Nat.	Oth.
England	35.5	30.5	43.5	18.4	–	7.6	18	51	2	–	–
Wales	43.1	14.6	55.9	8.7	17.1	3.7	–	5	–	–	–
Scotland	38.2	14.5	42.5	7.2	32.6	1.6	–	8	–	2	–
G.B.	36.2	27.9	44.2	16.7	4.3	6.9	18	64	2	2	–
N. Ireland	48.7	–	–	–	–	100.0	–	–	–	–	3
U.K.	36.8	26.9	42.6	16.1	4.1	10.2	18	64	2	2	3

Electorate 43,037,821   Votes cast 15,847,417

General Election Results by Regions

	1900	1906	Jan 1910	Dec 1910	1918*	1922	1923	1924	1929	1931	1935	1945
County of London												
Con	51	19	33	30	Coal.	43	29	39	24	53	39	12
Lib	8	38	25	26	53	9	11	3	2	4	1	–
Lab	–	2	1	3	Op.	9	22	19	36	5	22	48
Others	–	–	–	–	9	1	–	–	1	–	–	2
Rest of S. England												
Con	123	45	107	103	Coal.	130	89	150	111	156	147	88
Lib	32	107	46	49	149	23	48	5	18	4	3	3
Lab	–	3	2	2	Op.	9	27	10	35	5	15	91
Others	–	–	–	1	16	3	1	–	1	–	3	3
Midlands												
Con	60	27	49	50	Coal.	53	45	64	35	80	67	24
Lib	27	59	31	30	67	17	17	2	5	3	1	–
Lab	1	2	8	8	Op.	17	25	21	47	4	19	64
Others	–	–	–	–	20	–	–	–	·	–	–	2
Northern England												
Con	98	31	45	50	Coal.	82	57	101	51	146	106	43
Lib	55	102	86	82	121	27	48	9	10	9	5	2
Labour	–	20	22	21	Op.	60	64	59	108	15	60	128
Others	1	1	1	1	50	2	2	2	2	1	–	–
Wales												
Con	6	–	2	3	Coal.	6	4	9	1	11	11	4
Lib	27	33	27	26	20	10	12	10	9	8	6	6
Lab	1	1	5	5	Op.	18	19	16	25	16	18	25
Others	–	–	–	–	15	1	–	–	–	–	–	–
Scotland												
Con	36	10	9	9	Coal.	13	14	36	20	57	43	29
Lib	34	58	59	58	54	27	22	8	13	7	3	–
Lab	–	2	2	3	Op.	29	34	26	37	7	20	37
Others	–	–	–	–	17	2	1	1	1	–	5	5
Ireland												
Con	19	16	19	17	Coal.	10	10	12	10	10	10	9
Lib	1	3	1	11	–	–	–	–	–	–	–	–
Lab	–	–	–	–	Op.	–	–	–	–	–	–	–
Others	81	82	81	83	100	2	2	–	2	2	2	3
Universities												
Con	9	9	9	9	Coal.	8	9	8	8	8	9	4
Lib	–	–	–	–	13	3	2	3	2	2	1	1
Lab	–	–	–	–	Op.	–	–	–	–	–	–	–
Others	–	–	–	–	2	1	1	1	2	2	2	7
Totals												
Con	402	157	273	272	Coal.	345	258	419	260	521	432	213
Lib	184	400	275	272	478	116	159	40	59	37	20	12
Lab	2	30	40	42	Op.	142	191	151	288	52	154	393
Others	82	83	82	84	229	12	7	5	8	5	9	22
Total seats	670	670	670	670	707	615	615	615	615	615	615	640

* In 1918 all Coalition and all non-Coalition candidates are listed together. In fact a substantial number of the 48 Conservatives who were elected without the Coupon worked with the Government. Virtually no Coupons were issued to Irish candidates but 23 out of the 101 non-University seats in Ireland went to Unionists

The vertical lines indicate redistributions of seats.
Northern England includes Cheshire, Lancashire Yorkshire, and all counties to their north.
Midlands includes Hereford, Worcs., Warwickshire, Northants., Lincs., Notts., Leics., Staffs., Salop, Derbyshire.
Southern England includes the rest of England, except for the County of London.

General Election Results by Regions

	1950	1951	1955	1959	1964	1966	1970	Feb 1974	Oct 1974	1979	1983	1987	1992
County of London (GLC)													
Con	12	14	15	18	10	6	9	42	41	50	56	58	48
Lib	–	–	–	–	–	–	–	–	–	–	2	3	1
Lab	31	29	27	24	32	36	33	50	51	42	26	23	35
Others	–	–	–	–	–	–	–	–	–	–	–	–	–
Rest of S. England													
Con	144	153	163	171	157	134	169	136	128	146	168	170	161
Lib	1	–	–	1	3	4	2	5	5	3	5	3	6
Lab	54	46	42	34	46	67	34	21	29	13	3	3	10
Others	–	–	1	–	–	1	1	–	–	–	–	–	–
Midlands													
Con	35	35	39	49	42	35	51	43	40	57	70	67	57
Lib	–	–	–	–	–	–	–	–	–	–	–	–	–
Lab	59	59	57	47	54	61	45	54	58	41	30	33	43
Others	–	–	–	–	–	–	–	1	–	–	–	–	–
Northern England													
Con	61	69	75	77	53	44	63	47	44	53	68	63	53
Lib	1	2	2	2	–	2	–	4	3	4	6	4	3
Lab	107	99	90	88	114	121	104	112	117	107	89	96	107
Others	–	–	–	–	–	–	–	1	–	–	–	–	–
Wales													
Con	4	6	6	7	6	3	7	8	8	11	14	8	6
Lib	5	3	3	2	2	1	1	2	2	1	2	3	1
Lab	27	27	27	27	28	32	27	24	23	22	20	24	27
Others	–	–	–	–	–	1	2	3	2	2	2	3	4
Scotland													
Con	32	35	36	31	24	20	23	21	16	22	21	10	11
Lib	2	1	1	1	4	5	3	3	3	3	8	9	9
Lab	37	35	34	38	43	46	44	40	41	44	41	50	49
Others	–	–	–	1	–	–	1	7	11	2	2	3	3
Ireland													
Con	10	9	10	12	12	11	8	–	–	–	–	–	–
Lib	–	–	–	–	–	–	–	–	–	–	–	–	–
Lab	–	–	–	–	–	–	–	–	–	–	–	–	–
Other	2	3	2	–	–	1	4	12	12	12	17	17	17
Universities													
Con	–	–	–	–	–	–	–	–	–	–	–	–	–
Lib	–	–	–	–	–	–	–	–	–	–	–	–	–
Lab.	–	–	–	–	–	–	–	–	–	–	–	–	–
Other	–	–	–	–	–	–	–	–	–	–	–	–	–
Totals													
Con	298	321	344	365	304	253	330	297	277	339	397	376	336
Lib	9	6	6	6	9	12	6	14	13	11	23	22	18
Lab	315	295	277	258	317	363	287	301	319	269	209	229	271
Other	3	3	3	1	–	2	7	23	26	16	21	23	24
Total seats	625	625	630	630	630	630	630	635	635	635	650	650	651

The vertical lines indicate redistributions of seats.
Northern England includes Cheshire, Lancashire Yorkshire, and all counties to their north.
Midlands includes Hereford, Worcs., Warwickshire, Northants., Lincs., Notts., Leics., Staffs., Salop, Derbyshire.
Southern England includes the rest of England, except for the County of London (the old L.C.C. area), but from 1974 the seats in the outer areas of the Greater London Council are calssed with the County of London and not with the rest of S. England.

Party Changes between Elections

The party composition of the House of Commons changes continuously partly owing to Members changing their allegiance and partly owing to by-election results. The following table shows the net change due to both causes during the life of each Parliament. (Seats vacant at dissolution are included under the last incumbent's party.)

		Con.	Lib.	Lab.	Others
1895–1900	Dissolution	399	189	..	82
1900–05	Election	402	184	2	82
	Dissolution	369	215	4	82
1906–09	Election	157	400	30	83
	Dissolution	168	373	46	83
1910	Election	273	275	40	82
	Dissolution	274	274	40	82
1910–18	Election	272	271	42	85
	Dissolution	281	260	39	90
1918–22[a]	Election	383	161	73	90
	Dissolution	378	155	87	87
1922–23	Election	345	116	142	12
	Dissolution	344	117	144	10
1923–24	Election	258	159	191	7
	Dissolution	259	158	193	5
1924–29	Election	419	40	151	5
	Dissolution	400	46	162	7
1929–31	Election	260	59	288	8
	Dissolution	263	57	281[b]	14
1931–35	Election	521	37	52	5
	Dissolution	512	34	59	10
1935–45	Election	432	20	154	9
	Dissolution	398	18	166	33
1945–50	Election	213	12	393	22
	Dissolution	218	10	391	21
1950–51	Election	298	9	315	3
	Dissolution	298	9	314	4
1951–55	Election	321	6	295	3
	Dissolution	322	6	294	3

		Con.	Lib.	Lab.	Others
1955–59	Election	344	6	277	3
	Dissolution	340	6	281	3
1970–74	Election	330	6	287	7
	Dissolution	323	11	287	9
1959–64	Election	365	6	258	1
	Dissolution	360	7	262	2
1964–66	Election	304	9	317	–
	Dissolution	304	10	316	-
1966–70	Election	253	12	363	2
	Dissolution	264	13	346	7
1974	Election	297	14	301	23
	Dissolution	297	15	300	23
1974–79	Election	277	13	319	26
	Dissolution	284	14	309	28
1979–83	Election	339	11	269	16
	Dissolution	336	(42)	240	17
1983–87	Election	397	(23)	209	21
	Dissolution	393	(27)	208	22
1987–92	Election	376	23	229	23
	Dissolution	369	23	231	28
1992–	Election	336	20	271	24

M.P.s' Changes of Allegiance

The difficulties in compiling an exact and comprehensive list of all floor-crossings, Whip withdrawals, Whip resignations, and Whip restorations are enormous. The list which follows is probably fairly complete as far as floor-crossings go (except for 1918–22) but it certainly omits a number of Members who relinquished the Whip for a time. It also omits cases of M.P.s who stood without official party support in their constituencies but who remained in good standing with the Whips and some cases of M.P.s taking the Whip immediately before a General Election (as happened with several Members in 1918 and a few in 1945) or immediately after a General Election (as happened with the Lloyd George Group in 1935). No attempt has been made to record shifts between the various factions of Irish Nationalism. Throughout this list the test, in so far as it can be applied, is whether the M.P. was officially in receipt of the weekly documentary Whip.

Parliament of 1900–05

			from	to	
Nov 02	*J. Wason	Orkney & Shetland	L.U.	Ind.	Won by-el Nov 02 took Lib. Whip by 05
Apr 03	*J. W. Wilson	N. Worcs.	L.U.	Lib.	
Apr 03	Sir M. Foster	London Univ	L.U.	Lib.	
Jan 04	†W. Churchill	Oldham	Con.	Ind. ⎱	Con. Whip restored after
Jan 04	*Sir J. Dickson-Poynder	Chippenham	Con.	Ind. ⎰	2 weeks; Lib. Whip taken Apr 04
Feb 04	*T. Russell	S. Tyrone	L.U.	Lib.	
Feb 04	J. Wilson	Falkirk	L.U.	Lib.	
Mar 04	†J. Seely	I. of Wight	Con.	Ind.	Won by-el Apr 04 unop.; took Lib. Whip May 04
Apr 04	†I. Guest	Plymouth	Con.	Lib.	
Aug 04	E. Hain	St Ives	L.U.	Lib.	
Aug 04	G. Kemp	Heywood	L.U.	Lib.	
Jul 04	J. Jameson	W. Clare	I.Nat.	Con.	
Nov 04	R. Rigg	Appleby	Lib.	Ind.	Resigned seat Dec 04
Mar 05	E. Mitchell	N. Fermanagh	Ind.C.	Lib.	
Mar 05	J. Wood	E. Down	L.U.	Lib.	
Mar 05	E. Hatch	Gorton	Con.	Ind.	
Mar 05	Sir E. Reed	Cardiff D.	Lib.	L.U.	

Parliament of 1906–09

Feb 06	*J. W. Taylor	Chester-le-Street	Lib.	Lab.	
Feb 06	A. Taylor	E. Toxteth	Con.	Lib.	
Feb 07	*R. Hunt	Ludlow	Con.	–	Whip withdrawn. Whip restored Mar 07
Nov 07	L. Renton	Gainsboro'	Lib.	Con.	
Aug 08	*A. Corbett	Tradeston	L.U.	Ind.Lib.	
Mar 09	T. Kincaid Smith	Stratford-on-Avon	Lib.	Ind.	Lost by-el May 09
May 09	A. Cross	Camlachie	L.U.	Lib.	
Oct 09	C. Bellairs	King's Lynn	Lib.	L.U.	

Parliament of 1910

Nov 10	Sir J. Rees	Montgomery	Lib.	L.U.	

Parliament of 1911–18

Jan 14	D. Mason	Coventry	Lib.	Ind.	
Feb 14	*B. Kenyon	Chesterfield	Lab.	Lib.	Introduced as new M.P. by Lab. but resigned Whip after 2 weeks
Apr 14	W. Johnson	Nuneaton	Lab.	Lib.	Lab. Whip withdrawn
Apr 15	*J. Hancock	Mid-Derbys.	Lab.	Lib.	Lab. Whip withdrawn
Sep 17	*H. Page Croft	Christchurch	Con.	Nat.P.	
Sep 17	*Sir R. Cooper	Walsall	Con.	Nat.P.	
Jul 18	E. John	E. Denbigh	Lib.	Lab.	
Jul 18	J. Martin	St. Pancras E.	Lib.	Lab.	

In Nov 18 a number of Liberals became Independent or Labour and some Labour members accepted the label Coalition Labour or Coalition National Democratic Party shortly before the dissolution of Parliament.

* Relected for same seat at next General Election.
† Elected for different seat at next General Election.

Parliament of 1919–22

Throughout this parliament the confusion of party labels and the movements within and between the Coalition and non-Coalition wings of each party make it impossible to attempt any comprehensive listing of all switches. The following changes were, however, more clear cut.

Apr	19	*J. Wedgwood	Newcastle-under-Lyme	Co.Lib.	Lab.	Lab. Whip granted May 19
Oct	19	E. Hallas	Duddeston	Co.NDP	Lab.	
Nov	19	C. Malone	Leyton E.	Co.Lib.	Ind.	Joined Communist Party Jul 20
Oct	20	*O. Mosley	Harrow	Co.Con.	Ind.	
Oct	20	*Sir O. Thomas	Anglesey	Lab.	Ind.	
Feb	22	*A. Hopkinson	Mossley	Co.Lib.	Ind.	

Parliament of 1922–23

Jan	23	*J. Erskine	Westminster St. George's	I.Con.	Con.	
Jan	23	*H. Becker	Richmond	I.Con.	Con.	
Jan	23	*G. Hall Caine	Dorset E.	I.Con.	Con.	
Jul	23	A. Evans	Leicester E.N.	Lib.	Con.	
Oct	23	G. Roberts	Norwich	Ind.	Con.	

Parliament of 1923–24

Feb	24	G. Davies	Welsh Univ.	Ind.	Lab.	
May	24	O. Mosley	Harrow	Ind.	Lab.	

Parliament of 1924–29[1]

Jan	26	Sir A. Mond	Carmarthen	Lib.	Con.	Made peer Jun 28
Feb	26	E. Hilton Young	Norwich	Lib.	Ind.	Took Con. Whip May 26
Oct	26	*J. Kenworthy	Hull C.	Lib.	Lab.	Won by-el Nov 26
Nov	26	D. Davies	Montgomery	Lib.	Ind.	
Feb	27	G. Spencer	Broxtowe	Lab.	Ind.	Expelled from party
Feb	27	†W. Benn	Leith	Lib.	Ind.	Resigned seat Feb 27
Feb	27	L. Haden Guest	Southwark N.	Lab.	Ind.	Lost by-el Mar 27
Oct	27	*Sir R. Newman	Exeter	Con.	Ind.	
Jul	28	*Sir B. Peto	Barnstaple	Con.	–	Whip withdrawn; restored Nov 28

Parliament of 1929–31

Jun	29	Sir W. Jowitt	Preston	Lib.	Lab.	Won by-el Jul 29
Feb	30	*N. Maclean	Govan	I.Lab.	Lab.	
Feb	31	Sir O. Mosley	Smethwick	Lab.	N.P.	
Feb	31	Lady C. Mosley	Stoke	Lab.	N.P.	
Feb	31	R. Forgan	W. Renfrew	Lab.	N.P.	
Feb	31	W. Allen	Belfast W.	Con.	N.P.	⎫
Feb	31	C. R. Dudgeon	Galloway	Lib.	N.P.	⎬
Feb	31	J. Strachey	Aston	Lab.	N.P.	⎬ Became Ind. Jun 31
Feb	31	O. Baldwin	Dudley	Lab.	Ind.	⎬
Feb	31	W. Brown	Wolverhampton W.	Lab.	Ind.	⎭
Mar	31	*Sir W. Wayland	Canterbury	Con.	–	Whip withdrawn; restored Apr 31
Jun	31	*E. Brown	Leith	Lib.	Ind.	⎫
Jun	31	*Sir R. Hutchison	Montrose	Lib.	Ind.	⎬ Became L.Nat. Oct 31
Jun	31	*Sir J. Simon	Spen Valley	Lib.	Ind.	⎭
Sep	31	*E. Taylor	Paddington S.	Ind.	Con.	

[1] The 7 members, all former Liberal M.P.s, elected under the label 'Constitutional' never voted as a group. Two, *W. Churchill and Sir H. Greenwood, took the Conservative whip from the start and one, A. Moreing, later. Three reverted during the Parliament to their former Liberalism, J. Edwards, *A. England, and J. Ward. One, *Sir T. Robinson, became an Independent.

* Re-elected for same seat at next General Election.
† Elected for different seat at next General Election.

Parliament of 1929–31 (cont.)

In Oct 31, 23 Liberal Members broke with the party to form the Liberal National Group. A further 6 Liberals, most notably the Lloyd George family, became Independent Liberals. 15 Labour members under R.MacDonald formed the National Labour Group.

Parliament of 1931–35

Nov 31	*G. Buchanan	Gorbals	Lab.	ILP	
Nov 31	*J. McGovern	Shettleston	Lab.	ILP	
Nov 31	J. Maxton	Bridgeton	Lab.	ILP	
Nov 31	*D. Kirkwood	Dumbarton	Lab.	ILP	Returned to Lab. Aug 33
Nov 31	R. Wallhead	Merthyr	Lab.	ILP.	Returned to Lab. Sep 33
Nov 32	*J. Leckie	Walsall	Lib.	L.Nat.	
Dec 32	A. Curry	Bp Auckland	L.Nat.	Lib.	
Dec 32	F. Llewellyn Jones	Flint	L.Nat.	Lib.	
Feb 33	H. Nathan	Bethnal Gn NE	I.L.	Ind.	Took Lab. Whip Jun 34
Jun 34	W. McKeag	Durham	Lib.	L.Nat.	
Jun 34	J. Hunter	Dumfries	Lib.	L.Nat.	
Jun 34	J. Lockwood	Shipley	Con.	Ind.	
May 35	F. Astbury	Salford W.	Con.	Ind.	
May 35	L. Thorp	Nelson & C.	Con.	Ind.	
May 35	A. Todd	Berwick	Con.	Ind.	
May 35	*D'ess of Atholl	Kinross&W.P.	Con.	Ind.	Whip restored Sep 35
May 35	*Sir J. Nall	Hulme	Con.	Ind.	Whip restored Nov 35
Early 35	*G. Morrison	Scottish Un.	Lib.	L.Nat.	

Parliament of 1935–45

Jun 36	*H. Macmillan	Stockton	Con	Ind.	Whip restored Jul 37
Oct 36	R. Bernays	Bristol N.	Lib.	L.Nat.	
Apr 38	D'ess of Atholl	Kinross&W.P.	Con.	Ind.	Lost by-el Dec 38
Oct 38	H. Holdsworth	Bradford S	Lib.	L.Nat.	
Nov 38	A. Hopkinson	Mossley	Nat.	Ind.	
Jan 39	*Sir S. Cripps	Bristol E.	Lab.	–	Expelled from party; Whip restored Feb 45
Mar 39	*A. Bevan	Ebbw Vale	Lab.	–	Expelled from party; Whip restored Dec 39
Mar 39	*G. Strauss	Lambeth N.	Lab.	–	Expelled from party; Whip restored Feb 40
May 39	*G. Buchanan	Gorbals	ILP	Lab.	
Dec 39	*C. Davies	Montgomery	L.Nat.	Ind.	Took Lib. Whip Aug 42
Mar 40	*D. Pritt	Ham'smith N.	Lab.	–	Expelled from party
May 40	A. Ramsay	Peebles	Con.	Ind.	Detained until Dec 44
Feb 42	*E. Granville	Eye	L.Nat.	Ind.	Took Lib.Whip Apr 45
Feb 42	*Sir M. Macdonald	Inverness	L.Nat.	Ind.	Whip restored by 45
Feb 42	L. Hore-Belisha	Devonport	L.Nat.	Ind.	
Feb 42	S. King-Hall	Ormskirk	N.Lab.	Ind.	
Feb 42	*Sir H. Morris-Jones	Denbigh	L.Nat.	Ind.	Whip restored May 43
Feb 42	†K. Lindsay	Kilmarnock	N.Lab.	Ind.	
May 42	C. Cunningham-Reid	St M'lebone	Con.	–	Whip withdrawn
Sep 42	Sir R. Acland	Barnstaple	Lib.	C.W.	
Mar 43	A. Maclaren	Burslem	Lab.	Ind.	
Nov 44	*J. Loverseed	Eddisbury	C.W.	Ind.	Took Lab.Whip May 45
Jan 45	*T. Driberg	Maldon	Ind.	Lab.	
May 45	*J. Little	Down	U.U.	Ind.	
May 45	*C White	W.Derbyshire	Ind.	Lab.	

* Re-elected for same seat at next General Election.

Parliament of 1945–50

Apr 46	E. Millington	Chelmsford	C.W.	Lab.	
Oct 46	T. Horabin	N. Cornwall	Lib	Ind.	Took Lab.Whip Nov 47
Mar 47	*J. McGovern	Shettleston	ILP	Lab.	
Jul 47	C. Stephen	Camlachie	ILP	Ind.	Took Lab.Whip Oct 47
Oct 47	*J. Carmichael	Bridgeton	ILP.	Ind.	Took Lab.Whip Nov 47
Nov 47	E. Walkden	Doncaster	Lab.	Ind.	
Mar 48	*J. McKie	Galloway	Ind.Con.	Con.	
Apr 48	J. Platts-Mills	Finsbury	Lab.	–	Expelled from party
May 48	A. Edwards	Middlesbro'	Lab.	–	Expelled from party, took Con.Whip Aug 49
Oct 48	I. Bulmer-Thomas	Keighley	Lab.	Ind.	Took Con.Whip Jan 49
Nov 48	E. Gander Dower	Caithness & Sutherland	Con.	Ind.	
May 49	L. Solley	Thurrock	Lab.	–	Expelled from party
May 49	K. Zilliacus	Gateshead	Lab.	–	Expelled from party
Jul 49	L. Hutchinson	Rusholme	Lab.	–	Expelled from party

Parliament of 1950–51

Aug 50	R. Blackburn	Northfield	Lab.	Ind.	

Parliament of 1951–55

Jun 54	Sir J. Mellor	Sutton Coldf'd	Con.	Ind.	Whip restored Jul 54
Jul 54	*H. Legge-Bourke	Isle of Ely	Con.	Ind.	Whip restored Oct 54
Nov 54	*G. Craddock	Bradford S.	Lab.	–	⎫
Nov 54	*S. Davies	Merthyr	Lab.	–	⎪
Nov 54	*E. Fernyhough	Jarrow	Lab.	–	Whip withdrawn;
Nov 54	*E. Hughes	S. Ayrshire	Lab.	–	restored Feb 55
Nov 54	*S. Silverman	Nelson & C.	Lab.	–	⎪
Nov 54	*V. Yates	Ladywood	Lab.	–	⎭
Nov 54	*J. McGovern	Shettleston	Lab.	–	Whip withdrawn; restored Mar 55
Mar 55	*A. Bevan	Ebbw Vale	Lab.	–	Whip withdrawn; restored Apr 55
Mar 55	Sir R. Acland	Gravesend	Lab.	Ind.	Resigned seat to fight by-el; expelled from party

Parliament of 1955–59

Nov 56	C. Banks	Pudsey	Con.	Ind.	Whip restored Dec 58
May 57	P. Maitland	Lanark	Con.	Ind.	Whip restored Dec 57
May 57	Sir V. Raikes	Garston	Con.	Ind.	Resigned seat Oct 57
May 57	A. Maude	Ealing S.	Con.	Ind.	Resigned seat Apr 58
May 57	*J. Biggs-Davison	Chigwell	Con.	Ind.	⎫
May 57	*A. Fell	Yarmouth	Con.	Ind.	⎪
May 57	*Vt Hinchingbrooke	S.Dorset	Con.	Ind.	Whip restored Jul 58
May 57	L. Turner	Oxford	Con.	Ind.	⎪
May 57	P. Williams	Sunderland S.	Con.	Ind.	⎭
Nov 57	Sir F. Medlicott	C.Norfolk	Con.	Ind.	Whip restored Nov 58
Jan 59	*Sir D.Robertson	Caithness & Sutherland	Con.	Ind.	

Parliament of 1959–64

Mar 61	A. Brown	Tottenham	Lab.	Ind.	Took Con. Whip May 62
Mar 61	*W. Baxter	W. Stirling	Lab.	–	⎫
Mar 61	*S. Davies	Merthyr	Lab.	–	⎪
Mar 61	*M. Foot	Ebbw Vale	Lab.	–	Whip withdrawn;
Mar 61	*E. Hughes	S. Ayrshire	Lab.	–	restored May 63
Mar 61	*S. Silverman	Nelson & Colne	Lab.	–	⎭

* Re-elected for same seat at next General Election.

Parliament of 1959–64 (cont.)

Mar 61	*K. Zilliacus	Gorton	Lab.	–	Whip suspended; restored Jan 62
Oct 61	Sir W. Duthie	Banff	Con.	Ind.	Whip restored Nov 63
Jan 64	D. Johnson	Carlisle	Con.	Ind.	

Parliament of 1964–66

[None]

Parliament of 1966–70

Jul 66	G. Hirst	Shipley	Con.	Ind.	
Aug 66	*G. Fitt	Belfast W.	Rep.Lab.	SDLP	Expelled by Rep.Lab.
Dec 66	*R. Paget	Northampton	Lab.	Ind.	Whip restored Jun 67
Jan 68	D. Donnelly	Pembroke	Lab.	Ind.	Expelled from party Mar 68
Feb 68	24 M.P.s		Lab.	–	Whip suspended for one month

Parliament of 1970–74

Oct 71	*I. Paisley	N. Antrim	Prot.U.	Dem.U.	
Feb 72	R. Gunter	Southwark	Lab.	Ind.	
Oct 72	*D. Taverne	Lincoln	Lab.	Dem.Lab.	Won by-el Mar 73
Dec 72	S. Mills	Belfast N.	U.U.	Con.	Joined Alliance Party Apr 73

Parliament of 1974

Jul 74	C. Mayhew	Woolwich E.	Lab.	Lib.	

Parliament of 1974–79

Oct 75	W. Craig	Belfast E.	UUUC	Vanguard	Wound up Vanguard and rejoined UUUC Feb 78
Oct 75	*J. Kilfedder	N. Down	UUUC	Ind. U.	
Apr 76	J. Stonehouse	Walsall N.	Lab.	Ind.	
Jul 76	J. Sillars	S. Ayrshire	Lab.	Sc.Lab.	Formed Sc.Lab.P. Apr 76
Jul 76	J. Robertson	Paisley	Lab.	Sc.Lab.	Resigned Lab Whip Jul 76
May 77	*I. Paisley	N. Antrim	UUUC	Dem.U.	
May 77	J. Dunlop	Mid-Ulster	UUUC	Ind.	
Oct 77	†R. Prentice	Newham N E	Lab.	Con.	

Parliament of 1979–83

Nov 79	G. Fitt	Belfast W.	SDLP	Ind. Soc.	
Feb 81	T. Ellis	Wrexham	Lab.	SDP	
Feb 81	R. Crawshaw	Liv.Toxteth	Lab.	SDP	
Mar 81	T. Bradley	Leicester E.	Lab.	SDP	
Mar 81	*J. Cartwright	Woolwich E.	Lab.	SDP	
Mar 81	J. Horam	Gateshead W.	Lab.	SDP	
Mar 81	*R. Maclennan	Caithness & Sutherland	Lab.	SDP	
Mar 81	J. Roper	Farnworth	Lab.	SDP	
Mar 81	*D. Owen	Devonport	Lab.	SDP	
Mar 81	W. Rodgers	Stockton	Lab.	SDP	
Mar 81	N. Sandelson	Hayes & H.	Lab.	SDP	
Mar 81	M. Thomas	Newcastle E.	Lab.	SDP	
Mar 81	*I. Wrigglesworth	Thornaby	Lab.	SDP	
Mar 81	E. Lyons	Bradford W.	Lab.	SDP	
Mar 81	C. Brocklebank-Fowler	Norfolk N.W.	Con.	SDP	
Jul 81	J. Wellbeloved	Erith & C.	Lab.	SDP	
Sep 81	M. O'Halloran	Islington N.	Lab.	SDP	Became Ind. Lab. Mar 83
Oct 81	D. Mabon	Greenock	Lab.	SDP	

* Re-elected for same seat at next General Election.
† Elected for different seat at next General Election.

Parliament of 1979–83 (*cont.*)

Oct	81	R. Mitchell	Soton, Itchen	Lab.	SDP	
Oct	81	D. Ginsburg	Dewsbury	Lab.	SDP	
Oct	81	J. Dunn	Liv.Kirkdale	Lab.	SDP	
Oct	81	T. McNally	Stockport S.	Lab.	SDP	
Oct	81	E. Ogden	Liv. W.Derby	Lab.	SDP	
Nov	81	J. Grant	Islington C.	Lab.	SDP	
Nov	81	G. Cunningham	Islington S.	Lab.	Ind.Lab	Became SDP Jun 82
Dec	81	R. Brown	Hackney S.	Lab.	SDP	
Dec	81	J. Thomas	Abertillery	Lab.	SDP	
Dec	81	E. Hudson-Davies	Caerphilly	Lab.	SDP	
Dec	81	B. Douglas-Mann	Mitcham	Lab.	Ind.SDP	Lost by-elec. Jun 82
Jan	82	B. Magee	Leyton	Lab.	Ind.Lab	Became SDP Mar 82
Aug	82	R. Mellish	Bermondsey	Lab.	Ind.Lab	Resigned seat Jan 83

Parliament of 1983–87

[*None*]

Parliament of 1987–92

Mar	88	R. Maclennan	Caithness & Sutherland	SDP	(Lib)Dem	
Mar	88	C. Kennedy	Ross, Cromarty & Skye	SDP	(Lib)Dem	
May	88	R. Brown	Leith	Lab.	–	Whip withdrawn for 3 months
Mar	90	R. Douglas	Dunfermline W.	Lab.	Ind.Lab.	Joined SNP Oct 90
Dec	91	D. Nellist	Coventry S.E	Lab	–	Expelled from Party
Dec	91	T. Fields	Broad Green	Lab.	–	Expelled from Party
Mar	92	J. Browne	Winchester	Con.	–	Whip withdrawn

Parliament of 1992–

Jul	93	R. Allason	Torbay	Con.		Whip withdrawn Restored Jul 94

M.P.s elected under new label

In addition to the floor crossings recorded above there are the following instances of ex-M.P.s, after an interval out of Parliament, returning to the House under a designation basically different from the ones under which they had previously sat.

(Sir) R. Acland	Lib. 35–42,	C.W. 42–45,	Lab. 47–55
C. Addison	Lib. 10–22,	Lab. 29–31, 34–35	
P. Alden	Lib. 06–18,	Lab. 23–24	
W. Allen	Lib. 92–00,	Nat. 31–35	
C. Bellairs	Lib. 06–10,	Con. 15–31	
(Sir) A. Bennett	Lib. 22–23,	Con. 24–30	
(Sir) E. Bennett	Lib. 06–10,	Lab. 29–31,	N.Lab. 31–45
H. Bottomley	Lib. 06–12,	Ind. 18–22	
T. Bowles	Con. 92–06,	Lib. 10–10	
J. Bright	L.U. 89–95,	Lib. 06–10	
W. Brown	Lab. 29–31,	Ind. 42–50	
C. Buxton	Lib. 10–10,	Lab. 22–31	
N. Buxton	Lib. 05–06, 10–18,	Lab. 22–24, 29–30	
(Sir) W. Churchill	Con. 00–04,	Lib. 04–22,	Con. 24–64
(Sir) H. Cowan	Lib. 06–22,	Con. 23–29	
A. Crawley	Lab. 45–51,	Con. 62–67	
R. Denman	Lib. 10–18,	Lab. 29–31,	N.Lab. 31–45
(Sir) C. Entwistle	Lib. 18–24,	Con. 31–45	

M.P.s elected under new label (*cont.*)

R. Fletcher	Lib. 23–24,	Lab. 35–42	
(Sir) D. Foot	Lib. 31–45,	Lab. 57–70	
G. Garro-Jones	Lib. 24–29,	Lab. 35–47	
W. Grenfell	Lib. 80–82, 85–86, 92–93,	Con. 00–06	
Sir E. Grigg	Lib. 22–25,	Con. 33–45	
C. Guest	Lib. 10–18, 22–23,	Con. 37–45	
F. Guest	Lib. 10–22, 23–29,	Con. 31–37	
O. Guest	Co.Lib. 18–22,	Con. 35–45	
T. Harvey	Lib. 10–18, 23–24,	Ind. 37–45	
E. Hemmerde	Lib. 06–10, 12–18,	Lab. 22–24	
J. Horam	Lab. 70–81,	SDP 81–3,	Con. 92–
(Sir) B. Janner	Lib. 31–35,	Lab. 45–70	
R. Jenkins	Lab. 48–77,	SDP 82–87	
(Sir) W. Jowitt	Lib. 29–29,	Lab. 29–31,	Ind. 31–31,	Lab. 39–45
E. King	Lab. 45–50,	Con. 64–79	
H. Lawson	Lib. 85–92, 93–95,	L.U. 05–06, 10–16	
H. Lees-Smith	Lib. 10–18,	Lab. 22–23, 24–31, 35–42	
G. Lloyd-George	Lib. 22–24, 29–50,	Con. 51–57	
(Lady)M. Lloyd-George	Lib. 29–51,	Lab. 57–66	
F. Maddison	Lib. 97–00,	Lab. 06–10	
E. Mallalieu	Lib. 31–35,	Lab. 48–74	
C. Malone	Co.Lib. 18–19,	Ind. 19–22,	Comm. 22,	Lab. 28–31
(Sir) F. Markham	Lab. 29–31,	N.Lab. 35–45,	Con. 51–64	
H. Mond	Lib. 23–24,	Con. 29–30	
(Sir) O. Philipps	Lib. 06–10,	Con. 16–22	
A. Ponsonby	Lib. 08–18,	Lab. 22–30	
E. Powell	Con. 50–74,	U.U.U. 74–87	
S. Saklatvala	Lab. 22–23,	Comm. 24–29	
Sir A. Salter	Ind. 37–50,	Con. 52–54	
J. Seddon	Lab. 06–10,	Co.N.D.P. 18–22	
(Sir) C. Seely	L.U. 95–06,	Lib. 16–18	
J. Sillars	Lab. 70–76,	Sc.Lab. 76–9,	S.N.P. 88–92	
(Sir) E. Spears	Lib. 22–24,	Con. 31–45	
G. Spero	Lib. 23–24,	Lab. 29–31	
C. Stephen	Lab. 22–31,	I.L.P. 35–47,	Lab. 47	
J. Strachey	Lab. 29–30,	N.P.30–31,	Ind.31–31,	Lab. 45–63
(Sir) C. Trevelyan	Lib. 99–18,	Lab. 22–31	
P. Tyler	Lib. 74–74,	Lib.Dem 92–	
Mrs S.Williams	Lab. 64–79,	SDP 81–83	
J. (Havelock) Wilson	Lib. 92–00,	Lab. 06–10,	Co.N.D.P. 18–22	

M.P.s Denied Party Renomination since 1922

When a sitting M.P. does not stand again, it is often unclear whether the retirement is entirely voluntary. Irreparable conflicts with the local party may be behind formal statements about reasons of health or age or business. At least in the following cases, there is little doubt that the local party failed to renominate a sitting and willing M.P. who was still in receipt of the party whip at Westminster.[1] It is plain that in the overwhelming majority of cases the disagreement could be ascribed to personal rather than ideological considerations. In several of the 1983 cases, the M.P.s were seeking renomination in a substantially redrawn constituency, often against another sitting M.P.

---

[1] Up to 1983 this list does not include M.P.s whose seats were substantially changed by redistribution and who failed to secure renomination for any part of their old seat, e.g. in Feb 1974 Sir R. Russell and E. Bullus, Con. members for Wembley N. and Wembley S., were spurned for the successor seats, Brent North and Brent South, while W. Wells, Lab. member for Walsall N., was denied renomination in the redistribution seat of the same name.

Conservative

1923	Sir C. Warner (Lichfield)		1964	O. Prior-Palmer (Worthing)
1929	[a]Sir R. Newman (Exeter)		1964	[b]D. Johnson (Carlisle)
1935	[b]J. Lockwood (Shipley)		1964	J. Henderson (Glasgow, Cathcart)
1935	H. Moss (Rutherglen)		1970	R. Harris (Heston & Isleworth)
1938	[b]Duchess of Atholl (Perth & Kinross)		1974	Sir C. Taylor (Eastbourne)
1945	[a]J. McKie (Galloway)		1979	B. Drayson (Skipton)
1945	[b]C. Cunningham-Reid (St.Marylebone)		1979	R. Cooke (Bristol W.)
1945	H. Clifton Brown (Newbury)		1983	T. Benyon (Wantage)
1950	N. Bower (Harrow, West)		1983	M. Brotherton (Louth)
1950	C. Challen (Hampstead)		1983	J. Bruce-Gardyne (Knutsford)
1950	A. Marsden (Chertsey)		1983	R. Mawby (Totnes)
1950	Sir G. Fox (Henley)		1983	G. Morgan (Clwyd N.W.)
1951	E. Gates (Middleton & Prestwich)		1983	W. Rees-Davies (Thanet North)
1954	Lord M. Douglas Hamilton (Inverness)		1983	K. Stainton (Sudbury)
1959	N. Nicolson (Bournemouth E.)		1987	C. Murphy (Welwyn & Hatfield)
1959	Sir F. Medlicott (C. Norfolk)		1992	Sir A. Meyer (Clwyd N.W.)
1959	L. Turner (Oxford)		1992	[b]J. Browne (Winchester)
1964	M. Lindsay (Solihull)			

Ulster Unionist

1945	[a]D. Little (Down)		1970	G. Currie (Down, North)
1959	M. Hyde (Belfast N.)			

Labour

1929	[a]N. Maclean (Glasgow, Govan)		1983	F. Hooley (Sheffield, Heeley)
1929	E. Davies (Ebbw Vale)		1983	A. Lewis (Newham N.W.)
1945	[b]T. Groves (West Ham, Stratford)		1983	Mrs H. McElhone
1945	H. Charleton (Leeds S.)			(Glasgow, Queens Park)
1950	N. Maclean (Glasgow, Govan)		1983	A. McMahon (Glasgow, Govan)
1951	R. Adams (C. Wandsworth)		1983	C. Morris (Manchester Openshaw)
1951	J. Mack (Newcastle-under-Lyme)		1983	F. Mulley (Sheffield Park)
1955	J. Kinley (Bootle)		1983	E. Ogden (Liverpool W. Derby)
1955	J. Glanville (Consett)		1983	R. Race (Tottenham)
1959	E. Davies (Enfield E.)		1983	J. Sever (Birmingham Ladywood)
1964	J. Baird (Wolverhampton N.E.)		1983	A. Stallard (St Pancras N.)
1966	W. Warbey (Ashfield)		1983	J. Tilley (Lambeth & Vauxhall)
1970	M. McKay (Wandsworth. Clapham)		1983	D. Watkins (Consett)
1970	[a]S. O. Davies (Merthyr)		1987	R. Freeson (Brent E.)
1973	[a]D. Taverne (Lincoln)		1987	M. Maguire (Makerfield)
1974	[a]E. Milne (Blyth)		1987	N. Atkinson (Tottenham)
1974	[b]E. Griffiths (Sheffield, Brightside)		1987	M. Cocks (Bristol S.)
1974	W. Baxter (W. Stirlingshire)		1987	A. Woodall (Hemsworth)
1979	[c]Sir A. Irvine (Liverpool, Edge Hill)		1987	E. Roberts (Hackney N.)
1979	F. Tomney (Hammersmith N.)		1987	J. Forrester (Stoke N.)
1983	J. Barnett (Heywood & Royton)		1992	[b]D. Nellist (Coventry S.E.)
1983	S. Cohen (Leeds S.E.)		1992	[b]R. Brown (Edinburgh, Leith)
1983	S. C. Davies (Hackney C.)		1992	[b]T. Fields (Liverpool Broad Green)
1983	M. English (Nottingham W.)		1992	[b]J. Hughes (Coventry N.E.)
1983	[b]B. Ford (Bradford N.)		1992	[b]S. Bidwell (Southall)
1983	R. Fletcher (Ilkeston)			

[a] Stood as Independent and won.
[b] Stood as Independent and lost.
[c] Died before the ensuing election.

SOURCES.— R. J. Jackson, *Whips and Rebels* (1968); J. Pentney, 'Worms that Turned', *Parliamentary Affairs* (Autumn 1977), pp. 363–73.

By-elections

	Total* By-elections	Changes	Con. +	Con. −	Lib +	Lib −	Lab +	Lab −	Oth. +	Oth. −	No. per Year	% with Change
1900–05	113	30	2	26	20	4	3	–	5	–	22	27
1906–09	101	20	12	–	–	18	5	–	3	2	25	20
1910	20	–	–	–	–	–	–	–	–	–	20	–
1911–18	245	31	16	4	4	16	2	4	10	8	31	13
1918–22	108	27	4	13	5*	11*	14	1	4	2	27	25
1922–23	16	6	1	4	3	1	2	–	–	1	16	38
1923–24	10	3	2	1	–	1	1	1	–	–	10	30
1924–29	63	20	1	16	6	3	13	1	–	–	14	32
1929–31	36	7	4	1	–	1	2	4	1	1	15	19
1931–35	62	10	–	9	–	1	10	–	–	–	15	16
1935–45	219	30	–	29	–	–	13	1	17	–	23	14
1945–50	52	3	3	–	–	–	–	–	–	3	11	6
1950–51	16	–	–	–	–	–	–	–	–	–	10	–
1951–55	48	1	1	–	–	–	–	1	–	–	13	2
1955–59	52	6	1	4	1	1	4	–	–	1	12	12
1959–64	62	9	2	7	1	–	6	2	–	–	15	14
1964–66	13	2	1	1	1	–	–	1	–	–	9	15
1966–70	38	16	12	1	1	–	–	15	3	–	9	42
1970–74	30	9	–	5	5	–	2	3	2	1	9	30
1974	1	–	–	–	–	–	–	–	–	–	1	–
1974–79	30	7	6	–	1	–	–	7	–	–	6	23
1979–83	20	7	1	4	4	–	1	1	1	2	5	35
1983–87	31	6	–	4	4	–	1	1	1	1	8	19[a]
1987–92	23	8	–	7	3	–	4	1	1	–	4	35

* Up to 1918, and to a lesser extent to 1926, the number of by-elections is inflated by the necessity for Ministers to stand for re-election on appointment. In 53 such cases the returns were unopposed.
[a] 15 of the 31 by-elections were in N. Ireland. In mainland G.B. there were 16 by-elections – an annual incidence of 4 with a turnover rate of 31%.

Seats Changing Hands at By-elections

Date	Constituency	General Election	By-election	Date	Constituency	General Election	By-election
26 Sep 01	N.E. Lanark.	Lib.	Con.	30 Jan 04	[†]Ayr	Con.	Lib.
21 Nov 01	Galway	Con.	Nat.	12 Feb 04	[†]Mid-Herts.	Con.	Lib.
10 May 02	Bury	Con.	Lib.	17 Mar 04	E. Dorset	Con.	Lib.
29 Jul 02	Leeds N.	Con.	Lib.	6 Apr 04	Isle of Wight	Con.	Ind.Con.
1 Aug 02	Clitheroe	Lib.	Lab.	20 Jun 04	Devonport	{ Con. 02	Lib.
18 Aug 02	S. Belfast	Con.	Ind.U.			{ Lib. 00	
22 Oct 02	[†]Devonport	Lib.	Con.	26 Jul 04	[†]W. Shropshire	Con.	Lib.
19 Nov 02	Orkney & Shetland	Con.	Ind.Lib.	10 Aug 04	N.E. Lanark	{ Con. 01	Lib.
						{ Lib. 00	
2 Jan 03	E. Cambs.	Con.	Lib.	7 Jan 05	Stalybridge	Con.	Lib.
1 Mar 03	Woolwich	Con.	Lab.	26 Jan 05	N. Dorset	Con.	Lib.
17 Mar 03	[†]E. Sussex	Con.	Lib.	3 Mar 05	Bute	Con.	Lib.
20 Mar 03	[†]N. Fermanagh	Con.	Ind.Con.	5 Apr 05	Brighton	Con.	Lib.
24 Jul 03	Barnard Castle	Lib.	Lab.	1 Jun 05	[†]Whitby	Con.	Lib.
26 Aug 03	Argyll	Con.	Lib.	29 Jun 05	Finsbury E.	Con.	Lib.
17 Sep 03	[†]St Andrews	Con.	Lib.	13 Oct 05	[†]Barkston Ash	Con.	Lib.
15 Jan 04	Norwich	Con.	Lib.				

[a] Miners candidates standing as Lib–Lab, who only joined the Labour Party in 1909.
[†] Seats regained at subsequent General Election.

Date		Constituency	General Election	By-election
General Election 12 Jan–7 Feb 06				
3 Aug	06	Cockermouth	Lib.	Con.
31 Dec	06	Mid-Cork	Nat.	I.Nat.
30 Jan	07	N.E.Derbyshire[a]	Lib.	Lab.
26 Feb	07	†Brigg	Lib.	Con.
4 Jul	07	†Jarrow	Lib.	Lab.
18 Jul	07	†Colne Valley	Lib.	I.Lab.
31 Jul	07	N.W. Staffs[a]	Lib.	Lab.
17 Jan	08	†Mid-Devon	Lib.	Con.
31 Jan	08	S. Hereford	Lib.	Con.
24 Mar	08	Peckham	Lib.	Con.
24 Apr	08	†Manchester N.W.	Lib.	Con.
20 Jun	08	†Pudsey	Lib.	Con.
1 Aug	08	†Haggerston	Lib.	Con.
24 Sep	08	†Newcastle-o-T.	Lib.	Con.
2 Mar	09	Glasgow C.	Lib.	Con.
1 May	09	Cork City	Nat.	I.Nat.
4 May	09	Attercliffe	Lib	Lab.
4 May	09	Stratford-on-Avon	Lib.	Con.
15 Jul	09	Mid-Derbyshire	Lib.	Lab.
28 Oct	09	†Bermondsey	Lib.	Con.
General Election 14 Jan–9 Feb 10				
1910		no change		
General Election 2–19 Dec 10				
28 Apr	11	Cheltenham	Lib.	Con.
13 Nov	11	Oldham	Lib.	Con.
21 Nov	11	S. Somerset	Lib.	Con.
20 Dec	11	N. Ayrshire	Lib.	Con.
5 Mar	12	Manchester S.	Lib.	Con.
13 Jul	12	Hanley	Lab.	Lib.
26 Jul	12	Crewe	Lib.	Con.
8 Aug	12	Manchester N.W.	Lib.	Con.
10 Sep	12	Edinburghshire	Lib.	Con.
26 Nov	12	Bow & Bromley	Lab.	Con.
30 Jan	13	Londonderry	Con.	Lib.
18 Mar	13	S. Westmorland	Con.	Ind.Con.
16 May	13	E. Cambs.	Lib.	Con.
20 Aug	13	Chesterfield	Lab.	Lib.
8 Nov	13	Reading	Lib.	Con.
12 Dec	13	S. Lanarkshire	Lib.	Con.
19 Feb	14	Bethnal Green S.W.	Lib.	Con.
26 Feb	14	Leith	Lib.	Con.
20 May	14	N.E. Derbyshire	Lab.	Con.
23 May	14	Ipswich	Lib.	Con.
9 Dec	14	Tullamore	Nat.	I.Nat.
25 Nov	15	Merthyr Tydfil	Lab.	Ind.
9 Mar	16	E. Herts	Con.	Ind.
15 Nov	16	W. Cork	I.Nat.	Nat.
23 Dec	16	†Ashton-u-Lyne	Con.	Lib. (Unop.)
23 Dec	16	Sheffield, Attercliffe	Con.	Lib.
3 Feb	17	N. Roscommon	Nat.	S.F.
10 May	17	S. Longford	Nat.	S.F.
10 Jul	17	E. Clare	Nat.	S.F.
10 Aug	17	Kilkenny	Nat.	S.F.
2 Nov	17	Salford N.	Lib.	Lab.
19 Apr	18	Tullamore	{ I.Nat 14 / Nat. 10 }	S.F.
20 Jun	18	E. Cavan	Nat.	S.F.
General Election 14 Dec 18				
1 Mar	19	†Leyton W.	Co.U.	Lib.
29 Mar	19	Hull C.	Co.U.	Lib.
16 Apr	19	C. Aberdeen & Kincardine	Co.U.	Lib.
27 May	19	E. Antrim	Con.	Ind.U.
16 Jul	19	Bothwell	Co.U.	Lab.
30 Aug	19	†Widnes	Co.U.	Lab.
20 Dec	19	Spen Valley	Co.Lib.	Lab.
7 Feb	20	Wrekin	Co.Lib.	Ind.
27 Mar	20	†Dartford	Co.Lib.	Lab.
27 Mar	20	Stockport	Co.Lab.	Co.U.
6 Jun	20	Louth	Co.U.	Lib.
27 Jul	20	S. Norfolk	Lib.	Lab.
12 Jan	21	†Dover	Co.U.	Ind.
2 Mar	21	†Woolwich E.	Lab.	Co.U.
3 Mar	21	†Dudley	Co.U.	Lab.
4 Mar	21	†Kirkcaldy	Co.Lib.	Lab.
5 Mar	21	Penistone	Lib.	Lab.
7 Jun	21	Westminster, St George's	Co.U.	Ind.
16 Jun	21	Hertford	Ind.	Ind.
8 Jun	21	†Heywood & Radcliffe	Co.Lib.	Lab.
14 Dec	21	†Southwark, S.E.	Co.Lib.	Lab.
18 Feb	22	†Manchester, Clayton	Con.	Lab.
20 Feb	22	Camberwell N.	Co.U.	Lab.
24 Feb	22	Bodmin	Co.U.	Lib.
30 Mar	22	†Leicester E.	Co.Lib.	Lab.
25 Jul	22	Pontypridd	Co.Lib.	Lab.
18 Aug	22	Hackney S.	Ind.	Co.U.
18 Oct	22	Newport	Co.Lib.	Con.
General Election 15 Nov 22				
3 Mar	23	†Mitcham	Con.	Lab.
3 Mar	23	Willesden E.	Con.	Lib.
6 Mar	23	Liverpool, Edge Hill	Con.	Lab.
7 Apr	23	Anglesey	Ind.	Lib.
31 May	23	Berwick on Tweed	Nat.Lib.	Con.
21 Jun	23	Tiverton	Con.	Lib.
General Election 6 Dec 23				
22 May	24	Liverpool, W. Toxteth	Con.	Lab.
5 Jun	24	Oxford	Lib.	Con.
31 Jul	24	Holland with Boston	Lab.	Con.

[a] Miners candidates standing as Lib–Lab, who only joined the Labour Party in 1909.
† Seats regained at subsequent General Election.

Date	Constituency	General Election	By-election
General Election 29 Oct 24			
17 Sep 25	Stockport	Con.	Lab.
17 Feb 26	Darlington	Con.	Lab.
12 Mar 26	English Univs.	Lib.	Con.
29 Apr 26	East Ham N.	Con.	Lab.
28 May 26	Hammersmith N.	Con.	Lab.
29 Nov 26	Hull C.	Lib.	Lab.
23 Feb 27	Stourbridge	Con.	Lab.
28 Mar 27	†Southwark N.	Lab.	Lib.
31 May 27	Bosworth	Con.	Lib.
9 Jan 28	Northampton	Con.	Lab.
9 Feb 28	†Lancaster	Con.	Lib.
6 Mar 28	St Ives	Con.	Lib.
4 Apr 28	Linlithgow	Con.	Lab.
13 Jul 28	Halifax	Lib.	Lab.
29 Oct 28	Ashton-u-Lyne	Con.	Lab.
29 Jan 29	†N. Midlothian	Con.	Lab.
7 Feb 29	Battersea S.	Con.	Lab.
20 Mar 29	Eddisbury	Con.	Lib.
21 Mar 29	†N. Lanark	Con.	Lab.
21 Mar 29	Holland	Con.	Lib.
General Election 30 May 29			
31 Jul 29	Preston	Lib.	Lab.
14 Dec 29	Liverpool, Scotland	I.Nat.	Lab. (Unop.)
6 May 30	Fulham W.	Lab.	Con.
30 Oct 30	Paddington S.	Con.	Ind.
6 Nov 30	Shipley	Lab.	Con.
26 Mar 31	Sunderland	Lab.	Con.
30 Apr 31	Ashton-u-Lyne	Lab.	Con.
General Election 27 Oct 31			
21 Apr 32	Wakefield	Con.	Lab.
26 Jul 32	Wednesbury	Con.	Lab.
27 Feb 33	Rotherham	Con.	Lab.
25 Oct 33	†Fulham E.	Con.	Lab.
24 Apr 34	Hammersmith N.	Con.	Lab.
14 May 34	West Ham, Upton	Con.	Lab.
23 Oct 34	Lambeth N.	Lib.	Lab.
25 Oct 34	†Swindon	Con.	Lab.
6 Feb 35	†Liverpool, Wavertree	Con.	Lab.
16 Jul 35	Liverpool, W. Toxteth	Con.	Lab.
General Election 14 Nov 35			
18 Mar 36	Dunbartonshire	Con.	Lab.
6 May 36	Camberwell, Peckham	Con.	Lab.
9 Jul 36	Derby	Con.	Lab.
26 Nov 36	Greenock	Con.	Lab.
27 Feb 37	Oxford Univ.	Con.	Ind.Con.

Date	Constituency	General Election	By-election
19 Mar 37	English Univs.	Con.	Ind.
29 Apr 37	Wandsworth C.	Con.	Lab.
22 Jun 37	Cheltenham	Con.	Ind.Con.
13 Oct 37	Islington N.	Con.	Lab.
16 Feb 38	Ipswich	Con.	Lab.
6 Apr 38	Fulham W.	Con.	Lab.
5 May 38	Lichfield	Con.	Lab.
7 Nov 38	Dartford	Con.	Lab.
17 Nov 38	Bridgwater	Con.	Ind.
21 Dec 38	Kinross & W. Perth	Con. (Ind.)	Con.
17 May 39	Southwark N.	Con.	Lab.
24 May 39	Lambeth, Kennington	Con.	Lab.
1 Aug 39	Brecon & Radnor	Con.	Lab.
24 Feb 40	Cambridge Univ.	Con.	Ind.Con.
8 Jun 40	†Newcastle N.	Con.	Ind.Con.
25 Mar 42	Grantham	Con.	Ind.
29 Apr 42	Rugby	Con.	Ind.
29 Apr 42	†Wallasey	Con.	Ind.
25 Jun 42	Maldon	Con.	Ind.
9 Feb 43	Belfast W.	Un.	Eire Lab.
7 Apr 43	†Eddisbury	Con.	C.W.
7 Jan 44	†Skipton	Con.	C.W.
17 Feb 44	W. Derbyshire	Con.	Ind.
12 Apr 45	†Motherwell	Lab.	S.Nat.
13 Apr 45	Scottish Univs.	Con.	Ind.
26 Apr 45	Chelmsford	Con.	C.W.
General Election 5 Jul 45			
18 Mar 46	English Univs.	Ind.	Con.
6 Jun 46	Down	Ind.U.	Un.
29 Nov 46	Scottish Univs.	Ind.	Con.
28 Jan 48	†Glasgow, Camlachie	I.L.P.	Con.
General Election 23 Feb 50			
1950–51	no change		
General Election 25 Oct 51			
13 May 53	Sunderland, S.	Lab.	Con.
General Election 26 May 55			
11 Aug 55	Mid-Ulster	S.F.	Un.
8 May 56	Mid-Ulster	{ S.F. 55 / Un. 55 }	Ind.Un.
14 Feb 57	†Lewisham N.	Con.	Lab.
28 Feb 57	Carmarthen	Lib.	Lab.
12 Feb 58	Rochdale	Con.	Lab.
13 Mar 58	†Glasgow, Kelvingrove	Con.	Lab.
27 Mar 58	†Torrington	Con.	Lib.

† Seats regained at subsequent General Election.

Date	Constituency	General Election	By-election
General Election 8 Oct 59			
17 Mar 60	†Brighouse & Spenborough	Lab.	Con.
4 May 61	ªBristol S.E.	Lab.	Con.
14 Mar 62	Orpington	Con.	Lib.
6 Jun 62	Middlesbrough W.	Con.	Lab.
22 Nov 62	Glasgow, Woodside	Con.	Lab.
22 Nov 62	†S. Dorset	Con.	Lab.
23 Aug 63	Bristol S.E.	{ Lab.59 Conª61	Lab.
7 Nov 63	Luton	Con.	Lab.
14 May 64	Rutherglen	Con.	Lab.
General Election 15 Oct 64			
21 Jan 65	†Leyton	Lab.	Con.
24 Mar 65	Roxburgh Selkirk & Peebles	Con.	Lib.
General Election 31 Mar 66			
14 Jul 66	†Carmarthen	Lab.	P.C.
9 Mar 67	†Glasgow Pollok	Lab.	Con.
21 Sep 67	†Walthamstow W.	Lab.	Con.
21 Sep 67	Cambridge	Lab.	Con.
2 Nov 67	†Hamilton	Lab.	SNP
2 Nov 67	Leicester S.W.	Lab.	Con.
28 Mar 68	†Acton	Lab.	Con.
28 Mar 68	Meriden	Lab.	Con.
28 Mar 68	†Dudley	Lab.	Con.
13 Jun 68	†Oldham W.	Lab.	Con.
27 Jun 68	Nelson & Colne	Lab.	Con.
27 Mar 69	Walthamstow E.	Lab.	Con.
17 Apr 69	Mid-Ulster	U.U.	Ind.
26 Jun 69	†Birmingham, Ladywood	Lab.	Lib.
30 Oct 69	†Swindon	Lab.	Con.
4 Dec 69	Wellingborough	Lab.	Con.
General Election 18 Jun 70			
27 May 71	†Bromsgrove	Con.	Lab.
13 Apr 72	Merthyr Tydfil	I.Lab.	Lab.
26 0ct 72	Rochdale	Lab.	Lib.
7 Dec 72	†Sutton & Cheam	Con.	Lib.
1 Mar 73	Lincoln	Lab.	Dem.Lab.
26 Jul 73	Isle of Ely	Con.	Lib.
26 Jul 73	†Ripon	Con.	Lib.
8 Nov 73	†Glasgow Govan	Lab.	SNP
8 Nov 73	Berwick on Tweed	Con.	Lib.
General Election 28 Feb 74			
1974	no change		

Date	Constituency	General Election	By-election
General Election 10 Oct 74			
26 Jun 75	Woolwich W.	Lab.	Con.
4 Nov 76	†Walsall N.	Lab.	Con.
14 Nov 76	†Workington	Lab.	Con.
31 Mar 77	†Birmingham, Stechford	Lab.	Con.
28 Apr 77	†Ashfield	Lab.	Con.
2 Mar 78	Ilford N.	Lab.	Con.
29 Mar 79	Liverpool, Edge Hill	Lab.	Lib.
General Election 3 May 79			
9 Apr 81	Fermanagh & S. Tyrone	Ind.	Anti-H Block
22 Oct 81	†Croydon N.W.	Con.	Lib.
26 Nov 81	†Crosby	Con.	SDP
25 Mar 82	Glasgow, Hillhead	Con.	SDP
3 Jun 82	Mitcham & Morden	Ind. SDP	Con.
28 Oct 82	†Birmingham Northfield	Con.	Lab.
24 Feb 83	Bermondsey	Lab.	Lib.
General Election 9 June 83			
14 Jun 84	†Portsmouth S.	Con.	SDP
4 Jul 85	Brecon & Radnor	Con.	Lib.
26 Jan 86	Newry & Armagh	U.U.	SDLP
4 Apr 86	†Fulham	Con.	Lab.
8 May 86	†Ryedale	Con.	Lib.
26 Feb 87	Greenwich	Lab.	SDP
General Election 11 Jun 87			
10 Nov 88	†Glasgow, Govan	Lab.	SNP
4 Apr 89	†Vale of Glamorgan	Con.	Lab.
22 Mar 90	†Mid Staffs	Con.	Lab.
16 May 91	†Monmouth	Con.	Lab.
18 Oct 90	†Eastbourne	Con.	Lib.D.
7 Mar 91	†Ribble Valley	Con.	Lib.D.
7 Nov 91	†Langbaurgh	Con.	Lab.
7 Nov 91	†Kincardine & Deeside	Con.	Lib.D.
General Election 9 Apr 92			
6 May 93	Newbury	Con.	Lib.D.
29 Jul 93	Christchurch	Con.	Lib.D.
9 Jun 94	Eastleigh	Con.	Lib.D.

ª Seat awarded to Con. on petition.
† Seats regained at subsequent General Election.

In addition, there have over the years been a number of by-elections where the seat did not change hands, but which were seen as having great significance at the time. these are the outstanding examples:

19 Mar 24	Westminister (Abbey)	The official Conservative defeated the independent (W. Churchill) by 43 votes.
19 Mar 31	Westminster (St George's)	The official Conservative defeated an independent candidate supported by owners of popular newspapers.
27 Oct 38	Oxford	The official Conservative (Q. Hogg) defeated the independent anti-appeasement candidate.
24 Feb 49	Hammersmith South	Labour held on to a marginal seat – the Conservatives' best hope of a win during the post-war Lab govt. (1945–51).
27 Jan 66	Hull North	Swing of 4.5% to Lab encouraged govt. to call a general election.
28 Apr 77	Grimsby	Lab held seat unexpectedly when it was losing safer seats elsewhere.
16 Jul 82	Warrington	Lab held seat despite enormous swing to SDP (R. Jenkins).
28 Mar 83	Darlington	Lab held seat in three-cornered race when defeat could have ended M. Foot's leadership.

MPs seeking re-election

The following M.P.s on changing their party, or for other reasons, voluntarily resigned their seats to test public opinion in a by-election:

Date of by-election	M.P.	Constituency	Former label	New label	Whether successful
18 Nov 02	J. Wason	Orkney & Shetland	L.U.	Ind. L.	Yes
6 Apr 04	J. Seely	I. of Wight	Con.	Ind.	Yes (unop.)
19 Aug 04	W. O'Brien	Cork City	Nat.	Nat.	Yes
31 Dec 06	D. Sheehan	Mid-Cork	Nat.	Ind.Nat.	Yes (unop.)
21 Dec 08	C. Dolan	N. Leitrim	Nat.	Ind. Nat.	No
4 May 09	T. Kincaid-Smith	Stratford-on-Avon	Lib.	Ind.	No
26 Nov 12	G. Lansbury	Bow and Bromley	Lab.	Ind.	No
18 Feb 14	W. O'Brien	Cork City	Ind.Nat.	Ind.Nat.	Yes (unop.)
21 Jul 14	R. Hazleton	N. Galway	Nat.	Nat.	Yes (unop.)
29 Nov 26	J. Kenworthy	Hull C.	Lib.	Lab.	Yes
28 Mar 27	L. Guest	Southwark N.	Lab.	Const.	No
31 Jul 29	Sir W. Jowitt	Preston	Lib.	Lab.	Yes
21 Dec 38	Dss of Atholl	Kinross & W. Perth	Con.	Ind.	No
26 May 55[a]	Sir R. Acland	Gravesend	Lab.	Ind.	No
1 Mar 73	D. Taverne	Lincoln	Lab.	Dem. Lab.	Yes
3 Jun 82	B. Douglas-Mann	Mitcham & Morden	Lab.	Ind.SDP	No
23 Jan 86	15 M.P.s	Northern Ireland	Unionist	Unionist	14 Yes, 1 No

[a] Date of General Election which overtook the by-election.

Some members have been compelled to seek re-election – because they inadvertently held a government contract or appointment, or because they voted before taking the oath. This last happened in 1925.

Until the Re-election of Ministers Acts of 1919 and 1926 there were many cases of members having to seek re-election on appointment to ministerial office. In eight instances they were unsuccessful:

5 Apr	05	G. Loder	Brighton
24 Apr	08	W. Churchill	Manchester N.W.
20 Dec	11	A. Anderson	N. Ayrshire
5 Mar	12	Sir A. Haworth	Manchester S.
19 Feb	14	C. Masterman	Bethnal Green S.W.
23 May	14	C. Masterman	Ipswich
3 Mar	21	Sir A. Griffith-Boscawen	Dudley
25 Jul	22	T. Lewis	Pontypridd

The following ministers, defeated in a general election, stayed in office until a subsequent by-election.

Successful in by-election and continued in office		*Defeated in by-election and resigned office*	
Jan 1910	J. Seely	1922	Sir A. Griffith-Boscawen
Jan 1910	J. Pease	1922	J. Hills
Dec 1910	C. Masterman[a]	1922	G. Stanley
1935	R. Macdonald	1964	P. Gordon Walker
1935	M. Macdonald		
1950	Sir F. Soskice		

[a] Unseated on petition Jun 1911 but won by-election Jul 1911.

In 1959 J. Browne, a Scottish Office minister, was defeated in the general election but was given a peerage (Ld Craigton) and stayed in office. In 1983 H. Gray, an energy minister, was defeated in the general election but was given a peerage (Ld Gray of Contin) and stayed in office. In 1992 Lynda Chalker was defeated but was given a peerage and stayed in office.

See also p. 68 for Cabinet Ministers defeated while holding office.

Electoral Administration

From 1900 to 1918 electoral arrangements were governed primarily by the Representation of the People Act, 1867, as modified by the Ballot Act, 1872, the Corrupt Practices Act, 1883, the Franchise Act, 1884, the Registration Act, 1885, and the Redistribution of Seats Act, 1885. The Representation of the People Act, 1918, the Equal Franchise Act, 1928, and the Representation of the People Act, 1948 (consolidated in 1949), constitute the only major legislation in the century.

There have been seven major inquiries into electoral questions:

1908–10	Royal Commission on Electoral Systems
1917	Speaker's Conference on Electoral Reform
1930	Ullswater Conference on Electoral Reform
1943–44	Speaker's Conference on Electoral Reform
1965–68	Speaker's Conference on Electoral Law
1972–74	Speaker's Conference on Electoral Law
1977–78	Speaker's Conference on Electoral Law

The Franchise. From 1885 the United Kingdom had a system of fairly widespread male franchise, limited however by a year's residence qualification and some other restrictions. Voting in more than one constituency was permitted to owners of land, to occupiers of business premises, and to university graduates. The *Representation of the People Act, 1918,* reduced the residence qualification to six months and enfranchised some categories of men who had not previously had the vote. It also enfranchised women over 30. In 1928 the *Equal Franchise Act* lowered the voting age for women to 21. In 1948 the *Representation of the People Act* abolished the business and university votes for parliamentary elections; it also abolished the six months residence qualification.

In 1969 the Representation of the People Act provided votes for everyone as soon as they reached the age of 18.

Electorate

Year	Population	Population over 21	Electorate	Electorate as % of Adult Population[a]	
				Male	Total
1900	41,155,000	22,675,000	6,730,935	58	27
1910	44,915,000	26,134,000	7,694,741	58	28
1919	44,599,000	27,364,000	21,755,583	..	78
1929	46,679,000	31,711,000	28,850,870	..	90
1939	47,762,000	32,855,000	32,403,559	..	97
1949	50,363,000	35,042,000	34,269,770	..	98
1959	52,157,000	35,911,000	35,397,080	..	99
1970	55,700,000	40,784,000[b]	39,153,000	..	96
1979	55,822,000	42,100,000[b]	41,769,000	..	99
1990	57,801,000	44,503,000[b]	43,663,000	..	98

[a] This percentages makes allowance for plural voting. In the period before 1914 this amounted to about 500,000. After 1918 the business vote reached its peak in 1929 at 370,000. The university electorate rose from 39,101 in 1900 to 217,363 in 1945. See J. Todd and P. Butcher, *Electoral Registration 1981* (1982) for an estimate of the efficiency of the registration process.
[b] Population over 18.

Redistribution. The Redistribution of Seats Act, 1885, left the House of Commons with 670 members. The 1885 Act, while removing the worst of the anomalies, specifical rejected the principle that constituencies should be approximately equal in size. This principle was, however, substantially accepted in the Representation of the People Act,1918, on the recommendation of the Speaker's conference of 1917, although Wales, Scotland and Ireland were allowed to retain disproportionate numbers of seats. The 1918 Act increased the size of the House of Commons to 707 but this fell to 615 in 1922 on the creation of the Irish Free State. Population movements produced sustantial anomalies in representation and the *Redistribution of Seats Act, 1944,* authorised the immediate subdivision of constituencies with more than 100,000 electors, which led to 25 new seats being created for the 1945 election and raised the size of Parliament to 640. It also provided for the estabishment of Permanent Boundary Commissioners to report every three to seven years. The Boundary Commissioners' first recommendations were enacted in the *Representation of the People Act, 1948* (with the controversial addition by the Government of 17 extra seats as well as the abolition of the 12 University seats), and the 1950 Parliament had 625 members. The next reports of the Boundary Commissioners, given effect by resolutions of the House in December 1954 and january 1955, increased the number of constituencies to 630. The controversy caused by these changes led to the *Redistribution of Seats Act, 1958*, which modified the rules governing the Boundary Commissioners' decisions and asked them to report only every 10 to 15 years. The Boundary Commissioners started their revision in 1965; they reported in 1969, but the Labour Government secured the temporary rejection of their proposals. In November 1970 the Conservative Government gave effect to the 1969 proposals. The House of Commons elected in 1974 therefore had 635 constituencies. In 1977 the Boundary Commissioners began work on a fresh general revision of boundaries and in February 1978 a Speaker's Conference recommended that the representation of Northern Ireland should be increased from 12 to 17 seats. An Act authorising the Boundary Commissioners to proceed on this basis was passed in March 1979. In 1983 the general revision resulted in a House of Commons of 650. The laws on Redistribution were considated in the *Parliamentary Constituencies Act, 1986*. In 1992 the number of seats rose to 651 because of an extra seat created to cope with the overlarge constituencies around Milton Keynes. In 1991 the Boundary Commissions initiated a further redrawing of boundaries to be completed in 1995; but in 1992 a new *Redistribution Act* required them to report by the end of 1994; it also reduced the maximum interval between reviews from 15 to 12 years.

Election Expenses

Candidates' expenses were restricted by the *Corrupt Practices Act, 1883*, on a formula based on the number of electors. Candidates still had to bear the administrative costs of the election. The *Representation of the People Act, 1918*, removed from the candidates responsibility for the Returning Officers' fees and lowered the maximum limits on expenditure. This limit was further reduced by the *Representation of the People Act, 1948*, and only slightly increased by the *Representation of the People Act, 1969*; in February 1974 the *Representation of the People Act, 1974*, provided a further increase. In the following table the effect of variations in the number of unopposed candidates should be borne in mind (unopposed candidates seldom spent as much as £200). It is notable how the modifications in the law have kept electioneering costs stable despite a fivefold depreciation in the value of money and a fivefold increase in the size of the electorate.

Candidates' Election Expenses

Year	Total Expenditure	Candidates	Average per Candidate	Con.	Lib.	Lab
1900	777,429	1,002	776	731	831	419
1906	1,166,858	1,273	917	..	..	..
J.10	1,295,782	1,315	985	1,109	1,075	881
D.10	978,312	1,191	821	918	882	736
1918	No returns	1,625	..	..	..	..
1922	1,018,196	1,443	706	..	..	540
1923	982,340	1,446	679	845	789	464
1924	921,165	1,428	645	..	..	436
1929	1,213,507	1,730	701	905	782	452
1931	654,105	1,292	506	..	..	..
1935	722,093	1,348	536	777	495	365
1945	1,073,216	1,682	638	780	532	595
1950	1,170,124	1,868	626	777	459	694
1951	946,018	1,376	688	773	488	658
1955	904,677	1,409	642	692	423	611
1959	1,051,219	1,536	684	761	532	705
1964	1,229,205	1,757	699	790	579	751
1966	1,130,882	1,707	667	766	501	726
1970	1,392,796	1,786	761	949	828	667
F.74	1,780,542	2,135	951	1,197	745	1,127
O.74	2,168,514	2,252	963	1,275	725	1,163
1979	3,557,441	2,576	1,381	2,190	1,013	1,897
1983	6,145,264	2,579	2,383	3,320	2,520	2,927
1987	8,305,721	2,325	3,572	4,400	3,400	3,900
1992	10,443,407	2,948	3,542	5,840	3,169	5,090

These figures are based on the official returns from the candidates. What constitutes an election expense is a matter of judgement, particularly since there have been no petitions to test the law on expenses since 1929. Party headquarters have provided separate estimates of the amount spent centrally in general elections. (See also pp. 132–3 and 151.)

	Con. (£)	Lab. (£)		Con. (£)	Lab. (£)
1959	974,000	541,000	1979	2,300,000	1,038,000
1964	992,000	314,000	1983	3,800,000	2,258,000
1970	630,000	525,000	1987	9,000,000	4,200,000
1974 Feb	680,000	437,000	1992	10,100,000	7,100,000
1974 Oct	950,000	521,000			

European Referendum Expenses

In the 1975 Referendum each side was awarded £125,000 from public funds on condition that they published their accounts from 27 Mar 1975 onwards. Britain in Europe, the pro-Market 'umbrella organisation', reported an outlay of £1,481,583. On the other side the National Referendum Campaign reported £131,354. It has been estimated that Britain in Europe actually spent £1,850,000 in all.

Lost Deposits

The *Representation of the People Act, 1918* provided that any parliamentary candidate would have to deposit, on nomination, £150 in cash with the returning officer. This money would be forfeit to the state unless the candidate received one-eighth of the valid votes cast. In 1985 the deposit was raised from £150 to £500 but the condition of forfeiture was lowered from one eighth to one twentieth (5%).

	Con.	Lab.	Lib. (Alln.)	Comm.	Other	Total	% of all Candidates
1918	3	6	44	–	108	161	9.9
1922	1	7	31	1	12	52	3.6
1923	–	17	8	–	2	27	1.9
1924	1	28	30	1	8	68	4.7
1929	18	35	25	21	14	113	6.5
1931	–	21	6	21	37	85	6.6
1935	1	16	40	–	24	81	6.0
1945	5	2	76	12	87	182	10.8
1950	5	0	319	97	40	461	24.6
1951	3	1	66	10	16	96	7.0
1955	3	1	60	15	21	100	7.1
1959	2	1	55	17	41	116	7.6
1964	5	8	52	36	85	186	10.6
1966	9	3	104	57	64	237	13.9
1970	10	6	184	58	150	408	22.2
F.74	8	25	23	43	222	321	15.0
O.74	28	13	125	29	247	442	19.6
1979	3	22	303	38	635	1,001	38.1
1983	5	119	10	35	570	739	28.7
1987	–	–	1	19	288	289	12.4
1992	3	1	11	–	888	903	30.6
Gen.Elections							
1918–83	110	331	1,561	491	2,383	4,876	14.7
1987–92	3	1	12	19	1,176	1,192	22.6
	113	332	1,573	510	3,559	6,068	15.8
By-elections							
1918–85	23	19	94	37	439	612	22.5
1986–92	2	2	8	–	140	152	51.4
Lost deposits							
1918–92	138	353	1,675	547	4,138	6,832	15.3

Women Candidates and M.P.s

	Conservative		Labour		Liberal (Alln.)		Other		Total	
	Cands.	M.P.s	Cands.	M.P.s	Cands.	M.P.s	Cands.	M.P.s	Cands.	M.P.s
1918	1	..	4	..	4	..	8	1	17	1
1922	5	1	10	..	16	1	2	..	33	2
1923	7	3	14	3	12	2	1	..	34	8
1924	12	3	22	1	6	..	1	..	41	4
1929	10	3	30	9	25	1	4	1	69	14
1931	16	13	36	..	6	1	4	1	62	15
1935	19	6	35	1	11	1	2	1	67	9
1945	14	1	45	21	20	1	8	1	87	24
1950	28	6	42	14	45	1	11	..	126	21
1951	29	6	39	11	11	..	..	..	74	17
1955	32	10	43	14	12	..	2	..	89	24
1959	28	12	36	13	16	..	1	..	81	25
1964	24	11	33	18	25	..	8	..	90	29
1966	21	7	30	19	20	..	9	..	80	26
1970	26	15	29	10	23	..	21	1	99	26
F'74	33	9	40	13	40	..	30	1	143	23
O'74	30	7	50	18	49	..	32	2	161	27
1979	31	8	52	11	51	..	76	..	210	19
1983	40	13	78	10	(115)	..	87	..	280	23
1987	46	17	92	21	(106)	2	85	1	329	41
1992	59	20	138	37	144	2	227	1	568	60

Election Petitions

There have been 17 instances of election petitions leading to the original result being disallowed by the courts.

Jul	00	Maidstone (bribery by agent)
Jul	00	Monmouth (false expense statement)
Jan	06	Worcester (bribery)
Jan	06	Bodmin (treating by candidate)
Jan	10	E. Dorset (undue influence)
Jan	10	E. Kerry (intimidation)
Jan	10	Hartlepool (undue influence)
Dec	10	Cheltenham (irregular accounts) (candidate a felon)
Dec	10	E. Cork (treating)
Dec	10	Exeter (disallowed votes)
Dec	10	Hull C. (treating)
Dee	10	N. Louth (irregular accounts)
Dee	10	W. Ham N. (irregular accounts)
Nov	22	Berwick on Tweed (false expense return)
Dec	23	Oxford (false expense return)
May	55	Fermanagh and S. Tyrone (candidate a felon)
Aug	55	Mid-Ulster (candidate a felon)
May	61	Bristol S.E. (candidate a peer)

On 19 Oct 50 the House of Commons decided that the seat at West Belfast stood vacant because the successful candidate was ineligible as a minister of the Church of Ireland.

On 20 Jul 55 the House of Commons declared the Mid-Ulster seat vacant because the successful candidate was a felon; the same candidate was re-elected in the ensuing by-election; the defeated Unionist successfully petitioned for the seat as the only eligible candidate. However on 6 Feb 56 the seat was again declared vacant, as the Unionist too was found ineligible through holding an office of profit under the Crown.

Since 1918 there have been only two unsuccessful election petitions–by the defeated Conservative candidate in Plymouth, Drake, in 1929 and by Sir O. Mosley in Kensington North in 1959.

Sources on Electoral Matters

Official returns, listing candidates' votes and expenses, have been published as Parliamentary Papers about one year after every General Election, except 1918: 1901 (352) lix, 145; 1906 (302) xcvi, 19; 1910 (259) lxxiii, 705; 1911 (272) lxii, 701, 1924 (2) xviii, 681; 1924–5 (151) xviii, 775; 1926 (1) xxii, 523, 1929–30 (114) xxiv, 755; 1931–2 (109) xx, 1; 1935–6 (1 50) xx, 217; 1945–6 (128) xix, 539; 1950 (146) xviii, 311; 1951–2 (210) xxi, 841; 1955 (141) xxxii, 91 3; 1959–60 (173) xxiv, 1031; 1964–5 (220) xxv, 587; 1966–7 (162) liv, 1; 1970–1 (305) xxii, 41; 1974–5 (69); 1974–5 (478) ; 1979–80 (374), 1983–4 (130); 1987–8(426); 1992–3(408).

More usable returns, identifying candidates by party and supplying supplementary data, are to be found in the following works:

Dod's Parliamentary Companion, Vacher's Parliamentary Companion, and *Whitaker's Almanack*, all issued annually (or more often).

Parliamentary Poll Book, by F. H. McCalmont (7th ed. 1910). This gives all returns from 1832 to 1910 (Jan). In 1971 it was reprinted and updated to 1918.

Pall Mall Gazette House of Commons, issued in paperback form after each election from 1892 to 1910 (Dec).

The Times House of Commons, issued after every election since 1880 except for 1918, 1922, 1923 and 1924.

The Constitutional Year Book, issued annually from 1885 to 1939. Up to 1920 it gives all results from 1885. Up to 1930 it gives the results for all post- 1918 contests. Thereafter it records the latest four elections.

The Daily Telegraph Gallup Analysis of Election '66 provides an exhaustive statistical comparison of the 1964 and 1966 elections.

The most convenient and reliable source of constituency results, giving percentages as well as absolute figures, is provided by F. W. S. Craig i*n British Parliamentary Election Results 1885–1918* (1973*), British Parliamentary Election Results 1918–1949* (1969*), British Parliamentary Election Results 1950–1970* (1971) and *Britain Votes III* (1984) and *Europe Votes II*(1985). All by-election results are listed in C. Cook and J. Ramsden (eds.*), By-elections in British Politics* (1973), and in P. Norris*, British By-elections* (1990).

The 1975 Referendum results are set out in Cmnd 6105/1975.

From 1945, the results of each election have been analysed in statistical appendices to the Nuffield College series of studies, R. B. McCallum and Alison Readman*, The British General Election of 1945* (1947), H. G. Nicholas*, The British General Election of 1950.* (1951), D. Butler and other*s, The British General Election of 1951* (1952*), The British General Election of 1955* (1955*) The British General Election of 1959* (1960*), The British General Election of 1964* (1965*), The British General Election of 1966* (1966*), The British General Election of 1970* (1971*), The British General Election of February 1974* (1974*) The British General Election of October 1974* (1975*), The British General Election of 1979 (1980*), The British General Election of 1983,*(1984)*,The British General Election of 1987* (1988*) The British General Election of 1992* (1992*), The 1975 Referendum* (1975). See also A. K. Russell*, Liberal Landslide: The General Election of 1906* (1973) and N. Blewett*, The Peers, the Parties and the People; the General Elections of 1910* (1972). For 1983,1987 and 1992 see also R. Waller*, The Almanack of British Politics* (4th ed 1991); I. Crewe and A. Fox, *British Parliamentary Constituencies: A Statistical Compendium* (1984).

Further data is to be found in D. E. Butler*, The Electoral System in Britain since 1918,*(2nd ed. 1963), J. F. S. Ross *Parliamentary Representation,* (2nd ed. 1948) and J. F. S. Ross*, Elections and Electors,* (1955); R. Leonard*, Elections in Britain,* (2nd ed. 1992); F. W. S. Craig*, British Electoral Facts 1832–1987* (1988); M. Kinnear*, The British Voter 1885–*

1966, (1968); and H. Pelling, *Social Geography of British Elections 1885–1910,* (1967).
See also the Report of the Royal Commission on Electoral Systems (Cd. 5163/1910);
evidence Cd.5352/1910.

Census data arranged on a constituency basis is available for 1966 in *Census 1966; General
and Parliamentary Constituency Tables* (1969), and for 1971 in *Census 1971: General
and Parliamentary Constituency Tables* (1974);, in *Census 1981: General and Parliamentary Constituency Tables* (1983); and in *Census 1991: General and Parliamentary
Constituency Tables* (1994).

The problems of electoral administration are also dealt with in the reports of the Speaker's
Conferences on Electoral Reform of 1917, 1944, 1966,1972–4 and 1977–8 and the Ullswater Conference of 1930 (Cmnd. 8463/1917; Cmnd. 3636/1930; Cmnd. 6534 and
6543/1944. Cmnd. 2917 and 2932/1966, Cmnd. 3202 and 3275/1 967, Cmnd. 3550/
1968, Cmnd.5363/1973, Cmnd. 5547/1974 (minutes of evidence are available for the
1972–3 and 1977–8 Speaker's Conferences), Cmnd. 71 10/1978) and in the reports of
the Boundary Commissioners (Cmnd. 7260, 7274, 7270, 7231 of 1947, Cmnd. 9311–4 of
1954 and Cmnd. 4084–7 of 1969). See also H. L. Morris, *Parliamentary Franchise
Reform in England from 1885 to 1918* (New York 1921), D. E. Butler, 'The Redistribution of Seats', *Public Administration*, Summer 1955, pp. 125–47, and F. W. S. Craig,
Boundaries of Parliamentary Constituencies 1885–1972 (1972).

Public Opinion Polls

Gallup Poll

The British Institute of Public Opinion was established in 1937. Its name was changed in
1952 to Social Surveys (Gallup Poll) Ltd. Its poll findings were published exclusively in the
News Chronicle until October 1960. Since 1961 its findings have been published regularly in
the *Daily Telegraph* and the *Sunday Telegraph*. As the years advanced, its questions on
politics became increasingly systematic and detailed. Some of its early findings are collected in *Public Opinion, 1935–1946*, edited by H. Cantril (1951). Others may be found in
the *News Chronicle*, in occasional pamphlets, in *The Gallup International Public Opinion
Polls: Great Britain 1937–75*, and in the monthly Gallup Political Index available since 1960
from Social Surveys (Gallup Poll) Ltd. (now at 307 Finchley Road, London, N.W.3).

National Opinion Polls (N.O.P.)

National Opinion Polls were established in 1957 as an affiliate of Associated Newspapers
Ltd and Political findings were published in the *Daily Mail* intermittently until 1961 and
then regularly until 1979. In 1979 Associated Newspapers sold NOP to MAI; MAI merged
N.O.P with another research company under the name MAI Research. Political polls continue to be published under the NOP name, published intermittently by the *Daily Mail* and
the *Mail on Sunday* and later by the Independent and the BBC. Findings from the regular
political surveys and from other ad hoc political opinion polls were published in the bi-
monthly *N.O.P. Social Political and Economic Review* until 1992. Their address is now
Tower House, Southampton Street, London W.C.2.

Marplan Ltd/I.C.M.

Marplan (present address 5–13 Great Suffolk Street, London S.E.1) was founded in 1959 as
a subsidiary of Interpublic and later of Research International. It published opinion polls
for various newspapers from 1962 onwards. Since 1980 its polls have been reported regularly in the *Guardian*. In 1989 its principal political researchers left to form I.C.M.

Opinion Research Centre (O.R.C.)

The Opinion Research Centre was founded in 1965. It has conducted private polls for the Conservative Party ever since. It published a regular monthly poll in the *Evening Standard* and other newspapers from 1967 to 1976. It merged with Louis Harris in 1983 to form the Harris Research Centre.

Louis Harris Research Ltd/Harris Research Centre

In 1969 the *Daily Express* abandoned the poll which since the 1940s ithad run from within its own office and joined with the Opinion Research Centre and the American expert Louis Harris in setting up an independent new polling organisation, Louis Harris Research Ltd. In 1972 the Daily Express sold its shares. Louis Harris Research Ltd and the Opinion Research Centre share a single Managing Director, and merged with Opinion Research Centre in 1983 to form the Harris Research Centre. In addition to continuing to carry out private polling for the Conservative Party, it also publishes polls in the *Observer* and for London Weekend and Thames Television's current affairs programmes. (It is now based at Holbrooke House, Hill Rise, Richmond, Surrey.)

Market and Opinion Research International (MORI)

MORI (now at 32 Old Queen Street, London S.W.1), under the chairmanship of Robert Worcester, conducted extensive political surveys from 1969, including private studies for the Labour Party. from 1978 it published regular polls in the *(Evening) Standard* and the *Sunday Times*, as well as occasional polls for the *Times, Daily Express* and *Daily Star,* the *Scotsman,* the *Economist* and the B.B.C.

The following tables show in summary form the answers to the Gallup Poll question 'If there were a General Election tomorrow, how would you vote?' and to questions about approval of the government's record of the Prime Minister and of the Leader of the Opposition, as well as answers to the Party fortunes question 'Regardless of how you are going to vote yourself which party do you think is most likely to win?'

Polls on Voting Intention

Voting Intentions (Gallup Poll)

	Government %	Opposition %	Don't Know %
1939 Feb	50	44	6
1939 Dec	54	30	16
1940 Feb	51	27	22

Gallup Poll Findings

		Voting Intention				Approve Govt Record %	Approve P.M %	Approve Opposition Leader %	Party thought likely to win	
		Con. %	Lab. %	Lib. %	Other %				Con. %	Lab. %
1945	Jan	–	–	–	–	–	–	–	–	–
	Feb	27	47	12	12	–	–	–	22	33
	Mar	–	–	–	–	–	–	–	–	–
	Apr	28	47	14	11	–	–	–	–	–
	May	–	–	–	–	–	–	–	–	–
	Jun	32	45	15	8	–	–	–	–	–
	Jul	–	–	–	–	–	–	–	–	–
	Aug	–	–	–	–	–	66	–	–	–
	Sep	–	–	–	–	–	–	–	–	–
	Oct	–	–	–	–	57	–	–	–	–
	Nov	–	–	–	–	–	–	–	–	–
	Dec	–	–	–	–	–	–	–	–	–
1946	Jan	32	52	11	4	–	–	–	–	–
	Feb	–	–	–	–	–	–	–	–	–
	Mar	–	–	–	–	–	–	–	–	–
	Apr	–	–	–	–	–	–	–	–	–
	May	40	43	13	3	–	–	–	–	–
	Jun	–	–	–	–	42	–	–	–	–
	Jul	–	–	–	–	42	–	–	–	–
	Aug	–	–	–	–	46	–	–	–	–
	Sep	–	–	–	–	–	–	–	–	–
	Oct	–	–	–	–	44	53	–	–	–
	Nov	–	–	–	–	–	–	–	–	–
	Dec	–	–	–	–	43	52	–	–	–
1947	Jan	41	44	12	2	–	–	–	–	–
	Feb	–	–	–	–	–	–	–	–	–
	Mar	43	43	10	2	39	46	–	–	–
	Apr	–	–	–	–	–	–	–	–	–
	May	–	–	–	–	–	51	–	–	–
	Jun	42	42	12	2	42	–	–	–	–
	Jul	42	42	12	2	38	51	–	32	46
	Aug	44	41	11	3	–	–	–	–	–
	Sep	44	39	11	4	–	–	–	–	–
	Oct	–	–	–	–	36	41	–	–	–
	Nov	50.5	38	9	2	–	–	–	–	–
	Dec	–	–	–	–	41	44	–	–	–
1948	Jan	44	43	10	1	44	45	–	–	–
	Feb	46	42	8	3	–	–	–	–	–
	Mar	46	43	8	2	35	39	–	–	–
	Apr	42	41	10	6	–	–	–	–	–
	May	45	41	11	2	–	–	–	–	–
	Jun	–	–	–	–	–	–	–	–	–
	Jul	48	39	9	3	36	40	–	36	42
	Aug	48	41	8	2	–	–	–	–	–
	Sep	47	41	10	1	37	37	–	–	–
	Oct	46	41	9	2	–	–	–	–	–
	Nov	46	43	8	2	43	45	–	–	–
	Dec	–	–	–	–	–	–	–	–	–

Gallup Poll Findings

		Voting Intention				Approve Govt Record %	Approve P.M %	Approve Opposition Leader %	Party thought likely to win	
		Con. %	Lab. %	Lib. %	Other %				Con. %	Lab. %
1949	Jan	44	40	13	2	44	45	–	–	–
	Feb	44	43	9	2	–	–	–	–	–
	Mar	41	43	13	2	46	47	–	–	–
	Apr	42	43	13	1	–	–	–	–	–
	May	46	40	11	3	37	44	–	–	–
	Jun	46	41	10	2	–	–	–	–	–
	Jul	44	40	12	2	39	46	–	–	–
	Aug	46	40	11	1	–	–	–	–	–
	Sep	46	40	12	2	36	45	–	30	46
	Oct	45	39	12	2	–	–	–	–	–
	Nov	43	40	14	2	39	43	–	–	–
	Dec	45	41	12	1	–	–	–	–	–
1950	Jan	44	41	12	2	41	44	–	–	–
	Feb	43	44	12	–	–	–	–	20	40
	Mar	43	45	8	2	–	–	–	–	–
	Apr	45	47	7	–	–	–	–	–	–
	May	43	46	9	–	41	50	–	–	–
	Jun	43	46	9	1	–	–	–	–	–
	Jul	42	43	11	3	–	–	–	–	–
	Aug	44	46	8	1	44	49	–	–	–
	Sep	43	45	10	1	–	–	–	–	–
	Oct	42	45	10	2	45	47	–	–	–
	Nov	–	–	–	–	–	–	–	–	–
	Dec	43	44	11	1	38	49	–	–	–
1951	Jan	51	38	10	1	–	–	–	–	–
	Feb	51	37	9	1	31	44	–	–	–
	Mar	51	36	10	2	–	–	–	–	–
	Apr	50	38	9	2	32	49	–	–	–
	May	49	40	9	1	35	57	–	–	–
	Jun	48	41	10	1	–	–	–	–	–
	Jul	49	39	10	–	31	43	–	–	–
	Aug	50	38	10	1	–	–	–	45	32
	Sep	52	41	6	–	35	44	–	44	30
	Oct	50	44	4	1	–	–	–	45	29
	Nov	–	–	–	–	–	–	–	–	–
	Dec	47	45	6	1	44	55	–	–	–
1952	Jan	44	48	6	1	–	–	–	–	–
	Feb	41	47	10	1	44	53	–	–	–
	Mar	41	48	9	1	–	–	–	–	–
	Apr	–	–	–	–	–	–	–	–	–
	May	43	49	7	–	40	51	–	–	–
	Jun	40	49	9	1	–	–	–	16	63
	Jul	40	50	8	1	–	–	–	–	–
	Aug	40	48	6	5	–	–	–	–	–
	Sep	41	48	9	1	44	48	–	25	55
	Oct	41	48	9	1	–	–	–	–	–
	Nov	43	46	9	1	47	51	–	–	–
	Dec	44	45	9	1	51	–	–	–	–

Gallup Poll Findings

		Voting Intention			Approve Govt Record %	Approve P.M %	Approve Opposition Leader %	Party thought likely to win	
		Con. %	Lab. %	Lib. %	Other %				Con. %	Lab. %
1953	Jan	42	46	10	1	46	51	–	–	–
	Feb	42	46	10	1	–	–	–	–	–
	Mar	46	44	8	1	–	–	–	–	–
	Apr	47	45	7	–	60	–	–	–	–
	May	47	45	7	–	–	–	–	38	40
	Jun	46	46	7	1	–	–	–	–	–
	Jul	–	–	–	–	–	–	–	–	–
	Aug	45	46	8	1	49	–	–	–	–
	Sep	44	47	7	1	–	–	–	43	35
	Oct	45	45	7	–	54	56	–	–	–
	Nov	–	–	–	–	–	–	–	–	–
	Dec	45	47	7	1	–	–	–	–	–
1954	Jan	45	46	7	1	50	–	–	–	–
	Feb	45	47	7	–	50	–	–	36	34
	Mar	46	45	7	1	–	–	–	–	–
	Apr	46	46	7	–	–	48	–	–	–
	May	45	47	6	–	–	–	–	–	–
	Jun	45	47	7	–	47	–	–	–	–
	Jul	–	–	–	–	–	–	–	–	–
	Aug	42	48	8	1	–	–	–	–	–
	Sep	43	48	8	1	–	–	–	33	39
	Oct	45	45	8	1	–	–	–	–	–
	Nov	46	47	6	1	–	–	–	44	26
	Dec	49	49	2	–	–	–	–	–	–
1955	Jan	46	45	7	1	53	52	–	–	–
	Feb	46	44	8	1	–	–	–	–	–
	Mar	46	44	8	1	–	–	–	–	–
	Apr	48	44	7	1	–	73	–	52	22
	May	51	47	2	–	57	71	–	54	18
	Jun	–	–	–	–	–	–	–	–	–
	Jul	47	43	9	1	–	68	–	–	–
	Aug	44	47	7	1	–	–	–	–	–
	Sep	48	44	7	1	–	70	–	–	–
	Oct	46	44	8	1	–	63	–	–	–
	Nov	44	45	9	1	–	61	–	–	–
	Dec	45	46	7	–	44	60	–	–	–
1956	Jan	45	46	7	–	–	–	–	–	–
	Feb	44	46	9	1	–	50	–	–	–
	Mar	44	47	7	1	34	45	–	–	–
	Apr	43	48	8	1	–	41	–	–	–
	May	43	47	9	1	40	54	42	–	–
	Jun	–	–	–	–	–	–	–	–	–
	Jul	42	49	8	1	36	50	46	–	–
	Aug	43	49	6	1	–	–	–	–	–
	Sep	43	46	10	–	–	51	53	–	–
	Oct	42	47	9	1	–	47	–	–	–
	Nov	45	46	8	–	–	52	44	–	–
	Dec	45	46	8	1	–	56	–	–	–

OPINION POLLS
Gallup Poll Findings

		Voting Intention				Approve Govt Record %	Approve P.M %	Approve Opposition Leader %	Party thought likely to win	
		Con. %	Lab. %	Lib. %	Other %				Con. %	Lab. %
1957	Jan	43	48	7	1	–	50	–	–	–
	Feb	42	48	8	1	–	–	–	–	–
	Mar	40	51	7	1	–	45	–	–	–
	Apr	41	51	7	1	–	44	–	–	–
	May	41	50	7	1	–	54	41	–	–
	Jun	–	–	–	–	–	–	–	–	–
	Jul	41	49	8	1	–	–	–	–	–
	Aug	40	48	10	1	–	–	–	–	–
	Sep	33	52	14	–	–	44	39	24	51
	Oct	37	49	13	1	37	30	–	–	–
	Nov	38	49	12	–	–	39	–	–	–
	Dec	41	47	9	1	–	–	–	26	46
1958	Jan	40	47	12	–	38	46	40	–	–
	Feb	36	44	18	1	–	35	–	–	–
	Mar	–	–	–	–	–	–	–	–	–
	Apr	38	46	15	–	30	37	–	–	–
	May	34	47	19	–	30	37	–	–	–
	Jun	39	43	17	–	40	50	–	–	–
	Jul	–	–	–	–	41	–	37	–	–
	Aug	42	42	15	–	41	53	–	40	31
	Sep	44	43	13	–	43	55	32	–	–
	Oct	45	41	12	1	47	57	41	44	29
	Nov	46	42	10	1	48	55	42	–	–
	Dec	47	42	9	1	50	55	45	43	28
1959	Jan	45	45	8	1	48	53	47	39	28
	Feb	43	47	8	1	41	54	43	–	–
	Mar	45	47	6	1	44	57	46	–	–
	Apr	44	44	10	1	46	60	48	–	–
	May	45	44	10	1	47	62	47	–	–
	Jun	45	43	11	–	49	58	44	–	–
	Jul	45	41	12	–	53	62	42	–	–
	Aug	47	41	10	1	56	67	46	–	–
	Sep	50	43	5	–	–	–	–	56	20
	Oct	48	46	5	1	–	–	–	51	21
	Nov	48	44	7	1	–	–	–	–	–
	Dec	47	44	7	1	–	–	–	–	–
1960	Jan	47	43	8	1	–	–	–	–	–
	Feb	47	43	9	–	–	64	43	–	–
	Mar	47	42	10	1	–	57	40	–	–
	Apr	45	42	11	1	–	56	46	–	–
	May	45	42	11	1	–	79	47	–	–
	Jun	45	43	10	1	–	70	56	–	–
	Jul	47	43	9	1	–	65	43	–	–
	Aug	47	42	10	–	59	72	48	–	–
	Sep	47	40	11	1	59	74	43	–	–
	Oct	50	37	12	–	59	72	48	–	–
	Nov	46	40	13	–	56	69	44	–	–
	Dec	47	37	14	1	–	–	–	–	–

Gallup Poll Findings

		Voting Intention			Approve Govt Record %	Approve P.M %	Approve Opposition Leader %	Party thought likely to win	
		Con. %	Lab. %	Lib. %	Other %				Con. %	Lab. %
1961	Jan	45	41	12	1	59	72	35	–	–
	Feb	44	42	13	1	48	64	45	–	–
	Mar	44	40	15	1	51	63	45	–	–
	Apr	43	40	15	1	50	64	43	–	–
	May	44	40	14	1	49	58	45	–	–
	Jun	43	40	15	1	52	58	45	–	–
	Jul	44	41	14	–	49	54	51	–	–
	Aug	38	43	17	2	38	45	47	–	–
	Sep	40	45	13	1	39	43	46	–	–
	Oct	43	43	12	1	47	55	57	–	–
	Nov	41	43	14	1	43	54	42	–	–
	Dec	38	43	17	1	–	–	–	–	–
1962	Jan	42	42	15	1	43	53	50	–	–
	Feb	40	42	17	–	41	48	45	51	23
	Mar	39	44	16	–	41	50	50	41	17
	Apr	33	41	25	1	37	46	48	–	–
	May	34	39	25	–	38	47	48	36	36
	Jun	35	39	25	–	37	46	48	31	42
	Jul	35	41	22	1	41	47	47	28	42
	Aug	34	43	22	1	37	42	47	–	–
	Sep	34	45	20	1	38	42	51	30	39
	Oct	34	43	20	2	36	43	54	37	37
	Nov	39	47	13	1	41	47	51	29	42
	Dec	37	46	16	1	36	41	52	–	–
1963	Jan	35	48	16	–	34	42	49	–	–
	Feb	32	48	18	1	34	40	–	–	–
	Mar	33	50	15	1	30	35	44	26	52
	Apr	34	49	16	–	33	35	52	24	55
	May	36	47	16	1	38	41	53	25	57
	Jun	31	51	16	1	31	35	54	17	58
	Jul	33	51	14	1	32	37	57	16	68
	Aug	34	50	15	1	39	42	59	22	55
	Sep	33	49	16	1	38	40	56	23	55
	Oct	36	48	14	1	36	41	60	23	55
	Nov	37	49	12	1	44	42	67	30	53
	Dec	39	47	13	–	46	48	65	28	48
1964	Jan	39	47	13	–	41	43	63	29	45
	Feb	39	48	12	1	42	42	62	27	57
	Mar	39	48	12	–	41	44	64	31	47
	Apr	38	50	10	–	46	44	61	23	58
	May	39	50	10	–	41	44	62	21	65
	Jun	41	50	8	–	45	44	62	22	61
	Jul	40	49	9	–	43	46	56	26	56
	Aug	43	49	7	–	48	46	61	32	48
	Sep	44	47	8	–	42	47	58	41	38
	Oct	44	46	8	3	–	–	35	39	–
	Nov	38	50	11	–	49	60	39	–	–
	Dec	40	50	9	–	48	64	41	–	–

Gallup Poll Findings

		Voting Intention				Approve Govt Record %	Approve P.M %	Approve Opposition Leader %	Party thought likely to win	
		Con. %	Lab. %	Lib. %	Other %				Con. %	Lab. %
1965	Jan	42	46	10	–	39	56	38	27	46
	Feb	45	45	9	–	43	60	37	49	28
	Mar	43	46	9	1	47	58	38	41	34
	Apr	39	47	12	–	45	63	34	41	38
	May	44	43	12	–	39	56	36	40	34
	Jun	47	42	9	1	35	48	36	52	23
	Jul	46	45	8	–	36	51	32	44	30
	Aug	49	41	8	1	39	50	51	57	24
	Sep	42	48	8	1	42	54	49	56	24
	Oct	41	49	9	–	49	61	47	39	39
	Nov	42	48	8	1	50	65	48	35	44
	Dec	40	48	10	1	55	66	43	35	46
1966	Jan	42	47	9	1	51	65	48	32	42
	Feb	42	50	7	–	48	60	40	20	62
	Mar	40	51	8	1	–	–	–	11	69
	Apr	–	–	–	–	53	63	39	–	–
	May	35	53	10	1	54	69	44	–	–
	Jun	39	52	7	1	44	58	33	27	48
	Jul	41	48	8	2	42	61	33	25	55
	Aug	44	44	10	1	35	52	32	39	41
	Sep	42	45	11	1	34	49	37	37	37
	Oct	43	44	11	1	32	43	46	37	35
	Nov	44	42	12	1	33	46	32	41	34
	Dec	42	46	10	1	40	51	35	–	–
1967	Jan	42	45	10	1	40	51	29	–	–
	Feb	37	48	13	1	44	57	24	–	–
	Mar	42	42	12	2	40	53	26	–	–
	Apr	45	41	11	2	44	42	33	–	–
	May	46	40	12	1	38	43	35	–	–
	Jun	48	41	9	1	36	46	37	–	–
	Jul	43	41	13	2	35	48	32	–	–
	Aug	43	42	13	2	33	45	28	–	–
	Sep	45	41	10	3	29	40	31	–	–
	Oct	45	38	14	3	–	38	39	56	19
	Nov	46	36	11	6	28	41	44	62	63
	Dec	49	32	12	6	21	34	37	–	–
1968	Jan	45	39	11	4	23	33	32	–	–
	Feb	52	30	12	5	22	36	31	–	–
	Mar	50	31	15	4	18	35	29	–	–
	Apr	54	30	12	3	17	31	28	78	7
	May	56	28	11	5	19	27	31	73	11
	Jun	51	28	14	6	19	28	28	–	–
	Jul	50	30	13	7	18	30	28	76	13
	Aug	49	34	11	4	21	30	27	–	–
	Sep	47	37	11	4	24	33	27	–	–
	Oct	47	39	9	4	29	38	27	55	25
	Nov	50	32	14	3	20	31	37	–	–
	Dec	55	29	11	4	17	28	30	–	–

Gallup Poll Findings

		Voting Intention				Approve Govt Record %	Approve P.M %	Approve Opposition Leader %	Party thought likely to win	
		Con. %	Lab. %	Lib. %	Other %				Con. %	Lab. %
1969	Jan	53	31	11	4	23	34	31	–	–
	Feb	54	32	11	2	22	32	34	–	–
	Mar	52	34	10	3	22	35	31	–	–
	Apr	51	30	13	5	21	30	29	–	–
	May	52	30	13	4	19	29	28	76	9
	Jun	51	35	12	2	24	35	29	–	–
	Jul	55	31	11	2	23	30	40	–	–
	Aug	47	34	15	3	25	26	29	–	–
	Sep	46	37	13	3	29	39	29	–	–
	Oct	46	44	7	2	34	43	33	46	33
	Nov	45	41	10	3	35	41	33	48	31
	Dec	50	39	9	1	31	38	32	54	26
1970	Jan	48	41	7	3	32	42	38	54	25
	Feb	48	41	9	2	31	42	41	53	24
	Mar	46	41	9	3	35	42	39	54	27
	Apr	47	42	7	3	40	45	34	47	31
	May	42	49	7	1	42	49	28	26	56
	Jun	42	49	7	1	40	51	28	13	68
	Jul	–	–	–	–	–	–	–	–	–
	Aug	47	43	7	2	–	–	–	–	–
	Sep	46	44	8	1	21	35	59	–	–
	Oct	46	46	6	–	29	42	62	–	–
	Nov	43	48	6	2	31	39	66	–	–
	Dec	46	44	6	3	37	45	59	–	–
1971	Jan	42	47	8	2	35	41	61	–	–
	Feb	41	49	8	1	31	37	61	–	–
	Mar	38	50	8	3	33	38	59	–	–
	Apr	44	48	6	1	40	43	57	–	–
	May	38	50	9	2	31	35	61	–	–
	Jun	36	54	8	2	22	31	58	–	–
	Jul	33	55	8	3	36	32	58	–	–
	Aug	42	46	7	2	35	37	51	–	–
	Sep	35	54	8	2	30	32	57	–	–
	Oct	40	50	8	2	32	35	54	–	–
	Nov	42	48	7	2	35	38	52	–	–
	Dec	42	48	7	2	34	39	54	–	–
1972	Jan	40	48	9	2	37	39	54	–	–
	Feb	40	49	8	2	34	37	53	23	57
	Mar	39	48	9	2	35	36	51	–	–
	Apr	43	44	10	2	43	41	39	–	–
	May	40	46	11	2	36	39	45	35	40
	Jun	41	47	10	2	36	40	44	–	–
	Jul	39	49	9	2	31	35	45	–	–
	Aug	40	49	7	3	32	35	47	25	56
	Sep	38	49	9	2	30	33	43	23	57
	Oct	40	48	8	3	33	34	53	28	53
	Nov	37	45	15	2	32	37	50	28	52
	Dec	38	46	12	3	36	39	44	32	42

Gallup Poll Findings

		Voting Intention				Approve Govt Record %	Approve P.M %	Approve Opposition Leader %	Party thought likely to win	
		Con. %	Lab. %	Lib. %	Other %				Con. %	Lab. %
1973	Jan	38	44	15	2	33	38	40	31	46
	Feb	38	47	12	2	33	37	45	46	–
	Mar	39	43	16	2	38	41	41	–	–
	Apr	38	41	17	3	32	37	41	26	50
	May	38	43	14	4	35	38	40	26	51
	Jun	41	42	14	2	37	43	41	34	47
	Jul	35	45	17	2	31	37	45	22	55
	Aug	31	38	28	2	29	34	39	26	47
	Sep	33	43	22	1	29	36	42	23	51
	Oct	33	39	25	2	30	36	46	29	47
	Nov	36	38	22	2	31	39	37	35	36
	Dec	36	42	18	3	34	37	31	43	–
1974	Jan	40	38	19	3	36	39	38	40	35
	Feb	39	37	20	2	32	38	38	60	20
	Mar	35	43	19	3	–	–	–	–	–
	Apr	33	49	15	2	48	53	38	19	52
	May	33	46	17	3	40	50	35	26	48
	Jun	35	44	17	3	41	49	36	25	51
	Jul	35	38	21	6	32	41	33	32	36
	Aug	35	30	21	4	37	44	35	27	44
	Sep	37	40	18	4	28	41	29	18	55
	Oct	36	41	19	3	37	45	32	18	55
	Nov	35	46	14	4	40	50	32	–	–
	Dec	33	47	16	3	42	51	31	–	–
1975	Jan	34	48	13	4	37	49	29	–	–
	Feb	45	41	11	3	32	47	64	–	–
	Mar	42	44	11	3	37	51	60	–	–
	Apr	43	45	10	2	32	44	45	–	–
	May	45	39	11	4	26	40	41	45	29
	Jun	44	40	13	2	31	46	35	44	29
	Jul	43	40	12	4	27	46	37	46	28
	Aug	40	42	14	3	32	45	37	46	30
	Sep	38	41	16	3	30	45	39	44	29
	Oct	42	40	13	3	30	46	45	45	32
	Nov	39	44	12	4	31	45	42	43	35
	Dec	40	41	14	4	27	40	40	45	29
1976	Jan	40	42	14	3	29	42	42	45	32
	Feb	45	40	10	3	32	45	49	46	30
	Mar	44	41	9	5	30	46	43	49	30
	Apr	41	46	9	3	39	57	40	44	37
	May	44	41	10	4	32	43	36	51	28
	Jun	44	40	11	4	28	36	31	48	29
	Jul	41	41	13	5	32	46	33	44	32
	Aug	44	41	10	5	29	44	33	45	33
	Sep	42	42	11	4	29	46	40	44	34
	Oct	48	36	11	4	20	36	40	57	20
	Nov	55	30	11	3	19	33	41	66	18
	Dec	49	34	11	5	18	35	34	62	17

Gallup Poll Findings

		Voting Intention				Approve Govt Record %	Approve P.M %	Approve Opposition Leader %	Party thought likely to win	
		Con. %	Lab. %	Lib. %	Other %				Con. %	Lab. %
1977	Jan	47	34	14	4	21	37	39	57	21
	Feb	46	33	14	6	21	36	35	62	18
	Mar	49	33	13	4	22	37	35	62	20
	Apr	49	33	11	6	23	38	40	67	16
	May	53	33	8	5	23	43	45	74	12
	Jun	47	37	10	5	28	44	44	69	15
	Jul	49	34	10	6	24	45	42	71	13
	Aug	48	37	9	5	33	43	45	64	19
	Sep	45	41	8	5	32	49	47	54	28
	Oct	45	45	8	2	41	59	49	49	31
	Nov	45	42	8	4	41	55	47	46	35
	Dec	44	44	8	3	41	53	44	48	32
1978	Jan	43	43	8	4	43	57	42	46	38
	Feb	48	39	9	4	43	54	41	40	40
	Mar	48	41	8	3	41	51	45	52	30
	Apr	45	43	7	3	44	51	39	45	38
	May	43	43	8	4	41	54	40	48	33
	Jun	45	45	6	3	40	50	38	39	43
	Jul	45	43	8	3	40	52	38	40	42
	Aug	43	47	6	3	30	55	35	42	36
	Sep	49	42	6	2	39	51	40	42	36
	Oct	42	47	7	3	44	56	39	47	35
	Nov	43	48	6	3	44	54	33	36	41
	Dec	48	42	6	3	37	53	39	41	40
1979	Jan	49	41	6	3	34	48	38	44	35
	Feb	53	33	11	3	23	33	48	65	20
	Mar	51	37	8	3	27	39	47	61	23
	Apr	50	40	8	2	33	43	43	59	23
	May	43	41	13	2	–	–	–	–	–
	Jun	42	43	12	2	34	41	63	–	–
	Jul	41	46	11	1	34	41	61	–	–
	Aug	41	44	12	2	38	45	57	–	–
	Sep	40	45	12	2	36	45	53	–	–
	Oct	40	45	12	2	34	46	57	–	–
	Nov	39	43	15	2	38	44	55	–	–
	Dec	38	42	18	2	34	40	53	28	44
1980	Jan	36	45	16	3	33	39	53	29	45
	Feb	37	42	18	2	30	37	50	29	45
	Mar	37	49	11	2	30	38	53	27	55
	Apr	36	45	15	3	36	41	55	25	52
	May	39	43	15	2	37	44	51	24	57
	Jun	40	45	11	3	35	43	48	28	54
	Jul	40	43	14	2	33	41	46	28	55
	Aug	38	44	14	3	35	41	53	28	50
	Sep	35	45	16	3	29	37	48	22	58
	Oct	40	43	13	3	30	38	48	30	53
	Nov	36	47	15	1	29	34	38	22	60
	Dec	35	47	14	3	29	35	30	18	67

Gallup Poll Findings

		Voting Intention				Approve Govt Record %	Approve P.M %	Approve Opposition Leader %	Party thought likely to win	
		Con. %	Lab. %	Lib. %	Other %				Con. %	Lab. %
1981	Jan	33	46	18	2	26	31	26	17	65
	Feb	36	35	20	8	29	34	22	25	42
	Mar	30	34	32	4	23	30	23	17	50
	Apr	30	34	33	2	24	30	21	20	44
	May	32	35	29	3	29	35	26	18	56
	Jun	29	37	30	2	26	33	28	18	60
	Jul	30	40	26	3	23	30	25	13	63
	Aug	28	38	32	1	23	28	23	18	52
	Sep	32	36	29	2	26	32	28	19	46
	Oct	29	28	40	2	24	33	27	14	39
	Nov	26	29	42	2	23	28	16	17	31
	Dec	23	23	50	3	18	25	19	12	23
1982	Jan	27	29	39	3	24	32	18	16	27
	Feb	27	34	36	2	24	29	19	21	35
	Mar	31	33	33	2	29	34	21	32	33
	Apr	31	29	37	2	32	35	23	23	27
	May	41	28	29	1	42	44	18	43	21
	Jun	45	25	28	1	48	51	14	63	13
	Jul	46	27	24	2	47	52	16	66	12
	Aug	44	26	27	1	42	49	15	58	17
	Sep	44	30	23	2	40	48	?6	58	19
	Oct	40	29	27	3	40	46	20	58	20
	Nov	42	34	21	2	39	44	22	55	22
	Dec	41	34	22	2	37	44	20	54	25
1983	Jan	44	31	22	2	43	49	17	61	19
	Feb	43	32	22	2	39	45	17	62	19
	Mar	39	28	29	3	41	47	19	66	11
	Apr	40	35	22	2	38	44	21	59	21
	May	49	31	17	2	45	50	18	76	11
	Jun	45	26	26	2	44	48	17	87	5
	Jul	44	28	26	1	46	52	11	49	16
	Aug	44	25	29	1	44	51	10	56	10
	Sep	45	24	29	1	47	53	9	64	12
	Oct	42	35	20	2	41	48	58	48	28
	Nov	43	36	19	1	40	49	48	53	26
	Dec	42	36	19	2	38	47	40	49	27
1984	Jan	41	38	19	1	42	49	43	58	22
	Feb	43	33	21	2	41	48	45	59	23
	Mar	41	38	19	1	41	46	47	50	35
	Apr	41	36	20	2	42	46	42	52	28
	May	38	36	23	2	37	41	42	50	30
	Jun	37	38	23	1	36	41	43	49	31
	Jul	37	38	22	2	36	41	43	43	37
	Aug	36	39	22	2	34	39	37	49	29
	Sep	37	36	25	1	34	40	43	54	28
	Oct	44	32	21	2	43	50	35	64	19
	Nov	44.5	30	23.5	1	41	48	59	67	17
	Dec	39.5	31	27.5	2	34	43	36	67	16

Gallup Poll Findings

		Voting Intention				Approve Govt Record %	Approve P.M %	Approve Opposition Leader %	Party thought likely to win	
		Con. %	Lab. %	Lib. %	Other %				Con. %	Lab. %
1985	Jan	39	33	25.5	2	33	40	36	65	16
	Feb	35	32	31.5	1	31	37	31	63	19
	Mar	33	39.5	25.5	2	30	37	37	53	28
	Apr	34	34.5	26.5	2	32	38	36	54	28
	May	30.5	34	33.5	2	28	36	38	46	26
	Jun	34.5	34.5	30	1	31	38	37	44	31
	Jul	27.5	38	32.5	2	28	34	38	37	27
	Aug	24	40	34	2	23	30	34	34	33
	Sep	29	29.5	39	2.5	29	35	29	41	25
	Oct	32	38	28	2	29	33	50	39	28
	Nov	35	34	29.5	1.5	29	36	46	47	25
	Dec	33	32.5	32.5	2.5	34	39	47	47	24
1986	Jan	29.5	34	35	1.5	27	31	44	40	27
	Feb	29.5	35.5	33.5	1.5	25	29	40	35	30
	Mar	29.5	34	34.5	2	29	33	39	45	27
	Apr	28	38.5	31.5	2	23	28	40	36	40
	May	27.5	37	32.5	3	27	31	47	28	49
	Jun	34	39	24.5	2.5	27	30	41	35	43
	Jul	33	38	27	2	30	34	43	43	38
	Aug	30	36.5	30	3.5	25	28	38	38	39
	Sep	32.5	38	27.5	2	30	35	46	43	38
	Oct	37.5	37.5	22	2.5	33	36	47	49	32
	Nov	36	39.5	22	2.5	36	36	44	55	28
	Dec	41	32.5	22.5	3	34	38	36	65	18
1987	Jan	34.5	39.5	23.5	2.5	30	35	39	63	19
	Feb	36	34.5	27.5	2	32	35	37	65	19
	Mar	37.5	29.5	31.5	1.5	35	39	34	69	10
	Apr	40.5	28	29	2.5	41	43	26	74	8
	May	39	28	30	3	38	44	30	87	6
	Jun	41	34	23.5	1.5	36	41	45	77	11
	Jul	44.5	33	20.5	2	44	46	35	–	–
	Aug	45.5	35.5	17.5	1.5	42	46	36	–	–
	Sep	44	33	20	3	40	48	40	–	–
	Oct	52	31.5	13.5	3	46	52	39	–	–
	Nov	46.5	33	17	3.5	43	47	39	–	–
	Dec	46.5	34.5	16	3	42	47	40	69	15
1988	Jan	45.5	37	15	2.5	42	48	35	74	12
	Feb	46	36	15	3	40	45	36	71	14
	Mar	42	36.5	19.5	2	40	42	32	70	14
	Apr	40.5	41.5	15	3	35	40	39	74	16
	May	45	36	14.5	4.5	40	43	39	68	17
	Jun	42	43	11	4	39	42	38	71	17
	Jul	41.5	39	16	3.5	39	42	32	78	11
	Aug	45.5	33.5	17	4	41	45	27	79	9
	Sep	43	36.5	17.5	3	42	45	30	80	11
	Oct	45.5	34	17.5	3	43	48	33	83	8
	Nov	42.5	36	17	4.5	38	45	29	–	–
	Dec	43	32	19.5	5.5	38	44	26	78	13

OPINION POLLS

Gallup Poll Findings

| | | Voting Intention | | | | Approve Govt Record | Approve | | Party thought likely to win | |
		Con. %	Lab. %	Lib. %	Other %	%	Approve P.M %	Opposition Leader %	Con. %	Lab. %
1989	Jan	42.6	35.5	16.7	5.3	36.6	43.8	28.1	79	9
	Feb	41.0	36.4	17.9	4.7	34.2	41.6	28.7	74	10
	Mar	38.9	37.7	17.9	5.4	33.1	39.7	29.2	68	15
	Apr	39.2	38.4	17.0	5.5	34.6	40.6	31.7	70	17
	May	40.9	40.8	12.8	4.4	35.8	40.9	35.0	64	22
	Jun	38.2	41.3	11.0	9.4	32.8	37.7	37.5	47	40
	Jul	35.5	42.3	10.0	11.1	29.9	34.8	37.9	52	34
	Aug	36.8	42.3	9.3	11.3	31.8	35.6	36.2	56	22
	Sep	36.4	41.2	11.5	10.8	31.1	35.8	37.2	59	22
	Oct	36.2	47.0	8.3	8.6	29.0	33.1	45.1	45	42
	Nov	36.3	46.5	9.3	8.1	28.1	29.6	40.9	–	–
	Dec	37.3	46.2	9.4	7.1	30.1	32.2	42.7	52	36
1990	Jan	36.1	45.0	10.7	8.4	28.8	32.6	40.6	50	36
	Feb	32.7	47.3	11.6	8.5	24.9	29.2	39.6	38	48
	Mar	28.5	52.0	10.9	8.6	21.6	24.3	40.4	26	62
	Apr	28.1	51.8	11.6	8.4	22.2	23.2	40.1	33	56
	May	32.7	47.5	12.3	7.5	25.6	26.1	37.9	38	52
	Jun	33.7	49.5	8.8	8.1	26.1	27.7	38.2	48	41
	Jul	34.4	47.9	9.9	7.8	27.5	30.1	39.4	45	42
	Aug	35.1	47.6	9.3	7.9	28.8	31.8	38.8	48	40
	Sep	34.6	46.6	11.1	7.6	29.1	32.5	42.4	47	41
	Oct	34.3	46.4	13.0	6.3	28.1	31.5	44.1	43	40
	Nov	37.9	42.1	13.7	6.6	29.8	25.9	38.8	–	–
	Dec	44.6	39.1	10.5	5.8	34.3	49.3	33.5	60	27
1991	Jan	44.3	39.2	10.8	5.7	36.6	50.1	37.1	53	33
	Feb	44.3	39.3	11.0	5.4	37.0	59.3	38.3	62	27
	Mar	41.2	36.2	17.3	5.2	33.0	56.9	37.4	65	24
	Apr	40.9	37.1	16.5	5.6	33.2	53.9	34.8	53	42
	May	37.2	38.3	19.4	5.1	29.7	49.7	39.4	38	46
	Jun	36.5	39.5	18.7	5.0	29.8	47.8	34.9	42	25
	Jul	38.3	39.1	17.6	4.8	30.4	50.2	36.9	48	36
	Aug	38.5	38.8	17.1	5.5	31.4	52.1	35.8	52	31
	Sep	40.5	36.9	17.1	5.5	33.9	54.1	33.9	58	25
	Oct	41.0	40.4	13.8	4.8	33.2	52.0	39.3	47	37
	Nov	39.5	38.9	16.6	5.0	32.3	50.0	36.0	45	37
	Dec	40.6	38.9	15.0	5.6	33.2	49.6	33.4	45	35
1992	Jan	39.0	39.2	16.8	5.0	30.2	48.4	33.0	47	36
	Feb	38.9	37.6	18.3	5.2	29.7	48.5	33.6	56	26
	Mar	37.4	37.8	19.7	5.1	29.4	46.4	35.4	39	35
	Apr	38.5	38.0	20.0	3.5	33.8	48.5	40.0	55	22
	May	40.6	39.3	16.1	3.9	36.7	54.3	48.6	63	15
	Jun	39.8	40.4	15.2	4.5	34.0	51.7	47.0	62	16
	Jul	39.1	41.4	14.8	4.6	30.4	49.2	48.5	62	16
	Aug	38.4	42.6	14.1	4.9	26.2	45.2	38.8	56	23
	Sep	36.9	44.5	14.2	4.5	22.4	38.7	33.6	56	26
	Oct	32.0	48.4	14.4	5.3	14.0	25.6	45.1	43	37
	Nov	30.2	51.5	13.5	4.8	13.9	23.3	48.9	34	44
	Dec	32.2	48.1	14.6	5.1	15.9	27.0	46.3	33	46

Gallup Poll Findings

		Voting Intention			Approve Govt Record %	Approve P.M %	Approve Opposition Leader %	Party thought likely to win	
		Con. %	Lab. %	Lib. %	Other %				Con. %	Lab. %
1993	Jan	33.0	47.9	13.9	5.2	17.4	31.2	43.0	45	37
	Feb	31.9	47.4	15.4	5.4	16.0	27.9	45.1	39	43
	Mar	30.0	48.3	15.8	6.0	14.4	24.9	47.2	–	–
	Apr	30.9	47.4	16.0	5.8	16.0	26.0	47.0	45	37
	May	26.8	44.2	23.6	5.5	13.8	23.1	44.4	52	32
	Jun	24.2	45.8	24.5	5.6	11.0	18.4	43.0	35	42
	Jul	25.4	44.7	24.7	5.2	12.2	19.5	45.0	40	39
	Aug	23.7	42.9	28.3	5.1	12.0	19.5	43.7	36	37
	Sep	24.3	45.0	24.7	6.0	11.9	19.4	44.2	38	36
	Oct	26.2	45.6	22.6	5.5	13.1	22.6	53.1	41	34
	Nov	25.4	46.2	22.4	6.0	12.3	20.2	49.6	40	39
	Dec	26.8	46.4	21.3	5.4	14.0	22.9	50.1	41	38
1994	Jan	25.5	48.2	20.8	5.5	13.8	21.6	50.5	46	38
	Feb	26.3	47.6	21.0	5.1	14.0	23.2	52.5	34	43
	Mar	25.9	47.7	20.4	5.9	13.9	22.5	50.3	–	–
	Apr	24.4	48.3	22.3	4.9	12.0	19.3	48.5	35	45
	May	22.8	49.2	23.1	4.9	11.1	18.6	–	31	49
	Jun	21.6	51.8	20.3	6.3	10.7	18.8	–	–	–

Opinion Poll Accuracy in General Elections

The following is a list of all major poll predictions of general election results.

	Actual Result (G.B.)	Gallup Poll	NOP	Daily Express
1945				
Con	39.5	+1.5		
Lab	49.0	−2.0		
Lib	9.2	+1.3		
1950				
Con	43.1	+0.4	+1.4	
Lab	46.8	−1.8	−2.8	
Lib	9.3	+1.2	+1.7	
1951				
Con	47.8	+1.7	+2.2	+2.2
Lab	49.3	−2.3	−3.3	−6.3
Lib	2.6	+0.4	+0.9	(+4.1)[a]
1955				
Con	49.3	+1.7	+1.9	
Lab	47.3	+0.2	−0.1	
Lib	2.8	−1.3	−0.6	

	Actual Result (G.B.)	Gallup Poll	NOP	*Daily Express*	Research Services	
1959						
Con	48.8	−0.3	−0.8	+0.3		
Lab	44.6	+1.9	+0.5	+0.8		
Lib	6.1	−1.6	(+2.4)[a]	−1.1		
1964						
Con	42.9	+1.6	+1.4	+1.6	+2.1	
Lab	44.8	+1.2	+2.6	+1.1	+1.2	
Lib	11.4	+2.9	−3.5	−0.3	−2.4	
1966						
Con	41.4	−1.4	+0.2	−4.0	+0.2	
Lab	48.7	+2.3	−1.9	+5.9	+1.0	
Lib	8.6	−0.6	−1.2	−0.9	−0.3	
				Louis Harris	ORC	
1970						
Con	46.2	−4.2	−2.2	−0.2	+0.3	
Lab	43.8	+5.2	+4.3	+4.2	+1.7	
Lib	7.6	−0.1	−1.2	−2.6	−1.1	
1974 Feb						
Con	38.6	+0.9	+0.9	+1.6	+1.1	
Lab	38.0	−0.5	−2.5	−2.8	−1.3	
Lib	19.8	+0.7	+2.2	+1.4	+1.4	
Other	3.6	−1.1	−0.6	−0.9	−1.2	
1974 Oct						
Con	36.7	−0.7	−5.7	−2.1	−2.3	
Lab	40.2	+1.3	+5.3	+2.8	+1.6	
Lib	18.8	+0.2	+0.7	+0.5	+0.6	
Other	4.3	−0.8	−0.3	−1.2	+0.1	
				MORI	Marplan	
1979						
Con	44.9	−1.9	+1.1	−0.5	+0.1	
Lab	37.8	+3.2	+1.2	+1.0	+0.8	
Lib	14.1	−0.6	−1.6	−0.6	−0.6	
Other	3.2	−0.7	−0.7	+0.1	−0.3	
						Harris
1983						
Con	43.5	+2.0	+3.5	+0.3	+2.5	+3.5
Lab	28.3	−1.8	−3.3	−0.3	−2.3	−3.3
Alln	26.0	0.0	0.0	0.0	0.0	0.0
Other	2.2	−0.2	−0.2	−0.2	2.0	2.0
1987						
Con	43.3	−2.3	−1.3	+0.7	−1.3	−1.3
Lab	31.5	+2.5	+3.5	+0.5	+3.5	+3.5
Alln	23.1	+0.4	−2.1	−1.1	−2.1	−2.1
Other	2.1	−0.6	−0.1	−0.1	−0.1	−0.1

	Actual Result (G.B.)	Gallup Poll	NOP	MORI	ICM
1992					
Con	42.8	−4.3	−3.8	−4.0	−4.0
Lab	35.2	+2.8	+6.8	+3.8	+2.8
Lib.D.	18.3	+1.7	−1.3	−1.7	−1.7
Other	3.7	−0.2	−1.7	−1.7	+0.3

[a] Error in Liberal and Other vote combined.

In 1970 Marplan (on a U.K. not a G.B. basis) produced a forecast for *The Times* that overestimated Labour's lead by 9.6%.

In Oct 74 a Marplan poll in the *Sun* underestimated the Conservative lead by 1.1%. A Research Services poll in the *Observer* overestimated the Conservative lead by 4.4%. A separate MORI poll in the *Evening Standard* overestimated the Conservative lead by 0.9%.

The Common Market Referendum on 5 Jun 75 yielded a 67.2% 'yes' vote see p. 220. On that morning the opinion poll forecasts of a 'yes' vote were: Gallup 68%; ORC 73.7%; Louis Harris 72%; Marplan (decided voted) 58% 'yes', 27% 'no'.

SOURCES – For a comprehensive description of British opinion polling see F. Teer and J. D. Spence, *Political Opinion Polls* (1973); see also R. Hodder Williams, *Public Opinion Polls and British Politics* (1970). P. Rose, *The Polls and the 1970 Election* (1970) gives full documentation about the 1970 findings. Each of the Nuffield *British General Election Series* includes analyses of the polls. But R. Worester *British Public Opinion* (1991) provides the fullest record of political polling since 1945; see also Market Research Society's report on the 1992 performance of the polls (1994).

V

POLITICAL ALLUSIONS

The student of political history becomes familiar with allusive references to places, events, scandals, phrases and quotations. This chapter attempts to collect the most outstanding of these allusions.

Political Place-Names

At one time or another in the twentieth century the following place-names were sufficiently famous to be alluded to without further explanation. Any such list must necessarily be very selective. No foreign names are included here even though that means omitting Agadir, Chanak, Munich and Suez. No venues of party conferences are included, even though that means omitting Scarborough (Labour, 1960) and Blackpool (Conservative, 1963). No constituency names are included as such, even though that means omitting some, like Bewdley or Ebbw Vale, which are indelibly associated with individuals and others where sensational elections had a lasting national impact, like Colne Valley (1907), St George's Westminster (1931), East Fulham (1933), Orpington (1962), Smethwick (1964), Lincoln (1973), and Crosby (1981).

Abbey House, Victoria St, SW1. Conservative Party Headquarters 1946–58.
Abingdon St, SW1. Site of Liberal Party Headquarters 1910–34.
Admiralty House, SW1. Apartments of First Lord of Admiralty until 1960. Residence of H. Macmillan during Downing St repairs 1960–63 and since 1965 of Secretary of State for Defence and other ministers.
Aldermaston, Berkshire. Site of Atomic Weapons Research Establishment. Starting- or finishing-point of the Campaign for Nuclear Disarmament's Easter Marches 1958–63, 1967–.
Ashridge, Herts. Site of Conservative Party College, 1929–39.
Astley Hall. Worcestershire home of S. (Earl) Baldwin 1902–47.
Bachelor's Walk, Dublin. Scene (26 Jul 1914) of disturbance in which soldiers killed three rioters.
Balmoral Castle, Aberdeenshire. Summer home of the Sovereign since 1852.
Birch Grove, Sussex. Home of H. Macmillan 1906–86.
Blenheim Palace, Oxfordshire. Home of Dukes of Marlborough. Birthplace of (Sir) W. Churchill.
Bowood, Wiltshire. Home of Ms of Lansdowne.
Brixton, London, S.W.2. Scene of anti-police riots in April and July 1981.
Broadstairs, Kent. Birthplace and home of Edward Heath.
Buckingham Palace. Bought by George III in 1761. Official residence of the Sovereign since 1837.
Cable Street, Whitechapel, London. Scene of confrontations with the British Union of Fascists, 1935–36.
Carlton Club. London meeting place of Conservatives. Scene (19 Oct 1922) of gathering which brought down the Lloyd George Coalition.
Carmelite House, E.C.4. Long the Headquarters of the *Daily Mail* and *Evening News.*
Catherine Place. London home of T. Garel-Jones, and meeting place of ministers on 20 Nov 90.
Chartwell, Kent. Home of (Sir) W. Churchill 1923–65.
Chatsworth, Derbyshire. Home of Ds of Devonshire.
Chequers, Buckinghamshire. Country house given to the nation by Lord Lee of Fareham in 1917 and used as country residence for Prime Ministers from 1921.
Cherry Cottage, Buckinghamshire. Home of C. (Earl) Attlee 1951–61.
Cherkley Court, Surrey. Home of Ld Beaverbrook 1916–64.
Chevening, Kent. Country House bequeathed to the nation by Earl Stanhope. Now allocated by the Prime Minister to a Cabinet colleague. Site of Budget preparations in the 1980s and 1990s.
Church House, SW1. Meeting place of the Church Assembly since 1920; and of both Houses of Parliament, Nov–Dec 1940, May–Jun 1941, Jun–Aug 1944. Scene of United Nations preparatory meeting 1945 and of many Conservative gatherings.
Churt, Surrey. Home of D. Lloyd George (E) 1921–45.
Clay Cross, Derbyshire. Urban District Council which refused to implement 1972 Housing Act.

Cliveden, Buckinghamshire. Home of 2nd and 3rd Vt Astor. Alleged centre of 'Cliveden Set' in 1930s. Scene (1962) of events in the Profumo affair.

Coldharbour Lane, Brixton, London. Childhood home of J. Major, featured in 1991 Party conference speech and in party election broadcast in 1992.

Congress House, Gt. Russell St, W.C.1. Headquarters of Trades Union Congress 1960–.

Cowley St, London, SW1. Headquarters of the Social Democratic Party, 1981–88, and of the (Social and) Liberal Democrats 1988–.

Criccieth, Caernarvonshire. Welsh home of D. Lloyd George (E) 1880–1945.

Crichel Down, Dorset. The refusal to derequisition some land here led, ultimately, to the resignation of the Minister of Agriculture in Jul 1954.

Cross St, Manchester. Headquarters of the *(Manchester) Guardian* until 1970.

Curragh, The, Co. Kildare. Military camp; scene of 'mutiny' 20 Mar 1914.

Dalmeny, Midlothian. Home of Es of Rosebery.

Dorneywood, Buckinghamshire. Country house bequeathed to the nation in 1954 by Ld Courtauld-Thomson as an official residence for any Minister designated by the Prime Minister.

Downing St, SW1. No. 10 is the Prime Minister's official residence.[1] No. 11 is the official residence of the Chancellor of the Exchequer. No. 12 houses the offices of the Government Whips.

Dublin Castle. Offices of the Irish Administration until 1922.

Durdans, The, Epsom. Home of 5th E of Rosebery 1872–1929.

Eccleston Square, SW1. Site of Headquarters of the Labour Party and of the Trades Union Congress 1918–29.

Ettrick Bridge, Roxburgh. Constituency home of Sir D. Steel since 1966. Scene of meeting of Alliance leaders, 29 May 1983.

Euston Lodge, Phoenix Park, Dublin. Residence of the Ld-Lieutenant of Ireland.

Falloden, Northumberland. Home of Sir E. (Vt) Grey 1862–1933.

Fleet St, E.C.4. Location of *Daily Telegraph* and *Daily Express* until the late 1980s. Generic name for the London press.

Fort Belvedere, Berkshire. Country home of Edward VIII 1930–36.

Grand Hotel, Brighton. Scene of bombing on 11 Oct 1984 of Conservative Conference Headquarters.

Great George St, SW1. Site of the Treasury and, 1964–69, of the Department of Economic Affairs.

Greenham Common, Berkshire. Air base at which Cruise missiles were first sited (Nov 83). Women protesters camped outside it from Sep 81 until 1992.

Hampstead. London suburb which, during H. Gaitskell's leadership of the Labour Party, provided a generic name for the set of intellectuals associated with him.

Hatfield House, Hertfordshire. Home of Ms of Salisbury.

Highbury, Birmingham. Home of J. Chamberlain 1868–1914.

Hirsel, The, Berwickshire. Home of Es of Home.

Holy Loch, Argyll. Site of U.S. atomic submarine base 1962–92.

Howth, Co. Dublin. Scene of gun-running 26 Jul 1914.

Invergordon, Ross and Cromarty. Site of naval protest in Sep 1931 over proposed pay reductions.

Jarrow, Durham. Shipbuilding town where unemployment reached 73% in 1935. Start of Jarrow to London protest march, Oct 1936.

Kilmainham Jail, Dublin. Scene of execution of the leaders of the 1916 rising.

King St, W.C.2. Site of Communist Party Headquarters since early 1920s.

Knowsley, Lancashire. Home of Es of Derby.

Larne, Co. Antrim. Scene of gun-running 24 Apr 1914.

Limehouse, E.14. Scene of speech by D. Lloyd George 30 Jul 1909; became generic name for political vituperation. Also home of D. Owen 1965– and scene of meeting on 25 Jan 81, which produced 'The Limehouse Declaration' which anticipated the formation of the Social Democratic Party.

Londonderry House, W.1. London home of Ms of Londonderry until t946.

Lord North St SW1. Home of H. Wilson 1971–76.

Lossiemouth, Morayshire. Home of R. MacDonald, 1906- 1937.

Maze, The, County Antrim (formerly Long Kesh). Prison where many convicted terrorists were held from 1968 onwards. Scene of hunger strike in which 10 Republican prisoners died in 1981.

Molesworth, Cambridgeshire. Air base. Scene of demonstrations against Cruise missiles 1985–.

Notting Hill, W.11. Scene of racial disturbances in Aug 1958.

Old Queen St, SW1. Site of Conservative Party Headquarters 1941–46. Site of Conservative Research Department 1930–1981.

Olympia, W.14. Exhibition Hall; scene (7 Jun 1934) of Mosley meeting which provoked violence.

Palace Chambers, S.W.1. Headquarters of Conservative Party 1922–41.

Pembroke Lodge, W.8. Home of A. Bonar Law 1909–16.

---

[1] Since 1900, the only three Prime Ministers not to have lived at 10 Downing Street were M of Salisbury, up to 1902, H. Macmillan 1960–63, and H. Wilson 1974–76.

Poplar. London borough whose Poor Law Guardians (including G. Lansbury) were imprisoned in 1921 for paying more than national rates of relief.

Portland Place, W.1. Headquarters of the British Broadcasting Corporation 1932–.

Printing House Square, E.C.4. Headquarters of *The Times* 1785–1974.

Relugas, Morayshire. Fishing lodge of Sir E. Grey; scene of 'Relugas Compact' with H. Asquith and R. Haldane Sep 1905.

St James Palace, W.1. Royal Palace. Foreign Ambassadors continue to be accredited to the Court of St James.

St Paul's, Bristol. Scene of anti-police riot, Apr 1980.

St Stephen's Chambers, SW1. Site of Conservative Headquarters 1900–18.

Sanctuary Buildings, SW1. Site of Conservative Headquarters 1918–22.

Sandringham House, Norfolk. Royal residence since 1861.

Scapa Flow, Orkney. Naval anchorage where German Fleet was scuttled 21 Jun 1919. Scene of trouble at the time of the Invergordon 'mutiny' Sep 1931.

Scilly Isles, Cornwall. Location of H. Wilson's country cottage 1959–.

Selsdon Park. Hotel in Croydon. Scene of Conservative Shadow Cabinet's weekend meeting, 30 Jan–1 Feb 1970.

Shanklin, Isle of Wight. Scene (Feb 1949) of meeting of Labour Party leaders.

Sidney St, E.1. Scene of police siege of anarchists 3 Jan 1911.

Smith Square, SW1. Location of the Labour Party Headquarters (Transport House) 1928–1980; of the Conservative Party Headquarters since 1958; and of the Liberal Party Headquarters 1965–68.

Southall. West London suburb with large population of Asian origin. Scene of violent disturbances in anti-National Front riot, 23 Apr 1979.

Stormont, Belfast Site of Parliament and Government of Northern Ireland.

Sunningdale, Surrey. Location of Civil Service College where a Conference on Northern Ireland 6–9 Dec 73 produced the Sunningdale Agreement on power-sharing and a Council of Ireland.

Swinton, Yorkshire. Home of E of Swinton. Conservative Party College 1948–1971.

Taff Vale, Glamorgan. In 1901 the Taff Vale Railway Company successfully sued a trade union for loss due to a strike.

Threadneedle St, E.C.2. Site of the Bank of England.

Tonypandy. Scene of violent miners' strike to which W. Churchill sent troops in Nov 1910.

Toxteth, Liverpool 8. Scene of rioting, Jul 1981.

Transport House, SW1. Headquarters of the Transport and General Workers' Union and of the Labour Party 1928–80 and of the Trades Union Congress 1928–60.

Walworth Rd, London, S.E.17. In 1980 150 Walworth Rd became the headquarters of the Labour Party.

Wapping, East London. Site of headquarters of News International, where the *Times*, the *Sunday Times*, the *Sun* and the *News of the World* have been produced and printed since 1986.

Westbourne, Birmingham. Home of N. Chamberlain 1911–40.

Westminster, London. Parliament meets in the Palace of Westminster and Westminster has become a generic name for parliamentary activity.

Wharf, The, Sutton Courtenay, Berkshire. Home of H. Asquith 1912–28.

Whitehall, London. Many government departments are situated in Whitehall and it has become a generic name for civil service activity.

Whittingehame, East Lothian. Home of A. Balfour 1848–1930.

Windsor Castle, Berkshire. Official royal residence since 11th century.

Political Quotations

From time to time an isolated phrase becomes an established part of the language of political debate. Such phrases are frequently misquoted and their origins are often obscure. Here are a few which seem to have had an especial resonance. The list is far from comprehensive; it merely attempts to record the original source for some well-used quotations.

When was a war not a war? When it was carried on by *methods of barbarism* in South Africa?

SIR H. CAMPBELL-BANNERMAN, in a speech to National Reform Union, 14 Jun 01

For the present, at any rate, I must proceed alone. I must *plough my furrow alone*, but before I get to the end of that furrow it is possible that I may not find myself alone.

E of ROSEBERY, in a speech at the City Liberal Club, 19 Jul 01

To the distinguished representatives of the commercial interests of the Empire . . . I venture to allude to the impression which seemed generally to prevail among their brethren across the seas, that the old country must *wake up* if she [England] intends to maintain her old position of preeminence in her colonial trade against foreign competitors.

PRINCE of WALES (later GEORGE V) at a lunch at Guidhall on the completion of his tour of the Empire, 5 Dec 01

What is the advice I have to offer you? You have to *clear* your *slate*. It is six years since you were in office . . . The primary duty of the Liberal Party is to wipe its slate clean

E.of ROSEBERY, speaking to a Liberal audience at Chesterfield, 16 Dec 01. Sir H. CAMPBELL-BANNERMAN replied at Leicester 'I am no believer in the doctrine of the *clean slate.*'

I should consider that I was but ill-performing my duty if we were to profess a settled conviction when *no settled conviction exists.*

A.J. BALFOUR, House of Commons, 10 June 03

If I believed that there was the smallest reasonable chance of success, I would have no hesitation in advising my fellow-countrymen to endeavour to end the present system by *armed revolt.*

J. REDMOND, House of Commons, 12 Apr 05

It [the Chinese Labour Contract] cannot in the opinion of his Majesty's Government, be classified as slavery in the extreme acceptance of the word without some risk of *terminological inexactitude.*

W. CHURCHILL, House of Commons 22 Feb 06

You mean it is *Mr Balfour's poodle!* It fetches and carries for him. It barks for him. It bites anybody that he sets it on to.

D. LLOYD GEORGE, replying to H. Chaplin, M.P., who had claimed in a House of Commons debate on the House of Lords (Restoration of Powers) Bill, that the Lords was the watchdog of the Constitution, 26 Jun 07

If we believe a thing to be bad, and if we have a right to prevent it, it is our duty to try to prevent it and to *damn the consequences.*

LORD MILNER, in a speech at Glasgow in opposition to Lloyd George's 1909 Finance Bill, 26 Nov 09

Wait and see.

H. ASQUITH, repeated four times to Opposition members pressing for a statement when speaking on Parliament Act Procedure Bill, House of Commons, 4 Apr 10

We were beaten by *the Bishops and the rats.*

G. WYNDHAM, on the passing of the Parliament Bill by the House of Lords 10 Aug 11

La Grande Illusion.

Title of a book by N. ANGELL, first published in 1909 as *Europe's Optical Illusion* and republished as *The Great Illusion* in 1910

The lamps are going out all over Europe. We shall not see them lit again in our lifetime.

SIR E. GREY, 3 Aug 14, talking in his room at the Foreign Office, quoted in his autobiography *Twenty five Years*, vol. II, p. 20

Your King and Country Need YOU

Advertisement in *Daily Mail* and other papers 5 Aug 14. Basis for drawing on the cover of *London Opinion*, 5 Sep 14 designed by A. LEETE, depicting LORD KITCHENER with arresting eyes and pointing finger above the caption 'Your Country needs you'; reproduced by Parliamentary Recruiting Committee for use as recruiting poster and issued Sep 14

The maxim of the British people is *'business as usual'*.

W. CHURCHILL in a speech at the Guildhall, 9 Nov 14

To secure for the producers by hand or by brain the full fruits of their industry and the most equitable distribution thereof that may be possible upon the basis of *the common ownership of the means of production (distribution and exchange)*.

Listed under party objects in the Constitution of the Labour Party adopted at the Annual Conference in London 26 Feb 18 (words in brackets added at the 1928 Conference)

What is our task? To make Britain *a fit country for heroes to live in*.

D. LLOYD GEORGE, speech at Wolverhampton, 24 Nov 18

We will get everything out of her [Germany] that you can squeeze out of a lemon and a bit more . . . I will *squeeze* until you can hear the *pips squeak*.

SIR E. GEDDES, in a speech at the Drill Hall, Cambridge, 9 Dec 18

They are a lot of *hard-faced men* . . . who look as if they had done very well out of the war.

A Conservative politician (often said to be Baldwin), quoted by J.M. Keynes in *Economic Consequences of the Peace* (Macmillan, 1919), p. 133

First let me insist on what our opponents habitually ignore, indeed what they seem intellectually incapable of understanding, namely the *inevitable gradualness* of our scheme of change.

S. WEBB, in his Presidential Address to the Labour Party Conference Queen's Hall, Langham Place, 26 June 23

Until our educated and politically minded democracy has become predominantly *a property-owning democracy*, neither the national equilibrium nor the balance of the life of the individual will be restored.

A. SKELTON, in *Constructive Conservatism* (Blackwood, 1924), p. 17; subsequently used by A. EDEN at Conservative Conference, Blackpool, 3 Oct 46, and by W. CHURCHILL, 5 Oct 46

Although I know that there are those who work for different ends from most of us in this House, yet there are many in all ranks and all parties who will re-echo my prayer *'give us peace in our time, O Lord'*

S. BALDWIN speaking in House of Commons on Trade Unions (Political Fund) Bill, 6 Mar 25

Not a penny off the pay, not a second on the day.

Slogan coined by A.J. Cook, Secretary of the National Union of Mineworkers, and used frequently in the run-up to the miners' strike of 1926

We can conquer unemployment.

Title of a pamphlet which was a potted version of the Liberal *Yellow Book* (1929)

Safety first Stanley Baldwin, the man you can trust

Slogan on election posters used by the Conservative Party in 1929; the slogan 'Safety First' was previously used by the Conservatives in the 1922 Election

I remember when I was a child being taken to the celebrated Barnum's Circus . . . the exhibit which I most desired to see was the one described as 'the Boneless Wonder'. My parents judged that the spectacle would be too revolting for my youthful eyes, and I have waited fifty years to see *the Boneless Wonder* sitting on the Treasury Bench.

W. CHURCHILL, referring to R. MacDonald during a debate on Amendment Bill, 28 Jan 31

What the proprietorship of these papers is aiming at is power, and *power without responsibility, the prerogative of the harlot throughout the ages*

S. BALDWIN, attacking the Press Lords in a speech at Queen's Hall, London, during Westminster St George's by-election campaign, 18 Mar 31. The phrase was suggested by his cousin, Rudyard Kipling

I hope you have read the Election programme of the Labour Party. It is the most fantastic and impracticable programme ever put before the electors . . . This is not Socialism. It is *Bolshevism run mad.*

P. SNOWDEN, election broadcast, 17 Oct 31

I think it is well also for the man in the street to realise that there is no power on earth that can protect him from being bombed. Whatever people may tell him, *the bomber will always get through.*

S. BALDWIN, in the House of Commons, 10 Nov 32

That this House will in no circumstances *fight for its King and Country.*

Oxford Union motion, 9 Feb 33

[You are] placing . . . the Movement in an absolutely wrong position to be *hawking your conscience round* from body to body asking to be told what you ought to do with it.

E. BEVIN, attacking G. Lansbury at the Labour Party Conference, Brighton, 1 Oct 35

My lips are not yet unsealed.

S. BALDWIN, speaking in the House of Commons, on the Abyssinian crisis, 10 Dec 35, later quoted as 'My lips are sealed'

A Corridor for Camels.

Heading of a first leader in *The Times*, on the Hoare Laval Pact, written by G. Dawson, 16 Dec 35

I put before the whole House my own views with *appalling frankness* . . . supposing I had gone to the country and . . . said that we must rearm, does anybody think that this pacific democracy would have rallied to the cry? I cannot think of anything that would have made the loss of the election from my point of view more certain.

S. BALDWIN, speaking in the House of Commons, 12 Nov 36 (See W. Churchill in 1948)

Something ought to be done to find these people employment . . . *Something will be done.*

EDWARD VIII, On a visit to South Wales, 18 Nov 36

How horrible, fantastic, incredible it is that we should be digging trenches and trying on gas-masks here because of *a quarrel in a faraway country between people of whom we know nothing.*

N. CHAMBERLAIN, referring to Czechoslovakia in a Broadcast 27 Sep 38

Britain will *not* be involved in a European *war* this year, or next year either.

Daily Express headline, 30 Sep 38 inspired by LD BEAVERBROOK. Cited as basis for 'There will be no war' campaign in the *Daily Express*

This is the second time in my history that there has come back from Germany to Downing Street, peace with honour. I believe that it is *peace for our time.*

N. CHAMBERLAIN, referring back to Disraeli's comment on the Congress of Berlin (1878), in a speech from a window of 10 Downing Street on return from Munich, 30 Sep 38

Speak for England, Arthur.

L. AMERY, R. BOOTHBY; shouted out as Arthur Greenwood rose to speak in the House of Commons, 2 Sep 39

Whatever may be the reason, whether it was that *Hitler* thought he might get away with what he had got without fighting for it, or whether it was that, after all, the preparations are not sufficiently complete, one thing is certain; he *has missed the bus.*

N. CHAMBERLAIN, speaking at Conservative Central Council, 4 Apr 40

You have sat too long here for any good you have been doing. Depart, I say, and let us have done with you. *In the name of God, go!*

L. AMERY, quoting Cromwell (1653) to N. Chamberlain in the House of Commons, 7 May 40

I have nothing to offer but *blood, toil, tears and sweat.*

W. CHURCHILL, House of Commons, 13 May 40

We shall fight on the beaches, we shall fight on the landing grounds, we shall fight in the fields and in the streets.

W. CHURCHILL, House of Commons 4 Jun 40

If the British Empire and its Commonwealth last for a thousand years, men will still say, *'This was their finest hour'.*

W. CHURCHILL, broadcast to the nation when the fall of France was imminent, 18 Jun 40

Guilty Men

Political tract written by Michael Foot, Frank Owen and Peter Howard, using pseudonym Cato, published Jul 40

Never in the field of human conflict was *so much owed by so many to so few.*

W. CHURCHILL, House of Commons, 20 Aug 40

Give us the tools and we will finish the job.

W. CHURCHILL, broadcast to the nation, 9 Feb 41

When I warned them [the French] that Britain would fight on alone . . . their General told their Prime Minister, . . . in three weeks England will have her neck wrung like a chicken. *Some chicken, some neck.*

W. CHURCHILL, speaking to the Canadian Parliament, 30 Dec 41

I have not become the King's first Minister in order *to preside over the liquidation of the British Empire.*

W. CHURCHILL, speech at the Mansion House, 10 Nov 42

Pounds, shillings and pence have become quite *meaning-less* symbols.

A. GREENWOOD, in the House of Commons, 16 Feb 43

Let us face the future.

Title of Labour Party Manifesto, May 1945.

No *Socialist* system can be established without a political police . . . . They would have to fall back on some form of *Gestapo.*

W. CHURCHILL, election broadcast, 4 Jun 45

You have no right whatever to speak on behalf of the Government. Foreign Affairs are in the capable hands of Ernest Bevin. His task is quite sufficiently difficult without the embarrassment of irresponsible statements of the kind which you are making . . . *a period of silence on your part would be welcome.*

C. ATTLEE in a letter to H. Laski, Chairman of the Labour Party NEC 20 Aug 45

From Stettin in the Baltic to Trieste in the Adriatic, an *iron curtain* has descended across the Continent.

W. CHURCHILL, speaking at Westminster College, Fulton, U.S.A., 5 Mar 46. The phrase can be traced back to Mrs Snowden's visit to Russia in 1920

We are the masters at the moment and not only for the moment, but for a very long time to come.

SIR H. SHAWCROSS, in the House of Commons during third reading of the Trade Disputes and Trade Union Bill, 2 Apr 46

We know that you, the organised workers of the country, are our friends . . . . As for the rest, they do not matter *a tinker's curse.*

E. SHINWELL, speaking at E.T.U. Conference, Margate, 7 May 47

For in the case of nutrition and health, just as in the case of education, *the gentleman in Whitehall really does know better* what is good for people than the people know themselves.

D. JAY, from *The Socialist Case* (1947) p. 258

No attempt at ethical or social education can eradicate from my heart a deep burning hatred for the Tory Party . . . So far as I am concerned, they are *lower than vermin*.

A. BEVAN, at Manchester 4 Jul 48

I have authorised the relaxation of *controls* affecting more than 60 commodities for which the Board of Trade is responsible.

H. WILSON, House of Commons, 4 Nov 48

The Hon. Member asked two other questions. One of them was how many licences and permits are to be issued after the removal of the 200,000 Board of Trade licences and the 5,000 or 6,000 others which were as the result of yesterday's little *bonfire* . . .

H. WILSON, as President of the Board of Trade, House Commons, 5 Nov 48

Baldwin . . . confesses *putting party before country.*

W. CHURCHILL, entry in index to *The Gathering Storm*, Vol.I of *The Second World War* (1948) (see S.Baldwin 12 Nov 36)

The Right Road for Britain

Conservative Party policy statement, 1949

The language of priorities is the religion of socialism.

A. BEVAN, Labour Party Conference, Blackpool, 8 Jun 49

Whose finger on the trigger?

Daily Mirror, front-page headline on eve of the election, 24 Oct 51

We think it is a good thing to *set the people free,* as much as is possible in our complicated modern society, from the trammels of state control and bureaucratic management.

SIR W. CHURCHILL, in a BBC broadcast, 3 May 52

The right technique of economic opposition at the moment can be summed up in a slogan. The slogan is that the Opposition should keep itself on the constructive and sunny side of Mr Butskell's dilemma. Mr *Butskell[ism]* . . . is a composite of the present Chancellor and the previous one.

Article in the *Economist* refering to R. Butler and H. Gaitskell, 13 Feb 54

I know that the right kind of political leader for the Labour Party is *a desiccated calculating machine.*

A. BEVAN, taken as referring to H. Gaitskell, though Bevan subsequently denied this, at the *Tribune* meeting during Labour Party Conference at Scarborough, 29 Sep 54

There ain't gonna be no war.

H. MACMILLAN, at press conference, on return from Summit, 24 Jul 55

Reporter: Mr Butler, would you say that this is *the best Prime Minister we have?* R. Butler: Yes.

R. BUTLER, interviewed by the Press Association at London Airport, Dec 55

Most Conservatives, and almost certainly some of the wiser Trade Union Leaders, are waiting to feel *the smack of firm government.*

Daily Telegraph editorial written by the Deputy Editor D. MCLACHLAN, 3 Jan 56

And all these financiers, all the little *gnomes of Zurich* and the other financial centres about whom we keep on hearing, started to make their dispositions in regard to sterling.

H. WILSON, in the House of Commons Debate on the Address, 12 Nov 56

During the past few weeks I have felt sometimes that the *Suez Canal was flowing through my drawing-room.*

LADY EDEN, opening Gateshead Conservative Association Headquarters, 20 Nov 56

Let us be frank about it, most of our people *have never had it so good.*

H. MACMILLAN, speaking at Bedford to a Conservative Party rally, 21 Jul 57

If you carry this resolution . . . you'll send the British Foreign Secretary whoever he was *naked into the Conference Chamber.*

A. BEVAN, Labour Party Conference, Brighton, 3 Oct 57

And you call that statesmanship. I call it *an emotional spasm.*

A. BEVAN, speaking on unilateral disarmament, Labour Party Conference, Brighton, 3 Oct 57

I thought the best thing to do was to settle up *these little local difficulties,* and then turn to the wider vision of the Commonwealth.

H. MACMILLAN, referring to the resignation of Treasury Ministers in a statement at London Airport before leaving for Commonwealth tour, 7 Jan 58

Jaw-jaw is better than war-war.

H. MACMILLAN, Canberra, 30 Jan 58; echoing CHURCHILL, 'Talking jaw to jaw is better than going to war', White House lunch, 26 Jun 54

Introducing *Super-Mac.*

VICKY, caption of cartoon depicting H. Macmillan in a Superman outfit; first appeared in *Evening Standard,* 6 Nov 58

Life's better with the Conservatives. Don't let Labour ruin it.

Slogan on Conservative posters in the 1959 General Election

What matters is that Mr Macmillan has let Mr Lloyd know that at the Foreign Office, in these troubled times, *enough is enough.*

Article by David Wood, *The Times* Political Correspondent, 1 Jun 59

Britain belongs to you.

Title of Labour Party election manifesto, published 18 Sep 59

The *wind of change* is blowing through this Continent, and whether we like it or not, this growth of national consciousness is a political fact.

H. MACMILLAN, address to Joint Assembly of Union Parliament, Cape Town, 3 Feb 60

We have developed instead an *affluent,* open and democratic *society,* in which the class escalators are continually moving and in which people are divided not so much between 'haves' and 'have-nots' as between 'haves' and 'have-mores'.

R. BUTLER, at a Conservative Political Centre Summer School, 8 Jul 60

There are some of us, Mr Chairman, who will *fight and fight and fight again* to save the party we love.

H. GAITSKELL, Labour Party Conference, Scarborough, 3 Oct 60

The present Colonial Secretary . . . has been *too clever by half* . . . I believe that the Colonial Secretary is a very fine bridge player . . . It is not considered immoral, or even bad form to outwit one's opponents at bridge . . . It almost seems to me as if the Colonial Secretary, when he abandoned the sphere of bridge for the sphere of politics, brought his bridge technique with him.

M OF SALISBURY, referring to I. MACLEOD and his policies for Africa, House of Lords, 7 May 61

SCOTT: Do you think the Unions are going to respond to what amounts in effect to a 'wage freeze' in the public sector? LLOYD: Well, I said that I wasn't going to deal with every possible circumstance. This is a *pause* rather than a *wage freeze.*

S. LLOYD interviewed on B.B.C. Radio Newsreel by Hardiman Scott about the 'July measures'. 25 Jul 61

It does mean, if this is the idea, the end of Britain as an independent European state . . . it means the end of *a thousand years of history.*

H. GAITSKELL, Labour Party Conference, Brighton, 3 Oct 62

It is a moral issue.

Heading of *The Times* leader on the Profumo Affair, 11 Jun 63

A great party is not to be brought down because of a *squalid affair between a woman of easy virtue and a proven liar.*

LORD HAILSHAM, in a B.B.C interview with R. McKenzie about the Profumo Affair, 13 Jun 63

He would, wouldn't he?

Miss M. RICE-DAVIES in a Magistrates Court on 28 Jun 63, referring to a peer denying knowing her

And in bygone days, commanders were taught that, when in doubt, they should march their troops towards the sound of gunfire. *I intend to march my troops towards the sound of gunfire.*

J. GRIMOND, in a speech to the Liberal Assembly at Brighton, 15 Sep 63

We are re-defining and we are re-stating our socialism in terms of *the scientific revolution* . . . the Britain that is going to be forged in *the white heat* of this revolution will be no place for restrictive practices or out-dated methods on either side of industry.

H. WILSON, Labour Party Conference, Scarborough, 1 Oct 63

I hope that it will soon be possible for *the customary processes of consultation* to be carried on within the Party about its future leadership.

H. MACMILLAN, in the letter in which he announced his resignation as P.M.; read out to the Conservative Party Conference at Blackpool by the Earl of Home 10 Oct 63

After half a century of democratic advance, the whole process has ground to a halt with a *14th Earl.*

H. WILSON, speech at Belle Vue, Manchester, 19 Oct 63

When you come to think of it, he is the *14th Mr Wilson.*

Lord HOME in a television interview by Kenneth Harris on I.T.V., 21 Oct 63

Let's go with Labour.

Labour Party slogan used 1964

If the British public falls for this [Labour policies] *it will be stark staring bonkers.*

Q. HOGG, press conference at Conservative Central Office during the election campaign, 12 Oct 64

I have been given the *bed of nails.*

R. GUNTER, on his appointment as Minister of Labour, 18 Oct 64

Smethwick Conservatives can have the satisfaction of having topped the poll, of having sent a Member who, until another election returns him to oblivion, will serve his time here as *a Parliamentary leper.*

H. WILSON, referring Peter Griffiths, M.P., who defeated Patrick Gordon Walker in an allegedly racialist election campaign at Smethwick, House of Commons, 4 Nov 64

A week is a long time in politics.

Attributed to H. WILSON, probably first used in a lobby briefing late in 1964

In this connection [use of military force in Rhodesia] the Prime Ministers noted the statement by the British Prime Minister that on the expert advice available to him, the cumulative effects of the economic and financial sanctions might well bring the rebellion to an end within a matter of *weeks rather than months.*

Final communique of Commonwealth Prime Ministers' Conference at Lagos, released 12 Jan 66; referring back to unreported speech by H. WILSON also on 12 Jan 66

Action not words.

Title of Conservative manifesto, published 6 Mar 66

You KNOW *Labour Government works.*

Labour Party slogan used in 1966 election

Now one encouraging gesture from the French Government, which I welcome, and the Conservative leader *rolls on his back like a spaniel.*

H. WILSON, Bristol, 18 Mar 66

It is difficult for us to appreciate the pressures which are put on men . . . in the highly organised strike committees in the individual ports by this *tightly knit group of politically motivated men* . . . who are now determined to exercise back-stage pressures . . . endangering the security of the industry and the economic welfare of the nation.

H. WILSON, House of Commons 20 Jun 66

Sterling has been under pressure for the past two and a half weeks. After an improvement in the early weeks of May, we were *blown off course* by the seven weeks seamen's strike.

H. WILSON, House of Commons, 20 Jul 66

Every dog is allowed one bite, but a different view is taken taken of a *dog* that goes on biting all the time. He may not *get his licence* returned when it falls due.

H. WILSON, speech to Parliamentary Labour Party, 2 Mar 67

It does not mean, of course, that *the pound* here in Britain *in your pocket* or purse or in your bank has been devalued.

H. WILSON, television and radio broadcast announcing devaluation of the pound, 20 Nov 67

As I look ahead, I am filled with foreboding. Like the Roman, I seem to see *'the River Tiber foaming with much blood'*

E. POWELL, speech to a Conservative Political Centre Meeting in Birmingham, 20 Apr 68, referring to the Aeneid 'Thybrim multo spumantem sanguine cerno'

In Place of Strife.

Title of Government White Paper on industrial relations legislation, 19 Jan 69

Selsdon Man is designing a system of society for the ruthless and the pushing, the uncaring . . . . His message to the rest is: you're out on your own.

H. WILSON, at a Rally of the Greater London Party in Camden Town Hall, 21 Feb 70; referring to the Conservative policy-forming meeting at Selsdon Park, Croydon, 31 Jan 70

Nor would it be in the interests of the Community that its enlargement should take place except with the *full-hearted consent* of Parliament and people of the new member countries.

E. HEATH in a speech to the Franco British Chamber of Commerce in Paris, 5 May 70

I am determined, therefore, that a Conservative Government shall introduce *a new style of government.*

E. HEATH, in foreword to Conservative manifesto, published May 70

This would, *at a stroke,* reduce the rise in prices, increase productivity and reduce unemployment.

Wrongly reported in *The Times* as having been said by E. HEATH at a press conference at Central Office, 16 Jun 70; actually taken from a Conservative Press Release (No. G.E.228) distributed at the press conference

We believe that the essential need of the country is to gear its policies to the great majority of the people, who are not *lame ducks.*

J. DAVIES, speaking in a debate on public expenditure and taxation, House of Commons, 4 Nov 70; echoing a speech by A. BENN in the House of Commons ['the next question is what safeguards are there against the support of lame ducks'] on 1 Feb 68

Yesterday's Men.

Slogan on Labour poster caricaturing Conservative leaders,May 70; subsequently title of B.B.C. television programme about Labour leaders in opposition transmitted 17 Jun 71

We say that what Britain needs is a new *Social Contract.* That is what this document [Labour's Programe 1972] is all about.

J. CALLAGHAN, Labour Party Conference, 2 Oct Blackpool, 72; but A. Benn had used the phrase in a 1970 Fabian pamphlet *The New Politics.* J.-J. Rousseau's *Le Contrat Social* was published in 1762

It is the unpleasant and *unacceptable face of capitalism,* but one should not suggest that the whole of British industry consists of practices of this kind.

E. HEATH, replying to a question from J. Grimond about the Lonrho affair, House of Commons, 15 May 73

From 31 December, they [most industrial and commercial premises] will be limited [in the use of electricity] to *three* specified *days* each *week.*

E. HEATH, House of Commons, 13 Dec 73

Looking around the House, one realises that *we are all minorities now* – indeed, some more than others.

J. THORPE, House of Commons, after the election of the Speaker, 6 Mar 74

We believe that the only way in which the maximum degree of national cooperation can be achieved is for a *government of national unity* to be formed.

J. THORPE in a letter to E. Heath 4 Mar 74. Later in the year the phrase became a central theme in the Conservatives' October campaign.

With its [the local government world's] usual spirit of patriotism and its tradition of service to the community's needs, it is coming to realize that, for the time being at least, *the party is over.*

A. CROSLAND, at a civic luncheon at Manchester 9 May 1975

Ladies and Gentlemen, I stand before you tonight in my green chiffon evening gown, my face softly made up, my fair hair gently waved . . . *The Iron Lady* of the Western World. Me? A cold war warrior? Well, yes if that is how they wish to interpret my defence of values and freedoms fundamental to our way of life.

MRS M. THATCHER, speaking in her Finchley constituency 31 Jan 76, referring to a report in the Soviet *Red Star* 23 Jan 76

That part of his speech was rather like being *savaged by a dead sheep.*

D. HEALEY, 14 Jun 78, replying to a Commons attack by Sir G. Howe

Labour isn't working.

Slogan on Conservative poster designed by Saatchi and Saatchi, showing dole queue in Aug 1978 and widely used in the 1979 election

Crisis? What Crisis?
(Journalist: 'What . . . of the mounting chaos in the country at the moment?' Callaghan: 'I don't think that other people in the world would share the view that there is mounting chaos.')

Sun headline, 11 Jan 79, referring to J. CALLAGHAN at London airport on return home from Guadaloupe summit during widespread strikes, 10 Jan 1979

The Labour Way is the Better Way.

Title of Labour election manifesto published Apr 1979

I don't see how we can talk with Mrs Thatcher. . . . I will say to the lads, come on, *get your snouts in the trough.*

S. WEIGHELL, speaking in London, 10 Apr 79, echoing his speech at the Labour Party Conference, Blackpool, 6 Oct 78 'If you want it to go out . . . that you now believe in the philosophy of the pig trough those with the biggest snouts get the largest share, I reject it.'

There is no alternative.

A phrase widely attributed to Mrs M. THATCHER in 1979 and 1980

We are fed up with *fudging and mudging*, with mush and slush.

D. OWEN, at Labour Party Conference, Blackpool, 2 Oct 80

The Lady's not for turning

Mrs M. THATCHER, Conservative Party Conference, Brighton, 10 Oct 80

Breaking the mould of British politics

Phrase widely used after 1981 about the goals of the Alliance. Its origin seems to lie in R. JENKINS, *What Matters Now* (1972), quoting Andrew Marvell on Cromwell 'Casting Kingdoms of Old/Into another mould.'

Go back to your constituencies and *prepare for Government*.

D. STEEL addressing Liberal Party Conference in Llandudno, 18 Sep 81

He [his unemployed father in the 1930s] didn't riot. *He got on his bike* and looked for work.

N. TEBBIT, Conservative Party Conference, Blackpool, 15 Oct 81

'GOTCHA'

Sun headline on 4 May 82 on the sinking of the Argentine cruiser *Belgrano*

Let me make one thing absolutely clear. *The NHS is safe with us.*

MRS M THATCHER, addressing Conservative Party Conference, Brighton, 8 Oct 82

Heckler: 'At least Mrs Thatcher has got *guts*.'
N. Kinnock: 'And it's a pity that people had to leave theirs an the ground *at Goose Green* in order to prove it.'

N. KINNOCK during *TV South's* election programme 'The South Decides', 5 Jun 83

As one person said, it is perhaps *being economical with the truth.*

Sir R. ARMSTRONG, Permanent Secretary to the Cabinet, under cross examination in an Australian Court over the British Government's attempt to prevent publication of the book *Spycatcher*, 18 Nov 86. The phrase can be traced back to Mark Twain and Edmund Burke.

I'll tell you what happens with impossible promises. You start with implausible resolutions, which are then pickled into a rigid dogma or code. And you end up with *the grotesque chaos of a Labour Council* – a Labour Council – *hiring taxis to scuttle round a city handing out redundancy notices* to its own workers.

N. KINNOCK, addressing Labour Party Conference in Bournemouth, 1 Oct 85

I have a young family and for the next few years I should like to devote more while they are time to them while they are still so young.
I am naturally very sorry to see you go, but understand your reasons for doing so, particularly your wish to be able *to spend more time with your family.*

N. FOWLER in his letter of resignation to the Prime Minister, 3 Jan 90 and MRS M. THATCHER replying to N. FOWLER's resignation letter, 3 Jan 90.

The President of the Commission, M. Delors, said at this conference the other day that he wanted the European Parliament to be the democratic body of the Community, he wanted the Commission to be the Executive, and he wanted the Council of Ministers to be the Senate. *No. No. No.*

MRS M. THATCHER speaking in the House of Commons on her return from the Rome summit, 30 Oct 90

Britain has done itself no good by the distinction drawn between the skill of blue collar and white collar workers. . . . In the next ten years we will have to continue to make changes which will make the whole of this country *a genuinely classless society*.	J. MAJOR writing in *Today* 24 Nov 90
I want to see us build *a country that is at ease with itself*, a country that is confident and a country that is able and willing to build a better quality of life for all its citizens.	J. MAJOR speaking in Downing Street on becoming Prime Minister, 28 Nov 90.
Rising unemployment and the recession have been the price we've had to pay to get inflation down. But that is *a price well worth paying*.	N. LAMONT, House of Commons, 16 May 91.
The green shoots of economic spring are appearing once again.	N. LAMONT speaking at the Conservative Party Conference, 9 Oct 91.
Labour's Double Whammy.	Slogan attacking Labour tax plans coined by Conservative Central Office and used on pre-election publicity material, Feb 92
Je ne regrette rien.	N. LAMONT speaking at a press conference during the Newbury by-election campaign, 12 May 93.
Don't let the buggers get you down.	Inscription alleged to be on a watch given by M. MATES to fugitive businessman ASIL NADIR, Apr 93.
We don't want another three more of *the bastards* out there.	J. MAJOR explaining why he had not sacked right wing Cabinet members, 23 Jul 93 (Comments to a TV interviewer not intended for broadcast were leaked to the *Observer*, 25 Jul 93)

Political Scandals

The following list is not comprehensive but indicates most of the more celebrated examples. A few others are implicit in the list of ministerial resignations on pp. 68–70.

1904	Wyndham (Ministerial involvement with Irish Home Rule Schemes)
1912	Marconi (Ministers dealing in shares)
1918	Pemberton Billing (Libel action involing many public figures)
1918	Maurice (Army Council's disciplining of a General)
1921	Bottomley (M.P. and financial practice)
1922ff.	Maundy Gregory (Sale of honours)
1936	Budget leak (Minister telling M.P. of budget plans)
1940	Boothby (Minister influencing handling of blocked Czech assets)
1947	Allighan (M.P. leaking Parliamentary Labour Party meetings)
1948	Belcher/Stanley (Influencing peddling at the Board of Trade)
1951	Burgess/Maclean (spies fleeing to Moscow)
1955	Crichel Down (Minister's handling of sequestrated land)
1957	Bank Rate (Alleged leak)
1962	Vassall (Spy scandal)
1963	Profumo (Minister lying to the House)
1972	Poulson (Influence peddling in building)
1973	Jellicoe/Lambton (Sex scandal)

1976		Stonehouse (M.P.'s simulated drowning)
1976–9		Thorpe (Liberal Leader ultimately acquitted of conspiracy to murder).
1979		Blunt (Spy scandal)
1983		Parkinson (Sex scandal)
1986		Westland (Helicopter takeover)
1992		Mellor (Ministerial indiscretion)
1992		Matrix-Churchill (Arms for Iraq)
1993		Mates (involvement with Asil Nadir scandal)
1994		'Back to Basics' (a succession of six private scandals affecting Ministers and Conservative M.P.s)

Major Civil Disturbances and Demonstrations (in Great Britain)

8 Nov	1910	Tonypandy
16 Aug	1911	Liverpool ('Bloody Sunday' clash between police and strikers)
	1915–16	Anti-German riots in the East End
31 Jul	1919	Glasgow ('Bloody Friday' confrontation between police and strikers)
3–10 May	1926	General Strike
	Sep 1932	Unemployed demonstrations provoke violence in Birkenhead, Belfast and London
7 Jun	1934	Olympia (violence at Mosley rally)
4 Oct	1936	Cable Street (confrontation between police and anti-fascists)
	Nov 1936	Jarrow Hunger March
24 Aug	1958	Nottingham (race riot)
31 Aug	1958	Notting Hill Gate (race riot)
17 Mar	1968	Grosvenor Square (Demonstration against Vietnam War)
15 Jun	1968	Red Lion Square (confrontation between Nat.Front and opponents)
Jan–Mar	1972	Saltley (mass picketing of the coke depot)
Jul–Sep	1977	Grunwick, Dollis Hill (mass picketing of photographic factory)
23 Apr	1979	Southall (confrontation between police and anti-National Front demonstrators)
2 Apr	1980	St Paul's, Bristol (anti-police riots)
11–13 Apr	1981	Brixton (anti-police riot with racial overtones; more trouble Jul 81)
5–6 Jul	1981	Toxteth (major riot)
	1981–91	Greenham Common (women's protests against nuclear weapons)
Mar 1984–Mar	1985	Miners' Strike (many confrontations between police and pickets)
6 Oct	1985	Broadwater Farm, North London (riot)
Jan 1986–Feb	1987	Wapping (confrontation between police and pickets)
	Mar 1990	London and many other places (anti-poll tax demonstrations and riots)
	Apr 1990	Strangeways Prison, Manchester (prisoners' riot)

Political Assassinations
(Members of the House of Lords or House of Commons)

22 Jun	1922	Sir H. Wilson. Field Marshal and M.P. (shot in London by Sinn Fein).
5 Apr	1979	A. Neave (IRA bomb in his car at the House of Commons)
27 Aug	1979	Earl Mountbatten (killed by bomb on holiday in the Irish Republic)
14 Nov	1981	R. Bradford (Ulster M.P. shot in Belfast)
10 Oct	1984	Sir A. Berry (IRA bomb at Conservative Conference)
30 Jul	1990	I. Gow (IRA bomb at his Sussex home)

VI

CIVIL SERVICE

Heads of Departments and Public Offices

Except where stated otherwise, all these had the title of Permanent Secretary or Permanent Under-Secretary. The Permanent Secretary is the official head and usually the accounting officer of the Department and is responsible to the Minister for all the Department's activities. In some Departments, e.g. Defence since 1964, there are also Second Permanent Secretaries who are official heads and usually accounting officers for large blocks of work. Except where stated otherwise, all the following had the title of Permanent Secretary or Permanent Under-Secretary. The name is that by which they were known while in office; if a title was acquired while in office it is placed in brackets.

Admiralty

1884	Sir E. MacGregor
1907	Sir I. Thomas
1911	Sir G. Greene
1917	Sir O. Murray
1936	Sir R. Carter
1940	Sir H. Markham
1947	(Sir) J. Lang
1961	Sir C. Jarrett
1964	(see Defence)

Agriculture & Fisheries

1892	(Sir) T. Elliott
1913	Sir S. Olivier
1917	(Sir) D. Hall
1920	Sir F. Floud
1927	Sir C. Thomas
1936	(Sir) D. Fergusson
1945	Sir D. Vandepeer
1952	Sir A. Hitchman

(Agriculture, Fisheries & Food)

1955	Sir A. Hitchman
1959	Sir J. Winnifrith
1968	Sir B. Engholm
1973	Sir A. Neale
1978	(Sir) B. Hayes
1983	(Sir) M. Franklin
1987	(Sir) D. Andrews
1993	R. Packer

Air

1917	Sir A. Robinson
1920	(Sir) W. Nicholson
1931	(Sir) C. Bullock
1936	Sir D. Banks
1939	Sir A. Street
1945	Sir W. Brown
1947	Sir J. Barnes
1955	Sir M. Dean
1963	(Sir) M. Flett
1964	(see Defence)

Aircraft Production

(Director-General)

1940	Sir A. Rowlands
1943	Sir H. Scott
1945–45	Sir F. Tribe

Aviation

(see Transport & Civil Aviation)

1959	Sir W. Strath
1960	(Sir) H. Hardman
1963	Sir R. Way
1966	Sir R. Clarke
1966–67	Sir R. Melville

Burma

(see India & Burma)

Cabinet

(Secretary to the Cabinet)

1916	(Sir) M. Hankey
1938	Sir E. Bridges
1947	Sir N. Brook
1963	Sir B. Trend
1973	Sir J. Hunt
1979	Sir R. Armstrong
1988	Sir R. Butler

(Chief Scientific Adviser)

1964	Sir S. Zuckerman (Ld)
1971	Sir A. Cottrell
1974	(post vacant)

(Head of Government Statistical Service)

1968	(Sir) C. Moser
1978	(Sir) A. Boreham
1986	(Sir) J. Hibbert
1992	W. McLennan

Central Policy Review Staff

(Director-General)

1970	Ld Rothschild
1974	Sir K. Berrill
1980	R. Ibbs
1982	J. Sparrow
1983	(post vacant)

(see pp. 285 for *Economic Advisers*)

Civil Aviation

(Director-General)

1941	Sir W. Hildred
1946	Sir H. Self
1947	Sir A. Overton
1953	(see Transport & Civil Aviation)

Civil Service Commission

(First Commissioner)

1892	W. Courthope
1907	Ld F. Hervey
1910	(Sir) S. Leathers
1928	(Sir) R. Meiklejohn
1939	(Sir) P. Waterfield
1951	P. Sinker
1954	(Sir) L. Helsby
1959	Sir G. Mallaby
1965	Sir G. Abell
1968	J. Hunt
1971	K. Clucas
1974	F. Allen
1981	A. Fraser
1983	D. Trevelyan
1989	J. Holroyd
1994	Anne Bowtell

Head of the Home Civil Service

1919	Sir W. Fisher
1939	Sir H. Wilson
1942	Sir R. Hopkins

Head of the Home Civil Service
(*cont.*)

1945	Sir E. Bridges
1956	Sir N. Brook
1963	Sir L. Helsby
1968	Sir W. Armstrong
1974	Sir D. Allen
1978	Sir I. Bancroft
1981	{ Sir R. Armstrong
1981	{ Sir D. Wass
1983	Sir R. Armstrong
1988	Sir R. Butler

Civil Service Department

1968	Sir W. Armstrong
1974	Sir D. Allen
1978	Sir I. Bancroft
1981	(*post vacant*)

Colonial Office

1897	(Sir) E. Wingfield
1900	(Sir) M. Ommaney
1907	Sir F. Hopwood
1911	Sir J. Anderson
1916	Sir G. Fiddes
1921	Sir J. Masterton-Smith
1925	Sir S. Wilson
1933	Sir J. Maffey
1937	Sir C. Parkinson
1940	Sir G. Gater
1940	Sir C. Parkinson
1942	Sir G. Gater
1947	Sir T. Lloyd
1956	Sir J. Macpherson
1959	Sir H. Poynton
1966	(*see Commonwealth Affairs*)

Commonwealth Relations Office

1947	Sir E. Machtig
1947	Sir A. Carter
1949	Sir P. Liesching
1955	Sir G. Laithwaite
1959	Sir A. Clutterbuck
1962–66	Sir S. Garner

(Commonwealth Affairs)

1966	Sir S. Garner
1968–68	Sir M. James

Customs Establishment
(*Chairman*)

1900	(Sir) G. Ryder
1903	(Sir) T. Pittar

(Board of Customs and Excise)

1909	(Sir) L. Guillemard
1919	Sir H. Hamilton
1927	Sir F. Floud

1930	J. Grigg
1930	(Sir) E. Forber
1934	Sir E. Murray
1941	Sir W. Eady
1942	Sir A. Carter
1947	Sir W. Croft
1955	Sir J. Crombie
1963	Sir J. Anderson
1965	Sir W. Morton
1969	Sir L. Petch
1973	(Sir) R. Radford
1978	(Sir) D. Lovelock
1983	(Sir) A. Fraser
1987	(Sir) B. Unwin
1993	V. Strachan

Defence

1947	Sir H. Wilson Smith
1948	Sir H. Parker
1956	Sir R. Powell
1960	Sir E. Playfair
1961	Sir R. Scott
1964	Sir H. Hardman
1966	Sir J. Dunnett
1974	Sir M. Cary
1976	Sir F. Cooper
1983	(Sir) C. Whitmore
1988	Sir M. Quinlan
1993	Sir C. France

Defence (Procurement)
(*Chief Executive*)

1971	(Sir) D. Rayner
1972	Sir M. Cary
1974	(Sir) G. Leitch
1975	(Sir) C. Cornford
1980	(Sir) D. Cardwell
1983	D. Perry
1985	(Sir) P. Levene
1991	M. McIntosh

Dominions Office

1925	Sir C. Davies
1930	Sir E. Harding
1940	Sir C. Parkinson
1940–47	Sir E. Machtig

Economic Affairs

1964	Sir E. Roll
1966	(Sir) D. Allen
1968–69	Sir W. Nield

Economic Warfare
(*Director-General*)

1939	Sir F. Leith-Ross
1940	{ Sir F. Leith-Ross
	{ E of Drogheda
1942–45	E of Drogheda

Education (and Science)

1900	Sir G. Kekewich
1903	Sir R. Morant
1911	Sir A. Selby-Bigge
1925	Sir A. Symonds
1931	Sir H. Pelham
1937	(Sir) M. Holmes
1945	Sir J. Maud
1952	(Sir) G. Flemming
1959	Dame M. Smieton
1967	Sir H. Andrew
1970	(Sir) W. Pile
1976	(Sir) J. Hamilton
1983	(Sir) D. Hancock
1989	(Sir) J. Caines
1992	Sir D. Holland
1994	Sir T. Lankester

Employment
(*see Labour*)

Energy

1974	Sir J. Rampton
1980	Sir D. Maitland
1983	Sir K. Couzens
1985	(Sir) P. Gregson
1989	G. Chipperfield
1991–92	J. Guinness

Environment

1970	Sir D. Serpell
1972	Sir J. Jones
1975	Sir I. Bancroft
1978	Sir J. Garlick
1981	(Sir) G. Moseley
1985	(Sir) T. Heiser
1992	(Sir) R. Wilson
1994	A. Turnbull

Food (Director-General)

1918	Sir C. Fielding
1919–21	F. Coller
1939	Sir H. French
1945	Sir F. Tribe
1946	Sir P. Liesching
1949	(Sir) F. Lee
1951	Sir H. Hancock
1955	(*see Agriculture, Fisheries & Food*)

Foreign Office

1894	Sir T. Sanderson (Ld)
1906	Sir C. Hardinge (Ld)
1910	Sir A. Nicolson
1916	Ld Hardinge
1920	Sir E. Crowe
1925	Sir W. Tyrrell
1928	Sir R. Lindsay
1930	Sir R. Vansittart
1938	Sir A. Cadogan
1946	Sir O. Sargent

1949	Sir W. Strang
1953	Sir I. Kirkpatrick
1957	Sir F. Hoyer Millar
1962	Sir H. Caccia
1965	Sir P. Gore-Booth

(Foreign and Commonwealth Office)

(Also, from 1968, Head of Diplomatic Service)

1969	Sir D. Greenhill
1973	Sir T. Brimelow
1975	Sir M. Palliser
1982	Sir A. Acland
1986	Sir P. Wright
1991	Sir D. Gillmore

(Foreign Office, German Section)

1947	Sir W. Strang
1949	Sir I. Kirkpatrick
1950–51	Sir D. Gainer

Forestry Commission

(Chairman)

1920	Ld Lovat
1927	Ld Clinton
1929	Sir J. Stirling-Maxwell
1932	Sir R. Robinson (Ld)
1952	E of Radnor
1964	Earl Waldegrave
1966	L. Jenkins
1970	Ld Taylor of Gryfe
1976	J. Mackie
1979	Sir D. Montgomery
1989	(Sir) R. Johnstone

Fuel & Power

1942	Sir F. Tribe
1945	Sir D. Fergusson
1952	Sir J. Maud

(Power)

1957	Sir J. Maud
1958	(Sir) D. Proctor
1965	Sir M. Stevenson
1966	Sir D. Pitblado
1969	*(see Technology)*

Government Accountancy Service

1984	(Sir) A. Wilson
1989	Sir A. Hardcastle

Health

1919	Sir R. Morant
1920	Sir A. Robinson
1935	Sir G. Chrystal
1940	Sir J. Maude
1945	Sir W. Douglas
1951	(Sir) J. Hawton

1960	(Sir) B. Fraser
1964–68	(Sir) A. France

(Health & Social Security)

1968	Sir C. Jarrett
1970	Sir P. Rogers
1975	Sir P. Nairne
1981	Sir K. Stowe
1987	Sir C. France

(Health)

1988	Sir C. France
1992	G. Hart

Home Office

1895	Sir K. Digby
1903	Sir M. Chalmers
1908	Sir E. Troup
1922	Sir J. Anderson
1932	Sir R. Scott
1938	Sir A. Maxwell
1948	Sir F. Newsam
1957	Sir C. Cunningham
1966	Sir P. Allen
1972	Sir A. Peterson
1977	(Sir) R. Armstrong
1979	Sir B. Cubbon
1988	Sir C. Whitmore
1994	Sir R. Wilson

Home Security

1939	{ (Sir) T. Gardiner
	{ (Sir) G. Gater
1940	Sir G. Gater
1942	Sir H. Scott
1943–45	Sir W. Brown

Housing & Local Government

(see Town & Country Planning)

1951	Sir T. Sheepshanks
1955	Dame E. Sharp
1966	Sir M. Stevenson
1970	(see Environment)

India

1883	Sir A. Godley
1909	Sir R. Ritchie
1912	Sir T. Holderness
1920	Sir W. Duke
1924	Sir A. Hirtzel
1930	Sir F. Stewart

(India & Burma)

1937	Sir F. Stewart
1941–47	(Sir) D. Monteath

Industry

1974	Sir A. Part
1976–83	Sir P. Carey

(see Trade and Industry)

Information

(Director of Propaganda)

1918–1919	A. Bennett

(Director-General)

1939	Sir K. Lee
1940	F. Pick
1941	Sir C. Radcliffe
1945–46	E. Bamford

(Central Office of Information)

(Director-General)

1946	Sir E. Bamford
1946	Sir R. Fraser
1954	(Sir) T. Fife Clark
1971	F. Bickerton
1974	H. James
1978	J. Groves
1982	D. Grant
1985	N. Taylor
1989	G. Devereau

Board of Inland Revenue

(Chairman)

1899	Sir H. Primrose
1907	(Sir) R. Chalmers
1911	Sir M. Nathan
1914	Sir E. Nott-Bower
1918	W. Fisher
1919	Sir J. Anderson
1922	Sir R. Hopkins
1927	Sir E. Gowers
1930	(Sir) J. Grigg
1934	Sir E. Forber
1938	Sir G. Canny
1942	Sir C. Gregg
1948	Sir E. Bamford
1955	Sir H. Hancock
1958	Sir A. Johnston
1968	Sir A. France
1973	(Sir) N. Price
1976	Sir W. Pile
1980	Sir L. Airey
1986	Sir A. Battishill

Irish Office

1893	Sir D. Harrel
1902	Sir A. Macdonnell
1908	Sir J. Dougherty
1914	Sir M. Nathan
1916	Sir W. Byrne
1918	(Sir) J. Macmahon
1920–22	Sir J. Anderson

Labour

1916	(Sir) D. Shackleton
1920	Sir J. Masterton-Smith
1921	Sir H. Wilson
1930	Sir F. Moud
1935	Sir T. Phillips

(Labour & National Service)

1939	Sir T. Phillips
1944	(Sir) G. Ince
1956	Sir H. Emmerson

(Labour)

1959	Sir L. Helsby
1962	Sir J. Dunnett
1966	(Sir) D. Barnes

(Employment & Productivity)

1968	Sir D. Barnes

(Employment)

1970	Sir D. Barnes
1974	(Sir) C. Heron
1975	(Sir) K. Barnes
1983	(Sir) M. Quinlan
1988	(Sir) G. Holland
1993	(Sir) N. Monck

Land & Natural Resources

1964	F. Bishop
1965–66	Sir B. Fraser

Local Government Board

1898	(Sir) S. Provis
1910–19	(Sir) H. Monro

Secretary to the Ld Chancellor & Clerk of the Crown in Chancery

1885	(Sir) K. Mackenzie
1915	(Sir) C. Schuster
1944	(Sir) A. Napier
1954	(Sir) G. Coldstream
1968	(Sir) D. Dobson
1977	(Sir) W. Bourne
1982	(Sir) D. Oulton
1989	(Sir) T. Legg

Materials

1951	A. Hitchman
1952	Sir J. Helmore
1953–54	Sir E. Bowyer

Munitions

1915	Sir H. Llewellyn Smith
1916	E. Phipps
1917	Sir G. Greene
1920–21	{ Sir S. Dannreuther
	{ D. Neylan

National Health Service Management Board

(Chairman)

1985	V. Paige

National Heritage

1992	G. Phillips

National Insurance

1944	Sir T. Phillips
1949	Sir H. Hancock
1951	Sir G. King
1953	*(see Pensions & National Insurance)*

National Service

1917	S. Fawcett
1918–19	W. Vaughan

Northern Ireland

1972	Sir W. Nield
1973	(Sir) F. Cooper
1976	(Sir) B. Cubbon
1979	Sir P. Woodfield
1984	(Sir) R. Andrew
1988	Sir J. Blelloch
1990	J. Chilcot

Overseas Development

1964	Sir A. Cohen
1968	Sir G. Wilson
1970	*(see Foreign & Commonwealth Office)*
1974	(Sir) R. King
1976	(Sir) P. Preston
1982	Sir W. Ryrie
1984	Sir C. Tickell
1987	J. Caines
1989	(Sir) T. Lankester
1994	J. Vereker

Pensions

1916	Sir M. Nathan
1919	Sir G. Chrystal
1935	Sir A. Hore
1941	(Sir) A. Cunnison
1946	Sir H. Parker
1948	Sir A. Wilson

(Pensions & National Insurance)

1953	Sir G. King
1955	Sir E. Bowyer
1965–66	Sir C. Jarrett

(see Social Security)

Post Office

1899	Sir G. Murray
1903	Sir H. Babington-Smith
1909	Sir M. Nathan
1911	Sir A. King
1914	(Sir) E. Murray

(Director-General)

1934	(Sir) D. Banks
1936	Sir T. Gardiner
1946	Sir R. Birchall
1949	(Sir) A. Little
1955	(Sir) G. Radley
1960	Sir R. German
1966–68	(Sir) J. Wall
	(Deputy Chairman of Post Office Board)

Power

(see Fuel & Power)

Prices and Consumer Protection

1974–79	(Sir) K. Clucas

Privy Council

(Clerk of the Council)

1899	(Sir) A. FitzRoy
1923	Sir M. Hankey
1938	Sir R. Howorth
1942	(Sir) E. Leadbitter
1951	F. Fernau
1953	(Sir) W. Agnew
1974	(Sir) N. Leigh
1984	(Sir) G. de Deney
1992	N. Nicholls

Production

1942	Sir H. Self
1943	J. Woods

Property Services

1979	Sir R. Cox
1981	A. Montague
1984	Sir G. Manzie
1990	P. Brown
1991	(Sir) G. Chipperfield

Office of Public Service and Science

1992	R. Mottram

Reconstruction

1943–45	N. Brook

General Register Office

(Registrar-General for England and Wales)

1880	Sir B. Henniker
1900	R. MacLeod
1902	(Sir) W. Dunbar
1909	(Sir) B. Mallet
1921	(Sir) S. Vivian
1945	(Sir) G. North
1959	E. Firth
1964	M. Reed
1972	G. Paine
1978	A. Thatcher
1986	Mrs C. Banks
1990	P. Wormald

Department of Scientific and Industrial Research

(Secretary)

1916	(Sir) F. Heath
1927	H. Tizard
1929	(Sir) F. Smith
1939	(Sir) E. Appleton
1949	Sir B. Lockspeiser
1956	(Sir) H. Melville

(merged with Science Research Council 1965)

Office of the Minister for Science

1962–94	F. Turnbull

Scottish Office

1892	Sir C. Scott-Moncrieff
1902	Sir R. Macleod
1909	Sir J. Dodds
1921	Sir J. Lamb
1933	Sir J. Jeffrey
1937	J. Highton
1937	Sir H. Hamilton
1946	(Sir) D. Milne
1959	Sir W. Murie
1965	(Sir) D. Haddow
1973	(Sir) N. Morrison
1978	(Sir) W. Fraser
1988	(Sir) R. Hillmore

Shipping

1917	(Sir) J. Anderson
1919–20	T. Lodge
1939–41	Sir C. Hurcomb

Social Security

1966	Sir C. Jarrett
1968–88	*(see Health & Social Security)*
1988	(Sir) M. Partridge

Supply

1939	Sir A. Robinson
1940	Sir G. Gater
1940	Sir W. Brown
1942	Sir W. Douglas
1945	O. Franks
1946	Sir A. Rowlands
1953	Sir J. Helmore
1956	Sir C. Musgrave
1959–59	Sir W. Strath

Technology

1964	Sir M. Dean
1966	Sir R. Clarke
1970	*(see Trade & Industry*

Town & Country Planning

1943	Sir G. Whiskard
1946	Sir T. Sheepshanks

(Local Government & Planning)

1951	Sir T. Sheepshanks
1951	*(see Housing & Local Government)*

Board of Trade

1893	Sir C. Boyle
1901	Sir F. Hopwood
1907	(Sir) H. Llewellyn Smith
1913	{ Sir G. Barnes { Sir H. Llewellyn Smith
1916	{ Sir H. Llewellyn Smith { (Sir) W. Marwood
1919	{ Sir S. Chapman { Sir W. Marwood
1919	{ Sir S. Chapman { Sir H. Payne
1920	Sir S. Chapman
1927	Sir H. Hamilton
1937	Sir W. Brown
1941	Sir A. Overton
1945	Sir J. Woods
1951	Sir F. Lee
1960	Sir R. Powell
1968	Sir A. Part

(Trade & Industry)

1970	Sir A. Part

(Trade)

1974	Sir P. Thornton
1977	(Sir) L. Pliatzky
1979	Sir K. Clucas

(Trade and Industry)

1979	Sir P. Carey
1983	{ Sir B. Hayes { Sir A. Rawlinson
1985	Sir B. Hayes
1989	Sir P. Gregson

Transport

1919	Sir F. Dunnell
1921	Sir W. Marwood
1923	Sir J. Brooke
1927	C. Hurcomb
1937	Sir L. Browett

(Director-General of War Transport)

1941	Sir C. Hurcomb

(Transport)

1946	Sir C. Hurcomb
1947	Sir G. Jenkins

(Transport & Civil Aviation)

1953	Sir G. Jenkins

(Transport)

(and see Aviation)

1959	Sir J. Dunnett
1962	Sir T. Padmore
1968	Sir D. Serpell
1970–76	*(see Environment)*
1976	(Sir) P. Baldwin
1982	(Sir) P. Lazarus
1986	(Sir) A. Bailey
1991	A. Brown

Treasury

1894	Sir F. Mowatt
1902	{ Sir F. Mowatt { Sir E. Hamilton
1903	{ Sir E. Hamilton { Sir G. Murray
1908	Sir G. Murray
1911	{ Sir R. Chalmers { Sir T. Heath
1913	{ Sir J. Bradbury { Sir T. Heath
1916	{ Sir J. Bradbury { Sir R. Chalmers
1919	Sir W. Fisher
1939	Sir H. Wilson
1942	Sir R. Hopkins
1945	Sir E. Bridges
1956	{ Sir N. Brook { Sir R. Makins
1959	Sir N. Brook
1960	{ Sir F. Lee { Sir N. Brook
1962	{ W. Armstrong { Sir L. Helsby
1963	(Sir) W. Armstrong
1968	{ Sir W. Armstrong { Sir D. Allen
1968	Sir D. Allen
1974	(Sir) D. Wass
1983	(Sir) P. Middleton
1991	Sir T. Burns

Unemployment Assistance Board

(Chairman)

1934	Sir H. Betterton (Ld Rushcliffe)

(Assistance Board)

1940	Ld Rushcliffe
1941	Ld Soulbury

(National Assistance Board)

1948	G. Buchanan
1954	Sir G. Hutchinson (Ld Ilford)
1964–66	Ld Runcorn

University Grants Committee

(Chairman)

1919	Sir W. McCormick
1930	Sir W. Buchanan-Riddell
1935	Sir W. Moberly
1949	(Sir) A. Trueman
1953	(Sir) K. Murray
1968	(Sir) K. Berrill
1973	Sir F. Dainton
1978	(Sir) E. Parks
1983	Sir P. Swinnerton-Dyer

(Higher Education Funding Council)

1992	Sir R. Dearing

War Office

1897	Sir R. Knox
1901	Sir E. Ward

1914	Sir R. Brade
1920	Sir H. Creedy
1939	Sir J. Grigg
1942	{ Sir F. Bovenschen / Sir E. Speed
1945	Sir E. Speed
1949	Sir G. Turner
1956	Sir E. Playfair
1960	(Sir) R. Way
1963	(Sir) A. Drew
1964	*(see Defence)*

Welsh Office

1964	(Sir) G. Daniel
1969	(Sir) I. Pugh
1971	(Sir) H. Evans
1980	(Sir) T. Hughes
1985	(Sir) R. Lloyd-Jones
1993	M. Scholar

Works

1895	Sir R. Brett (Vt Esher)
1901	Sir S. McDonnell
1912	Sir L. Earle
1933	Sir P. Duff
1941	Sir G. Whiskard
1943	Sir P. Robinson
1946	Sir H. Emmerson
1956	Sir E. Muir

(Public Building & Works)

1962	Sir E. Muir
1965	(Sir) A. Part
1968	Sir M. Cary
1970	*(see Environment)*

Salary of Permanent Secretary to the Treasury

1900	£2,500
1910	£2,500
1920	£3,500
1930	£3,500
1940	£3,500
1950	£3,750
1960	£7,450
1970	£12,700
1980	£33,500
1990	£89,500

Prime Minister's Principal Private Secretary

1900	S. McDonnell	1939	A. Rucker	1964	D. Mitchell
1902	J. Sandars	1940	E. Seal	1966	A. Halls
1905	A. Ponsonby	1941	J. Martin	1970	A. Isserlis
1908	V. Nash	1945	L. Rowan	1970	R. Armstrong
1912	M. Bonham-Carter	1947	L. Helsby	1975	K. Stowe
1916	J. Davies	1950	D. Rickett	1979	C. Whitmore
1922	(Sir) R. Waterhouse	1951	D. Pitblado	1982	R. Butler
1928	R. Vansittart	1952	{ D. Pitblado / J. Colville	1985	N. Wicks
1930	P. Duff			1988	A. Turnbull
1933	J. Barlow	1955	D. Pitblado	1992	A. Allan
1934	H. Vincent	1956	F. Bishop		
1937	O. Cleverly	1959	T. Bligh		

Appointments Secretary

1947	(Sir) A. Bevir	1961	J. Hewitt	1984	(Sir) J. Catford
1956	D. Stephens	1972	C. Peterson	1993	J. Holroyd

Prime Minister's Staff

In addition to an official Civil Service Principal Private Secretary, all Prime Ministers have made their own arrangements for advice and help. These cannot be consistently categorised. The following have played significant roles.

Policy advisers

General advisers

1917–18	W. Adams
1918–21	P. Kerr
1921–22	E. Grigg
1940	F. Lindemann (Ld Cherwell)
1945–46	D. Jay
1946–48	W. Gorell Barnes

Head of Policy Unit

1974	B. Donoughue
1979	J. Hoskins
1982	F. Mount
1984	J. Redwood
1985	B. Griffiths
1990	Mrs S. Hogg

(See also Heads of Central Policy Review Staff p. 279)

Specialist Advisers

1935–39	Sir H. Wilson (Industrial Relations)
1982–83	Sir A. Parsons (Foreign Policy)
1984–90	Sir P. Cradock (Foreign Policy)
1982	Sir R. Jackling (Defence)
1983–89	Sir A. Walters (Economics)
1983–89	Sir D. (Ld) Rayner (Efficiency)
1983–88	Sir R. Ibbs (Efficiency)
1988–92	Sir A. Fraser (Efficiency)
1992	Sir P. Levene (Efficiency and Competition)
1992	Sir R. Braithwaite (Foreign Policy)

Political Secretary/Adviser

1929–35	H. D. Usher
1929–35	Miss R. Rosenberg
1957–63	J. Wyndham
1964–70	Mrs M. Williams
1964–68	T. Balogh
1970–74	D. Hurd
1974–74	W. Waldegrave
1974–76	Mrs M. Williams (Lady Falkender)
1976–79	T. McNally
1979–82	R. Ryder
1982–83	D. Howe
1983–88	S. Sherbourne
1988–90	J. Whittingdale
1990–92	Mrs J. Chaplin
1992–	J. Hill

Press Officers

Chief Press Liaison Officer

1931–44	G. Steward

Adviser on Public Relations

1945–47	F. Williams
1947–51	P. Jordan
1951–52	R. Bacon
1955–56	W. Clark
1957–64	S. Evans

Press Secretary

1964–69	T. Lloyd-Hughes
1969–70	J. Haines

Chief Press Secretary

1970–73	D. Maitland
1973–74	W. Haydon

Press Secretary

1974–76	J. Haines
1976–79	T. McCaffrey

Chief Press Secretary

1979–90	B. Ingham
1990–94	G. O'Donnell
1994–	C. Meyer

Special or Political Advisers to Ministers

Many Ministers have brought in unofficial advisers and secretaries but political advisers only became established in an official way after 1974 (although in 1970–74 six or seven Conservative ministers had full-time assistants paid from party funds). During Mr Wilson's 1974 ministry it was agreed that any Cabinet minister could appoint two political advisers with a tenure that lasted only as long as he or she continued in office.

In 1979 Mrs Thatcher limited Cabinet ministers to one political adviser – except for the Treasury and the Foreign Office.

Size of Civil Service

Adequate statistics of the number of civil servants engaged in each branch of government activity since 1900 are not readily available. Moreover, the transfer of functions between departments makes comparisons of one year with another potentially misleading. An analysis of civil service strength for certain years is to be found in *The Organisation of British Central Government, 1914–1956,* by D. N. Chester and F. M. G. Wilson. The figures in heavy type in the following table are taken from the statement *Staffs Employed in Government Departments* which has been published annually, or more frequently, by the Treasury as a Command Paper since 1919 (with retrospective figures for 1914 included in the first issue). The figures in light type in the table are taken from the Annual Estimates presented to Parliament by the Civil Service and Revenue Departments, and the East India House Accounts. These figures are liable to slight error as they are estimates and not reports of the actual staff employed. In each case they are estimates for the year ending March 31 of the following year (e.g. under the third column headed '1 Apr 1920' the estimates are for 1920–21). The source for the 1971 figures is the departmental returns made to the Civil Service Department. The figures in this table should be used with great caution because of the considerable differences in the sources.

Number of Civil Servants

	1901	1 Aug 1914	1 Apr 1920	1 Apr 1930	1 Apr 1938	1 Apr 1950	1 Apr 1960	1 Apr 1970	1 Apr 1980	1 Apr 1990	1 Apr 1993
Total Non-industrial Staff	n.a.	282,420	380,963	306,154	376,491	575,274	637,374	498,425	547,486	495,000	502,798
Total Industrial Staff	n.a.	497,100	n.a.	483,100	204,400	396,900	358,900	201,660	157,417	67,000	51,414
Total Civil Service Staff	n.a.	779,520	n.a.	789,254	580,891	972,174	996,274	700,085	704,903	562,388	554,212*
Admiralty[an]	n.a.	4,366	13,432	7,433	10,609	30,801	30,731	f	n	n	n
War Office	n.a.	1,636	7,434	3,872	7,323	33,493	47,244	f	n	n	n
Air	..	..	2,839	1,704	4,317	24,407	27,563	f	n	n	n
Aviation Supply	..	..	..	..	..	5,271	24,756	f	n	n	n
Defence (incl. Royal Ordnance Factories)	..	..	..	..	..	..	..	128,803	118,450	141,373	129,225
Foreign Office[an]	142	187	885	730	902	6,195	5,992	12,802	11,291	9,491	9,745
Colonial Off.	109	214	256	365	438	1,286	1,211	g	..	..	..
Dominions, CRO	..	..	..	52	91	904	847	g	..	..	..
India Office	589	554	342	n.a.	539	..	..	i	..	..	..
Irish Office	559	1,007	829	..	n.a.	749	887	..	208	194	219
Scottish Off.	159	401	517	68	..	..	..	5,651	9,990	10,274	10,906
Welsh Office[h]	..	..	..	..	..	..	..	903	2,324	2,284	2,426
Treasury[bq]	120	140	291	299	344	1,396	1,322	1,012	1,044	3,135	1,946
Home Office	297	773	926	1,024	1,688	3,953	3,534	21,743	30,289	42,721	51,370
Agriculture	182	2,976	3,446	2,463	4,388	16,842	14,938	14,874	13,273	9,881	10,038
Education	864	2,187	1,522	1,041	1,435	3,280	2,738	4,127	2,594	2,560	2,493
Energy	..	..	..	..	..	..	..	..	1,252	1,024	..
Environment	..	..	4,142	..	..	30,785	c	38,806	28,177	6,074[p]	7,537
Food	..	..	..	..	..	6,358	..	k	..	..	..
(Fuel &) Power	..	a	..	..	..	..	1,768	..	..	..	..
Health (& S.Sec)	..	..	5,820	6,711	6,771	5,893	4,993	71,811	95,923	5,422	4,845
Social Security	..	..	..	..	..	..	..	..	..	80,890	84,824
Labour (Employmt[m])	425	4,428	17,835[d]	18,076[d]	26,934[d]	29,902	21,394	31,099[j]	48,718	48,138	52,408
Housing and Local Govt	..	963	11,440	..	..	1,312	2,802	j	..	..	..
Munitions	..	..	2,263	..	..	..	..	..	..	..	..
Nat Insurance	..	1,250	24,169	6,175	3,147	10,954	36,323	n.a.	35,539[e]	i	..
Pensions	..	1,957	..	..	..	..	..	e	..	..	..
Post Office	79,482	88,890	209,269	194,933	224,374	249,869	254,919	..	..	..	..
Supply	..	..	..	..	..	13,312	..	k	..	..	..
Bd of Trade	1,359	2,535	5,410	4,398	4,611	10,136	6,735	..	..	..	..

	1901	1 Aug 1914	1 Apr 1920	1 Apr 1930	1 Apr 1938	1 Apr 1950	1 Apr 1960	1 Apr 1970	1 Apr 1980	1 Apr 1990	1 Apr 1993
Trade & Industry	..	..	..	..	..	..	..	24,549[k]	..	11,793	11,763
Trade	..	..	..	..	..	..	..	..	7,163	..	..
Industry	140	**679**	..	..	..	..	..	..	8,499	..	..
Transport	..	..	876	759	2,820	**6,906**	**6,909**	[p]	12,792	15,513	14,385
Works	..	..	580	2,054	3,584	**17,573**	**10,693**	..	..	..	..
Customs & Ex.	3,792	10,256	12,602	11,659	14,669	14,236	15,338	*17,949*	27,232	26,864	25,137
Exchequer	230	269	269	331	369	501	532	577	..	..	..
Inland Revenue	**5,345**	**9,753**	**19,446**	**21,059**	**24,342**	**49,740**	**56,026**	*69,765*	78,282	66,063	66,521
Nat. Assistance	..	..	..	..	8,105	8,516	10,509[e]	..	..	..	..
H.M.S.O.	100	517	728	1,660	1,947	3,241	2,903	3,480	3,070	3,201	3,080
Civil Serv. Dpt[q]	..	..	..	..	..	..		2,070	3,210	..	..
Cabinet Office	n.a.	n.a.	n.a.	n.a.	186	393	319	565	580	1,484	2,324
C.S.O.[r]	..	..	..	..	..	..	..	..	..	999	1,267
C.P.S.[s]	..	..	..	..	..	..	..	..	..	4,710	6,307
Ld Chancellor	..	..	..	..	..	..	..	..	..	10,454	11,924
Nat. Heritage[t]	..	..	..	..	..	..	..	..	..	[t]	965

[a] Home civil servants only.

[b] Not including subordinate departments (e.g. Committee of Imperial Defence, University Grants Commission).

[c] Combined with Ministry of Agriculture and Fisheries.

[d] The functions of the Local Government Board passed to the Ministry of Health in 1919. In 1943 the Ministry of Town and Country Planning (later becoming the Ministry of Housing and Local Government) took back many of these functions from the Ministry of Health.

[e] National Insurance merged with the Ministry of Pensions, and in 1966 together with the N.A.B. became the Ministry of Social Security.

[f] In 1964 the Admiralty, War Office and Air Office were combined into the Ministry of Defence.

[g] In 1965 the Foreign Office, Commonwealth Relations Office, and attaches abroad were combined into the Diplomatic Service, whose personnel appear under Foreign Office.

[h] The Welsh Office was set up in 1964.

[i] The Northern Ireland Office was set up in 1972.

[j] In 1970 the Ministry of Housing and Local Government, Ministry of Public Building and Works and the Ministry of Transport were combined into the Department of the Environment.

[k] In 1970 the Board of Trade and the the Ministry of Technology combined into the Department of Trade and Industry. In 1974 the DTI was broken up into four Departments (Trade, Industry, Energy and Prices & Consumer Protection). Prices was absorbed back into Trade in 1979. Trade and Industry merged in 1983. Energy was re-absorbed into the DTI in 1992.

[l] In 1968 the Ministry of Social Security and the Ministry of Health combined into the Department of Health and Social Security. They were split again in 1988.

[m] The Ministry of Labour became the Department of Employment in 1968.

[n] Staff of the Overseas Development Administration are included in the Foreign Office total throughout, although for a period after 1974 the Ministry of Overseas Development was technically a separate department.

[o] The Ministry of Transport became a separate department in 1976.

[p] The Civil Service Department was formed in 1968 by the merger of the Civil Service Commission, and the pay and management side of the Treasury. It was abolished in 1981 and its functions divided between the Cabinet Office and the Treasury.

[q] The Ministry of Transport became a separate department in 1976.

[r] The Central Statistical Office was established on 31 Jul 89.

[s] The Crown Prosecution Service was established on 20 Jul 87.

[t] The Department of National Heritage was established on 3 Jul 92.

Next Steps

In 1987 the Prime Minister commissioned a report into Civil Service reform, published in 1988 under the title '*Improving Management in Government: The Next Steps*' (the Ibbs Report). It proposed that many of the functions currently performed by the Civil Service could be performed more efficiently by semi-autonomous agencies managing themselves outside the main Civil Service structure. The programme began the same year, and was given legislative effect by the *Government Trading Act, 1990*. By 1 Apr 93 248,674 of the total of 554,212 Civil Service staff worked for agencies established under the Next Steps Initiative. The following such agencies have been created:

Responsible Department	Agency	Launch date
Lord Chancellor's	HM Land Registry	2 Jul 90
Lord Chancellor's	Public Record Office	1 Apr 92
Foreign Office	Wilton Park	1 Sep 91
Treasury	Central Statistical Office	19 Nov 91
Treasury	HM Customs & Excise	1 Apr 91
Treasury	Inland Revenue	1 Apr 92
Treasury	Paymaster	1 Apr 93
Treasury	Royal Mint	2 Apr 90
Treasury	Valuation Office	30 Sep 91
Home Office	Fire Service College	1 Apr 92
Home Office	Forensic Science Service	1 Apr 91
Home Office	HM Prison Service	1 Apr 93
Home Office	U.K. Passport Agency	2 Apr 91
Trade and Industry	Accounts Services Agency	1 Oct 91
Trade and Industry	Companies House	3 Oct 88
Trade and Industry	Insolvency Service	21 Mar 90
Trade and Industry	Government Chemist Lab.	30 Oct 89
Trade and Industry	National Physical Lab.	3 Jul 90
Trade and Industry	Nat. Weights & Measures Lab.	18 Apr 89
Trade and Industry	NEL	5 Oct 90
Trade and Industry	Patent Office	1 Mar 90
Trade and Industry	Radiocommunications Agency	2 Apr 90
Trade and Industry	Warren Spring Laboratory	20 Apr 89
Transport	Driver & Vehicle Licencing Ag.	2 Apr 90
Transport	Driving Standards Agency	2 Apr 90
Transport	DVOIT	1 Apr 90
Transport	Transport Research Laboratory	2 Apr 92
Transport	Vehicle Certification Agency	2 Apr 90
Transport	Vehicle Inspectorate	1 Aug 88
Defence	Army Base Repair Organisation	1 Apr 93
Defence	Chemical & Biological Def.ESt	1 Apr 91
Defence	Defence Accounts Agency	1 Apr 91
Defence	Defence Analytical Services	1 Jul 92
Defence	Defence Animal Centre	1 Jun 93
Defence	Defence Operational Analysis	1 Jul 92
Defence	Defence Postal & Courier Serv.	1 Jul 92
Defence	Defence Research Agency	2 Apr 91
Defence	D of York's Royal Military Sch.	1 Apr 92
Defence	Hydrographic Office	6 Apr 90
Defence	Meteorological Office	2 Apr 90
Defence	Military Survey	2 Apr 91
Defence	Naval Aircraft Repair Org.	1 Apr 92
Defence	Queen Victoria School	1 Apr 92
Defence	RAF Support Command's Maintenance Group Defence Agency	2 Apr 91
Defence	Service Children's Schools	24 Apr 91

Responsible Department	Agency	Launch date
Ag., Fish, & Food	ADAS	1 Apr 92
Ag., Fish, & Food	Central Science Laboratory	1 Apr 92
Ag., Fish, & Food	Central Veterinary Laboratory	2 Apr 90
Ag., Fish, & Food	Intervention Board	2 Apr 90
Ag., Fish, & Food	Pesticides Safety Directorate	1 Apr 93
Ag., Fish, & Food	Veterinary Medicines Directorate	2 Apr 90
National Heritage	Historic Royal Palaces Agency	1 Oct 89
National Heritage	Royal Parks Agency	1 Apr 93
Environment	Building Research Establishment	2 Apr 90
Environment	Ordnance Survey	1 May 90
Environment	Planning Inspectorate	1 Apr 92
Environment	QE II Conference Centre	6 Jul 89
Environment	Security Facilities Executive	15 Oct 91
Environment	Buying Agency	31 Oct 91
Wales	Cadw: Welsh Historic Monuments	2 Apr 91
Social Security	Benefits Agency	2 Apr 91
Social Security	Child Support Agency	5 Apr 93
Social Security	Contributions Agency	2 Apr 91
Social Security	Information Tech. Services Agency	2 Apr 90
Social Security	Resettlement Agency	24 May 89
Public Service	Central Office of Information	5 Apr 90
Public Service	Chessington Computer Centre	1 Apr 93
Public Service	Civil Service College	6 Jun 89
Public Service	HMSO	14 Dec 88
Public Service	Occupational Health Service	2 Apr 90
Public Service	Recruitment & Assessment Services Agency	2 Apr 91
Scotland	Historic Scotland	2 Apr 91
Scotland	Registers of Scotland	6 Apr 90
Scotland	Sc.Agricultural Science Agency	1 Apr 92
Scotland	Sc.Fisheries Protection Agency	12 Apr 91
Scotland	Sc. Office Pensions Agency	1 Apr 93
Scotland	Sc. Prison Service	1 Apr 93
Scotland	Scottish Record Office	1 Apr 93
Northern Ireland	Compensation Agency	1 Apr 92
Northern Ireland	Driver & Vehicle Licensing N.I.	2 Aug 93
Northern Ireland	Driver & Vehicle Testing Agency	1 Apr 92
Northern Ireland	N.I. Child Support Agency	5 Apr 93
Northern Ireland	Ordnance Survey of N.I.	1 Apr 92
Northern Ireland	Rate Collection Agency	1 Apr 91
Northern Ireland	Social Security Agency (N.I.)	1 Jul 91
Northern Ireland	Training & Employment Agency	2 Apr 90
Northern Ireland	Valuation and Lands Agency	1 Apr 93
Education	Teachers' Pensions Agency	1 Apr 92
Health	Medicines Control Agency	11 Jul 91
Health	NHS Estates	1 Apr 91
Health	NHS Pensions	20 Nov 92
Employment	Employment Service	2 Apr 90
Attorney General	Government Property Lawyers	1 Apr 93
Overseas Development	Natural Resources Institute	2 Apr 90

SOURCES – *Improving Management in Government: The Next Steps. A Report to the Prime Minister* (Ibbs Report), HMSO 1988. *National Audit Office: Report by the Comptroller and Auditor General – The Next Steps Initiative*, HMSO 1989. Public Accounts Committee. 38th Report. *The Next Steps Initiative*, HMSO 1989. *The Financing and Accountability of Next Steps Agencies* (Cm 914) 1989. *Making the most of Next Steps. A Report to the Prime Minister* (the Fraser Report), HMSO 1991. *Setting Up Next Steps – a short account of the origins, launch and implementation of the Next Steps Project in the British Civil Service*, HMSO 1991. *The Next Steps: review 1993*, HMSO 1993.

VII

ROYAL COMMISSIONS, COMMITTEES OF INQUIRY AND TRIBUNALS

Investigatory Process

The public investigation of problems can take a number of forms – Royal Commissions, Tribunals, *ad hoc* departmental Committees and special parliamentary conferences or committees. We do not deal here with purely parliamentary bodies like the Speaker's Conferences (on Electoral Reform – see p. 238 – and on Devolution – see p. 239) or like the Select Committees set up from time to time by the House of Commons and/or the House of Lords. But we attempt an exhaustive listing of all domestic Royal Commissions and of all Tribunals of Inquiry appointed under the *Tribunals of Inquiry Act*, 1921, as well as an arbitrary selection from the 1,000 or so *ad hoc* and statutory Committees of Inquiry appointed since 1900. It is, however, important to remember that the decision whether to refer a problem to a Royal Commission or a Committee is not necessarily determined by the importance of the subject. Royal Commissions are listed fully here because the number is not excessive. Departmental Committees, which have been much more numerous, often deal with relatively narrow and limited matters; we have selected only a few which seem plainly to be as important as the average Royal Commission. We have also omitted any reference to committees and sub-committees appointed by Royal Commissions and by standing governmental advisory bodies, though these include some reports of importance, such as the Report to the Central Advisory Council on Education by Lady Plowden's Committee on Primary Education (1967).

Advisory Committees appointed by the Government are of two basic types (apart from those which are just internal committees of Civil Servants): (a) standing committees, set up to give advice on such matters, usually within some general class of subjects, as may from time to time be referred to them or otherwise come to their attention; and (b) *ad hoc* committees, which are appointed to carry out some specific mandate and which come to an end when that mandate is discharged. These committees may be appointed directly by the Minister in his own name or indirectly in the name of the Crown. Finally, standing and *ad hoc* committees may both be appointed in two different ways: namely, by virtue of conventional or (in the case of the Crown) prerogative powers, or by virtue of authority conferred by Parliament by means of a statute.

Royal Commissions

Royal Commissions are *ad hoc* advisory committees formally appointed by the Crown by virtue of its prerogative powers. All such committees appointed since the turn of the century are listed in the table below, along with the name of their chairman, their size, the dates of their appointment and adjournment, and the Command number of their final report. There is no 'official' title for a Royal Commission, so that usage may vary slightly from that given below. Where there were two successive chairmen for a single committee, both are listed. The size of a Royal Commission is given as of the date of its appointment; subsequent changes in membership are not shown. The date of appointment is the date on which the Royal Warrant appointing the committee was signed, and the date of adjournment is the date of signature of the last report issued (or, failing that, the date of its presentation to the House of Commons). Command numbers in the twentieth century form part of four successive series, each of which is marked by a different abbreviation of the word 'Command' as follows:

1900–18:   Cd. 1 to Cd.9239
1919–56:   Cmd. 1 to Cmd. 9889
1956–86:   Cmnd. 1 to Cmnd.9927
1986–   :   Cm.1–

Title	Chairman	Size	Date appointed	Date of Report	Command number
Military and Civil Expenditure of India	Ld Welby	14	Apr 96	Aug 00	131
Local Taxation	Ld Balfour	14	Aug 96	May 01	638
University of London Act	Ld Davy	8	Aug 98	Feb 00	83
Newfoundland. Operation of Certain Treaties	Sir J. Bramston	2	Aug 98	Report not published	
Accidents to Railway Servants	Ld Hereford	14	May 99	Jan 00	41
Salmon Fisheries	E of Elgin	9	Mar 00	Jul 02	1188
Administration of the Port of London	Earl Egerton Ld Revelstoke	7	Jun 00	Jun 02	1151
South African Hospitals	Sir R. Romer	5	Jul 00	Jan 01	453
Poisoning by Arsenic (Arsenic in Beer and Other Articles of Diet)	Ld Kelvin	6	Feb 01	Nov 03	1848
University Education (Ireland)	Ld Robertson	11	Jul 01	Feb 03	1483
Tuberculosis	Sir M. Foster W. H. Power	5	Aug 01	Jun 11	5761
Coal Supplies	Ld Ailerton	15	Dec 01	Jan 05	2353
Alien Immigration	Ld James	7	Mar 02	Aug 03	1741
Physical Training (Scotland)	Ld Mansfield	9	Mar 02	Mar 03	1507
Martial Law Sentences in S. Africa	Ld Alverstone	3	Aug 02	Oct 02	136
South African War	E of Elgin	7	Sep 02	Jul 03	1789
Superannuation in the Civil Service	L. Courtney	9	Nov 02	Aug 03	1744
Locomotion and Transport in London	Sir D. Barbour	12	Feb 03	Jun 05	2597
Militia and Volunteer Forces	D of Norfolk	10	Apr 03	May 04	2061
Food Supply in Time of War	Ld Balfour of Burleigh	17	Apr 03	Aug 05	2643
Trade Disputes and Trade Combinations	A Murray (Ld Dunedin)	5	Jun 03	Jan 06	2825
Ecclesiastical Discipline	Sir M. Hicks Beach	14	Apr 04	Jun 06	3040
The Feeble-Minded	M of Bath	10	Sep 04	.. ..	
Churches (Scotland)	E of Elgin	3	Dec 04	Apr 05	2494
War Stores in South Africa	Sir G. Farwell	5	Jun 05	Jul 06	3127
Motor-car	Ld Selby	7	Sep 05	Jul 06	3080
Poor Laws	Ld Hamilton	18	Dec 05	Feb 09	4498
Canals and Inland Navigation of the United Kingdom	Ld Shuttleworth	15	Mar 06	Dec 09	4979
Duties of the Metropolitan Police	D. B. Jones A. Lyttelton	5	May 06	Jun 08	4156
Registration of Title	Ld Dunedin	8	May 06	Jul 10	5316
Safety in Mines	Ld Monkswell H. Cunynghame	9	Jun 06	.. ..	..
Trinity College Dublin	Sir E. Fry	9	Jun 06	Jan 07	311
Coast Erosion	I. Guest	13	Jul 06	reconstituted	
Congested Districts in Ireland	E of Dudley	9	Jul 06	May 08	4097
Lighthouse Administration	G. Balfour	5	Aug 06	Jan 08	3923
Vivisection	Ld Selby A. Ram	10	Sep 06	Mar 12	6114
Care and Control of the Feeble-Minded	E of Radnor	12	Nov 06	Jul 08	4202
Shipping 'Rings' or Conferences generally	A. Cohen	21	Nov 06	reconstituted	
Mines and Quarries	Ld Monkswell	9	May 07	Feb 11	5561

Title	Chairman	Size	Date appointed	Date of Report	Command number
Church of England in Wales and Monmouthshire	Sir R. Vaughan-Williams	9	Jun 07	Nov 10	5432
Indian Decentralisation	Sir H. Primrose C. Hobhouse	6	Sep 07	Feb 09	4360
Whisky and other Potable Spirits	Ld Hereford	8	Feb 08	Jul 09	4796
Coast Erosion and Afforestation	I. Guest	19	Mar 08	May 11	5708
Land Transfer Acts	Ld St Aldwyn	12	Jul 08	Jan 11	5483
Systems of Election	Ld R. Cavendish	8	Dec 08	May 10	5163
University Education in London	Ld Haldane	8	Feb 09	Mar 13	6717
Mauritius	Sir F. Swettenham	3	May 09	Apr 10	5185
Trade Relations between Canada and the West Indies	Ld Balfour	5	Aug 09	Aug 10	5369
Selection of Justices of the Peace	Ld James	16	Nov 09	Jul 10	5250
Divorce and Matrimonial Causes	Ld Gorell	14	Nov 09	Nov 12	6478
Metalliferous Mines and Quarries	Sir H. Cunynghame	9	May 10	Jun 14	7476
Public Records	Sir F. Pollock	9	Oct 10	Apr 18	367
Railways Conciliation and Arbitration Scheme of 1907	Sir D. Hamel	5	Aug 11	Oct 11	5922
Malta	Sir F. Mowatt	3	Aug 11	May 12	6090
Civil Service	Ld MacDonnell H. Smith	19	Mar 12	Nov 15	7832
The Natural Resources, Trade and Legislation of the Dominions	E. Vincent	10	Apr 12	Feb 17	8462
Public Services (India)	Ld Islington	12	Sep 12	Aug 15	8282
Housing of the Industrial Population of Scotland, rural and urban	G. Ballantyne	12	Oct 12	Sep 17	8731
Delay in the King's Bench Division	Ld St Aldwyn	11	Dec 12	Nov 13	7177
Finance and Currency (East A. Indies)	Chamberlain	10	Apr 13	Feb 14	7236
Venereal Diseases	Ld Sydenham	15	Nov 13	Feb 16	8189
Meat Export Trade of Australia	P. Street	1	Jun 14	Apr 15	7896
The circumstances connected with the Landing of Arms at Howth, 26 Jul 1914	Ld Shaw	3	Aug 14	Sep 14	7631
University Education in Wales	Ld Haldane	9	Apr 16	Feb 18	8991
The Rebellion in Ireland	Ld Hardinge	3	May 16	Jun 16	8729
The Arrest and subsequent treatment of Mr Francis Sheehy Skeffington, Mr Thomas Dickson, and Mr Patrick James McIntyre	Sir J. Simon	3	Aug 16	Sep 16	8376
Allegations against Sir John Jackson	A. Chamel	3	Nov 16	Mar 17	8518
Limited Proportional Representation	J. Lowther	5	Feb 18	Apr 18	944
Decimal Coinage	Ld Emmott	20	Aug 18	Feb 20	628
Income Tax	Ld Colwyn	21	Apr 19	Mar 20	615
Agriculture	H. Peat	23	Jul 19	Dec 19	473 [1]
Oxford and Cambridge Universities	H. Asquith	19	Nov 19	Mar 22	1588
The University of Dublin (Trinity College)	A. Geikie	5	Mar 20	Nov 20	1078
Fire Brigades and Fire Prevention	Sir P. Laurence	14	Jan 21	Jul 23	1945
The Importation of Store Cattle	Ld Finlay	5	May 21	Aug 21	1139
Local Government of Greater London	Vt Ullswater	8	Oct 21	Feb 23	1830
Honours	Ld Dunedin	7	Sep 22	Dec 22	1789
Local Government	E of Onslow	12	Feb 23	Nov 29	3436
Mining Subsidence	Ld Blanesburgh	13	Jun 23	Jun 27	2899
Superior Civil Services India	H. Lee	9	Jun 23	Mar 24	2128
Lunacy and Mental Disorder	H. Macmillan	10	Jul 24	Jul 26	2700

[1] Interim Report only: no final report was published.

Title	Chairman	Size	Date appointed	Date of Report	Command number
National Health Insurance	Ld Lawrence	13	Jul 24	Feb 26	2596
Food Prices	Sir A. Geddes	16	Nov 24	Apr 25	2390
Indian Currency and Finance	E. Hilton Young	9	Aug 25	Jul 26	*Parl. paper*
The Coal Industry	Sir H. Samuel	4	Sep 25	Mar 26	2600
Court of Session and the Office of Sheriff Principal (Scotland)	Ld Clyde	9	Jan 26	Jan 27	2801
Agriculture in India	M of Linlithgow	10	Apr 26	Apr 28	3132
Cross-River Traffic in London	Ld Lee of Fareham	6	Jul 26	Nov 26	2772
Land Drainage in England and Wales	Ld Bledisloe	11	Mar 27	Dec 27	2993
National Museums and Art Galleries	Vt d'Abernon	11	Jul 27	Jan 30	3463
London Squares	M of Londonderry	14	Aug 27	Sep 28	3196
Police Powers and Procedure	Ld Lee	8	Aug 28	Mar 29	3297
Transport	Sir A. Griffith-Boscawen	12	Aug 28	Dec 30	3751
Labour in India	J. Whitley	11	Jul 29	Mar 31	3583
Licensing (England and Wales)	Ld Amulree	19	Sep 29	May 31	3988
Civil Service	Ld Tomlin	16	Oct 29	Jul 31	3909
Licensing (Scotland)	Ld Mackay	14	Oct 29	May 31	3894
Unemployment Insurance	H. Gregory	7	Dec 30	Oct 32	4185
Malta	Ld Askwith	3	Apr 31	Jan 32	3993
Lotteries and Betting	Sir S. Rowlatt	12	Jun 32	Jun 33	4341
Newfoundland	Ld Amulree	3	Feb 33	at 33	4480
The University of Durham	Ld Moyne	8	Mar 34	Jan 35	4815
Tithe Rentcharge in England and Wales	J. Williams	4	Aug 34	Nov 35	5095
Despatch of Business at Common Law	Earl Peel	7	Dec 34	Jan 36	5065
Private Manufacture of and Trading in Arms	J. Bankes	7	Feb 35	Sep 36	5292
Local Government in the Tyneside Area	Sir A. Scott	5	May 35	Feb 37	5402
Merthyr Tydfil	Sir A. Lowry	2	May 35	Nov 35	5039
Safety in Coal Mines	Ld Rockley	10	Dec 35	Dec 38	5890
Palestine	Earl Peel	1	Aug 36	Jun 37	5479
The Distribution of the Industrial Population	Sir M. Barlow	13	Jul 37	Dec 39	6153
Rhodesia-Nyasaland	Vt Bledisloe	1	Mar 38	Mar 39	5949
West Indies	Ld Moyne	1	Aug 38	Dec 39	6607
Workmen's Compensation	Sir H. Hetherington	15	Dec 38	Dec 44	658
Population	Vt Simon	16	Mar 44	*reconstituted*	
	Sir H. Henderson	14	May 46	Mar 49	7695
Equal Pay	C. Asquith	9	Oct 44	Oct 46	6937
Justices of the Peace	Ld du Parcq	16	Jun 46	May 48	7463
The Press	Sir D. Ross	17	Apr 47	Jun 49	7700
Betting, Lotteries and Gaming	H. Willink	13	Apr 49	Mar 51	8190
Capital Punishment	Sir E. Gowers	12	May 49	Sep 53	8932
Taxation of Profits and Income	Ld Cohen	14	Jan 51		
	Ld Radcliffe	14	..	May 55	9474
University Education in Dundee	Ld Tedder	9	Mar 51	Apr 52	8514
Marriage and Divorce	Ld Morton of Henryton	18	Sep 51	Dec 55	9678
Scottish Affairs	E of Balfour	15	Jul 52	Jul 54	9212
East Africa	Sir H. Dow	8	Jan 53	May 55	9475
The Civil Service	Sir R. Priestley	12	Nov 53	Nov 55	9613
The Law Relating to Mental Illness and Mental Deficiency	Ld Percy of Newcastle	11	Feb 54	May 57	169
Common Land	Sir I. Jennings	12	Dec 55	Jul 58	462
Doctors' and Dentists' Remuneration	Sir H. Pilkington	9	Mar 57	Feb 60	939
Local Government in Greater London	Sir E. Herbert	7	Dec 57	Oct 60	1164
The Police	Sir H. Willink	15	Jan 60	Apr 62	1728

Title	Chairman	Size	Date appointed	Date of Report	Command number
The Press	Ld Shawcross	5	Mar 61	May 62	1811
The Penal System in England and Wales	Vt Amory	16	Jul 64	(wound up May 66)	
Reform of the Trade Unions and Employers' Associations	Ld Donovan	12	Apr 65	Jun 68	3623
Medical Education	Ld Todd	16	Jun 65	Mar 68	3569
Tribunals of Inquiry	Sir C. Salmon	7	Feb 66	Nov 66	3121
The Examination of Assizes and Quarter Sessions	Ld Beeching	8	Nov 66	Sep 69	4153
Local Government, England	Sir J. Maud (Ld)	11	May 66	Jun 69	4040
Local Government, Scotland	Ld Wheatley	9	May 66	Sep 69	4150
The Constitution	Ld Crowther Ld Kilbrandon	16	Apr 69	Oct 73	5460
Civil Liability and Compensation	Ld Pearson	16	Mar 73	Mar 78	7054
The Press	Sir M. Finer O. McGregor	11	Jun 74	Jul 77	6810
Standards of Conduct in Government	Ld Salmon	12	Jul 74	Jul 76	6526
Gambling	Vt Rothschild	10	Feb 76	Jul 78	7200
National Health Service	Sir A. Merrison	16	May 76	Jul 79	7613
Legal Services	Sir H. Benson	15	Jul 76	Oct 79	7648
Criminal Procedures	Sir C. Philips	16	Dec 77	Jan 81	8092
Criminal Justice	Ld Runciman	11	Jun 91	Jul 93	2263

Permanent and Operating Commissions

Certain Royal Commissions have an enduring existence:

The Royal Commission on Historical Manuscripts set up in 1869 sits under the *ex officio* Chairmanship of the Master of the Rolls. It was reconstituted with extended powers in 1959. Its task is to advise and assist in the preservation of historical manuscripts and to publish them.

The Royal Commission on Historical Monuments was set up for England in 1908 with similar bodies for Scotland (reconstituted 1948) and Wales and Monmouthshire. Their task is to maintain an inventory of Ancient Monuments.

The Royal Fine Arts Commission was set up in 1924 (reconstituted in 1933 and 1946) and the Royal Fine Art Commission for Scotland in 1927 (reconstituted 1948): their task is to inquire into questions of public amenity and artistic importance.

The Royal Commission for the Exhibition of 1851, surviving from the winding up of the affairs of the Great Exhibitions, still distributes the income from surplus funds to promote scientific and artistic education. There was also the Royal Commission for the Patriotic Fund (1854–1904). In addition, there have been operating Commissions for the Paris Exhibition of 1900, the St Louis Exhibition of 1904, and for the International Exhibitions at Brussels, Rome and Turin in 1910 and 1911. Another miscellaneous group of operating Royal Commissions covered Sewage Disposal (1898–1915), Horse-Breeding (1887–1911), and Crofter Colonisation (1888–1906).

War produced another group of operating or semi-permanent Royal Commissions, Sugar Supply (1914–21), Wheat Supplies (1916–25), Paper and Paper making materials (1917), Defence of the Realm Losses (1915–20), Compensation for Suffering Damage by Enemy Action (1921–24), Awards to Inventors (1919–35, 1946–56) and Foreign Compensation Commission (1950–). The Royal Commission on the Distribution of Incomes, set up under Ld Diamond in 1974, had a continuing existence until 1979.

Other Crown Committees

The Crown has also appointed a number of other advisory committees, some of which are called 'Royal Commissions' but all of which are different from those listed above. Some of them are different because they are standing, not *ad hoc*, in nature. Two of these appointed in the nineteenth century are still in existence: the Commission on the Exhibition of 1851 (appointed in 1850) and the Historical Manuscripts Commission (appointed in 1869). In the present century there have been thirteen others appointed (see table below), of which six are still in existence. All of them were appointed by virtue of prerogative powers. Other Crown advisory committees are different from those listed above because they were appointed by virtue of statutory, not prerogative, powers. Four, all of them *ad hoc* in nature, have been appointed in this century; they dealt with Property of the Free Church of Scotland (1905–10, Cd. 5060), the Election in Worcester in 1906 (1906, Cd. 3262), the Coal Industry (1919, Cmd. 360), and Indian Government (1927–30, Cmd. 3568). Finally, the Government in Ireland prior to 1922 appointed a special kind of committee in the name of the Crown called a 'Vice-Regal Commission'; thirteen were appointed in this century (see table below).

Standing Advisory Committees Appointed by the Crown since 1900
(including continuing Royal Commissions producing reports)

Title	Date of appointment	Date of adjournment	Report Cd.No.
Ancient and Historical Monuments and Constructions in Scotland	Feb 08	*	9404
Ancient Monuments and Constructions of Wales and Monmouthshire	Aug 08	*	8645
Ancient and Historical Monuments and Constructions in England	Oct 08	*	9351
Supply of Sugar	Aug 14	Apr 21	1300
Defence of the Realm Losses	Mar 15	Nov 20	1044
Supply of Paper	Feb 16	Feb 18	None issued
Supply of Wheat	Oct 16	Jul 25	2462
Awards to Inventors	Mar 19	Nov 37	5594
Compensation for Suffering and Damage by Enemy Action	Aug 21	Feb 24	2066
Fine Art	May 24	*	4832
Fine Art for Scotland	Aug 27	*	4317
Awards to Inventors	May 46	Apr 56	9744
Environmental Pollution	Feb 70	*	9149

Irish Vice-Regal Commissions

Title	Chairman	Size	Date appointed	Date of Report	Command number
Irish Inland Fisheries	S. Walker	7	Aug 99	Jan 01	448
Poor Law Reform in Ireland	W. L. Micks	3	May 03	Oct 06	3202
Trinity College, Dublin, Estates Commission	G. Fitzgibbon	3	Jun 04	Apr 05	2526
Arterial Drainage (Ireland)	A. Binnie	5	Sep 05	Feb 07	3374
Irish Railways, including Light Railways	C. Scotter	7	Jul 06	Jul 10	5247
Circumstances of the Loss of the Regalia of the Order of St Patrick	J. Shaw	3	Jan 08	Jan 08	3936
Irish Milk Supply	P. O'Neill	9	Nov 11	Oct 13	7129
Primary Education (Ireland) System of Inspection	S. Dill	8	Jan 13	Jan 14	7235
Dublin Disturbances	D. Henry	2	Dec 13	Feb 14	7269
Primary Education (Ireland) 1918	Ld Killanin	17	Aug 18	Feb 19	60
Intermediate Education (Ireland)	T. Molony	14	Aug 18	Mar 19	66
Under Sheriffs and Bailiffs (Ireland)	T. O'Shaughnessy	5	Oct 18	May 19	190
Reorganisation and Pay of the Irish Police Forces	J. Ross	6	Oct 19	Dec 19	603
Clerk of the Crown and Peace, Etc. (Ireland)	J. Wakely	7	Oct 19	Jun 20	805

Departmental Committees

Departmental Committees are *ad hoc* advisory committees appointed by Ministers by virtue of their conventional powers. As such they are the direct counterpart of Royal Commissions. In the table below are listed some of the more important Departmental Committees appointed since the turn of the century. As with Royal Commissions, there is no 'official' title for a Departmental Committee, so usage may vary slightly; where there were two successive chairmen, both are listed; and the dates of appointment and report as well as the Command number are derived in the same manner as for Royal Commissions.

A Select List of Departmental Committee 1900–

In the absence of any single official title for a Committee we have tried to select the most commonly used short title. The Command number given is that of the final report.

Title	Chairman	Date appointed	Date of Report	Cd. No.
Compensation for Injuries to Workmen	K. Digby	Nov 03	Aug 04	2208
Motor Cars	R. Hobhouse	Jan 04	Apr 04	2069
Income Tax	C. Ritchie	–	Jun 05	2575
Company and Commercial Law and Practice	C. Warmington	Feb 05	Jun 06	3052
Accounts of Local Authorities	W. Runciman	Jan 06	Jul 07	3614
Law of Copyright	Ld Gorell	Mar 09	Dec 09	4967
Probation of Offenders Act 1907	H. Samuel	Mar 09	Dec 09	5001
Procedure of Royal Commissions	Ld Balfour of Burleigh	Apr 09	Jun 10	5235
Railway Agreements and Amalgamations	R. Rea	Jun 09	Apr 11	5631

Title	Chairman	Date appointed	Date of Report	Cd. No.
Alien Immigrants at the Port of London	R. Lehmann	–	Mar 11	5575
Educational Endowments	C. Trevelyan	–	Mar 11	5662
National Guarantee for the War Risks of Shipping	A. Chamberlain	..	..	7560
Local Taxation	Sir J. Kempe	Nov 12	Mar 14	7315
Retrenchment in the Public Expenditure	R. McKenna	Jul 15	Sep 15	8068
Royal Aircraft Factory	R. Burbridge	Mar 16	Jul 16	8191
Increase of Prices of Commodities since the beginning of the War	J. Robertson	Jun 16	Sep 16	8358
Summer Time	J. Wilson	Sep 16	Feb 17	8487
Commercial and Industrial Policy, Imperial Preference	Ld Balfour of Burleigh	..	Feb 17	8482
Currency and Foreign Exchanges	Ld Cunliffe	Jan 18	Dec 19	464
National Expenditure	Ld Geddes	Aug 21	Feb 22	1589
Broadcasting	Sir M. Sykes	Apr 23	Aug 23	1951
Imperial Wireless Telegraphy	Sir R. Donald	Jan 24	Feb 24	2060
National Debt and Taxation	H. Colwyn	Mar 24	Nov 26	2800
Broadcasting	Ld Crawford & Balcarres	Aug 25	Mar 26	2599
Ministers' Powers	E of Donoughmore	Oct 29	Apr 32	4060
Finance and Industry	H. Macmillan (Ld)	Nov 29	Jun 31	3897
Regional Development	H. Chelmsford	Jan 31	Mar 31	3915
National Expenditure	Sir G. May	Mar 31	Jul 31	3920
Depressed Areas	(Three Area Chairmen)	Apr 34	Nov 34	4728
Broadcasting	Vt Ullswater	Apr 35	Mar 36	5091
Parliamentary Pensions	Sir W. Fisher	Jul 35	Nov 37	5624
Compensation and Betterment	Sir A Uthwatt	Jan 41	Sep 42	6291
Social Insurance and Allied Services	Sir W Beveridge	Jun 41	Nov 42	6404
Training of Civil Servants	R. Assheton	Feb 43	Apr 44	6525
Company Law Amendment	Sir L. Cohen	Jun 43	Jun 45	6659
Television	Ld Hankey	Sep 43	Dec 44	..
Rent Control	Vt Ridley	Nov 43	Feb 45	6621
Legal Aid and Legal Advice in England and Wales	Ld Rushcliffe	May 44	May 45	6641
Gas Industry	G. Heyworth	Jun 44	Nov 45	6699
Social and Economic Research	Sir J. Clapham	Jan 45	Jun 46	6868
Care of Children	Miss M. Curtis	Mar 45	Aug 46	6922
National Parks (England and Wales)	Sir A. Hobhouse	Jul 45	Mar 47	7121
New Towns	Ld Reith	Oct 45	Jul 46	6876
Port Transport Industry	R. Evershed	Nov 45	Dec 45	..
Shops and Non-Industrial Employment	Sir E. Gowers	Jan 46	Mar 49	7664
Resale Price Maintenance	Sir G. Lloyd-Jacob	Aug 47	Mar 49	7696
Higher Civil Service Remuneration	Ld Chorley	Jan 48	Sep 48	7635
Leasehold	Ld Uthwatt Ld Jenkins	Feb 48	Jun 50	7982
Political Activities of Civil Servants	J. Masterman	Apr 48	Apr 49	7718
Intermediaries	Sir E. Herbert	Feb 49	Oct 49	7904
Broadcasting	Ld Beveridge	Jun 49	Dec 50	8116
Fuel and Power Resources	Vt Ridley	Jul 51	Jul 52	8647
Departmental Records	Sir J. Grigg	Jun 52	May 54	9163
National Health Service	C. Guillebaud	May 53	Nov 55	9663
Air Pollution	Sir H. Beaver	Jul 53	Nov 54	9322
Crichel Down	A. Clark	Nov 53	May 54	9176
Electricity Supply Industry	Sir E. Herbert	Jul 54	Dec 55	9672
Homosexual Law Reform	Sir J. Wolfenden	Aug 54	Aug 57	247
Crown Lands	Sir M. Trustram Eve	Dec 54	May 55	9843
Dock Workers' Scheme	Sir P. Devlin	Jul 55	Jun 56	9813
Administrative Tribunals and Inquiries	Sir O. Franks	Nov 55	Jul 57	218
Children and Young People	Vt Ingleby	Oct 56	Oct 60	1191
Damage and Casualties in Port Said	Sir E. Herbert	Dec 56	Dec 56	47

Title	Chairman	Date appointed	Date of Report	Cd. No.
Working of the Monetary System	Ld Radcliffe	May 57	Jul 59	827
Interception of Communications	Sir N. Birkett	Jun 57	Sep 57	283
Preservation of Downing Street	E of Crawford	Jul 57	Mar 58	457
The Structure of the Public Library Service in England and Wales	Sir S. Roberts	Sep 57	Dec 58	660
The Youth Service in England and Wales	Ctss of Albemarle	Nov 58	Oct 59	929
Consumer Protection	J. Molony	Jun 59	Apr 62	1781
Control of Public Expenditure	Ld Plowden	Jul 59	Jun 61	1432
Company Law Committee	Ld Jenkins	Dec 59	May 62	1749
Broadcasting	Sir H. Pilkington	Jul 60	Jun 62	1753
Higher Education	Ld Robbins	Feb 61	Sep 63	2154
Major Ports of Great Britain	Vt Rochdale	Mar 61	Jul 62	1824
Security in the Public Service	Ld Radcliffe	May 61	Nov 61	1681
Economy of Northern Ireland	Sir R. Hall	May 61	Jun 62	1835
Sunday Observance	Ld Crathorne	Jul 61	Sep 64	2528
Decimal Currency	E of Halsbury	Dec 61	Jul 63	2145
Organisation of Civil Science	Sir B. Trend	Mar 62	Sep 63	2171
The Vassall Case	Sir C. Cunningham	Oct 62	Nov 62	1871
Security Service and Mr Profumo	Ld Denning	Jun 63	Sep 63	2152
Remuneration of Ministers and M.P.s	Sir G. Lawrence	Dec 63	Oct 64	2516
Social Studies	Ld Heyworth	Jun 63	Feb 65	2660
Housing in Greater London	Sir M. Holland	Aug 63	Mar 65	2605
Port Transport Industry	Ld Devlin	Oct 64	Nov 64	2523
Aircraft Industry	Ld Plowden	Dec 64	Dec 65	2853
Shipbuilding	R. Geddes	Feb 65	Feb 66	2939
Age of Majority	Sir J. Latey	Jul 65	Jun 67	3342
Local Authority Personal Social Services	F. Seebohm	Dec 65	Jul 68	3703
Death Certification and Coroners	N. Brodrick	Mar 65	Sep 71	4810
Civil Service	Ld Fulton	Feb 66	Jul 68	3638
Prison Security	Earl Mountbatten	Oct 66	Dec 66	3175
Fire Service	Sir R. Holroyd	Feb 67	May 70	4371
Shipping	Vt Rochdale	Jul 67	Feb 70	4337
Intermediate Areas	Sir J. Hunt	Sep 67	Feb 69	3998
Civil Air Transport	Sir E. Edwards	Nov 67	Apr 69	4018
Legal Education	Sir R. Ormrod	Dec 67	Jan 71	4595
Commercial Rating	D. Anderson	Aug 68	Apr 70	4366
Overseas Representation	Sir V. Duncan	Aug 68	Jun 69	4107
Consumer Credit	Ld Crowther	Sep 68	Dec 70	4596
Adoption of Children	Sir W. Houghton F. Stockdale	Jul 69	Jul 72	5107
Small Firms	J. Bolton	Jul 69	Sep 71	4811
One-Parent Families	Sir M. Finer	Nov 69	Oct 74	5629
Rent Acts	H. Francis	Oct 69	Jan 71	4609
Privacy	K. Younger	May 70	May 72	5012
Safety and Health at Work	Ld Roberts	May 70	Jun 72	5034
Defence Procurement	D. Rayner	Oct 70	Mar 71	4641
Dispersal of Government Work from London	Sir H. Hardman	Oct 70	Jun 73	5322
Lotteries	K. Witney	Jan 71	Dec 73	5506
Abuse of Social Security	Sir H. Fisher	Mar 71	Mar 73	5228
Liquor Licensing	Ld Erroll of Hale	Apr 71	Oct 72	5154
Scottish Licensing Laws	G. Clayson	Apr 71	Aug 73	5354
Official Secrets Act	Ld Franks	Apr 71	Sep 72	5104
Public Trustee Office	H. Hutton	May 71	Nov 71	4913
Contempt of Court	Ld Phillimore	Jun 71	Dec 74	5794
National Savings	Sir H. Page	Jun 71	Jun 73	5273
Brutality in Northern Ireland	Sir E. Compton	Aug 71	Nov 71	4823
Interrogation of Terrorists	Ld Parker of Waddington	Nov 71	Jan 72	4901
Probation Officers and Social Workers	J. Butterworth	Dec 71	Aug 72	5076
Psychiatric Patients	Sir C. Aarvold	Jun 72	Jan 73	5191

Title	Chairman	Date appointed	Date of Report	Cd. No.
Mentally Abnormal Offenders	Ld Butler	Sep 72	Oct 75	6244
Legal Procedures to deal with Terrorists in Northern Ireland	Ld Diplock	Oct 72	Nov 72	5185
Handling of Complaints against Police	A. Gordon-Brown	Apr 73	Mar 74	5582
Export of Animals for Slaughter	Ld O'Brien	Jul 73	Mar 74	5566
Conduct in Local Government	Ld Redcliffe-Maud	Oct 73	May 74	5636
Broadcasting	Ld Annan	Apr 74	Mar 77	6753
Pay of Non-University Teachers	Ld Houghton	Jun 74	Jan 75	5848
Civil Liberties in Northern Ireland	Ld Gardiner	Jun 74	Jan 75	5879
Local Government Finance	F. Layfield	Jun 74	Mar 76	6543
Ministerial Memoirs	Vt Radcliffe	Apr 75	Jan 76	6386
Tape Recording Police Interrogations	W. Hyde	Apr 75	Oct 76	6630
Industrial Democracy	Ld Bullock	Dec 75	Apr 77	6706
Recruitment of Mercenaries	Ld Diplock	Feb 76	Aug 76	6569
Age of Consent	Sir G. Waller	Dec 75	Apr 81	8216
Data Protection	Sir N. Lindop	Jun 76	Dec 78	7341
Political Activities of Civil Servants	Sir A. Armitage	Aug 76	Jan 78	7057
Genetic Manipulation	Sir G. Wolstenholme	Dec 76	Sep 82	8665
Insolvency Law	Sir K. Cork	Jan 77	Jun 82	8558
Functioning of Financial Institutions	Sir H. Wilson	Jan 77	Jun 80	7937
Financing of Small Firms	Sir H. Wilson	Jan 77	Mar 79	7503
Cabinet Document Security	Ld Houghton	Jul 77	Oct 77	6677
Obscenity and Film Censorship	B. Williams	Jul 77	Nov 79	7772
Ownership of Agricultural Land	Ld Northfield	Sep 77	Jul 79	7599
Police Pay	Ld Edmund-Davies	Oct 77	Jul 78	7283
Police Interrogation in Northern Ireland	H. Bennett	Jun 78	Mar 79	7497
Public Records	Sir D. Wilson	Aug 78	Mar 81	8204
U.K. Prison Service	Sir J. D. May	Nov 78	Oct 79	7673
Education of Ethnic Minority Children	A. Rampton Ld Swann	Mar 79	Feb 85	9403
Local Government in Scotland	Sir A. Stodart	Dec 79	Jan 81	8115
Postgraduate Education	Sir P. Swinnerton-Dyer	Dec 79	Apr 82	8537
University Scientific Research	Sir A. Merrison	Mar 80	Jun 82	8567
Police Complaints	Ld Plowden	Jul 80	Mar 81	8193
Brixton Disorders	Ld Scarman	Apr 81	Nov 81	8427
Civil Service Pay	Sir J. Megaw	Jun 81	Jul 82	8590
Review of 1976 Terrorism Act	Earl Jellicoe	Mar 82	Feb 83	8803
Cable Television	Ld Hunt of Tanworth	Apr 82	Oct 82	8679
Fertilisation of Human Embryos	Dame M. Warnock	Jul 82	Jul 84	9314
Falkland Islands Review	Ld Franks	Jul 82	Jan 83	8787
Protection of Military Information	Sir H. Beach	Feb 83	Dec 83	9112
Education of Children from Minority Groups	Ld Swann	Mar 87	Mar 85	9453
Crowd Safety at Football Grounds	Sir O. Popplewell	May 85	Jan 86	9710
Academic Valuation of Degree Courses	Sir N. Lindop	Apr 84	Apr 85	9501
Conduct of Local Authority Business	D. Widdecombe	Feb 85	Jun 86	9797
Financing the B.B.C.	A. Peacock	Mar 85	Jul 86	9824
Public Health in England	Sir D. Acheson	Jan 86	Jan 88	289
Child Abuse in Cleveland	Dame E. Butler-Sloss	Jul 87	Jul 88	412
King's Cross Underground Fire	D. Fennell	Nov 87	Nov 88	499
Parole System in England & Wales	Ld Carlisle of Bucklow	Sep 87	Feb 89	532
Banking Services	R. Jack	Jan 87	Feb 88	622
War Crimes	Sir T. Hetherington	Feb 88	Jul 89	744
Clapham Junction Railway Accident	A. Hidden	Dec 88	Nov 90	820
N.Ireland Emergency Provisions Acts	Vt Colville		Jul 90	1115
The Piper Alpha Disaster	Ld Cullen	Jul 88	Nov 90	1330
River Safety	J. Hayes	Dec 91	Jul 92	1991
Press Self-Regulation	Sir D. Calcutt	Jul 92	Jan 93	2135
Police Responsibilities and Rewards	Sir P. Sheehy	Jul 92	Jun 93	2263

Enquiries Held under the Tribunals of Inquiry (Evidence) Act, 1921

Upon a resolution of both Houses of Parliament on a matter of urgent public importance a tribunal might be appointed by the Sovereign or a Secretary of State with all the powers of the High Court as regards examination of witnesses and production of documents, for the objective investigation of facts.

Title	Members of Tribunal	Year	Command number
Destruction of documents by Ministry of Munitions officials	Ld Cave Ld Inchape Sir W. Plender	1921	1340
Royal Commission on Lunacy and Mental Disorder given powers under the Act	H. Macmillan (Ch)	1924	2700
Arrest of R. Sheppard, R.A.O.C. Inquiry into conduct of Metropolitan Police	J. Rawlinson	1925	2497
Allegations made against the Chief Constable of Kilmarnock in connection with the dismissal of Constables Hill and Moore from the Burgh Police Force	W. Mackenzie	1925	2659
Conditions with regard to mining and drainage in an area around the County Borough of Doncaster	Sir H. Monro (Ch)	1926/8	
Charges against the Chief Constable of St Helens by the Watch Committee	C. Parry T. Walker	1928	3103
Interrogation of Miss Irene Savidge by Metropolitan Police at New Scotland Yard	Sir J.E. Banks H. Lees-Smith J. Withers	1928	3147
Allegations of bribery and corruption in connection with the letting and allocation of stances and other premises under the control of the Corporation of Glasgow	Ld Anderson Sir R. Boothby J. Hunter	1933	4361
Unauthorised disclosure of information relating to the Budget	Sir J. Porter G. Simonds R. Oliver	1936	5184
The circumstances surrounding the loss of H.M. Submarine 'Thetis'	Sir J. Bucknill	1939	6190
The conduct before the Hereford Juvenile Court Justices of the proceedings against Craddock and others	Ld Goddard	1943	6485
The administration of the Newcastle upon Tyne Fire, Police and Civil Defence Services	R. Burrows	1944	6522
Bribery of Ministers of the Crown or other public servants in connection with the grant of licences, etc.	Sir J. Lynskey G. Russell Vick G. Upjohn	1948	7616
Allegations of improper disclosure of information relating to the raising of the Bank Rate	Ld Parker E. Holland G. Veale	1957	350
Allegations that John Waters was assaulted on 7th December 1957, at Thurso and the action taken by Caithness Police in connection therewith	Ld Sorn Sir J.Robertson J. Dandie	1959	718
The circumstances in which offences under the Official Secrets Act were committed by William Vassall	Ld Radcliffe Sir J. Barry Sir E. Milner Holland	1962	2009
The disaster at Aberfan	Sir E. Davies H. Harding V. Lawrence	1967	H.C.553
The events on Sunday, 30th January 1972 which led to loss of life in connection with the procession in Londonderry on that day	Ld Widgery	1972	H.C.220/72
The circumstances leading to the cessation of trading by the Vehicle and General Insurance Co. Ltd	Sir A. James M. Kerr S. Templeman	1972	H.C.133
The extent to which the Crown Agents lapsed from accepted standards of commercial or professional conduct or of public administration as financiers on their own account in the years 1967–74	Sir D. Croom-Johnson Sir W. Slimmings Ld Allen	1982	H.C.364

Tribunals and Commissions

A large number of statutory tribunals, with jurisdiction to decide quasi-legal disputes, have been created since 1900. By 1960 there were over 2,000 tribunals within the supervisory role of the Council on Tribunals. The fifteen-member Council on Tribunals was set up under the *Tribunals and Inquiries Act, 1958*, following the report of the Franks Committee (Cmnd. 218/ 1957). Its role is purely advisory, but it has to report annually to Parliament.

The reports list the tribunals that fall within its purview and the number of cases each type of tribunal has dealt with during the past year. In the following table some categories have been merged and appeals from lower to higher tribunals are not included nor are tribunals which have had no cases to deal with. Separate Scottish tribunals are also excluded.

Category	Latest enabling legislation	Number of Tribunals	Number of cases [decided and withdrawn]			
			1960	1970	1980	1990
Agriculture	1947	8	459	402	461	337
Air Transport	1982	12	..	3,537	1,002	1,754
Betting Levy	1963	1	..	196	–	97
Commons	1965	4	..	–	1,514	147
Compensation	1958	10	27	–	–	1,785
Education	1944	ad hoc	1	3	–	0
Immigration	1971	59	..	991	11,344	17,241
Industry and Employment	(1964)	84	..	10,318	31,736	30,751
Land	1949	1	1,121	1,511	1,237	992
Mental Health	1983	15	1	1,114	709	7,487
Milk and Dairies	1990	8	1	2	–	0
Misuse of Drugs	1971	53	..	..	–	0
National Assistance	1948	152	7,757	–	–	.a
(Non-Contrib.Benefits)	1966	151	..	28,717	..	.a
(Supplementary Benefit)	1975	123	..	..	45,471	.a
National Health Service	1977	91	1,235	979	1,137	2031
National Insurance	1946	228	60,914	54,787	–	.a
National Service	1948	83	5,954	–	–	1
Patents	1907	3	5,652	6,566	7,564	6,460
Pensions	1919	11	4,784	3,388	–	3,115
Performing Rights	1956	1	4	–	–	..
Rates, Valuation, Community Charge	1988	64	..	25,513	40,400	185,000
Rents	1980	53	4,652	14,923	5,086	315
Rent Assessment	1977	ad hoc	..	..	9,734	16,479
Revenue	1970	654	n.a.	6,562	n.a.	n.a.
Road Traffic	1985	1	22,110	23,205	29,528	47
Data Protection	1984	1	..	..	..	6
Finance	1989	4	..	..	..	5
Leasehold Valuation	1980	ad hoc	..	..	..	138
Copyright	1988	1	..	..	..	3
Social Security	1975	179	..	..	25,258	119,645a
Vaccine Damages	1979	6	..	..	897	16
Value Added Tax	1983	5	..	..	61	2,724
Residential Care Homes	1984	ad hoc	..	..	..	56

aFigures under 'National Assistance', included in 'Social Security' for 1990

Political Honours Scrutiny Committee

The Political Honours Scrutiny Committee was established in 1924, following scandals over the 'sale of honours'. It was to 'consider before they are submitted to the King, the names and particulars of persons recommended for appointment to any dignity or honours on account of political services . . . and to report . . . whether such persons . . . are fit and proper persons to be recommended'. Its activities were virtually never reported but they continued after H. Wilson announced the ending of 'political honours' in 1966 and again in 1974. In 1976, following agitation over Sir H. Wilson's resignation honours list, there was a complete change of membership. It has always had three members:

1923	Ld Dunedin (Ch)	1923	Ld Mildmay	1923	Sir E. Cecil
1923	Vt Ullswater	1924	T. Richards	1925	J. Rawlinson
1924	Ld Buckmaster	1925	W. Nicholson	1925	Ld Merrivale
	(Ch from 1929)	1925	Vt Novar (Ch)		
1929	H. (Ld) Macmillan			1929	G. Barnes
	(Ch from 1934)	1934	M of Crewe	1938	Ld Rushcliffe
		1945	J. Clynes	1949	Vt Templewood
1952	Ld Asquith (Ch)	1949	Ld Pethick-Lawrence		(Ch from 1954)
1954	Vt Thurso			1959	Ld Crookshank (Ch)
1961	C. Davies	1961	Ld Williams	1961	Ld Crathorne (Ch)
1962	Ld Rea	1967	Bness Summerskill		
1976	Ld Franks	1976	Ld Shackleton (Ch)	1976	Ld Carr
1987	Ld Grimond			1987	Ld Pym
1992	Ld Thomson of	1992	Ld Cledwyn		(Ch from 1992)
	Monifieth				

VIII

JUSTICE AND LAW ENFORCEMENT

Major Criminal Justice Legislation 1900–

Poor Prisoners' Defence Act, 1903. This was the first Act which made provision for legal aid, which was limited to trials on indictment.

The Probation of Offenders Act, 1907. This extended courts' probation powers and allowed appointment of official probation officers.

The Criminal Appeal Act, 1907. This created the Court of Criminal Appeal.

The Prevention of Crime Act, 1908. This provided for 'borstal training' of young recidivists and 'preventive detention' for adult habitual criminals.

The Children Act, 1908. This created 'places of detention' (later 'Remand Homes') and Juvenile Courts; it also prohibited imprisonment of those under 14, restricted imprisonment of those from 14–17 and abolished death sentence for those under 17.

The Criminal Justice Administration Act, 1914. This required Summary Courts to give time for payment of fines.

Poor Prisoners' Defence Act, 1930. This Act provided a comprehensive system of legal aid, extending aid to preliminary inquiries and to cases heard summarily before magistrates' courts.

Summary Jurisdiction (Appeals) Act, 1933. This Act made provision for free legal aid for criminal cases, payable out of county or borough funds at the discretion of the magistrates.

The Children and Young Persons Act, 1933. This Act, which followed the 1927 Report of the Cecil Committee on the treatment of young offenders, codified and extended 'care and protection' law; it also raised the age of criminal responsibility from 7 to 8.

The Administration of Justice (Miscellaneous Provisions) Act, 1933. This abolished Grand Juries.

The Criminal Justice Act, 1948. Following the lines of a 1938 Bill abandoned through the onset of war, this extended the fining powers of higher courts; it further restricted imprisonment of juveniles and abolished distinction between penal servitude, imprisonment, etc.; it also improved law on probation, introduced corrective training and a new form of preventive detention and it provided for remand centres, attendance centres and detention centres. It also abolished the right of peers to be tried by the House of Lords.

Legal Aid and Advice Act, 1949. This introduced a new system of aid for civil cases. It provided for the establishment of a network of local committees, composed of solicitors and some barristers to grant legal aid under regulations made by the Lord Chancellor. By this Act, aid was extended to cover all proceedings in civil courts and civil proceedings in magistrates' courts, except for certain types of action (of which defamation and breach of promise were the most important).

Cost in Criminal Cases Act, 1952. This Act empowered the courts, in the case of an indictable offence, to order reasonable defence costs to be paid out of public funds, when the accused was discharged or acquitted.

The Homicide Act, 1957. This amended the law on murder, distinguishing capital and non-capital murder and introducing the defence of diminished responsibility.

The First Offenders Act, 1958. This restricted imprisonment of adults by Summary Courts.

Administration of Justice Act, 1960.   This gave a greatly extended right of appeal to the House of Lords in criminal matters and reformed the law relating to habeas corpus and to contempt of court.

Legal Aid Act, 1960. This related financial conditions for legal aid and made further provision for the remuneration of counsel and solicitors.

The Criminal Justice Act, 1961.   This provided compulsory supervision after release from detention centres and rationalised custodial sentences for 17–21 age-group.

The Children and Young Persons Act, 1963.   This raised the age of criminal responsibility from 8 to 10, and redefined the need for 'care, protection, and control'.

The Criminal Injuries Compensation Board was set up in 1964, under an ex gratia State Scheme for compensating victims of crimes of violence.

The Murder (Abolition of Death Penalty) Act, 1965.   This suspended the death penalty until 1970, and substituted a mandatory 'life' sentence.
On 16 Dec 69 Parliament voted to continue the suspension indefinitely.
Motions for its restoration were rejected on 11 Dec 75, 19 Jul 79, 13 Jul 83, 13 Jan 87, 1 Apr 87, 7 Jun 88, 17 Dec 90 and on 21 Feb 94.

Criminal Appeal Act, 1966.   This amalgamated the Court of Criminal Appeal and the Court of Appeal.

The Criminal Justice Act, 1967.   This introduced suspended sentences, a Parole Board (see p. 320), a new type of sentence for recidivists and further restricted imprisonment of adults. It allowed majority verdicts (10–2) by juries.

The Theft Act, 1967.   This rationalised definitions of theft and other dishonesty.

The Criminal Law Act, 1967.   This replaced the distinction between felonies and misdemeanours, with a distinction between arrestable and non-arrestable offences.

The Children and Young Persons Act, 1969.   Redefined the circumstances in which juvenile courts could make orders dealing with children and young persons, and simplified the nature of such orders; it also provided for the raising of the minimum age of liability to prosecution (although this has not been implemented) and for the reorganisation of approved schools, children's homes, etc., into a system of 'community homes' controlled by local authorities.

The Courts Act, 1971.   Replaced Assizes and Quarter Sessions with a system of Crown Courts.

The Criminal Justice Act, 1972.   Provided courts with several new means of dealing with offenders, including criminal bankruptcy orders, community service orders, deferment of sentence, day centres for probationers; and further restricted the imprisonment of adults.

The Rehabilitation of Offenders Act, 1974.   This made it an offence to refer to criminal proceedings after the lapse of a certain period. This involved consequential amendments to the law of defamation.

Prevention of Terrorism (Temporary Provisions) Act, 1974.   This proscribed organisations concerned in terrorism and gave power to exclude certain persons from Great Britain in order to prevent acts of terrorism.

Criminal Jurisdiction Act, 1975.   This extended the jurisdiction of the criminal courts in Northern Ireland to allow them to try certain offences committed in the Irish Republic.

District Courts (Scotland) Act, 1975.   This set up a new system of courts of summary jurisdiction in Scotland.

Police Act, 1976.   This established a Police Complaints Board to deal with complaints from the public against members of the police.

Bail Act, 1976.   This extensively reformed the law on the granting of bail, requiring reasons to be given for refusal and creating a general presumption in favour of bail, particularly for offences not punishable with imprisonment.

Criminal Law Act, 1977. This simplified the rules governing the distribution of cases between the Crown Court and magistrates courts, with a view to allowing many more cases to be tried summarily rather than on indictment. It also raised the level of fines which can be imposed for many types of offence.

Judicature (Northern Ireland) Act, 1978. This modernised the structure of the superior courts in Northern Ireland, notably by abolishing the separate Court of Criminal Appeal and by setting up a new Crown Court to try all cases of indictment.

Criminal Attempts Act, 1981. This replaced the common law offence of attempt with a statutory offence and modified the statutory definition of criminal conspiracy. It also implemented the recommendation by the Home Affairs Committee of the House of Commons that the offence of 'sus' be repealed; it was partially replaced by a new offence of vehicle interference.

Criminal Justice Act, 1982. This created a completely new framework of custodial offences for offenders under 21, superseding imprisonment, Borstal training and detention in detention centres. It also amended the law on suspended sentences and introduced a new scale of standard maximum fines for summary offences.

Police and Criminal Evidence Act, 1984. This derived largely from various recommendations made by the Royal Commission on Criminal Procedure, the Criminal Law Revision Committee, and Lord Scarman's Report on the Brixton disorders. It reformed the law relating to police powers to stop and search, police powers of entry, search and seizure, powers of arrest and detention, the treatment, interrogation and identification of suspects, the admissibility of evidence obtained during police questioning, and public complaints against the police.

Prosecution of Offences Act, 1985. This established an independent Crown Prosecution Service under the Director of Public Prosecutions.

Public Order Act, 1986. This abolished the Common Law offences of riot, unlawful assembly and affray and established new statutory offences relating to public order.

Criminal Justice Act, 1987. Established the Serious Fraud Office.

Criminal Justice Act, 1988. This empowered the Attorney General to refer unduly light sentences to the Court of Appeal.

Criminal Justice Act, 1991. This set up a new structure for dealing with juvenile offenders, introduced a system of 'unit' fines related to ability to pay, and altered the rules on sentencing persistent offenders, making it harder for courts to take previous offences into account.

Criminal Justice Act, 1993. This repealed the provisions of the 1991 Act relating to unit fines and sentencing persistent offenders.

Criminal Justice and Public Order Act, 1994. This abolished the right of suspects to have no adverse inference drawn from silence in the police station, introduced changes to provisions for sites for travellers, gave police powers to stop 'rave' parties and lowered the age of consent below which homosexual acts are illegal from 21 to 18.

SOURCES. – R.M. Jackson, *Enforcing the Law* (1967); N.D. Walker, *Crime and Punishment in Britain* (2nd ed., 1968); K. Smith and D.J. Keenan, *English Law* (10th ed., 1992); G. Rose, *The Struggle for Penal Reform* (1961); J. Smith and B. Hogan, *Criminal Law* (7th ed., 1992); L. Blom-Cooper and G. Drewry, *Final Appeal: The House of Lords in its Judicial Capacity* (1972); C. McCrudden, *Individual Rights in the U.K.* (1993).

Major Legislation Relating to the Administration of Civil Justice, 1900–

Industrial Courts Act, 1919.   This Act provided a standing body for voluntary arbitration and inquiry in cases of industrial dispute.

Supreme Court of Judicature (Consolidation) Act, 1925.   This is still the principal Act defining the structure, composition and jurisdiction of the High Court and the Court of Appeal.

Administration of Justice (Miscellaneous Provisions) Act, 1933.   This restricted the right to jury trial in King's Bench civil proceedings.

Administration of Justice (Appeals) Act, 1934. This made it necessary to obtain leave to appeal to the House of Lords in civil matters arising in English courts.

County Courts Act, 1934.   This effectively abolished jury trials in county courts and rationalised the procedure for appointing registrars.

Summary Jurisdiction (Domestic Proceedings) Act, 1937.   This rationalised procedure in matrimonial, guardianship and affiliation proceedings before magistrates.

Administration of Justice (Miscellaneous Provisions) Act, 1938.   This Act made important changes relating in particular to the King's Bench Division of the High Court and to Courts of Quarter Sessions.

Juries Act, 1949.   This abolished special juries outside the City of London.

Justices of the Peace Act, 1949.   This Act brought about the extensive revision of the functions and organisation of magistrates' courts.

County Courts Act, 1955.   This fixed the general limit of county court jurisdiction at £400 (subsequently regularly raised by successive Orders in Council; abolished by the *Courts and Legal Services Act, 1990*).

County Courts Act, 1959.   This consolidated existing legislation on county courts.

Judicial Pensions Act, 1959.   This fixed a retiring age of 75 for the higher judiciary and revised the system of judicial pensions.

Legal Aid Act, 1964.   This gave limited powers for a non-legally aided litigant to be awarded his costs out of the legal aid fund where his unsuccessful opponent is in receipt of legal aid.

Justices of the Peace Act, 1968.   This abolished ex officio J.P.s and redefined the powers and functions of magistrates' clerks.

Administration of Justice Act, 1969.   This increased the jurisdiction of county courts to £750 and allowed certain categories of civil case in the High Court to 'leapfrog' directly to the House of Lords.

Administration of Justice Act, 1970.   This Act rearranged the jurisdictions of the three divisions of the High Court (the Probate, Divorce and Admiralty Division becoming the Family Division) and abolished imprisonment for debt.

Courts Act, 1971.   This replaced Courts of Assize and Quarter Sessions by Crown Courts staffed by Recorders and circuit judges; it rationalised the location of civil and criminal courts throughout England and Wales; it made sweeping changes in the administration of courts of intermediate jurisdiction and it abolished the use of juries in civil proceedings other than defamation.

Industrial Relations Act, 1971.   This established the National Industrial Relations Court (see p. 358).

Legal Aid and Advice Act, 1972.   This Act empowered solicitors to do up to £25 worth of work for a client without the latter first having to obtain a certificate from the Law Society.

Solicitors (Amendment) Act, 1974.   This made a number of changes in the administration of the solicitors' profession and made provision for a Lay Observer to examine the Law Society's handling of complaints against solicitors. *The Solicitors (Scotland) Act, 1976*, made similar changes in Scotland.

Litigants in Person (Costs and Expenses) Act, 1975. This enabled parties successfully conducting their own cases in civil proceedings to recover their costs and expenses from the other side.

The Legal Aid Act, 1979. This extended the 'green form' legal advice and assistance scheme to cover representation in inferior courts and tribunals.

The Contempt of Court Act, 1981. This implemented with modifications the Phillimore Report on Contempt of Court (Cmnd. 5794, 1974) and harmonised the law of England and Wales with the European Court's judgement in The *Sunday Times* (Thalidomide) case, 1973.

The Supreme Court Act 1981. This consolidated and significantly updated the legislation relating to the Supreme Court, superseding the Act of 1925 (see above).

Courts and Legal Services Act, 1990. This laid down a framework to give some solicitors rights of audience in the higher courts, removed the bar on solicitors becoming High Court judges, and allowed lawyers to take on cases on a 'no win, no fee' basis. It also removed the upper limit on the jurisdiction of the County Court in most cases.

SOURCES. – R.M. Jackson, *The Machinery of Justice in England* (8th edition, Ed. J.R. Spencer, 1989); D. Pannick, *Judges* (1987); J. Griffith, *The Politics of the Judiciary* (4th ed., 1991); M. Berlins and C. Dyer, *The Law Machine* (3rd ed., 1989).

Cases of Political Significance

The number of lawsuits that have had major domestic political implications is not great. Most of the celebrated ones have involved trade unions and are listed on pp. 356–8. Successful election petitions are listed on p. 238. Although the European Court of Justice is dealt with more fully on p. 476, two of the most significant rulings are included here. But these cases also seem to have left a significant mark on the political scene.

Bowles v. Bank of England [1913] 1 Ch.57 (Ch. D.). Collecting new taxes in advance of the Finance Act violates the Bill of Rights. This case led to the passage of the *Provisional Collection of Taxes Act, 1913.*

Viscountess Rhondda's Claim [1922] A.C. 339. The Sex Disqualification (Removal) Act 1919 did not entitle a peeress in her own right to sit in the House of Lords.

Vauxhall Estates Ltd v. Liverpool Corporation [1932] 1 K.B.733. Parliament cannot bind its successors as to the subject matter of legislation.

Liversidge v. Anderson [1942] A.C. 206 (H.L.). A Court of law may not inquire into whether a Minister has 'reasonable grounds' for exercising a statutory discretion.

Duncan v. Cammell Laird & Co. Ltd. [1942] A.C.624 (H.L.). The Crown may withhold documents or refuse questioning if a minister certifies that the answer would be injurious to the public interest.

R. v. Tronoh Mines Ltd. [1952] I All E.R., 697. Election expenditure has to be declared only if it is specifically directed to secure the election of a particular candidate.

MacCormick v. Lord Advocate ('The Royal Numeral Case') [1953] S.L.T. 225. A Scottish case laying down that the unlimited sovereignty of Parliament does not apply to Scotland.

Re Parliamentary Privilege Act, 1770 [1958] A.C. 331 (P.C.) (Strauss Case). Not every communication between an M.P. and a Minister is protected by parliamentary privilege.

Costa v. Enel [1964] CML Rep 425. Community law prevails over all existing inconsistent national law since 'the member States have restricted their sovereign rights, albeit within limited spheres'.

Burmah Oil Co. v. the Lord Advocate [1965] A.C. 75 (H.L.). Government held liable to compensate firm ordered to destroy its property to impede the advance of the enemy in wartime. (Reversed by the War Damage Act, 1965.)

Conway v. Rimmer [1968] A.C. 910 (H.L.). This judgement supersedes and amplifies Liversidge v. Anderson (above). The courts have a residuary power to inspect documents privately to determine whether the public interest in suppressing them outweighs the interests of parties, and of the public in the unfettered administration of justice.

Padfeld v. Minister of Agriculture [1968] A.C. 997 (H.L.). Where a statute confers a discretion on a minister it is beyond his power to exercise it in such a way as to frustrate the policy of Parliament, as interpreted by the court.

John v. Rees [1969] 2 W.L.R. 1294. Chairman may not adjourn meeting without consent of majority present, majority entitled to carry on and elect a new Chairman; Constituency Labour Parties not allowed to disaffiliate from the national Labour Party; a group of members may be suspended by the National Executive Committee only if natural justice is complied with by giving them an opportunity to put their case; all persons entitled to attend a meeting must be summoned or the meeting is improperly constituted and hence invalid. (The case concerned D. Donnelly and the Pembroke Constituency Labour Party.)

Anisminic Ltd. v. Foreign Compensation Commission [1969] 2 A.C. 147 (H.L.). A clause in a statute ousting the jurisdiction of the court to review administrative decisions will not be recognised and such decisions are a nullity ab initio.

The Hauptzollamt Hamburg Case [1970] CMLR 141. If Community law occupies a certain field in a matter within Community competence, the European Court of Justice does not recognise the right of Parliaments to pass any law on the matter, unless to implement this law.

McWhirter v. A.G. [1972] CMLR 882. The court will review the scope, but not the exercise, of the Crown's prerogative.

Attorney-General v. Jonathan Cape Ltd. [1976] Q.B. 752 (The Crossman Diaries case). The courts have power to prevent publication of Cabinet material in circumstances where such publication would be both a breach of confidence and a threat to the maintenance of the doctrine of collective responsibility. (In this instance injunctions were refused owing to the considerable time which had elapsed since the events described in the Diaries.)

Gouriet v. Post Office Union [1977] 3 All E.R. 70 (H.L.). The Attorney-General is not obliged to bring an action to prevent a breach of the law when required to by a member of the general public, as distinct from someone materially damaged by the breach. Neither is an injunction or declaration available without the Attorney-General's consent; and he need give no reasons for his decision. (The case concerned the blacking of mail to South Africa.)

Laker Airways v. Dept. of Trade [1977] Q.B. 643. Ministerial guidance, albeit approved by Parliament, is ultra vires if it conflicts with express policy objectives contained in an Act. (The case concerned the proposal for 'Skytrain' cheap flights to America.)

Sec. of State for Education v. Tameside Met B/C [1977] A.C. 1014 (H.L.). Where a statute gives a minister certain powers if he is satisfied that a local authority is acting unreasonably he may exercise them only if no reasonable authority would have done what was done, and never simply because he disagrees with the local authority's policy. (This case concerned the Tameside council's response to the Government's policy on comprehensive schools.)

Lewis v. Heffer [1978] T.L.R. 25 Jan 1978. In confirming a series of High Court judgements, arising from disputes in the Newham North-East Labour Party, the Court of Appeal ruled that the National Executive Committee of the Labour Party had the power to suspend the constituency party and, in general, argued that the courts should only be used as a very last resort in factional party controversies.

Mead v. Haringey [1979]. All E. R. 1016 A. C.   The Court of Appeal held that it was argu-able that a local authority might be in breach of its statutory duty to provide for children's education when it failed to do so by reason of the industrial action of School caretakers.

Duport Steels Ltd. v. Sirs [1980] 1 All E. R. 529.   In the course of a pay dispute with the British Steel Corporation, the trade unions involved took secondary industrial action against private steel firms in the hope of causing a total shutdown of the industry. The Court of Appeal granted injunctions to the private steel companies, but the House of Lords reversed the decision, holding that the secondary action was 'in furtherance of a trade dispute' within the meaning of the Trade Union and Labour Relations Act, 1974. The Thatcher Government subsequently reversed the decision by legislation (see p. 313).

Williams v. Home Office [1981] 1 All E. R. 151.   Following the principles laid down in Conway v. Rimmer (above), the judge ordered the disclosure of internal Home Office documents relating to experimental control units, in an action brought against the depart-ment by a prisoner.

Harman v. Home Office [1982] 2 All E. R. 151.   A solicitor was given confidential policy documents by way of discovery in the course of a civil action brought against the Home Office, and undertook not to disclose them outside the course of the proceedings. The documents were read out in open court and the solicitor then showed them to a journal-ist. The House of Lords affirmed, by a 3:2 majority, the lower courts' finding that this amounted to contempt of court.

Norwich City Council v. Secretary of State for the Environment [1982] 1 All E. R. 737.   The Court of Appeal upheld the exercise of default powers by a minister against a local author-ity in circumstances where the minister adjudged the authority to have been dilatory in fulfilling statutory obligations to sell council houses to tenants.

O'Reilly v. Mackman [1982] 3 All E. R. 1182 (H.L.)   There is a fundamental distinction between private law and public law proceedings which cannot be evaded by seeking a private law remedy against a public authority in circumstances where a public law remedy is appropriate.

Bromley London Borough Council v. GLC [1983] A. C. 768 (H.L.).   The GLC 'Fares Fair' case. The Council acted *ultra vires* the Transport (London) Act, 1969, and in breach of its fiduciary duty towards ratepayers by its decision to cut fares by 25%.

Pickwell v. Camden Borough Council [1983] 1 All E. R. 602.   A local authority, respond-ing to a strike by its employees, agreed a pay settlement that turned out to be more gener-ous than the settlement agreed nationally. The Queen's Bench Divisional Court denied the district auditor's claim that the action of the council was ultra vires.

Air Canada v. Secretary of State for Trade [1983] 1 All E. R. 910.   Action brought by for-eign airlines disputing increases in fees at Heathrow Airport. The House of Lords declined to order disclosure of ministerial documents on the grounds that the plaintiffs had failed to show that the documents were likely to assist their case.

The Council of Civil Service Unions v. Minister for the Civil Service [1984] Industrial Cases Reports 1985, 15.   The House of Lords decided that the 'reasonable expectations' of the Civil Service unions to be consulted before the Government banned union member-ship at GCHQ were overridden by considerations of national security. However, their Lordships held, contrary to the Government's contentions, that ministerial actions based on the royal prerogative could, in principle, be reviewed by the courts.

Attorney General v. Guardian Newspapers Ltd [1987] 3 All E. R. 316; Attorney General v. Guardian Newspapers (no. 2) [1988] 3 All E. R. 545.   The House of Lords first upheld by a 3–2 majority the Attorney General's efforts to prevent publication of extracts from the book *Spycatcher* on the grounds that a member of the Security Service owed a lifelong duty of confidentiality to the Crown. In the second case they removed the ban on the grounds that the material was now in the public domain.

Brind v. Secretary of State for the Home Department [1991] 1 All E. R. 720. The House of Lords upheld the decision of the Home Secretary banning the direct broadcasting of words spoken in support of terrorist organisations (in effect banning interviews with Sinn Fein).

Barber v. Guardian Royal Exchange Insurance Group [1990] 2 All E. R. 660; E. C. J. C–262/88. The European Court of Justice ruled since occupational pensions constitute a form of pay, any unjustified discrimation in benefits paid under the scheme are illegal (with implications for different pension ages). The ruling was modified in the case of *Neath v. Hugh Sleeper Ltd E. C. J. C–152/1991,* which ruled that actuarial factors such as women's longer life expectancy could be taken into account.

Factortame Ltd v. Secretary of State for Transport [1991] E. C. J. C–213/89. The European Court of Justice ruled in a case concerning a Spanish fishing firm that where a British Act of Parliament conflicts with European legislation the Act of Parliament is not enforceable in the courts.

Principal Judges

Lord Chancellor
(See p. 52)

Vice Chancellor

1971	Sir J. Pennycuik	1985	Sir N. Browne-Wilkinson
1974	Sir A. Plowman	1991	Sir D. Nicholls
1976	Sir R. Megarry	1994	Sir R. Scott

Master of the Rolls

1897	Sir N. Lindley (Ld)	1923	Sir E. Pollock
1900	Sir R. Webster		(Ld Hanworth)
	(Ld Alverstone)	1935	Ld Wright
1900	Sir A. Smith	1937	Sir W. Greene (Ld)
1901	Sir R. Collins	1949	Sir R. Evenshed
1907	Sir H. Cozens-Hardy (Ld)	1962	Ld Denning
1918	Sir C. Eady	1982	Sir J. Donaldson (Ld)
1919	Ld Sterndale	1992	Sir T. Bingham

President of the Probate, Divorce and Admiralty Division
(since 1971 the Family Division)

1892	Sir F. Jeune	1933	Sir B. Merriman (Ld)
1905	Sir G. Barnes	1962	Sir J. Simon
1909	Sir J. Bigham	1971	Sir G. Baker
1910	Sir S. Evans	1979	Sir J. Arnold
1918	Ld Sterndale	1988	Sir S. Brown
1919	Sir H. Duke (Ld Merrivale)		

Lord Chief Justice

1894	Ld Russell of Killowen	1946	Ld Goddard
1900	Ld Alverstone	1958	Ld Parker of Waddington
1913	Ld Reading (Vt) (E)	1971	Ld Widgery
1921	Ld Trevethin	1980	Ld Lane
1922	Ld Hewart	1992	Ld Taylor of Gosforth
1940	Vt Caldecote		

Lord Chief Justice of Ireland

1889	Ld O'Brien	1917	Sir J. Campbell
1914	R. Cherry	1918–24	T. Molony

Lord Chief Justice of Northern Ireland

1921	(Sir) D. Henry	1937	(Sir) J. Andrews	1971	Sir R. Lowry (Ld)
1925	(Sir) W. Moore	1951	Ld MacDermott	1988	Sir B. Hutton

Lord President of the Court of Session

1899	Ld Kinross	1920	Ld Clyde	1954	Ld Clyde
1905	Ld Dunedin	1935	Ld Normand	1974	G. Emslie (Ld)
1913	Ld Strathclyde	1947	Ld Cooper	1989	Ld Hope

Lord Justice Clerk

1888	Ld Kingsburgh	1933	Ld Aitchison	1962	Ld Grant
1915	Ld Dickson	1941	Ld Cooper	1972	Ld Wheatley
1922	Ld Alness	1947	Ld Thomson	1985	Ld Ross

Lords of Appeal in Ordinary

1887–1910	Ld Macnaghten	1954–1960	Ld Somervell of Harrow
1894–1907	Ld Davey	1957–1962	Ld Denning
1899–1909	Ld Robertson	1959–1963	Ld Jenkins
1899–1905	Ld Lindley	1960–1973	Ld Morris of Borth-y-Gest
1905–1928	Ld Atkinson	1960–1971	Ld Hodson
1907–1910	Ld Collins	1961–1971	Ld Guest
1909–1929	Ld Shaw	1961–1964	Ld Devlin
1910–1912	Ld Robson	1962–1969	Ld Pearce
1912–1921	Ld Moulton	1962–1965	Ld Evershed
1913–1918	Ld Parker	1963–1971	Ld Upjohn
1913–1930	Ld Sumner (Vt)	1963–1971	Ld Donovan
1913–1932	Ld Dunedin (Vt)	1964–1982	Ld Wilberforce
1918–1922	Vt Cave	1965–1974	Ld Pearson
1921–1929	Ld Carson	1968–1985	Ld Diplock
1923–1937	Ld Blanesburgh	1969–1980	Vt Dilhorne
1928–1944	Ld Atkin	1971–1977	Ld Cross of Chelsea
1929–1935	Ld Tomlin	1971–1977	Ld Simon of Glaisdale
1929–1946	Ld Russell of Killowen	1971–1977	Ld Kilbrandon
1929–1948	Ld Thankerton	1972–1980	Ld Salmon
1930–1939 / 1941–1947	Ld Macmillan	1974–1981	Ld Edmund-Davies
		1975–1985	Ld Fraser of Tullybelton
1932–1935 / 1937–1947	Ld Wright	1975–1982	Ld Russell of Killowen
		1977–	Ld Keith of Kinkel
1935–1938 / 1939–1941	Ld Maugham (Vt)	1977–1986	Ld Scarman
		1979–1980	Ld Lane
1935–1938	Ld Roche	1980–1986	Ld Roskill
1938–1944	Ld Romer	1980–1992	Ld Bridge of Harwich
1938–1954	Ld Porter	1981–1991	Ld Brandon of Oakbrook
1944–1951 / 1954–1962	Ld Simonds (Vt)	1982–1986	Ld Brightman
		1982–	Ld Templeman
1944–1946	Ld Goddard	1985–1993	Ld Griffiths
1946–1949	Ld Uthwatt	1985–1987	Ld Mackay of Clashfern
1946–1949	Ld du Parcq	1986–1993	Ld Ackner
1947–1951	Ld MacDermott	1986–	Ld Goff of Chieveley
1947–1953	Ld Normand	1986–1992	Lord Oliver of Aylmerton
1947–1957	Ld Oaksey	1988–	Ld Jauncey of Tullichettle
1947–1959	Ld Morton of Henryton	1988–	Ld Lowry
1948–1975	Ld Reid	1991–	Ld Browne-Wilkinson
1949–1950	Ld Greene	1992–	Ld Mustill
1949–1964	Ld Radcliffe	1992–	Ld Slynn of Hadley
1950–1961	Ld Tucker	1992–	Ld Woolf
1951–1954	Ld Asquith of Bishopstone	1993–	Ld Lloyd
1951–1960	Ld Cohen	1994–	Ld Nolan
1953–1961	Ld Keith of Avonholm	1994–	Ld Nicholls

Any peers of Parliament as are holding or have held, high judicial office are also entitled to take part in cases before the House of Lords.

JUDGES

Lords Justices of Appeal

1892–1900	Sir A. Levin Smith	1960–1961	Sir P. Devlin
1894–1901	Sir J. Rigby	1960–1965	Sir G. Upjohn
1897–1901	Sir R. Collins	1960–1963	Sir T. Donovan
1897–1914	Sir R. Williams	1961–1969	Sir H. Danckwerts
1899–1906	Sir R. Romer	1961–1974	Sir W. Davies
1900–1906	Sir J. Stirling	1961–1968	Sir K. Diplock
1901–1906	Sir J. Mathew	1962–1975	Sir C. Russell
1901–1907	Sir H. Cozens-Hardy	1964–1972	Sir C. Salmon
1906–1912	Sir J. Moulton	1965–1972	Sir E. Winn
1906–1913	Sir G. Farwell	1966–1974	Sir E. Davies
1906–1915	Sir H. Buckley	1966–1971	Sir E. Sachs
1907–1915	Sir W. Kennedy	1968–1971	Sir J. Widgery
1912–1913	Sir J. Hamilton	1968–1971	Sir F. Atkinson
1913–1918	Sir C. Eady	1968–1974	Sir H. Phillimore
1913–1916	Sir W. Phillimore	1968–1973	Sir S. Karminski
1914–1919	Sir W. Pickford	1969–1983	Sir J. Megaw
1915–1927	Sir J. Bankes	1970–1983	Sir D. Buckley
1915–1926	Sir T. Warrington	1970–1977	Sir D. Cairns
1916–1937	Sir T. Scrutton	1971–1978	Sir B. Stamp
1918–1919	Sir H. Duke	1971–1985	Sir J. Stephenson
1919–1928	Sir J. Atkin	1971–1980	Sir A. Orr
1919–1923	Sir R Younger	1971–1980	Sir E. Roskill
1923–1928	Sir C Sargant	1972–1986	Sir F. Lawton
1926–1934	Sir P Lawrence	1973–1977	Sir L. Scarman
1927–1938	Sir F Greer	1973–1976	Sir A. James
1928–1929	Sir J. Sankey	1974–1983	Sir R. Ormrod
1928–1929	F. Russell	1974–1983	Sir P. Browne
1929–1940	Sir H. Slesser	1974–1979	Sir G. Lane
1929–1938	Sir M. Romer	1975–1980	Sir W. Goff
1934–1935	Sir F. Maugham	1975–1980	Sir N. Bridge
1934–1935	Sir A. Roche	1975–1982	Sir S. Shaw
1935–1937	Sir W. Greene	1976–1984	Sir G. Waller
1935–1948	Sir L. Scott	1976–1985	Sir R. Cumming-Bruce
1937–1946	Sir F. MacKinnon	1977–1985	Sir E. Eveleigh
1938–1942	Sir A. Clauson	1978–1981	Sir H. Brandon
1938–1945	Vt Finlay	1978–1982	Sir S. Templeman
1938–1944	Sir F. Luxmoore	1979–1982	Sir J. Donaldson
1938–1944	Sir R. Goddard	1979–1982	Sir J. Brightman
1938–1946	Sir H. du Parcq	1980–1986	Sir D. Ackner
1944–1947	Sir G. Lawrence	1980–1984	Sir R. Dunn
1944–1947	Sir F. Morton	1980–1986	Sir P. Oliver
1945–1950	Sir F. Tucker	1980–1993	Sir T. Watkins
1945–1951	Sir A. Bucknill	1980–1989	Sir P. O'Connor
1946–1954	Sir D. Somervell	1980–1985	Sir H. Griffiths
1946–1951	Sir L. Cohen	1981–1992	Sir M. Fox
1946–1951	Sir C. Asquith	1981–1989	Sir M. Kerr
1947–1948	Sir F. Wrottesley	1982–1989	Sir J. May
1947–1949	Sir R. Evershed	1982–1991	Sir C. Slade
1948–1957	Sir I. Singleton	1982–1993	Sir F. Purchas
1948–1957	Sir A. Denning	1982–1986	Sir R. Goff
1949–1959	Sir D. Jenkins	1982–1994	Sir B. Dillon
1950–1957	Sir N. Birkett	1983–1988	Sir S. Brown
1951–1960	Sir F. Hodson	1983–1992	Sir R. Parker
1951–1960	Sir J. Morris	1983–1985	Sir N. Browne-Wilkinson
1951–1960	Sir C. Romer	1984–1989	Sir D. Croom-Johnson
1954–1958	Sir H. Parker	1984–1993	Sir A. Lloyd
1957–1968	Sir F. Sellers	1985–1992	Sir M. Mustill
1957–1963	Sir B. Ormerod	1985–	Sir B. Neill
1957–1962	Sir H. Pearce	1985–	Sir I. Glidewell
1958–1968	Sir H. Willmer	1985–	Sir M. Nourse
1959–1970	Sir C. Harman	1985–	Sir A. Balcombe

Lords Justices of Appeal (cont.)

1985–	Sir R. Gibson	1991–	Sir R. Scott
1986–1991	Sir D. Nicholls	1992–	Sir J. Steyn
1986–1992	Sir T. Bingham	1992–	Sir P. Kennedy
1986–1992	Sir J. Stocker	1992–	Sir L. Hoffman
1986–1992	Sir H. Woolf	1992–	Sir D. Hirst
1987–	Sir P. Russell	1992–	Sir Simon Brown
1988–1992	Sir P. Taylor	1992–	Sir A. Evans
1988–	Dame E. Butler-Sloss	1992–	Sir C. Rose
1988–	Sir M. Stuart-Smith	1993–	Sir J. Waite
1988–	Sir C. Staughton	1993–	Sir J. Roch
1988–	Sir M. Mann	1993–	Sir P. Gibson
1989–	Sir D. Farquharson	1993–	Sir J. Hobhouse
1989–	Sir A. McCowan	1993–	Sir D. Henry
1989–	Sir R. Beldam	1994–	Sir M. Saville
1990–	Sir A. Leggatt	1994–	Sir S. Thomas
1991–1994	Sir M. Nolan	1994	Sir A. Morritt

The Lord High Chancellor (President), the Lord Chief Justice, the Master of the Rolls, and the President of the Family Division serve *ex officio* on the Court of Appeal.

SOURCES. – *The Law List, 1900-; Who Was Who 1900-,* and *Who's Who; Whitaker's Almanack 1900–.*

Other Legal and Law Enforcement Officials

Law Commission
Chairman

1965	Sir L. Scarman
1973	Sir S. Cooke
1978	Sir M. Kerr
1981	Sir R. Gibson
1985	Sir R. Beldam
1990	Sir P. Gibson
1993	Sir H. Brooke

Police Complaints Board
Chairman

1977	Ld Plowden
1981	Sir C. Philips

(Police Complaints Authority)

1985	Sir C. Clothier
1989	F. Petre
1992	Sir L. Peach

Director of Public Prosecutions

1894	(H. Cuffe) E of Desart
1909	Sir C. Mathews
1920	Sir A. Bodkin
1930	Sir E. Atkinson
1944	Sir T Mathew
1964	(Sir) N. Skelhorn
1978	(Sir) T. Hetherington
1987	A. Green
1992	Mrs B. Mills

Serious Fraud Office, 1988–
Director

1988	Sir J. Wood
1990	Mrs B. Mills
1992	G. Staple

Monopolies and Restrictive Practices Commission
Chairman

1948	Sir A. Carter
1954	Sir D. Cairns

(Monopolies Commission)

1956	R. Levy
1965	(Sir) A. Roskill

(Monopolies and Mergers Commission)

1973	Sir A. Roskill
1975	(Sir) J. Le Quesne
1988	Sir S. Lipworth
1993	G. Odgers

Commissioner of Metropolitan Police

1890	Sir E. Bradford
1903	Sir E. Henry
1918	Sir N. Macready
1920	Sir W. Horwood
1928	Vt Byng
1931	Ld Trenchard
1935	Sir P. Game
1945	Sir H. Scott
1953	Sir J. Nott-Bower
1958	Sir J Simpson
1968	Sir J. Waldron
1972	(Sir) R. Mark
1977	(Sir) D. McNee
1982	Sir K. Newman
1987	(Sir) P. Imbert
1993	(Sir) P. Condon

Criminal Injuries Compensation Board 1964– *Chairman*		*Clerk of the Crown in Chancery*[1]	
1964	(Sir) W. Carter	1885	(Sir) K. Mackenzie
1975	M. Ogden	1915	(Sir) C. Schuster
1989	Ld Carlisle of Bucklow	1944	(Sir) A. Napier
		1954	(Sir) G. Coldstream
Procurator General and Treasury Solicitor		1968	(Sir) D. Dobson
		1977	(Sir) W. Bourne
1894	H. Cuffe (E of Desart)	1982	(Sir) D. Oulton
1909	(Sir) J. Mellor	1989	(Sir) T. Legg
1923	C. Lawrence		
1926	(Sir) M. Gwyer		
1934	Sir T. Barnes		
1953	Sir H. Kent		
1964	(Sir) H. Druitt		
1971	Sir H. Ware		
1975	(Sir) B. Hall		
1980	Sir M. Kerry		
1984	J. Bailey		
1988	J. Nursaw		
1992	G. Hooker		

[1] Full title, Permanent Secretary to the Chancellor and Clerk of the Crown in Chancery. See also p. 282.

Intelligence Services

MI5 (the Security Service) and MI6 (the Secret Intelligence Service) can trace their origins back to 1909, and the establishment of the Secret Service Bureau with domestic and foreign intelligence arms. In 1916 the internal arm, known as M.O. 5, was reorganised within the the Military Intelligence Directorate, and became known as MI5. The Secret Intelligence Service was given the acronym MI 1 (c) in 1916, but by the 1920s had become known as MI6. In 1989 MI5 was put on a statutory footing by the *Security Service Act*. In 1994 MI6 was put on a similar statutory footing by the *Intelligence Services Act*, which also established a joint committee of both houses to bring the intelligence services under parliamentary scrutiny for the first time.

Security Service (MI5) *Director General*		Secret Intelligence Service (MI6) *Director General*	
1909	(Sir) V. Kell	1909	(Sir) M. Smith Cumming
1940	Sir D. Petrie	1923	H. Sinclair
1946	(Sir) D. White	1939	(Sir) S. Menzies
1956	(Sir) R. Hollis	1952	Sir J. Sinclair
1965	(Sir) M. Furnival Jones	1956	Sir D. White
1972	(Sir) M. Hanley	1968	(Sir) J. Rennie
1979	Sir H. Smith	1973	(Sir) M. Oldfield
1981	(Sir) J. Jones	1978	(Sir) A. Franks
1985	Sir A. Duff	1981	(Sir) C. Figurres
1988	Sir P. Walker	1985	(Sir) C. Curwen
1992	Mrs S. Rimington	1989	(Sir) C. McColl
		1994	D. Spedding

SOURCES. – N. West, *A Matter of Trust: MI5 1945–72* (1983). N. West, *The Friends: Britain's Post-war Secret Intelligence Operations* (1988).

Security Commission

The Security Commission was set up by Sir A. Douglas-Home in Jan 1964. In a statement to the House of Commons (HC Deb vol 687, col 1271) he set out terms of reference 'If so requested by the Prime Minister, to investigate and report upon the circumstances in which a breach of security is known to have occurred in the public service, and upon any related failure of departmental security arrangements or neglect of duty; and in the light of any such investigation, to advise whether any change in security arrangements is necessary or desirable'. There were minor amendments to these terms of reference in 1965 and 1969 to take account of difficulties investigating matters which were before the courts. Its role was redefined under the Security Service Act, 1989.

Security Commission 1964–

Chairman

1964	Sir R. Winn
1971	Ld Diplock
1982	Ld Bridge of Harwich
1985	Ld Griffiths
1992	Sir A. Lloyd (Ld)

Judicial and Criminal Statistics

Number of Judges

(England and Wales)

Year	Lords of Appeal Lord Justices & ex officio judges	High Court Judges	County Court Judges
1910	12	24	57
1920	14	24	54
1930	15	26	57
1940	18	29	59
1950	20	35	60
1960	24	57	75
1970	26	68	103
1980	31	75	333
1990	40	83	420

SOURCES. – *Criminal Statistics, Civil Judicial Statistics.*

Volume of Civil Proceedings

Appellate Courts

	Privy Council	House of Lords	Court of Appeal	High Court
1938	107	43	574	263
1958	44	52	668	315
1968	37	52	948	776
1978	52	83	1,401	831
1988	61	90	1,645	2,151
1992	63	73	1,651	3,570

SOURCE. – *Civil Judicial Statistics.*

Civil Proceedings Commenced

	Chancery	Queen's Bench	County Court
1938	9,826		1,212,253
1958	10,071	89,284	1,300,942
1968	21,461	167,447	1,481,416
1978	13,813	151,003	1,467,545
1988	27,054	235,721	2,285,125
1992	47,597	270,305	3,741,804

SOURCE. – *Civil Judicial Statistics.*

The Growth of Judicial Review

Applications for leave to apply for judicial review of administrative action

Year	No.	Year	No.	Year	No.
1968	87	1977	376	1986	816
1969	184	1978	340	1987	1,529
1970	396	1979	410	1988	1,229
1971	227	1980	491	1989	1,580
1972	180	1981	533	1990	2,129
1973	140	1982	685	1991	2,089
1974	160	1983	850	1992	2,439
1975	270	1984	915	1993	2,886
1976	290	1985	1,169		

SOURCE. – *Civil Judicial Statistics.*

Criminal Statistics: England and Wales

Higher Courts All Ages

	Total	No. for trial Male	Female	No. found Guilty[b]	Death[l]	Custody[c]	Probation	Fine	Nom. pen.[d]	Other[a]
1900	10,149	8,928	1,219	7,975	0.3	90.5	–	1.1	8.1	2.2
1910	13,680	12,522	1,157	11,337	0.2	83.6	5.2	0.6	10.2	0.2
1920	9,130	8,141	989	7,225	0.5	76.5	8.1	0.8	13.4	0.7
1930	8,384	7,781	601	6,921	0.2	71.4	11.3	1.6	15.0	0.5
1938	10,003	9,322	681	8,612	0.3	62.4	19.2	1.3	16.0	0.8
1950	18,935	17,990	945	17,149	0.2	62.6	17.2	6.6	13.2	0.2
1960	30,591	29,462	1,129	27,830	0.1	53.8	22.5	13.8	9.3	0.6
1970	44,134	41,691	2,443	35,709	–	54.3[m]	10.7	13.9	3.5	2.7
1980	73,892	66,410	7,482	59,008	–	46.2[m]	6.2	14.6	5.7	8.6
1990	101,900	89,300	8,600	92,900	–	45.6[m]	10.4	9.4	5.2	13.2

For Notes see p. 319.

Summary Courts: Indictable Offences

	Adults[fg]		Sentences as a percentage of those found guilty				Juveniles[k]	
	No. proceeded against	No. found guilty or charge proved[b]	Custody[c]	Probation	Fine	Other[e]	No. proceeded against	No. found guilty or charge proved[b]
1900[h]	43,479	30,736	47.1	14.0	26.7	12.8	n.a.	n.a.
1910	40,434	36,094	47.5	11.3	22.1	19.1	12,275	10,786
1920	37,107	32,942	31.7	11.3	38.6	28.4	14,380	12,919
1930	43,464	38,709	25.6	21.1	28.3	25.0	12,198	11,137
1938	46,014	41,976	22.0	22.2	28.9	25.9	29,388	27,875
1950	61,701	57,102	18.5	11.9	48.8	20.8	43,823	41,910
1960	84,527	79,538	13.4	12.5	56.1	18.0	58,350	56,114
1970	227,072	201,017	8.2/9.9[m]	9.5	60.1	12.3	63,531	71,860
1980[k]	407,363	306,183	7.0/6.5[m]	7.9	59.2	19.4	98,082	89,192
1990[k]	433,000	256,200	2.8/2.8[m]	9.5	49.8	35.1	36,000	n.a.

[a] Including the Central Criminal Court and the Crown Courts.
[b] Excluding those found guilty but insane or (since 1964) acquitted by reason of insanity.
[c] Including imprisonment, or committal to a reformatory, approved school, remand home, or (since 1952) detention centre, or (in the case of Assizes and Quarter Sessions) borstal training.
[d] Includes absolute and conditional discharge and binding over with recognances.
[e] Includes whipping (abolished 1948), fit person orders (introduced 1934), as well as days in prison cells, admission to mental institutions, and other miscellaneous and numerically unimportant methods of disposal.
[f] Until 1932, persons aged 16 or older were tried and sentenced as adults (although in some cases sent to establishments reserved for younger offenders, e.g. borstals). From 1933, however, 'adult' means a person aged 17 or older.
[g] Includes small numbers of juveniles tried jointly with adults.
[h] The published tables for 1900 unfortunately do not distinguish adults from juveniles, although one table shows that those found guilty include 9,450 persons under 16. Consequently the figures showing the disposal of adult offenders in 1900 include unknown numbers of juveniles. Almost certainly most of the 3,218 who were whipped in 1900 were boys.
[i] From 1908 there were in effect 'juvenile courts', although lacking many special features which were introduced later.
[j] The death penalty was in practice, confined to murder throughout this period (except for war-time executions for treason or similar offences). 'Infanticides' were excluded from 'murder' from 1922, and from 1957 murders in certain circumstances became 'non-capital': the death penalty for murder was completely suspended from 1965. A large proportion of the murderers who were sentenced to death were subsequently reprieved.
[k] Figures for 1980 and 1990 are based on indictable and summary offences as redefined by the *Criminal Law Act, 1977*, and on a new counting procedure.
[l] Not including suspended sentences – 1970–14.9; 1980–18.6; 1990–15.9
[m] The second figure is for suspended prison sentences.

SOURCES. – N.D. Walker in A.H. Halsey (ed.) *Trends in British Society since 1900* (2nd ed., 1988), *Criminal Statistics*.

Recorded Crime, 1900–1990

Year	Murder, Other killing	Wounding	Robbery	Burglary	Rape	Theft
1900	312	1,212	256	3,812	231	63,604
1910	291	1,294	198	6,499	146	76,044
1920	313	791	235	6,863	130	77,417
1930	300	1,443	217	11,169	89	110,159
1950	315	5,177	1,021	29,834	314	334,222
1960	282	14,142	2,014	46,591	515	537,003
1970	393	38,735	6,273	190,597	884	952,666
1980	620	95,044	15,006	294,375	1,225	1,463,469
1990	664	177,200	36,200	529,200	3,400	2,374,400

SOURCE. – *Criminal Statistics*.

Traffic Offences

Highway / Motoring Offences[a]
(all courts)

1900	No. found guilty	As % of all found guilty of non-indictable offences
1900	2,548	0.4
1910	55,633	9.1
1920	157,875	24.9
1930	267,616	42.8
1938	475,124	60.3
1950	357,932	52.6
1960	622,551	60.1
1970	1,014,793	60.6
1980	1,309,992	74.9
1990	1,501,100	n.a.

[a] From 1900 to 1938 'highway offences' have been taken to include all offences under the Highway Acts together with offences against regulations etc., dealing with stage coaches, trams, trolleybuses and so on. For 1950 they have been taken to include offences numbered 123–38, 173 and 180 in the Home Office code, and for 1960 onwards offences numbered 124, 130, 135–8, 173 and 180.

Prison Sentences and Prison Populations, 1901–

England and Wales

	Prisoners received under sentence[a]	Daily average prison population[b]		
		Male	Female	Total
1901	149,397	14,459	2,976	17,435
1910	179,951	19,333	2,685	22,018
1920	35,439	8,279	1,404	9,683
1930	38,832	10,561	785	11,346
1940	24,870	8,443	934	9,377
1950	33,875	19,367	1,107	20,474
1960	42,810	26,198	901	27,099
1970	62,020	38,040	988	39,028
1980	75,896	42,180	1,580	43,760
1990	67,510	44,039	1,597	45,636

[a] This column excludes those sentenced by courts martial and those under sentence of death or recalled under licence; but includes sentences of penal servitude (which were abolished in 1948), borstal training and committals to detention centres from 1952. Civil prisoners are not included as they are not 'under sentence'.
[b] Figures are for daily average population of penal establishments in prisons, borstals and (from 1952) detention centres.

SOURCE. – *Annual Reports* of the Prison Commissioners (changed in 1964 to the Prison Department of the Home Office.) *Prison Statistics.*

Parole Board, 1967–

Chairman (see p. 306)

1967	Ld Hunt
1974	Sir L. Petch
1979	Ld Harris of Greenwich
1982	Ld Windlesham
1988	Vt Colville of Culross
1992	Ld Belstead

Police Force

1900	England & Wales		Scotland		Ireland (N.I. only from 1930)	
	No. of forces	No. of police	No. of forces	No. of police	No. of forces	No. of police
1900	179	41,900	64	4,900	1	12,300
1910	190	49,600	63	5,600	1	11,900
1920	191	56,500	59	6,500	1	11,600
1930	183	58,000	49	6,600	1	2,800
1940	183	57,300	48	6,800	1	2,900
1950	129	62,600	33	7,200	1	2,800
1960	125	72,300	33	8,700	1	2,900
1970	47	92,700	20	11,200	1	3,800
1980	43	115,900	8	13,200	1	6,900
1990	43	125,646	8	13,981	1	8,243

SOURCES. – *The War against Crime in England and Wales 1959–64,* Cmnd. 2296/1964; C. Reith, *A Short History of the British Police* (1948); J.M. Hart, *The British Police* (1951); B. Whitaker, *The Police* (1965); M. Banton, *The Police and the Community* (1964); Sir F. Newsam, *The Home Office* (2nd Ed. 1955); *Royal Commission on Police Powers and Procedure* Cmd. 3297/1929; *Royal Commission on the Police,* Cmnd. 1728/1962; G. Marshall, *Police and Government* (1965). R. Reiner, *The Politics of the Police* (2nd ed. 1992). Annual Reports of H.M. Inspectors of Constabulary for England and Wales. Further information from Scottish Office and Northern Ireland Office.

IX

SOCIAL CONDITIONS

Population

U.K. POPULATION 1901–
(thousands)

1901	41,459	1921	47,123	1941	48,216	1961	52,709	1981	56,352
1902	41,893	1922	44,372	1942	48,400	1962	53,274	1982	56,306
1903	42,237	1923	44,597	1943	48,789	1963	53,553	1983	56,347
1904	42,611	1924	44,916	1944	49,016	1964	53,885	1984	56,460
1905	42,981	1925	45,060	1945	49,182	1965	54,218	1985	56,618
1906	43,361	1926	45,233	1946	49,217	1966	54,500	1986	56,763
1907	43,738	1927	45,389	1941	49,571	1967	54,800	1987	56,930
1908	41,124	1928	45,578	1948	50,065	1968	55,049	1988	57,065
1909	41,519	1929	45,672	1949	50,363	1969	55,263	1989	57,236
1910	44,916	1930	45,866	1950	50,616	1970	55,421	1990	57,411
1911	45,222	1931	46,038	1951	50,225	1971	55,515	1991	57,649
1911	45,136	1932	46,335	1952	50,430	1972	55,781	1992	57,998
1913	45,648	1933	46,520	1953	50,593	1973	55,913		
1914	46,048	1934	46,666	1954	50,765	1974	55,922		
1915	44,333	1935	46,869	1955	50,946	1975	55,900		
1916	43,710	1936	47,081	1956	51,184	1976	55,886		
1917	43,280	1937	47,289	1957	51,430	1977	55,852		
1918	43,116	1938	47,494	1958	51,652	1978	55,822		
1919	44,599	1939	47,762	1959	51,956	1979	55,881		
1920	46,472	1940	48,226	1960	52,372	1980	55,945		

Census figures for 1901, 1911, 1921, 1931, 1951, 1961, 1971, 1981 and 1991. Figures for other years are mid-year estimates. Figures are for other years are mid-year estimates. Figures for 1901–21 are inclusive of S. Ireland. Figures for 1915–20 and for 1940–50 relate to civil population only.

SOURCES. - *Annual Reports of the Registrar-General for England and Wales, Scotland and Northern Ireland; Annual Abstract of Statistics; Monthly Digest of Statistics.*

INTERCENSAL CHANGES IN POPULATION
(thousands)

	Population at beginning of period	Total Increase	Average Annual Change		
			Excess of births over deaths	Net Civilian Migration	Other Adjustments
1901–1911	38,237	385	467	−82	
1911–1921	42,082	195	286	−92	
1921–1931	44,027	201	268	−67	
1931–1951	46,038	212	190	+22	
1951–1961	50,290	252	246	−7	+13
1961–1971	52,807	280	324	−32	−12
1971–1981	55,928	42	69	−44	+17
1981–1991	56,352	130	103	+21	+6

Census enumerated population up to 1951; mid-year estimates of home population from 1951 onwards.

SOURCE. - *Annual Abstract of Statistics.*

POPULATION OF COMPONENTS OF U.K.
(thousands)

	Area (sq.km.)	1911	1931	1951	1961	1971	1981	1991
England: Standard Regions								
North	19,349	2,815	3,038	3,137	3,250	3,296	3,104	3,109
Yorks & Humb	14,196	3,877	4,285	4,522	4,635	4,799	4,860	4,797
East Midlands	12,179	2,263	2,531	2,893	3,100	3,390	3,819	3,919
East Anglia	12,565	1,192	1,232	1,382	1,470	1,669	1,872	2,018
South East	27,408	11,744	13,539	15,127	16,271	17,230	16,796	16,794
South West	23,660	2,687	2,794	3,229	3,411	3,781	4,349	4,600
West Midlands	13,013	3,277	3,743	4,423	4,758	5,110	5,148	5,089
North West	7,993	5,796	6,197	6,447	6,567	6,743	6,414	6,147
Wales	20,763	2,421	2,593	2,599	2,664	2,731	2,792	2,812
Scotland	77,179	4,760	4,843	5,097	5,179	5,229	5,131	4,962
N. Ireland	13,570	1,251	1,280	1,371	1,425	1,536	1,482	1,578
Metropolitan counties, etc.								
Greater London	1,578	7,160	8,110	8,197	7,992	7,452	6,696	6,394
West Midlands	899	1,780	2,143	2,547	2,732	2,793	2,646	2,511
West Yorkshire	2,034	1,852	1,939	1,985	2,005	2,067	2,037	1,992
Greater Manch.	1,286	2,638	2,727	2,716	2,720	2,729	2,595	2,455
Merseyside	655	1,378	1,587	1,663	1,718	1,657	1,513	1,380
Tyne and Wear	540	1,105	1,201	1,201	1,244	1,212	1,143	1,090
Strathclyde	13,502	2,270	2,400	2,524	2,584	2,575	2,404	2,219

SOURCE. – *Annual Abstract of Statistics.*

BIRTH RATES, DEATH RATES, AND MARRIAGES IN THE U.K.
(per thousand population)

	Total Births per 1000 Population	Infant Mortality (under one year) per 1000 live births	Total Deaths per 1000 Population	Total Marriages per 1000 Population
1900	28.2	142.0	18.4	15.1
1910	25.0	110.0	14.0	14.3
1920	25.4	82.0	12.9	19.4
1930	16.8	67.0	11.7	15.5
1940	14.6	61.0	14.4	22.2
1950	16.2	31.2	11.8	16.1
1960	17.5	22.4	11.5	15.0
1970	16.3	18.5	11.8	17.0
1980	13.2	12.2	11.6	14.9
1990	13.9	7.9	11.1	13.1

Figures for 1900, 1910 and 1920 (except for infant mortality) include Southern Ireland. Death rate in 1940 based on civil deaths and population only.

SOURCE: *Annual Abstract of Statistics, OPCS Marriage and Divorce Statistics, Birth Statistics.*

AGE DISTRIBUTION OF THE POPULATION OF THE U.K.
(Percentages)

Age Group	1901	1911	1921[a]	1931	1939	1951	1961	1971	1981	1991
Under 10	22.2	21.0	18.2	16.1	14.1	16.0	15.1	16.6	12.6	13.0
10–19	20.3	19.1	19.0	16.8	16.3	12.9	14.9	14.6	16.3	12.6
20–29	18.3	17.3	16.2	17.1	15.6	14.2	12.7	14.3	14.1	15.4
30–39	13.9	15.1	14.5	14.5	16.0	14.5	13.7	11.6	13.8	13.9
40–49	10.5	11.4	13.1	12.9	13.1	14.8	13.5	12.3	11.3	13.4
50–59	7.3	7.9	9.6	11.1	11.3	11.9	13.2	11.9	11.7	10.6
60–69	4.7	5.1	6.0	7.3	8.5	8.9	9.4	10.6	10.2	10.1
70–79	2.2	2.5	2.7	3.4	4.1	5.3	5.6	5.9	7.2	7.3
80+	0.6	0.6	0.7	0.8	1.0	1.5	1.9	2.2	2.7	3.7
Total	100.0	100.0	100.0	100.0	100.0	100.0	100.0	100.0	100.0	100.0

[a] Percentages for 1921 are for England, Wales and Scotland only.

SOURCES. – Census figures except for 1939, which is mid-year estimate. Registrars-General of England and Wales, and Scotland, *Censuses of Population*, and the *Annual Abstract of Statistics*.

EXPECTATION OF LIFE
England and Wales
(Average future expected lifetime at birth)

Years	Male	Female		Years	Male	Female
1900–02	46	50		1950–52	66	72
1910–12	52	55		1960–62	68	74
1920–22	56	60		1969–71	69	75
1930–32	59	63		1978–80	70	77
1938	61	66		1988–90	73	79

SOURCES. – *Annual Reports of Registrars-General for England and Wales*, and the *Government Actuary's Department, Annual Abstract of Statistics*.

MAIN CAUSE OF DEATH
England and Wales
(000s)

	1900	1910	1920	1930	1940	1950	1960	1970	1980	1990
Total deaths	588	483	466	455	572	510	526	575	581	565
Due to:										
Tuberculosis	61	51	43	36	27	16	3	2	1	1
Cancer	27	35	44	57	69	83	96	114	131	145
Vascular lesions of the nervous system[a]	41	30	49	41	52	65	76	79	71	67
Heart diseases	n.a.	49	53	90	136	146	153	179	192	193
Pneumonia	44	40	37	28	29	18	24	43	54	27
Bronchitis	54	34	38	19	46	28	26	29	19	7
Violent causes	20	19	17	22	47[b]	19	23	23	20	18

[a] All diseases of the nervous system, 1900–30, cerebrovascular disease (including strokes), 1970 onwards.
[b] Including 22,000 deaths of civilians due to operations of war.

SOURCES. – *Annual Reports and Statistical Reviews of the Registrars-General for England and Wales; Annual Abstract of Statistics*.

POPULATION
AVERAGE AGE AT FIRST MARRIAGE

England and Wales

Year	Bachelors	Spinsters	Year	Bachelors	Spinsters
1901–05	26.9	25.4	1951–55	26.5	24.2
1911–15	27.5	25.8	1961–65	25.5	22.9
1921–25	27.5	25.6	1970	24.4	22.7
1931–35	27.4	25.5	1980	25.3	23.0
1941–45	26.8	24.6	1990	27.2	25.2

SOURCES. – *Annual Reports of the Registrars-General for England Wales;* figures since 1970 are from *OPCS Marriage and Divorce Statistics.*

DIVORCES
(Great Britain)

Decrees made absolute		Decrees made absolute	
1910	801	1960	25,672
1920	3,747	1970	62,010
1930	3,944	1980	158,829
1940	8,396	1990	165,658
1950	32,516		

SOURCE. – *Annual Reports of the Registrars-General for England, Wales and Scotland. OPCS Marriage and Divorce Statistics.*

The law on divorce was significantly relaxed by the *Matrimonial Causes Act*s of 1937, 1950 and 1967, and by the *Divorce Reform Act, 1969.*

NET EMIGRATION FROM GREAT BRITAIN AND IRELAND

Commonwealth citizens travelling by the long sea routes to non-European countries, 1900–59; all routes 1970–

	1900	1910	1920	1931	1938	1946	1950	1959	1970	1980	1990
All	71,188	241,164	199,047	−39,056	−6,467	103,504	54,153	28,400	92,700	55,400	−36,000
U.S.A.	47,978	75,021	60,067	−10,385	−1,432	45,151	8,541	4,500	4,500	11,800	13,000
Canada	7,803	115,955	94,496	−10,464	−3,974	43,414	6,464	−400	12,700	14,300	2,500
Australasia	6,259	34,657	28,405	−8,760	2,204	8,443	54,581	28,800	59,300	28,000	300
S. Africa	7,417	8,314	7,844	−1,263	2,037	2,242	1,912	−800	19,400	7,600	2,700

Southern Ireland excluded from 1938 onwards.

SOURCES. – 1900–1950: *External Migration 1815–1950*, N.H. Carrier and J.R. Jeffrey, *Studies on Medical and Population Subjects No. 6*, General Register Office (1953); figures from 1959 on are from the *Annual Abstract of Statistics.*

PEOPLE BORN OVERSEAS[a]

Great Britain

Birthplace	1931 000s	1931 % of pop.	1951 000s	1951 % of pop.	1961 000s	1961 % of pop	1971 000s	1971 % of pop.	1981 000s	1981 % of pop.	1991 % of 000s pop.	
Foreign countries[b]	347	0.8	722	1.5	842	1.6	984	1.7	1,274	2.3	1,288	2.3
Canada, Australia, New Zealand	75	0.2	99	0.2	110	0.2	136	0.4	152	0.3	177	0.3
Other Commonwealth	137	0.3	218	0.4	541	1.1	1,140	2.1	1,325	2.5	1,688	3.1
Irish Republic[c]	362	0.8	532	1.1	709	1.4	718	1.3	606	1.1	593	1.1
Total born overseas	921	2.0	1,571	3.2	2,202	4.3	2,976	5.5	3,360	6.2	3,775	6.9

[a] Persons resident in Great Britain at the time of the Census who had been born outside the United Kingdom; including United Kingdom citizens born overseas but excluding short-term visitors.
[b] Including South Africa.
[c] Including Ireland (part not stated).

SOURCES. – *Social Trends* 1972. Census for 1981 and 1991.

NATURALISATION

Total certificates granted by the Home Department or oaths taken in period

1901–10	7,997	1941–50	51,132	1981–90	23,108
1911–20	11,293	1951–60	44,977		
1921–30	9,849	1961–70	40,252		
1931–40	15,454	1971–80	28,717		

SOURCES. – 1900–1950: *External Migration 1815–1950*, N.H. Carrier and J.R. Jeffrey, *Studies on Medical and Population Subjects No. 6*, General Register Office (1953); and *Whitaker's Almanack*.

COMMONWEALTH IMMIGRATION

Commonwealth immigration came under systematic control under the *Commonwealth Immigrants Act, 1962*. This Act was strengthened by the *Commonwealth Immigrants Act, 1968* and largely replaced by the *Immigration Act, 1971*. The *British Nationality Act, 1981*, completely revised the definition of British nationality, introducing three classes of citizenship with the right to live in Britain largely restricted to those with a British grandparent.

MAIN SOURCES OF IMMIGRATION INTO THE UNITED KINGDOM 1956–62

Year	West Indians	Indians	Pakistanis (Bangladeshis)
1956	26,400	5,600	2,100
1957	22,500	6,000	5,200
1958	16,500	6,200	4,700
1959	20,400	2,900	900
1960	52,700	5,900	2,500
1961	61,600	23,750	25,100
1962	35,000	22,100	24,900

ACCEPTANCES FOR SETTLEMENT IN THE UNITED KINGDOM 1963–

	Foreign	Old Commonwealth	New Commonwealth	Total
1963	15,349	3,735	56,071	75,155
1964	19,211	3,060	52,840	75,111
1965	20,615	3,454	53,898	77,967
1966	18,948	4,214	48,104	71,266
1967	18,346	4,335	60,633	83,314
1968	20,093	3,761	60,620	84,474
1969	21,862	3,581	44,503	69,946
1970	20,917	4,497	37,893	63,307
1971	23,467	4,577	44,261	72,305
1972	19,681	3,989	68,519	92,189
1973	21,118	3,099	32,247	55,162
1974	26,800	3,948	42,531	68,878
1975	31,477	5,387	53,265	82,405
1976	31,464	5,967	55,013	80,745
1977	31,917	6,572	44,155	69,313
1978	34,364	7,453	30,514	72,331
1979	36,600	6,960	26,110	69,670
1980	38,410	6,900	24,610	69,920
1981	31,280	5,380	22,400	59,060
1982	26,080	5,150	22,650	53,880
1983	20,120	5,800	27,550	53,460
1984	18,720	7,440	24,800	50,950
1985	20,150	8,160	27,050	55,360
1986	17,740	6,560	22,520	46,820
1987	18,230	6,900	20,850	45,980
1988	19,100	7,380	22,800	49,280
1989	18,330	7,870	22,860	49,060
1990	20,700	6,030	25,660	52,400
1991	22,850	3,120	27,930	53,900

This table covers work permit holders admitted for more than one year. Voucher holders were admitted for settlement on arrival. Work permit holders may qualify for settlement after 4 years in approved employment.

SOURCE. – *Control of Immigration: Statistics.*

COMMONWEALTH IMMIGRANTS IN THE U.K.

Defined as those living in households whose head was born in the relevant area, according to the 1961, 1971, and 1981 Censuses.

Year	W.Indians	Bangladeshis, Indians and Pakistanis	Australians	Others in British Territories	Total
1961	173,076	115,982[a]	23,390[a]	285,962[b]	596,755
1971	302,970	462,125	32,400	496,410[b]	1,293,905
1981	295,179	628,589	61,916	280,466	1,666,120
1991	433,641	1,295,810	n.a.	n.a.	2,635,411[c]

[a] Persons born in these countries but British by birth or descent have been deducted for 1961.
[b] The largest contributors to this total are Cypriots, New Zealanders, Maltese, Canadians and South Africans.
[c] New Commonwealth only.

The 1991 Census was the first to ask respondents to categorize themselves in terms of colour; previous census questions about the birthplace of the head of household would now be less informative about race, since so many non-white people living in Britain are now second- or third-generation. This was the breakdown in 1991:

Black (Caribbean)	Black (Other)	Indian	Pakistani	Bangladeshi	Other non-white
499,964	290,763	840,255	476,555	162,835	644,678[1]

[1] of which the largest components are 'other Asian' and Chinese.

According to the 1991 Census, 837,464 people resident in Great Britain gave their place of birth as the Irish Republic, or simply Ireland.

SOURCE. – *Census*. See also Radical Statistics Race Group, *Britain's Black Population* (2nd ed., 1987).

Race Relations Legislation

Race Relations Act, 1965, set up the Race Relations Board to receive complaints of unlawful discrimination and to investigate them.

Race Relations Act, 1968, enlarged the Race Relations Board and extended its scope. It also set up the Community Relations Commission to establish harmonious race relations.

Race Relations Act, 1976, made discrimination unlawful in employment, training, education and in the provision of goods and services and made it an offence to stir up racial hatred. It extended discrimination to include indirect discrimination and discrimination by way of victimisation. It replaced the Race Relations and the Community Relations Commission by the Commission for Racial Equality.

Race Relations Board 1966–77

Chairman

17 Feb 66	M. Bonham Carter
1 Jan 71	Sir R. Wilson (Acting)
1 Oct 71	Sir G. Wilson

Community Relations Commission 1968–77

Chairman

17 Feb 68	F. Cousins
1 Jan 71	M. Bonham Carter
1 Mar 77	Ld Pitt

Commission for Racial Equality 1977–

Chairman

13 Jun 77	(Sir) D. Lane
1 Apr 82	P. Newsam
1 Feb 88	(Sir) M. Day
19 Apr 93	H. Ouseley

Housing

(a) Major Housing Acts

Housing and Town Planning Act, 1909. This amended the law relating to the housing of the working classes, and provided for town-planning schemes. It also provided for the establishment of public health and housing committees of county councils.

Housing Acts, 1919, 1923, and 1924. these Acts provided for varying subsidies to encourage the building of new houses for the working classes.

Housing Act, 1930. This Act extended subsidies and provided wider powers for slum clearance.

Housing (Financial Provisions) Act, 1933. This reduced the general subsidies, but presented subsidies for slum clearance.

Housing (Financial Provisions) Act, 1938. This Act regulated subsidies to housing.

Housing (Financial Provisions) Act, 1958. This Act provided grants for improvements to private houses.

House Purchase and Housing Act, 1959. This extended grants for improvements.

Housing Act, 1961. Laid down regulations for landlords leasing houses for less than 7 years to keep the structure, exterior, installations, etc., of the house in repair and proper working order.

Housing Act, 1964. Set up the Housing Corporation to assist Housing Associations to provide housing accommodation and conferred powers and duties on local authorities with regard to housing improvements.

Building Control Act, 1966. Controlled and regulated building and constructional work.

Housing Subsidies Act, 1967. Provided for financial assistance towards the provision, acquisition or improvement of dwellings and the provision of hostels.

Housing Act, 1969. Made further provision for grants by local authorities towards the cost of improvements and conversions; made provision as to houses in multiple occupation; altered the legal standard of fitness for human habitation; and amended the law relating to long tenancies.

Housing Act, 1971. Increased the amount of financial assistance available for housing subsidies in development or intermediate areas.

Housing Finance Act, 1972. Increased financial help to local authorities needing to clear slums, provided national rent rebate scheme for Council tenants and rent loans for private tenants of unfurnished accommodation, and based rent of public sector and private unfurnished accommodation on the 'fair rent' principle.

Housing Act, 1974. Extended functions of Housing Corporation, provided for the registration and giving of assistance to housing associations, introduced new powers for declaration of Housing Action Areas and made provisions for higher renovation grants.

Housing Finance (Special Provisions) Act, 1975. Prevented surcharges arising out of the Housing Finance Act 1972 (relating to refusal by Clay Cross Councillors to charge proper rents under the Act) and substituted other means of making up losses.

Housing Rents and Subsidies Act, 1975. Repealed provisions of Housing Finance Act 1972 relating to fixing of public sector rents; introduced new subsidies for local authorities and new town corporations and made certain housing associations eligible for housing association grant.

Housing (Homeless Persons) Act, 1977. Local authorities put under a duty to house homeless persons in 'priority need' unless the homelessness could be shown to be intentional.

Home Purchase Assistance and Housing Corporation Guarantee Act, 1978. Set up the 'Homeloan' scheme (to provide a reduction in the cost of house purchase for first-time purchasers).

Housing Act, 1980. Provided a new and much more flexible subsidy system; repealed the 'no-profit rule'; local authority tenants of 3 years' standing or more to have the right to buy their houses at discounts ranging from 33% to 50%.

Social Security and Housing Benefits Acts, 1982. Replaced rent rebates, rent allowances, rate rebates, and the 'rent' element in tenants' Supplementary Benefit by Housing Benefit.

Housing and Building Control Act, 1984. Maximum discount on 'right-to-buy' purchase increased to 60%; exercise of right to buy simplified and extended; new system of building control.

Housing Act, 1988. This established new forms of rented tenure – assured tenancies and assured shorthold tenancies. It provided for Housing Action Trusts in designated areas to take over run-down local authority housing, and pass on the ownership and management to new private sector landlords – subject to a ballot by local residents.

Local Government Act, 1988. This prevented local authorities from spending revenue from general funds on housing – effectively 'ring-fencing' the housing revenue account.

Local Government and Housing Act, 1989. This amended the rules for local government housing revenue, placed strict limits on housing improvement grants and extended the 'Right to Buy' to occupants of houses and flats designed for the elderly and disabled.

Leasehold Reform, Housing and Urban Development Act, 1993. This proposed new rights for leaseholders of flats and houses to buy the freehold of their buildings. It also established an Urban Regeneration Agency to promote the redevelopment of derelict land in cities.

(b) Major Rent and Mortgage Interest Restriction Acts

Increase of Rent and Mortgage Interest (Restrictions) Acts, 1915. These acts established a limit to the rent of small houses, and protected tenants from eviction.

Rent Acts, 1919–39. These altered the exact limits on rent.

Rent and Mortgage Interest (Restriction) Act, 1939. This extended rent restriction and security of tenure to houses which had become decontrolled and to new houses.

Furnished Houses (Rent Control) Act, 1947. This Act created rent tribunals to fix the prices of furnished lettings.

Landlord and Tenant Rent Control Act, 1949. Rent tribunals were authorised to determine 'reasonable' rents, on the application of the tenants, who could also apply for the recovery of premiums. The Act applied to unfurnished houses and flats.

Housing Repairs and Rents Act, 1954. This Act authorised landlords to increase rents where sufficient repairs to their property had been carried out. Rent could also be increased to cover the increase in cost since 1939 of other services provided by the landlord.

Rent Act, 1957. This decontrolled many houses in 1958 and permitted substantial increases on controlled rents.

Protection from Eviction Act, 1964. This prevented a landlord of residential premises from recovering possession without an order of the county court. (Consolidated in *Protection from Eviction Act, 1977.*)

Rent Act, 1965. Provided for the registration of rents, introduced controls, and provided security of tenure subject to certain conditions. A landlord cannot enforce a right to possession against a tenant without a court order.

Leasehold Reform Act, 1967. Enabled tenants of houses held on long leases at low rents to acquire the freehold or an extended lease.

Rent Act, 1968. Consolidated the statute law relating to protected or statutory tenancies, rents under regulated or controlled tenancies and furnished tenancies.

Rent Act, 1974. Extended indefinite security of tenure and access to rent tribunals to furnished tenants. Landlords resident on the premises exempt from provisions of the Act. It brought most residential furnished tenancies of absentee landlords into the full protection of the Rent Acts.

Finance Act, 1974. This introduced a 25,000 ceiling on the sum on which mortgage payers could get tax relief.

Rent (Agriculture) Act, 1976. Afforded security of tenure for agricultural workers housed by their employers and imposed duties on housing authorities in respect to agricultural workers.

Housing (Homeless Persons) Act, 1977. Made local authorities more fully responsible for providing accommodation for the homeless.

Rent Act, 1977. Consolidated law relating to control and regulation of rent, security of tenure, and powers and duties of Rent Officers, Rent Assessment Committees, and Rent Tribunals.

Housing Act, 1980. All remaining rent-controlled dwellings transferred to regulation. 'Shorthold' tenure introduced, with security of tenure for limited period only.

Finance Act, 1983. Raised the ceiling on mortgage interest tax relief from £25,000 to £30,000.

Housing Act, 1988. This abolished 'fair rent' assessment for new tenancies.

Finance Act, 1993. This further restricted mortgage interest tax relief by restricting it to 20% of the interest on the first £30,000.

Finance Act, 1994. This restricted mortgage interest tax relief to 15%.

Permanent Dwellings Completed

Great Britain: 1919–45; United Kingdom: 1945–

	Public Sector (000s)	Private Sector (000s)	Total (000s)		Public Sector (000s)	Private Sector (000s)	Total (000s)
1919/20	–	1	1	1947	148	41	189
1920/21	17	23	40	1948	217	34	251
1921/22	110	32	142	1949	177	28	205
1922/23	67	45	112	1950	175	30	205
1923/24	20	74	94	1951	176	25	202
1924/25	24	120	144	1952	212	37	248
1925/26	50	134	184	1953	262	65	327
1926/27	84	151	235	1954	262	92	354
1927/28	120	141	261	1955	208	116	324
1928/29	70	119	189	1956	181	126	308
1929/30	73	147	220	1957	179	129	308
1930/31	64	133	197	1958	148	130	278
1931/32	79	136	215	1959	128	153	282
1932/33	68	151	219	1960	133	171	304
1933/34	72	222	294	1961	122	181	303
1934/35	57	294	351	1962	135	178	314
1935/36	70	280	350	1963	130	178	308
1936/37	87	283	370	1964	162	221	383
1937/38	92	268	360	1965	174	217	391
1938/39	122	237	359	1966	187	209	396
1939/40	69	152	221	1967	211	204	415
1940/41	26	31	57	1968	200	226	426
1941/44[a]	8	3	11	1969	192	186	378
1945	11	1	12	1970	188	174	362
1946	109	31	140	1971	168	196	364

[a] Annual average

	Public Sector (000s)	Private Sector (000s)	Total (000s)		Public Sector (000s)	Private Sector (000s)	Total (000s)
1972	130	201	331	1982	54	129	183
1973	114	191	305	1983	56	153	209
1974	134	145	280	1984	55	166	221
1975	167	155	322	1985	44	163	208
1976	170	155	325	1986	39	178	216
1977	170	144	314	1987	35	191	226
1978	136	152	289	1988	35	207	242
1979	108	144	252	1989	34	187	221
1980	110	131	240	1990	35	163	198
1981	88	119	207	1991	31	153	185

NOTES. – From 1919/20 to 1944/45, the figures are combinations of England and Wales financial year figures and Scottish calendar year figures.

For 1946 onwards the figures are for the United Kingdom including Northern Ireland. 'Public sector' comprises local authorities, new towns, housing associations, and public bodies in their capacity as employers. Before 1945 the last two were included in the private sector.

SOURCES. – *Housing and Construction Statistics*; Department of the Environment.

Housing by Tenancy

Great Britain

	Owner Occupied %	Rented from Local Authority[a] %	Rented from Private Landlord %	Other[b] %	Total stock (millions)
1914	10[c]	–[d]		90	9.0
1938	25	10		65	12.7
1945	26	12	54	8	12.9
1951	29	18	45	8	13.9
1956	34	23	36	7	15.1
1960	42	26	26	6	16.2
1965	47	28	20	5	17.4
1970	50	30	15	5	18.7
1975	53	31	16		19.9
1980	55	32	13		21.0
1985	62	27	11		21.8
1990	67	22	11		22.9

[a] Includes New Towns.
[b] Includes dwellings rented with farm and business premises, or occupied by virtue of employment.
[c] Approximate only: true figure probably lies between 8% and 15%.
[d] Included under private landlord.

SOURCE. – *Housing and Construction Statistics*

Council House Sales

Under the *Housing Act, 1980,* tenants in local authority, new town and housing association properties were given the 'Right to Buy' their homes at substantial discounts:

Year	Sales Completed	Year	Sales Completed
1980	1,342	1987	108,033
1981	84,897	1988	167,609
1982	202,558	1989	185,791
1983	144,456	1990	132,437
1984	104,847	1991	76,993
1985	96,486	1992	65,148[1]
1986	93,162		

[1] Not including a small number of sales completed by Scottish housing associations.

SOURCES. – *Housing and Construction Statistics.*

Social Security

Old Age Pensions Act, 1908. This granted non-contributory pensions ranging from one to five shillings a week to be paid from national funds, subject to a means test, at the age of 70, where income was under £31 p.a.

National Insurance Act, 1911 (National Health Insurance, Pt. I). This was the first part of an act providing insurance against both ill-health and unemployment. The Act covered all those between the ages of 16 and 70 who were manual workers or earning not more than £160 p.a. (This income limit was raised in 1920 and 1942.) The self-employed, non-employed, and those already provided for by other health insurance schemes were not insurable under this Act. The scheme was administered through independent units, or 'approved societies'. Local insurance committees were set up. The insurance included benefits for sickness, maternity, and medical needs. A weekly contribution was made by the insured person, his employer, and the government. The basic weekly sickness benefit was 10s. for men, 7s. 6d. for women. It also set up general medical and pharmaceutical services.

Widows', Orphans' and Old Age Contributory Pensions Act, 1925. This provided for a contributory scheme, covering almost the same field as the national health insurance scheme. Pensions were payable to the widows of insured persons, and to insured persons and their wives over the age of 70. This age limit was reduced to 65 in 1928. The weekly rates were 10s. for widows, with additional allowances of 5s. for the first child and 3s. for each other child, 7s. 6d. for orphans and 10s. for old age pensioners.

Widows', Orphans' and Old Age Contributory Pensions Act, 1929. This Act provided a pension at age 55 for certain widows who could not satisfy the conditions of the 1925 Act.

Widows', Orphans' and Old Age Contributory Pensions (Voluntary Contributors) Act, 1937. This Act created a new scheme of voluntary insurance for old age, widows' and orphans' benefits open to certain persons who were not within the scope of the main scheme.

Old Age and Widows' Pensions Act, 1940. This reduced to 60 the age at which a woman who was herself insured or who was the wife of an insured man could become entitled to an old age pension. The Act also introduced supplementary pensions in cases of need for widow pensioners over the age of 60 and for old age pensioners. The Unemployment Assistance Board was renamed the Assistance Board and became responsible for payment of these supplementary pensions.

National Health Insurance, Contributory Pensions and Workmen's Compensation Act, 1941. This raised the income limit for compulsory insurance of non-manual workers for pensions purposes to £420 p.a.

Family Allowances Act, 1945. This granted a non-contributory allowance, to be paid to the mother, for each child other than the first. 1945–52 5s. per week; 1952–68 8s. per week; 1956–68 10s. per week for third and subsequent children; 1968 15s. (75p) per week for second, £1 per week for third and subsequent children.

National Health Service Act, 1946. By this Act, hospitals were transferred from local authorities and voluntary bodies and were to be administered by the Minister through regional hospital boards, general medical and dental services through executive councils, and other health services by county and county borough councils. Health centres were to be provided by local authorities for general, mental, dental, and pharmaceutical services, but few were built. Almost all services under the Act were to be free.

National Health Service (Amendment) Act, 1949, National Health Service Acts, 1951 and 1952, and National Health Service Contributions Acts, 1957–1958. These made modifications in the original scheme by imposing charges for certain parts of the scheme (prescriptions, dental treatment, etc.).

National Insurance Act, 1946. This Act provided a new scheme of insurance replacing the national health insurance and contributory pensions schemes with effect from 5 Jul 1948. All persons over school-leaving age, except certain married women, became compulsorily insurable. In addition to provisions for unemployment (see p. 000) benefits payable were retirement pension, widow's benefit, and death grant.

National Insurance Act, 1951. This Act introduced an allowance payable with widows' benefits for each dependent child in the family.

Family Allowances and National Insurance Act, 1956. Enabled allowances for dependent children to be paid in certain cases up to the age of 18; introduced new personal rate of widowed mother's allowance, reduced length of marriage condition for widow's pension, and introduced amendments to widows' pensions.

National Insurance Act, 1957. This introduced the child's special allowance for the children of divorced parents payable on the death of the father if he had been contributing towards their support and the mother had not remarried.

National Insurance Act, 1959. This introduced a state scheme of graduated pensions, requiring that both contributions and pensions should be graduated according to salary level.

Mental Health Act, 1959. The Board of Control was abolished and its functions passed to the new Mental Health Review Tribunals, local authorities, and the Minister of Health. The Act redefined the classifications of mental disorders, provided for further safeguards against improper detention, and extended the provisions for voluntary and informal treatment of patients.

Family Allowances and National Insurance Act, 1964. This increased from 18 to 19 the age limit up to which a person could be regarded as a child for the purposes of an increase of benefit or widowed mother's allowance.

Prescription Charges were ended in 1965. They were reimposed in 1968 with exemptions for some categories.

National Insurance Act, 1966. This extended the period of widow's allowance, introduced a scheme of earnings-related supplements to unemployment and sickness benefits and included a widow's supplementary allowance.

Ministry of Social Security Act, 1966. Repeated and amended much previous legislation. It provided for the abolition of the Ministry of Pensions and National Insurance and the National Assistance Board and the establishment of the Ministry of Social Security. The Act also provided for a scheme of supplementary benefits to replace the system of allowances which had previously been administered by the National Assistance Board. The benefits were paid as of right to those people whose incomes were below the levels set in the Act and not according to national insurance contribution records.

Chronically Sick and Disabled Persons Act, 1970. This placed more stringent obligations on local authorities to seek out and provide for the chronically sick and disabled.

National Insurance (Old Persons and Widows Pensions and Attendance Allowance) Act, 1970. Gave pensions to those of pensionable age in 1948. Reduced from 50 to 40 the qualifying age for widows' pensions.

Family Income Supplements Act, 1970. Created new benefit for families with small incomes.

Social Security Pensions Act, 1975. This provided for social security pensions and other related benefits to consist of a basic element and an additional component related to higher earnings and made various other provisions in relation to pensions. Made full National Insurance contributions obligatory for women except widows and women already on reduced rates.[1]

Child Benefits Act, 1975. Replaced family allowances with child benefit, and provided for an interim benefit for unmarried or separated parents with children.

Social Security Act, 1980. This ended discretion in supplementary benefits by introducing a detailed rule-based scheme. It also removed the obligation to uprate pensions in line with earnings.

Social Security (No. 2) Act, 1980. Phased out earnings-related supplements to unemployment and sickness benefits, and brought short-term benefits into tax.

Health Services Act, 1980. Made provision for increased access to Health Service facilities by private patients and made other alterations to the law regarding private health care.

Social Security and Housing Benefits Act, 1982. Made provision for the payment of statutory sick pay by the employers and amended rent and rate rebate procedure.

Social Security Act, 1986. This transformed supplementary benefit into income support, and family income supplement into family credit. It also restructured housing benefits, widows' benefits and the State Earnings Related Pension Scheme.

Social Security Act, 1988. This removed entitlement to Income Support from unemployed 16- and 17-year olds who refused to join a Youth Training Scheme. It also put the cold weather payment scheme on a statutory footing.

Social Security Act, 1989. This removed entitlement to benefit from claimants who were unable to satisfy officials they were genuinely seeking work, and from those who had been unemployed for three months and had turned down work on the grounds the pay was too low.

Social Security Act, 1990. This provided greater protection and right for members of occupational pension schemes. It also restructured disability benefits, increasing the scope of attendance allowance and severe disability allowance, but restricting payments under the industrial injuries scheme and earnings-related additions to invalidity benefits.

Statutory Sick Pay Act, 1991. This reduced the proportion of statutory sick pay recoverable by employers from the government.

On 1 Dec 93 the Social Security Secretary announced reforms of social security including a new job seekers' allowance which would replace unemployment benefit and income support from 1996. Pension ages would be equalised at 65, to be phased in between 2010 and 2020.

Statutory Sick Pay Act, 1994. This abolished the reimbursement of statutory sick pay by the government to all but the smallest employers.

---

[1] For further provisions see Women's Rights legislation below.

Old Age Pensions

Maximum rate for a single person

Jan 1909	5s.	14 Nov 1977	£17.50
Feb 1920	10s.	13 Nov 1978	£19.50
Oct 1946	26s.	12 Nov 1979	£23.30
Sep 1952	32s.6d.	24 Nov 1980	£27.15
Jan 1958	50s.	23 Nov 1981	£29.60
Apr 1961	57s.6d.	22 Nov 1982	£32.85
Mar 1963	67s.6d.	21 Nov 1983	£34.05
Mar 1965	81s.	26 Nov 1984	£35.80
Oct 1967	90s.	25 Nov 1985	£38.30
Nov 1969	100s.	28 Jul 1986	£38.70
Sep 1971	£6.00	6 Apr 1987	£39.50
Oct 1972	£6.75	11 Apr 1988	£41.15
Oct 1973	£7.35	10 Apr 1989	£43.60
Jul 1974	£10.00	9 Apr 1990	£46.90
Apr 1975	£11.60	8 Apr 1991	£52.00
Nov 1975	£13.30	6 Apr 1992	£54.15
15 Nov 1976	£15.30	4 Apr 1993	£57.60

In 1972 a £10 Christmas bonus for pensioners was instituted.

SOURCES. – Sir E. Wilson and G.S. Mackay, *Old Age Pensions* (1941); *Keesing's Contemporary Archives 1931–88*, and *Keesing's UK Record 1988-*; *Report on Social Insurance and Allied Services* (Beveridge), Cmd. 6404/1944, Appendix B, *National Superannuation and Social Insurance*, Cmnd. 3883/1969, and the Department of Social Security.

Women's Rights

Representation of the People Act, 1918. Gave women over 30 the right to vote.

Sex Disqualification (Removal) Act 1919. Abolished disqualification by sex or marriage for entry to the professions, universities, and the exercise of any public function.

Matrimonial Causes Act, 1923. Relieved a wife petitioner of necessity of proving cruelty, desertion etc. in addition to adultery as grounds for divorce. (Further acts in 1927 and 1950 extended grounds for divorce and codified the matrimonial law.)

Guardianship of Infants Act, 1924. Vested guardianship of infant children in the parents jointly. If parents disagreed either could apply to court, the Court's subsequent decision being guided solely by consideration of the infant's interest.

New English Law of Property, 1926. Provided that both married and single women may hold and dispose of their property, real and personal, on the same terms as a man.

Representation of the People Act, 1928. Gave women over 21 the right to vote.

Law Reform (Married Women and Tortfeasors) Act, 1935. Empowered a married woman to dispose by will of all her property as if she were single.

British Nationality of Women Act, 1948. Gave British women the right to retain British nationality on marriage to a foreigner, and ended right of alien women to acquire automatic British nationality when marrying.

Equal Pay Act, 1970. (See p. 355.)

Matrimonial Proceedings and Property Act, 1970. Empowered courts to order either spouse to make financial provision for the other spouse or a child of the family. Laid down that if either spouse had contributed money or money's worth to property during marriage, then a share in that property had been acquired.

Finance Act, 1971. Allowed husband's and wife's earnings to be taxed separately if they so applied.

Domicile and Matrimonial Proceedings Act, 1973. Allowed women to stay in the family home.

Matrimonial Causes Act, 1973. Gave effect to recommendations of the Law Commission on Matrimonial Proceedings, validity of marriage, nationality and maintenance. Gave British women married to foreigners the same right as men for their spouses to live in Britain.

Employment Protection Act, 1975. Made dismissal because of pregnancy unlawful, and made it obligatory for employers to offer a new contract when the pregnancy was over. Also made provisions for paid maternity leave.

Sex Discrimination Act, 1975. Equal Pay Act of 1970 amended and included in this Act. Together they outlawed discrimination on grounds of sex in all aspects of employment, education, provision of professional services, recreational facilities, banking, insurance and credit. Established Equal Opportunities Commission (see below).

Social Security Act, 1975. Set up a special maternity allowance fund, incorporated into Employment Protection Act, 1975, and included income supplements for divorced women.

Social Security Pensions Act, 1975. Stipulated that pension schemes must be open on an equal basis to women doing the same or broadly similar work as men. Abolished the 'half-test' by which women had to have twenty consecutive years in employment to qualify for a full state pension.

Equal Pay (Amendment) Act, 1984. Updated legislation in line with European law on equal pay for different work of equal value.

Sex Discrimination Act, 1986. This extended the provisions of the 1975 Sex Discrimination Act in line with European directives, and also removed some restrictions on women's hours of work.

Finance Act, 1988. Further amended tax law to remove disadvantage for married women by introducing independent taxation for all.

Employment Act, 1989. This removed further restrictions on women's conditions of employment, including the statutory bar on working in mines.

Trade Union Reform and Employment Rights Act, 1993. Introduced much stronger employment protection for pregnant women in line with European directives.

Equal Opportunities Commission, 1975–

Chairman

Dec 75	Betty Lockwood (Lady)
May 83	Lady Platt
May 88	Joanna Foster
Jun 93	Kamlesh Bahl

Maternity and Child Welfare

Midwives Act, 1902. This Act sought to improve the standards of midwifery. It only became fully operative in 1910. further Acts were passed in 1936 and 1951.

Notification of Births Act, 1908. This gave powers to local authorities to insist on compulsory notification of births.

Notification of Births Extension Act, 1915. This made notification universally compulsory.

Children Act, 1908. This Act consolidated the existing law and recognised the need for legal protection of children. It provided legislation covering negligence to children. Imprisonment of children was abolished, and remand homes were set up for children awaiting trial. This was to be only in special juvenile courts.

Education (Choice of Employment) Act, 1910. This empowered authorities to set up their own juvenile employment bureaux.

Maternity and Child Welfare Act, 1918. This empowered authorities to set up 'home help' schemes and clinics.

Children and Young Persons Act, 1933. This extended responsibility for children until the age of 17 and included a careful definition of the meaning of the need for care and protection. It established approved schools, and made detailed regulations about juvenile court procedure.

Children Act, 1948. This gave local authorities new responsibilities, with children's officers to administer the children's service (see Local Government section).

Children and Young Persons Act, 1963. This extended the power of local authorities to promote the welfare of children and dealt with children and young persons in need of supervision, ordered approved schools, employment of children and young persons (amended by *Children and Young Persons Act, 1969*).

Abortion Act, 1967. Made it legal for a registered medical practitioner to perform an abortion provided two registered practitioners are of the opinion termination is justifiable, either because continuance of the pregnancy would involve more risk to the life of the pregnant woman or injury to her physical or mental health or any existing children, than if the pregnancy were terminated, or because there would be a substantial risk that if the child were born it would be seriously physically or mentally handicapped.

Family Law Reform Act, 1969. This reduced the age of majority from 21 to 18. It also secured rights for illegitimate children.

Guardianship of Minors Act, 1971. Made some provision for equal rights for mothers and gave either spouse the right to appoint any person as guardian after his or her death.

Children Act, 1975. Gave new rights to children, foster-parents, local authorities and adoptive parents, and diminished rights of natural parents in care proceedings and adoption cases. Allowed adopted children over 18 access to information about their natural parents.

Children's Homes Act, 1982. Required children in the care of local authorities to be accommodated in registered and inspected homes.

Abortion (Amendment) Act, 1988. This reduced the time limit within which abortions had to be performed from 28 to 24 weeks.

Children Act, 1989. This put greater emphasis on nthe rights and wishes of children in cases of marriage break-up. It also made numerous changes to the law relating to adoption, and children's homes.

Child Support Act, 1991. Established a Child Support Agency to ensure that divorced and separated parents made financial contributions to the cost of raising the family, according to a formula laid down by Parliament rather than the courts.

Rates of Child Benefit

	First Child	Each other Child		First Child	Each other Child
5 Apr 77	£1.00	£1.50	25 Nov 85	£7.00	£7.00
3 Apr 78	£2.30	£2.30	28 Jul 86	£7.10	£7.10
13 Nov 78	£3.00	£3.00	6 Apr 87	£7.25	£7.25
2 Apr 79	£4.00	£4.00	8 Apr 91	£8.25	£7.25
24 Nov 80	£4.75	£4.75	7 Oct 91	£9.25	£7.50
23 Nov 81	£5.25	£5.25	6 Apr 92	£9.65	£7.80
22 Nov 82	£5.85	£5.85	5 Apr 93	£10.00	£8.10
21 Nov 83	£6.50	£6.50	5 Apr 94	£10.20	£8.25
26 Nov 84	£6.85	£6.85			

Legal Abortion, England and Wales
(residents only)

	Married	Single	Other[a]	Total
1968[b]	10,090	10,302	1,840	22,332
1969	22,979	22,287	4,563	49,829
1970	34,314	34,492	7,156	75,962
1971	41,536	44,302	8,732	94,570
1972	46,894	51,115	10,556	108,565
1973	46,766	52,899	10,903	110,568
1974	45,167	53,331	10,934	109,432
1975	43,322	52,423	10,903	106,648
1976	39,868	50,481	10,934	101,003
1977	39,445	51,604	11,188	102,237
1978	42,200	56,600	13,300	112,100
1979	42,800	61,700	14,500	119,000
1980	44,300	68,800	15,900	128,900
1981	42,400	70,000	16,100	128,600
1982	40,500	71,800	16,200	128,600
1983	38,400	73,200	15,400	127,200
1984	38,700	81,100	16,600	136,400
1985	37,700	87,200	16,200	141,100
1986	38,200	93,000	16,400	147,600
1987	38,200	100,700	17,300	156,200
1988	38,700	111,000	18,600	168,300
1989	38,100	113,000	19,300	170,500
1990	38,200	116,200	19,600	173,900
1991	37,800	110,900	18,700	167,400

[a] Widowed, divorced, separated, or women whose marital status was unknown.
[b] The 1968 figures are from 27 Apr when the Act came into effect.

SOURCE. – *Population Trends*

Education

Education Act, 1902. This abolished school boards, gave powers to local authorities to provide secondary education, and made provisions for rate aid to voluntary schools (see Local Government section).

Education (Provision of Meals) Act, 1906. By this Act cheap school meals for children attending public elementary schools were given statutory recognition. Local authorities were to use voluntary organisations, contributing only to the cost of administration. In 1914 half the cost of the meals was provided by the Exchequer.

Education (Administrative Provisions) Act, 1907. This provided for medical inspection for elementary schools. In 1912 the Board of Education made grants to Local Education Authorities to make the treatment of children possible.

Education Act, 1918. Compulsory attendance was made universal until the age of 14. Day continuation (part-time compulsory) education was introduced for children between school-leaving age and 18. This almost disappeared under the economies proposed by Geddes but was revived in 1944.

Free milk was supplied to children in need in 1921. In 1934 it was subsidised by the Milk Marketing Board. From 1946 to 1971 it was free to all.

Education Act, 1936. Provision was made for the school-leaving age to be raised to 15 in Sep 1939 but this was not implemented. In 1940–41, the school meal service was expanded and subsidised to meet war-time needs.

These provisions were continued after the war, by the *Education Act, 1944.*

Education Act, 1944. This Act changed the title of the President of the Board of Education to the Minister of Education. Primary and secondary education was divided at '11-plus', and secondary education was generally provided under this Act in three types of schools, grammar, technical, and modern. Some local authorities preferred to use their powers to amalgamate these into comprehensive schools. Provision was made for compulsory part-time education between the school-leaving age and, 18 in county colleges, but this was not implemented. The minimum school-leaving age was raised to 15 (in 1947) and provision was made for raising it to 16. Powers were granted under this Act, which led to a great expansion of technical colleges. No fees were to be charged in schools which were publicly provided or aided by grants from the local authority.

School-leaving Age. It was announced in 1964 that the school-leaving age would be raised to 16 in the educational year 1970–71. In 1968 this date was put back for four years. The change was eventually made in 1973.

Comprehensive Schools. In 1965 the Department of Education asked all local authorities to submit plans for reorganising secondary education on comprehensive lines, with a view to ending selection at 11-plus and the tripartite system. The policy of universal comprehensivisation was suspended in 1970 but revived in 1974 by Government Circular 4/74. In 1976 the Direct Grant system was phased out (119 of the 170 Direct Grant schools decided to become independent) and the Education Act, 1976, required Local Education Authorities to submit comprehensivisation proposals (7 had earlier refused. See the Tameside case, p. 310).

Nursery Schools. In 1972 the Department of Education (Cmnd 5174) accepted that within ten years it should provide nursery education for 90 per cent of 4-year-olds and 50 per cent of 3-year-olds.

Education Act, 1980. The Assisted Places Scheme was established to provide financial support for some students in independent education, and various other changes were made to increase parental choice and participation in the schooling of their children.

Education Reform Act, 1988. This introduced a National Curriculum to be followed by all pupils from the ages of 5 to 16. The governing bodies of all secondary schools and larger primary schools were given responsibility for their own budgets. All secondary schools as well as larger primary schools were given the right to apply for grant maintained status – 'opting out' of local education authority control, subject to a ballot by parents. Funding of higher education was transferred from local authorities to a Polytechnics and Colleges Funding Council. The University Grants Committee was replaced by a Universities Funding Council. The Act also abolished the Inner London Education Authority, vesting most of its responsibilities with the inner London boroughs.

Education (Student Loans) Act, 1990. This introduced 'top-up' loans for students in higher education as a partial replacement for maintenance grants.

Education (Schools) Act, 1992. This compelled schools and local education authorities to cooperate with the publication of information about exam results, including 'league tables'.

Further and Higher Education Act, 1992. This transferred further education colleges and sixth form colleges out of local authority control; they were to be funded instead by a new Further Education Funding Council. The Act also set up Higher Education Funding Councils for England and Wales, replacing the Universities Funding Council and the Polytechnics and Colleges Funding Council. Polytechnics were given the right to assume the title of university.

Education Act, 1993. This established a Funding Agency for schools which had opted out of local authority control. A machinery was established for dealing with 'failing' schools. The National Curriculum Council and the Schools Examination and Assessment Council were abolished and replaced by the School Curriculum and Assessment Authority.

Education Act, 1994. This restricted the role and funding of student unions and regulated teacher training.

SOURCES. – *Education of the Adolescent* (Hadow) (1926); *The Primary School* (Hadow) (1931); *Secondary Education* (Spens) (1938); *The School Curriculum* (Norwood) (1943); *Education Reconstruction* (Cmd. 6458/ 1942–3); *Public Schools* (Fleming) (1944); *Education from 15 to 18* (Crowther) (1959); *Half our Future* (Newsom) (1963); *Higher Education* (Robbins) (Cmnd. 2154/ 1963); *Primary Education* (Plowden) (1967). Since 1947 the Department of Education has published an *Annual Report* and *A Guide to the Educational Structure of England and Wales.* See also J. Vaizey and J. Sheehan, *Resources for Education* (1968); A.H. Halsey, A.F. Heath and J.M. Ridge, *Origins and Destinations* (1980); M. Scott, *Net Investment in Education in the United Kingdom,* in the Oxford Review of Education 1 (6): 21–30 (1980); K. Fogelman (ed.), *Growing Up in Britain: Papers from the National Child Development Study* (1983); Chapters on Schools and Higher Education in A.H. Halsey, *British Social Trends since 1900* (1988).

Pupils in Schools

England and Wales (000s)   (age 2–14)

	Public Elementary	Secondary Schools	Efficient Independent	Other Independent
1900	5,709	n.a.	n.a.	n.a.
1910	6,039	151	22	n.a.
1920	5,878	340	46	n.a.
1930	4,936	411	82	n.a.
	Primary & Secondary Maintained	Direct Grant		
1950	5,710	95	204	n.a.
1960	6,924	111	294	203
1970	7,960	143	304	110
	State Nursery and Primary	State Secondary	Special Schools	Independent Schools
1970	5,918	3,554	103	606
1980	5,143	4,606	147	629
1990	4,873	3,473	113	604

SOURCES. – G. Walford (ed.), *British Public Schools: Policy and Practice* (1984); *Annual Abstract of Statistics; Education Statistics.*

Percentage of Various Ages Receiving Full-Time Education

Great Britain 1870–1970; UK 1970–

	10-year olds	14-year olds	16-year olds	19-year olds
1870	4	2	1	1
1902	100	9	2	1
1938	100	38	4	2
1962	100	100	15	7
1970	100	100	20	13
1980	100	100	27	12[1]
1990	100	100	43	18[1]

[1] Figures for 1980 and 1990 cover 19 and 20 year olds and are not therefore strictly comparable.

SOURCES. – *Report on Higher Education* (Robbins), Cmnd. 2154/1963; *Education Statistics*.

Students in Full-Time Higher Education

Great Britain

	University	Teacher Training	Further Education[a]
1900/1	20,000	5,000	–
1924/5	42,000	16,000	3,000
1938/9	50,000	13,000	6,000
1954/5	82,000	28,000	12,000
1962/3	118,000	55,000	43,000
1970/1	235,000	124,000	98,000
1980/1[b]	307,000	228,000	
1990/1[b]	370,000	378,000	

[a] Advanced Courses only.
[b] Includes N. Ireland.

SOURCES. – *Report on Higher Education* (Robbins), Cmnd. 2154/1963; *Education Statistics*.

Expenditure on Education (U.K.)

(current prices)

	Net public current expenditure on education (£m)	(as % of National Income)	Private expenditure on education (£m)	Current expenditure of universities (£m)	% of university expenditure from parliamentary grants
1919/20	65.1	(1.2)	8.4	4.4	22
1929/30	92.8	(2.3)	8.3	6.6	29
1939/40	107.5	(2.0)	10.0	8.2	30
1949/50	272.0	(2.7)	27.8	23.0	56
1954/5	410.6	(2.8)	30.9	33.9	65
1964/5	1,114.9	(4.1)	60.0	123.9	72
1970/71	1,644.3	(5.2)	n.a.	317.7	72
1980/81	12,940.8	(5.5)	n.a.	1381.5[a]	76[b]
1990/91	26,677.8	(4.8)	n.a.	2476.0[a]	76

[a] Excluding Oxford and Cambridge college accounts.
[b] The fall is due to changes in the payment of tuition fees from Parliament to local authorities.

SOURCES. – 1919–1965 J. Vaizey and J. Sheehan, *Resources for Education* (1968); *Annual Abstract of Statistics* and *Education Statistics*.

Public Library Service

Year	Books in stock (000s)	Book issues (000s)	Total Expenditure (£000)
1906	4,450	26,255	286
1911	10,874	54,256	805
1924	14,784	85,668	1,398
1939	32,549	247,335	3,178
1953	56,056	359,700	11,183
1962	77,200	460,504	24,431
1971	114,472	628,000	73,436
1980–1	108,400	551,000	263,600
1989–90	109,500	475,000	525,300

SOURCE. – A.H. Halsey (ed.), *Trends in British Society* (1988). *Report by the Minister for the Arts on Library and Information Matters*, HC35. Annual CIPFA Reports.

Pressure Groups

There are a large number of groups in the social field representing causes or offering voluntary services. These may seek to influence public policy by direct contact with Parliament and Government Departments or indirectly through the publication of information and research or appeals to public opinion. Some notable examples of pressure groups are listed below. They include some registered charities which have also sought to direct public funds and attention to the causes they represent (e.g. the National Council for One-Parent Families); some which were founded to bring about a change in the law (e.g. Committee for Homosexual Law Reform)[1]; some which were formed to safeguard and promote the interests of a minority racial group (e.g. the Indian Workers' Association) or of a profession or trade (e.g. the Road Haulage Association); and some whose main target has been industry rather than government (e.g. the Campaign for Real Ale). Most are financed by voluntary contributions but some receive grants from central or local government and may, indeed, be directly involved in the implementation of public policy.

Abortion and Birth Control

Workers' Birth Control Group, 1924. Together with four other bodies became National Birth Control Council, 1930. Changed name to National Birth Control Association in 1931. Changed name to Family Planning Association, 1939–
Abortion Law Reform Association, 1967–
Society for the Protection of Unborn Children, 1967–
Life, 1970–

Animal Welfare

Society for the Prevention of Cruelty to Animals, 1824. Changed name to Royal Society for the Prevention of Cruelty to Animals, 1840–
League Against Cruel Sports, 1924–
National Anti-Vivisection Society, 1975–

[1] *Sexual Offences Act, 1967*, amended the law in England and Wales relating to homosexual acts and permitted homosexual acts in private by consenting adults over the age of 21.

Constitutional Questions

National Council for Civil Liberties, 1934–. Adopted short title Liberty, 1988.
Freedom Association, 1975–
Campaign for Press and Broadcasting Freedom, 1979–
Campaign for Freedom of Information, 1984–
Charter 88, 1988–
Anti-Federalist League, 1991–

Consumers

Consumers Association, 1946–
Campaign for Real Ale, 1971–
National Consumer Council, 1975–

Education

Advisory Centre for Education, 1960–
Confederation for the Advancement of State Education, 1961–

The Elderly

National Old People's Welfare Council, 1940. Changed name to Age Concern, 1971–
Help the Aged, 1961–
British Pensions and Trade Union Action Committee, 1972–

Environment

National Trust, 1895–
Council for the Protection of Rural England, 1926–
Civic Trust, 1957–
Council for Environmental Conservation (COENCO), 1969–
Friends of the Earth, 1970–
Greenpeace, 1971–
Campaign for Lead-free Air (CLEAR), 1982–

Family Welfare

National Council for the Unmarried Mother and her Child, 1918. Changed name to
    National Council for One Parent Families, 1973–
National Society for the Prevention of Cruelty to Children, 1884–
National Marriage Guidance Council (Relate), 1937–
Gingerbread, 1970–

Health

British and Foreign Society for Improving the Embossed Literature for the Blind, 1868.
   Changed name to British and Foreign Blind Association, 1870. Changed name to
   National Institute for the Blind, 1914. Changed name to Royal National Institute for
   the Blind, 1953–
National Bureau for Promoting the General Welfare of the Deaf, 1911. Changed name to
   the National Institute for the Deaf, 1924. Changed name to the Royal National Insti-
   tute for the Deaf, 1961–
The Voluntary Euthanasia Society, 1935–79, 1982- (Exit, 1979–82)
National Association for Mental Health, 1946. Changed name to Mind, 1973–
National Association of Parents of Backward Children, 1946. Changed name to The
   National Society for Mentally Handicapped Children, 1955. Became National
   Society for Mentally Handicapped Children and Adults, with the short title MEN-
   CAP, in 1980. Became the Royal Society for Mentally Handicapped Children and
   Adults (MENCAP), 1981–.
Samaritans, 1953–
Patient's Association, 1961–
Disablement Income Group, 1966–
Action on Smoking and Health (ASH), 1971–
Terence Higgins Trust, 1983–

Homosexuals

Committee for Homosexual Law Reform, 1967. Changed name to Campaign for Homo-
sexual Equality, 1970–
Stonewall, 1989–
OutRage, 1990–

Housing

Shelter, 1966–
Crisis at Christmas, 1967. Changed name to Crisis, 1989–
Campaign for the Homeless and Rootless (CHAR), 1972–

Legal System

Howard League for Penal Reform, 1886–
Central Discharged Prisoners' Aid Society, 1924. Changed name to National Association
   of Aid to Discharged Prisoners' Societies, 1960. Changed name to National Associa-
   tion for the Care and Resettlement of Offenders, (NACRO), 1966–
National Campaign for the Abolition of Capital Punishment, 1955–69
National Association of Victim Support Schemes, 1979–

Morality

Lord's Day of Observance Society, 1831–
The National Viewers' and Listeners' Council (Mary Whitehouse), 1964–
British Humanist Association, 1928– (formerly Ethical Association)
Keep Sunday Special, 1985–

Overseas Aid

War on Want, 1954–
Save the Children Fund, 1919–
Oxfam, 1942–
Christian Aid, 1945–

Poverty

Child Poverty Action Group, 1965–
Low Pay Unit, 1974–

Race

Indian Workers' Association, 1956–
West Indian Standing Conference, 1958–
Anti-Apartheid Movement, 1959–
Runnymede Trust, 1968–
Standing Conference of Pakistani Organisations, 1975–
Anti-Nazi League, 1992–
Anti-Racist Alliance, 1991–

Temperance

United Kingdom Alliance, 1853–

Transport

Royal Automobile Club, 1897–
The Automobile Association, 1905–
National Association of Railway Users, 1971–

Women's Rights

London Society for Women's Suffrage, 1866–1918 (now Fawcett Society)
Women's Freedom League, 1908–1961
National Federation of Women's Institutes, 1917–
Women's Social and Political Union, 1903-1918
Women's Liberation Workshop, 1969–
National Women's Aid Federation, 1975–
Women in Media, 1971–

SOURCES. – A. Butt Philip (ed.), *Directory of Pressure Groups in the European Community* (1991). *Directory of British Associations*.

Transport and Communications

Transport by mode – as percentage of miles travelled

	Bus & coach	Cars	Motor cycle	Cycle	All Road	Rail	Air
1952	42	27	3	11	82	18	0.1
1960	28	49	4	4	86	14	0.3
1970	15	74	1	1	91	9	0.5
1980	11	79	2	1	92	7	0.6
1990	7	85	1	1	93	6	0.7

SOURCE. – *Transport Statistics.*

CURRENT VEHICLE LICENCES IN GREAT BRITAIN[a]

Year	Cars[b]	Public Transport[c]	Goods Vehicles[d]	Total
1905	15,895	7,491	9,000	32,386
1910	89,411	24,466	30,000	143,877
1915	277,741	44,480	84,600	406,821[e]
1920	474,540	74,608	101,000	650,148[e]
1925	1,151,453	113,267	259,341	1,524,061
1930	1,760,533	114,796	391,997	2,287,326
1935	1,973,945	96,419	490,663	2,581,027
1938	2,406,769	96,718	590,397	3,093,884
1940	1,701,500	88,200	542,200	2,331,900
1945	1,795,700	110,800	740,500	2,647,000
1946	2,232,279	110,704	769,747	3,112,930
1950	3,009,611	141,091	1,263,131	4,413,833
1955	4,781,741	104,664	1,581,814	6,468,219
1960	7,387,075	93,942	1,958,856	9,439,873
1965	10,623,900	96,500	2,219,500	12,939,900
1970	12,687,000	103,000	2,161,000	14,950,000
1975	15,051,000	112,000	2,337,000	17,500,000
1980	16,545,000	110,000	2,555,000	19,210,000
1985	19,406,000	120,000	1,632,000	21,157,000
1990	22,822,000	115,000	1,736,000	24,673,000

[a] 1905–20 – Figures at 31 Mar 1925; and at 31 Aug 1930–38 and from 1946 during quarter ending 30 Sep.
[b] Cars, motor cycles, tricycles and pedestrian-controlled vehicles. In the figures for 1985 and 1990 Light Goods Vehicles are classified as cars.
[c] Buses, coaches, trams and taxis.
[d] Goods vehicles, haulage including agricultural vehicles, tax exempt vehicles including electric cars and government vehicles. In the figures for 1985 and 1990 Light Goods Vehicles are classified as cars.
[e] These figures do not include trams. In 1920 there were 14,000 trams.
[f] Figures before 1921 are estimates only, from *The Motor Industry of Great Britain, 1935.* They may be exaggerated.

SOURCES. – *Census of Mechanically Propelled Vehicles* (Ministry of Transport), 1926–62 *Highway Statistics* (Ministry of Transport), 1963 onwards, *The Motor Industry of Great Britain* (Soc. of Motor Manufacturers and Traders). Reports of the Steering Group appointed by the Ministry of Transport, *Traffic in Towns* (Buchanan Report, H.M.S.O.); D.L. Munby and A.A. Watson, *Inland Transport Statistics, Great Britain 1900–1970,* vol II. *Transport Statistics.*

RAILWAYS

Great Britain

	Standard Gauge Route Miles	Train Miles (millions)	Passengers Carried (millions)	Freight[a] Tons (millions)	Ton miles (millions)
1900	18,680	379.3	962.3	461.1	n.a.
1910	19,986	386.7	936.0	504.7	n.a
1920	20,147	355.7	1243.2	332.2	19.2
1930	20,243	397.7	1238.5	304.3	17.8
1938	19,934	420.9	1237.2	265.7	16.7
1950	19,471	384.1	981.7	281.3	22.1
1960	18,369	375.4	1036.7	248.5	18.6
1970	11,799	195.9	823.9	199.0	15.0
1980	10,964	246.4	760.2	152.2	10.8
1990	10,307	225.3	746.4	143.1	10.4

Excluding operations of London Electric Railway, London Passenger Transport Board, and London Transport throughout. Standard Gauge railways only (except 1900 and 1910).

[a] Excluding free hauled traffic.

SOURCES: – 1930–38 *Railway Returns*; 1950– *British Railways Annual Reports.*

SHIPPING

Tonnage registered

(United Kingdom)

	Gross tons (000s)	% of world tonnage
1900	11,514	51.5
1910	16,768	45.0
1920	18,111	33.6
1930	20,322	29.9
1939	17,891	26.1
1950	18,219	21.5
1960	21,131	16.3
1970	25,825	11.0
1980	27,135	6.4
1990	6,716	1.7

Steam and motor ships of 100 gross tons and over.

SOURCE. – *Lloyd's Register of Shipping* (Statistical Tables), published annually.

VOLUME OF AIR TRAFFIC

Terminal Passengers at U.K. Civil Aerodromes

1950	2,133,000
1960	10,075,000
1970	31,606,000
1980	57,822,000
1990	102,418,000

SOURCE. – *Transport Statistics.*

VOLUME OF POSTAL TRAFFIC

Letters, postcards, parcels, registered letters (excluding football pools).
Number of inland deliveries.

	millions
1903–04	4,300
1911–12	5,508
1922–23	5,638
1929–30	6,622
1935–36	7,569
1939–40	7,624
1946–47	6,601
1951–52	7,964
1956–57	8,753
1959–60	9,244
1965–66	10,461
1975–76	8,890
1983–84	10,793
1992–93	15,745[1]

[1] Excluding parcels, now carried by Parcelforce, a separate company.

COST OF LETTER MAIL

(inland)

	First Class	Second Class
May 1840	1d.	–
Jun 1918	1½d.	–
Jun 1920	2d.	–
May 1922	1½d.	–
May 1940	2½d.	–
Oct 1957	3d.	–
May 1965	4d.	–
Sep 1968	5d.[a]	4d.
Feb 1971	3p	2½p
Sep 1973	3½p	3p
Jun 1974	4½p	3½p
Mar 1975	7p	5½p
Sep 1975	8½p	6½p
Jun 1977	9p	7p
Aug 1979	10p	8p
Feb 1980	12p	10p
Jan 1981	14p	11½p
Feb 1982	15½p	12½p
Apr 1983	16p	12½p
Sep 1984	17p	13p
Nov 1985	17p	12p
Oct 1986	18p	13p
Sep 1988	19p	14p
Oct 1989	20p	15p
Sep 1990	22p	17p
Sep 1991	24p	18p
Nov 1993	25p	19p

[a] Two-tier postal pricing introduced.

TELEPHONES
United Kingdom[a]

	Total number of telephones[a]	Total number of connections
1900	3,000	n.a.
1910	122,000	n.a.
1920	980,000	n.a.
1930	1,996,000	1,196,000
1940	3,339,000	2,061,000
1950	5,171,000	3,140,000
1960	7,864,000	4,784,000
1970	13,844,000	8,551,000
1980	27,870,000	17,592,000
1990	..	25,013,000

[a] Including Southern Ireland, 1900–20

SOURCES. – General Post Office, *Post Office Commercial Accounts*, published annually; *Annual Abstract of Statistics; British Telecom Annual Reports.*

X

EMPLOYMENT AND TRADE UNIONS

Major Employment and Trade Union Legislation

Factory and Workshop Act, 1901. This consolidated, with amendments, all previous Factory and Workshop Acts.

Unemployed Workmen Act, 1905. This established 'Distress Committees' to investigate needs and to provide employment or assistance. Funds were to be partly voluntary, and partly from the local rates.

The Trade Disputes Act, 1906, reversed the Taff Vale decision and freed trade unions from liability caused by the calling of a strike.

Labour Exchanges Act, 1909. These were established in 1909 and renamed Employment Exchanges in 1919.

National Insurance Act, 1911. This Act covered all those between the ages of 16 and 70 years, but was limited to manual workers in industries known to be subject to severe and recurrent unemployment. (The Act covered about 2¼ million people.) Within these limits it was compulsory, and financed by a triple weekly levy, from the worker, the employer, and the government. Payment of benefit continued only for a limited period, after which responsibility for the unemployed person lapsed to the poor law. In 1916 the Act was extended to include munitions workers.

The Trade Union Act, 1913. Reversed the Osborne judgment and laid down the conditions under which political objects could be included in the rules of a Union by its members' consent.

Industrial Courts Act, 1919. This provided for the establishment of an Industrial Court and Courts of Inquiry in connection with Trade disputes, and made other provisions for the settlement of such disputes.

Unemployment Insurance Act, 1920. The scheme was extended to cover the same field as the National Health Insurance scheme, and included non-manual workers with an income of under £250 p.a. Workers in agriculture or domestic service were excluded from the insurance scheme until 1936–37. It was administered through the local employment exchanges of the Ministry of Labour. The basic unemployment benefit was 7s. in 1911, increased to 15s. in 1920. It was increased in 1921, and in 1924 was 18s. It was reduced in 1928 and 1931. Additional allowances for dependants were introduced in 1921.

Unemployment Insurance Act, 1927. By this Act the original scheme was completely revised in accordance with the recommendations of the Blanesburgh Committee Report. The new scheme was to provide unlimited benefits after the insured person had satisfied certain qualifying contribution conditions.

The Trades Disputes and Trade Unions Act, 1927. Made a sympathetic strike or a lockout designed to coerce the government illegal; it also severed the connection between civil service organisations and other unions; and it imposed new restrictions on the unions' political activities and their conduct of trade disputes. The political levy could only be raised from workers who 'contracted in'.

Local Government Act, 1929. This Act abolished the Poor Law Guardians, and their responsibilities passed to county councils and county borough councils, who were so far as possible to administer the specialised branches through separate committees.

Poor Law Act, 1930. By this Act Poor Law was renamed Public Assistance. The existing law was consolidated.

Unemployment Insurance Act, 1930. This made qualification easier for transitional benefit, and abolished the requirement that the unemployed receiving benefits should be 'genuinely seeking work'. Transitional benefits were made to claimants in need of assistance, but unable to fulfil the usual qualifying conditions. Responsibility for the long-term unemployed was placed directly on the Exchequer in 1931, though receipt of benefit was made subject to a 'means test'. Dependants' benefits were increased.

Unemployment Act, 1934. An amended scheme was introduced distinguishing between 'unemployed benefit' paid from the Fund (at the basic rate of 17s. a week) for a limited period to those satisfying contribution conditions, and 'unemployment assistance' which was paid, subject to a 'means test', to those still needing assistance after exhausting their title to benefit, or those who were not entitled. These long-term unemployed were paid directly by the Exchequer through the newly created Unemployment Assistance Board (known as Assistance Board from 1940 and from 1948 until 1966 as National Assistance Board). In 1937 juveniles between the ages of 14 and 16 were brought into the scheme for medical benefits only.

Unemployment Insurance (Agriculture) Act, 1936. A separate insurance scheme was set up for agricultural workers granting lower rates of benefit than the general scheme. In 1937, the benefits of voluntary insurance for widows, orphans, etc. (see Contributory Pensions Act, 1925), were extended to those with small incomes, without the qualifications of insurable employment essential to insurance under the main scheme. for the first time married women could become voluntary contributors for pensions.

Control of Employment Act, 1939. This gave the government wide powers for the organisation of labour in war-time. Its aim was to make the best use of labour and to direct it to the most vital work.

Determination of Needs Act, 1941. This abolished the household 'means test'.

National Insurance (Industrial Injuries) Act, 1946. This covered all those in insurable employment against injuries and industrial diseases arising from their employment. It was financed by contributions from the insured person, his employer, and the government.

National Insurance Act, 1946. This Act covered all contributors between school-leaving age and pensionable age, for benefits for unemployment, sickness, maternity, retirement, widows' pensions, guardians' allowances, and death grants. The self-employed and non-employed were entitled to fewer benefits. The basic weekly rate for unemployment benefit was raised to 26s.

The national insurance scheme has since been the subject of numerous minor amendments (for rates, see p. 360).

The Trade Unions Act, 1946. This repealed *The Trades Disputes and Trade Unions Act, 1927.*

National Assistance Act, 1948. This Act repealed all the poor law still in existence and it established a comprehensive scheme to be financed from government funds, to cover all the arrangements for assistance then in force. Provision was also made for those not qualified for benefits under national insurance schemes, or where the benefits were insufficient.

Local Employment Act, 1960. Made provision for promoting employment in areas of persistent or threatened unemployment.

Payment of Wages Act, 1960. Removed certain restrictions on methods of payment of wages and permits them to be paid otherwise than in cash by payment into a banking account in the name of the employee, by Postal Order, by Money Order or by Cheque.

The Contracts of Employment Act, 1963. Laid down the notice required to be given by an employer to terminate the contract of a person who had been continuously employed for 26 weeks or more (reduced to 13 weeks in 1974), the length of notice to be given varying according to the length of continuous employment.

Offices, Shops and Railway Premises Act, 1963. Contained sweeping provisions relating to the health, safety, and welfare of employees, fire precautions, accidents and other matters in connection with office, shop and railway premises.

The Industrial Training Act, 1964. Gave power to establish an industrial training board for the training of persons over compulsory school age for employment in any activities of industry or commerce.

Trade Disputes Act, 1965. Reversed the Rookes v. Barnard case and disallowed actions for tort or reparation being brought in respect of some kinds of activities in the conduct of industrial disputes.

Redundancy Payments Act, 1965. Obliged employers in certain industries to make payment to redundant workers and set up a Redundancy fund to which employers had to contribute.

Equal Pay Act, 1970. Made provision for the application to all workers of the principle of equal remuneration for men and women for work of equal value and required that terms and conditions of employment applicable to one sex should not be in any respect less favourable than those applicable to the other.

Industrial Relations Act, 1971. Established new legal rights for the individual worker, mainly in relation to trade union activity but also in protection from unfair dismissal, information about the terms of employment, and long duration of notice. Most of these rights were preserved and expanded in the *Trade Unions and Labour Relations Acts of 1974 and 1975.* It also introduced fundamental and wide ranging changes in the legal framework of industrial relations. It repealed the *Trade Union Acts, 1871 and 1876,* and the *Trade Disputes Acts, 1906 and 1965.* Its provisions established new legal rights for the individual mainly in relation to trade union membership and activity, protection from unfair dismissal, information about his employment, and improved terms of notice. The Act introduced a new concept of 'unfair industrial practice'. It established a National Industrial Relations Court which, together with the industrial tribunals, was required to maintain these standards and rights by hearing complaints of unfair industrial practice and determining rights and liabilities. The Act also provided for a new system of registration and restricted legal immunities to registered trade unions; new methods of settling disputes over trade union recognition to be administered by a Commission on Industrial Relations; and new powers to be exercised by the Secretary of State for Employment to deal with emergency situations (i.e. the 'cooling off period' and ballots of membership).

Employment and Training Act, 1973. Extended provisions for public authorities to provide work or training for unemployed persons.

Health and Safety at Work Act, 1974. Provided a comprehensive system of law to deal with health and safety at work and established a Health and Safety Commission and Executive.

Trade Unions and Labour Relations Act, 1974. Repealed the *Industrial Relations Act, 1971,* except for the provisions on unfair dismissal. The Act abolished the National Industrial Relations Court and the Commission on Industrial Relations.

Employment Protection Act, 1975. Amended the law relating to workers and employers and provided redress against arbitrary dismissal. It extended the scope of redundancy payments and guaranteed suspension pay to those whose work was interrupted for external causes. It also provided for the establishment of the Advisory Conciliation and Arbitration Service as an independent statutory body and of a Central Arbitration Commission, together with a Certification Officer to take over the functions previously exercised by the Registrar of Friendly Societies in monitoring Trade Unions.

Trade Union and Labour Relations (Amendment) Act, 1975. Amended the 1974 Act and provided for a charter on Freedom of the Press.

Sex Discrimination Act, 1975 (see p. 338).

Race Relations Act, 1976   (see p. 329).

Employment Act, 1980.   Provided for payment of public funds towards the costs of ballots among Trade Union members over strike action.

Employment Act, 1982.   Provided for compensation from public funds for employees dismissed as a result of closed shop agreements.

Trade Union Act, 1984.   Made legal immunity conditional on the conduct of strike ballots and made the continued existence of political funds dependent on ten-yearly votes by the membership.

Wages Act, 1986.   This reduced the powers and scope of wages councils by limiting them to determining a single minimum rate, and removing young people from their jurisdiction. Unauthorized deductions from wages became a civil matter rather than a criminal offence.

Sex Discrimination Act, 1986.   (see p. 338).

Employment Act, 1988.   This made dismissal for non-membership of a union unfair dismissal in all circumstances. It made it illegal for trade unions to discipline members for crossing picket lines or refusing to strike, even if the strike had been approved by a ballot. It gave members of trade unions the right to prevent union funds from being used for unlawful purposes.

Employment Act, 1989.   This removed restrictions on the hours and other employment terms of 16- and 17-year olds. It abolished some restrictions on women's employment, such as the ban on working in mines. The Training Commission, which had replaced the Manpower Services Commission, was abolished.

Employment Act, 1990.   This banned the pre-entry closed shop, and made it unlawful to refuse employment to someone for belonging or not belonging to a union. Trade unions lost their immunity from civil damages claims for all forms of secondary action.

Trade Union Reform and Employment Rights Act, 1993.   This introduced restrictions on deduction of union subscriptions from wages, compelled unions to publish fuller accounts, tightened rules on strike ballots, abolished wages councils, and gave workers the right to join any union regardless of whether it was organised in their workplace.

Major Trade Union Litigation

Taff Vale Railway Co. v. Analgamated Society of Railway Servants, [1901] A.C. 426 (H.L.). A trade union, registered under the Trade Union Acts, 1871 and 1876, may be sued in its registered name. Lord Halsbury said, 'If the legislature has created a thing which can own property, which can employ servants, or which can inflict injury, it must be taken, I think, to have impliedly given the power to make it suable in a court of law, for injuries purposely done by its authority and procurement.'

Amalgamated Society of Railway Servants v. Osborne, (1910) A.C. 87 (H.L.).   There is nothing in the Trade Union Acts from which it can reasonably be inferred that trade unions as defined by Parliament were meant to have the power of collecting and administering funds for political purposes. Exercise of such powers is ultra vires and illegal.

Bonsor v. Musicians' Union, [1956] A.C. 104 (H.L.).   A member of a registered trade union wrongfully expelled from it was entitled to maintain an action for damages for breach of contract against the union in its registered name.

Rookes v. Barnard, [1964] A.C. 1129.   Threats to strike in breach of a contractual agreement for the purpose of injuring a third party were unlawful and were, even if done in furtherance of a trade dispute, not protected by the *Trade Disputes Act, 1906.*

Stratford v. Lindley, [1964] 3 All E.R. 102.   Strike Action not taken in pursuance of a trade dispute about terms of employment with the plaintiff's firm was not prima facie protected by the *Trade Disputes Act of 1906.*

1971–4 Between 1971 and 1974 there were a series of confrontations under the terms of the *Industrial Relations Act.* The T.U.C. in Sep 1971 instructed all unions not to register under the Act and in Sep 1972 the 32 which had registered were suspended and 20 of them were expelled in Sep 1973. In Apr 1972 the T.G.W.U. was fined £55,000 for contempt of the N.I.R.C. (though the fine was quashed by the Court of Appeal in Jun 1972). In Dec 1972 the A.U.E.W. refused to pay £50,000 in the *Goad* case (over the individual rights of a union member). In Oct 1973 £75,000 of seized A.U.E.W. assets were used to pay a further £47,000 N.I.R.C. contempt fine in the *Con-Mech* case. In May 1974 a further seizure of A.U.E.W. assets was ordered to pay £47,000 compensation to Con-Mech (the money was then paid by an anonymous donor). On 17 Apr 1972 the N.I.R.C. ordered a 14-day cooling off period in a national railway dispute and on 13 May 1972 ordered a ballot which produced an 85% vote in favour of a railway strike. On 21 Jul 1972 the N.I.R.C. committed five docker shop stewards to prison over the blacking of London container depots. They were released on 26 Jul. On 6 Aug 1974 the *Industrial Relations Act* was repealed.

Gouriet v. Post Office Union, [1977] 3 All E.R. (H.L.).   An attempt to enjoin the Post Office Union from blacking mail to South Africa was frustrated because the Attorney-General refused his fiat to bring the case on the ground that the plaintiff was not directly involved (see p. 310).

Grunwick Processing Laboratories Ltd. v. Advisory Conciliation and Arbitration Service, [1977] T.L.R. 14 Dec 77.   The House of Lords ruled that an A.C.A.S. recommendation on union recognition was void because A.C.A.S. had not ascertained the opinions of two-thirds of the work force involved (this was due to the non-cooperation of the firm's management).

B. B. C. v. Hearn, [1977] I.R.L.R. 273; *Beaverbrook Newspapers v. Keys,* [1978], I.R.L.R. 34; *Star Sea Transport v. Slater,* [1978] I.R.L.R. 507; *McShane v. Express Newspapers,* [1979] I.R.L.R. 79; *United Biscuits v. Fall* [1979] I.R.L.R. 110; *Associated Newspaper Group v. Wade* [1979] I.R.L.R. 201..   The decisions in each of these cases reduced the area of legal immunity for actions taken in furtherance of an industrial dispute.

Thomas et al. v. Haringey [1979].   The Court of Appeal held that it was arguable that a local authority might be in breach of its duty to provide education when it failed to do so by reason of industrial action by school caretakers.

Messenger Newspaper Group Ltd v. NGA (1982) (Industrial Relations Law Reports 1984, 397).   The Court of Appeal endorsed the powers of sequestrators seeking to secure control of union funds when the union had been fined for contempt for its actions in seeking to enforce a closed shop.

Mercury Communications Ltd v. Scott Garer (Industrial Cases Reports 1984, 74).   The Court of Appeal ruled that it was possible under the *Employment Act 1982* to secure an interlocutory injunction against union actions that were not 'wholly or mainly' related to an industrial dispute.

Dimbleby & Sons Ltd. v. National Union of Journalists (Industrial Cases Reports 1984, 386).   The House of Lords endorsed the granting of an interlocutory injunction against preventing a union from instructing its members to break contracts of employment in pursuits of a trade dispute that, under the *Employment Act 1980,* was excluded from protection.

Barretts and Baird (Wholesale) Ltd v. IPCS [1987] IRLR 3.   Not only are union members liable in damages to their employer for breach of their employment contract, but the same breach of contract may give rise to further liabilities based on its 'unlawful' character.

Boxfoldia Ltd v. NGA [1988] ICR 752.   Although members may authorize their union to decide on official industrial action, it does not follow that the union is authorised to act as their agent in terminating their employment contracts.

Associated British Ports v. TGWU [1989] IRLR 305, 318 CA.   The Court issued an injunction against industrial action on the grounds that the union had no immunity against tort liability for inducing workers to breach their statutory duty with intent to injure. The judgement was subsequently reversed by the House of Lords on other grounds.

Dimskal Shipping Sa v. ITWF [1991] 3WLR 875 HL.   Industrial action could be ruled unlawful secondary action even if it took place in another country (in this case Sweden) under whose law it was legal, according to the commercial law principle of 'economic duress'

SOURCES. – Lord Wedderburn of Charlton, *The Worker and the Law* (3rd Ed., 1986). W.E.J. McCarthy (ed.), *Trade Unions* (2nd Ed., 1985). W.E.J. McCarthy, *Legal Intervention in Industrial Relations* (1992).

National Industrial Relations Court 1971–4

President

1971   Sir J. Donaldson

Commission on Industrial Relations 1971–4

Chairman

1969   G. Woodcock

(Made a Statutory Body, 1 Nov 71)

1971 (Sir) L. Neal

(Advisory) Conciliation and Arbitration Service (A.C.A.S.)[1] 1974–

Chairman

1974   J. Mortimer
1981   (Sir) P. Lowry
1987   (Sir) D. Smith
1993   J. Hougham

[1] The Conciliation and Arbitration Service was established within the Department of Employment in 1974. It was made an independent statutory body by the *Employment Protection Act, 1975*

Earnings and Hours Worked

United Kingdom

	Average Weekly Earnings				Average Weekly Hours			
	Manual workers		Non-manual workers		Manual workers		Non-manual workers	
	Men aged 21 and over	Women aged 18 and over	Males aged 21 and over	Females aged 18 and over	Men aged 21 and over	Women aged 18 and over	Males aged 21 and over	Females aged 18 and over
Year								
1924	2.8	1.4			n.a.	n.a.		
1935	3.2	1.6			n.a.	n.a.		
1938	3.5	1.6			47.7	43.5		
1940	4.5	1.9			n.a.	n.a.		
1941	5.0	2.2			n.a.	n.a.		
1942	5.6	2.7			n.a.	n.a.		
1943	6.1	3.1			52.9	45.9		
1944	6.2	3.2			51.2	44.6		
1945	6.1	3.2			49.7	43.3		
1946	6.0	3.3			47.6	42.5		
1947	6.4	3.5			46.6	41.4		
1948	6.9	3.7			46.7	41.4		
1949	7.1	3.9			46.8	41.5		
1950	7.5	4.1			47.6	41.8		

| | Average Weekly Earnings | | | | Average Weekly Hours | | | |
| | Manual workers | | Non-manual workers | | Manual workers | | Non-manual workers | |
Year	Men aged 21 and over	Women aged 18 and over	Males aged 21 and over	Females aged 18 and over	Men aged 21 and over	Women aged 18 and over	Males aged 21 and over	Females aged 18 and over
1951	8.3	4.5			47.8	41.3		
1952	8.9	1.8			47.7	41.7		
1953	9.5	5.1			47.9	41.8		
1954	10.2	5.4			48.5	41.8		
1955	11.1	5.8			48.9	41.6		
1956	11.9	6.2			48.5	41.3		
1957	12.6	6.5			48.2	41.0		
1958	12.8	6.7			47.7	41.0		
1959	13.6	7.0	18.0	9.7	48.5	41.4		
1960	14.5	7.4	19.1	10.2	48.0	40.5		
1961	15.3	7.7	20.0	10.7	47.4	39.7		
1962	15.9	8.0	21.1	11.3	47.0	39.4		
1963	16.7	8.4	22.3	12.0	47.6	39.7		
1964	18.1	9.0	23.5	12.6	47.7	39.4		
1965	19.6	9.6	25.5	13.7	47.0	38.7		
1966	20.3	10.1	26.7	14.2	46.0	38.1		
1967	21.4	10.6	27.9	14.9	46.2	38.2		
1968	23.0	11.3	29.8	15.8	46.4	38.3		
1969	24.8	12.1	32.1	17.0	46.5	38.1		
1970	26.7	13.3	35.1	17.7	45.9	38.6	39.0	36.9
1971	29.4	15.3	39.1	19.8	45.0	38.4	38.7	36.9
1972	32.8	17.1	43.5	22.2	46.0	39.9	38.7	36.8
1973	38.1	19.7	48.1	24.7	46.7	39.9	38.8	36.8
1974	43.6	23.6	54.4	28.6	46.5	39.8	38.8	36.8
1975	55.7	32.1	68.4	39.6	45.5	39.4	38.7	36.6
1976	65.1	39.4	81.6	48.8	45.3	39.3	38.5	36.5
1977	71.5	43.7	88.9	53.8	45.7	39.4	38.7	36.7
1978	80.7	49.4	100.7	59.1	46.0	39.6	38.7	36.7
1979	93.0	55.2	113.0	66.0	46.2	39.6	38.8	36.7
1980	111.7	68.0	141.3	82.7	45.4	39.6	38.7	36.7
1981	121.9	74.5	163.1	96.7	44.2	39.4	38.4	36.5
1982	133.8	80.1	178.9	104.9	44.3	39.3	38.2	36.5
1983	143.6	87.9	194.9	115.1	43.9	39.3	38.4	36.5
1984	152.7	93.5	209.0	124.3	44.3	39.4	38.5	36.5
1985	163.6	101.3	225.0	133.8	44.5	39.5	38.6	36.6
1986	174.4	107.5	244.9	145.7	44.5	39.5	38.6	36.7
1987	185.5	115.3	265.9	157.2	44.6	39.7	38.7	36.8
1988	200.6	123.6	294.1	175.5	45.0	39.8	38.7	36.9
1989	217.8	134.9	323.6	195.0	45.3	39.9	38.8	36.9
1990	239.5	148.4	346.4	214.3	45.4	40.0	38.9	36.9
1991	253.1	159.2	375.7	236.8	44.4	39.7	38.7	36.8
1992	268.3	170.1	400.4	256.5	44.5	39.8	38.6	36.8

The figures to 1969 cover manufacturing industry and some non-manufacturing industries and services, but exclude coal mining, dock labour, railways, agriculture, shipping, distributive trades, catering, entertainments and domestic service. In 1940–45, the figures are for July but otherwise up to 1969 they are for October. The figures to 1969 come from the *Ministry of Labour Gazette British Labour Statistics: Historical Abstract 1886–1968.* From 1970 the figures come from the New Earnings Survey of a sample of all employees in Great Britain and are not therefore strictly comparable with those for pre-1970. They relate to April in each year.

SOURCES. – *British Labour Statistics: Historical Abstract 1886–1968; Department of Employment Gazette: New Earnings Survey.*

Size of Labour Force

Great Britain
(to nearest 000)

Year	Total	Male	Female
1901	16,312	11,548	4,763
1911	18,354	12,930	5,424
1921	19,357	13,636	5,701
1931	21,055	14,790	6,265
1939	19,750	14,656	5,094
1960	24,436	16,239	8,197
1970	24,721	15,977	8,743
1980	26,198	15,637	10,561
1990	28,189	16,031	12,158
1993	27,684	15,564	12,119

1901, 1911, and 1921 figures cover Persons aged 10 years and over.
1931 and 1939 figures cover persons aged 14 years and over.
1951, 1960 and 1970 figures cover persons aged 15 years and over.
1980 onwards figures cover Persons 16 and over.

Rates of Unemployment Benefit

(other than agricultural)

	Men over 18	Women over 18		Men over 18	Women over 18
15 Jan 13	7s.	Nil			
25 Dec 19	11s.	Nil	22 Jul 74	£8.60	
8 Nov 20	15s.	12s.	7 Apr 75	£9.80	
3 Mar 21	20s.	16s.	20 Nov 75	£11.10	
30 Jun 21	15s.	12s.	18 Nov 76	£12.90	
14 Aug 24	18s.	15s.	17 Nov 77	£14.70	
8 Oct 31	15s.3d.	13s.6d.	16 Nov 78	£15.75	
26 Jul 34	17s.	15s.	15 Nov 79	£18.50	
1 Aug 40	20s.	18s.	27 Nov 80	£20.65	
2 Nov 44	24s.	22s.	26 Nov 81	£22.50	
3 Jun 48	26s.	26s.	25 Nov 82	£25.00	
24 Jul 52	32s.6d.	26s.	24 Nov 83	£27.05	
19 May 55	40s.	26s.	26 Nov 84	£28.45	
			28 Nov 85	£30.45	
6 Feb 58		50s.	31 Jul 86	£30.80	
6 Apr 61		57s.6d.	9 Apr 87	£31.45	
7 Mar 63		67s.6d.	14 Apr 88	£32.75	
28 Jan 65		80s.	10 Apr 89	£34.70	
30 Oct 67		90s.	9 Apr 90	£37.35	
6 Nov 69		100s.	11 Apr 91	£41.40	
23 Sep 71		£6.00	9 Apr 92	£43.10	
20 Oct 72		£6.75	5 Apr 93	£44.65	
4 Oct 73		£7.35	11 Apr 94	£45.45	

After 6 Oct 66 flat rate unemployment benefit was supplemented by earnings related benefit.

SOURCE. – Department of Health and Social Security. Department of Social Security. *Annual Abstract of Statistics.*

Industrial Analysis of the Occupied Population 1911–1981

Great Britain
(000s)

	1911	1921	1931	1951	1961	1971	1981
Total Working Population[a]	18,351	19,369	21,074	22,610	24,014	25,021	26,697
Total Out of Employment	n.a.	n.a.	2,524	476	676	1,289	2,176
Total in Employment	n.a.	n.a.	18,550	22,013	23,501	24,615	24,323
Agriculture & Fishing	1,493	1,373	1,180	1,126	855	635	352
Mining & Quarrying	1,308	1,469	1,040	841	722	391	336
Manufacturing Industries	6,147	6,723	5,981	7,902	8,383	8,136	5,974
Building & Contracting	950	826	970	1,404	1,600	1,669	1,117
Gas, Electricity & Water	117	180	224	358	377	362	338
Transport & Communications	1,260	1,359	1,430	1,705	1,673	1,564	1,422
Distributive Trades	n.a.	n.a.	2,697	2,742	3,189	3,016	2,715
Insurance, Banking & Finance[b]	n.a.	328	388	489	722	952	1,295
Public Administration:							
National (inc. Defence)	452	480	368	1,036	798	812	589
Local	555	457	541	602	629	760	931
Professional, Scientific	n.a.	868	1,018	1,536	2,120	2,901	3,649
Miscellaneous Services	n.a.	n.a.	2,713	2,393	2,270	2,534	2,522[c]
(of which domestic service)	n.a.	(1,390)	(1,509)	(499)	(362)	(239)	(n.a.)

The table shows only the changes in the general pattern of industry over the period. The figures are based on the Census of Population figures published by the Registrar-General. The figures for 1911 and 1921 are not completely comparable with those for the later years due to changes in classification and the inclusion of the unemployed who are excluded in the analysis from 1931 onwards.

[a] 1911, 12 and over; 1921, 1931, 14 and over; 1951 on, 15 and over.
[b] Including Business Services.
[c] Not Including private domestic service.

SOURCES. – *Department of Employment Gazette; Annual Abstract of Statistics.*

From 1981 a new system of classification was introduced which was no longer compatible with previous figures:

Employees in employment by industry, 1975–1993

Great Britain
(000s)
Figures for June of each year

	1975	1980	1985	1990	1993
Agriculture, Forestry, Fishing	388	352	321	277	255
Coal, Oil, Gas extraction	356	355	273	157	103
Gas, Electricity, Water supply	361	361	309	284	247
Metals, Mechanical Engineering[a]	4,159	3,867	2,840	2,646	2,156
Chemicals and man-made fibres	432	420	339	325	293
Food, drink, tobacco	731	705	575	524	459
Textiles, leather, clothing	875	716	550	477	401
Timber, rubber, plastics, furniture	602	554	473	540	438
Paper, printing, publishing	553	538	477	481	443
Construction	1,207	1,206	994	1,060	807
Wholesale, Retail, Hotels, Catering	3,906	4,204	4,213	4,756	4,452
Transport, Post, Telecommunications	1,480	1,464	1,308	1,361	1,248
Banking, Insurance, Finance	1,468	1,669	2,039	2,701	2,577
Public Administration	1,937	1,925	1,862	1,942	1,823
Education	1,534	1,586	1,557	1,735	1,806
Health	1,112	1,214	1,489	1,664	1,713

[a] SIC 1980 Classifications 21–24, 31–37

SOURCE. – *Department of Employment Gazette.*

Trades Union Congresses 1900–

Date	Place	President	General secretary	No. of Delegates	Members represented (000s)
3–8 Sep 00	Huddersfield	W. Pickles	S. Woods	386	1,250
2–7 Sep 01	Swansea	C. Bowerman	..	407	1,200
1–6 Sep 02	London	W. Steadman	..	485	1,400
6–11 Sep 03	Leicester	W. Hornidge	..	460	1,500
5–10 Sep 04	Leeds	R. Bell	..	453	1,423
4–9 Sep 05	Hanley	J. Sexton	W. Steadman	457	1,541
3–8 Sep 06	Liverpool	D. Cummings	..	491	1,555
2–7 Sep 07	Bath	A. Gill	..	521	1,700
7–12 Sep 08	Nottingham	D. Shackleton	..	522	1,777
6–11 Sep 09	Ipswich	..	..	598	1,705
12–17 Sep 10	Sheffield	J. Haslam	..	505	1,648
4–9 Sep 11	Newcastle	W. Mullin	C. Bowerman	523	1,662
2–7 Sep 12	Newport	W. Thorne	..	495	2,002
1–6 Sep 13	Manchester	W. Davis	..	560	2,232
6–11 Sep 15	Bristol	J. Seddon	..	610	2,682
4–9 Sep 16	Birmingham	H. Gosling	..	673	2,851
3–8 Sep 17	Blackpool	J. Hill	..	697	3,082
2–7 Sep 18	Derby	J. Ogden	..	881	4,532
8–13 Sep 19	Glasgow	G. Stuart-Bunning	..	851	5,284
6–11 Sep 20	Portsmouth	J. Thomas	..	955	6,505
5–10 Sep 21	Cardiff	E. Poulton	..	810	6,418
4–9 Sep 22	Southport	R. Walker	..	723	5,129
3–8 Sep 23	Plymouth	J. Williams	F. Bramley	702	4,369
1–6 Sep 24	Hull	A. Purcell	..	724	4,328
7–12 Sep 25	Scarborough	A. Swales	..	727	4,351
6–11 Sep 26	Bournemouth	A. Pugh	W. Citrine	696	4,366
5–10 Sep 27	Edinburgh	G. Hicks	..	646	4,164
3–8 Sep 28	Swansea	B. Turner	..	621	3,875
2–6 Sep 29	Belfast	B. Tillett	..	592	3,673
1–5 Sep 30	Nottingham	J. Beard	..	606	3,744
7–11 Sep 31	Bristol	A. Hayday	..	589	3,719
5–9 Sep 32	Newcastle	J. Bromley	..	578	3,613
4–8 Sep 33	Brighton	A. Walkden	..	566	3,368
3–7 Sep 34	Weymouth	A. Conley	..	575	3,295
2–6 Sep 35	Margate	W. Kean	Sir W. Citrine	575	3,389
7–11 Sep 36	Plymouth	A. Findlay	..	603	3,615
6–10 Sep 37	Norwich	E. Bevin	..	623	4,009
5–9 Sep 38	Blackpool	H. Elvin	..	650	4,461
4–5 Sep 39	Bridlington	J. Hallsworth	..	490	4,669
7–9 Oct 40	Southport	W. Holmes	..	667	4,867
1–4 Sep 41	Edinburgh	G. Gibson	..	683	5,079
7–11 Sep 42	Blackpool	F. Wolstencroft	..	717	5,433
6–10 Sep 43	Southport	Anne Loughlin	..	760	6,024
16–20 Oct 44	Blackpool	E. Edwards	..	730	6,642
10–14 Sep 45	Blackpool	..	..	762	6,576
21–25 Oct 46	Brighton	C. Dukes	V. Tewson	794	6,671
1–5 Sep 47	Southport	G. Thomson	..	837	7,540
6–10 Sep 48	Margate	Florence Hancock	..	859	7,791
5–9 Sep 49	Bridlington	Sir W. Lawther	..	890	7,937
4–8 Sep 50	Brighton	H. Bullock	Sir V. Tewson	913	7,883

Date	Place	President	General secretary	No. of Delegates	Members represented (000s)
3–7 Sep 51	Blackpool	A. Roberts	Sir V. Tewson	927	7,828
1–5 Sep 52	Margate	A. Deakin	..	943	8,020
7–11 Sep 53	Douglas	T. O'Brien	..	954	8,088
6–10 Sep 54	Brighton	J. Tanner	..	974	8,094
5–9 Sep 55	Southport	C. Geddes	..	984	8,107
3–7 Sep 56	Brighton	W. Beard	..	1,000	8,264
2–6 Sep 57	Blackpool	Sir T. Williamson	..	995	8,305
1–5 Sep 58	Bournemouth	T. Yates	..	993	8,337
7–11 Sep 59	Blackpool	R. Willis	..	1,017	8,176
5–9 Sep 60	Douglas	C. Bartlett	G. Woodcock	996	8,128
4–8 Sep 61	Portsmouth	E. Hill	..	984	8,299
3–7 Sep 62	Blackpool	A. Godwin	..	989	8,313
2–6 Sep 63	Brighton	F. Hayday	..	975	8,315
7–11 Sep 64	Blackpool	G. Lowthian	..	997	8,326
6–10 Sep 65	Brighton	H. Collison	..	1,013	8,771
5–9 Sep 66	Blackpool	J. O'Hagan	..	1,048	8,868
4–8 Sep 67	Brighton	Sir H. Douglass	..	1,059	8,787
2–6 Sep 68	Blackpool	Ld Wright	..	1,051	8,726
1–5 Sep 69	Portsmouth	J. Newton	..	1,034	8,875
7–11 Sep 70	Brighton	Sir S. Greene	V. Feather	1,064	9,402
6–10 Sep 71	Blackpool	Ld Cooper	..	1,064	10,002
4–8 Sep 72	Brighton	G. Smith	..	1,018	9,895
3–7 Sep 73	Blackpool	J. Crawford	..	991	10,001
2–6 Sep 74	Brighton	Ld Allen	L. Murray	1,032	10,002
1–5 Sep 75	Blackpool	Marie Patterson	..	1,030	10,364
6–10 Sep 76	Brighton	C. Plant	..	1,114	11,036
5–9 Sep 77	Blackpool	Marie Patterson	..	1,148	11,516
4–8 Sep 78	Brighton	D. Basnett	..	1,172	11,865
3–7 Sep 79	Blackpool	T. Jackson	..	1,200	12,128
1–5 Sep 80	Brighton	T. Parry	..	1,203	12,173
7–11 Sep 81	Blackpool	A. Fisher	..	1,188	11,601
6–10 Sep 82	Brighton	A. Sapper	..	1,163	11,006
5–9 Sep 83	Blackpool	F. Chapple	..	1,155	10,810
3–7 Sep 84	Brighton	R. Buckton	N. Willis	1,121	10,082
2–6 Sep 85	Blackpool	J. Eccles	..	1,124	9,855
1–5 Sep 86	Brighton	K. Gill	..	1,091	9,586
7–11 Sep 87	Blackpool	F. Jarvis	..	1,065	9,243
5–9 Sep 88	Bournemouth	C. Jenkins	..	1,052	9,127
4–8 Sep 89	Blackpool	A. Christopher	..	1,006	8,652
3–7 Sep 90	Blackpool	Anne Maddocks	..	985	8,405
2–6 Sep 91	Glasgow	A. Smith	..	937	8,193
7–11 Sep 92	Blackpool	R. Bickerstaffe	..	892	7,762
6–10 Sep 93	Brighton	A. Tuffin	J. Monks	874	7,303

SOURCE. – *Trades Union Congress Reports, 1900–*.

The Largest Unions

(Unions which, at some time, have had over 200,000 members)[a]

Amalgamated Engineering and Electrical Union 1920 (1992)

Amalgamated Society of Engineers (founded 1851) merged with other unions to form the Amalgamated Engineering Union (A.E.U.) in 1920. In 1968 the A.E.U. merged with the Amalgamated Union of Foundry Workers (A.E.F.) which in 1970 merged with the Construction Engineering Workers and the Draughtsmen and Allied Technicians Association, taking the title the Amalgamated Union of Engineering Workers. Merged in 1992 with EETPU and took its present title.

President

1920	J. Brownlie	1956	(Sir) W. Carron (Ld)
1930	W. Hutchinson	1967	H. Scanlon
1933	J. Little	1978	T. Duffy
1939	J. Tanner	1986	W. Jordan
1954	R. Openshaw		

Amalgamated Weavers' Association 1884–1974

An association of many small local unions in the Cotton Trade. In 1974 it merged with the National Union of Textile and Allied Workers to form the Amalgamated Textile Workers Union.

Secretary

1907	J. Cross	1953	L. Wright (Ld)
1925	J. Parker	1969	H. Kershaw
1929	(Sir) A. Naesmith	1972	F. Hague

Manufacturing, Science, Finance (MSF) 1917 (1988)

National Foreman's Association became Association of Supervisory Staff, Executives and Technicians (ASSET) in 1941. Became Association of Scientific, Technical and Managerial Staffs (ASTMS) in 1968 when it merged with the Association of Scientific Workers (founded in 1918 as National Union of Scientific Workers and became AScW in 1925). NFA joined TUC in 1919; AScW in 1942. Merged with TASS in 1988 to become MSF.

Secretary

1917	H. Reid (NFA)	1970	C. Jenkins
1939	T. Agar (NFA)	1988	{ C. Jenkins
1945	W. Bretherton (ASSET)		{ K. Gill
1946	H. Knight (ASSET)	1989	K. Gill
1960	C. Jenkins (ASSET)	1992	R. Lyons
1968	{ J. Dutton		
	{ C. Jenkins		

Civil and Public Service Association 1902 (1969)

Assistant Clerks Association became Clerical Officers Association in 1919 and Civil Service Clerical Association in 1922. Changed name to CPSA in 1969 (not in TUC 1927–46).

Secretary

1916	W. Brown	1976	K. Thomas
1942	L. White	1982	A. Kendall
1955	G. Green	1987	J. Ellis
1963	L. Wines	1992	B. Reamsbottom
1967	W. Kendall		

[a] Not including the Royal College of Nursing.

Confederation of Health Service Employees (COHSE) 1946–1992

Formed by a merger of various small hospital unions. Merged with NUPE and NALGO to form UNISON in 1992.

Secretary

1946	G. Gibson		1969	F. Lynch
1948	C. Comer		1974	A. Spanswick
1953	J. Waite		1983	D. Williams
1959	W. Jepson		1987	H. MacKenzie
1967	A. Akers			

Electrical, Electronics, Telecommunications and Plumbing Union (EETPU) 1889–1992

Originally Electrical Trades Union. In 1968 following mergers it became the Electrical, Electronic and Telecommunications Union Plumbing Trades Union and then the Electrical, Electronics, Telecommunications and Plumbing Union. Expelled from TUC in 1988. Merged with AUEW 1992; EEPTU wing readmitted to TUC 1993.

President/General Secretary

1907	J. Ball		1963	(Sir) L. Cannon
1931	E. Bussey		1971	F. Chapple
1940	H. Bolton		1984	E. Hammond
1944	F. Foulkes		1992	P. Gallagher

General Municipal Boilermakers and Allied Trades Union (GMB) 1924

National Union of General Workers (founded 1889 as the National Union of Gasworkers and General Labourers of G.B. and Ireland), National Amalgamated Union of Labour (founded 1889 as Tyneside and General Labourers' Union), and Municipal Employees' Association (founded 1894). Became National Union of General and Municipal Workers in 1924. Changed name to General and Municipal Workers Union for popular use in 1965. Merged with Amalgamated Society of Boilermakers, Shipwrights, Blacksmiths and structural workers to form GMB in 1982.

Secretary

1924	W. Thorne		1962	J. (Ld) Cooper
1934	C. Dukes		1972	D. Basnett
1946	(Sir) T. Williamson		1986	J. Edmonds

Graphical, Paper and Media Union (GPMU) 1847 (1991)

Established by amalgamation of the National Union of Bookbinders and Machine Rulers and the National Union of Printing and Paper Workers as the National Union of Printing Bookbinding and Paper Workers (NUPBPW). In 1968 merged with the National Society of Operative Printers (NATSOPA) to form SOGAT. In 1971 the merger was dissolved but NUPBPW section kept name of SOGAT. Merged with National Graphical Association in 1991 to form GPMU.

Secretary

1921	T. Newland		1974	W. Keys
1938	E. Spackman		1985	Brenda Dean
1946	V. Flynn		1991	A. Dubbins
1947	W. Morrison			
1959	T. Smith (1968–71 jointly with R. Briginshaw)			

National and Local Government Officers' Association 1905–1993

National Association of Local Government Officers. 1930 amalgamated with National Poor Law Officers' Association and in 1963 with the British Gas Staffs Association. 1952 changed name to National and Local Government Officers' Association (joined TUC 1965.) Merged with COHSE and NUPE to form UNISON in 1993.

General Secretary

1905	F. Ginn	1957	W. Anderson
1909	L. Hill	1973	G. Drain
1943	J. Simonds	1983	J. Daly
1945	H. Corser (Acting)	1990	A. Jinkinson
1946	J. Warren		

National Union of Mineworkers (NUM) 1889 (1945)

Formed as the Miners' Federation of G.B., amalgamated with specialist unions, and renamed NUM in 1945.

President		Secretary	
1912	R. Smillie	1920	F. Hodges
1921	H. Smith	1924	A. Cook
1929	T. Richards	1932	E. Edwards
1931	E. Edwards	1946	A. Homer
1932	P. Lee	1969	L. Daly
1934	J. Jones	1984	P. Heathfield
1938	W. Lawther	1992	(vacant)
1954	W. Jones		
1960	S. Ford		
1971	J. Gormley		
1982	A. Scargill		

National Union of Public Employees (NUPE) 1888 (1928)–1993

Formed as London County Council Protection Association; in 1894 became Municipal Employees Association; in 1920 the MEA and the National Union of Corporation Workers jointly affiliated to the TUC but in 1924 MEA was absorbed by NUGMW. The National Union of Corporation Workers became NUPE in 1928. Merged with COHSE and NALGO to form UNISON in 1993.

Secretary

1926	J. Wills	1968	A. Fisher
1934	B. Roberts	1982	R. Bickerstaffe
1962	S. Hill		

National Union of Rail, Maritime, and Transport workers (RMT) 1913 (1989)

The National Union of Railwaymen was formed in 1913 from the merger of the Amalgamated Society of Railway Servants, the General Railway Workers' Union, and others. In 1989 the NUR merged with the National Union of Seamen and took its present title.

Secretary

1920	J. Thomas and C. Cramp	1948	J. Figgins
1931	C. Cramp	1953	J. Campbell
1933	(Acting Secretary)	1958	(Sir) S. (Ld) Greene
1934	J. Marchbank	1975	S. Weighell
1943	J. Benstead	1982	J. Knapp

National Union of Teachers (NUT) 1870

Originally National Union of Elementary Teachers (till 1890). Affiliated to TUC in 1970.

Secretary

1892	(Sir) J. Yoxall	1970	(Sir) E. Britton
1924	F. Goldstone	1975	F. Jarvis
1931	(Sir) F. Mander	1989	D. McAvoy
1947	(Sir) R. Gould		

Transport and General Workers Union 1922

Dock, Wharf, Riverside and General Workers' Union, National Union of Dock Labourers and other dockers' unions, United Vehicle Workers, National Union of Vehicle Workers and others. 1928 amalgamated with the Workers' Union.

Secretary

1921	E. Bevin	1966	F. Cousins
1940	A. Deakin (Acting till 1946)	1969	J. Jones
1955	A. Tiffin	1977	M. Evans
1956	F. Cousins	1985	R. Todd
1964	H. Nicholas (Acting)	1992	B. Morris

Union of Construction, Allied Trades and Technicians (UCATT) 1860 (1971)

Amalgamated Society of Carpenters and Joiners became, in 1921 after mergers, Amalgamated Society of Woodworkers (ASW). ASW merged in 1971 with the Amalgamated Union of Building Trade Workers (formed 1921), the Amalgamated Society of Painters and Decorators and the Association of Building Technicians.

Secretary

1919	A. Cameron	1959	(Sir) G. Smith
1925	F. Wolstencroft	1978	L. Wood
1949	J. MacDermott	1985	A. Williams

Union of Communication Workers (Union of Post Office Workers) (UCW) 1920

Postal Telegraph Clerks' Association. U.K. Postal Clerks Association merged in 1914 to form Postal and Telegraph Clerks' Association. This merged in 1920 with Fawcett Association and other unions to form UPW. Name changed to Union of Communication Workers in 1980. (Legally banned from membership of TUC 1927–1946.). Note that the UCW is quite distinct from the National Communications Union (NCU – until 1975 the POEU), which represents telecommunications engineers.

Secretary

1920	J. Bowen	1957	R. Smith
1936	T. Hodgson	1966	T. Jackson
1944	C. Geddes	1982	A. Tuffin

UNISON 1993

See above entries for COHSE, NALGO and NUPE.

General Secretary

1993	A. Jinkinson

Union of Shop, Distributive and Allied Workers (USDAW) 1921 (1946)

Cooperative Employees, and Warehouse and General Workers amalgamated in 1921 to form the National Union of Distributive and Allied Workers. 1946 fusion with National Amalgamated Union of Shop Assistants, Warehousemen and Clerks.

Secretary

1921	J. Hallsworth and W. Robinson	1962	A. (Ld) Allen
1924	(Sir) J. Hallsworth	1979	W. Whatley
1947	(*Acting Secretary*)	1986	G. Davies
1949	(Sir) A. Birch		

SOURCE. – *Trades Union Congress Reports, 1920–.*

THE LARGEST UNIONS

Membership (to nearest 000) (at 31 December)

The Eight Largest Unions (in 1960)

Year	AUEW	ETU	NALGO	(NU)GMW	NUM	NUR	T&GWU	USDAW
1920	407	57	36	..	900	458	..	..
1921	357	46	36	..	800	341	300	100
1922	256	31	33	..	750	327	300	90
1923	246	26	33	..	750	327	300	90
1924	206	28	34	327	800	327	300	93
1925	205	29	37	320	800	327	300	95
1926	162	29	40	300	800	327	300	94
1927	146	26	44	278	725	327	300	100
1928	151	26	46	258	600	313	286	109
1929	155	29	49	261	600	310	389	115
1930	154	31	61	258	600	321	384	119
1931	146	31	65	240	600	310	390	121
1932	136	31	68	220	500	285	390	127
1933	135	31	73	230	500	272	370	131
1934	146	34	79	252	500	291	403	134
1935	164	40	86	280	500	306	460	145
1936	248	48	93	340	518	338	523	158
1937	299	58	101	405	538	365	611	172
1938	334	64	106	417	584	367	635	183
1939	376	70	114	430	589	350	648	194
1940	454	80	111	441	589	362	650	223
1941	550	97	113	548	580	376	680	234
1942	645	113	121	721	599	394	806	254
1943	825	124	127	726	603	406	1,089	268
1944	811	132	133	661	605	404	1,017	272
1945	704	133	134	605	533	410	975	275
1946	723	162	146	795	538	414	1,230	374
1947	742	170	171	824	572	448	1,264	343
1948	743	182	176	816	611	455	1,271	342
1949	714	188	189	805	609	421	1,253	340
1950	716	192	197	785	602	392	1,242	343
1951	756	198	212	809	613	396	1,285	348
1952	796	203	222	808	641	397	1,277	346
1953	810	212	225	790	669	378	1,259	339
1954	823	216	230	787	675	372	1,240	344
1955	854	223	236	805	675	368	1,278	347
1956	860	228	243	808	674	369	1,264	349
1957	900	239	247	804	681	371	1,244	352
1958	888	230	252	775	674	355	1,225	353
1959	908	233	263	769	639	334	1,241	351
1960	973	243	274	769	586	334	1,302	355
1961	982	253	285	786	545	317	1,318	351
1962	986	257	295	781	529	311	1,331	356
1963	981	272	226	782	501	283	1,374	355
1964	1,011	282	338	785	479	264	1,426	352
1965	1,049	293	349	796	446	255	1,444	349
1966	1,055	293	361	793	413	220	1,428	336
1967	1,107	352	367	782	380	218	1,451	321
1968	1,136	365	373	798	344	199	1,476	311
1969	1,195	392	397	804	297	191	1,532	316

Year	AUEW	ETU	NALGO	(NU)GMW	NUM	NUR	T&GWU	USDAW
1970	1,295	421	440	853	279	198	1,629	330
1971	1,284	420	464	842	276	194	1,643	319
1972	1,340	417	498	848	271	184	1,747	325
1973	1,173	420	518	864	261	174	1,785	326
1974	1,211	414	542	884	255	173	1,857	353
1975	1,429	420	625	881	262	180	1,856	377
1976	1,412	420	683	916	260	180	1,930	413
1977	1,423	420	709	945	258	180	2,023	441
1978	1,484	420	729	965	255	180	2,073	462
1979	1,499	420	753	967	253	180	2,086	470
1980	1,381	405	782	916	257	170	1,887	450
1981	1,290	395	796	865	250	160	1,696	438
1982	1,238	380	784	940	245	150	1,633	417
1983	1,220	365	780	875	208	143	1,547	403
1984	1,221	355	766	847	200	136	1,491	392
1985	975	348	752	840	135	130	1,434	385
1986	858	336	750	814	105	125	1,378	382
1987	815	330	759	803	91	118	1,349	387
1988	794	330	755	864	77	110	1,313	397
1989	742	360	751	823	59	123	1,271	376
1990	702	367	744	933	53	118	1,224	362
1991	702	357	760	860	44	110	1,127	341

SOURCE. – *Trades Union Congress Reports, 1920–*.

Other Unions Which Have Exceeded 200,000 Members

	ASTMS (MSF)	CPSA	COHSE	NUPE	NUT	SOGAT	UCATT	UCW
1950	12	134	53	175	192	124	197	149
1960	25	140	54	200	225	158	192	166
1970	221	185	90	373	311	192	221	209
1980	491	224	213	692	249	206	348	203
1990	653	123	203	579	169	166	207	201

The Amalgamated Weavers' Association had 219,000 members in 1920. It fell to 89,000 by 1940.

SOURCE. – *Trades Union Congress Reports, 1920–*.

Income, Expenditure and Funds of Registered Trade Unions

(in shillings per member)

Year	Income from Members	Expenditure Benefits			Other		Total
		Dispute benefit	Unemployment benefit	Other Welfare benefits	Working expenses	Political Funds	
1910	27.8	5.3	6.8	11.1	..	8.1	59.3
1920	32.4	9.3	4.5	5.1	0.5	17.2	45.8
1930	37.6	1.6	9.7	12.1	0.5	16.6	62.0
1940	36.0	0.2	3.0	10.4	0.4	14.8	92.2
1950	39.6	0.6	0.4	10.4	1.1	22.8	156.4
1960	58.8	1.1	0.4	15.5	1.2	34.9	211.6
1970	104.9	8.6	0.6	25.9	3.7	72.4	322.6
1980	365.2	14.4	4.1	35.2	6.4	302.4	500.2
1990	943.4	–	134.1	–	25.9	971.3	1,296.1

SOURCES. – A. Flanders, *Trade Unions* (1967); *Department of Employment Gazette; Annual Reports of the Certification Officer.*

Density of Union Membership in Total Labour Force (%)

United Kingdom

1901	12.6	1951	44.1
1911	17.7	1961	43.1
1920	45.2	1970	47.7
1933	22.6	1974	49.6
1938	29.5	1981	43.7
		1991	34.3

SOURCES. – G.S. Bain, *The Growth of White Collar Unionism* (1970); G.S. Bain and R. Price, 'Union Growth and Employment Trends in the U.K. 1964–70', *British Journal of Industrial Relations* (1972), pp. 366–81 and 'Union Growth Revisited 1948–70', *British Journal of Industrial Relations* (1976), pp. 339–55; *Annual Reports of the Certification Officer.*

Major Industrial Disputes

(strikes and lockouts in which more than 500,000 working days were lost)

Dispute Began		Industrial group	Area	Numbers affected (000s)	Working days lost (000s)[a]
1900	Apr	Potters	N. Staffs.	20	640
	Nov	Quarrymen	Bethesda	3	505
1902	Jul	Miners	UK	103	872
1906	Oct	Shipyard workers	Clyde	15	592
1908	Feb	Shipyard workers	Humber, Barrow, Birkenhead, Clyde, E. Scotland	35	1,719
	Feb	Engineers	N.E. Coast	11	1,706
	Sep	Cotton operatives	Lancs., Cheshire, Derby	120	4,830
1909	Jul	Miners	S. Wales and Mon.	55	660
1910	Jan	Miners	Durham	85	1,280
	Jan	Miners	Northumberland	30	1,080
	Apr	Miners	Rhondda	13	2,985
	Jun	Cotton operatives	Lancs. and Chesh.	102	600
	Sep	Shipyard workers	N.E. and Scotland	35	2,851

Dispute Began		Industrial group	Area	Numbers affected (000s)	Working days lost (000s)[a]
1911	Jun	Seamen and dockers	U.K.	120	1,020
	Aug	Dockers and carters	London	22	500
	Aug	Railwaymen	U.K.	145	500
	Dec	Cotton weavers	N.E. Lancs.	160	2,954
1912	Feb	Miners	U.K.	1,000	30,800
	Feb	Jute workers	Dundee	28	726
	May	Dockers and carters	Port of London and Medway	100	2,700
1913	Jan	Cab drivers	London	11	637
	Apr	Tube and metal workers	S. Staffs. and N. Worcs.	50	1,400
	Aug	Transport workers	Dublin	20	1,900
1914	Jan	Builders	London	20	2,500
	Feb	Miners	Yorks.	150	2,654
1915	Jul	Miners	S. Wales	232	1,400
1916	Mar	Jute workers	Dundee	30	500
1917	May	Engineers	U.K.	160	2,880
1918	May	Miners	S. Wales and Mon.	40	760
	Dec	Cotton spinners	Lancs. and Chesh.	100	900
1919	Jan	Miners	Yorks.	150	1,950
	Jan	Shipyard workers	N.E. Coast	40	820
	Mar	Miners	Various districts	100	600
	Jun	Cotton operatives	Lancs. and adjoining counties	450	7,500
	Jul	Miners	Yorks.	150	4,050
	Sep	Ironfounders	England, Wales, and Ireland	50	6,800
	Sep	Railwaymen	U.K.	500	3,850
1920	Sep	Cotton operatives	Oldham area	400	620
	Oct	Miners	U.K.	1,100	16,000
	Dec	Shipyard carpenters	U.K.	10	2,200
1921	Apr	Miners	U.K.	10	2,200
	Jul	Builders	U.K.	100	2,970
1925	Jul	Wool textile workers	W. Yorks, Lancs	165	3,105
1926	May	Miners	U.K.	1,050	145,200
	May	General Strike	U.K.	1,580[b]	15,000[b]
1928	May	Cotton weavers	Nelson	17	600
1929	Jul	Cotton operatives	Lancs. and adjoining counties	388	6,596
1930	Apr	Wool textile workers	W. Yorks, Lancs	120	3,258
1931	Jan	Cotton weavers	Lancs. and adjoining counties	145	3,290
	Jan	Miners	S. Wales, Mon.	150	2,030
1932	Aug	Cotton weavers	Lancs., Yorks.	148	4,524
	Oct	Cotton spinners	Lancs. and adjoining counties	130	760
1937	May	Busmen	London	24	565
1944	Mar	Miners	Wales and Mon.	100	550
	Mar	Miners	Yorkshire	120	1,000
1945	Sep	Dockers	Birkenhead, Hull, Manchester, Liverpool, London	50	1,100
1953	Dec	Engineers and Shipyard workers	U.K.	1,070	1,070
1954	Sep	Dockers	Port of London and sympathy strikes	45	726
1955	May	Dockers	English ports	21	673
	May	Railwaymen	U.K.	70	865
1957	Mar	Engineers	U.K.	615	4,000
	Mar	Shipyard workers	U.K.	165	2,150
	Jul	Busmen	Provinces	100	770
1958	Apr	Dockers, transport and market workers	London	24	515
	May	Busmen	Greater London	49	1,604
1959	Jun	Printing workers	U.K.	120	3,500

Dispute Began		Industrial group	Area	Numbers affected (000s)	Working days lost (000s)[a]
1962	Feb	Engineering & Shipbuilding	U.K.	1,750	1,750
	Mar	Engineering & Shipbuilding	U.K.	1,750	1,750
1966	May	Shipping	U.K.	30	850
1968	May	Engineering	U.K.	1,500	1,500
1969	Feb	Motor Vehicles	Various areas	38	561
	Oct	Miners	Various areas	121	979
1970	Jul	Dockers	U.K.	42	502
	Sep	Local authority workers	England and Wales	134	1,216
	Oct	Miners	Various	99	1,050
1971	Jan	Motor vehicles	Various areas	42	1,909
	Jan	Post Office workers	U.K.	180	6,229
1972	Jan	Miners	U.K.	309	10,726
	Jun	Construction	England and Wales	120	2,904
	Jun	Construction	Scotland	36	933
	Jul	Dockers	U.K.	35	548
1974	Feb	Miners	U.K.	250	5,567
1977	Nov	Firemen	U.K.	30	1,250
1978	Oct	Motor Vehicles (Ford)	U.K.	56	2,529
	Dec	Printworkers	London	3	592
1979	Jan	Lorry drivers	U.K.	85	950
	Jan	Public employees	U.K.	1,500	3,239
	Feb	Civil servants	U.K.	279	508
	Jul	Television staff	U.K.	12	600
	Aug	Engineers	U.K.	1,500	16,000
1980	Jan	Steelworkers	U.K.	151	8,800
1981	Mar	Civil servants	U.K.	318	867
1982	Jan	Railway footplatemen	U.K.	59	814
	Apr	Health service	U.K.	180	781
	May	All workers	U.K.	948	672
1983	Jan	Water workers	England, Wales, Northern Ireland	35	766
1984	Mar	Miners	U.K.	130	26,100
1985	Feb	Teachers	England & Wales	168	772
1987	Jan	Engineers	Various U.K.	113	1,471
	Apr	Civil servants	Various U.K.	14	624
1988	Jun	Shipbuilding	Cumbria	13	754
	Sep	Postmen	U.K.	119	1,036
1989	Jul	Local authority white collar	G.B.	350	2,004
	Oct	Engineers	Various G.B.	9	611

[a] Where figures for working days lost have not been given in the Gazettes, they have been estimated.
[b] Excluding miners.

SOURCES. – *The Board of Trade Labour Gazette*, (1900–17); *The Ministry of Labour Gazette* (1918–68); *Employment and Productivity Gazette* (1968–70); *Department of Employment Gazette* (1970–).

Emergency Powers

Under the *Emergency Powers Act, 1920*, the government may proclaim a State of Emergency if the essentials of life of the country are threatened. The Act then empowers the government to make regulations by Order-in-Council which have the full force of law. All the occasions on which States of Emergency have been proclaimed under the Act have been associated with strikes.

31 Mar	21	Coal
26 Mar	24	London Transport[1]
2 May	26	General Strike
29 Jun	48	Docks
11 Jul	49	Docks
31 May	55	Rail
23 May	66	Seamen
16 Jul	70	Docks
12 Dec	70	Electricity
9 Feb	72	Coal
3 Aug	72	Docks
13 Nov	73	Coal and Electricity (also Middle East oil crisis)

[1] It is doubtful whether this proclamation was ever made.

Unemployment, Industrial Disputes, and Trade Union Statistics

	Unemployment[b]		Industrial Disputes[c]				Total No. of Trade Union Members affiliated to TUC	Total No. of Trade Unions affiliated to TUC	No. of members of Trade Unions (000s)
	Maximum (000s)	Minimum (000s)	Working Days Lost[d] (000s)	No. of Stoppages beginning in year[e]	Total Workers involved[d] (000s)	No. of Trade Unions (000s)			
1900			3,088	633	185	1,325	1,911	184	1,250
1901			4,130	631	179	1,323	2,022	191	1,200
1902			3,438	432	255	1,322	2,025	198	1,400
1903			2,320	380	116	1,297	2,013	204	1,500
1904			1,464	346	87	1,285	1,994	212	1,423
1905			2,368	349	92	1,256	1,967	205	1,541
1906			3,019	479	218	1,244	1,997	226	1,555
1907			2,148	585	146	1,282	2,210	236	1,700
1908			10,785	389	293	1,283	2,513	214	1,777
1909			2,687	422	297	1,268	2,485	219	1,705
1910			9,867	521	514	1,260	2,477	212	1,648
1911			10,155	872	952	1,269	2,565		
1912			40,890	834	1,462	1,290	3,139	202	1,662
1913			9,804	1,459	664	1,252	3,416	201	2,002
1914			9,878	972	447	1,269	4,135	207	2,232
1915			2,953	672	448	1,260	4,145	215	2,682
1916			2,446	532	276	1,229	4,359	227	2,851
1917			5,647	730	872	1,225	4,644	235	3,082
1918			5,875	1,165	1,116	1,241	5,499	262	4,532
1919			34,969	1,352	2,591	1,264	6,533	266	5,284
1920			26,568	1,607	1,932	1,360	7,926	215	6,505
1921	2,038[a]		85,872	763	1,801	1,384	8,348	213	6,418
1922	2,015 Jan	1,443 Oct	19,850	576	552	1,275	6,633	206	5,129
1923	1,525 Jan	1,229 Dec	10,672	628	405	1,232	5,625	194	4,369
1924	1,374 Jan	1,087 Jun	8,424	710	613	1,192	5,429	203	4,328
1925	1,443 Aug	1,243 Dec	7,952	603	441	1,194	5,544	205	4,351
1926	1,432 Dec	1,094 Apr	162,233	323	2,734	1,176	5,506	207	4,366
1927	1,451 Jan	1,059 May	1,174	308	108	1,164	5,219	204	4,164
1928	1,375 Aug	1,127 Mar	1,388	302	124	1,159	4,919	196	3,875
1929	1,466 Jan	1,164 Jun	8,287	431	533	1,142	4,866	202	3,673

Notes: see p. 375.

	Unemployment[b]		Industrial Disputes[c]				Total No. of Trade Union Members affiliated to TUC (000s)	Total No. of Trade Unions affiliated to TUC	No. of members of Trade Unions (000s)
	Maximum (000s)	Minimum (000s)	Working Days Lost[d] (000s)	No.of Stoppages beginning in year[e]	Total Workers involved[d] (000s)	No. of Trade Unions (000s)			
1930	2,500 Dec	1,520 Jan	4,399	422	307	1,133	4,858	210	3,744
1931	2,880 Sep	2,578 May	6,983	420	490	1,121	4,842	210	3,719
1932	2,955 Jan	2,309 Nov	6,488	389	379	1,108	4,624	209	3,613
1933	2,407 Jan	1,858 Dec	1,072	357	136	1,081	4,444	208	3,368
1934	2,295 Jan	2,080 Sep	959	471	134	1,081	4,392	210	3,295
1935	2,333 Jan	1,888 Dec	1,955	553	271	1,063	4,590	211	3,389
1936	2,169 Jan	1,640 Aug	1,829	818	316	1,049	4,867	214	3,615
1937	1,739 Dec	1,373 Sep	3,413	1,129	597	1,036	5,295	214	4,009
1938	1,912 Dec	1,818 Apr	1,334	875	274	1,032	5,842	216	4,461
1939	2,032 Jan	1,230 Aug	1,356	940	337	1,024	6,053	217	4,669
1940	1,471 Jan	683 Dec	940	922	299	1,019	6,298	223	4,867
1941	653 Jan	151 Dec	1,079	1,251	360	1,004	6,613	223	5,079
1942	162 Jan	100 Dec	1,527	1,303	456	996	7,165	232	5,433
1943	104 Jan	..	1,808	1,785	557	991	7,867	230	6,024
1944	84 Jan	..	3,714	2,194	821	987	8,174	190	6,642
1945	111 Jan	..	2,835	2,293	531	963	8,087	191	6,576
1946	408 Jan	360 Jan	2,158	2,205	526	781	7,875	192	6,671
1947	1,916 Feb	262 Sep	2,433	1,721	620	757	8,803	187	7,540
1948	359 Dec	299 Jun	1,944	1,759	424	734	9,145	188	7,791
1949	413 Jan	274 Jul	1,807	1,426	433	735	9,319	187	7,937
1950	404 Jan	297 Jul	1,389	1,339	302	726	9,274	186	7,937
1951	367 Jan	210 Jul	1,694	1,719	379	732	9,289	186	7,828
1952	468 Apr	379 Jan	1,792	1,714	415	735	9,535	183	8,020
1953	452 Feb	273 Jul	2,184	1,746	370	719	9,583	183	8,088
1954	387 Feb	220 Jul	2,457	1,989	448	717	9,523	184	8,094
1955	298 Jan	185 Jul	3,781	2,419	659	703	9,556	183	8,107
1956	297 Dec	223 Jun	2,083	2,648	507	694	9,726	186	8,264
1957	383 Jan	244 Jul	8,412	2,859	1,356	685	9,829	185	8,305
1958	536 Nov	395 Jan	3,462	2,629	523	675	9,639	185	8,337
1959	621 Jan	395 Jul	5,270	2,093	645	668	9,623	186	8,176
1960	461 Jan	292 Jul	3,024	2,832	817	664	9,835	184	8,128
1961	419 Jan	259 Jul	3,046	2,686	771	646	9,897	183	8,299
1962	566 Dec	397 Jun	5,795	2,449	4,420	626	8,887	182	8,313
1963	878 Feb	449 Jul	1,755	2,068	591	607	9,934	176	8,315
1964	501 Jan	318 Jul	2,277	2,524	871	598	10,079	175	8,326
1965	376 Jan	276 Jun	2,925	2,354	871	630	10,325	172	8,771
1966	564 Dec	261 Jun	2,398	1,937	530	622	10,261	170	8,868
1967	603 Feb	497 Jul	2,787	2,116	734	603	10,110	169	8,787
1968	631 Jan	515 Jul	4,690	2,378	2,255	584	10,193	160	8,726
1969	595 Jan	499 Jun	6,846	3,116	1,654	563	10,472	155	8,875
1970	628 Jan	547 Jun	10,980	3,906	1,793	540	11,179	150	9,402
1971	868 Dec	655 Jan	13,551	2,228	1,776	523	11,128	142	10,002
1972[f]	929 Jan	745 Dec	23,909	2,497	1,722	503	11,353	132	9,895
1973	785 Jan	486 Dec	7,197	2,873	1,513	513	11,449	126	10,001
1974	628 Aug	515 Jun	14,750	2,922	1,622	498	11,756	109	10,002

Notes: see p. 375.

	Unemployment[b]		Industrial Disputes[c]				Total No. of Trade Union Members affiliated to TUC (000s)	Total No. of Trade Unions affiliated to TUC	No. of members of Trade Unions (000s)
	Maximum (000s)	Minimum (000s)	Working Days Lost[d] (000s)	No. of Stoppages beginning in year[e]	Total Workers involved[d] (000s)	No. of Trade Unions (000s)			
1975	1,152 Dec	738 Jan	6,012	2,282	789	488	12,184	111	10,364
1976	1,440 Aug	1,220 Jun	3,284	2,016	882	462	12,376	113	11,036
1977	1,567 Aug	1,286 May	9,985	2,627	1,143	485	12,719	112	11,516
1978	1,608 Aug	1,364 Dec	9,306	2,349	939	485		112	11,865
1979	1,464 Jul	1,299 May	29,474	4,583	2,080	462	13,112	112	12,128
1980	2,244 Dec	1,471 Jan	11,964	830	1,330	453	13,289	109	12,173
1981	2,772 Oct	2,271 Jan	4,266	1,499	1,338	438	12,947	108	11,601
1982	3,097 Dec	2,770 Jun	5,313	2,101	1,528	414	12,106	105	11,006
1983	3,225 Jan	2,984 Jun	3,754	571	1,352	408	11,593	102	10,810
1984	3,284 Sep	3,030 Jun	27,135	1,221	1,464	394	11,236	98	10,082
1985	3,346 Sep	3,179 Jun	6,402	903	791	375	10,994	91	9,855
1986	3,408 Jan	3,216 Nov	1,920	1,074	720	370	10,821	88	9,586
1987	3,297 Jan	2,686 Nov	3,546	1,016	887	335	10,539	87	9,243
1988	2,722 Jan	2,047 Dec	3,702	781	790	330	10,475	83	9,127
1989	2,074 Jan	1,612 Nov	4,128	701	727	315	10,376	78	8,652
1990	1,850 Dec	1,556 Jun	1,903	630	298	309	10,158	78	8,405
1991	2,552 Dec	1,960 Jan	761	369	176	287	9,947	74	8,193
1992	2,983 Dec	2,674 Jan	528	253	148	275	9,585	72	7,762
1993	3,062 Jan	2,679 Nov	649	211	385	268	9,048	..	..

[a] Figures for December available only.

[b] 1900–20, unemployment figures for certain skilled trade unions available in *Ministry of Labour Gazettes*. Figures are given as percentages. No comparable figures of total unemployed are available before 1921. Figures for insured workers registered as unemployed. Agricultural workers, insurable in 1936, are included from that date. Numerous changes in coverage throughout.

[c] Disputes involving less than 10 work people and those lasting less than one day are ommitted, except where aggregate duration exceeded 100 working days.

[d] S. Ireland included from 1900–07.

[e] Workers involved directly and indirectly. 'Indirectly' involved means those unable to work at establishments where disputes occurred, though not themselves parties to the dispute.

[f] After the passage of the *Industrial Relations Act, 1971*, many trade unions ceased to be registered and as a result many trade union statistics for the following four years are non-existent or non-comparable.

SOURCES. – *Annual Abstract of Statistics, Ministry of Labour Gazette, Employment Gazette* and *Abstract of Labour Statistics. TUC Congress Reports.*

BIBLIOGRAPHY: H. A. Clegg, *The Changing System of Industrial Relations in Great Britain*(1979); G. S. Bain (ed.), *Industrial Relations in Britain* (1983); H. Pelling, *A History of British Trade Unionism* (5th Ed., 1992); H. A. Clegg *et al.*, *A History of British Trade Unions since 1889* (1985); Lord Wedderburn, *The Worker and the Law* (4th Ed., 1994); N. Selwyn, *The Law of Employment* (8th Ed., 1993); Hepple and Fredman, *Labour Law and Industrial Relations in Great Britain* (2nd Ed., 1992); K. Coates and T. Topham, *Trade Unions in Britain* (3rd Ed., 1988); R. Hyman, *Strikes* (4th Ed., 1989); *Trade Unions and the Labour Party: Final Report of the Review Group on Links between the Trade Unions and the Labour Party* (1993).

XI

THE ECONOMY

Some Landmarks in the British Economy

1 Aug 14	War emergency measures, including temporary increase in Bank Rate to 10%.
Dec 16	Exchange rate pegged at $4.77 to £.
15 Aug 18	Report of Cunliffe Committee on Currency and Foreign Exchanges (Cd. 9182) recommended eventual return to an effective gold standard at pre-war par value.
20 Mar 19	Withdrawal of official peg from sterling-dollar exchange; exchange rates allowed to fluctuate.
Jan 21	Post-war trade slump. Unemployment exceeded 1 million (it remained above that level until 1939).
28 Apr 25	Return to fixed gold parity, at pre-1914 level ($4.86 = £1). Britain now on gold bullion standard.
3 May 26	General Strike.
23 Jun 31	Report of Macmillan Committee on Finance and Industry (Cmd. 3897).
24 Jul 31	Report of May Committee on National Expenditure (Cmd. 3920), recommended big cuts in Government expenditure.
21 Sep 31	Gold Standard suspended; sterling on fluctuating rate.
29 Feb 32	Import Duties Act set up Import Duties Advisory Council.
25 Apr 32	Exchange Equalisation Fund established to smooth variations in exchange rates.
30 Jun 32	Bank rate reduced to 2% and held at this level until 1939.
21 Aug 32	Ottawa Agreements on Imperial Preference.
21 Dec 33	Agricultural Marketing Act authorises quota controls on agricultural imports.
21 Dec 34	Special Areas (Development and Improvement) Act recognised problems of distressed areas.
3 Feb 36	Publication of J. M. Keynes, *General Theory of Employment, Interest and Money*.
12 Oct 36	Tripartite Agreement between Britain, France, and the U.S.A. to promote greater exchange stability by inter-Treasury Cooperation.
4 Sep 39	War emergency measures including imposition of exchange control with formal definition of the Sterling Area. Exchange rate fixed at $4.03 = £1.
21 Aug 41	Start of Lend-Lease.
22 Jul 44	Bretton Woods agreement leading to establishment of International Monetary Fund (27 Dec 1945).
26 Aug 44	White Paper on Employment Policy (Cmd. 6527) accepts Government responsibility for 'maintenance of a high and stable level of employment'.
21 Aug 45	End of Lend-Lease followed by U.S. and Canadian loans to Britain.
1 Jan 46	Nationalisation of Bank of England.
Feb 47	Fuel Crisis.
5 Jun 47	Gen. Marshall's speech leading to establishment of Marshall Aid (Jul 48) and of Organisation for European Economic Co-operation (Apr 48).
15 Jul 47	Sterling made convertible. Convertibility suspended 20 Aug.
4 Oct 47	Agriculture Act put the policy of agricultural subsidy and protection on a peranent basis.
4 Feb 48	'Wage Freeze' and dividend restraint.
30 Jul 48	Monopolies and Restrictive Practices (Inquiry and Control) Act established Monopolies Commission.
18 Sep 49	Devaluation of £ from $4.03 to $2.80.
13 Dec 50	Marshall Aid suspended as no longer necessary.
7 Nov 51	Bank rate increase from 2% to 2½% signals the revival of use of monetary policy. Import liberalisation rescinded to check record dollar drain.
25 Oct 55	Autumn budget following balance-of-payments crisis.
2 Aug 56	Restrictive Trade Practices Act established Restrictive Trade Practices Court.
11 Dec 56	Stand-by credits arranged following post-Suez balance-of-payments crisis.
12 Aug 57	Council on Prices Productivity and Incomes ('Three Wise Men') set up. (Disbanded 1961.)
19 Sep 57	Bank rate raised to 7% to meet sterling crisis.
27 Dec 57	Convertibility announced for non-resident sterling on current account.
20 Aug 59	Report of Radcliffe Committee on the working of the monetary system (Cmnd. 827).
20 Nov 59	European Free Trade Association Treaty signed.
4 Dec 60	O.E.E.C. reconstituted and broadened to include U.S.A. and Canada and retitled O.E.C.D.
20 Jul 61	Plowden Report on Control of Public Expenditure.
25 Jul 61	'Pay Pause' measures of S. Lloyd following balance-of-payments crisis. Establishment of National Economic Development Council.

10 Aug 61	Britain applies to join European Economic Community (negotiations terminated Jan 63).
16 Jul 64	Resale Prices Act greatly limits resale price maintenance.
26 Oct 64	New Government meets balance-of-payments deficit by imposing 15% import surcharge (reduced to 10% in Apr 65 and ended Nov 66).
18 Mar 65	Establishment of Prices and Incomes Board.
5 Aug 65	Monopolies and Mergers Act extended 1948 Monopolies Act to cover services as well as goods.
13 Sep 65	Publication of first National Economic Plan (Cmnd. 2764).
25 Jan 66	Industrial Reorganisation Corporation established to encourage 'concentration and rationalisation and to promote the greater efficiency and international competitiveness of British Industry'. (Cmnd. 2889.)
6 Mar 66	Announcement that Decimal Currency would be adopted in 1971.
20 Jul 66	Sterling crisis leads to Bank rate of 7%, tax increases, credit restraints, and prices and incomes standstill (Cmnd. 3073).
12 Aug 66	Prices and Incomes Act becomes law (Part IV activated 6 Oct 66).
7 Mar 67	First landing of North Sea Gas.
11 May 67	Britain applies (for second time) to join European Economic Community. (De Gaulle gives second veto 27 Nov 67).
18 Nov 67	Devaluation of £ from $2.80 to $2.40. Bank Rate 8%.
19 Jan 68	Major cuts in Government expenditure announced, followed by drastically deflationary Budget 19 Mar.
17 Mar 68	Two-tier Bold system announced by World Central Banks.
30 Mar 68	Agreement on Special Drawing Rights in International Monetary Fund.
27 Oct 70	Expenditure cuts of £330m. announced, together with tax cuts.
15 Feb 71	Changeover to decimal currency.
30 Mar 71	Budget announces switch from surtax to graduated tax and to adopt Value Added Tax in 1973.
15 Aug 71	U.S.A. ends dollar-gold convertibility and, thereby, the Bretton Woods era.
23 Aug 71	£ floated.
19 Dec 71	General currency realignment under the Smithsonian agreement.
18 Feb 72	Wilberforce Court of Enquiry (Cmnd. 4903) ends six-week miners' strike with 22% pay increase recommendation.
26 Sep 72	Anti-inflation programme announced including pay and prices freezes and establishment of Prices Commission and Pay Board.
1 Jan 73	Britain joins European Economic Community.
4 Mar 73	European currencies floated against £.
1 Apr 73	Value Added Tax supplants other excise duties and Selective Employment Tax.
6 Oct 73	Outbreak of Middle East War followed by short term cut in Middle East oil supplies and quadrupling of world oil prices.
8 Oct 73	Announcement of 'Phase 3' anti-inflation proposals.
13 Dec 73	Announcement of 3-day week for industry, starting in January, to cope with miners' overtime ban since 12 Nov.
11 Feb 74	Complete mine stoppage until 11 Mar. 3-day week ended 8 Mar.
31 Dec 74	End of year during which retail prices rose by 19% while wage rates by 29% while total industrial production fell by 3% (each figure a post-war record).
30 Jan 75	*Financial Times* Index of leading shares prices touched 252 having been at 146 on 9 Jan 75 and at 339 on 28 Feb 74.
5 Jun 75	Referendum on continued British membership of the EEC. 67.2% vote to stay in Community.
18 Jun 75	First landing of North Sea Oil.
11 Jul 75	Government publishes White Paper, *The Attack on Inflation*, which introduces a universal pay rise limit of £6 per week from 1 Aug 75. (In the year up to June 1975 earnings for manual workers had risen by 33.3%).
12 Aug 75	Monthly retail price index shows a 26.9% increase in a year – a post-war record.
20 Nov 75	Announcement that cash limits will be applied to most public expenditure in the financial year 1976/7.
19 Feb 76	Public expenditure White Paper published, showing cuts in spending of £1.0 billion in 1977/8 and £2.4 billion in 1978/9 compared with previous plans.
2 Mar 76	Sterling falls below $2 for first time.
6 Apr 76	In Budget £1.3 billion tax cuts are announced but made dependent on agreement by the T.U.C to a new low pay norm in Stage 2. 4½% pay formula agreed on 5 May and endorsed at special T.U.C. meeting on 16 Jun.
22 Jul 76	Announcement of further £1,000m. cut in public expenditure in 1977/8.
29 Sep 76	Government approaches IMF for a $3.9 billion stand-by credit.
7 Oct 76	Minimum Lending Rate increased to 15%.

28 Oct 76	Sterling closes at $1.5675 – its lowest ever.
15 Dec 76	A further cut in public expenditure of £1,000m. in 1977/8 and £1,500m. in 1978/9 is announced as part of the agreement with the IMF.
11 Aug 77	Unemployment reaches peak of 1,635,800.
7 Sep 77	T.U.C. supports 12-month rule for Stage 3. Government continues to seek voluntary 10% limit on earnings increases.
4 Jan 78	U.K. official reserves rise to $20.6 billion – the highest ever.
5 Jan 78	U.S. Treasury announces it will intervene in foreign exchange markets to halt decline in dollar.
17 Feb 78	Inflation (year on year) falls below 10% for first time since 1973.
12 Mar 79	European Monetary system starts.
12 Jun 79	New Conservative Government's budget cuts income tax from 33% to 30% and raises VAT from 8% to 15%.
24 Oct 79	Abolition of exchange controls.
15 Nov 79	Minimum lending rate touches 17%.
26 Mar 80	Announcement of Medium Term Financial Strategy (MTFS).
Jun 80	Britain becomes net exporter of oil.
2 Jun 80	Agreement on reduction of Britain's EEC budget contribution.
21 Nov 80	Youth Opportunities Programme doubled.
Oct 80	£ reaches peak exchange with $ (2.39).
Jan 81	Bottom of worst post-war slump for Britain.
20 Aug 81	Minimum lending rate abolished.
27 Jul 82	Hire purchase controls abolished.
9 Sep 82	Unemployment reaches three million.
13 Mar 84	Beginning of miners' strike.
26 Jun 84	Fontainebleau summit agrees permanent settlement of Britain's EEC contribution.
28 Nov 84	Government sells 33% of British Telecom.
3 Dec 84	Br Telecom Shares (sold in Nov) gain 45% premium in first Stock Exchange dealings.
19 Dec 84	Hong Kong Agreement for 1997 handover.
18 Jan 85	FT Index breaks 1000 for the first time.
4 Mar 85	End of year-long miners' strike (26.1m. days lost).
7 Mar 85	£ touches bottom level of $1.05.
10 Mar 86	Budget lowers basic income tax to 29%.
27 Oct 86	'Big Bang' revolutionises stock exchange mechanics.
17 Feb 86	Single European Act.
Jan 87	Guinness scandal leads to top City prosecutions.
5 Feb 87	Wapping strike ends and transforms newspaper finances.
17 Mar 87	Budget lowers basic income tax to 27%.
19 Oct 87	'Black Monday' collapse in stock market.
11 Mar 88	Budget reduces basic income tax to 25%; top rate to 40%.
Sep 88	Worst ever trade deficit announced.
29 Oct 89	Lawson resigns as Chancellor. Major succeeds.
1 Apr 90	Start of poll tax.
Apr 90	Unemployment begins strong upward rise.
2 Aug 90	Invasion of Kuwait starts 6 month Gulf War.
8 Oct 90	United Kingdom joins Exchange Rate Mechanism at £1 = 2.95DM.
1 Nov 90	Sir G. Howe resigns.
28 Nov 90	J. Major becomes Prime Minister with N. Lamont as Chancellor.
28 Feb 91	End of Gulf War.
Mar 91	End of poll tax announced.
11 Dec 91	Maastricht agreement signed with U.K. opt-outs.
25 Dec 91	Yeltsin succeeds Gorbachev in Russia.
10 Mar 92	Budget announces ending of April Budgets.
9 Apr 92	Conservatives win General Election with low tax promises.
16 Sep 92	'Black Wednesday': Britain leaves Exchange Rate Mechanism. £ at $1.90 on Sep 1 falls to $1.65 by Sep 30.
12 Nov 92	Chancellor predicts a £37bn. Public Sector Borrowing requirement for next year.
16 Mar 93	Last Spring Budget imposes V.A.T. on fuel.
Apr 92	After 8 negative Quarters recession officially ends.
27 May 93	K. Clarke replaces N. Lamont as Chancellor.
23 Jul 93	Maastricht treaty finally approved by Parliament.
29 Nov 93	House of Commons votes for Sunday shopping.
30 Nov 93	First unified Budget involves expenditure cuts and higher taxes.
15 Dec 93	GATT changes (Uruguay Round) approved by 117 countries.

Sources of Government Economic Advice

The Treasury and, from 1964–69, the Department of Economic Affairs have provided governments with their main official guidance (see p. 283 for Permanent Secretaries). In addition, under the Cabinet Office or the Treasury, there have been the following official economic advisers.

Economic Section of the Cabinet Office (1941–53)

Director

1941	J. Jewkes	1946	J. Meade
1941	L. Robbins	1947	R. Hall

Economic Adviser to the Government (1953–64)

1953	(Sir) R. Hall	1961	A. Cairncross

Head of Government Economic Service (1964–)

1964	(Sir) A. Cairncross	1976	Sir A. Atkinson
1969	Sir D. MacDougall	1980	(Sir) T. Burns
1973	Sir K. Berrill	1991	A. Budd
1974	Sir B. Hopkin		

Outside the Civil Service there have been the following official bodies:

Bank of England (1696)

Governor

1899	S. Gladstone	1920	M. Norman (Ld)
1901	(Sir) A. Prevost	1944	Ld Catto
1903	S. Morley	1949	C. Cobbold (Ld)
1905	A. Wallace	1964	E of Cromer
1908	R. Johnston	1966	(Sir) L. O'Brien (Ld)
1913	W. Cunliffe (Ld)	1973	G. Richardson (Ld)
1918	Sir B. Cokayne	1983	R. Leigh-Pemberton
	(Ld Cullen of Ashbourne)	1993	E. George

Economic Advisory Council (1930–39)

(No full meeting of this body was held after the first year, but until 1939 its Standing Committee on Economic Information was active under Sir J. Stamp (Ld).)

Import Duties Advisory Council (1932–39)

Chairman

1932 Sir F. May (Ld)

Economic Planning Board (1947–62)

Chairman

1947–53 Sir E. Plowden

(After 1953, when some of its functions were merged with the Economic Section of the Treasury, the Permanent Secretary of the Treasury was made *ex officio* Chairman of the Board of outside advisers.)

National Economic Development Council (1961–92)

Director-General of National Economic Development Office

1962	Sir R. Shone	1973	(Sir) R. McIntosh
1966	Sir F. Figgures	1983	J. Cassels
1966	(Sir) F. Catherwood	1988	W. Eltis

Council on Pay, Productivity, and Incomes (1957–61)

Chairman

1957	Ld Cohen
1960	Ld Heyworth

National Incomes Commission (1961–64)

Chairman

1962	Sir G. Lawrence

Prices and Incomes Board (1965–70)

Chairman

1965	A. Jones

Prices Commission (1973–79)

Chairman

1973	Sir A. Cockfield
1976	C. Williams

Pay Board (1973–74)

Chairman

1973	Sir F. Figgures

Industrial Adviser to the Government (1974–75)

1974	Sir D. Ryder (Ld)

Commission on Pay Comparability (1979–80)

Chairman

1979	H. Clegg

(See also Monopolies Commission, p. 417; Royal Commissions and Committees of Inquiry, pp. 292–300; Central Policy Review Staff, p. 279.)

Economic Interest Groups

Industrial and Commercial Organisations

Federation of British Industry (1916–1965)

President

1916	F. Docker	1930	Sir J. Lithgow	1945	Sir C. Ballieu
1917	Sir R. Vassar-Smith	1931	Sir A. Duckham	1947	Sir F. Bain
1918	Sir V. Gaillard	1932	Sir G. Beharrel	1949	Sir R. Sinclair
1919	Sir P. Rylands	1933	Sir G. Macdonough	1951	Sir A. Forbes
1921	O. Armstrong	1934	Ld H. Scott	1953	Sir H. Pilkington
1923	Sir E. Geddes	1935	Sir F. Joseph	1955	Sir G. Hayman
1925	V. Willey	1936	Ld Hirst	1957	Sir H. Beaver
1927	Sir M. Muspratt	1937	(Sir) P. Bennett	1959	Sir W. MacFadzean
1928	Ld Ebbisham	1940	Ld D. Gordon	1961	Sir C. Harrison
1929	L. Lee	1943	Sir G. Nelson	1963	Sir P. Runge

Director

1916	R. Nugent	1919	(Sir) R. Nugent	1946	(Sir) N. Kipping
1917	E. Hill	1932	(Sir) G. Locock		

Confederation of British Industry (1965)

Formed by a merger of the Federation of British Industries (FBI) (founded 1916), the National Association of British Manufacturers (1915) and the British Employers' Confederation (1919). It held its first Annual Conference at Brighton 13–15 Nov 77.

President

1965	Sir M. Laing	1974	Sir R. Bateman	1984	Sir J. Cleminson
1966	Sir S. Brown	1976	Vt Watkinson	1986	D. Nickson
1968	Sir A. Norman	1978	Sir J. Greenborough	1988	Sir T. Holdsworth
1970	Sir J. Partridge	1980	Sir R. Pennock	1990	Sir B. Corby
1972	Sir M. Clapham	1982	Sir C. Fraser	1992	Sir M. Angus

Director-General

1965	J. Davies	1976	(Sir) J. Mcthven	1987	(Sir) J. Banham
1969	(Sir) C. Adamson	1980	Sir T. Beckett	1992	H. Davies

Economic Pressure Groups

Adam Smith Institute (1977)
Aims of Industry (1942)
Association of British Chambers of Commerce (1860)
British Institute of Management (1947)
Building Societies Association (1860)
Free Trade League (1873)
National Chamber of Trade (1897)
National Farmers' Union (1908)
Tariff Reform League (1903)
Trades Union Congress (1868) (see p. 362)
Institute of Directors
National Federation of Small Business (1974)
Low Pay Unit
Child Poverty Action Group

Consumer Organisations

(a) **Official**

Consumer Council (1963–1970). Director 1963: (Dame) E. Ackroyd.
Office of Fair Trading (1973–). Director General: 1973 J. Methven; 1977 (Sir) G. Borrie.
National Consumer Council (1975–). Director: 1975 A. Kershaw; 1975 J. Hosker; 1975– J. Mitchell.

In 1972 Sir G. Howe was appointed Minister for Trade and Consumer Affairs in the Department of Trade and Industry, but with a seat in the Cabinet.

In 1974 the Department of Prices and Consumer Protection was established. (Secretaries of State: 1974, Mrs S. Williams; 1976, R. Hattersley) but in 1979 it was absorbed into the Department of Trade.

(b) **Unofficial**

Consumers' Association (1956–)

Select Statistics

NATIONAL INCOME, TAXES AND PRICES

	Net National Income (at factor cost)[a] (£m) 1	Income Tax (Standard rate in £) 2	Amount Retained of Bachelor's £10,000 earned income after Income Tax and Surtax 3	Wholesale Price Index Number 4	Retail Price Index Number (1963=100) 5	Purchasing Power of £ (1900=£1) 6	Real gross domestic product per head (1963=100) 7
1900	1,750	8d.	9,667	22	19	20/-	53
1901	1,727	1/-	9,500	21	19	19/9	54
1902	1,740	1/2	9,417	21	19	19/7	54
1903	1,717	1/3	9,375	21	19	19/4	52
1904	1,704	11d.	9,542	22	19	19/1	52
1905	1,776	1/-	9,500	21	19	19/4	53
1906	1,874	1/-	9,500	22	19	19/4	53
1907	1,966	1/-	9,500	23	20	18/8	53
1908	1,875	1/-	9,500	23	20	18/4	49
1909	1,907	1/-	9,500	23	20	18/4	51
1910	1,984	1/2	9,242	24	20	18/1	52
1911	2,076	1/2	9,242	24	21	17/11	53
1912	2,181	1/2	9,242	25	21	17/3	53
1913	2,265	1/2	9,242	26	21	17/3	54
1914	2,209	1/2	9,242	26	21	17/5	54
1915	(2,591)	1/8	8,669	31	26	14/2	..
1916	(3,064)	3/-	7,721	41	30	11/11	..
1917	(3,631)	5/-	6,721	53	37	9/11	..
1918	(4,372)	5/-	6,721	59	42	8/7	..
1919	(5,461)	6/-	5,813	66	46	8/1	..
1920	5,664	6/-	5,813	79	52	7/-	..
1921	4,460	6/-	5,672	50	47	7/8	48
1922	3,856	6/-	5,672	41	38	9/6	48
1923	3,844	5/-	6,150	41	37	10/-	49
1924	3,919	4/6	6,389	43	37	9/11	49
1925	3,980	4/6	6,389	41	37	9/11	54
1926	3,914	4/-	6,968	38	36	10/1	50
1927	4,145	4/-	6,968	36	35	10/5	54
1928	4,154	4/-	6,968	36	35	10/6	56
1929	4,178	4/-	6,968	35	35	10/7	57
1930	3,957	4/-	6,968	30	33	11/-	56
1931	3,666	4/6	6,487	27	31	11/10	52
1932	3,568	5/-	6,103	26	30	12/1	52
1933	3,728	5/-	6,103	26	30	12/5	52
1934	3,881	5/-	6,103	27	30	12/4	56
1935	4,109	4/6	6,340	27	30	12/2	59
1936	4,388	4/6	6,341	29	31	11/10	60
1937	4,616	4/9	6,222	33	32	11/4	63
1938	4,671	5/-	6,103	30	33	11/2	65
1939	5,037	5/6	5,867	31	34	10/10	..
1940	5,980	7/-	4,965	42	38	8/11	..
1941	6,941	8/6	3,921	47	42	8/-	..
1942	7,664	10/-	3,138	48	45	7/5	..
1943	8,171	10/-	3,138	50	47	7/2	..
1944	8,366	10/-	3,138	51	47	7/-	..

[a] Changes in sources at 1914 and 1947.

	Net National Income (at factor cost)[a] (£m) 1	Income Tax (Standard rate in £) 2	Amount Retained of Bachelor's £10,000 earned income after Income Tax and Surtax 3	Wholesale Price Index Number 4	Retail Price Index Number (1963=100) 5	Purchasing Power of £ (1900=£1) 6	Real gross domestic product per head (1963=100) 7
1945	8,340	10/-	3,138	53	49	6/10	..
1946	7,974	10/-	3,138	58	51	6/7	..
1947	8,587	9/-	3,637	67	54	6/2	..
1948	9,669	9/-	3,501	63	57	5/9	72
1949	10,240	9/-	3,587	66	59	5/7	73
1950	10,784	9/-	3,587	71	61	5/5	75
1951	11,857	9/-	3,598	80	67	5/-	78
1952	12,763	9/6	3,361	84	73	4/8	78
1953	13,766	9/6	3,411	84	75	4/8	81
1954	14,573	9/-	3,646	83	76	4/7	84
1955	15,511	9/-	3,646	86	80	4/5	86
1956	16,861	8/6	3,873	89	84	4/2	87
1957	17,863	8/6	3,873	92	87	4/1	89
1958	18,615	8/6	4,341	93	90	4/-	88
1959	19,559	8/6	4,341	93	90	4/-	90
1960	20,809	7/9	4,648	94	91	3/11	94
1961	22,268	7/9	4,648	97	94	3/10	97
1962	23,267	7/9	4,648	99	98	3/8	97
1963	24,810	7/9	4,648	100	100	3/7	100
1964	26,953	7/9	4,845	103	103	3/6	105
1965	28,807	8/3	5,922	107	108	3/5	107
1966	30,423	8/3	5,922	110	112	3/3	108
1967	32,037	8/3	5,715	111	115	3/2	111
1968	34,177	8/3	5,715	115	121	3/-	114
1969	36,056	8/3	5,715	120	127	2/10	116
1970	39,567	7/9	5,715	128	135	2/8	118
1971	44,674	38.75%	6,188	140	148	12.5	121
1972	49,984	38.75%	6,141	147	159	11.5	122
1973	58,588	30%	6,377	158	173	10.5	130
1974	67,379	33%	6,088	195	201	9p	129
1975	83,958	35%	5,930	242	250	7.5p	127
1976	99,504	35%	5,966	281	291	6.5p	132
1977	111,285	34%	6,580	335	337	5.5p	134
1978	128,001	33%	7,013	365	365	5p	138
1979	146,586	30%	7,387	..	414	4.5p	141
1980	167,042	30%	7,413	..	488	3.5p	138
1981	181,179	30%	7,413	..	546	3.5p	137
1982	206,192	30%	7,470	..	593	3p	139
1983	227,905	30%	7,536	..	620	3p	143
1984	246,239	30%	7,602	..	651	3p	146
1985	268,315	30%	7,661	..	691	3p	152
1986	287,809	29%	7,777	..	714	3p	158
1987	316,271	27%	7,955	..	744	2.5p	165
1988	353,229	25%	8,151	..	781	2.5p	173
1989	388,467	25%	8,196	..	841	2.5p	177
1990	419,316	25%	8,251	..	921	2p	178
1991	431,634	25%	8,324	..	975	2p	174
1992	456,387	25%	8,486	..	1015	2p	173
1993		25%	8,486	..	..	2p	..

[a] Changes in sources at 1914 and 1947.

SOURCES.-
1. 1990–14, C.H.Feinstein, 'Income and Investment in the U.K. 1856–1914', *Economic Journal*, June 1961. 1914–46, A.R.Prest, 'National Income of the U.K. 1870–1946', *Economic Journal*, March 1948. 1947 to 1985, *National Income and Expenditure* Annual Blue Books, renamed since 1985 *United Kingdom National Accounts* Annual Blue Books.
2. and 3. *Reports of the Commissioners for Inland Revenue* and *Inland Revenue Statistics*.
4. and 5. *The British Economy: Key Statistics 1900-1970* and *Annual Abstract of Statistics*.
6. 1900–14 based on unofficial price index compiled by G.H.Wood, in W.T.Layton and G.Crowther, *An Introduction to the Study of Prices* (1938); 1914–38 based on Ministry of Labour *Cost of Living Index (Min. of Labour Gazette)*; 1938 onwards based on figures in the *Annual Abstract of Statistics*.
7. Based on *The British Economy: Key Statistics 1900–1970* and *Economic Trends*.

PRODUCTION AND INTEREST RATES

	Index Number of Industrial Production (1963=100) 1	Steel[a] Prod-uction (000s) 2	Car Prod-uction (000s) 3	Coal[b] Prod-uction (000s) 4	Raw Cotton Consum-ption[c] (m.lbs) 5	Agriculture[d] Output (1963=100) 6	Employ-ment (000s) 7	Price of 2.5% Consols (Ave for year) 8	Bank Rate % (Max and Min for year) 9	
1900	27	4,900	..	225	1,737	52	2,243	99.6	6	3
1901	27	4,900	..	219	1,569	52	..	94.3	5	3
1902	28	4,910	..	227	1,633	53	..	94.4	4	3
1903	28	5,030	..	230	1,617	52	..	90.8	4	3
1904	28	5,030	..	232	1,486	52	..	88.3	4	3
1905	28	5,810	..	236	1,813	54	..	89.8	3	2.5
1906	29	6,460	..	251	1,855	54	..	88.3	6	3.5
1907	30	6,520	..	268	1,985	53	..	84.1	7	4
1908	28	5,290	..	262	1,917	53	..	86.0	7	2.5
1909	29	5,880	..	264	1,824	55	..	83.9	5	2.5
1910	29	6,370	..	264	1,632	56	..	81.1	5	3
1911	30	6,460	..	272	1,892	54	2,205	79.3	4	3.5
1912	31	6,800	..	260	2,142	55	..	76.2	5	3
1913	33	7,664	..	287	2,178	56	..	73.6	5	4.5
1914	31	7,835	..	266	2,077	54	..	74.8	10	3
1915	..	8,550	..	253	1,931	..	..	65.5	5	5
1916	..	8,992	..	256	1,972	..	..	58.0	6	5
1917	..	9,717	..	249	1,800	..	..	54.7	6	5
1918	..	9,539	..	228	1,499	..	..	56.9	5	5
1919	30	7,894	..	230	1,526	51	..	54.1	6	5
1920	33	9,067	..	230	1,726	49	1,553	47.0	7	6
1921	27	3,703	..	163	1,066	50	1,488	48.0	7	5
1922	31	5,801	..	250	1,409	50	1,453	56.5	5	3
1923	33	8,482	71	276	1,362	52	1,415	58.0	4	3
1924	36	8,201	117	267	1,369	50	1,423	57.0	4	4
1925	38	7,385	132	243	1,609	53	1,420	56.3	5	4
1926	36	3,596	154	126	1,509	55	1,407	55.0	5	
1927	41	9,097	165	251	1,557	55	1,389	54.8	5	4.5
1928	40	8,520	165	238	1,520	58	1,380	55.9	4.5	
1929	42	9,636	182	258	1,498	58	1,372	54.3	6	4.5
1930	40	7,326	170	244	1,272	60	1,340	55.8	5	3
1931	38	5,203	159	220	985	54	1,312	56.9	6	2.5
1932	37	5,261	171	209	1,257	57	1,300	66.8	6	2
1933	46	7,024	221	207	1,177	62	1,296	73.7	2	2
1934	44	8,850	257	221	1,322	62	1,279	80.6	2	2

[a] Great Britain only.
[b] including S. Ireland, 1900-21 inclusive.
[c] From 1958 a revised bale weight was used in calculations.
[d] Including forestry and fishing. From 1978 onwards the figures include only employees and not the farmers themselves.

	Index Number of Industrial Production (1963=100) 1	Steel[a] Production (000s) 2	Car Production (000s) 3	Coal[b] Production (000s) 4	Raw Cotton Consumption[c] (m.lbs) 5	Agriculture[d] Output (1963=100) 6	Agriculture[d] Employment (000s) 7	Price of 2.5% Consols (Ave for year) 8	Bank Rate % (Max and Min for year) 9	
1935	47	9,859	338	222	1,261	60	1,260	86.6	2	2
1936	52	11,785	354	228	1,366	60	1,232	85.1	2	2
1937	55	12,984	390	240	1,431	59	1,213	76.3	2	2
1938	53	10,398	341	227	1,109	58	1,180	74.1	2	2
1939	..	13,221	305	231	1,317	..	1,168	67.2	4	2
1940	..	12,975	2	224	1,389	..	1,128	73.5	2	2
1941	..	12,312	5	206	965	..	1,177	80.0	2	2
1942	..	12,942	5	205	939	..	1,192	82.6	2	2
1943	..	13,031	2	199	885	..	1,235	80.7	2	2
1944	..	12,142	2	193	804	..	1,226	79.6	2	2
1945	..	11,824	17	183	717	..	1,207	85.5	2	2
1946	55	12,695	219	190	813	65	1,240	96.3	2	2
1947	58	12,725	287	197	815	62	1,231	90.7	2	2
1948	62	14,877	335	209	977	67	1,274	78.0	2	2
1949	66	15,553	412	215	979	72	1,274	75.9	2	2
1950	70	16,293	523	216	1,017	73	1,258	70.5	2	2
1951	72	15,639	476	223	1,024	75	1,232	66.1	2.5	2
1952	71	16,418	448	227	686	77	1,203	59.1	4	2.5
1953	75	17,609	595	224	831	79	1,177	61.3	4	3.5
1954	79	18,520	769	224	892	81	1,164	66.6	3.5	3
1955	83	19,791	898	222	778	80	1,155	60.0	4.5	3
1956	83	20,659	708	222	714	84	1,121	52.8	5.5	4.5
1957	85	21,699	861	224	744	86	1,111	50.2	7	5.5
1958	84	19,566	1052	216	628	84	1,091	50.2	7	4
1959	88	20,186	1190	206	623	87	1,044	51.8	4	4
1960	95	24,305	1353	194	599	93	1,017	46.1	6	4
1961	96	22,086	1004	192	536	93	985	46.1	7	5
1962	97	20,491	1249	199	473	96	951	40.7	6	4.5
1963	100	22,520	1607	197	483	100	929	44.8	4.5	4
1964	108	26,230	1868	195	508	104	890	41.5	7	4
1965	112	27,006	1722	187	492	107	846	39.0	7	6
1966	114	24,315	1604	175	454	106	814	36.7	7	6
1967	115	23,895	1552	175	384	110	789	37.4	8	5.5
1968	122	25,862	1816	167	382	109	757	33.8	8	7
1969	125	26,422	1717	153	376	110	727	28.2	8	7
1970	125	27,868	1641	145	366	116	707	27.3	7.5	7
1971	126	23,792	1742	147	316	123	..	27.6	7	5
1972	128	24,921	1941	120	291	126	709	27.5	9	5
1973	138	26,228	1747	130	278	130	713	23.2	13	7.5
1974	133	22,072	1534	109	245	131	681	16.8	13	11.5
1975	126	19,879	1268	127	218	119	664	17.1	11.75	9.75
1976	129	21,922	1333	122	249	110	660	17.6	15	9
1977	134	20,088	1304	120	212	130	658	20.4	14.25	5
1978	139	19,989	1223	122	184	138	366	21.0	12.5	6.5
1979	144	21,125	1070	121	192	137	350	22.1	17	12
1980	135	11,077	924	128	138	151	345	21.1	17	14
1981	128	15,573	955	125	101	152	334	19.3	16	12
1982	131	13,705	888	122	101	167	331	21.4	14.5	9
1983	134	14,986	1045	116	101	159	326	24.5	11	9
1984	135	15,121	909	50	99	..	320	24.7	12	8.5

[a] Great Britain only.
[b] including S. Ireland, 1900–21 inclusive.
[c] From 1958 a revised bale weight was used in calculations.
[d] Including forestry and fishing. From 1978 onwards the figures include only employees and not the farmers themselves.

	Index Number of Industrial Production (1963=100) 1	Steel[a] Prod- uction (000s) 2	Car Prod- uction (000s) 3	Coal[b] Prod- uction (000s) 4	Raw Cotton Consum- ption[c] (m.lbs) 5	Agriculture[d] Output (1963=100) 6	Agriculture[d] Employ- ment (000s) 7	Price of 2.5% Consols (Ave for year) 8	Bank Rate % (Max and Min for year) 9
1985	..	15,722	1048	91	99	..	321	24.8	14 9.5
1986	..	14,725	1019	105	105	..	310	26.4	12.5 10
1987	..	17,414	1143	102	114	..	302	27.7	11 8.5
1988	..	18,950	1227	102	94	..	293	27.4	13 7.5
1989	..	18,740	1299	99	83	..	280	27.1	15 13
1990	..	17,841	1296	92	67	..	277	23.1	15 14
1991	..	16,474	1237	93	45	..	268	25.1	14 10.5
1992	..	16,212	1292	84	31	..	260	27.3	12 7

[a] Great Britain only.
[b] including S. Ireland, 1900-21 inclusive.
[c] From 1958 a revised bale weight was used in calculations.
[d] Including forestry and fishing. From 1978 onwards the figures include only employees and not the farmers themselves.

SOURCES.–
1. *The British Economy, Key Statistics 1900–1970* and *Annual Abstract of Statistics.*
2. British Iron and Steel Federation, *Annual Abstract of Statistics.*
3. B.R.Mitchell, *British Historical Statistics* (1988). *Annual Abstract of Statistics.*
4. Department of Trade and Industry, *Annual Abstract of Statistics.*
5. R.Robson, *The Cotton Industry in Britain* (1957), p. 332. *Annual Abstract of Statistics.*
6 and 7. *The British Economy, Key Statistics 1900-1970* and *Annual Abstract of Statistics. 1972* onwards *Economic Trends.*
8 and 9. Bank of England and *Annual Abstract of Statistics.*

INTERNATIONAL TRADE FIGURES

	Net Balance of Payments Current account[a] (£m) 1	Imports and Exports of the U.K. Terms of Trade Index[b] (1963=100) 2	Imports cif[c] (£m) 3	Exports of UK[c] Products (m) 4	Reexports f.o.b. (m) 5	Volume indices Imports[d] 6	Volume indices Exports 7	Foreign Exchange Rates USA ($) 8	Foreign Exchange Rates France (Francs) 9	Foreign Exchange Rates Germany (Marks) 10	Japan (Yen)
1900		72	523	291	63	48	44	4.84	25.1	20.4	
1901		71	522	280	68	49	44	4.85	25.2	20.4	
1902		69	528	283	66	51	47	4.85	25.2	20.5	
1903		67	543	291	70	51	48	4.85	25.1	20.4	
1904		69	551	301	70	52	49	4.85	25.2	20.4	
1905		68	565	330	78	53	54	4.85	25.2	20.5	
1906		68	608	376	85	54	58	4.82	25.1	20.5	
1907		68	646	426	92	55	63	4.84	25.1	20.5	
1908		69	593	377	80	53	58	4.85	25.1	20.4	
1909		65	625	378	91	54	60	4.86	25.2	20.4	
1910		65	678	430	104	56	65	4.84	25.2	20.4	
1911		67	680	454	103	57	68	4.84	25.3	20.4	
1912		66	745	487	112	61	72	4.85	25.2	20.5	
1913	237	69	769	525	110	64	75	4.83	25.2	20.4	
1914		..	697	431	95	..	..	4.87	25.2	20.5	

[a] changes in sources and methods in 1924.
[b] export price index as a percentage of import price index. A fall indicates an adverse price movement.
[c] 1900–22 inclusive, S.Ireland is included. From 1923 direct foreign trade of S.Ireland is excluded, and imports and exports include trade of Great Britain and N.Ireland with S.Ireland. There are small changes in coverage from time to time.
[d] 1900–23 inclusive, including S. Ireland.

	Net Balance of Payments Current account[a] (£m)	Imports and Exports of the U.K.			Volume indices		Foreign Exchange Rates			
		Terms of Trade Index[b] (1963=100)	Imports cif[c] (£m)	Exports of UK[c] Products (m)	Reexports f.o.b. (m)	Imports[d]	Exports	USA ($)	France (Francs)	Germany (Marks)	Japan (Yen)
	1	2	3	4	5	6	7	8	9	10	
1915		..	852	385	99	..	..	4.77	26.3	..	
1916		..	949	506	98	..	..	4.76	28.2	..	
1917		..	1,064	527	70	..	..	4.76	27.4	..	
1918		..	1,316	501	31	..	..	4.76	27.2	..	
1919	−128	79	1,626	799	165	56	41	4.60	29.7	..	
1920	235	86	1,933	1,334	223	56	53	3.97	47.9	145	
1921	119	87	1,086	703	107	47	37	3.73	46.7	268	
1922	173	90	1,003	720	104	54	51	4.41	52.8	1,654	
1923	169	89	1,096	767	119	59	56	4.58	75.2	720,000	
1924	72	86	1,277	801	140	66	57	4.33	81.8	18 bn.	
1925	46	85	1,321	773	154	69	56	4.86	106.1	20.4	
1926	−15	87	1,241	653	125	70	50	4.87	167.5	20.4	
1927	82	86	1,218	709	123	72	58	4.85	124.0	20.5	
1928	123	82	1,196	724	120	69	60	4.87	124.2	20.4	
1929	103	85	1,221	729	110	73	61	4.84	124.0	20.4	
1930	28	92	1,044	571	87	71	50	4.86	123.7	20.4	
1931	−104	102	861	391	64	72	38	4.86	124.2	20.5	
1932	−51	102	702	365	51	63	38	3.58	91.1	15.0	
1933	−	104	675	368	49	63	39	4.30	86.2	14.3	
1934	−77	103	731	396	51	66	41	5.04	76.6	13.3	
1935	32	100	756	426	55	67	45	4.94	74.5	12.2	
1936	−18	99	848	441	61	72	45	5.01	75.7	12.4	
1937	−56	93	1,028	521	75	76	49	4.94	120	12.3	
1938	−70	102	920	471	62	72	43	4.95	178	12.3	
1939	−250	99	886	440	46	69	40	4.68	177	11.7	
1940	−804	85	1,152	411	26	61	31	4.03	177	..	
1941	−816	93	1,145	365	13	50	21	4.03	..	..	
1942	−663	94	997	271	5	47	16	4.03	..	..	
1943	−680	94	1,234	234	6	50	12	4.03	..	..	
1944	−659	100	1,309	266	16	54	13	4.03	..	..	
1945	−875	94	1,104	399	51	44	20	4.03	203.8	..	
1946	−230	95	1,298	912	50	49	43	4.03	480.0	..	
1947	−381	88	1,798	1,142	59	55	47	4.03	480.0	..	
1948	26	85	2,075	1,578	61	57	60	4.03[e]	[f]	..	
1949	−1	86	2,279	1,789	58	61	66	[e]	[g]	..	
1950	307	80	2,609	2,174	85	61	75	2.80	980.0	..	
1951	−369	73	3,905	2,582	127	69	74	2.80	979.7	..	
1952	163	80	3,456	2,567	142	63	69	2.79	981.5	West Germany only	
1953	145	87	3,328	2,558	103	68	71	2.81	982.8	11.7	
1954	117	87	3,359	2,650	98	69	74	2.81	981.6	11.7	

[a] changes in sources and methods in 1924.
[b] export price index as a percentage of import price index. A fall indicates an adverse price movement.
[c] 1900–22 inclusive, S.Ireland is included. From 1923 direct foreign trade of S.Ireland is excluded, and imports and exports include trade of Great Britain and N.Ireland with S.Ireland. There are small changes in coverage from time to time.
[d] 1900–23 inclusive, including S. Ireland.
[e] 4.03 to 19 Sep, 2.80 thereafter.
[f] 480 to 25 Jan, 864 from 26 Jan to 17 Oct, 1,062 thereafter.
[g] 1,062 to 26 Apr, 1,097 from 27 Apr to 20 Sep, 980 thereafter.
[h] 984.9 to 19 Aug, 1,117.1 thereafter.
[i] 1,775.5 to 24 Dec, 13,74 from 29 Dec (in units of 100 francs).
[j] in units of 100 francs (100 francs = 1 New Franc).

	Net Balance of Payments Current account (£m)	Imports and Exports of the U.K.				Volume indices		Foreign Exchange Rates			
		Terms of Trade Index[b] (1963=100)	Imports cif[c] (£m)	Exports of UK[c] Products (m)	Reexports f.o.b. (m)	Imports	Exports	USA ($)	France (Francs)	Germany (Marks)	Japan (Yen)
	1	2	3	4	5	6	7	8	9	10	
1955	−155	84	3,861	2,877	116	76	80	2.79	978.1	11.7	
1956	208	86	3,862	3,143	144	75	84	2.80	982.7	11.7	
1957	233	87	4,044	3,295	130	78	86	2.79	h	11.7	
1958	346	95	3,748	3,176	141	79	83	2.81	i	11.7	
1959	158	97	3,983	3,330	131	84	86	2.81	13.77[j]	11.7	
1960	−244	97	4,557	3,536	141	94	90	2.81	13.77	11.7	
1961	27	99	4,398	3,682	158	93	93	2.80	13.74	11.17	
1962	130	101	4,492	3,792	158	96	95	2.81	13.76	11.22	
1963	129	100	4,820	4,080	154	100	100	2.80	13.72	11.16	
1964	−358	99	5,696	4,412	153	111	103	2.79	13.68	11.10	
1965	−45	101	5,751	4,724	173	111	108	2.80	13.70	11.17	
1966	109	103	5,949	5,047	194	114	112	2.79	13.72	11.17	
1967	−294	104	6,437	5,029	185	123	111	2.79[k]	13.68[l]	11.10[m]	
1968	−286	101	7,897	6,182	220	136	126	2.39	11.86	9.56	
1969	463	101	8,315	7,039	259	138	140	2.39	12.43[n]	9.38	
1970	731	103	9,051	7,741	323	144	143	2.40	13.24	8.74	
1971	1,090	104	9,799	9,071		153	154	2.44	13.47	8.61	864[o]
1972	135	106	11,073	9,602		171	154	2.50	12.61	7.97	794[p]
1973	−979	93	15,724	12,087		195	175	2.45	10.90	6.54	665
1974	-3,278	81	23,139	16,309		196	187	2.34	11.25	6.05	683
1975	-1,523	87	24,046	19,607		179	180	2.22	9.50	5.45	658
1976	−846	85	31,084	25,277		190	197	1.80	8.61	4.55	535
1977	53	87	36,219	31,990		193	213	1.75	8.57	4.05	468
1978	1,162	92	39,533	35,330		202	218	1.92	8.65	3.85	403
1979	- 525	96	46,925	40,637		224	229	2.12	9.03	3.89	466
1980	3,629	100	49,773	47,364		212	231	2.33	9.83	4.23	526
1981	7,221	100	51,169	50,998		204	229	2.03	10.94	4.56	445
1982	4,034	99	56,978	55,558		213	234	1.75	11.48	4.24	435
1983	3,336	98	66,101	60,684		233	236	1.52	11.55	3.87	360
1984	1,473	97	78,967	70,488		259	255	1.34	11.64	3.79	317
1985	2,888	97	85,027	78,392		268	273	1.30	11.55	3.78	307
1986	−871	92	86,176	72,988		287	284	1.47	10.16	3.18	247
1987	−4,983	93	94,026	79,849		309	301	1.64	9.84	2.94	237
1988	−16,617	94	106,571	81,655		351	308	1.78	10.60	3.12	228
1989	−22,512	94	121,699	93,771		380	326	1.64	10.45	3.08	226
1990	−18,268	95	126,086	103,692		380	346	1.79	9.69	2.88	257
1991	−7,652	95	118,786	104,877		360	350	1.77	9.95	2.93	238
1992	−8,547	97	125,867	108,508		383	358	1.77	9.32	2.75	224
1993								1.50	8.51	2.48	167

[b] export price index as a percentage of import price index. A fall indicates an adverse price movement.
[c] 1900–22 inclusive, S.Ireland is included. From 1923 direct foreign trade of S.Ireland is excluded, and imports and exports include trade of Great Britain and N.Ireland with S.Ireland. There are small changes in coverage from time to time.
[e] 4.03 to 19 Sep, 2.80 thereafter.
[j] in units of 100 francs (100 francs = 1 New Franc).
[k] 2.79 to 18 Nov, 2.40 thereafter.
[l] 13.68 to 18 Nov, 11.88 thereafter.
[m] 11.10 to 18 Nov, 9.50 thereafter.
[n] 11.86 to 11 Aug, 13.31 thereafter.
[o] 864 to 13 Aug, 811 to Dec 17, 803 therafter.
[p] 794 to Jun 23, 713 thereafter.

SOURCES.–
1. *Key Statistics* and *Balance of Payments Pink Books.*
2. *The British Economy, Key Statistics 1900–1970.*
3, 4 and 5. *Trade and Navigation Accounts of the UK*, Board of Trade, annually. From 1965, *Overseas Trade Accounts of the UK.*
6 and 7. *The British Economy, Key Statistics 1900–1970. Annual Abstract of Statistics.*
8, 9 and 10. 1900–1939, *The Economist*, figures for the end of June; 1940–1970 *Annual Abstract of Statistics.* 1970– *Financial Statistics.*

CENTRAL GOVERNMENT REVENUE

	Total Central Government Revenue[a] (£m) 1	Income Tax[b] (£m) 2	Surtax (£m) 3	Profits (Corporation) Tax (£m) 4	Customs & Excise (£m) 5	Death Duties (£m) 6	Capital Gains Tax[d] (£m) 7	Capital Transfer (Inheritance) Tax (£m) 8
				Main Sources of Revenue				
1900	140	28	..	..	65	17		
1901	153	35	..	..	68	19		
1902	161	39	..	..	72	18		
1903	151	31	..	..	71	17		
1904	153	31	..	..	72	17		
1905	154	31	..	..	70	17		
1906	155	31	..	..	69	19		
1907	157	31	..	..	68	19		
1908	152	34	..	..	63	18		
1909	132	13	..	..	61	22		
1910	204	60	3	..	73	25		
1911	185	42	3	..	72	25		
1912	189	41	4	..	71	25		
1913	198	44	3	..	85	27		
1914	227	59	10	..	81	28		
1915	337	112	17	..	121	31		
1916	573	186	19	140	127	31		
1917	707	216	23	220	110	32		
1918	889	256	36	285	162	30		
1919	1,340	317	42	290	283	41		
1920	1,426	339	55	220	334	48		
1921	1,125	337	62	48	324	52		
1922	914	315	64	21	280	57		
1923	837	269	61	23	268	58		
1924	799	274	63	19	234	59		
1925	812	259	69	14	238	61		
1926	806	235	66	8	240	67		
1927	843	251	61	2	251	77		
1928	836	238	56	2	253	81		
1929	815	238	56	2	247	80		
1930	858	256	68	3	245	83		
1931	851	287	77	2	256	65		
1932	827	252	61	2	288	77		
1933	809	229	53	2	286	85		
1934	805	229	51	2	290	81		
1935	845	238	51	1	303	88		
1936	897	257	54	1	321	88		
1937	949	298	57	1	335	89		
1938	1,006	336	63	22	340	77		
1939	1,132	390	70	27	400	78		

[a] Total national revenue includes ordinary and self-balancing revenue. Figures relate to year ending Mar 31 the following year.
[b] 1900–1910 'Income Tax' includes Property and Income Tax. 1910 figure includes arrears for 1909.
[c] Corporation tax replaced Profits Tax and Income Tax on Companies from 1966. Some Profits Tax is included in the figures for subsequent tax years (negligible by 1968).
[d] Capital Transfer Tax began to replace Estate Duty in 1975. It was renamed Inheritance Tax in 1986.

	Total Central Government Revenue[a] (£m)	Main Sources of Revenue						
		Income Tax[b] (£m)	Surtax (£m)	Profits (Corporation) Tax (£m)	Customs & Excise (£m)	Death Duties (£m)	Capital Gains Tax[d] (£m)	Capital Transfer (Inheritance) Tax (£m)
	1	2	3	4	5	6	7	8
1940	1,495	524	76	96	529	81	..	..
1941	2,175	770	75	269	704	91	..	..
1942	2,922	1,007	75	378	885	93	..	..
1943	3,149	1,184	76	500	1,043	100	..	..
1944	3,355	1,317	74	510	1,076	111	..	..
1945	3,401	1,361	69	466	1,111	120	..	..
1946	3,623	1,156	76	357	1,184	148	..	..
1947	4,011	1,189	91	289	1,421	172	..	..
1948	4,168	1,368	98	279	1,557	177	..	..
1949	4,098	1,438	115	297	1,520	190	..	..
1950	4,157	1,404	121	268	1,630	185	..	..
1951	4,629	1,669	130	315	1,752	183	..	..
1952	4,654	1,736	131	376	1,764	152	..	..
1953	4,606	1,731	132	188	1,764	165	..	..
1954	4,987	1,893	135	173	1,872	188	..	..
1955	5,160	1,943	139	193	2,014	176	..	..
1956	5,462	2,114	158	195	2,101	169	..	..
1957	5,679	2,208	157	251	2,149	171	..	..
1958	5,850	2,322	167	274	2,191	187	..	..
1959	6,016	2,243	181	261	2,282	227	..	..
1960	6,344	2,433	189	263	2,390	236	..	..
1961	6,644	2,727	224	335	2,595	262	..	..
1962	6,794	2,818	184	383	2,668	270	..	..
1963	6,890	2,745	177	390	2,766	310	..	..
1964	8,157	3,088	184	423	3,174	297	..	..
1965	9,144	3,678	203	438	3,401	292	..	..
1966	10,219	3,246	242	1,118	3,536	301	7	..
1967	11,177	3,826	239	1,253	3,721	330	15	..
1968	13,363	4,337	225	1,354	4,601	382	47	..
1969	15,266	4,900	255	1,689	4,933	365	127	..
1970	15,843	5,728	248	1,591	4,709	357	139	..
1971	16,932	6,449	348	1,560	5,325	451	156	..
1972	17,178	6,475	341	1,533	5,744	459	208	..
1973	18,226	7,136	307	2,263	6,220	412	324	..
1974	23,570	10,239	186	2,851	7,407	338	380	..
1975	29,417	15,054	109	1,998	9,176	212[d]	387	118[d]
1976	33,778	17,013	62	2,655	10,900	124[d]	323	260[d]
1977	38,773	17,420	30	3,343	12,284	87[d]	340	310[d]
1978	43,088	18,748	15	3,940	13,835	46[d]	353	317[d]
1979	54,331	20,599	11	4,646	18,032	32[d]	431	404[d]

[a] Total national revenue includes ordinary and self-balancing revenue. Figures relate to year ending Mar 31 the following year.
[b] 1900–1910 'Income Tax' includes Property and Income Tax. 1910 figure includes arrears for 1909.
[c] Corporation tax replaced Profits Tax and Income Tax on Companies from 1966. Some Profits Tax is included in the figures for subsequent tax years (negligible by 1968).
[d] Capital Transfer Tax began to replace Estate Duty in 1975. It was renamed Inheritance Tax in 1986.

	Total Central Government Revenue[a] (£m)	Main Sources of Revenue						
		Income Tax[b] (£m)	Surtax (£m)	Profits (Corporation) Tax (£m)	Customs & Excise (£m)	Death Duties (£m)	Capital Gains Tax[d] (£m)	Capital Transfer (Inheritance) Tax (£m)
	1	2	3	4	5	6	7	8
1980	66,213	24,295	5	4,645	22,095	27[d]	508	423[d]
1981	76,754	28,725	4	4,926	25,248	17[d]	525	480[d]
1982	83,270	30,474	2	5,564	27,895	12[d]	632	499[d]
1983	88,364	31,306	2	6,011	31,435	9[d]	671	571[d]
1984	95,194	32,063	1	7,124	33,883	6[d]	694	652[d]
1985	104,193	33,965	..	9,485	37,770	8[d]	855	846[d]
1986	110,867	39,283	..	12,647	40,259	..	971	939[d]
1987	119,517	40,040	..	14,510	43,474	..	1,230	1,053
1988	129,738	43,268	..	17,303	48,711	..	2,172	1,068
1989	141,388	46,546	..	22,430	52,160	..	2,002	1,171
1990	151,260	53,739	..	22,062	54,754	..	1,892	1,315
1991	177,659	57,417	..	19,346	59,382	..	1,359	1,263
1992	172,732	57,570	..	16,184	64,349	..	1,073	1,227
1993	173,262	57,363	..	15,284	66,039	..	788	1,268

[a] Total national revenue includes ordinary and self-balancing revenue. Figures relate to year ending Mar 31 the following year.
[b] 1900–1910 'Income Tax' includes Property and Income Tax. 1910 figure includes arrears for 1909.
[c] Corporation tax replaced Profits Tax and Income Tax on Companies from 1966. Some Profits Tax is included in the figures for subsequent tax years (negligible by 1968).
[d] Capital Transfer Tax began to replace Estate Duty in 1975. It was renamed Inheritance Tax in 1986.

SOURCE.– *Annual Abstract of Statistics* and *Financial Statistics*.

GOVERNMENT EXPENDITURE AND TARIFFS

	Main Heads of Expenditure			Specimen Tariffs			
	Defence (£m)	Health, Labour and Insurance[a] (£m)	Pensions[b] (£m)	Sugar[c] (per cwt) s. d.	Tea[c] (per lb.) s. d.	Excise Duty on Beer[d] (per barrel of 36 gallons) s. d.	National Debt[e] (£m)
	1	2	3	4	5	6	7
1900	121	..	..	..	6	6/9	628·9
1901	124	..	..	4/2	6	7/9	689·5
1902	101	..	..	4/2	6	7/9	745·0
1903	72	..	..	4/2	6	7/9	770·8
1904	66	..	..	4/2	8	7/9	762·6
1905	62	..	..	4/2	6	7/9	755·1
1906	59	..	..	4/2	5	7/9	743.3
1907	58	..	..	4/2	5	7/9	7245
1908	59	..	..	1/10	5	7/9	709.0
1909	63	..	..	1/10	5	7/9	702.7
1910	67	..	..	1/10	5	7/9	713.2
1911	70	..	..	1/10	5	7/9	685.2
1912	72	..	..	1/10	5	7/9	668.3
1913	77	14	1	1/10	5	7/9	656.5
1914	437	14	1	1/10	5	7/9	649.8
1915	1,424	14	1	1/10	8	23/-	1,105.0
1916	2,007	14	1	14/-	1/-	24/-	2,133
1917	2,436	14	1	14/-	1/-	25/-	4,011
1918	2,238	15	1	25/8	1/-	50/-	5,871
1919	692	74	100	25/8	1/-	70/-	7,434
1920	292	73	110	25/8	1/-	100/-	7,828
1921	189	73	96	25/8	1/-	100/-	7,574
1922	111	61	83	25/8	8	100/-	7,654
1923	105	59	72	25/8	8	100/-	7,742
1924	114	65	71	11/8	4	100/-	7,641
1925	119	65	70	11/8	4	100/-	7,597
1926	116	75	65	11/8	4	100/-	7,558
1927	117	73	62	11/8	4	100/-	7,554
1928	113	76	59	11/8	4	100/-	7,527
1929	113	86	56	11/8	..	100/-	7,500
1930	110	108	55	11/8	..	103/-	7,469
1931	107	121	52	11/8	..	103/-	7,413
1932	103	155	49	11/8	4	134/-	7,433
1933	107	151	49	11/8	4	24/-	7,643
1934	113	151	47	11/8	4	24/-	7,822

[a] 1900–13, the system of classification prevents entries comparable with those for later years. 1949–53, figures cover Housing, Local Government, Health, Labour, National Insurance and National Assistance. From 1954 figures cover Health, Housing and Local Government

[b] 1900–13, the system of classification prevents entries comparable with those for later years. Before 1954, 'Pensions' equivalent to 'non-effective' charges. 1954 onwards figures cover Pensions, National Insurance and National Assistance.

[c] Full Customs duty given. In many cases preferential rates apply to Commonwealth trade. Sugar: exceeding 98° of polarisation.

[d] 1900–32 beer of 1,055° specific gravity. 1933–49 beer of 1,027° specific gravity. 1950 beer of 1,030° specific gravity.

[e] Debt of U.K. Exchequer, debt created by N. Ireland Exchequer excluded. Bonds tendered for death duties and held by National Debt Commissioners excluded from 1920. External debt arising out of 1914–18 war, excluded from 1935, when it was £1,035.5m at 31 Mar.

| | Main Heads of Expenditure | | | Specimen Tariffs | | | |
	Defence (£m)	Health, Labour and Insurance[a] (£m)	Pensions[b] (£m)	Sugar[c] (per cwt) s. d.	Tea[c] (per lb.) s. d.	Excise Duty on Beer[d] (per barrel of 36 gallons) s. d.	National Debt[e] (£m)
	1	2	3	4	5	6	7
1935	136	162	46	11/8	4	24/-	6,763
1936	186	162	45	11/8	6	24/-	6,759
1937	197	162	44	11/8	6	24/-	6,764
1938	254	166	43	11/8	8	24/-	6,993
1939	626	167	42	11/8	8	24/-	7,130
1940	3,220	165	41	23/4	8	90/-	7,899
1941	4,085	170	41	23/4	8	90/-	10,366
1942	4,840	186	40	23/4	8	118/1	13,041
1943	4,950	199	39	23/4	8	138/4	15,822
1944	5,125	208	40	23/4	8	140/7	18,562
1945	4,410	219	42	23/4	8	140/7	21,365
1946	1,653	334	97	23/4	8	140/7	23,636
1947	854	380	91	23/4	8	140/7	25,630
1948	753	598	96	23/4	8	178/10	25,620
1949	741	806	97	11/8	2	157/10	25,167
1950	777	835	94	11/8	2	155/4	25,802
1951	1,110	810	91	11/8	2	155/4	25,921
1952	1,404	884	100	11/8	2	155/4	25,890
1953	1,365	903	97	11/8	2	155/4	26,051.
1954	1,436	619	419	11/8	2	155/4	26,583
1955	1,405	652	433	11/8	2	155/4	26,933
1956	1,525	750	463	11/8	2	155/4	27,038
1957	1,430	782	490	11/8	2	155/4	27,007
1958	1,468	794	575	11/8	2	155/4	27,232
1959	1,475	1,209	610	11/8	2	111/9	27,376
1960	1,596	1,384	634	11/8	2	111/9	27,732
1961	1,689	1,417	659	11/8[f]	2	111/9	28,251
1962	1,767	1,549	705	..	2	123/-	28,674
1963	1,792	1,716	772	..	2[g]	123/-	29,847
1964	1,909	1,897	792	..	..	147/-	30,226
1965	2,055	..[h]	..[h]	..	..	171/-	30,440
1966	2,145	..	..	..	..	171/-	31,340
1967	2,274	..	..	..	..	188/8	31,935
1968	2,232	..	..	..	..	188/8	34,193
1969	2,204	..	..	..	..	207/6	33,982

[a] 1900–13, the system of classification prevents entries comparable with those for later years. 1949–53, figures cover Housing, Local Government, Health, Labour, National Insurance and National Assistance. From 1954 figures cover Health, Housing and Local Government

[b] 1900–13, the system of classification prevents entries comparable with those for later years. Before 1954, 'Pensions' equivalent to 'non-effective' charges. 1954 onwards figures cover Pensions, National Insurance and National Assistance.

[c] Full Customs duty given. In many cases preferential rates apply to Commonwealth trade. Sugar: exceeding 98° of polarisation.

[d] 1900–32 beer of 1,055° specific gravity. 1933–49 beer of 1,027° specific gravity. 1950 beer of 1,030° specific gravity.

[e] Debt of U.K. Exchequer, debt created by N. Ireland Exchequer excluded. Bonds tendered for death duties and held by National Debt Commissioners excluded from 1920. External debt arising out of 1914–18 war, excluded from 1935, when it was £1,035.5m at 31 Mar.

[f] April 1962 Excise duty on sugar was repealed.

[g] June 1963 tariffs on tea ceased to be direct revenue and became chargeable under the Import Duties Act 1958.

[h] From 1965 onwards figures no longer collected in this form.

	Main Heads of Expenditure			Specimen Tariffs			
	Defence (£m)	Health, Labour and Insurance[a] (£m)	Pensions[b] (£m)	Sugar[c] (per cwt) s. d.	Tea[c] (per lb.) s. d.	Excise Duty on Beer[d] (per barrel of 36 gallons) s. d.	National Debt[e] (£m)
	1	2	3	4	5	6	7
1970	2.493	..	..	..	..	207/ 6	33,079
1971	2,799	..	..	..	..	£10.37	33,441
1972	3,083	..	..	..	..	£10.37	35,839
1973	3,495	..	..	..	..	£ 6.90[i]	36,910
1974	4,228	..	..	..	..	£ 9.36[i]	40,124
1975	5.458	..	..	..	..	£13.68[i]	45,925
1976	6,282	..	..	..	..	£15.84[i]	56.581
1977	6,965	..	..	..	..	£17.42[i]	67,165
1978	7,701[j]	..	..	..	..	£17.42i	79,179
1979	9,431	..	..	..	..	£21.35	86,884
1980	11,759	..	..	..	..	£29.45	95,314
1981	12,968	..	..	..	..	£33.37	113,036
1982	14,288	..	..	..	..	£33.37	118,390
1983	15,592	..	..	..	..	£35.33	127,727
1984	16,851	..	..	..	..	£39.26	142,885
1985	17,857	..	..	..	..	£42.20	158,127
1986	18,608	..	..	..	..	£42.20	171,456
1987	18,668	..	..	..	..	£42.20	185,796
1988	19,288	..	..	..	..	£44.17	197,441
1989	20,446	..	..	..	..	£44.17	197,232
1990	22,178	..	..	..	..	£47.60	192,553
1991	24,544	..	..	..	..	£52.01	198,698
1992	23,842	..	..	..	..	£54.38	214,528
1993	..	..	..	..	..	£57.07	248,626

[a] 1900–13, the system of classification prevents entries comparable with those for later years. 1949–53, figures cover Housing, Local Government, Health, Labour, National Insurance and National Assistance. From 1954 figures cover Health, Housing and Local Government.

[b] 1900–13, the system of classification prevents entries comparable with those for later years. Before 1954, 'Pensions' equivalent to 'non-effective' charges. 1954 onwards figures cover Pensions, National Insurance and National Assistance.

[c] Full Customs duty given. In many cases preferential rates apply to Commonwealth trade. Sugar: exceeding 98° of polarisation.

[d] 1900–32 beer of 1,055° specific gravity. 1933–49 beer of 1,027° specific gravity. 1950 beer of 1,030° specific gravity.

[e] Debt of U.K. Exchequer, debt created by N. Ireland Exchequer excluded. Bonds tendered for death duties and held by National Debt Commissioners excluded from 1920. External debt arising out of 1914–18 war, excluded from 1935, when it was £1,035.5m at 31 Mar.

[f] April 1962 Excise duty on sugar was repealed.

[g] June 1963 tariffs on tea ceased to be direct revenue and became chargeable under the Import Duties Act 1958.

[h] From 1965 onwards figures no longer collected in this form.

[i] Subject to VAT at standard rate from 1/4/73.

[j] From 1978, Defence figures cover expenditure in the year ending in April the following year.

SOURCES.–
1. *Annual Abstract of Statistics*. From 1970 *Financial Statistics*.
2 and 3. *Annual Abstract of Statistics*. Central Statistical Office.
4 and 5. *Customs Tariff of the U.K. (Annual Reports of Commissioners for Customs and Excise)*.
6. *Reports of Commissioners for Customs and Excise*.
7. *Finance Accounts of the U.K.*, from 1969 *Consolidated Fund and National Loans Fund Accounts* and *Financial Statistics*.

PERCENTAGE SHARES IN NET NATIONAL INCOME
(BASED ON CURRENT PRICES)
United Kingdom (percentages)

Year	Wages	Salaries	Income from self-employment	Private companies	Gross Trading Profits of: Public corporations	Rent
1900	41.4	9.1		36.4		12.5
1910	39.0	10.6		34.6		12.1
1921	43.6	17.9	13.4	5.7	0.5	5.8
1930	39.4	21.1	14.8	11.3	1.2	8.5
1938	40.8	21.9	13.4	14.3	1.4	9.3
1950	44.8	25.5	12.8	19.6	3.0	4.9
1960	42.8	29.2	9.5	17.7	3.4	5.9
1970	68.6		8.3	12.0	3.5	7.5
1980	68.5		9.0	13.8	3.1	7.1
1990	65.2		12.7	13.5	0.8	8.1

SOURCE.–*National Income and Expenditure*, Blue Books.

SELECTED ITEMS OF CONSUMER EXPENDITURE AS PERCENTAGES OF TOTAL CONSUMER EXPENDITURE
United Kingdom

Year	Food	Alcoholic drink	Tobacco	Furniture, electrical and other durables	Cars and motorcycles[a]	Clothing and footwear
1900	27.3	20.8	3.7	2.5	0.0	10.0
1910	28.7	16.0	4.0	2.5	0.1	10.1
1921	29.9	12.4	6.0	3.4	0.2	9.4
1930	30.2	8.4	5.7	4.7	0.8	9.8
1938	29.0	7.2	6.3	4.7	1.2	9.3
1950	31.1	6.2	6.6	4.0	0.7	9.8
1960	24.9	5.9	7.0	4.8	2.7	9.6
1970	20.3	7.4	5.5	4.3	3.1	8.5
1980	16.7	7.3	3.5	5.1	4.6	7.2
1990	12.0	6.2	2.5	4.5	5.5	6.0

[a] This does not include running costs.

INCOME DISTRIBUTION AFTER TAX
United Kingdom
(tax units–000s)

Year	£50– £250	£250– £500	£500– £750	£750– £1,000	£1,000– £2,000	£2,000– £6,000	£6,000– £10,000	£10,000 and over
1938	n.a.	1,940	375	132	142	66	7	0
1949	13,040	10,140	2,020	442	368	90	0	0
1959	6,200	7,440	6,630	3,880	2,052	295	3	0
1967	2,338	5,906	5,418	4,822	8,298	954[a]	63[b]	0
1972/3	7,465			4,164	11,138	5,474	101	9
1978/8	1,446				7,580	16,709	2,988	353
1990/1	6,350						7,840	12,101

[a] £2,000–£5,000
[b] £5,000–£10,000
[c] Under £750
SOURCE.–*National Income and Expenditure*, Blue Books.

DISTRIBUTION OF PERSONAL WEALTH AMONG ADULT[c] POPULATION

Percent of total wealth owned by top groups

Wealth Group	1911–13[a]	1924–30[a]	1936[a]	1951–56[a]	1960[b]	1970[b]	1980	1990
Top 1%	65.5	59.5	56.0	42.0	37.6	29.6	19	17
Top 5%	86.0	82.5	81.0	56.7	63.6	54.4	36	37
Top 10%	90.0	89.5	88.0	79.8	76.1	70.1	50	51
Top 20%	..	96.0	94.0	89.0	..	..	..	..
Top 25%	..	..	..	..	93.2	92.9	73	72

[a] England and Wales
[b] Great Britain
[c] Over 25, 1911–56. Over 18, 1960–.

SOURCES:– H.F. Lydall and D.G. Tipping, 'The Distribution of Personal Wealth in Britain', *Bulletin of the Oxford University Institute of Statistics* (1961); *Inland Revenue Statistics* (1978).

OUTPUT PER MAN 1900–1970

(1913=100)

	U.K	U.S	France	Germany (F.R.)	Italy	Sweden
1900	98.1	79.8	90.0	85.5	77.3	70.1
1913	100.0	100.0	100.0	100.0	100.0	100.0
1929	121.6	126.7	135.6	96.5	126.3	101.6
1938	143.6	136.0	125.7	122.4	145.2	127.5
1950	159.4	177.1	146.1	124.1	153.2	171.1
1960	193.1	217.3	215.8	207.5	229.4	223.6
1970	247.6	271.8	352.8	321.2	418.2	315.1
1970 (U.K.=100.0)	100.0	251	146	142	100	166

SOURCE:–Adapted from A. Maddison, *Economic Growth in the West* (1964) and updated with O.E.C.D. data.

INDUSTRIAL OUTPUT OF THE U.K.

(Census of Production figures)

All census Industries	Value of Production (Gross Output) (£m.)
1907[a]	1,765
1924	3,747[b]
1930	3,371[b]
1935	3,543[b]
1948[c]	12,961
1951	18,733
	___d
1958	26,980
1963	34,467
1968	48,216
1973	68,472[e]
1982	212,640[e]
1990	380,790

[a] Including firms in the Irish Republic.
[b] Firms employing more than 10 persons only.
c Great Britain only.
[d] Prior to 1951 classified according to the 1948 edition of the Standard Industrial Classification.
For 1958 and 1963 according to the 1958 edition, and 1968 and 1973 according to the 1968 edition.
[e] Excludes construction

SOURCE:– *Annual Abstract of Statistics*.

SURTAX, 1909–1972

Year of change	Income level at which Surtax Payable Exceeding £	Maximum Rate in £ Payable			£
1909	5,000	6d.	on amount in excess of		3,000
1914	3,000	1/9½	"	"	8,000
1915	3,000	3/6	"	"	10,000
1918	2,500	4/6	"	"	10,000
1920	2,000	6/-	"	"	30,000
1929	2,000	7/6	"	"	50,000
1930	2,000	8/3	"	"	50,000
1938	2,000	9/6	"	"	30,000
1939	2,000	9/6	"	"	20,000
1946	2,000	10/6	"	"	20,000
1951	2,000	10/-	"	"	15,000
1961	2,000[a]	10/-	"	"	15,000
1969	2.500	50%	"	"	15,000
1971	3,000	50%	"	"	15,000

[a] In 1961 special reliefs introduced for earned incomes made the surtax threshold effectively £5,000.
In 1973 the system of personal income tax and surtax was replaced by a single graduated tax. In consequence surtax ceased to be charged after 1972–3.

SOURCE:– *Annual Reports of Commisssioners of Inland Revenue.*

CAPITAL TRANSFER TAX

Following the abolition of Estate Duty in 1974, a Capital Transfer Tax of 45% became payable on property transferred from a £100,000 estate on death or within three years preceding death. The maximum rate of Capital Transfer Tax reached 75% for an estate over £2m. However, from 1984 the top brackets were abolished, leaving the highest rate at 60% on estates over £285,000. In 1986 Capital Transfer Tax was renamed Inheritance Tax.

CONSUMER CREDIT 1947–

Hire Purchase and other instalment credit (Finance Houses, Durable Goods, Shops and Department Stores)– total outstanding business at end of period (£m).

1947	68	1963	959	1979	6,901
1948	105	1964	1,115	1980	7,844
1949	128	1965	1,196	1981	8,481
1950	167	1966	1,104	1982	9,693
1951	208	1967	1,058	1983	15,905
1952	241	1968	1,089	1984	18,810
1953	276	1969	1,063	1985	22,229
1954	384	1970	1,127	1986	26,049
1955	461	1971	1,377	1987	30,150
1956	376	1972	1,769	1988	36,177
1957	448	1973	2,151	1989	42,546
1958	556	1974	1,944	1990	52,583
1959	849	1975	1,892	1991	53,765
1960	935	1976	2,163	1992	52,891
1961	934	1977	4,184		
1962	887	1978	5,499		

SOURCES:– *Key Statistics 1900–1970*; *Annual Abstract of Statistics 1970–*; *Economic Trends* (1977). The basis of calculations is different after 1977. The figures jump in 1983 with the inclusion of bank loans.

BUDGET DATES

1900	5 Mar	1926	26 Apr	1949	6 Apr		12 Nov
1901	18 Apr	1927	11 Apr	1950	18 Apr	1975	15 Apr
1902	14 Apr	1928	24 Apr	1951	10 Apr	1976	6 Apr
1903	23 Apr	1929	15 Apr	1952	11 Apr	1977	29 Mar
1904	19 Apr	1930	14 Apr	1953	14 Apr	1978	11 Apr
1905	10 Apr	1931	27 Apr	1954	6 Apr	1979	3 Apr
1906	30 Apr		10 Sep	1955	19 Apr		12 Jun
1907	18 Apr	1932	19 Apr		26 Oct	1980	26 Mar
1908	7 May	1933	25 Apr	1956	17 Apr	1981	10 Mar
1909	29 Apr	1934	17 Apr	1957	9 Apr	1982	9 Mar
1910	30 Jun	1935	15 Apr	1958	15 Apr	1983	15 Mar
1911	16 May	1936	21 Apr	1959	7 Apr	1984	13 Mar
1912	2 Apr	1937	20 Apr	1960	4 Apr	1985	19 Mar
1913	22 Apr	1938	26 Apr	1961	17 Apr	1986	18 Mar
1914	4 May	1939	25 Apr	1962	8 Apr	1987	17 Mar
	17 Nov		27 Sep	1963	3 Apr	1988	15 Mar
1915	4 May	1940	23 Apr	1964	14 Apr	1989	14 Mar
	21 Sep		23 Jul		11 Nov	1990	20 Mar
1916	4 Apr	1941	7 Apr	1965	6 Apr	1991	19 Mar
1917	3 May	1942	14 Apr	1966	5 May	1992	10 Mar
1918	22 Apr	1943	12 Apr	1967	11 Apr	1993	16 Mar
1919	3 Apr	1944	25 Apr	1968	19 Mar	1993	30 Nov
1920	19 Apr	1945	24 Apr	1969	15 Apr		
1921	25 Apr		23 Oct	1970	14 Apr		
1922	1 May	1946	9 Apr	1971	30 Mar		
1923	17 Apr	1947	15 Apr	1972	21 Apr		
1924	29 Apr		12 Nov	1973	6 Mar		
1925	28 Apr	1948	6 Apr	1974	26 Mar		

Occasionally *ad hoc* statements by the Chancellor of the Exchequer on revised fiscal and economic arrangements have been referred to by the media as 'Budgets', although not so regarded by the Treasury. Such statements or 'mini-Budgets' occurred on 22 Jul 74, 12 Nov 74, 11 Jul 75, 19 Feb 76, 22 Jul 76, 15 Dec 76, 15 Jul 77, 26 Oct 77, 8 Jun 78, and 15 Nov 80.

In 1982 the forecast required under the Industry Act, 1975 for decisions on public expenditure plans and proposed changes to National Insurance contributions were brought together in one 'Autumn Statement'. These took place on the following dates:

1982	8 Nov
1983	17 Nov
1984	11 Nov
1985	12 Nov
1986	6 Nov
1987	3 Nov
1988	8 Nov
1989	15 Nov
1990	8 Nov
1991	6 Nov
1992	12 Nov

The Chancellor announced in his 1992 Budget that as from November 1993, the Budget and the Autumn Statement would be brought together and announced on the same day, in late November or early December.

XII

THE PUBLIC SECTOR

Economic activity by the state – other than the core activity undertaken by the Civil Service – takes a range of forms which defy easy categorisation. Whereas a public corporation (or a limited company in which the state is a majority shareholder) can clearly be classified as being within the public sector, there have often been grey areas resulting from minority government shareholdings, 'golden shares', and changing accounting rules over the raising of private capital.

Public corporations, defined as public trading bodies which have a substantial degree of financial independence of the public authority which created them, include not only the major nationalised industries, but a number of other bodies listed on pp. 416–418. For practical purposes 'nationalised industries' can be defined as public corporations whose assets are in public ownership, whose boards are appointed by a Secretary of State, whose employees are not civil servants, which are engaged in trading activities, and which derive the greater part of their revenue directly from customers.

Main Landmarks

1908 **The Port of London Authority** was set up in 1909 under the *Port of London Act, 1908* (but it only followed the pattern of the Mersey Docks and Harbour Board, set up in 1874).

1914 The Government acquired a majority shareholding in Anglo-Persian Oil Company, with the intention of safeguarding the supply of fuel for the Admiralty.

1926 **The Central Electricity Board** was set up by the *Electricity (Supply) Act, 1926*, to control generation by purchasing all electricity output.

1926 **The British Broadcasting Corporation** was granted its first charter as a public corporation.

1933 **The London Passenger Transport Board** was established.

1943 **The North of Scotland Hydro-Electricity Board** was established.

1946 **The Bank of England** was taken into public ownership.

1946 **The Coal Industry** was nationalised by the *Coal Industry Nationalisation Act, 1946*, which set up the National Coal Board.

1946 **Civil Aviation** was reorganised by the *Civil Aviation Act, 1946*. This covered the British Overseas Airways Corporation (set up in 1939), and two new corporations, British European Airways and British South American Airways. B.S.A.A. was merged with B.O.A.C. in 1949. B.O.A.C. and B.E.A. were merged into British Airways in 1972–74.

1947 **Electricity** was fully nationalised by the *Electricity Act, 1947*, which set up the British Electricity Authority. The *Electricity Act, 1957*, set up the Electricity Council and the Central Electricity Generating Board. The twelve area boards remained financially autonomous.

1948 **Railways, Canals** (and some other transport) were nationalised by the *Transport Act, 1947*. The British Transport Commission was established, and the Docks and Inland Waterways, Hotels, Railways, London Transport, Road Haulage, and Road Passenger Transport were administered by six executive boards. The *Transport Act, 1953*, denationalised Road Haulage. The *Transport Act, 1962*, reorganised nationalised transport undertakings and provided for the establishment of separate Boards for Railways, London Transport, Docks and Waterways, and for a Transport Holding Company, as successors to the British Transport Commission.

1948 **Gas** was nationalised by the *Gas Act, 1948*, which established twelve Area Gas Boards and the Gas Council. The *Gas Act, 1972*, established the British Gas Corporation which replaced the Gas Council and Area Boards.

1949 **Iron and Steel** were nationalised by the *Iron and Steel Act, 1949*, and the Iron and Steel Corporation of Great Britain was established. The vesting date of the Act was 15 Feb 51. The *Iron and Steel Act, 1953*, denationalised the industry, and set up the Iron and Steel Board. In 1967 the *Iron and Steel Act* renationalised the industry, as from 28 Jul 67.

1954 **The U.K. Atomic Energy Authority** was established by the *Atomic Energy Authority Act, 1954.*

1969 **The Post Office** ceased to be a Government Department and became a public corporation.

1971–73   **Hiving-off.** The Conservative Government began to hive-off some concerns of nationalised industries. In 1971–72 some B.O.A.C. routes were allotted to British Caledonian. In 1973 Thomas Cook's travel agency and the Carlisle state breweries (which was nationalised in 1916) were sold to the private sector.

1971   **Rolls-Royce Ltd** was established following the company's bankruptcy. The shares were vested in the National Enterprise Board in February 1976.

1975   **British Leyland.** The majority of shares were acquired by the Government and later vested in the National Enterprise Board.

1975   **The National Enterprise Board** established by *Industry Act, 1975.*

1976   **British National Oil Corporation** established by *Petroleum and Submarines Pipelines Act, 1975.*

1977   **British Aerospace** and **British Shipbuilders** established by *Aircraft and Shipbuilding Industries Act, 1977.* In June 1977 the Labour Government sold off 17% of the shares in British Petroleum, leaving it with a 51% stake.

Privatisation

In May 1979 the Conservatives came to power pledged to 'roll back the frontiers of the state', although the objective of systematically selling off state-owned assets was not at that stage clearly spelled out. Below is a list of the main privatisations since 1979, and the proceeds; it does not include sales by public corporations which retained the proceeds themselves, such as BR's sale of Sealink in 1984.

		Assets sold	Net proceeds £m
Nov	1979	5% of British Petroleum	276
Dec	1979	25% of ICL Computers	37
		Suez Finance Company shares	22
		Miscellaneous (mainly land and property)	42
Total revenue for 1979/80 from privatisation			**377**
Jun	1980	100% of Fairey (NEB subsidiary)	22
Jul	1980	50% of Ferranti (NEB subsidiary)	55
Feb	1981	49% of British Aerospace	43
		North Sea Oil licences	195
		Miscellaneous (mainly property assets)	90
Total revenue for 1980/81 from privatisation			**405**
Oct	1981	49% of Cable and Wireless	182
Feb	1982	100% of Amersham International	64
Feb	1982	100% of National Freight Corporation	5
Feb	1982	24% of British Sugar	44
		NEB subsidiaries	2
		New Towns	73
		Oil stockpiles	50
		Miscellaneous	74
Total revenue for 1981/82 from privatisation			**494**
Nov	1982	51% of Britoil (first cash call)	334
Feb	1983	52% of Associated British Ports	46
		Oil stockpiles	33
		Miscellaneous	42

	Assets sold	Net proceeds £m
Total revenue for 1982/83 from privatisation		**455**
Apr 1983	Britoil (second cash call)	293
Sep 1983	7% of British Petroleum	543
Dec 1983	25% of Cable and Wireless	263
Mar 1984	Scott Lithgow shipyard	12
	Miscellaneous	31
Total revenue for 1983/84 from privatisation		**1,139**
Apr 1984	48% of Associated British Ports	51
Jun 1984	Enterprise Oil	384
Nov 1984	British Telecom (first installment)	1,358
	British Telecom (loan stock)	44
	NEB subsidiaries	168
	Forestry Commission land and miscellaneous	55
Total revenue for 1984/85 from privatisation		**2,050**
May 1985	British Aerospace	347
Jun 1985	British Telecom (second installment)	1,246
Aug 1985	Britoil	426
Dec 1985	Cable and Wireless	577
	British Telecom (loan stock)	61
	NEB subsidiaries	30
	Land and buildings	18
Total revenue for 1985/86 from privatisation		**2,706**
Apr 1986	British Telecom (third installment)	1,081
Dec 1986	British Gas (first installment)	1,820
Feb 1987	British Airways (first installment)	435
	British Gas (redemption of debt)	750
	British Telecom (loan stock)	53
	British Telecom (preference shares)	250
	NEB subsidiaries	34
	Wytch Farm	18
	Miscellaneous	16
Total revenue for 1986/87 from privatisation		**4,458**
Apr 1987	Royal Ordnance	186
May 1987	Rolls-Royce	1,029
Jun 1987	British Gas (second installment)	1,758
Jul 1987	BAA	534
Aug 1987	British Airways (second installment)	419
Aug 1987	Plant Breeding Institute	65
Oct 1987	British Petroleum (first installment)	863
	British Telecom (loan stock)	23
	British Telecom (preference shares)	250
	Miscellaneous	12
Total revenue for 1987/88 from privatisation		**5,140**
Apr 1988	British Gas (third installment)	1,555
May 1988	BAA	689
Aug 1988	British Petroleum (second installment)	3,030
Dec 1988	British Steel	1,138
Mar 1989	General Practice Finance Corporation	67
(May 1987)	Rolls-Royce	3
	British Gas (redemption of debt)	250
	British Telecom (loan stock)	85
	British Telecom (preference shares)	250
	Miscellaneous	2

Total revenue for 1988/89 from privatisation			7,069
Aug	1988	Rover Group	150
Apr	1989	British Petroleum (third installment)	1,363
Jun	1989	Short Brothers	30
Dec	1989	Water companies (first installment)	423
		British Gas (mainly redemption of debt)	804
		British Steel	1,289
		British Telecom (loan stock)	92
		Harland and Wolff	8
		Water companies (debt redemption)	73
		Miscellaneous	−3

Total revenue for 1989/90 from privatisation			4,226
Jul	1990	British Gas (sale of shares)	150
Jul	1990	Water companies (second installment)	1,487
Dec	1990	Electricity shares (England & Wales)	3,134
		British Gas (redemption of debt)	350
		British Telecom (loan stock)	100
		Wytch Farm	130
		Miscellaneous	−6

Total revenue for 1990/91 from privatisation			5,346
Jun	1991	Electricity shares (Scotland)	1,112
Jul	1991	Water companies (sale of shares)	1,483
Oct	1991	National Transcommunications	70
Dec	1991	British Telecom (first installment)	1,666
Dec	1991	Insurance Services Group	12
Mar	1992	British Technology Group	24
		British Telecom (loan stock)	106
		Electricity shares (England and Wales)	2.329
		Redemption of Electricity debt	1,106
		Miscellaneous	15

Total revenue for 1991/92 from privatisation			7,923
		British Gas (redemption of debt)	350
Jun	1992	British Telecom (second installment)	3,520
Aug	1992	Electricity shares (England and Wales)	1,457
		British Telecom (Loan stock)	113
		Electricity shares (Scotland)	825
		Redemption of Electricity debt	110
		Privatised companies' debt	1,337
Jun	1993	Northern Ireland Electricity	7,650
Jul	1993	22% of British Telecom	350
		Miscellaneous	−62

SOURCES.—R. Vernon (ed.), *The Promise of Privatisation* (1988). J. Vickers and G. Yarrow, *Privatisation: an Economic analysis* (1988). Also *Public Expenditure Analyses*, HM Treasury, Cm 2219 (Jan 1993).

Nationalised Industries

Air

British Overseas Airways Corporation (B.O.A.C.) 1939–74

Responsible Minister		*Chairman*	
1939	Sec. of State for Air	26 May 43	Vt Knollys
1944	Min. for Civil Aviation	1 Jul 47	Sir H. Hartley
1951	Min. for Transport and Civil	1 Jul 49	Sir M. Thomas
	Aviation	1 May 56	(Sir) G. d'Erlanger
1959	Min. of Civil Aviation	29 Jul 60	Sir M Slattery
1964	Min. of Aviation	1 Jan 64	Sir G. Guthrie
1968	Min. of State at Board of Trade	1 Jan 69	(Sir) C. Hardie
1970	Min. of Aviation at the Dept of Trade and Industry	1 Jan 71	K. Granville
1971	Min. for Aerospace (and Shipping 1972) at the	1 Sep 72	J. Stainton
	Dept. of Trade and Industry		
1974	Sec. of State for Trade		

Established under the *Air Corporations Act, 1939*, as successor to Imperial Airways. In 1946 became one of the three corporations set up under the *Civil Aviation Act, 1946*, to provide passenger and cargo flights to all parts of the world, other than Europe and Latin America. Under the *Civil Aviation Act, 1971*, merged with BEA in April 1974 to form British Airways.

British European Airways Corporation (B.E.A.), 1946–74

Responsible Minister		*Chairman*	
1946	Min. for Civil Aviation	1 Aug 46	Sir H. Hartley
1951	Min. of Transport and Civil Aviation	1 Apr 47	G. d'Erlanger
1959	Min. of Aviation	14 Mar 49	Ld Douglas
1968	Min. of State at the Board of Trade	3 May 56	(Sir) A. Milward
1970	Min. of Aviation Supply	1 Jan 71	H. Marking
1971	Min. for Aerospace (and Shipping 1972) at the	1 Sep 72	P. Lawton
	Dept. of Trade and Industry		
1974	Sec. of State for Trade		

Established under the *Civil Aviation Act, 1946*, to take over European, domestic and some North African flights. In April 1974, under the *Civil Aviation Act, 1971*, merged with BOAC to form British Airways.

British South American Airways Corporation (B.S.A.A.) 1946–49

Responsible Minister		*Chairman*	
1946	Min. for Civil Aviation	1 Aug 46	J. Booth
		1 May 49	Sir M. Thomas

Established under the *Civil Aviation Act, 1946*, to take over Central and South American routes from BOAC. Merged with BOAC 1949.

British Airways, 1974–87

Responsible Minister		*Chairman*	
1972	Min. for Aerospace and Shipping at the Dept. of	7 Oct 71	D. Nicolson
	Trade and Industry	1 Jul 76	Sir F. McFadzean
1974	Sec. of State for Trade	1 Jul 79	Sir R. Stainton
1983	Sec. of State for Transport	3 Jan 81	J. (Ld) King

Established under the *Civil Aviation Act, 1971*, to take overall responsiblility for the activities of BEA and BOAC from 1 Apr 72. Became fully operational from 1 Apr 74. Became Limited Company in 1983. Sold by share issue in 1987.

British Airports Authority, 1966–87 (BAA plc, 1986–87)

	Responsible Minister		Chairman	
1966	Min. of Aviation	3 Jun 65	(Sir) P. Masefield
1968	Min. of State at the Board of Trade	9 Jan 72	N. Foulkes
1970	Min of Aviation Supply at the Dept. of Trade and Industry	1 Mar 77	(Sir) N. Payne
1971	Min. for Aerospace (and Shipping 1972) at the Dept. of Trade and Industry		
1974	Sec. of State for Trade		
1983	Sec. of State for Transport		

Established under the *Airports Authority Act, 1965*, to run Gatwick, Heathrow and Stansted, and since 1971 Edinburgh Turnhouse airports. Aberdeen and Glasgow were acquired in 1975. Became BAA plc under *Airports Act, 1986*. Sold by public share issue Jul 87.

British Aerospace 1977–81

	Responsible Minister		Chairman	
1977	Sec. of State for Industry	22 Mar 77	Ld Beswick
1983	Sec of State for Trade and Industry	22 Mar 80	(Sir) A. Pearce

Established under the *Aircraft and Shipbuilding Act, 1977*, to promote the efficient and economical design, development, production, sale, repair and maintenance of civil and military aircraft, of guided weapons and of space vehicles. Became a public limited company under the *British Aerospace Act, 1980*. In 1981 51% of shares were sold to the private sector and employees. The remaining shares in government hands were sold in 1985.

Fuel and Power

British Electricity Authority (Central Electricity Authority 1955–57) 1947–55

	Responsible Minister	Chairman		
1947	Min. of Fuel and Power	15 Aug 47–31 Dec 57	Ld Citrine
1957	Min. of Power		

Established under the *Electricity Act, 1947*, to be responsible for generation and main transmission throughout Great Britain excluding the North of Scotland. There were 14 Area Boards responsible for distribution. Under *Electricity Reorganisation (Scotland) Act, 1954*, two of these Area Boards (S.E. Scotland and S.W. Scotland) merged and took over generation in their areas from British Electricity Authority which was now renamed Central Electricity Authority.

Electricity Council 1957–90

	Responsible Minister		Chairman	
1957	Min. of Power	1 Sep 57	Sir H. Self
1969	Min. of Technology	1 Sep 59	(Sir) R. King
1970	Sec. of State for Trade and Industry	1 Jan 66	Sir R. Edwards
1974	Sec. of State for Energy	1 Nov 68	Sir N. Elliott
		1 Apr 72	Sir P. Menzies
		1 Apr 77	(Sir) F. Tombs
		1 Jan 81	(Sir) A. Bunch
		1 Apr 83	(Sir) P. Jones

Established under the *Electricity Act, 1957*, to co-ordinate development of the industry. It consisted of 14 statutory corporations: the Electricity Council, the CEGB and 12 Area Electricity Boards. The Council was wound up in 1990, when the CEGB was broken up in anticipation of electricity privatisation.

Central Electricity Generating Board (CEGB) 1957–90

	Responsible Minister		Chairman
1957	Min. of Power	1 Sep 57	Sir C. Hinton
1969	Min. of Technology	1 Jan 65	(Sir) S. Brown
1970	See. of State for Trade and Industry	1 Jul 72	A. Hawkins
1974	Sec. of State for Energy	9 May 77	G. England
		9 May 82	(office vacant)
		1 Jul 82	Sir W. (Ld) Marshall
		18 Dec 89	(office vacant)

Established under the *Electricity Act, 1957*, to own and operate the power stations and the National Grid, and to provide electricity in bulk to the 12 Area Boards. Under the *Electricity Act, 1989*, the CEGB was broken up into four companies – National Power, PowerGen, National Grid and Nuclear Electric, with effect from 1 Apr 90.

North of Scotland Hydro-Electricity Board (Scottish HydroElectric, 1990–91) 1943–90

	Responsible Minister		Chairman
1943	Secretary of State for Scotland	1 Sep 43	E of Airlie
		1 Apr 46	T. Johnston
		1 Jul 59	Ld Strathclyde
		1 Sep 69	T. Fraser
		30 Apr 73	Sir D. Haddow
		1 Jan 79	Ld Greenhill
		1 Jan 84	M. Joughin

Established under the *Hydro-Electric Development (Scotland) Act, 1943*, to supply electricity and to develop water power in the Highlands and Islands. In 1947 became responsible for all public generation and distribution of electricity in the North of Scotland. Under *Electricity Act, 1989*, name changed to Scottish HydroElectric, in Apr 1990, in preparation for privatisation which took place in Jun 91.

South of Scotland Electricity Board (Scottish Power, 1990–91) 1955–90

	Responsible Minister		Chairman
1955	Secretary of State for Scotland	1 Dec 54	(Sir) J. Pickles
		20 Feb 62	N. Elliot
		1 Apr 67	C. Allan
		1 Jan 74	F. Tombs
		1 Apr 77	D. Berridge
		22 Mar 82	(Sir) D. Miller

Established under the *Electricity Reorganisation (Scotland) Act, 1954*, to generate and distribute electricity throughout south of Scotland. Became Scottish Power in Apr 90 under *Electricity Act, 1989*, and lost responsibility for nuclear power stations in Scotland. Sold by public share offer Jun 91.

National Coal Board (NCB) 1946–87; British Coal, 1987–

	Responsible Minister		Chairman
1946	Min. of Fuel and Power	15 Jul 46	Ld Hyndley (Vt)
1956	Min. of Power	1 Aug 51	Sir H. Houldsworth
1969	Min. of Technology	1 Feb 56	(Sir) J. Bowman
1970	Sec. of State for Trade and Industry	1 Feb 61	A. Robens (Ld)
1974	Sec. of State For Energy	3 Jul 71	(Sir) D. Ezra
1992	Pres. of Board of Trade	3 Jul 82	(Sir) N. Siddall
		1 Sep 83	I. MacGregor
		1 Sep 86	Sir R. Haslam
		1 Jan 91	N. Clarke

Established under the *Coal Industry Nationalisation Act, 1946*, to own and run the coal industry and certain ancillary activities. Changed name to British Coal under the *Coal Industry Act, 1987*.

Gas Council and Boards, 1948–73

	Responsible Minister		Chairman
1948	Min. of Fuel and Power	23 Nov 48	Sir E. Sylvester
1957	Min. of Power	1 Jan 52	(Sir) H. Smith
1969	Min. of Technology	1 Jan 60	Sir H. Jones
1970	Sec. of State For Trade and Industry	1 Jan 72	A. Hetherington

Established by the *Gas Act,1948*, to co-ordinate 12 Area Gas Boards which were set up to manufacture and retail town gas. The Gas Council was responsible for the purchase and distribution of natural gas. Under the *Gas Act, 1972*, replaced by British Gas Corporation.

British Gas 1973–86

	Responsible Minister		Chairman
1973	Sec of State For Trade and Industry	1 Jan 73	(Sir) A. Hetherington
1974	Sec. of State for Energy	1 Jul 76	(Sir) D. Rooke

Established under the *Gas Act, 1972*, to take over responsibilities of Gas Council and Area Gas Boards. In 1984 British Gas's offshore oil interests were hived off to form Enterprise Oil. Became a public limited company under *Gas Act, 1986*, and sold by public share offer in Dec 86.

United Kingdom Atomic Energy Authority 1954–
(U.K.A.E.A.)

	Responsible Minister		Chairman
1954	Ld President	1 Aug 54	Sir E. Plowden (Ld)
1956	Prime Minister	1 Jan 60	Sir R. Makins
1959	Min. of Science	10 Feb 64	Sir W. Penney (Ld)
1963	Ld President	16 Oct 67	(Sir) J.Hill
1964	Min. of Technology	7 Jul 81	Sir W. Marshall
1970	Sec. of State For Trade and Industry	1 Oct 82	Sir P. Hirsch
1974	Sec. of State for Energy	1 Oct 84	A. Allen
1992	President of the Board of Trade	1 Jan 87	J. Collier
		1 Jul 90	J. Maltby
		1 Jul 93	Sir A. Cleaver

Established under the *Atomic Energy Authority Act, 1954*, to be responsible for the development of nuclear energy and its applications. From May 1989 traded as AEA Technology.

British National Oil Corporation (B.N.O.C.) 1976–82

	Responsible Minister		Chairman
1976	Sec. of State for Energy	1 Jan 76	Ld Kearton

Established under the *Petroleum and Submarines Pipelines Act, 1975*, to search for and get, move, store and treat, buy, sell, and deal in petroleum. In Nov 1982 the government sold its majority shareholding to the private sector.

British Nuclear Fuels 1971–

	Responsible Minister		Chairman
1971	Sec. of State for Trade and Industry	1 Apr 71	(Sir) J. Hill
1974	Sec. of State for Energy	1 Apr 83	C. Allday
1992	Pres. of Board of Trade	1 Apr 86	(Sir) C. Harding
		1 Jul 92	J. Guinness

Established under the *Atomic Energy Act, 1971*, from the former production group of the UK Atomic Energy Authority, taking over responsibility for the production, enrichment and reprocessing of nuclear fuel. Became a public limited company in 1984, with the Government the sole shareholder.

Nuclear Electric 1990–

Responsible Minister	Chairman
1990 Sec. of State for Energy	1 Jan 90 J. Collier
1992 President of the Board of Trade	

Established by the CEGB to take over the running of the nuclear power stations following the decision to exclude nuclear power stations from privatisation.

Scottish Nuclear 1990–

Responsible Minister	Chairman
1990 Sec. of State for Scotland	1 Apr 90 J. Hann

Took over the running of Scottish nuclear power stations from the South of Scotland Electricity Board as the electricity industry was prepared for privatisation under the *Electricity Act, 1989.*

PowerGen 1990–91

Responsible Minister	Chairman
1990 Sec. of State for Energy	1 Apr 90 R. Malpas
	16 Nov 90 Sir G. Day

Formed when the CEGB was broken up prior to privatisation, with 39% of non-nuclear generating capacity. The Government sold 60% of the shares in February 1991.

National Power 1990–91

Responsible Minister	Chairman
1990 Sec. of State for Energy	1 Apr 90 Ld Marshall
	5 Jul 90 Sir T. Holdsworth

Formed when the CEGB was broken up prior to privatisation, with 61% of non-nuclear generating capacity. The Government sold 60% of the shares in Feb 91.

Transport

London Passenger Transport Board (L.P.T.B.) 1933–47

Responsible Minister	Chairman
1933 Min. of Transport	1933 Ld Ashfield
1941 Min. of War Transport	
1946 Min. of Transport	

Established under the *London Passenger Transport Act, 1933,* to take over railway, tramway, bus and coach undertakings within the London area. Under the *Transport Act, 1947,* responsibilities transferred to the British Transport Commission operating through a London Transport Executive.

London Transport Board 1963–70

Responsible Minister	Chairman
1963 Min. of Transport	1 Jan 63 (Sir) A. Valentine
	1 Apr 65 (Sir) M. Holmes

Established under the *Transport Act, 1962,* to replace part of the British Transport Commission, to provide an adequate and properly co-ordinated system of passenger transport for the London area. Under the *Transport (London) Act, 1969,* responsibilities transferred to the Greater London Council.

NATIONALISED INDUSTRIES

London Regional Transport (L.R.T.) 1984–

Responsible Minister			*Chairman*	
1984	Sec. of State for Transport		29 Jun 84	(Sir) K. Bright
			13 Mar 89	(Sir) W. Newton

Established under the *London Regional Transport Act, 1984*, to take over responsibility for transport in London from the GLC.

British Transport Commission (B.T.C.) 1947–62

Responsible Minister		*Chairman*	
1947	Min. of Transport	8 Sep 47	Sir C. Hurcomb (Ld)
1953	Min. of Transport and Civil Aviation	15 Sep 53	Sir B. Robertson
1959	Min. of Transport	1 Jun 61	R. Beeching (Ld)

Chairman of Executives of BTC

Docks and Inland Waterways Executive

1947–53	Sir R. Hill

Hotels Executive

1948–51	Ld Inman (*part-time from 1950*)
1951–53	Sir H. Methven (*part-time*)

Railway Executive

1947–51	Sir E. Missenden
1951–53	J. Elliot

Road Haulage Executive

1948–53	G. Russell

London Transport Executive

1947–53	Ld Latham
1953–59	(Sir) J. Elliot
1959–62	A. Valentine

Road Passenger Service

1948–52	G. Cardwell

Established under the *Transport Act, 1947*, to provide an integrated system of transport facilities (excluding air). The separate executives were wound up in 1953 (except for the London Transport Executive). The *Transport Act, 1962*, transferred the whole of the B.T.C. to new separate corporations.

British Railways Board (B.R.) 1963–

Responsible Minister		*Chairman*	
1962	Min. of Transport	1 Jan 63	R. Beeching (Ld)
1970	Sec. of State for the Environment	1 Jun 65	(Sir) S. Raymond
1976	Sec. of State for Transport	1 Jan 68	(Sir) H. Johnson
		13 Sep 71	(Sir) R. Marsh
		12 Sep 76	(Sir) P. Parker
		12 Sep 83	(Sir) R. (Robert) Reid
		1 Apr 90	(Sir) R. (Bob) Reid

Established under the *Transport Act, 1962*, to take over the B.T.C.'s rail services. The *Railways Act, 1993*, laid down plans for the franchising of some routes by the private sector.

Railtrack 1994–

Responsible Minister		*Chairman*	
1994	Sec. of State for Transport	1 Apr 94	B. Horton

Established under the *Railways Act 1993* to take over responsibility for track and signalling from British Rail in preparation for the franchising of services.

British Transport Docks Board 1963–84

Responsible Minister		*Chairman*	
1962	Min. of Transport	3 Dec 62	Sir A. Kirby
1970	Sec. of State for the Environment	15 Jun 67	S. Finnis
1976	Sec. of State for Transport	6 Aug 69	R. Wills
		25 Sep 69	C. Cory (acting)
		19 Jan 70	Sir C. Doye
		1 May 71	Sir H. Browne
		1 May 82	K. Stuart

Established under the *Transport Act, 1962*, to administer publicly owned ports throughout the country. Under *Docks and Harbours Act, 1966*, became licensing authority for all but three ports. Sold off in 1983 and 1984 under the *Tranport Act, 1981*, to form Associated British Ports.

British Waterways Board 1963–

Responsible Minister		*Chairman*	
1963	Min. of Transport	1 Jan 63	F. Arney
1970	Sec. of State for the Environment	1 Jul 63	Sir J. Hawton
		1 Jul 68	Sir F. Price
		1 Jul 84	Sir L. Young
		1 Jul 87	A. Robertson (acting)
		22 Oct 87	D. Ingman
		1 Nov 93	(*office vacant*)

Established under the *Transport Act, 1962*, to take over inland waterways from the B.T.C. *The Transport Act, 1968*, extended its powers particularly in regard to recreation and amenities.

National Bus Company, 1968–91

Responsible Minister		*Chairman*	
1968	Min. of Transport	28 Nov 68	A. Todd
1970	Sec. of State for the Environment	1 Jan 72	F. Wood
1976	Sec. of State for Transport	1 Jan 79	Ld. Shepherd
		1 Jan 85	R. Brook
		8 Apr 86	R. Lund
		1 Apr 88	Sir P. Harrup

Established under the *Transport Act, 1968*, to take over responsibility for state-owned bus companies and bus manufacturing interests from the Transport Holding Company. Broken up and sold off following *Transport Act, 1985*. Formally wound up in Apr 91.

National Freight Corporation 1968–82

Responsible Minister		*Chairman*	
1968	Min. of Transport	1 Jan 69	Sir R. Wilson
1970	Sec. of State for the Environment	1 Jan 71	(Sir) D. Pettit
1976	Sec. of State For Transport	1 Jan 79	Sir R. Lawrence

Established under the *Transport Act, 1968*, to take over road haulage and shipping interests of the Transport Holding Company. Shipping interests terminated in 1971. Sold to the National Freight Consortium in 1982.

Scottish Transport Group, 1968–

Responsible Minister		Chairman	
1968	Secretary of State for Scotland	18 Nov 68	(Sir) P. Thomas
		1 Jan 78	A. Donnet (Ld)
		1 Jan 81	W. Stevenson
		1 Jan 87	I. Irwin

Established under the *Transport Act, 1968*, to control various transport activities in Scotland, including road passenger, insurance, tourism and shipping. Under the *Transport (Scotland) Act, 1989*, the Scottish Office announced a programme to dispose of STG's assets. This was largely complete by 1991, although the Group still formally exists.

Transport Holding Company 1962–72

Responsible Minister		Chairman	
1962	Min. of Transport	15 Nov 62	Sir P. Warter
1970	Sec. of State for the Environment	15 Nov 67	Sir R. Wilson
		1 Jan 71	L. Whyte

Established by the *Transport Act, 1962*, to take over all B.T.C. investments not given to British Rail, London Transport, Docks or Waterways Boards. The *Transport Act, 1968*, transferred its road interests to the National Freight Corporation and the National Bus Company. Its residual interests (Thomas Cook, Lunn-Poly, etc.) were sold 1970–72.

Miscellaneous

Iron and Steel Corporation 1950–53

Responsible Minister		Chairman	
1950	Min. of Supply	2 Oct 50	S. Hardie
		25 Feb 52	Sir J. Green

Established under the *Iron and Steel Act, 1949*, to take over 298 companies in the iron and steel industries. Wound up by the *Iron and Steel Act, 1953*.

British Steel Corporation 1968–88

Responsible Minister		Chairman	
1967	Min. of Power	28 Jul 67	Ld Melchett
1969	Min. of Technology	18 Jun 73	(Sir) M. Finniston
1970	Sec. of State For Trade and Industry	10 Sep 76	Sir C. Villiers
1974	Sec. of State for Industry	1 Jul 80	I. MacGregor
1983	Sec. of State for Trade and Industry	1 Sep 83	(Sir) R. Haslam
		1 Apr 86	(Sir) R. Scholey

Established under the *Iron and Steel Act, 1967*, to take over the management of the major part of the steel industry. Sold by public share issue in Dec 1988 after becoming a public limited company under the terms of the *British Steel Act, 1988*.

Cable and Wireless Ltd 1947–81

Responsible Minister		Chairman	
1947	Postmaster-General	1 Jan 47	Sir A. Augwin
1969	Min. of Posts and Telecommunications	1 Apr 51	(Sir) L. Nicholls
1970	Sec. of State for Trade and Industry	1 Feb 56	Sir G. Ince
1974	Sec. of State for Industry	1 Jan 62	Sir J. Macpherson
1983	Sec. of State for Trade and Industry	1 Nov 67	D. McMillan
		1 Mar 72	H. Lillicrap
		1 Nov 76	E. Short (Ld Glenamara)
		15 Oct 80	(Sir) E. Sharp

Under the *Cable and Wireless Act, 1946*, the Government acquired all those shares of Cable and Wireless Ltd. not already in its possession. The company's U.K. assets were integrated into the Post Office and it continued to own and operate telecommunications services outside the U.K. In 1981 the Government sold the majority of its shares; the remainder were sold in 1983 and 1985.

Post Office Corporation 1970–

Responsible Minister		Chairman	
1970	Min. of Posts and Telecommunications	1 Oct 69	Vt Hall
1974	Sec. of State for Industry	22 Apr 71	(Sir) W. Ryland
1983	Sec. of State for Trade and Industry	31 Oct 77	Sir W. Barlow
		1 Sep 80	Sir H. Chilver
		1 Oct 81	(Sir) R. Dearing
		1 Oct 87	Sir B. Nicholson
		1 Jan 93	(Sir) M. Heron

Established under the *Post Office Act, 1969*, to take over from the office of the Postmaster General, responsibility for postal services, Giro and remittance services and telecommunications throughout the U.K. In March 1974 all broadcasting functions transferred to Home Office supervision. In 1981 all teleeommunications services were transferred to British Telecom.

British Telecom 1981–84

Responsible Minister		Chairman	
1981	Sec. of State for Industry	27 Jul 81	Sir G. Jefferson
1983	Sec. of State for Trade and Industry		

Established under the *British Telecommunications Act, 1981*, to take over the telecommunication functions of the Post Office prior to privatisation. 50.2% of shares were sold in Nov 1984; the government eventually sold its last 22% stake in the company in Jul 1993.

British Shipbuilders 1977–

Responsible Minister		Chairman	
1977	Sec. of State for Industry	1 Jul 77	Sir A. Griffin
1983	Sec. of State for Trade and Industry	1 Jul 80	(Sir) R. Atkinson
		1 Sep 83	G. Day
		1 May 86	P. Hares
		1 May 88	J. Lister
		4 Sep 89	C. Campbell

Established under the *Aircraft and Shipbuilding Industries Act, 1977*, to promote the efficient and economical design, development, production, sale, repair and maintenance of ships. Broken up from 1984. The last yard was sold in 1990, although the company still exists.

British Technology Group 1981–92

	Responsible Minister		Chairman
1981	Sec. of State for Industry	20 Jul 81	Sir F. Wood
1983	Sec. of State for Trade and Industry	1 Nov 83	C. Barker

Established in 1981 as an umbrella organisation for the National Enterprise Board and the National Research Development Corporation, which retained separate legal identities until merged by the *British Technology Group Act, 1991*. It acted as a holding company for shares in high technology firms and had a brief to develop the potential of inventions made within the public sector. The group was sold to a consortium of investors in March 1992.

Rolls Royce Ltd 1971–87

	Responsible Minister		Chairman
1971	Min. For Aerospace at the Dept. of Trade and Industry	22 May 71	Ld Cole
		5 Oct 72	Sir K. Keith (Ld)
1974	Sec. of State for Industry	22 Jan 80	Ld McFadzean
1983	Sec. of State for Trade	31 Mar 83	Sir W. Duncan
		13 Nov 84	Sir A. Hall (acting)
		31 Jan 85	Sir F. Tombs

Established in Feb 1971 under the *Companies Act, 1960*, with the Government as the sole shareholder to ensure the continuance of those activities of Rolls-Royce Ltd. which are essential to national defence and to air forces and airlines all over the world. Shares vested in N.E.B. from 1 Feb 76 to 12 Aug 80. The Government sold its shares in 1987.

BL (British Leyland) 1975–86; Rover Group 1986–8

	Responsible Minister		Chairman Minister responsible
1975	Sec. of State for Industry	30 Oct 75	Sir R. Edwards
1983	Sec. of State For Trade and Industry	14 Apr 76	Sir R. Dobson
		1 Nov 77	(Sir) M. Edwardes
		8 Nov 82	Sir A. Bide
		1 May 86	(Sir) G. Day

Majority of shareholdings were purchased in 1975, using *Companies Act, 1960*, following financial problems. Shares vested in N.E.B. from 30 Oct 75 to 31 Mar 81. Sold to British Aerospace, Aug 88.

Nationalised Industries: Assets and Employees, 1950–

	1950		1960		1970		1980		1990	
	Net Assets	Total Employed	Net Assets	Total Employed	Net Assets	Total Employed	Net Assets	Total Employed	Net Assets	Total Employed
BOAC	42	16	132	21	251	23	–	–	–	–
BEA	6	7	58	13	116	25	–	–	–	–
British Airways	–	–	–	–	–	–	880	57	–	–
British Airports Authority	–	–	–	–	73	4	748	7	–	–
British Aerospace	–	–	–	–	–	–	992	78	–	–
British Electricity Board, Electricity Council, CEGB, Area Boards	686	161	1,948	189	4,921	197	7,179	159	31,741[a]	130
N.S.H.E.B	53	3	197	3	267	4	610	4	2,203	4
S.S.E.B	–	–	153	13	418	15	828	14	827	10
Gas industry	269	132	585	127	1,658	119	2,576	104	–	–
National Coal Board	337	749	910	631	666	356	2,128	294	5,868	85
U.K.A.E.A.	–	–	488	39	256	30	98	14	134	11
B.N.O.C.	–	–	–	–	–	–	1,000	2	–	–
Brit.Trans. Comm.	1,226	889	1,828	729	–	–	–	–	–	–
British Rail	–	–	–	–	850	273	1,230	238	2,108	134
National Bus Company	–	–	–	–	93	84	214	51	–	–
National Freight Company	–	–	–	–	116	65	74	31	–	–
British Transport Docks	–	–	–	–	123	11	166	11	–	–
I.&S.C. / British Steel	492	292	–	–	1,222	250	2,056	121	–	–
Post Office Corporation	–	–	–	–	2,521	407	7,342	423	2,360	211
Cable and Wireless	38	13	46	10	70	10	248	12	–	–
British Shipbuilders	–	–	–	–	–	–	88	70	–	–

[a] The last available figures for the Electricity industry are 1989.

External Financing Requirements of Nationalised Industries

(excluding central government grants generally available to private sector)
Figures are billions of pounds. Year ending Apr.

Year	BA	Coal	Gas	BR	Shipb	Steel	BT	Elec	LRT.	PO	Water	Mis	Total
1977	–	0.4	−0.1	0.6	–	1.0		0.3	–	0.2	–	0.3	2.7
1978	0.1	0.3	−0.2	0.6	–	0.8	–	0.3	–	–	–	0.1	2.0
1979	0.1	0.6	−0.4	0.6	0.1	0.8	−0.1	−0.1	–	–	0.3	0.5	2.3
1980	0.2	0.7	−0.4	0.7	0.2	0.6	0.3	0.3	–	–	0.3	0.2	3.0
1981	0.3	0.8	−0.4	0.8	0.2	1.1	−0.1	0.2	–	–	0.3	–	3.2
1982	0.2	1.2	–	1.0	0.1	0.8	0.2	−0.1	–	–	0.3	−0.1	3.6
1983	–	1.0	−0.2	0.8	0.1	0.6	−0.3	−0.1	–	−0.1	0.3	–	2.1
1984	−0.2	1.2	–	0.8	0.3	0.3	−0.2	−0.3	–	−0.1	0.4	0.1	2.3
1985	−0.3	1.7	−0.2	1.0	0.2	0.5	−0.3	0.8	–	–	0.3	0.1	3.9
1986	−0.2	0.4	−0.2	0.9	–	0.4		−0.3	0.3	−0.1	0.2	0.1	1.7
1987	−0.1	0.9	−0.7	0.8	0.2	–		−1.2	0.3	−0.1	0.1	–	0.3
1988		0.9		0.5	0.1	−0.3		−1.1	0.2	−0.1	–	−0.1	0.2
1989		0.8		0.4	0.1	−0.4		−1.7	0.2	−0.1	–	0.1	−0.5
1990		1.3		0.7				−1.4	0.3	–	–	0.1	1.0
1991		0.9		1.1				−0.3	0.5	–	–	0.1	2.3
1992		0.6		1.5				−0.1	0.6	−0.1	–	0.1	2.5
1993		0.5		2.0				−0.3	1.1	−0.1	–	0.1	3.4

Inquiries into Nationalised Industries

The nationalised industries were frequently the subject of Government inquiries into different aspects of their organisation and performance. Later examples include *Report of the Post Office Review Committee*, July 1977 (Cmnd 6850), and *The Structure of the Electricity Supply Industry in England and Wales*, January 1976 (Cmnd 6388). In addition, the National Economic Development Office in June 1975 were invited to undertake a wide-ranging inquiry into the role of nationalised industries in the economy and 'the way in which they are to be controlled in future'. Their report published in 1976, together with an appendix volume and 7 background papers, add up to the most comprehensive analysis of the industries' post-war performance.

Between 1965 and 1970 the National Board for Prices and Incomes produced reports which, while primarily concerned with prices and wages, considered the efficiency of the industries. from 1967–70 all major price increase proposals by the nationalised industries were referred to the National Board for Prices and Incomes.

The Select Committee on Nationalised Industries (1956–79) also published regular reports.

Central Government Trading Bodies

Some central government trading bodies have raised revenue through the sales of goods and services, but have not been organised as public corporations:

Export Credits Guarantee Department 1975–
Forestry Commission 1918–
Her Majesty's Stationery Office (HMSO) 1786–[a]
Horserace Totalisator Board, 1963–
National Savings Bank 1969–
Land Authority for Wales 1975–
Royal Mint 11th cent, reorganised 1870–[a]
Royal Ordnance Factories (sold to British Aerospace 1987)
Crown Estate Commission 1762, reorganised 1961–
Land Registry 1862–[a]
National Audit Office, 1983–

Other Quasi-governmental Organisations

The dividing line between nationalised industries and other quasi-autonomous national government organisations is by no means a clear one. Many of the organisations listed below enjoy similar legal status to the public corporations listed above – the main difference in many cases being one of size. Most official and academic studies indicate that there are between 250 and 350 central non-Departmental bodies of a permanent nature in the U.K. The categories set out below do not purport to represent a comprehensive list, but do include some of the more notable examples.

1.   Those which act as agencies for the spending of government money

Regional Health Authorities
University Grants Committee 1919–89
Universities Funding Council 1989–93
Polytechnics and Colleges Funding Council 1989–93

[a] Now an agency under the Government's Next Steps programme.

Higher Education Funding Councils 1993–
Manpower Services Commission 1974–88
Sports Council 1972–
Agricultural (and Food) Research Council 1931–
NHS Hospital Trusts 1991–
Medical Research Council 1920–
Natural Environment Research Council 1965–
Arts Council 1946–
National Film Finance Corporation 1949–84
National Research Development Corporation 1967–91 *(see above entry for British Technology Group)*
National Enterprise Board 1975–91 *(see above entry for British Technology Group)*
Housing Corporation 1964–
Social Science Research Council 1965–83
Economic and Social Research Council 1983–
British Council 1934–
British Film Commission 1992–
Legal Aid Board 1989–

2. *Quasi-judicial and prosecuting bodies*

Prices and Incomes Board 1965–70
Monopolies Commission 1956–73
Monopolies and Mergers Commission 1973–
Price Commission 1973–79
Criminal Injuries Compensation Board 1964–
General and Special Commissioners of Income Tax
Parole Board 1967–
Mental Health Act Commission 1983–
Police Complaints Authority 1984–
Serious Fraud Office 1987–
Crown Prosecution Service 1986–

3. *Bodies with statutory powers of regulation and licensing*

H.M. Land Registry 1925–[a]
Charity Commission 1853–
Transport Tribunals
Independent Broadcasting Authority 1954–1990 (see p.)
Independent Television Commission 1991–
Radio Authority 1991–
Civil Aviation Authority 1971–
Office of Fair Trading 1973–
Commission for Local Authority Accounts in Scotland 1975–
Audit Commission 1983–
Office of the Data Protection Registrar 1984–
Office of Telecommunications (OFTEL) 1984–
Office of Gas Supply (OFGAS) 1986–
Office of Electricity Regulation (OFFER) 1989–
Office of Water Services (OFWAT) 1989–
Broadcasting Standards Council 1988–
National Rivers Authority 1989–

4. *Statutory advisory or consultative bodies nominated wholly or in part by Ministers*

Gaming Board for Great Britain 1968–
Metrication Board 1969–80
Consumer Councils of the Nationalised Industries
Health and Safety Commission and Executive 1974–
Law Commission 1965–
Industrial Reorganisation Corporation 1966–70
Countryside Commission 1968–
Equal Opportunities Commission 1975–
Commission for Racial Equality 1977–
Advisory, Conciliation and Arbitration Service 1975–

5. *Executive agencies administering specific activities*

National Dock Labour Board 1947–89
Covent Garden Market Authority 1961–
Northern Ireland Electricity 1973–92
Northern Ireland Transport Holding Company 1968–
National Ports Council 1964–81
Regional Water Authorities (until 1991)

6. *Development agencies*

New Town Development Corporations and Commission (see p.)
Scottish Development Agency 1975–91
Scottish Enterprise 1991–
Welsh Development Agency 1976–
Highlands and Islands Development Board 1965–91
Highlands and Islands Enterprise 1991–
Colonial Development Corporation 1948–63
Commonwealth Development Corporation 1963–
Development Commission (for Rural England) 1909–88
Rural Development Commission 1988–
Urban Development Corporations

Policy for Nationalised Industries

Four important White Papers on the control of Nationalised Industries have been issued since the war. They are:

Nationalised Industries: Financial and Economic Obligations (Cmnd 1337, 1961)
Nationalised Industries: A Review of Economic and Financial Objectives (Cmnd 3437, 1967)
Ministerial Control of Nationalised Industries (Cmnd 4027, 1969)
The Nationalised Industries (Cmnd 7131, 1978)

In addition a series of White Papers have been published on both Fuel Policy (1965, 1967) and Transport Policy (1952, 1966, 1977) which have had an important impact on the operation of the nationalised industries in these sectors.

SOURCES. – For an analysis of the statutory provisions of the nationalised industries, see D.N.Chester, *The Nationalised Industries* (1951). Other studies of the nationalised industries include: Action Society Trust, *Twelve Studies on Nationalised Industries* (1950–3); H.A.Clegg and T.E.Chester, *The Future of Nationalisation* (1953); D.Coombes, *The Member of Parliament and the Administration: The case of the Select Committee on Nationalised Industries* (1966); M. Rees, *The Public Sector in the Mixed Economy* (1973); R. Kelf-Cohen, *British Nationalisation 1945–73* (1973); R.Pryke, *The Nationalised Industries: Policy and Performance since 1968* (1981); R. Vernon (ed.), *The Promise of Privatisation* (1988). J.Vickers and G.Yarrow, *Privatisation: an Economic analysis* (1988). Also *Public Expenditure Analyses*, HM Treasury, Cm 2219 (Jan 1993).

XIII

ROYALTY

British Kings and Queens, 1900–

Name	Accession		Coronation		Died		Age	Reigned
Victoria	20 Jun	1837	28 Jun	1838	22 Jan	1901	81	63 yrs
Edward VII	22 Jan	1901	9 Aug	1902	6 May	10	68	9 yrs
George V	6 May	10	22 Jun	11	20 Jan	36	70	25 yrs
Edward VIII	20 Jan	36	..		(Abdicated)		..	325 days
George VI	11 Dec	36	12 May	37	6 Feb	52	56	15 yrs
Elizabeth II	6 Feb	52	2 Jun	53	..	..	..	

Use of Royal Power

Throughout this century great efforts have been made to avoid involving the Crown in politics. But there have been a few occasions when, unavoidably or deliberately, the Sovereign has been involved in decision making. No list of such occasions can be very satisfactory. It may omit times when in private audience the Sovereign expressed strong views to the Prime Minister. It may include times when, despite all the formality of consultation, the Sovereign had no real opportunity of affecting the outcome. The following list of incidents is compiled primarily from Sir Ivor Jennings, *Cabinet Government*; Sir Harold Nicolson, *King George V*; Sir J. W. Wheeler-Bennett, *King George VI*; F. Hardie, *The Political Influence of the Monarchy 1868–1952*; and *The Royal Encyclopaedia* (ed. R. Allison).

	1903	Edward VII's visit to France, on his own initiative; prelude to Entente Cordiale of 1904
Dec	1909	Edward VII's refusal to promise to create peers until after a second general election.
Jul	1910	George V's sponsorship of the Constitutional Conference.
Nov	1910	George V's secret pledge to create peers, if necessary.
Jul	1914	George V's sponsorship of Buckingham Palace Home Rule Conference.
	1915	Buckingham Palace meeting on conscription
Mar	1917	George V's support for General Haig, when in danger of being dismissed.
Dec	1916	Buckingham Palace Conference on choice of Prime Minister following H. Asquith's resignation.
	1917	Relinquishment of German titles. Proclamation of dynasty of Windsor.
May	1923	George V's summons of S. Baldwin as Prime Minister.
Jan	1924	George V's request to R. MacDonald to form government.
Oct	1924	George V's agreement to dissolution.
May	1926	George V blocks government proposal during General Strike to embargo trade union funds.
Aug	1931	George V's invitation to R MacDonald to form National Government.
Oct	1931	George V agrees to General Election.
Dec	1936	Edward VIII's decision to abdicate.
May	1940	George VI's invitation to W. Churchill to form Coalition Government.
Jun	1944	George VI's veto on W. Churchill's plan to accompany troops on D-Day invasion.
Jul	1945	George VI's advice on switching appointment of Bevin and Dalton (a disputed allegation).
Jan	1957	Elizabeth II's summons of H. Macmillan as Prime Minister.
Oct	1963	Elizabeth II's invitation to E of Home to form a Government.
Nov	1965	Elizabeth II's award of G.C.V.O. to Governor of Rhodesia.
May	1977	Elizabeth II's Silver Jubilee Speech to Parliament stressing her Coronation oath as Queen of the United Kingdom.
Jul	1986	Elizabeth II's reference to her role as head of the Commonwealth, interpreted as a reproach to the Prime Minister, Margaret Thatcher, over the issue of sanctions on South Africa.

Regency Acts, 1937 and 1953

These Acts provide that if the Sovereign is under 18 years of age, the royal functions shall be exercised by a Regent appointed under the provisions of the Acts. (Formerly the appointment of a Regent was *ad hoc.*) The Regent may not give assent to Bills altering the succession to the throne or repealing the Acts securing the Scottish Church.

The Acts provide for Counsellors of State to be appointed during the Monarch's absence from the U.K., or infirmity; and empower certain high officials of the state to declare that 'the Sovereign is by infirmity of mind or body incapable for the time being of performing the royal function'.

The Royal Family

Children of Queen Victoria

1. H.R.H. Princess Victoria (Princess Royal). Born 21 Nov 1840, married Prince Frederick of Prussia (1858), afterwards Kaiser Frederick III, died 5 Aug 1901.
2. **H.M. King Edward VII.** Born 9 Nov 1841, married H.R.H. Princess Alexandra (eldest daughter of King Christian IX of Denmark), 10 Mar 1863, succeeded to the throne 22 Jan 1901, crowned at Westminster Abbey 9 Aug 1902, died 6 May 1910 (*for children, see below*).
3. H.R.H. Princess Alice. Born 25 Apr 1843, married Prince Louis (1862), afterwards Grand Duke of Hesse, died 14 Dec 1878.
4. H.R.H. Prince Alfred, D of Edinburgh. Born 6 Aug 1844, married Marie Alexandrovna (1874) only daughter of Alexander II, Emperor of Russia. Succeeded as D of Saxe-Coburg and Gotha 22 Aug 1893, died 30 Jul 1900.
5. H.R.H. Princess Helena. Born 25 May 1846, married H.R.H. Prince Christian of Schleswig-Holstein (1866), died 9 Jun 1923.
6. H.R.H. Princess Louise. Born 18 Mar 1848, married M of Lorne (1871), afterwards 9th D of Argyll, died 3 Dec 1939.
7. H.R.H. Prince Arthur, D of Connaught. Born 1 May 1850, married H.R.H. Princess Louisa of Prussia (1879), died 16 Jan 1942.
8. H.R.H. Prince Leopold, D of Albany. Born 7 Apr 1853, married Princess Helena of Waldeck (1882), died 28 Mar 1884.
9. H.R.H. Princess Beatrice. Born 14 Apr 1857, married H.R.H. Prince Henry of Battenberg (1885), died 26 Oct 1944.

Children of Edward VII

1. H.R.H. Prince Albert, D of Clarence and Avondale (1891). Born 8 Jan 1864, died 14 Jan 1892.
2. **H.M. King George V.** H.R.H. Prince George, D of York (1893), Prince of Wales (1901–1910). Born 3 Jun 1865, married (6 Jul 1893) H.R.H. Princess Mary of Teck (Queen Mary, died 24 Mar 1953), succeeded to the throne 6 May 1910, crowned at Westminster Abbey 22 Jun 1911, assumed by Royal Proclamation (17 Jun 1917) the name of Windsor for his House and family, died 20 Jan 1936 (*for children, see below*).
3. H.R.H. Princess Louise (Princess Royal). Born 20 Feb 1867, married to 1st D of Fife (1889), died 4 Jan 1931. Children: (i) H.H. Princess Alexandra, Duchess of Fife. Born 17 May 1891, married H.R.H. Prince Arthur of Connaught (1913), died 26 Feb 1959. Child:

Alastair, D of Connaught, born 9 Aug 1914, died 26 Apr 1943. (ii) H.H. Princess Maud. Born 3 Apr 1893, married to 11th E of Southesk (1923), died 14 Dec 1945. Child: D of Fife, born 23 Sep 1929, married (1956) Hon. Caroline Dewar.

4. H.R.H. Princess Victoria. Born 6 Jul 1868, died 2 Dec 1935.
5. H.R.H. Princess Maud. Born 26 Nov 1869, married Prince Charles of Denmark (1896), afterwards King Haakon VII of Norway, died 20 Nov 1938. Child: H.M. Olaf V, King of Norway. Born 2 Jul 1903, married (1929) H.R.H. Princess Marthe of Sweden. Died 17 Jan 1991. Children: (i) H.R.H. Princess Ragnhild, born 9 Jun 1930, married (1953) to E. Lorentzen. (ii) H.R.H. Princess Astrid, born 12 Feb 1932. (iii) H.M. Harald V, King of Norway, born 21 Feb 1937, married (1968) Miss S. Haraldsen. Children: (i) H.R.H. Princess Martha Louise, born 22 Sep 1971. (ii) H.R.H. Prince Haakon Magnus, Crown Prince of Norway, born 20 Jul 1973.

Children of George V

1. H.R.H. Prince Edward, D of Windsor (1936), Prince of Wales (1910–36). Born 23 Jun 1894, succeeded to the throne as **King Edward VIII** on 20 Jan 1936, abdicated 11 Dec 1936. Married Mrs W. Simpson on 3 Jun 1937. Died 28 May 1972.
2. **H.M. King George VI**. H.R.H. Prince Albert, D of York (1920). Born 14 Dec 1895, married Elizabeth Bowes-Lyon, daughter of 14th E of Strathmore and Kinghorne on 26 Apr 1923, succeeded to the throne on 11 Dec 1936, crowned at Westminster Abbey 12 May 1937, died 6 Feb 1952 (*for children, see below*).
3. H.R.H. Princess Victoria (Princess Royal). Born 25 Apr 1897, married (1922) to 6th E of Harewood, died 28 Mar 1965. Children: (i) George, 7th E of Harewood. Born 7 Feb 1923, married (1949) Marion, daughter of E. Stein. Divorced, 7 Jul 1967. Married (1967) Patricia Tuckwell. Children: David, Vt Lascelles, born 21 Oct 1950; J. Lascelles, born 5 Oct 1953; R. Lascelles, born 14 Feb 1955; M. Lascelles, born 5 Jul 1964. (ii) G. Lascelles, born 21 Aug 1924, married (1952) Miss A. Dowding. Children: H. Lascelles, born 19 May 1953; M. Lascelles, born 9 Feb 1962. Divorced July 1978. Married Mrs E. Colvin 1978.
4. H.R.H. Prince Henry, D of Gloucester (1928). Born 31 Mar 1900, married (1935) Lady A. Montagu-Douglas-Scott, daughter of 7th D of Buccleuch, died 10 Jun 1974. Children: (i) H.R.H. Prince William, born 18 Dec 1941, died 28 Aug 1972. (ii) H.R.H. Prince Richard, D of Gloucester, born 26 Aug 1944, married (1972) Birgit Van Deurs. Children: Alexander, Earl of Ulster, born 28 Oct 1974. Lady Davina Windsor, born 19 Nov 1977. Lady Rose Windsor, born 1 Mar 1980.
5. H.R.H. Prince George, D of Kent (1934). Born 20 Dec 1902, married (1934) H.R.H. Princess Marina of Greece and Denmark, killed on active service 25 Aug 1942. Children: (i) H.R.H. Prince Edward, D of Kent, born 9 Oct 1935, married (1961) Katherine, daughter of Sir W. Worsley. Children: George, E of St Andrews, born 26 Jun 1962, married (1988) Sylvana Tomaselli. Children: Edward, Lord Downpatrick, born 2 Dec 1988; Lady Marina Windsor, born 13 Sep 1992; Lady Helen Windsor, born 28 April 1964, married (1992) Timothy Taylor. Child: Colombus, born 6 Aug 1994; Lord Nicholas Windsor, born 25 Jul 1970. (ii) Princess Alexandra, born 25 Dec 1936, married (1963) Hon.(Sir) Angus Ogilvy. Children: James Ogilvy, born 29 Feb 1964, married (1988) Julia Rawlinson; Marina Ogilvy, born 31 Jul 1966, married (1990) Paul Mowatt. Child: Zenouska Mowatt, born 26 May 1990. (iii) H.R.H. Prince Michael, born 4 July 1942, married (1978) Baroness Marie-Christine von Reibnitz. Children: Lord Frederick Windsor, born 6 Apr 1979. Lady Gabriella Windsor, born 23 Apr 1981.
6. H.R.H. Prince John. Born 12 Jul 1905, died 18 Jan 1919.

Children of George VI

1. **H.M. Queen Elizabeth II**. Born 21 Apr 1926, married to Philip, D of Edinburgh on 20 Nov 1947, succeeded to the throne 6 Feb 1952, crowned at Westminster Abbey 2 Jun 1953. Children: (i) H.R.H. Prince Charles, Prince of Wales (26 Jun 1958), D of Cornwall, born 14 Nov 1948, married Lady Diana Spencer 29 Jul 1981. Children: Prince William Arthur Philip Louis, born 21 Jun 1982; Prince Henry Charles Albert David, born 15 Sep 1984. Separated 9 Dec 1992. (ii) H.R.H. Princess Anne, the Princess Royal (13 Jun 1987), born 15 Aug 1950, married Mark Phillips 14 Nov 1973. Divorced 23 Apr 1992. Children: Peter Mark Andrew Phillips, born 15 Nov 1977; Zara Anne Elizabeth, born 15 May 1981. Married Timothy Lawrence 12 Dec 1992. (iii) H.R.H. Prince Andrew, Duke of York (23 Jul 1986), born 19 Feb 1960, married Sarah Ferguson 23 Jul 1986. Separated 19 Mar 92. Children: Princess Beatrice of York, born 8 Aug 1988; Princess Eugenie of York, born 23 Mar 1990. (iv) Prince Edward, born 10 Mar 1964.
2. H.R.H. Princess Margaret. Born 21 Aug 1930, married on 6 May 1960 to Antony Armstrong-Jones (created E of Snowdon, 1961). Divorced 24 May 1978. Children: (i) David, Vt Linley, born 3 Nov 1961, married Serena Stanhope 2 Oct 1993. (ii) Lady Sarah Armstrong-Jones, born 1 May 1964, married Daniel Chatto, 14 Jul 1994.

Private Secretaries to the Sovereign

1895–1901	Sir A. Bigge (Ld Stamfordham)	1953–72	Sir M. Adeane
1901–13	Sir F. Knollys (Ld) (Vt)[1]	1972–77	Sir M. Charteris
1910–31	Ld Stamfordham[1]	1977–86	Sir P. Moore
1931–36	Sir C. Wigram (Ld)	1986–90	Sir W. Heseltine
1936–43	Sir A. Hardinge	1990–	Sir R. Fellowes
1943–52	Sir A. Lascelles		

Lord Chamberlains

1898	E of Hopetoun	1938	6th E of Clarendon
1900	5th E of Clarendon	1952	E of Scarborough
1905	Vt Althorp (Earl Spencer)	1963	Ld Cobbold
1912	Ld Sandhurst (Vt)	1971	Ld Maclean
1921	D of Atholl	1984	E of Airlie
1922	E of Cromer		

Poets Laureate

1896	A. Austin	1968	C. Day Lewis
1913	R. Bridges	1971	Sir J. Betjeman
1930	J. Masefield	1984	E. Hughes

Civil List of the Crown

The annuities payable to the Sovereign and Members of the Royal Family are known as the Civil List which is granted by Parliament upon the recommendation of a Select Committee. Specific sums are allocated to named members of the Royal Family. In 1981 the Queen undertook to bear the cost of the Civil List vote to three of her cousins (the Duke of Kent, the Duke of Gloucester and Princess Alexandra), by refunding to the Exchequer an equivalent sum. On 11 Feb 93 the Prime Minister announced that from 6 Apr 93 the Queen would refund the Civil List payments to all other members of her family except

---

[1] Ld Stamfordham and Ld Knollys were joint private secretaries 1910–13 to King George V.

the Queen Mother, the Duke of Edinburgh and herself. At the same time he announced that the Queen's personal income from investments and other sources would henceforth be taxed, along with such revenues from the Privy Purse and the Duchy of Cornwall as were to be used for personal purposes.

Year	Privy Purse	Total voted	Total retained by Queen
1900	£60,000	£385,000	
1901	£110,000	£470,000	
1931[a]	£97,000	£420,000	
1938	£110,000	£410,000	
1952	£60,000	£475,000	
1972	..[b]	£980,000	
1975	..	£1,400,000	
1976	..	£1,614,575	
1977	..	£1,905,000	
1978	..	£2,394,962	
1979	..	£2,609,200	
1980	..	£3,527,550	
1981	..	£4,249,200	£3,964,200
1982	..	£4,612,883	£4,308,183
1983	..	£4,833,900	£4,515,600
1984	..	£5,017,000	£4,686,000
1985	..	£5,180,000	£4,838,000
1986	..	£5,387,300	£5,031,700
1987	..	£5,661,200	£5,289,500
1988	..	£5,922,300	£5,535,700
1989	..	£6,195,300	£5,795,200
1990	..	£6,762,000	£6,327,000
1991	..	£10,420,000	£9,790,000
1993	..	£10,420,000	£8,900,000

[a] By command of the King the Civil List was reduced by £50,000 p.a. as from 1 Oct 1931, in view of the national economic situation.
[b] In 1972 the Privy Purse, as a separate head, was abolished.

SOURCES. – *Imperial Calendar; Whitaker's Almanack; Dictionary of National Biography; Who Was Who; Who's Who; Keesing's UK Record.*

XIV

THE BRITISH ISLES

Scotland

Under the *Treaty of Union, 1707,* Scotland preserved her independent legal and judicial systems, under which developed her system of education and local government which have never been assimilated to those of England and Wales. The established (Presbyterian) Church was also recognised by the Union settlement. From the abolition of the post of Secretary of State for Scotland in 1746 until the establishment of the Secretaryship for Scotland in 1885 (which became a full Secretaryship of State in 1926), Scotland had been controlled into the nineteenth century by a 'Manager', then the Lord Advocate acting through the Home Secretary, and, for a short period from 1881, by an Under Secretary at the Home Office with responsibility for Scottish Affairs, as well as by the developing system of Boards.

The continued existence of the Boards was criticised as anachronistic, maintaining a system of patronage and lacking direct responsibility to Parliament in practice, if not in theory, in Reports of the Royal Commission on the Civil Service in 1914[1] and the Haldane Committee on the Machinery of Government in 1918.[2] Under the Reorganisation of Offices (Scotland) Act, 1928, the Boards of Agriculture and Health for Scotland became Departments statutorily defined independent of, though in reality responsible to, the Scottish Secretary of State.

This constitutional peculiarity disappeared along with the remaining Boards after a general review of the Scottish administration by the Gilmour Committee[3] which led to the *Reorganisation of Offices (Scotland) Act, 1939.* This Act brought into being four Departments of the Scottish Office: Agriculture, Education, Health, and Home Affairs, each with their permanent head and with a Permanent Under Secretary of State over them. Further responsibilities were allocated to the Scottish Office during and after the Second World War such as the Crown Estates in 1943 and Forestry in 1945. Following the Report of the Royal Commission on Scottish Affairs,[4] published in 1954, there were further transfers to the Scottish Departments such as the responsibility for roads, bridges and ferries, Justices of the Peace, animal health, and the duties of the defunct Ministry of Food. Functions withdrawn from the Scottish Office have been fewer; roads were lost to the Ministry of Transport in 1911, though regained in 1956, but the most notable function transferred from the Scottish Office was that of pensions and national insurance in 1948. In 1962 the Scottish Development Department was created and the Scottish Economic Planning Department was established in 1973. A Scottish Development Agency, responsible to the Scottish Office, was set up in 1975. By 1977 most 'United Kingdom' Departments had regional offices in Scotland. Over the period from 1885, the Scottish Office has gained additional Ministers including Under Secretaries in 1919, 1940, and 1952. A Minister of State was added to assist the Secretary of State in 1952. By 1983 the Scottish Office was organised into five Departments; the Department of Agriculture and Fisheries for Scotland, the Scottish Development Department, the Scottish Economic Planning Department, the Scottish Education Department, and the Scottish Home and Health Department. The office's headquarters in Edinburgh is complemented by a liaison office in Dover House, Whitehall.

[1] Cmd.7338/ 1914.
[2] Cmnd. 9320/ 1918.
[3] Cmnd. 5563/ 1936–37.
[4] Cmnd. 9212/ 1953–4.

Scotland has its own separate legal and judicial systems, its bar, its established church, and its heraldic authority, Lord Lyon King-at-Arms. A Scottish Grand Committee was established by the House of Commons on an experimental basis in 1894/5 and then from 1907 had a continued existence. Scottish Standing Committees dealing with peculiarly Scottish legislation were created in 1957 and 1962, and a Select Committee on Scottish Affairs was established in 1969 (see p. 193), although it went into abeyance in 1972, but in 1979 the Select Committee on Scottish Affairs was reconstituted (see p. 202). After the passage of the Scotland Act, 1978, a referendum was held on 1 Mar 1979 to ascertain the electorate's views on the provisions for legislative devolution contained in the Act. In the referendum 1,230,937 voted 'Yes' and 1,153,502 voted 'No' but as the 'Yes' majority represented 32.9% of the registered electorate, failing to overcome the 40% provision of the enactment, an Order to Repeal the Scotland Act, 1978, was successfully moved on 20 Jun 1979, following the General Election of 3 May.

SOURCES: – Sir D. Milne. *The Scottish Office (1957)*; G. Pryde, *Central and Local Government in Scotland Since 1707* (1960); H. Hanham, *Scottish Nationalism* (1969); J.G.Kellas, *The Scottish Political System* (3rd.ed 1885); G. Pottinger, *The Secretaries of State for Scotland* (1979); M. Keating and A. Midwinter, *The Government of Scotland* (1983); A. Midwinter et al., *Politics and Public Policy in Scotland* (1991); M. Linklater and x. Denniston (eds.) *Anatomy of Scotland* (1992); A. Marr, *The Battle for Scotland* (1992); See also *The Scottish Government Year Book (1975–91)* which was replaced by the *Scottish Quarterly* (1992–).

See also Govermental Reports: (Gilmour) *Scottish Administration* (Cmd 5563/ 1937; (Balfour) *Royal Commission on Scottish Affairs,* (Cmnd.9212/ 1954); (Wheatley) *Royal Commission on Local Governmernt in Scotland,* (Cmnd. 4150/ 1969); (Kilbrandon) *Royal Commission on the Constitution,*,Cmnd. 5460–1/ 1973.

Wales

The only significant devolution of administrative responsibility from Westminster to Wales has taken place since 1950, and this to a much more limited extent than in Scotland. In 1907 a Welsh Department of the Board of Education (now part of the Ministry of Education) was established. A Welsh Board of Health was set up in 1919, but was only to exercise such powers in Wales as the Minister thought fit. A Welsh Office in the Ministry of Housing and Local Government was also established. In 1951 a Minister for Welsh Affairs was appointed, holding the office jointly with the Home Office from 1951 to 1957. From 1957 to 1964 the Minister for Welsh Affairs was also the Minister of Housing and Local Government. A second parliamentary secretary was appointed at the Home Office from 1951 to 1957 to be responsible for Welsh Affairs; in 1957 a Minister of State for Welsh Affairs was appointed and in 1964 a Welsh Office was established with a Secretary of State for Wales. Since 1964 in many detailed ways powers have been devolved from Whitehall to the Welsh Office in Cardiff. In 1960 a Welsh Grand Committee analogous to the Scottish Grand Committee was appointed by the House of Commons to consider all Bills and other parliamentary business relating exclusively to Wales. In 1979 a Select Committee on Welsh Affairs was appointed (see p. 209).

Welsh national or separatist feeling has, however, expressed itself in forces other than the movement for home rule or devolution. The most important aspects of this have been the campaigns on such matters as the Church, education, land, temperance reform and the Welsh language. The *Welsh Sunday Closing Act, 1881* and the *Intermediate Education (Wales) Act, 1889* were the beginning of separate legislation for Wales. In 1961, 1968, 1975, 1982 and 1989 referendums were held throughout Wales on Sunday opening of licensed premises. The *Elections (Welsh Forms) Act, 1964*, provided for the use of Welsh on election forms and following the recommendations of the Hughes Parry committee, the *Welsh Language Act, 1967*, paved the way for the removal of restrictions on the use of the Welsh language in official documents and in the administration of justice in Wales. In 1978 the Wales Act provided for the establishment of a devolved Welsh Assembly in Cardiff, subject to a referendum. In the referendum on 1 Mar 1979 243,048 (11.9 per cent or 20.2 per cent of valid votes) voted 'yes', 956,330 (46.9 per cent or 79.8 per cent of valid votes) voted 'no' and 41.2 percent did not vote; the highest 'yes' vote (34.5 per cent) was in Gwynedd and the lowest (12.1 per cent) was in Gwent.

In 1901 50 per cent of the population spoke Welsh; in 1931 the figure was 37 per cent; in 1951, 29 per cent; in 1961, 26 per cent; in 1971, 21 per cent; in 1981, 19 per cent; and in 1991, 19 per cent. A Welsh language television channel was established in 1982.

SOURCES: – J. Davies, *A History of Wales* (1993); K. Morgan, *Wales in British Politics 1868–1922*(3rd. ed. 1980); K. Morgan, *Rebirth of a Nation: Wales 1880–1980* (1981); D. Foulkes et al (eds.) *The Welsh Veto: The Wales Act 1978 and the Referendum* (1983); D. Balsom and M. Burch, *A Political and Electoral Handbook for Wales; 1959–1979* (1980).

Ireland 1900–1922

From 1900 to 1921 the Lord-Lieutenant of Ireland was responsible for the administration of Irish affairs, with an office in Dublin. His Chief Secretary was a member of the House of Commons, and assisted him in carrying on the parliamentary business of the department, for which he was the responsible minister. At the same time there were several departments in Dublin, working under the presidency of the Chief Secretary: the Department of Agriculture and Technical Instruction, the Irish Congested Districts Board, and the Local Government Board for Ireland. There were three boards of education commissioners, all of whom were appointed by the Lord-Lieutenant or the Government, and there was the Irish Land Commission. The Irish Public Works Board was controlled by the Treasury in London, and not by the Irish Government. There was scarcely any further devolution of administrative authority to Ireland between 1900 and 1922.

The Irish Office remained in existence until 1924 after the partition of Ireland, though the posts of Chief Secretary and Lord-Lieutenant lapsed in 1922, with the recognition of the Irish Free State. The functions previously exercised by the Irish Office became the responsibility of the Home Office (for Northern Ireland) and the Colonial Office handled relations with the Free State (in 1937 renamed Eire). When Ireland became a republic in 1949, the Commonwealth Relations Office continued to be the department responsible for relations with her. In 1966 this responsibility was transferred to the Commonwealth Affairs Office (since 1968 the Foreign and Commonwealth Office).

Lord-Lieutenant of Ireland 1900–22		Chief Secretary for Ireland 1900–22	
1895	Ld Cadogan	1900	G. Balfour
8 Aug 02	E of Dudley	7 Nov 00	G. Wyndham
3 Feb 06	E of Aberdeen	12 Mar 05	W. Long
19 Feb 15	Ld Wimborne	10 Dec 05	J. Bryce
12 May 18	Vt French	23 Jan 07	A. Birrell
2 May 21	Vt FitzAlan	31 Jul 16	(Sir) H. Duke
	(Office in cabinet only	5 May 18	E. Shortt
	June 95–8 Aug 02	10 Jan 19	I. Macpherson
	and 28 Oct 19–2 Apr 21)	2 Apr 20	S. H. Greenwood
			(Irish Office wound up 1922)

(See p. 56 for Lord Chancellor of Ireland and Irish Law Officers.)

Northern Ireland 1922–1972

The Northern Ireland Parliament was created by the *Government of Ireland Act, 1920*. The powers of the Crown were exercised by the Governor, appointed by the Crown. Provision was made in the Act for the continued representation of Northern Ireland constituencies in the House of Commons of the United Kingdom. The constitutional position of Northern Ireland was thus unique in that it was part of the United Kingdom and sent representatives to the United Kingdom Parliament but was subject in most internal matters to the jurisdiction of a Parliament and Government of its own. The Government of Ireland Act conferred on that Parliament extensive powers for the regulation of the affairs of Northern Ireland, but excluded a number of specified matters from its jurisdiction. In respect of these excluded matters executive power remained with the United Kingdom Government, and only the United Kingdom Parliament could legislate. Consequently Northern Ireland was subject to two jurisdictions, and although most of Northern Ireland's public services were administered by Ministers who were members of the Northern Ireland Government, there were some public services, such as, for example, the Post Office services, the Customs and Excise service, and the Inland Revenue service, for which Ministers of the United Kingdom Government were responsible.

In respect of all matters on which the Northern Ireland Parliament was empowered to make laws, executive powers were exercisable by the Government of Northern Ireland. At the head of this Government was the Governor appointed by the Crown who formally summoned, prorogued and dissolved the Parliament, appointed the members of the Privy Council, and appointed Ministers to administer such Government departments as the Northern Ireland Parliament might establish. The departments were the Prime Minister's Department, the Ministry of Finance, the Ministry of Home Affairs, the Ministry of Development, the Ministry of Education, the Ministry of Agriculture, the Ministry of Commerce, and the Ministry of Health and Social Services. The Ministers in charge of these eight departments (together with the Minister in the Senate, the Minister of State in the Ministry of Development, and the Minister who was Leader of the House) formed an Executive Committee of the Privy Council which aided and advised the Governor in the exercise of his executive powers.

The Parliament of Northern Ireland consisted of a Senate and a House of Commons. The House of Commons had 52 members. Proportional Representation was used in the elections of 1921 and 1925 but after 1929, except for 4 members for Queen's University, Belfast, they were chosen directly by single-member constituencies. In 1969 the University constituency was abolished and four new territorial seats were created. The Senate had 26 members, 24 being elected by the House of Commons by proportional representation, and two being ex officio, the Lord Mayor of Belfast and the Mayor of Londonderry. The main differences between the Northern Ireland law relating to elections to the Northern Ireland Parliament and the United Kingdom law relating to elections to the United Kingdom Parliament were that, after 1950, Northern Ireland law retained the University seats (until 1963) and the 'business premises' qualification for a vote (until 1968), and required qualified electors either to have been born in Northern Ireland or to have been resident in the U.K. for seven years and to possess the requisite residence, business premises or service qualification. The Parliament of Northern Ireland could legislate on all matters except certain fields that were permanently excepted by the 1920 Act, such as the succession to the Crown, making of peace or war, the armed forces of the Crown, the making of treaties, honours, naturalisation and aliens, and certain functions that were reserved such as postal and telegraph services, the Supreme Court, and the important forms of taxation. It was also prohibited from making laws which would interfere with religious freedom or might discriminate against any religious body, and until 1961, from taking property without compensation. All United Kingdom bills applied to Northern Ireland unless there was express provision to the contrary. In general, legislation at Stormont followed very closely legislation in Westminster. The revenue of the Government of Northern Ireland was derived partly from taxes imposed by the United Kingdom Parliament (known as 'reserved' taxes) and partly from taxes imposed by the Northern Ireland Parliament (known as 'transferred taxes'). The powers of the Northern Ireland Parliament were similar to those of the United Kingdom Parliament as regards the appropriation of revenue. The Treasury was responsible for financial relations with Northern Ireland, and other departments were concerned with trade, commerce, and employment, but the Home Office retained the major responsibility for Northern Ireland.

Governors of Northern Ireland 1922–73		Prime Ministers of Northern Ireland 1921–72	
11 Dec 22	D of Abercorn	7 Jun 21	Sir J. Craig
7 Sep 45	Earl Granville		(1927 Vt Craigavon)
1 Dec 52	Ld Wakehurst	26 Nov 40	J. Andrews
1 Dec 64	Ld Erskine	6 May 43	Sir B. Brooke
2 Dec 68	Ld Grey		(1952 Vt Brookeborough)
(office abolished 19 Jul 73)		25 Mar 63	T. O'Neill
		1 May 69	J. Chichester-Clark
		23 Mar 71	B. Faulkner
		(office suspended 30 Mar 72)	

Members of Northern Ireland Cabinet 1921–72

Minister of Finance

1921	H Pollock	1956	G. Hanna	1968	W. Long
1937	J. M. Andrews	1956	T. O'Neill	1969	R. Porter
	(also PM 1940–1)	1963	J. L. Andrews	1970	J. Chichester-Clark *(PM)*
1941	J. Barbour	1964	I. Neill	1971	B. Faulkner *(PM)*
1943	J. Sinclair	1965	H. Kirk		
1953	W. Maginess	1966	W. Craig		

Minister of State (Finance)

1971	J. Brooke

Minister of Home Affairs

1921	(Sir) D. Bates	1956	T. O'Neill	1965	W. Morgan
1943	W. Lowry	1956	W. Topping	1969	R. Porter
1944	J. Warnock	1959	B. Faulkner	1969	W. Fitzsimmons
1949	W. Maginess	1963	W. Craig		
1953	G. Hanna	1964	R. McConnell		

Minister of Health (and Local Government)

1944	W. Grant	1964	W. Craig	1966	W. Fitzsimmons
1949	Dame D. Parker		*(1965 became Minister of*	1968	I. Neill
1957	J. L. Andrews		*Development)*	1969	W. Long
1961	W. Morgan	1965	W. Craig	1969	B. Faulkner
				1971	R. Bradford

Minister of Education

1921	M of Londonderry	1950	H. Midgely	1966	W. Long
1926	Vt Charlemont	1957	W. May	1969	P. O'Neill
1937	J. Robb	1962	I. Neill	1969	W. Long
1943	R. Corkey	1964	H. Kirk		
1944	S. Hall-Thompson	1965	W. Fitzsimmons		

Minister of Public Security

1940	J. MacDermott
1941	W. Grant
1943	H. Midgely

Minister of Labour (and National Insurance 1949)

1921	J. M. Andrews	1945	W. Maginess	1962	H. Kir
1938	J. Gordon	1949	W. McCleery	1964	W Morgan
1943	W. Grant	1949	H. Midgely	*(1965 became Minister of Health*	
1944	H. Midgely	1950	I. Neill	*and Social Services)*	

Minister of Agriculture (and Commerce 1921–5)

1921	(Sir) E. Archdale	1943	R. Moore	1969	P. O'Neill
1933	Sir B. Brooke	1960	H. West	1971	H. West
1941	Ld Glentoran (1st)	1967	J. Chichester-Clark		

Minister of Commerce

1925	J. Barbour	1949	W. Maginess	1963	B. Faulkner
1941	Sir B. Brooke	1949	W. McCleery	1969	R. Bradford
	(also PM 43–5)	1953	Ld Glentoran (2nd)	1971	R. Bailie
1945	Sir R. Nugent	1961	J. L. Andrews		

Minister without Portfolio

1944–44	Sir R. Nugent
1966–67	J. Chichester-Clark
1969–71	J. Dobson

Minister in the Senate

1949	Sir R. Nugent	1951	A. Gordon	1964	J. L. Andrews
1950	*(office vacant)*	1961	Ld Glentoran (2nd)		

Minister of State (PM's Office)

1971	G. Newe

Minister of Community Relations

1970	R. Simpson
1971	D. Bleakley
1971	B. McIvor

Minister of State (Development)

1966	B. McConnell
1969	N. Minford

Minister of State (Home Affairs)

1971	J. Taylor

General Elections of Northern Ireland 1921–69

Date	Unionist	Ind. Unionist	Lib.	Lab.	Nat.	Sinn Fein Republican Abstentionist	Irish Lab Rep.Lab. Soc.Rep. Ind.Lab.	Ind.& Other
24 May 21	40	..	..	..	6	6	..	..
28 Apr 25	32	4	..	3	10	2	..	1
22 May 29	37	3	..	1	11	..	..	..
30 Nov 33	36	2	..	2	9	2	..	1
9 Feb 38	39	3	..	1	8	..	1	..
14 Jun 45	33	2	..	2	9	..	3	3
10 Feb 49	37	2	..	..	9	..	2	2
22 Oct 53	38	1	..	..	7	2	3	1
20 Mar 58	37	..	..	4	8	..	2	1
31 May 62	34	..	1	4	9	..	3	1
25 Nov 65	36	..	1	2	9	..	2	2
24 Feb 69	36	3	..	2	6	..	2	3

Northern Ireland 1972–

After sectarian troubles and terrorist activities which from 1969 onwards cost several hundred lives and led to the sending of substantial British military forces, the British Government on 30 Mar 72 passed the Northern Ireland (Temporary Provisions) Act. This Act suspended Stormont and transferred all the functions of the Government and Parliament of Northern Ireland to a new Secretary of State for Northern Ireland, acting by Order-in-Council, for one year (extended in Mar 1973 for a further twelve months).

Secretary of State for Northern Ireland

24 Mar 72	W.Whitelaw		14 Sep 82	J. Prior
2 Dec 73	F. Pym		11 Sep 83	D. Hurd
5 Mar 74	M. Rees		3 Sep 84	T. King
10 Sep 76	R.Mason		24 Jul 89	P. Brooke
5 May 79	H.Atkins		11 Apr 92	Sir P. Mayhew

On 8 Mar 73 on a 58.1 % poll, the electors of Northern Ireland voted, 591,820 for the province to remain part of the U.K. and 6,463 for it to be joined with the Republic of Ireland, Eire. following a White Paper (Cmnd.5259 published on 2 Mar 73) the Northern Ireland Constitution Act 1973 was passed; this abolished the office of Governor and the Northern Ireland Privy Council; vested the executive power in the Crown, exercisable by the Secretary of State; provided for a complex system of power-sharing in a new Assembly (to be elected by proportional representation from multi-member constituencies) with an Executive to be appointed by the Secretary of State after consulting with the parties, and also authorised any department in Northern Ireland 'to consult' or 'enter into agreements with any authority of the Republic of Ireland in respect of any transferred matter'. Local elections were held on 30 May 1973 for 26 district councils (using proportional representation) in place of the old local government bodies. On June 28 1973 the 78-member Assembly was elected; its composition was 22 Ulster Unionist (B. Faulkner) 13 other Unionist (12 anti-White Paper) 15 Loyalist Coalition (7 Vanguard (W. Craig) 8 Democratic Unionist (I. Paisley)), 3 Alliance (O. Napier) 1 Northern Ireland Labour Party (D. Bleakley) and 19 Social Democratic and Labour Party (G. Fitt).

The election was followed by prolonged negotiations over the formation of a Northern Ireland Executive, which was finally agreed in December. The Executive which took over on 1 Jan 1974 consisted of 6 Ulster Unionists accepting the leadership of B. Faulkner, the Chief Executive, 4 S.D.L.P. members under G. Fitt, the Deputy Chief Executive, and 1 Alliance Party member. Opposition to the Sunningdale agreement of Dec 1973 (which provided, among other things, for the establishment of a Council of Ireland) led to Mr Faulkner's repudiation by the Unionist Party. In May 1974 a strike of Protestant workers forced the ending of the Northern Ireland Executive and the return to direct rule from Westminster.

On 1 May 75 elections were held for a Northern Ireland constitutional Convention. 46 of the 78 seats went to the Ulster Unionists (H. West), 5 to the Unionist Party of Northern Ireland (B. Faulkner) and one to an Independent Loyalist; there were 8 Alliance members, one from the Northern Ireland Labour Party and 17 from the Social Democratic and Labour Party. The Convention discussions proved abortive.

On 7 Nov 75 it submitted a majority (42–31) draft final report to the Secretary of State, and then adjourned. It reconvened 3 Feb 76, at the request of the Secretary of State, to reconsider the report. The Convention was finally dissolved by Order in Council on 6 Mar 76 because, as reported in the House of Commons on 5 Mar (H. C. Deb. 906 c. 1715–1727), the debates and resolutions in the Convention had made it plain that there was no prospect of agreement between the parties and that no further progress could be made.

The *Northern Ireland Act, 1982*, again attempted to restore devolved institutions to the province. On 25 Oct 1979, the Secretary of State, H. Atkins had announced that the new Conservative Government favoured devolution in Northern Ireland. In Nov 1979 a White Paper was published, *The Government of Northern Ireland: A Working Paper for a Conference* (Cmnd. 7763) setting out principles to be observed in the transfer of power, and issues for discussion at a round-table conference. The conference held between Jan and Mar 1980 failed to reach agreement. A further White Paper, *The Government of Northern Ireland – Proposals for Further Discussion* (Cmnd. 7950), published in Jul 1980 put forward further proposals for discussion.

In Feb 1982, J. Prior, the new Secretary of State, held further discussions with the Northern Ireland parties, and in Apr 1982, a third White Paper, *Northern Ireland – A Framework for Devolution* (Cmnd. 8451), was published, proposing a scheme of 'rolling devolution' given legislative effect by the Northern Ireland Act which was placed on the statute book on 23 Jul 1982. This provided for the election of a Northern Ireland Assembly whose functions would initially be limited to scrutiny, deliberation and advice, pending cross-community agreement on the transfer of certain legislative powers.

The election for the Assembly was held on 20 Oct 1982, and of the 78 seats, 26 went to the Official Unionists, 21 to the Democratic Unionists, 14 to the SDLP, 10 to Alliance, 5 to Sinn Fein, 1 to a Popular Unionist and 1 to an Independent Unionist. However, Sinn Fein and the SDLP refused to take their seats in the Assembly, while on 21 Nov 83 most of the Official Unionists withdrew after some murders in Armagh.

The SDLP took part in a New Ireland forum with the leaders of the three main parties in the Irish Republic – Fine Gael, Fianna Fail and the Labour Party – which met for the first time on 30 May 1983 in Dublin, and produced a report on 2 May 84 advocating fresh approaches.

On 15 Nov 85 an Anglo-Irish Agreement was signed at Hillsborough. Article 1 restated the British Government's commmitment to N.Ireland remaining part of the United Kingdom as long as that was the wish of the majority of the population. Article 2 provided for regular inter-governmental conferences. The 15 Unionist M.P.s resigned their seats in protest against the Agreement; 14 of them were returned in the subsequent by-elections.

In January 1990 Peter Brooke launched the 'Brooke Initiative', a series of 'talks about talks'; these collapsed in July 1991 but were resuscitated by Sir P. Mayhew in April 1992. Secret negotiations with the I.R.A. took place and there were increased contacts between the London and Dublin governments which resulted in the Downing Street Declaration of 15 Dec 93 offering talks about reform to all parties that would renounce violence. In March 1994 the House of Commons established a permanent Select Committee for Northern Ireland (see p. 202).

(See p. 484 for Army activities.)

SOURCES: – N. Mansergh, *The Government of Northern Ireland* (1936); T. Wilson (ed.) *Ireland under Home Rule* (1955); R.Lawrence, *The Government of Northern Ireland* (1965); M. Wallace, *Northern Ireland: 50 years of Self-Government* (1971); R. Rose, *Governing without Consensus: an Irish Perspective* (1971); S. Elliott, *Northern Ireland Parliamentary Election Results 1921– 72* (1973); A. Maltby, *The Government of Northern Ireland 1922–1972: a Catalogue and Breviate of Parliamentary Papers* (1974); P. Bew *et al.*, *The State in Northern Ireland 1921–1972* (1979); P. Buckland, *Northern Ireland: A Short History* (1980); W.D. Flackes (ed.) *Northern Ireland: A Political Directory 1968–79* (1980).

The Channel Islands

The Channel Islands which were originally part of the Duchy of Normandy have been associated with England since 1066. They have their own legislative assemblies, systems of local administration, fiscal systems, and courts of law. The Islanders have general responsibility for the regulation of their local affairs subject to the prerogative of the Crown over appointment to the chief posts in the local administrations and the necessity of Royal Assent to legislative measures passed by the insular assemblies. Most of the laws by which they are governed emanate from their representative assemblies and although they cannot be regarded as local authorities most of their public services are provided by these assemblies in the same way as local government services are provided and administered in Great Britain.

The Channel Islands are divided into 2 Bailiwicks, one comprising Jersey and the other, Alderney, Sark, and Guernsey with its dependants, Herm and Jethou. Each Bailiwick has a Lieutenant Governor appointed by the Crown for a period of 5 years, through whom all official communications between the U.K. Government and the Islands pass, and in whom certain executive functions are vested. A Bailiff also appointed by the Crown presides over the local legislatures, the States, and over the sittings of the Royal Court. Since 1948 all members of the States who have the right to vote are elected directly or indirectly by the electorate. The Islands have their own Courts of Law, but there remains leave to appeal to the Judicial Committee of the Privy Council.

The Island Assemblies may initiate legislation but they must then petition the Sovereign in Council to give these measures force of law. Acts of the U.K. Parliament do not apply to the Channel Islands unless by express provision or necessary application. As a general rule Parliament refrains from legislating on matters with which these assemblies can deal unless for some special reason a U.K. act must be preferred to local legislation.

The public revenues of the Islands are raised by duties on imported goods, by income taxes and other taxes. Proposals made by the States for raising revenue require authorisation by Order in Council but responsibility for determining how the revenue shall be spent is, in practice, left to the States. Immunity from taxation for Crown purposes has been a privilege of the Islanders since the time of Edward VI.

SOURCE: – *Report of the Commission on the Constitution* (Cmnd.5460–1/ 1973)

Jersey

Lieutenant-Governor

1895	(Sir) E. Hopton	1929	Ld Ruthven	1963	Sir M. Villiers
1900	H. Abadie	1934	(Sir) H. Martelli	1969	Sir J. Davis
1904	H. Gough	1939	R. Harrison	1974	Sir D. Fitzpatrick
1910	(Sir) A. Rochfort	1940	(Office vacant)	1979	Sir P. Whiteley
1916	Sir A. Wilson	1945	Sir A. Grassett	1985	Sir W. Pillar
1920	Sir D. Smith	1953	Sir R. Nicholson	1990	Sir J. Sutton
1924	Sir F. Bingham	1958	Sir G. Erskine		

Bailiff

1899	(Sir) W. Venables-Vernon	1961	C. Harrison	1988	(Sir) P. Crill
1931	C. Malet de Carteret	1962	(Sir) R. le Masurier		
1935	(Sir) (Ld) A. Coutanche	1973	(Sir) F. Ereaut		

Guernsey

Lieutenant-Governor

1899	M. Savard	1929	E. Willis	1969	Sir C. Mills
1903	B. Camphell	1990	Sir M. Wilkins	1974	Sir J. Martin
1908	R. Auld	1934	(Sir) E. Broadbent	1980	Sir P. Le Cheminant
1911	Sir E. Hamilton	1939	J. Minshull-Ford	1985	Sir A. Boswell
1914	Sir R. Hart	1940	(office vacant)		
1918	Sir F. Kiggell	1945	Sir P. Neame		
1920	Sir J. Capper	1953	Sir T. Elmhirst		
1925	Sir C. Sackville-West	1958	Sir G. Robson		
	(Ld Sackville)	1964	Sir C. Coleman		

Bailiff

1895	(Sir) T. Carey	1929	A. Bell	1973	(Sir) J. Loveridge
1902	W. Carey	1935	(Sir) V. Carey	1982	(Sir) C. Frossard
1915	(Sir) E. Chepnell Ozanne	1946	(Sir) A. Sherwill	1992	G. Dorey
1922	Sir H. de Sausmarez	1960	(Sir) W. Arnold		

The Isle of Man

This island was successively under the rule of Norway, of Scotland, of the Stanley family and of the Dukes of Atholl before it became a Crown Dependency in 1765. For over 1000 years the internal affairs of the island have been regulated by the Tynwald, which has evolved from the Lord of Man's Council composed of his chief officials and other persons of importance and the House of Keys. The latter comprises 24 representatives elected by all over the age of 18 who have resided in the island for 6 months. The consent of both the Legislative Council and the Keys is requisite for any Act of Tynwald except when in two successive sessions of a Parliament the Keys pass the same Bill, or a essentially similar one, which is once rejected by the Council. In that case the Bill is deemed to have been passed by the Council. All legislation by Tynwald depends for its validity on confirmation by Royal Assent granted by the Lieutenant Governor or, in certain rare cases, in the form of orders made by the Queen in Council.

Most of the public services are provided by Tynwald and administered by Boards of Tynwald, but the Lieutenant Governor is still the executive authority for certain services, including the administration of justice. In 1866, Tynwald was granted certain financial powers which had been removed from it in 1765. This process continued through the following decades until, by Tynwald's Isle of Man Contribution Act of 1958 the Treasury's control over the Island's finance was removed enabling the Tynwald to regulate its own finances and Customs, although under the Act, the Island continues to make an annual contribution to the Exchequer for defence and common services. There is a statutory body of members of Tynwald known as the Executive Council the duty of which is to consider and advise the Lieutenant Governor upon all matters of principle and policy and legislation.

SOURCE: – Report of the *Commission on the Constitution* (Cmnd.5460–1/1973); D. Kermode, *Devolution at Work: A Case Study of the Isle of Man* (1979)

Lieutenant-Governor

1899	Ld Henniker	1937	W. Leveson-Gower	1966	Sir P. Stallard
1902	Ld Raglan		(Earl Granville)	1973	Sir J. Paul
1919	(Sir) W. Fry	1945	Sir G. Bromet	1980	Sir N. Cecil
1926	Sir C. Hill	1952	Sir A. Dundas	1985	(Sir) L. New
1933	Sir M. Butler	1959	Sir R. Garvey	1990	Sir L. Jones

Devolution

Main Landmarks

1906–14	Scottish Home Rule Bills given First or Second Readings 6 times in House of Commons, though never reaching Committee Stage.
1912	First draft of Government of Ireland Bill proposed that all Bills referring exclusively to England, Scotland, or Ireland should be dealt with by national Grand Committees. This was to be a prelude to full legislative devolution but was abandoned to avoid overloading the Government of Ireland Bill.
4 Jun 19	Resolution in favour of devolution carried by 187 to 34.
12 May 20	Speaker's Conference reported (Cmd 692/1920) in favour of either full legislative devolution or devolution to Grand Committees.
7 Jun 21	Devolved powers transferred to Northern Ireland government at Stormont under Government of Ireland Act 1920.
12 Apr 45	First Scottish Nationalist M.P. elected (defeated 5 Jul 45).
1949–51	Scottish Covenant attracts 1,100,000 signatures in Scotland.
1950	Parliament for Wales Campaign.
14 Jul 66	First Plaid Cymru M.P. elected.
2 Nov 67	S.N.P. win Hamilton by-election.
9 May 68	E. Heath in Declaration of Perth proposes directly elected Scottish Assembly. (Endorsed by Douglas-Home Committee 1970)
11 Jun 69	Royal Commission on Local Government (Redcliffe-Maud, Cmnd 4040/1969) envisages eight provincial Councils for England.
15 Apr 69	Committee on the Constitution set up under Ld Crowther (Lord Kilbrandon from 1970).
30 Mar 72	Suspension of Stormont.
18 Jul 73	Northern Ireland Constitution Act provides for a power-sharing Executive.
31 Oct 73	Kilbrandon Commission report (Cmnd 5460/1973) rejects separatism or federation but unanimously favours directly elected Scottish Assembly and approves devolution in general.
1 Jan 74	Power-sharing Executive established in Northern Ireland.
28 Feb 74	General Election results in 7 S.N.P. and 2 Plaid Cymru M.P.s.
28 May 74	Power-sharing Executive resigns, following strike (see p. 431).
3 Jun 74	Privy Council Office publishes discussion document Devolution in the U.K.
17 Jul 74	Northern Ireland Act confirms suspension of Northern Ireland Executive.
17 Sep 74	Government announces decision to set up elected assemblies (Cmnd 5732/1974).
10 Oct 74	General Election results in 11 S.N.P. M.P.s (with 30% of Scottish vote) and 3 Plaid Cymru M.P.s.
27 Nov 75	Government outlines detailed proposals in Our Changing Democracy (Cmnd 6348/1975, modified by Cmnd 6585/1976).
16–19 Jan 76	Four-day debate on devolution in House of Commons.
9 Dec 76	Consultative document published, Devolution.– the English Dimension.

16 Dec 76	Second Reading of Scotland and Wales Bill carried 292–247.
22 Feb 77	Government fails (312–283) to secure guillotine on Scotland and Wales Bill.
5 Mar 77	Abortive all-party talks on devolution started.
16 Jun 77	Scotland and Wales Bill 1976 withdrawn by government.
14 Nov 77	Second Reading of Scotland Bill carried 307–263.
15 Nov 77	Second Reading of Wales Bill carried 295–264.
23 Nov 77	House of Commons rejects Proportional Representation for Scottish Assembly Elections 290- 107.
25 Jan 78	Amendments setting referendum condition (40% of electorate voting 'Yes') carried against Government (confirmed 298–243 15 Feb 78).
22 Feb 78	Scotland Bill gets Third Reading, 297–257.
31 Jul 78	Scotland Bill and Wales Bill receive Royal Assent.
1 Mar 79	Scotland votes 'yes' in Referendum (33% to 31% with 36% not voting); Wales votes 'no' (12% to 47% with 41% not voting).
28 Jun 79	Parliament passes resolution nullifying Scotland Act, 1978.
5 Jul 79	Parliament passes resolution nullifying Wales Act, 1978.
5 Apr 82	Government outlines new Northern Ireland proposals in *Northern Ireland.– A framework for Devolution* (Cmnd. 8451).
26 Oct 82	Northern Ireland Assembly elected (see p. 432).
2 May 84	Irish Forum proposals published in Dublin.
15 Nov 86	Anglo-Irish Agreement.
30 Mar 89	First meeting of Scottish Convention – an interparty discussion on forms of devolution, boycotted by the Conservatives and the Nationalists.
Jan 90	'Brooke Initiative' on Northern Ireland.
Feb 92	Scottish Convention endorses Scottish Parliament elected by P.R.
15 Dec 93	Downing Street Declaration on Northern Ireland.
Mar 94	Northern Ireland Select Committee established.

SOURCE: – Wan-Hsuan Chiao, *Devolution in Great Britain* (1926): J. Mackintosh, *The Devolution of Power* (1968); J.Banks, *Federal Britain* (1973); A.Birch, *Political Integration in the British Isles* (1977); V. Bogdanor, *Devolution* (1979); see also the White Papers listed in the chronology above.

XV

LOCAL GOVERNMENT

Structure[a]

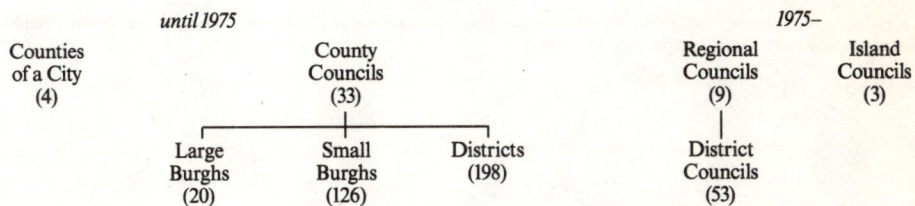

London

until 1965	1965–86
London County Council	Greater London Council
Metropolitan Boroughs (28)	Greater London Boroughs (32)

Rest of England & Wales

until 1974			1974–86	since 1974
County Boroughs (83)	County Councils (58)		Metropolitan County Councils[b] (6)	County Councils (47)
Non-County Boroughs (270)	Urban Districts (535)	Rural Districts (471)	Metropolitan District Councils (36)	District Councils (333)

[a] In 1993 a Committee was set up under Sir J. Banham to reconsider local government structure in England. Its work was proceeding in 1994 and it had recommended the abolition of some shire counties, substituting singl tier authorities but leaving the two-tier county and district structure elsewhere. Wales was to be redivided into single tier authorities in 1995. The Scottish map was also redrawn in 1995.

[b] Metropolitan County Councils were abolished in 1986 and the Metropolitan Districts became single purpose authorities.

Scotland

until 1975			1975–	
Counties of a City (4)	County Councils (33)		Regional Councils (9)	Island Councils (3)
Large Burghs (20)	Small Burghs (126)	Districts (198)	District Councils (53)	

Number of Councils in England & Wales[a]

	County Councils inc. London and Met. Counties	County Boroughs	Non-County Boroughs	Urban District Councils	Rural District Councils	London Boroughs & City of London
1900	62	67	250	800	663	29
1910	62	75	249	812	657	29
1920	62	82	246	799	649	29
1930	62	83	300	780	638	29
1940	61	83	256	581	476	29
1950	61	83	309	572	475	29
1960	62	83	319	564	473	29
1973	58	83	270	535	471	33
				Metropolitan Councils	District Councils	
1974	54	–	–	36	333	33
1986	47	–	–	36	333	33

[a] This table does not include parish councils. No exact figures for their numbers are available. In 1900 there were about 8,000; in 1920 about 7,000 and in 1966 about 7,700. Following the 1974 reorganisation of local government a number of the local authorities that had been abolished applied for parish council status.

[b] The figures in this column are deceptively constant. In the 1960s a few County Boroughs disappeared through local government amalgamation while a few more Non-County Boroughs were promoted to county status.

Local Government Finance England and Wales

Year (ending 31 Mar)	Total Receipts from Rates (£000s)	Assessable Values of all Rateable Property (£000s)	Average Rates collected per £ Assessable Value	Government Grants[b] (£000s)	Total Expenditure (£000s)
1900	40,734	175,623	4s. 11d.	12,249	100,862
1910	63,261	215,310	6s. 2d.	20,915	166,105
1920	105,590	220,714	9s. 6d.	48,263	289,353
1930	156,312	284,937	11s 6d.	107,828	423,655
1940	200,567	318,834	12s. 7d.	181,900	578,798[c]
1950	280,195	325,262	17s. 3d.	294,358	849,099[c]
1960	646,608	687,618	18s. 10d.	705,590	,865,718[c]
1965	988,054	2,099,034	9s. 6d.[a]	1,102,989	2,902,829[c]
1970	1,515,184	2,440,500	12s. 4d.[a]	1,954,931	5,405,264[c]
1975	2,927,262	6,659,700	43.95p.[d]	5,651,767	12,253,941[c]
1980	6,122,518	7,441,233	100.3p.	11,845,505	29,979,700
1985	11,792,986	7,915,100		17,165,363	46,602,700
1990	18,943,436	32,915,600	not comparable	21,379,347	61,731,800

[a] This spectacular fall was partly due to the de-rating of industry and partly to the general revaluation on 1 Apr 63.
[b] Consisting partly of grants-in-aid and partly of receipts from the Local Taxation Account and from the local Taxation Licence Duties, not including capital receipts.
[c] Expenditure other than loans for capital works. Including the repayment of loans by various local authorities to the L.C.C. Consolidated Loans Fund.
[d] A revised system of returns after 1969 may invalidate comparisons with earlier years. In 1973 a general revaluation of rateable values may account for the sharp changes shown here.

SOURCES: – *Annual Abstract of Statistics*.

Major Legislation Affecting Local Government

Education Act, 1902.   This transferred the responsibility for education from school boards and school attendance committees to county councils, county borough councils, and some of the larger county districts.

Housing Acts.   A series of acts from 1919 onwards provided for the building of houses by local authorities with varying rates of subsidy from the Exchequer and from the rates.

Local Government Act, 1929.   This abolished the guardians of the poor, and transferred their responsibilities for poor law and registration to county councils and county borough councils. It also reorganised the system of grants in aid, creating the general grant, partly as compensation for the complete de-rating of agriculture and the de-rating of industry to 25%.

Town and Country Planning Act, 1932.   This established a general system of planning control which could be adopted by second tier local authorities.

Local Government Act, 1933.   This was a codifying Act covering the structure and constitution of local authorities of all sorts, but making no fundamental change in the law.

Local Government (Boundary Commission) Act, 1945.   This provided for the establishment of a local government boundary commission, which was later abolished by the *Local Government Boundary Commission (Dissolution) Act*, 1949. (But see *Local Government Boundary Commission Act, 1958.*)

New Towns Act, 1946.   This provided for the establishment of new towns to be built by development corporations appointed by the Ministry, and was succeeded by further Acts which were consolidated in the *New Towns Act, 1965.*

National Health Service Act, 1946.   This transferred local authority hospitals to the Ministry of Health. It made counties and county boroughs responsible for ambulance service, maternity and child welfare, health visiting, home helps, prevention of illness, and after-care, etc.

Town and Country Planning Act, 1947.   This applied planning control to the whole country, transferred responsibility to county councils and county borough councils, and introduced development charges balanced by a compensation fund of £300m. Development charges and the £300m. fund were abolished by the *Town and Country Planning Act, 1953.*

Children Act, 1948.   After the Curtis Committee Report, this Act made counties and county boroughs responsible for all children without proper homes.

National Assistance Act, 1948.   This repealed the existing poor law. It made counties and county boroughs responsible for accommodation of the aged and those temporarily homeless, also for welfare services for the blind, deaf, dumb, etc. financial assistance and residual responsibilities were passed to the National Assistance Board.

Local Government Act, 1948.   This replaced the block grant by theExchequer Equalisation grant. It transferred responsibility for valuation from local authorities to Inland Revenue and it provided for revaluation: small houses being valued on pre-war building costs, other houses by reference to pre-war rents.

Local Government Act, 1958.   This abolished most percentage grants and the Exchequer Equalisation grant, substituting a general grant and a rate deficiency grant.

Local Government Boundary Commission Act, 1958.   This set up local boundary commissions, producing a number of reports before being wound up in 1966. The main recommendations put into effect were in the Black Country and Teesside.

Town and Country Planning Act, 1959.   This Act altered the basis of compensation for compulsory acquisition.

Public Bodies (Admission to Meetings) Act, 1960.   This extended the rights of members of the public and press to be admitted to local authority meetings. These have since been extensions to meetings of Regional Water Authorities, Regional Health Authorities and Community Councils.

Rating and Valuation Act, 1961.   This Act ended the derating of industrial and freight-transport property, empowered the Minister to reduce by order the rateable value of dwellings in valuation lists, offered 50% relief from rates on property occupied by charities, and introduced a new method of rating statutory water undertakings. Industry and Commerce re-rated to 100% values.

Town and Country Planning Act, 1962.   This consolidated enactments for England and Wales from 1944 onwards and incorporated planning sections of other Acts.

Local Authorities (Land) Act, 1963.   This introduced a new 'positive planning'–power for local authorities to acquire land by agreement in advance of requirements; and powers to develop their land and to make advances to promote developments by others on land released by them.

London Government Act, 1963.   This Act replaced the old LCC with a Greater London Council which covered, in addition to the old LCC area, almost all of Middlesex and some suburban portions of Surrey, Kent, Essex, and Hertfordshire. All the existing 85 local authorities in the GLC area were merged into 32 new boroughs (the City of London alone preserved its complete independence). The first GLC election took place on 9 Apr 64, two, three and four councillors being chosen en bloc from each of the 32 boroughs. The GLC formally took over from the LCC on 1 Apr 65.

Local Government (Financial Provision) Act, 1963.   This extended the powers of local authorities to defray expenses incurred by their members and officers, and to contribute to other local authorities and to bodies having activities connected with local government, and made further provision with respect to borrowing by local authorities; the management of local authority debt, the application by local authorities of capital funds, renewal and repair funds, unexpected balances of loans, and capital money received by way of financial adjustment.

Housing Act, 1964.   This set up a new Housing Corporation to assist Housing Societies, conferred new compulsory powers on local authorities to secure improvement of houses, amended the improvement grant system and strengthened the powers of local authorities in dealing with houses in multi-occupation.

Rating Act, 1966.   This conferred on rateable occupiers of dwellings the right to pay rates in monthly instalments and provided for the granting of rebates in respect of such rates.

Town and Country Planning Act, 1968.   This introduced a fundamental change in the land-use planning system in the direction of greater flexibility and speed of action and a greater degree of public participation. The development plan was replaced by the 'structure, action area' and 'local'plans.

Local Authority Social Services Act, 1970.   This required counties and county boroughs to combine, under one social services department, the child care, personal health, and welfare services.

Local Government Act, 1972.   This was the first full-scale reorganisation of the local government structure of England and Wales since 1889. It abolished the existing system entirely (outside Greater London) and replaced it with a top tier of metropolitan counties in the six conurbations and 47 non-metropolitan counties in the rest of the country. The new second tier comprised 36 metropolitan districts within the areas of the metropolitan counties and 333 districts in the rest of the country.

Local Government Act, 1974.   This provided for a Commissioner for Local Administration (an Ombudsman) to be established (see p. 441).

Lotteries Act, 1975.   This gave power to local authorities to conduct lotteries under certain restricted conditions.

Inner Urban Areas Act, 1978.   This provided for designated urban districts to lend money for land acquisition or for works on land within their areas. Other powers are exercisable in declared 'improvement areas' and by 'partnership' authorities (to make loans for site preparation, grants for industrial and commercial rents, and for small firms' interest-payments).

Local Government, Planning and Land Act, 1980.   This complex and diverse Act relaxed certain Ministerial controls on authorities and required them to publish reports and information about the performance of their functions (as prescribed by the Secretary of State). It brought the operations of direct labour organisations under control to secure more regulated working, separate accounting, open tendering, and prescribed rates of return. It extended arrangements for the payment of rates by instalments and added rate rebates for the disabled. It provided for registers of under-used land owned by public authorities in designated areas. The Act also provided for a new control system for local authority capital expenditure giving expenditure allocations a switching of resources between authorities and between financial years. A new system for the distribution of rate support grant with a single block grant in place of the previous 'needs' and 'resources'elements was a major change.

Local Government Finance Act, 1982.   This provided for the abolition of supplementary rates and precepts and required them to be levied for complete financial years. By amendment of the 1980 Act it provided expressly for adjustments in block grant payable to an authority to be made by reference to central government guidance. This was designed to encourage reductions in expenditure on account of general economic conditions. The Act also established the Audit Commission for Local Authorities in England and Wales which would appoint the auditors (whether from the private sector or from the Commission). The

Commission is also responsible for studies of the economy, efficiency and effectiveness of local services (and the impact on them of statutory provisions and Ministerial initiatives). It is appointed by the Security of State, who may direct it in the discharge of its functions.

Local Authority (Expenditure Powers) Act, 1983.   This was intended to facilitate the aid which local authorities could give to industry in particular to top up expenditure by the 'free two pence' powers in S.137 of the *Local Government Act 1972.*

Rates Act, 1984.   This allowed for rate limitation 'rate capping' by a selection scheme or by one of general limitation. It also required authorities to consult industrial and commercial ratepayers before reaching decisions on expenditure and its financing and to provide additional information to ratepayers.

Local Government Act, 1985.   This abolished the Greater London Council and the six Metropolitan County Councils and distributed their functions and responsibilities among their component boroughs and some joint authorities.

Local Government Finance Act 1988.   This replaced the domestic rates with a community charge (or 'poll tax'). Non-domestic rates were made uniform across the country and the systems of grant reformed. Changes were to take effect in 1990.

Education Reform Act, 1988.   This transferred control of polytechnics from local to central government as well as allowing schools to opt out of local authority control.

Local Government Act, 1989.   This required local authorities to expose their provision of services to compulsory competitive tender.

Local Government Act, 1992.   This abolished the poll tax and replaced it with a 'council tax'. It provided for a structural reorganisation of local government in Scotland, Wales and the non-metropolitan areas of England.

(*See also Housing*, pp. 330–4.)

Local Authority Interest Groups

The interests of the local authorities have been represented by two main kinds of groups. First, there are the associations of each tier of local authorities. Most powerful amongst these have been the Association of Municipal Corporations (1873–1974) and the County Councils Association (1889–1974). They were replaced in 1974 by the Association of Metropolitan Authorities and the Association of County Councils; a new District Council Association was also formed. In addition, there are associations representing each of the professions in local government services. Examples would be the Institute of Municipal Engineers (1873) and the Institute of Municipal Treasurers and Accountants (1885), renamed in 1973 the Chartered Institute of Public Finance and Accountancy. All kinds of municipal employees were represented by the National and Local Government Officers Association (1905) and National Union of Public Employees (1886) which merged in 1993 to form UNISON and by other unions .

Many pressure groups which have focused on Local Authorities are listed on pp. 344–7.

Commission for Local Administration in England

Chairman

1974	Lady Serota
1982	(Sir) D. Yardley

Commission for Local Administration in Wales

Chairman

1974	D. Jones-Williams	1985	H. Jones
1979	A. Jones	1992	E. Moseley

Commission for Local Administration in Scotland

Chairman

1975	R. Moore	1982	E. Gillett
1978	J. Russell	1986	R. Peggie

New Towns

The *New Towns Act, 1946*, with subsequent amendments as consolidated in the *New Towns Act, 1965*, provided for New Towns to be built by development corporations appointed by the Minister. *The New Towns Act, 1959*, provided for a Commission for the New Towns to take over responsibility for New Towns as soon as the development corporations' purposes were substantially achieved. The *New Towns (Amendment) Act, 1976*, and the *New Towns Act, 1981*, provided for the transfer to local authorities of certain of the New Towns Commission's housing and related assets. By 1992 all the English and Welsh corporations had been wound up. The wind-up of the Scottish Corporations was under consideration in 1994. The New Towns Commission continues to dispose of the Corporations' remaining assets and liabilities

New Towns	Development Corporation Formed	Handed over to Commission	Area (acres)	Population (000s)				
				1951	1961	1971	1981	1988
Aycliffe[a], Durham	1947	1988	2,508	0.6	12	24	26	25
Basildon. Essex	1949	1986	7,818	24	54	85	100	n.a.
Bracknell, Berks.	1949	1982	3,303	5	20	34	48	n.a.
Central Lancs.	1970	1986	35,225			25	247	n.a.
Corby, Northants.	1950	1980	4,296	15	36	48	48	51
Crawley, Sussex	1947	1962	6,047	10	54	68	76	87
Cwmbran, Gwent	1949	1988	3,157	13	30	46	45	42
Harlow, Essex	1947	1980	6,395	5	53	71	79	75
Hatfield, Herts.	1948	1966	2,340	9	20	26	25	n.a.
Hemel Hempstead, Herts	1947	1962	5,910	21	55	70	81	n.a.
Milton Keynes, Bucks.	1967	1992	22,000			46	97	137
Northampton	1968	1985	19,966			148	162	170
Peterborough	1968	1988	15,940			87	121	146
Peterlee, Durham	1948	1988	2,799	0.2	14	22	23	25
Redditch, Worcs.	1964	1985	7,200			38	64	76
{ Runcorn, Cheshire	1964	1989	7,234			36 }	198	214
{ Warrington (Merged 1981)	1968	1989	19,000			125 }		
Skelmersdale, Lancs.	1962	1985	4,100			27	41	n.a.
Stevenage, Herts.	1946	1980	6,256	7	42	68	74	74
Telford, Salop.	1963	1991	10,243			80	104	111
Warrington (see Runcorn)								
Washington, Durham	1964	1988	5,300			25	52	57
Welwyn, Herts.	1948	1966	4,317	19	35	44	42	n.a.
Cumbernauld, Dunbarton	1956		7,788		5	32	51	49
East Kilbride, Lanarks	1947		13,679	6	32	64	76	70
Glenrothes, Fife	1948		5,696	2	13	27	38	38
Irvine, Ayrshire	1966		3,989			42	60	59
Livingston, W.Lothian	1962		3,641			14	39	41

In 1973 Stonehouse, Lanarks., was designated a New Town, but its status was cancelled in 1977. In 1967 Newtown, Powys, was designated a New Town, but in 1977 its status was cancelled and it fell under the Development Board for Rural Wales.

SOURCE.– F. J. Osborn and J. Whittick, *The New Towns* (1963). See also *Annual Reports* of the New Towns and of the Commission for New Towns.

New Towns Commission

Chairman

1961	Sir D. Anderson	1971	(Sir) D. Pilcher	1982	Sir N. Shields
1964	Sir M. Wells	1978	C. Macpherson		

Local Government Elections

After the Second World War the results of Local Government Elections became increasingly accepted as barometers to the national political mood. They could be misleading. The custom of fighting under national party labels spread only gradually and sporadically. The fact that, under the triennial system, only a third of the seats on borough and district councils were fought each year caused much confusion (a party might claim a great trend in its favour because it was gaining compared to three years before, even though it was losing compared to the previous year). Moreover the results were very patchily reported and no altogether satisfactory statistics are available. However, the results in the boroughs of England and Wales (excluding London), both county and non-county, provided some pointer to the national mood (even though the smaller non-county boroughs introduced a very distorting element). Between 3,300 and 3,500 seats used to be fought each year, usually on a party basis; after 1964 the number of seats at risk was between 3,000 and 3,200 owing to the merging of councils under the London Government Act. After 1946 the outcome of these borough contests was fairly accurately reported, although it was not until 1965 that the first really detailed analyses of the voting figures appeared (see The *Economist* for the Saturday nine days after the elections each year since 1965).

Borough Council Election Results 1949–72

	Conservative and Conservative-supported Independent	Independent without Conservative Support	Labour	Liberal	Total	Labour % of vote (County Boroughs only)	Turnout % (County Boroughs)
1947	1,892	359	776	97	3,124	41.7	52.6
1949	1,749	426	1,091	79	3,345	43.2	52.2
1950	1,610	510	1,132	72	3,324	46.2	45.5
1951	1,893	548	883	79	3,403	n.a.	44.4
1952	1,138	488	1,718	53	3,397	55.4	49.9
1953	1,571	447	1,448	60	3,562	52.0	45.2
1954	1,498	511	1,438	74	3,521	49.2	42.8
1955	1,604	514	1,470	56	3,644	47.6	43.8
1956	1,358	454	1,614	72	3,498	51.1	37.6
1957	1,292	435	1,642	89	3,458	50.0	40.0
1958	1,307	460	1,705	118	3,590	49.3	40.3
1959	1,545	441	1,399	103	3,488	45.5	41.0
1960	1,750	449	1,137	130	3,466	40.0	35.4
1961	1,453	470	1,387	196	3,506	43.3	40.6
1962	995	465	1,571	454	3,485	42.4	40.2
1963	973	524	1,733	255	3,485	46.0	41.3
1964	967	474	1,494	149	3,084	47.0	40.5
1965	1,140	476	1,027	154	2,797	38.3	37.7
1966	1,107	467	1,259	151	2,984	43.1	35.6
1967	1,690	466	846	148	3,150	36.4	40.3
1968	2,184	436	450	152	3,222	29.8	35.8
1969	1,972	453	542	168	3,135	33.1	35.6
1970	1,382	406	1,207	133	3,128	44.0	37.6
1971	823	391	1,848	128	3,180	55.7	39.2
1972	890	375	1,643	155	3,063	52.6	36.7

Party Control in Major Cities 1945–

Party politics in many cities goes back to the first half of the nineteenth century but, although in most sizeable towns (practically all over 50,000) councillors have worn political labels throughout this century, in only a few larger councils did a majority of councillors of one party mean that that party exercised control. Labour successes after the first World War introduced a more organised form of party politics into some councils. After the Second World War, the local government franchise was extended to practically the same basis as that for parliamentary elections (it had hitherto been confined to ratepayers) and, with sweeping Labour successes in the 1945 municipal elections and an organised Conservative counter-attack in the succeeding years, party politics extended their hold to most urban authorities, including practically all those with more than 20,000 inhabitants. Here is the record since 1945 of the party control in cities which in 1972 had more than 200,000 inhabitants: 'Citizen' in Bristol, 'Ratepayers' in Southampton and ' Progressive' (also called 'Moderate') in Scottish cities and Newcastle refers to local anti-Socialist, Conservative-supported parties. for England and Wales the 1974 entries refer to the district councils elected in 1973 (in some cases on enlarged boundaries).

Belfast.
1945–Unionist.
Birmingham
1945 No clear majority.[1] 1946–47 Labour. 1947–49 No majority. 1949–52 Conservative. 1952–66 Labour. 1966–72 Conservative. 1972–75 Labour. 1975–76 No clear majority. 1976–79 Conservative. 1979–80 No clear majority. 1980–82 Labour. 1982–84 Conservative. 1984– Labour.
Bradford
1945–51 Labour. 1951–52 No clear majority. 1952–59 Labour. 1959–61 No clear majority. 1961–62 Conservative and National Liberal. 1962–63 No clear majority. 1963–67 Labour. 1967–72 Conservative. 1972–74 Labour. 1974–80 Conservative. 1980–82 Labour. 1982–86 No clear majority. 1986–88 Labour. 1988–90 Conservative. 1990– Labour.
Bristol
1945–49 Labour. 1949–51 No clear majority. 1951–52 Citizen. 1953–60 Labour. 1960–63 Citizen. 1963–67 Labour. 1967–72 Citizen. 1972–83 Labour. 1983–86 No clear majority. 1986– Labour.
Cardiff
1945–58 anti-Labour coalition. 1958–61 Labour 1961–63 No clear majority. 1963–66 Labour. 1967–74 Conservative. 1974–76 Labour. 1976–79 Conservative. 1973–83 Labour. 1983–87 Conservative. 1987–91 No clear majority. 1991– Labour.
Coventry
1945–67 Labour. 1967–72 Conservative. 1972–75 Labour. 1975–79 Conservative. 1979– Labour.
Edinburgh
1945–62 Progressive. 1962–65 No clear majority. 1965–71 Progressive.[2] 1971–77 No clear majority. 1977–84 Conservative. 1984–92 Labour. 1992– No clear majority.
Glasgow
1945–47 Labour. 1947–50 No clear majority. 1950–52 Progressive. 1952–68 Labour. 1968–69 No clear majority. 1969–70 Progressive. 1970–77 Labour. 1977–80 No clear majority. 1980– Labour.
Leeds
1945–51 Labour. 1951–53 Conservative. 1953–67 Labour. 1967–72 Conservative. 1972–74 Labour. 1974–76 No clear majority. 1976–79 Conservative. 1979–80 No clear majority. 1980– Labour.
Leicester
1945–49 Labour. 1949–52 Conservative. 1952–61 Labour. 1961–62 Conservative. 1962–63 No clear mahority. 1963–66 Labour. 1966–67 No continuous majority. 1967–72 Conservative. 1972–76 Labour. 1976–79 Conservative. 1979– Labour.

---

[1] 'No clear majority' is shown wherever no party had a clear overall majority of seats; frequently a party holding half the seats was able to exercise some control in this situation with the aid of the mayoral vote and in other cases a party exercised control in alliance with a minor group.
[b] The position in Ediburgh and Glasgow is complicated by two *ex officio* councillors who make clear definition of overall majority difficult.

Liverpool
 1945–54 Conservative. 1954–55 Conservative with Protestant support. 1955–61 Labour. 1961–63 Conservative. 1963–67 Labour. 1967–72 Conservative. 1972–74 Labour. 1974–83 No clear majority (Liberal largest party 1974–76. Labour 1976–83). 1983– Labour.

Manchester
 1945–47 Labour. 1947–49 No clear majority. 1949–52 Conservative. 1952–53 No clear majority. 1953–67 Labour. 1967–71 Conservative. 1971– Labour.

Newcastle
 1945–49 Labour, 1949–58 Progressive. 1958–67 Labour. 1967–74 Conservative. 1974– Labour.

Nottingham
 1945–50 Labour. 1950–51 No clear majority. 1951–52 Conservative. 1952–53 No clear majority. 1953–60 Labour. 1960–61 No clear majority. 1961–63 Conservative. 1963–67 Labour. 1967–72 Conservative. 1972–76 Labour. 1976–79 Conservative. 1979–87 Labour. 1987–9 Conservative. 1989–91 No clear majority. 1991– Labour.

Plymouth
 1945–53 Conservative. 1953–59 Labour. 1959–63 Conservative. 1963–66 Labour. 1966–91 Conservative. 1991– Labour.

Portsmouth
 1949–64 Conservative. 1964–65 Labour. 1965–90 Conservative. 1990– No clear majority.

Sheffield
 1945–68 Labour. 1968–69 Conservative. 1969– Labour.

Southampton
 1945–50 Labour. 1950–54 Ratepayers. 1954–61 Labour. 1961–62 Conservative. 1962–67 Labour. 1967–72 Conservative. 1973–76 Labour. 1976–84 Conservative. 1984–87 Labour. 1987–8 No clear majority. 1988– Labour.

Stoke on Trent
 1945–70 Labour. 1970–71 Conservative. 1971– Labour.

Sunderland
 1945–68 Labour. 1968–72 Conservative. 1972– Labour.

Teesside (created 1967, abolished 1974)
 1967–72 Conservative. 1972–74 Labour.

Wolverhampton
 1945–49 Labour. 1949–52 Conservative and allies. 1952–67 Labour. 1967–72 Conservative. 1972–78 Labour. 1978–79 No clear control. 1979–87 Labour. 1987–88 No clear majority; 1988–92 Labour; 1992–94 No clear majority. 1994– Labour.

Local Government Elections 1973–

	Party Control				Seats				
	Con.	Lab.	Lib.	No Clear Control	Con.	Lab.	Lib./Alln	Other	Nat. or Ind.
Metropolitan Counties[1]									
12 Apr 73	–	6	–	–	141	402	49	9	–
5 May 77	4	2	–	–	360	213	19	8	–
7 May 81	–	6	–	–	122	425	50	3	–
Other Counties									
12 Apr 73	18	11	–	18	1484	1397	210	513	18
5 May 77	36	3	–	8	2524	641	71	445	37
7 May 81	19	14	1	13	1560	1376	340	371	23
2 May 85	10	9	1	27	1370	1269	640	360	21
4 May 89	17	13	..	17	1456	1297	458	273	25
6 May 93	1	14	3	29	966	1389	867	237	41

[1] Not including GLC.

	Party Control				Seats				
	Con.	Lab.	Lib.	No Clear Control	Con.	Lab.	Lib./Alln	Other	Nat. or Ind.
Metropolitan Districts									
10 May 73	5	26	–	5	716	1566	183	48	–
7 May 75[2]	9	22	–	5	919	1361	173	58	–
6 May 76[2]	15	18	–	3	1088	1199	151	75	–
4 May 78[2,4]	18	14	–	4	1169	1127	124	82	–
3 May 79[2,4]	11	18	–	7	986	1317	116	87	–
May 80	6	27	–	3	770	1548	133	75	–
6 May 82	7	24	–	5	751	1457	222	42	–
5 May 83	7	24	–	5	745	1481	213	39	–
3 May 84	5	25	–	6	690	1523	228	40	–
1 May 86	1	27	–	8	560	1663	228	30	–
7 May 87	1	27	–	8	552	1632	271	26	–
5 May 88	2	28	–	6	537	1656	268	20	–
3 May 90	2	31	——	3	505	1721	238	17	–
2 May 91	1	32	–	3	460	1748	244	29	–
7 May 92	1	24	–	11	556	1612	273	40	–
6 May 94	1	23	–	12	522	1606	329	16	–
Other Districts (England)									
7 Jun 73	86	73	–	137					
6 May 76	176	29	–	91					
4 May 78[3]	176	30	–	90					
3 May 79[3,4]	4166	49	–	81					
1 May 80	148	53	3	82					
6 May 82	139	59	2	96					
5 May 83	145	55	3	93					
3 May 84	140	53	3						
8 May 86	123	64	5	104					
7 May 87	123	56	9	108					
6 May 88	128	58	8	102					
3 May 90	116	65	5	110					
2 May 91	72	78	20	126					
7 May 92	76	74	21	125					
6 May 94	64	77	28	125					
Other districts (Wales)[a]									
7 Jun 73	1	19	–	17					
6 May 76	4	9	–	24					
3 May 79[4]	2	16	–	17					
5 May 83	3	14	–	20					
7 May 87	2	18	–	17					
1 May 91	–	20	–	17					
Scottish Regions									
9 May 74	1	2	–	6	115	171	11	18	19
2 May 78	2	4	–	3	135	174	7	96	17
6 May 82	2	3	–	4	119	186	25	88	23
8 May 87	–	4	–	5	65	223	40	117	
3 May 92	–	4	–	5	52	233	82	78	

[2] From 1975 onwards one-third of Metropolitan District Councillors came up for re-election in each year, except those in which there are county elections. The seats are the totals for both continuing and newly elected councillors.

[3] 44 of the 316 non-metropolitan districts in England opted that after 1976 one-third of their councillors would retire at a time. 1978 saw the first such elections.

[4] The 1979 elections took place simultaneously with the General Election.

[a] A few Welsh authorities have annual elections which are not reported here.

SOURCES.– D. Clark, *Battle for the Counties* (1977); and the series by J.; Bochel and D. Denver, *The Scottish Local Government Elections* (1974, 1977, 1980, 1984); *The Scottish Regional Elections* (1978, 1982).

	Party Control				Seats				
	Con.	Lab.	Lib.	No Clear Control	Con.	Lab.	Lib./Alln	Other	Nat. or Ind.
Scottish Districts									
9 May 74	5	17	–	31	241	428	17	335	62
3 May 77	8	5	–	40	277	299	31	335	170
1 May 80	6	24	–	23	229	494	40	307	54
3 May 84	4	25	1	23	189	545	78	278	59
5 May 88	3	24	2	24	162	553	84	355	
7 May 92	4	19	2	28	204	468	94	392	

Metropolitan Counties

2 Apr 1973	Councillors					% of vote			
	Con.	Lab.	Lib	Other		Con.	Lab.	Lib.	Other
Greater Manchester	24	69	13	–		38.7	45.1	14.9	1.3
Merseyside	26	53	19	1		33.7	41.3	22.0	3.0
South Yorkshire	13	82	1	4		25.5	55.8	11.3	7.4
Tyne & Wear	27	74	1	2		36.3	55.7	4.6	3.4
West Midlands	27	73	4	–		48.3	42.5	7.7	1.5
West Yorkshire	25	51	11	1		37.3	44.8	14.6	3.3
Greater London	32	58	2	–		38.0	47.4	12.5	2.1
5 May 1977									
Greater Manchester	82	23	–	1		56.6	34.6	7.5	1.9
Merseyside	67	26	6	–		47.7	32.0	19.1	1.2
South Yorkshire	31	62	2	5		39.7	44.7	6.3	9.4
Tyne & Wear	44	54	4	2		49.4	40.7	6.4	3.4
West Midlands	82	18	3	1		56.5	31.7	4.1	6.1
West Yorkshire	54	30	4	–		50.3	35.4	10.3	4.1
Greater London	64	28	–	–		52.6	32.9	7.8	6.3
7 May 1981									
Greater Manchester	19	78	9	–		30.6	49.8	18.0	1.7
Merseyside	27	56	15	–		29.3	45.6	24.2	1.0
South Yorkshire	14	82	3	1		25.8	58.2	12.8	3.2
Tyne & Wear	23	72	7	2		29.4	55.9	12.2	2.5
West Midlands	25	74	5	–		36.0	50.3	9.8	3.9
West Yorkshire	14	63	11	–		30.2	47.5	21.0	1.3
Greater London	41	50	1	–		39.4	41.4	15.0	4.2

Party Representation on the London County Council, 1898–1964

| Year | Councillors (elected) | | | | | Aldermen | | | | | |
	Pr.	MRM	Lab.	Ind.	Total	Pr.	MRM	Lab.	Ind.	Total	Majority
1898	84	34	..	..	118	13	6	..	..	137	Pr.
1901	87	31	..	..	118	14	5	..	..	137	Pr.
1904	83	35	..	..	118	15	4	..	..	137	Pr.
1907	38	79	..	1	118	9	10	..	..	137	MRM
1910	55	60	3	..	118	2	15	..	2	137	MRM
1913	50	67	1	..	118	3	14	..	2	137	MRM
1919	40	68	15	1	124	6	12	2	..	144	MRM
1922	25	82	17	..	124	5	12	3	..	144	MRM
1925	6	83	35	..	124	3	13	4	..	144	MRM
1928	5	77	42	..	124	1	12	6	1	144	MRM
1931	6	83	35	..	124	..	13	6	1	144	MRM
1934	..	55	69	..	124	..	9	11	..	144	Lab.
1937	..	49	75	..	124	..	8	12	..	144	Lab.
	Lib.	Con.	Lab.	Comm.		Lib.	Con.	Lab.	Comm.		
1946	2	30	90	2	124	..	6	14	..	144	Lab.
1949	1	64	64	..	129	..	5	16	..	150[a]	Lab.
1952	..	37	92	..	129	..	6	15	..	150	Lab.
1955	..	52	74	..	126	..	8	13	..	147	Lab.
1958	..	25	101	..	126	..	7	14	..	147	Lab.
1961	..	42	84	..	126	..	7	14	..	147	Lab.

[a] Plus Chairman, an outsider and Labour nominee.

Pr.	Progressives (Lib.)		Ind.	Independent
MRM	Municipal Reform Moderates (Con.)		Comm.	Communist
Lab.	Labour		Lib.	Liberal

SOURCES.– Sir G. Gibbon and R.W. Bell, *History of the London County Council, 1889–1939* (1939); *General Election of County Councillors* (published after each election by the L.C.C.), 1919–61.

Greater London Council, 1964–1981[a]

| 1980 | Councillors | | | Aldermen | | |
	Con.	Lab.	Lib.	Con.	Lab.	Lib.
1964	36	64	–	5	11	–
1967	82	18	–	10	6	–
1970	65	35	–	11	5	–
1973	32	58	2	6	9	–
1977	64	28	–	(Aldermen abolished)		
1981	41	50	1			

[a] From 1964 to 1986 the Inner London Education Authority (ILEA), covering the former LCC area, was a special committee of the GLC. It was controlled by Labour 1964–67, Conservative 1967–70 and Labour 1970–86. Following the abolition of the GLC in 1985, ILEA members were directly elected on 8 May 1986. Labour won 45 seats, the Conservatives 11 and the Liberals 2. ILEA was abolished on 1 Apr 1990.

Control and Representation in London Boroughs, 1964–

	Control				Councillors			
	Con.	Lab.	Lib.	No clear control	Con.	Lab.	Lib/Alln	Other
1964	9	20		3	668	1,112	13	66
1968	27	4		1	1,441	350	10	57
1971	10	21		1	601	1,221	9	32
1974	13	18		1	713	1,090	27	37
1978	17	14		1	960	882	30	36
1982	17	12		3	984	781	124	25
1986	11	15	2	4	685	957	249	23
1990	12	14	3	3	731	925	229	29
1994	5	17	3	7	519	1044	323	31

SOURCES: – J. Redlich and F. Hirst (ed. B. Keith-Lucas) *The History of Local Government in England* (1958); *Report of the Royal Commission on Local Taxation* (1901); *Report of the Royal Commission on the Poor Law* (1909); *Report of the Royal Commission on the Poor Law* (1925); *Social Insurance and Allied Services* (Beveridge Report) 1942; *Report of the Committee on Care of Children* (Curtis Report) (1946); *Local Government Functions of County Councils and District Councils* (Cmnd 161/1957) *Local Government Finance* (Cmnd 209/1957); *Report of the Royal Commission on Local Government in Greater London* (Cmnd 1164/1960); *Report of the Royal Commission on Local Government in England (Redcliffe-Maud Report);* (Cmnd 4040/ 1969); P. Richards, *The Reformed Local Government System* (1973) J. Stewart and G. Stoker, *The Future of Local Government* (1989); T. Travers, *The Politics of Local Government Finance* (1987); T. Byrne, *Local Government* (5th ed. 1990); D. Butler et al., *Failure in British Government: the Politics of the Poll Tax* (1994); C. Rallings and M. Thrasher, *The Local Elections Handbook* (annually from 1985); C. Rallings and M. Thrasher, (eds), *Local Elections in Britain* (1993) gives summary election results for all local authorities in Great Britain 1973–1992.

XVI

THE COMMONWEALTH

Main Territories under British Rule since 1900

Commonwealth Status Aug 1994		Original entry to British rule and Status (1900)	Changes of Status
	Aden	Colony (1839) and adjacent Protectorate	Acceded to South Arabian Federation 1963. Became People's Republic of South Yemen 1967 and merged with North Yemen in 1990.
Dependency	Anguilla	*See* St. Kitts	Became separate Dependency 1980
Member	Antigua and Barbuda	Colony (1663)	*See* Leeward Isles
Dependency of St Helena	Ascension	Admiralty administered territory (1815)	Became dependency of Colony of St Helena 1922.
Member	Australia	First settled 1788 6 self-governing colonies (1855 and later)	Federal government formed 1901. Dominion status recognised 1907
Member	Bahamas	First settled 1646. Colony (1783)	Independence granted 1973
Member	Bangladesh		Became East Pakistan 1947. Broke away from Pakistan 1971. Commonwealth Member 1972.
Member	Barbados	Settled 1627 Colony (1662)	Part of West Indies Federation 1958–62; Independence granted 1966.
	Basutoland	Protectorate (1871) Colony (1884)	Independence granted 1966. Now Lesotho.
	Bechuanaland	Protectorate (1885)	Independence granted 1966. Now Botswana.
Member	Belize	Formerly Br. Honduras	Independence granted 1981.
Colony	Bermuda	First settled 1609. Colony (1684)	
Member	Botswana		Formerly Bechuanaland Protectorate. Independence granted 1966 as Republic.
Dependency	British Antarctic Territory	Discovered (1819)	Became a Territory 1982. Part was devolved to Australia 1933.
	British Guiana	Ceded Colony (1814)	Independence granted 1966. Now Guyana.
	British Honduras	First settled 1638. Colony (separated from Jamaica 1884)	Changed name to Belize 1973.
Dependency	British Indian Ocean Territory	Dependencies of Mauritius or Seychelles	The Chagos Archipelago and Aldabra, Farquhar and Desroches Islands were formed into a single British Dependency in 1965.
	British North Borneo	Protectorate (1888)	Administered by Chartered Company 1882–1946. Became part of North Borneo Colony 1946. Entered Malaysian Federation as Sabah 1963

Commonwealth Status Aug 1994		Original entry to British rule and Status (1900)	Changes of Status
Member	British Solomon Islands	Protectorate (1893)	Independence granted 1978 as Solomon Islands.
	British Somaliland	Protectorate (1887)	Independence granted 1960 when it became part of Somalia, a Republic outside the Commonwealth.
	British Togoland		Administered by Britain under League of Nations mandate 1922–46 and U.N. Trusteeship 1946–57. Merged with Ghana 1957.
Member	Brunei	Protectorate (1888)	Independence granted 1984 as indigenous Monarchy.
	Burma	Indian Province (1852)	Separated from India 1937. Independence granted in 1948 when it became a Republic outside the Commonwealth
	Cameroons (British)		Administered as part of Nigeria under League of Nations mandate 1922. Northern Cameroons incorporated in Nigeria 1961. Southern Cameroons joined Cameroun Republic, outside the Commonwealth.
Member	Canada	Ceded Colonies from 1714 onwards. Self-governing Federation (1867)	Dominion status recognised 1907.
	Cape of Good Hope	Ceded Colony (1814)	Dominion status recognised 1907. Province of Union of South Africa.
Dependency	Cayman, Turks and Caicos	Ceded (1670) Dependencies of Jamaica (1848)	Separate dependencies following Jamaican Independence 1962.
Member	Ceylon	Ceded Colony	Independence granted 1948. Became Republic and changed name to Sri Lanka 1972.
	Christmas Island	Annexed (1888)	Part of Straits Settlements 1900 by incorporation with Singapore. Separate Colony Jan 1958. Transferred to Australia Oct 1958.
	Cocos-Keeling Islands	Annexed (1857)	Part of Straits Settlement 1903. Incorporated in Singapore Colony 1946. Transferred to Australia 1958.
Ass. state	Cook Islands of N.Z.	Protectorate (1888)	Annexed 1900. Administered by New Zealand since 1901.
Member	Cyprus	British administered territory (1878)	Annexed by Britain 1914. Colony 1925. Independence granted as a Republic 1960.
Member	Dominica	Colony (1763)	Part of Leeward Islands till 1940. Separate Colony 1940. Associated State 1967. Independent Republic 1978.
	East African Protectorate	Protectorate (1895)	Became a Colony and protectorate of Kenya 1920. See Kenya.

Commonwealth Status Aug 1994		Original entry to British rule and Status (1900)	Changes of Status
	Egypt	Occupied by British 1882	British Protectorate 1922.
	Eire	(see Ireland)	
Dependency	Falkland Islands	Colony (1833)	Invaded by Argentina, then recaptured 1982
	Fiji	Colony (1874)	Independence granted 1970. Republic and out of Commonwealth 1987.
Member	Gambia	Settlement began 1618. Colony (1843) and adjacent Protectorate (1888)	Independence granted 1965. Republic 1970.
Member	Ghana		Formerly Gold Coast. Independence granted 1957. Republic 1960.
Dependency	Gibraltar	Ceded Colony (1713)	
	Gilbert and Ellice Islands	Protectorate (1892)	Colony 1915. Ellice Islands separated 1975. See Tuvalu. Independence granted to Gilbert Islands as Republic 1979 with name of Kiribati.
	Gold Coast	Settlement began 1750. Colony (1821 and 1874)	Independence granted 1957. Now Ghana.
Member	Grenada	Ceded Colony (1763)	Part of Leeward Isles 1871–1974. Independence granted 1974.
Member	Guyana		Formerly British Guiana. Independence granted 1966. Republic 1970.
Dependency	Hong Kong	Ceded Colony (1843)	Kowloon ceded to Britain in 1860. New Territories leased to Britain for 99 years in 1898. 1997 reversion to China agreed 1984.
Member	India	Settlement began 1601. Indian Empire (1876)	Independence granted 1947. Republic 1950.
	Iraq		Administered by Britain under League of Nations Mandate 1922–32.
	Ireland	Union with Great Britain (1801)	26 counties became Irish Free State 1922 with Dominion Status. 1937 Constitution asserted Sovereign Independence. Became Republic of Ireland (Eire) outside Commonwealth in 1949.
Member	Jamaica	Colony (seized 1655 and ceded 1670)	Part of West Indies Federation 1958–62. Independence granted 1962.
Member	Kenya		Formerly East African Protectorate. Colony and Protectorate of Kenya (1920). Independence granted 1963. Republic 1964.
Member	Kiribati		Formerly Gilbert Islands. Independence granted as Republic 1979.
	Labuan	Colony (1848) governed by North Borneo Company (1890)	Administered by Straits Settlement 1907. Became separate Straits Settlement 1912. Part of North Borneo (1946) now Sabah (1963).

Commonwealth Status Aug 1994		Original entry to British rule and Status (1900)	Changes of Status
	Lagos	Colony (1861)	Amalgamated with protectorate of Southern Nigeria 1906.
	Leeward Isles	Colonies federated (1871)	Federated Colony dissolved 1956.(Antigua, Montserrat, St Kitts-Nevis and until 1940 Dominica and Virgin Is.) Part of West Indies Federation (except for Virgin Is.) 1958–62. See separate entries.
Member	Lesotho		Formerly Basutoland Colony. Independence granted 1966 with indigenous monarch.
Member	Malawi		Formerly Nyasaland. Part of Federation of Rhodesia and Nyasaland 1953–63. Independence granted 1964. Republic 1966.
	Malay States	9 Protectorates, 4 of which were federated	
	Malaya		Formerly Malay States (federated and unfederated) and Straits Settlements. Independence granted in 1957 as elective monarchy. Merged in Malaysia Federation 1963
Member	Malaysia		Formed in 1963 by a federation of Malaya, Singapore, Sabah (North Borneo),and Sarawak; Singapore seceded in 1965. An indigenous elective monarchy.
Member	Maldives	Protectorate (1887)	Independence granted 1965. Republic 1980.
Member	Malta	Ceded Colony (1814)	Independence granted 1964. Republic 1974.
Member	Mauritius	Ceded Colony (1814)	Independence granted 1968.
Dependency	Montserrat	First settled (1642) as Colony	*See* Leeward Isles. Separately administered since 1962.
Member	Namibia		Formerly South-West Africa. Became independent and joined Commonwealth 1990.
	Natal	Colony (1843)	Province of South Africa 1910.
Member	Nauru		Administered by Australia under League of Nations mandate 1920–47 and under U.N. Trusteeship 1947–68. Independent Republic 1968.
	New Guinea		Administered by Australia under League of Nations mandate 1921–46 and under U.N. Trusteeship since 1946. United with Papua 1946 as Papua-New Guinea
Member	New Hebrides		Administered as Anglo-French condominium 1906. Independence granted as Republic of Vanuatu 1980
Member	New Zealand	Colony (1840)	Dominion status recognised 1907.
	Newfoundland	Settlement began 1623. Self-governing Colony (1855)	Dominion Under Commission government 1933–1949. Acceded to Canada 1949.

Commonwealth Status Aug 1994		Original entry to British rule and Status (1900)	Changes of Status
Member	Nigeria	Protectorates	Colony of Lagos joined Southern Nigeria 1906. Protectorates of Northern and Southern Nigeria joined 1914. Independence granted 1960. Republic 1963.
	Norfolk Island	Settled 1788. Under New South Wales (1896)	Became dependency of Australian Government 1914
	North Borneo		Colony created in 1946 mainly from British North Borneo. Entered Malaysian Federation as Sabah 1963.
	Northern Rhodesia	Chartered Company territory (1889)	Administered by British South Africa Company. Became Protectorate 1924. Part of Federation of Rhodesia and Nyasaland 1953–63. Independence granted 1964. Now Zambia.
	Nyasaland	Protectorate (1891)	Part of Federation of Rhodesia and Nyasaland 1953–63. Independence granted 1964. Now Malawi.
	Orange Free State	Colony (1902)	Province of Union of South Africa 1910
(Member)	Pakistan	Part of Indian Empire	Independence granted 1947. Republic 1950. Left Commonwealth 1972. Rejoined 1989.
	Palestine		Administered by Britain under League of Nations mandate 1922–48. Achieved Independence as State of Israel 1948.
	Papua	Protectorate (1884) Colony (1888)	Administered by Australia since 1906. United with New Guinea 1946.
Member	Papua-New Guinea		Papua and New Guinea were united under Australian Trusteeship 1946. Independence granted 1975.
Dependency	Pitcarn Islands	Settled 1790 Colony (1898)	
Member	Rhodesia		Formerly Southern Rhodesia. Part of Federation of Rhodesia and Nyasaland 1953–63. Resumed status as a self-governing colony with name of Rhodesia 1964. Unilateral declaration of independence 1965. Granted independence as Zimbabwe 1980.
	Rhodesia and Nyasaland		Federation of Northern Rhodesia, Nyasaland, and Southern Rhodesia established in 1953 and dissolved in 1963.
	Sabah		Formerly North Borneo. Part of Malaysian Federation since 1963.
Member	St Christopher (St Kitts) and Nevis	Colony (1625)	*See* Leeward Isles.
Colony	St Helena	Administered by E. India C. 1673 Colony (1834)	Ascension (1922) and Tristan da Cunha (1938) are its dependencies.

Commonwealth Status Aug 1994		Original entry to British rule and Status (1900)	Changes of Status
Member	St Lucia	Ceded Colony (1814)	(*See* Windward Isles) Independence granted 1979.
Member	St. Vincent and the Grenadines	Ceded Colony (1763)	*See* Windward Isles.
	Sarawak	Protectorate (1888)	Ceded to Britain in 1946 as Colony. Part of Malaysian Federation since 1963.
Member	Seychelles	Dependency of Mauritius (1810)	Separate Colony 1903. Independence granted 1976. Republic 1976.
Member	Sierra Leone	Colony (1808) Protectorate (1896)	Independence granted 1961. Republic 1971.
Member	Singapore	Under Indian government 1824	Separate Colony 1946. Part of Malaysian Federation 1963–65. Seceded to form Republic 1965.
Member	Solomon Is.	Protectorate (1893)	Formerly British Solomon Islands. Independence granted 1978.
(Member)	South Africa		Union of South Africa formed 1910 from the Colonies of Cape of Good of Hope, Natal, Orange Free State and Transvaal. Dominion status 1910. Became Republic 1961 and left the Commonwealth. Rejoined 1994.
	South Arabia		Federation formed in 1959 from 6 states or sheikhdoms. A further 16 subsequently acceded together with (1963) the Colony of Aden. Became Republic of South Yemen 1967.
	South-West Africa		Administered by South Africa under League of Nations mandate 1920–46 and under U.N. Trusteeship since 1946. Unilaterally incorporated in South Africa 1949. Became independent as Namibia 1990.
	South Yemen		Formerly Aden Protectorate. Merged with North Yemen 1990.
	Southern Rhodesia	Chartered Company (1889)	Administered by British South Africa Company. Self-governing Colony 1923. Part of Federation of Rhodesia and Nyasaland 1953–63. Rhodesia 1963–80. Now Zimbabwe.
Member	Sri Lanka	Formerly Ceylon	Independence granted 1948. Became Republic and changed name 1972.
	Straits Settlements (Singapore, Penang, Malacca)	Colonies (1867)	Part of Straits Settlements. Malacca, Labuan added 1912. Labuan and Penang joined Malay States 1948. Singapore joined Malaysian Federation 1963 but seceded 1965.
	Sudan	Condominium with Egypt (1899)	Independence granted 1956 when it became a Republic outside the Commonwealth.
Member	Swaziland	British Protectorate 1903	Independence granted 1968. Indigenous monarchy.

Commonwealth Status Aug 1994	Original entry to British rule and Status (1900)	Changes of Status
	Tanganyika	Administered by Britain under League of Nations mandate 1920–46 and under U.N. Trusteeship 1946–61. Independence granted 1961. Republic 1962. Merged with Zanzibar to form Tanzania 1964.
Member	Tanzania	Formed by merging Tanganyika and Zanzibar 1964.
Dependency of N.Z.	Tokelau	Protectorate (1877)	Annexed by U.K. 1916. Administration transferred to New Zealand 1925.
Member	Tonga	Protectorate (1900)	Independence granted under indigenous monarchy 1970.
	Transjordan	Administered by Britain under League of Nations mandate 1922–28. Full independence recognised 1946.
	Transvaal	Annexed 1902	Responsible Government 1906. Province of Union of South Africa 1910.
Member	Trinidad and Tobago	Ceded Colony (1802, 1814). (Combined 1889)	Part of West Indies Federation. Independence granted 1962.
	Tristan da Cunha	British settlement (1815) (Evacuated 1961–63)	Dependency of Colony of St Helena 1938.
Dependency	Turks and Caicos Islands	Annexed 1766 Dependency of Jamaica (1873)	Dependency following Jamaican independence 1962.
Member	Tuvalu		Protectorate (1892) Formerly Ellice Islands. Part of Gilbert and Ellice Islands. Separated 1975. Independence granted 1978.
Member	Uganda	Protectorate (1894)	Independence granted 1962. Sovereign State 1963.
Member	Vanuatu		Formerly New Hebrides. Administered as Anglo-French condominium 1906. Independence granted as Republic of Vanuatu 1980.
Dependency	Virgin Islands West Indies Federation	Colonies (1666)	See Leeward Isles Independence was granted in 1958 to a Federation of the colonies of Jamaica, Trinidad and Tobago, Barbados, the Leeward Isles (except for the Virgin Isles) and the Windward Isles. The Federation broke up in 1962 when Jamaica and Trinidad and Tobago became independent. Some common institutions were continued by the other members of the Federation.
Member	Western Samoa		Administered by New Zealand under League of Nations mandate 1920–46 and under U.N. Trusteeship 1946–62. Independent Republic 1962. Full Commonwealth member 1970.

Commonwealth Status Aug 1994		Original entry to British rule and Status (1900)	Changes of Status
Members	Windward Isles	Colonies (1763 and 1814, federated 1885)	The colonies Grenada, Dominica, St Lucia, and St Vincent. Part of West Indies Federation 1958–62. Attained Associated Statehood 1967. Independence granted to Grenada 1974; Dominica 1978; St Lucia 1979; St Vincent 1979.
Member	Zambia		Formerly Northern Rhodesia. Part of Federation of Rhodesia and Nyasaland 1953–63. Independence granted as Republic 1964.
	Zanzibar	Protected State (1890)	Independence granted 1963. Republic 1964. Merged with Tanganyika as Tanzania 1964.
Member	Zimbabwe	Chartered Company (1889)	Formerly Rhodesia. Independence granted as Republic 1980.

Independent Self-Governing Members of the Commonwealth

United Kingdom
1856 New Zealand
1867 Canada[1]
1901 Australia[1]
1909–61, 1994– South Africa[1] (Republic 1960)
1907–33 Newfoundland[1, 2]
1922–49 Ireland (Eire)
1947 India[3] (*Republic 1950*)
1947–72, 1989– Pakistan (*Republic 1956*)
1948 Ceylon (Sri Lanka 1972) (*Republic 1972*)
1953–63[4] Federation of Rhodesia and Nyasaland
1957 Ghana (*Republic 1960*)
1957 Malaya (Malaysia 1963) (*Elective Monarchy*)
1958–62[5] West Indies Federation
1960 Nigeria (*Republic 1963*)
1961 Cyprus (*Republic 1960*)
1961 Sierra Leone (*Republic 1971*)
1961 Tanganyika (Tanzania 1964) (*Republic 1962*)
1962 Jamaica
1962 Trinidad and Tobago (*Republic 1976*)
1962 Uganda (*Republic 1963*)
1963–64 Zanzibar (*See* Tanzania)
1963 Kenya (*Republic 1964*)
1964 Zambia (*Republic 1964*)
1964 Malta (*Republic 1974*)
1964 Malawi (*Republic 1966*)
1965 The Gambia (*Republic 1970*)
1965 Singapore (*Republic 1965*)
1966 Botswana (*Republic 1966*)
1966 Guyana (*Republic 1970*)

1966 Lesotho (*Indigenous Monarchy*)
1966 Barbados
1968 Nauru (*Republic 1968*)
1968 Swaziland (*Indigenous Monarchy*)
1968 Nauru (*Republic 1968*)
1968 Mauritius (*Republic1992*)
1970–87 Fiji (*Republic 1987*)
1970 Tonga (In*digenous Monarchy*)
1970 Western Samoa (*Indigenous Monarchy*)
1972 Bangladesh (*Republic 1972*)
1973 Bahamas
1974 Grenada
1975 Papua-New Guinea
1976 Seychelles (*Republic 1976*)
1978 Dominica
1978 Solomon Islands
1978 Tuvalu
1979 St Lucia
1980 Vanuatu (*Republic 1980*)
1979 Kiribati (*Republic 1979*)
1979 St Vincent and the Grenadines
1980 Vanuatu (*Republic 1980*)
1980 Zimbabwe (*Republic 1980*)
1981 Antigua and Barbuda
1981 Belize
1982 Maldive Islands (*Republic 1982*)[6]
1983 St Christopher and Nevis
1984 Brunei (*Indigenous Monarchy*)
1990 Namibia (*Republic 1990*)

[1] These were recognized as having 'Dominion Status' in 1907.
[2] From 1933 to 1949 Newfoundland was governed by a U.K. Commission of Government. In 1949 Newfoundland joined the Canadian confederation as the tenth province.
[3] Indian representatives were invited to attend Imperial Conferences and Prime Ministers' Meetings 1917–47.
[4] Although the Central African Federation, set up in 1953, and composed of N. Rhodesia, S. Rhodesia, and Nyasaland, was not a fully independent member of the Commonwealth, her Prime Ministers were invited to the Prime Ministers' Meetings 1955–62 and the Prime Minister of Rhodesia was invited 1962–65.
[5] Barbados, Jamaica, Trinidad, Tobago, the Leeward and the Windward Islands all formed the West Indies Federation between 1958 and 1962.
[6] Special membership.

Commonwealth Prime Ministers' Meetings, 1900–1970

(All took place in London)

30 Jun–11 Aug 02	Colonial Conference
15 Apr–9 May 07	Colonial Conference
23 May–20 Jun 11	Imperial Conference
Mar–May 17	Imperial War Conference
Jun–Aug 18	Imperial War Conference
1 Oct- 8 Nov 23	Imperial Conference
19 Oct–23 Nov 26	Imperial Conference
1 Oct–14 Nov 30	Imperial Conference
14 May–15 Jun 37	Imperial Conference
1–16 May 44	Commonwealth Prime Ministers' Meeting
23 Apr–23 May 46	Commonwealth Prime Ministers' Meeting
11–22 Oct 48	Commonwealth Prime Ministers' Meeting
21–28 Apr 49	Commonwealth Prime Ministers' Meeting
4–12 Jan 51	Commonwealth Prime Ministers' Meeting
3–9 Jun 53	Commonwealth Prime Ministers' Meeting
31 Jan–8 Feb 55	Commonwealth Prime Ministers' Meeting
27 Jun–6 Jul 56	Commonwealth Prime Ministers' Meeting
26 Jun–5 Jul 57	Commonwealth Prime Ministers' Meeting
3–13 May 60	Commonwealth Prime Ministers' Meeting
8–17 Mar 61	Commonwealth Prime Ministers' Meeting
10–19 Sep 62	Commonwealth Prime Ministers' Meeting
8–13 Jul 64	Commonwealth Prime Ministers' Meeting
17–25 Jan 65	Commonwealth Prime Ministers' Meeting
6–15 Sep 66	Commonwealth Prime Ministers' Meeting
7–15 Jan 69	Commonwealth Prime Ministers' Meeting

Commonwealth Heads of Government Meetings 1971–

14–22 Jan 71	Commonwealth Heads of Government Meeting (Singapore)
2–10 Aug 73	Commonwealth Heads of Government Meeting (Ottawa)
29 Apr–6 May 75	Commonwealth Heads of Government Meeting (Kingston, Jamaica)
8–15 Jun 77	Commonwealth Heads of Government Meeting (London)
1–10 Aug 79	Commonwealth Heads of Government Meeting (Lusaka)
30 Sep–7 Oct 81	Commonwealth Heads of Government Meeting (Melbourne)
23–29 Nov 83	Commonwealth Heads of Government Meeting (New Delhi)
16–22 Oct 85	Commonwealth Heads of Government Meeting (Nassau, Bahamas)
13–17 Oct 87	Commonwealth Heads of Government Meeting (Vancouver)
18–24 Oct 89	Commonwealth Heads of Government Meeting (Kuala Lumpur)
16–22 Oct 91	Commonwealth Heads of Government Meeting (Harare)
21–25 Oct 93	Commonwealth Heads of Government Meeting (Nicosia)

Certain other meetings of comparable status have been held.

20 Jun–5 Aug 21	Conference of Prime Ministers and London Representatives of the United Kingdom, the Dominions, and India, London.
21 Jul–20 Aug 32	Imperial Economic Conference, Ottawa.
4–13 Apr 45	British Commonwealth Meeting, London.
27 Nov–11 Dec 52	Commonwealth Economic Conference, London.
11–12 Jan 66	Commonwealth Prime Ministers' Conference on Rhodesia, Lagos.

SOURCES: – Commonwealth Relations Office List 1951, pp. 56–58; Annual register 1900-; Keesing's Archives 1931–.

Commonwealth Secretariat

As a result of the Commonwealth Prime Ministers' Meeting of Jul 1964 a Commonwealth Secretariat was established in London with its own civil servants seconded from Commonwealth Governments.

Secretary-General

Aug 65	A. Smith (Canada)
Jul 75	(Sir) S. Ramphal (Guyana)
Jul 90	E. Anyaoku (Nigeria)

Viceroys and Governors-General

Antigua and Barbuda 1981–

1 Nov 81	Sir W. Jacobs
1 Jun 93	J. Carlisle

Australia 1901–

1 Jan 01	E of Hopetoun	8 Oct 25	Ld Stonehaven	22 Sep 65	Ld Casey
9 Jan 03	Ld Tennyson	22 Jan 31	Sir I. Isaacs	30 Apr 69	Sir P. Hasluck
21 Jan 04	Ld Northcote	23 Jan 36	Ld Gowrie	11 Jul 74	Sir J. Kerr
9 Sep 08	E of Dudley	30 Jan 45	D of Gloucester	8 Dec 77	Sir Z. Cowan
31 Jun 11	Ld Denman	11 Mar 47	Sir W. McKell	9 Jul 82	Sir N. Stephen
18 May 14	Sir R. Munro-Ferguson	8 May 53	Sir W. Slim	16 Feb 89	W. Hayden
6 Oct 20	Ld Forster	2 Feb 60	Vt Dunrossil		
		3 Aug 61	Vt de L'Isle		

Bahamas 1973–

10 Jul 73	Sir J. Paul	22 Jan 76	Sir G. Cash (*acting*)	26 Jun 88	Sir H. Taylor (*acting*)
1 Aug 73	Sir M. Butler	24 Sep 79	Sir G. Cash	1 Mar 91	Sir H. Taylor
				2 Jan 92	Sir C. Darling

Barbados 1966–

30 Nov 66	Sir J. Stow	17 Nov 76	Sir D. Ward	24 Feb 84	Sir H. Springer
15 May 67	Sir W. Scott	23 Jan 79	Sir G Cash (*acting*)	6 Jun 90	Dame N. Barrow
				16 Nov 93	C. Young

Belize 1981–

21 Sep 81	Dame M. Gordon

Canada 1900–

1898	E of Minto	4 Apr 31	E of Bessborough	4 Apr 67	R. Michener
10 Dec 04	Earl Grey	2 Nov 35	Ld Tweedsmuir	14 Jan 74	J. Leger
13 Oct 11	D of Connaught	21 Jun 40	E of Athlone	22 Jan 79	E. Schreyer
11 Nov 16	D of Devonshire	12 Apr 46	Vt Alexander	14 May 84	Jeanne Sauve
11 Aug 21	Ld Byng	28 Feb 52	V. Massey	29 Jan 90	R. Hnatyshyn
2 Oct 26	Vt Willingdon	15 Sep 59	G. Vanier		

Ceylon 1948–71

4 Feb 48	Sir H. Moore	17 Jul 54	Sir O. Goonetilleke	*22 May 72*	*Declared Republic*
6 Jul 49	Ld Soulbury	2 Mar 62	W. Gopallawa		

Fiji 1970–1986

10 Oct 70	Sir R. Foster
13 Jan 73	Sir G. Cakobau
12 Feb 83	Sir P. Ganilau
7 Oct 87	*Declared Republic*

The Gambia 1965–70

18 Feb 65	Sir F. Singhateh
24 Apr 70	*Declared Republic*

Ghana 1957–60

6 Mar 57	E of Listowel
1 Jul 60	*Declared Republic*

Grenada 1974

7 Feb 74	(Sir) L. de Gale
30 Sep 78	Sir P. Scoon
93	Sir R. Palmer

Guyana 1966–70

26 May 66	Sir R. Luyt
16 Dec 66	Sir D. Rose
23 Feb 70	*Declared Republic*

Viceroys of India 1900–47

1899	Ld Curzon	10 Apr 25	E of Lytton	18 Apr 36	M of Linlithgow
30 Apr 04	Ld Ampthill		*(officiating)*	25 Jun 38	Ld Brabourne
	(officiating)	3 Apr 26	Ld Irwin		*(officiating)*
13 Dec 04	Ld Curzon	29 Jun 29	Vt Goschen	25 Oct 38	M of Linlithgow
18 Nov 05	E of Minto		*(officiating)*	20 Oct 43	Vt Wavell
23 Nov 10	Ld Hardinge of	24 Oct 29	Ld Irwin	24 Mar 47	Vt Mountbatten
	Penshurst	18 Apr 31	E of Willingdon		(Earl)
4 Apr 16	Ld Chelmsford	16 May 34	Sir G. Stanley		
2 Apr 21	E of Reading		*(officiating)*		

Dominion of India Governors-General 1947–50

15 Aug 47	Earl Mountbatten
21 Jun 48	C. Rajagopalachari
26 Jan 50	*Declared Republic*

Ireland 1922–37

6 Dec 22	T. Healy
15 Dec 27	J. McNeill
30 Nov 32	D. O'Buachalla
29 Dec 37	*Declared Republic*

Jamaica 1962–

6 Aug 62	Sir C. Campbell
27 Jun 73	(Sir) F. Glasspole
14 Aug 91	(Sir) H. Cooke

Kenya 1963–64

12 Dec 63	M. Macdonald
12 Dec 64	*Declared Republic*

Malawi 1964–66

6 Jul 64   Sir G. Jones
6 Jul 66   Declared Republic

Malta 1964–74

21 Sep 64   Sir M. Dorman
5 Jul 71   Sir A. Mamo
13 Dec 74   Declared Republic

Mauritius 1968–1992

1 Sep 68	Sir A. Williams	15 Mar 78	(Sir) D. Burrenchobay
27 Dec 72	Sir R. Osman	27 Dec 83	Sir S. Ramgoolam
19 Nov 77	Sir W. Garrioch *(acting)*		

17 Jan 86	Sir V. Ringadoo
22 Mar 92	*Declared Republic*

New Zealand 1900–

(*Governors*)

1897   E of Ranfurly
20 Jun 04   Ld Plunkett
22 Jun 10   Ld Islington
19 Dec 12   E of Liverpool

(*Governors-General*)

28 Jun 17	E of Liverpool	16 Jun 46	Ld Freyberg
27 Sep 20	Earl Jellicoe	1 Dec 52	Sir C. Norrie (Ld)
13 Dec 24	Sir C. Fergusson	3 Sep 57	Vt Cobham
18 Mar 30	Ld Bledisloe	9 Nov 62	Sir B. Fergusson
12 Apr 35	Vt Galway	19 Oct 67	Sir A. Porritt
21 Feb 41	Ld Newall	26 Sep 72	Sir D. Blundell

26 Oct 77	Sir K. Holyoake
26 Oct 80	(Sir) D. Beattie
10 Nov 85	Sir P. Reeves
20 Nov 90	Dame K. Tizard

Nigeria 1960–63

1 Oct 60   N. Azikwe
1 Oct 63   Declared Republic

Dominion of Pakistan 1947–56

15 Aug 47   M. Jinnah
14 Sep 48   Khwaja Nazimuddin
19 Oct 51   Ghulam Mohammed
6 Oct 55   Iskander Mirza
23 Mar 56   Declared Republic

Papua-New Guinea 1975–

15 Sep 75   Sir J. Guise
1 Mar 76   Sir T. Lokoloko
28 Feb 83   Sir K. Dibela
28 Feb 89   Sir I. Kilage
12 Dec 90   V. Eri
12 Nov 91   (Sir) W. Korowi

Federation of Rhodesia and Nyasaland 1957–63

8 Oct 57   E of Dalhousie
31 Dec 63   Federation dissolved

St Christopher-Nevis 1983

19 Sep 83   Sir C. Arrindell

St Lucia 1979–

22 Feb	79	Sir A. Lewis
21 Feb	80	B. Williams
13 Dec	82	Sir A. Lewis
16 May	87	Sir V. Floissac (*acting*)
21 Feb	88	(Sir) S. James

St Vincent and the Grenadines 1979–

27 Oct	79	Sir S. GunMunro
1 Mar	85	Sir J. Eustace
20 Sep	90	Sir D. Jack

Sierra Leone 1961–71

27 Apr	61	Sir H. Lightfoot-Boston
(*In Mar 67 the Constitution was suspended*)		
7 Apr	68	B. Tejan-Sie (*acting*)
19 Apr	*71*	*Declared Republic*

Solomon Islands 1978–

7 Jul	78	(Sir) B. Devesi
7 Jul	88	Sir G. Lepping

South Africa 1910–61

31 May	10	Vt Gladstone	21 Jan	24	E of Athlone	1 Jan	46	G. van Zyl
8 Sep	14	Vt Buxton	26 Jan	31	E of Clarendon	1 Jan	51	E. Jansen
20 Nov	20	Prince Arthur of Connaught	5 Apr	37	Sir P. Duncan	25 Nov	59	C. Swart

The Union of South Africa became an independent republic outside the British Commonwealth on 31 May 61.

Tanganyika 1961–62

9 Dec	61	Sir R. Turnbull
9 Dec	*62*	*Declared Republic*

Trinidad and Tobago 1962–76

31 Aug	62	Sir S. Hochoy
31 Jan	73	Sir E. Clarke
1 Aug	*76*	*Declared Republic*

Tuvalu 1978–

1 Oct	78	(Sir) P. Teo
1 Feb	86	Sir T. Leupena
1 Oct	90	(Sir) T. Lauti
28 Nov	93	(Sir) T. Sione

Uganda 1962–63

9 Oct	62	Sir F. Crawford
9 Oct	*63*	*Declared Republic*

West Indies 1957–62

10 May	57	Ld Hailes
Feb	*62*	*Federation dissolved*

SOURCES: – C. Cook and J. Paxton, *Commonwealth Political Facts; Statesman's year-book* (1900–).

XVII

INTERNATIONAL RELATIONS

Major Treaties and Documents Subscribed to by Britain since 1900[1]

30 Jan 02	Anglo-Japanese Alliance
8 Apr 04	Anglo-French Entente
31 Aug 07	Anglo-Russian Entente
18 Mar 15	Anglo-Russian Agreement over Constantinople
25 Apr 15	Treaty of London (Italy)
May 16	Sykes-Picot Agreement (Middle East)
31 Oct 17	Balfour Declaration (Palestine)
28 Jun 19	Treaty of Versailles (Germany) and League of Nations Covenant[2]
10 Sep 19	Treaty of St Germain (Austria)
27 Nov 19	Treaty of Neuilly (Bulgaria)
9 Feb 20	Spitzbergen Treaty (status and sovereignty of Spitzbergen Archipelago)
4 Jun 20	Treaty of Trianon (Hungary)
10 Aug 20	Treaty of Sèvres (Turkey)
6 Dec 21	Articles of Agreement for an Irish Peace
13 Dec 21	Washington Four Power Treaty (Pacific)
6 Feb 22	Washington Nine Power Treaty (China)
6 Feb 22	Washington Five Power Treaty (Naval)
23 Aug 23	Treaty of Lausanne (Middle East and the Straits)
17 Jun 25	Geneva Protocol on the use of Asphyxiating and Poisonous Gases
15 Oct 25	Locarno Pact
27 Aug 28	General Pact for the Renunciation of War (Briand-Kellogg)
22 Apr 30	London Naval Treaty
18 Jun 35	Anglo-German Naval Agreement
25 Mar 36	London Naval Treaty
20 Jul 36	Montreux Agreement (Straits)
7 Aug 36	Non-Intervention Agreement (Spain)
26 Aug 36	Anglo-Egyptian Treaty
29 Sep 38	Munich Agreement
31 Mar 39	Franco-British Guarantee to Poland
13 Apr 39	British Guarantee to Roumania and Greece
12 May 39	British Guarantee to Turkey
25 Aug 39	Anglo-Polish Agreement of Mutual Assistance
14 Aug 41	Atlantic Charter
23 Feb 42	Anglo-American Aid Mutual Agreement (Lend-Lease 'Master Agreement')
26 May 42	Anglo-Soviet Treaty
22 Jul 44	Bretton Woods Agreement (International Finance)
7 Dec 44	Chicago Convention on International Civil Aviation
11 Feb 45	Yalta Agreement
26 Jun 45	United Nations Charter[3]
2 Aug 45	Potsdam Agreement
16 Oct 45	Institution of the Food and Agriculture Organisation
6 Dec 45	Anglo-American Financial Agreement
9 Feb 47	Peace Treaties with Italy, Hungary, Roumania, Bulgaria, and Finland
17 Mar 48	Brussels Treaty Organisation
16 Apr 48	Organisation for European Economic Co-operation
6 Jul 48	Economic Co-operation Agreement (Marshall Aid)

[1] See also the section on the Commonwealth (pp.451–63) and on Britain and Europe (pp. 471–7).
[2] The *International Labour Organisation* (I.L.O) was created by the Treaty of Versailles, as a semi-autonomous organisation association with the League of Nations. on 16 Dec 20 a statute was drawn up for the establishment of the *Permanent Court of International Justice* at the Hague. The Hague Court had its preliminary session on 30 Jan 22. It was dissolved by resolution of the League Assembly in Apr 1946.
[3] The Charter made provision for the continuance of the *International Court of Justice* at the Hague. The I.L.O continued to function as one of the specialised agencies of the United Nations. (Among the other subsidiary organisations were F.A.O., U.N.E.S.C.O., W.H.O., I.M.F., etc see *The Statesman's Year-Book*, pp. 10–23, for a brief summary of the organisations and their member countries).

4 Apr 49	North Atlantic Treaty Organisation (Nato)
5 May 49	Council of Europe
12 Aug 49	Red Cross Convention on the protection of civilians in wartime
4 Nov 50	Convention for the protection of Human Rights and Fundamental Freedom (U.N. Declaration on Human Rights)
28 Nov 50	Colombo Plan (South and South-East Asia)
8 Sep 51	Treaty of Peace with Japan
20 Jul 54	Geneva Conventions on Indo-China
8 Sep 54	South-East Asia Defence Treaty (Seato)
3 Oct 54	London Nine Power Agreement (European security and integration)
23 Oct 54	Western European Union (formerly Brussels Treaty Organisation)
21 Dec 54	European Coal and Steel Community (Britain made an agreement of association). Community formed on 18 Apr 51.
4 Apr 55	Special agreement whereby Britain joined the Baghdad Pact (defence). (Pact signed 24 Feb 55).
5 May 55	Bonn/Paris Conventions terminating the Occupation Regime in West Germany
15 May 55	Austrian State Treaty (occupation ended and declaration of neutrality)
29 Jul 57	International Atomic Energy Agency
29 Apr 58	Law of the Sea Convention (Continental Shelf)
4 Feb 59	European Atomic Energy Community (Euratom). Britain made an agreement of association. (Euratom formed 1 Jan 58)
21 Aug 59	Central Treaty Organisation (Cento). Formerly the Baghdad Pact
20 Nov 59	European Free Trade Association
31 May 59	Antarctic Treaty
14 Dec 60	Organisation for Economic Co-operation and Development (formerly Organisation for European Economic Cooperation)
18 Apr 61	Vienna Convention on Diplomatic Relations
30 Sep 62	Convention on the High Seas
6 Apr 63	Polaris Sales Agreement with the U.S.A.
5 Aug 63	Test-ban Treaty
30 Aug 63	European Space Research Organisation
9 Mar 64	European Fisheries Convention
20 Aug 64	INTELSAT agreement (interim arrangements for a global commercial communications satellite system)
27 Jan 67	Outer Space Treaty
25 Aug 67	'Hotline' Agreement with U.S.S.R.
22 Apr 68	Agreement on the Rescue and Return of Astronauts and Space Vehicles
1 Jul 68	Nuclear Non-Proliferation Treaty
13 Aug 70	Ratification by U.K. of the Hague Convention on the Pacific Settlement of International Disputes (originally signed 29 Jul 1889)
11 Feb 71	Treaty on prohibition of weapons of mass destruction on sea-bed
20 Aug 71	Revised INTELSAT Agreement and INTELSAT operating Agreement
3 Sep 71	Quadripartite Agreement on Berlin
22 Jan 72	Treaty of Accession to European Economic Community and European Atomic Energy Community
10 Apr 72	Convention on the Prohibition of the Development, Production and Stockpiling of Bacteriological (Biological) and Toxic Weapons
9 Nov 72	Quadripartite Declaration on the entry of the Federal Republic of Germany and the German Democratic Republic into the U.N.
2 Feb 75	Lome Convention (E.E.C. with 46 African, Caribbean and Pacific Territories)
1 Aug 75	Final Act of Conference on Security and cooperation in Europe (Helsinki Conference)
20 May 76	International (U.N.) Covenants on Economic and Social Rights and on Civil and Political Rights
18 May 77	Convention on the Prohibition of military or any other hostile use of environmental modification techniques
21 Dec 79	Lancaster House agreement between Britain and the leaders of the main parties in Zimbabwe-Rhodesia.
19 Dec 84	Hong Kong treaty between Britain and China signed in Peking.
17 Feb 86	Single European Act.
17 Feb 92	Maastricht Treaty on European Union agreed.
12 Jun 92	Rio biodiversity Treaty.
1 Jan 93	Completion of single market.
15 Apr 94	New Protocols to General Agreement on Tariffs and Trade.

League of Nations, 1919–1946

Britain was a founder member of the League of Nations. Between 1919 and 1922 the British Government conducted its relations with the League through its cabinet secretariat. After 1922 the Foreign Office was responsible for British representation at the League. A member of the Government was generally deputed to act as British representative at meetings of the League. No permanent national delegation stayed at Geneva. A. Eden was the only Minister appointed officially for League of Nations Affairs (7 Jun–22 Dec 35). Vt Cranborne was Parliamentary Under-Secretary at the Foreign Office with special responsibility for League of Nations Affairs from 6 Aug 35 until 20 Feb 38. The League was formally dissolved in 1946 although in practice it ceased to meet during the war.

United Nations, 1946–

Britain was one of the original signatories of the Charter of the United Nations. Since 1946 the British Government has had a permanent representative at the United Nations in New York. In addition, a Minister of State at the Foreign Office has usually been given special responsibility for United Nations affairs. From 1964 to 1970 the permanent representative was a Minister of State at the Foreign Office.

Foreign Affairs Pressure Groups

The League of Nations Union (1920–45) and the United Nations Association (1945–) have provided nationwide forums for the discussion of foreign affairs. Other bodies concerned with the country's international involvements include the Royal Institute of International Affairs (Chatham House) (1920), the European Movement (1949), Amnesty International (1960) and the Campaign for Nuclear Disarmament (1958).

British Ambassadors to Leading Powers, 1900–

Austria-Hungary (–1914)

1896	Sir H. Rumbold	1 Nov 08	Sir F. Cartwright	12 Aug 14	*War declared by*
9 Sep 00	Sir F. Plunkett	1 Nov 13	Sir M. de Bunsen		*G.B. on Austria-*
7 May 05	Sir W. Goschen				*Hungary*

France

1896	Sir E. Monson	24 Apr 37	Sir E. Phipps	11 Feb 65	Sir P. Reilly
1 Jan 05	Sir F. Bertie (Ld)	1 Nov 39	Sir R. Campbell	17 Sep 68	(Sir) C. Soames
19 Apr 18	E of Derby	24 Jun 40	*Diplomatic mission*	13 Nov 72	Sir E. Tomkins
27 Nov 20	Ld Hardinge of		*withdrawn*	8 Dec 75	Sir N. Henderson
	Penhurst	23 Oct 44	A. Duff Cooper	20 Apr 79	Sir R. Hibbert
31 Dec 22	M of Crewe	9 Jan 48	Sir O. Harvey	4 Mar 82	Sir J. Fretwell
30 Jul 28	Sir W. Tyrrell (Ld)	13 Apr 54	Sir G. Jebb	22 Jun 87	Sir E. Fergusson
17 Apr 34	Sir G. Clerk	11 Apr 60	Sir P. Dixon	29 Jan 93	Sir C. Mallaby

Germany

1895	Sir F. Lascelles	12 Oct 26	Sir R. Lindsay		*(Military Governors)*
1 Nov 08	Sir W. Goschen	1 Aug 28	Sir H. Rumbold	1945	Sir B. Montgomery
4 Aug 14	*War declared by*	2 Aug 33	Sir E. Phipps	1946	Sir S. Douglas
	G.B. on Germany	29 Apr 37	Sir N. Henderson	1947	Sir B. Robertson
10 Jan 20	Ld Kilmarnock	3 Sep 39	*War declared by*		
	(ch. d'aff.)		*G.B. on Germany*		
29 Jun 20	Ld D'Abernon				

(*British High Commissioners*)

1949	Sir B. Robertson
1950	Sir I. Kirkpatrick
1953	Sir F. Hoyer Millar

(*Ambassadors to West Germany*)

5 May 55	Sir F. Hoyer Millar
7 Feb 57	Sir C. Steel
15 Feb 63	Sir F. Roberts
15 May 68	Sir R. Jackling
25 Jul 72	Sir N. Henderson
30 Sep 75	Sir O. Wright

17 Mar 81	Sir J. Taylor
1 Sep 84	Sir J. Bullard
20 Mar 88	Sir C. Mallaby
17 Jan 93	(Sir) N. Broomfield

Italy

1898	Sir P. Currie (Ld)
17 Jan 03	Sir F. Bertie
1 Jan 05	Sir E. Egerton
1 Dec 08	Sir J. Rennell Rodd
21 Oct 19	Sir G. Buchanan
25 Nov 21	Sir R. Graham
26 Oct 33	Sir E. Drummond (E of Perth)
1 May 39	Sir P. Loraine

11 Jun 40	*War declared by Italy on G.B.*
5 Apr 44	Sir N. Charles
	(1944, *High Commissioner,* 1945, *Representative of H.M. Government with the personal rank of Ambassador*)
9 Oct 47	Sir V. Mallet
12 Nov 53	Sir A. Clarke

19 Sep 62	Sir J. Ward
17 Dec 66	Sir E. Shuckburgh
16 Sep 69	Sir P. Hancock
14 Oct 76	Sir A. Campbell
12 Jul 79	Sir R. Arculus
1 Mar 83	Ld Bridges
3 Dec 87	Sir D. Thomas
14 Nov 89	Sir S. Egerton
5 Jul 92	Sir P. Fairweather

Russia (U.S.S.R.)

1898	Sir C. Scott
28 Apr 04	Sir C. Hardinge (Ld)
10 Feb 06	Sir A. Nicolson
23 Nov 10	Sir G. Buchanan
1917	*Diplomatic mission withdrawn*
1 Feb 24	Sir R. Hodgson (ch. d'aff.)
3 Jun 27	*Suspension of diplomatic relations*
7 Dec 29	Sir E. Ovey

24 Oct 33	Vt Chilston
19 Jan 39	Sir W. Seeds
12 Jun 40	Sir S. Cripps
4 Feb 42	Sir A. Kerr (Ld Inverchapel)
17 May 46	Sir M. Peterson
22 Jun 49	Sir D. Kelly
18 Oct 51	Sir A. Gascoigne
1 Oct 53	Sir W. Hayter
19 Feb 57	Sir P. Reilly
29 Apr 60	Sir F. Roberts
27 Nov 62	Sir H. Trevelyan

27 Aug 65	Sir G. Harrison
3 Oct 68	Sir D. Wilson
9 Sep 71	Sir J. Killick
13 Nov 73	Sir T. Garvey
18 Jan 76	(Sir) H. Smith
1 Apr 78	(Sir) C. Keeble
16 Sep 82	Sir I. Sutherland
18 Jul 85	Sir B. Cartledge
23 May 88	Sir R. Braithwaite
3 Jun 92	Sir B. Fall

Turkey

1898	Sir N. O'Conor
1 Apr 08	Sir G. Barclay (*Min. plen. ad. int.*)
1 Jul 08	Sir G. Lowther
10 Oct 13	Sir L. Mallet
5 Nov 14	*War declared by G.B. on Turkey*
1 Nov 20	Sir H. Rumbold
2 Feb 24	(Sir) R. Lindsay
(*H.M. Representative*)	
1 Mar 25	Sir R. Lindsay

(*Ambassador*)	
12 Nov 26	Sir G. Clerk
16 Dec 33	Sir P. Loraine
25 Feb 39	Sir H. Knatchbull-Hugessen
29 Sep 44	Sir M. Peterson
10 May 46	Sir D. Kelly
20 Apr 49	Sir N. Charles
6 Dec 51	Sir K. Helm
13 Jan 54	Sir J. Bowker
15 Nov 58	Sir B. Burrows

7 Mar 63	Sir W. Allen
16 Mar 67	Sir R. Allen
8 Feb 73	Sir H. Phillips
15 Jun 77	Sir D. Dodson
30 Jan 80	Sir P. Laurence
28 Feb 83	(Sir) M. Russell
1 Nov 86	(Sir) T. Dault
23 Oct 92	J. Goulden

U.S.A.

1893	Sir J. Pauncefote (Ld)
4 Jun 02	(Sir) M. Herbert
23 Oct 03	Sir M. Durand
3 Feb 07	J. Bryce
19 Apr 13	Sir A. Spring-Rice
1 Jan 18	E of Reading
25 Mar 20	Sir A. Geddes
2 Feb 24	Sir E. Howard

11 Mar 30	Sir R. Lindsay
29 Aug 39	M of Lothian
24 Jan 41	Vt Halifax (E of)
23 May 46	Ld Inverchapel
22 May 48	Sir O. Franks
31 Dec 52	Sir R. Makins
2 Nov 56	Sir H. Caccia
18 Oct 61	Sir W. Ormsby-Gore (Ld Harlech)

6 Apr 65	Sir P. Dean
21 Feb 69	J. Freeman
4 Jan 71	E of Cromer
3 Mar 74	Sir P. Ramsbotham
21 Jul 77	P. Jay
9 Jul 79	Sir N. Henderson
2 Sep 82	Sir O. Wright
28 Aug 86	Sir A. Acland
20 Aug 91	Sir R. Renwick

North Atlantic Council

18 Aug	53	Sir C. Steel	15 Nov	66	Sir B. Burrows	15 Feb	82	Sir J. Graham
7 Feb	57	Sir F. Roberts	17 Apr	70	Sir E. Peck	30 Jun	86	(Sir) M. Alexander
20 Oct	60	Sir P. Mason	17 Oct	75	Sir J. Killick	25 Jan	91	(Sir) J. Weston
7 Jan	63	Sir E. Shuckburgh	14 Sep	79	Sir C. Rose			

The United Nations

1 Feb	46	Sir A. Cadogan	15 Nov	64	Ld Caradon	9 Sep	79	Sir A. Parsons
27 Jun	50	Sir G. Jebb	4 Sep	70	Sir C. Crowe	17 Aug	82	Sir J. Thomson
13 Mar	54	Sir P. Dixon	7 Aug	73	Sir D. Maitland	29 May	87	Sir C. Tickell
7 Sep	60	Sir P. Dean	25 Mar	74	I. Richard	7 Sep	90	Sir D. Hannay

SOURCES: – *United Nations Year-books, 1946–; Foreign Office List 1953–66; Diplomatic Service List 1967–.*

Among the major works on international relations since 1900 are: A.J.P. Taylor, *Struggle for Mastery in Europe, 1848–1918* (1954); C.R.M.F. Crutwell, *A History of the Great War, 1914–18* (1936); E.H. Carr, *International Relations between the Two World Wars* (1947); E.H. Carr, Twenty years' *Crisis* (1947); G.F. Hudson, *The Far East in World Politics* (1939); W.M. Joran, *Great Britian, France and the German Problem, 1919–39* (1943); A.J.P. Taylor, *Origins of the Second World War* (1961); J.W. Wheeler-Bennett, *Munich: Prologue to Tragedy* (1948); A. Wolfers, *Britain and France between the two wars* (1940); Sir L. Woodward, *British Foreign Policy in the Second World War* (1962); W. McNeill, *American, Britain and Russia: Their Co-operation and Conflict 1941–46* (1953); F.S. Northedge, *The Troubled Giant, Britain among the Great Powers 1916–1939* (1974); J. Frankel, *British Foreign Policy 1945–73* (1975); W. Wallace, *The Foreign Policy Process in Britain* (1976).

Among the main works on Britain and the international organisations are: F.P. Walters, *History of the League of Nations* (2 vols. 1951); G.L. Goodwin, *Britain and the United nations* (1957); and A.H. Robertson, *European Institutions* (1966).

The Royal Institute of International Affairs has published the *Survey of Internal Affairs* annually since 1920. since 1915 the texts of major public documents have been printed in the *Annual Register*. For reference only, see *The Statesman's Year-book*, and the *Year Book of International Organisations, 1951–*.

XVIII

BRITAIN AND EUROPE

A Chronology of Events

17 Mar 48   Treaty signed establishing Western European Union
7 May 48   Churchill's speech at Hague Congress leads to formation of European Movement
5 May 49   Council of Europe established at Strasbourg
9 May 50   Schuman Plan launched leading to establishment of European Coal and Steel Community
30 Aug 54   Final abandonment of Pleven Plan for European Defence Community
2 Jun 55   Messina meeting at which Economic Community negotiations begin (British observer withdrawn Nov 55)
25 Mar 57   Treaty of Rome signed by the Six establishes E.E.C. and Euratom
20 Nov 59   EFTA established following failure to agree with E.E.C. on free-trade area
31 Jul 61   Conservative Government initiates negotiations to join E.E.C.
14 Jan 62   E.E.C. agrees Common Agricultural Policy
14 Jan 63   General de Gaulle vetoes British entry
29 Jan 66   'Luxembourg Compromise' preserves veto on issues of 'vital national interest'.
1 Jan 67   Merger treaty comes into effect creating common institutions for the the European communities (E.C.S.C., E.E.C., and Euratom)
2 May 67   Labour Government announces intention to apply following winter exploratory talks
27 Nov 67   General de Gaulle delivers second veto
1 Dec 69   Hague E.C. summit agrees in principle to open negotiations for British entry
8 Jun 70   E.C. invites Britain to apply and negotiations start on 30 Jun
7 Jul 71   White Paper (Cmnd 4715) sets out agreement reached on almost all major points
28 Oct 71   Parliament endorses (by 356 to 244) Decision in principle to join on the terms negotiated
22 Jan 72   Treaty of Accession signed
17 Oct 72   Royal Assent to European Communities Act
1 Jan 73   Britain becomes member of E.C.
1 Apr 74   'Renegotiation' of British membership opened at Brussels
11 Mar 75   'Renegotiation' concluded at Dublin meeting of E.C. Heads of Government
9 Apr 75   Parliament endorses (by 396 to 170) 'renegotiation'
5 Jun 75   Britain votes 67.2% 'Yes' in Referendum on continued E.C. membership
7 Jul 75   Labour party delegates take seats in European Parliament for first time
29 Jun 76   Foreign ministers agree to start negotiations with Greece
13 Jul 76   Heads of Governments agree to 410 seat Parliament with direct elections in 1978
6 Jan 77   R. Jenkins becomes first British President of Commission
7 Jul 77   House of Commons gives Second Reading to European Elections Bill 394–147. Vote repeated in new session Nov 77, 381–98
13 Dec 77   Proportional representation for European elections defeated 319–222
31 Dec 77   Transitional period for U.K. ends
7 Apr 78   Copenhagen summit Decides on Jun 79 for first Direct Elections to European Parliament
5 May 78   Royal Assent to European Elections Bill
6 Dec 78   Brussels summit approves European Monetary System (commenced 12 Mar 79) but Britain does not participate
4 May 79   Conservatives under Mrs Thacher win U.K.election
7 Jun 79   60 Con; 17 Lab; 4 Other U.K. members elected to European Parliament
2 Dec 79   Dublin summit: Mrs Thatcher asks for her money back
14 Dec 79   European Parliament rejects the Community budget for spending too much on agriculture and not enough on the Regional and Social funds
18 May 80   E.C. states impose economic sanctions against Iran in support of the United States
30 May 80   Agreement is reached among E.C. foreign ministers in dispute over Britain's budget contribution (Britain gets 2/3 rebate for three years). The Commission is asked to report on long-term reform (the Mandate)
6 Jan 81   Greece enters the Community. New Commission takes office under Gaston Thorn
27 Nov 81   London summit of E.C. leaders fails to reach agreement on the Commission's Mandate report. Britain's hopes of getting a long-term solution to her budget problems fade
2 Apr 82   Argentina invades the Falklands. The EEC states swiftly back Britain in a programme of economic sanctions against Argentina

18 May 82	The British veto over farm price increases is overruled in the Agriculture Council, but France states that Luxembourg Compromise still stands
24 Dec 82	European Parliament rejects supplementary budgets containing British and West German rebates
9 Jun 83	Mrs Thatcher's Government returned with an increased majority
3 Oct 83	Labour make withdrawal 'an option' rather than a certainty should Labour Government be returned
20 Dec 83	The European Parliament freezes British and West German rebates again after the failure of the Athens summit to come to a long-term solution to the budget problem
14 Jun 84	Second direct elections to the European Parliament. Conservatives lose 15 seats: Con. 45, Lab. 32, SNP 1
14 Jun 84	Commmission publishes Cockfield White Paper on completing Single Market by 31 Dec 92
29 Jun 84	At Milan Summit U.K., Danish and Portugese veto overridden on calling an intergovernmental conference to reform treaties
26 Jun 84	British Budget settlement agreed at Fontainebleau
6 Jan 85	New Commission takes office under Jacques Delors
3 Dec 85	Luxembourg summit agrees Single European Act
1 Jan 86	Spain and Portugal join Community
11 Jun 87	Mrs Thatcher wins third U.K. election
1 Jul 87	Single European Act comes into force
20 Sep 88	Mrs.Thatcher criticises European integration in Bruges speech
6 Jan 89	Second Delors Commission takes office
15 Jun 89	Third direct elections to the European Parliament.Conservatives lose 13 seats: Con.32, Lab 45, SNP 1.
9 Nov 89	Fall of Berlin Wall.
8 Dec 89	Intergovernmental Conference convened for December 1991. 11 states adopt Social Charter.
3 Oct 90	German Unification takes place.
8 Oct 90	Britain joins Exchange Rate Mechanism at 2.95 Dm to £.
28 Oct 90	Rome Summit leaves Mrs Thacher isolated on monetary union, provoking Sir G.Howe to resign from U.K.cabinet
28 Nov 90	J.Major replaces Mrs Thatcher as PM
10 Dec 91	Maastricht Summit endorses IGC proposals
9 Apr 92	Conservatives win fourth successive U.K. election
2 Jun 92	Danish referendum narrowly rejects Maastricht Treaty
16 Sep 92	'Black Wednesday'. U.K. leaves Exchange Rate
20 Sep 92	French referendum narrowly endorses Maastricht Treaty
4 Nov 92	Commons vote 319–316 for further consideration of Maastricht Bill.
6 Jan 93	Third Delors Commission takes office
17 May 93	Danish referendum endorses Maastricht Treaty
22 Jul 93	U.K. Government position on Social Chapter rejected by Commons, 324–316; wins vote of confidence next day 339–299
1 Nov 93	Maastricht Treaty comes into force. European Community become European Union
29 Mar 94	Agreement on enlargement of Community by admitting Austria, Finland, Norway and Sweden
9 Jun 94	First direct elections to European Parliament. Con. lose seats; Con. 18, Lab. 62, Lib.D. 2, SNP 2

Summits 1975–

Meetings of European Heads of Governemnt occurred quite frequently but on an ad hoc basis until 1975. Since 1975 there has always been at least one 'European Council' during each member state's six-month Presidency of the Council of Ministers. The following summits have taken place since the United Kingdom joined the Community in 1973.

14–15 Dec 73	Copenhagen	29–30 Nov 76	The Hague	4–5 Dec 78	Brussels
9–10 Dec 74	Paris	25–26 Mar 77	Rome	12–13 Mar 79	Paris
10–11 Mar 75	Dublin	29–30 Jun 77	*London	21–22 Jun 79	Strasbourg
1–2 Dec 75	Rome	5–6 Dec 78	Brussels	29–30 Nov 79	Dublin
13–15 Jun 76	Brussels	7–8 Apr 78	Copenhagen	27–28 Apr 80	Luxembourg

* UK Presidency

12–13 Jun 80	Venice	3–4 Dec 84	Dublin	25–26 Jun 90	Dublin II
1–2 Dec 80	Luxembourg	29–30 Mar 85	Brussels	27–28 Oct 90	Rome I
23–24 Mar 81	Maastricht	28–29 Jun 85	Milan	14–15 Dec 90	Rome II
29–30 Jun 81	Luxembourg	2–3 Dec 85	Luxembourg	28–29 Jun 91	Luxembourg
26–27 Nov 81	*London	26–27 Jun 86	The Hague	9–10 Dec 91	Maastricht
29–30 Mar 82	Brussels	5–6 Dec 86	*London	26–27 Jun 92	Lisbon
28–29 Jun 82	Brussels	23–24 Jun 87	Brussels	16 Oct 92	*Birmingham
3–4 Dec 82	Copenhagen	4–5 Dec 87	Copenhagen	11–12 Dec 92	*Edinburgh
21–23 Mar 83	Brussels	27–28 Jun 88	Hanover	2–0–22 Jun 93	Copenhagen
17–19 Jun 83	Stuttgart	2–3 Dec 88	Rhodes	29 Oct 93	Brussels
4–6 Dec 83	Athens	26–27 Jun 89	Madrid	10–11 Dec 93	Brussels
19–20 Jun 84	Brussels	8–9 Dec 89	Strasbourg	24–25 Jun 94	Corfu
14–17 Jun 84	Fontainebleau	28 Apr 90	Dublin I	15 Jul 94	Brussels

* UK Presidency

European Organisations with British Membership

Western European Union (W.E.U.), 1947–

The U.K., France, the Netherlands, Belgium and Luxembourg signed a 50 year treaty in Brussels, 17 Mar 48, for collaboration in economic, cultural and social matters and for collective self-defence. Western Union's defence functions were formally transferred to NATO 20 Dec 50. In 1954 Italy and West Germany were invited to join and W.E.U. was formally inaugurated 6 May 55. Its social and cultural functions were transferred to the Council of Europe 1 Jul 60 but the W.E.U. Council continued to hold regular consultative meetings.

European Free Trade Association (ETA), 1960–72

After failure to agree on a Free Trade Area with the European Economic Community in 1959 Britain joined with Austria, Denmark, Norway, Portugal, Sweden and Switzerland in EFTA under the Stockholm Convention, 20 Nov 59 signed in May 1960. Iceland joined EFTA 27 Mar 70 and Finland became an Associate on 27 Mar 61. All inter-EFTA tariffs were removed by 31 Dec 67, three years earlier than planned. Britain and Denmark left EFTA 1 Jan 73 on joining the Common Market but on 27 Jul 72 the remaining EFTA countries had signed Free Trade Agreements with the E.E.C. and by 1 Jul 77 there was a complete free trade area between E.E.C. and EFTA.

Council of Europe, 1949–

Following the 1948 Congress of Europe at the Hague, the Council of Europe came into being in May 1949. Its founder members were Belgium, Denmark, France, Ireland, Italy, Luxembourg, the Netherlands, Norway, Sweden and the U.K. Turkey and Greece joined later in 1949, Iceland in 1950, West Germany in 1951, Austria in 1956, Cyprus in 1961, Switzerland in 1963 and Malta in 1965. It is run by a Committee of Ministers and Consultative Assembly (147 members, 18 from U.K.). The Council of Europe aims to foster European co-operation in every field and about 80 Conventions have been concluded, ranging from extradition rules to equivalence of degrees. One of its main achievements was the European Convention on Human Rights signed in 1950 (with violations examinable by the European Court of Human Rights set up in 1959).

European Court of Human Rights, 1959–

Britain has been involved in a number of cases brought under the European Convention of Human Rights. In the following cases some or all of the complainant's argument has been found proved against the British authorities.

21 Feb 75	Golder (Prisoner: Access to a solicitor)
18 Jan 78	Ireland (Internment and interrogation in N. Ireland)
25 Apr 78	Tyrer (Isle of Man: corporal punishment)
26 Apr 79	Sunday Times (Press freedom: Contempt of Court in Thalidomide case)
13 Aug 81	Young, James and Webster (Closed shop)
22 Oct 81	Dudgeon (Homosexuality in N. Ireland)
5 Nov 81	X (Review of mental patient's detention)
25 Feb 82	Campbell and Cosans (Corporal punishment in schools)
25 Mar 83	Silver and others (Censorship of prisoners' correspondence)
28 Jun 84	Campbell and Fell (Prison visitors: conduct of disciplinary proceedings)
2 Aug 84	Malone (Telephone tapping)
28 May 85	Abdulaziz, Cabales, & Balkanadali (Sex discrimination in immigration law)
24 Nov 86	Gillow (Residence rules in Guernsey)
2 Mar 87	Weeks (Re-detention of prisoner released on licence)
8 Jul 87	O., H., W., B., and R. (Access to children in local authority care)
27 Apr 88	Boyle and Rice (Prisoners' letters and visits)
29 Nov 88	Brogan and others (Length of detention under terrorism law)
7 Jul 89	Gaskin (Access to personal records)
7 Jul 89	Soering (Extradition to USA on murder charge)
28 Mar 90	Granger (Legal aid for prisoner's appeal)
30 Aug 90	Fox, Campbell & Hartley (Detention in N. Ireland)
30 Aug 90	McCallum (Prisoner's letters)
25 Oct 90	Thynne, Wilson & Gunnell (Discretionary life sentences)
26 Nov 91	*Observer* & others, *Guardian* & others (Spycatcher)
26 Nov 91	*Sunday Times* (No. 2) (Spycatcher)
25 Mar 92	Campbell (Censorship of prisoner's correspondence with solicitor)
26 Oct 93	Darnell (Medical discipline – length of proceedings)

In all but one of the above cases the British Government undertook to take necessary measures to comply with the Convention. The exception was the Brogan case in 1988, when the Government derogated from the Convention.

European Communities, 1973–

Britain subscribed to the Treaty of Rome 22 Jan 72 and joined the Communities 1 Jan 73. British membership was confirmed in a nationwide Referendum 5 Jun 75 (see p. 220).

European [Economic] Community (E.[E.]C.), 1973–93; European Union (EU), 1993–

The E.E.C. was established 1 Jan 1958 (under the Treaty of Rome 25 Mar 1957) with France, Germany, Italy, Belgium, Holland and Luxembourg as members. It achieved a complete customs union by 1 Jul 1968. On 1 Jan 1973 Britain, Denmark and Ireland joined and, following transitional arrangements, the customs union of the enlarged Community was complete by 1 Jul 1977. Greece joined the Community in January 1981. Spain and Portugal joined in January 1986. It became the European Union when the Maastricht Treaty came into effect on 1 Nov 1993.

The European Commission situated in Brussels (currently comprised of seventeen members, two from each of the larger nations and one each from the smaller ones) initiates all Community laws and is responsible for ensuring that they are put into operation. The laws themselves are primarily made by the Council of Ministers on which the national Minister responsible for the subject under discussion sits. Decisions are sometimes taken unanimously but in certain areas can be made by a weighted majority. Since the Single

European Act and the Maastricht Treaty the European Parliament has had an increased share of law-making power in certain areas. The European Court of Justice has the final say on any dispute relating to the implementation of EU laws. Committees and Sub-committees of the House of Commons and House of Lords scrutinise the work of the European institutions (see p. 194).

The fundamental policies of the European Union stemming from the Treaty of Rome have been the creation of a customs union and its transformation into a single market, the common external trade policy, and the common agricultural policy. However, an increasing number of other policy areas have been developed at European level including regional and social funds, environmental policy, scientific research and development programmes and the move to create economic and monetary union in Europe. The Maastricht Treaty added two other areas of activity to run alongside the main work carried out under the Treaty of Rome. These are a common foreign and security policy and co-operation in justice and law enforcement.

Net U.K. payments to European Community institutions[a]

U.K. Financial Year	Gross Payments	Public Sector Receipts	Negotiated Refunds and Abatements	Total Net Payments
1973–4	200	104	–	96
1974–5	197	232	–	−35
1975–6	370	354	–	16
1976–7	544	320	–	244
1977–8	941	382	–	540
1978–9	1,323	555	–	743[b]
1979–80	1,665	781	–	837
1980–1	1,900	1,022	645	168
1981–2	2,330	1,161	959	103
1982–3	2,820	1,323	774	576
1983–4	3,097	1,885	239	853
1984–5	3,614	1,892	589	977
1985–6	3,745	1,930	823	819
1986–7	5,121	2,557	1,343	1,074
1987–8	4,906	1,958	1,137	1,661
1988–9	5,167	2,400	1,600	1,006
1989–90	5,804	2,035	1,317	2,316
1990–1	6,411	2,388	1,838	2,027
1991–2	6,129	2,757	2,428	705
1992–3	6,970	2,810	1,993	1,898
1993–4	8,961	4,295	2,500	1,778

[a] These figures are on a 'payments' basis – that is, it shows the net payments actually made during U.K. financial years, regardless of the Community budget to which they relate or from which they are financed.
[b] From 1978–9 onwards the net payments column excludes the U.K.'s contribution to multilateral overseas aid.

European Coal and Steel Community (E.C.S.C.), 1973–

E.C.S.C. was established 10 Apr 52 (following Paris Treaty 18 Apr 51) with France, West Germany, Italy and the Benelux countries as members.Britain, Denmark and Ireland joined on 1 Jan 73.

European Atomic Energy Community (Euratom), 1973–

Euratom was established 1 Jan 58 for E.E.C. members to cooperate in the peaceful uses of atomic energy. Britain joined 1 Jan 73 on joining the E.E.C.

European Parliament, 1973–

Under the Treaty of Rome, each member country's Parliament nominated delegates from its own members to serve in a European Parliament which meets monthly in Strasbourg or Luxembourg. Its main functions have been advisory and supervisory. It has to be consulted on the Community Budget and it can, by a two-thirds majority, dismiss the Commissioners en bloc. After the enlargement of the Community in 1973 it had 198 members. The U.K. was entitled to send 36 members but, in the absence of Labour representation, it at first sent only 22 (18 Conservatives, 2 Liberal, 1 Scottish National Party and 1 Independent). After the 1975 Referendum a Labour delegation was selected and until 1979 there were 18 Labour, 16 Conservative, 1 Liberal and 1 Scottish National representative. (26 were M.P:s and 10 peers.)

On 7–10 Jun 1979, on 15–18 Jun 1984, and on 15 to 18 Jun 89 Community-wide elections took place for a directly elected Parliament which expanded by stages from 410 members to 518 members (see pp. 221–2). In 1991 it was decided to expand the Parliament to 567 members. The UK delegation was to rise from 81 to 87 at the 1994 elections. The powers of the Parliament were also increased.

Leaders of the British Party Groups

Conservative		*Labour*	
Jan 73	(Sir) P. Kirk	Jul 75	M. Stewart
Feb 77	G. Rippon	Nov 76	J. Prescott
Jun 79	(Sir) J. Scott-Hopkins	Jun 79	Mrs B. Castle
Jun 82	Sir H.(Ld) Plumb	Jun 85	A. Lomas
Jul 87	Sir C. Prout	Jun 87	D. Martin
Jul 94	Ld Plumb	Jun 88	B. Seal
		Jun 90	G. Ford
		Jun 93	Ms P. Green
		Jun 94	W. David

European Court of Justice, 1973–

This was established under the Treaty of Rome to adjudicate on disputes arising out of the application of the Community treaties. Its regulations are enforceable on all member countries. After 1973 it had 9 judges and 4 advocates-general. With the accession of Spain, Portugal and Greece the Court grew to 12 Judges. It has become increasingly important as the powers of the Community have widened. It has ruled against Britain on numerous occasions, some of which are listed on pp. 310–11.

British Members of European Commission

1 Jan 73	Sir C. Soames	1 Jan 81	C. Tugendhat	1 Jan 89	B. Millan
1 Jan 73	G. Thomson	1 Jan 81	I. Richard	1 Jan 93	Sir L. Brittan
1 Jan 77	R. Jenkins	1 Jan 85	Ld Cockfield	1 Jan 93	B. Millan
	(President)	1 Jan 85	S. Clinton Davies	1 Jan 95	Sir L. Brittan
1 Jan 77	C. Tugendhat	1 Jan 89	Sir L. Brittan	1 Jan 95	N. Kinnock

British Ambassadors to the European Communities (1960–72)

17 Jul 60	Sir A. Tandy	7 Apr 65	Sir J. Marjoribanks	17 Oct 71	(Sir) M. Palliser
18 Apr 63	Sir C. O'Neill	30 May 71	(*post vacant*)		

Ministers with special E.E.C. Responsibilities

(Cabinet Ministers)

19 Sep 57–14 Oct 59	R. Maudling	28 Jul 70–5 Nov 72	G. Rippon
27 Jul 60–20 Oct 63	E. Heath	5 Nov 72–4 Mar 74	J. Davies
7 Jan 67–29 Aug 67	G. Thomson	5 May 79–11 Sep 81	Sir I. Gilmour
19 Jun 70–25 Jul 70	A. Barber	11 Sep 81–5 Apr 82	H. Atkins

(Ministers of State at the Foreign Office)

Mar 74–Aug 76	R. Hattersley		Jan 86–Jul 89	Mrs L.Chalker
Aug 76–Feb 77	D. Owen		Jul 89–Jul 90	F. Maude
Feb 77–May 79	F. Judd		Jul 90–May 93	T. Garel-Jones
May 79–Jun 83	D. Hurd		May 93–Jul 94	D. Heathcoat-Amory
Jun 83–Jan 86	M. Rifkind		Jul 94–	D. Davis

Permanent British Representative to the European Communities

1 Jan 73	(Sir) M. Palliser	5 May 79	(Sir) M. Butler	2 Sep 90	(Sir) J. Kerr
1 Jul 75	Sir D Maitland	14 Oct 85	(Sir) D. Alexander		

British Member of the European Court

1 Jan 73	Ld Mackenzie-Stuart
1 Jan 88	Sir G. Slynn
1 Jan 92	D. Edward

SOURCES.– M.Camps, *Britain and the European Communities, 1955–63* (1964); D. Butler and U. Kitzinger, *The 1975 Referendum* (1976); D. Butler and D. Marquand, *European Elections and British Politics* (1980); D. Butler and P. Jowett, *Party Strategies in Britain: A Study of the 1984 European Elections* (1985). See also *The Times Guides to the European Parliament* (1979, 1984 and 1989).

XIX

ARMED FORCES

Service Chiefs

Royal Navy		Army		Royal Air Force	
First Naval Lord		*Commander in Chief*		*Chief of Air Staff*	
1899	Ld W. Kerr	1895	Vt Wolseley	1918	Sir H. Trenchard
		1900	Ld Roberts (Earl)	1918	Sir F. Sykes
First Sea Lord				1919	Sir H. Trenchard
1904	Sir J. Fisher (Ld)	*Chief of General Staff*		1930	Sir J. Salmond
1910	Sir A. Wilson	1904	Sir N. Lyttelton	1933	Sir G. Salmond
1911	Sir F. Bridgeman	1908	Sir W. Nicholson	1933	Sir E. Ellington
1912	Prince Louis of			1937	Sir C. Newall
	Battenberg	*Chief of Imperial General Staff*		1940	Sir C. Portal
1914	Ld Fisher	1909	Sir W. Nicholson	1946	Sir A. Tedder (Ld)
1915	Sir H. Jackson	1912	Sir J. French	1950	Sir J. Slessor
1916	Sir J. Jellicoe	1914	Sir C. Douglas	1953	Sir W. Dickson[1]
1917	Sir R. Wemyss	1914	Sir J. Wolfe-Murray	1956	Sir D. Boyle
1919	Earl Beatty	1915	Sir A. Murray	1960	Sir T. Pike
1927	Sir C. Madden	1915	Sir W. Robertson	1964	Sir C. Elworthy
1930	Sir F. Field	1918	Sir H. Wilson	1968	Sir J. Grandy
1933	Sir E. Chatfield (Ld)	1922	E of Cavan	1971	Sir D. Spotswood
1938	Sir R. Backhouse	1926	Sir G. Milne	1973	Sir A. Humphrey
1939	Sir D. Pound	1933	Sir A. Montgomery	1976	Sir N. Cameron
1943	Sir A. Cunningham(Ld)		Massingberd	1977	Sir M. Beetham
1946	Sir J. Cunningham	1936	Sir C. Deverell	1982	Sir K. Williamson
1948	Ld Fraser of North Cape	1937	Vt Gort	1985	Sir D. Craig
1951	Sir R. McGrigor	1939	Sir E. Ironside	1988	Sir P. Harding
1955	Earl Mountbatten	1940	Sir J. Dill	1992	Sir M. Graydon
1959	Sir C. Lambe	1941	Sir A. Brooke		
1960	Sir C. John		(Ld Alanbrooke)		
1964	Sir D. Luce	1946	Vt Montgomery	**Defence Staff**	
1966	Sir V. Begg	1948	Sir W. Slim		
1968	Sir M. Le Fanu	1952	Sir J. Harding	*Chief of Defence Staff[1]*	
1970	Sir P. Hill-Norton	1955	Sir G. Templer	1958	Sir W. Dickson
1971	Sir M. Pollock	1958	Sir F. Festing	1959	Earl Mountbatten
1974	Sir E. Ashmore	1963–4	Sir R. Hull	1965	Sir R. Hull
1977	Sir T. Lewin			1967	Sir C. Elworthy
1979	Sir H. Leach			1971	Sir P. Hill-Norton
1982	Sir J. Fieldhouse	*Chief of General Staff*		1973	Sir M. Carver
1985	Sir W. Staveley	1964	Sir R. Hull	1976	Sir A. Humphrey
1989	Sir J. Oswald	1965	Sir J. Cassels	1977	Sir E. Ashmore
1993	Sir B. Bathurst	1968	Sir G. Baker	1979	Sir T. Lewin
		1971	Sir M. Carver	1982	Sir E. Bramall
		1973	Sir P. Hunt	1985	Sir J. Fieldhouse
		1976	Sir R. Gibbs	1988	Sir D. Craig
		1979	Sir E. Bramall	1991	Sir R. Vincent
		1982	Sir J. Stanier	1993	Sir P. Harding
		1985	Sir N. Bagnall	1994	Sir P. Inge
		1988	Sir J. Chapple		
		1992	Sir P. Inge		
		1994	Sir C. Guthrie		

[1] Before the post of Chief of the Defence Staff was established in 1958, Sir W. Dickson acted as Chairman of the Chief of Staffs Committee (1955–58).

Defence Organisation

Committee of Imperial Defence (C.I.D.), 1904–1946

The committee was first established in 1902 on a temporary basis to advise the Prime Minister, as a result of British experience in the Boer War of the need for planning and co-ordination of the Empire's defence forces. The C.I.D. was established permanently in 1904, as a small flexible advisory committee to the Prime Minister. Members were usually cabinet ministers concerned with defence, military leaders, and key civil servants. The Dominions also had representatives sitting on the committee occasionally. The Prime Minister was the chairman of the committee, which had no executive power, but exercised considerable influence. A secretariat was set up to assist the C.I.D., which was later adopted by the cabinet itself. During the First World War the C.I.D. was suspended. Its functions between 1914 and 1919 were taken over by the War Council (Nov 1914), the Dardanelles Committee (May 1915), the War Committee (Nov 1916), and finally the War Cabinet (Dec 1916–Nov 1919). The C.I.D. resumed plenary sessions in 1922. In the 1930s membership of the C.I.D. rose from about 11 to 18, and the committee became unwieldy. This led to the establishment of a Minister for the Co-ordination of Defence (1936–40), who was without a department, but worked through the Committee Secretariat. On the outbreak of the Second World War the C.I.D. was again suspended, and its responsibilities taken over by the War Cabinet. In 1946 the decision to make the suspension permanent was published in a White Paper on the C.I.D. (Cmd. 6923).

Secretaries to the C.I.D. 1904–1946

1904	G. Clarke
1907	Sir C. Ottley
1912	(Sir) M. Hankey[1]
1938	(Sir) H. Ismay (Ld)

Ministry of Defence. The C.I.D. was replaced by a cabinet defence committee, with executive power, and the Ministry of Defence was set up as a regular department on 1 Jan 47. It existed as an administrative body, responsible for liaison between the Service Ministries and co-ordination of defence policy until 31 Mar 64.

On 1 Apr 64 the complete reorganisation of the three Service Departments (Admiralty, War Office and Air Ministry) under the Secretary of State for Defence took place. A Defence Council was also established under the Secretary of State to exercise the powers of command and administrative control previously exercised by the separate Service councils, which became subordinate to it. Further reorganisation on 6 Jan 67 reduced the status of the administrative heads of the three Services from Ministers to Under-Secretaries of State, while creating two new posts: Minister of Defence (Administration) and Minister of Defence (Equipment). In June 1970 further reorganisation of these two posts later reduced them to that of a single Minister of State for Defence. In May 1981 a major reorganisation abolished the three Service Under-Secretaries of State and divided the Ministry of Defence between a Minister of State and Under-Secretary of State for Defence Procurement, and a Minister of State and Under-Secretary of State for Armed Forces. The present membership of the Defence Council consists of the Secretary of State for Defence, the two Ministers of State and their Parliamentary Under-Secretaries, the Chiefs of Defence, Naval, General and Air Staffs, the Chief of Personnel and Logistics, the Chief Scientific Adviser, the Chief Executive of the Procurement Executive and the Permanent Under-Secretary of State.

---

[1] Sir M. Hankey (later Ld Hankey) became the Joint Secretary to the C.I.D. and the Cabinet in 1916, and in 1923 he was also appointed Clerk to the Privy Council.

Defence Pressure Groups

Pressure on the Service Departments and the Cabinet about the nature and scale of forces and armaments has always been informal. But arguments for the expansion of particular services has been sustained by the Navy League (founded 1895) and the Air League (1909). More recently the Institute of Strategic Studies (1958) has provided an influential forum for the discussion of defence questions. See also the Foreign Affairs pressure groups listed on p. 467.

Total Forces Serving[a] (Year ending 31 March)

	1900	1910	1920	1930	1940[b]	1950[b]	1960	1970	1980	1990
Army	661	522	435	333	1,688	360	252	174	159	153
Royal Navy[d]	98	128	133	97	282	135	93	86	64	63
R.A.F.	..	..	28	33	303	193	158	113	90	90
Total	759[c]	650	596	463	2,273[e]	688	503	373	321	312

[a] Men locally enlisted abroad are excluded, except that the figures for the army include those whose documents are held in the U.K.
[b] Including Women's Auxiliaries. The figures for the war years include a number of casualties that had not been reported on the dates to which the figures relate. They also include men and women locally enlisted.
[d] the Navy figure includes Royal Marines.
[e] The total strength of the Armed Forces reached its war-time peak in 1945 with 5,098,100 men and women serving.

Under current defence plans it is envisaged that service strengths will fall by the late 1990s to Army 119,000, Navy 52,000, R.A.F. 70,000.

Total Expenditure on Defence[a] (year ending 31 March) 1900–1960

	1900	1910	1920	1930	1940	1950	1960
Army	43.6	27.2	395.0	40.5	81.9	291.8	428.2
Navy	26.0	35.8	156.5	55.8	69.4	186.8	364.6
Air Force	..	..	52.5	16.8	66.6	201.6	485.1
Total[b]	69.8	63.0	604.0	113.1	626.4[c]	740.7	1475.7

[a] The figures refer to the Exchequer of the U.K. and included Northern Ireland up to 1972 only to the extent that services, taxes, etc., are reserved to the U.K. Parliament.
[b] The discrepancies between the service votes and the totals are due to the expenditures of the Ministries of Defence and Civil Aviation (1950 and 1960), and the Army Ordnance Factories.
[c] Including votes of credit of £408.5 m. Defence expenditure reached its war-time peak in 1944–5 at £5,125.0 m.

SOURCES.–The *Annual Abstract of Statistics*, 1900–; for a brief summary of the statistics. The *Army, Navy and Air Estimates* giving the full figures are published annually as government white papers up to 31 Mar 64. From 1 Apr 64 figures are those given in Ministry of Defence estimates.

Total Expenditure on Defence (year ending 31 March) 1970–90

	1970	1980	1990
Armed Forces Personnel	1,009	3,912	8,099
Equipment	822	3,640	8,536
Other (land, stores etc)	435	1,625	4,120
Total	2,266	9,178	20,755

Conscription

After a long controversy about conscription, H. Asquith announced the introduction of the first Military Service Bill on 5 Jan 16. Military service lapsed in 1919. It was first introduced in peace time on 26 Apr 39. The period of compulsory service was to have been six months, but war intervened. Conscription was extended to women from Dec 1941 until Jan 1947, but few women were called up after Nov 1944. The National Service Act, 1947, provided for the continuation of military service after the war. The period of service was twelve months. It was increased to eighteen months in Dec 1948, and to two years in Sep 1950. A government White Paper published on 5 Apr 571 announced a progressive reduction in the national service intake. No men were to be called up after the end of 1960, so that by the end of 1963 there were no national servicemen left in the forces. (This was slightly modified by the Army Reserves Bill, introduced in 1962.)

Rationing

The first national rationing scheme in this country came into operation on 31 Dec 17, with the rationing of sugar. This was followed in Jul 1918 by national schemes for meat, lard, bacon, ham, butter and margarine. The abolition of rationing began on 28 Jul 18 and was completed on 29 Nov 20. Butter and meat rations were most severely restricted in Apr-May 1918 and sugar in 1919. There was much controversy during the course of World War 1 over the form that rationing should take. National rationing was preceded by local schemes and even after Jul 1918 rationing was, in many cases, wider in extent locally than nationally. The characteristic feature of the World War I scheme was the tie to the retailer of each customer.

When World War II broke out in Sep 1939, prearranged plans for commodity control were at once put into effect. Rationing was introduced on 8 Jan 40 when bacon, butter, and sugar were put under control and extended during the following two years to meat, tea, margarine, lard, jam, marmalade, cheese, eggs, and milk. In Dec 1941 the 'points' system was introduced to ration such items as tinned meat and biscuits and from Jul 1942 sweets and chocolate were rationed under a system of 'personal points'. During the war animal feedstuffs, fertilizers, farm machinery, petrol, domestic coal, clothing and textiles were also rationed. Rationing was at its most stringent, however, in the immediate post-war years. In Jul 46, bread rationing, which in 1939 the Minister of Food had described as 'the last resort of a starving nation', was introduced for the first time ever and this was followed in Nov 1947 by the rationing of potatoes. In Dec 1947 the distribution of nearly all important foods was controlled with the exception of some fresh fruit and vegetables, fish and coffee; the bacon, butter, meat and fats rations were at their lowest ebbs and the basic petrol ration had been suspended altogether. The gradual abolition of rationing began in Apr 1948; it was not completed until the abolition of butter rationing in May 1954, of meat rationing in July 1954 and of coal rationing in 1958. During the Suez crisis of 1956, petrol rationing was re-introduced. It lasted from 17 Dec 56 to 14 May 57.

Principal Military Operations

Boer War, 1899–1902

Following the rejection by the British Government of the Boer ultimatum, the Transvaal and Orange Free State declared war on Britain in October 1899. Major operations against the Boers ended in the summer of 1900, but guerrilla warfare continued. Peace was finally concluded at Vereeniging on 31 May 02.

Costs and Casualties

1. Total Engaged (000s)	2. Killed[a] (000s)	Percentage Col.2 to Col.1	(£m.)
448	22	4.9	217

[a] Killed includes dying of wounds or as prisoners of war

First World War, 1914–1918

4 Aug	14	Britain declares war on Germany	27 Mar	17	Turks defeated at Gaza
12 Aug	14	Britain declares war on Austria-Hungary	6 Apr	17	U.S.A. enters War
23 Aug	14	Retreat from Mons begins	4 Oct	17	British victory at Passchendaele
12 Oct	14	First Battle of Ypres	20 Nov	17	Tanks used in Cambrai victory
20 Jan	15	First Zeppelin Raid on Britain	21 Nov	17	Russia asks for peace
22 Apr	15	Second Battle of Ypres	9 Dec	17	Jerusalem captured by British
25 Apr	15	Gallipoli landing	21 Mar	18	German Somme offensive
6 Sep	15	Bulgaria joins Central Powers	15 Jul	18	Last German offensive
25 Sep	15	British attack at Loos	11 Sep	18	Allies break Hindenburg Line
8 Jan	16	Evacuation of Gallipoli completed	2 Oct	18	British capture Damascus
31 May	16	Battle of Jutland	30 Oct	18	Turkey signs Armistice
1 Jul	16	Battle of the Somme	3 Nov	18	Austria-Hungary signs Armistice
			11 Nov	18	Germany signs Armistice
			28 Jun	19	Treaty of Versailles

Military Costs and Casualties

(Empire figures)

1. Total Engaged	2. Killed[a]	Percentage	Cost (£m.)
9,669,000	947,000	9.8	3,810

[a] Killed includes dying of wounds or as prisoners of war

Intervention in Russia, 1918–1919

British troops landed at Murmansk and Archangel in June and August of 1918. Troops also entered the Transcaucasus in August 1918. The withdrawal of troops from the Transcaucasus was completed by 5 Apr 19; and from Murmansk and Archangel by 28 Sep 19.

Second World War, 1939–1945

1 Sep	39	Germany invades Poland	27 May	41	Bismarck sunk
3 Sep	39	Britain and France declare war	29 May	41	German N. Africa offensive halted
17 Sep	39	Russia invades Poland	22 Jun	41	Germany invades Russia
30 Nov	39	Russia invades Finland	16 Jul	41	British occupy Syria
9 Apr	40	Germany invades Denmark and Norway	18 Nov	41	Second British Libyan offensive
10 May	40	Germany invades Holland and Belgium	7 Dec	41	Japan attacks Pearl Harbour
4 Jun	40	Dunkirk evacuation complete	8 Dec	41	U.S.A. and Britain declare war on Japan
22 Jun	40	France capitulates	9 Dec	41	British relieve Tobruk
10 Jul	40	Italy declares war on Britain	11 Dec	41	Germany and Italy declare war on U.S.A. and vice versa
15 Sep	40	Climax of Battle of Britain	15 Feb	42	Japanese take Singapore
20 Nov	40	Hungary joins axis powers	21 Jan	42	German offensive in Libya
7 Feb	41	British reach Benghazi	30 Jun	42	German held at El Alamein
1 Mar	41	Bulgaria joins axis powers			

19 Aug 42	Dieppe raid	25 Aug 44	Allies enter Paris
23 Oct 42	British attack at El Alamein	17 Sep 44	Arnhem assault
23 Jan 43	British enter Tripoli	16 Dec 44	German Ardennes offensive
12 May 43	Axis surrenders N. Africa	22 Mar 45	Rhine crossing
10 Jul 43	Allies invade Sicily	8 May 45	VE day, final German surrender
3 Sep 43	Allies invade Italy	6 Aug 45	Atomic bomb on Hiroshima
22 Jan 44	Allied landing at Anzio	9 Aug 45	Second atomic bomb on
4 Jun 44	Allies take Rome		Nagasaki
6 Jun 44	D Day landing in Normandy	14 Aug 45	VJ Day Hostilities end
13 Jun 44	V I Bombardment begins	2 Sep 45	Final Japanese surrender signed

Military Costs and Casualties

(Great Britain)

1. *Total engaged* (000s)	2. *Killed[a]* (000s)	*Percentage Col.2 to Col.1*	*Cost* (£m)
5,896	265	4.5	34,423

[a] Killed includes dying of wounds or as prisoners of war

Korean War 1950–1953

Britain declared her support for the United States' action in Korea on 28 Jun 50, following the invasion of South Korea by North Korean troops, and the call for a cease fire by an emergency session of the United Nations Security Council. The intervention of Chinese troops fighting with the North Koreans was confirmed on 6 Nov 50. An armistice was signed between the United Nations and the Communist forces on 27 Jul 53. British casualties in the Korean war were 749 killed (H.C. Deb., 1952–53, Vol. 518, Cols. 221–222). The total expenditure incurred by Britain was about £50m. (H.C. Deb., 1952–53, Vol. 517, Col. 1218).

Suez, 1956

Following the Egyptian nationalisation of the Suez Canal on 26 Jul 56, tension grew in the Middle East. The Israeli army attacked the Egyptians on 29 Oct 56 in the Sinai peninsula. The rejection of a British and French ultimatum by Egypt resulted in a combined British and French attack on Egypt on 1 Nov 56. Operations were halted at midnight on 6–7 Nov 56. On 26 Jan 61 full diplomatic relations were resumed between Britain and Egypt. British casualties were 21 men killed (H.C. Deb., 1956–57, Vol. 561, Col. 36). The military expenditure incurred was about £30m. (H.C. Deb., 1956–57, Vol. 575, Col.51).

Northern Ireland, 1969–

On 14 Aug 69 the Government of Northern Ireland informed the U.K. Government that as a result of the severe rioting in Londonderry it had no alternative but to ask for the assistance of the troops at present stationed in Northern Ireland to prevent a breakdown in law and order. British troops moved into Londonderry that day, and into Belfast on 15 Aug 69. On 19 Aug 69 G.O.C. Northern Ireland assumed overall responsibility for security in the Province.

Costs and Casualties

	Regular Army		U.D.R.[b]		Expenditure	Civilian	RUC
	Strength[a]	Deaths	Strength	Deaths	(£m.)	Deaths	Deaths
1969	7,495	0	..	..	..	11	1
1970	7,170	0	4,008	0	1.5	21	2
1971	13,762	43	6,786	5	6.5	104	11
1972	16,661	103	9,074	24	14	305	17
1973	15,342	58	7,982	8	29	158	13
1974	14,067	28	7,795	7	33	151	15
1975	13,913	14	7,861	6	45	205	11
1976	13,672	14	7,769	15	60	222	23
1977	13,632	15	7,843	14	65	55	14
1978	13,600	14	7,862	7	69	40	10
1979	13,000	38	7,623	10	81	37	14
1980	11,900	8	7,373	8	96	41	9
1981	11,600	10	7,479	13	111	36	21
1982	10,900	21	7,111	7	149	45	12
1983	10,200	5	6,925	10	143	44	19
1984	10,000	9	6,468	10	141	36	9
1985	9,700	2	6,494	4		25	23
1986	10,500	4	6,408	8		37	12
1987	11,400	3	6,531	8		66	16
1988	11,200	21	6,393	12		54	6
1989	11,200	12	6,230	2		39	9
1990	11,500	7	6,043	8		49	12
1991	11,200	5	6,276	8		75	6
1992	12,600	6	n.a.	0		76	3

[a] Figure for Regular Army strength is at 31 Dec up until 1982; 1 Jul thereafter. It does not include any UDR or Royal Irish Regiment personnel.
[b] The Ulster Defence Regiment was formed on 1 Apr 70. The figures include permanent, part-time, male and female members. On 1 Jul 92 the UDR merged with the Royal Irish Rangers to form the Royal Irish Regiment. Up to that date no UDR soldiers had been killed in that year.
[c] After 1984 it becomes impossible to disentangle Northern Ireland military expenditure from Defence accounts in any meaningful way.

SOURCES.– Ministry of Defence and Northern Ireland Office.

Falklands, 1982

On 2 Apr 1982 Argentine forces landed on the Falklands and took over the Islands and South Georgia. An expeditionary force was despatched and on 25 Apr South Georgia was recaptured. British forces landed on West Falkland on 20 May and by 14 Jun Port Stanley was recaptured and all the Argentine forces surrendered. The British forces under Rear-Admiral J. Woodward lost six ships and twenty aircraft. The total casualties were 254 killed and 777 wounded. The cost of the operation from Apr to Jun was estimated at £350m.

Gulf, 1990–91

On 2 Aug 90, Iraqi armed forces invaded and occupied Kuwait. The same day the Security Council of the United Nations passed Resolution 660 demanding unconditional Iraqi withdrawal. US, British and other forces were deployed in Saudi Arabia and the Persian Gulf. On 29 Nov 90 the UN Security Council authorised the use of 'all necessary means' to free Kuwait if the Iraqis failed to withdraw by 15 Jan 91 (Resolution 678). On 16 Jan 91

American, British and other allied planes began an aerial bombardment of Iraq. On 24 Feb 91 Allied ground forces crossed the Iraqi and Kuwaiti borders from Saudi Arabia. On 26 Feb 91 Kuwait City fell to Allied troops and on 28 Feb 91 Allied and Iraqi forces agreed a ceasefire. British forces under Sir P. de la Billiere lost 24 killed and 43 wounded. The total cost was estimated at £2,094 million, although contributions from allies who took no military part in operations amounted to £2,023 million.

SOURCES: *Whitaker's Almanack; First Report on the Defence Estimates by House of Commons Select Committee on Defence, 1992.478*

Major War Commanders

World War I

Allenby, E. 1st Vt (1919). 1861–1936
    Field-Marshal. C-in-C Egyptian Expeditionary Force 1917–19.
Beatty, D. 1st E (1919). 1871–1936
    Admiral of the Fleet. Commanded Grand Fleet 1916–19.
Fisher, J. 1st Ld (1909). 1841–1920
    Admiral of the Fleet. 1st Sea Lord 1914–15.
French, J. 1st E of Ypres (1922). 1852–1925
    Field-Marshal. C-in-C British Expeditionary Force in France 1914–15. C-in-C Home Forces 1916.
Haig, D. 1st E (1919). 1861–1928
    Field-Marshal. Commanding 1st Army 1914–15. C-in-C Expeditionary Forces in France and Flanders 1915–19.
Hamilton, I. Sir (1915). 1853–1947
    General. C-in-C Mediterranean Expeditionary Force 1915.
Jellicoe, J. 1st E (1925). 1859–1935
    Admiral of the Fleet. Commanded Grand Fleet 1914–16.
Plumer, H. 1st Vt (1929). 1857–1932
    Field-Marshal. General Officer Commanding Italian Expeditionary Force 1917–18. 2nd Army British Expeditionary Force 1918–19.
Robertson, W. Sir. 1st Bt (1919). 1860–1933
    Field-Marshal. Chief of Imperial General Staff 1915–18. C-in-C Eastern Command 1918. Great Britain 1918–19. B.A.O.R. 1919–20.
Trenchard, H. 1st Vt (1936). 1873–1956
    Marshal of the RAF. Assistant Commandant Central Flying School 1913–14. G.O.C. Royal Flying Corps in the Field 1915–17. Chief of Air Staff 1918. Commanded Independent Force 1918. Chief of Air Staff 1919–29.
Wilson, H. Sir. 1st Bt (1919). 1864–1922
    Field-Marshal. Assistant Chief of General Staff to Ld French 1914. Commanded 1st Army Corps 1915–16. Eastern Command 1917. British Military Representative Versailles 1917. Chief of Imperial General Staff 1918–22.

World War II

Alanbrooke, 1st Ld (1945). 1st Vt (1946). 1883–1963, Sir A. Brooke.
    Field-Marshal. G.O.C.-in-C Southern Command 1939 and 1940. C of Second Army Corps B.E.F. 1939–40. C-in-C Home Forces 1940–41. Chief of Imperial General Staff 1941–46.

Alexander, H. 1st E (1952). 1891–1969
> Field-Marshal. C-in-C Middle East 1942–43. C-in-C North Africa 1943. C-in-C Allied Armies in Italy 1943–44. Supreme Allied Commander Mediterranean Theatre 1944–45.

Auchinleck, C. Sir. 1884–1981.
> Field-Marshal. C-in-C India 1941 and 1943–47. C-in-C Middle East 1941–42.

Cunningham, A. 1st Vt of Hyndhope (1946). 1883–1962
> Admiral of the Fleet. Ld Commissioner of the Admiralty and Deputy Chief of Naval Staff 1938–39. C-in-C Mediterranean 1939–42. Naval C-in-C Expeditionary Force North Africa 1942. C-in-C Mediterranean 1943. 1st Sea Ld and Chief of Naval Staff 1943–46.

Dill, J. Sir. 1881–1944
> Field-Marshal. Commanded 1st Corps in France 1939–40. Chief of Imperial General Staff 1940. British Representative on Combined Chief of Staffs' Committee in U.S. 1941.

Douglas,W. 1st Ld (1948). 1893–1969
> Marshal of the RAF. C-in-C Fighter Command 1940–43. Air Officer C-in-C Middle East 1943–44. Air Officer C-in-C Coastal Command 1944–45. Air C-in-C British Air Forces of Occupation in Germany 1945–46.

Dowding, H. 1st Ld (1943). 1882–1970
> Air Chief Marshal. Air Officer C-in-C Fighter Command 1936–1940.

Fraser, B. 1st Ld (1946). 1888–1981
> C-in-C Home Fleet 1943–44. C-in-C Eastern Fleet 1944–45.
> Gort, J. 6th Vt (Ireland) (1902). 1st Vt (U.K.) (1945) 1886–1946 Field-Marshal. C-in-C British Expeditionary Force 1939–40. Commanded B.E.F. in withdrawal towards Dunkirk 1940.

Harris, A. Sir. 1st Bt (1953). 1892–1984.
> Marshal of the RAF. Air Officer. C-in-C Bomber Command 1942–45.

Ironside,W. 1st Ld (1941). 1880–1959
> Field-Marshal. C.I.G.S. 1939–40. C-in-C Home Forces 1940.

Leigh-Mallory, T. Sir. 1892–1944
> Air Chief Marshal. Air Officer C-in-C Fighter Command 1942. Air C-in-C Allied Expeditionary Force 1943–44. Lost while flying to take up appointment as Allied Air C-in-C South-East Asia.

Montgomery, B. 1st Vt of Alamein (1946). 1887–1976
> Field-Marshal. Commander 8th Army 1942 in N. Africa, Sicily and Italy. C-in-C British Group of Allied Armies N. France 1944. British Commander Allied Expeditionary Forces in Europe 1944–46.

Mountbatten, L. 1st E of Burma (1947). 1900–1979
> Admiral of the Fleet. Chief of Combined Operations 1942–43. Supreme Allied Command S.E. Asia 1943–46.

Newall, C. 1st Ld (1946). 1886–1963
> Marshal of the RAF. Chief of Air Staff 1937–40. Governor- General and C-in-C New Zealand 1941–46.

Park, K. Sir. 1892–1975
> Air Chief Marshal. Air Officer Commanding RAF Malta 1942–43. Air Officer C-in-C 1944. Allied Air C-in-C South-East Asia Command 1945–6.

Peirse, R. Sir. 1892–1970
> Air Chief Marshal. Air Officer C-in-C Bomber Command 1940–42. Air Officer C-in-C India 1942–43. Allied Air C-in-C South-East Asia Comand 1943–44.

Percival, A. 1887–1966
    Lieutenant-General. G.O.C. Malaya 1941–42.
Portal, C. 1st Vt (1946). 1893–1971
    Marshal of the RAF. Air Officer C-in-C Bomber Command 1940. Chief of the Air Staff 1940–45.
Pound, D. Sir. 1877–1943
    Admiral of the Fleet. C-in-C Mediterranean 1936–39. 1st Sea Lord 1939–43.
Ramsay, B. Sir. 1883–1945
    Admiral. Flag Officer commanding Dover 1939–42. Naval Commander Eastern Task force Mediterranean 1943.
Ritchie, N. Sir. 1897–1984.
    General. Commander of 8th Army, Libya, 1941–42.
Slessor, J. Sir. 1897–1979
    Marshal of the RAF. Air Officer C-in-C Coastal Command 1943–44. C-in-C RAF Mediterranean and Middle East 1944–45.
Slim, W. 1st Vt (1960). 1891–1970
    Field-Marshal. C-in-C Allied Land Forces S.E. Asia 1945–46.
Tedder, A. 1st Ld (1946). 1890–1967
    Marshal of the RAF. Air Officer C-in-C Middle East 1941–43. Air C-in-C Mediterranean Air Command 1943. Deputy Supreme Commander under Gen. Eisenhower 1943–45.
Wavell, A. 1st E (1947). 1883–1950
    Field-Marshal. Formed Middle East Command 1939. C-in-C India 1941. Supreme Commander S.W. Pacific 1941–43.
Wilson, H. 1st Ld (1946). 1881–1964
    Field-Marshal. C-in-C Egypt 1939–41. C-in-C Greece 1941. C-in-C Persia-Iraq Command 1942–43. C-in-C Middle East 1943. Supreme Commander Mediterranean Theatre 1944.

XX

THE PRESS[1]

National Daily Newspapers

The following national newspapers have been published at some time in this century. Those which are now defunct are in parenthesis.

(British Gazette), 5–13 May 1926
Proprietors: His Majesty's Stationery Office. Printed at offices of *Morning Post*.
Policy: Strong opposition to the general strike.
Editor: W. Churchill.

(Daily Chronicle), 1869–1930
Proprietors: E. Lloyd, 1871–1918. Frank Lloyd and family trading as United Newspapers Ltd. Lloyd family parted with their interest in 1918. Bought by D. Lloyd George and associates 1918. Sold to Sir T. Catto and Sir D. Yule, 1926. Bought by Inveresk Paper Co., 1928. Sold and incorporated with *Daily News* as the *News Chronicle*, 1930.
Policy: Liberal.
Editor: W. Fisher, 1899. R. Donald, 1902. E. Perris, 1918–30.

(Daily Citizen), 1912–Jan 1915
Proprietors: Labour Newspapers Ltd.
Policy: Official Labour.
Editor: F. Dilnot, 1912–15.

Daily Express, 1900
Proprietors: A. Pearson, Daily Express (1900) Ltd. Acquired by London Express Newspaper Ltd, 1915. Ld Beaverbrook assumed control in 1916. In 1954 he relinquished it to Beaverbrook Newspapers Ltd and transferred controlling shares to the Beaverbrook Foundations. In 1977 Beaverbrook Newspapers were taken over by Trafalgar House property group (Chairman: V. (Ld) Matthews). In 1985 Express Newspapers were taken over by United Newspapers (Chairman: D. (Ld) Stephens).
Policy: Independent conservative.
Editors: A. Pearson, 1900. R. Blumenfeld, 1902. B. Baxter, 1929. A. Christiansen, 1933. E. Pickering, 1957. R. Wood, 1962. R. Edwards, 1964. D. Marks, 1965. I. MacColl, 1971. A. Burnet, 1974. R. Wright, 1977. D. Jameson, 1977. A. Firth, 1980. C. Ward, 1981. Sir L. Lamb, 1983. (Sir) N. Lloyd 1986.

(Daily Graphic), 1890–1926. 1946–52
Proprietors: Founded by W. L. Thomas. Owned by H. Baines & Co. Amalgamated with *Daily Sketch* in 1926 (Kemsley Newspapers). Appeared as *Daily Sketch and Daily Graphic* 1926–46, as *Daily Graphic* 1946–52, then as *Daily Sketch*.
Policy: Independent conservative.
Editors: H. Hall, 1891. H. White, 1907. W. Ackland, 1909. A. Hutchinson, 1912. A. Netting, 1917. H. Lawton, 1919. E. Tebbutt, 1923. H. Heywood, 1925–26. A. Thornton, 1946. N. Hamilton, 1947. H. Clapp, 1948–52 (*See Daily Sketch*).

(Daily Herald), 1912–1964
Proprietors: Daily Herald Printing and Publishing Society in association with Odhams Press Ltd. Formed Daily Herald (1929) Ltd (Chairman: Ld Southwood). 49% of shares held by T.U.C., 51% by Odhams Press. 1960 new agreement between Odhams Press and T.U.C. 1961 Daily Mirror Newspapers, Ltd take over Odhams Press. T.U.C. sign agreement for the paper to be published by the Mirror Group (International Publishing Corporation). 1964 T.U.C. sold their 49% holding to I.P.C. 1964, replaced by the *Sun*.
Policy: General support to Labour Movement, 1912–23, 1960–4. Official Labour 1923–60.
Editors: R. Kenny, 1912. W. Seed, 1912. S. Jones, 1912. C. Lapworth, 1913. G. Lansbury, 1913. W. Ryan, 1922. H. Fyfe, 1923. W. Mellor, 1926. W. Stevenson, 1931. F. Williams, 1937. P. Cudlipp, 1940. S. Elliott, 1953. D. Machray, 1957. J. Beavan, 1960. S. Jacobson, 1962–64. (Issued as a weekly paper during 1st World War, launched again as a daily in 1919.)

[1] The policies of national newspapers between 1900 and 1994 have inevitably fluctuated. Policy should be taken only as a general indication of the nature of the paper. In very few cases have newspapers been the official organ of a political party.

Daily Mail, 1896
Proprietors: A. Harmsworth (Ld Northcliffe), Associated Newspapers Ltd (Chairman: 1st (1922), 2nd (1932), 3rd (1971) Lds Rothermere).
Policy: Independent. Right-wing Conservative.
Editors: T. Marlowe, 1899. W. Fish, 1926. O. Pulvermacher, 1929. W. McWhirter, 1930. W. Warden, 1931. A. Cranfield, 1935. R. Prew, 1939. S. Horniblow, 1944. F. Owen, 1947. G. Schofield, 1950. A. Wareham, 1955. W. Hardcastle, 1959. M. Randall, 1963. A. Brittenden, 1966. (Sir) D. English, 1971. P. Dacre, 1992.

Daily Mirror, 1903
Proprietors: A. Harmsworth, Sir H. Harmsworth (Ld Rothermere), 1914. Pictorial Newspaper (1910) Co. Daily Mirror Newspapers Ltd. 1961, bought by International Publishing Corporation (Chairman: C. King. H. Cudlipp, 1968). Control acquired by Reed International 1970 (Chairman: (Sir) D. Ryder. (Sir) A. Jarratt, 1974). Control of Mirror Group Newspapers acquired by Maxwell Foundation 1984 (Chairman R. Maxwell; I. Maxwell 1991). Control acquired by creditor banks, 1992.
Policy: Independent. Since 1940s Labour-supporting.
Editors: Mary Howarth, 1903. H. Fyfe, 1904. A. Kinealy, 1907. E. Mynn, 1915. A. Campbell, 1919. L. Brownlee, 1931. C. Thomas, 1934. S. Bolam, 1948. J. Nener, 1953. L. Howard, 1960. A. Miles, 1971. M. Christiansen, 1974. M. Molloy, 1975. R. Stott, 1985. R. Greenslade, 1990. R. Stott, 1991. D. Banks, 1992. C. Myler, 1994.

(Daily News), 1846–1930
Proprietors: Daily News Ltd, 1901 (Chairman: G. Cadbury, 1901–11). Amalgamated with *Morning Leader,* as *Daily News and Leader,* 1912. Amalgamated with *Westminster Gazette,* 1928. Amalgamated with *Daily Chronicle,* 1930. Continued as *News Chronicle (See below).*
Policy: Liberal.
Editors: E. Cook, 1896. R. Lehmann, 1901. A. Gardiner, 1902. S. Hodgson, 1920–30.

(Daily Paper), 1904 (32 issues only)
Proprietor: W. Stead.
Policy: 'A paper for the abnormally scrupulous'.
Editor: W. Stead.

(Daily Sketch), 1908–1971
Proprietors: E. Hulton and Co. Ltd. Daily Mirror Newspapers Ltd, and Sunday Pictorial Newspapers (1920) Ltd. Bought by the Berry brothers, 1926, and merged with the *Daily Graphic.* Name changed to *Daily Graphic,* 1946–52. Subsidiary of Allied Newspapers Ltd. Kemsley Newspapers Ltd. Bought by Associated Newspapers Ltd, 1952. Renamed *Daily Sketch,* 1953. Merged with *Daily Mail,* 1971.
Policy: Independent Conservative.
Editors: J. Heddle, 1909. W. Robinson, 1914. H. Lane, 1919. H. Gates, 1922. H. Lane, 1923. A. Curthoys, 1928. A. Sinclair, 1936. S. Carroll, 1939. L. Berry, 1942. A. Thornton and M. Watts, 1943. A. Thornton, 1944. N. Hamilton, 1947. H. Clapp, 1948. H. Gunn, 1953. C. Valdar, 1959. H. French, 1962. D. English, 1969–71.

Daily Sport, 1992 (previously three times a week)
Proprietors: Sport Newspapers Ltd (Chairman D. Sullivan).
Policy: Independent.
Editor: P. Grimsditch, 1992. W. Robertson, 1992. W. Carson, 1993. J. McGowan, 1993.

Daily Star, 1978
Proprietors: Beaverbrook Newspapers (Chairman: V. Matthews). At first printed in Manchester and distributed only in North. Acquired by United Newspapers (Ld Stevens) in 1985.
Policy: Independent.
Editor: P. Grimsditch, 1978. L. Turner, 1982. M. Gabbert, 1987. B. Hitchen, 1987.

Daily Telegraph, 1855
Proprietors: Ld Burnham and family. Sold to Sir W. Berry (Ld Camrose), Sir G. Berry (Ld Kemsley) and Sir E. Iliffe (Ld) in 1928. Absorbed *Morning Post,* as *Daily Telegraph and Morning Post* in 1937. Ld Camrose acquired Ld Kemsley's and Ld Iliffe's interests in 1937. M. Berry (Ld Hartwell) succeeded him as Editor-in-Chief in 1968. Acquired by C. Black, 1987.
Policy: Conservative.
Editors: (Sir) J. le Sage, 1885. F. Miller, 1923. A. Watson, 1924. (Sir) C. Coote, 1950. M. Green, 1964. W. Deedes, 1974. M. Hastings, 1986.

(Daily Worker), 1930–1966
Proprietors: Daily Worker Cooperative Society Ltd. Descendant of the Sunday Worker, 1925–30. Publication suppressed 1941–42. Changed name to *Morning Star,* 1966.
Policy: Communist.
Editors: W. Rust, 1930. J. Shields, 1932. I. Cox. 1935. R. Palme Dutt, 1936. W. Rust, 1939. J. Campbell, 1949. G. Matthews, 1959–1966.

(Financial News), 1884–1945
Proprietors: Financial News Ltd, 1898 (H. Marks). Incorporated with the *Financial Times* in 1945.
Policy: Finance, independent.
Editors: H. Marks, 1884. Dr Ellis, 1916. H. O'Neill, 1921. W. Dorman and W. Lang, 1921. Sir L. Worthington-Evans, 1924. Sir E. Young, 1925. O. Hobson, 1929. M. Green, 1934. H. Parkinson, 1938–45.

Financial Times, 1888
Proprietors: Financial Times Ltd. Incorporated *Financier and Bullionist*. Incorporated the *Financial News* in 1945. Controlling interest held by Pearson plc since 1957.
Policy: Finance, independent.
Editors: W. Lawson. A. Murray, 1901. C. Palmer, 1909. D. Hunter, 1924. A. Chisholm, 1938. A. Cole, 1940. H. Parkinson, 1945. (Sir) G. Newton, 1950. F. Fisher, 1973. (Sir) G. Owen, 1981. R. Lambert, 1991.

Independent, 1986.
Proprietors: Newspaper Publishing Co. Ltd.
Policy: Independent.
Editors: A. Whittam-Smith.

(Manchester) Guardian, 1821
Proprietors: The Manchester Guardian & Evening News Ltd. Renamed *Guardian*, 1959. The Scott Trust.
Policy: Independent liberal.
Editors: C. P. Scott, 1872. E. Scott, 1929. W. Crozier, 1932. A. Wadsworth, 1944. A. Hetherington, 1956. P. Preston 1975.

(Majority), 1906 (10–14 Jul only)
Proprietors: Majority Ltd.
Policy: 'The organ of all who work for wage or salary'.

(Morning Herald), 1892–1900
Proprietors: Morning Newspaper Co. Became *London Morning* in 1898, and *Morning Herald* in 1899. Merged with *Daily Express* in 1900.
Policy: Independent.
Editor: D. Murray, 1892–1900.

(Morning Leader), 1892–1912
Proprietors: Colman family of Norwich. Merged with *Daily News,* as *Daily News and Leader* in 1912 (See *Daily News*).
Policy: Liberal.
Editor: E. Parke, 1892–1912.

(Morning Post), 1772–1937
Proprietors: Sir A. Borthwick (W Glenesk), 1876–1908. Lady Bathurst, 1908–24. Absorbed in *Daily Telegraph* in 1937 (Ld Camrose).
Policy: Conservative.
Editors: J. Dunn, 1897. S. Wilkinson, 1905. F. Warr, 1905. H. Gwynne, 1911–37.

(Morning Standard), 1857–1917
Proprietors: Bought from Johnston family by A. Pearson, 1904. Sold to D. Dalziel (Ld) in 1910.
Policy: From 1904 supporter of tariff reform.
Editors: W. Mudford, 1874. G. Curtis, 1900. H. Gwynne, 1904. H. White, 1911–17.

Morning Star, 1966
Proprietors: Morning Star Co-operative Society. Successor to the *Daily Worker*.
Policy: Communist.
Editor: G. Matthews, 1966. T. Chater, 1974.

(New Daily), 1960–1966
Proprietors: The British Newspaper Trust Ltd. Sponsored by the People's League for the Defence of Freedom,
        the Free Press Society, and the Anti-Socialist Front.
   Policy: 'The only daily newspaper in Great Britain independent of combines and trade unions'.
   Editor: E. Martell, 1960–66.

(News Chronicle), 1930–60
Proprietors: Amalgamation of *Daily News and Leader* and *Daily Chronicle* in 1930 (Cadbury family). Bought
        by Associated Newspapers Ltd in 1960, and merged with *Daily Mail.*
   Policy: Liberal.
   Editors: T. Clarke, 1930. A. Vallance, 1933. G. Barry, 1936. R. Cruikshank, 1948. M. Curtis, 1954. N. Cursley, 1957.

Post, 1988 (10 Nov – 17 Dec only)
Proprietors: Messenger Group Newspapers (E. Shah).
   Policy: Independent.
   Editor: L. Turner.

(Recorder), 27 Oct 1953–17 May 1954
Proprietors: The Recorder Ltd. (Managing Director:
        E. Martell). A weekly suburban newspaper 1870–1939, continued as a weekly after 1954.
   Policy: Independent. 'Keynote:
        pride in Britain and the British Empire.'
   Editor: W. Brittain, 1953–4.

Sun, 1964
Proprietors: International Publishing Corporation (Chairman: C. King. H. Cudlipp, 1968). 1969 News Interna-
        tional Ltd (R. Murdoch).
   Policy: Labour. Independent since 1969.
   Editors: S. Jacobson, 1964. R, Dinsdale, 1965. A. Lamb, 1969. B. Shrimsley, 1972. (Sir) L. Lamb, 1975. K.
        McKenzie, 1981. S. Higgins, 1994.

The Times, 1785[1]
Proprietors: Founded as the Daily Universal Register, became The Times in 1788. Owned by the Walter family,
        1785–1908. Bought by Ld Northcliffe in 1908. Owned by J. Astor and J. Walter in 1922. 7 Aug 24,
        Times Association formed (comprising Lord Chief Justice, Warden of All Souls, Oxford, Presi-
        dent of the Royal Society, President of the Institute of Chartered Accountants and Governor of
        the Bank of England). 21 Dec 66, Monopolies Commission approved common ownership of *The
        Times* and the *Sunday Times* by the Thomson Organisation. Times Newspapers Ltd formed. Pre-
        sident:
        G. Astor (Ld). Chairman: Sir W. Haley. 1967 K. Thomson (Ld). Acquired by News International,
        1981 (Chairman: R. Murdoch).
   Policy: Independent conservative.
   Editors: G. Buckle, 1884. G. Dawson, 1912. H. Steed, 1919. G. Dawson, 1922. R. Barrington-Ward, 1941. W.
        Casey, 1948. Sir W. Haley, 1952. W. Rees-Mogg, 1967. H. Evans, 1981. C. Douglas-Home, 1983. C.
        Wilson, 1985. S. Jenkins, 1990. P. Stoddart, 1992.

Today, 1986
Proprietors: Messenger Group (E. Shah). Bought by Lonrho, 1986. Bought by News International (Chairman:
        R Murdoch) 1987.
   Policy: Independent.
   Editors: B. MacArthur 1986. D. Montgomery, 1987. M. Dunn, 1991.

(Tribune), 1906–1908
Proprietors: F. Thomasson.
   Policy: Liberal.
   Editors: W. Hill and S. Pryor, 1906.

(Westminster Gazette), 1921–1928 issued as a morning paper.
        (*See Evening Papers*).

---

[1] *The Times* suspended publication from 1 Dec 1978 to 12 Nov 79.

National Sunday Newspapers

(excluding all those not published in London)

((Illustrated) Sunday Herald), 1915–1927
Proprietors: Sir E. Hulton. Renamed *Illustrated Sunday Herald*. Bought by Berry family in 1926 and renamed *Sunday Graphic* in 1927 *(See below)*.
Policy: Independent conservative.
Editors: J. E. Williams. T. Hill, 1926–27.

Independent on Sunday, 1988.
Proprietors: Newspaper Publishing Co Ltd.
Policy: Independent.
Editor: A. Whittam-Smith.

Mail on Sunday, 1982
Proprietors: Associated Newspapers Ltd (Chairman: 3rd Ld Rothermere).
Policy: Independent Conservative.
Editors: B. Shrimsley, 1982. Sir D. English, 1982. S. Steven, 1982. J. Holborow, 1992.

(National News), 1917–1918
Proprietors: Odhams Press Ltd.
Policy: Independent.
Editor: A. de Beck, 1917–18.

News of the World, 1843
Proprietors: News of the World Ltd. (Sir) G. Riddel) (Ld), 1903–34. The Carr family 1934–69. 1969 News International Ltd (R. Murdoch).
Policy: Independent conservative.
Editors: Sir E. Carr, 1891. D. Davies, 1941. R. Skelton, 1946. A. Waters, 1947. R. Cudlipp, 1953. S. Somerfield, 1959. C. Lear, 1970. P. Stephens, 1974. B. Shrimsley, 1975. K. Donlan, 1980. B. Askew, 1981. D. Jameson, 1981. N. Lloyd, 1984. D.Montgomery, 1985. Wendy Henry, 1987. Patsy Chapman, 1988. P. Morgan 1994.

(News on Sunday), 1987 (Apr–Nov only).
Proprietors: News on Sunday Ltd (Chairman N. Horsley; shares held largely by local authority pension funds and trade unions, notably TGWU). Acquired by Growfar Ltd (owned by O. Oyston) Jun 1987.
Policy: Left-wing.
Editors: K. Sutton, D. Jones, B. Whitaker, W. Nutting.

Observer, 1791
Proprietors: F. Beer. Bought by Ld Northcliffe in 1905. Bought by W. Astor (Vt) in 1911. Sold to Atlantic Richfield, 1976. 10 shares to remain with Observer Trustees. Sold to Lonrho, 1980 (Chairman: R. Rowland). Taken over by Guardian and Evening News Group, 1993.
Policy: Conservative. Independent since 1942.
Editors: F. Beer, 1894. A. Harrison, 1905. J. Garvin, 1908. I. Brown, 1942. D. Astor, 1948. D. Trelford, 1976. J. Fenby, 1993.

People, 1881
Proprietors: W. Madge and Sir G. Armstrong. Sir W. Madge, 1914–22. M. L. Publishing Co. Ltd. The People Ltd. Odhams Press. 1961 amalgamated with International Publishing Corporation (Chairman: C. King. H. Cudlipp, 1968). Control acquired by Reed International 1970 (Chairman: (Sir) D. Ryder. A. Jarratt, 1974). Control acquired by R. Maxwell, 1984. I. Maxwell, 1991. Control acquired by creditor banks, 1992.
Policy: Independent.
Editors: J. Hatton. J. Sansome 1913. H. Swaffer, 1924. H. Ainsworth, 1925. S. Campbell, 1958. R. Edwards, 1966. G. Pinnington, 1972. R. Stott, 1984. E. Burrington, 1985. J. Blake, 1988. Wendy Henry, 1989. R. Stott, 1990. W. Haggerty, 1991. Bridget Rowe, 1992.

(Reynolds News), 1850–1967
Proprietors: Originally Reynold's Weekly Newspaper, and later Reynold's Illustrated News. Owned by J. Dicks and family since 1879. H. Dalziel (Ld) appointed business manager in 1907. He became the sole proprietor in 1914. Bought by the National Co-operative Press Ltd. Incorporated the *Sunday Citizen.* 1962. Changed name to *Sunday Citizen and Reynolds News.*
Policy: Support for the Labour and Co-operative movements.
Editors: W. Thompson, 1894. H. Dalziel, 1907. J. Crawley, 1920. S. Elliott, 1929. (Sir) W. Richardson, 1941–67.

(Sunday Correspondent), 1989–90.
Proprietors: Sunday Publishing Co plc
Policy: Independent
Editors: P. Cole, 1989. J. Bryant 1990.

(Sunday Citizen), 1962–1967.
    (See above, Reynolds News)

(Sunday Dispatch), 1801–1961
Proprietors: Sir G. Newnes (1900–10). Originally the *Weekly Dispatch* until 1928. Bought by the Harmsworth family. Ld Northcliffe, Ld Rothermere from 1928. Associated Newspapers Ltd. Absorbed by the *Sunday Express* in 1961.
Policy: Independent conservative.
Editors: M. Cotton, H. Swaffer, 1915. B. Falk, 1919. W. McWhirter, 1930. H. Lane, 1933. W. Brittain, 1934. C. Brooks, 1936. C. Eade, 1938. H. Gunn, 1959–61.

Sunday Express, 1918
Proprietors: Sunday Express Ltd. (Ld Beaverbrook; From 1954 Beaverbrook Newspapers Ltd.) Taken over by Trafalgar House property group, 1977. Chairman: V. (Ld) Matthews. Acquired by United Newspapers, 1985 (Chairman D. (Ld) Stevens).
Policy: Independent conservative.
Editors: J. Douglas, 1920. J. Gordon, 1928. (Sir) J. Junor, 1954. R. Esser, 1986. R. Morgan, 1989. Eve Pollard, 1991.

(Sunday Graphic (and Sunday News)), 1915–60
Proprietors: Sir E. Hulton. Originally called the *Sunday Herald*, renamed the *Illustrated Sunday Herald.* Bought by the Berry family in 1926, and renamed the *Sunday Graphic* in 1927. Daily Graphic and Sunday Graphic Ltd., a subsidiary of Ld Kemsley's newspapers. Incorporated the *Sunday News* in 1931. Bought by R. Thomson in 1959. Ceased publication in 1960.
Policy: Independent.
Editors: T. Hill, 1927. A. Sinclair, 1931. R. Simpson, 1935. M. Watts, 1947. N. Hamilton, 1947. L. Lang, 1948. A. Josey, 1949. B. Horniblow, 1950. P. Brownrigg, 1952. M. Randell, 1953. G. McKenzie, 1953. A. Hall, 1958. R. Anderson, 1959. A. Ewart, 1960.

(Sunday Illustrated), 1921–23
Proprietor: H. Bottomley.
Policy: Independent.
Editor: H. Bottomley.

(Sunday (Illustrated) News), 1842–1931
Proprietors: Originally *Lloyd's Sunday News.* Sunday News Ltd. United Newspapers Ltd (W. Harrison). Merged with the *Sunday Graphic* in 1931.
Policy: Independent liberal.
Editors: T. Catling. W. Robinson, 1919. E. Perris, 1924. E. Wallace, 1929–31.

Sunday Mirror, 1963
Proprietors: International Publishing Corporation (Chairman: C. King. H. Cudlipp, 1968) Control acquired by Reed International 1970 (Chairman: (Sir) D. Ryder. 1974, A. Jarratt). Bought by R. Maxwell, 1984. I. Maxwell, 1991. Control acquired by creditor banks, 1992.
Policy: Independent.
Editor: M. Christiansen, 1963. R. Edwards, 1972. M. Molloy, 1986. Eve Pollard, 1988. Bridget Rowe, 1991. C. Myler, 1992. P. Connew, 1994.

(Sunday Pictorial), 1915–1963
Proprietors: The Harmsworth family. Taken over by Ld Rothermere in 1922. Sunday Pictorial Newspapers
(1920) Ltd. 1961 absorbed by International Publishing Corporation (Cecil King). 1963. Became
Sunday Mirror (See above).
Policy: Independent.
Editors: F. Sanderson, 1915. W. McWhirter, 1921. D. Grant, 1924. W. McWhirter, 1928. D. Grant, 1929. H.
Cudlipp, 1938. R. Campall, 1940. H. Cudlipp, 1946. P. Zec, 1949. H. Cudlipp, 1952. C. Valdar, 1953. L.
Howard, 1959. R. Payne, 1960.

((Sunday) Referee), 1877–1939
Proprietors: Printed by the Daily News Ltd. Owned by I. Ostrer. Incorporated in the *Sunday Chronicle* in 1939
(which was published in Manchester and ceased independent publication in 1955).
Policy: Conservative.
Editors: R. Butler. (Sir) R. Donald, 1922. A. Laber, 1924. M. Joulden, 1933.

(Sunday Special), 1897–1904
Proprietor: H. Schmidt.

Sunday Sport, 1986
Proprietor: Sport Newspapers Ltd (D. Sullivan).
Policy: Independent.
Editors: P. Grimsditch, 1986. M. Gabbert, 1987. D. Robertson, 1987. I. Pollock, 1990. G. Thompson, 1993. D.
Mohan, 1993.

Sunday Telegraph, 1961
Proprietors: The Sunday Telegraph Ltd (M. Berry (Ld Hartwell)). Bought by C. Black 1987.
Policy: Independent conservative.
Editor: D. McLachlan, 1961. B. Roberts, 1966. J. Thompson, 1976. P. Worsthorne, 1986. T. Grove, 1989.
C. Moore, 1992.

Sunday Times, 1822
Proprietors: Mrs. F. Beer. Bought by H. Schmidt. Amalgamated with the *Sunday Special* in 1904. Bought by the
Berry family in 1915. Bought by R. Thomson in 1959 (Thomson Allied Newspapers). Times News-
papers Ltd, formed in 1967 to run *The Times* and *Sunday Times*. Control acquired by News Inter-
national, 1981 (Chairman: R. Murdoch).
Policy: Indepndent conservative.
Editors: L. Rees, 1901. W. Hadley, 1932. H. Hodson, 1950. C. D. Hamilton, 1961. H. Evans, 1967. F. Giles, 1981. A.
Neil, 1983. J. Witherow (*acting*) 1994.

(Sunday Today), 1986–7
Proprietors: Messenger Group Newspapers (E. Shah). Control acquired by Lonrho, 1986. Bought by News Inter-
national (Chairman R. Murdoch) 1987.
Policy: Independent
Editor: B. MacArthur

(Sunday Worker), 1925–30
Proprietors: The Communist Party through nominees. Published daily as the *Daily Worker* from 1930.
Policy: Communist.
Editors: W. Paul, 1925. W. Holmes, 1927.

London Evening Newspapers

(Evening Echo and Chronicle), 22 Mar–4 May 1915
Proprietor: E. Lloyd. Merged with Star.
Policy: Liberal.

(Echo), 1868–1905
Proprietors: Consolidated Newspapers. F. Pethick-Lawrence in control, 1901–5.
Policy: Radical, progressive.
Editors: W. Crook, 1898. T. Meech, 1900. P. Alden, 1901 . F. Pethick-Lawrence, 1901–5.

(Evening News), 1881–1980, 1987 (Mar–Oct only).
Proprietors: A. Harmsworth (Evening News Ltd), 1894. Associated Newspapers Ltd, 1905. Merged with Evening Standard, 1980. Briefly re-launched by Associated Newspapers in 1987.
Policy: Conservative.
Editors: W. Evans, 1896. C. Beattie, 1922. F. Fitzhugh, 1924. G. Schofield, 1943. J. Marshall, 1950. R.Willis, 1954. J. Gold, 1967. D. Boddie, 1973. L. Kirby, 1974–80. J. Lees, 1987.

Evening (New) Standard, 1827
Proprietors: Bought by A. Pearson from Johnston family in 1904. Absorbed *St James Gazette* in 1905. D. Dalziel (Ld)[1], 1910. Hulton and Co. 1915–23. Incorporated with *Pall Mall Gazette* and *Globe*, 1923. Bought by Ld Beaverbrook in 1923. In 1954 he relinquished it to Beaverbrook Newspapers Ltd and transferred controlling shares to the Beaverbrook Foundations. In 1977 Beaverbrook Newspapers were taken over by Trafalgar House property group. Chairman: V. Matthews. Sold to Associated Newspapers, 1980 (Chairman: Ld Rothermere) and merged with *Evening News* as *(New) Standard*. Reverted to name *Evening Standard* in 1987.
Policy: Independent conservative.
Editors: S. Pryor, 1897. W. Woodward, 1906. J. Kilpatrick, 1912. D. Sutherland, 1914. A.Mann, 1916. D. Phillips, 1920. E. Thompson, 1923. G. Gilliat, 1928. P. Cudlipp, 1933. R. Thompson, 1938. F. Owen, 1939. M. Foot, 1942. S. Elliott, 1943. H. Gunn, 1944. P. Elland, 1950. C. Wintour, 1959. S. Jenkins, 1977. C. Wintour, 1978. L. Kirkby, 1980. J. Lees, 1986. P. Dacre, 1991. S. Steven, 1992.

(Evening Times), 1910–1911
Proprietors: London Evening Newspaper Co. (J. Morrison, Sir S. Scott, J. Cowley).
Policy: Conservative.
Editors: C. Watney, E. Wallace.

(Globe), 1803–1921
Proprietors: (Sir) G. Armstrong, 1871–1907. H. Harmsworth, 1907–11. W. Madge, 1912–14. Absorbed by *Pall Mall Gazette* in 1921, incorporated with *Evening Standard* in 1923.
Policy: Conservative.
Editors: Sir G. Armstrong, 1895. P. Ogle, 1907. J. Harrison, 1908. C. Palmer, 1912. W. Peacock, 1915–21.

(London Daily News), 1987 (Feb–Jul only)
Proprietors: Mirror Group Newspapers (Chairman: R. Maxwell).
Policy: Independent Labour-leaning.
Editor: M.Linklater.

(Pall Mall Gazette), 1865–1923
Proprietors: W. Astor (Ld), 1892. Sir H. Dalziel, 1917. Sir J. Leigh, 1923. Incorporated with *Evening Standard* in 1923.
Policy: Conservative.
Editors: Sir D. Straight, 1896. F. Higginbottom, 1909. J. Garvin, 1912. D.Sutherland, 1915–23.

(St James's Gazette), 1880–1905
Proprietors: E. Steinkopff, 1888. W. Dallas Ross. A. Pearson, 1903. Amalgamated with Evening Standard in 1905.
Policy: Conservative.
Editors: H. Chisholm, 1897. R. McNeill, 1900. G. Fiennes, 1903. S. Pryor,1904–5.

(Star), 1887–1960
Proprietors: Star Newspaper Co. Owned by Daily News Ltd. Bought by Associated Newspapers Ltd, and incorporated in *Evening News*, 1960.
Policy: Liberal.
Editors: E. Parke, 1891. J. Douglas, 1908. W. Pope, 1920. E. Chattaway, 1930. R. Cruikshank, 1936. A. Cranfield, 1941. R. McCarthy, 1957–60.

---

[1] Later Lord Dalziel of Wooler, not to be confused with Ld Dalziel of Kirkcaldy who was proprietor of *Reynolds News*, 1914–62.

(Sun), 1893–1906
Proprietors: T. P. O'Connor. H. Bottomley, 1900. Sir G. Armstrong and W. Madge, 1904–6.
   Policy: Literary, non-political.
  Editors: T. P. O'Connor. T. Dahle.

(Westminster Gazette), 1893–1928
Proprietors: Sir G. Newnes, 1893. Liberal Syndicate (Chairman: Sir A. Mond), 1908–15. A. Pearson, 1915–28. Last issue as evening paper 5 Nov 21. First issue as morning paper 7 Nov 21. Incorporated with *Daily News* in 1928.
   Policy: Liberal.
  Editors: J. Spender, 1896. J. Hobman, 1921–28.

National Newspapers Printing in More than One City 1900–1985[1]

	London	Manchester	Glasgow
Daily Chronicle	1869–1930	1925–1930[2]	–
Daily Express	1900–	1927–	1928–1974
Daily Herald (Sun)	1912–	1930–1969	–
Daily Mail	1896–	1900–	1946–1966[3]
Daily Mirror[4]	1903–	1955–	–
Daily News	1846–1930	1921–1924, 1929–30	–
Daily Star	1978–	1978–	–
Daily Sketch (Graphic)	1911–1971	1908–1953	–
Daily Telegraph	1855–	1940–	–
News Chronicle	1930–1960	1930–1960	–
(Manchester) Guardian	1961–	1821–	–
News of the World	1843–	1941–	–
Summary Dispatch	1801–1961	1930–1961	–
Sunday Express	1918–	1927–	1927–1974
Sunday Graphic	1915–1960	1932–1952[5]	–
Sun. Pictorial/Sun. Mirror	1955–	1955–	–
(Sunday) People	1881–	1930–	–
Sunday Times	1822–	1940–1964	–
Sunday Chronicle	1939–1955	1885–1955	–

[1] From the mid-1980s new technology made printing in many different centres the norm rather than the exception.
[2] The *Daily Chronicle* was printed in Leeds, not Manchester, 1925–30.
[3] The Scottish *Daily Mail* was printed in Edinburgh, not Glasgow, 1946–66.
[4] The *Daily Mirror* was also printed in Belfast, 1966–71.
[5] The Manchester printing of the *Sunday Graphic* was suspended from 1936–50.

Partisan Tendencies and Circulations of National Daily Newspapers in British General Elections, 1945–92

Circulation in millions; Party support

Newspaper	1945	1950	1951	1955	1959	1964	1966	1970	Feb 1974	Oct 1974	1979	1983	1987	1992
D. Express	3.3 Con Coal.	4.1 Con	4.2 Con	4.0 Con	4.1 Con	4.2 Con	4.0 Con	3.6 Con	3.2 Con	3.1 Con	2.5 Con	1.9 Con	1.7 Con	1.5 Con
D. Herald/The Sun[1]	1.9 Lab	2.0 Lab	2.0 Lab	1.8 Lab	1.5 Lab	1.3* Lab	1.2 Lab	1.5 Lab	3.3 Con	3.5 All-Pty	3.9 Con	4.2 Con	4.0 Con	3.6 Con
D. Mail	1.7 Con	2.2 Con	2.3 Con	2.1 Con	2.1 Con	2.4 Con	2.4 Con	1.9 Con	1.8 Con	1.7 Con-Lib Coal.	2.0 Con	1.8 Con	1.8 Con	1.7 Con
D. Mirror	2.4 Lab	4.6 Lab	4.5 Lab	4.7 Lab	4.5 Lab	5.1 Lab	5.1 Lab	4.7 Lab	4.2 Lab	4.2 Lab	3.8 Lab	3.3 Lab	3.1 Lab	2.9 Lab
D. Sketch/ D. Graphic[2]	0.9 Con	0.8 Con	0.8 Con	1.0 Con	1.2 Con	0.8 Con	0.8 Con	0.8 Con	–	–	–	–	–	–
D. Telegraph	0.8 Con	1.0 Con	1.0 Con	1.1 Con	1.2 Con	1.3 Con	1.4 Con	1.4 Con	1.4 Con	1.4 Con	1.4 Con	1.3 Con	1.1 Con	1.0 Con
(Manchester) Guardian[3]	0.1 Lib	0.1 Lib	0.2 Lib/Con	0.2 Lib/Con	0.3 Lab/Lib	0.3 Lab	0.3 Lab/Lib	0.4 Lab/Lib	0.4 Party Balance	0.4 More Lib.	0.3 Lab.	0.4 All./Con.	0.5 Lab.	0.4 Lab./Lib.Dem.
Independent	–	–	–	–	–	–	–	–	–	–	–	–	0.3 None	0.4 None
News Chronicle[4]	1.5 Lib	1.5 Lib	1.5 Lib	1.3 Lib	1.2 Lib	–	–	–	–	–	–	–	–	–
The Times	0.2 Lab	0.3 Con	0.2 Con	0.2 Con	0.3 Con	0.3 Con	0.3 ?/Lib	0.4 Con/Lib	0.3 Con/Lib	0.3 Con-Lib Coalition	..	0.3 Con.	0.4 Con.	0.4 Con.
Today	–	–	–	–	–	–	–	–	–	–	–	–	0.3 Coal.	0.5 Con.
Daily Star	–	–	–	–	–	–	–	–	–	–	n.a. Neutral	1.3 Con.	1.3 Con.	0.8 Neutral/Con.

PARTISANSHIP IN ELECTIONS

	1945	1950	1951	1955	1959	1964	1966	1970	Feb 1974	Oct 1974	1979	1983	1987	1992
Total circulation	12,799	16,632	16,623	16,224	16,067	15,679	15,419	14,642	14,633	14,573	13,789⁵	14,527	14,824	13,546
Total Conservative circulation	6,713 (52%)	8,333 (50%)	8,599† (52%)	8,487† (52%)	8,715 (54%)	9,016 (57%)	8,538 (55%)	8,133† (55%)	10,441† (71%)	6,898† (47%)	9,731 (71%)	11,260† (78%)	10,914† (74%)	8,728⁵ (64%)
Total Conservative vote	9,578 (40%)	12,503 (43%)	13,718 (48%)	13,312 (50%)	13,750 (49%)	12,001 (43%)	11,418 (42%)	13,145 (46%)	11,872 (38%)	10,465 (36%)	13,698 (44%)	13,012 (42%)	13,763 (42%)	14,093 (42%)
Total Labour circulation	4,454 (35%)	6,633 (40%)	6,517 (39%)	6,484 (40%)	6,145† (38%)	6,663 (42%)	6,608† (43%)	6,509† (44%)	4,557 (31%)	4,572† (31%)	4,058 (29%)	3,267 (22%)	3,924† (26%)	3,332† (25%)
Total Labour vote	11,633 (48%)	13,267 (46%)	13,949 (49%)	12,405 (46%)	12,216 (44%)	12,206 (44%)	13,065 (48%)	12,178 (43%)	11,646 (37%)	11,457 (39%)	11,532 (37%)	8,457 (28%)	10,030 (31%)	11,560 (34%)
Total Liberal circulation	1,632 (13%)	1,666 (10%)	1,646† (10%)	1,409† (9%)	1,390† (9%)	–	556† (4%)	705† (5%)	716† (5%)	2,432† (17%)	–	417 (3%)	307† (2%)	429† (3%)
Total Liberal vote	2,197 (9%)	2,622 (9%)	731 (2%)	722 (3%)	1,639 (6%)	3,093 (11%)	2,327 (8%)	2,117 (7%)	6,059 (19%)	5,347 (18%)	4,314 (14%)	7,781 (25%)	7,341 (23%)	5,999 (18%)

[1] Name changed to the Sun in 1964.
[2] Named Daily Graphic, 1946–52.
[3] 'Manchester' dropped from title in 1959.
[4] Ceased publication in 1960.
[5] Not including the Daily Star.
* Figure uncertain due to relaunching at that time.
† Including paper(s) with divided support, but omits The Sun in October 1974.

SOURCE of circulation figures: 1945, 1950: Nuffield election studies; thereafter, Audit Bureau of Circulation, excepting *The Daily Telegraph* figures for 1951, 1955, 1959 (London Press Exchange). Circulation figures are for the period of the year in which the election was held. The *Daily Worker*, the Communist daily paper, which changed its name to the *Morning Star* in 1966, is omitted: comparable circulation figures are not available. The number of Communist candidates at election was as normally under fifty.

SOURCES. – *Royal Commission on the Press*; Working Paper No. 3. Cmnd 6810.

Circulations of National Newspapers, 1910–

National Daily Newspapers

(to nearest 000)

	1910	1930	1939	1951	1960	1965	1970	1980	1990	1993
D. Express	400	1,603	2,486	4,193	4,130	3,981	3,607	2,325	1,585	1,359
D. Herald/Sun	..	750[b]	2,000	2,071	1,467	1,274	1,509	3,837	3,855	3,737
D. Mail	900	1,968	1,510	2,245	2,084	2,464	1,917	1,985	1,708	1,701
D. Mirror[h]	630	1,071	1,367[d]	4,567	4,545	4,957[i]	4,697	3,651	3,083	2,424
D. News	320	900	..	..	..	..	..	..	..	..
D. Sketch	750[a]	1,013	850[d]	777	1,152	844	806	..	..	..
D. Star	..	..	..	..	..	..	..	1,033	833	731
D. Telegraph	230	222[c]	640[d]	976[e]	1,155[e]	1,351	1,402	1,456	1,076	1,008
D.Worker/M. Star	..	n.a.	100[d]	115	73[f]	..	..	34	26	20
Guardian	40	47	51	140	190	270	303	375	424	389
Independent	..	..	..	..	..	..	..	..	411	302
M. Leader	250	..	..	..	..	..	..	..	..	..
M. Post	n.a.	119	..	..	..	..	..	..	..	..
N. Chronicle[g]	800[a]	967	1,317	1,583	1,206	..	..	..	..	..
Times	45	187	213	254	255	258	402	316	420	439
Today	..	..	..	..	..	..	..	..	540	541

Unless otherwise stated the figures are taken from *T.B.Browne's Advertisers' ABC*, 1910–40, and figures after 1950 are from the Audit Bureau of Circulation.

[a] Circulation figure for 1915, *T.B.Browne*
[b] P.E.P.: Report on the British Press (1938) gives 1,082 for 1930.
[c] From the P.E.P. Report.
[d] From the P.E.P. Report. Figure for 1938.
[e] *Daily Telegraph* audited circulation figures.
[f] ABC circulation in 1956. Latest available figure.
[g] 1910 and 1930 figures are for *Daily Chronicle*.
[h] This does not include circulation of *Daily Record* (Glasgow) acquired by *Daily Mirror* in 1955.
[i] For a period in 1964 the *Daily Mirror* became the only daily newspaper ever to top 5m. circulation.

National Sunday Newspapers

(to nearest 000)

	1900	1910	1930	1937	1951	1960	1965	1970	1980	1990	1993
Independent on S.	..	..	..	..	..	..	..	..	..	352	335
Lloyd's Weekly	1,250	1,250	1,450[b]	..	..	..	..	..	..	..	..
News of the World	400	1,500	3,250[b]	3,850	8,407	6,664	6,176	6,215	4,472	5,056	4,612
Observer	60	n.a.	201	208	450	738	829	848	1,018	551	482
Mail on Sunday	..	..	..	..	1,903	1,903	..	..	..	..	..
People	n.a.	n.a.	2,535	3,406	5,181	5,468	5,538	5,242	3,856	2,566	2,038
Reynolds News	2,000[a]	2,000[a]	420	426	712	329	236	..	..	..	..
Sunday Dispatch	n.a.	n.a.	1,197	741	2,631	1,520	..	..	..	..	..
Sunday Express	..	..	958[b]	1,350	3,178	3,706	4,187	4,281	3,100	1,664	1,602
Sunday Graphic	..	..	1,100[b]	651	1,121	890	..	..	..	..	..
Sunday Mirror	..	..	..	..	..	..	5,022	4,885	3,856	2,894	2,471
Sunday Pictorial	..	..	1,883	1,345	5,170	5,461	..	..	..	..	..
Sunday Referee	n.a.	n.a.	73	342	..	..	..	..	..	..	..
Sunday Sport	..	..	..	..	..	..	..	..	..	402	226
Sunday Telegraph	..	..	..	..	..	..	662	756	1,032	594	626
Sunday Times	n.a.	n.a.	153	270	529	1,001	1,290	1,464	1,419	1,165	1,209

Unless otherwise stated, these figures are taken from *T.B.Browne's Advertiser's ABC*, 1900–30; the figures for 1937 are from the *Report of the Royal Commission on the Press*, 1947–49 (Cmd. 7700 and 7690/1949). From 1951, Audit Bureau of Circulation.

[a] These figures should be treated with caution. They are from an advertisement in *T.B.Browne's Advertiser's ABC* for 1901 and 1911.
[b] From *Sell's World Press*

London Evening Newspapers

(to nearest 000)

	1905	1910	1930	1939	1951	1960	1965	1970	1980	1990
E. News	300	300	667	822	1,752	1,153	1,238	1,017	..	..
E. Standard	n.a.	160	n.a.	390	862	586	680	550	608	502
Star	250	327	744	503	1,228	744	..	..	..	..

All circulation figures for evening newspapers exclude Sporting Editions. 1905–39 figures from *T. B. Browne's Advertiser's ABC*; from 1951 figures are from the Audit Bureau of Circulation, published in the *Newspaper Press Directory*. Information on the circulation of other evening papers is not available.

Provincial Morning Daily Newspapers, 1900–

Sporting newspapers and publications such as the *Hull Shipping Gazette* and the *Hartlepool Daily Shipping List* have been omitted. Bold type indicates newspapers still being published on 1 Jan 1994.

ABERDEEN – *Aberdeen Daily Journal* (1746). Merged with *Aberdeen Free Press* (1853) Nov 1922 and became **Aberdeen Press and Journal**.

BATH – *Bath Daily Argus* (1870). Merged with local evening paper, *Bath Daily Chronicle*, in Jan 1900.

BEDFORD – *Bedford Daily Circular* (1903). Merged with *Bedford Record* July 1939.

BELFAST – **Belfast News-Letter** (1737).
    Northern Whig (1824). Changed name to *Northern Whig and Belfast Post* Jun 1919. Ceased publication 1963.
    Irish Daily Telegraph (1904). Merged with local evening paper, *Belfast Telegraph*, Apr 1952.
    Irish News and Belfast Morning News (1881).

BIRMINGHAM – *Daily Argus* (1891). Merged with local evening paper, *Birmingham Evening Dispatch*, Jan 1902.
    Birmingham Daily Post (1857). Changed name to *Birmingham Post* May 1918. Became *Birmingham Post and Gazette* Nov 1956. Changed name to **Birmingham Post** 1973.
    Birmingham Daily Gazette (1862). Merged with *Midland Express* and changed name to *Birmingham Gazette and Express* 1904. Merged with *Birmingham Post* Nov 1956.

BRADFORD – *Bradford Observer* (1834). Changed name to *Yorkshire Daily Observer* Nov 1901. Changed name to *Yorkshire Observer* Jan 1909. Merged with local evening paper, *The Telegraph and Argus*, Nov 1956.

BRIGHTON – *Morning Argus* (1896). Ceased publication as morning paper May 1926.[1]
    Sussex Daily News (1868). Merged with *Evening Argus* Mar 1956.

BRISTOL – *Bristol Western Daily Press* (1858). Changed name to **Western Daily Press** 1928.
    Bristol Mercury (1790). Changed name to *Bristol Daily Mercury* Dec 1901. Ceased publication Nov 1909.
    Bristol Times and Mirror (1713). Merged with *Western Daily Press* 1932.

CARDIFF – *South Wales Daily News* (1872). Changed name to *South Wales News* Apr 1928. Merged with *Western Mail* Aug 1928.
    Western Mail (1869).
    Cardiff Journal of Commerce (1904). Changed name to *Cardiff and South Wales Journal of Commerce* July 1914. Changed name to *South Wales Journal of Commerce* June 1918. Ceased publication Apr 1935.

CROYDON – *Surrey Morning Echo* (1908). Ceased publication Jan 1910.

DARLINGTON – *North Star* (1881). Merged with *Newcastle Daily Journal* 1926.
    Northern Echo (1870).

DUNDEE – *Dundee Advertiser* (1861). Merged with *Courier and Argus* 1926 and became *Dundee Advertiser and Courier*.
    Courier and Argus (1861). Merged with the daily edition of *Dundee Advertiser* 1926 and became *Dundee Advertiser and Courier*.
    Dundee Advertiser and Courier (1926). Changed name to **Courier and Advertiser** 1926.

EDINBURGH – **Scotsman** (1817).

EXETER – *Devon and Exeter Daily Gazette* (1772). Merged with *Western Morning News* Mar 1932.
    Western Times (1827). Became weekly paper 1922.

GLASGOW – **Glasgow Herald** (1783).
    North British Daily Mail (1847). Became *Glasgow Daily Mail* 1901. Merged with *Daily Record* 1901.
    Daily Record (1895). Incorporated *Glasgow Daily Mail* 1901 and became *Daily Record and Daily Mail*. Changed name to *Daily Record and Mail* 1902. Changed name to **Daily Record** 1954.

---

[1] Localised editions of the Argus were published in Battle, Chichester, Eastbourne, East Grinstead, Hastings, Horsham, Hove, Lewes, Littlehampton, Rye, Tunbridge Wells, and Worthing. Those still publishing in 1926 were merged with the Brighton Morning Argus into the evening Argus.

GLASGOW (*cont.*)
  Bulletin (1915). Became *Bulletin and Scots Pictorial* Jan 1924. Ceased publication July 1960.
  Scottish Daily News (Apr 75). Workers' Cooperative, using *Scottish Daily Express* plant. Ceased publication Nov 1975.
HUDDERSFIELD – *Huddersfield Daily Chronicle* (1871).[2] Ceased publication Dec 1915.
HULL – *Daily Mail* (1787). Became an evening paper 1902.
  Eastern Morning News (1861). Ceased publication Nov 1929.
IPSWICH – **East Anglian Daily Times** (1874).
LEAMINGTON – **Leamington, Warwick, Kenilworth and District Morning News** (1896). Originally *Leamington, Warwick, Kenilworth and District Daily Circular.* Changed name and started morning publication in 1919.
LEEDS – *Leeds Mercury* (1718). Changed name to *Leeds and Yorkshire Mercury* Oct 1901-Nov 1907. Merged with *Yorkshire Post* Nov 1939.
  Yorkshire Post (1754).
LEICESTER – *Leicester Daily Post* (1872). Ceased publication Mar 1921.
LIVERPOOL – *Liverpool Courier* (1808). Changed name to *Liverpool Daily Courier* Sep 1922. Changed name to *Daily Courier* Oct 1922. Ceased publication Dec 1929.
  Liverpool Mercury (1811). Merged with *Liverpool Daily Post* Nov 1904.
  Liverpool Daily Post (1855).
  Journal of Commerce (1861).
MANCHESTER – *Manchester Courier* (1825). Ceased publication Jan 1916.
  Daily Dispatch (1900). Merged with *News Chronicle* Nov 1955.
  (Manchester) **Guardian** (1821). (*See under National Daily Newspapers.*)
  Manchester Journal of Commerce. Ceased publication 1911.
  Telegraphic News. Ceased publication 1901.
  Daily Citizen (1912). Ceased publication Jun 1915.
  Daily Sketch (1909). Ceased publication Apr 1911.
NEWCASTLE – *Illustrated Chronicle* (1910). Ceased publication June 1925.
  Newcastle Daily Chronicle (1858). Merged with *North Mail* Mar 1923.
  Newcastle Daily Journal (1832). Became *Newcastle Journal and North Mail* Sep 1939. Changed name to **Journal** Jul 1958.
  North Mail (1901). Incorporated *Newcastle Daily Chronicle* Mar 1923 and became *North Mail and Newcastle Daily Chronicle.* Merged with *Newcastle Journal* in Sep 1939.
  Newcastle Morning Mail (1898). Changed name to *Morning Mail* Feb 1901. Ceased publication Aug 1901.
NEWPORT – *South Wales Daily News* (1872). Changed name to *South Wales News* 1928. Merged with *Western Mail* 1928.
NORWICH – **Eastern Daily Press** (1870).
  Norfolk Daily Standard (1855). Became an evening paper in 1900.
NOTTINGHAM – *Nottingham Daily Express* (1860). Changed name to *Nottingham Journal and Express* Apr 1918. Changed name to *Nottingham Journal* 1921. Merged with *Nottingham Guardian* Sep 1953 to become *Nottingham Guardian Journal.* Ceased publication Jan 1973.
  Nottingham Daily Guardian (1861). Changed name to *Nottingham Guardian* Oct 1905. Merged with *Nottingham Journal* Sep 1953.
OXFORD – *Oxford Morning Echo* (1860). Ceased publication Jan 1900.
PLYMOUTH – *Western Daily Mercury* (1860). Merged with *Western Morning News* Jan 1921.
  Western Morning News (1860).
PORTSMOUTH – *Southern Daily Mail* (1884). Ceased publication 1905.
SHIELDS – *Shields Morning Mail* (1889). Ceased publication Feb 1901.
SHEFFIELD – *Yorkshire Early Bird* (1899). Became morning paper in 1929. Changed named to *Early Bird* Mar 1938. Merged with local evening paper, *Chronicle Midday,* May 1950.
  Sheffield Daily Telegraph (1855). Changed name to *Sheffield Telegraph* Jun 1934: to *Sheffield Telegraph and Daily Independent* Oct 38-May 39; to *Telegraph and Independent* Jun-Jul 42; to *Sheffield Telegraph* Jul 42-Sep 65; to *Sheffield Morning Telegraph* Sep 65. Closed 1987.
  Sheffield and Rotherham Independent (1819). Changed name to *Sheffield Independent* Jan 1901. Changed name to *Sheffield Daily Independent* Feb 01-Oct 09. Changed name to *Daily Independent* June 1922. Amalgamated with *Sheffield Telegraph* Oct 1938.
SWANSEA – *Swansea Gazette.* Changed name to *Swansea Daily Shipping Register* 1900. Ceased publication 1918.
YORK – *Yorkshire Herald* (1790). Became weekly 1936.

[2] Not published on Saturdays.

SOURCE. – *Willing's Press Guide 1900-*; the catalogue of the British Museum Newspaper Library at Colindale.

Main Political Weeklies

Economist, The, 1843
Proprietors: The Economist Newspaper Limited. (Since 1928 50% of shares held by Financial Newspaper Proprietors Limited,later Financial News Ltd.)
Policy: Independent.
Editors: E. Johnstone, 1883. F. Hurst, 1907. H. Withers, 1916. W. Layton, 1922. G. Crowther, 1938. D. Tyerman, 1956. A. Burnet, 1965. A.Knight, 1974. R. Pennant-Rea, 1986. B.Emmott, 1993.

(Nation), 1907
Proprietors: The Nation. 1931 Amalgamated with the *New Statesman*.
Policy: Independent radical.
Editors: H. Massingham, 1907. H.Henderson, 1923. H. Wright, 1930–1931.

New Statesman (and Society), 1913
Proprietors: Statesman Publishing Company. 1931 Amalgamated with the Nation, The Statesman and Nation Publishing Company. Merged with *New Society* in 1988 and adopted full title *New Statesman and Society*.
Policy: Independent radical.
Editors: C. Sharp, 1913. K. Martin, 1931. J. Freeman, 1961. P. Johnson, 1965. R. Crossman, 1970. A. Howard, 1973. B. Page, 1978. H. Stephenson, 1982. J. Lloyd, 1986. S. Weir, 1988. S. Platt, 1990.

The Spectator, 1828
Proprietors: The Spectator Limited since 1898. J. St. L. Strachey, 1898. (Sir) E. Wrench, 1925. I. Gilmour, 1954. H. Creighton, 1967. H. Keswick,1975. A. Clough, 1981.
Policy: Independent conservative.
Editors: J. St. L. Strachey, 1897. (Sir) Evelyn Wrench, 1925. W. Harris, 1932.W.Taplin, 1953.I.Gilmour, 1954. B.Inglis, 1959. I.Hamilton, 1962. I. Macleod, 1963. N. Lawson, 1966. G. Gale, 1970. H. Creighton, 1973. A. Chancellor, 1975. C. Moore, 1984. D. Lawson, 1989.

(Time and Tide), 1920
Proprietors: Lady Rhondda, 1920–1958. L. Skevington, 1958. T. Beaumont, 1960. W. Brittain, 1962. Time and Tide Ltd, 1977. Re-named Time and Tide Business News 1977 and published fortnightly. From 1978 published monthly.
Policy: Independent.
Editors: Lady Rhondda, 1920. A. Lejeune, 1957. L. Skevington, 1958. J. Thompson, 1960. W. Brittain, 1962. I. Lyon, 1977.

Tribune, 1937
Proprietors: Tribune Publications, Ltd.
Policy: Left-wing.
Editors: W. Mellor, 1937. J. Hartshorn, 1938. R. Postgate, 1940. A. Bevan, 1942. J. Kimche, 1945. M. Foot, 1948. R. Edwards, 1952. M. Foot, 1956. R. Clements, 1959. C. Mullin, 1982. N. Williamson, 1984. P. Kelly, 1986. P. Anderson, 1990. M. Seddon, 1993.

The Press Council, 1953–1990

Chairman

(General Council of the Press)		(The Press Council)	
1953	W. Astor (Ld)	1963	Ld Devlin
1955	Sir L. Andrews	1969	Ld Pearce
1959	G. Murray	1974	Ld Shawcross
		1978	(Sir) P. Neill
		1983	Sir Z. Cowen
		1989	L. Blom-Cooper

The General Council of the Press was formed in 1953 in response to a recommendation of the Royal Commission on the Press (Cmd. 7700). It consisted of 15 editorial representatives and 10 managerial representatives. Its objects were to preserve the freedom of the press, to review any developments likely to restrict the supply of information of public interest and importance, to encourage training of journalists and technical research and to study developments in the press tending towards greater concentration or monopoly.

In 1963 it was reorganised to bring in lay members and the title was changed to the Press Council. The objects of the Council were extended to include considering complaints about the conduct of the press or the conduct of persons and organisations towards the press, and publishing relevant statistical material.

In 1977 the Press Council accepted the recommendation of the Royal Commission on the Press that in addition to its independent lay Chairman, it should consist of equal numbers of press and lay members. From 1978 to 1990, the composition was 12 representatives from newspaper and magazine management, 4 from the National Union of Journalists, 2 from the Institute of Journalists, 18 lay representatives, 8 non-voting consultative members and a lay Chairman. Lay members were appointed by an independent body, the Press Council Appointments Commission. The NUJ representatives withdrew from the Council in 1980, and only returned in May 1990, seven months before the Council was wound up.

Press Complaints Commission, 1991–

Chairman
1991   Ld McGregor of Durris

The Press Complaints Commission was established by the newspaper industry to take over from the Press Council following the report of the Committee on Privacy and Related Matters chaired by Sir D. Calcutt, published in Jun 90 (Cm 1102). It is responsible for adjudicating on complaints of unfair treatment, maintaining high professional standards and implementing a code of practice drafted by editors. Seven of its members are editors of national and local newspapers and magazines; nine, including the Chairman, are drawn from other fields. In Jan 93 a review of the operation of the Press Complaints Commission, the Calcutt Review of Press Self-Regulation (Cm 2135), concluded that the Commission had not been an effective regulator of the press and a statutory authority was needed.

SOURCES. – *The Cambridge Bibliography of English Literature,* Vol. III pp. 797–8, lists all press directories, pp. 798–846 lists all newspapers and magazines. *The History of the Times,* Pt II, pp. 1130–36 gives a chart of the metropolitan morning and evening press from 1884–1947. There are several press directories which cover all or part of the period: *T.B. Browne's Advertiser's ABC,* 1900–1932; *Sell's Dictionary of the World's Press,* 1900–1921 (including a *Who's Who* of notabilities of the British Press in 1914–21 editions); *Mitchell's Newspaper Press Directory* (became *Benn's* in 1946), 1900–61; *Willing's Press Guide,* 1900–. PEP: *Report on the British Press* (1938); *Report of the Royal Commission on the Press* (Cmd. 7700 of 1949, Minutes of Evidence, Cmd. 7317 of 1948); *Report of the Royal Commission on the Press* (Cmnd. 1811 of 1962); N. Kaldor and R. Silverman, *A Statistical Analysis of Advertising Expenditure and of the Revenue of the Press* (1948); A.P. Wadsworth, 'Newspaper Circulations' (in *Proceedings of the Manchester Statistical Society* 1954). J.L. Hammond, *C.P. Scott of the Manchester Guardian* (1934); J.W.Robertson Scott, *The Life and Death of a Newspaper (The Pall Mall Gazette)* (1952); A. Gollin, *The Observer and J.L. Garvin* (1960); S. Jenkins, *The Market for Glory: Fleet Street Ownership in the Twentieth Century* (1986); F. Williams, *Dangerous Estate* (1957); C. Seymour-Ure, *Politics, the Press and the Public* (1968); C.Seymour-Ure, *The Political Impact of the Mass Media* (1974); C.Seymour-Ure, *The British Press and Broadcasting since 1945* (1991); J.Whale, *The Politics of the Media* (1977); J. Tunstall and M. Palmer, *Media Moguls* (1991); Press Council Annual Reports, *The Press and the People;* H.P. Levy, *The Press Council* (1967). *Hutton Readership Surveys,* J.W. Hobson and Harry Henry, came out annually between 1947 and 1955. See also *Royal Commission on the Press* (Cmnd. 6810) and companion papers Cmnd. 6811–16; R. Harris, *Gotcha: The Media, The Government and the Falklands Crisis* (1983); D. McQuail, *Review of Sociological Writing on the Press* (1976); C. Seymour-Ure, Oliver Boyd Barrett and Jeremy Tunstall, *Studies on the Press* (1977); J.Tunstall, *The Media in Britain* (1983); S. Jenkins, *Newspapers* (1980); R.Snoddy, *The Good, the Bad, and the Unacceptable* (1993).

XXI

BROADCASTING AUTHORITIES

The British Broadcasting Corporation

The British Broadcasting Company Ltd was formed by some 200 manufacturers and shareholders on 18 Oct 22, registered on 15 Dec 22, and received its licence on 18 Jan 23. A system of paid licences for owners of radio receivers was started in 1922. London, Manchester, Birmingham, and Newcastle stations began to operate in November and December, 1922. This was followed by the establishment of the *British Broadcasting Corporation* under royal charter (20 Dec 26), which came into operation on 1 Jan 27. It was to be a public service body 'acting in the national interest' and financed by licence fees paid by all owners of radio receivers. (A formal agreement with the Postmaster General had been drawn up on 9 Nov 26.) Under the royal charter the B.B.C. was granted a licence for ten years and was to be directed by a board of governors nominated by the government. The charter was renewed and modified 1 Jan 37, 1 Jan 47, 1 Jul 52, 30 Jul 64. It was extended until 31 July 1979 in 1976 (Cmnd. 6581). In Jul 1979 it was extended for a further period until 31 Jul 1981, when it was replaced by a new charter (Cmnd 8313) to last until 31 Dec 1996. On 6 Jul 94 the National Heritage Secretary P. Brooke announced in the White Paper 'The Future of the BBC – Serving the Nation, Competing Worldwide' (Cm. 2621) that the Charter would be renewed for another ten years until 2006, and that the licence fee would remain the basis of B.B.C. funding for at least the next five years.

British Broadcasting Company, 1923–1926

Chairman: Ld Gainford   **Managing Director**:   (Sir) J. Reith
                                                            (formerly **General Manager**)

Board members:

G. Isaacs (*Marconi*), Sir W. Noble (*General Electric*), B. Binyon (*Radio Communication Co.*), H. Pease (*Western Electric*), A. McKinstry (*Metropolitan Vickers*), W. Burnham (*Burndept*), J. Gray (*British Thomson-Houston Co.*), Sir W. Bull (*M.P.*).

British Broadcasting Corporation, 1927–

Board of Governors

Chairmen		Vice-Chairmen	
1 Jan 27	E of Clarendon	1 Jan 27	Ld Gainford
2 Jun 30	J. Whitley	1 Jan 33	R. Norman
28 Mar 35	Vt Bridgeman	25 Oct 35	H. Brown
3 Oct 35	R. Norman	8 Jun 37	C. Millis
19 Apr 39	Sir A. Powell	1 Jan 47	Marchioness of Reading
1 Jan 47	Ld Inman	7 Jan 51	Ld Tedder
9 Jun 47	Ld Simon	1 Jul 54	Sir P. Morris
1 Aug 52	Sir A. Cadogan	1 Jul 60	Sir J. Duff
1 Dec 57	Sir A. fforde	19 Sep 65	Ld Fulton
1 Feb 64	Sir J. Duff (*acting*)	11 Jun 66	R. Lusty
14 May 64	Ld Normanbrook	31 Jul 67	Ld Fulton
1 Sep 67	Ld Hill of Luton	1 Jan 68	R. Lusty
1 Jan 73	Sir M. Swann	15 Feb 68	Ld Fulton
1 Aug 80	G. Howard (Ld)	12 Nov 70	Lady Plowden
1 Aug 83	S. Young	26 Jun 75	M. Bonham Carter
29 Aug 86	(*vacant*)	1 Aug 81	Sir W. Rees-Mogg
6 Nov 86	M. Hussey	1 Aug 86	Ld Barnett
		1 Aug 93	Ld Cocks

Governors

1927–31	Sir G.Nairne		1962–67	Sir A. Clarke
1927–32	M Rendall		1966–67	Ld Fulton
1927–32	Mrs P. Snowden (Vtess)		1966–68	J. Trower
1932–36	H. Brown		1967–73	Sir R. Murray
1933–35	Vt Bridgeman		1968–71	Sir R. Bellenger
1933–37	Mrs M. Hamilton		1968–72	P. Wilson
1935–39	Lady Bridgeman		1968–73	T. Jackson
1935–39	H.Fisher		1968–71	Sir L. Constantine (Ld)
1937–39	Sir I. Fraser		1968–73	Dame M. Green
1937–39	J. Mallon		1969–71	Sir H. Greene
1938–39	Miss M Fry		1971–76	R. Allan (Ld)
(From 1939–41 the Board was reduced to two			1972–76	R. Fuller
members, the Chairman and Deputy Chairman)			1972–76	T. Morgan
1941–46	Lady V. Bonham-Carter		1972–80	G. Howard
1941–46	Sir I. Fraser		1973–76	V. Feather (Ld)
1941–46	J.Mallon		1973–78	Sir D. Greenhill (Ld)
1941–46	A. Mann		1974–81	Mrs S. Clarke
1941–46	H. Nicolson		1976–81	P. Chappell
1946–49	Miss B. Ward		1976–82	Ld Allen
1946–49	G. Lloyd		1977–82	Lady Serota
1946–49	Sir R. Peck		1978–85	Sir J. Johnston
1946–50	E. Whitfield		1979–84	C. Longuet-Higgins
1946–50	Marchioness of Reading		1981–83	P. Moons
1947–52	J. Adamson		1981–83	S. Young
1950–54	Ld Tedder		1981–88	Miss J. Barrow
1950–52	Ld Clydesmuir		1982–87	Miss D. Park
1951–52	F. Williams		1982–87	Sir J. Boyd
1950–56	Mrs Barbara Wootton		1983–88	M. McAlpine
1952–54	Sir P. Morris		1984–89	Lady Parkes
1951–55	C. Stedeford		1985–87	E of Harewood
1952–56	Lady Rhys Williams		1985–90	Sir C. Keeble
1954–59	Ld Rochdale		1988–93	J. Roberts
1955–60	Sir E. Benthall		1988–	W. Jordan
1956–61	Mrs T. Cazalet-Keir		1988–93	(Lady) P. D. James
1956–62	Dame F. Hancock		1988–93	K. Oates
1959–60	Sir J. Duff		1990–	Ms J. Glover
1960–62	E of Halsbury		1990–	Mrs Shawhar Sadeque
1960–65	R. Lusty		1990–	Ld N. Gordon-Lennox
1961–66	G. Cooke		1993–	Mrs M. Spurr
1962–68	Dame A. Godwin			

Governors appointed to represent national interests

N. Ireland		*Scotland*		*Wales*	
1952	Sir H. Mulholland	1952	Ld Clydesmuir	1952	Ld Macdonald
1958	J. McKee	1955	T. Johnston	1960	Mrs R. Jones
1962	Sir P. Pim	1956	E of Balfour	1965	G. Williams
1968	Ld Dunleath	1960	Sir D. Milne	1971	G. Hughes
1973	W. O'Hara	1965	Lady Baird	1979	A. Roberts
1978	Lady Faulkner	1971	Lady Avonside	1986	J. Parry
1985	J. Kincade	1976	A. Thompson	1992	G. Jones
1991	Sir K. Bloomfield	1979	(Sir) R. Young		
		1984	W. Peat		
		1989	Sir G. Hills		

Director-General

1 Jan 27	Sir J. Reith	17 Jul 52	B. Nicholls	1 Aug 82	A. Milne
1 Oct 38	F. Ogilvie		(*acting*)	29 Jan 87	(*vacant*)
1 Jan 42	Sir C. Graves	1 Dec 52	Sir I. Jacob	26 Feb 87	(Sir) M. Checkland
	& R. Foot	31 Dec 59	(Sir) H. Greene	23 Dec 92	J. Birt
24 Jun 43	R. Foot	1 Apr 68	(Sir) C. Curran		
31 Mar 44	(Sir) W. Haley	1 Oct 77	(Sir) I. Trethowan		

B.B.C. Radio

The B.B.C. originally offered one basic radio service, known as the National Programme, together with variant Regional Services. In 1939 these services were all replaced by a single Home Service; the Forces Programme, providing a lighter alternative, began in 1940. In 1945 Regional Home Services, as variants of the Home Service, were restarted, and the Light Programme replaced the Forces Programme. In 1946 the Third Programme was introduced to provide a second alternative service. Very high frequency (VHF) transmissions began in 1955, in order to improve the quality and coverage of the existing services. In 1964 the Music Programme was added, using the Third Programme wavelengths in the daytime, and in 1967 a fourth network came into being to provide a pop music service replacing the offshore 'pirate' stations; this was called Radio 1, and the existing national services were renamed Radio 2 (Light Programme), Radio 3 (Third and Music Programmes) and Radio 4 (Home Service).

In 1970 the radio networks were reorganised as 'generic' services following publication of the B.B.C.'s proposals in Broadcasting in the Seventies, and the English regional radio services were then gradually wound down, though the regional centres continued to provide programmes for the networks. The regional radio broadcasts in the three National Regions started to develop as autonomous services with the opening of Radio Ulster in 1975. In 1978 there was a major reorganisation of the radio frequencies used for the national networks, and Radio 4 became available throughout the United Kingdom on the long-wave band. This enabled the national services Radio Scotland, Radio Wales, Radio Cymru (Welsh language, on VHF only) and Radio Ulster to become fully independent of Radio 4. Regular network services of sports programming were carried on Radio 2 and, for cricket, on Radio 3. Radios 3 and 4 carried Open University programmes on their VHF-FM bands and Radio 4 also carried Schools and Continuing Education output. In 1978 also the B.B.C. began regular broadcasting on radio of recorded material from Parliamentary proceedings (see pp. 173–4). On 27 Aug 90 a fifth network, Radio 5, began broadcasting using medium wave frequencies to carry youth and education programmes, and take over sports broadcasting from Radio 2. In Mar 94 Radio 5 was abolished and replaced by a News and Sport Network, Radio 5 Live.

B.B.C. Local Radio

The B.B.C. first began a limited experiment in Local Radio in 1967. The following stations broadcast in England and the Channel Islands.

Three Counties Radio (formerly Radio Bedfordshire)	1985
Radio Berkshire	1992
Radio Bristol	1970
Radio Cambridgeshire	1982
Radio Cleveland (formerly Radio Teesside)	1970
Radio Cornwall	1983
Radio Cumbria (formerly Radio Carlisle)	1975
CWR (Coventry & Warwickshire Radio)	1990
Radio Derby	1971
Radio Devon	1983
Dorset FM	1993
Radio Durham	1968–72
Radio Essex	1986
Radio Furness	1982
Radio Gloucestershire	1988

GLR (formerly Radio London)	1970
GMR (formerly Radio Manchester)	1970
Radio Guernsey	1982
Radio Hereford & Worcester	1989
Radio Humberside	1971
Radio Jersey	1982
Radio Kent (formerly Radio Medway)	1970
Radio Lancashire (formerly Radio Blackburn)	1971
Radio Leeds	1968
Radio Leicester	1967
Radio Lincolnshire	1980
Radio Merseyside	1967
Radio Newcastle	1971
Radio Norfolk	1980
Radio Northampton	1982
Radio Nottingham	1968
Radio Oxford	1970
Radio Sheffield	1967
Radio Shropshire	1985
Radio Solent	1970
Somerset Sound	1988
Radio Stoke-on-Trent	1968
Radio Suffolk	1990
Radio Surrey	1991
Radio Sussex (formerly Radio Brighton)	1968
Radio WM (formerly Radio Birmingham)	1970
Wiltshire Sound	1989
Radio York	1983

B.B.C. Television

On 2 Nov 1936 the first scheduled public service television was started from Alexandra Palace. The service was suspended from September 1939 until June 1946. The first stations outside London, in the Midlands and the North, began transmitting in 1949 and 1951 respectively. By 1966, with more than 100 transmitting stations, B.B.C. Television was within the range of more than 99 per cent of the population of the United Kingdom on a 405-line standard. In April 1964 a second B.B.C. Channel was opened in the London area. In 1967 it began broadcasting in colour; by this time it was available to more than two-thirds of the population of the U.K. It was transmitted on 625 lines. In 1969 the first channel began to be transmitted on 625 lines as well as 405, and colour transmissions were started on BBC1. Transmission on 405 lines ceased in 1986. Well over 99% of the U.K. population are now within range of 625-line transmissions.

BBC1 began breakfast-time broadcasting in 1983, and by 1991 the BBC was broadcasting 240 hours of television a week. World Service Television began broadcasting in Mar 91, using local transmitters and satellites to reach a large audience principally in South and South-east Asia.

Broadcast Receiving Licences and B.B.C. Expenditure

Since 1922 the BBC has been financed mainly by the issue of licences. In 1939–45 all licence revenue went to the Government and the B.B.C. was financed by an annual grant-in-aid. The external services have continued to be financed in this way. Except for 1950–51 the Treasury retained part of the licence fee every year until 1961.

Year	Sound only	Sound/black & white	Colour
1922	10s	..	..
1946	£1	£2	..
1954	£1	£3	..
1957	£1	£4	..
1965	£1 5s	£5	..
1968	£1 5s	£5	£10
1969	£1 5s	£6	£11
1971	–	£7	£12
1975	–	£8	£18
1977	–	£9	£21
1978	–	£10	£25
1979	–	£12	£34
1981	–	£15	£46
1985	–	£18	£58
1988	–	£21	£62.50
1989	–	£22	£66
1990	–	£24	£71
1991	–	£25.50	£77
1992	–	£26.50	£80
1993	–	£27.50	£83
1994	–	£28	£84.50

	Total Licences issued 000s	Sound only 000s	Sound & Monochrome TV 000s	Colour TV 000s	Expenditure on revenue account £000s	
1925	1,654	1,654	..	..	..	
1927	2,270	2,264	..	..	902	
1930	3,092	3,076	..	..	1,224	
1935	7,012	6,970	..	..	2,473	
1940	8,951	8,898	..	..	4,350	
1945	9,710	9,663	..	..	9,001	
					Home	External
1947	10,778	10,713	15	..	7,273	3,878
1950	12,219	11,819	344	..	9,579	4,471
1955	13,980	9,414	4,504	..	17,964	5,093
1960	15,005	4,480	10,470	..	30,560	6,408
1965	16,047	2,759	13,253	..	55,642	8,499
1970	18,184	2,279	15,609	273	81,134	10,565
1975	17,701	..	10,120	7,580	152,771	19,625
1980	18,285	..	5,383	12,902	363,400	40,100
1985	18,716	..	2,896	15,820	808,700	83,900
1990	19,645	..	1,681	17,964	1,261,900	132,500
1992	19,631	..	1,205	18,426	1,443,100	163,600

The difference between the total and other licences column is explained by the issue of free licences to the blind.

The expenditure figures from 1940 onwards are for the year ending the following 31 Mar. The figures from 1947 onwards are for operational expenditure only.

SOURCE: *BBC Annual Report & Accounts. Annual Abstract of Statistics.*

Independent Broadcasting

The Independent Television Authority was set up by the Postmaster-General under section 1 (3) of the *Television Act, 1954,* on 4 Aug 1954 for a period of ten years. The Authority was to licence programme contracting companies and to regulate their output. The whole of the finance of Independent Television was to depend on advertising revenue though the Act specifically prohibited the 'sponsoring' of programmes by advertisers. The first Independent Television programmes were transmitted on 22 Sep 1955. The following Acts have since been passed significantly affecting Independent Broadcasting:

Television Act, 1963. This extended the life of the I.T.A. until 1976.

Television Act, 1964. This consolidated the *Television Acts of 1954 and 1963* and increased the I.T.A.'s power over programmes and advertising.

Sound *Broadcasting Act, 1972.* This Act renamed the I.T.A. the Independent Broadcasting Authority and extended its functions to include the provision of local commercial sound broadcasting services.

Independent Broadcasting Authority Act, 1973. This consolidated the *Television Act, 1964* and the *Sound Broadcasting Act, 1972.*

Independent Broadcasting Authority Act, 1974. This Act made provision for 'additional payments' to be made by television programme contractors to the I.B.A.

Independent Broadcasting Authority Act (No 2), 1974. This extended the I.B.A.'s life until July 1979.

Independent Broadcasting Authority Act, 1978. This further extended the I.B.A. until the end of 1981.

Independent Broadcasting Authority Act, 1979. This Act gave the I.B.A. responsibility for establishing transmitters for a fourth television channel.

Broadcasting Act, 1980. This Act extended the life of the I.B.A. until 1996. It laid down the operating condition of the fourth television channel, which was to be separately established in Wales by the Welsh Fourth Channel Authority, and also established a Broadcasting Complaints Commission.

Broadcasting Act, 1981. This consolidated the *Independent Broadcasting Authority Acts, 1973, 1974, and 1978,* and the *Broadcasting Act, 1980.*

Cable and Broadcasting Act, 1984. This made provision for the establishment of a Cable Authority to provide cable programmes and amended the *Broadcasting Act, 1981,* to provide for the establishment of a Satellite Broadcasting Board.

Broadcasting Act, 1987. This extended the period of the contracts between the IBA and the ITV companies, now expiring on 31 Dec 1992, to give more time for the consideration of a new licensing system.

Broadcasting Act, 1990. This replaced the Independent Broadcasting Authority and the Cable Authority with the Independent Television Commission and the Radio Authority, and laid down new procedures for licensing and regulating commercially funded television services.

Independent Television Authority 1954–1972
and Independent Broadcasting Authority 1972–90

Chairman

31 Mar 55	Sir K. Clark		1 Sep 67	Ld Aylestone
8 Nov 57	Sir I. Kirkpatrick		1 Apr 75	Lady Plowden
6 Nov 62	Sir J. Carmichael (*acting*)		1 Jan 81	Ld Thomson of Monifieth
1 Jul 63	Ld Hill of Luton		1 Jan 89	(Sir) G. Russell

Director-General

1 Oct 54	Sir R. Fraser		31 Oct 82	J. Whitney
15 Oct 70	(Sir) B. Young		1 Apr 89	Mrs S. Littler (Lady)

Independent Television Commission, 1991–

Chairman		Chief Executive	
1 Jan 91	Sir G. Russell	1 Jan 91	D. Glencross

Radio Authority, 1991–

Chairman		Chief Executive	
1 Jan 91	Ld Chalfont	1 Jan 91	P. Baldwin

Channel 3 – I.T.V Programme Contracting Companies

The following programme companies have held ITV franchises in the UK. In 1964 all were re-appointed to provide programmes until July 1968. On 11 June 1967 new contractors were announced to operate from 30 July 1968 to 29 July 1974. In 1972 the Authority made plain its intention to renew the existing contracts with the programme companies for two years from 31 July 1974, subject to satisfactory performance and subject to review of rentals and areas. A further reallocation of contracts was announced on 28 Dec 1980, and took effect in Jan 1982. The Broadcasting Act, 1990, laid down a new procedure under which the newly established Independent Television Commission awarded licences to the highest bidder, subject to programme proposals meeting a quality threshold, and the proposals being considered financially sustainable. In 1992 Yorkshire Television merged with Tyne Tees, although they retained separate identities on air. In Nov 93 the Government announced a limited relaxation of the ITV ownership rules, enabling one ITV company to hold two large regional licences, except in London. A number of proposed mergers were subsequently announced.

On air	Off air	Company	Franchise Areas
22 Sep 55	29 Jul 68	Ass. Rediffusion	London (weekday)
24 Sep 55	28 Jul 68	Associated (ATV)	London (weekend)
17 Feb 56	31 Dec 81	Associated (ATV)	Midlands (weekday)
18 Feb 56	28 Jul 68	ABC	Midlands (weekend)
3 May 56 –		Granada	N.W. England (weekday)
5 May 56	28 Jul 68	ABC	N.W. England (weekend)
31 Aug 57 –		Scottish (STV)	Central Scotland
14 Jan 58	3 Mar 68	TWW	Wales & W. England
30 Aug 58	31 Dec 81	Southern	South of England
15 Jan 59 –		Tyne-Tees	N.E. England
27 Oct 59 –		Anglia	East of England
31 Oct 59 –		Ulster	Northern Ireland
29 Apr 61	11 Aug 81	Westward	S.W. England
1 Sep 61 –		Border	The Borders
30 Sep 61 –		Grampian	N.E. of Scotland
1 Sep 62 –		Channel	Channel Islands
14 Sep 62	26 Jan 64	Wales (W & N)	West & North Wales
4 Mar 68 –		Harlech (HTV)	Wales & W. England
29 Jul 68 –		Yorkshire	Yorkshire
30 Jul 68	31 Dec 92	Thames	London (weekday)
2 Aug 68 –		London Weekend (LWT)	London (weekend)
12 Aug 81	31 Dec 92	TSW	S. W. England
1 Jan 81	31 Dec 92	TVS	South of England
1 Jan 81 –		Central	Midlands
1 Feb 83	31 Dec 92	TV-am	(breakfast)
1 Jan 93 –		Carlton	London (weekday)
1 Jan 93 –		GMTV	(breakfast)
1 Jan 93 –		Meridian	South of England
1 Jan 93 –		Westcountry	S. W. England

Channel Four

The fourth television channel in the UK is provided by Channel Four Television Corporation in England, Scotland and Northern Ireland, and in Wales by S4C.

The Channel 4 Television Company was established as a subsidiary of the IBA under the *Broadcasting Act, 1980*. It went on air on 2 Nov 82. It became an independent corporation as a result of the *Broadcasting Act, 1990*, selling its own advertising airtime from 1 Jan 93. Chairman: E. Dell, 1981. Sir R. Attenborough, 1987. Sir M. Bishop, 1992.

The S4C Authority, the regulatory body for the fourth channel in Wales, was also established under the *Broadcasting Act, 1980*. S4C began transmission on 1 Nov 1982. Chairman: Sir G. Daniel, 1981. J. Davies, 1986.

Finances of Independent Broadcasting, 1955–

(£000s)

Year	ITV Revenue	ILR Revenue	ITA/IBA/ITC	Govt. Levy
1955		..	55	..
1956	13,024	..	500	..
1957	31,986	..	1,702	..
1958	48,671	..	2,284	..
1959	58,359	..	2,871	..
1960	76,960	..	3,757	..
1961	93,276	..	4,213	..
1962	99,794	..	4,693	..
1963	62,931	..	5,464	..
1964	74,433	..	5,623	..
1965	82,840	..	7,246	8,350
1966	85,825	..	8,381	21,186
1967	91,776	..	8,697	22,855
1968	98,759	..	8,697	24,811
1969	97,540	..	7,556	25,779
1970	94,742	..	6,936	26,102
1971	108,634	..	7,793	24,811
1972	134,221	..	11,248	10,839
1973	160,831	..	13,054	18,243
1974	149,245	..	13,641	22,763
1975	176,532	8,535	14,897	19,163
1976	230,807	14,700	15,614	22,162
1977	299,887	23,100	17,876	47,878
1978	363,005	29,845	21,304	65,388
1979	346,796	44,587	22,317	70,018
1980	529,311	44,858	24,443	45,380
1981	611,223	50,824	30,243	55,495
1982	697,170	60,748	36,441	59,110
1983	824,417	70,800	53,769	38,673
1984	912,265	75,700	58,253	28,321
1985	982,603	72,100	62,595	41,409
1986	1,183,000	79,006	65,331	22,090
1987	1,325,871	99,400	68,052	76,225
1988	1,508,400	125,000	71,531	87,553
1989	1,613,537	145,000	74,919	100,139
1990	1,613,672	143,400	74,759 (55,714*)	108,298
1991	1,587,453	133,500	20,928	135,462

*IBA closing account, April–Dec 1990.

SOURCE. – B. MacDonald, *'Broadcasting in the United Kingdom - a guide to information sources'* (2nd ed., 1993).

Cable Television

There were experiments with cable television as early as the 1950s, with localised relay operators offered wired television in areas of poor reception. In 1972 community cable television services were established in Greenwich, Bristol, Swindon, Sheffield and Wellingborough, but most turned out not to be financially viable. In 1983 a Government White Paper took up the recommendations of the Hunt Committee and proposed granting interim licences for new cable services providing new programming material, financed by private enterprise. This was the basis of the *Cable and Broadcasting Act, 1984*, which established the Cable Authority as the regulatory body. Under the *Broadcasting Act, 1990*, the I.T.C took over these functions with effect from 1 Jan 91. There are restrictions on ownership of cable operators which bar existing terrestrial TV companies or political or religious organisations from gaining control.

Cable Authority, 1984–90

Chairman	Director-General
1984 R. Burton	1984 J. Davey

Satellite Television

The origins of direct broadcasting by satellite can be traced back to the first live television transmissions by the Telstar satellite on 11 Jul 62. But the development of a service direct into people's homes was hampered by the limitations of the technology and the large capital cost.

Chronology of development of Direct Broadcast by Satellite

22 Nov 82	Home Office accepts Part Report's findings on satellite system technology.
Jul 84	BBC and ITV companies are joined by other companies in 'Club of 21' to plan for DBS services.
Jun 85	Satellite Broadcasting Board tells Government the consortium cannot proceed, due to prohibitive cost of using British-made satellite stipulated by Government.
8 Jul 85	S.B.B. wound up after less than a year.
Apr 86	I.B.A. advertises for 15 year contract for DBS on system of contractor's choice.
11 Dec 86	British Satellite Broadcasting wins contract, proposing to transmit from the Marcopolo high-power satellite using the latest D-MAC transmission technology and 'squarial' home dish aerials. Major shareholders include Anglia, Granada and Pearson.
8 Jun 88	R. Murdoch announces plans for Sky Television on Astra satellite.
5 Feb 89	Sky Television begins transmission.
29 Apr 90	B.S.B. begins DBS transmissions.
2 Nov 90	B.S.B. and Sky announce merger to form British Sky Broadcasting (BSkyB).

Independent Local Radio

These companies have been franchised by the I.B.A. and the Radio Authority.

Aberdeen	Jul 81	NorthSound Radio	Bradford	Sep 75	The Pulse (formerly Pennine Radio)
Alton	Nov 92	Wey Valley 102			
Ayr	Oct 81	West Sound	Bradford	Dec 89	Sunrise FM
Belfast	Mar 76	Downtown Radio	Brighton	Aug 83	Southern Sound
Belfast	Feb 90	Cool FM	Bristol	Oct 81	GWR (formerly Radio West)
Birmingham	Feb 74	BRMB Radio			
Birmingham	May 90	Buzz FM	Bristol	Apr 90	Galaxy Radio (formerly FTP)
Blackpool	May 92	Radiowave			
Borders	Jan 90	Radio Borders	Bury St	Nov 82	SGR (formerly Saxon Radio)
Bournemouth	Sep 80	Two Counties Radio	Edmunds		

Location	Date	Station
Cambridge	Feb 89	CN.FM
Cardiff	Apr 80	Red Dragon FM (formerly CBC)
Ceredigion	Dec 92	Radio Ceredigion
Cheltenham	Mar 93	603 Radio
Cornwall	Apr 92	Pirate FM
Coventry	May 80	Mercia Sound
Coventry	Aug 90	Radio Harmony
Devon	Oct 92	Lantern Radio
Dumfries	May 90	South West Sound
Dundee	Oct 80	Radio Tay
Edinburgh	Jan 75	Radio Forth
Exeter	Nov 80	Devonair Radio
Glasgow	Dec 73	Radio Clyde
Glasgow	Jun 90– Aug 91	East End Radio
Gloucester	Oct 80	Severn Sound
Great Yarmouth	Oct 84	Radio Broadland
Guernsey	Oct 92	Island FM
Guildford	Apr 83	Premier Radio (formerly County Sound)
Harlow	May 93	Ten 17
Hereford	Oct 82	Radio Wyvern
High Wycombe	Dec 93	Eleven Seventy
Humberside	Apr 84	Viking Radio
Inverness	Feb 82	Moray Firth Radio
Ipswich	Oct 75	SGR (formerly Radio Orwell)
Isle of Wight	Apr 90	Isle of Wight Radio
Jersey	Oct 92	Channel FM
Kettering	Apr 90	KCBC
King's Lynn	Jul 92	KL.FM
Leeds	Sep 81	Radio Aire
Leicester	Sep 81– Oct 83	Centre Radio
Leicester	Sep 84	Leicester Sound
Lincoln	Mar 92	Lincs FM
Liverpool	Oct 74	Radio City
London	Oct 73	Capital Radio
London	Oct 73– Mar 94	LBC
London	Nov 89	Sunrise Radio
London	Nov 89	WNK
London	Nov 89	London Greek Radio
London	Mar 90	Jazz FM
London	Mar 90	RTM
London	Mar 90	Choice FM
London	Jun 90	Spectrum Radio
London	Jun 90– Feb 92	Airport Information Radio
London	Jul 90	Melody Radio
London	Sep 90	Kiss FM
Ludlow	Oct 92	Sunshine 855
Luton	Oct 81	Chiltern Radio
Maidstone	Oct 84	Invicta Radio
Manchester	Apr 74	Piccadilly Radio
Manchester	Oct 89	Sunset Radio
Milton Keynes	Oct 89	Horizon Radio
Montgomery	Jul 93	Radio Maldwyn
Morecambe	Mar 93	The Bay
Newport	Jun 83– Apr 85	Gwent Broadcasting
Northampton	Oct 86	Northants Radio
Nottingham	Jul 75	Radio Trent
Oxford	Sep 89	Fox FM
Paisley	Sep 92	Q96
Peterborough	Jul 80	Hereward Radio
Pitlochry	Mar 92	Heartland FM
Plymouth	May 75	Plymouth Sound
Portsmouth	Oct 75– Jun 86	Radio Victory
Portsmouth	Oct 86	Ocean Sound
Preston	Oct 82	Red Rose Radio
Reading	Mar 76	Radio 210
Reigate	Oct 84	Radio Mercury
Salisbury	Sep 92	Spire FM
Sheffield	Oct 74	Radio Hallam
Shetland Isles	Oct 91	SIBC
Southend	Sep 81	Essex Radio
Stirling	Jun 90	Central FM
Stockport	Feb 90	Signal Cheshire
Stoke-on-Trent	Sep 83	Signal Radio
Sunderland	Nov 90	Wear FM
Swansea	Sep 74	Swansea Sound
Swindon	Oct 82	GWR (formerly Wiltshire Radio)
Teesside	Jun 75	TFM Radio (formerly Radio Tees)
Tendring	Oct 90	Mellow 1557
Tyne & Wear	Jul 74	Metro Radio
Weymouth	Sep 93	Wessex FM
Windsor	May 93	Star FM
Wolverhampton	Apr 76	Beacon Radio
Wrexham	Sep 83	Marcher Sound
Yeovil	Nov 89	Orchard FM
York	Jul 92	Minster FM

Independent National Radio

The Radio Authority has approved the establishment of two music-based national radio stations, using frequencies given up by the BBC. They are

| 7 Sep 92 | Classic FM |
| 30 Apr 93 | Virgin 1215 |

Independent Radio News (I.R.N), a wholly owned subsidiary of LBC, has since October 1973 provided a news service, available to all the independent local radio stations.

Broadcasting Complaints Commission

This was established under the *Broadcasting Act, 1980* (amended by the *Broadcasting Act, 1981* and the *Cable and Broadcasting Act, 1984*, and replaced by the *Broadcasting Act, 1990*) to consider and adjudicate on complaints of unfair treatment or invasion of privacy by BBC, ITC or Radio Authority licensed services. Its findings are published in the *Radio Times*, *TV Times* etc. where appropriate, or broadcast on air.

Chairman

1981	Lady Pike
1985	Sir T. Skyrme
1987	Lady Anglesey
1992	Mrs B. Wells
1992	P. Pilkington

Broadcasting Standards Council

This was established by the Home Secretary in 1988, and put on a statutory footing by the *Broadcasting Act, 1990*, to consider standards in portrayal of sex and violence, and matters of taste and decency on TV, radio and video.

Chairman

1988	Sir W. Rees-Mogg
1993	Lady Howe

Inquiries into Broadcasting

Committee Chairman	Date appointed	Date of report	Command Number	Estimated Cost (£)
Sir F. Sykes	Apr 23	Aug 23	1951	320
E of Crawford and Balcarres	Aug 25	Mar 26	2599	106
Ld Selsdon	May 34	Jan 35	4793	965
Vt Ullswater	Apr 35	Feb 36	5091	564
Ld Hankey	Sep 43	Mar 45	Non-parl.	..
Ld Beveridge	Jun 49	Jan 51	8116	15,415
Sir H. Pilkington	Jul 60	Jun 62	1753	45,450
Ld Annan	Apr 74	Mar 77	6753	315,000
Ld Hunt of Tanworth	Apr 82	Oct 82	8679	47,388
Sir A. Part	Jul 82	Nov 82	8751	34,625
A. Peacock	May 85	Jul 86	9824	268,761
J. Sadler	Feb 89	Mar 91	1436	215,000

SOURCES.– A. Briggs, *The BBC: The First Fifty Years* (1985); A. Briggs, *The History of Broadcasting in the United Kingdom* (4 vols, 1961–79); J. Cain, *The BBC: 70 Years of Broadcasting* (1992); A. Davidson, *Under the Hammer: The Inside Story of the 1991 ITV Franchise Battle* (1992); B. Henny, *British Television Advertising: The First Thirty Years* (1986); B. MacDonald, *Broadcasting in the United Kingdom: A Guide to Information Sources* (1993); N. Reville, *Broadcasting: A Guide to the New Law* (1991); B. Sendall, *Independent Television in Britain* (4 vols, 1982–90).

XXII

RELIGION

Church Membership Statistics

Extreme caution should be observed in making use of church membership statistics, as no entirely reliable sources exist giving information about membership or attendance. The last reasonably authoritative figures of religious affiliations in Britain were taken from the 1851 census, though even then there was no compulsion to answer the questions on religion. Since then no census has included questions on religious affiliation. Strictly comparable figures are impossible to obtain for church membership and church attendance since 1900. Indeed, there are at least three equally sustainable measures of affiliation to churches. First, there is the community to which a person considers themself belonging; thus someone who never goes to church, who is asked when they go into hospital 'what is your religion?' may reply they are 'C of E' or 'Catholic'. Secondly, there is membership as defined by the individual groups. Anglicans can join their parish Electoral Roll if they are over 16 and live within the parish, whereas Baptists teach the importance of adult baptism, and Pentecostalists the necessity to speak in tongues. These membership statistics are not therefore strictly comparable. Finally, and most restrictively, there is regular weekly church attendance.

The *UK Christian Handbook* publishes regular figures for the first two, community and membership, updated every two years. As for churchgoing, extensive church censuses have been undertaken in England in 1979 and 1989, Wales in 1982 and Scotland in 1984 and 1994. The 1989 English Church Census report was published under the title *'Christian' England*, and gave details of churchgoing by denomination, county, type of area and so on.

Christianity by Numbers published by MARC Europe in 1989 gives a bibliography of books with church data on subjects like church growth, church leadership, and the unreached, as well as listing the various denominational yearbooks and comparable works for Europe and further afield. Similar material is now collected and published by the Christian Research Association. Earlier information on statistical sources for religion is given in Volume XX *Religion* of *Reviews of UK Statistical Sources* published jointly by the ESRC and the Royal Statistical Society.

More general works on religion in Britain in the twentieth century are: R. B. Braithwaite, *The State of Religious Belief* (1927); E. O. James, *History of Christianity in England* (1949); R. Lloyd, *The Church of England in the Twentieth Century* (2 vols, 1948–50); G. Spinks (ed.), *Religion in Britain since 1900* (1952); R. F. Wearmouth, *The Social and Political Influence of Methodism in the Twentieth Century* (1957); J. Highet, *The Scottish Churches* (1960); R. Currie (ed), *Churches and Churchgoers* (1977). Maps on the strength of religion in Britain are given in *The Reader's Digest Atlas of Britain* (1965), and in John D. Gay, *The Geography of Religion in England* (1971).

The most convenient summary of facts and statistics is to be found in P. Brierley's chapter in A. H. Halsey (ed.), *Social Trends in Britain since 1900* (1988).

THE CHURCH OF ENGLAND

Principal degrees of membership for the Provinces of Canterbury and York.

(Totals for 43 dioceses[a])

Year	Home pop. of the two provinces	Estimated baptised membership		Estimated confirmed membership		Membership of parochial electoral rolls	
		(000s)[d]	Per 1,000 home pop.	(000s)[d]	Per 1,000 pop. 13+[e]	(000s)[d]	Per 1,000 adults
1901	30,673[b]	n.a.		n.a.		n.a.	
1911	33,807[b]	n.a.		n.a.		n.a.	
1921	35,390[b]	22,000	622	8,100	301	3,537[f]	140
1931	37,511[b]	23,800	634	9,000	302	3,686	145
1941	39,173[c]	24,900	636	9,200	294	3,423[g]	120
1951	41,330[b]	25,800	624	9,400	284	2,923[h]	95
1960	43,296	27,323	631	9,792	281	2,862	89
1970	46,429	27,736	597	9,514	205	2,559	73
1980	46,660[j]	27,113	581	8,700	185	1,815	52
1990	48,208[j]	26,855	557	n.a.	n.a.	1,540	44

[a] In 1910 there were 15,864 parochial churches. In 1966 there were 17,755.
[b] Enumerated in the Registrar General's censuses of ecclesiastical areas.
[c] Estimates based on the Registrar General's annual estimates of population at 30 Jun.
[d] Calculated by the Statistical Unit of the Central Board of Finance of the Church of England by reference to the age composition of the home population, born and resident in the two provinces, and to the respective rates of infant baptisms at Anglican fonts per 1,000 live births; and to the respective rates of Anglican confirmations per 1,000 males and females living at age 15 years (it is not possible to include in these estimates baptised and confirmed Anglicans who were born abroad but are now resident in the two provinces).
[e] In the Church of England very few boys and girls are confirmed before the age of 13 years.
[f, g, h] Figures for 1924, 1940, and 1953 respectively.
[i] 1957 was the first year that persons of 17 years and over were included in the electoral rolls. In previous years the minimum age was 18 years.
[j] Population figures for 1980 and 1990 are based on the census figure the following year.

SOURCES. – *Facts and Figures about the Church of England*, Nos. 1–3. Edited by R.F. Neuss, published by the Church Information Office (1966). *UK Christian Handbook*. The Statistical Unit, Central Board of Finance of the Church of England.

Archbishops and leading Bishops of the five principal Dioceses in the Church of England[1]

(These are the only Sees automatically represented in the House of Lords)

Archbishops of Canterbury

1896	F. Temple (Frederick Cantuar:)
1903	R. Davidson (Randall Cantuar:)
1928	C. Lang (Cosmo Cantuar:)
1942	W. Temple (William Cantuar:)
1945	G. Fisher (Geoffrey Cantuar:)
1961	A. Ramsey (Michael Cantuar:)
1974	F. Coggan (Donald Cantuar:)
1980	R. Runcie (Robert Cantuar:)
1991	G. Carey (George Cantuar:)

Archbishops of York

1891	W. Maclagan (William Ebor:)
1909	C. Lang (Cosmo Ebor:)
1929	W. Temple (William Ebor:)
1942	C. Garbett (Cyril Ebor:)
1956	A. Ramsey (Michael Ebor:)
1961	F. Coggan (Donald Ebor:)
1974	S. Blanch (Stuart Ebor:)
1983	J. Habgood (John Ebor:)

Bishops of London

1897	M. Creighton (Mandell Londin:)
1901	A. Winnington-Ingram (A. F. Londin:)
1939	G. Fisher (Geoffrey Londin:)
1945	J. Wand (William Londin:)
1956	H. Campbell (Henry and in:)
1961	R. Stopford (Robert Londin:)
1973	G. Ellison (Gerald Londin:)
1981	G. Leonard (Graham Londin:)
1991	D. Hope (David Londin:)

Bishop of Durham

1890	B. Westcott (B. F. Dunelm:)
1901	H. Moule (Handley Dunelm:)
1920	H. Henson (Herbert Dunelm:)
1939	A. Williams (Alwyn Dunelm:)
1952	A. Ramsey (Michael Dunelm:)
1956	M. Harland (Maurice Dunelm:)
1966	I. Ramsey (Ian Dunelm:)
1973	J. Habgood (John Dunelm:)
1984	D. Jenkins (David Dunelm:)
1994	M. Turnbull (Michael Dunelm)

[1] Names in brackets are those used as signature.

Bishops of Winchester

1895	R. Davidson (Randall Winton:)
1903	H. Ryle (Herbert E. Winton:)
1911	E. Talbot (Steuart Edward Winton:)
1924	F. Woods (Theodore Winton:)
1932	C. Garbett (Cyril Winton:)
1942	M. Haigh (Mervyn Winton:)
1952	A. Williams (Alwyn Winton:)
1961	S. Allison (Falkner Winton:)
1974	J. Taylor (John Winton:)
1985	C. James (Colin Winton:)

THE CHURCH IN WALES

The Church in Wales was disestablished from 31 March 1920

Year	Parochial Easter Day Communicants Estimated No. (000s)	No. of Churches
1920	160	1,755
1930	185	1,774
1940	175	1,766
1950	168	n.a.
1960	183	1,783
1970	155	1,720
1980	132	1,675
1990	108	1,142

SOURCE: – HMSO *Social Trends*; *Whitaker's Almanack*; *UK Christian Handbook*; and the Secretary, the Representative Body of the Church in Wales.

EPISCOPAL CHURCH IN SCOTLAND

Year	Permanent Members (000s)	No. of Church Buildings
1900	116	354
1910	142	404
1920	144	416
1930	134	415
1940	124	404
1950	109	397
1960	97	369
1970	86	341
1980	71	311
1990	58	310

SOURCES. – *The Year Book for the Episcopal Church in Scotland; Whitaker's Almanack; The Statesman's Year-Book; UK Christian Handbook.*

BAPTIST UNION

British Isles

Year	Members (000s)	No. of Places of Worship
1900	366	2,579
1910	419	2,889
1920	405	2,866
1930	406	2,965
1940	382	3,044
1950	338	3,110
1960	318	3,053
1970	293	3,657
1980	240	3,344
1993	232	3,627

These are statistics actually received from churches; no estimates are made for churches omitting to return figures. Figures cover the Baptist Union of Great Britain, the Baptist Unions of Wales, Scotland and Ireland, the Grace Baptist Assembly, Gospel Standard Strict Baptists and other Baptist Churches.
SOURCES.– *The Baptist Handbook, 1900– . Whitaker's Almanack. The UK Christian Handbook.*

CONGREGATIONAL UNION

United Kingdom[a]

Year	Members (000s)	No. of Places of Worship
1900	436	4,607[b]
1910	494	4,721
1930	490	3,556
1939	459	3,435
1950	387	3,173
1959	212	2,984
1965	198	2,799
1971	165	2,266

On 5 Oct 72 the Congregational Union merged with the Presbyterian Church of England to form the United Reformed Church.
[a] 1900 and 1910 figures for British Isles.
[b] Figure for 1901.
SOURCE.– *The Congregational Year Book, 1900–1972.*

PRESBYTERIAN CHURCH

England

Year	Members (000s)
1900	76
1911	87
1922	84
1930	84
1940	82
1950	82
1960	71
1965	70
1971	57

On 5 Oct 72 the Presbyterian Church in England merged with the Congregational Union to form the United Reformed Church.
SOURCES.– 1900 and 1911, *The Official Handbook of of the Presbyterian Church of England;* 1922–72, *The Statesman's Year Book.*

UNITED REFORMED CHURCH

	Members (000s)	No. of Church Buildings
1973	192	2,139
1980	147	1,936
1990	120	1,813

METHODIST CHURCH[a]

Great Britain and Ireland

Year	Members and Probationers (000s)	No of Church Buildings
1900	794	9,037
1910	868	n.a.
1920	826	9,013
1930	868	9,070
1940	830	n.a.
1950	772	n.a.
1960	766	n.a.
1970	642	9,972
1980	531	8,492
1990	468	7,591

[a] These are aggregate figures for all the major branches of Methodism. The Methodist Church was formed in 1932 by a union of the Wesleyan, Primitive and United Methodist Churches. The United Methodists were themselves formed by the union of three separate bodies in 1907.

SOURCES. – *Minutes of the Methodist Conference, 1900–*. HMSO *Social Trends. Whitaker's Almanack. UK Christian Handbook.*

THE CHURCH OF SCOTLAND[a]

(Presbyterian)

Year	Total Communicants On Rolls (000s)	No. of Places of Worship
1900	662	n.a.
1910	714	1,703
1920	739	1,704
1930	1,271	2,795
1940	1,278	2,507
1951	1,271	2,348
1960	1,248	2,212
1970	1,154	2,088
1980	954	1,936
1990	787	1,813

[a] In 1929 the United Free Church of Scotland rejoined the Church of Scotland, which accounts for the jump in figures.

SOURCE: – *The Church of Scotland Year Book. Whitaker's Almanack. UK Christian Handbook.*

THE ROMAN CATHOLIC CHURCH

United Kingdom

Year	Estimated Catholic Population (000s)	Catholic Baptisms (000s)	No. of Public Churches and Chapels
1900	2,466	n.a.	1,536
1910	2,661	n.a.	1,773
1920	2,922	n.a.	1,408
1930	3,212	66	1,564
1940	3,471	70	1,802
1950	3,970	92	1,971
1960	4,845	123	3,204
1970	5,419	108	n.a.
1980	5,539	76	4,132
1990	5,624	80	4,297

SOURCES. – Census reports quoted in *The Statesman's Year-Book, 1900–*. *UK Christian Handbook*.

Roman Catholic Archbishops of Westminster

1892	H. Vaughan (Cardinal, 1893)	1956	W. Godfrey (Cardinal, 1958)
1903	F. Lourne (Cardinal, 1911)	1963	J. Heenan (Cardinal, 1965)
1935	A. Hinsley (Cardinal, 1937)	1976	B. Hume (Cardinal, 1976)
1943	B. Griffin (Cardinal, 1946)		

SOURCE. – *The Catholic Directory, 1900–*.

NORTHERN IRELAND

Religious Affiliations

Year	Roman Catholic	Presbyterian	Church of Ireland	Methodist	Other Denomination
1901	430	397	317	44	48
1911	430	395	327	46	50
1926	420	393	339	50	52
1937	428	391	345	55	58
1951	471	410	353	67	63
1961	498	413	345	72	71
1971	478	406	334	71	88
1981	415	340	281	59	113
1991	606	337	279	60	122

The figures for 1971, 1981 and 1991 are affected by much higher numbers giving 'no religion', or leaving the relevant questions blank. The totals in these categories rose from around 20,000 to 143,000 in 1971, 275,000 in 1981, and 174,000 in 1991.

SOURCE.– *Census reports*.

OTHER CHRISTIAN DENOMINATIONS

Data on the smaller denominations is of very uneven quality. However, some recent figures are worth recording.

Assemblies of God	49,381	(1992)		
Elim Pentecostal Church	42,901	(1992)		
Greek Orthodox	260,000	(1992)		
Jehovah's Witnesses	55,876	(1969)	126,173	(1992)
Mormons	145,000	(1992)		
(Plymouth) Brethren	81,000	(1992)		
Presbyterian Church of Wales	57,876	(1993)		
Salvation Army	58,687	(1992)		
Scientologists	80,000	(1992)		
Seventh-Day Adventists	17,873	(1992)		
Society of Friends (Quakers)	18,072	(1992)		
Unitarians	8,500	(1992)		
Welsh Independents	49,850	(1992)		

The Church of Christ, Scientist does not publish estimates of its membership, but in 1991 it had 215 branch churches in the United Kingdom.

SOURCES.– *Whitaker's Almanack, UK Christian Handbook.*

THE JEWISH COMMUNITY[a]

Great Britain

Year	Estimated No. of Jews (000s)	Approx. No. of Synagogues
1900	160	80[d]
1910	243	200[d]
1920	287	200[d]
1929[b]	297	300[e]
1940	385[c]	200[e]
1950	450	240[e]
1960	450	240[e]
1970	450	240[e]
1980	410	321
1990	326	330

[a] Statistics for 1900 for GB and Ireland, 1910 for British Isles, 1920 for UK, 1929 for GB, 1940 onwards for UK.
[b] No Jewish statistics available 1930–34.
[c] Including about 35,000 refugees.
[d] From Whitaker's Almanack.
[e] From The Statesman's Year-Book.

SOURCES.- *Whitaker's Almanack, the Statesman's Year-Book, the UK Christian Handbook.*

BUDDHISTS

	Members	Priests	Buildings
1970	6,000	38	8
1980	17,000	210	50
1990	28,000	350	105

MARRIAGES

HINDUS

	Members	Priests	Buildings
1970	50,000	80	60
1980	120,000	120	125
1990	140,000	150	140

MUSLIMS

	Members	Priests	Buildings
1970	204,000	1,000	75
1980	306,000	1,540	193
1990	505,000	2,500	350

SIKHS

	Members	Priests	Buildings
1970	75,000	100	40
1980	150,000	140	105
1990	250,000	180	149

Marriages by Manner of Solemnisation

England and Wales

	1901	1911	1919	1934	1952	1962	1974	1980	1990
Total (000s)	259	275	369	342	349	348	384	370	331
	%	%	%	%	%	%	%	%	%
C. of E.	66.6	61.1	59.7	53.5	49.6	47.4	35.8	33.3	34.8
R.C.	4.1	4.4	5.2	6.5	9.4	12.3	8.8	7.7	6.8
Jewish	0.7	0.7	0.5	0.7	0.5	0.4	0.4	0.3	0.3
Baptist			1.9	1.8	1.5	1.7	1.2	1.2	1.1
Cong.	12.8	13.0	2.3	2.1	2.0	1.9	1.6	2.0	2.3
Methodist			5.6	5.3	4.8	4.9	4.1	4.5	5.1
Other Religion			1.6	1.8	1.6	1.8	1.6	1.5	2.2
All Religious	84.2	79.1	76.9	71.6	69.4	70.4	53.5	50.4	52.6
Secular	15.8	20.9	23.1	28.4	30.6	29.6	46.5	49.6	47.4
	100	100	100	100	100	100	100	100	100

[a] The Congregationalist figures since 1973 include United Reformed Church.

SOURCE. – *Annual Reports of the Registrar General.*

BIBLIOGRAPHICAL NOTE

This book does not attempt to provide an extensive bibliography of works on British politics since 1900. That would demand a separate volume and much of its contents would duplicate bibliographies already available. The main sources of factual data used in compiling this book are listed separately in the appropriate sections. There are, however, some works of reference of such major importance and reliability that it seems useful to collect them together as a help or reminder to those involved in research.

Many of the standard and most useful sources for reference are Stationery Office publications. Summaries, guides, and short-cuts to these publications are provided in the *Annual Catalogue of Government Publications*, the Sectional Lists of Government Publications, published by the H.M.S.O. for individual departments, the *List of Cabinet Papers* 1880-1914 (P.R.O. handbook), the *General Index* to Parliamentary Papers, 1900–1949 (H.M.S.O.), the three volumes by P. and G. Ford, *Breviate of Parliamentary Papers* (1900–16, 1917–39, 1940–54), and C. Hughes, *The British Statute Book* (1957). An H.M.S.O. *Guide to Official Statistics* has been published occasionally since 1976. J. G. Olle, *An Introduction to British Government Publications*, although dated, is still very useful as is the *Directory of British Official Publications: a guide to sources* (ed. S. Richard, 2nd ed 1984). *A Guide to non-H.M.S.O. Government Publications* has been published by Chadwick-Healey. The CD-ROM database UKOP gives comprehensive coverage of British parliamentary and non-parliamentary official publications from 1980 onwards.

For reference to day-to-day political events the Official Index to *The Times* is the most complete guide, though before 1906 Palmer's Index to *The Times* is difficult to use successfully and is by no means complete. In recent years the *Independent* and the *Financial Times* have also compiled indexes and they and other newspaper offices preserve cuttings from their own and other papers on very accessible CD-ROM files. *Keesing's Contemporary Archives* since 1931 give a concise summary of news reported in the national Press, though they were not published in their present fuller form until 1937; since 1988 Keesings have published a separate set dealing exclusively with British Politics. Brief chronologies of the year's major events (including some very minor ones) are printed in the *Annual Register*, which also covers them in greater detail in the main text of the book. Still briefer summaries of the year's events are to be found in *Whitaker's Almanac* and in G. Foote, *A Chronology of British Post-War Politics 1945–1987* (1988). Since 1990 the Institute of Contemporary British History has published a comprehensive volume *Contemporary Britain: an Annual Review*.

For biographical details of leading figures in British politics since 1900 the main sources are the *Dictionary of National Biography* (1901–11, 1912–21, 1922–30, 1931–40, 1941–50, 1951–60, 1961–70, 1971–80, 1981–85 and *Missing Names*), the *Concise Dictionary of National Biography*, 1901–80, *Who Was Who* (1897–1915, 1916–28, 1929–40, 1941–50, 1951–60, 1961–70, 1971–80, 1981–90) and *Who's Who*, for those still alive. As supplements to these, for lesser-known figures in the Labour and Co-operative movement see also the *Labour Who's Who*, 1924 and 1927 (The Labour Publishing Company), the *Herald Book of Labour Members* (1923, with a supplement in 1924, ed. S. Bracher), and the *Dictionary of Labour Biography* (eds J. Bellamy and J. Saville). Appointments are recorded in many official sources. The major annual publications are: the *Imperial Calendar and Civil Service List* (replaced in 1973 by two works, *Civil Service Year Book and Diplomatic List*), *H.M. Ministers and Heads of Public Departments* (published 1946–77, from four to six times a year and after 1973 renamed *H.M. Ministers and Senior Staff in Public Departments*), and the *London Gazette*, where appointments are announced officially, which appears about once a fortnight. Since 1978 the House of Commons has published a *Weekly Information Bulletin* and since 1983 a *Sessional Information Bulletin*. Official appointments are also recorded in the annual Lists of the Foreign Office, the Colonial Office, and the Commonwealth Relations Office, the *Army, Navy and Air Force Lists*, the *Law Lists*, and the *Annual Estimates* of the civil, revenue, and service departments. There are three handbooks on Parliament, giving the names of M.P.s, details of procedure and officials: *Dod's Parliamentary Companion* (annually), Vacher's *Parliamentary Companion* (published from four to six times a year) and F. W. S. Craig's *The Political Companion* (published quarterly 1968– 1983). Since 1992 the annual *Whitehall Companion* offers a comprehensive guide to personnel and functions. Up to 1931 Debrett's Illustrated *House of Commons and the Judicial Bench* is particularly useful. Extremely valuable sources of reference for the House of Commons are the books *House of Commons* published by the *Pall Mall Gazette* in 1906, 1910 and 1911, and since 1885 by *The Times* after each General Election (1922–4 excepted) – in 1885–1900 as *The New House of Commons* and since 1970 as *The Times Guide to the House of Commons*. M. Stenton and S. Lees, *Who's Who* of British Members of Parliament, vols 2–4: 1886–1979 (1978–81) offers the most compact single source of M.P.s' biographies. Other sources of biographical information are *Debrett's Peerage* and *Burke's Peerage*, *Burke's New Extinct Peerages* (1972) and Burke's *Dictionary of the Landed Gentry*, L. G. Pine, *The New Extinct Peerage, 1884–1971* (1972), the *Directory of Directors*, the Authors' and Writers' *Who's Who*, and other directories or registers devoted to the members of particular professions, or to the alumni of particular schools and universities. C. Hazlehurst and C. Woodland, *A Guide to the Papers of British Cabinet Ministers* 1900–51 (1975, now under revision) can lead to much recherche material. See also *Councils, Committees and Boards* (7th ed. 1989) and the Directory of British Associations (11th ed. 1992)

The annual almanacs are also an extremely useful source of information. Amongst these the most notable are: the *Constitutional Year Book* (published until 1939), *Whitaker's Almanac*, the *Statesman's Year-Book*, the *Yearbook of International Organisations*, the *United Nations Yearbook*, and *Britain: An Official Handbook* (published by the Central Office of Information).

The major sources for British statistics are already quoted in notes to the tables throughout the book. The most readily available is the *Annual Abstract of Statistics* (H.M.S.O.). The *Monthly Digest of Statistics* can be very helpful; so can the monthlies, *Economic Trends* and *Financial Statistics*. The reports of the major revenue departments, the Commissioners for Customs and Excise, the Commissioners for Inland Revenue, and the Registrars-General for England and Wales and for Scotland, are major sources of statistical information – as are the *Reports* of the other Government Departments, and especially the Ministry of Labour / Dept. of Employment (and Productivity) with its monthly *Employment Gazette* (formerly the *(Board of Trade) Labour Gazette*), and, up till 1975, the *Annual Abstract of Labour Statistics*). Another major source of information is B. R. Mitchell, *Abstract of British Historical Statistics* (2nd ed. 1988) and C. Feinstein, *National Income Expenditure and Output of the U.K. 1855–1965)* (1972). Much statistical information is presented in A. H. Halsey (ed.), *British Social Trends* since 1900 (1988).

A useful guide to works on British politics is to be found in the subject index of the British Museum Library. Bibliographical references can be checked through the *British National Bibliography* and the *Cumulative Book Index*; there is also the *London Bibliography of the Social Sciences* (published annually since 1931) and the *International Bibliography of the Social Sciences* (annually since 1953). For information on many aspects of British politics the *Encyclopaedia Britannica* or *Chambers' Encyclopaedia* may give a lead; see also V. Bogdanor, *The Blackwell Encyclopaedia of Political Institutions* (1987). Weekly journals, especially the *Economist*, may provide much additional information.

The learned journals with most material on British politics are the *Political Quarterly* (1930–), *Parliamentary Affairs* (1947–), *Political Studies* (1953–), the *British Journal of Political Science* (1971–) and *Contemporary Record* (1987–). *The Table* (the Journal of the

Commonwealth Parliamentary Association, 1931), *Government and Opposition* (1965–) and the Journal of *Contemporary History* (1986–) also contain much that is relevant. *International Political Science Abstracts* published regularly since 1951 gives a classified abstract of journal articles.

The *Bulletin* of the Society for the Study of Labour History contains an annual bibliography. So does the *British Journal of Industrial Relations* and several other specialist journals. The Royal Historical Society has produced an annual bibliography since 1976.

No attempt has been made to provide a bibliography for the whole of this century. But P. Catterall, *British History 1945–87* (1990) deals comprehensively with the second half of the century. For the early years, a valuable guide is H. J. Hanham, *Bibliography of British History 1851–1914* (1976); see also C. Cook, *Sources on British Political History 1900–1951* (6 vols. 1975–85). An extensive bibliography is available for the middle of the period by C. L. Mowat in *Britain between the Wars* (1955) and in his article, 'Some Recent Books on the British Labour Movement', *Journal of Modern History*, xvii, No. 4, Dec 1945. He also published *British History since 1926: A Select Bibliography* (The Historical Association, 1960). Another critical bibliography is supplied by A. J. P. Taylor, *English History 1914–45* (1965). See also R. M. Punnett, *British Government and Politics* (6th ed. 1994). Other bibliographies include J. Palmer, *Government and Parliament in Britain: A Bibliography* (1960, The Hansard Society), E. J. Hobsbawm, 'Twentieth-Century British Politics', *Past and Present*, No. 11, Apr 1957, and H. R. Winkler, 'Some Recent Writings on Twentieth-Century Britain', *Journal of Modern History*, xxxii, No. 1 , Mar 1960. See also 'Bibliography of British Labour History' in the *Journal of Modern History*, Vol. 41, No. 3, Sep 1969, compiled by William H. Maehl Jr. Other good bibliographies are to be found in A. F. Havinghurst, *Modern England 1901–70* (1976), and J. Westergaard, A. Weyman and P. Wiles, *Modern British Society, a Bibliography* (1977).

Abortions, 337–41
Aden, 451
Admiralty:
    First Lords of, 1–26, 50, 53
    Permanent Secretaries, 279
    number of civil servants, 287
Aerospace, Minister for, 34, 50, 53, 405, 406
    see also Air, Transport and Aviation
Africa, Ministers Resident in, 18, 51, 61
Age Concern, 345
Age of ministers, 67
Agriculture (see also Food),
    Ministry of, 1–49, 50, 53–4, 192, 279, 287
    policy, resignations over, 69
    National Farmers' Union, 151, 382
    Select Committee on, 192, 202
    Royal Commission on, 293
    Unemployment Insurance Scheme, 354
    employment, 361, 385–6
    import controls, 377
    output, 385–6
    as a pressure group, 382
    Research Council, 417
Air (see also Aviation, British Airports Authority,
        British Airways Board and Aerospace):
    Board, 7, 50, 54
    Council, 7, 50, 54
    Ministry, 8–26, 50, 54, 279, 287, 405–6
    Aircraft Production, Ministry of, 18, 20, 50, 54, 279
    Force, 69, 479–88; resignations over, 69; see also
        Defence
    Aircraft Industry, Committee on, 299
    Civil air transport, Committee on, 299
    Nationalisation, 401–6
    Airways (B.O.A.C., B.E.A., etc.), 401–6
Alliance Party of Northern Ireland, 161–2, 431–2
Alliance, Liberal/SDP, 152, 167, 209
Amalgamated Union of Engineering Workers, 150,
        364, 368–9
Amalgamated Weavers' Association, 364, 369
Ambassadors, 467–9, 476–7
Amersham International, 402
Animal welfare, 344
Archbishops:
    C. of E., 518
    Roman Catholic, 522
Armed Forces, Minister for, 39–44
Army (see also Defence and War):
    Under-Secretary for, 27–39
    Commanders-in-Chief, 479
    Chiefs of General Staff, 479
    total forces serving, 481
    expenditure, 481
    war commanders, 486–8
Arts, Minister for, 30–44, 50, 54
Arts Council, 417
Assassinations, 277
Assistance Board, National, 288, 354
Association of County Councils, 441

Association of Scientific, Technical and Managerial
        Staffs, 150, 364, 368–9
Atomic Energy Authority, 401, 408, 415, 471
Attorneys-General, 2–49, 50, 54
Australia, 327–8, 451, 455, 458
Austria-Hungary, 467
Aviation (see also Transport and Aerospace)
    Ministry of, 27–30, 50, 54, 279, 287
    Supply, Ministry of, 33, 50, 55, 287, 406
    Civil Authority, 417

Bahamas, 451, 458, 460
Balance of Payments, 377–9, 387–9
Bangladesh, 327–9, 451, 458
Bank of England, 192, 380, 401
Bank rate, 301, 377–9, 385–6
Baptist Union, 520, 524
Barbados, 451, 458, 460
Beer, 291, 393–5
Belize, 451, 458, 460
Bibliographical Note, 525–7
Bills, parliamentary, 176–8, 183–5
Biographies of Ministers, 71–6
Birth control, 344
Birth rates, 324
Bishops, 518
Blockade, Minister of, 7, 50, 54
Boer War, 263, 292, 482–3
British Aerospace, 402, 403, 405, 405
British Airports Authority, 405, 406, 415
British Airways Board, 401, 405–6, 415
British Broadcasting Company, 505
British Broadcasting Corporation:
    Headquarters, 263
    formation, 505
    Governors, 505–6
    Directors-General, 506
    radio, 507
    television, 508
    licences, 508
    expenditure, 509
British Employers' Confederation, 382
British European Airways Corporation, 401, 405, 415
British Leyland, 402, 414
British National Oil Corporation, 402, 403, 408
British National Party, 157, 164
British Overseas Airways Corporation, 403, 405, 415
British Shipbuilders, 402, 413, 415
British South American Airways Corporation, 401,
        405
British Steel Corporation, see Steel
British Telecom, 413, 415 (see also Post Office)
British Waterways Board, 411
Broadcasting (see also British Broadcasting
        Corporation and Independent Television):
    of parliament, 173
    quotations from broadcasts, 268–276
    departmental committees, 297–300, 515
    nationalisation, 401

Broadcasting (contd.)
  British Broadcasting Company, 505
  British Broadcasting Corporation, 505–9
  Independent Broadcasting, 510–14
  legislation, 510
Bryce Report, 211
Budgets, 69, 301, 377–9, 399
Buddhists, 523
Burma, 16–22, 50, 57, 281, 452
Bus Company, 411, 415
Business pressure groups, 381–2
By-elections, 234–7

Cabinet (see also Ministers):
  death in office, 68
  defeat in office, 68
  education of, 66
  Ministers, 1–48
  size, 66
  social composition, 66
  secretary to, 279
  Office staff, 288
  Office, Economic Section, 380
Cable and Wireless Ltd, 192, 402, 413, 415
Canada, 326–8, 377, 452, 458, 460
Capital punishment, 306, 318, 346
Capital transfer tax, 398
Cars, see Motor cars
Central Electricity Generating Board, 401, 407, 415
Central Policy Review Staff, 279
Ceylon, 452, 456, 458, 460
Chancellors of the Exchequer, 1–48, 51, 53, 71–6; see
  also Treasury
Channel Islands, 433–4
Children (see also Education):
  departmental committees on, 300
  legislation (criminal justice), 305–7
  legislation (welfare), 339–40
  pressure groups, 345
Churches:
  Assembly, 263
  Royal Commissions, 293
  in Wales, 426, 519
  membership statistics, 517–524
  Church of England, 517–19, 524
  buildings, 519–24
  Episcopal, in Scotland, 519
  Baptist, 520
  Congregational, 520
  Presbyterian, 520
  United Reformed, 521
  Methodist, 521
  of Scotland, 521
  Roman Catholic, 522
  in Northern Ireland, 522
  other Christian denominations, 523
  marriages in, 524
Civil Aviation, see Aviation
Civil Liability, 295, 308–9
Civil Liberties, 300, 345
Civil List, 422–3
Civil & Public Service Association, 364, 369

Civil Service:
  Department, 33–45, 50, 55
  heads of departments, 279–283
  size of, 286–8
  salary levels, 286–8
  Royal Commissions, 291–4
  Select Committee, 202
  political activities of, 298
  training, 298
  Fulton Committee on, 298
Clerk of the Crown in Chancery, 315, 318
Coal (see also Mines and National Union of
  Mineworkers):
  disputes, 265, 371–2, 379
  Royal Commissions, 294
  production, 385–7
  nationalisation, 401, 407
  National Coal Board, 407, 415
  European Coal and Steel Community, 471, 475
Coalition Labour, 214
Coalition Liberal, 214
Coalition Unionist, 214
Colonial Office, 2–30, 50, 55, 280, 287
  Development Corporation, 418
  see also Dominions and Commonwealth
Commission for Racial Equality, 329
Committees:
  Nineteen Twenty-Two, 130
  Labour Representation, 138
  National Executive, 138
  Ways and Means, 171
  of Selection, 189
  Public Accounts, 190
  Estimates, 190–1
  on National Expenditure, 191
  on Nationalised Industries, 192
  Agriculture, 192
  Science and Technology, 192
  Overseas Aid, 193
  Race Relations and Immigration, 193
  Scottish Affairs, 193, 201
  Services, 194–5
  Domestic Committees, 195–6
  Members' Interests, 196
  of Privileges, 196–8
  on Parliamentary Commissioner, 200
  Specialist Select Committees, 201
  of Inquiry, 291, 301
  Departmental, 297–300
  Standing Advisory, 296
  Political Honours Scrutiny, 303
  of Imperial Defence, 480
Common Wealth Party, 157, 159
Commons, House of, 171–204 (see also Parliament
  and Members of Parliament):
  Leaders, 65
  Speakers, 171
  Chairmen of Ways and Means, 171
  Officers of, 172
  Sessions, 172
  Emergency recalls, 173
  hours of sitting, 172
  broadcasting, 173–4

allocation of time, 176–8
dates of dissolution, 176–8
prorogations, 176–8
Fathers of, 179
critical votes in, 186
Government and Private Members time, 173
confidence motions, 186
guillotine motions, 187
suspension of Members, 187
Select Committees of, 188–202
quotations from, 265–276
Commonwealth (*see also* Colonial Office and
    Dominions Office):
Department, 22–30, 50, 56, 280, 287
emigration to, 327
Development Corporation, 418
territories since 1900, 451–8
Members, 458
Prime Ministers' Meetings, 459
Secretariat, 460
Viceroys and Governors-General, 460–3
Communist Party:
history, 157, 159
election results, 215–19
lost deposits, 157, 242
headquarters, 264
on the L.C.C., 448
Community Relations Commissions,
    see Race
Compensation, legal, 294, 306, 310–11, 316
Conduct of M.P.s, 187
Confederation of British Industry, 382
Confederation of Health Service Employees, 365,
    369
Confidence votes, 186
Congregational Church, 520, 524
Conscription, 69, 482
Conservative Party (*see also* National Party):
Leaders, 127; in the House of Lords, 128
Deputy Leaders, 127
officials, 128–9
Chief Whips, 130
Research Department, 129, 130
Nineteen Twenty-Two Committee, 130
Shadow Cabinet, 130–2
membership, 132
finance, 132–3
annual conferences, 133–4, 263
in the House of Lords, 206–7
election results, 213–223
M.P.s changes of allegiance, 225–31
in by-elections, 234–8
election expenses, 241
lost deposits, 242
women candidates and M.P.s, 243
rating in opinion polls, 247–61
headquarters, 263–5
quotations from, 266–76
in local elections, 443–9
in the press, 489–503
sponsored M.P.s, 149, 151
Consols, 385–6
Constitution, Commission on, 295

Consumers:
(Trade and) Consumer Affairs, Minister of, 42, 50,
    55, 60
Prices and Consumer Protection, Ministry of, 37,
    51, 60, 282
protection, 299, 382
credit, 299
expenditure, 396
pressure groups, 345, 382
councils, 418
Cook, Thomas, 402
Co-operative Party, 157, 159–60
Co-ordination of Defence, 15, 50, 55
Co-ordination of Transport, Secretary of State, 24, 50
Copyright, 297
Cotton, 364, 385–7
Council of Europe, 466, 473
Council for the Protection of Rural England, 345
Councils, *see* Local Government
Covent Garden Market Authority, 418
Crime statistics, 318–20
Criminal procedure, 295, 305–7
Criminal Injuries Compensation Board, 306, 315
Critical votes, 183–5, 210
Crown Estates Commission, 416
Crown Lands, 298
Customs and Excise:
Board, 280
civil servants, 288
revenue, 390–2
tariffs, specimen, 393–5
Cyprus, 452, 458

Death:
certification, committee on, 299
penalty, 308, 319, 346
rates, 324
main causes of, 325
death duties, 390–2, 398
Decimal currency, 293, 299, 378
Defence (*see also* War, Army, Navy and Air):
Co-ordination of, Minister for, 15, 50, 55
Ministry of, 17–49, 50, 55, 480
Minister of, for Administration, 30, 50, 55, 480
Minister of, for Equipment, 30, 50, 55, 480
Air Force, Minister for, 27, 30, 50, 55
Army, Minister for, 27, 30, 50, 55
Navy, Minister for, 27, 30, 50, 55
Procurement, Minister of, 30, 39, 44, 50, 55
Committee on Procurement, 299
Select Committee on Defence, 202
permanent secretaries, 280
civil servants, 287
of the Realm, Standing Advisory Committee
    on, 296
expenditure, 393–5, 481
Service Chiefs, 479
Committee of Imperial Defence, 480
pressure groups, 481
total forces serving, 481
military operations, 482–6
war commanders, 486–8
Democratic Labour, 230, 238

Democratic Unionist Party, 161–2, 431–3
Demonstrations, 277
Departmental Committees, 297–300
Development Commission, 418
Devolution, 425–36
Diplomatic Service, 467–9
Disturbances and demonstrations, major civil, 277
Divorce, 293, 294, 326, 337–8
Docks, 292, 298, 299, 357, 401–3, 410
  (see also Ports, Transport, and Transport and
        General Workers' Union)
Dominica, 452, 458
Dominions Office, 11–22, 50, 55, 280, 287; (see also
  Commonwealth)
Duchy of Lancaster, 2–48, 50, 58
Dual mandate, 182

Earnings, 357—8; see also Pay
Economic:
  Warfare, Ministry of, 16, 50, 56, 280
  Affairs, Ministry of, 21, 24, 29, 50, 53, 280
  policy, resignations over, 69, 70
  Departmental Committees, 297–300
  statistics, 358–9, 383–98
  landmarks, 377–9
  policy, 377–81
  National Plan, 378
  European Economic Community, 378, 471–7
  and Social Research Council, 417
  advice, sources of, 380–1
  National Economic Development Council, 377,
        381
  Service, Head of, 380
  Advisory Council, 380
  Planning Board, 380
  Section of the Cabinet Office, 380
Education:
  Board of, 1–18, 50, 54, 341
  Ministry of, 18–27, 44, 50, 56, 280, 299
  and Science, Ministry of, 27–44, 50, 56, 280, 299
  policy, resignations over, 69, 70
  and Science, Select Committee on, 193, 202
  Central Advisory Council on, 291
  departmental committees on, 298–300
  legislation, 341–2, 438
  finance, 341, 343
  statistics, 342–3
  expenditure, 343
  pressure groups, 344
Eire, 427–9, 453; see also Ireland
Elderly, see Pensions
Elections:
  resignations over, 68
  statistics, 213–22
  results, 213–19
  European Parliament, 220
  regional results, 222–3
  party changes between elections, 224–5
  by-elections, 234–7
  administration, 239
  Speakers' Conferences, 239
  franchise, 240
  redistribution, 240

  expenses, 241–2
  lost deposits, 240
  women candidates and M.P.s, 243
  petitions, 243
  Royal Commissions, 293
  women's rights in, 337–8
  Local Government, 443–9
Electrical Trades Union, 150, 364, 368–9
Electricity:
  Union, 150, 364, 368–9
  Departmental Committees on, 298, 301
  employees, 361
  nationalisation, 401–2
  British Electricity Authority, 406, 415
  Central Electricity Generating Board, 401, 407
  Council, 406, 415
  North of Scotland Hydro-Electricity Board, 407,
        415
  South of Scotland Electricity Board, 407, 415
  Central Electricity Board, 401
Emergency Powers, 372
Emigration, 326
Employment (see also Labour and Unemployment):
  (and Productivity), Ministry of, 31–49, 54, 56
  Select Committee on, 202
  Permanent Secretaries, 280
  civil servants, 287
  legislation, 353–6
  statistics, 358–61, 373–5
  government responsibility for, 377
Energy (see also Fuel and Power):
  Department of, 34–46, 50, 56, 280, 287
  Select Committee on, 202
  atomic, 401, 408, 415
Environment (see also Housing, Local Government
        and Transport):
  Department of, 34–46, 50, 56, 410–12
  Select Committee on, 202
  Permanent Secretaries, 280
  civil servants, 287
  Environmental Pollution, Standing Advisory
        Committee, 296
  pressure groups, 345, 441
Equal pay, 294, 337, 355
Equal Opportunities Commission, 338
Estate Duty, 392, 398
Estimates Committee, 190–1
European:
  Economic Community, 69–70, 378, 471–7
  Secondary Legislation, Select Committee on, 194
  Referendum on, 222, 242
  Parliament, 220–1, 471, 475
  Free Trade Association, 377, 471, 473
  European Economic Co-operation, Organisation
        for, 377, 471, 473
  Council of Europe, 471–3
  Coal and Steel Community, 475
  Atomic Energy Community, 475
  Budgetary contribution, 475
  Court of Justice, 476
  Commission, British members of, 476
  Cabinet Ministers, 476
  ambassadors, 477

Exchange rates, 377, 387–9
Exchequer and Audit Department, 288
Excise (*see also* Customs and Excise):
    Board, 280
    revenue, 390–2
    duty on beer, 383–5
Exports, 387–9
Export Credits Guarantee Department, 416

Factory Acts, 353
Falkland Islands, 70, 453, 485
Family Allowances, 334–6
Family Division, 312
Family Welfare, 345
Farmers, 151, 382
Fascists, British Union of, 157, 165
Fathers of the House of Commons, 189
Federation of British Industries, 379
Fiji, 453, 458, 461
First Secretary of State, 26, 29, 51, 62
Fisheries, *see* Agriculture and White Fish Authority
Food:
    Ministry of Food Control, 7, 50, 56
    Ministry of, 15, 24, 50, 56, 280, 287
    Director-General, 280
    Royal Commissions, 292
    specimen tariffs, 393–5
    percentage of consumer expenditure, 396
Foreign:
    Office, 2–30, 50, 53, 280–1
    Secretaries, 2–49, 50, 53, 71–6
    (and Commonwealth Office), 30–49, 50, 53, 281
    policy, resignations over, 69–70
    Affairs, Select Committee, 202
    pressure groups, 467
    policy quotations, 265–75
    Permanent Secretaries, 280–1
    civil servants, 287–8
    United Nations affairs, 467, 469
Forestry Commission, 281, 416
France, 377, 387–9, 397, 465–7
Franchise, 239
Free Trade, 69
Fuel (*see also* Gas, Electricity, Coal and Power): (Light and Power),
    Ministry of, 18, 50, 56
    (and Power), Ministry of, 22–6, 50, 56, 57, 281, 287
    Co-ordination of Transport, Fuel & Power, Secretary of State for, 24, 50
    Resources, Committee on, 298
    work force, 361
    crises, 373, 377–9
    nationalised industries, 401–4, 406–9, 415
    rationing, 482

Gallup Poll, 245, 246–61
Gambia, 453, 458, 461
Gambling, 294, 299, 418
Gas:
    Industry, Committee on, 298
    employees, 365
    nationalisation, 401, 408, 415
    Council, 401, 408, 415

Area Gas Boards, 401, 408, 415
    Corporation, 401, 403–4, 408, 415
General and Municipal Workers' Union, 150, 365, 368–9
General Dental Council, 199
General Elections, *see* Elections
General Register Office, 282
General Strike, 371, 373
Germany, 387–9, 397, 465–7
Ghana, 453, 458, 461
Gibraltar, 453
Gold, 377
Government (*see also* Cabinet *and* Ministers):
    in chronological order, 1–48
    size of, 66
    Economic Service, 380
    revenue, 390–2
    expenditure, 393–5
Greater London Council, 437, 439, 441, 448
Grenada, 453, 458, 461
Gross Domestic Product, 383–4
Guernsey, 433–4
Guyana, 453, 458, 461

Harris Poll, *see* Public Opinion Polls
Health (and Social Security) (*see also* Social Services):
    Department of, 7–49, 50, 57
    ministerial salaries, 47
    policy, resignation over, 69
    Permanent Secretaries, 281
    civil servants, 287
    Royal Commission, 292–5
    Departmental Committees, 298
    tribunals, 302
    legislation, 334–6; industrial, 353–6
    expenditure, 393–4
    local authority responsibility for, 437
    pressure groups, 441
Her Majesty's Stationery Office, 416
Hindu religion, 524
Hire Purchase, 398
Hiving-off of nationalised industries, 402
Home Office:
    Ministers, 1–49, 50, 53
    Secretaries, 1–49, 50, 53
    Select Committee on, 202
    Permanent Secretaries, 281
    civil servants, 279–80, 287
Home Security, Ministry of, 15–8, 50, 281
Homosexuals, 346
Hong Kong, 453, 466
Honours scrutiny, 293, 303
Horserace Totalisator Board, 416
House of Commons, *see* Commons, House of
House of Lords, see Lords, House of
Housing:
    (and Local Government), Ministry of, and Construction, Ministry of, 34–49, 50, 57
    policy, resignation over, 69
    Permanent Secretaries, 281
    civil servants, 287
    Royal Commission, 293
    Departmental Committee on, 298–9

Housing (*contd.*)
  legislation, 330–2
  Corporation, 330–1, 417
  Local Authorities, 331, 438–41
  statistics, 332–4
  pressure groups, 346

Immigration, 292, ; *see also* Race, 327–9
Imperial Preference, 69
Imports:
  Duties Advisory Council, 380
  statistics, 388–9
  statistics, 388–9
India:
  Office, 1–16, 50, 57, 281, 287
  and Burma Office, 16–22, 50, 57, 281
  Royal Commissions, 293–4
  immigration from, 327–9
  independence, 453, 458
  Governors-General, 461
  Viceroys, 461
Independent Broadcasting Authority, 417, 510
Independent Labour Party (I.L.P.), 157, 160, 216
Independent M.P.s, 167–8
Independent Television (*see also* Television and
    Independent Broadcasting Authority):
  Select Committee investigation, 192
  Authority, 510
  programme contracting companies, 511–12
  Commission, 511
Industry (*see also* Trade):
  (and Trade) Department of, 35–41, 50, 57, 405–8,
    412–19
  Industrial Development, Ministry of, 34, 50, 57
  Department of, 36–41, 50, 57, 412–14
  Select Committee investigation, 202
  Authority, 505
  Industrial Development, Ministry of, 34, 50, 57
  Department of, 36–41, 50, 57, 412–14
  Select Committee on, 202
  Finance and, Committee on, 298, 377
  Courts of Inquiry, 302
  industrial relations, 303–8, 351–4, 357
  industrial injuries, 354–6
  work force, 360–1
  disputes, 370–2.373–6
  Reorganisation Corporation, 378, 418
  production, 385–7
  output, 397
  nationalised, 401–16
  Confederation of British Industry, 382
Inflation, 377–9, 383–4
Information:
  Ministry of, 8, 16–22, 50, 57, 281
  Central Office of, 281
  Ministry of Information Technology, 41, 50 68
Inland Revenue, 281, 288, 390–2
Insurance, *see* National Insurance and Social
    Insurance
Interest groups, *see* Pressure groups
International:
  Monetary Fund, 377, 378
  relations, 465–9

Ireland (*see also* Eire and Northern Ireland):
  Chief Secretaries for, 1–7, 50, 57, 427
  Lord Chancellors, 1–9, 50, 57
  Lords Lieutenant of, 2, 50, 57, 427
  Attorneys-General, 1–9, 50, 57–8
  Solicitors-General, 1–9, 51, 57–8
  Permanent Secretaries, 281
  Civil Service, 287
  Ministerial resignations over, 69, 70
  parties, 160–2
  election results, 213–24
  Royal Commission, 292–3
  Vice-Regal Commissions, 297
  Lords Chief Justice, 312
  emigrations from, 326, 329
  government of (1900–22), 427
  Governors-General, 461
  independence of, 453
Irish Nationalist Party, 157, 160–2
Irish Office, *see* Ireland
Iron, *see* Steel
Italy, 397, 465, 468

Jamaica, 453, 458, 461
Jersey, 433–4
Jewish community, 517, 518
Judges, 312–15
  number, 317
Junior Lords of the Treasury, *see* Whips
Justice (*see also* Judges, Law and Legislation):
  Royal Commission relating to, 292
  administration of, 305–22
  criminal legislation, 305–8
  civil legislation, 308–9
  Law Commission, 315
  statistics, 318–20

Kenya, 453, 458, 461
Kings, 419–23; *see also* Royal
Kiribati, 453, 458
Korean War, 484

Labour (*see also* Employment):
  (and National Service) Ministry of, 7–31, 51, 58,
    281–2, 287–8
  force, size of, 360
Labour Party (*see also* Independent Labour Party and
    National Labour Party):
  leaders, 135–7
  Chief Whips, 138
  Representation Committee, 138
  National Executive Committee, 138
  Parliamentary Committee, 139
  Parliamentary Labour Party 140–44
  Annual Conferences, 144–5
  membership, 146–7
  organisation and constitutions, 148–9
  sponsored M.P.s, 149–51
  finance, 151
  dissidents, 168
  in the House of Lords, 206–7
  election results, 213–23
  M.P.s' changes of allegiance, 225–31

in by-elections, 234–8
election expenses, 241
lost deposits, 242
women candidates and M.P.s, 243
rating in opinion polls, 247–61
headquarters, 263–5
quotations from, 267–76
in local elections, 443–9
and the press, 489–503
Lancaster, Duchy of, 1–49, 51, 57
Land:
    and National Resources, Ministry of, 31, 51, 57
    Permanent Secretaries, 282
    Royal Commissions, 293, 294
    Lands tribunal, 302
    Registry, 417
Law (*see also* Judges, Justice and Legislation):
    Officers, 2–48, 50, 52, 54, 57–8, 61, 62
    Society, 198
    Company, Committees on, 299
    Commission, 315
    pressure groups, 346
League of Nations, 16, 469
Leasehold, 298, 331–2
Leeward Islands, 454
Legal Aid, 305–9
Legal System, *see* Law
Legislation:
    criminal justice, 305–8
    civil justice, 308–9
    housing, 330–1
    rent and mortgage interest restriction, 331–2
    social security, 334–7
    women's rights, 337–9
    maternity and child welfare, 339
    education, 341–2
    employment, 352–6
    trade union, 353–6
    monopolies, 377–8
    economic, 377–9
    local government, 438–41
Lend-Lease, 377, 465
Liberal Democrat Party:
    Leaders, 156
    officers, 156
    Conferences, 156
    election results, 219
Liberal National Party, 163, 215
Liberal Party:
    Leaders, 152
    National Liberal Federation, 152
    party organisation, 153
    Chief Whips, 154
    Annual Conferences, 154–5
    in the House of Lords, 152
    election results, 213–23
    M.P.s' changes of allegiance, 225–31
    sponsored M.P.s, 149
    in by-elections, 234–8
    election expenses, 241
    lost deposits, 242
    women candidates and M.P.s, 243
    rating in opinion polls, 247–61

headquarters, 263–5
quotations, 265–75
in local elections, 443–9
in the press, 489–503
Liberal Unionist Party, 163, 207, 213, 226
Libraries, 299, 344
Licensing laws, 294, 299
Life, expectation of, 325
Litigation:
    political, 309–12
    Trade Union, 356–8
Local Government (*see also* National and Local
        Government Officers'
    Association and Town and Country Planning):
    Board, President of, 1–8, 51, 58
    and Planning, 23, 36, 51, 58
    and Housing, Ministry of, 24–34, 51, 58
    and Regional Planning, 31, 51
    and Development, 34, 51, 59
    and Environmental Services, 69, 76
    Permanent Secretaries, 281, 282, 283
    civil servants, 287
    Royal Commissions, 294
    committees on, 298–300
    finance, 298–300
    housing, responsibilities for, 339
    children, responsibilities for, 339
    industrial dispute, 372
    structure, 437
    legislation, 438–41
    health, responsibilities for, 439
    elections, 443–9
    pressure groups, 441
London, 294, 401, 403, 410, 448–9
Long tenure of office, 67
Lords Advocate, 2–48, 51, 61
Lord Chancellors, 1–47, 51, 52, 282, 316
    Secretaries to, 282, 316
Lord Chancellors of Ireland, 2–9, 51, 57
Lord Chief Justices, 312
Lords, House of:
    Leaders, 65
    Officers, 205
    Lord Chairmen of Committees, 205
    composition of, 205
    attendance, 207
    Party organisation, 206
    Party strengths, 207
    sittings, 208–9
    business, 208–9
    critical votes, 210
    reform of, 211–12
    appeals heard, 318
Lords in Waiting, *see* Whips
Lord Justice Clerk, 312
Lords Justices of Appeal, 314–15
Lords of Appeal in Ordinary, 313
Lord Presidents of the Council, 1–49, 51, 52
Lord Presidents of the Court of Session, 313
Lords Privy Seal, 1–49, 52–3

Malawi, 454, 458, 462
Malaya, 454, 458

Malta, 293, 454, 458, 462
Man, Isle of, 434–5
Manpower Services Commission, 417
Market & Opinion Research International, 246, 260–1
Marplan Ltd, 245, 260–1
Marriage (*see also* Divorce):
  Royal Commission, 293–4
  rates, 324
  average age at, 326
  legislation, 337–8
  by solemnisation, 524
Marshall Aid, 377
Master of the Rolls, 312
Materials, Ministry of, 25, 51, 59, 282
Maternity and child welfare, 339–40
Mauritius, 293, 454, 458, 462
Members of Parliament:
  sponsored, 149–51
  education, 175
  occupations, 175
  longest serving, 179–180
  oldest, 180
  youngest, 180
  family connections of, 180–1
  spouse's succession, 181
  final succession, 182
  payment of, 203–4, 299
  pensions, 203–4, 299
  seats forfeited, 204
  suspensions, 187
  changes of allegiance, 225–31
  seeking re-election, 238
  women, 243
  creation of peerages, 206
  denied renomination, 232–3
Methodist Church, 521, 522, 524
Metrication Board, 418
Metropolitan Police, 315
Militant, 163
Military operations, 482–6
Mines, 8–16, 51, 292, 293, 294, 361, 366, 368–9, 370–2, 378–97; *see also* Coal *and* National Union of Mineworkers
Ministers (*see also* Government and Cabinet):
  by Governments, 1–49
  salaries, 49, 299
  ministerial officers, 50–1
  holders of ministerial office, 52–64
  number of, 66
  longest serving, 67
  dying in office, 68
  losing seats, 68
  powers, 298
  resignations, 68–70
  biographical notes, 71–6
  index of, 77–125
  re-election of, 238–9
  memoirs of, 300
  Northern Ireland, 429–30
  resident overseas, 18, 51, 61
Minor parties, 157–69
  representation, 169

election results, 213–21
Monetary system, 299, 379
Monopolies:
  Commission, 315, 377, 378, 417
  and Restrictive Practices Commission, 315, 378
  and Mergers Commission, 315, 417
  legislation, 377, 378
Morality pressure groups, 346
Mortgage Interest (Restriction) Acts, 331
Motor cars (*see also* Transport and Traffic):
  Royal Commission, 292
  licences, 349
  industrial disputes, 372
  percentage of consumer expenditure, 396
Munitions, Ministry of, 6–8, 51, 59, 282, 287
Museums, 294
Muslim religion, 524

National and Local Government Officers' Association, 366, 368–9
National Assistance, 283, 288, 335–6, 439
National Association of British Manufacturers, 382
National Bus Company, 411, 415
National Debt, 298, 393–4
National Democratic Party, 163–4
National Dock Labour Board, 418
National Economic Development Council, 377, 381
National Enterprise Board, 402, 403, 414, 417
National Executive Committee, 138–9
National Expenditure Committee, 191, 298, 377
National Farmers' Union, 151, 382
National Film Finance Corporation, 417
National Freight Corporation, 402, 411, 415
National Front, 158, 164
National Health Service, 294, 296, 298, 302;
  see also Health and Social Security Management Board, 286
National Heritage Department, 45, 51, 59
National Income, 383–4, 396
  Commission, 381
National Insurance (*see also* Social Insurance and Pensions):
  (and Pensions) Ministry of, 19–31, 51, 60
  Permanent Secretaries, 282
  civil servants, 287
  Royal Commission, 294
  committee on, 298
  tribunals, 302
  legislations, 334–6, 353–6
  expenditure, 393–4
  National Labour Party, 158, 164, 215, 228
National Opinion Poll, 245, 259–61
National Party, 158, 164
National Research Development Corporation, 414
National Savings Bank, 416
National Service:
  Ministry of, 68, 51, 59
  (Labour and) Ministry of, 16–25, 51, 58
  resignation over, 69
  Permanent Secretaries, 282
  history of, 482
National Union of General and Municipal Workers, 150, 365, 368–9

National Union of Mineworkers (N.U.M.), 150, 366, 368–9

National Union of Public Employees (N.U.P.E.), 150, 366, 368–9

National Union of Railwaymen (N.U.R.), 150, 366, 368–9

National Union of Teachers (N.U.T.), 151, 366, 363–9

Nationalisation, 401–16

Nationalised Industries, Select Committee, 196, 416
  policy for, 418

Naturalisation, 327

Nauru, 454, 458

Navy (*see also* Admiralty *and* Defence)
  Under-Secretaries for, 27–39
  First Sea Lords, 479
  total forces serving, 481
  expenditure, 481
  war commanders, 485–8

New Party, 158, 165, 215, 228

New Towns, 333, 418, 438, 442–3

New Zealand, 327–9, 454, 458, 462

Newfoundland, 294, 454, 458

Newspapers (*see also* Press):
  headquarters, 263–5
  national daily, 489–92, 497–500
  national Sunday, 493–5, 500
  London evening, 495–7, 521
  printing in more than one city, 498–9
  partisan tendencies, 498–9
  circulation, 498–501
  provincial morning daily, 501
  readership, 499–500
  weekly, 503

Nigeria, 455, 458, 462

Nineteen Twenty-Two Committees, 130

North Atlantic Council, 469

North Atlantic Treaty Organisation (N.A.T.O.), 466

Northern Ireland (*see also* Stormont, S.D.L.P., Sinn Fein and Ulster
  Unionist Party):
  Department, 34–49, 51, 59, 282
  resignation over, 70
  committees on, 299–300
  tribunals of inquiry, 301
  Lords Chief Justice, 313
  judicature, 307
  quangos, 418
  Government of, 428–33
  Governors of, 428–9
  Prime Ministers, 428, 429
  Ministers, 34–48, 51, 59, 429–30
  General Elections, 218–23, 430
  civil disturbances, 431, 484–5
  B.B.C., Governor for, 506
  religious affiliations, 522

Oil, 19, 51, 402, 403, 408; *see also* Power

Oldest M.P.s, 180

Oldest Ministers, 67

Ombudsman, *see* Parliamentary Commissioner for the Administration

One-parent families, 299, 339, 345

Opinion Research Centre, 246, 259–60

Opposition, Leader of, 49, 71–6

Organisation for European Economic Co-operation (and Development), 377, 465

Output per man, 397

Overseas:
  Trade Department of, 8–25, 51
  Development, Ministry of, 31–49, 51, 59, 282, 287–8
  Development, Select Committee, 193, 202
  Aid, Select Committee, 193
  people born, 327

Pakistan, 327–9, 455, 458, 462

Palestine, 69, 294, 455

Papua-New Guinea, 454, 455, 458, 462

Parliament, 171–212; *see also* Members of Parliament, Commons, House of, and Lords, House of,

Parliamentary Commissioner for Administration, 201–2

Parliamentary Labour Party, 135–44

Parliamentary Private Secretaries, 66, 70

Parliamentary Secretary to the Treasury, *see* Whips

Parliamentary time, allocation of, 172–3, 176–8

Parole Board, 320

Party Conferences:
  Conservative, 133–4
  Labour, 144–5
  Liberal, 154–5
  quotations from, 265–76

Party finance, 132–3, 151

Pay:
  Board, 378, 381
  Productivity and Incomes, Council on, 381
  percentage of national income, 396
  Comparability Commission, 381

Paymaster-General, 1–49, 51, 60

Peerages, 206

Pensions:
  Ministry of, 8, 25, 51, 60
  and National Insurance, Ministry of, 25–31, 51, 60
  Permanent Secretaries, 282
  civil servants, 287
  tribunals, 302
  legislation, 334–6
  old age, 334–7
  widows', 334
  pressure groups, 345
  expenditure, 393–4

Permanent Secretaries, 279–84; salary, 284

Petroleum Department, 19, 51; *see also* Fuel

Place-names, political, 265–7

Plaid Cymru, 158, 165

Planning and Land, Minister for, 31, 51

Planning and Local Government, *see* Local Government

Poets Laureate, 422

Police, 294, 297, 300, 301, 307, 315, 321

Police Commissioners, 315

Police Complaints Board, 307, 315

Political advisers, 286

Political honours, 293, 303

Political litigation, 309–12

Polls, *see* Public Opinion Polls

Pollution, 296, 298

Population:
 Royal Commissions, 292
 regional distribution, 294, 324
 in prison, 320
 statistics, 323–4
 intercensal change, 323
 main conurbations, 323
 age distribution, 325
 wealth distribution, 396
 in agriculture, 361, 385–7
Portfolio, Minister without, 5–49, 51, 60
Ports (see also Docks):
 Royal Commissions on, 292
 Departmental Committees on, 299
 Port of London Authority, 401
 nationalised, 410, 411
Post Office:
 Postmaster General, 1–31, 51, 61, 413
 Posts and Telecommunications, Ministry of, 31–4, 51, 61, 413
 Union, 150, 367, 369
 Permanent Secretaries, 282
 Directors-General, 282
 civil servants, 287
 postal traffic, 350; costs, 350
 telephones, 351
 industrial dispute, 372
 nationalisation, 401, 413
 Corporation, 413, 415, 416
Power (see also Fuel):
 Ministry of, 28–31, 51, 61, 281, 287
 crises, 373, 377–8
 nationalised industries, 401–15
Presbyterian Church, 520, 522, 524
Prescription charges, 335–6
Presidents of Probate, Divorce and Admiralty Division, 312
Press, 294; see also Newspapers
Press Council, 503–4
Pressure groups, 169, 344–7, 380, 441, 467, 481
Prices:
 and Consumer Protection, Ministry of, 37, 51, 60, 298
 Royal Commissions, 294
 departmental committees, 300
 Council on, 378
 Commission, 378, 381
 and Incomes Board, 381
 indices, 383–4
Prime Ministers:
 by Government, 1–48, 51, 52, 66
 salary, 49
 chronological list of, 52
 P.P.S.s to, 70
 biographical details, 71–6
 homes of, 265–6
 Private Secretaries to, 285
 staff, 285
 Atomic Energy, responsibility for, 408
 durability of, 67
Prisons:
 Committee on, 298, 299 301, 302
 sentences, 318–20

 prisoners, 320
 reform, 346
Privacy, Committee on, 299
Privatisation, 402–4
Privileges, Committee of, 196–8
Privy Council:
 Minister of State for, 35, 38, 51
 Counsellors, 77–125
 Clerk of the Council, 282
Probate, Divorce and Admiralty Division, 312
Probation, 297, 299, 305–7, 318, 319
Procedure, Parliamentary Committee on, 194
Procurator-General, 316
Production, Ministry of, 19, 51, 282
Proportional representation, 293
Prorogations of Parliament, 176–8
Prosecutions, Director of Public, 315
Public Accounts Commission, 201
Public Accounts Committee, 190
Public Building and Works, Ministry of, 28–34, 51, 61, 284; see also Works
Public opinion polls:
 Gallup Poll, 245–262
 National Opinion Poll, 245, 259–61
 Opinion Research Centre, 246, 259–61
 Louis Harris Research Ltd, 245, 259–61
 Marplan Ltd, 245, 259–61
 Market & Opinion Research International, 246, 259–61
Public Petitions, Select Committee on, 198–200
Public schools:
 ministers educated at, 66, 71–6; see also Index of Ministers, 77–125
 M.P.s educated at, 175
Public Transport, Minister of, 42, 51, 61
Public Trustee Office, 299

Quakers, 523
Quangos, 416–8
Queens, 415–18; see also Royal
Questions, parliamentary, 176–8
Quotations, political, 265–76

Race:
 Select Committee on Race Relations and Immigration, 193, 329
 riots, 277
 Race relations Board, 329
 pressure groups, 347
Radio, 507–8, 513–14; see also Broadcasting
Railways (see also Transport):
 unions, 150, 356, 367
 Royal Commissions on, 293, 294
 departmental committees on, 297
 statistics, 349
 disputes, 371, 373
 nationalisation, 401–2
 British Railways Board, 404, 410, 415
Rationing, 482
Reconstruction, Ministry of, 8, 19, 51, 61, 282
Redistribution of seats, 240–1
Re-election, 238–9

Referendums:
  on Europe, 220, 242, 472
  in Scotland, 426
  in Wales, 427
  in Northern Ireland, 432
Regional Development, 298
Registrars-General, 278
Regnal years, 187–8
Religion (*see also* Churches and Sunday Observation):
  Christian, 517–24
  other, 523, 524
Rent:
  departmental committees, 298–9
  tribunals, 302
  legislation, 331–2
  percentage of national income, 396
Resale Price Maintenance, 298, 378
Resident Overseas, Ministers, 18, 51, 61
Resignations, Ministerial, 68–9
Restrictive Trade Practices Court, 377
Rhodesia (*see also* Zimbabwe), 455, 458, 462
Rolls-Royce Ltd, 402, 403, 414
Roman Catholics, 522, 524
Rosebery Committee Report, 210
Royal:
  Household, 1–49, 423
  Assent, 176–8, 420, 434
  homes, 262–4
  quotations from, 266
  power, 419
  Regency Acts, 420
  family, 420–3
  Private Secretaries, 423
  Chamberlains, 423
  payment, 424
Royal Commissions:
  description, 291
  lists of, 291–4
  permanent and operating commissions, 295–6
  Irish and Vice-Regal Commissioners, 297
Royal Mint, 416
Royal Ordnance Factories, 416
R.S.P.C.A., 344
Runnymede Trust, 347; *see also* Race
Russia, 465, 468

Safety and Health at Work, Committee on, 302
St Lucia, 456, 458, 463
Salaries:
  Ministers, 49
  M.P.s', 203
  Permanent Secretaries to the Treasury, 284
Salvation Army, 523
Scandals, political, 276–7 280–1
Schools, 341–3; *see also* Public Schools and Education
Science (*see also* Education):
  Ministry of, 28, 51, 61
  and Technology, Committee on, 192
  Chief Scientific Advisers, 279
  Research Council, 283
  Scientific and Industrial Research
    Department, 283

Scotland:
  Secretary (of State) for, 1–49, 51, 61, 421—2
  Lords Advocate, 2–49, 51, 61
  Solicitors-General, 2–49, 52, 61
  Scottish Affairs, Committee on, 193, 202
  election results, 223–4, 426, 446
  Scottish Office, Permanent Secretaries, 283; civil
    servants, 287
  Electricity Boards, 407, 415
  Scottish Transport Group, 412
  Local Government, 437, 441, 446
  Development Agency, 418
  government of, 425–6
  B.B.C. Governors for, 506
  Scottish Television, 511
  churches in, 519, 521
Scottish Labour Party, 158, 166
Scottish National Party, 158, 166
Seats forfeited, 204
Select Committees, 189–202
Selection, Committee of, 189
Service Chiefs, 479
Seychelles, 456, 458
Shadow Cabinets:
  Conservative, 130–32
  Labour (Parliamentary Committee), 139–43
Shipbuilding, 402, 403, 413, 415
Shipping:
  Ministry of, 8, 16, 19, 51, 62, 283
  Royal Commission, 292
  departmental committees, 298
  tonnage registered, 349
  industrial disputes, 372–3
  nationalisation proposals, 402, 403
Sierra Leone, 452, 458, 463
Sikh religion, 524
Singapore, 456, 458
Sinn Fein, 161, 169
Social and Liberal Democrats, 156
Social Democratic Party, 156, 158, 167, 219, 230–1, 237,
  264
Social Democratic and Labour Party, 161, 230, 431–2
Social Insurance (*see also* Pensions *and* National
    Insurance):
  Ministry of, 19, 51, 60
  Beveridge Committee on, 298
  tribunals, 304
  legislation, 334–7, 353–7
Social Security, *see* Health and Social Security
Social Services, *see also* Health and Social Security
  Secretary of State for, 32–41, 51, 62
  Select Committee on, 202
  Pressure groups, 345–7
Society of Friends, 523
Society of Graphical & Allied Trades, 365, 369
Solicitors-General, 2–49, 51, 62
  for Ireland, 2–9, 51, 58
  for Scotland, 2–47, 51, 61
Solomon Isles, 452, 456, 458, 463
South Africa, 292, 456, 458; *see also* Boer War
Speaker of House of Commons, 171
Speakers' Conferences, 239, 245
Sponsored M.P.s, 149–51

Sport, Minister of State for, 30–47, 51, 62
Sri Lanka, *see* Ceylon
Standing Advisory Committees, 296
State:
    Ministers of, 19, 21, 24, 51, 62
    First Secretary of, 26, 29, 51, 62
Statistical Service, 279
Statute Law Commission, *see* Law Commission
Statutory Instruments Committee, 198–9
Steel:
    production, 385–7
    nationalisation, 401–2
    Iron and Steel Corporation, 401, 412
    British Steel Corporation, 401, 412
    European Coal and Steel Community, 471, 475
Sterling, 377–9, 387–9
Stormont, 428–31
Strikes, 370–5; *see also* General Strike
Students (*see also* Universities *and* Education):
    in full-time higher education, 347
Suez, 70, 270, 484–5
Sugar tariffs, 393–4
Summer time, 298
Sunday observance, 299, 346
Sunningdale Agreement, 432
Supplementary benefits tribunals, 304
Supply, Ministry of, 8, 16–28, 51, 62
Sweden, 397
Swinton Committee Report, 211

Tanganyika, 457, 458, 463
Tanzania, 457
Tariffs, specimen, 393–4
Taxation (*see also* Inland Revenue):
    Income Tax, 293, 297, 379, 383–4, 390–2
    Royal Commission, 293, 294, 295
    local, 292, 300
    departmental committees on, 297
    Value Added Tax, 378, 379
    Profits Tax, 390–2
    Capital Transfer Tax, 390–2
    Capital Gains Tax, 390–2
    Selective Employment Tax, 378
    Surtax, 390–2, 398
    Death Duty, 390–2, 398
    Estate Duty, 398
Tea tariffs, 393–4
Technical Cooperation, Secretary for, 28, 51, 62
Technology, Minister of, 32–4, 57, 62
Telephones, 351
Television:
    Independent, 192, 417, 510–14
    Committees on, 298, 299, 515
    B.B.C., 401, 505–9
    pressure groups, 346
Temperance, 348
Tenancy, 333
Town and Country Planning. Ministry of, 19–23, 51, 62, 283, 438–40
    see also Local Government
Trade (*see also* Restrictive Trade Practices Court):
    Board of, 1–48, 51, 63

and Industry, Department of, 34–5, 42, 45, 51, 63, 401, 405–14
and Consumer Affairs. Minister of, 34, 51, 63
Department of, 37–42
Free Trade, 68–9
Permanent Secretaries, 283
civil servants, 287–8
Royal Commission, 293
statistics, 387–9
terms of, 387–9
Central Government Trading Bodies, 417
Select Committee, 202
Trade Unions (*see also* Employment and Industry):
    M.P.s, 149–51
    places associated with, 263–5
    quotations from and about, 265–75
    Royal Commissions, 292–5
    legislation, 353–5
    litigation, 356–7
    Congresses, 362–3
    largest unions, 364–9
    income, expenditure and funds, 370
    membership statistics, 368–70, 373–5
Traffic (*see also* Transport):
    offences, 320
    road, 349
    railway, 349
    postal, 350
Transport (*see also* War Transport, Railways, Motor cars *and* Traffic):
    Ministry of, 8–49, 51, 63, 405–14
    Co-ordination of Transport, Fuel & Power, Secretary of State for, 24, 50
    and Civil Aviation, Ministry of, 25–8, 51, 63, 405–6
    Industries, Minister for (under Environment), 34, 51, 63
    Minister for (under Environment), 36, 51, 63
    Select Committee on, 202
    and General Workers' Union, 150, 367–9
    Permanent Secretaries, 283
    civil servants, 288
    Royal Commissions, 292, 294
    tribunals, 304, 417
    pressure groups, 346
    statistics, 348–51
    employment in, 361, 415
    industrial disputes, 371–2
    nationalisation, 401–2, 405–14
    privatisation, 402–4
    London Passenger Transport Board, 401, 409
    London Transport Board, 409
    British Transport Commission, 401, 410, 415
    British Transport Docks Board, 411, 415
    Scottish Transport Group, 412
    Transport Holdings Company, 401, 412
Treasury (*see also* Chancellors of the Exchequer, Whips and Economy):
    Ministers, 1–49, 51, 63, 68–70
    Select Committee on, 202
    Permanent Secretaries, 283
    civil servants, 288
    Solicitor, 316
    role in economic policy, 380–2

Economic Section of, 380
Treaties, 465–6
Tribunals of Inquiry, 291, 294, 298, 301–3
Trinidad and Tobago, 457, 458, 463
Turkey, 69, 468
Tuvalu, 457, 458, 465
Tynwald, 434

Uganda, 457, 458, 463
Ullswater Conference on Electoral Reform, 239
Ulster Unionist Party, 161–2, 230, 431–2
Unemployment:
  resignation over, 69
  Assistance Board, 283, 354
  benefits, 353–6, 360, 370
  legislation, 353–6
  statistics, 373–6
Union of Construction, Allied Trades and
  Technicians, 150, 367, 369
Union of Shop, Distributive and Allied Workers, 150,
  367–9
Union Movement, 158, 165
Unitarians, 523
United Kingdom Atomic Energy Authority, 401, 408,
  415
United Nations, 465, 466, 467
United Reformed Church, 520, 521
United States of America, 326, 377–9, 387–9, 397, 466,
  468
United Ulster Unionist Council, 161, 432
Universities:
  Ministers educated at, 66, 71–6 83, 88—94; see also
    Index of Ministers, 77–125
  University seats, 167, 222, 172, 230–1
  M.P.s educated at, 175
  University Grants Committee, 284, 416
  Royal Commissions, 292–4
  Committee on, 292
  removal of sex disqualification, 337
  students at, 343
  expenditure on, 343
  Urban Affairs, Minister of State, 51
U.S.S.R., 465, 468

Value Added Tax, 378, 379
Vanguard Movement, 161–2, 431
Vanuatu, 457, 458
Virgin Islands, 457
Vivisection, 292, 344
Voting intention, 246–59

Wales (see also entries for subjects where England and
    Wales are taken together):
  Minister for Welsh Affairs, 24–28, 51, 64, 426–7
  Secretary of State for, 32–49, 51, 64, 420–7
  disestablishment, 68
  election results, 22–3
  Welsh Office, Permanent Secretaries, 284
  civil servants, 287
  government of, 426–7
  Church in, 426, 519
  B.B.C. Governors for, 506
  Development Agency, 418

Commission for Local Government, 4411
Select Committees, 202
War (see also Economic Warfare, Defence and Army):
  Office, 2–28, 51, 63–4, 286, 287, 480
  Transport Ministry, 51, 63, 283
  ministerial resignations over, 69
  quotations: (1914–18), 267–8; (1939–45), 268–9
  Royal Commissions, 294
  emergency measures, 372–3, 482
  Boer, 482
  First World, 483
  intervention in Russia, 483
  Second World, 484
  Korean, 484
  Suez, 484
  Falklands, 484
  Gulf, 484
  commanders, 486–8
  costs and casualties in, 483–5
Water Authorities, 417, 418
Waterways, 401, 411, see also Transport
Ways and Means Committee, 171
Welsh, see Wales
Welsh Nationalist Party, see Plaid Cymru
Wesleyan, see Methodist
West Indies, 328–9, 451, 458, 463
Western European Union, 473
Western Samoa, 457, 458
Whips:
  P.S. to Treasury (Chief Whips), 1–48, 65
  Junior Lords of Treasury (Government
    Whips), 1–49
  Government Chief Whip in the Lords (Capt. Gents
    at Arms), 1–49, 65
  Lords in Waiting (Government Whips in the
    Lords), 1–49
  Assistant Government Whips, 32–48
  Opposition, 49
  Conservative, 130
  Labour, 138
  Liberal, 154
Women (see also Marriage, Divorce and
  Abortion):
  candidates and M.P.s, 243
  votes for, 240
  rights of, 337–9
  pressure groups, 344
  welfare legislation, 337–40
Works:
  First Commissioner of, 2–19, 51, 64
  Ministry of, 19–28, 51, 64
  and Buildings, Ministry of, 19, 51, 64
  and Planning, Ministry of, 19, 51, 64
  Public Building and Works, Ministry of, 28–34, 51,
    61
  Permanent Secretaries, 284
  civil servants, 288

Youngest M.P.s, 180
Youngest Ministers, 67

Zambia, 459
Zimbabwe, 459, 460, 464; see also Rhodesia